L. L. Guy   Henry D. Tho...

E. Flourad   Countee Cullen   D H Lawrence

Charles Dickens   Jonathan Swift   Daniel Defoe

G. Bernard Shaw   Phillis Wheatley   Stephen Crane

Langston   Bret Harte   Henry W. Longfellow

oscar wilde   Thornton Wilder   Edgar A Poe

[signature]   Ernest Hemingway   J. Austen

Sinclair Lewis   Herman Melville   R Emerson

Ed [signature]   Ivan Turgeneur   A Bradstreet

T. S. Eliot   Jack London   Thomas Hardy

MACMILLAN LITERATURE SERIES

WORLD LITERATURE

SIGNATURE EDITION

TEACHER'S ANNOTATED EDITION

GLENCOE
Macmillan/McGraw-Hill

Lake Forest, Illinois   Columbus, Ohio   Mission Hills, California   Peoria, Illinois

Send all inquiries to:
GLENCOE DIVISION
Macmillan/McGraw-Hill
15319 Chatsworth Street
P.O. Box 9609
Mission Hills, CA 91346-9609

ISBN 0-02-635081-5/10–12 (Student's Edition)
ISBN 0-02-635082-3/10–12 (Teacher's Annotated Edition)

Printed in the United States of America.

1 2 3 4 5 6 7 8 9   99 98 97 96 95 94 93 92 91

Macmillan Literature Series

SIGNATURE EDITION

TABLE OF CONTENTS

Student Edition Features

IV

Teacher's Annotated Edition Features

X

Teacher's Classroom Resources

XVI

Additional Support

XVIII

Scope and Sequence

XX

Student's Edition

 ake literature the heart of your Language Arts program with *Macmillan Literature Series,* Signature Edition.

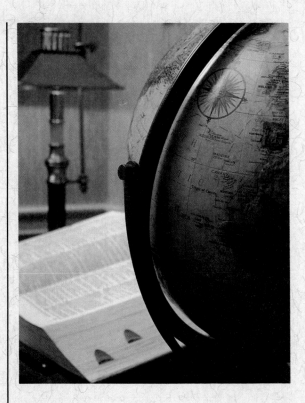

The Unit Preview

1 provides a frame of reference for the selection

2 offers a springboard for classroom discussion

3 opens students' minds to learning about themselves through the experiences of others

Before each selection, students will find

1 a brief biography of the author and notes on the author's contributions to literature

2 a purpose-setting question that links the students' experiences to concepts in the selection

PEARL BUCK
1892–1973

Buck was born in West Virginia but grew up in China. Many of her works, such as *The Good Earth*, take place in China. The stories by this Nobel Prize recipient create better understanding among people.

Student's Edition

From Beowulf to James Michener, from Emily Dickinson to Dante, *Macmillan Literature Series* presents the most thought-provoking classic and contemporary selections, crossing periods, cultures, and genres. Selections were chosen and organized in response to surveys of 5,200 English teachers.

STUDENTS BECOME ACTIVE READERS THROUGH STUDY AND RESPONSE ACTIVITIES.

After each selection, a three-part questioning strategy leads students through various levels of thinking:

1 Recalling: students recall literal facts.
2 Interpreting: students apply critical thinking skills.
3 Extending: students explore selection ideas.

Challenge and Viewpoint activities encourage different types of response.

Comparing Activities encourage students to look at literature in new ways.

SPEAKING AND LISTENING HANDBOOK *Grades 7–12*

Includes lessons on how to present orally, listen effectively, and interact in collaborative learning activities.

THINKING SKILLS HANDBOOK *Grades 7–12*

Provides lessons on how to apply higher order thinking skills.

READING AND STUDY SKILLS HANDBOOK *Grades 7–10*

Lessons reinforce the skills essential to demonstrating comprehension.

BENJAMIN
FRANKLIN

1706–1790

·

Franklin educated himself

by reading widely. He

published his first essay

as a teenager. He moved

penniless from Boston to

Philadelphia, where he

became a civic leader.

Student's Edition

riting assignments challenge students at different levels. At the end of selections, students have a choice of two different writing assignments—an analytical composition about the selection or a creative writing project.

The *Writing About Literature Handbook* encourages writing about the selections.

The Research Paper Casebook
Grades 11–12
Guides students through the specific steps needed to produce a successful research paper.

EVALUATE STUDENT PROGRESS WITH UNIT REVIEWS AND ACTIVITIES TO ENSURE COMPREHENSION.

The *Model for Active Reading* and follow-up activities help students extract meaning and enjoyment from the selections in each unit.

Literary Skills Reviews and *Themes Reviews* reinforce the unit lessons.

Student's Resources
Lessons in Active Learning
In the Student Resources handbooks at the back of the Student's Edition are guides for independent learning and evaluation.

ROBERT FROST
1874–1963

•

Frost is closely identified

with New England even

though he was born in

San Francisco and moved

to New Hampshire as a

child. He received many

honors, including four

Pulitzer Prizes.

Teacher's Annotated Edition

very feature in the Teacher's Annotated Edition can be immediately used and applied in the classroom.

On-the-page annotations

1 provide on-the-spot help in directing class discussion

2 include ideas that can be shared with students of various abilities

3 save time for busy teachers rather than demand more time

INTRODUCE STUDENTS TO GREAT LITERATURE WITH EFFECTIVE PREREADING STRATEGIES.

Lead students into the literature with the help of these prereading features:

1 *At a Glance* summarizes major developments on the page; teachers can see "what happens where" without having to read the entire selection.

2 *Literary Options* lists the most obvious literary elements associated with the selection allowing teachers to focus on one or more dominant elements or techniques.

3 *Thematic Options* lets teachers select one or more themes to focus on in the teaching of the selection.

GWENDOLYN
BROOKS

1917–

Brooks was the first black woman to win a Pulitzer Prize. She began writing poetry that was quite traditional, but in her later work she often uses free verse and open forms.

Teacher's Annotated Edition

 eyed-to-text annotations highlight passages in the selection for the teacher. Similar to marginal notes that any teacher keeps, these annotations

1 give insight about the passage and its relation to the selection as a whole
2 enrich class discussion
3 are brief enough to be used while teaching

These keyed-to-text annotations include literary elements, background, vocabulary, paraphrases, reading skills, and response journal.

Response Journal offers suggestions for student writing about a specific passage in a selection.

Reflecting on the Selection suggests overview questions that allow students to respond in general before beginning a detailed post-selection analysis.

Guided Reading questions address thinking skills and check students' comprehension page by page, helping prepare them for end-of-selection study questions.

CHALLENGE STUDENTS WITH ACTIVITIES AND REVIEWS THAT DEVELOP THEIR THINKING SKILLS AS THEY RESPOND TO LITERATURE.

Unit teaching notes offer activities for the *Model for Active Reading* feature in the student text.

Answers to themes review help to encourage class discussion.

Answers to end-of-selection questions appear on the Teacher's Annotated Edition page, so there's no more juggling separate answer keys.

Annotations at the beginning of each Student's Resources handbook explain the philosophy, structure, or application of the lessons.

ANTON CHEKHOV

1860–1904

Chekhov was the grandson

of a Russian serf. While

at medical school he

began to write, launching

a brilliant literary career.

Teacher's Annotated Edition

O n-the-page *Suggestions for Critiques* of the two-part composition assignments suggested in the student text save you time in assessing student writing.

It is easy to assess student achievement with a variety of reviews and checkpoints:

1   Selection End: three-level study questions feature recall, interpretation, and extension.
2   Unit End: Literary Skills Review encourages students to look at literature in a broad context.

WILLIAM
SHAKESPEARE
1564–1616

Shakespeare, poet and

playwright, is said to be

the world's favorite author.

No other writer's plays

have been produced so

often and read so widely

all over the world.

Teacher's Classroom Resources

hese booklets in the Teacher's Classroom Resources specify when to use each component while teaching a selection.

1   One-page lesson plans begin with clearly stated objectives.

2   Each lesson plan lists materials and activities by lesson elements: *Prereading, Reading and Response, Composition, Closure and Transfer, Reteaching, Enrichment and Extension, and Evaluation.*

The *Macmillan Literature Series* Lesson Plans make teaching manageable by providing step-by-step management of each and every component.

UNIT BOOKLETS HELP STUDENTS BECOME ACTIVE READERS AND IN-DEPTH THINKERS.

For teaching each selection, teachers will find in the Unit Booklets:

A *Teaching Chart* to identify features in the Student's Edition, Teacher's Annotated Edition, and Teacher's Classroom Resources (including Overhead Transparencies) for use before, during, and after reading a selection.

Teaching Notes

1   Author notes to help teachers provide additional background and context for the selection.

2   A Statement of Theme or Main Idea and Synopsis.

3   Motivation suggestions to engage students' interest before reading.

4   Words in Glossary to show teachers the selection words that appear in the Glossary in the Student's Edition.

5   Additional Projects to help students work in a novel, often nonverbal, way to further explore the selection.

A *Prereading Vocabulary blackline master* to introduce and provide practice with difficult words from the selection using various strategies.

A *Reading Guide blackline master* to keep less-able readers focused on the selection and help them note key points as they read.

A *Check Test blackline master* to give teachers a quick sense of students' grasp of the selection on a literal level.

A *Writing Process Guide blackline master* to help students complete the analytical composition assignments in the Student's Edition.

A *Selection Test blackline master* including vocabulary test items to help teachers evaluate the students' understanding.

TEACHER'S CLASSROOM RESOURCES

These resources offer everything a teacher needs for planning and teaching lessons for Grades 6–12.

Teacher's Classroom Resources

 Literary Skills and *Active-Learning Guides* provide opportunities for students to become actively involved with literary terms and elements as well as reinforcement of *Student's Resources Lessons in Active Learning.*

An *Answer Key booklet* is a quick reference that provides answers and guidelines for evaluation.

Overhead Transparencies provide an alternative medium for instruction while students are actively involved with great literature.

Teacher's Professional Resources booklet contains helpful articles about the teaching of literature.

Models of Student Writing cover twelve types of writing and exemplify the writing process and the teacher's evaluation of that process.

Additional Teaching Materials complete a comprehensive literature program.

Macmillan Literature Series Test Generator provides individual test items that can be selected from the computer data bank so that tests can be customized.

Macmillan Literature Novel and Drama Guides enable students to apply independently their literary and vocabulary skills.

The Macmillan Literature Series Video Library supports classroom instruction and brings literature to life by showing how to integrate videotapes with reading.

The Macmillan Literature Series Audiotapes expand students' literary experiences with outstanding presentations and active reader comments.

MARK TWAIN

1835–1910

Mark Twain, who was

born Samuel Clemens,

did not just write a story.

He told it. His mastery

of American speech and

his ability to spin a yarn

are unsurpassed.

Scope and Sequence

MACMILLAN LITERATURE SERIES

All the components fit together to make MACMILLAN LITERATURE SERIES,
Signature Edition, a comprehensive language arts program.

Reading and Literary Skills	Discovering Literature	Introducing Literature	Enjoying Literature	Understanding Literature	Appreciating Literature	American Literature	English Literature with World Masterpieces	World Literature
allegory						181, 936	56, 120, 287, 290, 893	281
alliteration	355, 626	219, 274, 598	224, 282, 628, 630, 646	195, 720, 724, 730	200, 788, 792	131, 936	18, 26, 430, 996, 1020	328, 608, 612
allusion		430, 598	453, 646	487, 724	200, 792	29, 936	276, 285, 286; 656, 1020	156, 166, 612
analogy					332, 792	39, 936	1020	612
antagonist					792	665, 936	1020	612
assonance			227, 646	195, 720, 724	192, 788, 792	131, 937	430, 996, 1020	302, 328, 608, 612
atmosphere	342, 626	131, 172, 598	92, 165, 646	75, 304, 724	58, 792	148–149	225, 756, 1020	128, 612
audience	434, 626	47, 289, 322, 598	25, 297, 330, 486, 646	233, 261, 327	263, 353	68	236	
autobiography, biography	51, 125, 463, 626	21, 289, 295, 303, 333, 598	11, 297, 304, 312, 646	234, 240, 245, 251, 716, 724	264, 270, 277, 346, 792	58, 244, 937	365, 498, 1021	378, 397, 612
ballad, song				171, 724	225, 792	7, 12–14, 170–171, 236–238, 286	5, 49, 52, 55, 141, 143, 266, 313, 366, 372, 394–395, 554, 651, 804, 1021	323, 349, 358, 612
blank verse				356, 724	196, 491, 793	123, 937	165, 277, 285, 286, 1021	612
cause and effect	233, 626	72, 479, 598	47, 318, 341, 494, 646					
character	106, 170, 194, 251, 266, 413, 467, 470, 513, 582, 605, 616, 618, 626, 630	105, 171, 368, 404, 434, 447, 498, 574, 598	67, 77, 430, 462, 468, 496, 566, 622, 624, 646	53, 63, 145, 157, 326–327, 374, 428, 613, 708, 724	44, 134, 432, 512, 612, 772, 793	114, 323, 339, 710, 937	78, 225, 502, 510, 640, 701, 712, 724, 731, 904, 913, 1021	43, 55, 71, 166, 510, 538, 596, 613, 615, 616
characterization	266, 605, 626	95, 109, 170, 404, 434, 498, 532, 574, 598	67, 85, 160, 406, 430, 622, 624, 646, 647	40, 47, 613, 725	39, 793	323, 512, 600–601, 937	78, 79, 104, 698, 712, 724, 819, 1021–1022	43, 613
chronological order	206, 313, 535, 627	72, 308, 599	47, 159, 318, 332, 647					
Classicism						101, 937	311–313, 1022	584 (Neo-)
climax	14, 225, 407, 612, 627	65, 172, 308, 332, 404, 599	41, 166, 430, 647	10, 273, 326, 427, 725	20, 448, 793	323, 711, 937	224, 711, 1022, 1028	10, 526, 594, 613
comedy			349, 350, 647	293, 725	353, 384, 793	665, 667	132–133, 242–243, 313, 569, 913, 1022	463, 613
comparison/contrast	627	143, 519, 599	211, 647	708	345, 346	92, 896–897	986	
concrete language		235, 599	238, 647	277, 725	320			422, 613
conflict	14, 107, 225, 321, 407, 467, 582, 612, 627	79, 85, 170, 308, 330, 404, 451, 508, 599	52, 165, 430, 647	26, 33, 273, 326, 427, 458, 592, 725	28, 134, 448, 491, 793	323, 365–366, 938	224, 701, 1022, 1028	17, 22, 526, 613
consonance				720	192, 788	131, 938	430, 996, 1022	302, 608
description	385, 627	289, 312, 327, 599	297, 323, 333, 648	240, 725	794	92, 311, 938	1023	613
details	78, 275, 385, 420, 627	100, 138, 202, 282, 312, 406, 599	73, 96, 212, 290, 291, 292, 323, 432, 434, 618, 648	69, 158, 240	58, 103, 174, 296, 320	92, 150	42, 78, 79, 104	
dialogue	170, 627	45, 161, 171, 341, 355, 600	22, 189, 344, 349, 364, 642, 648	33, 273, 293, 326, 726	309, 354, 382, 794	665, 939	52, 476, 933, 1023	452, 614
drama	170, 627	44, 341, 404, 592, 594, 600	22, 349, 364, 430, 432, 433, 640, 642, 648	293, 726	353, 354, 794	665, 710–711, 753, 939	144–145, 236, 242, 391, 826, 1023	452, 453, 462, 494, 614, 617
dramatic monologue					235, 794	414, 419, 939	502, 507, 1023	614
elegy						261	38, 274, 366, 371, 498, 1024	
epic				433, 726	225, 576, 794	939	5, 8, 120, 277, 285, 351, 786, 820, 1024, 1027	268, 274, 614
essay	309, 624, 628	21, 289, 317, 600	11, 297, 318, 323, 327, 331, 648	263, 273, 277, 280, 285, 726	290, 296, 309, 313, 319, 325, 339, 346, 794	664, 939	228, 332, 339, 461, 466, 1024	408, 422, 433, 614
exposition (in plot)				10, 273, 326, 427, 726	20, 296, 448, 794	323, 710, 848, 939	224, 711, 1024, 1028	10, 526, 594, 614
fable	275, 628	145, 455, 600	471, 649	114, 727	90, 795	303, 939–940	732, 1024	241, 614

Scope and Sequence

The heart of your language arts program.

Reading and Literary Skills	Discovering Literature	Introducing Literature	Enjoying Literature	Understanding Literature	Appreciating Literature	American Literature	English Literature with World Masterpieces	World Literature
style		47	25	233, 277, 731	263, 800	3, 23, 384, 464, 496, 772–773, 946	243, 246, 277, 285, 286, 653, 683, 752, 1031	196, 218, 619
symbol			287	436	114, 134, 173, 219, 782, 800	190–191, 650–651, 902–903, 947	376, 382, 383, 640, 650, 717, 992, 1031	151, 218, 355, 538, 604, 619
theme	170, 275, 365, 413, 447, 513, 605, 633	145, 156, 174, 178, 186, 200, 209, 267, 269, 342, 368, 371, 404, 605	4, 7, 139, 145, 157, 276, 277, 279, 282, 287, 350, 366, 430, 502, 654	114, 118, 126, 145, 157, 188, 327, 428, 540, 714, 731	90, 98, 134, 536, 612, 780, 800	323, 384, 534, 650–651, 710–711, 904–905, 947	225, 514, 698, 764, 994, 1031	133, 139, 218, 352, 538, 602, 620
thesis statement		317, 324, 606	327, 335, 618, 654	285, 702	339, 769, 800	894	984	433, 592, 620
tone					82, 134, 178, 186, 263, 778, 800	474, 870, 947	246, 265, 285, 312, 640, 658, 676, 756, 1002, 1031	111, 196, 218, 339, 620
topic sentence	633	322, 331, 606	305, 335, 655	285, 703	769			593
total effect	513, 605, 633	178, 186, 200, 277, 323, 404, 532	157, 178, 211, 285, 331, 430, 581, 628	127, 220, 222, 227, 286, 427, 540, 668	134, 247, 253, 346, 459, 569, 605, 661, 734, 790	306, 908–909	224–225, 639, 998	225, 538, 610
tragedy			350, 655	293, 331, 731	353, 462, 568, 800	665	133, 146, 224, 313, 826, 861, 1031	620
Transcendentalism						154–155, 260, 947		
word choice	333, 633	47, 238	25, 243, 655	181, 728, 731	178, 181, 249, 800	211	395, 502, 554, 569, 651, 663, 679, 683, 756	343, 620

Composition Skills	Discovering Literature	Introducing Literature	Enjoying Literature	Understanding Literature	Appreciating Literature	American Literature	English Literature with World Masterpieces	World Literature
ANALYTICAL (Students are asked to write about the following literary genres, techniques, elements, and terms.)								
autobiography, biography	125, 624	295, 586	305, 634	240, 245, 251, 257, 716	270, 277, 281	64		391
character	67, 107, 180, 194, 266, 352, 467, 559, 614, 617	105, 115, 156, 174, 369, 447, 472, 574	67, 77, 107, 270, 365, 468, 622	40, 47, 53, 63, 109, 126, 145, 157, 429, 669, 706, 708	39, 44, 52, 154, 460, 570, 662, 772	211, 339, 441, 512	41, 79, 103, 726, 731	22, 47, 62, 71, 166, 171, 256, 539, 597
comparison/contrast	505	265, 369	67	63, 669, 708	52, 570, 662, 772	29, 39, 95, 391, 496, 588, 605, 621, 632, 896–897	127, 269, 507, 650, 701, 893, 913, 937, 951, 986	38, 71, 76, 111, 119, 133, 139, 151, 196, 225, 241, 256, 289, 292, 295, 303, 306, 310, 314, 317, 320, 331, 339, 343, 346, 355, 367, 402, 416, 596
diction and sentence structure	333					171, 827	249	
drama	171	45, 405, 592	23, 431, 640		383	711	225, 640	539
figures of speech				205	114, 117	220		314, 336, 346
imagery		233, 240	238, 247, 628	216	207, 213, 251	227	143	306, 336, 346, 355
irony					129, 784	391	351	207
nonfiction	51, 309, 385, 624	295, 312, 586	305, 323, 328, 634	262, 273, 277, 280, 285, 289, 718	296, 309, 320, 323, 326, 332, 339, 349, 786	180, 244, 844, 853, 900–901	231, 339, 465, 705, 990	391, 402, 416, 419, 433, 606
plot	14, 185, 206, 407, 612	57, 72, 85, 126, 167, 279, 443, 461, 572	41, 52, 243, 273, 620	26, 138, 151, 704	28, 770	113, 583	764	17, 171, 594
poetry	292, 376, 622	218, 269, 277, 281, 580	225, 234, 285, 289, 628	167, 173, 178, 205, 212, 215, 217, 225, 226, 720	181, 194, 198, 206, 215, 217, 227, 230, 233, 235, 239, 255, 788	134, 273, 287, 387, 413, 420, 426, 449, 463, 779, 906–907	452, 527, 537, 545, 646, 671, 679, 685, 996	260, 268, 295, 297, 299, 303, 306, 314, 328, 331, 334, 336, 343, 346, 349, 355, 363, 367, 608
point of view				85, 94, 151, 178, 712	75, 776	801		82, 95, 103, 119, 600
purpose				245, 257, 280, 285	270	653, 660, 853	339, 990	260, 416
review of a book or drama	606	45, 405, 533, 592	23, 431, 582, 640					
setting	78, 239, 342	131, 182	92, 167, 482	69, 75, 80, 710	58, 68, 774	324		133, 156, 160, 171, 598
symbol					114, 117, 345, 782	333, 627, 832, 840, 902–903	431, 501, 667, 688, 724, 992	151, 363, 604
theme	275, 365, 420, 457	145	189	114, 118, 157, 540, 714	90, 99, 108, 780	124, 475, 535, 810, 904–905	285, 756, 803, 873, 994	144, 171, 355, 602
tone					86, 154, 289, 778	305	656	111, 203
total effect	513		189, 628	16, 429, 540, 669, 722	141, 167, 259, 570, 735, 790	149, 637, 651, 908–909	225, 640, 998	225, 610

Scope and Sequence

MACMILLAN LITERATURE SERIES

CREATIVE (Students are asked to create the following kinds of written materials.)

Composition Skills	Discovering Literature	Introducing Literature	Enjoying Literature	Understanding Literature	Appreciating Literature	American Literature	English Literature with World Masterpieces	World Literature
anecdote	275			126	270	588		
aphorisms						64		203
article	185			145	108, 114, 606			10, 43, 260, 268, 349
description	292, 333, 342, 385, 467	156, 182, 216, 265, 269, 312, 447, 466, 472, 477	67, 77, 92, 273, 323, 462, 482, 493	69, 75, 94, 151, 205, 216, 277, 289	58, 68, 99, 117, 141, 192, 206, 207, 251, 320, 323, 383	45, 92, 118, 149, 191, 339, 366, 463, 475, 512, 621, 660	41, 103, 294, 406, 431, 527, 545	22, 103, 128, 144, 160, 187, 336, 346
dialogue	67	150, 423, 443	243, 468	109	20, 52, 570	711	933	55, 218
diary, journal entry	180, 206, 457, 606	105	52, 582	33, 47, 262	133	29, 252, 651	305, 711, 756	151, 171, 299
drama		45, 126, 369, 594	23, 189, 431, 468, 642	138, 304	75	420, 711	507, 861, 877, 913	38, 452, 539
essay	275, 309, 420	295, 312, 322	305, 323, 328	273, 280, 285	296, 309, 326, 339, 349	171, 180, 844, 869	231, 339, 705	144, 297, 361, 408, 416, 422
fable		145, 455	139	118	90	305		241, 245
figurative language, imagery		238		63	213, 217	220, 387	143, 342, 667	306, 336, 339, 343
narrative, story	14, 51, 125, 194, 239, 352, 395, 407, 559, 618	14, 72, 115, 174, 279, 308, 451, 461, 576	5, 107, 167, 624	53, 80, 85, 151, 157, 225, 429, 540	150, 281, 309	449, 482, 496, 613	286, 514, 724, 893	28, 76, 82, 95, 119, 139, 156, 160, 166, 179, 196, 233, 236, 251, 256, 281
opinion	395, 447			245, 280	129	69, 353, 653		144, 297, 352, 361, 429
persuasion		238, 322	365	280	44, 167, 326, 332	39, 84, 605		429
poem	80, 376, 447	131, 218, 226, 233, 240, 257, 277, 281, 582	229, 265, 275, 279, 285, 630	167, 215, 217, 226, 327	181, 183, 186, 194, 198, 213, 215, 227, 230, 233, 235, 239, 244, 251, 255, 259	273, 413, 426, 459, 552, 765	127, 646, 650, 656, 662, 671, 679, 683, 825, 937	289, 292, 295, 297, 306, 314, 317, 320, 323, 334, 336, 339, 343, 346, 352, 355, 358, 361, 367, 412, 416, 462
point of view				173, 178, 669	309	113	685, 873	82, 95, 119, 236
setting	78, 239, 618		92, 487	304	68, 320	333, 637		128, 156
sketch	107, 266, 505, 513, 616			240, 251, 487	270	118, 211, 324	365, 701	274, 378, 397
speech	365			114	44, 332, 460	257, 420, 827	225, 507	429, 539

Vocabulary Skills	Discovering Literature	Introducing Literature	Enjoying Literature	Understanding Literature	Appreciating Literature	American Literature	English Literature with World Masterpieces
analogies	112, 268, 413	182, 317	73, 328	262	154, 309, 662	287, 560, 660	469, 501, 925, 937, 961
antonyms	54, 236	135, 150, 447	156, 232, 449	26, 114, 157	114, 296, 332	39, 124, 366, 601, 711	286, 358, 540, 764, 913, 955
connotation/denotation			453	213	200	149, 211	
context clues	395, 463	22, 95, 201	11, 86, 365, 458, 581	85	99, 150, 320		
dialect		238	102	126, 210	606	324	640
dictionary	45, 189	80	58, 482				
etymology	45, 289	267, 385, 477	260, 318	75, 151, 487	39, 270, 339, 460	14, 92, 420, 773, 785	97, 305, 873
glossary	189, 372	138	96				
jargon, technical words, slang	482	369	305	181, 728	735	512	
pronunciation key	45, 189, 372	303	393				
sentence completions	321, 376, 434, 505	65, 115, 161, 186, 265, 279, 461	47, 227	273	44, 133, 326	29, 87, 535, 651	861
synonyms	6, 200, 251, 400, 582	14, 58, 107, 221, 295	5, 41, 130, 312	10, 40, 245	20, 75, 345	22, 64, 455, 832	89, 231, 331, 481, 650, 929
thesaurus	251	252	179				
word choice	251	252	179	185, 251, 280	129, 188, 200, 227, 232, 289, 735	80, 171, 227, 257, 366, 512, 563	371, 431, 679
word development, invention	107, 125, 217, 289, 352, 447, 467, 494			190	167, 246, 270, 339	273	903

World Literature, which focuses on language study, includes Word Origins features based on the following languages:

African Languages 391	**Greek**	241, 346, 429	**Latin**	274	**Spanish**	203
Arabic 251	**Greek and Roman Mythology**		**Malayo-Polynesian Languages**	90	**Turkish**	352
Celtic Languages 95	**Hebrew**	317	**Middle English**	17	**Yiddish**	408
Chinese 187	**Indian Languages**	55, 378	**Native Languages of Mexico, South America, and the Caribbean**	236		
French 17, 397, 538	**Italian**	225	**Old English**	260		
German 336	**Japanese**	187, 462	**Scandinavian Languages**	71		

MACMILLAN LITERATURE SERIES

SIGNATURE EDITION

DISCOVERING LITERATURE

INTRODUCING LITERATURE

ENJOYING LITERATURE

UNDERSTANDING LITERATURE

APPRECIATING LITERATURE

AMERICAN LITERATURE

ENGLISH LITERATURE
WITH WORLD MASTERPIECES

WORLD LITERATURE

GENERAL ADVISERS

WORLD LITERATURE

SIGNATURE EDITION

GLENCOE

Macmillan/McGraw-Hill

Lake Forest, Illinois   Columbus, Ohio   Mission Hills, California   Peoria, Illinois

ACKNOWLEDGMENTS

Grateful acknowledgment is given authors, publishers, and agents for permission to reprint the following copyrighted material. Every effort has been made to determine copyright owners. In the case of any omissions, the Publisher will be pleased to make suitable acknowledgments in future editions.

Aguilar S. A.
FEDERICO GARCÍA LORCA: "La guitarra" from *Obras Completas.* Used by permission of the publisher.

Aiken and Stone Ltd.
V. S. NAIPAUL: Specified excerpt from "The Crocodiles of Yamoussoukro" from *Finding the Center, Two Narratives.* Copyright © 1984 by V. S. Naipaul. Reprinted by permission of Aiken and Stone Ltd.

Vicente Aleixandre
VICENTE ALEIXANDRE: "On the Way to School" translated by Stephen Kessler from *A Longing for the Light: Selected Poems of Vicente Aleixandre* edited by Lewis Hyde. Spanish texts © 1979 by Vicente Aleixandre. This translation appeared originally in the *Iowa Review.* © 1978 by Iowa Review.

Edward Arnold
JAMES ENE HENSHAW: "The Jewels of the Shrine" from *This Is Our Chance.* Reprinted by permission of the publisher, the educational, academic and medical publishing division of Hodder & Stoughton, London.

The Asia Society
NGUYEN TRAI: "The Bamboo Hut" from *A Thousand Years of Vietnamese Poetry* edited by Nguyen Ngoc Bich. Copyright © 1962, 1967, 1968, 1969, 1970, 1971, 1972, 1974 by Asia Society, Inc. Reprinted by permission of The Asia Society.

Elizabeth Barnett
CHARLES BAUDELAIRE: Excerpt from "Parisian Dream" translated by Edna St. Vincent Millay. From *Flowers of Evil* by Charles Baudelaire, translated from the French by George Dillon and Edna St. Vincent Millay, Harper & Brothers. Copyright © 1936, 1963 by Edna St. Vincent Millay and Norma Millay Ellis. Reprinted by permission of Elizabeth Barnett, Literary Executor.

Hayyim (Chaim) Nachman Bialik
HAYYIM (CHAIM) NACHMAN BIALIK: "Summer Is Dying" translated by L. V. Snowman from *Bialik, Poems from the Hebrew*, London 1924.

Robert Bly
FEDERICO GARCÍA LORCA: "The Guitar" translated by Robert Bly in *Lorca and Jiménez, Selected Poems.* Copyright © 1973 by Robert Bly. Used by permission of Robert Bly.

Copyrights and Acknowledgments continue on pages 628–632, which represent a continuation of the copyright page.

Send all inquiries to:
Glencoe Division, Macmillan/McGraw-Hill
15319 Chatsworth Street
P.O. Box 9609
Mission Hills, CA 91346-9609

ISBN 0-02-635081-5

2   3   4   5   6   7   8   9   96   95   94   93   92   91

CONTENTS

Alternate Contents by Country . . . *xv*

A Note on the Special Features in This Book . . . *xx*

Map of the Contemporary World . . . *xxii*

World Events Time Line . . . *xxiv*

Reading Literature in Translation . . . *xxvi*

THE SHORT STORY ... *1*

Stories About Life's Surprises

Barbara Kimenye . . . . The Winner ... *3*
UGANDA

Guy de Maupassant . . . . The Piece of String ... *12*
FRANCE

Rumer Godden . . . . You Need to Go Upstairs ... *19*
ENGLAND / INDIA

Anton Chekhov . . . . The Beggar ... *24*
RUSSIA

Stan Barstow . . . . The Actor ... *30*
ENGLAND

This Table of Contents readily indicates both the contents and the organization of *World Literature*. Note that the selections are divided into five units based on literary genre—"The Short Story"; "Myths, Folk Tales, and Epics"; "Poetry"; "Nonfiction"; and "Drama." Selections in two units, "The Short Story" and "Poetry," are further grouped by broad literary theme.

Nationalities are indicated beneath each author's name. For a quick overview of the diverse nations and cultures represented in the anthology, consult the Alternate Contents by Country, which begins on page xv.

The selections in *World Literature* were carefully chosen to illustrate different literary skills as well as a diversity of cultures and themes. The annotations in this column indicate the chief literary skill or skills that each selection illustrates. These literary skills are taught in Literary Focuses or highlighted in other study aids that accompany the selections.

. . . . Plot; foreshadowing

. . . . External conflict

. . . . Internal conflict

. . . . . Irony and surprise endings

. . . Situational and dramatic irony

Characterization ....

Characterization ....

Character motivation ....

Character motivation ....

Flat and round characters; static
and dynamic characters ....

Static and dynamic characters ...

First-person point of view ....

Limited third-person point of
view ....

Limited third-person point of
view ....

Omniscient point of view ....

Tone ....

Omniscient point of view ....

Setting and atmosphere ....

Theme ....

Stated and unstated themes ....

Stories About Human Relationships

Chinua Achebe .... Dead Men's Path ... *40*
NIGERIA

Bjørnstjerne Bjørnson .... The Father ... *45*
NORWAY ▪ NOBEL PRIZE ▪

Rabindranath Tagore .... The Kabuliwallah ... *49*
INDIA ▪ NOBEL PRIZE ▪

Manuel Rojas .... The Glass of Milk ... *57*
CHILE

Selma Lagerlöf .... The Rat Trap ... *64*
SWEDEN ▪ NOBEL PRIZE ▪

Tu Peng-cheng .... Lingkuan Gorge ... *73*
PEOPLE'S REPUBLIC OF CHINA

Stories About Growing Up

Tayeb Salih .... A Handful of Dates ... *78*
SUDAN

N. V. M. Gonzalez .... On the Ferry ... *84*
PHILIPPINES

Sean O'Faolain .... The Trout ... *92*
IRELAND

Alan Paton .... The Quarry ... *97*
SOUTH AFRICA

Katherine Mansfield .... The Doll's House ... *105*
NEW ZEALAND / ENGLAND

Thomas Mann .... The Infant Prodigy ... *113*
GERMANY ▪ NOBEL PRIZE ▪

Stories About Personal Values

Gabrielle Roy .... Hoodoo Valley ... *121*
CANADA

Åsta Holth .... Salt ... *130*
NORWAY

Giovanni Boccaccio .... Federigo's Falcon ... *135*
ITALY

R. K. Narayan........................... Like the Sun ... *141*
INDIA

Jan Neruda .... Hastrman ... *146*
CZECHOSLOVAKIA

Stories About Reality and Fantasy

Gerardo María .... Matusalén, the Village Without Time ... *153*   .... Realistic fiction and fantasy; allusion
MEXICO

Naguib Mahfouz .... A Tale of Our Quarter ... *158*   .... First-person narrator
EGYPT ■ NOBEL PRIZE ■

Miguel de Cervantes .... *from* Don Quixote ... *162*   .... Character foils
SPAIN

Thomas Wolfe .... The Far and the Near ... *168*   .... Title and meaning
UNITED STATES

Françoise Mallet-Joris .... Air des Clochettes ... *173*   .... Stream of consciousness
BELGIUM / FRANCE

Akutagawa Ryūnosuke .... Autumn Mountain ... *181*   .... Frame story
JAPAN

Stories About Cultures and Conflicts

Alphonse Daudet .... The Last Lesson ... *189*   .... Point of view
FRANCE

Ernest Hemingway .... Old Man at the Bridge ... *194*   .... Style and tone
UNITED STATES ■ NOBEL PRIZE ■

Gabriel García Márquez .... Tuesday Siesta ... *198*   .... Atmosphere
COLOMBIA ■ NOBEL PRIZE ■

Heinrich Böll .... The Laugher ... *205*   .... Single effect; irony
GERMANY ■ NOBEL PRIZE ■

Albert Camus .... The Guest ... *209*   ..... Elements of the short story
ALGERIA / FRANCE ■ NOBEL PRIZE ■

Grazia Deledda .... The Shoes ... *220*   .... Total effect
ITALY ■ NOBEL PRIZE ■

.... Theme

.... Symbol

■ C U L T U R E   L I N K :   The Tradition of Oral Storytelling ... *226* ■

Contents **vii**

MYTHS, FOLK TALES, AND EPICS ... *229*

Metamorphosis ....

Myth ....

Fable ....

Fable ....

Fable ....

Legend ....

Folk tale ....

Folk tale ....

Epic ....

Epic hero ....

Allegory ....

Ovid .... *from the* Metamorphoses ... *231*
ANCIENT ROME

Zapotec Traditional .... The Bat ... *235*
MEXICO

Aesop .... The Fox and the Grapes ... *238*
ANCIENT GREECE   The Goatherd and the Wild Goats ... *238*

Jean de La Fontaine .... The Fox and the Crow ... *240*
FRANCE

Indian Traditional .... *from the* Panchatantra ... *243*
INDIA

Arabian and Persian Traditional ..... *from* The Thousand and One Nights ... *247*
MIDDLE EAST

Kabyle Traditional .... The Story of the Chest ... *253*
ALGERIA / TUNISIA

Johann Wolfgang von Goethe .... The Erl-King ... *258*
GERMANY

Homer .... *from the* Iliad ... *262*
ANCIENT GREECE

Virgil .... *from the* Aeneid ... *270*
ANCIENT ROME

Dante Alighieri .... *from* The Divine Comedy ... *276*
ITALY

■ C U L T U R E L I N K : Saving the Past ... *282* ■

viii *Contents*

POETRY ... *285*

Poems About Love

Tu Fu .... The Emperor ... *286*
CHINA

William Butler Yeats .... Politics ... *288*
IRELAND ▪ NOBEL PRIZE ▪

Sappho .... Fragment of a Lullaby ... *290*
ANCIENT GREECE

Gabriela Mistral .... Rocking ... *291*
CHILE ▪ NOBEL PRIZE ▪

Lady Ōtomo .... My Heart, Thinking ... *293*
JAPAN

Yevgeny Yevtushenko .... Colors ... *294*
SOVIET UNION

Léopold S. Senghor .... And We Shall Be Steeped ... *296*
SENEGAL

Anna Akhmatova .... Lot's Wife ... *298*
SOVIET UNION

Special Feature on the Sonnet

Petrarch .... Sonnet 3 (It Was That Very Day on Which the
ITALY   Sun) ... *300*

William Shakespeare .... Sonnet 29 (When, in Disgrace with Fortune
ENGLAND   and Men's Eyes) ... *301*

Types of poetry; narrative poetry

.... Types of poetry; lyric poetry

.... Lyric poetry

.... Lyric poetry

.... Speaker

.... Speaker

.... Lyric poetry

..... Rhyme and rhyme scheme;
stanza form

Slant rhyme; Petrarchan sonnet

.... Slant rhyme; Shakespearean
sonnet

Contents **ix**

Imagery and mood ....

Imagery and mood ....

Figurative language: simile and
metaphor; implied metaphor ....

Figurative language: simile and
metaphor; implied metaphor ....

Extended simile ....

Extended metaphor ....

Personification ....

Personification ....

Haiku ....

Onomatopoeia; repetition ....

Alliteration and assonance;
parallelism ....

Alliteration and assonance ......

Imagery ....

Rhythm and meter ....

Poems About Nature

Antonio Machado .... Winter Sun ... *304*
SPAIN

Victor Hugo .... June Nights ... *305*
FRANCE

Nelly Sachs .... The Swan ... *307*
GERMANY ▪ NOBEL PRIZE ▪

Pablo Neruda .... The Horses ... *308*
CHILE ▪ NOBEL PRIZE ▪

Oswald Mbuyiseni Mtshali .... Sunset ... *311*
SOUTH AFRICA

João Cabral de Melo Neto .... Weaving the Morning ... *312*
BRAZIL

Chaim Nachman Bialik .... Summer Is Dying ... *315*
RUSSIA / ISRAEL

Octavio Paz .... Wind and Water and Stone ... *316*
MEXICO ▪ NOBEL PRIZE ▪

Special Feature on Haiku

Bashō, Jōsō, Chiyo, Shiki .... Four Japanese Haiku ... *318*
JAPAN

Poems of Delight

Gabon Pygmy Traditional .... All That Dances ... *321*
GABON

Sarojini Naidu .... Street Cries ... *324*
INDIA

Jorge Carrera Andrade .... Reaping the Barley ... *326*
ECUADOR

Nguyen Trai .... The Bamboo Hut ... *329*
VIETNAM

Emily Dickinson .... How Happy Is the Little Stone ... *330*
UNITED STATES

x   *Contents*

Vicente Aleixandre . . . . On the Way to School ... *332*
SPAIN ▪ NOBEL PRIZE ▪

Rainer Maria Rilke . . . . Spanish Dancer ... *335*
AUSTRIA

. . . . Free verse
. . . . Imagery and figurative
language

Poems of Sorrow

Li Po . . . . Taking Leave of a Friend ... *337*
CHINA

Czeslaw Milosz . . . . Encounter ... *338*
POLAND / UNITED STATES ▪ NOBEL PRIZE ▪

Special Feature on Translation

Federico García Lorca . . . . The Guitar ... *340*
SPAIN

George Seferis . . . . I Am Sorry ... *344*
GREECE ▪ NOBEL PRIZE ▪

Jorge Luis Borges . . . . Afterglow ... *345*
ARGENTINA

Heinrich Heine . . . . The Lorelei ... *347*
GERMANY

. . . . Tone
. . . . Tone

. . . . Translation and word choice

. . . . Imagery and figurative
language
. . . . Imagery

. . . . Ballad

Poems About Values and Ideals

Nazim Hikmet . . . . The World, My Friends, My
TURKEY   Enemies, You, and the Earth ... *350*

C. P. Cavafy . . . . Che Fece ... Il Gran Rifiuto ... *353*
GREECE

Jaime Torres Bodet . . . . The Window ... *354*
MEXICO

A. B. ("Banjo") Paterson . . . . Waltzing Matilda ... *356*
AUSTRALIA

Horace . . . . Ode: Better to Live, Licinius ... *359*
ANCIENT ROME

José Martí . . . . *from* Versos Sencillos ... *362*
CUBA

. . . . Theme
. . . . Theme
. . . . Symbolism
. . . . Folk song and refrain
. . . . Ode and apostrophe
. . . . Symbolism

Total effect ....

Total effect ....

Alexander Pushkin .... Message to Siberia ... *364*
RUSSIA

Joseph Brodsky .... The Monument ... *365*
SOVIET UNION / UNITED STATES ▪ NOBEL PRIZE ▪

▪ C U L T U R E   L I N K :   The Bible's Influence on World Literature ... *368* ▪

NONFICTION ... *371*

Autobiography and author's
purpose ....

Autobiography ....

Biography ....

Sayings ....

Maxims ....

Narrative essay ....

Sensory language ....

Santha Rama Rau .... By Any Other Name ... *373*
INDIA

Camara Laye .... The Snake and the Goldsmith ... *380*
GUINEA

Colette .... Two Memories of Sido ... *393*
FRANCE

Confucius .... Sayings *from* The Analects ... *399*
CHINA

François de La Rochefoucauld .... *from* Maxims ... *401*
FRANCE

Isaac Bashevis Singer .... Shosha ... *404*
POLAND / UNITED STATES ▪ NOBEL PRIZE ▪

Aleksandr Solzhenitsyn .... Three Prose Poems ... *410*
SOVIET UNION ▪ NOBEL PRIZE ▪

Juan Ramón Jiménez . . . . *from* Platero and I . . . *414*
SPAIN ▪ NOBEL PRIZE ▪   . . . . Author's purpose

Camilo José Cela . . . . Traveling in the Alcarria . . . *418*
SPAIN ▪ NOBEL PRIZE ▪   . . . . Figurative language

Isak Dinesen . . . . The Iguana . . . *421*
DENMARK / KENYA   . . . . Descriptive essay

Thucydides . . . . Pericles' Funeral Oration . . . *424*
ANCIENT GREECE   . . . . Speech

V. S. Naipaul . . . . The Crocodiles of Yamoussoukro . . . *431*
TRINIDAD / ENGLAND   . . . . Expository essay

■ C U L T U R E   L I N K :   International Travel Writing . . . *434* ■

DRAMA... *437*

James Ene Henshaw . . . . The Jewels of the Shrine . . . *439*
NIGERIA   . . . . Dialogue; staging

Seami Motokiyo . . . . The Dwarf Trees . . . *454*
JAPAN   . . . . Japanese No play

Edmond Rostand . . . . Cyrano de Bergerac . . . *464*
FRANCE   . . . . Dramatic irony; staging and
                                                                         character; dramatic plot; total
                                                                         effect

■ C U L T U R E   L I N K :   From Literature into Film . . . *540* ■

Contents **xiii**

Dramatically illustrated overviews of ten significant regions of the world, providing connections between each region's literature and its culture. Each lesson also contains outlines of the region's literary history, sample translations, and collaborative research projects for students.

Summary of major world literary movements, chronological listing of anthology's authors, and identification of Nobel Prize laureates

Special lessons that reinforce prewriting, writing, and revising skills. Composition assignments throughout the text refer to these lessons, which may be used in conjunction with the Composition assignments or independently.

Definitions and illustrations of literary terms taught in the text

Pronunciations and definitions of difficult vocabulary words

STUDENT'S RESOURCES ... 542

Literature and Culture Sourcebook
Classical Greece and Rome ... 544

Italy ... 548

France ... 552

Spain ... 556

Latin America ... 560

Germany ... 564

Russia and Eastern Europe ... 568

China and Japan ... 572

Africa ... 576

India and the Middle East ... 580

Guide to Literary Movements ... 584

Author Time Line ... 586

Winners of Nobel Prize for Literature ... 590

Writing About Literature Handbook ... 592
Lesson 1: Writing a Response to Literature ... 592

Lesson 2: Writing About Plot ... 594

Lesson 3: Writing About Character ... 596

Lesson 4: Writing About Setting ... 598

Lesson 5: Writing About Point of View ... 600

Lesson 6: Writing About Theme ... 602

Lesson 7: Writing About a Symbol ... 604

Lesson 8: Writing About Nonfiction ... 606

Lesson 9: Writing About Poetry ... 608

Lesson 10: Writing About the Total Effect ... 610

Literary Terms Handbook ... 612

Glossary ... 621

Index of Skills ... 633

Index of Fine Art ... 637

Index of Authors and Titles ... 641

ALTERNATE CONTENTS BY COUNTRY

This Alternate Table of Contents lists selections according to authors' nationality and groups them by continent or region of the world. Using this table of contents, you can see at a glance the national literatures represented in the anthology. This table of contents readily enables you to group selections from the perspective of national or regional literatures, should you prefer to teach world literature in this manner.

This Alternate Table of Contents groups selections according to authors' nationalities. Some authors are listed under two countries because they spent a substantial part of their lives in each country.

You will find the continents or regions of the world listed alphabetically. Each country is listed under the continent or region of the world where it is located.

AFRICA

ALGERIA / TUNISIA	**Albert Camus**	The Guest	*209*
	Kabyle Traditional	The Story of the Chest	*253*
EGYPT	**Naguib Mahfouz**	A Tale of Our Quarter	*158*
GABON	**Gabon Pygmy Traditional**	All That Dances	*321*
GUINEA	**Camara Laye**	The Snake and the Goldsmith	*380*
KENYA	**Isak Dinesen**	The Iguana	*421*
NIGERIA	**Chinua Achebe**	Dead Men's Path	*40*
	James Ene Henshaw	The Jewels of the Shrine	*439*
SENEGAL	**Léopold S. Senghor**	And We Shall Be Steeped	*296*
SOUTH AFRICA	**Oswald Mbuyiseni Mtshali**	Sunset	*311*
	Alan Paton	The Quarry	*97*
SUDAN	**Tayeb Salih**	A Handful of Dates	*78*
UGANDA	**Barbara Kimenye**	The Winner	*3*

AUSTRALIA AND NEW ZEALAND

AUSTRALIA............ **A. B. ("Banjo") Paterson**.......... Waltzing Matilda ... *356*

NEW ZEALAND ...... **Katherine Mansfield** .... The Doll's House ... *105*

CLASSICAL GREECE AND ROME

GREECE............... **Aesop**................................. The Fox and the Grapes ... *238*
                                          The Goatherd and the Wild
                                          Goats ... *238*
                Homer................................ *from the* Iliad ... *262*
                Sappho .... Fragment of a Lullaby ... *290*
                Thucydides .... Pericles' Funeral Oration ... *424*

ROME.................. **Horace** .... Ode: Better to Live, Licinius ... *359*
                Ovid .... *from the* Metamorphoses ... *231*
                Virgil .... *from the* Aeneid ... *270*

EASTERN EUROPE AND THE BALKANS

CZECHOSLOVAKIA .. **Jan Neruda**.......................... Hastrman ... *146*

GREECE............... **C. P. Cavafy** .... Che Fece . . . Il Gran Rifiuto ... *353*
                George Seferis .... I Am Sorry ... *344*

POLAND .... **Czeslaw Milosz** .... Encounter ... *338*
                Isaac Bashevis Singer .... Shosha ... *404*

THE FAR EAST

CHINA .... **Confucius** .... Sayings *from* The Analects ... *399*
                Li Po .... Taking Leave of a Friend ... *337*
                Tu Fu.................................. The Emperor ... *286*
                Tu Peng-cheng .... Lingkuan Gorge ... *73*

JAPAN .... **Akutagawa Ryūnosuke** .... Autumn Mountain ... *181*
                Bashō, Jōsō, Chiyo, Shiki .... Four Japanese Haiku ... *318*
                Lady Ōtomo .... My Heart, Thinking ... *293*
                Seami Motokiyo .... The Dwarf Trees ... *454*

PHILIPPINES .... **N. V. M. Gonzalez** .... On the Ferry ... *84*

VIETNAM .... **Nguyen Trai** .... The Bamboo Hut ... *329*

LATIN AMERICA

ARGENTINA .... **Jorge Luis Borges** .... Afterglow ... *345*

BRAZIL .... **João Cabral de Melo Neto** .... Weaving the Morning ... *312*

CHILE .... **Gabriela Mistral** .... Rocking ... *291*
                           Pablo Neruda .... The Horses ... *308*
                           Manuel Rojas .... The Glass of Milk ... *57*

COLOMBIA .... **Gabriel García Márquez** .... Tuesday Siesta ... *198*

CUBA .... **José Martí** .... *from* Versos Sencillos ... *362*

ECUADOR .... **Jorge Carrera Andrade** .... Reaping the Barley ... *326*

MEXICO .... **Jaime Torres Bodet** .... The Window ... *354*
                           Gerardo María .... Matusalén, the Village Without Time ... *153*
                           Octavio Paz .... Wind and Water and Stone ... *316*
                           Zapotec Traditional .... The Bat ... *235*

TRINIDAD .... **V. S. Naipaul** .... The Crocodiles of Yamoussoukro ... *431*

THE MIDDLE EAST AND INDIA

EGYPT .... **Naguib Mahfouz** .... A Tale of Our Quarter ... *158*

INDIA .... **Rumer Godden** .... You Need to Go Upstairs ... *19*
                           Sarojini Naidu .... Street Cries ... *324*
                           R. K. Narayan .... Like the Sun ... *141*
                           Santha Rama Rau .... By Any Other Name ... *373*
                           Rabindranath Tagore .... The Kabuliwallah ... *49*
                           Indian Traditional .... *from the* Panchatantra ... *243*

ISRAEL .... **Chaim Nachman Bialik** .... Summer Is Dying ... *315*

MIDDLE EAST .... **Arabian** .... *from* The Thousand and One
                           and Persian Traditional   Nights ... *247*

TURKEY .... **Nazim Hikmet** .... The World, My Friends, My Enemies, You, and the Earth ... *350*

Alternate Contents by Country **xvii**

RUSSIA

Anna Akhmatova	Lot's Wife ...	*298*
Chaim Nachman Bialik	Summer Is Dying ...	*315*
Joseph Brodsky	The Monument ...	*365*
Anton Chekhov	The Beggar ...	*24*
Alexander Pushkin	Message to Siberia ...	*364*
Aleksandr Solzhenitsyn	Three Prose Poems ...	*410*
Yevgeny Yevtushenko	Colors ...	*294*

UNITED STATES AND CANADA

UNITED STATES	Joseph Brodsky	The Monument ...	*365*
	Emily Dickinson	How Happy Is the Little Stone ...	*330*
	Ernest Hemingway	Old Man at the Bridge ...	*194*
	Czeslaw Milosz	Encounter ...	*338*
	Isaac Bashevis Singer	Shosha ...	*404*
	Thomas Wolfe	The Far and the Near ...	*168*
CANADA	Gabrielle Roy	Hoodoo Valley ...	*121*

WESTERN EUROPE

AUSTRIA	Rainer Maria Rilke	Spanish Dancer ...	*335*
BELGIUM	Françoise Mallet-Joris	Air des Clochettes ...	*173*
DENMARK	Isak Dinesen	The Iguana ...	*421*
ENGLAND	Stan Barstow	The Actor ...	*30*
	Rumer Godden	You Need to Go Upstairs ...	*19*
	Katherine Mansfield	The Doll's House ...	*105*
	V. S. Naipaul	The Crocodiles of Yamoussoukro ...	*431*
	William Shakespeare	Sonnet 29 (When, in Disgrace with Fortune and Men's Eyes) ...	*301*
FRANCE	Albert Camus	The Guest ...	*209*
	Colette	Two Memories of Sido ...	*393*
	Alphonse Daudet	The Last Lesson ...	*189*
	Victor Hugo	June Nights ...	*305*
	Jean de La Fontaine	The Fox and the Crow ...	*240*
	Françoise de La Rochefoucauld	*from* Maxims ...	*401*
	Françoise Mallet-Joris	Air des Clochettes ...	*173*
	Guy de Maupassant	The Piece of String ...	*12*
	Edmond Rostand	Cyrano de Bergerac ...	*464*

GERMANY............. **Heinrich Böll**........................ The Laugher ... *205*
               Johann Wolfgang von Goethe .. The Erl-King ... *258*
               Heinrich Heine .... The Lorelei ... *347*
               Thomas Mann .... The Infant Prodigy ... *113*
               Nelly Sachs .... The Swan ... *307*

IRELAND.............. **Sean O'Faolain** .... The Trout ... *92*
               William Butler Yeats .... Politics ... *288*

ITALY.................... **Giovanni Boccaccio** .... Federigo's Falcon ... *135*
               Dante Alighieri .... *from* The Divine Comedy ... *276*
               Grazia Deledda .... The Shoes ... *220*
               Petrarch .... Sonnet 3 (It Was That Very Day on
                                     Which the Sun) ... *300*

NORWAY.............. **Bjørnstjerne Bjørnson** .... The Father ... *44*
               Åsta Holth .... Salt ... *129*

SPAIN.................. **Vicente Aleixandre** .... On the Way to School ... *332*
               Camilo José Cela .... Traveling in the Alcarria ... *418*
               Miguel de Cervantes.............. *from* Don Quixote ... *162*
               Federico García Lorca .... The Guitar ... *340*
               Juan Ramón Jiménez .... *from* Platero and I ... *414*
               Antonio Machado .... Winter Sun ... *304*

SWEDEN.............. **Selma Lagerlöf**..................... The Rat Trap ... *64*

At the start of the semester, it will be helpful to spend ten or fifteen minutes introducing students to the anthology and its various special features. This page introduces students to four of those special features, as follows:

Map of the Contemporary World

A large, up-to-date map of the world

Preview: The Author and the World

Ask students to turn to page 2, the first of the special preview pages that precede most selections. Point out that the author biography on the left includes a small world map that pinpoints the location of the author's homeland. The Geography and Culture feature on the right provides valuable background on the setting of the story—usually the same as the author's homeland—and a more detailed map of the area.

Culture Link

Each unit ends with a Culture Link, a feature that focuses on a cultural issue relevant to the genre taught in the unit. For example, the Culture Link that follows "Myths, Folk Tales, and Epics" encourages students to think about different ways of preserving the past.

Literature and Culture Sourcebook

The Literature and Culture Sourcebook, which appears in the Student's Resources section at the back of this anthology, contains valuable cultural information about ten significant regions of the world. You may want to draw on this information when you teach the selections associated with each region.

Other Features

In addition, point out the other special features that students can find in the front and back of the book. You might direct them to the Contents (pp. v–xiv) for a listing of these features. Encourage students to turn to each feature as they find it in the Table of Contents. To enhance their familiarity with the text, you might have students complete the worksheet on Previewing the Anthology (Teacher's Classroom Resources 1, pp. 1–2).

A NOTE ON THE SPECIAL FEATURES IN THIS BOOK

People around the world share many common traits, but they also enjoy unique cultural differences. To help you better understand world literature, this book offers four special ways of getting to know the countries and peoples of the world. Each of the following features acknowledges that in order to understand literature from around the world, you have to know something about the part of the world the literature is from.

Map of the Contemporary World *(pages xxii–xxiii)*

Here you'll find an up-to-date map that you can use as a reference whenever you read a selection. This large, accurate map will provide context for the many specialized maps that you'll find throughout the book.

Preview: The Author and the World *(preceding most selections)*

Most selections in this book begin with a special Preview page. Here you'll learn where the author is from and find that country highlighted on a locator map of the world.

Then you'll find a Geography and Culture feature that gives you background on the geography, culture, and history of the country in which the selection takes place. This background will help you to immerse yourself in the piece of literature. Below this information you'll find a detailed map of the country or area.

On the facing page is a list of all the Geography and Culture features that appear on the Preview pages. Looking down the list, you should get a sense of how much the world's literature—and this book—have to offer you.

Culture Links *(at the end of each unit)*

At the end of each unit you'll be able to stand back and look at its literature from a fresh point of view in the Culture Link.

Literature and Culture Sourcebook *(pages 544–583)*

Here you'll find dynamically written and dramatically illustrated overviews of ten significant regions of the world. This section provides insights and connections between a region's literature and its culture. You'll find yourself turning to these pages time and time again as you move from one literature selection to another.

The topics covered in the Literature and Culture Sourcebook are Classical Greece and Rome, Italy, France, Spain, Latin America, Germany, Russia and Eastern Europe, China and Japan, Africa, and India and the Middle East.

GEOGRAPHY AND CULTURE FEATURES

Uganda and Buganda ... *2*

France and the Region of Normandy ... *11*

England and Its Gardens ... *18*

Poverty in Nineteenth-Century Russia ... *23*

Yorkshire and the English Class System ... *29*

Nigeria and the Ibo ... *39*

The Nation of Norway ... *44*

Calcutta and the Indian Subcontinent ... *48*

Chile and Its Coastline ... *56*

Värmland and Its Ironworks ... *63*

The Changing Face of China ... *72*

Sudan and the Nile ... *77*

The Philippine Islands ... *83*

Ireland and Its Countryside ... *91*

South Africa and Its People ... *96*

New Zealand's British Ties ... *104*

German Music Traditions ... *112*

Canada and the Dukhobors ... *120*

Finland and the Finns of Norway ... *129*

Florence and the Great Plague ... *134*

India and Its Music ... *140*

Bohemia and Prague's Little Quarter ... *145*

Mexico and Its "Lost" Villages ... *152*

Cairo and the "Old Quarter." ... *157*

Don Quixote and the Age of Chivalry ... *161*

America's Railroads ... *167*

Belgium and Paris, France ... *172*

Japan, China, and Oriental Painting ... *180*

The Region of Alsace ... *188*

The Spanish Civil War ... *193*

Colombia and Its Caribbean Coastline ... *197*

West Germany and the Postwar Era ... *204*

Algeria and Its Colonial Past ... *208*

The Island of Sardinia ... *219*

Greek and Roman Mythology ... *230*

Mexico and the Zapotecs ... *234*

Ancient Greece: The Cradle of Western Civilization ... *237*

The Palace of Versailles ... *239*

Ancient India and Its Storytelling Traditions ... *242*

Medieval Arabia and the City of Baghdad ... *246*

The Kabyles of North Africa ... *252*

Folk Tales from Germany's Black Forest ... *257*

The Trojan War ... *261*

The Founding of Rome ... *269*

Medieval Florence ... *275*

India's British Colonial Legacy ... *372*

Guinea's Economy and Culture ... *379*

The French Countryside ... *392*

Ancient Chinese Civilization ... *398*

France in the Age of Louis XIV ... *400*

Poland and Its Jewish Community ... *403*

The Soviet Union's Cultural Diversity ... *409*

Spain and Andalusia ... *413*

Spain and the Alcarria ... *417*

Kenya: Preserve of Natural Beauty ... *420*

Athens and the Peloponnesian War ... *423*

The Ivory Coast and Yamoussoukro ... *430*

Nigerian Rural Village Life ... *438*

Japan's Former Feudal Society ... *453*

France in the Seventeenth Century ... *463*

GEOGRAPHY AND CULTURE FEATURES

This page lists the titles and page numbers of all of the book's Geography and Culture features in the order in which they appear. These features, which are unique to *World Literature*, provide background on the geography, culture, and history of the countries in which the selections take place. Each feature appears as part of the preview page that precedes most of the selections and will enhance students' understanding and appreciation of the selection they are about to read. In addition, the features may be examined as a group to increase students' overall familiarity with world geography, cultures, and history.

Accompanying each Geography and Culture feature is a detailed map of the country or area in which the selection takes place. These maps can appreciably increase students' knowledge of world geography, especially if students examine the maps in conjunction with the large map of The Contemporary World (pp. xxii–xxiii).

THE CONTEMPORARY WORLD

This large, up-to-date map of the world should prove an important reference tool for students of *World Literature*. It offers a broad look at the geography of the nations whose literature students will be reading. It also clarifies the location of the nations pinpointed on the small world maps that accompany the author biographies preceding each selection. Finally, this map provides a context for the regional and national maps that appear in the Geography and Culture features throughout the anthology.

At the beginning of the semester, spend some class time going over the map to increase students' overall familiarity with world geography. Later, as students work on individual selections, encourage them to turn from smaller or more specific maps to this large world map so that they gain further insight into world geography and practice in placing individual nations and regions in their global context.

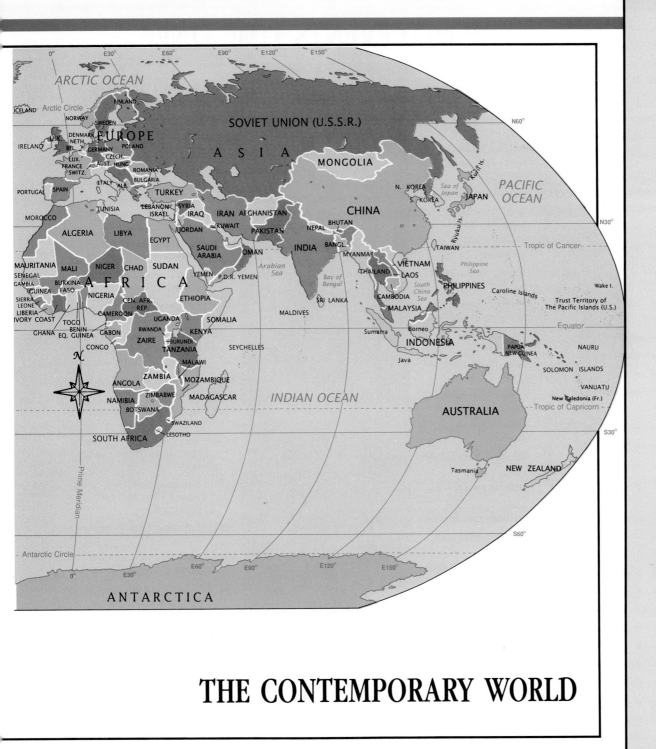

THE CONTEMPORARY WORLD

This time line, which lists major events and achievements in world history and culture, provides a broad chronological context for the world literature that students are about to read. You may wish to spend a few minutes highlighting and discussing particular entries.

Note that students' chronological perspective on world literature may be further enhanced by their examination of the outlines of regional or national literatures that appear throughout the Literature and Culture Sourcebook (pp. 544–583), the Guide to Literary Movements (pp. 584–585), and the Author Time Line (pp. 586–588).

WORLD EVENTS TIME LINE

c. 3100 B.C.	Sumeria: Invention of writing
c. 3000 B.C.	Egypt: Development of papyrus
c. 1850 B.C.	Sumeria: Oldest surviving Gilgamesh poems
c. 1193 B.C.	Asia Minor: Trojan War
c. 1100 B.C.	Israel: King David composes Psalms
c. 850 B.C.	Greece: Homer's *Iliad* composed
c. 600 B.C.	Mexico: Beginnings of Mayan civilization
c. 595 B.C.	Greece: Sappho composes lyrics
551 B.C.	China: Birth of Confucius
528 B.C.	India: Buddha begins teaching
443 B.C.	Greece: Sophocles, *Antigone*
c. 30 B.C.	Rome: Virgil begins *Aeneid*
4 B.C.	Palestine: Birth of Jesus
A.D. 5	Rome: Ovid, *Metamorphoses*
381	Rome: Christianity becomes state religion
449	Britain: Anglo-Saxon invasions
476	Fall of western Roman Empire
527	Byzantium: Justinian becomes emperor (to 565)
c. 700	England: *Beowulf* composed
c. 750	Western Europe: Beginnings of feudalism

800	Peru: Incas build Machu Picchu
1054	Europe: Roman Catholic and Eastern Orthodox churches split
1066	England: Norman Conquest
1075	Persia: Omar Khayyám writes poems
1096	Europe and Mideast: Crusades begin (to 1291)
1271	China: Marco Polo of Italy visits court of Kublai Khan
1307	Italy: Dante begins *Divine Comedy*
1325	Italy: Beginning of Renaissance
1345	Black Death kills one third of population from India to Ireland (to 1351)
1387	England: Chaucer begins *Canterbury Tales*
1428	France: Joan of Arc lifts siege of Orléans
1450	North America: Iroquois unite under Great Binding Law
1453	Germany: Gutenberg prints Bible on Europe's first printing press
1492	Columbus lands in New World
1503	Italy: Leonardo da Vinci paints *Mona Lisa*
1517	Germany: Luther posts Ninety-five Theses; Protestant Reformation begins
1519	Mexico: Cortés conquers Aztecs
1567	Brazil: Portuguese found Rio de Janeiro
1590	Italy: Galileo experiments with falling objects

xxiv *World Events Time Line*

1605	Spain: Cervantes, *Don Quixote,* Part I
1606	England: Shakespeare, *Macbeth*
1607	North America: British establish colony at Jamestown
1609	Canada: Champlain founds Québec
1659	France: Molière, *The Flying Doctor*
1675	Japan: Bashō publishes poetry
1687	England: Isaac Newton, *Principia Mathematica*
1690	India: British found Calcutta
1721	Germany: Bach composes *Brandenberg Concertos*
1760	Britain: Industrial Revolution begins
1776	America: Independence declared
1789	France: Bastille stormed; revolution begins
1798	England: Wordsworth and Coleridge, *Lyrical Ballads*
1808	Germany: Goethe, *Faust,* Part I
1815	Belgium: French emperor Napoleon defeated at Waterloo
1823	Germany: Beethoven, Symphony No. 9
1831	America: Edgar Allan Poe, *Poems*
1837	Britain: Victoria becomes queen
1848	Belgium: Marx and Engels, *Communist Manifesto*
1856	France: Flaubert, *Madame Bovary*
1859	England: Charles Darwin, *On the Origin of Species*
1861	France: Pasteur proposes theory of germs

1876	America: Alexander Graham Bell patents telephone
1889	Germany: Daimler builds first practical automobile
1900	Austria: Sigmund Freud, *Interpretation of Dreams*
1903	America: Wright brothers build first successful airplane
1905	Switzerland: Einstein proposes theory of relativity
1907	Germany: Rilke, *New Poems*
1913	India: Tagore wins Nobel Prize for Literature
1914	World War I begins (to 1918)
1917	Russian Revolution
1924	Chile: Pablo Neruda, *Twenty Poems*
1925	Austria: Franz Kafka, *The Trial* Britain: Baird transmits first television broadcasts
1939	World War II begins (to 1945)
1945	Chile's Gabriela Mistral wins Nobel Prize for Literature
1947	India and Pakistan gain independence
1949	China: People's Republic established
1960	Argentina: Jorge Luis Borges, *El hacedor (Dreamtigers)*
1969	America's *Apollo 11* lands on moon
1982	Colombia's Gabriel García Márquez wins Nobel Prize for Literature
1987	America: Brodsky wins Nobel Prize for Literature
1989	Spain's Camilo José Cela wins Nobel Prize for Literature
1990	East Germany and West Germany vote for unification

World Events Time Line **XXV**

This essay, which is written on a nonscholarly level, discusses the nature of translating a piece of literature and the special problems that arise in trying to convert an author's ideas and style from one language to another.

At the start of the semester, have students read and discuss the essay, and make sure they understand that the act of translation transforms a text to some degree. To stress that much of the literature in the anthology has been translated from its original language, you might have students thumb through the text and note the translator's credit that appears under the title of translated selections.

You may also use this essay in conjunction with the Special Feature on Translation (pp. 340–343), which asks students to compare the original Spanish-language version and three different English translations of "The Guitar" by Federico García Lorca, and The Original Language sections in the Literature and Culture Sourcebook (pp. 544–583), which present passages from various languages together with translations.

READING LITERATURE IN TRANSLATION

Almost all the literary works in this book are translations. From ancient times to the present, translation has enabled individuals from all over the world to understand one another. Translators make everything from political meetings and current events to television shows and fashion trends available to people who speak different languages. Whether we talk of ancient Greek translated into Latin by the Romans, or present-day Japanese and Swahili translated into English, Spanish, and Hebrew, translation allows the people of the world to understand one another's lives, values, and traditions.

The act of translating has been compared to painting. Just as the painter cannot reproduce an actual house on a canvas, the translator cannot reproduce a description of a house when moving from one language into another. The painter can use color and form to create an image that looks like a house, but that image will never include all the details of the original, and the house on the canvas will always be two-dimensional, not three-dimensional. Like the painter, the translator can never reproduce the full experience of an original piece of writing. Nevertheless, just as the painter tries to capture the essence of the house, the translator tries to capture the essence of the original literature.

In general, prose is easier to translate than poetry. While grammatical structure and vocabulary differ from language to language, the prose translator attempts to convey the meaning and mood of the original, as well as the writer's use of language. Though the translated description of the path leading up to the house will not be exactly the same as the original description, the translator can incorporate details from the original so that the reader will have a fairly accurate picture and understanding of the writer's intentions. In poetry, however, a translator must deal with many other elements. The essential qualities of poetry—rhyme, meter, sound, and form—are extremely difficult, and sometimes impossible, to imitate across languages.

When you think about translation, it is helpful to remember that one translator will translate a piece of literature differently from another translator. Each translator's interpretation of the original text will almost always come through in his or her translation. The following three translations of the first sentence of Miguel de Cervantes' *Don Quixote* show some of the differences that can exist among the works of several translators.

ORIGINAL SPANISH
En un lugar de la Mancha, de cuyo nombre no quiero acordarme, no ha mucho tiempo que vivía un hidalgo de los de lanza en astillero, adarga antigua, rocín flaco y galgo corredor.

TRANSLATIONS
In a certain corner of la Mancha, the name of which I do not choose to remember, there lately lived one of those country gentlemen, who adorn their halls with a rusty lance and worm-eaten target, and ride forth on the skeleton of a horse, to course with a sort of starved greyhound.

—translated by Tobias Smollett

At a village of La Mancha, whose name I do not wish to remember, there lived a little while ago one of those gentlemen who are wont to keep a lance in the rack, an old buckler, a lean horse and a swift greyhound.

—translated by Walter Starkie

In a village of La Mancha the name of which I have no desire to recall, there lived not so long ago one of those gentlemen who always have a lance in the rack, an ancient buckler, a skinny nag, and a greyhound for the chase.

—translated by Samuel Putnam

Each translator's choice of vocabulary and grammatical structures reflects the personal preference of the translator as well as the time in which the translator wrote. Words such as "wont," "buckler," and "nag" may be part of the translator's familiar vocabulary or may be the translator's way of bringing the reader closer to the time of Cervantes' original. Notice that only Smollett uses the words "corner" and "starved" in his translation. If the translations of one sentence can differ, imagine how the translations of an entire novel, play, or epic poem can vary.

Robert Fitzgerald, translator of the *Odyssey* by Homer, addressed the subject of translating this great work from ancient Greek into English: "It can no more be translated into English than rhododendron can be translated into dogwood. You must learn Greek if you want to experience Homer, just as you must go to the Acropolis and look at it if you want to experience the Parthenon." In his statement Fitzgerald points out that the original beauty in a work of literature cannot be translated into another language. What can happen, however, is that through the act of translation, the original work can be transformed, and in that transformation the original can acquire a new and different kind of beauty through the sounds of another language. The wealth of literature offered and the beauty sustained within each transformed text is well worth the sacrifice made in the act of translation.

Reading Literature in Translation **xxvii**

Sunday Afternoon on the Island of La Grande Jatte is one of seven major works that Georges Seurat (1859–1891) painted in the style called Pointillism. He used the tip of his brush to apply countless dots of paint in a formulaic matrix of color. Seurat painstakingly applied varying combinations of primary colors (red, yellow, and blue) and secondary colors (orange, green, and violet) to create a rich brocade of statuesque images. The resulting painting presents a stylized tableau of human forms awaiting a viewer's imagination to bring it to life.

■ Ask students to fill in the lives of some of the characters in Seurat's painting. What do they see beyond the shore? What is it about this small island that seems to fill these people with a feeling of quiet contemplation? Is it the artist who creates this feeling?

Sunday Afternoon on the Island of La Grande Jatte, 1884–1886, Georges Seurat.

xxviii   *The Short Story*

THE SHORT STORY

I *think that a writer's purpose is to make sense of life.*
—NADINE GORDIMER
South Africa

STORIES ABOUT LIFE'S SURPRISES

STORIES ABOUT HUMAN RELATIONSHIPS

STORIES ABOUT GROWING UP

STORIES ABOUT PERSONAL VALUES

STORIES ABOUT REALITY AND FANTASY

STORIES ABOUT CULTURES AND CONFLICTS

Ask students what they like to read. Encourage them to explain why they like fiction better than poetry, for instance, or nonfiction better than fiction. Help them define fiction as prose in which situations and characters are invented by the writer. Then explain that a short story is a brief work of fiction that usually can be read in a single sitting.

Note that in the upcoming unit students will be reading short stories from all over the world. Some of the stories are very old—for example, "Federigo's Falcon" by the Italian Giovanni Boccaccio, one of the world's first short story writers. Many of the other stories come from our own century and help display the diversity of cultures that constitute today's world.

Point out that the unit is divided into six thematic groupings:

- Stories About Life's Surprises
- Stories About Human Relationships
- Stories About Growing Up
- Stories About Personal Values
- Stories About Reality and Fantasy
- Stories About Cultures and Conflicts

By exploring these universal concerns and comparing and contrasting selections, students will see that while the peoples of the world share many ideas and traditions, they also have unique qualities that enhance and typify their individual cultures.

PREVIEW: THE AUTHOR AND THE WORLD

Barbara Kimenye

(born 1940)

Uganda

Journalist and fiction writer Barbara Kimenye is famous throughout East Africa for her columns published in the paper *Uganda Nation.* Born in Uganda, Kimenye [kə men′ yā] worked as a private secretary for the king of Buganda. Located on the northern shore of Lake Victoria, Buganda is the traditional homeland of the Ganda people and was once Uganda's largest tribal kingdom.

Kalasanda, her best known work of fiction, is a series of interconnected stories titled after a Buganda village so small that strangers "often travel straight through Kalasanda without realizing it, since at no place is there any indication that the village as such exists."

Kalasanda was published in 1965; a year later came a sequel, *Kalasanda Revisited.* Shortly thereafter, Kimenye moved first to Nairobi, Kenya, and then to London, England. There Kimenye still writes, although she has also been employed as a social worker since 1974. She has written many works for children, including a series of books about an adventurous young boy named Moses.

Uganda and Buganda

Located in East Africa, Uganda is a small but densely populated agricultural nation. It was a British colony for many decades, and English is widely spoken there. In fact, because Ugandans descend from various African tribes that each speak a different language, English, which is more commonly known, is Uganda's official language. Barbara Kimenye, a native Ugandan, writes in English.

After Uganda won independence from Great Britain in 1962, the new nation was divided into districts along tribal lines. The largest and most powerful district was the ancient tribal kingdom of Buganda, homeland of the Ganda tribe and location of the village of Kalasanda, where "The Winner" takes place. Until 1967, when Uganda's regional districts were abolished, Buganda had its own parliament and was allowed to keep its tribal king. "The Winner" takes place before 1967, when Buganda was still a district.

See LITERATURE AND CULTURE SOURCEBOOK: Africa

This witty story, set in Uganda, relates the tribulations of Pius Ndawula, a bachelor in his sixties. When Pius wins the football pools, his tiny home is swamped by relatives hoping for money. The capable Sarah seems to take over, and Pius at first suspects her of fortune hunting. He later comes to admire her, and the story reverses our expectation that Pius will be a victim of his own good fortune.

LITERARY SKILLS FOR THIS SELECTION

- plot
- foreshadowing
- characterization

THEMES IN THIS SELECTION

- life's surprises: coping with good fortune
- marriage and companionship
- exploiting others

LESSON OBJECTIVES

1. to recognize plot structure
2. to identify foreshadowing
3. to write a response to a story

Teacher's Classroom Resources 1

- Teaching Notes 15
- Prereading Vocabulary 16
- Reading Guide 17
- Check Test 18
- Responding to World Cultures 19
- Literary Focus: Plot; Foreshadowing 20
- Writing Process Guide: Writing a Response to a Story 21
- Grammar in Literature: Writing with Vivid Verbs 22
- Selection Test 23

TEACHING STUDENTS OF DIFFERENT ABILITIES

- **For less advanced students:** After students read the first few sentences, ask them to predict whether Pius will be happy at the story's end. Have students complete the Reading Guide for this selection.
- **For more advanced students:** Ask students to identify the mixture of cultures in this story, for example, African and Christian names and the combination of tribal customs and modern technology.

Small-Town Life Around the World

Like many African nations Uganda is overwhelmingly rural; only 8 percent of the population live in cities. Most Ugandans, like those depicted in this story, live on farms or in small villages.
- Ask students to describe life in a small town. What do small towns have in common? (Students might mention neighborliness, a slower pace, and limited cultural activities.)

Barbara Kimenye

The Winner

When Pius Ndawula[1] won the football pools,[2] overnight he seemed to become the most popular man in Buganda.[3] Hosts of relatives converged upon him from the four corners of the kingdom: cousins and uncles, of whose existence he had never before been aware, turned up in Kalasanda by the bus-load, together with crowds of individuals who, despite their down-trodden appearance, assured Pius that they, and they alone, were capable of seeing that his money was properly invested—preferably in their own particular business. Also lurking around Pius's unpretentious mud hut were newspaper reporters, slick young men weighed down with cameras, and sporting loud, check caps or trilbies, worn at a consciously jaunty angle, and serious young men from Radio Uganda, who were anxious to record Pius's delight at his astonishing luck for the general edification of the Uganda listening public.

The rest of Kalasanda were so taken by surprise that they could only call and briefly congratulate Pius before being elbowed out of the way by his more garrulous relations. All, that is to say, except Pius's greatest friend, Salongo, the custodian of the Ssabalangira's tomb.[4] He came and planted himself firmly in the house, and nobody attempted to move him. Almost blind and very lame, he had tottered out with the aid of a stout stick. Just to see him arrive had caused a minor sensation in the village for he hadn't left the tomb for years, but recognizing at last a chance to house the Ssabalangira's remains in a state befitting his former glory, made the slow, tortuous journey worthwhile to Salongo.

Nantondo hung about long enough to have her picture taken with Pius. Or rather she managed to slip beside him just as the cameras clicked and so it was that every Uganda newspaper, on the following day, carried a front-page photograph of "Mr. Pius Ndawula and his happy wife," a caption that caused Pius to shake with rage and threaten legal proceedings, but over which Nantondo gloated as she proudly showed it to everybody she visited.

"Tell us, Mr. Ndawula, what do you intend to do with all the money you have won?"

"Tell us, Mr. Ndawula, how often have you completed the pools coupon?"

"Tell us . . . Tell us . . . Tell us . . ."

Pius's head was reeling under this bombardment of questions, and he was even more confused by Salongo's constant nudging and muttered advice to "Say nothing!" Nor did the relatives make things easier. Their persistent clamoring for his attention, and the way they kept shoving their children under his nose, made it impossible for him to think, let alone talk.

It isn't at all easy, when you have lived for sixty-five years in complete obscurity, to adjust yourself in a matter of hours to the role of a celebrity, and the strain was beginning to tell.

Behind the hut—Pius had no proper kitchen—gallons of tea were being boiled, whilst several of the female cousins were employed in ruthlessly hacking down the bunches of *matoke*[5]

---

1. **Ndawula** [n də wōō'lə]
2. **football pools:** popular gambling venture based on soccer scores.
3. **Buganda** [bōō gän'də]: former kingdom of the Ganda tribe and a province of Uganda at the time the story takes place. (See the Geography and Culture feature that precedes the story.)
4. **Ssabalangira's** [sä bä läng gē'rəz] **tomb:** tomb maintained to honor a local hero said to have been an adviser of Buganda's early kings.

5. *matoke* [mə tō'kā]: fruit of the plantain, a type of banana tree, often cooked into a traditional dish widely eaten in Buganda.

The Winner 3

MOTIVATION: PRIOR KNOWLEDGE

Ask students to recall a movie or story in which someone unexpectedly became wealthy. How did others react? Have students consider why people often change under such circumstances.

PAGE SUMMARY: AT A GLANCE

■ Pius Ndawula wins the football pools.
■ People seeking funds descend on him.
■ Pius is bewildered by all the activity and attention.

IN THE GLOSSARY

■ unpretentious: modest
■ edification: enlightenment
■ garrulous: talkative
■ clamoring: crying out
■ obscurity: lack of fame

1 TEACHING PLOT: EXPOSITION

Point out that this long sentence comically describes the actions at the opening of the story, as people flock to Pius' hut. Ask what important information we learn at the end of the sentence. (All of the people want money.)

2 TEACHING CHARACTERIZATION

Ask students what sort of person they think Salongo is. Help them see that he is something of a recluse but is just as self-serving as Pius' other visitors.

CRITICAL THINKING: GUIDED READING QUESTIONS

LITERAL

1a. How does each of Pius' relatives want Pius to invest his money? (They want him to invest in their own business.)

2a. How has Pius lived his sixty-five years? (He has lived in complete obscurity.)

INFERENTIAL

1b. What opinion do you think the author wants us to have of these relatives? (She wants us to see them as opportunistic and insincere.)

2b. How do you predict Pius will handle the change from obscurity to celebrity? (Many students will suggest that Pius will be bewildered and perhaps frightened by the change. Some may feel that he will be exploited by a fortune seeker.)

- Sarah, who claims to be a cousin, says Pius needs a woman in his house.
- Pius is wary of Sarah.
- A flashback reveals how Pius first heard of his good fortune.
- Pius is touched at first by people's interest but is soon overrun by clamoring relatives.
- A young man tries to interview Pius.

IN THE GLOSSARY

- veranda: open porch
- effusively: emotionally

3 TEACHING PLOT: FORESHADOWING

Call attention to the way Sarah is singled out from among the other women at the hut. What might this foreshadow? (Sarah will prove important to the plot.)

4 TEACHING TONE

Note that the narrator seems to use the old men's words without actually quoting them. This indirect discourse creates a gently mocking tone in which the narrator reports but does not necessarily agree with Pius and Salongo's fussy, old-fashioned disapproval.

5 CULTURAL BACKGROUND

Pius' age sets him apart among Ugandans. Only 4 percent of Uganda's population is over sixty, compared with 16 percent in America. The relative rarity of older Ugandans may in part explain Pius' friendship with Salongo, probably one of the few neighborhood men over sixty.

6 TEACHING SETTING

Ask students what picture the narrator creates by likening Pius' hut to a "political meeting." (The comparison helps us see the unruly crowds, hear the argument and hubbub, and smell the stale cigarette smoke. The general impression is oppressive.)

from his meager plantains, to cook for everybody. One woman, she had introduced herself as Cousin Sarah, discovered Pius's hidden store of banana beer, and dished it out to all and sundry as though it were her own. Pius had become very wary of Cousin Sarah. He didn't like the way in which she kept loudly remarking that he needed a woman about the place, and he was even more seriously alarmed when suddenly Salongo gave him a painful dig in the ribs and muttered, "You'll have to watch that one—she's a sticker!"

Everybody who came wanted to see the telegram that announced Pius's win. When it arrived at the Ggombolola Headquarters,[6] Musizi had brought it personally, delighted to be the bearer of such good tidings. At Pius's request, he had gone straightaway to tell Salongo, and then back to his office to send an acknowledgment on behalf of Pius to the pools firm, leaving the old man to dream rosy dreams. An extension of his small coffee *shamba*,[7] a new roof on his house— or maybe an entirely new house, concrete blocks this time, with a veranda, perhaps. Then there were hens. Salongo always said there was money in hens these days, now that the women ate eggs and chicken: not that either of them agreed with the practice. Say what you liked, women eating chicken and eggs were fairly asking to be infertile. That woman Welfare Officer who came snooping occasionally tried to say it was all nonsense, that chicken meat and eggs made bigger and better babies. Well, they might look bigger and better, but nobody could deny that they were fewer, which only goes to show.

But it is surprising how news leaks out in Africa. Perhaps the newspapers have contacts in the pools offices. Anyway, before the telegram actually reached Pius, there was a small an-

nouncement in all the local papers, and Pius was still quietly lost in his dream when the first batch of visitors arrived. At first he was at a loss to understand what was happening. People he hadn't seen for years and only recognized with difficulty fell upon him with cries of joy. "Cousin Pius, the family are delighted." "Cousin Pius, why have you not visited us all this time?"

Pius was pleased to see his nearest and dearest gathered around him. It warmed his old heart once more to find himself in the bosom of his family, and he welcomed them effusively. The second crowd to arrive were no less well-received, but there was a marked coolness on the part of the forerunners.

However, as time went by, and the flood of strange faces gained momentum, Pius's *shamba* began to resemble a political meeting. All to be seen from the door of the house were white *kanzus*[8] and brilliant *busutis*,[9] and the house itself was full of people and cigarette smoke.

The precious telegram was passed from hand to hand until it was reduced to a limp fragment of paper with the lettering partly obliterated, not that it mattered very much, for only a few members of the company could read English.

"Now, Mr. Ndawula, we are ready to take the recording." The speaker was a slight young man wearing a check shirt. "I shall ask you a few questions, and you simply answer me in your normal voice." Pius looked at the leather box with its two revolving spools, and licked his lips.

"Say nothing," came a hoarse whisper from Salongo. The young man steadfastly ignored him and went ahead in his best B.B.C. manner.[10]

"Well, Mr. Ndawula, first of all let me con-

---

6. **Ggombolola** [gom bə lō′lə] **Headquarters:** local administrative headquarters. A *ggombolola* is similar to a township in the United States.
7. **coffee shamba:** piece of cultivated land used for growing coffee, the chief cash crop of Uganda.

---

8. *kanzus:* ankle-length cotton garments traditionally worn by males in Buganda.
9. *busutis:* [boo soo′tēz]: long cotton dresses traditionally worn by females in Buganda. By custom the men's garments were white, while the women's were multicolored.
10. **best B.B.C. manner:** imitating the well-spoken, professional style of a broadcaster for B.B.C., the British Broadcasting Corporation.

4 *The Short Story*

CRITICAL THINKING: GUIDED READING QUESTIONS

LITERAL

1a. What does Salongo say about Sarah? ("You'll have to watch that one—she's a sticker!")

2a. How do the earliest arrivals at Pius' hut react to the second crowd that comes? (They react coolly.)

INFERENTIAL

1b. What does Salongo mean? (He probably means that Sarah is after Pius' fortune.)

2b. Why do the earliest arrivals react in this way? (They do not want to compete with more people for Pius' money.)

gratulate you on your winning the pools. Would you like to tell our listeners what it feels like to suddenly find oneself rich?" There was an uncomfortable pause, during which Pius stared as if mesmerized at the racing spools and the young man tried frantically to cover the gap by asking, "I mean, have you any plans for the future?" Pius swallowed audibly, and opened his mouth to say something, but shut it again when Salongo growled, "Tell him nothing."

7 The young man snapped off the machine, shaking his head in exasperation. "Look here, Sir, all I want you to do is say something—I'm not asking you to make a speech! Now, I'll tell you what. I shall ask you again what it feels like to suddenly come into money, and you say

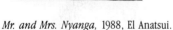
Mr. and Mrs. Nyanga, 1988, El Anatsui.

The Winner **5**

PAGE SUMMARY: AT A GLANCE

- Whenever the interviewer asks a question, Salongo tells Pius, "Say nothing."
- The interviewer becomes impatient with Pius.

7 READING SKILL: PREDICTING OUTCOMES

Ask students to predict whether Pius will be able to give the reporter a satisfactory answer. (Most likely Pius will remain tongue-tied because he is cowed by Salongo.)

ART AND LITERATURE

Born in Ghana, El Anatsui has spent most of his artistic career working in Nigeria. Drawing on his African heritage, in which ritual objects represent deities and mythical ancestors, Anatsui also brings the Western world's focus on individuality and personal creativity into his own art. In this wood carving, *Mr. and Mrs. Nyanga,* he carved curved wood, cut it into small sections, coated each with an oily resin, and then pieced them together in a different order, like a totem pole.

- After they have finished the story, ask students what the use of Anatsui's sculpture as an illustration for this story might hint about the story's outcome. (Pius' windfall might win him a bride.)

CRITICAL THINKING: GUIDED READING QUESTIONS

LITERAL

1a. What does Pius do when Salongo orders him to tell the interviewer nothing? (He shuts his mouth.)

INFERENTIAL

1b. Why do you think Pius reacts in this way? (He is easily intimidated and manipulated by Salongo, whom he respects a great deal, and he is dazzled by the sudden attention from the media.)

- Pius parrots what the interviewer says.
- Cousin Sarah steps in and gives the interview.
- Pius wearies of his numerous guests—in particular, of Sarah.
- His friends Yosefu Mukasa and Kibuka arrive and are alarmed at Pius' exhaustion.

IN THE GLOSSARY

- incredulity: disbelief

8 TEACHING TONE

Ask students whether the narrator is making fun of Pius here or whether she seems sympathetic toward him. Whichever way they feel, students should see that Pius' parroting of the reporter's words is both comic and touching, for it shows that he wants to please but is terribly unsure of himself.

9 TEACHING CHARACTERIZATION

Remind students that Sarah is the "sticker," according to Salongo. Ask students what impression they have of Sarah from her "interview." (She seems commanding, very sure of herself in contrast with Pius, and more protective of Pius than anyone else who has appeared so far.)

10 CRITICAL THINKING: LOGICAL REASONING

Ask students what they can deduce about Pius' life style from the fact that he has only three plates in his household. (His life is spare and simple, and he is unused to many visitors.) How is great wealth going to fit into such a life? (Pius will not become accustomed to it easily.)

11 TEACHING CHARACTERIZATION

Help students see that Yosefu Mukasa and Kibuka are different from Pius' other visitors, for they seem to care only about their friend's well-being.

---

something like 'It was a wonderful surprise, and naturally I feel very pleased'—and will you ask your friend not to interrupt! Got it? O.K., off we go."

The machine was again switched on, and the man brightly put his question, "Now Mr. Ndawula, what does it feel like to win the **8** pools?" Pius swallowed, then quickly chanted in a voice all off key, "It was a wonderful surprise and naturally I feel very happy and will you ask your friend not to interrupt!"

Tears came to the young man's eyes. This happened to be his first assignment as a radio interviewer, and it looked like being his last. He switched off the machine and gazed sadly into space. At that moment, Cousin Sarah caught sight of him. "Perhaps I can help you," she said. "I am Mr. Ndawula's cousin." She made this pronouncement in a manner that suggested Pius had no other. The young man brightened considerably. "Well, Madam, if you could tell me something about Mr. Ndawula's plans, I would be most grateful."

9 Cousin Sarah folded her arms across her imposing bosom, and when the machine again started up, she was off. Yes, Mr. Ndawula was very happy about the money. No, she didn't think he had any definite plans on how to spend it—with all these people about, he didn't have time to think. Yes, Mr. Ndawula lived completely alone, but she was prepared to stay and look after him for as long as he needed her. (Here a significant glance passed between the other women in the room, who clicked their teeth and let out long "Eeeeeehs!" of incredulity.) Yes, she believed she was Mr. Ndawula's nearest living relative by marriage. . . .

Pius listened to this tirade with growing horror, whilst Salongo frantically nudged him and whispered, "There! what did I tell you? That woman's a sticker!"

10 Around three in the afternoon, *matoke* and tea were served, the *matoke* on wide, fresh plantain leaves, since Pius only owned three plates,

and the tea in anything handy—tin-cans, jars, etc., because he was short of cups, too. Pius ate very little, but he was glad of the tea. He had shaken hands so much that his arm ached, and he was tired of the chatter and of the comings and goings in his house of all these strangers. Most of all he was tired of Cousin Sarah, who insisted on treating him like an idiot invalid. She kept everybody else at bay, as far as she possibly could, and when one woman plonked a sticky, fat baby on his lap, Cousin Sarah dragged the child away as though it were infectious. Naturally, a few cross words were exchanged but by this time Pius was past caring.

11 Yosefu Mukasa and Kibuka called in the early evening, when some of the relatives were departing with effusive promises to come again tomorrow. They were both alarmed at the weariness they saw in Pius's face. The old man looked utterly worn out, his skin gray and sickly. Also, they were a bit taken aback by the presence of Cousin Sarah, who pressed them to take tea and behaved in every respect as though she were mistress of the house. "I believe my late husband knew you very well, Sir," she told Yosefu. "He used to be a Miruka Chief[11] in Buyaga County. His name was Kivumbi."

"Ah, yes," Yosefu replied, "I remember Kivumbi very well indeed. We often hunted together. I was sorry to hear of his death. He was a good man." Cousin Sarah shrugged her shoulders, "Yes, he was a good man. But what the Lord giveth, the Lord taketh away." Thus was the late Kivumbi dismissed from the conversation.

Hearing all this enabled Pius to define the exact relationship between himself and Cousin Sarah, and even by Kiganda standards[12] it was virtually non-existent, for the late Kivumbi had been the stepson of one of Pius's cousins.

---

11. **Miruka** [mə rōō′kə] **Chief:** local village chief.
12. **Kiganda standards:** the standards of the Ganda tribe. *Ki-* is a prefix meaning "type."

6 *The Short Story*

CRITICAL THINKING: GUIDED READING QUESTIONS

LITERAL

1a. What is Pius' reaction to Sarah's "tirade" during the interview? (He becomes increasingly horrified.)

2a. When Yosefu Mukasa and Kibuka arrive in the evening, what is their response to what they see? (They are alarmed at Pius' weariness.)

INFERENTIAL

1b. Why do you think Pius reacts in this way? (He is afraid that Sarah is taking over his life, especially when she says she is prepared to "look after him.")

2b. How do these two friends differ from Pius' other visitors? (They are not interested in his money and are concerned only with his well-being.)

"Your stroke of luck seems to have exhausted you, Pius," Kibuka remarked, when he and Yosefu were seated on the rough wooden chairs brought forth by Cousin Sarah.

12 Salongo glared at the world in general and snarled, "Of course he is exhausted! Who wouldn't be with all this carrion collected to pick his bones?" Pius hushed him as one would a child. "No, no, Salongo. It is quite natural that my family should gather round me at a time like this. Only I fear I am perhaps a little too old for all this excitement." Salongo spat expertly through the open doorway, narrowly missing a group of guests who were on their way out, and said, "That woman doesn't think he's too old. She's out to catch him. I've seen her type elsewhere."

13 Yosefu's mouth quirked with amusement at the thought that "elsewhere" could only mean the Ssabalangira's tomb, which Salongo had guarded for the better part of his adult life. "Well, she's a fine woman," he remarked. "But see here, Pius, don't be offended by my proposal, but wouldn't it be better if you came and stayed with us at Mutunda for tonight? Miriamu would love to have you, and you look as though you need a good night's rest, which you wouldn't get here, because those relatives of yours outside are preparing a fire and are ready to dance the night away."

"I think that's a wonderful idea!" cried Cousin Sarah, bouncing in to remove the teacups. "You go with Mr. Mukasa, Cousin Pius. The change will do you as much good as the rest. And don't worry about your home—I shall stay here and look after things." Pius hesitated. "Well, I think I shall be all right here—I don't like to give Miriamu any extra work. . . ."

Salongo muttered, "Go to Yosefu's. You don't want to be left alone in the house with that woman—there is no knowing what she might get up to. . . ."

"I'll pack a few things for you, Pius." Cousin Sarah bustled off before anything more could be said, pausing only long enough to give Salongo a look that spoke volumes.

14 So Pius found himself being driven away to Mutunda in Yosefu's car, enjoying the pleasant sensation of not having to bother about a thing. Salongo too had been given a lift to as near the tomb as the car could travel, and his wizened old face was contorted into an irregular smile, for Pius had promised to help him build a new house for the Ssabalangira. For him the day had been well spent, despite Cousin Sarah.

Pius spent an enjoyable evening with the Mukasas. They had a well-cooked supper, followed by a glass of cool beer as they sat back and listened to the local news on the radio. Pius had so far relaxed as to modestly tell the Mukasas that he had been interviewed by Radio Uganda that morning, and when Radio Newsreel was announced, they waited breathlessly to hear his voice. But instead of Pius, Cousin Sarah's came booming over the air. Until that moment, the old man had completely forgotten the incident of the tape-recording. In fact he had almost forgotten Cousin Sarah. Now it all came back to him with a shiver of apprehension. Salongo was right. That woman did mean business. It was a chilling thought. However, it didn't cause him to lose any sleep. He slept like a cherub that night, as if he hadn't a care in the world.

Because he looked so refreshed the following morning, Miriamu insisted on keeping him at Mutunda for another day. "I know you feel better, but after seeing you yesterday, I think a little holiday with us will do you good. Go home tomorrow, when the excitement has died down a bit," she advised.

Soon after lunch, as Pius was taking a nap in a chair on the veranda, Musizi drove up in the Landrover, with Cousin Sarah by his side. 15 Miriamu came out to greet them, barely disguising her curiosity about the comely woman of whom she had heard so much. The two women sized each other up and decided to be friends.

Meanwhile, Musizi approached the old man.

The Winner **7**

- Salongo says that Sarah is out to "catch" Pius.
- Yosefu Mukasa invites Pius to stay at his home, away from the clamor.
- Pius enjoys staying at Yosefu's, except when he hears Sarah's "interview" on the radio.
- On Pius' second day at Yosefu's, Sarah arrives with Musizi, a local government representative.

IN THE GLOSSARY

- cherub: innocent child

12 TEACHING CHARACTERIZATION

Help students note the contrast between Pius' innocent, generous nature and Salongo's bitter, suspicious one.

13 TEACHING STUDENTS OF LIMITED ENGLISH PROFICIENCY

Expressions such as *the better part of his adult life* are idioms that students less proficient in English may have trouble interpreting. Some other idioms in this story are *to dance the night away, a look that spoke volumes, did mean business,* and *sized each other up.* Ask students to define these idioms, and have them look for others in the selection.

14 CULTURAL BACKGROUND

The fact that Yosefu has an automobile and (as mentioned later) a radio suggests that he is relatively prosperous.

15 TEACHING PLOT: FORESHADOWING

Ask students what they make of the fact that Yosefu's kind wife, Miriamu, decides she likes Sarah. (It hints that we, too, are going to like Sarah, since Miriamu is a positive character who has Pius' interests at heart.)

CRITICAL THINKING: GUIDED READING QUESTIONS

LITERAL

1a. Why is Salongo's face "contorted into an irregular smile" when he leaves Pius' hut? (Pius promised to help build a new tomb for the Ssabalangira.)

2a. How does Pius feel when he hears Sarah's interview, and how does he sleep that night? (He has a "shiver of apprehension"; he sleeps like a "cherub.")

INFERENTIAL

1b. What does Salongo's reaction suggest about his feelings for Pius? (Salongo is chiefly interested in what he can get from his friend.)

2b. Why do you think Pius manages to sleep well that night despite his apprehension? (He is exhausted, and the idea of being taken care of, even by Sarah, is perhaps not as disturbing as it seemed at first.)

- Musizi informs Pius that he will win only a thousand shillings from the pools, not seventeen thousand pounds.
- Pius says he does not need the larger sum at his age.
- Sarah agrees and offers to arrange the cleanup of Pius' home.
- When Pius returns home, the other relatives have left, and he and Sarah discuss plans for his winnings.

16 TEACHING PLOT: CLIMAX

Help students see that the story takes its most significant turn here. Pius' relief at having won only a thousand shillings suggests that his life will return to normal. The fortune hunters will now leave him alone. But what will Sarah do?

17 TEACHING CHARACTERIZATION

Ask students what Sarah's reaction reveals. (Since she is not upset, she must not be after Pius' fortune.)

18 GRAMMAR IN LITERATURE

Point out the author's use of adverbs of manner, such as *weakly* and (also in this column) *energetically, merely,* and *optimistically,* to clarify her meaning. Ask students to point out other telling adverbs of manner. (Examples include *expertly, modestly,* and *breathlessly* on page 7 and *expectantly* on this page.)

"Sit down, son." Pius waved him to a chair at his side. "Miriamu feeds me so well, it's all I can do to keep awake."

"I am glad you are having a rest, Sir," Musizi fumbled in the pocket of his jacket. "There is another telegram for you. Shall I read it?" The old man sat up expectantly and said, "If you'll be so kind."

Musizi first read the telegram in silence, then he looked at Pius and commented, "Well, Sir, I'm afraid it isn't good news."

"Not good news? Has anybody died?"

Musizi smiled. "Well, no. It isn't really as bad as that. The thing is the pools firm say they have discovered that the prize money has to be shared among three hundred other people."

Pius was stunned. Eventually he murmured, "Tell me, how much does it mean I shall get?"

16 "Three hundred into seventeen thousand pounds won't give you much over a thousand shillings."[13]

To Musizi's amazement, Pius sat back and chuckled. "More than a thousand shillings!" he said. "That is a lot of money!"

"But it's not, when you expected so much more!"

"I agree. And yet, son, what would I have done with all those thousands of pounds? I am getting past the age when I need a lot."

Miriamu brought a mat onto the veranda and she and Cousin Sarah made themselves comfortable near the men, whilst Musizi explained what had happened. "What a disappointment," cried

17 Miriamu, but Cousin Sarah sniffed and said, "I agree with Cousin Pius. He wouldn't know what to do with seventeen thousand pounds, and the family would be hanging round his neck for ever more."

At mention of Pius's family, Musizi frowned, "I should warn you, Sir, those relatives of yours have made a terrific mess of your *shamba*— your plantains have been stripped—and Mrs.

13. **pounds . . . shillings:** units of money in Uganda.

Kivumbi here," nodding at Sarah, "was only just in time to prevent them digging up your sweet potatoes."

"Yes, Cousin Pius," added Sarah, "it will take us some time to put that *shamba* back in order. They've trodden down a whole bed of young beans."

18 "Oh, dear," said Pius weakly. "That is dreadful news."

"Don't worry. They will soon disappear when I tell them there is no money and then I shall send for a couple of my grandsons to come and help us do some replanting." Pius could not but help admire the way Sarah took things in her stride. Musizi rose from his chair. "I'm afraid I can't stay any longer, so I will go now and clear the crowd, and see you tomorrow to take you home." He and Sarah climbed back into the Landrover and Sarah waved energetically until the house was out of sight.

"Your cousin is a fine woman," Miriamu told Pius before going indoors. Pius merely grunted, but for some odd reason he felt the remark to be a compliment to himself.

All was quiet at Pius's house when Musizi brought him home next day. He saw at once that his *shamba* was well nigh wrecked, but his drooping spirits quickly revived when Sarah placed a mug of steaming tea before him, and sat on a mat at his feet, explaining optimistically how matters could be remedied. Bit by bit he began telling her what he had planned to do with the prize money, ending with: "Of course, I shan't be able to do everything now, especially since I promised Salongo something for the tomb."

Sarah poured some more tea and said, "Well, I think the roof should have priority. I noticed last night that there are several leaks. And whilst we're about it, it would be a good idea to build another room on and a small outside kitchen. Mud and wattle is cheap enough, and then the whole place can be plastered. You can still go ahead and extend your coffee, and as for hens,

CRITICAL THINKING: GUIDED READING QUESTIONS

LITERAL

1a. How does Pius react when he learns Musizi's "bad news"? (He sits back, chuckles, and says that a thousand shillings is a lot of money.)

2a. How does Sarah react to the news? (She agrees with Pius and says he wouldn't know what to do with seventeen thousand pounds—his relatives would badger him forever.)

INFERENTIAL

1b. Why might Pius be happy with the news? (The smaller windfall is more appropriate to his life.)

2b. What does Sarah's reaction suggest about her feelings regarding Pius? (She is not after his fortune but is interested in him for another reason.)

well, I have six good layers at home, as well as a fine cockerel. I'll bring them over."

Pius looked at her in silence for a long time. "She is a fine looking woman," he thought, "and that blue *busuti* suits her. Nobody would ever take her for a grandmother—but why is she so anxious to throw herself at me?"

"You sound as if you are planning to come and live here," he said at last, trying hard to sound casual. Sarah turned to face him and replied, "Cousin Pius, I shall be frank with you. Six months ago my youngest son got married and brought his wife to live with me. She's a very nice girl, but somehow I can't get used to having another woman in the house. My other son is in Kampala,[14] and although I know I would be welcome there, he too has a wife, and three children, so if I went there I wouldn't be any better off. When I saw that bit about you in the paper, I suddenly remembered—although I don't expect you do—how you were at my wedding and were so helpful to everybody. Well, I thought to myself, here is somebody who needs a good housekeeper, who needs somebody to keep the leeches off, now that he has come into money. I **19** came along right away to take a look at you, and I can see I did the right thing. You do need me." She hesitated for a moment and then said, "Only you might prefer to stay alone. I'm so used to having my own way, I never thought about that before."

Pius cleared his throat. "You're a very impetuous woman," was all he could find to say.

A week later, Pius wandered out to the tomb and found Salongo busily polishing the Ssabalangira's weapons. "I thought you were dead," growled Salongo. "It is so long since you came here—but then, this tomb thrives on neglect. Nobody cares that one of Buganda's greatest men lies here."

"I have been rather busy," murmured Pius,

---

14. **Kampala** [käm pä′lə]: capital and largest city of Uganda.

"but I didn't forget my promise to you. Here! I've brought you a hundred shillings, and I only wish it could have been more. At least it will buy a few cement blocks."

Salongo took the money and looked at it as if it were crawling with lice. Grudgingly he thanked Pius and then said, "Of course, you will find life more expensive now that you are keeping a woman in the house."

"I suppose Nantondo told you?" Pius smiled sheepishly.

"Does it matter who told me? Anyway, never say I didn't warn you. Next thing she'll want will be a ring marriage."

Pius gave an uncertain laugh. "As a matter of fact, one of the reasons I came up here was to invite you to the wedding—it's next month."

Salongo carefully laid the spear he was rubbing down on a piece of clean barkcloth and stared at his friend as if he had suddenly grown another head. "What a fool you are! All this stems from your writing circles and crosses[15] on a bit of squared paper. I knew it would bring no good. At your age you ought to have more sense. Well, all I can advise is that you run while you still have a chance."

For a moment, Pius was full of misgivings. Was he, after all, behaving like a fool? Then he thought of Sarah, and the wonders she had worked with his house and his *shamba* in the short time they had been together. He felt reassured. "Well, I'm getting married, and I expect you at both the church and at the reception, and if you don't appear, I shall want to know why!" He secretly delighted at the note of authority in his voice, and Salongo's face was the picture of **20** astonishment. "All right," he mumbled, "I shall try and come. Before you go, cut a bunch of bananas to take home to your good lady, and there might be a cabbage ready at the back. After all, it seems she is the winner!"

---

15. **circles and crosses:** o's and x's; a reference to the football pools' entry coupon.

The Winner **9**

PAGE SUMMARY: AT A GLANCE

- Pius cannot understand Sarah's interest in him.
- Sarah says she is not happy with her living arrangements and hoped to be Pius' housekeeper.
- A week later Pius visits Salongo and reveals that he will soon marry Sarah.
- Salongo grumbles, but Pius insists that he come to the wedding.
- Salongo agrees and tells Pius to take some bananas to Sarah, since she seems to be the winner.

IN THE GLOSSARY

- impetuous: impulsive
- misgivings: doubts

19 TEACHING CHARACTERIZATION

Ask students to summarize Sarah's reasons for coming to Pius. How does she surprise us in her final sentence? (She shows a new sensitivity, an awareness that her aggressiveness may be intrusive.)

20 TEACHING PLOT: RESOLUTION

Help students see that Salongo, who tries to hold out against Pius' happiness, grudgingly chimes in with an almost cheerful note to make the happy ending unanimous.

COLLABORATIVE LEARNING: ENRICHMENT ACTIVITY

Dialogue The author never shows the moment at which Pius and Sarah decide to marry. Ask students to work in pairs to create the dialogue that leads to Pius and Sarah's betrothal. Students should try to imagine how the issue came up, who actually proposed to whom, and what the answer was.

CRITICAL THINKING: GUIDED READING QUESTIONS

LITERAL

1a. For what reasons has Sarah come to Pius? (She is uncomfortable living with her son's family and feels Pius needs her.)

2a. When Salongo calls him a fool, what does Pius feel at first, and what does he then feel when he thinks of Sarah? (At first he has doubts; then he feels reassured.)

INFERENTIAL

→ **1b.** What do you think of Sarah's motives? (Some students may feel that she is imposing on Pius for selfish reasons, even if she is less mercenary than the others. Many will see nothing wrong with her seeking a more independent, satisfying life.)

→ **2b.** How has his attitude toward Salongo changed, and why? (He stands up to Salongo for the first time, probably because his new-found happiness has given him confidence.)

READER'S RESPONSE

Do you think Pius and Sarah will be happy? Why or why not?

ANSWERS

STUDY QUESTIONS

1. visit him and eat his food; Salongo seeks a donation for the Ssabalangira's tomb.
2. He thinks she wants to take advantage of him. She acts "as though she were mistress of the house."
3. He chuckles and says he didn't need more than he won. Sarah agrees.
4. She was uncomfortable with her son and his wife and felt Pius needed help.
5. He will marry Sarah; Sarah.
6. when he learns that he has won less than expected and Sarah takes the news in stride; Many students will share his new, positive opinion.
7. Pius wins the football pools, while Sarah wins the "contest" between her and Salongo over Pius' affection. Sarah and Pius win happiness together.
8. The author pokes fun at the relatives' greed and hypocrisy and some bachelors' prejudices against women.
9. Many students will feel that despite different customs human nature is similar. They may cite the relatives' behavior, the intrusive media, and the human need Pius and Sarah fulfill by marrying.

LITERARY FOCUS

Plot

Exposition—Pius wins the pools; relatives appear. *Rising action*—Salongo criticizes Sarah; she is overly helpful. *Climax*—Pius learns he has won less money, and Sarah stays on. *Falling action*—Pius announces he will marry Sarah. *Resolution*—Salongo accepts the news.

Foreshadowing

Possible answers: "He slept like a cherub that night. . . ." "Pius could not help but admire the way Sarah took things in her stride." "'Your cousin is a fine woman,' Miriamu told Pius. . . ." Students may suspect the outcome when Pius first feels comfortable about Sarah.

STUDY QUESTIONS

Recalling

1. What do Pius' relatives do when the news spreads that Pius has won the football pools? For what reason does Salongo find it "worthwhile" to visit?
2. Why is Pius wary of Sarah at first? How does Sarah behave when Yosefu and Kibuka arrive?
3. What does Pius say and do when he learns that he won much less than he expected? What does Sarah say?
4. What does Sarah tell Pius about why she came to visit him?
5. What news does Pius announce when he visits Salongo? According to Salongo, who is the real winner?

Interpreting

6. When and why does Pius' opinion of Sarah begin to change? Did your opinion of her change as well?
7. Explain the multiple meanings of the story's title. Is there only one real winner at the end? If not, who are the winners, and why?
8. What human weaknesses does the author make fun of in the story?

Extending

9. Did you find Buganda society, as portrayed in the story, very different from contemporary American society? Cite story details to support your opinion.

LITERARY FOCUS

Plot

The **plot** is the sequence of events in a story. The plot usually follows the pattern below.

In the **exposition** the author introduces the story's characters, setting, and situation. The **narra-**

tive hook is the point at which the author catches our attention and establishes the basic conflict that the story will eventually resolve. The narrative hook begins the **rising action,** which adds complications to the story. The rising action builds to a **climax,** the point of greatest tension or reader involvement. The climax usually gives an indication of how the conflict will be resolved. The **falling action** reveals the outcome of the climax and brings the story to a **resolution,** or logical conclusion.

Thinking About Plot

- In "The Winner" the narrative hook is Cousin Sarah's appearance on the scene. Make a chart indicating the other parts of the plot, listing events that represent the exposition, rising action, climax, falling action, and resolution.

Foreshadowing

Authors often use clues known as **foreshadowing** to prepare readers for later developments in the plot. These clues usually take the form of minor incidents or statements that hint at events to come. Foreshadowing builds suspense and increases our involvement in the story because it encourages us to make predictions about what will happen. We then continue reading to see if our predictions are correct.

Thinking About Foreshadowing

- Identify at least three statements about Pius or Sarah that hint at the story's resolution. When did you begin to suspect the outcome of the story?

COMPOSITION

Writing a Response to a Story

- Write an evaluation of "The Winner." First decide whether you like the story. Then explain your response, considering the following questions: Did the story arouse your interest at the beginning and sustain it? What questions did it raise? Did it lead toward a logical solution? Support your opinion with examples from the story. *For help with this assignment, refer to Lesson 1 in the Writing About Literature Handbook at the back of this book.*

COMPOSITION: GUIDELINES FOR EVALUATION

WRITING A RESPONSE TO A STORY

Objective
To write an evaluation of a story

Guidelines for Evaluation
- suggested length: three or four paragraphs

- should state the student's overall opinion of the story
- should indicate whether the story aroused interest and led to a logical conclusion
- should support ideas with story details

GEOGRAPHY AND CULTURE

Guy de Maupassant

(1850–1893)

France

Guy de Maupassant ranks with the world's greatest short story writers. Though he was the child of wealthy parents, Guy de Maupassant [gē′ də mō′pə sänt′] grew up among the children of peasants and sailors who lived near his mother's estates in northwestern France. When he went away to school, he spent occasional Sundays with the great French novelist Gustave Flaubert [gōōs täv′ flō bār′], his mother's childhood friend. Flaubert encouraged the young Maupassant's literary efforts and suggested that he experiment with poetry in order to practice clarity and conciseness.

After serving in the Franco-Prussian War of 1870 to 1871, Maupassant became a government clerk but devoted his free time to writing. He continued to perfect his craft under Flaubert's guidance and published his first volume of stories in 1881, the year after Flaubert died.

In all, Maupassant produced nearly three hundred short stories. He is widely praised for his portraits of peasant life and his keen understanding of human nature. Most of Maupassant's tales take place in Normandy, the region of France where he grew up.

France and the Region of Normandy

Located in western Europe, France is a nation of many historic regions. One of these regions is Normandy, on the coast of northwestern France. Centuries ago, Normandy was colonized by Vikings from Scandinavia, who with time adopted the French language and other French customs. The people of Normandy are called Normans, which means "north men." Today, the region is famous for its historic fairs and festivals, its dairy products, and its apple cider.

In the nineteenth century, when "The Piece of String" takes place, most Norman men were sailors, fishermen, or farmers. The most eagerly awaited part of the week was market day, when people traveled to a large nearby town to sell their crops or livestock, buy needed goods, and catch up on the latest gossip. "The Piece of String" opens on market day in a bustling Norman town.

See LITERATURE AND CULTURE SOURCEBOOK: France

The Piece of String **11**

In this ironic tale a Norman peasant is destroyed by a seemingly trivial event. When thrifty Maître Hauchecome retrieves a piece of string from the mud, he is seen by a man with whom he has quarreled. Embarrassed, he tries to mask his actions. Later he is accused of picking up a pocketbook, not the string. Obsessed with proving his innocence, he grows ill and dies.

LITERARY SKILLS FOR THIS SELECTION

- conflict
- setting
- tone

THEMES IN THIS SELECTION

- life's surprises: grave results from trivial events
- the importance of reputation
- the dangers of small-mindedness

LESSON OBJECTIVES

1. to identify external conflicts
2. to understand the meanings and origins of words from French and Middle English
3. to trace a story's plot

Teacher's Classroom Resources 1

- Teaching Notes — 25
- Prereading Vocabulary — 26
- Reading Guide — 27
- Check Test — 28
- Responding to World Cultures — 29
- Literary Focus: External Conflict — 30
- Language Study: French and Middle English — 31
- Writing Process Guide: Writing About Plot — 32
- Grammar in Literature: Using Sensory Details — 33
- Selection Test — 34

IN THE CLASSROOM

TEACHING STUDENTS OF DIFFERENT ABILITIES

- **For less advanced students:** Have students list Maître Hauchecome's main actions and reactions and consider what they show about him. Also ask students to complete the Reading Guide for this selection.
- **For more advanced students:** Have students explain how the conflicts, resolution, and narrator's tone help convey ideas of Naturalism, discussed on page 585 of their text.

DISCUSSING GEOGRAPHY AND CULTURE

The Costumes of Normandy

In addition to its apples, Camembert cheese, and lace, Normandy is renowned for its regional dress. Norman women wore tall, starched white hats, triangular shawls, and long, full skirts. Men wore long, loose smocks and white tassled caps. Today these costumes are most commonly worn during the region's many folk festivals.

- Ask students to describe the traditional dress of the American West.

Ask students to describe different ways in which people react to being teased or laughed at. How do they think people *should* re-act to such situations? Why?

PAGE SUMMARY: AT A GLANCE

- All roads to Goderville are crowded with peasants coming to the town for market day.
- The men's physical appear-ance shows the effects of hard labor, and all look and dress alike.

1 TEACHING PLOT: EXPOSITION

Note that the exposition begins by identifying the setting and the people who inhabit it. Ask what the details stress about the life of a typical Norman peasant. (It was hardened by labor.)

2 TEACHING TONE

Point out that the narrator's tone, which at first seems sympathetic to the peasants' labors, changes here. Help students see that these details, especially the com-parison to balloons, create a hu-morous, mocking tone.

ART AND LITERATURE

In 1880, after failing as an art dealer and as a missionary to Belgian miners, Vincent van Gogh turned to painting as a means of synthesizing his artistic and religious yearnings. In a short time van Gogh developed his well-known sinuous, undulat-ing brush strokes and vibrant use of raw color, imbuing the most everyday scene with vivid, emo-tional force.

- Ask students to find phrases in the opening paragraph that recall van Gogh's forceful painting. ("proceeding with slow steps, the whole body bent forward . . . deformed"; "shining as if varnished")

The Auvers Stairs with Five Figures, Vincent van Gogh (1853–1890).

Guy de Maupassant

The Piece of String

Translated from the French by Raymond R. Canon

1   Along all the roads around Goderville[1] the peasants and their wives were coming toward the town because it was market day. The men were proceeding with slow steps, the whole body bent forward at each movement of their long twisted legs, deformed by their hard work, by the weight on the plow which, at the same time, raised the left shoulder and swerved the figure, by the reaping of the wheat which made the knees spread to make a firm "purchase,"[2] by all the slow and painful labors of the country. Their blouses, blue, "stiff-starched," shining as if varnished, ornamented with a little design in white at the neck and wrists, puffed about their 2 bony bodies, seemed like balloons ready to carry them off. From each of them a head, two arms, and two feet protruded.

   Some led a cow or a calf by a cord, and their

---

1. **Goderville** [gō der vēl′]: town in Normandy. (See the Geography and Culture feature that precedes the story.)

2. **firm "purchase":** position of the body appropriate for moving a large weight.

12   *The Short Story*

CRITICAL THINKING: GUIDED READING QUESTIONS

LITERAL

1a. What sort of blouses, or shirts, do the peasant men wear? (They wear highly starched blue blouses with a white design at the borders.)

INFERENTIAL

1b. What do the details suggest about the peasants' individuality? (They lack individuality; they all look and dress alike.)

wives, walking behind the animal, whipped its haunches with a leafy branch to hasten its progress. On their arms they carried large baskets from which, in some cases, chickens and, in others, ducks thrust out their heads. And they walked with a quicker, livelier step than their husbands. Their spare straight figures were wrapped in scanty little shawls, pinned over their flat bosoms, and their heads were enveloped in white cloths glued to the hair and surmounted by caps.

Then a wagon passed at the jerky trot of a nag, shaking strangely, two men seated side by side and a woman in the bottom of the vehicle, the latter holding onto the sides to lessen the hard jolts.

3 In the public square of Goderville there was a crowd, a throng of human beings and animals mixed together. The horns of the cattle, the tall hats with the long nap of the rich peasant, and the headgear of the peasant women rose above the surface of the assembly. And the clamorous, shrill, screaming voices made a continuous and savage din which sometimes was dominated by the robust lungs of some countryman's laugh, or the long lowing of a cow tied to the wall of a house.

All that smacked of the stable, the dairy and the dirt heap, hay and sweat, giving forth that unpleasant odor, human and animal, peculiar to the people of the field.

Maître[3] Hauchecome, of Bréauté,[4] had just arrived at Goderville, and he was directing his steps toward the public square, when he perceived upon the ground a little piece of string. Maître Hauchecome, economical like a true Norman, thought that everything useful ought to be picked up, and he bent painfully, for he suffered from rheumatism. He took the bit of thin cord from the ground and began to roll it carefully

when he noticed Maître Malandain, the harness maker, on the threshold of his door, looking at him. They had heretofore had business together on the subject of a halter, and they were on bad terms, being both good haters. Maître Hauchecome was seized with a sort of shame to be seen thus by his enemy, picking a bit of string
4 out of the dirt. He concealed his "find" quickly under his blouse, then in his trousers' pocket; then he pretended to be still looking on the ground for something which he did not find, and he went toward the market, his head forward, bent double by his pains.

He was soon lost in the noisy and slowly
5 moving crowd, which was busy with interminable bargainings. The peasants milked, went and came, perplexed, always in fear of being cheated, not daring to decide, watching the ven-
6 dor's eye, ever trying to find the trick in the man and the flaw in the beast.

The women, having placed their great baskets at their feet, had taken out the poultry which lay upon the ground, tied together by the feet, with terrified eyes and scarlet crests.

They heard offers, stated their prices with a dry air and impassive face, or perhaps, suddenly deciding on some proposed reduction, shouted to the customer who was slowly going away: "All right, Maître Authirne, I'll give it to you for that."

7 Then little by little the square was deserted, and when the Angelus[5] rang at noon, those who had stayed too long scattered to their shops.

At Jourdain's the great room was full of people eating, as the big court was full of vehicles of all kinds, carts, gigs, wagons, dump carts, yellow with dirt, mended and patched, raising their shafts to the sky like two arms, or perhaps with their shafts in the ground and their backs in the air.

Just opposite the diners seated at the table,

---

3. **Maître** [mātr]: French for "master"; used as a title of respect.
4. **Bréauté** [brā ō tā′]: village near Goderville.

---

5. **Angelus** [an′jə ləs]: church bell rung at morning, noon, and night to signal prayer recitations.

The Piece of String **13**

- Men, women, and farm animals crowd the open-air market.
- As thrifty Maître Hauchecome picks up a piece of string, he sees his enemy, Maître Malandain, watching him.
- Ashamed to be so seen, Hauchecome tries to mask his actions.
- By noon the crowd has dispersed, and many gather at Jourdain's for lunch.

IN THE GLOSSARY

- lowing: mooing
- interminable: endless
- impassive: showing no emotion

3 TEACHING SETTING

Point out details that describe the setting, and help students see that these details create a noisy, hectic atmosphere.

4 READING SKILL: PREDICTING OUTCOMES

Ask students what they think Maître Malandain, Hauchecome's enemy, is likely to make of these actions. (He will find them suspicious.)

5 CULTURAL BACKGROUND

Point out that market day in Normandy involved haggling, or bargaining over prices. You might have volunteers recount any experiences they have had with haggling.

6 TEACHING CHARACTERIZATION

Ask what this detail implies about the vendor's and peasants' attitude toward human nature. (They are cynical; they always think they are being cheated.)

7 CULTURAL BACKGROUND

Point out that on market day many shopkeepers set up stalls in the open-air market in the public square. This practice was easier than selling from a shop, which would have become crowded with peasants and their livestock on market day but would have gone unused on non-market days.

CRITICAL THINKING: GUIDED READING QUESTIONS

LITERAL

1a. What sort of haters are Maître Hauchecome and Maître Malandain? (They are good haters.)

2a. What seizes Maître Hauchecome when he realizes that his enemy has seen him picking up the string? (He is seized by a sort of shame.)

INFERENTIAL

1b. What does this detail suggest about both men's personalities? (They are petty, vindictive people.)

2b. Why would he feel shame? (He realizes that he is doing something petty and demeaning in front of someone who already has a low opinion of him.)

8 the immense fireplace, filled with bright flames, cast a lively heat on the backs of the row on the right. Three spits were turning on which were chickens, pigeons, and legs of mutton; and an appetizing odor of roast beef and gravy dripping over the nicely browned skin rose from the hearth, increased the jovialness, and made everybody's mouth water.

9 All the aristocracy of the plow ate there, at Maître Jourdain's, tavern keeper and horse dealer, a rascal who had money.

The dishes were passed and emptied, as were the jugs of yellow cider. Everyone told his affairs, his purchases and sales. They discussed the crops. The weather was favorable for the green things but not for the wheat.

Suddenly the drum beat in the court before the house. Everybody rose except a few indifferent persons, and ran to the door, or to the windows, their mouths still full and napkins in their hands.

10 After the public crier had ceased his drum-beating, he called out in a jerky voice, speaking his phrases irregularly:

"It is hereby made known to the inhabitants of Goderville, and in general to all persons present at the market, that there was lost this morning, on the road to Benzeville, between nine and ten o'clock, a black leather pocketbook containing five hundred francs[6] and some business papers. The finder is requested to return same with all haste to the mayor's office or to Maître Fortune Houlbreque of Manneville. There will be twenty francs reward."

Then the man went away. The heavy roll of the drum and the crier's voice were again heard at a distance.

Then they began to talk of this event, discussing the chances that Maître Houlbreque had of finding or not finding his pocketbook.

And the meal concluded. They were finishing

_____

6. **five hundred francs:** French money worth about a hundred dollars at the time the story takes place.

their coffee when a chief of the gendarmes[7] appeared upon the threshold.

He inquired: "Is Maître Hauchecome, of Bréauté, here?"

Maître Hauchecome, seated at the other end of the table, replied: "Here I am."

And the officer resumed: "Maître Hauchecome, will you have the goodness to accompany me to the mayor's office? The mayor would like to talk to you."

The peasant, surprised and disturbed, swallowed at a draft his tiny glass of brandy, rose, and, even more bent than in the morning, for the first steps after each rest were especially difficult, set out, repeating: "Here I am, here I am."

11 The mayor was awaiting him, seated on an armchair. He was the notary[8] of the vicinity, a stout, serious man, with pompous phrases.

"Maître Hauchecome," said he, "you were seen this morning to pick up, on the road to Benzeville, the pocketbook lost by Maître Houlbreque, of Manneville."

The countryman, astounded, looked at the mayor, already terrified by this suspicion resting on him without his knowing why.

"Me? Me? Me pick up the pocketbook?"

"Yes, you, yourself."

"Word of honor, I never heard of it."

"But you were seen."

"I was seen, me? Who says he saw me?"

"Monsieur[9] Malandain, the harness maker."

12 The old man remembered, understood, and flushed with anger.

"Ah, he saw me, the clodhopper, he saw me pick up this string, here, M'sieu'[10] the Mayor." And rummaging in his pocket, he drew out the little piece of string.

_____

7. **gendarmes** [zhän′därm]: French police officers.
8. **notary** [nō′tər ē]: public official who certifies documents, takes people's sworn statements, and attends to other legal matters.
9. **Monsieur** [mə syœ′]: French for "mister."
10. **M'sieu'** [m'syœ′]: Maître Hauchecome's clipped pronunciation of *monsieur*.

CRITICAL THINKING: GUIDED READING QUESTIONS

LITERAL

1a. What do the peasants in Jourdain's discuss after the public crier makes his announcement? (They discuss Maître Houlbreque's chances of finding his missing pocketbook.)

2a. What is Maître Hauchecome's reaction when he learns that Maître Malandain has accused him? (He remembers, understands, and flushes with anger.)

INFERENTIAL

1b. In view of their earlier attitudes at the market, what do you suppose the peasants think of Maître Houlbreque's chances? (They think that they are not good.)

2b. What does Maître Hauchecome "understand" about Maître Malandain's accusation? (It stems from his animosity toward Hauchecome and from Hauchecome's furtive behavior with the string, which an enemy would find suspicious.)

13 But the mayor, incredulous, shook his head.

"You will not make me believe, Maître Hauchecome, that Monsieur Malandain, who is a man worthy of credence, mistook this cord for a pocketbook."

The peasant, furious, lifted his hand, spat at one side to attest his honor, repeating: "It is nevertheless the truth of the good God, the sacred truth, M'sieu' the Mayor. I repeat it on my soul and my salvation."

The mayor resumed: "After picking up the object, you stood like a stilt, looking a long while in the mud to see if any piece of money had fallen out."

The good, old man choked with indignation and fear.

"How anyone can tell—how anyone can tell—such lies to take away an honest man's reputation! How can anyone—"

14 There was no use in his protesting; nobody believed him. He was confronted with Monsieur Malandain, who repeated and maintained his affirmation. They abused each other for an hour. At his own request, Maître Hauchecome was searched; nothing was found on him.

Finally the mayor, very much perplexed, discharged him with the warning that he would consult the public prosecutor and ask for further orders.

The news had spread. As he left the mayor's office, the old man was surrounded and questioned with a serious or bantering curiosity in which there was no indignation. He began to tell the story of the string. No one believed him. They laughed at him.

He went along, stopping his friends, beginning endlessly his statement and his protestations, showing his pockets turned inside out to prove that he had nothing.

They said: "Old rascal, get out!"

15 And he grew angry, becoming exasperated, hot, and distressed at not being believed, not knowing what to do and always repeating himself.

Night came. He must depart. He started on his way with three neighbors to whom he pointed out the place where he had picked up the bit of string; and all along the road he spoke of his adventure.

In the evening he took a turn in the village of Bréauté, in order to tell it to everybody. He only met with incredulity.

It made him ill at night.

The next day about one o'clock in the afternoon, Marius Paumelle, a hired man in the employ of Maître Breton, husbandman[11] at Ymanville, returned the pocketbook and its contents to Maître Houlbreque of Manneville.

This man claimed to have found the object in the road; but not knowing how to read, he had carried it to the house and given it to his employer.

16 The news spread through the neighborhood. Maître Hauchecome was informed of it. He immediately went the circuit[12] and began to recount his story completed by the happy climax. He was in triumph.

"What grieved me so much was not the thing itself, as the lying. There is nothing so shameful as to be placed under a cloud on account of a lie."

He talked of his adventure all day long; he told it on the highway to people who were passing by, in the wine shop to people who were drinking there, and to persons coming out of church the following Sunday. He stopped strangers to tell them about it. He was calm now, and yet something disturbed him without his knowing exactly what it was. People had the air of joking while they listened. They did not seem convinced. He seemed to feel that remarks were being made behind his back.

On Tuesday of the next week he went to the market at Goderville, urged solely by the necessity he felt of discussing the case.

---

11. **husbandman:** farmer.
12. **went the circuit:** traveled an accustomed route.

The Piece of String **15**

CRITICAL THINKING: GUIDED READING QUESTIONS

LITERAL

1a. According to the mayor, what did Hauchecome do after picking up an object in the street? (He stood like a stilt and looked at the mud to see whether any money had fallen out.)

2a. How does Maître Hauchecome feel after he learns that the pocketbook and its contents have been returned? (He feels happy and triumphant.)

INFERENTIAL

→ **1b.** Although Hauchecome is not a thief, what character flaw *did* he display when he acted in this way? (pride; He did not want his enemy to see him picking up a mere piece of string.)

→ **2b.** What do you think will happen to these happy, triumphant feelings when he returns to Goderville? Why? (They will be dispelled when he is met by more teasing disbelief; such disbelief is already evident among the people with whom he talks.)

- Everyone continues to laugh at Maître Hauchecome and believes he used an accomplice to return the pocketbook.
- Aware that he is capable of such trickery, he finds it impossible to prove his innocence.
- Obsessed with the matter, he wastes away and dies, still protesting that it was a piece of string he picked up.

IN THE GLOSSARY

- sharper: cheat
- confederate: accomplice
- wags: jokers
- reiterating: saying repeatedly

17 TEACHING CONFLICT

Point out that Hauchecome's conflict with his society is now full-blown. No one seems to believe or sympathize with him.

18 TEACHING PLOT: CLIMAX

Elicit that the climax occurs when a triumphant Hauchecome, certain his innocence is proved, returns to Goderville and finds he is still considered guilty.

19 TEACHING THEME

Elicit that Hauchecome's situation is not completely unjust: His petty enmity toward Malandain, miserliness in picking up the string, and reputation for sharp dealing have all contributed to it. Ask what his experiences show about life. (Small-mindedness can ruin a person's reputation, and a bad reputation can ruin a person's life.)

20 TEACHING IRONY

Point out that the final line stresses the story's irony: Great misfortune results from a seemingly trivial event.

COLLABORATIVE LEARNING: ENRICHMENT ACTIVITY

Dramatic Reading Working in groups, students might stage one of the confrontations in this story. Each group should script, act, and direct its chosen scene.

---

17 Malandain, standing at his door, began to laugh on seeing him pass. Why?

He approached a farmer from Crequetot, who did not let him finish, and giving him a thump in the stomach said to his face: "You big rascal."

Then he turned his back on him.

Maître Hauchecome was confused. Why was he called a big rascal?

When he was seated at the table in Jourdain's tavern, he commenced to explain "the affair."

A horse dealer from Monvilliers called to him: "Come, come, old sharper,[13] that's an old trick; I know all about your piece of string!"

Hauchecome stammered: "But since the pocketbook was found."

But the other man replied: "Shut up, papa, there is one that finds, and there is one that re-
18 ports. At any rate you are mixed up with it."

The peasant stood choking. He understood. They accused him of having had the pocketbook returned by a confederate, by an accomplice.

He tried to protest. All the table began to laugh.

He could not finish his dinner and went away, in the midst of jeers.

He went home ashamed and indignant, choking with anger and confusion, the more dejected

---

13. **sharper:** sharp customer.

---

that he was capable with his Norman cunning of doing what they had accused him of, and even
19 boasting of it as of a good turn. His innocence to him, in a confused way, was impossible to prove, as his sharpness was known. And he was stricken to the heart by the injustice of the suspicion.

Then he began to recount the adventures again, prolonging his history every day, adding each time new reasons, more energetic protestations, more solemn oaths which he imagined and prepared in his hours of solitude, his whole mind given up to the story of the string. He was believed so much the less as his defense was more complicated and his arguing more subtle.

"Those are lying excuses," they said behind his back.

He felt it, consumed his heart over it, and wore himself out with useless efforts. He wasted away before their very eyes.

The wags now made him tell about the string to amuse them, as they make a soldier who has been on a campaign tell about his battles. His mind, touched to the depth, began to weaken.

Toward the end of December he took to his bed.

He died in the first days of January, and in the delirium of his death struggles he kept claiming his innocence, reiterating:
20 "A piece of string, a piece of string—look— here it is, M'sieu' the Mayor."

CRITICAL THINKING: GUIDED READING QUESTIONS

LITERAL

1a. At Jourdain's what does Maître Hauchecome find people believe about the returned pocketbook? (They believe that he had the pocketbook returned by an accomplice and is still involved in the matter.)

2a. What wears Maître Hauchecome out and eventually causes his death? (He is worn out by, and dies from, his useless efforts to prove his innocence.)

INFERENTIAL

1b. What do these beliefs suggest about the effects of false accusations? (Many people will continue to believe them.)

2b. What does the outcome suggest can cause a person's downfall? (the contempt of one's society and obsessive concern for one's reputation, as well as seemingly trivial events)

STUDY QUESTIONS

Recalling

1. According to the sixth paragraph of the story, why does Maître Hauchecome pick up the piece of string? Why does he hide it?
2. Of what is Maître Hauchecome accused? Who believes his story about the string?
3. What do people accuse Maître Hauchecome of when the pocketbook is returned? What do the horse dealer and the farmer from Crequetot call him?
4. What finally happens to Maître Hauchecome? What are his last words?

Interpreting

5. Why does no one in the town believe in Maître Hauchecome's innocence? What does the story suggest about the power of a person's reputation?
6. What is surprising about the events that overtake Maître Hauchecome? Is his fate completely unfair, or does he in any way bring it upon himself? Explain.
7. Based on the story, how would you describe the author's view of human nature? Cite story details to support your answer.

Extending

8. Is it important to be concerned about your reputation? Is it possible to be overly concerned about what people think of you? Discuss your opinions.

LITERARY FOCUS

External Conflict

The events of a plot focus on a **conflict**, or struggle between two opposing forces. An **external conflict** occurs between a character and an outside force, such as nature, another character, society in general, or fate. For example, a character may struggle to survive a blizzard (nature), to defeat an enemy (another character), to fight an unfair law (society), or to escape the effects of circumstances he or she cannot control (fate). Whatever form the conflict takes, it is usually resolved by the story's end.

Thinking About External Conflict

1. Maître Hauchecome's chief conflict is with his society. What is the conflict? How is it resolved?
2. Does Maître Hauchecome also have a conflict with fate? Explain.

LANGUAGE STUDY

French and Middle English

Almost a thousand years ago, the Normans invaded and conquered England, bringing with them the old form of French that they spoke. As a result, so many French words were added to English that the language changed drastically. This changed form is known as Middle English to distinguish it from the Old English spoken previously and the modern English we speak today.

French is one of several languages that descend from Latin, the language of ancient Rome. If you look up the history of an English word that entered the language as a result of the Norman invasion, you will usually find its Middle English form, the Old or Middle French from which it came, and the Latin from which the French term arose.

Each of the following story words entered English as a result of the Norman invasion. Use the story context and a dictionary to help you determine the meaning and history of each word.

1. peasant	6. credence
2. clamorous	7. indignation
3. poultry	8. affirmation
4. pompous	9. accomplice
5. perplexed	

COMPOSITION

Writing About Plot

■ In a brief composition trace the plot of "The Piece of String." First tell what information is given in the exposition and identify the point where the conflict is introduced. Then explain how the action builds to a climax and falls to a resolution.

COMPOSITION: GUIDELINES FOR EVALUATION

WRITING ABOUT PLOT

Objective

To trace the parts of a plot

Guidelines for Evaluation

■ suggested length: one or two paragraphs
■ should identify the exposition, conflict, climax, and resolution of the story
■ should discuss events in correct sequence

How would you have behaved if you were Maître Hauchecome?

ANSWERS

STUDY QUESTIONS

1. He saves everything useful. He feels shame that an enemy has seen him pick it up.
2. finding and keeping a missing pocketbook; no one
3. having an accomplice return it; "rascal" and "sharper"
4. He grows ill and dies; he speaks of the piece of string.
5. His behavior was suspicious, and he is known as a sharp dealer; a bad reputation can lead to contempt and ruin.
6. They stem from a trivial event. His petty feuding, miserliness, sharp dealing, and obsessive behavior help bring it about.
7. knowing and cynical; Details include everyone's looking for the "trick in the man and the flaw in the beast" and their treatment of Hauchecome.
8. Answers will vary. Students may stress the importance of a good reputation, or they may feel that overconcern can cause the loss of freedom.

LITERARY FOCUS

1. to clear himself of a false accusation; He dies uncleared.
2. Yes; he has no control over being seen by an enemy the day the pocketbook is lost.

LANGUAGE STUDY

1. "small farmer"; from Middle English (ME) *paissaunt*, from French (Fr) *pais*, "country," from Latin (L) *pagus*, "district"
2. "noisy"; from ME *clamour*, via Fr, from L *clamare*, "cry out"
3. "farm birds raised for food"; from ME *pultrie*, via Fr, from L *pullus*, "chicken"
4. "self-important"; from ME, via Fr and L, from Greek *pompē*, "solemn procession"
5. "puzzled"; from ME, via Fr, from L *perplexus*, "entangled"
6. "belief"; from ME, via Fr, from L *credere*, "believe; trust"
7. "righteous anger"; from ME *indignacion*, via Fr, from L *indignari*, "consider unworthy"
8. "positive declaration"; from ME *affermen*, via Fr, from L *affirmare*, "present as fixed"
9. "partner in crime"; from ME, via Fr, from L *complexus*, "encircled; embraced"

In this realistic story set in modern England, a young girl learns self-reliance when she faces an everyday experience made difficult because she is blind. Spurred by an oversolicitous visitor, Ally insists on going alone from the garden to the upstairs lavatory. The author puts the reader in the blind girl's place by describing only what Ally can sense and by using the pronoun *you* to refer to Ally.

LITERARY SKILLS FOR THIS SELECTION

- conflict
- character motivation
- point of view

THEMES IN THIS SELECTION

- life's surprises: everyday experience from an unusual point of view
- self-reliance
- overcoming physical hardship

LESSON OBJECTIVES

1. to identify the conflicts in a story
2. to examine a story's use of sensory details
3. to recount a new incident involving a character in a story

Teacher's Classroom Resources 1

- Teaching Notes   37
- Prereading Vocabulary   38
- Reading Guide   39
- Check Test   40
- Responding to World Cultures   41
- Literary Focus: Internal Conflict   42
- Writing Process Guides: Writing About Sensory Details   43
  Writing About a Character's Experiences   44
- Grammar in Literature: Using Personal Pronouns   45
- Selection Test   46

TEACHING STUDENTS OF DIFFERENT ABILITIES

- **For less advanced students:** Because readers must use the details in the story to infer that

Rumer Godden

(born 1907)

England/India

Rumer Godden [roo'mər god'ən] has spent her life going back and forth between England and India, "perpetually homesick for one or the other." Born Margaret Rumer Godden in Sussex, England, as a child she went to live in India, where her father managed a shipping company. Later she returned to England to complete her education; she then went back to India and opened a school for dance in the city of Calcutta. Her teaching experience gave her keen insight into the problems of childhood and adolescence, frequent subjects of her fiction.

Godden's interest in writing began early: At five she was scribbling poems on her mother's notepaper; at seven she produced a "fictional autobiography." After publishing her first successful novel, *Black Narcissus,* in 1939, she sold her school and devoted herself to writing.

Godden's stories have appeared in magazines such as *The New Yorker,* and several of her novels have been adapted for the screen. Most of her works take place in England or India. "You Need to Go Upstairs" is set in England.

18 *The Short Story*

England and Its Gardens

England occupies most of the southern part of the island of Great Britain, which also includes Scotland and Wales. All three, together with Northern Ireland, are part of the country known as the United Kingdom.

Located off the west coast of Europe, Great Britain is often buffeted by storms, but temperatures are moderate, especially in England. Its mild, moist climate is excellent for growing a wide variety of plants, and English gardens are justifiably famous.

The English seldom speak of "front yards" or "back yards"; instead, they call the entire area around a home "the garden." Lawns tend to be smaller than they are in the United States, and narrow walks often lead between trees, flower beds, and carefully pruned hedges and borders. "You Need to Go Upstairs" opens on a day in early spring in a typical English garden.

Ally is blind, it may help to have students find dialogue and other details that point to this inference. Also have students complete the Reading Guide for this selection.

- **For more advanced students:** Encourage students to read and report on other works by Godden—fiction and nonfiction set in India as well as England.

DISCUSSING GEOGRAPHY AND CULTURE

Gardens and Privacy

In this story a young English girl is sitting in her garden—or yard, as we say in the United States. Although many of us take yards for granted, not everyone enjoys the luxury of this private space.

- Have students think of people who do not enjoy the luxury of a yard. Does a park serve the same purpose? What makes private yards and gardens special?

Rumer Godden

You Need to Go Upstairs

1 And just when everything is comfortably settled you need to go upstairs.

You are sitting in the garden for the first time this year, sitting on a cushion on the grass by Mother. The feel of the grass is good; when you press it down and lift your hand the blades spring up again at once as strong as ever; they will not be kept lying down.

2 You sit with your legs straight in front of you; they have come out from their winter stockings and are very thin and knobbly, but the sun is beginning to warm them gently as if it were glad to see them again.

Your back is against Mother's chair and occasionally she puts her finger between your collar and your skin, to feel if you are warm; you are warm and you pick up your knitting because you can knit; with your finger you follow the wool along the big wooden pins and you say, "Knit one—knit another"; with the slow puffs of wind. The wind brings the garden scents and the sounds to you; sounds of birds and neighbors and the street.

"I like it, Mother."

"So do I."

Then Doreen, who comes in the afternoons to help, brings out a visitor; voices and footsteps; Mother has to get up but you hang your head and go on knitting. Voices creaking and rustling and a sign. The visitor has sat down. Presently she whispers to Mother, "What is her name?"

3 "Her name is Alice," says Mother loudly and clearly to blot out the whisper. "We call her Ally. Ally, stand up and say how do you do."

"Ah, don't!" says the visitor and you do not stand up; you press the grass down flat with

4 your hand. It is then that you know you need to go upstairs. The cloakroom is out of order; you have to go upstairs.

The visitor's voice falls from high up, almost into your lap, cutting off the wind and the birds, cutting off Mother, so that you have to stand up.

"Yes, Ally?"

5 "Mother, I need to go upstairs," and you hurry to say, "I can go by myself, Mother."

Mother is looking at your face—you cannot look yourself, yet you can always feel Mother's look; now she is doubtful, but she is proud, and after a moment she says, "Very well, dear." You understand what she does not say, *Be careful! Be careful!*

"Alone?" breathes the visitor, and prickles seem to rise up all over you. You have said you will do it alone, and you will. You turn your back on the visitor.

From the chairs to the poplars is easy; you can hear them straining and moving their branches just enough to tell you where they are. There are two, and when you are up to them, you separate your hands the distance apart you think they will be and you do not hit them, you find them; their trunks are under your hands and you stay to feel those trunks; they are rough and smooth together; they are like people, they are alive.

On the other side of the trees is a smell of cinders where, last winter, ashes were thrown down on the snow. The smell warns you. Move your feet along the grass, don't lift them, because the path is there and it has a little brick-edge hidden in the grass. You fell over it last summer; suddenly you were down on the grass and you have a fright about falling. You won't

You Need to Go Upstairs **19**

Have students name the five senses (sight, hearing, smell, taste, and touch) and discuss which they consider most important.

PAGE SUMMARY: AT A GLANCE

- Ally (called *you* in the narrative) sits in the garden with her mother, knitting and enjoying an early spring day.
- Doreen, who works for Ally's family part time, brings out a visitor, who is shocked when Ally insists on going upstairs alone.
- Ally uses her memory and the senses of hearing, smell, and touch to cross the garden.

IN THE GLOSSARY

- prickles: sharp points
- poplars: trees in the willow family
- cinders: ashes

1 TEACHING PLOT: EXPOSITION

Point out that many modern stories dispense with lengthy exposition and instead open *in medias res,* or in the middle of the action.

2 TEACHING POINT OF VIEW

Note the story's unusual second-person point of view, in which the pronoun *you* is used to refer to the main character.

3 TEACHING DIALOGUE

Point out that the author uses dialogue to provide information about the main character, including her name.

4 CULTURAL BACKGROUND

In modernizing older English homes, second toilets were often installed in downstairs coat closets, called *cloakrooms.*

5 GRAMMAR IN LITERATURE

In conjunction with discussing point of view, you may want to review personal pronouns. Have students identify examples of first-, second-, and third-person pronouns in this passage. (*I, you,* and *she,* respectively)

CRITICAL THINKING: GUIDED READING QUESTIONS

LITERAL

1a. What does the visitor first do when she sits down? (She whispers, "What is her name?" to Ally's mother.)

2a. Why is it easy for Ally to travel from the chairs to the poplars? (She hears the poplars' branches moving.)

INFERENTIAL

1b. What is rude about the visitor's behavior? (She acts as if Ally is not present or cannot hear her.)

2b. From the senses that she does and does not use, what can you infer about Ally? (She is blind.)

PAGE SUMMARY: AT A GLANCE

- As she watches Ally, the visitor continues to express excessive emotion, but Ally's mother is matter-of-fact.
- Anticipating Ally's fear of tripping on Schiff, the pet tortoise, the mother casually but loudly remarks that he has not come out.
- Ally nearly falls on the front steps, where someone has thoughtlessly left the scraper.
- Greeted by familiar sounds and smells in the house, she crosses the hall to the stairs, which she can climb with the aid of tactile signals that her mother has put under the rail.

IN THE GLOSSARY

- pagodas: pyramid-shaped towers
- tortoise: land turtle
- rustle: soft sound

6 CRITICAL THINKING: CLASSIFICATION

You might have students classify common flowers by their shape or smell, using the clues that would help a blind person recognize them.

7 TEACHING STUDENTS OF LIMITED ENGLISH PROFICIENCY

Students may need help with the different meanings of *catch,* especially the expressions "catch at" and "catch your breath."

8 TEACHING CHARACTER MOTIVATION

Elicit that much of Ally's independence and persistence stems from her desire to show the over-solicitous visitor that she is capable of performing everyday tasks.

9 CULTURAL BACKGROUND

Point out that *drawing-room* is an Anglicism, a term used in England but rarely or never in America. Ask what other Anglicism is used in this passage. (*loo*)

10 TEACHING POINT OF VIEW

Note that the setting is described from Ally's point of view, with details that appeal to senses other than sight.

---

fall, the cinder smell has warned you. You find the path. Lift your feet—one—two. The cinders are crunching, now you can go along the path to where the flowers are.

"It's wonderful," says the visitor and her voice sounds like tears. "Her . . . little blue . . . jacket."

"It's a nice jacket, isn't it?" says Mother. "We got it at Pollards' bargain counter. Ally feels it's warm and gay."

That visitor there would be surprised if you picked the flowers, one by one, and took them to her and told her what they were. "I see no reason why you should not know your flowers," **6** Mother has often told you. "Flowers have shapes and smells as well as colors." This is the hyacinth bed; hyacinths are easy, strong in scent and shaped like little pagodas—"Remember, I told you about pagodas"—and these are crocuses and these are aconites—but Mother is not close and you remember that Schiff may be out on the path.

Schiff! You stop. Schiff is so small that you might easily step on him, but Schiff is large enough for you to fall over. Mother . . . but you must not call, you must go on. You think of falling, you can't help thinking of falling—down—into nothing until you get hit. Mother! Schiff! Mother! But you have not called and Mother is saying in what seems an ordinary voice to the visitor, but is her special loud voice for you. "How strange! With all this sun, our tortoise has not come out on the path today."

At the end of the path are two orange bushes with bitter-smelling leaves; they are bad little bushes, with twigs that catch on your coat; you don't like them and you think you will hurry past. There are two bushes in two tubs, and there are four steps; you can remember that, **7** twice two are four. One—two—three—four, and your foot is on the last step, but you catch at the air, catch at the door with a sharp pain ringing in your shin, catch your breath and catch the door and save yourself.

20 *The Short Story*

8 Someone, somebody, has left the scraper[1] on the step. It has been pulled right out. You stand there shaking, boiling with anger, the pain hurting in your leg, but there is no sound from the garden; the visitor has not seen.

Now you are in the house. At first it is always curiously still; and then always out of the stillness you find it. This is the hall and in it are the smells and sounds of all the rooms: furniture cream and hot pipes, carpet and dried roses **9** from the drawing-room,[2] tobacco and a little of pickles from the dining-room, mint and hot cake from the kitchen, and down the stairs comes soap from the bathroom. The loo[3] is up, next door to the bathroom—it has a piece of pine-smelling brick in a wire holder on the wall.

10 With the smells come the house sounds, all so familiar: Doreen's footsteps in the kitchen, a whirring like insects from the refrigerator and the clocks, a curtain flapping in the wind and a tapping, a tiny rustle from the canary. You know all these things better than anyone else.

Now you let go of the door—like this—and you go across the hall. Of course you could have gone round by the wall to the stairs, feeling around the hat rack and chest, but you would not do that any more than you would go up the stairs on your hands and knees. No, you go across—like this—like this—and the big round knob at the bottom of the stair is in your hands. Dear knob. You put your cheek against the wood; it is smooth and firm. Now you can go upstairs.

You are not at all afraid of the stairs. Why? Because Mother has put signals there for you, under the rail where no one can find them, and they guide you all the way up; now your legs go

---

1. **scraper:** small metal plate placed near an entrance and used for scraping mud off shoes and boots.
2. **drawing-room:** usually formal room for greeting and entertaining guests.
3. **loo:** British term for a lavatory. In many English homes, the lavatory is in a separate small room adjoining the bathroom, which contains the bathtub.

CRITICAL THINKING: GUIDED READING QUESTIONS

LITERAL

1a. What has Ally's mother often told her about flowers? ("I see no reason why you should not know your flowers. . . . Flowers have shapes and smells as well as colors.")

2a. What does Ally know better than anyone else? (She knows the smells and sounds of the house better than anyone else does.)

INFERENTIAL

1b. By teaching Ally to knit and identify flowers, what is Ally's mother encouraging in Ally? (independence, confidence, and personal fulfillment)

2b. Why does she know these things so well? (Since she relies on the senses other than sight, her perceptions of smell and sound are heightened.)

Detail. *Camille at Her Window, Argenteuil,* 1873, Claude Monet.

up the stairs as quickly as notes up a piano—almost. At the top is a small wooden heart for you to feel with your fingers; when you reach it, it is like a message and your own heart gets steady. It was not quite steady up the stairs.

"Ally, always, always be careful of the landing." Mother has said that so many times. The landing feels the same to you as the hall but it isn't. Once you dropped a ball over, and the sound came from far away down; if you tripped on the landing you might drop like the ball.

11   Now? Or not now? Are you facing the right way? That is an old fright. Did you turn round without noticing? You feel the stairs behind you with your foot and they are still there but now you are afraid to let go in case you can't step away. It is steep—steep behind you. Suppose you don't move away? Suppose you hit something—like the chair—and pitch down back-

wards? Little stickers come out along your back and neck; the back of your neck is cold, your fingers are sticky too, holding the heart signal. Suddenly you can't move away from the stairs. **12** Mother. Mother, but you bite your lips. You must not call out.

Through the window you hear voices—voices from the path.

Drops of water burst out on your neck and under your hair, and you leave the rail and step out on to the carpet and walk very boldly towards the verbena[4] and warm toweling and the hot-metal-from-the-bath-taps smell.

13   "Is she all right? Is she?"

"Ally, are you managing?" calls Mother.

"Perfectly," you answer, and you shut the loo door.

----

4. **verbena** [vər bē′nə]: plant with a pleasant smell.

You Need to Go Upstairs   **21**

CRITICAL THINKING: GUIDED READING QUESTIONS

LITERAL

1a. What is the last of the wooden signals that help Ally climb the stairs? (a small wooden heart)

2a. What dangerous area must Ally cross to reach the "loo"? (She must cross the upstairs landing.)

INFERENTIAL

1b. Why is this signal especially appropriate? (When she reaches it, Ally's own heart steadies after the ordeal of climbing the stairs. It also reminds Ally of her mother's loving confidence in her.)

2b. Why is this area especially dangerous? (If she makes a wrong turn, Ally could fall over the landing and hurt or even kill herself.)

ANSWERS

STUDY QUESTIONS

1. Ally enjoys the feel of the grass, the smells and sounds, and her knitting. She must go to the "loo."
2. "Very well, dear"; "Alone?"
3. Ally fears tripping over the tortoise and falling over the upstairs landing. Under the rail her mother has put little signals that Ally can feel.
4. "Perfectly."
5. The trip is perilous because she is blind. She feels triumphant.
6. She relies on smell, hearing, and touch. She relies on things being in their usual place, but Schiff moves around, and the scraper has been left out.
7. Ally's mother treats her normally and shows confidence in her, but the visitor treats her as handicapped and shows no confidence in her abilities. Ally insists on going alone to prove her independence and capability to the visitor.
8. It puts the reader in Ally's frame of mind and helps the reader experience what Ally experiences.
9. Answers will vary. Possibilities include tactile indicators on the landing and a bell on the tortoise.

LITERARY FOCUS

Ally's struggle to overcome her fears and triumph over her disability is the internal conflict. It is related to her battle to master the environment alone and her struggle to overcome the visitor's demeaning opinion of her, both external conflicts.

STUDY QUESTIONS

Recalling

1. Which specific things does Ally enjoy in the garden? To which upstairs room must she go?
2. What does Ally's mother say when Ally decides to go upstairs? What does the visitor say?
3. Identify two dangers that Ally fears as she makes her journey. Why is she not afraid of climbing the stairs?
4. What does Ally answer when her mother asks whether she is managing?

Interpreting

5. Why is Ally's trip upstairs so perilous? What feeling does she experience when she reaches her goal?
6. On which senses does Ally rely in making her journey? Why do Schiff and the scraper represent special dangers to her?
7. Contrast the way Ally's mother treats Ally with the way the visitor treats her. Why does Ally insist on going upstairs alone?
8. Instead of using *she* to refer to Ally or having Ally tell the story herself, Godden uses the pronoun *you*. How does this method influence the reader's response to the story?

Extending

9. If you knew Ally's family, what household devices or adaptations would you recommend that the family install for Ally's benefit?

LITERARY FOCUS

Internal Conflict

Every plot centers on a **conflict,** or a struggle between two opposing forces. While an **external con-**flict occurs between a character and some outside force, an **internal conflict** takes place within a character's mind. For example, the character may struggle mentally to face an unpleasant truth or to be strong in the face of adversity. He or she may be mentally torn between two conflicting emotions or two opposing goals.

When a story has more than one conflict, the conflicts are often related in some way. A character involved in an external conflict with a powerful enemy, for example, may also experience an internal conflict over whether he or she has the courage to face that enemy.

Thinking About Internal Conflict

■ The chief conflict in "You Need to Go Upstairs" is an internal one, since it takes place in Ally's mind. What is that conflict? To what external conflicts is it related?

COMPOSITION

Writing About Sensory Details

■ In preparing to write this story, the author blindfolded herself and walked around her house. What details in the story involve senses other than sight? How do these details make the story more realistic and emotionally satisfying? Answer these questions in a brief composition.

Writing About a Character's Experiences

■ In a few paragraphs describe another everyday struggle Ally might confront, and show how she overcomes it. Reveal Ally's perceptions by focusing on details that appeal to senses other than sight.

COMPOSITION: GUIDELINES FOR EVALUATION

WRITING ABOUT SENSORY DETAILS

Objective
To examine the use of sensory details

Guidelines for Evaluation
■ suggested length: two or three paragraphs
■ should cite perceptions described in the story
■ should explain how such details help readers share the main character's experiences

WRITING ABOUT A CHARACTER'S EXPERIENCES

Objective
To recount a new incident about a character in a story

Guidelines for Evaluation
■ suggested length: three or four paragraphs
■ should describe an everyday struggle for Ally
■ should include nonvisual sensory details

Anton Chekhov

(1860–1904)

Russia

Anton Chekhov [an' ton chek'ôf] of Russia is considered one of the grand masters of the short story. Born into a poor family in the seaport city of Taganrog, Chekhov was the son of a grocer who eventually went bankrupt. "There was no childhood in my childhood," Chekhov once said; his own financial struggles gave him a lifelong sympathy for the poor.

Chekhov began writing to support himself while attending medical school. Once he became a doctor, he chose to practice among the lower classes, even though that meant he could earn little himself. He continued to supplement his income by writing plays and stories, winning acclaim both at home and abroad.

Chekhov's work is known for its realistic blend of comedy and tragedy and for its strong moral tone. Many of his plays—including *Uncle Vanya, The Cherry Orchard,* and *The Three Sisters*—are considered classics. His stories are short and simple yet powerful, illustrating his belief that "conciseness is the sister of talent."

GEOGRAPHY AND CULTURE

Poverty in Nineteenth–Century Russia

The country we now know as the Soviet Union or U.S.S.R. was in the nineteenth century known as the Russian Empire. Poverty was an issue that concerned many nineteenth-century Russian writers, for the gulf between rich and poor was very wide. Until 1861 a large part of the rural Russian population—including Chekhov's own grandfather—was composed of serfs, or peasants legally bound to work land owned by the wealthy and unable to own land themselves. In 1861 the serfs were technically freed, but they still had to pay rent to their landlords or pay back the government for the small plots of land they were now allowed to own. If they gave up farming and tried to open small businesses using their meager savings, they often went bankrupt, as Chekhov's father did.

Many former serfs or their children moved to Russia's cities, swelling the ranks of the urban poor. The title character of the next story is typical of the many urban beggars who lived from hand to mouth and often sank into despair.

THE RUSSIAN EMPIRE (Late Nineteenth Century)

See LITERATURE AND CULTURE SOURCEBOOK: Russia and Eastern Europe

The Beggar 23

LESSON PREVIEW

A wastrel is reformed through unexpected means in this ironic nineteenth-century Russian tale. Self-righteous Skvortsoff shames a beggar, Lushkoff, into working for him and is sure he puts Lushkoff "on the right path." Later he learns that it was the kindness of his cook that motivated Lushkoff to change his ways.

LITERARY SKILLS FOR THIS SELECTION

- irony and surprise endings
- point of view
- characterization

THEMES IN THIS SELECTION

- life's surprises: false impressions of human behavior
- kindness versus harsh discipline
- social and personal reform

LESSON OBJECTIVES

1. to examine an ironic ending
2. to understand transliteration
3. to write a brief story with a surprise ending

Teacher's Classroom Resources 1

- Teaching Notes   49
- Prereading Vocabulary   50
- Reading Guide   51
- Check Test   52
- Responding to World Cultures   53
- Literary Focus: Irony and Surprise Endings   54
- Language Study: Writing Systems and Transliteration   55
- Writing Process Guide: Writing About Life's Surprises   56
- Grammar in Literature: Periods, Exclamation Points, and Question Marks   57
- Selection Test   58

IN THE CLASSROOM

TEACHING STUDENTS OF DIFFERENT ABILITIES

- **For less advanced students:** Preview the glossary words, and point out that the names *Skvortsoff* and *Lushkoff,* despite unusual consonant combinations, are phonetic. Have

students complete the Reading Guide for this selection.
- **For more advanced students:** Have students consider the values Chekhov endorses in this story and discuss whether or not they agree with him.

DISCUSSING GEOGRAPHY AND CULTURE

The Plight of the Russian Peasantry
Even after the emancipation of the serfs in 1861, most Russian peasants lived in crude wooden huts and subsisted largely on bread. Infant mortality was high, and epidemics of cholera, typhoid, and other diseases raged. Famines, such as the one that struck western Russia in 1891, were common.
- Some say that in the United States the gap between the rich and the poor is widening. Have students discuss their views of this trend.

Anton Chekhov

The Beggar

Translated from the Russian by Marian Fell

"Kind sir, have pity; turn your attention to a poor, hungry man! For three days I have had nothing to eat; I haven't five kopecks[1] for a lodging, I swear it before God. For eight years I was a village school-teacher and then I lost my place through intrigues. I fell a victim to calumny. It is a year now since I have had anything to do—"

1 The advocate[2] Skvortsoff looked at the ragged, fawn-colored overcoat of the suppliant, at his dull, drunken eyes, at the red spot on either cheek, and it seemed to him as if he had seen this man somewhere before.

"I have now had an offer of a position in the province of Kaluga,"[3] the mendicant went on, "but I haven't the money to get there. Help me kindly; I am ashamed to ask, but—I am obliged to by circumstances."

Skvortsoff's eyes fell on the man's overshoes, one of which was high and the other low, and he suddenly remembered something.

"Look here, it seems to me I met you day before yesterday in Sadovaya Street," he said; "but you told me then that you were a student who had been expelled, and not a village school-teacher. Do you remember?"

"N-no, that can't be so," mumbled the beggar, taken aback. "I am a village school-teacher, and if you like I can show you my papers."

2 "Have done with lying! You called yourself a student and even told me what you had been expelled for. Don't you remember?"

---
1. **kopecks** [kō′peks]: Russian coins of small value.
2. **advocate** [ad′və kit]: lawyer who argues cases in court.
3. **Kaluga** [kə lōō′gə]: area in west-central Russia.

24 *The Short Story*

Skvortsoff flushed and turned from the ragged creature with an expression of disgust.

"This is dishonesty, my dear sir!" he cried angrily. "This is swindling! I shall send the police for you! Even if you are poor and hungry, that does not give you any right to lie brazenly and shamelessly!"

The waif caught hold of the door-handle and looked furtively round the antechamber, like a detected thief.

"I—I'm not lying—" he muttered. "I can show you my papers."

"Who would believe you?" Skvortsoff continued indignantly. "Don't you know that it's a low, dirty trick to exploit the sympathy which society feels for village school-teachers and students? It's revolting!"

3 Skvortsoff lost his temper and began to berate the mendicant unmercifully. The impudent lying of the ragamuffin offended what he, Skvortsoff, most prized in himself: his kindness, his tender heart, his compassion for all unhappy beings. That lie, an attempt to take advantage of the pity of its "subject," seemed to him to profane the charity which he liked to extend to the poor out of the purity of his heart. At first the waif continued to protest innocence, but soon he grew silent and hung his head in confusion.

"Sir!" he said, laying his hand on his heart, "the fact is I—was lying! I am neither a student nor a school-teacher. All that was a fiction. Formerly I sang in a Russian choir and was sent away for drunkenness. But what else can I do? I can't get along without lying. No one will give me anything when I tell the truth. With truth a

---

CRITICAL THINKING: GUIDED READING QUESTIONS

LITERAL

1a. What does the beggar now pretend to be, and what did he pretend to be before? (He now pretends to be an out-of-work teacher who lost his job through intrigue; before, he pretended to be a poor student who had been expelled.)

2a. According to Skvortsoff's view of himself, why does he extend charity to the poor? (He does so out of the purity of his heart.)

INFERENTIAL

1b. Why does the beggar pretend to be a poor teacher and a poor student? (He does so to arouse the sympathy of others and thereby get a handout from them.)

2b. By evaluating himself with phrases such as "tender heart" and "the purity of his heart," what does Skvortsoff reveal about himself? (He has an exaggerated opinion of his own benevolence.)

man would starve to death or die of cold for lack of a lodging. You reason justly, I understand you, but—what can I do?"

4 "What can you do? You ask what you can do?" cried Skvortsoff, coming close to him. "Work! That's what you can do! You must work!"

"Work—yes, I know that myself; but where can I find work?"

"Rot! You're young and healthy and strong; you could always find work if you only wanted to, but you're lazy and spoiled and drunken! There's a smell about you like a tap-room. **5** You're rotten and false to the core, and all you can do is to lie. When you consent to lower yourself to work, you want a job in an office or in a choir or as a marker at billiards—any employment for which you can get money without doing anything! How would you like to try your hand at manual labor? No, you'd never be a porter or a factory hand; you're a man of pretensions, you are!"

"By God, you judge harshly!" cried the beggar with a bitter laugh. "Where can I find man- **6** ual labor? It's too late for me to be a clerk because in trade one has to begin as a boy; no one would ever take me for a porter because they couldn't order me about; no factory would have me because for that one has to know a trade, and I know none."

"Nonsense! You always find some excuse! How would you like to chop wood for me?"

"I wouldn't refuse to do that, but in these days even skilled wood-cutters find themselves sitting without bread."

"Huh! You loafers all talk that way. As soon as an offer is made you, you refuse it. Will you come and chop wood for me?"

"Yes, sir; I will."

"Very well; we'll soon find out. Splendid—we'll see—"

7 Skvortsoff hastened along, rubbing his hands, not without a feeling of malice, and called his cook out of the kitchen.

"Here, Olga," he said, "take this gentleman into the wood-shed and let him chop wood."

The tatterdemalion[4] scarecrow shrugged his shoulders, as if in perplexity, and went irresolutely after the cook. It was obvious from his gait that he had not consented to go and chop wood because he was hungry and wanted work, but simply from pride and shame, because he had been trapped by his own words. It was obvious, too, that his strength had been undermined by vodka and that he was unhealthy and did not feel the slightest inclination for toil.

Skvortsoff hurried into the dining room. From its windows one could see the wood-shed and everything that went on in the yard. Standing at the window, Skvortsoff saw the cook and the beggar come out into the yard by the back door and make their way across the dirty snow to the shed. Olga glared wrathfully at her companion, shoved him aside with her elbow, unlocked the shed, and angrily banged the door.

"We probably interrupted the woman over her coffee," thought Skvortsoff. "What an ill-tempered creature!"

Next he saw the pseudo-teacher, pseudo-student seat himself on a log and become lost in thought with his red cheeks resting on his fists. **8** The woman flung down an ax at his feet, spat angrily, and, judging from the expression of her lips, began to scold him. The beggar irresolutely pulled a billet of wood toward him, set it up between his feet, and tapped it feebly with the ax. The billet wavered and fell down. The beggar again pulled it to him, blew on his freezing hands, and tapped it with his ax cautiously, as if afraid of hitting his overshoe or of cutting off his finger. The stick of wood again fell to the ground.

Skvortsoff's anger had vanished and he now began to feel a little sorry and ashamed of himself for having set a spoiled, drunken, perchance

---

4. **tatterdemalion** [tat′ər di māl′yən]: dressed in rags; tattered in appearance.

The Beggar **25**

Below are the sidebar and bottom teaching sections.

CRITICAL THINKING: GUIDED READING QUESTIONS

LITERAL

1a. What feeling is Skvortsoff "not without" as he calls Olga to supervise the beggar's wood-chopping duties? (He is "not without" malice.)

2a. What sort of creature does Skvortsoff consider Olga to be? (He thinks she is ill-tempered.)

INFERENTIAL

1b. What does the author's remark about malice reveal about Skvortsoff's earlier view of himself? (He is really not the pure-hearted person he considers himself to be.)

2b. Since he feels malice when he calls Olga, what does Skvortsoff probably expect the "ill-tempered" Olga to do? (He expects her to make the beggar's wood chopping a highly unpleasant experience.)

- Skvortsoff dismisses his shame at making a weak man work in the cold.
- The beggar returns often to earn money doing various odd jobs.
- Later he is hired to help Skvortsoff move, and Skvortsoff learns that his name is Lushkoff.
- Skvortsoff recommends him for a job copying documents.
- Two years later he encounters Lushkoff, now a notary.
- When Skvortsoff expresses delight in the reformation he effected, Lushkoff says that, strictly speaking, it was Olga who saved him.

IN THE GLOSSARY

- menial: degrading
- gallery: theater balcony

9 TEACHING CHARACTERIZATION

Elicit that Skvortsoff actually does very little; it is his cook, Olga, who supervises the beggar's wood-chopping duties.

10 CULTURAL BACKGROUND

Point out that before the advent of typewriters and photocopying machines, hand copying of written documents was a widely performed, necessary task.

11 READING SKILL: INFERENCE

Note that the value of copper coins—like pennies in America—is generally small. Elicit that paying in copper coins shows that Lushkoff is still relatively poor, though now he can afford to attend the theater.

12 TEACHING PLOT: CLIMAX

Point out that the climax comes with the revelation of a surprise: It was Olga, not Skvortsoff, who changed Lushkoff.

---

sick man to work at menial labor in the cold.

"Well, never mind," he thought, going into 9 his study from the dining room. "I did it for his own good."

An hour later Olga came in and announced that the wood had all been chopped.

"Good! Give him half a ruble,"[5] said Skvortsoff. "If he wants to he can come back and cut wood on the first day of each month. We can always find work for him."

On the first of the month the waif made his appearance and again earned half a ruble, although he could barely stand on his legs. From that day on he often appeared in the yard and every time work was found for him. Now he would shovel snow, now put the wood-shed in order, now beat the dust out of rugs and mattresses. Every time he received from twenty to forty kopecks, and once, even a pair of old trousers were sent out to him.

When Skvortsoff moved into another house he hired him to help in the packing and hauling of the furniture. This time the waif was sober, gloomy, and silent. He hardly touched the furniture, and walked behind the wagons hanging his head, not even making a pretense of appearing busy. He only shivered in the cold and became embarrassed when the carters jeered at him for his idleness, his feebleness, and his tattered, fancy overcoat. After the moving was over Skvortsoff sent for him.

"Well, I see that my words have taken effect," he said, handing him a ruble. "Here's for your pains. I see you are sober and have no objection to work. What is your name?"

"Lushkoff."

"Well, Lushkoff, I can now offer you some other, cleaner employment. Can you write?"

"I can."

10 "Then take this letter to a friend of mine tomorrow and you will be given some copying to do. Work hard, don't drink, and remember what I have said to you. Good-bye!"

Pleased at having put a man on the right path, Skvortsoff tapped Lushkoff kindly on the shoulder and even gave him his hand at parting. Lushkoff took the letter, and from that day forth came no more to the yard for work.

Two years went by. Then one evening, as Skvortsoff was standing at the ticket window of a theater paying for his seat, he noticed a little man beside him with a coat collar of curly fur 11 and a worn sealskin cap. This little individual timidly asked the ticket seller for a seat in the gallery and paid for it in copper coins.

"Lushkoff, is that you?" cried Skvortsoff, recognizing in the little man his former woodchopper. "How are you? What are you doing? How is everything with you?"

"All right. I am a notary[6] now and get thirty-five rubles a month."

"Thank Heaven! That's fine! I am delighted for your sake. I am very, very glad, Lushkoff. You see, you are my godson, in a sense. I gave you a push along the right path, you know. Do you remember what a roasting I gave you, eh? I nearly had you sinking into the ground at my feet that day. Thank you, old man, for not forgetting my words."

"Thank you, too," said Lushkoff. "If I hadn't come to you then I might still have been calling myself a teacher or a student to this day. Yes, by flying to your protection I dragged myself out of a pit."

"I am very glad, indeed."

"Thank you for your kind words and deeds. You talked splendidly to me then. I am very grateful to you and to your cook, Olga. God bless that 12 good and noble woman! You spoke finely then, and I shall be indebted to you to my dying day; but, strictly speaking, it was your cook, Olga, who saved me."

---

5. **ruble** [rōō′bəl]: chief unit of currency in Russia. One hundred kopecks equal one ruble.

6. **notary** [nō′tər ē]: public clerk responsible for authenticating and certifying legal documents.

26 *The Short Story*

CRITICAL THINKING: GUIDED READING QUESTIONS

LITERAL

1a. What reason does Skvortsoff use to dismiss his shame at sending a weak man to work in the cold? ("I did it for his own good.")

2a. What important fact does Skvortsoff learn about the beggar when the beggar comes to help him move? (He learns his name.)

INFERENTIAL

1b. In view of this idea, what does Skvortsoff apparently feel is the way to change people for the better? (He seems to believe that harsh treatment leads to reform.)

2b. Why is it significant that he learns the beggar's name only after several months? (It stresses how little interest he has taken in Lushkoff as a human being.)

La Casa Grigia, 1917, Marc Chagall.

PAGE SUMMARY: AT A GLANCE

■ Lushkoff explains that Olga used to berate him at first, then weep for him, and—most significantly—chop all the wood for him.

■ He does not know why her behavior saved him, but it did.

IN THE GLOSSARY

■ sot: drunkard

13 TEACHING IRONY AND SURPRISE ENDINGS

Elicit that Olga is not the "ill-tempered" creature Skvortsoff thought her to be and that her "scolding" was far more sympathetic than he imagined.

14 READING SKILL: COMPARISON AND CONTRAST

Point out that while Olga, like Skvortsoff, was critical of Lushkoff's dissipated behavior, she took pity on him and did not force him to chop wood in his weakened state.

COLLABORATIVE LEARNING: ENRICHMENT ACTIVITY

Evaluation Divide the class into small groups, and ask each group to evaluate Olga's method of helping Lushkoff versus Skvortsoff's method. Each group should decide which method seems more likely to succeed with most individuals in need of help. Each group should present to the class its decision and the reasons behind that decision.

ART AND LITERATURE

The Russian-born painter Marc Chagall (1887–1985) lived most of his life in France, but most of his work reflects his Russian and Orthodox Jewish heritage. In *La Casa Grigia,* painted at the time of the Russian Revolution, when the peasantry rose up against the aristocracy, Chagall contrasted a peasant cabin with the more elaborate architecture of the town beyond.

■ Have students list other instances of imagery Chagall uses to portray the conflict between poverty and privilege. (The swirling sky suggests turmoil; the man clutching his bosom indicates the peasant's isolation and the hardship of poverty.)

"How is that?"

"Like this. When I used to come to your house to chop wood she used to begin: 'Oh, you sot, you! Oh, you miserable creature! There's nothing for you but ruin.' And then she would sit down opposite me and grow sad, look into **13** my face and weep. 'Oh, you unlucky man! There is no pleasure for you in this world and there will be none in the world to come. You drunkard! You will burn in hell. Oh, you unhappy one!' And so she would carry on, you know, in that strain. I can't tell you how much misery she suffered, how many tears she shed for my sake. **14** But the chief thing was—she used to chop the wood for me. Do you know, sir, that I did not chop one single stick of wood for you? She did it all. Why this saved me, why I changed, why I stopped drinking at the sight of her I cannot explain. I only know that, owing to her words and noble deeds a change took place in my heart; she set me right and I shall never forget it. However, it is time to go now; there goes the bell."

Lushkoff bowed and departed to the gallery.

The Beggar **27**

CRITICAL THINKING: GUIDED READING QUESTIONS

LITERAL

1a. Who actually chopped the wood that Lushkoff was paid to chop? (Olga)

2a. What can Lushkoff not explain? (He cannot explain why Olga's behavior saved him.)

INFERENTIAL

1b. Why did Olga chop the wood? (She was too considerate to let him chop wood in the cold when he was in such a weakened state.)

2b. What can *we* conclude is the reason for Lushkoff's reformation? (Olga's kindness and caring in words and actions touched him, prompting him to change for the better.)

Did Skvortsoff learn anything? Why or why not?

STUDY QUESTIONS

1. Lushkoff lies about his background and his reasons for begging; his kindness, tender heart, and compassion for all unhappy beings
2. Skvortsoff offers him work chopping wood; malice
3. He is ashamed at first but then certain it was done "for his own good." Later he is pleased at having put someone "on the right path."
4. He is a notary. He credits Olga with saving him: She chopped all the wood for him and wept to see his sorry state, and this caused his change.
5. No; in contrast to Olga, he is a hard taskmaster who makes a weakened man work in the cold.
6. Skvortsoff considers her an ill-tempered, scolding woman, but she was very kind to Lushkoff; her caring prompts him to feel better about himself, and she sets a good example.
7. Society should treat them with kindness and concern. The story suggests that human beings often surprise us, especially if we have made little effort to know them.
8. Answers will vary, but many students will say that there are more Skvortsoffs; they may disagree as to whether the author's compassionate approach would really work.

LITERARY FOCUS

At first we think Lushkoff has reformed because of Skvortsoff's tough-minded treatment, but he actually changes because of Olga's kindness. Chekhov manipulates details by telling the story from Skvortsoff's point of view, giving an inaccurate impression of Olga and of Skvortsoff's own effectiveness until he learns the truth from Lushkoff at the end.

LANGUAGE STUDY

1. Possible responses: Anton Chekov; Leo Tolstoi; Fyodor Dostoyevsky
2. Possibilities include Arabic, Chinese, Greek, Hebrew, Hindi, and Japanese.

STUDY QUESTIONS

Recalling

1. At the beginning of the story, what does Lushkoff, the beggar, do that angers Skvortsoff? What qualities does Skvortsoff most prize in himself?
2. When Lushkoff says he has no trade, what work does Skvortsoff offer him? What feeling does Skvortsoff have as he calls for his cook to put Lushkoff to work?
3. How does Skvortsoff feel when he sees Lushkoff trying to chop wood? How does he feel after Lushkoff helps him move?
4. What job does Lushkoff have two years later? Whom does he credit for saving him? Why?

Interpreting

5. Considering what Skvortsoff prizes in himself, is his self-image accurate? Explain.
6. Contrast Skvortsoff's earlier impressions of Olga with Lushkoff's impression of her near the end of the story. Why do you think Olga's actions motivate Lushkoff to change whereas Skvortsoff's actions do not?
7. What does the story suggest about the way society should treat people like Lushkoff in order to motivate them to change for the better? What does the story suggest about life's surprises?

Extending

8. In your opinion, are there more Olgas or more Skvortsoffs in the world? What do you think is the best way to motivate people to change for the better? Discuss your opinions.

LITERARY FOCUS

Irony and Surprise Endings

Irony exists when there is a contrast between the way things seem and the way they really are. When a story has a surprise ending, the ending is ironic because what seems likely to happen is not what actually occurs. Surprise endings are popular in fiction, in part because readers find them entertaining and memorable but also because most fiction attempts to reflect life, and life is often full of surprises. In order to create a surprise ending, authors must carefully manipulate the information they reveal earlier in the story, withholding information that could give away the ending but still providing enough information so that the surprise, when it comes, seems plausible.

Thinking About Irony and Surprise Endings

■ Explain the irony behind Chekhov's surprise ending by contrasting what we think has happened with what has actually happened to Lushkoff. How does Chekhov manipulate details of the story to create the surprise ending?

LANGUAGE STUDY

Writing Systems and Transliteration

English is written using the Roman alphabet, which several European languages employ. Other languages use different alphabets or writing systems; for example, Russian is written using the Cyrillic alphabet. To show how a foreign language that does not use the Roman alphabet sounds, the foreign language is **transliterated,** or spelled phonetically using Roman letters. This process is most frequently employed with names of persons and places, which are rarely translated into English.

Transliterated names and other words often have more than one acceptable spelling. The transliterated name of this story's author, for example, is usually spelled *Anton Chekhov,* but it is sometimes spelled *Anton Tchekhov.*

1. Use a dictionary to find at least one more acceptable spelling of *Anton Chekhov* and alternative spellings of the names of the Russian authors *Leo Tolstoy* and *Fyodor Dostoevski.*
2. What are some other languages that do not use the Roman alphabet? Use an encyclopedia or another reference work to help you identify at least five.

COMPOSITION

Writing About Life's Surprises

■ Think of a real-life incident you know about that ended in a surprising way. Write a brief short story based on the incident. Withhold the surprise from readers until the end of your story.

COMPOSITION: GUIDELINES FOR EVALUATION

WRITING ABOUT LIFE'S SURPRISES

Objective

To write a brief story with a surprise ending

Guidelines for Evaluation

■ suggested length: one to two pages
■ should be based on a true incident
■ should withhold details to ensure that the ending comes as a surprise

Stan Barstow

(born 1928)

England

With his stories, novels, and award-winning television dramas, England's Stan Barstow has won celebrity at home and an ever-growing audience abroad. Born in Yorkshire, England, Barstow worked as a sales executive for an engineering company until 1962, when he gave up that job to dedicate himself to writing. His television dramatizations have won awards from the Royal Television Society and the Writers' Guild of Great Britain.

Barstow's fiction is praised for its depictions of his native surroundings and for the honesty and compassion with which he describes his characters. His descriptions of Yorkshire's wild scenery and of the citizens who inhabit its towns are sharp and vivid.

"His people are mostly working or lower middle class," notes critic Isabel Quigley. "He speaks for urban provincial life with piercing vividness" and "for a particular outlook and morality that few other writers touch, let alone understand and feel for, today."

GEOGRAPHY AND CULTURE

Yorkshire and the English Class System

For centuries England was a nation with marked class distinctions based on geography as well as family background. Yorkshire, a region of rugged moors and dales located hundreds of miles north of London, was seen as backward by more sophisticated city dwellers to the south. The well-born and wealthy in Yorkshire might visit London frequently and receive polished educations at England's universities. However, the average Yorkshire native rarely journeyed far from home and usually spoke in a dialect that seemed peculiar and unrefined to England's educated upper classes. Many people in modern Yorkshire continue to speak in dialect, though its more obscure words and expressions have gradually begun to disappear.

In the twentieth century an increased belief in the equality of all people, as well as vast improvements in transportation and communications, has greatly diminished England's social and regional differences. Nevertheless, the old class distinctions have not entirely vanished, and many contemporary English authors—including Barstow—explore those distinctions in their work.

The Actor **29**

LESSON PREVIEW

A working-class Yorkshireman is offered a role in a local theatrical production. Albert Royston, a grocery clerk, overcomes his shyness and enjoys the endeavor. At the performance, however, the other actors accidentally skip his scene. He masks his disappointment and never again tries anything of the kind.

LITERARY SKILLS FOR THIS SELECTION

- irony
- characterization
- theme

THEMES IN THIS SELECTION

- life's surprises: coping with life's ironic disappointments
- appearance versus reality
- class differences

LESSON OBJECTIVES

1. to examine situational and dramatic irony
2. to understand dialect and Anglicisms
3. to write a scene for a play
4. to compare and contrast stories

Teacher's Classroom Resources 1

- Teaching Notes   61
- Prereading Vocabulary   62
- Reading Guide   63
- Check Test   64
- Responding to World Cultures   65
- Literary Focus: Situational and Dramatic Irony   66
- Language Study: Dialect and Anglicisms   67
- Writing Process Guide: Expanding a Scene   68
- Grammar in Literature: Some Uses of the Apostrophe   69
- Selection Test   70

TEACHING STUDENTS OF DIFFERENT ABILITIES

- **For less advanced students:** Preview the Literary Focus for this selection, making sure students understand the difference between situational and dramatic irony. Have students complete the Reading Guide for the selection.
- **For more advanced students:** Have students discuss how "The Actor" illustrates Thoreau's famous statement, "The mass of men lead lives of quiet desperation."

DISCUSSING GEOGRAPHY AND CULTURE

Regional Distinctions
This story takes place in Yorkshire, a region in northern England with its own customs and dialect. The United States also has regional differences—distinctions based not just on geography but on perceived character traits. Southerners, for instance, are traditionally considered polite and hospitable, whereas New Englanders are thought to be taciturn.
- Ask students to describe the personality traits associated with other American regions.

Stan Barstow

The Actor

1 He was a big man, without surplus flesh, and with an impassivity of face that hid extreme shyness, and which, allied with his striking build, made him look more than anything else, as he walked homewards in the early evening in fawn mackintosh[1] and trilby hat, like a plain-clothes policeman going quietly and efficiently about his business, with trouble for someone at the end of it.

All his adult life people had been saying to him, "You should have been a policeman, Mr. Royston," or, more familiarly, "You've missed your way, Albert. You're cut out for a copper, lad." But he would smile in his quiet, patient way, as though no one had ever said it before, and almost always give exactly the same reply: "Nay, I'm all right. I like my bed at nights."

In reality he was a shop assistant and could be found, in white smock, on five and a half days of the week behind the counter of the Moorend branch grocery store of Cressley Industrial Co-operative Society, where he was assistant manager. He had been assistant manager for five years and seemed fated to occupy that position for many more years to come before the promotion earmarked for him would become fact. For the manager was of a settled disposition also, and still comparatively young and fit.

2 But Albert did not apparently worry. He did not apparently worry about anything; but this again was the deception of his appearance. Quiet he might be, and stolid and settled in his ways; but no one but he had known the agony of shyness that was his wedding day; and no one but he had known the pure terror of the premature birth of his only child, when the dead baby

---

1. **mackintosh:** chiefly British term for "raincoat"; called *mac* for short.

30 *The Short Story*

he had longed for with so much secret yearning had almost cost the life of the one person without whom his own life would hardly have seemed possible—Alice, his wife.

3 So it was the measure of his misleading appearance and his ability to hide his feelings that no one ever guessed the truth, that no one was ever led from the belief that he was a taciturn man of unshakable placidity. "You want to take a leaf out of Albert's book," they would say. "Take a lesson from him. Never worries, Albert doesn't."

4 Thus Albert, at the age of thirty-seven, on the eve of his small adventure.

Amateur drama was a popular pastime in Cressley and varied in standard from rather embarrassing to really quite good. Generally considered to be among the best of the local groups was the C.I.C.S. Players—the drama group of Cressley Industrial Co-operative Society. They restricted their activities to perhaps three productions a year and worked hard to 5 achieve a professional finish. It was about the time of the casting for the Christmas production, perhaps the most important of the year, since at this time each group was shown in direct comparison with all the other bodies who joined together in the week-long Christmas Festival of Amateur Drama in the Co-operative Hall, that the rather fierce-looking lady from General Office, who was said to be the backbone and mainstay of the C.I.C.S. Players, happened to visit the shop and, seeing Albert on her way out as he towered over a diminutive woman customer, stopped abruptly and, waiting only till he was free, crossed over to him and said, "Tell me, have you ever acted?"

As it was the oddest thing anyone had ever asked him, Albert simply stared at the woman

---

CRITICAL THINKING: GUIDED READING QUESTIONS

LITERAL

1a. What does Albert's impassivity hide, and what is also "the deception of his appearance"? (His impassivity hides extreme shyness. That he seems not to worry is also deceptive.)

2a. What "agony" and "pure terror" has Albert known? (He has known the agony of shyness on his wedding day and the pure terror of nearly losing his beloved wife when she lost a premature baby.)

INFERENTIAL

1b. On the basis of these details, what generalization can you make about Albert's relationship with others? (They do not know his true nature because he hides his feelings from them.)

2b. What do these details reveal about the true Albert? (He is a sensitive person with strong feelings.)

while a colleague said, "He's always acting, Albert is. Make a cat laugh, the antics he gets up to."

"Take no notice of him," Albert said. "He's kiddin'."

6 "What I mean," the lady said, "is, have you had any experience of dramatics?"

"Dramatics?" Albert said.

"Taking part in plays."

Albert gave a short laugh and shook his head.

"There's a chap coming from M.G.M.[2] to see him next week," the facetious colleague said. "Cressley's answer to Alan Ladd."[3]

7 Ignoring the irrepressible one, the lady continued her interrogation of Albert with: "Has anyone ever told you you look like a policeman?"

"I believe it has been mentioned," said Albert, wondering if the woman had nothing better to do than stand here asking him daft questions all morning.

8 She now looked Albert over in silence for some moments until, unable to bear her scrutiny for another second, he bent down and pretended to look for something under the counter. He had his head down there when she spoke again and he thought for a moment he had misheard her.

"Eh?" he said, straightening up.

"I said, would you be interested in a part in our new production? You know, the C.I.C.S. Players. We're doing R. Belton Wilkins's *The Son of the House* for the Christmas Festival and there's a part in it for a police constable. We've no one in the group who fits the role nearly so well as you."

"But I can't act," Albert said. "I've never done anything like that before."

"It's only a small part—about a page. You'd soon learn it. And you'd find it great fun to be part of a group effort. There's nothing quite like the thrill of the stage, you know."

"Aye, happen[4] it's all right if you're that way inclined," Albert said, and was relieved to see a customer at the lady's elbow.

"Well, I won't keep you from your work," she said; "but think it over. We'd love to have you, and you'd never regret it. We start rehearsals next week. I'll pop in and see you again later. Think it over."

"Aye, aye," Albert said. "I'll think it over." Meaning that he would dismiss it from his mind for the nonsense it was as soon as she was gone. Acting! Him!

But he did not dismiss it from his mind. A part of his mind was occupied with it all morning as he attended to his customers; and at lunch-time, when the door had been locked, he went over to one of the young lady assistants from the opposite counter.

"You're mixed up with this acting thing, aren't you?"

9 "The Players?" the girl said. "Oh yes. It's grand fun. We're doing R. Belton Wilkins's latest West End[5] success for our next production."

"Aye," Albert said, "I've been hearin' so. I've had yon' woman on to me this morning."

"You mean Mrs. Bostock. I saw her talking to you. A real tartar,[6] she is. Terrifically keen and efficient. I don't know what we'd do without her."

"She's been doin' a bit o' recruitin' this morning," Albert said. "Been on to me to take a part in this new play. Don't know what she's thinkin' about." All morning a new feeling had been growing in him and now he realized that he was pleased and flattered by Mrs. Bostock's approach, nonsense though it undoubtedly was. "I always thought you wanted these la-di-da

---

4. **happen:** Yorkshire dialect for "perhaps."
5. **West End:** referring to London's theater district, in the western part of the city.
6. **tartar** [tär′tər]: stubborn, demanding, or quick-tempered person.

---

2. **M.G.M.:** Metro-Goldwyn-Mayer, famous Hollywood movie studio.
3. **Alan Ladd** (1913–1964): American movie star.

The Actor **31**

PAGE SUMMARY: AT A GLANCE

- Mrs. Bostock asks Albert to play a policeman in an upcoming production.
- When Albert protests that he cannot act, she says the part is small enough to learn quickly and mentions the fun of the group effort.
- Although Albert says he will consider her offer, he intends to forget it; he cannot, however.
- He questions a co-worker who is a member of the theater company.

IN THE GLOSSARY

- facetious: joking, sometimes inappropriately
- irrepressible: unable to be restrained
- interrogation: questioning

6 READING SKILL: PREDICTING OUTCOMES

On the basis of earlier details, have students predict the role Albert will most likely be offered. (that of a policeman)

7 GRAMMAR IN LITERATURE

Clarify that the "irrepressible one" here refers to the facetious colleague. You might then review pronoun referents, asking students which nouns "her" and "you" refer to. ("the lady" and "Albert," respectively)

8 TEACHING CHARACTERIZATION

Point out that here we have indirect characterization, revealing Albert's shyness, which was directly stated earlier.

9 CULTURAL BACKGROUND

Note that the dialogue of the "young lady" assistant reflects a more educated background than Albert's dialogue. Albert uses dialect ("Aye"), simple slang ("on to me"), and clipped pronunciations ("hearin'"). The young lady uses inflated expressions ("grand fun"), more fashionable slang ("terrifically keen"), and standard English pronunciation.

CRITICAL THINKING: GUIDED READING QUESTIONS

LITERAL

1a. What does Albert respond when Mrs. Bostock says, "Has anyone ever told you you look like a policeman?" ("I believe it has been mentioned.")

2a. What does Albert plan to do when he says, "I'll think it over," and what actually happens? (He plans to forget the woman's request, but he keeps thinking about it.)

INFERENTIAL

1b. How do Albert's thoughts as he responds show his masked feelings in action? (He actually thinks the lady is "daft," but he replies politely.)

2b. Why do you think Albert cannot dismiss the woman's request from his mind? (He is probably flattered that she considers him capable of acting and is tempted by a new, creative, and sociable experience that would be a change from his routine.)

- Albert voices several objections to the possibility of his acting, but the young woman is encouraging.
- Although he tells her not to bother, she gives him her copy of the play, and he begins reading it with interest.
- He asks whether he can take it home, saying only that it is interesting and he wants to see how it ends.
- That evening he tells Alice, his wife, what happened, and she readily guesses the role he has been offered.

10 TEACHING SYMBOLS

Note that Albert represents the common man and working-class Englishmen, not "la-di-da chaps" of the upper class. Ask what the title and the details thus far suggest that he also represents. (He is representative of people who hide their feelings.)

11 TEACHING STUDENTS OF LIMITED ENGLISH PROFICIENCY

Have students use context clues to determine meanings of expressions like "type-casting" ("casting someone who looks the part") and "put it on" ("pretend").

12 TEACHING IRONY

Elicit that Albert's actions belie his words: He is in fact "thinkin' o' doin' it."

13 CULTURAL BACKGROUND

Note that in England tea is more popular than coffee. The English often have tea instead of coffee after dinner, break for tea rather than coffee on the job, and have tea with snacks in a light afternoon meal that is called tea.

14 READING SKILL: INFERENCE

The author expects us to infer that Alice knows Albert was asked to be a policeman. Ask what we can infer she knows when she later says, "Oh, ho!" (He is interested in the acting offer.)

10 chaps for play-actin'," he said; "not ord'nary chaps like me."

"I don't know," the girl said, unbuttoning her overall. "What part does she want you for?"

"The policeman."

11 "Well, there you are. Perfect type-casting. You look the part exactly."

"But they'd know straight away 'at I wasn't an actor, soon as I opened me mouth."

"They don't want to know you're an actor. They want to think you're a policeman."

"But I can't put it on."

"Policemen don't put it on, do they? You'd just have to be yourself and you'd be perfect."

"And I've no head for remembering lines," Albert said.

"How do you know if you've never tried?"

"Hmm," Albert said.

"Look," the girl said, "I'll bring my copy of the play back after dinner and you can have a look at the part. As far as I remember, it's not very long."

12 "Oh, don't bother," Albert said. "I'm not thinkin' o' doin' it."

"No bother," the girl said. "You just have a look at it and see."

That afternoon, in the intervals between attending to customers, Albert could be seen paying great attention to something slightly below the level of the counter; and when the shop had closed for the day he approached the girl who had lent him the book and said, "Will you be wantin' this tonight? I thought I might take it home an' have a look at it."

"It's getting you, then?"

"Well, I've read it about halfway through," Albert said, "an' I've got interested like. In the story, I mean. I'd like to see how it ends, if you can spare the book."

"You can borrow it," the girl said. "You'll find it very gripping near the end. It ran for over two years in London."

"You don't say so," Albert said. "That's a long time."

32   *The Short Story*

"Of course, we're only doing one performance," the girl said, "so you needn't get the wind up."[7]

13 "What d'you think happened at the shop today?" Albert asked Alice after tea that evening.

Alice said she couldn't imagine.

"We had that Mrs. Bostock down from General Office an' she asked me if I'd like a part in this new play they're getting up."

"You?" Alice said. "She asked you?"

"Aye, I knew it," Albert said. "I knew you'd think it was daft an' all."

"I don't think it's daft at all," Alice said. "I'm surprised, but I don't think it's daft. What part does she want you to play?"

14 "Guess," Albert said. "She took one look at me an' offered me the part."

Alice began to laugh. "Why not? Why ever shouldn't you?"

"Because," Albert said, "there's a difference in walkin' the streets lookin' like a bobby an' walkin' on to a stage an' reckonin' to be one. I don't think I could do it, not with maybe hundreds o' people watchin' me."

"Oh, I don't know. They tell me you forget the audience once you start saying your lines."

"Aye, an' supposin' you forget your lines? What then?"

"Well, you just have to learn them. And you have rehearsals and what not. I don't suppose it's a long part, is it?"

Albert fingered the book. "Only a page. I have it here."

"Oh, ho!" Alice said.

"Well, young Lucy Fryer would bring it for me, an' I started readin' it and got interested. It's a real good play, y'know. They ought to do it on the telly. It ran for two years in London."

Alice took the book and looked at the title. "Yes, I've heard of this."

"It's all about a young feller and his dad's

---

7. **get the wind up:** become nervous or scared.

CRITICAL THINKING: GUIDED READING QUESTIONS

LITERAL

1a. What objections does Albert make about the possibility of his acting? (He is an ordinary chap, he can't "put it on," and he has no head for remembering lines.)

2a. What reason does Albert give for taking home a copy of the play? (He has read it halfway and wants to see how it ends.)

INFERENTIAL

1b. Why do you think Albert states so many objections? (He is too modest to admit his interest in acting and is accustomed to thinking of himself in self-deprecating terms.)

2b. What is Albert's real reason for taking the play home? (He is interested in performing in it.)

ever so rich and dotes on the lad. Thinks the sun shines out of him; an' all the time this lad's a real nasty piece o' work. A proper nowter."[8]

"Where's the policeman's part?"

"In the second act. Here, let me show you. This lad an' his brother are havin' a row,[9] see, because he's run some'dy down in his car and not stopped, because he was drunk. An' right in the middle of this I come in an' —"

"*You* come in?" Alice said. "I thought you weren't interested in the part?"

15 Albert looked sheepish. "I haven't said I am," he said. "I sort o' tried to imagine myself as I was reading it, that's all."

"I see," Alice said.

"Aye, that's all. . . . What you lookin' at me for?"

"I'm just looking," Alice said.

It was two days later that Mrs. Bostock came in again.

"Well," she said with ferocious brightness, "did you think it over?"

"He's read the play, Mrs. Bostock," Lucy Fryer said, coming over. "I lent him my copy."

"Splendid, splendid."

"Yes, a very entertainin' play indeed," Albert said. "But I haven't said owt[10] about playin' that part. I don't think it's owt in my line, y'see. She thinks so, an' my missis; but I'm not sure."

"Nonsense," Mrs. Bostock said.

"Y'see, I'm not the sort o' feller to show meself off in front of a lot o' people."

16 "Rubbish," Mrs. Bostock said.

"Oh, it's all right for you lot. You've done it all before. You're used to it."

"Come to rehearsal Monday evening," Mrs. Bostock commanded.

"Well, I don't know."

---

8. **a proper nowter** [nou′tər]: a real good-for-nothing. *Nowt* is Yorkshire dialect for "nothing."

9. **row** [rou]: quarrel; argument.

10. **owt** [out]: Yorkshire dialect for "anything."

"My house, seven-thirty. I won't take no for an answer till you've seen us all and given it a try. Lucy will tell you the address." And she was gone.

"A bit forceful, isn't she?" Albert said.

"A tartar," Lucy said.

17 "Oh, heck," Albert said, "I don't like this at all."

But secretly now he was beginning to like it enormously.

At seven twenty-five on Monday evening he presented himself, dressed carefully in his best navy blue and shaved for the second time that **18** day, at the front door of Mrs. Bostock's home, a large and rather grim-looking Victorian terrace house with big bay windows on a long curving avenue off Halifax Road, and was joined on the step by Lucy Fryer.

Mrs. Bostock herself let them in and showed them into a large and shabbily comfortable drawing-room[11] furnished mostly with a varied **19** assortment of easy chairs and settees, and more books than Albert had ever seen at one time outside the public library. He was introduced to a thin, distinguished-looking pipe-smoking man who turned out to be Mr. Bostock, and then the members of the drama group began to arrive.

There were only seven speaking parts in the play, but several people who would be responsible for backstage production turned up too, and soon the room was full of men and women whose common characteristic seemed to be that they all talked at the top of their voices. Albert was bewildered, and then smitten with acute embarrassment when Mrs. Bostock, standing on the hearthrug, clapped her hands together and saying, "Listen, everybody; I'd like you all to meet our new recruit," directed all eyes to him.

"I'm trying to talk Mr. Royston into playing the policeman in *Son of the House* and I want

---

11. **drawing-room:** usually formal room for greeting and entertaining guests.

The Actor **33**

PAGE SUMMARY: AT A GLANCE

- In summarizing the play for Alice, Albert revealingly uses the pronoun *I* in referring to the policeman's role.
- He continues to deny his interest when Mrs. Bostock visits the store, but she insists he come to a rehearsal before making a final decision.
- Secretly his interest in playing the part increases.
- At the rehearsal Mrs. Bostock embarrasses him by singling him out as "our new recruit."

15 READING SKILL: INFERENCE

Elicit that Albert is sheepish because his wife has caught him using the revealing pronoun *I*, and his excuse does not convince her that he is not interested in playing the part.

16 TEACHING CHARACTERIZATION

Point out that Mrs. Bostock is a confident, rather overbearing person. Ask why she might be a valuable member of the theater company. (She is the kind of person who gets things done.)

17 TEACHING IRONY

Note that once again Albert's words belie his true feelings.

18 CULTURAL BACKGROUND

Explain that homes typical of Queen Victoria's reign (1837–1901) were large and ornately decorated, in imitation of Gothic architecture of the Middle Ages. Owning such a large home suggests that the Bostocks are fairly wealthy.

19 TEACHING THEME

Ask what this detail reveals about the Bostocks and Albert. (They are educated intellectuals; he is not.) Point out that this contrast shows the effects of class differences, a central theme of the story.

CRITICAL THINKING: GUIDED READING QUESTIONS

LITERAL

1a. What does Albert say happens right in the middle of the brothers' quarrel in the second act of the play? ("I come in.")

2a. How is Albert dressed when he presents himself at Mrs. Bostock's house? (He wears his best navy-blue suit.)

INFERENTIAL

1b. What does his use of the pronoun *I* indicate? (He is indeed considering performing in the play.)

2b. Why does Albert wear his best clothing and shave twice? (He wants to look his best when he mixes with the acting company, whose members are better educated and higher class.)

- Members of the company praise Mrs. Bostock for her "find."
- Albert is relieved when attention turns from him, but his tension returns when he must perform the policeman's role.
- Later he performs his lines far better for Alice than he did at the rehearsal.
- He admits that acting "sort of gets you," and Alice encourages him to continue and "show" the others.
- He becomes committed to perfecting his part, and the weekly rehearsals open a new vista in his life.

IN THE GLOSSARY

- vista: broad view

20 TEACHING THEME

Elicit that the others view Albert not as a person but as a specimen, of interest only because he is so suited to the policeman's role. Ask what this behavior suggests about people like Albert. (Society uses but otherwise overlooks them.)

21 TEACHING WORD CHOICE

Note that the expression "dramatic climaxes" is not characteristic of Albert's choice of words and background. Elicit that he is probably repeating a term he heard at the rehearsal.

22 CULTURAL BACKGROUND

Point out that dropping an *h* sound is characteristic of several working-class English dialects and is not considered "proper English."

23 TEACHING CONFLICT

Elicit that Albert's effort to show society his true value is a central conflict of the plot.

24 READING SKILL: COMPARISON AND CONTRAST

Note that Albert's life has been dull and that he has always suppressed his feelings, but acting is an interesting experience in which the expression of one's feelings is encouraged.

---

you all to be nice to him because he isn't completely sold on the idea yet."

"But my dear Effie," said a stocky young man in a tweed jacket and yellow shirt, "you're a ge-
20 nius. You really are. Where on earth did you find him?" And Albert stood there feeling very uncomfortable while everybody looked at him as though he were an antique which Mrs. Bostock had uncovered in an obscure shop and was now presenting for their admiration.

"Mr. Royston is the assistant manager in Moorend Grocery," Mrs. Bostock told them. "I took one look at him and knew he was our man."

To Albert's relief attention turned from him and he was able for a time to sit in his corner and watch what went on without being called upon to do or say anything. But not for long. A first group-reading of the play was started upon and Albert followed the action in his copy, amazed at the way the actors let themselves go in their parts, delivering the most embarrassing lines without the least sign of self-consciousness. "'You know I love you,'" the young man in the yellow shirt said to a pretty dark girl sitting next to Albert. "'*Do* you love me?'" she replied. Albert blushed.

At the entrance of the policeman a silence fell upon the room and Mrs. Bostock, still directing operations from the hearthrug, said, "Now, Mr. Royston, this is where you come in."

Oh, it was terrible. His heart thumped sickeningly. He found his place, put his forefinger under the line, swallowed thickly, and said in a faint voice:

"'Is one of you gentlemen the owner of that car standing outside?'"

"Weak," Mrs. Bostock said. "Come now, Mr. Royston, a little more authority. Can't you imagine the impact of your entrance? . . ."

"Just imagine it, Alice," Albert said, getting up out of his chair with the book in his hand. "Here's this rotter of a bloke, who's had one too

many an' been drivin' like mad an' hit somebody an' left 'em in the road. He's scared out of his wits an' now he's telling his brother an' pleadin' with him to help him, when the maid comes in and says there's a policeman come—and I walk in.

"'Is one of you gentlemen the owner of that car standing outside?' An' this 'ere young chap nearly passes out with fright, thinkin' they're onto him. And really, y'see, all I'm doin' is pinchin' him[12] for parking without lights. Just
21 imagine it. It's . . . it's one of the dramatic climaxes of the play."

"It's ever so thrilling, Albert," Alice said. "Did you say it like that tonight?"

"What?"

"'Is one of you gentlemen the owner of that car outside?'"

"Well, happen not quite like that. It's not so
22 bad when there's only you listening to me, but it sort o' puts you off with all them la-di-da fellers there. You're scared to death you'll drop an aitch[13] or say a word wrong. . . . It'll be easier when I'm a bit more used to it."

"You're really taking it on, then?"

"Well," Albert said, scratching his head, "I don't seem to have much option, somehow. She's a very persuasive woman, that Mrs. Bostock. Besides," he went on, "it sort of gets you, you know. If you know what I mean."
23 Alice smiled. "I know what you mean. You do it, Albert. You show them."

Albert looked at her and in a moment a slow grin spread across his face. "I think I will, Alice," he said. "I think I will."

24 Once committed, Albert sank himself heart and soul into the perfecting of his part. Attendance at Mrs. Bostock's house on Monday evenings opened up a new vista of life to him. It was his first contact with the artistic temperament

---

12. **pinchin' him:** here, getting him; catching him.
13. **drop an aitch:** drop an *h* sound.

CRITICAL THINKING: GUIDED READING QUESTIONS

LITERAL

1a. According to Albert, why does he say his lines better to Alice than he did at the rehearsal? (Among all the "la-di-da fellers" at the rehearsal, he was scared that he would "drop an aitch" or say a wrong word.)

2a. What is Albert's final explanation for taking on the role? ("It sort of gets you.")

INFERENTIAL

1b. What differences between Albert and the others do these fears point out? (He is a member of the working class and is inexperienced with acting; they are members of an upper class and are experienced performers.)

2b. What does Albert mean by the statement he makes? (The experience of acting has gripped his imagination.)

Quantrell II, Judy North.

PAGE SUMMARY: AT A GLANCE

- Albert is both fascinated and repelled by the more pretentious members of the company.
- On the night of the dress rehearsal, he comes to his front door in costume and gruffly asks for himself.
- Until the light falls on his face, Alice does not recognize him.

IN THE GLOSSARY

- gruff: deep and rough
- indulgently: leniently

25 **TEACHING FIGURATIVE LANGUAGE**

Have volunteers explain the actual meaning of these figurative expressions. (The performers act friendly to find out how dangerous the others are and to lull the others' suspicions so that it is easier to attack or trick them.)

26 **TEACHING WORD CHOICE**

Point out that here Albert characteristically avoids the jargon "dress rehearsal" in contrast to his earlier use of "dramatic climax."

ART AND LITERATURE

In this watercolor by California artist Judy North (born 1937), the physical characteristics of a man are blurred, as if photographically manipulated or computer generated. Using highly contrasted, stippled colors, North dissolves the image of a particular person nearly to the point of abstraction.

- Ask students what aspects of North's picture remind them of Albert. (Answers will vary. Some may suggest that the man's bland expression masks unexpressed feelings; others may feel that the man resembles a policeman.)

and he soon realized that very often the amount of temperament varied in inverse ratio to the amount of talent. He was fascinated.

25 "You've never met anybody like 'em." he said to Alice one night. "They shake hands to feel how long the claws are an' put their arms round one another so's it's easier to slip the knife in."

"Oh, surely, Albert," said Alice, a person of sweetness and light, "they're not as bad as all that."

"No," he admitted; "some of 'em's all right; but there's one or two proper devils." He shook his hand. "They're certainly not sort o' folk I've been used to. Three quarters of 'em don't even work for t'Co-op."

"How is it coming along?" Alice asked.

26 "Pretty fair. We're trying it out on the stage next week, with all the actions an' everything."

On the night of the dress rehearsal Alice answered a knock on the door to find a policeman on the step.

"Does Albert Royston live here?" a gruff official voice asked.

Alice was startled. "Well, he does," she said, "but he's not in just now."

She opened the door a little wider and the light fell across the man's face. Her husband stepped toward her, laughing.

"You silly fool, Albert," Alice said indulgently. "You gave me a shock."

The Actor **35**

CRITICAL THINKING: GUIDED READING QUESTIONS

LITERAL

1a. What does Albert observe about three quarters of the acting company members? (They do not work for the Cressley Co-op.)

2a. What trick does Albert play on Alice on the night of the dress rehearsal? (To see if she will recognize him, he arrives at the front door in costume and asks for himself.)

INFERENTIAL

1b. Why might so many members not work for the organization that sponsors its acting company? (The company is one of the best in Cressley and apparently solicits experienced actors and other members likely to meet its high standards.)

2b. What does Alice's initial failure to recognize Albert indicate about his mastery of the role? (He has mastered it well.)

- Albert enjoys the joke he plays on Alice, who praises his appearance and expresses excitement about the upcoming performance.
- Albert arrives early for the performance and learns from Mrs. Bostock that the audience is receptive.
- In his dressing room he is seized by stage fright, although Mrs. Bostock speaks reassuringly.
- She accompanies him from the dressing room to the wings.

IN THE GLOSSARY

- guttural: rasping
- appraising: evaluating

27 READING SKILL: CAUSE AND EFFECT

Have a volunteer explain what could have caused Albert to get in trouble. (He might have got in trouble for impersonating a police officer.)

28 TEACHING IRONY

Point out that while Albert avoids expressing his excitement to his wife, his early arrival shows that he is actually quite excited.

29 CRITICAL THINKING: PROBLEM SOLVING

Ask students how they would solve the problem of Albert's stage fright if they were the play's director. Then tell them to continue reading to see how Mrs. Bostock tries to solve it.

30 TEACHING MOTIVATION

Elicit that Mrs. Bostock's kindness and perception are tied to her desire to ensure a good performance.

31 TEACHING PLOT: FORESHADOWING

Ask students what upcoming event this remark about Shirley, the prompter, may hint at. (Something may go wrong later, presenting a problem for the prompter.)

Albert was still chuckling as he walked through into the living room. "Well, how do I look?"

27 "You look marvelous," Alice said. "But you've never come through the streets like that, have you? You could get into trouble."

"It's all right," Albert told her. "I had me mac on over the uniform and the helmet in a bag. I just had to give you a preview like. An' Mrs. Bostock says could you put a little tuck in the tunic: summat[14] they can take out before it goes back. It's a bit on the roomy side."

"It must have been made for a giant," Alice said as she fussed about behind him, examining the tunic. "Ooh, Albert, but isn't it getting exciting! I can't wait for the night."

28 "Well, like it or lump it," Albert said, "there's only another week."

He was at the hall early on the night of the play and made up and dressed in the police constable's uniform by the end of the first act. As the second act began he found himself alone in the dressing room. He looked into the mirror and squared the helmet on his head. He certainly looked the part all right. It would be a bit of a lark to go out in the street and pinch somebody for speeding or something. He narrowed his eyes, looking fiercely at himself, and spoke his opening line in a guttural undertone.

Well, this was it. No good looking in the book. If he didn't know the part now he never would. Out there the second act was under way, the players doing their very best, reveling in a hobby they loved, giving entertainment to all those people; and in return the audience was thrilling to every twist and climax of the plot, and not letting one witty phrase, one humorous exchange go by without a laugh. A good audience, Mrs. Bostock had said: the sort of audience all actors, professional or amateur, loved: at one

---

14. **summat:** Yorkshire dialect for "something."

36 *The Short Story*

---

with the players, receptive, responsive, appreciative. And soon its eyes would be on him.

29 He was suddenly seized by an appalling attack of stage fright. His stomach was empty, a hollow void of fear. He put his head in his hands. He couldn't do it. How could he ever have imagined he could? He couldn't face all those people. His mouth was dry and when he tried to bring his lines to memory he found nothing but a blank.

A knock on the door made him look up. He felt panic grip him now. Had he missed his entrance? Had he ruined the performance for everybody by cringing here like a frightened child? The knock was repeated and Mrs. Bostock's voice said from outside, "Are you there, Mr. Royston?"

Albert took his script in his hand and opened the door. She smiled brightly up at him. "Everything all right?" She gave him an appraising look. "You look wonderful. You're not on for a little **30** while yet but I should come and stand in the wings and get the feel of the action. You look a bit pale about the gills. What's wrong—stage fright?"

"It's all a bit new to me," Albert said feebly.

"Of course it is. But you know your lines perfectly and once you're out there you'll forget your nervousness. Just remember the audience is on your side."

They went up the narrow steps to the level of the stage. The voices of the actors became more distinct. He caught the tail-end of a line he recognized. There already? Recurrent fear gripped his stomach.

He looked out onto the brightly lit stage, at the actors moving about, talking, and across to where the girl who was acting as prompter sat **31** with an open script on her knee. "Shirley hasn't had a thing to do so far," Mrs. Bostock murmured. "The whole thing's gone like a dream." She took the script from Albert's hands and found the place for him. "Here we are. Now you

---

CRITICAL THINKING: GUIDED READING QUESTIONS

LITERAL

1a. What is Albert's response to his wife's "Ooh, Albert, but isn't it getting exciting"? ("Well, like it or lump it, there's only another week.")

2a. What suddenly attacks Albert as he waits in the dressing room on the night of the performance? (stage fright)

INFERENTIAL

1b. What difference between Alice and Albert do these remarks stress? (Alice readily shows her feelings of excitement; Albert does not show his.)

2b. Why might Mrs. Bostock's advice to watch the play from the wings help Albert? (If he becomes absorbed in the action of the play, he may forget his fears.)

just follow the action in there and relax, take it easy. You'll be on and off so quick you'll hardly know you've left the wings."

"I'm all right now," Albert told her.

He realized to his own surprise that he was; and he became increasingly so as the action of the play absorbed him, so that he began to feel himself part of it and no longer a frightened amateur shivering in the wings.

Two pages to go. The younger son was telling his brother about the accident. The row was just beginning and at the very height of it he would make his entrance. He began to feel excited. What was it Mrs. Bostock had said? "From the second you step on you dominate the stage. Your entrance is like a thunder-clap." By shots! **32** He realized vaguely that Mrs. Bostock had left his side, but he didn't care now. He felt a supreme confidence. He was ready. He'd show them. By shots he would!

One page, "'You've been rotten all your life, Paul,'" the elder brother was saying. "'I've never cherished any illusions about you, but this, this is more than even I dreamed you were capable of.'"

"'I know you hate me, Tom. I've always known it. But if only for father's sake, you must help me now. You know what it will do to him if he finds out. He couldn't stand it in his condition.'"

"'You swine. You utter swine . . .'"

The girl who was the maid appeared at his side. She gave him a quick smile. No nerves about her. She'd been on and off the stage all evening, living the part. Albert stared out, fascinated. Not until this moment had he known the true thrill of acting, of submerging one's own personality in that of another.

"'Where are you going?'"

"'I'm going to find that man you knocked down and get him to a hospital. And you're coming with me.'"

"'But it's too late, Tom. It was hours ago.

Someone's sure to have found him by now. Perhaps the police . . .'"

Any minute, now. They were working up to his entrance. *Like a thunder-clap.* Albert braced his shoulders and touched his helmet. He glanced down at the script and quickly turned a **33** page. He had lost his place. Panic smote him like a blow. They were still talking, though, so he must be all right. And anyway the maid gave him his cue and she was still by his side. She had gone. He fumbled with his script. Surely . . . not so far . . .

He felt Mrs. Bostock at his elbow. He turned to her in stupid surprise.

34 "But," he said, "they've . . . they've—"
She nodded. "Yes. They've skipped three pages. They've missed your part right out."

He was already at home when Alice returned.

"Whatever happened, Albert?" she said anxiously. "You weren't ill, were you?"

He told her. "I went and got changed straight away," he said, "and came home."

"Well, isn't that a shame."

"Oh, they just got carried away," Albert said. "One of 'em lost his place and skipped and the other had to follow him. They did it so quick nobody could do owt about it." He smiled as he began to take off his shoes. "Looks as though I'll never know whether I'd've stood up to it or not," he said.

35 He never did anything of the kind again.

A long time after, he was able to face with equanimity his wife's request, in the presence of acquaintances, that he should tell them about his "acting career," and say, "No, you tell 'em, Alice. You tell it best." And the genuine smile on his honest face during the recounting of the story of the unspoken lines, which never failed to provoke shouts of laughter, always deceived **36** the listeners. So that never for one moment did they guess just how cruel, how grievous a disappointment it had been to him at the time.

The Actor **37**

CRITICAL THINKING: GUIDED READING QUESTIONS

LITERAL

1a. What happens to Albert's scene on the night of the performance? (The other actors accidentally skip it.)

2a. What facial expression accompanies Albert's explanation of events in the third-to-last paragraph? (a smile)

INFERENTIAL

1b. What seems to be Mrs. Bostock's attitude toward this turn of events? (She takes it matter-of-factly, showing little concern, since the show is still running smoothly; she expresses no sympathy for Albert.)

2b. What does Albert's smile mask? (his great disappointment)

PAGE SUMMARY: AT A GLANCE

- As Albert watches the action, his confidence returns.
- When his cue fails to come, he grows confused.
- Mrs. Bostock explains that the other actors accidentally skipped his scene.
- As he tells his wife what happened, Albert seems to take the incident in stride.
- He never again tries anything of the kind.
- Later, when he smiles at the recounting of the story, no one ever guesses how grievous the disappointment was to him.

IN THE GLOSSARY

- grievous: hurtful

32 TEACHING CONFLICT

Point out that the upcoming climax will reveal the outcome of Albert's struggle to "show them."

33 TEACHING IRONY

Note that these and earlier details make us think that Albert's failure onstage, if it comes, will be his own fault. The actual outcome surprises us.

34 TEACHING THEME

Elicit that the ironic outcome also has thematic significance: The common man has been overlooked by society.

35 TEACHING SYMBOLS

Note that "anything of the kind" refers not only to acting but also to anything creative or exciting that allows Albert to express his true nature.

36 TEACHING THEME

Ask what this sentence stresses about people in general. (Many people secretly suffer from life's disappointments.)

COLLABORATIVE LEARNING: ENRICHMENT ACTIVITY

Dramatizations Working in groups, students might perform some of the scenes they wrote for the Composition assignment or scenes from the plays of modern British dramatists, such as J. B. Priestley and George Bernard Shaw.

Are there many Alberts in to-day's world? Explain.

ANSWERS

STUDY QUESTIONS

1. his feelings; He is an assistant grocery manager, but people think he should be a po-liceman.
2. He thinks they are daft but is pleased and flattered by them.
3. He uses *I* in discussing the policeman's role. He begins to like the idea enormously.
4. He fears "dropping an aitch" or saying a wrong word.
5. The others skip it. Others never guess how cruel and grievous the disappointment was for him.
6. Albert acts in a play; in every-day life, he hides his feelings, thus "acting" in a different sense.
7. They are from a higher class and are arty and experienced in amateur theater. He finds them odd and "la-di-da" (pre-tentious) and fears speaking improperly in front of them.
8. He is an overlooked "common man" whose fling at creativity is thwarted. He was devas-tated and never again had the courage to try fulfilling himself.
9. Answers will vary. Students may stress the value of dis-cretion or the dangers of re-pressed feelings.

LITERARY FOCUS

1. We are led to wonder whether Albert will perform well or poorly, but he does neither.
2. The author uses dramatic irony wherever he tells us Al-bert's true feelings. It shows us the sadness of Albert's life and of others' misunderstand-ing of him.

LANGUAGE STUDY

1. They gave rise to the dialect terms *owt* ("anything") and *nowter* ("one who is nothing").
2. "cop"; "fellow"; "crazy"; "po-liceman"; "TV"; "living room"; "sofa"; "guy"; "police officer"

COMPARING STORIES

Answers will vary. For example, students may find the surprises in "The Winner" the most realistic and those in "The Beggar" the most memorable.

STUDY QUESTIONS

Recalling

1. According to the opening paragraphs of the story, what is Albert able to hide? What is Albert's actual job, and what job do people think he should hold?
2. At first, what does Albert think of Mrs. Bostock's questions and her suggestion that he act in a play? How does he begin to feel about the idea after she leaves?
3. What does Albert say that makes his wife realize he is interested in playing the part of the police-man? How does he secretly feel when Mrs. Bos-tock insists he come to a rehearsal?
4. After the first rehearsal, what fears does Albert confess to his wife?
5. What happens to Albert's part on the night of the performance? According to the final paragraphs of the story, what do listeners never guess when Al-bert's wife describes the incident later?

Interpreting

6. Explain at least two meanings behind the story's title.
7. How are other members of the dramatic society different from Albert? How do you know that Albert is strongly aware of those differences?
8. What does the author think is sad about Albert's life? What is sad about the line "He never did any-thing of the kind again" (page 37)?

Extending

9. Do you think it is important for people to hide their true feelings? Why or why not?

LITERARY FOCUS

Situational and Dramatic Irony

Irony exists when there is a contrast between the way things seem and the way they really are. In **situ-ational irony** what seems likely to happen is not what actually occurs. For example, a detective story uses situational irony if it keeps a criminal's identity secret to the end and surprises us by making the criminal an unlikely suspect.

In **dramatic irony** the reader or audience has important information that the characters do not have. A detective story uses dramatic irony if we learn the criminal's identity early on, before the characters dis-cover it. As the plot unfolds, events that seem per-

fectly innocent to the other characters have special meaning to us. Dramatic irony is often used in plays.

Thinking About Situational and Dramatic Irony

1. Why is the outcome of the story an example of situational irony?
2. Where in the story does the author use dramatic irony? What effect does it have on the reader?

LANGUAGE STUDY

Dialect and Anglicisms

A **dialect** is a version of a language spoken in a particular region or by a particular group of people. Dialects of English often contain vocabulary, pronun-ciations, and grammatical structures that are not part of **standard English,** the widely accepted form of the language. For example, Albert's Yorkshire dialect in-cludes the nonstandard term *summat* for "some-thing." In addition to the terms in Yorkshire dialect, "The Actor" contains other **Anglicisms,** words and expressions used in England but rarely or never used in the United States. For example, few Americans say *mackintosh;* instead, we say *raincoat.*

1. Look up *aught* and *naught* in a dictionary. Then explain how these words are probably related to terms in Yorkshire dialect in the story.
2. Use the context of the story to help you determine the meanings of these Anglicisms: *copper, chap, daft, bobby, telly, drawing room, settee, bloke, constable.* Check your answers in a dictionary.

COMPOSITION

Expanding a Play Scene

■ Try writing your own full version of the scene in the play in which the brothers quarrel and the po-liceman arrives at the house. The scene should involve dramatic irony, since the policeman is unaware of the true circumstances. To make the dialogue realistic, include Anglicisms and have the policeman speak in Yorkshire dialect.

COMPARING STORIES

■ Compare and contrast this story to other stories about life's surprises that you have read in this section or elsewhere. In which stories did you find the surprises most realistic? Most memorable? Cite story details to support your opinions.

COMPOSITION: GUIDELINES FOR EVALUATION

EXPANDING A PLAY SCENE

Objective

To write a scene from a play based on information about it in a story

Guidelines for Evaluation

■ suggested length: three to four pages

■ should use play form, with dialogue and stage di-rections
■ should include and expand on the play's dialogue given in the story
■ should include Anglicisms and, for the policeman, Yorkshire dialect

PREVIEW: THE AUTHOR AND THE WORLD

GEOGRAPHY AND CULTURE

Chinua Achebe

(born 1930)

Nigeria

Chinua Achebe [chē noō'ə ə chä'bā], a Nigerian, is one of Africa's best-known fiction writers. A member of the Ibo [ē'bō] tribe, Achebe grew up in the village of Ogidi, where his father taught at the local school. At the University College at Ibadan, Achebe majored in English literature and soon decided he wanted to become a writer: "At the university I read some appalling European novels about Africa . . . and realized that our story could not be told for us by anyone else."

In 1958 Achebe won fame with his first novel, *Things Fall Apart;* like much of his fiction, it explores the traumatic effects of African contact with Western ways. A decade later, after Nigeria had gained independence from England, Achebe was one of many Ibos who grew disillusioned with the new government and attempted to establish a separate nation called Biafra. As chairman of the Biafra National Guidance Committee, he traveled abroad with other writers, seeking support for the Biafran cause. The collapse of Biafra in 1970 prompted Achebe to retire from political life and devote most of his time to writing and teaching.

Nigeria and the Ibo

The West African nation of Nigeria is the homeland of more than two hundred different native tribes. The largest of these are the Hausa and Fulani, who live mainly in the north; the Yoruba, in the southwest; and the Ibo, in the southeast. Each group has its own language, but their common language is English, reflecting close to a century of British rule that ended in 1960. Chinua Achebe, though fluent in the Ibo language, usually writes in English.

Most Nigerians are Moslems or Christians, although ancient tribal beliefs still persist. The Ibos, for example, traditionally believed in a god so powerful that he had to be approached through lesser deities, each affiliated with a different Ibo village. Today most Ibos are Christians; however, especially when Achebe was growing up, many Ibo villagers still showed respect for their local deity. Sometimes, as in the upcoming story, the old ways came into conflict with new Western ideas.

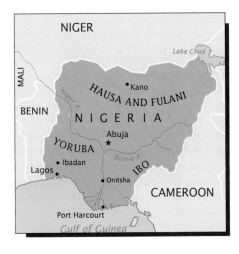

See LITERATURE AND CULTURE SOURCEBOOK: Africa

Dead Men's Path **39**

LESSON PREVIEW

In this tale of modern Nigeria, a "progressive" schoolmaster clashes with community tradition. The ambitious new headmaster, Michael Obi, forces local villagers to stop using their traditional footpath through the school's gardens. When a woman's death is blamed on Obi's actions, villagers destroy the gardens, and a visiting school supervisor writes a negative report about Obi.

LITERARY SKILLS FOR THIS SELECTION

- characterization
- conflict

THEMES IN THIS SELECTION

- human relationships: tolerance and insensitivity
- clash of cultures

LESSON OBJECTIVES

1. to make inferences from details of characterization
2. to understand proverbs and figurative language
3. to write a job-related report based on details in the story

Teacher's Classroom Resources 1

- Teaching Notes 73
- Prereading Vocabulary 74
- Reading Guide 75
- Check Test 76
- Responding to World Cultures 77
- Literary Focus: Characterization 78
- Language Study: Proverbs and Figurative Language 79
- Writing Process Guide: Writing a Job-Related Report 80
- Grammar in Literature: Adjectives 81
- Selection Test 82

IN THE CLASSROOM

TEACHING STUDENTS OF DIFFERENT ABILITIES

- **For less advanced students:** Ask students to read the opening paragraph and predict whether Obi will be successful. Also have them complete the Reading Guide for this selection.

- **For more advanced students:** Have students consider how the story illustrates the recent trends in African literature as described on page 578 of the Literature and Culture Sourcebook in their textbook.

DISCUSSING GEOGRAPHY AND CULTURE

Male and Female Roles

In traditional African cultures the tasks assigned to men and women are distinct and separate. Among most West African tribes, for instance, cloth is spun and dyed by women but woven by men. Among the Ibo, women cultivate all the crops except yams, which have a religious significance and are tended by men.

- Ask students to discuss the issue of the division of labor between men and women in our society.

Dead Men's Path

1 Michael Obi's hopes were fulfilled much earlier than he had expected. He was appointed headmaster of Ndume Central School[1] in January 1949. It had always been an unprogressive school, so the Mission authorities decided to send a young and energetic man to run it. Obi accepted this responsibility with enthusiasm. He had many wonderful ideas and this was an opportunity to put them into practice. He had had sound secondary school education which designated him a "pivotal teacher" in the official records and set him apart from the other headmasters in the mission field. He was outspoken in his condemnation of the narrow views of these older and often less-educated ones.

"We shall make a good job of it, shan't we?" he asked his young wife when they first heard the joyful news of his promotion.

"We shall do our best," she replied. "We shall have such beautiful gardens and everything will be just *modern* and delightful. . . ." In their two years of married life she had become completely infected by his passion for "modern methods" and his denigration of "these old and superannuated people in the teaching field who would be better employed as traders in the Onitsha[2] market." She began to see herself already as the admired wife of the young headmaster, the queen of the school.

The wives of the other teachers would envy her position. She would set the fashion in everything. . . . Then, suddenly, it occurred to her that there might not be other wives. Wavering between hope and fear, she asked her husband, looking anxiously at him.

---

1. **Ndume** [n dōō′mā] **Central School:** part of the network of Nigerian schools originally established by Christian missionaries.
2. **Onitsha** [ō nēt′shə]: city in southeastern Nigeria.

"All our colleagues are young and unmarried," he said with enthusiasm which for once she did not share. "Which is a good thing," he continued.

"Why?"

"Why? They will give all their time and energy to the school."

Nancy was downcast. For a few minutes she became skeptical about the new school; but it was only for a few minutes. Her little personal misfortune could not blind her to her husband's happy prospects. She looked at him as he sat folded up in a chair. He was stoop-shouldered and looked frail. But he sometimes surprised people with sudden bursts of physical energy. In his present posture, however, all his bodily strength seemed to have retired behind his deep-set eyes, giving them an extraordinary power of penetration. He was only twenty-six, but looked thirty or more. On the whole, he was not unhandsome.

4 "A penny for your thoughts, Mike," said Nancy after a while, imitating the woman's magazine she read.

"I was thinking what a grand opportunity we've got at last to show these people how a school should be run."

Ndume School was backward in every sense of the word. Mr. Obi put his whole life into the work, and his wife hers too. He had two aims. A high standard of teaching was insisted upon, and the school compound was to be turned into a place of beauty. Nancy's dream-gardens came to life with the coming of the rains, and blossomed. Beautiful hibiscus and allamanda hedges in brilliant red and yellow marked out the carefully tended school compound from the rank neighborhood bushes.

CRITICAL THINKING: GUIDED READING QUESTIONS

LITERAL

1a. What ideas of Michael Obi's have "infected" his wife? (his passion for "modern methods" and denigration of "superannuated" people in the teaching field)

2a. What "grand opportunity" does Obi say he has? (He has the opportunity to show people how a school should be run.)

INFERENTIAL

1b. From his ability to "infect" his wife, what positive qualities of Obi's can you infer? (He is persuasive and enthusiastic.)

2b. From this attitude toward others, what negative qualities of Obi's can you infer? (He is insensitive and abrasive.)

One evening as Obi was admiring his work he was scandalized to see an old woman from the village hobble right across the compound, through a marigold flower-bed and the hedges. On going up there he found faint signs of an almost disused path from the village across the school compound to the bush on the other side.

"It amazes me," said Obi to one of his teachers who had been three years in the school, "that you people allowed the villagers to make use of this footpath. It is simply incredible." He shook his head.

6 "The path," said the teacher apologetically, "appears to be very important to them. Although it is hardly used, it connects the village shrine with their place of burial."

"And what has that got to do with the school?" asked the headmaster.

"Well, I don't know," replied the other with a shrug of the shoulders. "But I remember there was a big row³ some time ago when we attempted to close it."

"That was some time ago. But it will not be used now," said Obi as he walked away. "What will the Government Education Officer think of this when he comes to inspect the school next week? The villagers might, for all I know, decide to use the schoolroom for a pagan ritual during the inspection."

7 Heavy sticks were planted closely across the path at the two places where it entered and left the school premises. These were further strengthened with barbed wire.

Three days later the village priest of Ani⁴ called on the headmaster. He was an old man and walked with a slight stoop. He carried a stout walking-stick which he usually tapped on the floor, by way of emphasis, each time he made a new point in his argument.

"I have heard," he said after the usual ex-

---

3. **row** [rou]: argument; quarrel.
4. **Ani** [ä′nē]: the local village deity.

change of cordialities, "that our ancestral footpath has recently been closed. . . ."

"Yes," replied Mr. Obi. "We cannot allow people to make a highway of our school compound."

8 "Look here, my son," said the priest bringing down his walking-stick, "this path was here before you were born and before your father was born. The whole life of this village depends on it. Our dead relatives depart by it and our ancestors visit us by it. But most important, it is the path of children coming in to be born. . . ."

Sculpture of Man, Felix Eboigbe.

- In using their traditional path, villagers trample some of the school's flower beds.
- A colleague tells Obi of the fuss when the school once tried to close the path.
- Obi nevertheless fences it in.
- The village priest explains that the dead depart and return by the path, and babies use it to enter the world.

6 TEACHING CONFLICT

Note that Obi's problem with the path is a social conflict between his modernism and the community's traditional beliefs.

7 CRITICAL THINKING: PROBLEM SOLVING

Ask why Obi's solution to his problem may prove unsatisfactory. (It will probably cause a "row," as happened in the past.) What would students do? (Perhaps they would move the flower beds.)

8 GRAMMAR IN LITERATURE

Note that parallel grammatical structures make the priest's words more powerful. Have students identify examples here and on the next page. ("Our dead relatives depart by it and our ancestors visit us by it"; "let the hawk perch and let the eagle perch.")

ART AND LITERATURE

Contemporary African sculptor Felix Eboigbe combines modern portraiture (characterized by defined personal features) with traditional, or tribal, wood carving. Before Western colonization, there was no interest among African artists in describing the traits of an individual. Artists were interested in archetypal representation in which a figure symbolizes all men, as in *Sculpture of Man.*

- After students have read the selection, ask them how the combination of modern portraiture and traditional dress in this sculpture illustrates a theme of the story. (Traditions should not be abandoned heedlessly.)

CRITICAL THINKING: GUIDED READING QUESTIONS

LITERAL

1a. Whose upcoming visit increases Obi's concern about the villagers' use of the path? (the Government Education Officer's)

2a. What does the priest say about how long the path has been there? (It was there before Obi was born and before Obi's father was born.)

INFERENTIAL

1b. What does this detail reveal about Obi's concerns? (He is far more concerned about his superiors than about the villagers.)

2b. What does this remark suggest that the priest values? (He values tradition.)

- Obi says that the school's purpose is to end such beliefs; he refuses to reopen the path.
- When a woman's death in childbed is blamed on the fence, villagers destroy part of the school grounds.
- A supervisor writes a nasty report about the "tribal-war situation" Obi's "misguided zeal" has helped create.

IN THE GLOSSARY

- eradicate: do away with
- diviner: one who discovers or interprets hidden knowledge
- propitiate: appease; pacify
- zeal: great enthusiasm

9 TEACHING CHARACTERIZATION

Elicit that the priest shows far more tolerance than Obi.

10 TEACHING THEME

Ask what theme this outcome suggests. (Lack of respect for others' beliefs causes social disharmony.)

11 TEACHING IRONY

Note the story's ironies: Obi zealously tries to do a good job, but his zeal leads to failure; he closes the path in part to avoid problems, but closing the path causes problems.

COLLABORATIVE LEARNING: ENRICHMENT ACTIVITY

Social Studies Have a group of students prepare and present an oral report on the religious customs of Nigeria. Each student should research and report on a different people—the Hausa, Fulani, Yoruba, Ibo, and so on.

ART AND LITERATURE

Born in Ghana in 1934, Ablade Glover has expressively painted this landscape, which shows dark, ghostlike plants branded in an atmosphere of warm earth tones. Working in the modern vein of interpreting the world from a private perspective, he depicts an imagined or spectral landscape, not an actual garden.

- Have students relate Glover's imagined garden to Obi's hedges. (They might note that in a sense the path is more real and permanent than the hedges, which were the dream child of the unrealistic headmaster.)

The Garden Imagined, 1986, Ablade Glover.

Mr. Obi listened with a satisfied smile on his face.

"The whole purpose of our school," he said finally, "is to eradicate just such beliefs as that. Dead men do not require footpaths. The whole idea is just fantastic. Our duty is to teach your children to laugh at such ideas."

9 "What you say may be true," replied the priest, "but we follow the practices of our fathers. If you reopen the path we shall have nothing to quarrel about. What I always say is: let the hawk perch and let the eagle perch." He rose to go.

"I am sorry," said the young headmaster. "But the school compound cannot be a thoroughfare. It is against our regulations. I would suggest your constructing another path, skirting our premises. We can even get our boys to help in building it. I don't suppose the ancestors will find the little detour too burdensome."

42 *The Short Story*

"I have no more words to say," said the old priest, already outside.

Two days later a young woman in the village died in childbed.[5] A diviner[6] was immediately consulted and he prescribed heavy sacrifices to propitiate ancestors insulted by the fence.

10 Obi woke up next morning among the ruins of his work. The beautiful hedges were torn up not just near the path but right round the school, the flowers trampled to death and one of 11 the school buildings pulled down. . . . That day, the white Supervisor came to inspect the school and wrote a nasty report on the state of the premises but more seriously about the "tribal-war situation developing between the school and the village, arising in part from the misguided zeal of the new headmaster."

---

5. **in childbed:** while giving birth to a child.
6. **diviner:** one who interprets mysterious events.

CRITICAL THINKING: GUIDED READING QUESTIONS

LITERAL

1a. What does Obi say is the school's duty? (Its duty is to teach the villagers' children to laugh at ideas like the one about the path.)

2a. After villagers damage the school grounds, what sort of report does the visiting Supervisor file? (He files "a nasty report.")

INFERENTIAL

1b. What do Obi's remarks to the priest show? (They show Obi's tactless contempt for tradition and his rudeness.)

2b. How has Obi brought about his own problems? (His problems arise from his contempt for others' beliefs and his refusal to compromise.)

STUDY QUESTIONS

Recalling

1. Why have the Mission authorities decided to send a "young and energetic" man to run the Ndume Central School? About what is the new headmaster, Michael Obi, "outspoken"?
2. What does the path through the school compound connect?
3. What explanation for closing the path does Mr. Obi give the village priest? After the priest explains the path's significance, what does Mr. Obi say about "the whole purpose" of the school?
4. What does the visiting supervisor write about the new headmaster after villagers damage the school grounds?

Interpreting

5. Contrast Mr. Obi's attitudes with those of the village priest. Which character shows more tolerance toward the other's attitudes?
6. What does the story suggest about the way people should treat the beliefs of others? What does it suggest about the way people should go about making changes?
7. Based on the priest's remarks, what can you infer about traditional Ibo attitudes toward their ancestors and their heritage?

Extending

8. If you were in a situation similar to Mr. Obi's, how would you handle the clash of new ways with the old?

LITERARY FOCUS

Characterization

Characterization refers to the personality of a character and the means by which that personality is revealed. Authors use **direct characterization** when they make direct statements about a character's personality; for example, "Alice was a kind person." We can accept as the truth an author's direct statement about a character. Authors use **indirect characterization** when they provide details from which readers infer a character's personality traits. Among the de-tails that can suggest personality are the character's speech, actions, and thoughts; details about the character's appearance; and the opinions that other characters express about the character.

Indirect characterization adds to our reading pleasure because it encourages us to participate actively in the reading process by interpreting the character's words and actions.

Thinking About Characterization

1. Reexamine the first several paragraphs of the story, and list details about Nancy Obi's actions, speech, thoughts, and appearance. What personality traits can you infer from these details?
2. Based on details in the story, what would you identify as Michael Obi's chief personality traits?

LANGUAGE STUDY

Proverbs and Figurative Language

Almost every culture has characteristic **proverbs** and other sayings that express rules of conduct or make general observations about life. Often these sayings use **figurative language**—language not meant to be taken literally—to express or imply ideas in more striking, imaginative terms. For example, the proverb "Don't put all your eggs in one basket" is not usually recited as literal advice to a poultry farmer. Rather, it is used figuratively to advise someone not to risk everything on a single method or situation.

■ Achebe is famous for incorporating Ibo proverbs and other sayings into his fiction. Find an example of a figurative saying used by the village priest. What does the saying actually mean? To what specific story circumstances does it refer?

COMPOSITION

Writing a Job-Related Report

■ Write what you imagine might have been the full report of the visiting school supervisor. First present the facts; then give conclusions and opinions. Express views clearly and firmly, but in language appropriate for a school employee reporting to his or her superiors.

Dead Men's Path **43**

Was Michael Obi a good headmaster? Why or why not?

ANSWERS

STUDY QUESTIONS

1. The school is unprogressive. Obi is outspoken about the narrow views of older, often less educated headmasters.
2. The path connects the village shrine with burial grounds.
3. "We cannot allow people to make a highway of the school compound." Obi says that the purpose of the school is to end beliefs like that of the villagers about the path.
4. He writes that the premises are damaged and a "tribal-war situation" is developing, in part because of the new headmaster's "misguided zeal."
5. Obi is modern, Westernized, and contemptuous of traditional beliefs, while the priest is old-fashioned and respectful of Ibo traditions. The priest shows more tolerance.
6. People should treat the beliefs of others with respect. Changes should be made slowly and diplomatically.
7. The Ibo traditionally show great respect for both.
8. Answers will vary, but students should see the need to make changes slowly and tactfully.

LITERARY FOCUS

1. Details include her thoughts and speech in the third, fourth, and eighth paragraphs and her remark imitating a woman's magazine. She is optimistic, loyal, materialistic, shallow, and easily influenced.
2. He is self-important, opinionated, zealously efficient, insensitive, and abrasive.

LANGUAGE STUDY

"Let the hawk perch and let the eagle perch" means live and let live. It refers to the priest's willingness to tolerate the school's presence despite the new ideas it teaches if Obi will refrain from interfering with traditional village practices.

COMPOSITION: GUIDELINES FOR EVALUATION

WRITING A JOB-RELATED REPORT

Objective

To write a job-related report based on the details of the story

Guidelines for Evaluation

■ suggested length: three or four paragraphs
■ should include facts from the story as well as opinions
■ should express views firmly
■ should use language appropriate for a school employee's report to superiors

In this tale of Norwegian peasant life, a farmer learns compassion and piety only through personal tragedy. Over the years Thord Överaas visits the local priest to arrange for his son's baptism and confirmation and the reading of the banns announcing his wedding. On each visit Thord shows a preoccupation with money and status. Then, just before the wedding, the son drowns. When he next visits the priest, Thord has sold his farm and is donating half the proceeds to charity.

LITERARY SKILLS FOR THIS SELECTION

- characterization
- theme

THEMES IN THIS SELECTION

- human relationships: parents and children
- spiritual versus material concerns
- personal growth and change

LESSON OBJECTIVES

1. to recognize cognates
2. to write about methods of characterization

Teacher's Classroom Resources 1

- Teaching Notes 85
- Reading Guide 86
- Check Test 87
- Responding to World Cultures 88
- Language Study: Cognates 89
- Writing Process Guide: Writing About Character 90
- Grammar in Literature: Writing Concisely 91
- Selection Test 92

TEACHING STUDENTS OF DIFFERENT ABILITIES

- **For less advanced students:** Students should have few difficulties with this brief, accessible story. You might have them summarize each of Thord's visits to the priest or complete the Reading Guide for this selection.
- **For more advanced students:** Have students re-

Bjørnstjerne Bjørnson

(1832–1910)

Norway

Bjørnstjerne Bjørnson [byurn′styär′nə byurn′sən] is one of Norway's most prominent authors. The eldest son of a Lutheran minister, Bjørnson grew up in the Romsdal district of western Norway. As a child he showed an early talent for writing: He composed poems and even created his own handwritten newspaper. In 1850 Bjørnson began his university studies in the Norwegian city of Christiania (now Oslo, Norway's capital). There he met the playwright Henrik Ibsen and other influential members of Norway's literary and theatrical communities. Fascinated by the theater, Bjørnson left college to become a playwright and drama critic. At the same time he began writing his famous series of "peasant tales," brief, realistic stories of Norwegian rural life. "The Father" is an example of this type of tale.

Employing his skills as a dramatist, Bjørnson told his stories through action and speech instead of merely describing events, as earlier European fiction had often done. His work had a major impact on Scandinavian fiction, and in 1903 Bjørnson became one of the first winners of the Nobel Prize for Literature.

The Nation of Norway

Norway is the westernmost nation on the Scandinavian peninsula in northern Europe. For much of its history, it was ruled by Denmark. Early in the nineteenth century, however, Norway was united with Sweden in an unequal partnership that spurred many Norwegians to press for independence. This independence movement lasted for most of Bjørnson's life, until Norway became an independent nation in 1905. In fact, Bjørnson wrote his ground-breaking tales of Norwegian peasant life in part because of his own patriotic feelings about being a Norwegian.

The Norwegian people are remarkably homogeneous. Many are tall and blonde, and nearly 70 percent have blue eyes. They speak a language that is related to German, and many dialects are spoken in the countryside.

Many millennia ago, slow-moving glaciers gouged and corrugated much of Norway's land. These glaciers have left an enduring mark on Norway's landscapes. They created tens of thousands of lakes and many fiords [fyôrdz], the narrow, cliff-lined inlets that cut into Norway's western coast. The Romsdal district, where Bjørnson grew up, adjoins one of these picturesque fiords, and a Norwegian lake figures prominently in "The Father."

search and report on Bjørnson's achievements as a dramatist or the influence of the Norwegian dramatist Henrik Ibsen on Bjørnson.

DISCUSSING GEOGRAPHY AND CULTURE

Politics and Power

Living standards in Norway are high, and the population is overwhelmingly middle-class. In Bjørnson's lifetime the lines between rich and poor were more sharply drawn, and some powerful individuals, such as the father described in this story, exerted great influence over local affairs.

- Ask students to describe the kind of influence wielded by the most powerful members of their community.

Bjørnstjerne Bjørnson

The Father

Translated from the Norwegian by James McFarlane and Janet Garton

The most powerful man in the parish, of whom this story tells, was called Thord Över-aas.[1] One day he stood in the priest's study, tall and serious.

1 "I have got a son," he said. "And I want him baptized."

"What is he to be called?"

"Finn, after my father."

"And the godparents?"

Their names were named; they were the best men and women of the village belonging to the man's family.

"Is there anything else?" asked the priest. He looked up.

2 The peasant stood for a while. "I would like to have him baptized on his own," he said.

"That means on a weekday?"

"On Saturday next, 12 noon."

"Is there anything else?" asked the priest.

"There is nothing else." The peasant twisted his cap as though about to go.

Then the priest rose. "Just this," he said and went over to Thord, took his hand and looked him straight in the eyes. "May God grant that the child will be a blessing to you!"

Sixteen years after that day Thord stood in the room of the priest.

"You are looking well, Thord," said the priest. He saw no change in him.

"I have no worries," answered Thord.

To this the priest was silent; but a moment later he asked: "What is your errand this evening?"

"I come this evening about my son who is to be confirmed tomorrow."

"He is a clever lad."

3 "I did not want to pay the priest until I'd heard what place he had been given in the ceremony."

"He is in first place."

4 "I am glad to hear it—and here is ten *daler* for the priest."

"Is there anything else?" asked the priest. He looked at Thord.

"There is nothing else." Thord left.

A further eight years passed, and then a commotion was heard outside the priest's study. For many men had come, with Thord at the head. The priest looked up and recognized him.

"You come with many men this evening."

"I want to ask for the banns to be called[2] for my son. He is to marry Karen Storliden, daughter of Gudmund, who is standing here."

"She is the richest girl in the parish."

"What you say is right," answered the peasant. He brushed his hair back with one hand. The priest sat a while as though in thought. He said nothing, but entered the names in his books, and the men signed. Thord placed three *daler* on the table.

"I only want one," said the priest.

"I know. But he is my only child. I wanted to do well by him."

The priest accepted the money. "This is the third time you stand here on your son's behalf, Thord."

5 "But this marks the finish," said Thord. He folded his pocketbook, said farewell and left. The men followed slowly.

---

1. **Överaas** [œ'vər ôs]

2. **banns to be called:** marriage proclamations to be made. Announcements were traditionally made in the church for three successive Sundays before the wedding.

The Father 45

- Before the wedding Thord's son drowns as he and his father row across a lake.
- A year later Thord visits the priest. He has sold his farm and now donates half the proceeds to charity.
- The priest says that the son has finally been a blessing to Thord, and Thord sadly agrees.

6 GRAMMAR IN LITERATURE

Point out that the concise narrative uses prepositional phrases to tell where and when. Have students identify the prepositions and their objects here. (across—water; in—weather; to—Storliden)

7 TEACHING CHARACTERIZATION

Ask what these actions stress about Thord. (They stress his deep love for his son.)

8 TEACHING THEME

Elicit that Thord's change in values points to a central theme of the story: Spiritual concerns are more meaningful than material concerns.

COLLABORATIVE LEARNING: ENRICHMENT ACTIVITY

Foreign Languages In conjunction with the Language Study activity, have students list words in foreign languages that have English cognates. Each group should focus on a different language.

ART AND LITERATURE

A melancholy boy is portrayed in this painting by the Norwegian artist Jean Heiberg (1884–1976). Combining dark outlines with mottled patches of color, Heiberg displays a common northern European preference for emotional self-searching over intellectual or stylistic content.

- Have students find passages in the story that evoke the atmosphere of Heiberg's portrait. (Possible answers: ". . . The son rolled over on his back, looked long at his father, and sank"; "They sat there a while, Thord with his eyes on the floor. . . .")

---

6 Fourteen days after that day, father and son were rowing across the water in calm weather to Storliden to discuss the wedding.

"This boat seat is not very secure under me," the son said, and he stood up to put it right. That same moment the floorboard he was standing on gave way; he threw up his arms, uttered a cry and fell into the water.

"Catch hold of the oar!" shouted the father. He stood up and held it out. But after the son had swum a few strokes, he got a cramp.

"Wait!" cried the father, and began rowing. But then the son rolled over on his back, looked long at his father, and sank.

Thord could not rightly believe it. He held the boat steady and stared at the spot where his son had gone down, as though he might come up again. A few bubbles rose, then more, then one single big one which burst—then the lake lay once again as smooth as a mirror.

7 For three days and three nights people watched the father row round that spot without food and without sleep. He was dragging for his son.[3] And on the morning of the third day he found him; and he went and carried him up the hill to his homestead.

A year or so might have passed following that day. Then late one autumn evening the priest heard a rattling at the door in the entrance, a cautious fumbling at the latch. The priest opened the door and in stepped a tall bent man, lean and white of hair. The priest looked long at him before he recognized him. It was Thord.

"You come late," said the priest and stood quietly before him.

"Ah, yes! I come late," said Thord. He sat down. The priest also sat down, as though waiting. There was a long silence.

Then Thord said, "I have something here I would like to give to the poor." He rose, placed

---

3. **dragging for his son:** pulling a net or another object across the bottom of the lake in search of his son's body.

Nordlandsgutt "Boy From Norland," 1910, Jean Heiburg.

money on the table, and sat down again. The priest counted it.

8 "This is a lot of money," he said.

"It is half of my farm. I sold it today."

The priest remained sitting a long time in silence. At length he asked gently: "What will you do now?"

"Some better thing."

They sat there a while, Thord with his eyes on the floor, the priest with his eyes on him. Then the priest said, slowly and quietly: "Now I think your son has finally been a blessing to you."

"Yes, now I think so too," said Thord. He looked up, and two tears ran sadly down his face.

CRITICAL THINKING: GUIDED READING QUESTIONS

LITERAL

1a. On his final visit to the priest, how has Thord changed physically? (Before he was "the most powerful man in the parish"; now he is "a tall bent man, lean and white of hair.")

2a. What does the priest say the son has finally been to Thord? (He says, "Your son has finally been a blessing to you.")

INFERENTIAL

1b. What does this change signify? (This signifies Thord's change from an overly confident man to a sadder but wiser one.)

2b. What does the priest mean? (The son's death has finally taught Thord the compassion and piety he lacked.)

STUDY QUESTIONS

Recalling

1. On his first visit to the priest, what special request does Thord make about his son's baptism? On his next visit, what does Thord want to know before donating money on the occasion of his son's confirmation?

2. What information do we learn about the girl Thord's son is to marry? What happens to Thord's son shortly before the wedding?

3. What does Thord give the priest on his final visit? In what way has Thord's appearance changed, and what has happened to his farm?

4. What is the priest's final observation, and how does Thord respond?

Interpreting

5. What social concerns and what attitude toward his son does Thord reveal through his actions and remarks on his first three visits to the priest?

6. What might the priest be thinking when Thord says, "I have no worries" and "this marks the finish [of my visits to you]"? In light of later story events, why are these remarks ironic?

7. How is Thord's attitude toward his final donation different from his attitude toward the money he has given earlier? In what way has Thord's son finally become a "blessing" to him?

Extending

8. Why do you think most people make charitable contributions? In your opinion, what are the best reasons for making such gifts?

LANGUAGE STUDY

Cognates

Cognates are words in different languages that are similar in appearance and meaning because they derive from a common source. For example, the English word *dollar* and the *daler* [dä′lər] that Thord gives the priest are cognates. Both are these words for money derive from the same earlier form, the old German word *thaler* [tä′lər], short for *Joachimsthaler* [yō ä′кнim stä′lər], a coin first made in 1519 in the Eastern European town of St. Joachimsthal.

1. The chief currency of Norway today is the *krone*. With what English word might *krone* be a cognate? (Hint: What royal symbol do you think the *krone* pictures or once pictured?)

2. Check an almanac, dictionary, or encyclopedia to learn the names of the chief currency units of two other European nations, Austria and the Netherlands. With what English words might these names of foreign currency be cognates?

COMPOSITION

Writing About Character

■ Write a brief composition explaining how Bjørnson uses both direct and indirect characterization to reveal Thord's personality to readers. First discuss what we learn about Thord from the details about his appearance, actions, and speech. Then explain how Thord changes in the course of the story, and discuss the details that help reveal those changes.

The Father 47

READER'S RESPONSE

Do you think the father needed to be taught such a severe lesson? Why or why not?

ANSWERS

STUDY QUESTIONS

1. He asks the priest to baptize his son on his own on Saturday at noon. On his next visit he asks to know the place his son has in the confirmation ceremony.

2. She is the richest girl in town. He drowns.

3. He gives the priest a large donation for the poor. He is now bent, lean, and white of hair; he has sold his farm and is donating half the proceeds to charity.

4. "I think your son has finally been a blessing to you." Thord sadly agrees.

5. He reveals his concerns with social status and wealth and his desire to have the "best" things for his son.

6. "Everyone has worries, and there is one more church rite for which you may need to visit—a funeral." When the son dies, Thord does indeed have great worries and does visit the priest one more time.

7. He is now pious and compassionate. His son's death has made him realize what is important in life.

8. Answers will vary. Students are likely to contrast contributions made for show or tax purposes with those made out of compassion and piety.

LANGUAGE STUDY

1. *crown*
2. Austria—schilling, cognate—*shilling*; Netherlands—guilder, cognates—*gold, golden, gilt*

COMPOSITION: GUIDELINES FOR EVALUATION

WRITING ABOUT CHARACTER

Objective

To analyze methods of characterization

Guidelines for Evaluation

■ suggested length: two or three paragraphs

■ should show how both direct and indirect characterization reveal Thord's personality
■ should cite details about Thord's appearance, actions, and speech
■ should cite details that show how Thord changes

Set in India, this touching story tells of a wandering peddler who befriends the narrator's young daughter, Mini. Their friendship breaks off when the Kabuliwallah is jailed. He reappears on Mini's wedding day only to find the grown-up Mini awkward with him. He moves the narrator by telling of his own daughter, whom he has not seen for years.

LITERARY SKILLS FOR THIS SELECTION

- character motivation
- point of view

THEMES IN THIS SELECTION

- human relationships: parents and children
- the end of childhood
- tolerance and prejudice

LESSON OBJECTIVES

1. to recognize character motivation
2. to understand the meaning and origin of words from Indian languages
3. to write a dialogue between characters in a story

Teacher's Classroom Resources 1

- Teaching Notes   95
- Prereading Vocabulary   96
- Reading Guide   97
- Check Test   98
- Responding to World Cultures   99
- Literary Focus: Character Motivation   100
- Language Study: Words from Indian Languages   101
- Writing Process Guide: Writing a Dialogue   102
- Grammar in Literature: Varying Sentence Openers   103
- Selection Test   104

Rabindranath Tagore

(1861–1941)

India

Rabindranath Tagore [rə bin'drə nät' tə gôr'] is one of India's most celebrated authors. Born in Calcutta, India, Tagore was the grandson of a prince and had a highly privileged childhood. After briefly studying law in England, he returned to India to manage his father's estate. Here he worked closely with the tenants and was deeply moved by the sufferings of the poor. The experience inspired much of his fiction; it also made him a supporter of Indian nationalism, although he always stressed social reform over political independence.

A prolific author, Tagore published his first volume of poetry in 1878 and went on to produce sixty more poetry collections before he died. He also wrote short stories, novels, and more than forty plays. He was also a painter and an educator, and founded what is now India's Visva-Bharati University.

Tagore wrote mainly in Bengali but was fluent in English and assisted in translating his works. His international reputation was enormous; in 1913 he became the first Asian writer to be awarded the Nobel Prize for Literature.

GEOGRAPHY AND CULTURE

Calcutta and the Indian Subcontinent

The south-central peninsula of the vast continent of Asia is often called the Indian subcontinent. It includes the present-day nations of India, Pakistan, Bangladesh, Nepal, Bhutan, and Sri Lanka. This area was known as British India and controlled by Britain until 1947. Until 1912, the capital of British India was Calcutta, a port city in the eastern Indian region called Bengal [ben gôl']. Today Calcutta is India's largest city, and a portion of Bengal that lies east of Calcutta is part of the nation of Bangladesh.

"The Kabuliwallah" takes place in late nineteenth-century Calcutta. Like many Calcutta natives, the story's narrator practices the Hindu religion and speaks the language of Bengali, Tagore's native tongue. The title character of the story, however, is not a native of Calcutta. He has traveled more than a thousand miles from Kabul [kä'bool], the capital of Afghanistan, a mountainous country northwest of what is now the nation of Pakistan.

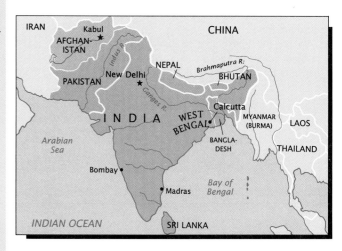

See LITERATURE AND CULTURE SOURCEBOOK:
India and the Middle East

TEACHING STUDENTS OF DIFFERENT ABILITIES

- **For less advanced students:** Help students see that the Kabuliwallah arouses prejudice because of people's fear of the unknown. Ask students to complete the Reading Guide for this selection.

- **For more advanced students:** Ask students what the story shows about the way relationships between children and parents change over time.

DISCUSSING GEOGRAPHY AND CULTURE

Living in a Metropolis

Calcutta, the setting for this story, is the largest city in India. Many people from different ethnic groups, speaking different languages and practicing different religions, have flocked to this metropolis throughout its history.

- Have students discuss a big city that they know well. What ethnic groups live there?

Rabindranath Tagore

The Kabuliwallah[1]

Translated from the Bengali by C. F. Andrews and Rabindranath Tagore

My five-year-old daughter Mini cannot live without chattering. I really believe that in all her life she has not wasted a minute in silence. Her mother is often vexed at this, and would stop her prattle, but I would not. To see Mini quiet is unnatural, and I cannot bear it long. And so my own talk with her is always lively.

One morning, for instance, when I was in the midst of the seventeenth chapter of my new novel, my little Mini stole into the room, and putting her hand into mine, said: "Father! Ramdayal the door-keeper calls a crow a *crew!* He doesn't know anything, does he?"

Before I could explain to her the differences of language in this world, she was embarked on the full tide of another subject. "What do you think, Father? Bhola says there is an elephant in the clouds, blowing water out of his trunk, and that is why it rains!"

And then, darting off anew, while I sat still making ready some reply to this last saying, "Father! what relation is Mother to you?"

"My dear little sister in the law!" I murmured involuntarily to myself, but with a grave face contrived to answer: "Go and play with Bhola, Mini! I am busy!"

The window of my room overlooks the road. The child had seated herself at my feet near my table, and was playing softly, drumming on her knees. I was hard at work on my seventeenth chapter, where Pratap Singh,[2] the hero, had just caught Kanchanlata, the heroine, in his arms, and was about to escape with her by the third

story window of the castle, when all of a sudden Mini left her play, and ran to the window, crying, "A Kabuliwallah! a Kabuliwallah!" Sure enough in the street below was a Kabuliwallah, passing slowly along. He wore the loose soiled clothing of his people, with a tall turban; there was a bag on his back, and he carried boxes of grapes in his hand.

I cannot tell what were my daughter's feelings at the sight of this man, but she began to call him loudly. "Ah!" I thought, "he will come in, and my seventeenth chapter will never be finished!" At which exact moment the Kabuliwallah turned, and looked up at the child. When she saw this, overcome by terror, she fled to her mother's protection, and disappeared. She had a blind belief that inside the bag, which the big man carried, there were perhaps two or three other children like herself. The peddler meanwhile entered my doorway, and greeted me with a smiling face.

So precarious was the position of my hero and my heroine that my first impulse was to stop and buy something, since the man had been called. I made some small purchases, and a conversation began about Abdur Rahman, the Russians, the English, and the Frontier Policy.[3]

As he was about to leave, he asked: "And where is the little girl, sir?"

And I, thinking that Mini must get rid of her false fear, had her brought out.

---

1. **Kabuliwallah** [kä′bool ē wä′lə]: fellow from Kabul, capital of Afghanistan. (See the Geography and Culture feature that precedes the story.)
2. **Singh:** [sing′hə]

3. **Abdur Rahman** [äb′dər rə män′] . . . **Frontier Policy:** Abdur Rahman Khan (1844?–1901), leader of Afghanistan from 1880 to 1901, opposed interference by the English, who sought to extend the frontiers of British India into Afghanistan, and by the Russian Empire, which also sought to extend its borders into Afghanistan.

The Kabuliwallah **49**

CRITICAL THINKING: GUIDED READING QUESTIONS

LITERAL

1a. What different attitudes do the narrator and his wife have toward Mini's "prattle"? (It entertains the narrator but vexes his wife.)

2a. What "blind belief" does Mini seem to hold regarding the Kabuliwallah? (She thinks he holds children captive in his bag.)

INFERENTIAL

1b. What do these attitudes reveal about the two characters' relationship with Mini? (The narrator has a good rapport with Mini but also indulges her; his wife is more of a disciplinarian.)

2b. What do you think led to this strange belief? (Mini could be reacting to the man's foreign and shabby appearance; she may also have based her belief on the comments and prejudices of others.)

- The Kabuliwallah does not succeed in winning Mini over this time.
- On another day the narrator finds Mini and the Kabuliwallah talking like old friends.
- The Kabuliwallah and Mini share private jokes.

IN THE GLOSSARY

- demur: object
- judicious: using good judgment
- behindhand: late
- trifle: somewhat
- euphemism: mild expression in place of a harsher one
- discomfited: confused

3 TEACHING CHARACTER MOTIVATION

Ask students about Mini's motives for becoming friendly with the Kabuliwallah. (He is her rapt audience.)

4 READING SKILL: INFERENCE

Ask students why Mini's mother is so distressed at the idea that Mini has taken money from the Kabuliwallah. (She probably objects to her daughter's accepting gifts from strangers.)

5 TEACHING THEME

Help students see the special relationship that each man has with this child. Each seems to revel in her unguarded spontaneity and liveliness.

6 TEACHING STUDENTS OF LIMITED ENGLISH PROFICIENCY

Point out that the narrator is explaining an idiom, or special saying. Elicit some particularly colorful American idioms (for example, "putting your foot in your mouth" for "saying something awkward"). Ask students who are not native speakers of English for examples of idioms from their own language.

She stood by my chair, and looked at the Kabuliwallah and his bag. He offered her nuts and raisins, but she would not be tempted, and only clung the closer to me, with all her doubts increased.

3 This was their first meeting.

One morning, however, not many days later, as I was leaving the house, I was startled to find Mini, seated on a bench near the door, laughing and talking, with the great Kabuliwallah at her feet. In all her life, it appeared, my small daughter had never found so patient a listener, save her father. And already the corner of her little sari[4] was stuffed with almonds and raisins, the gift of her visitor. "Why did you give her those?" I said, and taking out an eight-anna bit,[5] I handed it to him. The man accepted the money without demur, and slipped it into his pocket.

Alas, on my return an hour later, I found the unfortunate coin had made twice its own worth of trouble! For the Kabuliwallah had given it to Mini, and her mother, catching sight of the bright round object, had pounced on the child with: "Where did you get that eight-anna bit?"

"The Kabuliwallah gave it to me," said Mini cheerfully.

4 "The Kabuliwallah gave it to you!" cried her mother, much shocked. "Oh, Mini! how could you take it from him?"

I, entering at the moment, saved her from impending disaster, and proceeded to make my own inquiries.

It was not the first or second time, I found, that the two had met. The Kabuliwallah had overcome the child's first terror by a judicious bribery of nuts and almonds, and the two were now great friends.

They had many quaint jokes, which afforded

them much amusement. Seated in front of him, looking down on his gigantic frame in all her tiny dignity, Mini would ripple her face with laughter, and begin: "O Kabuliwallah, Kabuliwallah, what have you got in your bag?"

5 And he would reply, in the nasal accents of the mountaineer: "An elephant!" Not much cause for merriment, perhaps; but how they both enjoyed the witticism! And for me, this child's talk with a grown-up man had always in it something strangely fascinating.

Then the Kabuliwallah, not to be behindhand, would take his turn: "Well, little one, and when are you going to the father-in-law's house?"

Now most small Bengali maidens have heard long ago about the father-in-law's house; but we, being a little new-fangled,[6] had kept these things from our child, and Mini at this question must have been a trifle bewildered. But she would not show it, and with ready tact replied: "Are *you* going there?"

6 Amongst men of the Kabuliwallah's class, however, it is well known that the words *father-in-law's house* have a double meaning. It is a euphemism for jail, the place where we are well cared for, at no expense to ourselves. In this sense would the sturdy peddler take my daughter's question. "Ah," he would say, shaking his fist at an invisible policeman, "I will thrash my father-in-law!" Hearing this, and picturing the poor discomfited relative, Mini would go off into peals of laughter, in which her formidable friend would join.

These were autumn mornings, the very time of year when kings of old went forth to conquest; and I, never stirring from my little corner in Calcutta, would let my mind wander over the

---

4. **sari** [sär′ē]: traditional Hindu women's garment. According to custom, it is worn wrapped around the body and draped over the shoulder.
5. **eight-anna** [än′ə] **bit**: former coin of India, worth about eight cents at the time of the story.

6. **Bengali maidens . . . new-fangled:** Traditionally, Bengali marriages were arranged early, and the female went to live in her father-in-law's home. Among more modern Bengali families at the time of the story, however, "newfangled" Western customs were being adopted.

CRITICAL THINKING: GUIDED READING QUESTIONS

LITERAL

1a. How does the Kabuliwallah overcome Mini's "first terror"? (He bribes her with treats.)

2a. To what group does "father-in-law's house" mean "jail"? (to men of the Kabuliwallah's class)

INFERENTIAL

1b. Why does the Kabuliwallah enjoy being with Mini? (She makes him laugh and perhaps accepts him more completely than do other people in the region. Perhaps he has a special fondness for children.)

2b. What does the use of this expression suggest about men of the Kabuliwallah's class? (They are poor, live roughly, and are probably prone to trouble with the law.)

whole world. At the very name of another country, my heart would go out to it, and at the sight of a foreigner in the streets, I would fall to weaving a network of dreams—the mountains, the glens, and the forests of his distant home, with his cottage in its setting, and the free and independent life of far-away wilds. Perhaps the scenes of travel conjure themselves up before me, and pass and repass in my imagination all 7 the more vividly, because I lead such a vegetable existence that a call to travel would fall upon me like a thunderbolt. In the presence of this Kabuliwallah, I was immediately transported to the foot of arid mountain peaks, with narrow little defiles twisting in and out amongst their towering heights. I could see the string of camels bearing the merchandise, and the company of turbaned merchants carrying some of their queer old firearms, and some of their spears, journeying downward towards the plains. I could see—but at some such point Mini's mother would intervene, imploring me to "beware of that man."

Mini's mother is unfortunately a very timid lady. Whenever she hears a noise in the street, or sees people coming towards the house, she always jumps to the conclusion that they are either thieves, or drunkards, or snakes, or tigers, or malaria, or cockroaches, or caterpillars, or an English sailor. Even after all these years of experience, she is not able to overcome her terror. 8 So she was full of doubts about the Kabuliwallah, and used to beg me to keep a watchful eye on him.

I tried to laugh her fear gently away, but then she would turn round on me seriously, and ask me solemn questions.

Were children never kidnapped?

Was it, then, not true that there was slavery in Kabul?

Was it so very absurd that this big man should be able to carry off a tiny child?

I urged that, though not impossible, it was highly improbable. But this was not enough, and her dread persisted. As it was indefinite, however, it did not seem right to forbid the man the house, and the intimacy went on unchecked.

Once a year in the middle of January Rahmun, the Kabuliwallah, was in the habit of returning to his country, and as the time approached he would be very busy, going from house to house collecting his debts. This year, however, he could always find time to come and see Mini. It would have seemed to an outsider that there was some conspiracy between the two, for when he could not come in the morning, he would appear in the evening.

9 Even to me it was a little startling now and then, in the corner of a dark room, suddenly to surprise this tall, loose-garmented, much bebagged[7] man; but when Mini would run in smiling, with her, "O! Kabuliwallah! Kabuliwallah!" and the two friends, so far apart in age, would subside into their old laughter and their old jokes, I felt reassured.

One morning, a few days before he had made up his mind to go, I was correcting my proof sheets[8] in my study. It was chilly weather. Through the window the rays of the sun touched my feet, and the slight warmth was very welcome. It was almost eight o'clock, and the early pedestrians were returning home, with 10 their heads covered. All at once, I heard an uproar in the street, and, looking out, saw Rahmun being led away bound between two policemen, and behind them a crowd of curious boys. There were blood-stains on the clothes of the Kabuliwallah, and one of the policemen carried a knife. Hurrying out, I stopped them, and inquired what it all meant. Partly from one, partly from another, I gathered that a certain neighbor

---

7. **bebagged:** laden with bags.
8. **proof sheets:** printer's copies of an author's writing, sent to the author to check before final printing and publication.

The Kabuliwallah **51**

- The narrator's wife expresses concern that the peddler will harm Mini; the narrator disagrees.
- The Kabuliwallah goes home once a year, in January.
- One January day the narrator sees the peddler being led away by police officers.

IN THE GLOSSARY

- **arid:** dry
- **defiles:** mountain passes
- **imploring:** begging
- **malaria:** a tropical disease
- **intimacy:** close friendship

7 TEACHING SYMBOLS

Ask students what the Kabuliwallah seems to represent to the sedentary narrator. (freedom, the spirit of adventure)

8 TEACHING THEME

Remind students of Mini's "blind fear" that the Kabuliwallah carries children in his bag. The narrator's wife is expressing an adult version of this prejudice, based on the peddler's foreign looks.

9 GRAMMAR IN LITERATURE

Call attention to the string of modifiers here. In particular, the participial adjectives "loose-garmented" and "much bebagged" create an impression of eccentricity.

10 TEACHING PLOT: RISING ACTION

Point out that something important is about to happen to the Kabuliwallah, something that will probably change his relationship with the narrator's family.

CRITICAL THINKING: GUIDED READING QUESTIONS

LITERAL

1a. What fear regarding the Kabuliwallah does the narrator's wife express? (The Kabuliwallah might kidnap Mini.)

2a. How often does the Kabuliwallah go home? (He returns home only once a year.)

INFERENTIAL

1b. Why does the narrator say that this act is "highly improbable"? (The Kabuliwallah always treats Mini kindly and has never shown any sign of menace.)

2b. Why might he go home so seldom, and what does this fact suggest about the hardships of his life? (He is probably too poor to go home more often. He spends most of his time in foreign places, sees his family only briefly, and so leads a lonely existence.)

- The Kabuliwallah struck a customer who had tried to cheat him.
- Mini sees the Kabuliwallah being arrested.

11 TEACHING THEME

Note that it is the Kabuliwallah alone who is being punished; the Calcuttan who tried to cheat him is not held. Help students see that in this case the law itself may be prejudiced, favoring the dishonest local man over the foreigner.

ART AND LITERATURE

Since ancient times glass has been made by firing sand, flint, and ashes. Glass was thought to combine three of the four basic elements—fire, air, and earth (the fourth is water). In India copper and iron were added to yield a blue or green tint. The glass was then painted or incised.

- Although Indian painting is naturalistic in appearance, much Indian art, as represented by this glass bottle, is best described as idealized. Personal characteristics are formalized into an archetype that represents all the members of a particular culture. The figures on this bottle depict an ideal married couple, a two-in-one unity. The stylized tree in the background represents the family tree, the symbol for genealogical continuity.
- After students have read the story, ask them to identify two wedding traditions observed by Mini. (She wears red silk and has sandal paste on her forehead.)

Indian glass bottle, eighteenth century.

11 had owed the peddler something for a Rampuri[9] shawl, but had falsely denied having bought it, and that in the course of the quarrel, Rahmun

9. **Rampuri** [räm pōōr′e]: made in the city of Rampur.

52 *The Short Story*

had struck him. Now in the heat of his excitement, the prisoner began calling his enemy all sorts of names, when suddenly in a veranda of my house appeared my little Mini, with her usual exclamation: "O Kabuliwallah! Kabuliwal-

CRITICAL THINKING: GUIDED READING QUESTIONS

LITERAL

1a. Why is the Kabuliwallah being led away? (He struck a man who had tried to cheat him.)

INFERENTIAL

1b. What do you think will happen to the Kabuliwallah? (Many students will expect that he will go to jail. Some students may expect that the narrator will intervene to help the peddler.)

lah!" Rahmun's face lighted up as he turned to her. He had no bag under his arm today, so she could not discuss the elephant with him. She at once therefore proceeded to the next question: **12** "Are you going to the father-in-law's house?" Rahmun laughed and said: "Just where I am going, little one!" Then seeing that the reply did not amuse the child, he held up his fettered hands. "Ah," he said, "I would have thrashed that old father-in-law, but my hands are bound!"

On a charge of murderous assault, Rahmun was sentenced to some years' imprisonment.

Time passed away, and he was not remembered. The accustomed work in the accustomed place was ours, and the thought of the once-free mountaineer spending his years in prison seldom or never occurred to us. Even my light-hearted Mini, I am ashamed to say, forgot her old friend. New companions filled her life. As she grew older, she spent more of her time with **13** girls. So much time indeed did she spend with them that she came no more, as she used to do, to her father's room. I was scarcely on speaking terms with her.

Years had passed away. It was once more autumn and we had made arrangements for our **14** Mini's marriage. It was to take place during the Puja Holidays.[10] With Durga returning to Kailas,[11] the light of our home also was to depart to her husband's house, and leave her father's in the shadow.

The morning was bright. After the rains, there was a sense of ablution in the air, and the sun-rays looked like pure gold. So bright were they that they gave a beautiful radiance even to the sordid brick walls of our Calcutta lanes. Since early dawn today the wedding-pipes had been sounding, and at each beat my own heart throbbed. The wail of the tune, "Bhairavi,"[12] seemed to intensify my pain at the approaching separation. My Mini was to be married tonight.

From early morning noise and bustle had pervaded the house. In the courtyard the canopy had to be slung on its bamboo poles; the chandeliers with their tinkling sound must be hung in each room and veranda. There was no end of hurry and excitement. I was sitting in my study, looking through the accounts, when someone entered, saluting respectfully, and stood before me. It was Rahmun the Kabuliwallah. At first I did not recognize him. He had no bag, nor the long hair, nor the same vigor that he used to have. But he smiled, and I knew him again.

"When did you come, Rahmun?" I asked him.

"Last evening," he said, "I was released from jail."

The words struck harsh upon my ears. I had never before talked with one who had wounded his fellow, and my heart shrank within itself, when I realized this, for I felt that the day would have been better-omened had he not turned up.

"There are ceremonies going on," I said, "and I am busy. Could you perhaps come another day?"

15 At once he turned to go; but as he reached the door he hesitated, and said: "May I not see the little one, sir, for a moment?" It was his belief that Mini was still the same. He had pictured her running to him as she used, calling "O Kabuliwallah! Kabuliwallah!" He had imagined too that they would laugh and talk together, just as of old. In fact, in memory of former days he had brought, carefully wrapped up in paper, a few almonds and raisins and grapes, obtained somehow from a countryman, for his own little fund was dispersed.

I said again: "There is a ceremony in the house, and you will not be able to see anyone today."

---

10. **Puja Holidays:** autumn festival celebrating the Hindu mother goddess.
11. **Durga returning to Kailas** [kī läs′]: the Hindu mother goddess returning to her husband, Shiva, who, according to Hindu tradition, sits atop Mount Kailas, a high mountain north of India in Tibet. *Durga* is only one of many names for the Hindu mother goddess.

12. **"Bhairavi"** [bī rä′vē]: song about loss named for the Hindu goddess who leads souls to the afterlife.

The Kabuliwallah **53**

PAGE SUMMARY: AT A GLANCE

- The Kabuliwallah jokes with Mini about his "father-in-law's house."
- He is sentenced to several years in prison.
- Over time the narrator and Mini forget the peddler.
- Mini grows up and hardly sees her father anymore.
- It is Mini's wedding day.
- The Kabuliwallah comes to visit Mini, and the narrator tries to dismiss him.

IN THE GLOSSARY

- fettered: in chains
- ablution: cleansing
- sordid: filthy
- pervaded: spread throughout

12 TEACHING IRONY

Point out that Mini's reference to the father-in-law joke creates irony here because what was once a joke has become a sad reality.

13 TEACHING POINT OF VIEW

Ask students how the narrator seems to feel about the change in Mini. (He seems to miss the chattering child whom he so adored.)

14 CULTURAL BACKGROUND

Durga, the Hindu mother goddess, is usually portrayed holding deadly weapons in her eight or ten arms. The Durga-Puja to which the story refers is northeastern India's greatest religious festival, observed with nine days of festivities and processions.

15 READING SKILL: INFERENCE

Ask students why the peddler believes that Mini is still a little girl. (Perhaps he was not fully aware of the passage of time while he was in prison. Perhaps he clung to the image of the child as a happy memory during a sad time.)

CRITICAL THINKING: GUIDED READING QUESTIONS

LITERAL

1a. Do the narrator and Mini remember the Kabuliwallah while he is imprisoned? (No, they forget about him and go on with their lives.)

2a. What does the narrator say when the Kabuliwallah returns on Mini's wedding day? ("There are ceremonies going on . . . and I am busy. Could you perhaps come another day?")

INFERENTIAL

1b. Do you think the narrator and Mini *should* have thought about the Kabuliwallah? (Although their forgetting is natural, the narrator and Mini seem somewhat self-centered, since the Kabuliwallah visited frequently.)

2b. What do you think of the narrator's attempt to send the Kabuliwallah away? (Many students will find the narrator brusque, given the peddler's tender feelings for Mini.)

- The Kabuliwallah talks about his own daughter and shows the narrator her handprint.
- The narrator takes pity on him and summons Mini.
- When she appears in her wedding dress, the peddler is stunned but jokes about her father-in-law's house.
- She blushes and leaves.
- The narrator gives the peddler money so that he may go home to his own daughter.

IN THE GLOSSARY

- wares: items for sale
- curtail: cut back

16 TEACHING CHARACTER MOTIVATION

Point out that this is the first time we hear about the Kabuliwallah's daughter. Now we understand his special affection for Mini.

17 TEACHING PLOT: CLIMAX

Help students see that showing the little handprint brings the story to its climax, or emotional high point. Now the narrator sees the peddler in a new light, as a heartsick father.

18 TEACHING THEME

Encourage students to explain what the change in Mini shows about what children lose as they grow up. (They often lose spontaneity or liveliness.)

19 TEACHING PLOT: RESOLUTION

Help students see that the narrator, who has not always treated the kind peddler as he deserves, finally does right by him.

COLLABORATIVE LEARNING: ENRICHMENT ACTIVITY

Sociology "The Kabuliwallah" provides some description of traditional Hindu wedding customs. Divide students into groups, and ask each group to focus on wedding customs of a different culture or ethnic group.

The man's face fell. He looked wistfully at me for a moment, said "Good morning," and went out.

I felt a little sorry, and would have called him back, but I found he was returning of his own accord. He came close up to me, holding out his offerings, and said: "I brought these few things, sir, for the little one. Will you give them to her?"

16 I took them and was going to pay him, but he caught my hand and said: "You are very kind, sir! Keep me in your recollection. Do not offer me money!—You have a little girl; I too have one like her in my own home. I think of her, and bring fruits to your child, not to make a profit for myself."

Saying this, he put his hand inside his big loose robe, and brought out a small and dirty piece of paper. With great care he unfolded this, and smoothing it out with both hands on my

17 table. It bore the impression of a little hand. Not a photograph. Not a drawing. The impression of an ink-smeared hand laid flat on the paper. This touch of his own little daughter had been always on his heart, as he had come year after year to Calcutta, to sell his wares in the streets.

Tears came to my eyes. I forgot that he was a poor Kabuli fruit-seller, while I was—but no, what was I more than he? He also was a father.

That impression of the hand of his little Parvati[13] in her distant mountain home reminded me of my own little Mini.

I sent for Mini immediately from the inner apartment. Many difficulties were raised, but I would not listen. Clad in the red silk of her wedding-day, with the sandal paste on her forehead,[14] and adorned as a young bride, Mini

---

13. **Parvati** [pär vä´tē]: another name for the Hindu mother goddess; used here as a term of affection.
14. **sandal paste on her forehead:** decorative ointment made from the bark of the fragrant sandalwood tree and used by Brahmins to make distinguishing caste marks on their forehead. Brahmins are the highest of the four castes, or hereditary social classes, into which Hindus are traditionally divided.

---

came, and stood bashfully before me.

The Kabuliwallah looked a little staggered at the apparition.[15] He could not revive their old friendship. At last he smiled and said: "Little one, are you going to your father-in-law's house?"

18 But Mini now understood the meaning of the word "father-in-law," and she could not reply to him as of old. She flushed up at the question, and stood before him with her bride-like face turned down.

I remembered the day when the Kabuliwallah and my Mini had first met, and I felt sad. When she had gone, Rahmun heaved a deep sigh, and sat down on the floor. The idea had suddenly come to him that his daughter too must have grown in this long time, and that he would have to make friends with her anew. Assuredly he would not find her as he used to know her. And besides, what might not have happened to her in these eight years?

The marriage-pipes sounded, and the mild autumn sun streamed round us. But Rahmun sat in the little Calcutta lane, and saw before him the barren mountains of Afghanistan.

I took out a bank-note[16] and gave it to him, saying: "Go back to your own daughter, Rahmun, in your own country, and may the happiness of your meeting bring good fortune to my child!"

19 Having made this present, I had to curtail some of the festivities. I could not have the electric lights I had intended, nor the military band, and the ladies of the house were despondent at it. But to me the wedding feast was all the brighter for the thought that in a distant land a long-lost father met again with his only child.

---

15. **apparition:** here, someone who appears suddenly and unexpectedly. Mini is a startling vision because the Kabuliwallah doesn't recognize her as a grown woman.
16. **bank-note:** the equivalent of paper money, and worth substantially more than a coin. This represents a very generous gift.

CRITICAL THINKING: GUIDED READING QUESTIONS

LITERAL

1a. How does the narrator react when the Kabuliwallah shows him the handprint? (He is moved to tears and sends for Mini.)

2a. What idea does the narrator say suddenly comes to the Kabuliwallah after Mini leaves the room? (The peddler realizes that his own daughter is grown and that he must get to know her all over again.)

INFERENTIAL

1b. Why is the narrator so moved? (The Kabuliwallah has cherished the handprint through his long imprisonment. Also, the handprint reminds him of the younger Mini, who in a sense is now far away.)

2b. What emotions do you think the Kabuliwallah feels? (He probably fears that he will be unable to resume his relationship with his cherished child, just as he has been unable to resume his relationship with Mini.)

STUDY QUESTIONS

Recalling

1. What does the Kabuliwallah sell? From where does he come and, when the story opens, how often does he go home?
2. How old is Mini when the story begins? About what do she and the Kabuliwallah joke?
3. Why does the Kabuliwallah disappear for so long? On what special occasion does he return?
4. What memento does the Kabuliwallah show the narrator?
5. How does Mini behave when she sees the Kabuliwallah again? What happens after Mini leaves?

Interpreting

6. Why does Mini's mother fear the Kabuliwallah, and how are her fears proved wrong?
7. What is the double meaning of "going to your father-in-law's house"? At what point in the story does the expression become ironic, and at what point does it become touching?
8. What does the story suggest about the way people perceive children whom they do not see for a long time?
9. What messages about tolerance does the story convey?

Extending

10. Why might it sometimes be difficult to resume your affections for someone you have not seen in a long time?

LITERARY FOCUS

Character Motivation

Motivation is the reason or reasons that a character in a story acts or thinks in a certain way. For fictional characters to appear true to life, their motivation, or reasons behind their behavior, must seem believable to readers. Sometimes a character's motivation is directly stated in a story, either by the char-

acter or elsewhere in the narrative. At other times we must infer motivation from details the author provides about the character.

Thinking About Character Motivation

1. Why does the Kabuliwallah spend so much time with young Mini? Where in the story is his motivation stated?
2. Why does the Kabuliwallah work so far away from home? What details in the story lead you to infer this motivation?

LANGUAGE STUDY

Words from Indian Languages

Bengali, Tagore's native tongue, is only one of many languages spoken in India. The term *wallah* comes from Hindi, the most widely spoken of India's native languages. Originally a Hindi suffix, *wallah* became part of the English spoken in India. The word then traveled to Britain, where it is more widely used than in the United States. *Wallah* means "a person connected with a particular thing or function." Thus, someone who sells tea might be called a "tea wallah," and someone who works for an employment agency might be called a "job wallah."

1. In a movie released several years ago called *Shakespeare Wallah*, the main characters travel around India and do something. Based on the film's title, what do you think they do?
2. Use a dictionary to find the origins of these common English words: *loot, pajamas, shampoo.*

COMPOSITION

Writing a Dialogue

■ Write the dialogue that you imagine might take place between the Kabuliwallah and his daughter when the Kabuliwallah finally returns home. Make the characters' feelings and motivation clear, and show how the characters or their situations may have changed with the passage of time.

The Kabuliwallah **55**

COMPOSITION: GUIDELINES FOR EVALUATION

WRITING A DIALOGUE

Objective

To write a dialogue between characters

Guidelines for Evaluation

■ suggested length: one to two pages
■ should show characters' feelings and motives
■ should show how characters change over time
■ should be written in dialogue form

ANSWERS

STUDY QUESTIONS

1. fruits and nuts; Kabul, Afghanistan; once a year
2. She is five. They joke about the contents of the Kabuliwallah's bag and going to Mini's "father-in-law's house."
3. He is jailed for beating someone who cheated him. He returns on Mini's wedding day.
4. He shows the narrator a print of his daughter's hand, made long ago.
5. She blushes when he talks of her father-in-law's house. The narrator gives the Kabuliwallah money.
6. He is a foreigner, and she fears he will harm Mini. He loves Mini, who reminds him of his own daughter.
7. It means "to get married" and is slang for "going to prison." It is ironic when Mini asks the Kabuliwallah if he is going to his father-in-law's house when in fact he is going to jail; it is touching when he revives the joke on Mini's wedding day.
8. They think of children as young and innocent and forget that they become adults.
9. All people share the same feelings and should be treated with tolerance; children are often more tolerant than adults.
10. Answers will vary. People change and sometimes forget the past.

LITERARY FOCUS

1. She reminds him of his daughter, who is far away. This is revealed when the Kabuliwallah says, "I too have one like her."
2. He is poor and must go away to earn money; his soiled clothes, his job as a peddler, and the fact that he goes home only once a year

LANGUAGE STUDY

1. They put on plays by Shakespeare.
2. *loot*--Hindi *lut,* from Sanskrit *lunt,* "to rob"; *pajamas*--Hindi *pajama* from Persian *pai,* "a leg," and *jama,* "garment"; *shampoo*--Hindi *champo,* from *champna,* "to knead"

In this realistic Chilean story a starving young sailor finds kindness and sustenance. In the dock area of a busy port, a youth who ran off to sea has not eaten for three days. Nevertheless, he is too ashamed to accept several offers of charity. Famished, he wanders off to a quiet milk bar, where the food and kindness of a motherly waitress sustain him.

LITERARY SKILLS FOR THIS SELECTION

- character motivation
- atmosphere
- style

THEMES IN THIS SELECTION

- human relationships: kindness to strangers
- poverty and need
- the lure of adventure

LESSON OBJECTIVES

1. to understand sailors' jargon
2. to analyze a character's motivation
3. to write a letter of thanks from a story character

Teacher's Classroom Resources 1

- Teaching Notes   107
- Reading Guide   108
- Check Test   109
- Responding to World Cultures   110
- Language Study: Jargon   111
- Writing Process Guide: Writing About Character Motivation   112
- Writing a Letter of Thanks   113
- Grammar in Literature: Combining Sentences Using Participles   114
- Selection Test   115

PREVIEW: THE AUTHOR AND THE WORLD

Manuel Rojas

(1896–1973)

Chile

Manuel Rojas [män wel' rō'häs] is one of Chile's highly regarded fiction writers. Rojas wrote seven novels and four short-story collections and in 1957 won Chile's prestigious National Prize for Literature. He also had a distinguished academic career, including positions as Director of Publications at the University of Chile and as visiting professor at several American colleges.

Rojas' success did not come overnight, however. As a young man he took an odd assortment of jobs to support himself, working as a prompter in a theater, a longshoreman in the port of Valparaíso, and a laborer on the construction of the Trans-Andean Railway. His endeavors took him to many parts of Chile, which is one of the most geographically diverse countries in the world.

"The Glass of Milk," Rojas' most widely anthologized story, was inspired by his experiences as a longshoreman. The story paints a vivid picture of the bustle of activity at a busy international port, and it also reveals Rojas' compassionate understanding of life lived on the edge of poverty.

GEOGRAPHY AND CULTURE

Chile and Its Coastline

Located on the west coast of South America, Chile is a long and narrow nation, more than twenty times as long as it is wide. Running along much of Chile's eastern border are the rugged Andes Mountains. These craggy, often snow-capped mountains bear a marked resemblance to the Teton Range in the western United States. The Andes helped isolate Chile from its South American neighbors, especially before completion of the Trans-Andean Railway.

Scattered along Chile's Pacific coastline to the west, however, are many ports through which Chile has always maintained contact with the world. Chief among these ports are Punta Arenas in the south, Antofagasta and Arica in the north, and, in between, Chile's largest port, Valparaíso [val'pə rī'zō]. Rojas worked in Valparaíso as a longshoreman and probably set "The Glass of Milk" there.

See LITERATURE AND CULTURE SOURCEBOOK: Latin America

TEACHING STUDENTS OF DIFFERENT ABILITIES

- **For less advanced students:** Have students list in chronological order the information about the youth presented in the story's first section. Also have them complete the Reading Guide for this selection.

- **For more advanced students:** Have students research *criollismo,* or Latin American Regionalism, an offshoot of twentieth-century Realism, and then explain how the story illustrates *criollismo.*

DISCUSSING GEOGRAPHY AND CULTURE

Imagining an Ocean Voyage

In 1520 a Portuguese navigator named Ferdinand Magellan sailed through a narrow strait in what is now southern Chile to the Pacific Ocean. With this voyage Magellan became the first explorer to sail around the world.

- Have students look at the map on pages xxii–xxiii and plan an imaginary sailing trip around the world. Which countries would they most like to visit, and why?

Manuel Rojas

The Glass of Milk

Translated from the Spanish by Zoila Nelken

1   Propped on the starboard[1] rail, the sailor seemed to be waiting for someone. A bundle wrapped in white paper, grease-spotted, was in his left hand; his right tended his pipe.

From behind some freight-cars, a thin youth appeared; he paused a moment, looked out to sea, and then walked on along the edge of the wharf with his hands in his pockets, idling or thinking.

When he passed in front of the ship, the sailor called out to him in English:

"I say, look here!"

The youth raised his head, and without stopping, answered in the same language:

"Hello! What?"

"Are you hungry?"

2   There was a brief silence during which the youth seemed to be thinking, and took one shorter step as if to stop, but then replied, smiling feebly at the sailor:

"No, I'm not hungry. Thanks, sailor."

"All right."

The sailor took his pipe out of his mouth, spat, and replacing it, looked away. The youth, ashamed that he had seemed to need charity, walked a little faster, as if afraid he might change his mind.

A moment later, a gaudy tramp with a long, blond beard and blue eyes, dressed in odd rags and oversized, torn shoes, passed before the sailor, who without greeting called to him:

"Are you hungry?"

He had not yet finished the phrase when the tramp looked with shining eyes at the package the sailor held in his hand and answered hurriedly:

"Yes, sir; I'm very much hungry!"

The sailor smiled. The package flew through the air and landed in the eager hands. The hungry fellow did not even say "thanks," but sat right down on the ground, opened the still-warm bundle, and happily rubbed his hands as he saw what it contained. A port loafer might not speak English well, but he would never forgive himself if he didn't know enough to ask food from someone who did speak it.

The youth who passed by first had stopped nearby, and had seen what happened.

3   He was hungry too. He had not eaten for exactly three days, three long days. And more from timidity and shame than from pride, he refused to wait by the gangways at mealtimes, hoping the generosity of the sailors would produce some package of left-overs and bits of meat. He could not do it, he would never be able to do it. And when, as just now, someone did offer him a handout, the boy refused it heroically, though he felt his hunger increase with the refusal.

4   He had been wandering for six days around the side-streets and docks of that port. An English vessel had left him there after bringing him from Punta Arenas,[2] where he had jumped a previous ship on which he had served as captain's mess boy. He had spent a month there helping an Austrian crabber and then had stowed away on the first ship bound north.

---

1. **starboard** [stär′bərd]: referring to the right side of a ship as one faces forward.

2. **Punta Arenas** [pōōn′tä ä rā′näs]: one of Chile's southernmost ports. (See the Geography and Culture feature.)

The Glass of Milk   57

CRITICAL THINKING: GUIDED READING QUESTIONS

LITERAL

1a. Why does the youth walk faster after refusing the English sailor's offer of food? (He is ashamed that he seems to need charity.)

2a. To whom does the English sailor then give the food? (He gives it to a "gaudy" tramp.)

INFERENTIAL

1b. What does his shame reveal about him? (He is idealistic, and accepting charity is not in keeping with his ideals or self-image.)

2b. How is the tramp's attitude different from the youth's? (The tramp feels no shame in accepting charity and in fact subsists by doing so; he is far more pragmatic than the youth.)

MOTIVATION: PRIOR KNOWLEDGE

Ask why some people are attracted to a life of adventure. What jobs attract such people? What are the drawbacks to such a life?

PAGE SUMMARY: AT A GLANCE

- When a sailor offers him food, a youth refuses because he is ashamed to accept charity.
- A "gaudy" tramp readily accepts the handout.
- The youth had been serving as a captain's mess boy but jumped ship in Punta Arenas and stowed away on the first vessel heading north.
- That ship left him at this busy port six days ago, and he has not eaten for three days.

1 TEACHING PLOT: EXPOSITION

Point out that this story, like many modern stories, opens *in medias res,* or in the middle of the action, with background information gradually revealed later. Have students identify paragraphs of background information on this page. (the last two)

2 TEACHING STYLE

A detached, matter-of-fact tone is part of Rojas' style. Note that he achieves detachment by not telling us the youth's name and by reporting many of the youth's experiences from the outside: "He *seemed to be* thinking," for example, and "*as if* to stop."

3 TEACHING CHARACTER MOTIVATION

Point out that these words help explain the reason the youth refuses handouts despite his hunger. Ask what adverb later in the paragraph also touches on his motives. (*heroically*)

4 CULTURAL BACKGROUND

Note that sailors, in South America and elsewhere, usually come into contact with many different cultures. Ask what earlier evidence we have of the youth's international experiences. (his ability to speak English)

- To the youth the streets of the dock area are a place of slavery.
- Fascination with the sea has gripped the youth's life.
- Now, knowing he must eat, he takes a job as a stevedore but soon grows tired and dizzy.
- The foreman says it is customary not to pay workers until their second day but offers to lend the youth a bit of money.

IN THE GLOSSARY

- drudgery: tedious or lowly work
- rosary: string of beads used in reciting prayers

5 TEACHING STYLE

Figurative language, repetition, and parallel structure are strong elements of Rojas' style. Have students identify the similes here and below ("like a bale without a label," "as a strong arm a thin rod," etc.), and elicit that repetition and parallel structure ("without a label . . .") help stress the desperation of the youth's situation.

6 TEACHING CHARACTER MOTIVATION

Note that the youth left home because he was lured by a life at sea, which seemed to offer him adventure and freedom.

7 TEACHING ATMOSPHERE

Point out that details of the setting help give the dock area a hectic, oppressive atmosphere, in contrast to the "grand sweep of the sea" mentioned above.

8 TEACHING STYLE

In conjunction with the Language Study, note the many examples of sailors' jargon that add to the story's realism. Have volunteers give examples of jargon in another field, such as baseball, gardening, or medicine.

9 TEACHING STUDENTS OF LIMITED ENGLISH PROFICIENCY

Have students use context clues to determine the meaning of "at the end of his rope." ("at the end of one's endurance")

He was discovered the day after sailing, and put to work in the boiler room. At the first large port of call, he had been put off, and there he 5 had remained, like a bale without a label, without an acquaintance, without a penny, and without a trade.

As long as the ship was in port, the boy managed to eat, but after that . . . The great city that rose up beyond the back streets with their taverns and cheap inns did not attract him; it seemed a place of slavery: stale, dark, without the grand sweep of the sea; among its high walls and narrow streets people lived and died bewildered by agonizing drudgery.

6 The boy was gripped by that fascination of the sea which molds the most peaceful and orderly lives as a strong arm a thin rod. Although very young, he had already made several trips along the coast of South America on various ships, doing odd jobs and tasks, tasks and odd jobs which were almost useless on land.

After the ship left him, the boy walked and walked, hoping to chance upon something that would enable him to live somehow until he could get back to his home grounds; but he found nothing. The port was not very busy, and the few ships that had work would not take him on.

7 The docks were swarming with confirmed tramps: sailors on the beach, like himself, who had either jumped ship or were fleeing some crime; loafers given to idleness, who kept alive one knows not how, by begging or stealing, spending their days as if they were the beads of some grimy rosary, waiting for who knows what extraordinary events, or not expecting anything; people of the strangest and most exotic races and places, and even some in whose existence one doesn't believe until one sees a living example.

The following day, convinced that he could not hold out much longer, the youth decided to resort to any means to get some food.

58 *The Short Story*

Walking along, he found himself in front of a ship that had docked the night before, and was loading wheat. A line of men, heavy sacks on their shoulders, shuttled from the freight-cars, 8 across the gangplank to the hatchways of the ship's hold, where the stevedores[3] received the cargo.

He watched for a while, until he dared to speak to the foreman, offering his services. He was accepted, and enthusiastically he took his place in the long line of dock workers.

During the first period of the day he worked well; but later, he began to feel tired and dizzy; he swayed as he crossed the gangplank, the heavy load on his shoulder, on seeing at his feet the opening between the side of the ship and the thick wall of the wharf, at the bottom of which the sea, stained with oil and littered with garbage, lapped quietly.

There was a brief pause at lunch time, and while some of the men went off to the nearby eating places, and others ate what they had brought, the boy stretched out on the ground to rest, hiding his hunger.

9 He finished the day's work feeling completely exhausted, covered with sweat, at the end of his rope. While the laborers were leaving, the boy sat on some sacks, watching for the foreman, and when the last man had gone, approached him; confused and stuttering, he asked, without explaining what was happening to him, if he could be paid immediately, or if it were possible to get an advance on his earnings.

The foreman answered that it was customary to pay at the end of a job, and that it would still be necessary to work the following day in order to finish loading the ship. One more day! On the other hand, they never paid a cent in advance.

"But," he said, "if you need it, I could lend you about forty cents . . . That's all I have."

---

3. **stevedores:** longshoremen; people who load or store cargo on a ship.

CRITICAL THINKING: GUIDED READING QUESTIONS

LITERAL

1a. What sort of place do the back streets of the dock area seem to be to the youth? (a place of slavery)

2a. What happens to the youth after he works his first period as a stevedore? (He feels tired and dizzy and finishes the day exhausted.)

INFERENTIAL

1b. In contrast, what do the details suggest that the youth values in and associates with the sea? (freedom)

2b. Why is the youth so tired and dizzy? (He still has not eaten.)

The boy thanked him for his offer with an anguished smile, and left.

Then the boy was seized by acute despair. He was hungry, hungry, hungry! Hunger doubled him over, like a heavy, broad whiplash. He saw everything through a blue haze, and he staggered like a drunk when he walked. Nevertheless, he would not have been able to complain or to shout, for his suffering was deep and exhausting; it was not pain, but anguish, the end! It seemed to him that he was flattened out by a great weight.

Suddenly he felt his entrails on fire, and he stood still. He began to bend down, down, doubling over forcibly like a rod of steel, until he thought that he would drop. At that instant, as if a window opened before him, he saw his home, the view from it, the faces of his mother, brothers and sisters, all that he wanted and loved appeared and disappeared before his eyes shut by fatigue . . . Then, little by little, the giddiness passed and he began to straighten up, while the burning subsided gradually. Finally, he straightened up, breathing deeply. One more hour and he would drop unconscious to the ground.

He quickened his step, as if fleeing another dizzy spell, and, as he walked, he made up his mind to eat anywhere, without paying, even if they shamed him, beat him, sent him to jail, anything; the main thing was to eat, eat, eat. A hundred times he mentally repeated the word: eat, eat, eat, until it lost its meaning, leaving his head feeling hot and empty.

He did not intend to run away; he would simply say to the owner, "Sir, I was hungry, hungry, hungry, and I can't pay. . . . Do what you want."

He came to the outskirts of the city, and on one of the first streets he found a milk bar. It was a small, clean, and airy place, with little tables with marble tops. Behind the counter stood a blonde lady in a very white apron.

He chose that place. There were few passersby. He could have eaten at one of the cheap grills near the wharves but they were always full of people who gambled and drank.

There was only one customer in the milk bar. He was a little old man with glasses, who sat reading, his nose stuck between the pages of a newspaper, motionless, as if glued to his chair. On the little table there was a half-empty glass of milk.

While he waited for him to leave, the boy walked up and down the sidewalk; he felt the burning sensation in his stomach returning little by little; and he waited five, ten, up to fifteen minutes. He grew tired, and stood to one side of the door, from where he cast glances like stones at the old man.

What the devil could he be reading with such attention? The boy even imagined the old man was his enemy, who knew his intentions and had decided to frustrate them. He felt like entering and saying something insulting that would force the old man to leave, a rude word or phrase that would show him he had no right to sit there reading for an hour for so small a purchase.

Finally, the client finished what he was reading, or at least interrupted it. He downed the rest of the milk in one gulp, rose slowly, paid, and walked toward the door. He went out. He was a stoop-shouldered old man, probably a carpenter or varnisher.

Once in the street, the old man put on his glasses, stuck his nose in the newspaper again, and walked slowly away, stopping every ten steps to read more closely.

The youth waited until he was some distance away, and then entered. For a moment the boy stood by the entrance, undecided, not knowing where to sit. Finally, he chose a table and walked toward it, but halfway there he changed his mind, walked back, tripped over a chair, and finally installed himself in a corner.

The lady came, wiped the tabletop with a

The Glass of Milk **59**

PAGE SUMMARY: AT A GLANCE

- The youth politely refuses the foreman's offer.
- Giddy with hunger, he mentally sees the people he loves—his mother, brothers, and sisters.
- He decides to eat anywhere, without paying, even if it means that he will go to jail for it.
- He chooses a small, clean milk bar on the outskirts of the city and before going in waits for its one customer to leave.

IN THE GLOSSARY

- entrails: bowels; inner organs

10 TEACHING CHARACTER MOTIVATION

Elicit that the boy left the people he loved when he went to sea, and ask why he might think of them now. (Since his life of adventure is at a low point, he is homesick and probably regrets his decision to leave home.)

11 TEACHING CONFLICT

Note that up until now the youth's hunger has been countered by the shame he feels at accepting charity. Here he decides to assuage his hunger in a way that will result in a different kind of shame.

12 CRITICAL THINKING: EVALUATION

Have students discuss whether the youth's planned course of action is morally wrong, given his hunger. How would they treat him if they were the owner of the restaurant?

13 TEACHING ATMOSPHERE

Elicit the contrast between the quiet, pleasant atmosphere of the milk bar and the hectic, oppressive atmosphere of the dock area the youth chooses to leave.

14 GRAMMAR IN LITERATURE

Point out the use of compound predicates to capture the rhythm of the characters' actions. Have students find another example in the next paragraph. (". . . He changed his mind, walked back, tripped over a chair, and finally installed himself in a corner.")

CRITICAL THINKING: GUIDED READING QUESTIONS

LITERAL

1a. What does the youth refuse to accept from the foreman? (He refuses a small loan until his wages are paid the next day.)

2a. For what is the youth waiting as he stands outside the milk bar? (He is waiting for the one customer to leave.)

INFERENTIAL

1b. Why does the youth refuse the loan? (As before, he is probably too ashamed to accept charity.)

2b. Why do you think he waits until there are no customers? (He is planning to eat without paying and is too ashamed or afraid to do so in front of another customer.)

- The waitress takes the youth's order: a large glass of milk and vanilla wafers.
- He eats and drinks slowly and, desperate with the knowledge that he cannot pay, cries as never before.
- The waitress strokes his head and says, "Cry, son, cry."
- His second bout of crying is a cleansing one, and when the waitress brings him a second helping, he accepts as if nothing happened and the waitress were his own mother.
- When he is finished, he thanks her politely and leaves.

15 TEACHING PLOT: CLIMAX

Point out that this exchange begins the story's climax, in which the starving youth will finally eat, no matter what the consequences may be.

16 TEACHING CONFLICT

Stress that the youth's hunger battles here with "the reality of his desperate situation"—the likelihood of public humiliation or even beating or arrest because he will eat without paying.

17 READING SKILL: CONTRAST

Elicit that this second crying spell is different from the one two paragraphs above: There he cries in despair; here, in a joyous, cleansing way. Ask what causes this change in attitude. (the woman's kindness)

18 TEACHING CHARACTER MOTIVATION

Ask why the youth now accepts the woman's charity when he was too ashamed to accept anyone else's. (He does so in part because he has become desperate and in part because the woman shows more genuine understanding of his plight, and she reminds him of his mother, whose presence he has longed for earlier.)

---

rag, and in a soft voice that had a trace of Castilian[4] accent, asked him:

15 "What will you have?"

"A glass of milk."

"Large?"

"Yes, large."

"Is that all?"

"Are there any biscuits?"

"No. Vanilla wafers."

"Well, vanilla wafers."

When the lady had turned away, he wiped his hands on his knees, rejoicing, as if he were cold and were about to drink something hot.

The lady returned, and placed before him a large glass of milk, and a dish full of vanilla wafers; then she went back to her place behind the counter.

His first impulse was to drink the milk in one gulp and then eat the vanilla wafers; but he immediately changed his mind. He felt the woman's eyes watching him with curiosity and attention. He did not dare to look at her; he felt that if he did she would guess his situation and his shameful intentions, and he would have to get up and leave without touching what he had ordered.

16 Slowly, he took a vanilla wafer and moistening it in the milk, he took a bite; he took a sip of milk, and he felt the burning in his stomach diminishing, dying away. But he became aware of the reality of his desperate situation at once, and he felt something tight and hot well up inside, choking him. He realized that he was about to cry, to sob aloud, and although he knew that the lady was looking at him, he could neither hold back nor undo the burning knot of tears that grew tighter and tighter. He fought it, and as he fought he ate hurriedly, as if frightened, afraid that crying would keep him from eating. When he had finished the milk and the wafers, his eyes

---

4. **Castilian** [kas til′yən]: referring to the standard form of Spanish as spoken in Castile, a region in central Spain.

60   *The Short Story*

---

clouded and something hot rolled down his nose and into the glass. A terrible sob racked his whole body.

He held his head in his hands, and for a long time he cried, cried with rage, cried with shame, crying as he had never cried before.

He was hunched over crying when he felt a hand caress his tired head, and heard a woman's voice with a sweet Castilian accent say to him:

"Cry, son, cry . . ."

17 Again his eyes filled with tears and he cried as intensely as before, but this time not with pain but with joy; he felt a great refreshing sensation spread inside him, extinguishing the hot something that had nearly strangled him. As he cried, it seemed to him that his life and feelings were cleansed like a glass under a stream of water, recovering the clearness and firmness of former days.

When the crying spell passed, he wiped his eyes and face with his handkerchief, feeling relieved. He raised his head and looked at the lady, but she was no longer looking at him, she was gazing out at the street, at a distant point in space, and her face seemed sad.

18 On the table before him there was another glass of milk and another dish heaped with vanilla wafers. He ate slowly, without thinking about anything, as if nothing had happened to him, as if he were at home and his mother were that woman who was standing behind the counter.

When he had finished, it had grown dark, and the place was lit by an electric light. He remained seated for a while, wondering what he would say to the lady when he left, without thinking of anything appropriate.

At last he got up and said simply,

"Thank you very much, ma'am; goodbye . . ."

"Goodbye, son," she answered.

He went out. The wind blowing from the sea refreshed his face, still hot from crying. He walked about aimlessly for a while, then went

---

CRITICAL THINKING: GUIDED READING QUESTIONS

LITERAL

1a. When the waitress first brings his order, why does the youth avoid looking at her? (He is afraid she will guess his situation and his shameful intentions.)

2a. When the youth cries "as never before," what does the waitress do? (She strokes his head and says, "Cry, son, cry.")

INFERENTIAL

1b. What are the youth's "shameful intentions"? (his decision to eat without paying, even if doing so means public humiliation, beating, or arrest)

2b. What chief quality does the woman display? (kindness; motherliness)

<u>19</u> down a street that led to the docks. It was a very beautiful night, and large stars gleamed in the summer sky.

He thought about the blonde lady who had treated him so generously, resolving to repay her, to reward her as she deserved, when he got some money. But these thoughts of gratitude vanished with the burning of his face, until not one remained, and the recent event receded and was lost in the recesses of his past life.

Suddenly, he surprised himself humming. He straightened up happily, strode on with assurance and determination.

<u>20</u> He came to the edge of the sea, and walked back and forth with a spring in his step; he felt like a new man, as if his inner forces, previously scattered, had reassembled and united solidly.

Then he sat down on a pile of burlap sacks; fatigue, like a tingling sensation, climbed up his legs. He looked at the sea. The lights of the wharf and ships spread over the water in a reddish-gold ripple, trembling softly. He stretched out on his back, looking up at the sky for a long time. He did not feel like thinking, or singing, or talking. He just felt alive, that was all. Then he fell asleep with his face toward the sea.

Evening by the Sea, 1919, Karl Schmidt-Rottluff.

The Glass of Milk **61**

CRITICAL THINKING: GUIDED READING QUESTIONS

LITERAL

1a. How does the youth now stride as he walks to the edge of the sea? (He walks with assurance and determination.)

2a. How does the youth fall asleep? (He falls asleep with his face to the sea.)

INFERENTIAL

1b. What change do his humming and his assured, determined stride reflect? (He has lost his despair and feels renewed joy, hope, and confidence.)

2b. What does this detail suggest that the youth will probably do in the future? (He will go to sea again.)

If the youth had accepted the charity offered earlier, would he have behaved then as he does later in the milk bar? Why or why not?

ANSWERS

STUDY QUESTIONS

1. a sailor's handout of food; a loan of forty cents
2. After jumping ship, he worked on a crabber and then stowed away on a northbound ship until he was discovered and dropped at the next port. He has always been fascinated with the sea.
3. He chooses a clean, quiet milk bar. He cries as never before.
4. She strokes his head, does not charge him, and gives him a second portion. She reminds him of his mother.
5. He is younger, more innocent, and too ashamed to accept charity. The details of his past life show his regret at leaving home and the reason for leaving—his love of the sea.
6. kindness; People are capable of great kindness to strangers.
7. He probably did so to suggest that the youth represents any youth lured by a life of adventure, and the port is any city. No, ample details make him seem like an individual.
8. It stresses the tedious, prolonged nature of the youth's hunger and isolation. Examples include "He was hungry, hungry, hungry" and "without a label, without . . . trade."
9. Answers will vary. Some students may have felt glad to help but sad to see misfortune.

LANGUAGE STUDY

1. "the right side of a ship as one faces forward"
2. "a ship's passageway"
3. "left without permission a ship where one worked"
4. "young employee of a ship, who helps prepare or serve food"
5. "hid on a ship to get free passage"
6. "opening on a ship's deck through which entrance is made and cargo lowered"
7. "area below decks for storing cargo"
8. "dock worker who loads and unloads cargo"

STUDY QUESTIONS

Recalling

1. What does the youth refuse that the "gaudy tramp" accepts readily? After performing a day's labor, what does the youth refuse to take from the foreman?
2. How did the youth come to be alone and penniless in a large port city? What fascination has always gripped him?
3. Briefly describe the place the youth chooses for his first meal. What is the youth's emotional response to this meal?
4. What generous acts does the blonde lady perform? Of whom does she remind the boy?

Interpreting

5. How is the youth different from the other tramps who roam the dock area? What do the details about his past life reveal about his character?
6. What seems to motivate the blonde lady's actions at the story's end? What does her behavior suggest about human nature?
7. Why do you think Rojas chose not to tell us the youth's name or the city where story events take place? Is the youth less of an individual because his name is omitted? Explain.
8. Rojas is often praised for his rhythmic repetition of words. Why is word repetition especially suited to the experiences that this story recounts? Cite examples to support your answer.

Extending

9. Have you ever had the experience of helping someone in need? Why did you do it? How did you feel afterward?

LANGUAGE STUDY

Jargon

Jargon is the special terminology or vocabulary of a particular profession, activity, or group of people. Sailors and others involved with the sea use their own particular jargon. For example, they call the front of a ship the *bow* or *prow* and the back the *stern*.

Use the story context or a dictionary to explain the following examples of sailors' jargon.

1. starboard
2. gangway
3. jumped ship
4. mess boy
5. stowed away
6. hatchway
7. (ship's) hold
8. stevedore

COMPOSITION

Writing About Character Motivation

■ Write a brief composition in which you trace the youth's motives, or reasons behind his actions. First explain his motives for going to sea and the reasons he finds himself alone and penniless in a large port. Then discuss his motives for refusing the offers of both the English-speaking sailor and the foreman. Next identify his chief motive for visiting the milk bar. Finally, explore the possible motivations for his behavior in the milk bar and after he leaves it.

Writing a Letter of Thanks

■ Assuming the point of view of the youth, write a letter of thanks to the blonde lady that you would send several weeks later. Mention the feelings you experienced as a result of her kindness. Be sure to write the letter in the first person from the point of view of the youth.

COMPOSITION: GUIDELINES FOR EVALUATION

WRITING ABOUT MOTIVATION

Objective

To analyze a character's motivation

Guidelines for Evaluation

■ suggested length: three to five paragraphs
■ should explain why the youth goes to sea
■ should explore the possible reasons for his initial refusals of help and his subsequent actions

WRITING A LETTER OF THANKS

Objective

To write a letter of thanks from a story character

Guidelines for Evaluation

■ suggested length: two to four paragraphs
■ should be written in the first person as if by the youth
■ should treat the youth's motives, feelings, and reactions to the woman's kindness

PREVIEW: THE AUTHOR AND THE WORLD

GEOGRAPHY AND CULTURE

Selma Lagerlöf (1858–1940)

Sweden

The fiction of Sweden's Selma Lagerlöf [lä'gər lœf'] often features miraculous transformations, no doubt inspired by the near miracles of her own life. Struck by a paralyzing illness when she was three, Lagerlöf surprised everyone with her recovery. During her recuperation she was placed in the care of her grandmother, who entertained her with folk tales and legends of the Swedish countryside. Fascinated by these tales, young Selma became a voracious reader and soon began writing stories of her own. When the Lagerlöfs were forced to sell their family estate, Mårbacka [môr bäk'yä], Selma took a job as a teacher; she also entered an incomplete novel in a contest and was astonished when she won first prize.

With her subsequent novels, stories, and updated legends, Lagerlöf brought fame to Värmland [värm'länd], the region in western Sweden where she grew up. Most of her books were best sellers, and with her earnings she joyfully repurchased Mårbacka for her family. In 1906 Lagerlöf published Sweden's most beloved children's classic, *The Wonderful Adventures of Nils.* Three years later she became the first woman to win the Nobel Prize for Literature.

Värmland and Its Ironworks

Sweden is located on the Scandinavian Peninsula in northern Europe. The fourth largest nation in Europe, it can be divided into four geographical regions: the mountainous area of the north (Norrland), the lake district (Svealand), the heavily forested highlands (Småland), and the fertile, densely populated plains of the south (Skåne).

Like most of Europe, Sweden began shifting from an agricultural to an industrial economy in the second half of the nineteenth century. Because Värmland, in western Sweden, was a well-forested region rich in iron ore, it became an important center of Sweden's iron, lumber, and paper industries. Factories called ironworks, where iron was smelted and heavy iron goods produced, became a powerful force in the local economy. Often an ironworks acquired much of the local land and rented portions out to tenant farmers. Many farm families were displaced by the growing industry, and some people were reduced to lives of extreme poverty. These sweeping changes are evident in "The Rat Trap," which takes place in Värmland toward the end of the nineteenth century.

The Rat Trap **63**

LESSON PREVIEW

The owner of an ironworks mistakes a cynical, thieving peddler for an old friend and invites him home for Christmas. The kindness of the owner's daughter leads him to change his dishonorable ways.

LITERARY SKILLS FOR THIS SELECTION

- flat and round characters
- static and dynamic characters
- theme

THEMES IN THIS SELECTION

- human relationships: charity
- personal growth and change

LESSON OBJECTIVES

1. to distinguish between flat, round, static, and dynamic characters
2. to understand words from Scandinavian languages
3. to compare and contrast characters in a story
4. to compare and contrast stories

Teacher's Classroom Resources 1

- Teaching Notes 117
- Prereading Vocabulary 118
- Reading Guide 119
- Check Test 120
- Responding to World Cultures 121
- Literary Focus: Flat, Round, Static, and Dynamic Characters 122
- Language Study: Words from Scandinavian Languages 123
- Writing Process Guide: Writing About Character 124
- Grammar in Literature: Combining Sentences Through Coordination 125
- Selection Test 126

IN THE CLASSROOM

TEACHING STUDENTS OF DIFFERENT ABILITIES

- **For less advanced students:** Have students explain the peddler's analogy between the world and a rattrap and the reasons he developed such a negative view. Have them
complete the Reading Guide for this selection.

- **For more advanced students:** Have students read northern European folk tales, such as those collected or written by the Grimm brothers, Hans Christian Andersen, Sigrid Undset, and Lagerlöf herself, and compare them with "The Rat Trap."

DISCUSSING GEOGRAPHY AND CULTURE

The Industrial Revolution

Sweden was changed profoundly by the Industrial Revolution. In many parts of Sweden, workers left their farms for jobs in industry. The price of industrialization was often high: Pollution, labor conflicts, and poor working conditions were common.

- Ask students to discuss the ways in which modern technology has changed the nineteenth-century factory environment. (Examples include the installation of safety devices and pollution controls.)

Have students discuss the kinds of experiences that might cause someone to form a negative view of life, as well as the behavior we might expect from such a person.

PAGE SUMMARY: AT A GLANCE

- A poor peddler who sells rat-traps must resort to begging and petty thievery to survive.
- His life has led him to theorize that the world is a rattrap, offering riches and joys as bait but snapping shut when anyone tries to enjoy them.
- One evening he finds lodging with a talkative old crofter who treats him kindly.
- The crofter shows the peddler money he earned the previous month from his milk cow.

IN THE GLOSSARY

- vagabond: wanderer; tramp
- unwonted: unusual
- incredulous: unbelieving

1 TEACHING STYLE

Point out that Lagerlöf establishes a folk-tale quality with this standard opening.

2 TEACHING CHARACTER MOTIVATION

Note that the main motive for the peddler's dishonesty is survival.

3 TEACHING FLAT CHARACTERS

Elicit that the old man is a flat character whose main personality traits are kindness, loneliness, and garrulousness.

4 CRITICAL THINKING: EVALUATION

Ask students whether they feel that the old man has behaved "knowingly" or naively in showing his money. (the latter) Have students predict the likely results of his naiveté. (The peddler will rob him.)

Selma Lagerlöf

The Rat Trap

Translated from the Swedish by Florence and Naboth Hedin

1 Once upon a time there was a man who went around selling small rat traps of wire. He made them himself at odd moments, from material he got by begging in the stores or at the big farms. 2 But even so, the business was not especially profitable, so he had to resort to both begging and petty thievery to keep body and soul together. Even so, his clothes were in rags, his cheeks were sunken, and hunger gleamed in his eyes.

No one can imagine how sad and monotonous life can appear to such a vagabond, who plods along the road, left to his own meditations. But one day this man had fallen into a line of thought which really seemed to him entertaining. He had naturally been thinking of his rat traps when suddenly he was struck by the idea that the whole world about him—the whole world with its lands and seas, its cities and villages—was nothing but a big rat trap. It had never existed for any other purpose than to set baits for people. It offered riches and joys, shelter and food, heat and clothing, exactly as the rat trap offered cheese and pork, and as soon as anyone let himself be tempted to touch the bait, it closed in on him, and then everything came to an end.

The world had, of course, never been very kind to him, so it gave him unwonted joy to think ill of it in this way. It became a cherished pastime of his, during many dreary ploddings, to think of people he knew who had let themselves be caught in the dangerous snare, and of others who were still circling around the bait.

One dark evening as he was trudging along the road he caught sight of a little gray cottage by the roadside, and he knocked on the door to ask shelter for the night. Nor was he refused. Instead of the sour faces which ordinarily met him, 3 the owner, who was an old man without wife or child, was happy to get someone to talk to in his loneliness. Immediately he put the porridge pot on the fire and gave him supper; then he carved off such a big slice from his tobacco roll that it was enough both for the stranger's pipe and his own. Finally he got out an old pack of cards and played *mjölis*[1] with his guest until bedtime.

The old man was just as generous with his confidences as with his porridge and tobacco. The guest was informed at once that in his days of prosperity his host had been a crofter at Ramsjö Ironworks[2] and had worked on the land. Now that he was no longer able to do day labor, it was his cow which supported him. Yes, that bossy[3] was extraordinary. She could give milk 4 for the creamery every day, and last month he had received all of thirty kronor[4] in payment.

The stranger must have seemed incredulous, for the old man got up and went to the window, took down a leather pouch which hung on a nail in the very window frame, and picked out three wrinkled ten-kronor bills. These he held up before the eyes of his guest, nodding knowingly, and then stuffed them back into the pouch.

The next day both men got up in good season. The crofter was in a hurry to milk his cow,

---

1. *mjölis* [myœ′lis]: Swedish card game.
2. **crofter at Ramsjö** [räm′shyœ] **Ironworks:** small tenant farmer on land owned by the Ramsjö Ironworks. (See the Geography and Culture feature that precedes the story.)
3. **bossy:** pet name for a cow.
4. **thirty kronor:** about six dollars at the time of the story. The krona (plural, *kronor*) is the chief monetary unit of Sweden.

CRITICAL THINKING: GUIDED READING QUESTIONS

LITERAL

1a. According to the peddler, in what way is the world like a rattrap? (It offers riches and joys as tempting bait but snaps shut when anyone tries to touch them.)

2a. What does the old crofter give the peddler? (He gives him food, tobacco, confidences, and lodging for the night.)

INFERENTIAL

1b. In what way have his life's experiences led him to make this analogy? (His impoverished, isolated, and miserable life has made him very cynical.)

2b. How is the crofter different from the people the peddler usually encounters? (He treats the peddler much more kindly.)

and the other man probably thought he should not stay in bed when the head of the house had gotten up. They left the cottage at the same **5** time. The crofter locked the door and put the key in his pocket. The man with the rat traps said good-bye and thank you, and thereupon each went his own way.

But half an hour later the rat-trap peddler stood again before the door. He did not try to get in, however. He only went up to the window, smashed a pane, stuck in his hand, and got hold of the pouch with the thirty kronor. He took the money and thrust it into his own pocket. Then he hung the leather pouch very carefully back in its place and went away.

As he walked along with the money in his pocket he felt quite pleased with his smartness. He realized, of course, that at first he dared not continue on the public highway, but must turn off the road, into the woods. During the first few **6** hours this caused him no difficulty. Later in the day it became worse, for it was a big and confusing forest which he had gotten into. He tried, to be sure, to walk in a definite direction, but the paths twisted back and forth so strangely! He walked and walked, without coming to the end of the wood, and finally he realized that he had only been walking around in the same part of the forest. All at once he recalled his thoughts about the world and the rat trap. Now his own turn had come. He had let himself be fooled by a bait and had been caught. The whole forest, with its trunks and branches, its thickets and fallen logs, closed in upon him like an impenetrable prison from which he could never escape.

7 It was late in December. Darkness was already descending over the forest. This increased the danger, and increased also his gloom and despair. Finally he saw no way out, and he sank down on the ground, tired to death, thinking that his last moment had come. But just as he laid his head on the ground, he heard a sound— a hard, regular thumping. There was no doubt as to what that was. He raised himself. "Those are

the hammer strokes from an iron mill," he thought. "There must be people near by." He summoned all his strength, got up, and staggered in the direction of the sound.

8 The Ramsjö Ironworks, which are now closed down, was, not so long ago, a large plant, with smelter, rolling mill, and forge. In the summertime long lines of heavily loaded barges and scows slid down the canal which led to a large inland lake, and in the wintertime the roads near the mill were black from all the coal dust which sifted down from the big charcoal crates.

During one of the long dark evenings just before Christmas, the master smith and his helper sat in the dark forge near the furnace waiting for the pig iron, which had been put in the fire, to be ready to put on the anvil. Every now and then one of them got up to stir the glowing mass with a long iron bar, returning in a few moments, dripping with perspiration, though, as was the custom, he wore nothing but a long shirt and a pair of wooden shoes.

9 All the time there were many sounds to be heard in the forge. The big bellows groaned and the burning coal cracked. The fire boy shoveled charcoal into the maw of the furnace with a great deal of clatter. Outside roared the waterfall, and a sharp north wind whipped the rain against the brick-tiled roof.

It was probably on account of all this noise that the blacksmith did not notice that a man had opened the gate and entered the forge, until he stood close up to the furnace.

Surely it was nothing unusual for poor vagabonds without any better shelter for the night to be attracted to the forge by the glow of light which escaped through the sooty panes, and to come in to warm themselves in front of the fire. The blacksmiths glanced only casually and indifferently at the intruder. He looked the way people of his type usually did, with a long beard, dirty, ragged, and with a bunch of rat traps dangling on his chest.

The Rat Trap **65**

CRITICAL THINKING: GUIDED READING QUESTIONS

LITERAL

1a. What does the peddler come back to the cottage to do? (He returns to steal the crofter's money.)

2a. Where does the peddler become lost? (He loses his way in the woods.)

INFERENTIAL

1b. Why is it especially unjust for the peddler to steal from the crofter? (The crofter has been especially kind to him.)

2b. Why does the peddler not dare to take the public highway? (Once the robbery is reported, he would most likely be apprehended there.)

- The ironmaster, on one of his nightly inspections, mistakes the peddler for an old army friend, Nils Olof von Ståhle.
- Hoping the error will mean a handout, the peddler goes along with it and is nonplused when the ironmaster invites him home for Christmas.
- Fearful of staying in the neighborhood and being arrested, the peddler refuses to go.
- The ironmaster assumes his "old friend" is ashamed of his miserable clothing.
- The ironmaster leaves but soon sends his daughter to persuade the man to visit.

IN THE GLOSSARY

- deigned: condescended
- valet: servant who cares for a person's clothes

10 TEACHING CHARACTER MOTIVATION

Note the peddler's mercenary reason for at first going along with the ironmaster's error.

11 TEACHING ALLUSION

Point out that this figurative expression for "going right where the danger is" refers to the biblical story of Daniel, who was cast into a lion's den.

12 TEACHING POINT OF VIEW

Note that this statement tells us the ironmaster's thoughts. Have students find examples of other characters' thoughts that the omniscient narrator provides on this page. (the peddler's in the sixth, ninth, and eleventh paragraphs; the blacksmith's in the sixteenth paragraph)

13 TEACHING SETTING AND THEME

Note the story's Christmas setting, which enhances its theme of kindness and charity.

He asked permission to stay, and the master blacksmith nodded a haughty consent without honoring him with a single word.

The tramp did not say anything, either. He had not come there to talk but only to warm himself and sleep.

In those days the Ramsjö iron mill was owned by a very prominent ironmaster whose greatest ambition was to ship out good iron to the market. He watched both night and day to see that the work was done as well as possible, and at this very moment he came into the forge on one of his nightly rounds of inspection.

Naturally the first thing he saw was the tall ragamuffin who had eased his way so close to the furnace that steam rose from his wet rags. The ironmaster did not follow the example of the blacksmiths, who had hardly deigned to look at the stranger. He walked close up to him, looked him over very carefully, then tore off his slouch hat to get a better view of his face.

"But of course it is you, Nils Olof!" he said. "How you do look!"

10 The man with the rat traps had never before seen the ironmaster of Ramsjö and did not even know what his name was. But it occurred to him that if the fine gentleman thought he was an old acquaintance, he might perhaps throw him a couple of kronor. Therefore he did not want to undeceive him all at once.

"Yes, God knows things have gone downhill with me," he said.

"You should not have resigned from the regiment," said the ironmaster. "That was the mistake. If only I had still been in the service at the time, it never would have happened. Well, now of course you will come home with me."

To go along up to the manor house and be received by the owner like an old regimental comrade—that, however, did not please the tramp.

"No, I couldn't think of it!" he said, looking quite alarmed.

He thought of the thirty kronor. To go up to the manor house would be like throwing himself

11 voluntarily into the lions' den. He only wanted a chance to sleep here in the forge and then sneak away as inconspicuously as possible.

12 The ironmaster assumed that he felt embarrassed because of his miserable clothing.

"Please don't think that I have such a fine home that you cannot show yourself there," he said. "Elizabeth is dead, as you may already have heard. My boys are abroad, and there is no one at home except my oldest daughter and myself.

13 We were just saying that it was too bad we didn't have any company for Christmas. Now come along with me and help us make the Christmas food disappear a little faster."

But the stranger said no, and no, and again no, and the ironmaster saw that he must give in.

"It looks as though Captain von Ståhle[5] preferred to stay with you tonight, Stjernström,"[6] he said to the master blacksmith, and turned on his heel.

But he laughed to himself as he went away, and the blacksmith, who knew him, understood very well that he had not said his last word.

It was not more than half an hour before they heard the sound of carriage wheels outside the forge, and a new guest came in, but this time it was not the ironmaster. He had sent his daughter, apparently hoping that she would have better powers of persuasion than he himself.

She entered, followed by a valet, carrying on his arm a big fur coat. She was not at all pretty, but seemed modest and quite shy. In the forge everything was just as it had been earlier in the evening. The master blacksmith and his apprentice still sat on their bench, and iron and charcoal still glowed in the furnace. The stranger had stretched himself out on the floor and lay with a piece of pig iron under his head and his hat pulled down over his eyes. As soon as the young girl caught sight of him she went up and lifted his hat. The man was evidently used to

---

5. **von Ståhle** [fôn stô′lə]: apparently, Nils Olof's surname.
6. **Stjernström** [styern′strœm]

CRITICAL THINKING: GUIDED READING QUESTIONS

LITERAL

1a. In what way does the ironmaster "not follow the example of the blacksmiths"? (The blacksmiths barely deign to look at the ragged peddler, but the ironmaster inspects the stranger closely.)

2a. For whom does the ironmaster mistake the peddler? (He mistakes him for an old army acquaintance, Captain Nils Olof von Ståhle.)

INFERENTIAL

1b. What does the ironmaster's initial interest in the stranger reveal about his character, in contrast to the master blacksmith's? (He is kinder, more curious, and more open-minded.)

2b. Why is the peddler afraid to accompany the ironmaster to his home? (If his identity is discovered while he is in a prominent neighborhood home, it is likely he will be arrested for robbery.)

sleeping with one eye open. He jumped up abruptly and seemed to be quite frightened.

"My name is Edla Willmansson," said the young girl. "My father came home and said that you wanted to sleep here in the forge tonight, and then I asked permission to come and bring you home to us. I am so sorry, Captain, that you are having such a hard time."

<u>14</u> She looked at him compassionately, with her heavy eyes, and then she noticed that the man was afraid. "Either he has stolen something or else he has escaped from jail," she thought, and added quickly, "You may be sure, Captain, that you will be allowed to leave us just as freely as <u>15</u> you came. Only please stay with us over Christmas Eve."

She said this in such a friendly manner that the rat-trap peddler must have felt confidence in her.

"It would never have occurred to me that you would bother with me yourself, miss," he said. "I will come at once."

He accepted the fur coat, which the valet handed him with a deep bow, threw it over his rags, and followed the young lady out to the carriage, without granting the astonished blacksmiths so much as a glance.

<u>16</u> But while he was riding up to the manor house he had evil forebodings.

"Why the devil did I take that fellow's money?" he thought. "Now I am sitting in the trap and will never get out of it."

The next day was Christmas Eve, and when the ironmaster came into the dining room for breakfast he probably thought with satisfaction of his old regimental comrade whom he had run across so unexpectedly.

"First of all we must see to it that he gets a little flesh on his bones," he said to his daughter, who was busy at the table. "And then we must see that he gets something else to do than to run around the country selling rat traps."

"It is queer that things have gone downhill with him as badly as that," said the daughter. "Last night I did not think there was anything about him to show that he had once been an educated man."

"You must have patience, my little girl," said the father. "As soon as he gets clean and dressed

Detail. *Interior of a Factory* ("Une Forge"), Fernand Cormon (1854–1924).

The Rat Trap **67**

CRITICAL THINKING: GUIDED READING QUESTIONS

LITERAL

1a. What does Edla say when she suspects the "captain" of criminal activity? ("You may be sure, Captain, that you will be allowed to leave us just as freely as you came.")

2a. What plans does the ironmaster have for his "old friend"? (He plans to get some "flesh on his bones" and find him something better to do than peddle rattraps.)

INFERENTIAL

1b. Why is her remark compassionate? (She wants to reassure the man and welcome him into her home, something few people would do for someone they suspect of criminal activity, even if he were a friend of the family.)

2b. What qualities of the ironmaster do these plans reveal? (kindness, loyalty, and confidence)

- When the peddler appears clean and well dressed, the ironmaster realizes that the man is not his old friend.
- At first he questions the peddler's honesty and mentions calling the sheriff, but when the peddler amuses him with his rattrap theory, the ironmaster merely asks him to leave.
- Edla, however, in the spirit of Christmas, insists that the unfortunate man stay.

IN THE GLOSSARY

- dissimulate: pretend

17 TEACHING IRONY

Elicit that the ironmaster's confident words create dramatic irony because what he thinks is true is not what the reader knows to be true.

18 CULTURAL BACKGROUND

Point out that to a poor peddler in nineteenth-century Europe, staying in the home of a factory owner would be totally unfamiliar and splendid indeed. Stress that class differences were quite pronounced in Europe at the time. These differences help explain the ironmaster's shock and suspicion when he learns that his guest is not a down-on-his-luck army officer and friend but a stranger born to the lower class.

19 TEACHING THEME

Note that Edla's plea touches on a central theme of the story, the need to show kindness and charity, especially at Christmas.

20 READING SKILL: CAUSE AND EFFECT

Ask students why the ironmaster might be unable to oppose his daughter's wishes. (perhaps because he loves and pampers her, perhaps because he sees the validity of her arguments)

21 READING SKILL: PREDICTING OUTCOMES

Have students predict whether Edla will come to regret her invitation.

---

17 up, you will see something different. Last night he was naturally embarrassed. The tramp manners will fall away from him with the tramp clothes."

Just as he said this the door opened and the stranger entered. Yes, now he was truly clean and well dressed. The valet had bathed him, cut his hair, and shaved him. Moreover he was dressed in a good-looking suit of clothes which belonged to the ironmaster. He wore a white shirt and a starched collar and whole shoes.

But although his guest was now so well groomed, the ironmaster did not seem pleased. He looked at him with puckered brow, and it was easy enough to understand that when he had seen the strange fellow in the uncertain reflection from the furnace he might have made a mistake, but that now, when he stood there in broad daylight, it was impossible to mistake him for an old acquaintance.

"What does this mean?" he thundered.

The stranger made no attempt to dissimulate. **18** He saw at once that all the splendor had come to an end.

"It is not my fault, sir," he said. "I never pretended to be anything but a poor trader, and I pleaded and begged to be allowed to stay in the forge. But no harm has been done. At worst I can put on my rags again and go away."

"Well," said the ironmaster, hesitating a little, "it was not quite honest, either. You must admit that, and I should not be surprised if the sheriff would like to have something to say in the matter."

The tramp took a step forward and struck the table with his fist.

"Now I am going to tell you, Mr. Ironmaster, how things are," he said. "This whole world is nothing but a big rat trap. All the good things that are offered you are nothing but cheese rinds and bits of pork, set out to drag a poor fellow into trouble. And if the sheriff comes now and locks me up for this, then you, Mr. Ironmaster, must remember that a day may come when you yourself may want to get a big piece of pork, and then you will get caught in the trap."

The ironmaster began to laugh.

"That was not so badly said, my good fellow. Perhaps we should let the sheriff alone on Christmas Eve. But now get out of here as fast as you can."

But just as the man was opening the door, the daughter said, "I think he ought to stay with us today. I don't want him to go." And with that she went and closed the door.

"What in the world are you doing?" said the father.

The daughter stood there quite embarrassed and hardly knew what to answer. That morning she had felt so happy when she thought how homelike and Christmassy she was going to make things for the poor hungry wretch. She could not get away from the idea all at once, and that was why she had interceded for the vagabond.

19 "I am thinking of this stranger here," said the young girl. "He walks and walks the whole year long, and there is probably not a single place in the whole country where he is welcome and can feel at home. Wherever he turns he is chased away. Always he is afraid of being arrested and cross-examined. I should like to have him enjoy a day of peace with us here—just one in the whole year."

The ironmaster mumbled something in his **20** beard. He could not bring himself to oppose her.

"It was all a mistake, of course," she continued. "But anyway I don't think we ought to chase away a human being whom we have asked to come here, and to whom we have promised Christmas cheer."

21 "You do preach worse than a parson," said the ironmaster. "I only hope you won't have to regret this."

The young girl took the stranger by the hand and led him up to the table.

"Now sit down and eat," she said, for she

68 *The Short Story*

CRITICAL THINKING: GUIDED READING QUESTIONS

LITERAL

1a. After realizing the peddler's true identity, what does the ironmaster first threaten to do? (He threatens to call the sheriff.)

2a. What is the ironmaster's reaction to the peddler's rattrap theory? (He laughs, remarks, "That was not so badly said," and says he will not call the sheriff.)

INFERENTIAL

1b. Why would mention of the sheriff especially trouble the peddler? (He fears his theft of the crofter's money will be discovered, and he will be punished.)

2b. What does his reaction show about the differences between him and Edla? (His amusement suggests that he is less understanding than she of the misery of the peddler's life.)

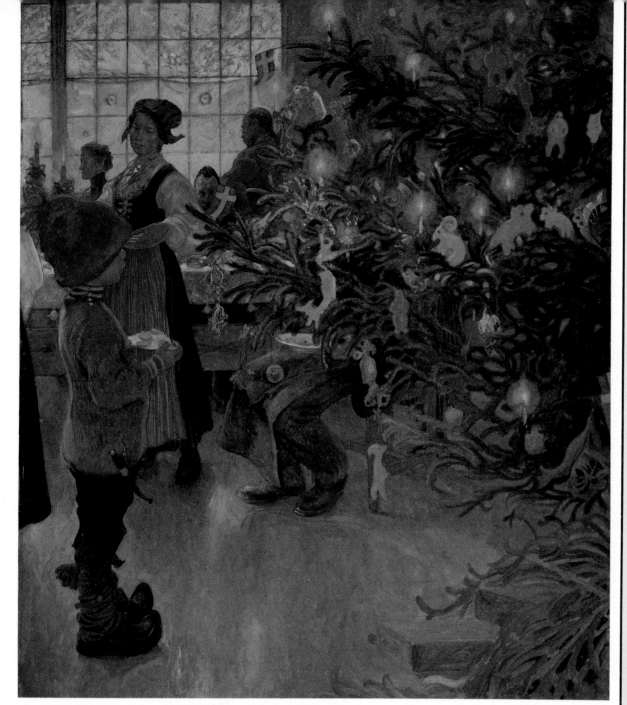

Christmas at Sanborn, from *The Christmas Triptych,* 1907, Carl Larsson.

ART AND LITERATURE

The Swedish painter and illustrator Carl Larsson (1853–1919) painted sentimental caricatures of everyday life. The atmosphere of his works is generally soft and sensual; the warm candles, soft light, and generous offerings in *Christmas at Sanborn* are typical features. Larsson's warm holiday atmosphere sharply contrasts with Cormon's painting of the iron forge on page 67.

- Have students compare the atmosphere of the painting with the atmosphere of Edla's house. (Students might recall how "homelike and Christmassy [Edla] was going to make things for the poor hungry wretch.")

- He cannot understand Edla's kindness, especially when she tells him to keep the suit and spend the next Christmas with them.
- At church the next morning the Willmanssons learn that the peddler robbed the crofter.
- They return home to find a package containing a rattrap, the crofter's money, and a letter signed "Captain von Ståhle."
- The letter asks Edla to return the money and explains that her kindness has led the peddler to change his behavior and his view of the world.

22 TEACHING CHARACTER MOTIVATION

Elicit that Edla is motivated by kindness and charity, motives the peddler's past experiences make him unable to understand.

23 READING SKILL: INFERENCE

Ask what the ironmaster means here. (He wonders whether the peddler has stolen from him.)

24 TEACHING THEME

Elicit that the peddler's new attitude reflects a central theme of the story: Great kindness can change people for the better.

25 TEACHING SYMBOLS

Point out that the rattrap is a symbol. Ask what it represents. (It represents the peddler's previous cynical world view.)

26 TEACHING DYNAMIC CHARACTERS

Note that the peddler is a dynamic character, one who changes and grows in the course of the story. To stress the change, he signs the letter "Captain von Ståhle," symbolizing the nobler attitude that now governs his actions.

COLLABORATIVE LEARNING: ENRICHMENT ACTIVITY

Theater Design Have students work in groups to design sets and costumes for a stage adaptation of the story. They should begin by researching set design or nineteenth-century Swedish costumes.

---

could see that her father had given in.

The man with the rat traps said not a word; he only sat down and helped himself to the food. **22** Time after time he looked at the young girl who had interceded for him. Why had she done it? What could the crazy idea be?

After that, Christmas Eve at Ramsjö passed just as it always had. The stranger did not cause any trouble because he did nothing but sleep. The whole forenoon he lay on the sofa in one of the guest rooms and slept at one stretch. At noon they woke him up so that he could have his share of the good Christmas fare, but after that he slept again. It seemed as though for many years he had not been able to sleep as quietly and safely as here at Ramsjö.

In the evening, when the Christmas tree was lighted, they woke him up again, and he stood for a while in the drawing room,[7] blinking as though the candlelight hurt him, but after that he disappeared again. Two hours later he was aroused once more. He then had to go down into the dining room and eat the Christmas fish and porridge.

As soon as they got up from the table he went around to each one present and said thank you and good-night, but when he came to the young girl she gave him to understand that it was her father's intention that the suit which he wore was to be a Christmas present—he did not have to return it; and if he wanted to spend next Christmas Eve in a place where he could rest in peace, and be sure that no evil would befall him, he would be welcomed back again.

The man with the rat traps did not answer anything to this. He only stared at the young girl in boundless amazement.

The next morning the ironmaster and his daughter got up in good season to go to the early Christmas service. Their guest was still asleep, and they did not disturb him.

---

7. **drawing room:** usually formal room for greeting and entertaining guests.

70 *The Short Story*

When, at about ten o'clock, they drove back from church, the young girl sat and hung her head even more dejectedly than usual. At church she had learned that one of the old crofters of the ironworks had been robbed by a man who went around selling rat traps.

23 "Yes, that was a fine fellow you let into the house," said her father. "I only wonder how many silver spoons are left in the cupboard by this time."

The wagon had hardly stopped at the front steps when the ironmaster asked the valet whether the stranger was still there. He added that he had heard at church that the man was a thief. The valet answered that the fellow had gone and that he had not taken anything with him at all. On the contrary, he had left behind a little package which Miss Willmansson was to be kind enough to accept as a Christmas present.

The young girl opened the package, which was so badly done up that the contents came into view at once. She gave a little cry of joy. She found a small rat trap, and in it lay three wrinkled ten-kronor notes. But that was not all. In the rat trap lay also a letter written in large, jagged characters:

Honored and noble Miss:

24 *Since you have been so nice to me all day long, as if I was a captain, I want to be nice to you, in return, as if I was a real captain: for I do not want you to be embarrassed at this Christmas season by a thief; but you can give back the money to the old man on the roadside, who has the money pouch hanging on the window frame as a bait for poor wanderers.*

25 *The rat trap is a Christmas present from a rat who would have been caught in this world's rat trap if he had not been raised to captain, because in that way he got power to clear himself.*

Written with friendship and high regard,
26 *Captain von Ståhle*

CRITICAL THINKING: GUIDED READING QUESTIONS

LITERAL

1a. What does Edla tell the peddler at supper? (She instructs him to keep the new suit as a Christmas present and spend the next Christmas with them, if he likes.)

2a. In his letter what reason does the peddler give for returning the crofter's money? (He wants to be as nice as Edla was to him and not spoil her Christmas by embarrassing her for harboring a thief.)

INFERENTIAL

1b. Why is the peddler amazed by Edla's behavior? (No one has ever before treated him with such kindness and trust.)

2b. By the end of the story, in what way have the peddler's outlook and behavior changed? (He no longer holds a cynical view of the world, and cynicism no longer prompts him to treat others dishonestly.)

STUDY QUESTIONS

Recalling

1. What theory about the world has the peddler developed? What does he take from the old man? How does he feel afterwards?
2. For whom does the ironmaster mistake the peddler?
3. What reasons does Edla give for allowing the peddler to stay after his identity is learned? What does she say when he says good night?
4. After learning how the peddler treated the old man, what does the ironmaster wonder on the way home from church? What do he and his daughter find at home?

Interpreting

5. What feelings about the world does the peddler's "rat-trap" theory express? What experiences have led him to evolve the theory?
6. Based on the peddler's final actions, what seems to have become of his theory? Why does he sign his letter "Captain von Ståhle"?
7. What message about human behavior does the story convey?

Extending

8. Do you think that one act of kindness can really change a person's view of the world? Discuss

LITERARY FOCUS

Flat and Round Characters

Depending on how much information we are given about them, characters can be either flat or round. **Flat characters** seem simple, as if they could be summed up with only one or two personality traits. On the other hand, **round characters** have several different and often conflicting personality traits. Because they are many-sided, round characters can do and say surprising things, just as real people can.

Thinking About Flat and Round Characters

■ Is the peddler a flat character or a round character? Explain. How would you classify the old man? Edla? The ironmaster?

Static and Dynamic Characters

Besides being flat or round, story characters may be classified as either static or dynamic. A **static character** remains the same throughout the story, displaying no change in personality or behavior. In contrast, a **dynamic character** changes and grows, often as a result of story events or the behavior of other story characters. Sometimes this change is the most important event of the story.

Thinking About Static and Dynamic Characters

■ What causes the peddler to change? Is Edla also a dynamic character? Explain.

LANGUAGE STUDY

Words from Scandinavian Languages

Swedish belongs to the group of modern Scandinavian languages that also includes Danish, Norwegian, and Icelandic. These languages have common ancestors, including Old Norse, the language spoken by the Vikings. English has borrowed many words from Scandinavian languages, some from Old Norse and others from modern Scandinavian languages.

Use a dictionary to help you determine the meanings and origins of the following English words.

1. gremlin
2. ransack
3. rutabaga
4. scant
5. scruff
6. slalom

COMPOSITION

Writing About Character

■ Compare and contrast the characters of the peddler and the ironmaster. Identify a number of points of comparison and contrast related to key character traits, character motivation, and character change. For each point explain how the characters are similar or different. *For help with this assignment, refer to Lesson 3 in the Writing About Literature Handbook at the back of this book.*

COMPARING STORIES

■ Compare and contrast this story with two other stories in which a character undergoes a transformation. For example, you might compare and contrast it with two of the following stories, which appear earlier in this book: "The Winner," "The Beggar," and "The Father." In which stories are the changes in dynamic characters the most similar? In which do you find the changes most believable? Cite story details to support your opinions.

The Rat Trap **71**

COMPOSITION: GUIDELINES FOR EVALUATION

WRITING ABOUT CHARACTER

Objective

To compare and contrast characters in a story

Guidelines for Evaluation

■ suggested length: two or three paragraphs
■ should explain similarities and differences between the peddler and the ironmaster
■ should treat character traits, motivation, and any changes in character

Is the peddler's change believable? Why or why not?

ANSWERS

STUDY QUESTIONS

1. The world is a rattrap offering riches and joys as bait but closing when one tries to touch them; thirty kronor; pleased with his "smartness"
2. an old army friend
3. She wants him to enjoy a peaceful Christmas. He should keep the suit and spend the next Christmas with them.
4. He wonders whether the peddler has stolen anything. They find a rattrap, a letter, and the crofter's money.
5. cynicism and discontent; poverty, isolation, and cruelty
6. He has abandoned it; to show that he wants to behave nobly and prove himself worthy of Edla's kindness
7. Kindness can cause people to change for the better.
8. Answers will vary. Students may feel the effects depend on the extent of the kindness.

LITERARY FOCUS

Flat and Round Characters

round; He has several conflicting traits; the old man, flat; Edla, round; the ironmaster, flat

Static and Dynamic Characters

Edla's kindness leads the peddler to change. No; she shows the same personality throughout.

LANGUAGE STUDY

1. "mischievous imaginary creature"; from Danish *græmling*
2. "search thoroughly"; from Old Norse *rann,* "house," and *sækja,* "to seek"
3. "turnip"; from Swedish dialect *rotabagge*
4. "meager"; from Old Norse *skammr,* "short"
5. "nape"; from Old Norse *skrufr,* "tuft of hair"
6. "zigzag course in skiing"; from Norwegian *slalom,* "ski track with an even slope"

COMPARING STORIES

Answers will vary. For example, students may say Lushkoff's change in "The Beggar" is most like the peddler's, and Pius' change in "The Winner" is the most believable.

The Rat Trap **T-71**

LESSON PREVIEW

In this modern Chinese story a grown man learns responsibility from a precocious boy. During the construction of a railroad, a cold and tired department chief on his way to a job site stops to rest in Lingkuan Gorge. He meets young Cheng-yu, whose parents are outside working in the snow. Inspired by Cheng-yu and his family, the man recaptures his sense of responsibility, and he leaves for his destination.

LITERARY SKILLS FOR THIS SELECTION

- theme
- point of view

THEMES IN THIS SELECTION

- human relationships: adults and children
- work and responsibility

LESSON OBJECTIVES

1. to understand transliteration from Chinese
2. to write a brief story based on a model
3. to compare and contrast stories

Teacher's Classroom Resources 1

- Teaching Notes   129
- Reading Guide   130
- Check Test   131
- Responding to World Cultures   132
- Language Study: Transliterating Chinese   133
- Writing Process Guide: Writing a Brief Short Story   134
- Grammar in Literature: Using Common and Proper Nouns   135
- Selection Test   136

Tu Peng-cheng (born 1921)

People's Republic of China

Like other contemporary Chinese writers, Tu Peng-cheng has seen his popularity wax and wane under the Communists. After growing up in a poor family in the province of Shenshi (also spelled Shaanxi), Tu* worked as a correspondent for the *New China News* during China's civil war in the late 1940s. His many notes about battles he witnessed became important sources for his later fiction, including his acclaimed war novel *Defend Yenan,* published in 1954.

Winning praise throughout China for his vivid depiction of military life, Tu enjoyed a flourishing career throughout the 1950s. In 1958 he published his next major novel, *In Peacetime,* which describes workers constructing the Paoki-to-Chengtu (Baoji-to-Chengdu) Railway. Tu fell from favor in the 1960s, when the increasingly repressive Communist government rewrote its history and condemned several former leaders whom Tu had praised in his fiction. His work was banned in China until 1978, when a thaw in the nation's totalitarian regime allowed Tu to resume his writing career.

---

* his surname. In Chinese names, the surname traditionally precedes the given name.

72   *The Short Story*

The Changing Face of China

Occupying much of eastern Asia, China is the world's most populated country and the third largest country in size. An ancient civilization, China has in the twentieth century experienced enormous upheaval. Major earthquakes have rocked the nation; so too has warfare—first with the Japanese from 1937 to 1945 and then during the civil war that brought the Communists to power in 1949.

During the 1950s the Chinese government developed a number of plans for rebuilding the countryside. Many workers were mobilized to help build new railroads to provide vital links between distant regions. So important were these railroads that laborers working on them often named their children after the railway lines. One major project was the Paoki-to-Chengtu (Baoji-to-Chengdu) Railway, featured in Tu Peng-cheng's second novel as well as in "Lingkuan Gorge."

See LITERATURE AND CULTURE SOURCEBOOK: China and Japan

IN THE CLASSROOM

TEACHING STUDENTS OF DIFFERENT ABILITIES

- **For less advanced students:** Students should have few difficulties with this brief, accessible story. Have them decide whether the two main characters are static or dynamic. They might also complete the Reading Guide for this selection.

- **For more advanced students:** In conjunction with the Language Study, students might find out more about the Pinyin system of transliteration.

DISCUSSING GEOGRAPHY AND CULTURE

The Life of a Pioneer

This story depicts construction workers in the Tsinling Mountains in central China. These mountains reach heights of ten thousand feet and are bisected by deep canyons. The region is sparsely populated, and its winters are harsh.

- The Chinese workers depicted in the story could be called pioneers. Ask students to define a pioneer and describe the qualities that pioneers in every culture need.

Tu Peng-cheng

Lingkuan Gorge

Translated anonymously from the Chinese

1 The snow, already more than half a foot deep, obliterated the line between earth and sky behind a hazy white curtain. I had been following the path of the future railway for forty kilometers. Although I could hear the roar of machinery further back in the hills, I had seen 2 neither work sites nor workers.

Entering Lingkuan Gorge, my irritation increased. Even in clear weather, in this gorge the sun never shone. It didn't matter where you looked up along the twisting course—the most you could see of the sky was a patch no bigger than the palm of your hand. Now it was dusk, and the swirling snowflakes and the gale made every step a struggle.

Construction in the gorge was very busy. Everywhere people were at work. Generators, cement-mixers, air compressors shook the ground. Hundreds of light bulbs gleamed dim and yellow. Electric wires, criss-crossing like a giant spider web, were scarcely visible, but I could see the overhead cables and their pulley cars sliding back and forth loaded with materials.

3 Hungry, cold, I tripped and fell, scraping my hands. Enough! I'd find some place under a cliff, out of the wind, and rest a few hours. If I reached the materials depot tomorrow morning by ten o'clock, that still wouldn't be too late. Stumbling around in the dark like this, I was liable to fall into some deep ravine, and that would be the end of this Materials Department chief. I'd have to be put on the "used up" list!

I noticed a path leading to a cave in the cliffside. A door curtain hanging in the entrance way showed that the cave was undoubtedly occupied by workers. Grasping branches along the steep path, I hauled myself up to the door and entered.

Strange! Seated on a small stool in the doorway was a little boy, seven or eight years old, elbows on his knees, supporting his face in his hands. His cheeks were red with cold. He had been peering at the opposite cliffside through a rent in the curtain. He glanced at me briefly as I came in, then went back to his observation.

4 The cave was large, but quite warm. It had a stove and eating utensils. On the wall above a bed was a colored New Year picture of "Chubby Children Pulling the Turnip." All the walls had been papered with old newspapers, now blackened by smoke from the stove.

"Why isn't anybody home?" I asked, shaking the snow from my coat and hat.

The little boy turned his head. His eyes flashed. "Aren't I anybody, uncle?"[1] He rose and walked towards me, his hands behind his back, his chest extended, as if to say: Not only am I somebody, I'm a very grown-up somebody!

I cupped his round little face in my hands. "You're pretty sharp, young imp!"

He pushed my hands aside. Doubling up his fists, he cocked his head to one side and demanded: "Who are you calling imp! I have a name!" Pointing at the baby girl asleep on the bed, he informed me: "Her name is Pao-cheng, mine is Cheng-yu."

No doubt about it. These kids were like thousands of others I had met, born and raised on construction sites. The workers liked to name

---

1. **uncle:** here, "mister." In China the words for *uncle* and *aunt* are often used to address older people who are not actual relatives.

Lingkuan Gorge **73**

CRITICAL THINKING: GUIDED READING QUESTIONS

- Cheng-yu proudly speaks of his father, who is outside dynamiting the mountains to open them for railway construction.
- Cheng-yu sits near the cave entrance because his father can see him from there.
- His own job is to watch his baby sister until his mother, who directs traffic, comes home.
- His mother is also outside working, even though traffic in the snow is light.

IN THE GLOSSARY

- discern: recognize

5 READING SKILL: INFERENCE

Elicit that the workers' practice of naming children after railway projects shows pride in their jobs and the importance with which these projects are viewed.

6 TEACHING THEME

Note that the value of work is stressed in this exchange. Cheng-yu, despite his age, is concerned not with playing but with seeing the work continue. His use of the pronoun *we* shows that he considers himself part of the work.

7 GRAMMAR IN LITERATURE

Point out that Tu uses several interrogative and exclamatory sentences for variety. Have students find examples here ("How can you tell . . . at this distance?" "Ah, so that was it!") and elsewhere.

8 TEACHING STUDENTS OF LIMITED ENGLISH PROFICIENCY

Have students use context clues to determine that the slang expression "knock off" means "stop." Ask them to find in the left-hand column an informal synonym for the expression. ("Quit" in the fourth paragraph)

9 TEACHING THEME

Elicit that the mother's responsible attitude again stresses the importance of doing one's job. Contrast the mother's remaining in the snow and the narrator's earlier decision to seek shelter.

5 their children after the projects where they were born. Cheng-yu probably had first seen the light of day on the railway project between Chengtu and Chungking, also known as Yu. His baby sister Pao-cheng very likely had been born right here—the site of the future Paoki-Chengtu Railway.[2]

I sat by the stove, smoking and rubbing the drying mud from my hands.

Cheng-yu crawled on to my lap and looked into my eyes, "Is it going to snow tomorrow, uncle?"

I pressed his icy red little nose. "As soon as we get our telephone line connected up with heaven, I'll ask for you. . . ."

Angrily, he leaped down and stood a meter away, scowling at me. "Quit your kidding! You've got a newspaper in your pocket. Why don't you look at the weather report?"

He resumed his seat in the doorway, clamped his elbows on his knees, rested his face in his hands, and peered out through the rent in the curtain. When I asked him where the kettle was, he ignored me. I certainly was sorry I had offended my small host!

6 "Why do you want to know about the snow, Cheng-yu?" I asked him. "Is it because you can't go out and play when it's snowing?"

He didn't even bother to look at me. "Papa says if it's still snowing tomorrow, we'll have to quit work."

"What does your pa do?"

"He opens up mountains!" the child replied proudly.

"Where?"

Cheng-yu pointed with pursed lips at the work site opposite.

I looked. All I could see was a searchlight beam, shining through the drifting snowflakes straight up into the heavens. In its light I could

---

2. **Paoki-Chengtu Railway:** now sometimes spelled Baoji-Chengdu. (See the Geography and Culture feature that precedes the story.)

74   *The Short Story*

vaguely discern a few dozen men, who seemed pasted to the side of the towering cliff, drilling holes for dynamite charges. The holes were like the steps of a ladder to the sky.

7 "How can you tell which one is your father at this distance?" I asked.

"I can't see him plainly, but pa says he can see me. He says all he has to do is turn around. I often sit here so he can see me."

Ah, so that was it!

The icy snow melted from my boots. My numbed legs, thawing out, ached painfully. I stamped to help the circulation.

Cheng-yu waved his hand warningly. I understood. He was afraid I'd wake his baby sister.

"You really take good care of sister," I commended.

8 "Mama says my job is to look after her. When mama comes home, I can knock off."

"So. You're on the job every day?" I hugged him to me. "What does mama do?"

He pointed to the road below the cave.

I could see a person standing by a telephone pole beside the road. Covered with snow, she looked like a white stone image. Apparently she was directing traffic. The road, not very wide, had been blasted through the rock. Ordinarily, carts, mules, donkeys, people . . . no doubt streamed in both directions along that road twenty-four hours a day. Someone had to keep the traffic in order.

9 Today, because of the big snow, there weren't many people or vehicles on the road. She could very well have spent the day at home. But there she stood, and there she would remain, three months, five months, or three years, five years, if need be. Perhaps, from time to time, she raised her head to gaze up at her child, or at her husband—that husband scaling the cliffs between the mountains and the sky. When he paused to wipe the sweat from his brow, could he see the determined figure of his wife, or the tiny image of his little boy? Even though it was a snowy, windy night, even though the

---

CRITICAL THINKING: GUIDED READING QUESTIONS

LITERAL

1a. In what aspects of the railway construction are → Cheng-yu's parents involved? (His father handles explosives to open the mountains for railroad construction; his mother directs traffic.)

2a. What is Cheng-yu's job? (His job is to look after → his baby sister until his mother comes home.)

INFERENTIAL

1b. What is Cheng-yu's attitude toward his parents? (He is affectionate, respectful, and proud.)

2b. What is Cheng-yu's attitude toward his job? (He is serious and responsible.)

Winter Landscape, Wang Jian (1598-1677).

PAGE SUMMARY: AT A GLANCE

- The narrator senses the family's love.
- Though Cheng-yu dozes, he will not go to bed because "a man should never leave his post."
- The narrator hugs him and then leaves, now wanting to reach his job without further delay.

10 TEACHING POINT OF VIEW

Point out that the first-person narrator must infer the family's feelings and work ethic from his own observations.

11 CRITICAL THINKING: EVALUATION

Explain that authors in totalitarian regimes must produce literature that fosters values approved by the government. Have students decide whether Tu's story suffers as a result. Do students find it too didactic, or does it still retain literary grace and charm?

COLLABORATIVE LEARNING: ENRICHMENT ACTIVITY

Literature and Social Studies Have a group of students prepare an oral report on writers whose works were banned in their homelands for political reasons. Each student should report on a different author—for example, Anna Akhmatova, Joseph Brodsky, Federico García Lorca, Nazim Hikmet, Victor Hugo, Pablo Neruda, Thomas Mann, and Nelly Sachs.

ART AND LITERATURE

In the late Ming dynasty (1368–1644) Wang Jian painted in an ink-wash style practiced by "literati," or poetry painters. Most academic painters combined calligraphy—a pictographic form of writing—with painting. The literati added a poetic element with their loose, "spilled-ink" style. In this watercolor the ancient mountains rise up above fragile houses, and leafless trees stand bent but unmoved from the frigid weather.

- Have students find words and phrases in the story that might describe this watercolor. ("The snow, already more than half a foot deep, obliterated the line between the earth and sky"; "a path leading to a cave in the cliffside"; "scaling the cliffs between the mountains and the sky," etc.)

10 worker, his wife and children couldn't see one another clearly, I was sure they could feel a mutual loving encouragement and sense that each was looking forward to the moment of family reunion.

I glanced at Cheng-yu. The child had placed his hands in his sleeves and pulled his neck into his collar. He kept dozing off.

"You're liable to catch a chill. Better get into bed and go to sleep."

He looked at me dreamily for a moment, probably thinking that his parents had returned.

When he realized who I was, he shook his head violently. "No. I won't!"

"Why not?"

He rubbed his eyes with his fists. "Papa and mama say a man should never leave his post."

I hugged him tightly and pressed my cheek against his. Then I rose, buttoned my coat, pulled my hat down firmly, left the cave, and walked down the path. Following the road that had been blasted through the rock, I pushed on. **11** A job was waiting for me. I wanted to reach my destination without any further delay.

Lingkuan Gorge **75**

CRITICAL THINKING: GUIDED READING QUESTIONS

LITERAL

1a. What does Cheng-yu say to explain his refusal to go to bed even though he keeps dozing? ("Papa and mama say a man should never leave his post.")

2a. At the end what reason does the narrator state for leaving? ("A job was waiting for me. I wanted to reach my destination without further delay.")

INFERENTIAL

1b. What does this statement stress about him? (It stresses his sense of responsibility, his obedience, and his desire to be considered mature.)

2b. What has caused the narrator to rethink his earlier decision to stop and rest? (his observations of Cheng-yu and his parents, who show a strong sense of responsibility)

What did you like about the character of Cheng-yu? Why?

ANSWERS

STUDY QUESTIONS

1. He is a Materials Department chief traveling to a materials depot on a railway construction site. The darkness, snow, and cold and his hunger and exhaustion persuade him to rest.
2. Cheng-yu is seven or eight. He says, "Aren't I anybody, uncle?"
3. His father is a railroad construction worker who blasts open mountains, and his mother directs traffic. Cheng-yu must watch his baby sister while his mother is gone. He says, "Papa and mama say a man should never leave his post."
4. He continues his journey. He realizes that a job is waiting for him.
5. Cheng-yu is precocious, serious, and proud. He displays a serious, respectful, responsible attitude.
6. In the beginning he decides to delay his mission, but in the end he is determined to continue. Observing Cheng-yu and his family, who take their responsibilities seriously and continue working despite discomfort, causes the narrator to change his attitude.
7. Work can be a source of pride and is important for society's general welfare. The story also suggests that family love and responsibility are valuable.
8. Answers may vary. The story entertains with the charming, humorous character of Cheng-yu and reveals its messages through action and speech instead of stating them directly.
9. Answers will vary. Students may say that children often inadvertently point out adults' compromised values.

LANGUAGE STUDY

Du Beng-cheng

COMPARING STORIES

Answers will vary. For example, students may find the characters in "The Kabuliwallah" the most developed and the relationships in "Dead Men's Path" the most realistic.

STUDY QUESTIONS

Recalling

1. What is the narrator's job and the purpose of his journey? What physical conditions persuade him to rest for a few hours?
2. About how old is Cheng-yu? What does he respond when the narrator asks, "Why isn't anybody home?"
3. What work do Cheng-yu's parents do? What "job" has Cheng-yu been assigned, and what explanation does he give for refusing the narrator's advice to go to sleep?
4. What does the narrator do in the final paragraph? What does he realize is waiting for him?

Interpreting

5. What sort of child is Cheng-yu? What attitude does he display toward his parents and his responsibilities?
6. What change in mood or outlook does the narrator experience in the course of the story? What causes the change?
7. What ideas about work does the story convey? What else does the story suggest is valuable?
8. Do you think the story is overly moralistic? How does Tu make his story entertaining despite its rather heavy-handed message?

Extending

9. Do young children often teach important lessons to their elders? Discuss.

LANGUAGE STUDY

Transliterating Chinese

Because Chinese is not traditionally written in the Roman alphabet that we use in English, various systems have been devised for **transliterating** Chinese words, that is, spelling them out in Roman letters. For many years the most popular transliteration system for Chinese was the Wade-Giles system; more recently the Chinese government introduced the Pinyin system, which attempts to capture Chinese pronunciations more accurately. In 1979 China asked that English publications adopt the Pinyin system, and many newspapers and recent reference works have done so. In the field of literature, however, Wade-Giles forms are still better known, since so much great Chinese literature was published before 1979.

Study the following examples of Chinese names in Wade-Giles and Pinyin forms.

Wade-Giles	Pinyin
Li Po	Li Bo
Tu Fu	Du Fu
Mao Tse-tung	Mao Zedung
Paoki	Baoji

- Based on these examples, how would you transliterate the author's name, *Tu Peng-cheng,* in the new Pinyin system?

COMPOSITION

Writing a Brief Short Story

- Recall a visit with someone that changed your mood or outlook, and use it as the basis of a brief story. Do not state the change in attitude. Instead, like the narrator of "Lingkuan Gorge," provide details that help readers infer the change.

COMPARING STORIES

- Compare and contrast this story with other stories about human relationships that you have read in this section or elsewhere. In which stories were the characters most fully developed? In which stories did the relationships between characters seem most realistic? Cite details from the stories to support your opinions.

COMPOSITION: GUIDELINES FOR EVALUATION

WRITING A BRIEF SHORT STORY

Objective
To write a brief story based on a model

Guidelines for Evaluation
- suggested length: one to two pages
- should be a fictionalized account based on personal experience
- should recount an incident that changes the narrator's mood or outlook
- should allow readers to infer the change rather than state it directly

PREVIEW: THE AUTHOR AND THE WORLD

GEOGRAPHY AND CULTURE

In this coming-of-age tale from Sudan, the narrator recalls his childhood love of his grandfather. He also liked their neighbor Masood, a debtor who had lost much land to the grandfather. After witnessing the grandfather's harsh treatment of Masood, the narrator is unable to eat the dates his grandfather claimed as payment of Masood's debts.

LITERARY SKILLS FOR THIS SELECTION

- point of view
- symbols

THEMES IN THIS SELECTION

- growing up: facing the harsh realities of life
- the need for compassion

LESSON OBJECTIVES

1. to examine first-person point of view
2. to write about the first-person narrator of a story
3. to rewrite a story from another character's point of view

Teacher's Classroom Resources 1

- Teaching Notes 139
- Prereading Vocabulary 140
- Reading Guide 141
- Check Test 142
- Responding to World Cultures 143
- Literary Focus: First-Person Point of View 144
- Writing Process Guides: Writing About a First-Person Narrator 145 Rewriting from Another Point of View 146
- Grammar in Literature: Using Precise and Vivid Language 147
- Selection Test 148

Tayeb Salih

(born 1929)

Sudan

Although he has worked in London and Paris, Tayeb Salih [tə yēb′ sä′ lā] writes mainly about the rural villages of northern Sudan where he grew up. Salih comes from a family of small farmers and initially planned to study agriculture. While attending Khartoum [kär toom′] University, however, he grew interested in broadcasting and decided to make that his field.

After completing his studies in England, he became director of drama for the British Broadcasting Corporation's Arabic-language service, a job that he held for twelve years. He later worked for the Sudan Broadcasting Service and took a Paris-based job with UNESCO, the United Nations Educational, Scientific, and Cultural Organization.

In the meantime Salih began making a name for himself as a writer of Arabic fiction. His fame spread in the late 1960s when his collection *The Wedding of Zein and Other Stories* and his novel *Season of Migration to the North* were translated into English. "A Handful of Dates," from *The Wedding of Zein,* is one of Salih's most widely anthologized stories.

Sudan and the Nile

Located in northeast Africa, Sudan is the largest nation on the continent. For centuries it has been a cultural crossroads between Africa and the Mediterranean countries. Its population is about three-quarters Moslem, and Arabic is the official language. Other languages spoken are English and tribal dialects. Most of the Moslem population lives in the north; in the south, native African languages and customs thrive. Khartoum, where Salih went to college, is the nation's capital.

Much of northern Sudan, where Salih grew up, is desert. The Libyan Desert fills the northwest; the Nubian Desert, the northeast. In between flows the world's longest river, the Nile. Its waters irrigate a wide strip of land in northern Sudan, making farming possible. It is on the fertile banks of the Nile that "A Handful of Dates" takes place.

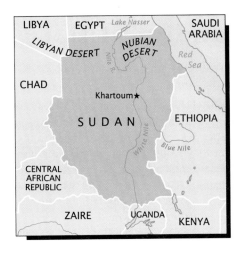

See LITERATURE AND CULTURE SOURCEBOOK: Africa

A Handful of Dates 77

TEACHING STUDENTS OF DIFFERENT ABILITIES

- **For less advanced students:** Have students explain what the handful of dates and the narrator's rejection of them stand for. Ask them to complete the Reading Guide for this selection.

- **For more advanced students:** Students might research and present reports on the Koran. Reports should include oral readings of famous passages from the Chapter of the Merciful as well as background information about the Koran.

Desert Survival Skills

The Nubian people who settled in the Sudan thousands of years ago found inhospitable territory: The deserts of northern Sudan receive less than two inches of rain per year. Recently, severe drought and famine have ravaged much of the Sudan.

- Ask students to discuss the skills people need to survive in a desert. (finding and conserving water, raising crops and animals with few resources, and learning to adapt to a shifting terrain)

The Great Mosque at Medina, manuscript.

Tayeb Salih

A Handful of Dates

Translated from the Arabic by Denys Johnson-Davies

1   I must have been very young at the time. While I don't remember exactly how old I was, I do remember that when people saw me with my grandfather they would pat me on the head and give my cheek a pinch—things they didn't do to my grandfather. The strange thing was that I never used to go out with my father, rather it was my grandfather who would take me with him wherever he went, except for the mornings when I would go to the mosque[1] to learn the Koran.[2] The mosque, the river[3] and the fields—these were the landmarks in our life. While most of the children of my age grumbled at having to go to the mosque to learn the Koran, I used to love it. The reason was, no doubt, that I was 2 quick at learning by heart and the Sheikh[4] always asked me to stand up and recite the Chapter of the Merciful[5] whenever we had visitors, who would pat me on my head and cheek just as

___

2. **Koran** [kô rän′]: the Moslem holy book.
3. **river:** that is, the Nile River. (See the Geography and Culture feature that precedes the story.)
4. **Sheikh** [shĕk]: tribal and religious leader.
5. **Chapter of the Merciful:** section of the Koran.

___

1. **mosque** [mosk]: Moslem house of worship.

78   *The Short Story*

people did when they saw me with my grandfather.

Yes, I used to love the mosque, and I loved the river too. Directly we finished our Koran reading in the morning I would throw down my wooden slate and dart off, quick as a genie,[6] to my mother, hurriedly swallow down my breakfast, and run off for a plunge in the river. When tired of swimming about I would sit on the bank and gaze at the strip of water that wound away eastwards and hid behind a thick wood of acacia trees. I loved to give rein to my imagination and picture to myself a tribe of giants living behind that wood, a people tall and thin with white beards and sharp noses, like my grandfather. Before my grandfather ever replied to my many questions he would rub the tip of his nose with his forefinger; as for his beard, it was soft and luxuriant and as white as cotton-wool—never in my life have I seen anything of a purer whiteness or greater beauty. My grandfather must also have been extremely tall, for I never saw anyone in the whole area address him without having to look up at him, nor did I see him enter a house without having to bend so low that I was put in mind of the way the river wound round behind the wood of acacia trees. I loved him and would imagine myself, when I grew to be a man, tall and slender like him, walking along with great strides.

I believe I was his favorite grandchild: no wonder, for my cousins were a stupid bunch and I—so they say—was an intelligent child. I used to know when my grandfather wanted me to laugh, when to be silent; also I would remember the times for his prayers and would bring him his prayer-rug[7] and fill the ewer for his ablutions[8] without his having to ask me. When he had nothing else to do he enjoyed listening to

6. **genie** [jē'nē]: in Moslem mythology, spirit that can appear and disappear quickly.
7. **prayer-rug:** Moslems traditionally kneel on rugs while praying.
8. **ablutions:** a ritual washing of the body.

me reciting to him from the Koran in a lilting voice, and I could tell from his face that he was moved.

One day I asked him about our neighbor Masood. I said to my grandfather: "I fancy you don't like our neighbor Masood?"

To which he answered, having rubbed the tip of his nose: "He's an indolent man and I don't like such people."

I said to him: "What's an indolent man?"

My grandfather lowered his head for a moment, then looking across at the wide expanse of field, he said: "Do you see it stretching out from the edge of the desert up to the Nile bank? A hundred feddans.[9] Do you see all those date palms? And those trees—*sant,* acacia, and *sayal*? All this fell into Masood's lap, was inherited by him from his father."

Taking advantage of the silence that had descended upon my grandfather, I turned my gaze from him to the vast area defined by his words. "I don't care," I told myself, "who owns those date palms, those trees or this black, cracked earth—all I know is that it's the arena for my dreams and my playground."

My grandfather then continued: "Yes, my boy, forty years ago all this belonged to Masood—two-thirds of it is now mine."

This was news to me for I had imagined that the land had belonged to my grandfather ever since God's Creation.

"I didn't own a single feddan when I first set foot in this village. Masood was then the owner of all these riches. The position has changed now, though, and I think that before Allah[10] calls me to Him I shall have bought the remaining third as well."

I do not know why it was I felt fear at my grandfather's words—and pity for our neighbor

9. **feddans** [fə däns']: units of land measurement used in many North African nations. One feddan equals 1.038 acres.
10. **Allah:** Moslem name for God.

A Handful of Dates **79**

CRITICAL THINKING: GUIDED READING QUESTIONS

LITERAL

1a. What does the narrator imagine he will be like when he is older? (He expects to be tall and slender, like his grandfather.)

2a. From whom did the grandfather get his land, and what does he expect in the future? (He got it from Masood and expects to get the rest of Masood's land.)

INFERENTIAL

1b. What does this detail show about the narrator's feelings for his grandfather? (He admires him and wants to be like him.)

2b. Considering the land he already has, what do the grandfather's future plans reveal about him? (He is acquisitive.)

PAGE SUMMARY: AT A GLANCE

- The narrator loves the mosque, the Nile, and giving rein to his imagination; he also loves and admires his grandfather.
- One day he asks why his grandfather dislikes their neighbor Masood.
- Calling Masood indolent, the grandfather explains that all his land once belonged to Masood and that before the grandfather dies, he expects to acquire the rest of Masood's land.
- These words make the narrator fearful, and he pities Masood.

IN THE GLOSSARY

- acacia: tree of the mimosa family
- luxuriant: abundant; thick
- fancy: imagine
- indolent: lazy

3 TEACHING STUDENTS OF LIMITED ENGLISH PROFICIENCY

Students may have difficulty with the British translator's construction here. Point out that most Americans would say "Directly *after* we finished. . . ."

4 TEACHING CHARACTERIZATION

Point out that this detail stresses the narrator's love of imagination and creativity, a trait that later helps explain his appreciation of Masood.

5 TEACHING IRONY

Note that the grandfather is moved by religious teachings that his subsequent words and actions ironically contradict: He does not show mercy toward Masood.

6 READING SKILL: CONTRAST

Elicit the contrast between the narrator's innocent values and his grandfather's more grasping ones.

7 TEACHING POINT OF VIEW

Note that here the first-person narrator reports feelings that as a child he cannot understand. Ask what the cause of the fear might be. (He may have an inkling that his grandfather may not be the loving, admirable man the narrator has known.)

- The narrator recalls Masood's singing and laughter; his grandfather never laughs.
- When Masood reluctantly asks the grandfather to the harvesting of his dates, the grandfather's eyes gleam.
- At the harvesting Masood warns a boy not to cut the heart of a date palm, and the narrator recalls that Masood once said that palm trees, like humans, experience joy and suffering.

IN THE GLOSSARY

- **aloof:** remote; reserved
- **sickle:** tool with a crescent-shaped blade, used for cutting plants, branches, and so on

8 TEACHING CHARACTERIZATION

Elicit the recognition that these details show Masood to be a warmhearted person who loves life and feels emotions strongly.

9 CULTURAL BACKGROUND

Note that Moslem men are permitted more than one wife but are expected to provide for them.

10 CULTURAL BACKGROUND

Explain that dates, the fruit of a type of palm tree, are an important crop of the area. They are harvested or gathered when ripe and then sold in markets.

11 READING SKILL: INFERENCE

Have students discuss the likelihood that Masood is inviting the grandfather to the harvesting because he owes the grandfather money and will pay the debt with proceeds from the sale of the dates. Ask what quality the grandfather's gleaming eyes reveal. (acquisitiveness)

12 TEACHING SYMBOLS

Point out that the palm trees are a symbol, and ask what they represent. (They represent human beings, especially those who feel strong emotion, like Masood.)

---

8 Masood. How I wished my grandfather wouldn't do what he'd said! I remembered Masood's singing, his beautiful voice and powerful laugh that resembled the gurgling of water. My grandfather never used to laugh.

I asked my grandfather why Masood had sold his land.

"Women," and from the way my grandfather pronounced the word I felt that "women" was 9 something terrible. "Masood, my boy, was a much-married man. Each time he married he sold me a feddan or two." I made the quick calculation that Masood must have married some ninety women. Then I remembered his three wives, his shabby appearance, his lame donkey and its dilapidated saddle, his djellaba[11] with the torn sleeves. I had all but rid my mind of the thoughts that jostled in it when I saw the man approaching us, and my grandfather and I exchanged glances.

10 "We'll be harvesting the dates today," said Masood. "Don't you want to be there?"

I felt, though, that he did not really want my 11 grandfather to attend. My grandfather, however, jumped to his feet and I saw that his eyes sparkled momentarily with an intense brightness. He pulled me by the hand and we went off to the harvesting of Masood's dates.

Someone brought my grandfather a stool covered with an ox-hide, while I remained standing. There was a vast number of people there, but though I knew them all, I found myself, for some reason, watching Masood: aloof from that great gathering of people, he stood as though it were no concern of his, despite the fact that the date palms to be harvested were his own. Sometimes his attention would be caught by the sound of a huge clump of dates crashing down from on high. Once he shouted up at the

---

11. **djellaba** [jə lä′bə]: loose-fitting hooded robe worn by men and women in some North African countries.

80   *The Short Story*

---

boy perched on the very summit of the date palm who had begun hacking at a clump with his long, sharp sickle: "Be careful you don't cut the heart of the palm."

No one paid any attention to what he said and the boy seated at the very summit of the date palm continued, quickly and energetically, to work away at the branch with his sickle till the clump of dates began to drop like something descending from the heavens.

12 I, however, had begun to think about Masood's phrase "the heart of the palm." I pictured the palm tree as something with feeling, something possessed of a heart that throbbed. I remembered Masood's remark to me when he had once seen me playing about with the branch of a young palm tree: "Palm trees, my boy, like humans, experience joy and suffering." And I had felt an inward and unreasoned embarrassment.

When I again looked at the expanse of ground stretching before me I saw my young companions swarming like ants around the trunks of the palm trees, gathering up dates and eating most of them. The dates were collected into high mounds. I saw people coming along and weighing them into measuring bins and pouring them into sacks, of which I counted thirty. The crowd of people broke up, except for Hussein the merchant, Mousa the owner of the field next to ours on the east, and two men I'd never seen before.

I heard a low whistling sound and saw that my grandfather had fallen asleep. Then I noticed that Masood had not changed his stance, except that he had placed a stalk in his mouth and was munching at it like someone surfeited with food who doesn't know what to do with the mouthful he still has.

Suddenly my grandfather woke up, jumped to his feet and walked towards the sacks of dates. He was followed by Hussein the mer-

---

CRITICAL THINKING: GUIDED READING QUESTIONS

LITERAL

1a. In contrast to Masood, what does the grandfather never do? (He never laughs.)

2a. What did Masood once tell the narrator about palm trees? ("Like humans, [they] experience joy and suffering.")

INFERENTIAL

1b. What does this detail suggest about the grandfather? (He is a cold person.)

2b. What qualities of Masood's does this remark stress, and why would having such qualities make him appeal to the narrator? (It stresses his poetic imagination and strong feelings, qualities the narrator shares.)

chant, Mousa the owner of the field next to ours, and the two strangers. I glanced at Masood and saw that he was making his way towards us with extreme slowness, like a man who wants to retreat but whose feet insist on going forward. They formed a circle round the sacks of dates and began examining them, some taking a date or two to eat. My grandfather gave me a fistful, which I began munching. I saw Masood filling the palms of both hands with dates and bringing them up close to his nose, then returning them.

13 Then I saw them dividing up the sacks between them. Hussein the merchant took ten; each of the strangers took five. Mousa the owner of the field next to ours on the eastern side took five, and my grandfather took five. Understanding nothing, I looked at Masood and saw that his eyes were darting about to left and right like two mice that have lost their way home.

14 "You're still fifty pounds¹² in debt to me,"

_____

12. **fifty pounds:** a fair amount of money at the time the story takes place. The pound is the chief monetary unit of Sudan.

said my grandfather to Masood. "We'll talk about it later."

Hussein called his assistants and they brought along donkeys, the two strangers produced camels, and the sacks of dates were 15 loaded on to them. One of the donkeys let out a braying which set the camels frothing at the mouth and complaining noisily. I felt myself drawing close to Masood, felt my hand stretch out towards him as though I wanted to touch the hem of his garment. I heard him make a noise in his throat like the rasping of a lamb being slaughtered. For some unknown reason, I experienced a sharp sensation of pain in my chest.

I ran off into the distance. Hearing my grandfather call after me, I hesitated a little, then continued on my way. I felt at that moment that I hated him. Quickening my pace, it was as though I carried within me a secret I wanted to rid myself of. I reached the river bank near the bend it made behind the wood of acacia trees. 16 Then, without knowing why, I put my finger into my throat and spewed up the dates I'd eaten.

A Handful of Dates **81**

PAGE SUMMARY: AT A GLANCE

- As the men inspect Masood's dates, the grandfather hands the narrator a fistful, which he begins munching.
- The men divide Masood's dates between them, and the grandfather reminds Masood that Masood still owes him fifty pounds.
- The narrator feels closer to Masood and feels a strange pain in his chest.
- He runs to the river, puts his finger in his mouth, and spews up the dates he ate.

IN THE GLOSSARY

- spewed: vomited

13 **TEACHING POINT OF VIEW**

Note that the youthful narrator does not understand the reason behind the actions he reports. Have students find in the next paragraphs instances in which the narrator expresses uncertainty of his *own* motives. ("For some unknown reason" in the next-to-last paragraph and "without knowing why" in the last sentence)

14 **CRITICAL THINKING: EVALUATION**

Have students evaluate the grandfather's treatment of Masood here and earlier.

15 **GRAMMAR IN LITERATURE**

Note the author's frequent use of gerunds to name activities— "braying," "frothing," and "complaining." Have students cite an example from below. ("rasping")

16 **TEACHING SYMBOLS**

Elicit the idea that the dates symbolize the grandfather's acquisitiveness and his harsh treatment of Masood.

COLLABORATIVE LEARNING: ENRICHMENT ACTIVITY

Social Studies Have a group of students prepare an oral report on the Nile River. Each student should research and report on a different aspect of the river: geography, exploration, economic importance, religious importance, role in music and art, and so on. Have the students use visual aids in their presentations.

CRITICAL THINKING: GUIDED READING QUESTIONS

LITERAL

1a. How does the narrator feel, momentarily, about his grandfather in the final paragraph? (He hates him.)

2a. What does the narrator do with the handful of dates his grandfather gave him to eat? (He sticks his finger down his throat and spews them out.)

INFERENTIAL

1b. Why does the narrator feel this way? (His grandfather has brought great pain to Masood, whom the narrator likes.)

2b. What is suggested by the narrator's not knowing why he does this? (His rejection of his grandfather's harshness is based on his feelings, not on reasoning.)

Were you as sympathetic to Masood as the narrator was? Why or why not?

STUDY QUESTIONS

1. He loves the mosque, the Nile, giving rein to his imagination, and his grandfather.
2. He got it from Masood and expects to get the rest of Masood's land. The narrator remembers Masood's singing and laughter.
3. They and two strangers divide Masood's dates. The grandfather reminds Masood that Masood owes him fifty pounds.
4. He spews them up.
5. In rejecting the dates, he rejects the means by which the grandfather acquired them.
6. He goes from idolizing him to hating him momentarily and considering him unmerciful and wrong. The grandfather's acquisitiveness and harsh treatment of Masood causes the change.
7. He is warmhearted and romantic but careless in practical matters; he, too, suffers from the harsh treatment of others.
8. That the grandfather is moved by the narrator's recitations but shows little mercy in his business dealings stresses his hypocrisy.
9. Answers will vary. Students may mention firmness, leadership, cleverness, and acquisitiveness; some of these may conflict with compassion.

LITERARY FOCUS

1. Instances include the opening and closing of the second paragraph, his thoughts about the heart of the palm, and the remark about hating his grandfather in the last paragraph. Readers would miss the narrator's growing awareness of his grandfather's imperfections and of life's harsh realities.
2. No, he is too involved with them emotionally; moreover, a child would likely exaggerate people's flaws and virtues.

STUDY QUESTIONS

Recalling

1. According to the story's opening, what four things does the narrator love as a young boy?
2. What does the grandfather explain about the land he now owns and his plans for the future? What does the narrator remember about Masood then?
3. What do the grandfather, Mousa, and Hussein do after Masood's dates are harvested? About what does the grandfather remind Masood?
4. In the last paragraph, what does the narrator do with the dates his grandfather gave him?

Interpreting

5. Explain the significance of the narrator's actions in the final paragraph.
6. What change occurs in the narrator's opinion of his grandfather? What causes the change?
7. What qualities make Masood a good person but a bad businessman? In what way might Masood's remarks about the heart of the palm apply to his own experiences in the story?
8. Why is it significant that at the start of the story the narrator often recites from the Koran, especially from the Chapter of the Merciful, to his grandfather and others?

Extending

9. What qualities make someone a good businessman or businesswoman? Can a person who is good at business also be compassionate? Explain.

LITERARY FOCUS

First-Person Point of View

Point of view is the relationship between the storyteller, or *narrator,* and the story. In a story told from the **first-person point of view,** the narrator is one of the characters and refers to himself or herself with the first-person pronoun *I.* The first-person narrator relates events in which he or she was involved and may also tell readers his or her most private thoughts and feelings. Because the narrator is so close to the action and so intimate with readers, the first-person point of view can seem especially vivid and authentic. On the other hand, because the first-person narrator can report only what he or she thinks and experiences and is often emotionally involved in story events, we cannot get an objective picture of other characters.

Thinking About First-Person Point of View

1. Describe three instances in which the first-person narrator of "A Handful of Dates" reveals his thoughts and feelings to readers. What changes in the boy would readers miss if the story were told from another character's point of view?
2. Is it likely that the narrator gives an objective picture of his grandfather and Masood? Explain.

COMPOSITION

Writing About a First-Person Narrator

■ Write a brief composition about the narrator of "A Handful of Dates" and the changes he undergoes. Begin with a general statement about the type of change the narrator experiences. Next discuss the narrator's specific attitudes and behavior at the start of the story. Then trace the narrator's experiences and his feelings about them, and show how these experiences and feelings lead to his change in attitude and behavior by the story's end.

Rewriting from Another Point of View

■ Retell the story of "A Handful of Dates" from the point of view of the grandfather. Describe events and other characters as the grandfather would see them, and refer to yourself with the first-person pronoun *I.*

COMPOSITION: GUIDELINES FOR EVALUATION

WRITING ABOUT A FIRST-PERSON NARRATOR

Objective

To write about a story's first-person narrator

Guidelines for Evaluation

■ suggested length: two or three paragraphs
■ should describe the narrator at the start
■ should trace the narrator's experiences and changes in attitude and behavior

REWRITING FROM ANOTHER POINT OF VIEW

Objective

To rewrite a story from another point of view

Guidelines for Evaluation

■ suggested length: four to six pages
■ should be told in the first person by the grandfather
■ should include events and details from the story

PREVIEW: THE AUTHOR AND THE WORLD

N. V. M. Gonzalez
(born 1915)

Philippines

Nestor Vicente Madali Gonzalez has received virtually every major writing award in his native country, the Philippines. Born on the small Philippine island of Romblon, Gonzalez attended English-language schools at home and later studied at several American universities.

He began his literary career as a staff writer for Manila's *Graphic Weekly* and later worked as editor of the *Manila Evening News Magazine.* After winning fame with his first novel, *The Winds of April,* Gonzalez became an assistant professor at the University of the Philippines and later received Rockefeller grants to study and travel in the United States and the Far East.

Gonzalez's continued literary output has been honored in his own country, earning him literary prizes such as the Republic Cultural Heritage Award and the 1964 *Philippine Free Press* prize for the year's best short story. Almost all of his fiction is set in the Philippines, but his characters make the same voyages of self-discovery that people make everywhere.

GEOGRAPHY AND CULTURE

The Philippine Islands

Located in the western Pacific Ocean east of continental Southeast Asia, the Philippines is a nation of eleven large islands and several thousand smaller ones. Together the islands form an *archipelago,* or island chain, that stretches more than a thousand miles from north to south. The inhabitants—called *Filipinos*—descend from various Asian peoples and speak several native languages. The official and most widely used language is Pilipino, which is based on a native language called Tagalog. In addition, since the Philippine Islands are former possessions of Spain and the United States, both Spanish and English are spoken there. N. V. M. Gonzalez writes in English.

The largest Philippine island and one of the northernmost is Luzon. Much of the Philippine population is concentrated in Luzon, and the nation's capital, Manila, is located there. Some fifty miles south of Manila is the port city of Batangas. Ferries to and from Batangas link Luzon to the island of Mindoro, just across the bay to the south. The characters in "On the Ferry" are making the crossing from Batangas to Calapan, a port city in northern Mindoro.

On the Ferry **83**

LESSON PREVIEW

In this contemporary Filipino story a father learns to let his teen-age son face life on his own. Mr. Lopez is traveling home with his son Nilo, who must leave college for financial reasons. Passing an abandoned, sinking boat helps Mr. Lopez realize he can no longer shelter his son from harsh realities.

LITERARY SKILLS FOR THIS SELECTION

- point of view
- characterization

THEMES IN THIS SELECTION

- growing up: parents and children
- facing harsh realities

LESSON OBJECTIVES

1. to examine the limited third-person point of view
2. to understand words from Malayo-Polynesian languages
3. to interpret a quotation

Teacher's Classroom Resources 1

- Teaching Notes — 151
- Prereading Vocabulary — 152
- Reading Guide — 153
- Check Test — 154
- Responding to World Cultures — 155
- Literary Focus: Limited Third-Person Point of View — 156
- Language Study: Words from Malayo-Polynesian Languages — 157
- Writing Process Guide: Writing About a Quotation — 158
- Grammar in Literature: Using the Past Perfect Tense — 159
- Selection Test — 160

IN THE CLASSROOM

TEACHING STUDENTS OF DIFFERENT ABILITIES

- **For less advanced students:** Have students explain what Mr. Lopez realizes during the crossing. Have them complete the Reading Guide for this selection.

- **For more advanced students:** Have students compare the parent-child relationship in this story with that of another story, such as "You Need to Go Upstairs," "The Father," or "The Kabuliwallah."

DISCUSSING GEOGRAPHY AND CULTURE

Exploring an Uninhabited Island

There are more than 7,000 islands in the Philippines. Fewer than half of them have names, and only 350 of them have an area greater than one square mile. Most are coral or volcanic rock.

- Ask students to imagine that they have claimed one of the unnamed islands in the Philippines. What would they name it? What sort of structures would they build? How would they spend their time on it?

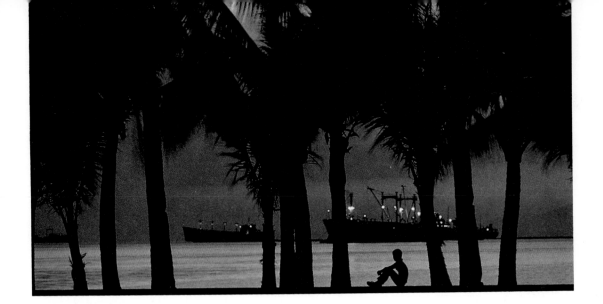

N. V. M. Gonzalez

On the Ferry

During the entire two and a half hour ride from Manila to Batangas[1] they had suffered enough. No seats had been available except those over at the rear, which was the part of the bus called Hollywood. It used to be known as the Kitchen; and, to say the least, it was hardly comfortable there. But some things just couldn't be helped—like getting to the bus station late, or being unable to raise enough money to keep your son in school. You had to accept all that— well, like Hollywood.

Except for the bus seats, Mr. Lopez had run through these things before. Now in the comparative comfort of the ferry, he could run through them again. But he didn't care to; and,

hoping he could cast them out of his mind, he turned to Nilo.

"Have you checked our luggage?"

The thin bespectacled boy who sat on the wooden bench beside him replied: "Yes, Pa."

"Check again," Mr. Lopez said.

The boy got up and peeked under his seat where the *cargador*[2] had pushed in an old suitcase, two boxes of books and magazines, and two grocery paperbags.

It was almost sailing time. During the quarter of an hour they had been on board—"Pa, let's avoid the rush," Nilo had said—a steady stream of people had, like them, arrived on passenger trucks that had raced like huge red beetles through the dust from Manila. Mr. Lopez and his son had taken one of the starboard[3] benches,

---

1. **Manila . . . Batangas:** two cities on the Philippine island of Luzon, which is the largest island in the Philippines. Manila is the capital of the Philippines; Batangas, a port city south of Manila, is the capital of the province of Batangas. (See the Geography and Culture feature that precedes the story.)

2. *cargador* [kär gä dôr′]: Spanish for stevedore, or longshoreman, the person who loads or stores cargo on a ship.
3. **starboard** [stär′bərd]: referring to the right side of the ship as one faces forward.

84 *The Short Story*

hoping they could have it all to themselves, but, presently, a big party—three elderly ladies and two young girls—occupied the other end of the bench. Tangerine-shirted *cargadores* followed after them, piling up baskets of fruit, suitcases, and grocery paperbags, too, before them and then shoving these under the seat. One of the ladies sat beside Nilo, while the two others at the far end of the bench let the two young girls sit between them. The latter were plain-looking and dressed in the uniform of St. Bridget's College and were perhaps spending the weekend with relations at Calapan.[4]

Mr. Lopez, who had been assistant district engineer in his day, hoped he would not meet any acquaintances from Calapan. That he did not know who the women were pleased him. He was afraid he would only embarrass himself in the presence of former associates in the government service, or even with business friends. Lopez & Co., Builders, had won many a public works bid in its time, had constructed bridges and river control projects all over Mindoro. But what people would remember, Mr. Lopez feared, was the Badjao Dam. If foreign-owned timber concessions had not denuded, through indiscriminate cutting, the once heavily forested hills around Mt. Halcon,[5] nobody would instantly see where the Dam came in. The fact was that the big flood of December 1956 had washed it away. Contracts had since then been difficult to come by.

The *cargadores* had stopped running up and down the deck. A shudder shook the ferry, accompanied by shouts from the pier, where the red buses were backing out in a steady grinding whirr. And then, finally, there was the whistle; and the boat put out toward the open sea.

It was a clear day, unusual for early July. Although Mr. Lopez had made this trip many times before, it had never quite ceased to fascinate him. Today Batangas receded slowly in the mid-morning sun, with the dome of the old church and that of the provincial capitol flashing like twin gems of a pendant in its original box of green suede that you had snapped open.

As the ferry turned toward the Mindoro coast, the view from Mr. Lopez' side of the deck was obstructed by gray canvas awnings rudely flapping in the breeze. He found himself, shortly, crossing over and leaning from the larboard[6] rail. Hardly eighteen years ago, as a young engineer, he had married a girl from St. Bridget's, and it was on a ferry such as this one that the two of them had crossed over to Mindoro. He could not remember, though, whether the two of them had stood at the railings together, their future literally before them, and let some fragment of the Batangas skyline share, too, in their daydreaming.

Nilo had remained on the bench and had pulled out a magazine from somewhere. The bookworm, Mr. Lopez thought, as he returned to his seat, picking his way through the scattered baggages along the deck. The boy had his mother's forehead and chin; he was delicately built. The eyeglasses added two or three years to his sixteen, but he was very much a boy still. A year away from school—and hoping his luck improved, Mr. Lopez told himself—Nilo would be ready for the heavier work of a sophomore engineering student. A sudden recollection of the boy's letters the year before, in which he had described how he had scrimped on food, sometimes limiting himself to a bottle of coke for breakfast, touched in Mr. Lopez something tender and deep. The appalling fact that Lopez & Co., Builders, had been an utter failure moved him to pity for the boy, for this full year he would lose, for his having gotten himself a bankrupt father.

---

4. **Calapan** [kä lä pän′]: Philippine city on the island of Mindoro, just across the bay from Luzon.
5. **Mt. Halcon:** mountain near Calapan.

---

6. **larboard:** referring to the left side of the ship as one faces forward.

On the Ferry **85**

- Three older women and two girls in school uniforms sit on the same bench as Mr. Lopez and Nilo.
- Mr. Lopez hopes he will not meet anyone from Calapan who might remember the dam, engineered by his company, that washed away in a flood.
- He recalls the ferry ride he took eighteen years ago with his bride.
- He regrets that Nilo, a delicately built boy, scrimped on food at school and now must leave school for a year because of his father's bankruptcy.

IN THE GLOSSARY

- denuded: stripped bare
- indiscriminate: random

3 TEACHING STUDENTS OF LIMITED ENGLISH PROFICIENCY

Students may have trouble with compound adjectives before a noun, a construction that is rare in other languages. Help them decipher this phrase as "*cargadores* in shirts of tangerine." Since *cargadores* is a Spanish word, you might ask any Spanish speakers how they would say the entire phrase in Spanish.

4 CULTURAL BACKGROUND

Point out that most Filipinos are Roman Catholics and that St. Bridget's College is a Catholic secondary school.

5 READING SKILL: INFERENCE

Elicit the fact that Lopez & Co. is Mr. Lopez's business. Then help students infer what Mr. Lopez feels was the cause of the dam's failure. (Indiscriminate logging denuded the forests and helped cause a terrible flood that swept the dam away.)

6 TEACHING CHARACTERIZATION

Ask what this physical description suggests about Mr. Lopez's overall view of his son. (Nilo is delicate and needs protection.)

7 READING SKILL: CAUSE AND EFFECT

Ask students what seems to have caused the company's bankruptcy. (the failure of the dam)

CRITICAL THINKING: GUIDED READING QUESTIONS

LITERAL

1a. Why will it embarrass Mr. Lopez to meet acquaintances from Calapan? (They will remember that his company built the dam near Calapan that washed away.)

2a. At school that year what was Nilo's diet like? (He had to scrimp on food.)

INFERENTIAL

1b. What does this detail stress about Mr. Lopez's attitudes toward unpleasant situations? (He prefers to avoid unpleasantness instead of facing it.)

2b. Why did Nilo have to scrimp on food? (He had little money because his father's business went bankrupt.)

- After the two girls lend Nilo a magazine, Mr. Lopez cannot avoid introductions.
- He is surprised by the well-informed conversation of the girls' three aunts.
- He sends Nilo to buy everyone soda and watches Nilo count his meager pocket change.
- The ladies converse about engineering, which Nilo has been studying at school.

IN THE GLOSSARY

- **chided:** criticized
- **heartening:** encouraging
- **surmised:** guessed
- **apposite:** appropriate

8 TEACHING IRONY

Point out the irony of the topic of the article: It is about the engineer of a very successful building project, while Mr. Lopez is a failed engineer whose dam collapsed. Ask what Mr. Lopez must feel as he hears Goethals discussed. (He must feel embarrassment.)

9 TEACHING POINT OF VIEW

Note that in this limited third-person narrative, we are given only Mr. Lopez's impressions of the other characters.

10 READING SKILL: INFERENCE

Ask who *is* embarrassed by Nilo's lack of pocket money. (his father)

11 CULTURAL BACKGROUND

Point out that Spanish words, part of the legacy of Spanish rule, permeate Filipino culture. *Peso* is a Spanish word that originally meant "weight." Characters' surnames also show the influence of Spanish.

12 TEACHING CHARACTERIZATION

Elicit the idea that this remark reveals Mr. Lopez's paternal pride in Nilo's scholastic achievements.

But Mr. Lopez caught himself, as it were, and, remarking on the magazine that Nilo was reading, he said: "Must be interesting!" He tried to sound cheerful. "What's it? A *Reader's Digest*?"

"It's theirs," Nilo said, pointing to the two St. Bridget girls. He had turned the pages up and Mr. Lopez read the title of the article that the young fellow had been reading: "My Most Unforgettable Character."

"Who's it about?" he said.

8 "Go-e-thals," Nilo said. "He built the Panama Canal." He turned to the two girls and asked: "Isn't that how you pronounce it?"

"Go-thals!" the girls corrected him.

They were surprisingly not shy, and there was no avoiding introductions now. Mr. Lopez chided his son lightly: "Keeping your friends all to yourself, eh?"

The two young ones were Mary and Rose. The three elderly ladies were aunts of theirs, and the amazing thing was that they were all Miss Adevas and elementary school teachers.

"Ah," said one Miss Adeva, "What they demand of us nowadays that science's very much in the air!"

"But we have no vocabulary for science in the National Language," the second Miss Adeva protested. She was obviously a Tagalog teacher.[7]

"Hmm, isn't it true that you have to be good these days in math?" asked the third Miss Adeva, the most innocent of the three apparently.

"I don't know much about these things," Mr. Lopez demurred. "I'm only a business man now."

"You're being very modest, Engineer," said the first Miss Adeva.

9 The three ladies were a complete surprise. Judging by their appearance, Mr. Lopez could not have guessed they were abreast with the times and were troubled in their own way by some idea of progress. It was all very heartening.

"Look, Nilo," Mr. Lopez said to his son, "there's a canteen at the other end of the boat. Why don't you run over and get some cokes?"

The ladies begged him not to bother. The second Miss Adeva tugged motherly at Nilo's sleeve, urging the boy not to leave his seat.

Meanwhile, Nilo had returned the magazine to the girl called Rose; and, pushing his eyeglasses up the bridge of his nose, he stood up **10** and got out the coins in his pocket. He counted them unembarrassedly, the two St. Bridget girls unable to hide their amusement.

"You have enough money there, haven't **11** you?" Mr. Lopez asked, as if ready to offer Nilo a peso[8] of his own.

"It's all right, Pa," the boy said.

"He's such a kid, really," said Mr. Lopez after Nilo had left them. "You go wrong these days, though, if you leave boys too much pocket money."

"There's a wise father," said the first Miss Adeva.

To merit the remark, Mr. Lopez told the ladies what he surmised they needed to know about Nilo. He was an engineering student at **12** U.P.[9] "The highest standards, you know," he couldn't help adding.

On discovering that the ladies were very enthusiastic about engineering and that the profession was in their view getting deservedly popular, Mr. Lopez realized he had to say something similarly apposite.

"A wise choice for Nilo," the second Miss Adeva was saying.

"It used to be the law," the third Miss Adeva said with conviction.

"Oh, you school people," Mr. Lopez said, still casting about, "—well, you've certainly begun to produce a new type of student these days!"

---

7. **Tagalog** [tä gä′ləg] **teacher:** teacher who conducts classes in the chief native language of the Philippines, where English-language classes are also common.

8. **peso:** chief monetary unit of the Philippines.

9. **U.P.:** short for University of the Philippines, which is located just outside Manila.

CRITICAL THINKING: GUIDED READING QUESTIONS

LITERAL

1a. What does Mr. Lopez find "heartening" about the Misses Adeva? (They are abreast of the times and "troubled in their own way by some idea of progress.")

2a. What topic do the ladies discuss after learning what Nilo has been studying at school? (engineering)

INFERENTIAL

1b. Why would Mr. Lopez be heartened by the ladies' being "troubled . . . by some idea of progress"? ("Progress" led to the denuded forests that caused the flood that swept away his company's dam.)

2b. Why is this topic awkward for Mr. Lopez? (He would be embarrassed if the ladies learned that his engineering firm had built the failed dam and is now bankrupt.)

"Thank you, thank you," the second Miss Adeva said, flattered by the remark.

13 The third Miss Adeva declared that times had changed; for one thing, education had become too costly.

"Don't I know," said Mr. Lopez. This was a subject about which he had a direct and personal knowledge. "And I with only one college student in the family. . . ."

"How many do you expect to have?" the second Miss Adeva asked. "Don't tell us, if it will embarrass you. . . ."

"It's nothing to be secretive about, let me assure you, ladies," Mr. Lopez said. "I've three boys, and a little daughter. . . ."

"That's all?" said the third Miss Adeva skeptically.

Mr. Lopez whispered something to her. Lest the two others feel left out, he said: "What I said was merely that Mrs. Lopez is in the family way."

14 He was surprised on hearing his own words. One more moment and he could have told the ladies the whole story of his life. But he checked himself from this excess of familiarity, judiciously limiting himself to his son's student career.

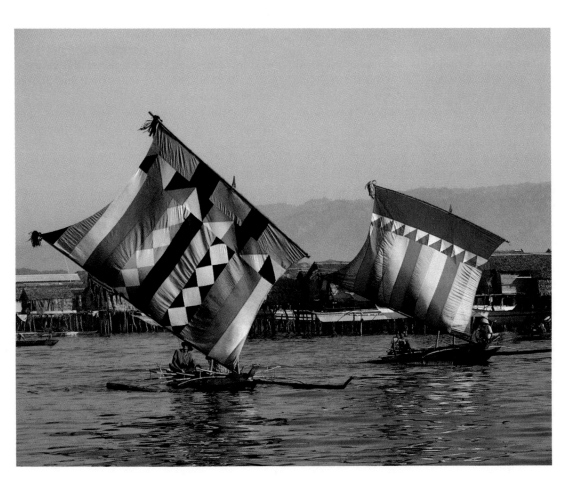

On the Ferry **87**

PAGE SUMMARY: AT A GLANCE

■ The third Miss Adeva observes that education has become too costly, a remark that really strikes home for Mr. Lopez.

■ Inspired by a sympathetic audience, Mr. Lopez finds himself telling intimate details of his life, but then he checks himself and draws back.

13 CRITICAL THINKING: CLASSIFICATION

Have students list the characters' observations about Filipino life and then decide which of them also apply to American life today and which do not. For example, is the cost of education also a problem in America today?

14 TEACHING CHARACTERIZATION

Point out that throughout this scene Mr. Lopez has difficulty conversing with the Misses Adeva despite his appreciation of their intelligence and sympathy. This awkwardness stresses his general awkwardness with society and his desire to avoid anything unpleasant or embarrassing.

CRITICAL THINKING: GUIDED READING QUESTIONS

LITERAL

1a. What does the third Miss Adeva say about education? (It has become too costly.)

INFERENTIAL

1b. Why is her remark ironic? (Although she does not know it, Mr. Lopez has had to take Nilo out of college for a year because he could not afford the tuition.)

- The Misses Adeva are sympathetic when Mr. Lopez tells them about Nilo's delicate health.
- When they assume Nilo left college for health reasons, Mr. Lopez does not correct them.
- Nilo and the girls blush when the topic of age comes up, and we learn that Nilo will soon be sixteen and that the girls, who are twins, are also sixteen.
- When the ferry runs into rough waters, only Nilo becomes seasick, and the first Miss Adeva is especially solicitous for his condition.

IN THE GLOSSARY

- precariously: uncertainly
- dormant: sleeping or inactive

15 READING SKILL: INFERENCE

Ask students why they think Mr. Lopez may have discussed Nilo's health when he went to see the dean. (He probably used Nilo's health as an excuse for removing Nilo from school instead of revealing the embarrassing facts about his bankruptcy.)

16 GRAMMAR IN LITERATURE

Point out the author's use of a semicolon to connect two closely related groups of clauses. Have students find another example in the next column. ("He ought never . . . they said.")

17 TEACHING SYMBOLS

Note that the rough waters are a symbol of the rough times Nilo and his father are experiencing and that the entire ferry ride is a symbolic journey for both of them.

18 TEACHING CHARACTERIZATION

Elicit the insight that this detail stresses the first Miss Adeva's sympathetic attitude, an attitude all three sisters have displayed.

"He's his mother's favorite," Mr. Lopez said. He told them about Nilo's health, which had always been delicate; and he described his interview with the dean of the engineering college, who had given him a cigar and remarked: "Health's wealth, as well we know, Mr. Lopez," clapping him on the shoulder.

The ladies warmed up to the new subject. They were certain that living conditions in Manila were not particularly wholesome for young people. They complained about the dust and the noise, the crowded boarding houses, and jam-packed movies. All these must have contributed to Nilo's poor health, they decided. To which Mr. Lopez wholeheartedly agreed.

"But where else can we send our boys these days?" he added, in the tone of one used to generous doses of compassion.

The question made the ladies sad. The first Miss Adeva, in particular, flicked her long eyelids. "In any case," she said, "a boy such as yours—why, Mr. Lopez, you really ought not to work him too hard."

"That's what his mother always says," Mr. Lopez replied.

"And you must watch out," warned the second Miss Adeva. "Boys his age easily get pleurisy[10] or something like that. I had a nephew, you know . . ."

And they were discussing the luckless nephew when Nilo returned with seven bottles of coke clasped together precariously, with straws already stuck into them. The deck heaved under his feet; the bench slid forward. It was all he could do to deliver the bottles safely.

As the ladies sipped their cokes quietly Mr. Lopez revealed that Nilo's mother had studied at St. Bridget's. But while this proved to be interesting in itself, especially to the two young ones, Mary and Rose—who asked Mr. Lopez: "Did Mrs. Lopez wear a different uniform from ours?"—

---

10. **pleurisy** [ploor'ə sē]: an ailment characterized by inflammation of the lungs.

88 *The Short Story*

---

the Adeva ladies returned to the problem of Nilo's health, expressing their great concern unequivocally. It was as if Nilo's return from the ship's canteen with the bottles of coke awoke in them feelings that had long been dormant. He ought never to prefer his studies to his health; no, Nilo shouldn't, they said. The college was right in sending him home for awhile. The first Miss Adeva said, addressing Nilo directly:

"You're only sixteen, as your father says . . ."

It was neither a question nor a statement of fact—to judge from the tone this Miss Adeva used. Before the boy, who looked puzzled, could say something for himself, Mr. Lopez clarified the issue of his son's age: "Next September, to be exact."

Now Nilo was blushing from being made too much of, and perhaps because Mary and Rose were blushing, too. Still on the matter of ages, the first Miss Adeva revealed that her nieces were also sixteen, both of them.

"They're twins, you see," she said, as if to explain whatever it was that might be thought of as inexplicable about youth.

The ferry was running into some rough sea, which meant they had reached the middle of Verde Island Passage. For a good half hour until the ferry came directly in the shelter of the island, it ran into the three-foot waves which occasionally caused the benches to slip again or tilt back against the railings. The Adevas were wonderful sailors, so used as they were to crossing the Passage. It was Nilo who looked every inch the poor sailor. Attentively, the first Miss Adeva, who had taken it upon herself to look after him, bade the seasick boy rest his head on the bench, giving him all the room he needed.

"He'll be all right," Mr. Lopez said. "Don't be bothered by him."

"In fifteen years or so—oh, who knows?—" said the second Miss Adeva, dreamily, "there'll be a tunnel through here. We'll all be going by train."

"That's one reason we'll be needing more

CRITICAL THINKING: GUIDED READING QUESTIONS

LITERAL

1a. What does Mr. Lopez tell the Misses Adeva about Nilo's health? (It has always been delicate.)

2a. What does the Misses Adeva assume is the reason Nilo left school? (He was sent home for health reasons.)

INFERENTIAL

1b. What does this detail stress about Mr. Lopez's attitude toward his son? (He has always been very protective of Nilo.)

2b. Why does neither Mr. Lopez nor Nilo correct their assumption? (Mr. Lopez is ashamed to admit his financial problems and the events that led to them, and Nilo is apparently unaware of the real reason he has been forced to leave school.)

engineers," the third Miss Adeva said.

19 Now Nilo raised his head off the back of the bench, as if surprised to hear someone speak so confidently about the future. The sea had become smooth again. The sound of water like falling rain ran through the length of the ferry. It was a school of tuna, Mr. Lopez saw, caught unawares in the path of the prow. An island, one of the three that girded Calapan harbor, swung forward, and the twins cried out: "A boat!"

Mr. Lopez turned quickly to landward, and there it was: a five-ton *lanchon,* or one-masted sailboat, listing precipitously in the sheltered cove where the small island rose from a sheet of white sand into thick underbrush fringed with coconuts.

The Adevas were excited and exchanged all sorts of conjectures, their breaths quivering. One said a leak had sprung, causing the boat to list; another said that it sat on a rock right there. The third Miss Adeva averred she could see no **20** signs of a crew. The *lanchon* had been mysteriously abandoned. Mr. Lopez wished that the ferry had come closer, although he knew it would be something of an impertinence, especially as he himself could see no signs of a crew.

Nilo remarked just about this time that the ladies had said all they had to say: "It seems, Pa," he spoke solemnly—"I can actually see it sinking!"

Mary and Rose sighed. They agreed with Nilo, and watched breathlessly, clutching each other on the arm.

"Pa, isn't it sinking? Inch by inch!" Nilo said, almost begging to be believed.

"Why, that's right! Of course, it's sinking!" the three Adevas exclaimed, dramatically.

"And nobody's doing anything about it!" Nilo seemed terror-stricken. "What could have happened, Pa?"

What could he say? He could not explain this if he tried. His mind turned to Nilo, to the note of insistence in the boy's words, to the claim that he must be believed, and the little dere-**21** lict[11] explained away. But Mr. Lopez had no explanation to make here any more than for all he had made up to conceal having failed him. He knew he could not lie to him or about him any more. The time must come when he could protect him no more with excuses and fabrications. How far could he go? He would run short of college deans and cigars and Panama Canals, and the little half-truths you said about them that made each day pass sufferably. You could fashion make-believe to order; but, oh, not life, complete with its mystery and loneliness. And he had other sons to see through, to say nothing of the young girl now in grade school. A sixth lay as yet unidentifiable deep in its mother's womb, but one thing was certain: with all six of them to look after, you could grow hardened enough. And once you've developed the callousness, how dreadful it would be, Mr. Lopez thought. Thank God, he could see that.

The ferry was cutting through the channel beyond the tip of the island now: he could see that, too. The green underbrush, the white beach, the derelict itself—was it the mast that you could see above the water?—all these slipped away, and the Calapan pier emerged. The iron roofing of the buildings on the shore were garishly white in the sunshine, against the palms on the shoulder of the hill. For a moment Mr. Lopez watched his son Nilo, who stood with his two new friends, their hands on the railings, their eyes shining. A sudden beauty to his being father to this boy possessed him; and he felt that his own eyes were shining, too. The deck began to sway under him—the waves were getting just a bit frisky again—and he sat steady on the **22** wooden bench, aware of something hard gathering at the core of his being.

"No, not yet," he prayed silently, frightened by perhaps the same terror that had seized Nilo before.

But he felt it was already there.

———————
11. **derelict:** here, a boat that has been abandoned at sea.

On the Ferry **89**

CRITICAL THINKING: GUIDED READING QUESTIONS

LITERAL

1a. What two things does Mr. Lopez realize he cannot explain to Nilo about the abandoned boat? (the boat's situation and everything he has made up to conceal "having failed" Nilo)

2a. As he sits on the wooden bench, what is Mr. Lopez aware of? (He is aware of something hard gathering at the core of his being.)

INFERENTIAL

1b. What has Mr. Lopez made up to conceal "having failed" Nilo? (He has fabricated excuses to mask the real reason Nilo had to leave school.)

2b. What does Mr. Lopez realize he must do? What prompts this realization? (He must stop protecting Nilo from harsh realities. His inability to explain the boat and the conversation in which he evaded truths prompt this realization.)

---

19 READING SKILL: INFERENCE

Ask why Nilo might find others' confidence in the future surprising. (He himself probably has felt little confidence since he was forced to leave school.)

20 TEACHING SYMBOLS

Note that the abandoned boat symbolizes several things: the individual nature and mystery of human experience, on which it is an "impertinence" to intrude; life's harsh realities, from which Mr. Lopez realizes he can no longer protect Nilo; and Nilo and Mr. Lopez, who in a sense must abandon each other.

21 TEACHING THEME

Elicit the idea that Mr. Lopez's realizations are experiences that all parents have when their children reach maturity.

22 TEACHING DYNAMIC CHARACTERS

Point out that Mr. Lopez is a dynamic character who changes and grows in the story.

COLLABORATIVE LEARNING: ENRICHMENT ACTIVITY

Social Studies Have a group of students prepare a written report on the Philippines, with each student contributing a different section—on geography, peoples, education, economy, the arts, and so on.

Mr. Lopez feels that he has failed his son. Do you agree?

ANSWERS

STUDY QUESTIONS

1. His company built a dam near there that washed away.
2. Mr. Lopez went bankrupt and cannot afford to keep Nilo in school; the memory of Nilo's scrimping on food at school
3. Nilo's health; they blame conditions at school
4. why a boat is sinking and abandoned; the time when he can no longer protect Nilo.
5. He feels sad and ashamed.
6. He must let Nilo face life on his own. He is thinking of the toughness he must project to stop protecting his son.
7. Their sympathy and his evasions show him that he must not avoid painful truths.
8. harsh realities and mysteries, individuality, and "abandoning" offspring; Mr. Lopez's discovery of the limits of parental protection or Nilo's passage into adulthood
9. Answers will vary. Students may feel parents need to be less protective.

LITERARY FOCUS

Mr. Lopez's; He may have chosen the limited third-person point of view to convey a distance from the other characters, perhaps in keeping with the theme of parents distancing themselves from children.

LANGUAGE STUDY

1. "backwoods"; from Tagalog *bundok,* "mountain"
2. "dyed, usually striped or checked cotton cloth"; from Malay *ginggang,* "striped"
3. "tailless New Zealand bird or subtropical fruit"; from a Maori name imitating the bird's cry
4. "tree-dwelling ape of Borneo and Sumatra"; from Malay *orang utan,* "man of the forest"
5. "sheathlike garment"; from Malay *sarung,* "sheath"
6. "religious or social restriction"; from Polynesian (Tongan) *tabu,* "sacred; set apart"
7. "mark from inserting colored pigment in skin"; from Polynesian (Tahitian) *tatau*
8. "small, guitarlike instrument"; from Hawaiian *ukulele,* "insect jumping," derived from the movement of fingers

STUDY QUESTIONS

Recalling

1. Why does Mr. Lopez hope not to be recognized by anyone from Calapan?
2. Why is Nilo going to lose a year in school? What memory touches something "tender and deep" in Mr. Lopez?
3. What new subject does Mr. Lopez discuss with the Misses Adevas after nearly telling the whole story of his life? What do the women blame for Nilo's condition?
4. As the ferry nears Calapan harbor, what does Nilo ask his father to explain? What time does Mr. Lopez recognize has come?

Interpreting

5. How does Mr. Lopez feel about his business failures and the way he has provided financially for his son?
6. Explain in your own words what Mr. Lopez eventually realizes about his relationship with his son. What does he mean by "something hard gathering at the core of his being"?
7. How might Mr. Lopez's experiences with the Misses Adevas help prompt his realizations at the end of the story?
8. What aspects of life might the abandoned boat represent? What inner journey might the ferry crossing represent?

Extending

9. Do you think parents really need to harden their tender feelings toward their children as the children get older? Explain.

LITERARY FOCUS

Limited Third-Person Point of View

Point of view is the relationship between the narrator and the story. In a story told from the **limited third-person point of view,** the narrator reveals the thoughts and feelings of only one story character but refers to that character with the third-person pronoun *he* or *she.* The narrator lets readers know everything this character thinks and feels—the same information we might know if the character were telling his or her own story. Nevertheless, because the narrator is not

personally involved in the story, the limited third-person point of view achieves a degree of detachment and objectivity that would not be possible if the character were telling his or her own story.

Thinking About Limited Third-Person Point of View

■ To which character's thoughts and feelings is the point of view limited in "On the Ferry"? Why do you think Gonzalez chose to use limited third-person point of view instead of having that character tell his own story in the first person?

LANGUAGE STUDY

Words from Malayo-Polynesian Languages

Tagalog, the Filipino native language mentioned in the story, is one of many Asian and Pacific languages that belong to the Malayo-Polynesian language family. This large family also includes Malay, a language spoken in Malaysia, Singapore, and parts of Indonesia; and Polynesian, a subfamily of very closely related languages that includes Hawaiian and Maori, a language spoken by some native inhabitants of New Zealand.

Use a dictionary to help you determine the meanings and origins of these English words, which all come from Malayo-Polynesian languages.

1. boondocks
2. gingham
3. kiwi
4. orangutan
5. sarong
6. taboo
7. tattoo
8. ukulele

COMPOSITION

Writing About a Quotation

■ Scholar Leonard Casper has suggested that Gonzalez's view of humanity has been shaped by the island geography of the Philippines, since Gonzalez sees every human being as "an island in an archipelago [island chain] of human striving." In a brief composition tell what you think the quotation means and explain how "On the Ferry" reflects this view of humanity. Discuss Mr. Lopez's relationship with other characters in the story, and consider other relevant story details—the abandoned boat, for example.

COMPOSITION: GUIDELINES FOR EVALUATION

WRITING ABOUT A QUOTATION

Objective

To interpret a quotation and apply it to a story

Guidelines for Evaluation

■ suggested length: two to three paragraphs
■ should interpret the quotation's implications about independence and isolation
■ should apply these ideas to the relationships of the characters and other details of the story

PREVIEW: THE AUTHOR AND THE WORLD

Sean O'Faolain

(born 1900)

Ireland

John Whelan took the Irish Gaelic form of his name, Sean O'Faolain, to show support for Ireland's political and cultural independence from Great Britain. His name is pronounced as [shôn′ ō fā′lin]. As a young man he participated in Ireland's struggle for independence; later he created vivid prose portraits of Irish life.

The son of a policeman, O'Faolain was raised in the town of Cork, where his first literary interests centered around the local theater. He attended college in Cork and later completed his studies at Harvard University in the United States. After graduation he taught literature in the United States, England, and Ireland until he began to make a name for himself as an author. His first popular success was his novel *A Nest of Simple Folk,* published in 1933.

Over the years O'Faolain produced additional novels, travel books, and biographies of famous Irish men and women, but he is best known for his short stories. These carefully crafted tales, usually set in an Irish landscape, deal with universal human concerns.

GEOGRAPHY AND CULTURE

Ireland and Its Countryside

The Republic of Ireland occupies the southern portion of an island located just west of Great Britain off the Atlantic coast of Europe. Ruled by Britain for centuries, the southern part of the island became a wholly independent nation in 1949. (The northern part of the island still belongs to the United Kingdom.) As part of the independence movement, the Irish people attempted to revive their native language, called Irish or Irish Gaelic, which the British government had tried to suppress in the past. Nevertheless, while Irish is taught in public schools, English remains the first language of most of Ireland's population. Sean O'Faolain studied Irish and experimented with it in some of his writings, but he wrote his best-known works in English.

Ireland is a rainy, largely rural island, so green that it is often called "The Emerald Isle." City dwellers often take holidays in the summer to visit scenic spots in the Irish countryside. As "The Trout" opens, a girl named Julia and her family arrive at a picturesque country spot that they have visited several times before.

The Trout **91**

LESSON PREVIEW

In this Irish tale a girl learns to accept responsibility. When twelve-year-old Julia finds a trout trapped in a well, she is not satisfied with the stories her mother invents to explain its presence to Julia's younger brother. Julia realizes that she must resolve the trout's problems herself.

LITERARY SKILLS FOR THIS SELECTION

- point of view
- atmosphere
- characterization

THEMES IN THIS SELECTION

- growing up: learning self-reliance
- childhood myths versus reality

LESSON OBJECTIVES

1. to understand words from Celtic languages
2. to evaluate an author's choice of point of view
3. to write a story using limited third-person point of view

Teacher's Classroom Resources 1

■ Teaching Notes	163
■ Prereading Vocabulary	164
■ Reading Guide	165
■ Check Test	166
■ Responding to World Cultures	167
■ Language Study: Words from Celtic Languages	168
■ Writing Process Guides: Writing About Point of View	169
Writing in Limited Third-Person Point of View	170
■ Grammar in Literature: Creating Coherence with Transition Words	171
■ Selection Test	172

IN THE CLASSROOM

TEACHING STUDENTS OF DIFFERENT ABILITIES

- **For less advanced students:** Review the Literary Focus on page 55, and ask students to consider Julia's motivation as they read "The Trout." Have them complete the Reading Guide for this selection.

- **For more advanced students:** Have students compare this story with other coming-of-age stories, films, or plays that they have read or seen.

DISCUSSING GEOGRAPHY AND CULTURE

Country Homes

This story takes place in a country retreat in Ireland. Irish country houses are usually one story high and made of stone; the roofs are thatched or tiled with slate. Many farmhouses in Ireland are being abandoned as poor families quit the countryside to search for work in the city.

- Have students describe farms and farmhouses in the United States.

PAGE SUMMARY: AT A GLANCE

- Twelve-year-old Julia likes running through the Dark Walk, a terrifying experience she now introduces to her younger brother, Stephen.
- She refuses to believe that there is a well in the walk until she sees it herself.
- In the well she finds a trapped trout, whose presence there puzzles everyone.
- Julia returns to view it and ponder the mystery in private.

IN THE GLOSSARY

- lofty: towering
- sinewy: powerful; strong
- squabbled: argued noisily
- shrouded: covered; concealed

1 TEACHING ATMOSPHERE

Elicit the insight that words such as *midnight* and *sinewy* help give the Dark Walk an eerie atmosphere.

2 TEACHING CHARACTERIZATION

Point out that Julia takes her brother to the Dark Walk because she likes scaring him as well as herself and that her behavior reveals a degree of immaturity.

3 TEACHING POINT OF VIEW

Note that the third-person limited narrator focuses on Julia's impressions but still maintains a distant, adult perspective.

4 CULTURAL BACKGROUND

Explain that larger Irish houses traditionally have kitchen gardens where vegetables are grown. Julia and her family are apparently visiting a country home where Martin works as a gardener.

5 TEACHING STUDENTS OF LIMITED ENGLISH PROFICIENCY

Students may need help in deciphering Martin's dialect, such as "divil a'" for "devil I."

Sean O'Faolain

The Trout

One of the first places Julia always ran to when they arrived in G—— was The Dark Walk. It is a laurel walk, very old, almost gone wild, a lofty midnight tunnel of smooth, sinewy branches. Underfoot the tough brown leaves are never dry enough to crackle: there is always a suggestion of damp and cool trickle.

She raced right into it. For the first few yards she always had the memory of the sun behind her, then she felt the dusk closing swiftly down on her so that she screamed with pleasure and raced on to reach the light at the far end; and it was always just a little too long in coming so that she emerged gasping, clasping her hands, laughing, drinking in the sun. When she was filled with the heat and glare she would turn and consider the ordeal again.

This year she had the extra joy of showing it to her small brother, and of terrifying him as well as herself. And for him the fear lasted longer because his legs were so short and she had gone out at the far end while he was still screaming and racing.

When they had done this many times they came back to the house to tell everybody that they had done it. He boasted. She mocked. They squabbled.

"Cry babby!"

"You were afraid yourself, so there!"

"I won't take you any more."

"You're a big pig."

"I hate you."

Tears were threatening, so somebody said, "Did you see the well?" She opened her eyes at that and held up her long lovely neck suspiciously and decided to be incredulous. She was twelve and at that age little girls are beginning to suspect most stories: they have already found

out too many, from Santa Claus to the stork. How could there be a well! In The Dark Walk? That she had visited year after year? Haughtily she said, "Nonsense."

But she went back, pretending to be going somewhere else, and she found a hole scooped in the rock at the side of the walk, choked with damp leaves, so shrouded by ferns that she uncovered it only after much searching. At the back of this little cavern there was about a quart of water. In the water she suddenly perceived a panting trout. She rushed for Stephen and dragged him to see, and they were both so excited that they were no longer afraid of the darkness as they hunched down and peered in at the fish panting in his tiny prison, his silver stomach going up and down like an engine.

Nobody knew how the trout got there. Even old Martin in the kitchen garden laughed and refused to believe that it was there, or pretended not to believe, until she forced him to come down and see. Kneeling and pushing back his tattered old cap he peered in.

"Be cripes, you're right. How the divil in hell did that fella get there?"

She stared at him suspiciously.

"You knew?" she accused; but he said, "The divil a' know," and reached down to lift it out. Convinced, she hauled him back. If she had found it, then it was her trout.

Her mother suggested that a bird had carried the spawn. Her father thought that in the winter a small streamlet might have carried it down there as a baby, and it had been safe until the summer came and the water began to dry up. She said, "I see," and went back to look again and consider the matter in private. Her brother remained behind, wanting to hear the whole

---

Jumping Trout, 1889, Winslow Homer.

story of the trout, not really interested in the actual trout but much interested in the story which his mummy began to make up for him on [6] the lines of, "So one day Daddy Trout and Mammy Trout . . ." When he retailed it to her she said, "Pooh."

It troubled her that the trout was always in the same position; he had no room to turn; all the time the silver belly went up and down; otherwise he was motionless. She wondered what he ate, and in between visits to Joey Pony and the boat, and a bathe to get cool, she thought of his hunger. She brought him down bits of dough; once she brought him a worm. He ignored the food. He just went on panting. Hunched over him she thought how all the winter, while she was at school, he had been in there. All the winter, in The Dark Walk, all day,

all night, floating around alone. She drew the leaf of her hat down around her ears and chin [7] and stared. She was still thinking of it as she lay in bed.

It was late June, the longest days of the year. [8] The sun had sat still for a week, burning up the world. Although it was after ten o'clock it was still bright and still hot. She lay on her back under a single sheet, with her long legs spread, trying to keep cool. She could see the D of the moon[1] through the fir tree—they slept on the ground floor. Before they went to bed her mummy had told Stephen the story of the trout again, and she, in her bed, had resolutely presented her back to them and read her book. But she had kept one ear cocked.

──────────

1. **D of the moon:** shape of the half-full moon.

The Trout **93**

PAGE SUMMARY: AT A GLANCE

- Stephen is less interested in the actual trout than in childish stories about it.
- Julia scoffs at these stories.
- She is troubled by the trout's situation and brings it food.
- She lies in bed thinking about the trout.

IN THE GLOSSARY

- retailed: retold; repeated
- resolutely: with determination

6 READING SKILL: CONTRAST

Elicit the contrast between Julia's scoffing at stories of "Daddy Trout and Mammy Trout" and her still calling the pony Joey Pony. Julia fluctuates between childish and more mature behavior while moving toward maturity.

7 CRITICAL THINKING: PROBLEM SOLVING

Ask students what they would do to solve the problem of the trout. (They may suggest moving it to a larger body of water or learning more about the behavior of trout.)

8 GRAMMAR IN LITERATURE

Point out the use of the past perfect tense to show action that began before another past action: "The sun *had sat* still for a week" before the actions of this night took place.

ART AND LITERATURE

The American painter and watercolorist Winslow Homer (1836–1910) captured with a direct and unsentimental visual poetry many diverse aspects of American life. An outdoorsman, he often made watercolors on hunting and fishing trips. Like *Jumping Trout* these watercolors are accurate, vivid, carefully designed portraits of nature.

- Have students contrast the trout in the story with the trout in the painting. (The trout in the story is "panting in his tiny prison, his silver stomach going up and down," whereas Homer's *Jumping Trout* is free.)

CRITICAL THINKING: GUIDED READING QUESTIONS

LITERAL

1a. In what is Stephen not really interested? (He is not interested in the actual trout.)

2a. What troubles Julia about the trout? (It is always in the same position, with no room to turn.)

INFERENTIAL

1b. In contrast, what is Julia's attitude toward the trout? (She shows concern for its plight and wants to help it survive.)

2b. What do her troubled feelings reveal about how she is changing? (She is growing more mature and considerate.)

- Annoyed by yet another childish story about the trout, Julia now realizes that there are no fairy godmothers and that the real trout is suffering.
- Stealing out to the Dark Walk, she manages to put the trout in a ewer of water and release it into the river.
- The next morning, when Stephen asks how the trout vanished, Julia superciliously replies, "Fairy godmother, I suppose?"

IN THE GLOSSARY

- ewer: large pitcher
- scuttled: moved with short, rapid steps
- superciliously: arrogantly

9 TEACHING THEME

Stress Julia's new awareness: She realizes that neither magical intervention nor adults will help the trout and that she can help it only by acting herself.

10 TEACHING CHARACTERIZATION

Remind students of Julia's fears of the Dark Walk by day, and elicit the insight that it is brave of her to go there at night.

11 TEACHING STYLE

Note that vivid terms like "slimy hole" and the long, action-packed final scene help capture Julia's fear and excitement.

12 TEACHING CHARACTER FOILS

Point out that the still immature Stephen is a foil for his sister and that she herself recognizes the difference when she notes that he still believes in fairy godmothers.

COLLABORATIVE LEARNING: ENRICHMENT ACTIVITY

Travel Brochure Have a group of students prepare a travel brochure on Ireland. Each student should contribute a section on a different place or subject of interest, such as Dublin, the Aran Islands, fishing, castles, and poetry festivals.

"And so, in the end, this naughty fish who would not stay at home got bigger and bigger and bigger, and the water got smaller and smaller. . . ."

Passionately she had whirled and cried, "Mummy, don't make it a horrible old moral story!" Her mummy had brought in a fairy godmother then, who sent lots of rain, and filled the well, and a stream poured out and the trout floated away down to the river below. Staring at the moon she knew that there are no such things as fairy godmothers and that the trout, down in The Dark Walk, was panting like an engine. She heard somebody unwind a fishing reel. Would the *beasts* fish him out!

She sat up. Stephen was a hot lump of sleep, lazy thing. The Dark Walk would be full of little scraps of moon. She leaped up and looked out the window, and somehow it was not so lightsome[2] now that she saw the dim mountains far away and the black firs against the breathing land and heard a dog say *bark-bark*. Quietly she lifted the ewer of water and climbed out the window and scuttled along the cool but cruel gravel down to the maw of the tunnel. Her pajamas were very short so that when she splashed water it wet her ankles. She peered into the tunnel. Something alive rustled inside there. She raced in, and up and down she raced, and flur-

---

2. **lightsome:** lighthearted; lively.

---

ried, and cried aloud, "Oh, gosh, I can't find it," and then at last she did. Kneeling down in the damp she put her hand into the slimy hole. When the body lashed they were both mad with fright. But she gripped him and shoved him into the ewer and raced, with her teeth ground, out to the other end of the tunnel and down the steep paths to the river's edge.

All the time she could feel him lashing his tail against the side of the ewer. She was afraid he would jump right out. The gravel cut into her soles until she came to the cool ooze of the river's bank where the moon mice on the water crept into her feet. She poured out, watching until he plopped. For a second he was visible in the water. She hoped he was not dizzy. Then all she saw was the glimmer of the moon in the silent-flowing river, the dark firs, the dim mountains, and the radiant pointed face laughing down at her out of the empty sky.

She scuttled up the hill, in the window, plonked down the ewer, and flew through the air like a bird into bed. The dog said *bark-bark*. She heard the fishing reel whirring. She hugged herself and giggled. Like a river of joy her holiday spread before her.

In the morning Stephen rushed to her, shouting that "he" was gone, and asking "where" and "how." Lifting her nose in the air she said superciliously, "Fairy godmother, I suppose?" and strolled away patting the palms of her hands.

CRITICAL THINKING: GUIDED READING QUESTIONS

LITERAL

1a. What does Julia leave the house to do? (She goes to take the trout from the well and release it into the river.)

2a. What does Julia do after returning to bed? (She hugs herself and giggles.)

INFERENTIAL

1b. Why does she do this? (She is troubled by the trout's suffering and wants to help it survive.)

2b. Why is she so happy? (She has helped the trout on her own and has returned safely from an exciting, secret adventure.)

STUDY QUESTIONS

Recalling

1. What "extra joy" involving the Dark Walk does Julia have this year?
2. What is Julia's first reaction when she hears about the well where she later finds the trout? Instead of the actual trout, what interests Julia's little brother, Stephen?
3. What troubles Julia about the trout? What does she bring it?
4. Summarize the events of the last five paragraphs. What does Julia answer when Stephen asks how the trout escaped?

Interpreting

5. Contrast Julia's new understandings about life with her younger brother's view of the world.
6. Why does Julia free the trout? How is her action related to her sharpened awareness of life's realities?
7. What definition of maturity, or growing up, does the story convey? What does the story suggest about the relationship between maturity and reality?
8. Did you find Julia a true-to-life character? Cite details in the story to support your opinion.

Extending

9. How do you think most children feel when they begin to question the fairy tales and other stories they were told when they were very young?

LANGUAGE STUDY

Words from Celtic Languages

Irish, or Irish Gaelic, is one of the Celtic [sel'tik or kel'tik] languages, a group that also includes Scottish Gaelic, spoken in parts of Scotland; Welsh, spoken by some people in Wales; and Breton, spoken by some people in the region of France called Brittany. Of these languages the one most closely related to Irish is Scottish Gaelic. Both descend from a common ancestor called Gaelic, which was spoken in Ireland centuries ago.

Use a dictionary to help you determine the meanings and origins of these English words, which all come from Celtic languages.

1. banshee	5. coracle	9. shamrock
2. bog	6. galore	10. slogan
3. cairn	7. glen	11. smithereens
4. clan	8. plaid	12. trousers

COMPOSITION

Writing About Point of View

■ Write a brief composition about the point of view the author uses in "The Trout." First identify the point of view as first-person or limited third-person. Then explain why this point of view is effective and how it influences the reader's response to the story. Be sure to cite specific story details to support general statements you make about the story. *For help with this assignment, refer to Lesson 5 in the Writing About Literature Handbook at the back of this book.*

Writing in Limited Third-Person Point of View

■ Using limited third-person point of view, write a short-short story in which a child or a teen-ager comes to an important understanding about the world. Focus the story on the child's or teen-ager's experiences, and provide only that character's thoughts and feelings.

The Trout **95**

COMPOSITION: GUIDELINES FOR EVALUATION

WRITING ABOUT POINT OF VIEW

Objective

To evaluate an author's choice of point of view

Guidelines for Evaluation

■ suggested length: two or three paragraphs
■ should identify the story's point of view as limited third person
■ should explain why the point of view is effective

WRITING IN LIMITED THIRD-PERSON POINT OF VIEW

Objective

To write a story in limited third-person point of view

Guidelines for Evaluation

■ suggested length: one or two pages
■ should treat a maturing child or teen-ager
■ should reveal only that character's thoughts

How do you think Julia will treat Stephen in the future?

ANSWERS

STUDY QUESTIONS

1. She can scare Stephen as well as herself.
2. She thinks it is "Nonsense"; his mother's childish stories about the trout
3. It has no room to move about and is nearly motionless; food
4. Julia slips from the house and frees the trout. She says, "Fairy godmother, I suppose?"
5. Julia accepts the real world; Stephen sees life through a haze of childhood fantasies.
6. She recognizes its suffering and wants to help it. She sees that life is not a fantasy in which problems are solved by magic.
7. recognizing reality, having compassion, and taking actions to solve problems; to be mature one must not soften unpleasant realities
8. Most students will find her realistic. Details include her squabbling with Stephen and her contempt for fantasies.
9. Answers will vary; perhaps confusion, anger, or pride

LANGUAGE STUDY

1. "female spirit"; from Irish *bean*, "woman," and *sith*, "fairy"
2. "small marsh"; from Gaelic *bog*, "soft; moist"
3. "small stone pile used as a monument"; from Gaelic *carn*, "elevation"
4. "group sharing descent or interests"; from Gaelic *clann*, "tribe"
5. "short, wide boat of covered wood"; from Welsh *corwg*
6. "in abundance"; from Irish *go*, "to," and *leor*, "enough"
7. "valley"; from Scottish Gaelic *glenn*
8. "cloth with a crossbarred pattern"; from Gaelic *plaide*, "blanket"
9. "three-leaf Irish clover"; from Irish *seamrog*
10. "catchword; rallying cry"; originally, a cry used by Scottish Highland and Irish clans in battle or assembly, from Gaelic *sluagh*, "army," and *gairm*, "call"
11. "fragments"; from the Irish *smidirin*
12. "pants"; from the Scottish Gaelic *triubhas*

Concern over a boy in danger unites a South African community. Johnny Day, a white South African, climbs a quarry wall and reaches a point from which he can go neither up nor down. A racially mixed crowd puts aside its differences to show concern for the boy, and a young black man, Thomas Ndhlovu, climbs up to him. After the police rescue them, Johnny insists on thanking Thomas in public.

LITERARY SKILLS FOR THIS SELECTION

- point of view
- theme

THEMES IN THIS SELECTION

- growing up: wise and unwise choices
- the evils of racial prejudice
- the common bond of humanity

LESSON OBJECTIVES

1. to examine the omniscient point of view
2. to evaluate an author's choice of point of view
3. to explain the steps in a process

Teacher's Classroom Resources 1

- Teaching Notes   175
- Prereading Vocabulary   176
- Reading Guide   177
- Check Test   178
- Responding to World Cultures   179
- Literary Focus: Omniscient Point of View   180
- Writing Process Guides: Writing About Point of View   181
  Describing a Process   182
- Grammar in Literature: Using Subordinate Clauses   183
- Selection Test   184

TEACHING STUDENTS OF DIFFERENT ABILITIES

- **For less advanced students:** Preview the themes for this selection, and ask students to consider how they are conveyed. Also have them complete the Reading Guide.

Alan Paton (1903–1988)

South Africa

Alan Paton [pā′tən] was one of South Africa's first writers to bring the tragedy of his nation's racial policies to the world's attention. An internationally celebrated author, Paton might easily have settled abroad and lived in comfort. Instead he chose to remain in his troubled homeland and struggle to bring about social change.

Born in what is now the South African province of Natal, Paton worked as the principal of a boys' reformatory. His bold innovations at the reform school reflected his sympathy for the problems of young people, sympathies that are also apparent in his fiction.

While visiting prisons in Europe and the United States, Paton wrote his novel *Cry, the Beloved Country,* his most famous attack on his government's racial policies. At home he helped found and later led the Liberal Party of South Africa, which sought to win voting rights for the nation's nonwhite majority. Even after the party was banned in 1968, Paton continued to press for reform. When he died, he was mourned not only as a fine writer but as a champion of human rights.

- **For more advanced students:** Have students view the entire story as an allegory of South African life and explain the symbolic relevance of characters, places, objects, and events, including Johnny's climb itself.

GEOGRAPHY AND CULTURE

South Africa and Its People

Located at the southern tip of the African continent, South Africa is a nation of vast mineral resources. In addition to its famous diamond deposits and gold mines, South Africa has many quarries from which stones such as limestone are cut. "The Quarry" takes place at an abandoned quarry in eastern South Africa, in a coastal city that borders the Indian Ocean.

The inhabitants of eastern South Africa include whites of English and Dutch descent, blacks mainly of Zulu descent, and Asians whose families emigrated from India in the late nineteenth century. Both blacks and Asians have suffered under the South African government's policy of apartheid [ə pär′tīd], or racial separation. Alan Paton was among the liberal whites who joined with blacks and Asians to protest South Africa's apartheid laws. Behind the suspenseful plot of "The Quarry" is a quiet plea for racial understanding.

See LITERATURE AND CULTURE SOURCEBOOK: Africa

DISCUSSING GEOGRAPHY AND CULTURE

Striking It Rich

Twenty years after the California gold rush of 1849, the first diamonds were discovered in South Africa. Gold was first unearthed in large quantities in South Africa in 1886. The early South African mining camps were similar to those in the American West: crowded, lawless, and feverishly busy.

- Ask students whether they have ever been tempted by get-rich-quick schemes. Can they identify with the miners of yesteryear?

Alan Paton

The Quarry

1   Everywhere the city was driving back nature, to the south and the west and the north. Only the east was safe, for there lay the ocean. Skyscrapers stood on the places where elephants had crashed through the forest. Hippopotamus Pool was a city square full of the smells of buses, Lions' River ran down a straight concrete channel into the Bay.

    Only Mitchell's Quarry had resisted the march of the city. It was a stony scar cut out of the side of Pigeon Hill, and though it was ugly it was a piece of nature. The large green pigeons had long since gone, but small birds and animals still clung to it, and lived in the trees and grass that ran down each side of the scar. Frogs and very small fish lived in the pools. Children were attracted there, for it was the only bit of wildness in the city.

    It was Johnny Day's favorite place. Sometimes he sat by the pools for hours, watching the fish. Sometimes he climbed up through the trees, and sat on the very edge of the quarry, in the cool exciting wind from the dancing ocean.

2 He more than once wondered whether anyone could climb down, but Tom Hesketh, who was sixteen and very manly, told him it was impossible, and had never been done, and never would be done unless one came down on a rope. One could climb up from the bottom and Tom had done it once with two of his friends.

    "Which way did you take, Tom?"

    "I'm not telling you," said Tom, "it's not for kids. Can't you see the notice?"

3   The notice said, NO CLIMBING, BY ORDER, only whose order it was, no one knew.

    "And I'm not doing it again," said Tom, "because when I was halfway up, all I wanted to do was to come down again, and I couldn't."

    Sitting by one of the pools, Johnny looked at the quarry face, wondering which way Tom had **4** taken. All he knew was that Tom had begun by the noticeboard NO CLIMBING, BY ORDER, and that is where he would begin too, on the day after Christmas Day. He would climb in a direction half-right, where it seemed there was a track of footholds made for just such a purpose. Halfway up the quarry face the track seemed to peter out, but another track bearing half-left could be seen some feet higher. All that he must do was to find the way from one to the other.

    On the morning of the day after Christmas Day Johnny arrived at the quarry and found nobody there. Confident of success he took off his jacket and cap, and laid them on a stone under the noticeboard. He was wearing sandshoes, because that was what Tom Hesketh had worn. He looked up at the quarry face, which was roughly a perpendicular plane. He placed his right foot in a niche that seemed to have been made for it. He drew his left foot up and now stood about a foot above the level floor and the pools. The climb had begun, and the feeling of the climber was not nervousness but pure ambition, strong in one so young, for he was only twelve.

    It certainly seemed that the track had been cut deliberately, perhaps to enable the quarry workers to climb the face. There was always a place for the foot, and the rock face inclined away from him a few degrees from the perpendicular, so that he had a feeling of security. There was no need so far for skill or ingenuity, for the method was simple—a hold with the hands, right foot up, left foot up, an inching forward on the same small ledge if possible, a searching for another hold with the hands and another small ledge for the right foot. He was about twenty feet up, and could see that he

The Quarry **97**

CRITICAL THINKING: GUIDED READING QUESTIONS

LITERAL

1a. What does Johnny consider sixteen-year-old Tom Hesketh to be? (He considers him "very manly.")

2a. What does Tom tell Johnny about climbing the quarry wall? ("It's not for kids" and "I'm not doing it again because when I was halfway up, all I wanted to do was to come down again, and I couldn't.")

INFERENTIAL

1b. What does his opinion of Tom suggest about Johnny's motives for making the climb? (He wants to prove his manhood.)

2b. Based on Tom's remarks, do you think Johnny should be as confident of success as he is? Why or why not? (No; if an older, bigger boy had difficulty making the climb, a smaller boy may well find it impossible.)

- As Johnny continues up the quarry wall, he recalls Tom Hesketh's advice about how to make the climb.
- Johnny reaches a point where the rock face grows dangerously perpendicular, but he decides to continue even though doing so probably means passing the point of no return.
- From below an Indian man, accompanied by some Indian boys, tries to persuade Johnny to climb down.
- Johnny refuses—to the despair of the man and the admiration of the boys.
- As a crowd gathers, Johnny reaches a place where the trail stops dead.

IN THE GLOSSARY

- exhilaration: excitement; high spirits
- invoked: called on; prayed for

5 READING SKILL: PREDICTING OUTCOMES

Have students predict whether the rock face is likely to be so "obliging" as Johnny progresses. (No, the earlier descriptions suggest that the climb will get very difficult.)

6 TEACHING CHARACTERIZATION

Elicit the idea that Johnny's behavior shows stubborn determination and foolhardiness.

7 TEACHING CHARACTER MOTIVATION

Ask students what motivates the Indian man to invent his story. (He is concerned for Johnny's welfare.)

8 TEACHING STUDENTS OF LIMITED ENGLISH PROFICIENCY

Help students understand the meanings of familiar words used in less familiar ways, such as *addressed* meaning "applied" and *generous* meaning "ample."

9 TEACHING STYLE

Point out Paton's occasional use of a short sentence for emphasis, and ask what "Then it stopped dead" emphasizes. (the danger)

could return safely, if it was necessary. He looked down, and this gave him a feeling of exhilaration. He looked up, but decided not to do it again, because it seemed to reveal his own insignificance against the vast wall of the quarry, and above that the vast emptiness of the sky. 5 From now on he would confine his attention to the handhold, the foothold and the rock face that so obligingly allowed him to lean against it.

The track continued as before for a short distance and he was at a height of about thirty feet when he reached a place where the rock face became suddenly perpendicular for a length of some three feet, so that he would not be able to lean against it. He wondered if he could take a step direct from safety to safety, but knew that the step would be too big for him. His only hope was a good hold for hands and feet. He was the slightest bit nervous, because he knew something else too, that if he decided to take the next two steps it would be twice as hard to return.

Tom Hesketh had said to him, "If you're frightened to take the next step, don't take it, just climb down, if you can. If you can't climb down, then you've got to take the next step, that's all. And I can tell you, kid, it's dangerous getting frightened up there."

6 Well, he might be a bit nervous but he wasn't climbing down. He could see the trail clearly, and it looked easy except for this one next step. There was a place for the hands and a place for the right foot, just as good as any he had used so far.

Someone shouted at him from below. It was a big Indian[1] man who was shouting with some Indian boys.

"Come down, sonny," shouted the big Indian man.

Johnny shook his head. Without looking he pointed at the sky.

---

1. **Indian:** someone whose ancestors came from India.

98   *The Short Story*

The big Indian man shook his head too.

"No, no," he shouted. "It's too dangerous, sonny. Come down."

Again Johnny shook his head, and pointed up. The Indian man tried warnings.

7 "Last year," he shouted, "an Indian boy was killed here. He was climbing the same way you are climbing now." This wasn't true. There never had been such an Indian boy, but the Indian man believed that if the end was good, one shouldn't worry too much about the means. When the warnings failed, he invoked divine aid.

"God sent me here," he shouted, "to tell you to come down. He is telling you now to come down. He does not mean for you to be up there. If you don't come down, He will be plenty angry." He added a clever afterthought. "Just like He was angry with that Indian boy."

"Don't let anything take your mind off your hands and feet," said Tom, "or off the rock face. Don't think of the height, or of the spectators. Don't look at birds or ships on the sea. Just think of the climb."

That is what Johnny did. To the despair of the big Indian man, and the admiration of the 8 Indian boys, he addressed himself to the task of finding a place for his right hand and a place for his right foot, and when he had found them, he took the dangerous step. It was done. The ledge was generous, and he brought up his left foot. Tom's instruction was immediately forgotten, and he looked down at the growing crowd of Indian men and women and boys and girls, and African men from the factory near the quarry.

The big Indian man shouted at him again to come down, and it was this very shouting that brought Tom's instruction back to Johnny's mind, so that the louder and more desperate the warnings and the threats, the less he paid atten- 9 tion to them. He took his next step with confidence, and the trail before him was now straightforward and easy for at least seven steps. Then it stopped dead. He braced himself to look

---

CRITICAL THINKING: GUIDED READING QUESTIONS

LITERAL

1a. Why does Johnny decide not to look up? (Looking up seems to reveal his own insignificance against the vast quarry wall and against the vast emptiness of space.)

2a. What contrasting feelings do the big Indian man and the Indian boys have when Johnny continues the climb? (The man feels despair; the boys, admiration.)

INFERENTIAL

1b. What does this revelation make Johnny recognize for the first time in the story? (He realizes the great danger and his mortality.)

2b. What do the Indian boys' feelings show that they share with Johnny? (They share a boyish, if unwise, sense of adventure.)

up, and there, about ten or twelve feet above him, he could see the second trail that ran half-left, and would take him to the top. He could see [10] almost at once that he could go no further in a half-right direction, that he would have to climb straight up. He could also see toeholds for the first five feet, for that was his own height. It would all depend whether there were handholds also, and that he would have to tell by feeling for them, partly because he was apprehensive about looking up, and partly because the rock face seemed to be nearer the perpendicular when one thought of climbing it perpendicularly.

These thoughts and speculations took him some minutes, so that the crowd below knew that he was facing some kind of crisis. He was nearly fifty feet up, about one-third of the height of the quarry face. There were now a hundred people watching him, talking to each other, but not loudly, because they were subdued by con-[11]templation of the dangers that lay ahead. The boys were filled with admiration and awe, and the women with tender feeling and care. It was a white boy, it is true, but there in the danger and excitement of his journey up the quarry face he had become one of their own. The boys wished him luck and the women shook their heads,

Mont Sainte-Victoire Seen from the Bibemus Quarry, c. 1897, Paul Cézanne.

The Quarry **99**

PAGE SUMMARY: AT A GLANCE

■ Johnny can see a second trail ten or twelve feet above him, but he sees only the first set of toeholds he would need to reach it and no handholds.
■ About a hundred people have gathered below, most of them blacks and Indians full of feeling for the white boy who has "become one of their own."

IN THE GLOSSARY

■ speculations: guesses made after thinking about something

10 **READING SKILL: CONTRAST**

Note that up until now Johnny, climbing at a gradual angle ("half right"), found it easier than going straight up, as he now must go.

11 **TEACHING POINT OF VIEW AND THEME**

Point out that the omniscient narrator jumps in and out of the different characters' minds, in part to convey the theme of the common bond of humanity.

ART AND LITERATURE

The French Impressionist Paul Cézanne (1839–1906) is considered the pioneer of modern abstract art. His short brushstrokes and unblended colors create a patchwork surface of paint with an almost unreceding depth of field. Cézanne's frequently painted subject Mont Sainte-Victoire is a lone peak in southern France within walking distance of the town of Aix-en-Provence, where the artist grew up and lived.
■ Ask students what words and phrases from page 97 might describe the quarry in the painting. (Possible answers: The quarry wall was "a stony scar cut out of the side of Pigeon Hill"; "the quarry face . . . was roughly a perpendicular plane.")

CRITICAL THINKING: GUIDED READING QUESTIONS

LITERAL

1a. What feelings fill the women and boys as Johnny faces his crisis? (The boys feel admiration and awe; the women, tenderness and care.)

INFERENTIAL

1b. What does their attitude suggest about human nature? (In times of crisis, human beings draw together and forget their differences.)

- As Johnny begins the precarious ascent, the big Indian man again pleads that he stop, but Johnny continues.
- His actions create a drama new to the city, witnessed by "a crowd of every color and class and tongue."
- Finally Johnny reaches a nine-inch ledge, where he is able to rest and even turn to face the onlookers, many of whom cheer.

IN THE GLOSSARY

- ascent: act of climbing
- reprieve: release; relief

12 TEACHING POINT OF VIEW

Point out that the omniscient narrator not only can tell us what characters say but can explain what they really mean.

13 GRAMMAR IN LITERATURE

Note that throughout this paragraph Paton omits the introductory *there* and the verb *was* or *were* in several of his sentences. For example, here one would ordinarily write "Then again *there were* the hands exploring. . . ." Elicit the insight that this short-hand style helps build suspense.

14 TEACHING SYMBOLS

Ask students what the stone face of the quarry might symbolize. (the implacable forces of nature or anything else that is not human and lacks concern for human feelings and misfortunes)

15 TEACHING THEME

Elicit the understanding that these details stress the human ability to rise above hatred and revenge and show compassion for someone formerly viewed as an enemy or alien.

---

unable to be indifferent to either his naughtiness or his plight.

Johnny lifted his right foot to make the first step of the ascent, and this action put the big Indian man into a panic.

"Sonny," he cried, "true's God, don't go up any more. You'll die, sonny, and no one here wants you to die. Sonny, I ask you to come down." He went down on his knees on the quarry floor, and said, "I pray God to make you come down. I pray God not to be angry with you." The women there, both Indian and African, **seeing him kneeling there, cried out, "Shame," but not because they thought his action was shameful; they were merely saying how sad the whole thing was.**

The Indian man was now struck by a new idea, and he shouted, "Sonny, what's your address?" Johnny heard him but he tried to pay no attention, needing it all for the dangerous piece ahead. However, the question disturbed him slightly, and he brought his right foot down again, causing the crowd to give a composite groan, with many meanings. The Indian man took it as a reprieve, and shouted, "Sonny, I pray to God, give me your address."

It was now clear to all but his would-be rescuer that the small boy intended to continue the climb. His small exploratory movements showed that he meant to go up, not down. Again he placed his right foot, but this time he pulled himself up, causing the Indian man to rise from his knees and to collapse groaning on to a rock with his hands covering his eyes. So was silenced his vocal opposition to the climb, but the rest were quiet too, speaking in low voices, even whispers, as Johnny placed his hands and his foot, and pulled himself up, two feet now above **the safety of the sloping trail. Then again the hands exploring, the right foot testing, the body bracing, the small boy like a fly on a cinema screen, except that he was no intruder, rather the creator of a drama never before witnessed in this city, of a crowd of every color and class and** tongue, **bound all of them together for these moments by unbreakable bonds, to a small white boy climbing a quarry face made of a stone that knew nothing of admiration or anxiety or pity.** And again a step, and again the low talking, and again the exploring hands and the testing foot, and again the bracing of the body. And down below silence, and silent prayers, and silent apprehension. The Indian man took his hands from his eyes, and watched despairingly; it was clear **he was in an agony of care and pity over this child of an alien race, many of whose members had shown neither care nor pity for himself or his people.** And up above again the winning of another step, again the murmur from below, from a crowd growing every moment, swollen by people streaming over the waste ground between the quarry and the tarred road. There they stood, shoulder to shoulder, ruler and ruled, richer and poorer, white and black and yellow and brown, with their eyes fixed on a small piece of whiteness halfway up the quarry face, and those of them who knew a thing or two knew that the boy was in a position of considerable danger.

Fortunately Johnny himself did not know it. He was surprised that his right hand searching above his head had found another generous ledge, at least nine inches wide. Once he had reached it, he would be able to rest, even perhaps to look upward to plan the last piece of climbing that would enable him to reach the half-left trail. Therefore he set out to reach it, alternately terrifying and gratifying the watching crowd below.

The crowd did not realize the achievement when at last Johnny's feet were both planted on the nine-inch ledge. He himself decided not only to rest, but to allow his attention to be diverted from the climb. The ledge was so wide that he could turn himself about for the first time, stand with his back to the quarry face, and look down on the hundreds of people below. Some of them clapped and cheered him, some of them looked

---

CRITICAL THINKING: GUIDED READING QUESTIONS

LITERAL

1a. What question disturbs Johnny slightly? ("Sonny, what's your address?")

2a. What sort of people stand "shoulder to shoulder" watching Johnny? ("ruler and ruled, richer and poorer, white and black and yellow and brown")

INFERENTIAL

1b. Why do you think the question bothers Johnny? (He no doubt does not want his family to be informed of his dangerous and disobedient behavior.)

2b. What does the phrase "shoulder to shoulder" stress about the crowd? (Despite everyone's differences, they are united in their concern for Johnny.)

at him out of troubled eyes. The big Indian man stood up from the rock onto which he had collapsed, and called out, in a less assured voice than hitherto, for the small boy to come down, but after another man had spoken quietly to him, he desisted and it was generally understood that the second man had told him that the small boy had reached a point of no return, and it were better to leave him alone, and to pray rather for his salvation.

For three minutes, four minutes, it must have been, Johnny stood with his back to the quarry face. After acknowledging the crowd's cheers, he had cut them off from attention, and stood there reassembling his small boy's powers. Everything was silent when again he turned his face to the quarry wall. The foothold was there, the handhold for the left hand was there, but of handhold for the right hand there was no sign whatsoever. At first he could not believe it, but when he tried again he knew there was no doubt __16__ of it. Had the handhold been perpendicularly above the toehold he might have done it, but it was at least a foot to the left of his body line. No one could pull himself up from such a position.

A growl went up from the crowd, of defeat and frustration, and from the more knowledgeable, of sharpened anxiety. Again the questing hands, again the finding of nothing. The small boy, leaving his two arms in this upstretched position, but his face to the face of the quarry, almost as if he were weeping or praying, which indeed is what some thought he was doing. He brought down his arms and caused the crowd to groan and shudder as his left foot explored the rock below him, trying to find the foothold he had used to reach the ledge.

In complete silence they watched him put his foot on it, but after a moment he withdrew and again laid his face against the face of the quarry. It was then clear that his ambition to climb had gone, and in its place was the frightenedness of a small boy. Again he turned himself round so that he faced the crowd, who could see clearly his loneliness and despair. His movements, so splendidly co-ordinated until now, gave alarming signs of randomness, and for one terrible moment it seemed that he might panic and fall.

This was the signal for a young African man of about twenty to take charge.

"Hi, sonny," he shouted, waving with outstretched arm to the small boy, "don't be frightened. Thomas Ndhlovu[2] is coming."

__17__ On his way to the starting-point by the noticeboard, Thomas spoke to a white man who seemed to be senior to the others.

"Get the police, master, or the fire brigade. I go up to stay with the small boy."

Then he started his climb, amid a new noise of laughs, cheers, approval, and advice. Thomas soon showed himself to be vigorous and unskilled, and his friends below, who had been so anxious about the first climber, made jokes about the second. As for Thomas himself, whenever he had brought off what he thought a piece of good climbing, he would turn to the crowd and raise his clenched fist, to be greeted by __18__ cheers and laughter. Every few steps he would shout at the small boy, urging him to be of good heart, because one Thomas Ndhlovu was coming. The small boy himself had recovered from his panic and watched absorbedly the progress of his savior. What had been a tense and terrifying affair had become a kind of festival. Jests and laughter had replaced groans and sighs, and Thomas, with intention somewhat foolish, climbed flamboyantly and wildly, shouting encouragement in English to the small boy and __19__ exchanging banter in Zulu[3] with his friends on the ground. It was only when he reached the end of the first trail and began to inspect the sharp perpendicular ascent that the crowd again fell silent.

_____

2. **Ndhlovu** [n′də lŏ′vōō]
3. **Zulu** [zōō′lōō]: Bantu language of the Zulu tribe. Many black South Africans are of Zulu descent, especially those in eastern South Africa, where the story takes place.

The Quarry **101**

CRITICAL THINKING: GUIDED READING QUESTIONS

LITERAL

1a. When it is clear that Johnny is in grave trouble, what does Thomas Ndhlovu tell a "senior white man" to do? (get the police or fire brigade)

2a. In what manner does Thomas climb up to Johnny? (flamboyantly and jokingly)

INFERENTIAL

1b. Why does Thomas climb up to stay with Johnny instead of waiting below until the rescuers arrive? (Realizing that Johnny has panicked and may fall, Thomas goes up to calm and comfort him.)

2b. What are the positive effects of Thomas' flamboyant behavior? (It eases the crowd's tension and helps Johnny overcome his panic.)

■ When he finally reaches the nine-inch ledge, Thomas comforts Johnny, who thanks him.

■ Thomas is amused by the thought of Johnny's mother's seeing her son in a newspaper photo with a "native boy."

■ The crowd greets the police with uncustomary warmth, and everyone cheers after the police lower Johnny and Thomas to safety.

■ Johnny insists on thanking Thomas in public.

IN THE GLOSSARY

■ ovation: enthusiastic demonstration of public acclaim

20 TEACHING THEME

Elicit the fact that because Johnny's rescuer is black, the story effectively illustrates the evils of racial prejudice and the common bond of humanity.

21 CULTURAL BACKGROUND

Explain that the police, as an arm of the government, have treated black South Africans harshly and unfairly over the years.

22 CRITICAL THINKING: EVALUATION

Note that "under the eyes of authority" refers here to the police. Then remind students that Johnny disobeyed authority and climbed the wall because he wanted to show "manliness," or courage and maturity. Ask why he shows *true* courage and maturity here. (Climbing the wall was foolhardy; here he bravely goes against the social taboos of his homeland in order to do what is morally correct.)

COLLABORATIVE LEARNING: ENRICHMENT ACTIVITY

Journalism Have a group of students create the local newspaper articles that might have appeared after Johnny's climb. Articles can include an objective news account, profiles of Johnny and Thomas, interviews with Tom Hesketh and the Indian man, and editorials and letters focusing on social lessons the event helped teach.

Thomas however would not tolerate this new respect. Turning round he shouted something at his friends that caused much laughter. He too made the exploratory motions of hands and it was very clear that he was caricaturing the small boy's motions. Nevertheless the laughter died away as he began the ascent and the atmosphere was tense, without being fearful. When at last he placed his foot on the nine-inch ledge, rulers and ruled, richer and poorer, joined in an ovation of shouting and clapping, which was doubled and redoubled when he too **20** turned to face the crowd. He smiled down at the small white boy and put his hand on his shoulder, as if to assure him that no one fell from a ledge when Thomas Ndhlovu was on it.

"Now be quiet," he said, "some time the police come, and the fire brigade, and you go home to your mother."

The small boy said, "Thanks a million," and Thomas said, "What your mother say?"

"I won't tell my mother," said Johnny.

Thomas laughed uproariously, and pointed at the crowd below, where newspapermen were taking photographs and interviewing spectators.

"Tomorrow," said Thomas, "big picture in paper, you and me. Your mother open paper, she say, what you doing there with that native boy?"

He thought this very funny, and for a time occupied himself with it. Then he asked, "What's your name, sonny?"

"Johnny Day."

"Johnny Day, eh? Very good name. My name **22** Thomas Ndhlovu."

"Very good name too," said Johnny.

21 "Police coming," said Thomas pointing. "When police coming other times, Thomas running. Now police coming, Thomas staying."

The arrival of the police was greeted with great good humor, for here was an occasion on which their arrival was welcome. Words in Zulu were shouted at them, compliments tinged with satire, for the crowd was feeling happy and free. The policemen grasped the whole situation

102 *The Short Story*

immediately. Two of them, armed with ropes, set off up through the trees that grew at the side of the quarry and in a few minutes had reached the upper edge, where they took up a position directly above the man and the boy. Instructions were shouted and a rope was lowered to Thomas, who, once he had the cradle-like end in his hand, laughed with uproarious delight. To the end of this rope was attached another which Thomas threw to the policemen below. More instructions were shouted and Thomas soon had the small boy in the cradle. The policemen above lowered the cradle down the quarry wall. The policemen below held it away from the stony face. In one minute Johnny was on the quarry floor, lost to sight in a swirling multicolored mass, shouting their joy and congratulation. This celebration was still in progress as Thomas Ndhlovu landed on the quarry floor, when it transferred itself to him. Everybody, white, yellow, brown, black, wanted to shake hands with him, to thank him for his splendid act, to ask God to bless him. The Indian man, now fully restored, was one of the most enthusiastic of these participators.

"Come, sonny," said the senior white man. "Tell me where you live and I'll take you home."

"I must thank Thomas first," said Johnny.

The senior white man looked at the tumultuous scene. "How are you going to do that?" he said.

"I'll wait," said Johnny.

But he did not need to wait. The policemen cleared a way through the mob of congratulators, and there, under the eyes of authority, Johnny Day put out his hand and thanked Thomas Ndhlovu again for the act which, for all we know, saved his life. This second evidence of gratitude was extremely pleasurable to Thomas and, moved to great heights by it, he led the small white boy to the noticeboard which said, NO CLIMBING, BY ORDER. What he said, no one heard, for it was lost in an outburst of catcalls, laughter, jeering and cheering.

CRITICAL THINKING: GUIDED READING QUESTIONS

LITERAL

1a. According to Thomas, what will Johnny's mother say when she sees Johnny and Thomas' picture in the paper? ("What you doing with that native boy?")

2a. What does Johnny insist on doing before he goes home? (He thanks Thomas again.)

INFERENTIAL

1b. Why does Thomas feel she may say that? (He thinks she is likely to show the typical white South African prejudice against blacks.)

2b. Why do you think he insists on thanking him again? (He wants to acknowledge openly—in a society where blacks are too often the victims of unfair treatment—the debt he owes Thomas and the courage and kindness that Thomas displayed.)

STUDY QUESTIONS

Recalling

1. What notice at the quarry does Johnny disobey? Who points out the notice to him?
2. What kinds of people gather to watch Johnny's climb?
3. How do the boys and the women in the crowd feel as they watch Johnny climb? How does the Indian man feel?
4. When does Johnny become frightened and show signs of panic? Who comes to his aid until the police arrive?
5. After his rescue, what does Johnny insist on doing before he goes home?

Interpreting

6. Why does Johnny attempt to climb the quarry wall?
7. What happens to the crowd's usual ethnic ties as they watch the boy try to climb the wall? What does their attitude suggest about people in general?
8. Explain the significance of Thomas Ndhlovu's ethnic background and Johnny's behavior in the final paragraphs. What does the story suggest about racial prejudice?

Extending

9. Did you find the crowd's reactions and attitudes in this story typical of group behavior during a crisis? Cite examples to support your opinion.

LITERARY FOCUS

Omniscient Point of View

A story told from the **omniscient point of view** is told by an all-knowing narrator who stands outside the story and looks into the minds of all its characters.

The omniscient narrator reveals the thoughts and feelings of several characters and may even reveal information that none of the characters could know. The omniscient narrator usually provides a more objective account of events than narrators with more limited points of view.

Thinking About Omniscient Point of View

■ Which characters' thoughts are revealed in "The Quarry"? As a result, what things do readers find out that they might not otherwise know?

COMPOSITION

Writing About Point of View

■ Write a brief composition about the omniscient point of view used in "The Quarry." Explain why you think Paton chose to narrate the story from this point of view instead of providing only one character's thoughts or having that character tell the story himself. Tell how the point of view affects the reader's response to the story. Be sure to support your ideas with specific details from the story. *For help with this assignment, refer to Lesson 5 in the Writing About Literature Handbook at the back of this book.*

Describing a Process

■ Some of the paragraphs in "The Quarry" give a step-by-step description of the way Johnny climbs up the quarry wall. Describe another process or activity that involves several steps. For example, you might tell how to perform an athletic activity or explain how to build something or take it apart. Provide a clear, step-by-step explanation, using time-order words such as *first, next,* and *last* and expressions that clarify movement or direction, such as *on the right, above,* and *below*.

What effects do you think this experience will have on Johnny Day's behavior in the future?

ANSWERS

STUDY QUESTIONS

1. "NO CLIMBING, BY ORDER"; Tom Hesketh, an older boy who made the climb, points out the sign.
2. "A crowd of every color and class and tongue" gathers.
3. The boys feel admiration and awe; the women feel tenderness and care. The Indian man feels "an agony of care and pity."
4. Thomas becomes frightened when he cannot find a right handhold and can neither pull himself up farther nor return; Thomas Ndhlovu, a young black man.
5. He thanks Thomas in public.
6. He wants to show that he is as "manly" as Tom Hesketh.
7. They abandon their differences in a unified concern for Johnny; nonwhites forget their oppression and find that Johnny's racial identity does not matter. In times of crisis, people can overcome prejudice and fear and show unity.
8. As a black victim of white oppression, Thomas overcomes his resentment to help a white boy and with his kindness and courage shows that color does not matter. Johnny recognizes this idea when he breaks social taboos and thanks Thomas in public. Racial prejudice is wrong and ignores the good qualities found in all people.
9. Answers will vary. Students might describe groups who band together and behave nobly, crowds who panic, and people who ignore pleas for help.

LITERARY FOCUS

Johnny's, the big Indian man's, Thomas Ndhlovu's, and those of several unnamed people in the crowd; how much onlookers of different ethnic backgrounds care about what happens to Johnny

---

COMPOSITION: GUIDELINES FOR EVALUATION

WRITING ABOUT POINT OF VIEW

Objective

To evaluate an author's choice of point of view

Guidelines for Evaluation

■ suggested length: two or three paragraphs
■ should evaluate the advantages of telling the story from an omniscient point of view
■ should support ideas with story details

DESCRIBING A PROCESS

Objective

To explain the steps in a process

Guidelines for Evaluation

■ suggested length: one to three paragraphs
■ should explain a process involving several steps and provide the steps in correct sequence
■ should include words that clarify sequence and direction

LESSON PREVIEW

This story, set in New Zealand, concerns a young girl who overcomes class prejudice. The Burnell girls are given a doll's house, and Kezia is especially taken with its realistic lamp. The girls are allowed to show the house to all their schoolmates except the Kelveys, the socially shunned daughters of a washerwoman. After the schoolmates taunt the Kelveys, Kezia shows them the doll's house, to the fury of her aunt.

LITERARY SKILLS FOR THIS SELECTION

- tone
- characterization
- symbols

THEMES IN THIS SELECTION

- growing up: overcoming social pressure and class differences
- value of kindness and fairness

LESSON OBJECTIVES

1. to understand and examine tone
2. to describe a story's changes in tone
3. to compare and contrast stories

Teacher's Classroom Resources 1

■ Teaching Notes	187
■ Prereading Vocabulary	188
■ Reading Guide	189
■ Check Test	190
■ Responding to World Cultures	191
■ Literary Focus: Tone	192
■ Writing Process Guide: Writing About Tone	193
■ Grammar in Literature: Writing Dialogue	194
■ Selection Test	195

IN THE CLASSROOM

TEACHING STUDENTS OF DIFFERENT ABILITIES

- **For less advanced students:** Have students point out some sentences on the first page that show a child's perspective and several that show a more adult viewpoint. Also have them complete the Reading Guide.

- **For more advanced students:** Refer students to the Guide to Literary Movements (pages 584–585). Ask them to identify the movement into which Mansfield's writing best fits.

Katherine Mansfield

(1888–1923)

New Zealand/England

Unlike many other modern writers of fiction, Katherine Mansfield decided to concentrate on short stories. Her well-crafted tales helped establish the short story as a major literary form.

Mansfield, whose real name was Kathleen Mansfield Beauchamp [bē′chəm], grew up in Karori, a rural New Zealand village not far from the nation's capital, Wellington. The daughter of a wealthy banker, she nevertheless attended local New Zealand schools, rubbing elbows with children from families far less privileged than her own.

In 1903 Mansfield went to study in England, where she fell in love with London's cosmopolitan atmosphere. After a brief return to New Zealand, she settled in London, but she did not win fame until she began writing about her homeland. This she did with *Bliss, and Other Stories,* a 1920 collection inspired by her New Zealand childhood, followed two years later by *The Garden Party,* another story collection. "The Doll's House," one of Mansfield's best-known stories, is based on her childhood experiences in New Zealand.

GEOGRAPHY AND CULTURE

New Zealand's British Ties

Located in the South Pacific Ocean, New Zealand consists of two main islands, North Island and South Island, and several smaller ones. New Zealand became a British colony in 1840. Today it is an independent nation; however, as members of the British Commonwealth, New Zealanders still hold allegiance to Britain's queen. Almost ninety percent of all New Zealanders are of European, mostly British, background and speak English as their native tongue.

Three-quarters of New Zealand's citizens live on the North Island, where most of the country's industry is located. Traditionally, New Zealand was a rural country, and it is still famous for its butter and cheese. In recent years, however, many New Zealanders have drifted away from their farms and have settled in cities. Even the Maori, the native Polynesian minority, have become increasingly urban.

Katherine Mansfield grew up at a time when class differences were far more pronounced than they are in New Zealand today. Because there were few schools in rural areas, wealthy New Zealanders sent their young children to the same schools the poor attended; but they still made harsh judgments based on social status. In "The Doll's House," two young girls suffer from such social tensions.

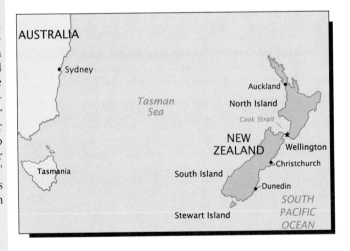

DISCUSSING GEOGRAPHY AND CULTURE

Place Names and Culture

In 1769 New Zealand was explored by Captain James Cook, who was also the first Englishman to visit Hawaii. Cook spent six months mapping New Zealand's coasts; he then claimed the territory for the British. The names of New Zealand's towns and cities reflect Cook's English heritage.

- Have students identify the first European nations to explore and settle their region. Which place names in the area reflect the influence of these nations?

Katherine Mansfield

The Doll's House

1   When dear old Mrs. Hay went back to town after staying with the Burnells she sent the children a doll's house. It was so big that the carter and Pat carried it into the courtyard, and there it stayed, propped up on two wooden boxes beside the feed-room door. No harm could come of it; it was summer. And perhaps the smell of paint would have gone off by the time it had to be taken in. For, really, the smell of paint coming from that doll's house ("Sweet of old Mrs. Hay, of course; most sweet and generous!")—but the smell of paint was quite enough to make anyone seriously ill, in Aunt Beryl's opinion. Even before the sacking[1] was taken off. And when it was . . .

There stood the doll's house, a dark, oily, spinach green, picked out with bright yellow. Its two solid little chimneys, glued on to the roof, were painted red and white, and the door, gleaming with yellow varnish, was like a little slab of toffee. Four windows, real windows, were divided into panes by a broad streak of green. There was actually a tiny porch, too, painted yellow, with big lumps of congealed paint hanging along the edge.

2   But perfect, perfect little house! Who could possibly mind the smell? It was part of the joy, part of the newness.

"Open it quickly, someone!"

The hook at the side was stuck fast. Pat pried it open with his penknife, and the whole house-front swung back, and—there you were, gazing at one and the same moment into the drawing-room[2] and dining-room, the kitchen and two bedrooms. That is the way for a house to open! Why don't all houses open like that? How much more exciting than peering through the slit of a door into a mean little hall with a hatstand and two umbrellas! That is—isn't it?—what you long to know about a house when you put your hand on the knocker. Perhaps it is the way God opens houses at dead of night when He is taking a quiet turn with an angel. . . .

"O-oh!" The Burnell children sounded as though they were in despair. It was too marvelous; it was too much for them. They had never

3   seen anything like it in their lives. All the rooms were papered. There were pictures on the walls, painted on the paper, with gold frames complete. Red carpet covered all the floors except the kitchen; red plush chairs in the drawing-room, green in the dining-room; tables, beds with real bedclothes, a cradle, a stove, a dresser with tiny plates and one big jug. But what Kezia liked more than anything, what she liked frightfully, was the lamp. It stood in the middle of the dining-room table, an exquisite little amber lamp with a white globe. It was even filled, all ready for lighting, though, of course, you couldn't light it. But there was something inside that looked like oil, and that moved when you shook it.

4   The father and mother dolls, who sprawled very stiff as though they had fainted in the drawing-room, and their two little children asleep upstairs, were really too big for the doll's house. They didn't look as though they belonged. But the lamp was perfect. It seemed to smile at Kezia, to say, "I live here." The lamp was real.

The Burnell children could hardly walk to school fast enough the next morning. They burned to tell everybody, to describe, to—

---

1. **sacking:** brown paper packing.
2. **drawing-room:** a usually formal room that was used for greeting and entertaining guests. The word is rarely used today.

The Doll's House **105**

MOTIVATION: PRIOR KNOWLEDGE

Have students define and discuss peer pressure and describe the kind of person who does not succumb to it.

PAGE SUMMARY: AT A GLANCE

■ After visiting the Burnells, Mrs. Hay sends the children a doll's house.
■ The doll's house is put in the courtyard because Aunt Beryl complains of the smell of its paint.
■ The Burnell children are captivated by it, and Kezia is especially taken with the realistic little lamp.

IN THE GLOSSARY

■ congealed: thickened

1 TEACHING SETTING

Point out that Mrs. Hay's visiting from "town" and details of setting, such as "courtyard" and "feed-room," suggest that the Burnells live on a prosperous farming estate in the country.

2 TEACHING POINT OF VIEW AND TONE

Elicit the point that the omniscient narrator here takes on a tone of childlike wonder that expresses the children's attitude toward the doll's house.

3 TEACHING SYMBOLS

Note that the doll's house symbolizes the luxurious, sheltered, constricted, and somewhat artificial life of the Burnells.

4 READING SKILL: CONTRAST

Elicit the contrast between the dolls, whose stiffness makes them seem artificial, and the little lamp, which Kezia finds homey and "real."

CRITICAL THINKING: GUIDED READING QUESTIONS

LITERAL

1a. What does Aunt Beryl say of Mrs. Hay, and what is her opinion of the paint on the doll's house? (She says, "Sweet of old Mrs. Hay, of course; most sweet and generous!" but she finds the smell of the paint enough to make anyone seriously ill.)

2a. What does Kezia like about the little lamp? (It seems real and seems to smile and say, "I live here.")

INFERENTIAL

1b. What does this contradiction reveal about Aunt Beryl? (She is something of a hypocrite.)

2b. What does her attitude toward the lamp suggest about Kezia? (She dislikes pretense and displays a child's innocence and sense of wonder.)

- Isabel Burnell, as the oldest sister, has the privilege of telling her schoolmates about the doll's house and inviting the first two to view it.
- The Burnells' schoolmates may see the doll's house two at a time but may not stay to tea or enter the Burnells' home.
- Isabel is treated as a "special friend" by everyone at school except the Kelveys, who know better than to approach the Burnells.
- The Burnells are forbidden even to speak to the Kelveys, the poorly dressed daughters of a washerwoman and a man rumored to be in jail.

IN THE GLOSSARY

- traipsing: walking aimlessly
- spry: nimble

5 TEACHING CHARACTERIZATION

Elicit the insight that Isabel's remarks show she is bossy and self-important.

6 CULTURAL BACKGROUND

Point out the custom in England and many of its former colonies of taking tea, a light afternoon meal usually consisting of tea and small sandwiches or pastries. Inviting guests to tea is also customary.

7 TEACHING CHARACTER MOTIVATION

Elicit that the girls want to be Isabel's "special friend" only because she has something special to offer them.

8 TEACHING THEME

Point out that the theme of class distinctions is conveyed in the girls' treatment of the Kelveys.

9 TEACHING TONE

Note the shifting tone of the narrator: First she gives her own positive impression of Mrs. Kelvey, calling her "spry" and "hardworking"; then she lapses into the tone of Aunt Beryl and Kezia's parents: "This was awful enough."

well—to boast about their doll's house before the school-bell rang.

5 "I'm to tell," said Isabel, "because I'm the eldest. And you two can join in after. But I'm to tell first."

There was nothing to answer. Isabel was bossy, but she was always right, and Lottie and Kezia knew too well the powers that went with being eldest. They brushed through the thick buttercups at the road edge and said nothing.

"And I'm to choose who's to come and see it first. Mother said I might."

For it had been arranged that while the doll's house stood in the courtyard they might ask the girls at school, two at a time, to come and look. **6** Not to stay to tea, of course, or to come traipsing through the house. But just to stand quietly in the courtyard while Isabel pointed out the beauties, and Lottie and Kezia looked pleased. . . .

But hurry as they might, by the time they had reached the tarred palings[3] of the boys' playground the bell had begun to jangle. They only just had time to whip off their hats and fall into line before the roll was called. Never mind. Isabel tried to make up for it by looking very important and mysterious and by whispering behind her hand to the girls near her, "Got something to tell you at playtime."

7 Playtime came and Isabel was surrounded. The girls of her class nearly fought to put their arms round her, to walk away with her, to beam flatteringly, to be her special friend. She held quite a court under the huge pine trees at the side of the playground. Nudging, giggling together, the little girls pressed up close. And the only two who stayed outside the ring were the two who were always outside, the little Kelveys. They knew better than to come anywhere near the Burnells.

For the fact was, the school the Burnell children went to was not at all the kind of place

---

3. **palings:** fence posts; pickets.

their parents would have chosen if there had been any choice. But there was none. It was the only school for miles. And the consequence was all the children in the neighborhood, the Judge's little girls, the doctor's daughters, the storekeeper's children, the milkman's, were forced to mix together. Not to speak of there being an equal number of rude, rough little boys as well. But **8** the line had to be drawn somewhere. It was drawn at the Kelveys. Many of the children, including the Burnells, were not allowed even to speak to them. They walked past the Kelveys with their heads in the air, and as they set the fashion in all matters of behavior, the Kelveys were shunned by everybody. Even the teacher had a special voice for them, and a special smile for the other children when Lil Kelvey came up to her desk with a bunch of dreadfully common-looking flowers.

9 They were the daughters of a spry, hardworking little washerwoman who went about from house to house by the day. This was awful enough. But where was Mr. Kelvey? Nobody knew for certain. But everybody said he was in prison. So they were the daughters of a washerwoman and a jailbird. Very nice company for other people's children! And they looked it. Why Mrs. Kelvey made them so conspicuous was hard to understand. The truth was they were dressed in "bits" given to her by the people for whom she worked. Lil, for instance, who was a stout, plain child with big freckles, came to school in a dress made from a green art-serge table-cloth of the Burnells', with red plush sleeves from the Logans' curtains. Her hat, perched on top of her high forehead, was a grown-up woman's hat, once the property of Miss Lecky, the postmistress. It was turned up at the back and trimmed with a large scarlet quill. What a little guy[4] she looked! It was impossible not to laugh. And her little sister, our Else, wore

---

4. **little guy:** little rag doll; from the rag dolls representing Guy Fawkes (1570–1606), British traitor.

CRITICAL THINKING: GUIDED READING QUESTIONS

LITERAL

1a. What invitation will *not* be extended to the girls who come to see the doll's house? (They may not stay to tea or come "traipsing" through the house.)

2a. What does Mrs. Kelvey do for a living, and how do her daughters dress? (She is a washerwoman. Her daughters dress in makeshift clothes and hand-me-downs.)

INFERENTIAL

1b. What does this rule imply about the Burnells? (They are not hospitable, and they impose severe social restrictions.)

2b. What do these details reveal about the reason for the daughters' treatment? (They are shunned because they are poor and deemed "low-class.")

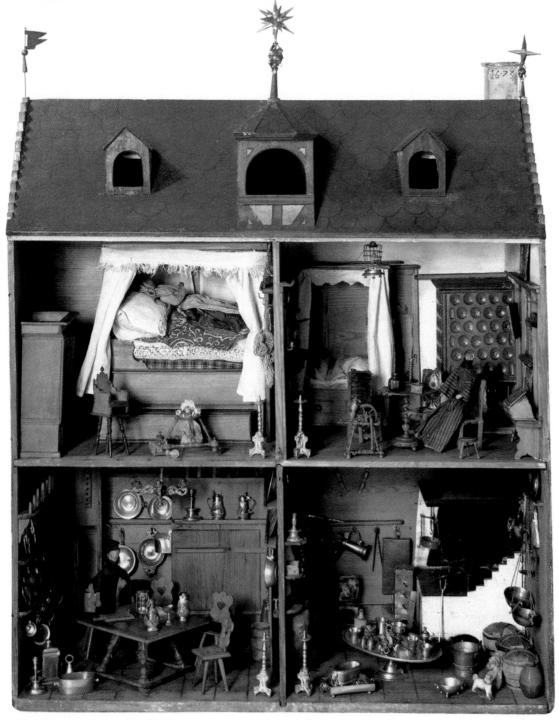

Doll House from Nuremberg, 1673.

- The shy Else Kelvey and her older sister, Lil, listen from afar as Isabel tells the others about the doll's house.
- Kezia feels that Isabel does not do justice to the lamp.
- Isabel chooses the first two girls to view the doll's house.
- As more girls see it, it becomes the talk of the neighborhood.
- Kezia asks her mother for permission to invite the Kelveys but is refused.
- At school several girls taunt the Kelveys about their background.

IN THE GLOSSARY

- flagged: lost vigor; weakened

10 READING SKILL: INFERENCE

Elicit the fact that the Kelveys, though excluded, seem as interested in the doll's house as the others.

11 TEACHING STUDENTS OF LIMITED ENGLISH PROFICIENCY

Note that the first *Isabel's* here is a possessive, whereas the second is a contraction for "Isabel is." Have students identify in the lines above other words in which an apostrophe and *s* form a contraction. (*there's, lamp's*)

12 CULTURAL BACKGROUND

Explain that mutton, or lamb, is widely eaten in Britain and its former colonies, where sheep are raised. Johnny cake, which is called corn bread in America, is made of wheat in Australia and New Zealand, where wheat is the chief grain.

13 TEACHING CHARACTERIZATION

Elicit the insight that Kezia shows kindness, thoughtfulness, and courage in going against the distinctions made by her peers and adult society.

14 TEACHING THEME

Stress that contempt for the Kelveys is something the girls have learned from their elders.

---

a long white dress, rather like a nightgown, and a pair of little boy's boots. But whatever our Else wore she would have looked strange. She was a tiny wishbone of a child, with cropped hair and enormous solemn eyes—a little white owl. Nobody had ever seen her smile; she scarcely ever spoke. She went through life holding on to Lil, with a piece of Lil's skirt screwed up in her hand. Where Lil went our Else followed. In the playground, on the road going to and from school, there was Lil marching in front and our Else holding on behind. Only when she wanted anything, or when she was out of breath, our Else gave Lil a tug, a twitch, and Lil stopped and turned round. The Kelveys never failed to understand each other.

10 Now they hovered at the edge; you couldn't stop them listening. When the little girls turned round and sneered, Lil, as usual, gave her silly, shamefaced smile, but our Else only looked.

And Isabel's voice, so very proud, went on telling. The carpet made a great sensation, but so did the beds with real bedclothes, and the stove with an oven door.

When she finished Kezia broke in. "You've forgotten the lamp, Isabel."

"Oh, yes," said Isabel, "and there's a teeny little lamp, all made of yellow glass, with a white globe that stands on the dining-room table. You couldn't tell it from a real one."

"The lamp's best of all," cried Kezia. She thought Isabel wasn't making half enough of the little lamp. But nobody paid any attention. Isabel was choosing the two who were to come back with them that afternoon and see it. She chose Emmie Cole and Lena Logan. But when the others knew they were all to have a chance, they couldn't be nice enough to Isabel. One by one 11 they put their arms round Isabel's waist and walked her off. They had something to whisper to her, a secret. "Isabel's *my* friend."

Only the little Kelveys moved away forgotten; there was nothing more for them to hear.

Days passed, and as more children saw the doll's house, the fame of it spread. It became the one subject, the rage. The one question was, "Have you seen Burnells' doll's house? Oh, ain't it lovely!" "Haven't you seen it? Oh, I say!"

Even the dinner hour was given up to talking about it. The little girls sat under the pines eat- 12 ing their thick mutton sandwiches and big slabs of johnny cake spread with butter. While always, as near as they could get, sat the Kelveys, our Else holding on to Lil, listening too, while they chewed their jam sandwiches out of a newspaper soaked with large red blobs. . . .

13 "Mother," said Kezia, "can't I ask the Kelveys just once?"

"Certainly not, Kezia."

"But why not?"

"Run away, Kezia; you know quite well why not."

At last everybody had seen it except them. On that day the subject rather flagged. It was the dinner hour. The children stood together under the pine trees, and suddenly, as they looked at the Kelveys eating out of their paper, always by themselves, always listening, they wanted to be horrid to them. Emmie Cole started the whisper.

"Lil Kelvey's going to be a servant when she grows up."

"O-oh, how awful!" said Isabel Burnell, and she made eyes at Emmie.

14 Emmie swallowed in a very meaning way and nodded to Isabel as she'd seen her mother do on those occasions.

"It's true—it's true—it's true," she said.

Then Lena Logan's little eyes snapped. "Shall I ask her?" she whispered.

"Bet you don't," said Jessie May.

"Pooh, I'm not frightened," said Lena. Suddenly she gave a little squeal and danced in front of the other girls. "Watch! Watch me! Watch me now!" said Lena. And sliding, gliding, dragging one foot, giggling behind her hand, Lena went over to the Kelveys.

CRITICAL THINKING: GUIDED READING QUESTIONS

LITERAL

1a. What do the Kelvey sisters never fail to do? (They never fail to understand each other.)

2a. Which two girls does Isabel invite first to view the doll's house, and what do these two later do? (Emmie Cole and Lena Logan; They later taunt the Kelveys about their background.)

INFERENTIAL

1b. Why do you think they share this kind of understanding? (As outcasts they have only each other's company and rely on each other more than siblings usually do.)

2b. From these details what can you infer about Emmie and Lena's status or role in the group of schoolgirls? (They are leaders who maintain their power or "popularity" by humiliating others.)

Lil looked up from her dinner. She wrapped the rest quickly away. Our Else stopped chewing. What was coming now?

15 "Is it true you're going to be a servant when you grow up, Lil Kelvey?" shrilled Lena.

Dead silence. But instead of answering, Lil only gave her silly, shamefaced smile. She didn't seem to mind the question at all. What a sell[5] for Lena! The girls began to titter.

Lena couldn't stand that. She put her hands on her hips; she shot forward. "Yah, yer father's in prison!" she hissed, spitefully.

This was such a marvelous thing to have said that the little girls rushed away in a body, deeply, deeply excited, wild with joy. Someone found a long rope, and they began skipping. And never did they skip so high, run in and out so fast, or do such daring things as on that morning.

In the afternoon Pat called for the Burnell children with the buggy and they drove home. There were visitors. Isabel and Lottie, who liked visitors, went upstairs to change their pina-
16 fores.[6] But Kezia thieved out at the back. Nobody was about; she began to swing on the big white gates of the courtyard. Presently, looking along the road, she saw two little dots. They grew bigger, they were coming towards her. Now she could see that one was in front and one close behind. Now she could see that they were
17 the Kelveys. Kezia stopped swinging. She slipped off the gate as if she was going to run away. Then she hesitated. The Kelveys came nearer, and beside them walked their shadows, very long, stretching right across the road with their heads in the buttercups. Kezia clambered back on the gate; she had made up her mind; she swung out.

"Hullo," she said to the passing Kelveys.

They were so astounded that they stopped.

---

5. **sell:** slang for "disappointment."
6. **pinafores:** sleeveless garments worn by young girls over dresses; they are worn here as a type of school uniform.

Lil gave her silly smile. Our Else stared.

"You can come and see our doll's house if you want to," said Kezia, and she dragged one
18 toe on the ground. But at that Lil turned red and shook her head quickly.

"Why not?" asked Kezia.

Lil gasped, then she said, "Your ma told our ma you wasn't to speak to us."

"Oh, well," said Kezia. She didn't know what to reply. "It doesn't matter. You can come and see our doll's house all the same. Come on. Nobody's looking."

But Lil shook her head still harder.

"Don't you want to?" asked Kezia.

Suddenly there was a twitch, a tug at Lil's skirt. She turned round. Our Else was looking at her with big, imploring eyes; she was frowning; she wanted to go. For a moment Lil looked at our Else very doubtfully. But then our Else twitched her skirt again. She started forward. Kezia led the way. Like two little stray cats they followed across the courtyard to where the doll's house stood.

"There it is," said Kezia.

There was a pause. Lil breathed loudly, almost snorted; our Else was still as a stone.

"I'll open it for you," said Kezia kindly. She undid the hook and they looked inside.

"There's the drawing-room and the dining-room, and that's the—"

"Kezia!"

Oh, what a start they gave!

"Kezia!"

19 It was Aunt Beryl's voice. They turned round. At the back door stood Aunt Beryl, staring as if she couldn't believe what she saw.

"How dare you ask the little Kelveys into the courtyard?" said her cold, furious voice. "You know as well as I do, you're not allowed to talk to them. Run away, children, run away at once. And don't come back again," said Aunt Beryl. And she stepped into the yard and shooed them out as if they were chickens.

The Doll's House **109**

CRITICAL THINKING: GUIDED READING QUESTIONS

LITERAL

1a. What do the other girls think of Lena's taunt about the Kelveys' father being in prison? (It is "such a marvelous thing to have said.")

2a. What does Kezia decide to do for the Kelveys? (She decides to show them the doll's house.)

INFERENTIAL

1b. Why do they consider it "marvelous"? (It goes beyond the girls' everyday level of cruelty to the Kelveys and is something they wish they had the nerve to say.)

2b. How might the events at school have prompted Kezia's decision? (The others' cruelty makes Kezia feel sorry for the Kelveys and reinforces her desire not to exclude them.)

---

15 CRITICAL THINKING: EVALUATION

Have students evaluate the girls' behavior and the values that underlie it: for example, their thinking it so shameful to be a servant.

16 TEACHING WORD CHOICE

Note that "thieved out" implies that Kezia's nonconformity is the equivalent of criminal behavior in her constricted world.

17 TEACHING CONFLICT

Point out that Kezia's external conflict with her society parallels an internal conflict in which she is torn between obeying society's dictates or heeding those of her conscience. She resolves her inner conflict at the end of the paragraph, when she makes up her mind.

18 TEACHING CHARACTERIZATION

Elicit the fact that Lil lacks Kezia's courage: She has been intimidated into going along with social restrictions that make her and Else outcasts. Ask why Mrs. Kelvey might want her daughters to heed these restrictions. (Going against her employers' orders might cost her her job.)

19 CRITICAL THINKING: CLASSIFICATION

Have students classify as sympathetic or unsympathetic all the characters named in the story.

- When the Kelveys run off, Aunt Beryl scolds Kezia.
- Scaring the Kelveys and scolding her niece make Beryl feel more lighthearted after having received an unpleasant letter.
- The Kelveys rest near a field, and Else happily tells Lil, "I seen the little lamp."

IN THE GLOSSARY

- ghastly: terrible; horrible

20 GRAMMAR IN LITERATURE

Have students identify participial adjectives. (*burning, shrinking, huddling, dazed*)

21 TEACHING IRONY

Point out the ironic contrast between Aunt Beryl's contemptible behavior and the positive view she has of it.

22 TEACHING SYMBOLS

Note that the lamp represents Kezia's kindness, the sense of wonder she and Else share, the splendid life Else has never known, and perhaps hope for the future.

COLLABORATIVE LEARNING: ENRICHMENT ACTIVITY

Literary Discussion Have groups of students read different stories by Katherine Mansfield and then discuss the author's style, settings, characters, and themes.

Detail. *Doll House from Nuremberg,* 1673.

"Off you go immediately!" she called, cold and proud.

20 They did not need telling twice. Burning with shame, shrinking together, Lil huddling along like her mother, our Else dazed, somehow they crossed the big courtyard and squeezed through the white gate.

"Wicked, disobedient little girl!" said Aunt Beryl bitterly to Kezia, and she slammed the doll's house to.

The afternoon had been awful. A letter had come from Willie Brent, a terrifying, threatening letter, saying if she did not meet him that evening in Pulman's Bush, he'd come to the front 21 door and ask the reason why! But now that she had frightened those little rats of Kelveys and given Kezia a good scolding, her heart felt lighter. That ghastly pressure was gone. She

went back to the house humming.

When the Kelveys were well out of sight of Burnells', they sat down to rest on a big red drain-pipe by the side of the road. Lil's cheeks were still burning; she took off the hat with the quill and held it on her knee. Dreamily they looked over the hay paddocks,[7] past the creek, to the group of wattles where Logan's cows stood waiting to be milked. What were their thoughts?

Presently our Else nudged up close to her sister. But now she had forgotten the cross lady. She put out a finger and stroked her sister's quill; she smiled her rare smile.

22 "I seen the little lamp," she said, softly.

Then both were silent once more.

7. **paddocks:** New Zealand term for fields.

110 *The Short Story*

CRITICAL THINKING: GUIDED READING QUESTIONS

LITERAL

1a. What "lightens" Aunt Beryl's heart after she receives the unpleasant letter? (scaring "those little rats of Kelveys" and giving Kezia a good scolding)

2a. What does Else do after she and her sister stop to rest? (She strokes the feather on her sister's hat, smiles her rare smile, and says, "I seen the little lamp.")

INFERENTIAL

1b. What do these details show about the kind of person she is? (She is a cruel, shallow person who takes her problems out on others and bullies children.)

2b. What does her remark show that she shares with Kezia? (She shares Kezia's sense of wonder.)

STUDY QUESTIONS

Recalling

1. What do the Burnell children think of their new doll's house? What does Kezia like best about it?
2. Under what conditions are the girls' school friends allowed to see the doll's house?
3. What rule must the Burnell girls obey regarding the Kelvey sisters? About what aspects of the Kelveys' background does Lena taunt Lil Kelvey?
4. Summarize what happens when Kezia lets Lil and Else see the doll's house. What does the usually silent Else tell her sister at the end of the story?

Interpreting

5. What does the story suggest about the effects adult prejudices can have on children? What does it suggest about the way economic or class differences can affect people?
6. In what sense can Kezia's family be said to live in a "doll's house" of their own? How is Kezia different from the rest of her family?
7. What abstract qualities or values might the little lamp represent? Why is it significant that, at the end of the story, Else smilingly recalls the lamp?

Extending

8. What do you think Kezia will be like when she grows up? Why?

LITERARY FOCUS

Tone

Tone is the attitude that an author takes toward his or her subject. We often think of tone as something that can be heard—for instance, a tone of voice. Written words also express tone. The tone of a story may be serious or lighthearted, restrained or excited, angry or mocking.

Sometimes the tone changes in the course of a story. In addition, the author may present one character's experiences in a different tone than he or she uses to recount another character's experiences. In such a case, the contrasts in tone will usually reflect different attitudes toward the two characters.

Thinking About Tone

1. What tone does the author use to describe the arrival of the doll's house? For which character, in particular, does this tone reflect the author's sympathy?
2. What tone does the author use to describe Aunt Beryl? What attitude do you think the author has toward Aunt Beryl?

COMPOSITION

Writing About Tone

■ Write a brief composition about the changes in tone in "The Doll's House." Show how the changing tone reflects different attitudes toward different story characters. Give examples of words the author uses to describe different characters and tell what tones the words convey. Among the characters you may want to discuss are Kezia, Lena Logan, Aunt Beryl, and the Kelvey sisters.

COMPARING STORIES

■ Compare and contrast this story to another story you have read about economic or class differences and the problems they can cause. For example, you might compare and contrast it to "The Actor," which appears earlier in this book. What is similar and different about the societies portrayed in each story? About the behavior and reactions of the characters?

The Doll's House **111**

ANSWERS

STUDY QUESTIONS

1. It is "perfect" and "marvelous." Kezia likes the little lamp best.
2. They can see it two at a time, and they cannot enter the Burnell home.
3. They cannot speak to the Kelveys. Lena taunts Lil about her mother's job as a washerwoman and her father's supposed stay in prison.
4. They are interrupted by Aunt Beryl, who chases off the Kelveys and scolds Kezia. Else says, "I seen the little lamp."
5. They can cause children to adopt the same prejudices. They can create great unhappiness and injustice.
6. They live easy, sheltered, and constricted lives. Kezia is thoughtful, kind, and not preoccupied with social status.
7. The lamp might represent Kezia's kindness, her and Else's sense of wonder, the splendid life Else has never known, and perhaps hope for the future. It shows that Else shares Kezia's sense of wonder and stresses the kindness Kezia has shown and the cruelty and unfairness of society.
8. Answers will vary. Some students might think that Kezia will retain her independence; others might think that she will lose her innocence and kindness and conform to her society.

LITERARY FOCUS

1. a tone of wonder; Kezia
2. a mocking, ironic tone; contempt

COMPARING STORIES

Answers will vary. For example, students may feel that similar class differences are treated more satirically in "The Doll's House."

COMPOSITION: GUIDELINES FOR EVALUATION

WRITING ABOUT TONE

Objective

To describe a story's changes in tone

Guidelines for Evaluation

■ suggested length: three or four paragraphs
■ should examine tone changes showing different attitudes toward different characters
■ should cite examples of word choice that help convey tone

A young pianist manipulates his public in this satiric exploration of art and artifice. Young Bibi, an infant prodigy, performs for an elegant crowd in a palatial hall. Though he loves his music, he holds his audience in contempt. Audience members focus on their own concerns instead of the beauty of the music. After the performance, however, Bibi is lionized as the great talent he was billed to be.

LITERARY SKILLS FOR THIS SELECTION

- point of view
- tone
- characterization

THEMES IN THIS SELECTION

- growing up: the loss of childhood innocence
- art and artifice
- mass behavior versus individuality

LESSON OBJECTIVES

1. to analyze a story's point of view
2. to write a narrative using the omniscient point of view
3. to compare and contrast stories

Teacher's Classroom Resources 1

- Teaching Notes 197
- Prereading Vocabulary 198
- Reading Guide 199
- Check Test 200
- Responding to World Cultures 201
- Writing Process Guides: Writing About Point of View 202
  Writing with an Omniscient Narrator 203
- Grammar in Literature: Organization and Coherence 204
- Selection Test 205

IN THE CLASSROOM

TEACHING STUDENTS OF DIFFERENT ABILITIES

- **For less advanced students:** Preview the Glossary words, and help students define other unfamiliar words in this story.

Thomas Mann (1875–1955)

Germany

Thomas Mann is widely considered one of the greatest writers of the twentieth century. Mann came from a middle-class background and probably would have joined his family's grain business had it not been sold after his father's untimely death. Soon afterward, the Manns moved to Munich, where young Thomas became active in the city's cultural life. He worked for a literary journal, began writing his own stories, and in 1901 published his best-selling novel *Buddenbrooks*. There followed other major works of both fiction and nonfiction, and by 1929 Mann's international esteem was high enough to earn him the Nobel Prize.

In 1933 Mann chose to leave his homeland rather than live under Nazi rule. Stripped of his German citizenship, he spent the last decades of his life in Switzerland and the United States, though he visited his homeland frequently after the Nazi defeat in World War II.

"The Infant Prodigy," one of Mann's most famous stories, takes place in an earlier era. It deals with a subject Mann often examines: the conflict between artistic values and the more mundane concerns of society.

Then have them complete the Reading Guide.
- **For more advanced students:** Ask students to consider how the story reflects the ideas of German Modernism as described on page 566 of their text.

German Music Traditions

The German people have a long tradition as lovers of music. Many of the world's greatest composers—Bach, Beethoven, Brahms, Mendelssohn, Schumann, and Wagner, to name a few—were German. These composers made great contributions to such musical forms as the sonata, the symphony, and the opera.

Concerts have traditionally drawn great crowds, and before World War I German royalty and aristocrats were often patrons of concert halls.

"The Infant Prodigy" opens in an elegant recital hall in the years before World War I. The musician the audience has come to hear is a child prodigy, an artist who displays his genius at a remarkably early age. Such youthful talents were often idolized by audiences. The great Austrian composer Wolfgang Amadeus Mozart, for example, made his concert debut in Munich when he was five years old.

See LITERATURE AND CULTURE SOURCEBOOK: Germany

DISCUSSING GEOGRAPHY AND CULTURE

Cities and Music

This tale is probably set in Munich, the cultural capital of Germany and Mann's home for many years. The city was founded in the twelfth century by Henry the Lion, Duke of Bavaria. The Bavarian royalty built splendid museums and theaters in Munich, where concert music is still renowned for its brilliant quality.
- Ask students whether they play an instrument. In which cities would they choose to perform if they went on a concert tour?

Thomas Mann

The Infant Prodigy

Translated from the German by H. T. Lowe-Porter

The infant prodigy entered. The hall became quiet.

It became quiet and then the audience began to clap, because somewhere at the side a leader of mobs, a born organizer, clapped first. The audience had heard nothing yet, but they applauded; for a mighty publicity organization had heralded the prodigy and people were already hypnotized, whether they knew it or not.

The prodigy came from behind a splendid screen embroidered with Empire[1] garlands and great conventionalized flowers and climbed nimbly up the steps to the platform, diving into the applause as into a bath, a little chilly and shivering, but yet as though into a friendly element. He advanced to the edge of the platform and smiled as though he were about to be photographed; he made a shy, charming gesture of greeting, like a little girl.

He was dressed entirely in white silk, which the audience found enchanting. The little white jacket was fancifully cut, with a sash underneath it, and even his shoes were made of white silk. But against the white socks his bare little legs stood out quite brown, for he was a Greek boy.

He was called Bibi Saccellaphylaccas. And such indeed was his name. No one knew what Bibi was the pet name for, nobody but the impresario,[2] and he regarded it as a trade secret. Bibi had smooth black hair reaching to his shoulders; it was parted on the side and fastened back from the narrow domed forehead by a little silk bow. His was the most harmless childish countenance in the world, with an unfinished nose and guileless mouth. The area beneath his pitch-black mouselike eyes was already a little tired and visibly lined. He looked as though he were nine years old but was really eight and given out for seven. It was hard to tell whether to believe this or not. Probably everybody knew better and still believed it, as happens about so many things. The average man thinks that a little falseness goes with beauty. Where should we get any excitement out of our daily life if we were not willing to pretend a bit? And the average man is quite right, in his average brains!

The prodigy kept on bowing until the applause died down, then he went up to the grand piano, and the audience cast a last look at its programs. First came a *Marche solennelle*,[3] then a *Rêverie*,[4] and then *Le Hibou et les moineaux*[5]— all by Bibi Saccellaphylaccas. The whole program was by him; they were all his compositions. He could not score them, of course, but he had them all in his extraordinary little head and they possessed real artistic significance, or so it said, seriously and objectively, in the program. The program sounded as though the impresario had wrested these concessions from his critical nature after a hard struggle.

The prodigy sat down upon the revolving stool and felt with his feet for the pedals, which were raised by means of a clever device so that Bibi could reach them. It was Bibi's own piano,

---

1. **Empire** [om pĕr′]: referring to a French style of decoration developed during the first French Empire (1804–1815) under Napoleon I.
2. **impresario** [im′prə sär′ē ō]: organizer or manager of live entertainments.

3. **Marche solennelle** [märsh′ sô lə nel′]: French for "solemn march."
4. **Rêverie** [re ver ē′]: brief, quiet musical composition.
5. **Le Hibou et les moineaux** [lə ē bo͞o′ ā lā mwa nō′]: French for "The Owl and the Sparrows."

The Infant Prodigy **113**

CRITICAL THINKING: GUIDED READING QUESTIONS

LITERAL

1a. Why does the audience begin clapping? ("A leader of mobs, a born organizer, clap[s] first.")

2a. What sort of gesture does the prodigy make at the edge of the platform? (He makes a "shy, charming gesture.")

INFERENTIAL

1b. What does this suggest about audiences, or at least this audience? (They are easily manipulated.)

2b. Do you think he is really shy? Why or why not? (Shyness is unlikely in a small child who is able to perform in such a serious, elegant milieu and who performs his own compositions in public.)

MOTIVATION: PRIOR KNOWLEDGE

Ask what thoughts students might "overhear" if they could read the minds of a concert audience.

PAGE SUMMARY: AT A GLANCE

- Bibi Saccellaphylaccas, billed as a child prodigy, enters an elegant concert hall.
- After enchanting the audience, he seats himself at a special grand piano designed to accommodate his small size.
- The program consists of all Bibi's compositions.

IN THE GLOSSARY

- prodigy: very gifted person, usually a child
- heralded: announced
- countenance: face
- score: arrange the music for various instruments to play
- wrested: extracted with effort

1 TEACHING POINT OF VIEW AND TONE

Note that the story has an omniscient narrator, able to report the thoughts and motives of the whole audience. He immediately establishes a mocking, satirical tone by revealing the way in which the audience has been manipulated.

2 TEACHING CHARACTERIZATION

Ask what the detail about Bibi's eyes suggests. (Performing has prematurely aged and hardened him.)

3 CULTURAL BACKGROUND

Tell students that in the past French was the international language of upper-class, cultured Europeans. Naming the pieces in French suggests culture—or pretension.

4 CRITICAL THINKING: LOGICAL REASONING

Note the ironic use of "objectively," since the program promoting the star is unlikely to be objective. Elicit the insight that this irony—part of the narrator's mocking tone—should logically make us suspect the "real artistic significance" of Bibi's compositions.

PAGE SUMMARY: AT A GLANCE

- Though Bibi has an artificial pose for the audience, he also takes joy in playing the piano.
- He starts his first piece with a powerful blast and ends with a grand climax.
- In the palatial concert hall every seat is taken, and the front seats are very costly.
- In the audience is an elderly princess, the "picture of elegant composure."

IN THE GLOSSARY

- artful: clever; cunning
- abysmal: very deep
- palatial: like a palace
- belabored: thrashed; beat
- infectious: contagious

5 TEACHING TONE

Note that *artful,* with its connotations of artifice as well as art, helps convey the narrator's knowing, mocking tone. Pairing it with *little* stresses the incongruity between Bibi's seeming innocence and actual cynicism.

6 TEACHING STUDENTS OF LIMITED ENGLISH PROFICIENCY

Encourage students to use their knowledge of cognates to understand unfamiliar words. Spanish or Italian speakers, for example, may recognize that the *oct* in *octave* means "eight" and that an octave is thus "eight notes."

7 TEACHING SETTING

Discuss the fact that the "fashionable" setting is part of the showmanship aimed at impressing the audience.

8 TEACHING CHARACTERIZATION

Point out that this is the impresario's rationale: Hypocritical and greedy, he sets high prices to realize high profits.

9 READING SKILL: COMPARISON

Note that the princess, like Bibi, is a performer, presenting to the public the "picture" that the public expects of her.

he took it everywhere with him. It rested upon wooden trestles and its polish was somewhat marred by the constant transportation—but all that only made things more interesting.

5 Bibi put his silk-shod feet on the pedals; then he made an artful little face, looked straight ahead of him, and lifted his right hand. It was a brown, childish little hand; but the wrist was strong and unlike a child's, with well-developed bones.

Bibi made his face for the audience because he was aware that he had to entertain them a little. But he had his own private enjoyment in the thing too, an enjoyment which he could never convey to anybody. It was that prickling delight, that secret shudder of bliss, which ran through him every time he sat at an open piano—it would always be with him. And here was the 6 keyboard again, these seven black and white octaves, among which he had so often lost himself in abysmal and thrilling adventures—and yet it always looked as clean and untouched as a newly washed blackboard. This was the realm of music that lay before him. It lay spread out like an inviting ocean, where he might plunge in and blissfully swim, where he might let himself be borne and carried away, where he might go under in night and storm, yet keep the mastery: control, ordain—he held his right hand poised in the air.

A breathless stillness reigned in the room—the tense moment before the first note came. . . . How would it begin? It began so. And Bibi, with his index finger, fetched the first note out of the piano, a quite unexpectedly powerful first note in the middle register, like a trumpet blast. Others followed, an introduction developed—the audience relaxed.

7 The concert was held in the palatial hall of a fashionable first-class hotel. The walls were covered with mirrors framed in gilded arabesques,[6]

------

6. **arabesques** [ar′ə besks′]: elaborate designs of intertwined patterns.

114 *The Short Story*

between frescoes[7] of the rosy and fleshly school. Ornamental columns supported a ceiling that displayed a whole universe of electric bulbs, in clusters darting a brilliance far brighter than day and filling the whole space with thin, vibrating golden light. Not a seat was unoccupied, people were standing in the side aisles and at the back. 8 The front seats cost twelve marks;[8] for the impresario believed that anything worth having was worth paying for. And they were occupied by the best society, for it was in the upper classes, of course, that the greatest enthusiasm was felt. There were even some children, with their legs hanging down demurely from their chairs and their shining eyes staring at their gifted little white-clad contemporary.

Down in front on the left side sat the prodigy's mother, an extremely obese woman with a powdered double chin and a feather on her head. Beside her was the impresario, a man of oriental appearance with large gold buttons on his conspicuous cuffs. The princess was in the middle of the front row—a wrinkled, shriveled little old princess but still a patron of the arts, especially everything full of sensibility.[9] She sat in a deep, velvet-upholstered arm-chair, and a Persian carpet was spread before her feet. 9 She held her hands folded over her gray striped-silk breast, put her head on one side, and presented a picture of elegant composure as she sat looking up at the performing prodigy. Next her sat her lady-in-waiting, in a green striped-silk gown. Being only a lady-in-waiting she had to sit up very straight in her chair.

Bibi ended in a grand climax. With what power this wee manikin[10] belabored the keyboard! The audience could scarcely trust its ears. The march theme, an infectious, swinging tune, broke out once more, fully harmonized,

------

7. **frescoes:** paintings executed directly on plaster.
8. **marks:** German units of money. At the time of the story, a mark was worth about twenty-five cents.
9. **sensibility:** here, delicate feeling.
10. **manikin:** little man.

CRITICAL THINKING: GUIDED READING QUESTIONS

LITERAL

1a. Why does Bibi make his face for the audience? (He is aware that he has to entertain them a little.)

2a. What runs through Bibi every time he sits at the piano? ("Prickling delight, that secret shudder of bliss," runs through him.)

INFERENTIAL

1b. What does this detail stress about Bibi's childlike innocence? (It is false; he is actually manipulative and quite cynical.)

2b. What may hamper Bibi's ability to communicate his private love for the piano? (his false showmanship and resulting scorn for the public)

10 GRAMMAR IN LITERATURE

Note the vivid modifiers that help us picture Bibi and mentally hear the applause. Have students distinguish between the adverbs and adjectives. (*Fourth, unanimously,* and *enthusiastically* are adverbs; *demure, little, maidenly,* and *front* are adjectives.)

11 CULTURAL BACKGROUND

Have students list the story's terms from music—such as *bass* here and *treble* on the next page—and then consult a dictionary for each term's definition and etymology. Note that many terms in music come from Italy, where many classical-music forms and instruments were developed.

ART AND LITERATURE

The Finnish artist Alvar Cawen (1886–1935) studied the brightly colored works of the French artist Henri Matisse but preferred to work with more somber tones to create a mood of introspection. In *Grand Piano* he combines dark colors with a loose rendering of a recitalist to produce a sober, contemplative mood.
- After reading the story ask students which of the musical pieces named in the selection—*méditation, étude, fantaisie,* or rhapsody—Cawen's painting suggests to them. (Answers will vary; some may suggest *méditation* or *étude*.)

Grand Piano, 1919, Cawen.

bold and showy; with every note Bibi flung himself back from the waist as though he were marching in a triumphal procession. He ended *fortissimo*,[11] bent over, slipped sideways off the stool, and stood with a smile awaiting the applause.

10 And the applause burst forth, unanimously, enthusiastically; the child made his demure little maidenly curtsy and people in the front seat thought: "Look what slim little hips he has! Clap, clap! Hurrah, bravo, little chap, Saccophylax or whatever your name is! Wait, let me take off my

gloves—what a little devil of a chap he is!"

Bibi had to come out three times from behind the screen before they would stop. Some late-comers entered the hall and moved about looking for seats. Then the concert continued. Bibi's *Rêverie* murmured its numbers, consisting almost entirely of arpeggios,[12] above which a bar of melody rose now and then, weak-winged. Then came *Le Hibou et les moineaux*. This piece was brilliantly successful, it made a strong impression; it was an effective childhood fantasy, remarkably well envisaged. The bass repre-

11. *fortissimo* [fôr tēs′ē mō′]: Italian for "very loud"; a musical direction.

12. **arpeggios** [är pej′ē ōz′]: notes of a musical chord played in succession instead of together.

The Infant Prodigy **115**

CRITICAL THINKING: GUIDED READING QUESTIONS

LITERAL

1a. How does Bibi acknowledge the enthusiastic applause? (He makes a "demure little maidenly curtsy.")

INFERENTIAL

1b. What is the purpose of this behavior? (It stresses his youth and shows a false modesty and innocence, all aimed at making the audience more appreciative by eliciting a sense of astonishment at his accomplishments.)

- *Le Hibou* prompts an ovation, which Bibi knowingly prolongs, although he considers the audience "idiots" for liking the simple piece more than his own favorite, the *Fantaisie*.
- As he plays the more complex *Fantaisie*, he occasionally loses himself in the music.
- Listening from their "regular rows," the audience members think all sorts of thoughts in their "regular brains."

IN THE GLOSSARY

- ovation: enthusiastic demonstration of public acclaim
- oblivion: state of forgetfulness

12 READING SKILL: CONTRAST

Elicit the contrast between Bibi's thoughts and actions. (He does not show the contempt he really feels.)

13 TEACHING THEME

Note that this description of the audience and the contrast with Bibi stress the lack of individuality in mass behavior, an important theme of the story.

14 TEACHING CHARACTERIZATION

Stress that Bibi is not all false showmanship: He does have a love for the music.

15 READING SKILL: INFERENCE

Elicit the idea that this description, like the term "drawing card" learned from the impresario, is probably not original to Bibi. Here he most likely is quoting the impresario or the program.

16 TEACHING POINT OF VIEW

Note that here and in the next paragraphs the omniscient narrator reveals the thoughts of several members of the audience.

sented the owl, sitting morosely rolling his filmy eyes, while in the treble the impudent, half-frightened sparrows chirped. Bibi received an ovation when he finished; he was called out four times. A hotel page with shiny buttons carried up three great laurel wreaths onto the stage and proffered them from one side while Bibi nodded and expressed his thanks. Even the princess shared in the applause, daintily and noiselessly pressing her palms together.

Ah, the knowing little creature understood how to make people clap! He stopped behind the screen—they had to wait for him—lingered a little on the steps of the platform, admired the long streamers on the wreaths—although actually such things bored him stiff by now. He bowed with the utmost charm; he gave the audience plenty of time to rave itself out, because applause is valuable and must not be cut short. "*Le Hibou* is my drawing card," he thought—this expression he had learned from the impresario. "Now I will play the fantasy, it is a lot better than *Le Hibou,* of course, especially the

12 C-sharp passage. But you idiots dote on the *Hibou,* though it is the first and the silliest thing I wrote." He continued to bow and smile.

Next came a *Méditation*[13] and then an *Étude*[14]—the program was quite comprehensive. The *Méditation* was very like the *Rêverie*—which was nothing against it—and the *Étude* displayed all of Bibi's virtuosity, which naturally fell a little short of his inventiveness. And then the *Fantaisie.*[15] This was his favorite; he varied it a little each time, giving himself free rein and sometimes surprising even himself, on good evenings, by his own inventiveness.

He sat and played, so little, so white and shining, against the great black grand piano,

13 elect and alone, above that confused sea of faces, above the heavy, insensitive mass soul, upon

---

13. *Méditation* [mā dē tä syŏɴ′]: short musical piece.
14. *Étude* [ā tōōd′]: solo musical piece intended to demonstrate a special technique.
15. *Fantaisie* [fän tä zē′]: improvised musical piece.

116 *The Short Story*

---

which he was laboring to work with his individual, differentiated soul. His lock of soft black hair with the white silk bow had fallen over his forehead; his trained and bony little wrists pounded away; the muscles stood out visibly on his brown childish cheeks.

14 Sitting there he sometimes had moments of oblivion and solitude, when the gaze of his strange little mouselike eyes with the big rings beneath them would lose itself and stare through the painted stage into space that was peopled with strange vague life. Then out of the corner of his eye he would give a quick look back into the hall and be once more with his audience.

15 "Joy and pain, the heights and the depths—that is my *Fantaisie*," he thought lovingly. "Listen, here is the C-sharp passage." He lingered over the approach, wondering if they would notice anything. But no, of course not, how should they? And he cast his eyes up prettily at the ceiling so that at least they might have something to look at.

16 All these people sat there in their regular rows, looking at the prodigy and thinking all sorts of things in their regular brains. An old gentleman with a white beard, a seal ring[16] on his finger and a bulbous swelling on his bald spot, a growth if you like, was thinking to himself: "Really, one ought to be ashamed." He had never got any further than "Ah, thou dearest Augustin"[17] on the piano, and here he sat now, a gray old man, looking on while this little hop-o'-my-thumb[18] performed miracles. Yes, yes, it is a gift of God, we must remember that. God grants His gifts, or He withholds them, and there is no shame in being an ordinary man. Like with the Christ Child.—Before a child one may kneel

---

16. **seal ring:** ring with an embossed design, usually of the wearer's family emblem. Such rings were used to make imprints in sealing wax that served as a letter's signature.
17. **Augustin:** that is, "Ach, du lieber Augustin," a simple German song.
18. **hop-o'-my-thumb:** very small person.

CRITICAL THINKING: GUIDED READING QUESTIONS

LITERAL

1a. How does the princess share in the applause for *Le Hibou*? (She "daintily and noiselessly press[es] her palms together.")

2a. What does Bibi realize is "valuable and must not be cut short"? (applause)

INFERENTIAL

1b. What does her manner of applauding reveal about the princess? (She is too proud and too concerned with her dignity to applaud with any enthusiasm.)

2b. Why is applause valuable to Bibi and the impresario? (It signals popularity and helps members of the audience feel as if they are enjoying themselves, thus enhancing Bibi's prospects for fame and profit.)

17 without feeling ashamed. Strange that thoughts like these should be so satisfying—he would even say so sweet, if it was not too silly for a tough old man like him to use the word. That was how he felt, anyhow.

Art . . . the business man with the parrot-nose was thinking. "Yes, it adds something cheerful to life, a little good white silk and a little tumty-ti-ti-tum. Really he does not play so badly. Fully fifty seats, twelve marks apiece, that makes six hundred marks—and everything else besides. Take off the rent of the hall, the lighting and the programs, you must have fully a thousand marks profit. That is worthwhile."

18 That was Chopin[19] he was just playing, thought the piano-teacher, a lady with a pointed nose; she was of an age when the understanding sharpens as the hopes decay. "But not very original—I will say that afterwards; it sounds well. And his hand position is entirely amateur. One must be able to lay a coin on the back of the hand—I would use a ruler on him."

Then there was a young girl, at that self-conscious and chlorotic[20] time of life when the most ineffable ideas come into the mind. She was thinking to herself: "What is it he is playing? It is expressive of passion, yet he is a child. If he kissed me it would be as though my little brother kissed me—no kiss at all. Is there such a thing as passion all by itself, without any earthly object, a sort of child's-play of passion? What nonsense! If I were to say such things aloud they would just be at me with some more cod-liver oil. Such is life."

An officer was leaning against a column. He looked on at Bibi's success and thought: "Yes, you are something and I am something, each in **19** his own way." So he clapped his heels together and paid to the prodigy the respect which he

---

19. **Chopin** [shō′pan]: Frédéric Chopin (1810–1849), Polish composer and pianist who spent much of his life in France.
20. **chlorotic** [klō rot′ik]: referring to a type of anemia that affects adolescent girls.

felt to be due to all the powers that be.

Then there was a critic, an elderly man in a shiny black coat and turned-up trousers splashed with mud. He sat in his free seat and thought: "Look at him, this young beggar of a Bibi. As an individual he has still to develop, but as a type he is already quite complete, the artist **20** *par excellence.*[21] He has in himself all the artist's exaltation and his utter worthlessness, his charlatanry and his sacred fire, his burning contempt and his secret raptures. Of course I can't write all that; it is too good. Of course, I should have been an artist myself if I had not seen through the whole business so clearly."

Then the prodigy stopped playing and a perfect storm arose in the hall. He had to come out again and again from behind his screen. The man with the shiny buttons carried up more wreaths: four laurel wreaths, a lyre made of violets, a bouquet of roses. He had not arms enough to convey all these tributes; the impresario himself mounted the stage to help him. He hung a laurel wreath round Bibi's neck, he tenderly stroked the black hair—and suddenly as though overcome he bent down and gave the prodigy a kiss, a resounding kiss, square on the mouth. And then the storm became a hurricane. That kiss ran through the room like an electric shock; it went direct to peoples' marrow and made them shiver down their backs. They were carried away by a helpless compulsion of sheer noise. Loud shouts mingled with the hysterical clapping of hands. Some of Bibi's commonplace little friends down there waved their handkerchiefs. But the critic thought: "Of course that kiss had to come—it's a good old gag. Yes, good Lord, if only one did not see through everything quite so clearly—"

21 And so the concert drew to a close. It began at half past seven and finished at half past eight. The platform was laden with wreaths and two

---

21. *par excellence* [pär ek′sə läns′]: French expression meaning "beyond comparison."

The Infant Prodigy **117**

- As they view the performance, audience members indulge their personal concerns and soon forget the music itself.
- After the performance—which is only an hour long—Bibi is showered with floral tributes.
- The impresario bestows a stagy kiss that sends the audience into even greater raptures.

IN THE GLOSSARY

- ineffable: difficult to express in words

17 READING SKILL: GENERALIZATION

As they read these lines and the next five paragraphs, have students make a generalization about the audience's reactions to Bibi. (Everyone relates Bibi's performance to his or her own concerns and does not appreciate the music itself.)

18 CRITICAL THINKING: LOGICAL REASONING

Point out that the compositions are all Bibi's own; therefore, when the piano teacher thinks, "That was Chopin he was just playing," she means that Bibi wrote something that resembles a work by Chopin.

19 CULTURAL BACKGROUND

Explain that in the German military, clapping or clicking one's heels was a sign of respect.

20 TEACHING CHARACTERIZATION

Note that this is the critic's rationalization for not becoming an artist; the more likely reason was a lack of talent or perseverance. Elicit the insight that he, like the others, is hypocritical.

21 TEACHING TONE AND IRONY

Point out that this seemingly simple fact is steeped in irony, given the high prices paid and the great fuss made over so brief a concert.

CRITICAL THINKING: GUIDED READING QUESTIONS

LITERAL

1a. As he reacts to the music, what does the business man calculate? (the profit made that evening)

2a. Why does the piano teacher decide to say "not very original" afterward? (It sounds good.)

INFERENTIAL

1b. What does his reaction show about his appreciation of the music? (He does not really appreciate it.)

2b. What does this motive reveal that she has in common with Bibi? (They share a concern for appearances that prompts false behavior.)

- After taking many curtain calls, Bibi is surrounded by members of the audience.
- Others encircle the princess, and it is hard to tell who receives more homage.
- When Bibi is introduced and the princess asks about his creative process, he thinks, "Oh, what a stupid old princess!"
- As the audience leaves, a girl with untidy hair remarks, "We are all infant prodigies, we artists," and then she stares enviously at an elegant group whom she "rather despises."

IN THE GLOSSARY

- homage: respect; honor
- critique: critical assessment

22 TEACHING CHARACTERIZATION

Ask what valuing criticism more than art reveals about the critic. (He is vain and self-promoting.)

23 CRITICAL THINKING: EVALUATION

Ask whether students agree with Bibi—are the princess' questions stupid? (Composers of classical music usually have extensive training and do not compose intuitively, but the princess may be knowingly insulting Bibi's efforts.)

24 TEACHING FLAT CHARACTERS

Note that the audience members are easily labeled flat characters because they behave predictably: the profit-hungry business man and the sour-grapes critic, for example. Ask how students would label the girl with untidy hair. (radical artist; Bohemian type)

COLLABORATIVE LEARNING: ENRICHMENT ACTIVITY

Music Have a group of students research some of Germany's famous composers of classical music and prepare an oral report or series of tapes that include biographical data and recordings of their works.

little pots of flowers stood on the lamp-stands of the piano. Bibi played as his last number his *Rhapsodie grecque,*[22] which turned into the Greek national hymn at the end. His fellow-countrymen in the audience would gladly have sung it with him if the company had not been so august. They made up for it with a powerful noise and hullabaloo, a hot-blooded national demonstration. And the aging critic was thinking: "Yes, the hymn had to come too. They have to exploit every vein—publicity cannot afford to neglect any means to its end. I think I'll criticize that as inartistic. But perhaps I am wrong, perhaps that is the most artistic thing of all.

[22] What is the artist? A jack-in-the-box. Criticism is on a higher plane. But I can't say that." And away he went in his muddy trousers.

After being called out nine or ten times the prodigy did not come any more from behind the screen but went to his mother and the impresario down in the hall. The audience stood about among the chairs and applauded and pressed forward to see Bibi close at hand. Some of them wanted to see the princess too. Two dense circles formed, one round the prodigy, the other round the princess, and you could actually not tell which of them was receiving more homage. But the court lady was commanded to go over to Bibi; she smoothed down his silk jacket a bit to make it look suitable for a court function, led him by the arm to the princess, and solemnly indicated to him that he was to kiss the royal

[23] hand. "How do you do it, child?" asked the princess. "Does it come into your head of itself when you sit down?" "*Oui, madame,*"[23] answered Bibi. To himself he thought: "Oh, what a stupid old princess!" Then he turned round shyly and uncourtier-like and went back to his family.

Outside in the cloak-room there was a

___

22. *Rhapsodie grecque* [rap′sō dē′ grek′]: French for "Greek Rhapsody." A rhapsody is a musical piece of free, irregular form.
23. *Oui, madame* [wē′ mə däm′]: French for "Yes, ma'am."

118   *The Short Story*

crowd. People held up their numbers and received with open arms furs, shawls, and galoshes. Somewhere among her acquaintances the piano-teacher stood making her critique. "He is not very original," she said audibly and looked about her.

In front of one of the great mirrors an elegant young lady was being arrayed in her evening cloak and fur shoes by her brothers, two lieutenants. She was exquisitely beautiful, with her steel-blue eyes and her clean-cut, well-bred face. A really noble dame. When she was ready she stood waiting for her brothers. "Don't stand so long in front of the glass, Adolf," she said softly to one of them, who could not tear himself away from the sight of his simple, good-looking young features. But Lieutenant Adolf thinks: What cheek![24] He would button his overcoat in front of the glass, just the same. Then they went out on the street, where the arc-lights[25] gleamed cloudily through the white mist. Lieutenant Adolf struck up a little dance on the frozen snow to keep warm, with his hands in his slanting overcoat pockets and his collar turned up.

[24] A girl with untidy hair and swinging arms, accompanied by a gloomy-faced youth, came out just behind them. A child! she thought. A charming child. But in there he was an awe-inspiring . . . and aloud in a toneless voice she said: "We are all infant prodigies, we artists."

"Well, bless my soul!" thought the old gentleman who had never got further than Augustin on the piano, and whose boil was now concealed by a top hat. "What does all that mean? She sounds very oracular." But the gloomy youth understood. He nodded his head slowly.

Then they were silent and the untidy-haired girl gazed after the brothers and sister. She rather despised them, but she looked after them until they had turned the corner.

___

24. **What cheek:** What nerve!
25. **arc-lights:** high-intensity light produced by an electric arc and used to illuminate outdoor nighttime events.

CRITICAL THINKING: GUIDED READING QUESTIONS

LITERAL

1a. After the concert how do members of the audience treat the princess? (They flock around her to pay homage.)

2a. What does Bibi think when he meets the princess? ("Oh, what a stupid old princess!")

INFERENTIAL

1b. What does this behavior suggest about their artistic values? (They are as interested in wealth and social status as they are in art.)

2b. What does the discrepancy between his thoughts and actions show about Bibi? (He is still "performing," or behaving falsely.)

STUDY QUESTIONS

Recalling

1. Why does Bibi make "an artful little face" when he begins to play? What "private enjoyment" does he feel he can never share?
2. What does Bibi think and how does he act after playing *Le Hibou*?
3. Cite three examples of people's thoughts as Bibi plays the *Fantaisie*.
4. What does Bibi think as he meets the princess and kisses her hand?
5. What does the girl with untidy hair think about Bibi in the third-to-last paragraph?

Interpreting

6. What aspects of Bibi's performance are truly impressive and what aspects are false or exaggerated? What effect has fame had on Bibi?
7. Does most of the audience really appreciate Bibi's performance? Explain.
8. Why is it significant that the crowd surrounds the princess as well as Bibi after the concert?
9. What do you think the girl means when she says that all artists are infant prodigies like Bibi?

Extending

10. To what extent do you think today's artists or entertainers and their audiences share the attitudes of Bibi and his audience?

COMPOSITION

Writing About Point of View

■ How does the use of the omniscient point of view add to the effectiveness of "The Infant Prodigy"? Does the story have a true main character, or is the entire audience, along with Bibi, the main character? Answer these questions in a brief composition that uses details from the story to support your ideas.

Writing with an Omniscient Narrator

■ Write a narrative in which you use an omniscient narrator, recounting an event through the eyes of several characters. Reveal the thoughts and feelings of the characters as they witness or take part in the event. If you like, create contrasts between the characters' attitudes and their perceptions of the event.

COMPARING STORIES

■ Compare and contrast this story to other stories you have read about growing up, either in this section or elsewhere. What is similar and different about the children or teen-agers portrayed? What is similar and different about the relationships of the characters to their societies, as portrayed in the stories?

The Infant Prodigy **119**

ANSWERS

STUDY QUESTIONS

1. He knows he must entertain the audience. He feels he can never share the "prickling delight, that secret shudder of bliss" when he plays the piano.
2. He thinks the members of the audience are idiots for enjoying the silliest thing he ever wrote, but he bows and smiles anyway.
3. Examples include the old gentleman's shame for his own poor progress on the piano, the business man's calculations of the night's profits, and the piano teacher's decision that Bibi's music is not original.
4. He thinks, "Oh, what a stupid old princess!"
5. "A child! . . . A charming child. But in there he was an awe-inspiring . . ."
6. His talent and feeling for the music are impressive, his manipulation of the applause is false, and his youth and innocence are exaggerated. Fame has made him jaded and hypocritical at an early age.
7. No; though many enjoy it, they relate it to their own concerns and soon forget the music.
8. It shows they are as impressed with rank and wealth as they are with art.
9. Answers may vary. She probably means that she considers herself a great talent, too.
10. Answers will vary. Students may say many artists today are "hyped" and some audience members are more interested in the performers' private lives than in their performance.

COMPARING STORIES

Answers will vary. For example, students may find Bibi cynical and the narrator of "A Handful of Dates" naive; they may think Bibi is less protected but far more manipulative than Kezia in "The Doll's House."

COMPOSITION: GUIDELINES FOR EVALUATION

WRITING ABOUT POINT OF VIEW

Objective

To analyze a story's point of view

Guidelines for Evaluation

■ suggested length: one or two paragraphs
■ should explain how the omniscient point of view adds to the story's effectiveness
■ should consider whether the entire audience, along with Bibi, is the main character

WRITING WITH AN OMNISCIENT NARRATOR

Objective

To write a narrative using an omniscient point of view

Guidelines for Evaluation

■ suggested length: two or three pages
■ should focus on a single event
■ should be told in the third person and reveal many characters' thoughts and feelings

LESSON PREVIEW

In this Canadian tale a group of immigrants who have fled Russia because of religious persecution seek to settle in a place that reminds them of home. Finally they come upon Hoodoo Valley, whose sunset mirages duplicate the lush, hilly terrain they seek. Though the soil is poor and they realize the beauty is an illusion, they feel that they have found a good home.

LITERARY SKILLS FOR THIS SELECTION

- setting and atmosphere
- character motivation

THEMES IN THIS SELECTION

- personal values: material versus spiritual concerns
- immigration and homesickness

LESSON OBJECTIVES

1. to examine setting and atmosphere in a story
2. to understand the meanings and origins of borrowed words
3. to write a description of a setting

Teacher's Classroom Resources 1

- Teaching Notes   207
- Prereading Vocabulary   208
- Reading Guide   209
- Check Test   210
- Responding to World Cultures   211
- Literary Focus: Setting and Atmosphere   212
- Language Study: Borrowed Words   213
- Writing Process Guide: Describing a Setting   214
- Grammar in Literature: Combining with Appositives   215
- Selection Test   216

IN THE CLASSROOM

TEACHING STUDENTS OF DIFFERENT ABILITIES

- **For less advanced students:** Have students list and contrast the Dukhobors' values with those of McPherson. Have them complete the Reading Guide for this selection.

PREVIEW: THE AUTHOR AND THE WORLD

GEOGRAPHY AND CULTURE

Gabrielle Roy (1909–1983)

Canada

One of the most popular French Canadian authors of the twentieth century, Gabrielle Roy was born to a pioneer family in Manitoba. As a young woman she taught in rural schools until she saved enough money to travel to Europe, where she studied drama in Paris and London. When she returned to Canada in 1939 she found she could support herself better by writing.

Settling in Montreal, Roy contributed articles to French Canadian magazines. In 1945 she completed her first novel, *Bonheur d'occasion* (later translated as *The Tin Flute*), a powerful portrait of a poverty-stricken Montreal family. A best seller in Canada, the novel was also the first Canadian work to win France's noted literary award, the Prix Fémina.

Over the years Roy produced a string of additional novels and stories, many of them exploring western Canada's pioneer past. Her novel *Rue Deschambault* (translated as *Street of Riches*) describes country life in the province of Manitoba. *Ces enfants de ma vie (Children of My Heart)* draws on her experiences as a school teacher. "Hoodoo Valley" is from her story collection *Garden in the Wind*.

Canada and the Dukhobors

Canada is the largest country in North America and the second largest country in the world, after the Soviet Union. Once ruled by both France and Britain, Canada reflects its history in the languages of its people. Canada has two official languages, French—the language in which Gabrielle Roy wrote—and English. The country is divided into provinces just as the United States is divided into states. During the nineteenth and early twentieth centuries, Canada's western provinces—Manitoba, Saskatchewan, Alberta, and British Columbia—attracted pioneers just as the western United States did. Most of these Canadian pioneers came to raise wheat.

Among the immigrant groups to settle in western Canada were the Dukhobors [dōō′kə bôrz′] of "Hoodoo Valley." The Dukhobors were members of a devout Russian religious sect that split with the Russian Orthodox Church in the late 1700s. They were exiled to southern Russia in the 1840s and periodically persecuted until the great writer Leo Tolstoy persuaded Russia's czar [zär], or emperor, to allow them to emigrate. More than 7,000 Dukhobors settled in western Canada in the 1890s.

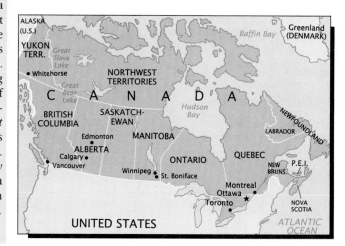

DISCUSSING GEOGRAPHY AND CULTURE

- **For more advanced students:** Have students research and report on Roy's place in French Canadian literature.

Local Geography: A Bird's-Eye View

The events of this tale unfold in the vast plains of western Canada, a region that is very similar to the Great Plains of the United States. If you flew over this part of Canada today, you would see small towns laid out in neat grids near grain elevators or railroad tracks and great rectangles of land planted with wheat, oats, and alfalfa.

- Ask students what they would see if they flew in a plane over their home state.

Gabrielle Roy

Hoodoo Valley

Translated from the French by Alan Brown

I

The group of Dukhobors newly arrived in Verigin,[1] a prairie hamlet, were living for the time being in the round tents and converted railway cars that had been provided for them: a melancholy encampment on a hostile terrain invested by marshes, mosquitoes and, worse still, every evening, by boredom. Then, gathered like an immense family around a fire of branches, you could hear them intoning, all with the same low-pitched, afflicted voice, some song of their people.

No Dukhobor was ready to say it right out loud, but they were desolate.

"It's nothing like our Humid Mountains."

"Oh, no! Far it is from our green Caucasus!"[2]

From the very start the plain had set about rebuffing them with its flat immensity, naked under the sky, this endless space, this too-vast exaggeration of a land where in winter, they said, it was cold enough to freeze your breath in your throat, and in summer hot enough to put an end to your days. And the people here, the ones who'd been living in this solitude awhile, what strange ones they were! Eaters of meat and other forbidden foods, they squabbled among themselves as if life wasn't hard enough already; or, carried away by a different madness, they'd dance till the tavern tables jumped. They couldn't be Christians, these folk who used alco-

hol and tobacco and never seemed to tire of spatting viciously among themselves.

The Dukhobor women, their blond hair carefully hidden under kerchiefs doubled to a point, had perhaps less time for boredom than their men. They cooked over little piles of embers, did the washing, laid it to dry on the grass, and went off across the naked plain, sometimes quite a distance, searching for bits of wood to burn. But their husbands, these great stalwarts, upright as oaks, with heavy mustaches, their blue eyes childlike and astonished, had all the leisure they needed for sighing and lamenting.

Their leaders, Streliov, Zibinov and Strekov, went out every day with their guide McPherson, the settlement agent, sometimes to the north, sometimes to the south, in search of land for their community. Up to now they had nowhere found a concession[3] that in their eyes combined the qualities they obscurely felt would suit them.

The man McPherson, an ambitious and enterprising little Scot, had wagered that he'd settle his Dukhobors in no time, intending to use their success on Canadian soil as a stepping stone to promotion in his career.

The women, the children, the old men, would surround the three leaders on their return to the encampment and ask: "What did you see today, Zibinov, Streliov, Strekov?"

And these three, the men in whom they had placed their confidence, would reply: "Just the flat land. The same as here."

---

1. **Dukhobors . . . Verigin:** The Dukhobors have named the hamlet after their spiritual leader, Peter Verigin (d. 1924), then serving a sentence as an exile back in Russia.
2. **Caucasus** [kô′kə səs]: mountains in southern Russia. The Dukhobors had lived in the Caucasus region since the 1840s, when they were sent there by the Russian government.

3. **concession:** a subdivision of land granted by a government to a group of settlers.

Hoodoo Valley **121**

CRITICAL THINKING: GUIDED READING QUESTIONS

LITERAL

1a. What do the Dukhobors find strange about the area's other inhabitants? (They eat meat, drink alcohol, use tobacco, dance vigorously, and fight among themselves.)

2a. What do the three Dukhobor leaders report every night about the land they have seen? ("Just the flat land. The same as here.")

INFERENTIAL

→ **1b.** From these details, what can you infer about the Dukhobors' customs and beliefs? (They are vegetarians, do not use alcohol or tobacco, do not dance, and believe in nonviolence.)

→ **2b.** What sort of land are they looking for, and why? (They are looking for green, mountainous land that resembles the Russian area from which they came and which they miss.)

IN THE GLOSSARY

- tenacity: firmness
- incessant: continuous
- plaintive: sad; mournful
- arable: fit for cultivation

5 GRAMMAR IN LITERATURE

Remind students that an appositive is a noun or noun phrase that further explains an adjacent noun or noun phrase. Have students identify the two appositives in this sentence. ("a handful of neighbors" and "immigrants . . . land")

6 TEACHING THEME

Elicit that the Dukhobors are impractical because to them kinship and other spiritual values are more important than material concerns.

7 CULTURAL BACKGROUND

Point out that to attract settlers, land developers often spread exaggerated reports about the beauties and opportunities in the New World. Ask why the Dukhobors would be likely to believe such reports. (They are a naive and dreamy people.)

8 READING SKILL: CAUSE AND EFFECT

Ask what has caused the Dukhobors' "hearts" to forget the persecution and feel only nostalgia. (They are disappointed with the new land to which they have come.)

"And that was all?"

"Just prairie, I tell you. Nothing but prairie."

McPherson was fuming. What else did they expect to find here in the flattest stretch of all Canada?

A strange folk, gentle, dreaming, with only one foot in this world; but in their refusal, their disillusion, they had a tenacity that could outlast the most energetic. 5 The people of the village, a handful of neighbors, immigrants themselves but resigned with good grace to their new land, began to grow impatient with these long-faced Dukhobors whose incessant plaintive songs reached them night after night in their scattered shacks. As if singing could change the prairie! It had heard other sighs, seen other regrets, this plain of exile and homesickness. In the end it always brought people around. Others, many others, had been through the same thing. The Dukhobors too would have to give in.

They didn't want to break up or settle in small groups as others did. That would have solved many problems, for the good land was by no means all in one place. Most often it was a patchwork created by ancient alluvia[4] or waterways. But they absolutely refused to separate. 6 They insisted on settling in a single region, old and young, grandchildren and grandparents together, along with nephews, cousins and friends—in short, the whole lost folk in one place.

So they sought a big stretch of arable land. At some distance from the camp such tracts of land were still to be found. McPherson took Strekov, Streliov and Zibinov to see them, across miles and miles of silent plain, often serene and inviting under the high, clear sky. Where the road stopped the wagon made its own trail through the grasses. In this way they'd seen a good part of the countryside: sandy, desert-like

spaces overrun by the wind; others with a stubby growth like wire twisted and rolled together; others made almost livable by pretty groups of trees that showed from afar the presence of water. Nowhere did the Dukhobor leaders consent to stop.

"Nyet,[5] nyet."

Here the country seemed too wild, too isolated; there they would spy tents or trappers' huts and suddenly were unwilling to have neighbors.

"Nyet, nyet!"

They shook their heads. Their eyes, blue and candid, wide with astonishment, always expressed the same tenacious estrangement.

And this had been going on for weeks.

The women were constantly on the lookout for the party's return.

"Come now, you must have seen something today that would suit us!"

"Nyet. We saw nothing but the flat land. Always the same."

They could find no other way to express their disappointment. 7 Before they left the Caucasus, someone must have told them a very fancy story to attract them to the Canadian West, and they'd swallowed it whole. They always ended up singing their songs of lamentation. At such times the gentle landscape they had left behind, the land of acacias, of lemon trees and tender grass, came to life again behind 8 their closed eyelids. For each new evil chases out the last; having forgotten the persecutions that had forced them to leave their native soil, their hearts retained nothing of it but the most tender recollections.

Oh, what nostalgia!

By now even the women were almost all infected by it.

This wretched plain all around! (At times

---

4. **alluvia** [ə lōō'vē ə]: mud or sand deposited by flowing water.

5. **Nyet:** Russian for "no."

CRITICAL THINKING: GUIDED READING QUESTIONS

LITERAL

1a. What is McPherson's reaction to the Dukhobors' stubborn refusal to accept the prairie land? (It makes him fume.)

2a. What have the Dukhobors' "hearts" forgotten about their homeland? (They have forgotten the persecution that forced them to leave.)

INFERENTIAL

1b. Why does he grow angry? (He hoped to settle them quickly, and he finds absurdly unrealistic their desire for something other than prairie land.)

2b. What does this detail stress about the role emotions play in the Dukhobors' behavior? (They are more emotional than logical.)

Snow Flurries, 1953, Andrew Wyeth.

Andrew Wyeth (born 1917), the son of the famous American illustrator N. C. Wyeth, was largely self-taught. Working in egg tempera, which allowed for a subtle range of color and fine brushstrokes, Wyeth created an austere, at times sentimental naturalism using a subtle, nearly sunless palette of colors. Wyeth carefully composed his landscapes and portraits to capture psychological and often ominous drama. In works such as *Snow Flurries,* he sets a desolate scene at an odd visual angle to convey a feeling of looming suspense.

■ Ask students whether they think the Dukhobors would settle the land in the painting. Why or why not? (Answers will vary, but on the basis of descriptions of rejected land on page 122, most students will probably say no.)

■ Makaroff, the oldest, notes that their lush Caucasus homeland was originally barren land that the first Dukhobor settlers planted themselves.
■ He and several women feel it is time to make the best of a bad situation and settle down.
■ When some younger women question the move to Canada, an angry babushka (grand-mother) reminds them that their spiritual leader back in Russia promised them peace and religious freedom in Canada, not an easy life.

IN THE GLOSSARY

■ enigmatic: puzzling

9 TEACHING STUDENTS OF LIMITED ENGLISH PROFICIENCY

Help students use context clues to determine that the expression "make the best of a bad job" means "do as well as one can with a bad situation."

10 READING SKILL: INFERENCE

Elicit that the "cruel indifference" to which Streliov refers may be that of the harsh landscape or its rugged pioneer inhabitants.

11 READING SKILL: GENERALIZATION

Note that the narrator often gen-eralizes about the Dukhobors' feelings and actions or those of segments within the group. For example, here she tells us what the young mothers *in general* think and do. Have students find more examples of such gener-alizations. (Examples include the thoughts and behavior of the pregnant women at the end of this paragraph and the old women in the next.)

12 TEACHING CHARACTER MOTIVATION

Ask why the pregnant women would show the most disappoint-ment. (They care most about the future because of their maternal concern for their unborn children.)

you could see one of them stoop to pick up a pebble and hurl it violently as if to strike the immense countryside and take vengeance on its numb expanse.)

"What did you see today, Streliov?" asked Makaroff, the oldest and wisest, who thought the time had come to make the best of a bad job. Life wasn't so long, he often said. If we have to use up so much of it regretting the past, what's left for doing what's still to be done?

And Streliov, the oldest of the three leaders, a solid man with all the strength of his thirty years, began to sigh like a stripling.

"The same thing as here, Grandfather. The naked plain, always. And always, it seems, the same cruel indifference."

The old man drew nearer to poke the fire.

"I remember when I was young and we'd just been exiled to the Caucasus, life didn't seem so easy there either at the start. Did you say 'indif-ference,' Streliov? Do you have any idea how many trees—lemon trees and cherry trees and acacias—we had to plant there for every one that lived? Do you know that, Streliov?"

The immigrants, seated in a circle in the growing dark, were suddenly as struck by his words as they had been by their recurrent long-ing for their lost homeland. At once their eyes turned outward toward the plain, which their imagination saw as endless: the mute, the enig-matic land. They did their best to see it covered with little whitewashed houses, with pens for the chickens, vegetable gardens, fences, milk pails upside down on the fence posts, busy com-ings and goings, and even their seesaw wells like the ones at home in the Caucasus, punctuating the prairie with the long strokes of their lever poles drawn dark against the sky. For awhile they were all comforted by the vision of the tre-mendous work to be redone and they burned with impatience to get started.

"True enough, you know," some of the more realistic women grumbled, "it's more than time we started in somewhere. You leaders, go off on

your search again. And try to come back with some good news. It's high time to get on with our work."

But others, lulling their babies, held them tight to their breast as if defying the dark plain to steal them away. And suddenly they would begin to weep, doubtless because of some vague perception that the plain would finally take their children, would take thousands of others, would absorb as many lives as there were grains of sand, before this would even show. Still others, a few about to bear children, had an even stronger hatred of the stark land and the giant sky which their eyes probed in terror.

The ones with the most common sense were the very old women, tottering babushkas,[6] come to this country with just enough time left to die and sleep in its foreign soil.

They scolded the younger ones: "What would our holy little father Verigin think, and him in exile in the wilds of Siberia,[7] if he saw you now, downcast and fearful and always sniveling?"

And the others would reply: "Our little fa-ther Verigin promised we'd find peace at the end of the world, and harmony, and that in the place we went to we'd be of one heart and mind. Per-haps we didn't understand his orders. Did he really mean us to come to Canada?"

A very angry babushka scolded back: "There's no such thing as a country where we can be of one mind unless we try, each one of us, to make it so. Our little father Verigin prom-ised us a land where they'd let us live in peace according to our ideal of non-violence and free conscience. He didn't promise the grass would be trimmed and the house all built and the bread on the table. Have you all gone mad? Tell me! The old Dukhobors of my time put more heart in their work and whined less. And they'd

---

6. **babushkas** [bə boosh′kəz]: Russian for "grandmothers."
7. **Siberia** [sī bir′ē ə]: cold, remote region in northeastern Asia; the traditional Russian place of exile.

CRITICAL THINKING: GUIDED READING QUESTIONS

LITERAL

1a. What does Makaroff say earlier Dukhobors had to do when they settled in the Caucasus? (They had to plant many trees.)

2a. What vision momentarily brings the Dukhobors comfort? (They find comfort in the vision of the tre-mendous amount of work they will have to do.)

INFERENTIAL

1b. On the basis of his remarks, how was the lushness and beauty of the Caucasus homeland achieved? (It was achieved through hard work.)

2b. If hard work does not bother them, what is making them so unhappy? (They are disappointed with the new land and homesick for the old.)

seen something of cruelty and injustice, before our good Lukeria,[8] in those dark years when they wandered over Russia. What about those who fell under the knout[9] of the Czarist soldiers rather than take arms against their brothers? Did you ever hear that they grumbled? Shame to these Dukhobors around me!"

In the end they prayed together under the great starlit sky. At least the stars were still familiar. Their eyes raised on high, they asked for a light to guide them on their earthly path.

"Little mother, it's not the work we're afraid of. It's the silence here. It's as if God no longer wanted to give us a sign. As if from now on he would be silent forever."

The wrinkled face, furrowed by life, was absorbed in contemplation of the flames.

"It is true. Since we came to Canada he has seldom spoken to us. But he is there, behind all that silence. Just wait, my lambs. Tomorrow, the next day, one day soon, he will surely give us a sign."

II

Forty miles north of the railway a great stretch of grassy plain, formerly pastureland to a herd of buffalo, was still there for the taking. That was the destination of the expedition that set out on a certain July morning.

The heavy wagon lumbered along at the trot—often a slow one—of the four prairie horses, all small but solidly built. Six men were in the party: the three Dukhobor leaders, then McPherson, flanked by his interpreter, James Craig, and the half-Indian driver. They had left at dawn accompanied by particularly fervent women's

---

8. **Lukeria** [lōō kir′ē ə]: Lukeria Kalmykova, spiritual leader of the Dukhobors from 1864 until her death, in 1886. Under her able leadership, the Dukhobors saw a temporary lessening in tension with the Russian government.
9. **knout** [nout]: whip that was the traditional means of inflicting punishment in Russia under the czar [zär], or emperor.

---

voices raised in song, for after the long evening of prayer everyone had risen with the conviction that this day, at last, would be marked by divine favor.

At first they drove across a plain where a reddish grass waved as far as you could see; then others where a thick growth of weeds rose to the wagon's axles; saline patches harbored the noxious smells of many carcasses of young deer and dead birds; brushwood country, and muskegs[10] where everyone had to get off and help the horses; morose landscapes where there was nothing living but the wind; and, from time to time, fresh little stands of elder trees or poplar. Almost everywhere the plain seemed uninhabited and silent.

Each patch of green in this limitless landscape could be seen for miles around, and this was all that kept the tired beasts going or altered the men's unblinking stare.

Evening was not far off. Still nothing hinted that they might be nearing the former buffalo pasture. McPherson was growing worried. Had they taken the wrong fork at the last faint crossing of the ways?

No path was visible now. They were navigating by guesswork across rocky soil or through virgin grass. The half-Indian driver seemed as uncertain as the little horses themselves. Their ears pricked up anxiously from time to time. The leaders, impassive in the back, pretended to ignore these disturbing developments.

Suddenly McPherson exclaimed loudly in vexation. The land was changing without warning. For in fact, on emerging from a gulley of shadows that had hemmed them in for several minutes, they were met by an intense and gleaming light. There a new landscape stood revealed, one of surprising beauty, unsuspected even a moment ago.

It was Hoodoo Valley, so named by the

---

10. **muskegs:** mossy bogs or marshes in western Canada and Alaska.

Hoodoo Valley **125**

PAGE SUMMARY: AT A GLANCE

- When someone explains that it is not work they fear but God's failure to provide a sign, the old grandmother predicts that God's sign will soon appear.
- As McPherson takes the three Dukhobor leaders to inspect a former buffalo pasture, they accidentally go through Hoodoo Valley.

IN THE GLOSSARY

- fervent: passionate
- morose: gloomy

13 READING SKILL: CONTRAST

Elicit that this statement stresses the unfamiliarity that the Dukhobors feel with everything else—only the stars are familiar.

14 READING SKILL: PREDICTING OUTCOMES

Have students predict what sort of sign, if any, the Dukhobors may receive.

15 TEACHING SETTING AND ATMOSPHERE

Point out that the vivid details of the setting help us picture the landscape and recognize its bleakness.

16 TEACHING POINT OF VIEW

Elicit that the omniscient narrator here indirectly provides McPherson's thoughts: The question is McPherson's.

17 CULTURAL BACKGROUND

In conjunction with the Language Study, point out that *hoodoo* is a North Americanism; it is not used in Britain. An alteration of *voodoo*, a West African word that entered English from Creole (Louisiana) French, *hoodoo* means "something bringing bad luck" but is sometimes applied to anything frightening and eerie. For example, in parts of western America, a fantastically shaped rock formation is sometimes called a hoodoo.

CRITICAL THINKING: GUIDED READING QUESTIONS

LITERAL

1a. In response to the babushka, what does one of the Dukhobors explain about the reasons for their unhappiness? (It is not work they fear but the silent prairie and God's failure to give them a sign. They feel God has forsaken them.)

2a. What does the babushka predict? (God will give them a sign.)

INFERENTIAL

1b. Why do most of the Dukhobors feel as if they are literally in a God-forsaken place? (They feel this way because the barren landscape is so alien to their experience.)

2b. What does the babushka's prediction show that she has not lost? (She has not lost faith.)

- The setting sun makes Hoodoo Valley a place of exotic splendor.
- Even McPherson is affected, though he will not admit it and hates the place.
- The Dukhobors want to stop here, for they feel they have at last received God's sign.
- The sun creates optical illusions in which the clouds seem like mountains and a streak of light seems like a river.
- The Dukhobors feel the place has everything needed to "rejoice the heart of man."

18 TEACHING SETTING AND ATMOSPHERE

Elicit that the vivid details of the setting, which help us picture the valley, work together to create a mysterious, exotic atmosphere.

19 TEACHING PLOT: CLIMAX

Help students recognize that the Dukhobors' excited affirmation, a reversal of their previous attitude, represents the story's climax, or turning point.

20 TEACHING CHARACTER MOTIVATION

Elicit the Dukhobors' reasons for loving Hoodoo Valley. (It reminds them of their home in the Humid Mountains, and they believe its beauty and mystery are the signs they were awaiting from God.)

21 READING SKILL: CAUSE AND EFFECT

Ask students what has produced the "mountains" and "river." (The setting sun has created optical illusions that make the clouds seem like mountains and a streak of light seem like a river.)

Indians who were frightened of its strangeness and the curious power it had—precisely at this hour of day—over the unstable souls of men.

18 With an exotic splendor, more reminiscent of the Orient than of the plain with its assortment of quiet shades, it flamed up before them in the floods of copper light the sun spilled over it at this day's end. Countless flowers, pushing up through brambles and tall, sharp-bladed grass, gave off a glow in that light almost not to be borne. Flowers among which not one, so people said, was without its sting, its poison sap, its capacity to wound, but all strangely sumptuous, in umbels[11] of garnet velvet, bunched heads of somber gold, purple or milky corollas[12] with stiff, smooth leaves shining with their lacquer.

In the distance clouds tinted blazing red enclosed this odd valley, surrounding it as with a chain of hills whose folds held an indefinable attraction. Each one appeared to open into the reddened sky a secret and mysterious passage toward a place where certainty and happiness must reign at last. From one minute to the next, moreover, beneath the constant flaming of the sky, the more distant clouds took on further depth and issued their silent call.

McPherson, almost caught in the spell for a moment, though he'd have been the last to admit it, got hold of himself. He hated this place above all others. He was about to give the order to leave at once when the three leaders, on their feet in the back of the wagon, began encourag-**19** ing each other excitedly: "Da, da!"

This was the first time McPherson had heard them say yes.

Further words seemed torn from them by their excess of emotion and the infinite joy of being there together, all three unanimous.

---

11. **umbels:** blooms that consist of clusters of many tiny flowers whose stems stretch up from a common point.
12. **corollas** [kə rōl′əz]: flower petals, especially circular ones.

126 *The Short Story*

"What's that they're saying?" asked McPherson.

The interpreter smiled with some commiseration.

20 "They want to get off here. They're talking about the Humid Mountains, something about receiving a sign at last . . . and I don't know what-all, it doesn't make much sense. . . ."

As if under a spell, they were barely recognizable, their faces lit up and transformed, their eyes gleaming. With one accord they leapt from the wagon and advanced toward the valley. Stones rolled beneath their feet, a fine dust rose from the earth where they walked, and this alone should have told them of the poverty of the soil; but the Dukhobors paid no attention, their eyes dazzled, advancing in line toward the brilliance the setting sun had managed to extract from an inextricable tangle of thorn and thistle.

They stopped. One raised his arm and pointed to the mass of clouds resting on the sky's edge, forming enchanting hills that rolled back to beyond this world. Another pointed at the long streak of light that wound across the valley like a river of pale waters. The third fervently stared out at the fiery horizon.

"What do they say?"

"That there's all you need here to rejoice the **21** heart of man," the interpreter said. "Mountains in the distance, a river in the grass, a rare kind of peace and birds everywhere."

True enough, for look! The burning air was filled with the presence of birds! Nesting in the serried[13] thickets, calling from bush to bush, then, all at once, with great cries and whirring of wings, bursting into flight; creatures with flaming throats, crested with red or light yellow, thronged into the air. But these were unsociable birds and fled from men: their presence here,

---

13. **serried:** closely packed.

CRITICAL THINKING: GUIDED READING QUESTIONS

LITERAL

1a. What place does McPherson hate above all others? (Hoodoo Valley)

2a. What things in Hoodoo Valley do the Dukhobors feel "rejoice the heart of man"? (mountains in the distance, a river in the grass, a rare kind of peace, and birds everywhere)

INFERENTIAL

1b. Why do you think he hates it so much? (He is a realist who hates the illusions that Hoodoo Valley creates and the romantic, impractical ideas that it inspires.)

2b. How does Hoodoo Valley seem different from all the other land the Dukhobors have seen? (It seems lush, colorful, and mountainous, not bleak and flat.)

like that of the strange flowers, spoke further of the wildness of the place.

"But those aren't mountains yonder," McPherson tried to explain, "and that's no river in the valley. Tell them, Craig, that it's all mirage and trumpery. It's the sun and the time of day that make the cursed valley turn this way at sunset!"

But it was no use. The three Dukhobors had removed their hats as if to salute one of the most moving encounters of their lives. They stayed motionless a long time, their eyes moist, contemplating the landscape and listening to their conquered hearts.

22 "They know, at least I think they do," the interpreter reported, "that the mountains and rivers aren't real, but they say, 'What's the difference, as long as we can see them? And if the three of us, by God's grace, can see again in this place the mountains and river of our sweet homeland, why should it be any different for our wives and children and old men? Won't they see these things too? And when they've seen them, won't they be reassured, as we are?'"

23 Then McPherson, forgetting that they couldn't understand him, shouted: "Just scratch that soil! See how poor it is! Look at that confounded brush, it's all that'll grow here. I can give you a hundred times better, a thousand times better! I can give you lovely flat fields where the grass is so tasty your horses'll whinny a mile away. Or if you want I'll find you land that's half woods and a real river running through it. Just a few hours from here, all that's waiting for you!"

But the Dukhobors would hear none of it.

Beyond the call of reason now, exiled in elation, assured that they alone understood the world's mystery, they stood there, hat in hand, imagining that they had perhaps been shown an infallible sign of destiny. They took one pace forward and struck up a song of thanksgiving. The song found its way down the valley and echoed back twice, three times. The great, wild birds, and the dry leaves rustling at their passage, seemed shaken with surprise at hearing an old, exalted hymn rolling all the way from ancient Russia.

At last the three men ended their song. McPherson saw that they were weeping. Tears rushed impetuously from their eyes, washing the dust from their cheeks and disappearing in their blond mustaches. They wept without raising a hand to wipe their cheeks, in abandon and confidence, relieved once and for all of the cruelty of expectation.

McPherson waited yet awhile. Soon there would be an end to the fugitive beauty of the place. In a moment now it would be left bare: when the great footlight on the horizon dimmed, perhaps they would see that this was nothing but a wasteland under false, flamboyant colors.

But now the Dukhobors were showing their impatience to be gone. They were in a hurry to bring the good news to the others.

They sat on one side of the wagon, facing the same way. They were looking back when suddenly the valley dimmed into twilight and what **24** was perhaps its true and poignant gloom. But in the shadow there still glowed on their inscrutable faces the flaming sky that their eyes had seen and their souls now bore away.

Hoodoo Valley **127**

PAGE SUMMARY: AT A GLANCE

■ McPherson explains that the mountains and river are illusions caused by the setting sun, but the Dukhobors say, "What's the difference, as long as we can see them?"

■ They speak of God's grace in enabling them to "see" again the mountains and river of their homeland.

■ McPherson shouts about the poor soil, but the Dukhobors will hear none of it.

■ They are impatient to return to the others and tell them the good news.

IN THE GLOSSARY

■ elation: great happiness
■ poignant: evoking compassion
■ inscrutable: mysterious

22 TEACHING THEME

Note that the Dukhobors' attitude stresses the value they place on spiritual concerns, an important theme of the story. Ask what their attitude also suggests about reality and illusion. (Reality may not be important if an illusion brings spiritual comfort.)

23 TEACHING CHARACTER FOILS

Point out that the practical McPherson cannot understand the motives and values of the impractical Dukhobors.

24 CRITICAL THINKING: EVALUATION

Have students evaluate the Dukhobors' decision about Hoodoo Valley, keeping in mind the Dukhobors' needs and goals.

COLLABORATIVE LEARNING: ENRICHMENT ACTIVITY

Science Ask a group of students to prepare an informational exhibit on natural optical illusions, such as ignis fatuus (will-o'-the-wisp), rainbows, and mirages in the desert and at sea.

CRITICAL THINKING: GUIDED READING QUESTIONS

LITERAL

1a. What does McPherson point out about the soil in Hoodoo Valley? (It is poor for farming.)

2a. Why are the Dukhobors in a hurry to leave? (They want to bring the good news to the others.)

INFERENTIAL

1b. What difference between McPherson and the Dukhobors is stressed by the Dukhobors' lack of concern about the soil? (He is practical and places great importance on material concerns; they are impractical and place more importance on spiritual concerns.)

2b. What is this good news? (They have received what they feel is God's sign and have found the place to settle.)

How do you think the Dukhobors will feel when they see Hoodoo Valley at another time?

ANSWERS

STUDY QUESTIONS

1. It is "nothing like our Humid Mountains"—flat, too cold in winter, and too hot in summer. They refuse to settle in smaller groups.
2. They remember the beautiful landscape and gentle climate. They have forgotten their persecution.
3. He promised peace and religious freedom, not an easy life. They pray for God's sign, which the babushka predicts will come soon.
4. They see bright-colored flowers and birds, mountains, and a river. He says these are illusions, and they say they know, but it does not matter.
5. the valley's true appearance; the flaming sky they saw "still glow[s]" on the Dukhobors' faces
6. devout faith, pacifism, vegetarianism, and avoidance of alcohol, tobacco, and dancing
7. It reminds them of their home, and its mystery seems to have spiritual significance.
8. He is practical. They were diverse and had different goals.
9. Answers will vary. Some students may think it wise, since it brings them joy and they do not mind hard work; others may find it too impractical.

LITERARY FOCUS

1. The story is set in the western Canadian hamlet of Verigin in the late nineteenth century. The mood is bleak. Details include "marshes," "mosquitoes," and the "flat immensity" of the plain.
2. Hoodoo Valley at sunset; mysterious
3. The first reflects their despondency and homesickness; the second, their revitalized spirits. They choose Hoodoo Valley because it reminds them of their home, unlike anything else they have seen.

LANGUAGE STUDY

1. the Ojibwa Indians
2. the French; large area of flat or slightly rolling grassland
3. kerchief; They traditionally wore such kerchiefs.

STUDY QUESTIONS

Recalling

1. In the beginning of the story, what do the desolate Dukhobors say and think about the prairie? What solution to the problem of finding good land do they refuse to consider?
2. What tender recollections of their homeland do the Dukhobors have? What have they forgotten about their homeland?
3. What does the angry babushka tell the younger Dukhobors about their leader Verigin's promise? What do the Dukhobors pray for, and what prediction does the babushka make?
4. What do the Dukhobors see, or think they see, as they reach Hoodoo Valley at sunset? What does McPherson try to explain to them about the valley, and what answer do they give?
5. What does McPherson hope the Dukhobors will see when the sun goes down? What remains on the Dukhobors' faces after the gloom of twilight falls on the valley?

Interpreting

6. From the story details, list four inferences you can make about the Dukhobors' customs, beliefs, and attitudes toward community life.
7. What makes Hoodoo Valley so appealing to the Dukhobors?
8. In contrast to the Dukhobors, what sort of person is McPherson? What does the contrast suggest about the kinds of people who immigrated to western Canada and the reasons that prompt immigrants to travel to a new land?

Extending

9. Do you think the Dukhobors made a wise decision at the end of the story? Discuss your opinion and give reasons to support it.

LITERARY FOCUS

Setting and Atmosphere

The **setting** of a story is the time and place in which the events of the story occur. The author usually describes the setting early in the narrative, using several vivid details to draw us into the world of the story. The details used in the setting description often work together to create an **atmosphere,** or mood, that can color the entire story. For example, the atmos-

128   *The Short Story*

phere may be exotic or homey, forbidding or comforting, hopeful or bleak, intimate or grand.

Once the setting is described, it may simply become a background for the plot and characters. In many stories, however, the setting actually affects plot events and the way characters behave. If a new setting is introduced and described in detail, it is usually important to the plot and characters. Sometimes the description of the new setting creates an atmosphere that contrasts with the original atmosphere.

Thinking About Setting and Atmosphere

1. What is the opening setting of "Hoodoo Valley"? What atmosphere, or mood, does the description of this setting create? List at least three details that help to create this atmosphere.
2. What later setting is very important in the story? What atmosphere does that setting create?
3. How do both settings reflect the feelings of the Dukhobors, and how do they affect their decision at the end of the story?

LANGUAGE STUDY

Borrowed Words

English-speaking immigrants settling in a new place often borrow words from the languages of those people native to the area. Similarly, immigrants who speak different languages often introduce new words to English when they settle in English-speaking areas. Use a dictionary to help you answer these questions about words in "Hoodoo Valley."

1. From whom did English speakers borrow the word *muskeg* to refer to the mossy bogs or marshes in western Canada and Alaska?
2. What early European immigrants to North America gave English the word *prairie*? What is a prairie?
3. With what meaning has the Russian word *babushka* entered English? What does this origin reveal about the garb of Russian peasant women?

COMPOSITION

Describing a Setting

■ In a paragraph or two, describe an unusual setting. The setting may be real or fictional. Use details to make your setting description vivid and to create a particular atmosphere, as Roy does in her setting descriptions in "Hoodoo Valley."

COMPOSITION: GUIDELINES FOR EVALUATION

DESCRIBING A SETTING

Objective

To write a description of a setting

Guidelines for Evaluation

■ suggested length: one or two paragraphs
■ should include vivid sensory details
■ should create an atmosphere

PREVIEW: THE AUTHOR AND THE WORLD

Åsta Holth

(born 1904)

Norway

Åsta [ôs′tə] Holth is a Norwegian of Finnish ancestry, and she grew up in a community where her Finnish roots remained always strong. As a child, she heard tales of her Finnish ancestors in Norway; later she won fame by writing about them.

Holth is from Finnskogen, an area of Norway settled by Finns more than two centuries ago. She began writing in the 1920s, when she became interested in drama. First she wrote plays, some of which were performed by local theater groups. She then branched out, producing children's books, poetry, and short stories.

"Salt" is from Holth's first story collection, *Gamble bygdevegen (Old Country Roads).* Among her many novels are *Gullsmeden (Goldsmith),* about a gold worker in sixteenth-century Norway; *Kornet og freden (Grain and Peace),* a trilogy about Finnskogen; *Steinen blømer (The Stone Is Blooming);* and *Kapellet (The Chapel).*

Almost all Holth's stories look at the experiences and traditions of Norway's Finnish settlers. Many of the stories take place in the past; "Salt" is set in nineteenth-century Finnskogen.

GEOGRAPHY AND CULTURE

Finland and the Finns of Norway

Located in northern Europe between Sweden and the Soviet Union, Finland was often ruled by one of its neighbors. It was also the site of frequent warfare between them, forcing many Finns to leave their homeland. During the seventeenth and eighteenth centuries many Finns settled west of Sweden in Norway, in a wooded area near the Swedish border that became known as Finnskogen, or "The Finns' Forest." Here Finnish settlers cleared land for their small farms and struggled to survive in a harsh environment. Winters in Finnskogen are cold and dark—in December and January the sun appears for only a few hours—and summer storms are frequent. Towns are few and far between, and the settlers had few amenities to comfort them.

"Salt" takes place several decades after the settlers' arrival, at a time when wealthy landowners were buying up the small farms of Finnskogen. It was also a time when movements for national independence and ethnic pride were sweeping northern Europe. The Finns in Norway eagerly awaited contact with Finnish nationalists, but it was slow in coming. Meanwhile Finnskogen's farmers, like those in the story, had to face their hardships on their own.

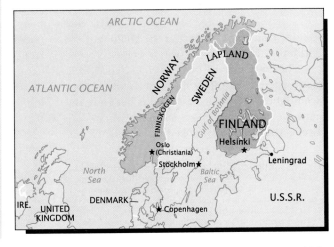

Salt **129**

In this tale of Norway's Finnish community, a woman's resistance to pressure sets an example. When Marit Karhinen refused to sign a document, she was not allowed to buy salt. Now she and her husband are desperate for salt. After a Finnish nationalist wakens the community's ethnic pride and explains that by signing the document the Finns gave away their land, four neighbors bring Marit salt.

LITERARY SKILLS FOR THIS SELECTION

- theme
- setting and atmosphere

THEMES IN THIS SELECTION

- personal values: heritage and community spirit
- physical and economic hardship
- acting independently

LESSON OBJECTIVES

1. to analyze theme
2. to explain how setting relates to the author's purpose
3. to compare and contrast stories

Teacher's Classroom Resources 1

■ Teaching Notes	219
■ Prereading Vocabulary	220
■ Reading Guide	221
■ Check Test	222
■ Responding to World Cultures	223
■ Literary Focus: Theme	224
■ Writing Process Guide: Writing About Setting	225
■ Grammar in Literature: Using Parallelism for Effect	226
■ Selection Test	227

IN THE CLASSROOM

TEACHING STUDENTS OF DIFFERENT ABILITIES

- **For less advanced students:** Have students consider, as they read, the significance of the story's title. Have them complete the Reading Guide.

- **For more advanced students:** Have students discuss historical fiction: its purposes and the qualities that make it successful. What problems might writers of historical fiction encounter?

DISCUSSING GEOGRAPHY AND CULTURE

Comparing Women's Roles

The main character in "Salt" is a strong-minded woman of Finnish descent. In Finland women are prominent in society: Finland was the first European country to allow women to vote, and today Finnish women occupy high posts in business and government. More than three-fourths of the women in Finland work outside the home.
- Ask students to discuss the roles women play in contemporary American society.

Åsta Holth

Salt

Translated from the Norwegian by Katherine Hanson

"I had imagined that she would be a mean old witch, but she was a gentle, sweet and sensible woman."

—C. A. Gottlund[1]

Heikki Karhinen[2] stood sniffing the air like an animal. Surely there wouldn't be a thaw now? It had been cold all fall, the rimy trees looked mangy and unkempt. But when such long rime fringes hung from the birches, it was never long before the cold broke. Oh well—just as long as the thaw didn't last too long.

"You'd better come in and eat," his wife said quietly. In a tone as if she were asking him to do something unpleasant, but necessary.

He sat down at the table, his face dark. Unsalted porridge with unsalted pork. They didn't look forward to meals at Honkamäk.[3] Marit looked pained, but as always her mouth was firm. They were in a bad way these days. There was something missing, their mouths watered when they thought the word, their bodies cried for it, it felt like a kind of hunger or thirst—yes, they actually thirsted for *salt*. Marit had scrimped and saved as well as she could, but the bottom of the salt box was now empty.

"There's going to be a thaw," Heikki said. Marit offered no reply; her mouth was drawn even tighter. It sounded as if it was her fault, the mild weather too. Every morning when they awoke, they anxiously looked at the window and were glad when the frost lay thick on the windowpane. Because if it thawed, the meat would spoil. The brine was so thin that there may as well not have been any.

Heikki ate slowly; the food grew in his mouth.

"Couldn't you have signed?" he said after a while.

"No." It sounded curt and hard. And afterwards a threatening question mark hung in the air: Is there anything else you'd like to say?

Marit Karhinen had gone to Grue[4] to trade this fall instead of Heikki. He had cut his foot. She rode the long journey to Grue Parish with four or five men from Finnskogen. They made these trips every fall, sold meat and hides and wrought iron and bought seed, salt, sugar and other things. This time they were met at Gruset[5] by a stranger. He was a refined and distinguished man who said he was Mr. Anker's secretary as he spread out huge documents that they were to sign. They were informed that Anker owned Finnskogen, the land and the forest, and that he was a good and understanding man who took their interests to heart and gave them good terms. The folk from Finnskogen looked long and hard at the white documents but didn't understand a thing. They could understand and speak both Norwegian and Swedish after a fashion, but this was a convoluted, legal Danish[6]—they couldn't make anything out of it.

"I can't sign something when I don't know what it is," Marit Karhinen said.

---

1. **C. A. Gottlund** [gôt′lōnd]: Carl Aksel (Kaarle Akseli) Gottlund (1796–1875), Finnish writer and nationalist influential in the development and promotion of Finnish literature and the Finnish language.
2. **Heikki Karhinen** [hä′kē kar′hēn en]
3. **Honkamäk** [hôn′kə mäk′]: the Karhinens' farm. The name is Finnish dialect for "Pine Hill."

---

4. **Grue** [grōō′e]: village in Finnskogen. (See the Geography and Culture feature that precedes the story.)
5. **Gruset** [grōō′set]: another nearby village.
6. **legal Danish:** Because Denmark ruled Norway for many years, some legal documents were written in Danish.

CRITICAL THINKING: GUIDED READING QUESTIONS

LITERAL

1a. When Heikki says there will be a thaw, how does Marit take his remark? (She takes it as a suggestion that the mild weather is her fault, too.)

2a. What did Mr. Anker's secretary say about Mr. Anker's character? (He is a "good and understanding man.")

INFERENTIAL

1b. What has actually made Heikki so critical and Marit so defensive? (lack of salt in their diet and Heikki's annoyance over Marit's refusal to sign the document)

2b. Why can we not accept the secretary's opinion? (An employee is not likely to be objective, and failure to explain the documents in detail seems like an attempt at trickery.)

But when she went to trade, she was told that, unfortunately, they didn't have any more seed and salt. She ought to speak with Mr. Anker's secretary, however. Maybe he could help her. So she had to go back to the secretary who smiled and bowed and put the paper in front of her once again. She understood very little of the document and very little of what he said. Her eyes, questioning and alert, were on the secretary. All the others had signed. But they were men. And it's the feminine instinct that is always on the alert, always smells danger. She shook her head. Wasn't it true that she wanted seed and salt? Yes, could he please help her buy those things? Once again he tried to get her to **6** sign. But Marit was stubborn as a mule. His face grew taut and he said that he was sorry, but he could not get her the goods she wanted. Marit began to feel confused. But she wasn't stupid and gradually she understood how everything fit **7** together. If she signed, there would probably be a way for her to buy seed and salt, but she understood that putting her name there could be dangerous. She fixed her gaze on the elegant man. There was a faint, yet unmistakable glint in the Finnish woman's good-natured eyes. She turned her back to him—a fine, stubborn woman's back—and left.

And that is how there came to be a salt shortage at Honkamäk. Her father had given them a little rye seed, enough that they could do some planting in the spring, though less than usual. But with the salt it was worse. She could borrow from the neighbors, but perhaps they would say: "Why didn't you sign? What if we had been as **8** obstinate as you?" Besides, salt was a precious commodity at Finnskogen; it was thirty to forty kilometers to the merchant, on roads that were not always passable. And no one was so rich that they could buy as much as they wanted at any one time.

9 The sky was gray and mangy; it ran together with the scruffy forest. No doubt about it, it was going to thaw. Heikki took his gun and headed for the forest. Not because they needed meat,

but because he was unhappy with himself and everything else and was in no mood to talk with people. It was the lack of salt that was to blame. Now it had come between him and Marit. They were peevish and mean toward each other. He knew so well that Marit had done what was right and even so he had to rebuke her by asking: Couldn't you have signed? And Marit turned a stubborn back—it was her back he saw most often these days—and her mouth, which could be so soft, was firm, showing clearly that she fully realized what she had done.

Marit fed the animals and then put on her kerchief and shawl and walked to Revholt[7] to **10** listen to the visitor who had come: the student from Finland, who spoke to the people at Finnskogen in their own language and who worked for their rights.

A delicate shower of hoarfrost needles[8] drifted down from the forest. Grouse wings flapped in among the spruce trees. Strange—until now people at Finnskogen had believed they owned both the spruce and the bird. Most of them had bought and paid for the ground they built on. Before their forefathers came a couple hundred years ago, no human foot had trodden here. The gigantic spruce trees had stood until they rotted. Large herds of moose grazed in the vast marsh. They roamed at will. Now when the wind rustled through rye fields and cows shared the pasture with the moose, now fancy gentlemen came and said, "This is ours!"

11 Heikki's parents came by foot to Honkamäk when it was covered with forest. With them they had a cow, an ox and a little pouch of rye. They tied the cow to a tree and started to clear! Now Honkamäk was a farm, with luxuriant fields of rye and cows and a horse. And here came that swell gentleman Anker saying it was his.

Poverty grew and many Finnskogen folk had

---

7. **Revholt** [rev′hōlt]: another village in the area.
8. **hoarfrost** [hôr′frôst′] **needles**: pine needles covered with frozen dew.

- At the store Marit was told there was no salt or seed, but she soon realized these things would be available if she signed the document.
- All her neighbors did sign documents, and they would criticize her now if she asked to borrow salt, a precious commodity.
- That evening, as she goes to hear a speaker from Finland, Marit recalls the struggle of Heikki's parents to build the farm she and Heikki now run.

IN THE GLOSSARY

- commodity: product
- mangy: shabby
- peevish: ill-tempered
- grouse: fowllike bird
- luxuriant: abundant

6 TEACHING CHARACTERIZATION

Note this example of direct characterization, and have students find another a few lines below. ("But she wasn't stupid.")

7 TEACHING CONFLICT

Ask what conflict the salt shortage is tied to. (It is tied to Marit's struggle with Mr. Anker and his goals.)

8 CULTURAL BACKGROUND

Explain that salt was once very valuable because it was so hard to get. In fact, in some societies people were paid with salt, the origin of our word *salary*.

9 TEACHING ATMOSPHERE

Note that negative words such as *mangy* and *scruffy* contribute to the bleak atmosphere.

10 GRAMMAR IN LITERATURE

Have students identify the adjective clauses used here. ("who had come," "who spoke . . . language," and "who worked . . . rights")

11 TEACHING THEME

Note that pride in one's heritage is an important theme of the story.

CRITICAL THINKING: GUIDED READING QUESTIONS

LITERAL

1a. What does Marit gradually understand is the reason she cannot buy salt and seed? (She has refused to sign the document.)

2a. What does Marit recall about Heikki's parents? (They came to Honkamäk on foot and worked hard to establish the farm.)

INFERENTIAL

→ **1b.** What can we infer about Mr. Anker's relationship with the store and his method of doing business? (He controls the store, and he bullies and coerces people to get his way.)

→ **2b.** How do her recollections make her feel about the Karhinen land and Mr. Anker's acquisition of local land? (proud and angry)

- The visitor offers the vision of a future in which community members share their common Finnish heritage and work together for their rights.
- Marit learns that those who signed Mr. Anker's documents signed away their land.
- The next day four Finnish neighbors bring the Karhinens salt and acknowledge Marit's wisdom in not signing the document.

12 CRITICAL THINKING: EVALUATION

Remind students that Gottlund was quoted in the epigraph, or the story's opening quotation. Have students evaluate the appropriateness of the epigraph to the story.

13 TEACHING STUDENTS OF LIMITED ENGLISH PROFICIENCY

Have nonnative speakers describe any social gatherings at which their native tongue is spoken and explain the benefits of such gatherings.

14 TEACHING SYMBOLS

Note that the salt represents not only a physical need but also the spiritual nourishment Gottlund offers the community.

15 READING SKILL: CONTRAST

Note the contrast between the neighbors' behavior before, when they kept to themselves, and now.

16 TEACHING THEME

Elicit the insight that Marit's joyous reaction to the neighbors' aid points to the value of community spirit, an important theme of the story.

COLLABORATIVE LEARNING: ENRICHMENT ACTIVITY

Interviews and Oral History Have a group of students record interviews to create an oral history of the immigrant experience. Interviewers should have family members or neighbors describe personal experiences or those that are part of family lore.

---

no choice but to become cotters[9] for Anker and others just like him. Actually, they were worse off than cotters, for they had no rights; they could neither clear land nor fell trees to build their homes.

Marit Karhinen had a heavy heart. Life at Finnskogen had become so dark and difficult. Everyone kept to himself. Though it had always been that way since the distance between neighbors was great. The young people were growing restless and longed to leave the forest. Here they found no answers to the thousand questions that torment youth. Here they had only the forest and the animals and the Bible—and their own inexpressible longing.

For that reason they inhaled every word the visiting fellow said. For that reason the boys flocked around him and the girls blushed and **12** gave him their trust. Carl Aksel Gottlund was his name.

Marit and Heikki came home at the same time at dusk. Both of them were happier than when they left. Heikki had shot a hare and sucked the blood from the warm animal throat—*salt* blood. And Marit's cheeks were warm from everything she had heard.

"We can't be sure the thaw will last long," Heikki said. Then the two of them went out to taste the brine.

"It *does* quench our thirst," Heikki said and licked his index finger. Marit did the same. Two times they tasted. Good, very good.

Marit had many things to tell about. They'd better sit down a while on the couch. She took his arm and put it around her waist. And then she told about the wonderful visions, dreams of the future, Gottlund had unveiled. A church here in the forest, with a Finnish minister and Finnish songs, teachers who taught the children in the cherished, soft and trilling language of **13** their native country. A little Suomi[10] for themselves in the midst of this foreign land.

---

9. **cotters:** tenant farmers.
10. **Suomi** [sōō′ō mē]: Finnish name for Finland and the Finnish language.

132 *The Short Story*

"I did the right thing by not signing, Heikki. They have signed away the right to their land; Anker can force them to leave their farms any time he wishes! Gottlund explained to us what it said in those papers."

"Of course you did the right thing."

Later they read the little book Gottlund had given her, *Pieniä Runoja.*[11] It awakened a new hunger in them. They could feel that they had been living in spiritual darkness. But Gottlund had said he would help them get Finnish maga- **14** zines and books—for spiritual nourishment, the salt of life.

The next day four neighboring Finnish **15** women came to Honkamäk. After they had chatted a good, long while about the weather, about encroachment from Grue Parish, about the wolf that had torn apart Lehomoinen's goat over in Revholt—right outside the barn!—and, most particularly, about Carl Gottlund, they got around to the real reason for their visit: a small bag of salt from each of them—they hoped she didn't think it too modest a gift. It occurred to them that Marit might be without salt, not having been able to trade this fall. They knew what a shortage of salt meant at Finnskogen.

"You did the right thing by not signing. If we all held together, it wouldn't be so easy for these bigwigs to do as they please with us."

16 *"Monda kosti Jumala!"*[12] Marit's eyes filled with tears as she thanked them.

Outdoors the mangy sky was falling in a drizzle. Salt-white snow covered forest and field. But the winter solstice was not far off. . . .

As she stood grinding the salt with a round stone, Marit had to taste it. She smiled warmly at Heikki, like in the old days.

"Better times are coming, you'll see."

"We certainly don't need to worry about a thaw now."

Heikki kissed a tiny grain of salt from her lips.

---

11. *Pieniä Runoja* [pē′en ē ä rōō′nô yə]: Finnish title meaning *Small Poems*.
12. *Monda kosti Jumala* [ūm′ə lə]: God bless you!

CRITICAL THINKING: GUIDED READING QUESTIONS

LITERAL

1a. What does Heikki tell Marit when she says she did the right thing by not signing? ("Of course you did the right thing.")

2a. What do four Finnish neighbors do on the day after Gottlund's visit? (They bring the Karhinens the salt they need.)

INFERENTIAL

1b. What change in the Karhinens' relationship does this remark show? (Warmth and approval have returned.)

2b. How has Gottlund's visit prompted their actions? (He reminded them of shared Finnish ties, prompting them to help a Finnish neighbor, and he showed them the wisdom of standing up for their rights, as Marit had done.)

STUDY QUESTIONS

Recalling

1. How did there come to be a salt shortage at Honkamäk? What does Marit think the neighbors will say if she tries to borrow salt?
2. As she walks to Revholt to hear the visitor, what does Marit recall about her Finnish forefathers and Heikki's parents?
3. What "wonderful visions" of the future does Gottlund unveil? What does he say is the "salt of life"?
4. What have the other farmers signed away?
5. After Gottlund's visit, what do four neighbor women do? What do they say to Marit?

Interpreting:

6. How is Marit different from the other people in the community? Why does she value the family land?
7. Why is Gottlund's visit important to the villagers? What link is there between his visit and the neighbor women's kindness?

Extending

8. What benefits do people enjoy today when they value their cultural or ethnic heritage?

LITERARY FOCUS

Theme

The **theme** of a work of literature is the main idea that the author expresses. The specific details of a story point to the theme, which is usually an insight into life or human experience. For example, in a story about a gymnast named Jan who trains for years before she wins an Olympic medal, the theme may be "Persistence is eventually rewarded" or "Athletes must train hard to win." Notice that the theme does not relate *only* to the story, such as "Jan is a good athlete." It moves beyond the story to say something about experience in general.

Usually a theme can be expressed in a single sentence. To find a story's theme, ask the following questions:

- What ideas about life does the *title* convey?
- What do the particular *events, conflicts,* and *resolution* of the *plot* reveal about life?
- What might the qualities of these particular *characters* tell us about people in general?
- What does seeing the events from this specific *point of view* tell us about life?
- What view of the world does the *setting* offer?

Thinking About Theme

1. Considering Gottlund's remark about the "salt of life," what is the full meaning of the story's title? What ideas about life does the double meaning convey?
2. What does Marit's conflict with Mr. Anker reveal about life in general? What does the story's resolution reveal?
3. State in a single sentence what you believe the story's theme to be.

COMPOSITION

Writing About Setting

■ Write a brief composition about the setting of "Salt." Show how the choice of setting reveals the author's purpose. First decide what Holth's purpose was in writing the story. Then consider how the setting affects the story's plot, conflicts, and characters and how it helps point to the story's theme. *For help with this assignment, see Lesson 4 in the Writing About Literature Handbook at the back of this book.*

COMPARING STORIES

■ Compare and contrast this story with other stories about land and wealth that you have read in this book or elsewhere. For example, you might compare it to "Hoodoo Valley," the first story in this section. What does land mean to the characters at the start of each story and at the story's end? What is similar and different about the stories' themes?

Salt **133**

COMPOSITION: GUIDELINES FOR EVALUATION

WRITING ABOUT SETTING

Objective

To explain how setting relates to the author's purpose

Guidelines for Evaluation

■ suggested length: three or four paragraphs

■ should state Holth's purpose
■ should explain how the choice of setting reflects this purpose
■ should show how setting affects plot, conflicts, and characters and helps point to theme

---

What did you admire most about Marit?

ANSWERS

STUDY QUESTIONS

1. When Marit refused to sign a document, she was not allowed to buy salt. "Why didn't you sign? What if we had been as obstinate as you?"
2. They worked hard to establish farms in the wilderness.
3. He envisions a Finnish church, Finnish schools, and use of the Finnish language. He says that spiritual nourishment from their heritage is the "salt of life."
4. They have signed away the right to their land.
5. They bring Marit salt. They say that she was right not to sign and that if they all stuck together, they could protect their rights better.
6. She is courageous and not easily fooled. She recognizes her ancestors' achievements in settling it.
7. He makes them feel less isolated by awakening ethnic pride and championing their rights. He prompts them to help a compatriot and to recognize that Marit was right in not signing the document.
8. Answers will vary. Possible responses include pride, community feeling, and better understanding of the past.

LITERARY FOCUS

1. It refers to the salt the Karhinens need and the spiritual nourishment of ethnic pride. The spiritual rewards of pride in one's heritage are as important as physical well-being.
2. The wealthy and powerful may infringe on the rights of the poor and weak. Working together helps people overcome hardship.
3. When nourished by their shared heritage, people may work together to overcome hardship.

COMPARING STORIES

Answers will vary. For example, the characters in both "Salt" and "Hoodoo Valley" come to feel happier than they were in a foreign land; but while spiritual concerns are paramount to the Dukhobors, the material value of the land is also of concern to the Finns.

Salt **T-133**

LESSON PREVIEW

A Florentine cavalier is rewarded for his selfless love in this tale from the *Decameron.* Hoping to win Monna Giovanna's love, Federigo spends his fortune and must move to the country with little but his prized falcon. When Monna's son falls ill and begs her for the bird, Monna visits Federigo, prompting him to kill the falcon to feed her. After the son dies and Monna is urged to remarry, she recalls Federigo's generosity and chooses him.

LITERARY SKILLS FOR THIS SELECTION

- stated and unstated themes
- irony
- frame story

THEMES IN THIS SELECTION

- personal values: rewards of unselfishness
- fate versus free will

LESSON OBJECTIVES

1. to determine a story's stated and unstated themes
2. to examine Romance languages
3. to update a story
4. to compare and contrast stories

Teacher's Classroom Resources 1

- Teaching Notes   229
- Prereading Vocabulary   230
- Reading Guide   231
- Check Test   232
- Responding to World Cultures   233
- Literary Focus: Stated and Unstated Themes 234
- Language Study: The Romance Languages 235
- Writing Process Guide: Writing a Modern Version of a Story 236
- Grammar in Literature: Combining with Subordinate Clauses 237
- Selection Test   238

IN THE CLASSROOM

TEACHING STUDENTS OF DIFFERENT ABILITIES

- **For less advanced students:** To help with the old-fashioned style and language, have stu-

---

Giovanni Boccaccio

(1313–1375)

Italy

Sometimes considered the father of all modern fiction, Giovanni Boccaccio [jō vä′nē bō kä′chē ō′] was one of the world's first writers to tell his tales in prose instead of verse. Boccaccio grew up in the Italian city of Florence. His father, a wealthy merchant, hoped his son would also become a businessman and sent him to the city of Naples to study business and law. While these studies were not at all to Boccaccio's liking, living in Naples gave him the chance to attend the court of King Robert of Naples, a ruler who supported many writers and artists. Boccaccio became a popular figure, entertaining the court with his stories and poems.

Returning to Florence in 1340, Boccaccio met the poet Petrarch (see the Poetry unit), who encouraged Boccaccio's literary pursuits. By 1348 Boccaccio was writing his masterpiece, the *Decameron,* a collection of one hundred tales that took five years to complete. Never adept at handling finances, Boccaccio spent his last years in poverty and ill health. Petrarch's death in 1374 was a great loss to him, and Boccaccio died one year later.

Florence and the Great Plague

The southern European nation of Italy was in Boccaccio's day not a unified nation but a group of independently governed kingdoms and cities. Among these was Florence, a city in north-central Italy. In 1348, when Boccaccio began the *Decameron,* Florence was struck by the Great Plague, an outbreak of bubonic plague that swept through Europe, killing about a quarter of the population. Since this highly contagious disease spread most rapidly in cities, many people fled to the country.

Boccaccio drew on this event when he wrote the frame story that ties the tales of the *Decameron* together. A **frame story** is a story in which one or more smaller tales unfold. In the *Decameron*'s frame story, ten young people, hoping to escape the plague, leave Florence for the country. To entertain one another, they each tell a tale a day for ten days —*Decameron* means "Ten Days' Work." Among the storytellers is the young queen who narrates "Federigo's Falcon."

*See LITERATURE AND CULTURE SOURCEBOOK:
Italy*

---

dents paraphrase different paragraphs of the story. Also ask them to complete the Reading Guide.

- **For more advanced students:** Have students consider how the story expresses ideas of the Italian Renaissance described on page 550 of their text.

DISCUSSING GEOGRAPHY AND CULTURE

Doctors and Diseases

In the Middle Ages physicians knew little about the way diseases spread or how to treat them. The result was devastating: Between 1347 and 1350 bubonic plague infected more than fifty million Europeans, half of whom died. Today doctors better understand diseases, and mortality rates have fallen sharply.

- Discuss twentieth-century advances in conquering disease. (Examples include vaccines against polio, measles, etc., and genetically engineered cures.)

Giovanni Boccaccio

Federigo's Falcon

from the **Decameron**

Translated from the Italian by Richard Aldington

Filomena had ceased speaking, and the queen, seeing that nobody was left to speak except Dioneo (who had his privilege[1]) and herself, began cheerfully as follows:

It is now my turn to speak, dearest ladies, and I shall gladly do so with a tale similar in part to the one before, not only that you may know the power of your beauty over the gentle heart, but because you may learn yourselves to be givers of rewards when fitting, without allowing Fortune always to dispense them, since Fortune most often bestows them not discreetly but lavishly.

You must know then that Coppo di Borghese Domenichi,[2] who was and perhaps still is one of our fellow citizens, a man of great and revered authority in our days both from his manners and his virtues (far more than from nobility of blood), a most excellent person worthy of eternal fame, and in the fullness of his years, delighted often to speak of past matters with his neighbors and other men. And this he could do better and more orderly and with a better memory and more ornate speech than anyone else.

Among other excellent things, he was wont to say that in the past there was in Florence a young man named Federigo, the son of Messer[3] Filippo Alberighi,[4] renowned above all other young gentlemen of Tuscany[5] for his prowess in arms and his courtesy. Now, as most often happens to gentlemen, he fell in love with a lady named Monna Giovanna,[6] in her time held to be one of the gayest and most beautiful women ever known in Florence. To win her love, he went to jousts and tourneys,[7] made and gave feasts, and spent his money without stint. But she, no less chaste than beautiful, cared nothing for the things he did for her nor for him who did them.

Now as Federigo was spending far beyond his means and getting nothing in, as easily happens, his wealth failed and he remained poor with nothing but a little farm, on whose produce he lived very penuriously, and one falcon which was among the best in the world. More in love than ever, but thinking he would never be able to live in the town any more as he desired, he went to Campi[8] where his farm was. There he spent his time hawking,[9] asked nothing of anybody, and patiently endured his poverty.

Now while Federigo was in this extremity it happened one day that Monna Giovanna's husband fell ill, and seeing death come upon him, made his will. He was a very rich man and left his estate to a son who was already growing up. And then, since he had greatly loved Monna

---

1. **his privilege:** It has been agreed that Dioneo will have the privilege of being each day's last storyteller. (For more on the storytellers of *The Decameron*, see the Geography and Culture feature that precedes the story.)
2. **Coppo di Borghese Domenichi** [kōp′ō dē bôr gā′zē dō mā nē′kē]: *Coppo* is an Italian title of respect.
3. **Messer:** Mister.
4. **Filippo Alberighi** [fē lēp′po äl′bä rē′gē]

5. **Tuscany:** the region of north-central Italy where the city of Florence is located.
6. **Monna Giovanna** [mōn′ə jō vän′ə]
7. **jousts and tourneys:** festival contests in which knights displayed their skill in combat.
8. **Campi** [käm′pē]: town in Tuscany.
9. **hawking:** hunting with falcons, hawks trained to capture and retrieve smaller birds and other small animals.

Federigo's Falcon **135**

CRITICAL THINKING: GUIDED READING QUESTIONS

LITERAL

1a. Who is the Coppo di Borghese Domenichi? (He is the upstanding Florentine from whom the queen says she heard the story of Federigo.)

2a. Why does Federigo spend money lavishly? (He is attempting to impress Monna and win her love.)

INFERENTIAL

1b. Why do you think Boccaccio describes the Coppo in such detail when he is not a character in the story? (He does so to show the Coppo's reliability as a source and to make Federigo's story seem more authentic.)

2b. Why is the outcome of Federigo's spending ironic? (Instead of winning Monna's love, he impoverishes himself and is forced to leave the city where Monna lives.)

- After Monna's husband dies, she and her son retire to a country house near Federigo's farm.
- When the son falls ill, he says his health will improve if he has Federigo's falcon.
- Overcoming her scruples about asking for the bird, Monna goes to Federigo.
- He welcomes her warmly and apologizes for his impoverished circumstances.

5 CULTURAL BACKGROUND

Explain that in the past wives in Europe were not necessarily heirs to their husbands' estates. If there was no son or the son died, the estate often went to the closest male relative.

6 READING SKILL: INFERENCE

Ask in what ways the falcon is Federigo's "support in life." (It is his chief source of happiness and companionship and also helps him obtain food.)

7 TEACHING CHARACTERIZATION

Elicit that Monna displays courtesy and honor by going in person, despite her embarrassment, to ask for the bird.

8 GRAMMAR IN LITERATURE

Point out that the translator tries to capture Boccaccio's style by using old-fashioned or archaic phrasing, such as "on the morrow." Ask what we would now usually say. ("the next day")

9 CRITICAL THINKING: EVALUATION

Have students evaluate Federigo's attitude here, given what has happened in the past. What do they admire or find wrong in it?

---

5 Giovanna, he made her his heir in case his son should die without legitimate children; and so died.

Monna Giovanna was now a widow, and as is customary with our women, she went with her son to spend the year in a country house she had near Federigo's farm. Now the boy happened to strike up a friendship with Federigo, and delighted in dogs and hawks. He often saw Federigo's falcon fly, and took such great delight in it that he very much wanted to have it, but did not dare ask for it, since he saw how much Federigo prized it.

While matters were in this state, the boy fell ill. His mother was very much grieved, as he was her only child and she loved him extremely. She spent the day beside him, trying to help him, and often asked him if there was anything he wanted, begging him to say so, for if it were possible to have it, she would try to get it for him. After she had many times made this offer, the boy said:

"Mother, if you can get me Federigo's falcon, I think I should soon be better."

The lady paused a little at this, and began to think what she should do. She knew that Federigo had loved her for a long time, and yet had never had one glance from her, and she said to herself:

6 "How can I send or go and ask for this falcon, which is, from what I hear, the best that ever flew, and moreover his support in life? How can I be so thoughtless as to take this away from a gentleman who has no other pleasure left in life?"

Although she knew she was certain to have the bird for the asking, she remained in embarrassed thought, not knowing what to say, and did not answer her son. But at length love for her child got the upper hand and she determined that to please him in whatever way it 7 might be, she would not send, but go herself for it and bring it back to him. So she replied:

"Be comforted, my child, and try to get bet-

ter somehow. I promise you that tomorrow morning I will go for it, and bring it to you."

The child was so delighted that he became a 8 little better that same day. And on the morrow the lady took another woman to accompany her, and as if walking for exercise went to Federigo's cottage, and asked for him. Since it was not the weather for it, he had not been hawking for some days, and was in his garden employed in certain work there. When he heard that Monna Giovanna was asking for him at the door, he was greatly astonished, and ran there happily. When she saw him coming, she got up to greet him with womanly charm, and when Federigo had courteously saluted[10] her, she said:

"How do you do, Federigo? I have come here to make amends for the damage you have suffered through me by loving me more than was needed. And in token of this, I intend to dine today familiarly[11] with you and my companion here."

9 "Madonna,"[12] replied Federigo humbly, "I do not remember ever to have suffered any damage through you, but received so much good that if I was ever worth anything it was owing to your worth and the love I bore it. Your generous visit to me is so precious to me that I could spend again all that I have spent; but you have come to a poor host."

So saying, he modestly took her into his house, and from there to his garden. Since there was nobody else to remain in her company, he said:

"Madonna, since there is nobody else, this good woman, the wife of this workman, will keep you company, while I go to set the table."

Now, although his poverty was extreme, he had never before realized what necessity he had fallen into by his foolish extravagance in spending his wealth. But he repented of it that morning when he could find nothing with which to

---

10. **saluted:** here, made a sign of greeting; bowed to.
11. **familiarly:** here, informally; in the manner of families.
12. **Madonna:** Italian for "my lady."

CRITICAL THINKING: GUIDED READING QUESTIONS

LITERAL

1a. Why does Monna decide to ask for the falcon despite her embarrassment? (She asks out of love for her son.)

2a. What is Federigo's reaction to Monna's remark about the damage he suffered by loving her? (He says he recalls no such damage but only good coming from her worth and the love he bore her.)

INFERENTIAL

1b. Why is she embarrassed? (Since Federigo lost his wealth and happiness out of love for her while she remained indifferent to him, she knows it is presumptuous to appear suddenly and ask for his prized possession.)

2b. What does this reaction show about Federigo's character? (He is generous and neither vindictive nor bitter.)

do honor to the lady, for love of whom he had entertained vast numbers of men in the past. In his anguish he cursed himself and his fortune and ran up and down like a man out his senses, unable to find money or anything to pawn. The hour was late and his desire to honor the lady extreme, yet he would not apply to anyone else, even to his own workman; when suddenly his eye fell upon his falcon, perched on a bar in the <u>10</u> sitting room. Having no one to whom he could appeal, he took the bird, and finding it plump, decided it would be food worthy of such a lady. So, without further thought, he wrung its neck, made his little maid servant quickly pluck and prepare it, and put it on a spit to roast. He spread the table with the whitest napery,[13] of which he had some left, and returned to the lady in the garden with a cheerful face, saying that the meal he had been able to prepare for her was ready.

<u>11</u>   The lady and her companion arose and went to table, and there together with Federigo, who served it with the greatest devotion, they ate the good falcon, not knowing what it was. They left the table and spent some time in cheerful conversation, and the lady, thinking the time had now come to say what she had come for, spoke fairly to Federigo as follows:

"Federigo, when you remember your former life and my chastity, which no doubt you considered harshness and cruelty, I have no doubt that you will be surprised at my presumption when you hear what I have come here for chiefly. But if you had children, through whom you could know the power of parental love, I am certain that you would to some extent excuse me.

"But, as you have no child, I have one, and I cannot escape the common laws of mothers. Compelled by their power, I have come to ask you—against my will, and against all good manners and duty—for a gift, which I know is some-

Ginevra de'Benci, c. 1474, Leonardo da Vinci.

thing especially dear to you, and reasonably so, because I know your straitened fortune has left you no other pleasure, no other recreation, no other consolation. This gift is your falcon, which has so fascinated my child that if I do not take it to him, I am afraid his present illness will grow so much worse that I may lose him. Therefore I beg you, not by the love you bear me (which <u>12</u> holds you to nothing), but by your own nobleness, which has shown itself so much greater in all courteous usage than is wont in other men, that you will be pleased to give it to me, so that through this gift I may be able to say that I have saved my child's life, and thus be ever under an obligation to you."

When Federigo heard the lady's request and knew that he could not serve her, because he had given her the bird to eat, he began to weep in her presence, for he could not speak a word. The lady at first thought that his grief came from having to part with his good falcon, rather than from anything else, and she was almost on the point of retraction. But she remained firm and

---

13. **napery** [nā′pə rē]: tablecloths, cloth napkins, and other cloth items used in table settings.

Federigo's Falcon **137**

■ Seeking a meal that will "do honor" to Monna Giovanna, Federigo is at his wits' end until he sees his falcon, which he promptly kills and has cooked.

■ Monna Giovanna eats the bird without knowing what it is.

■ Afterward, when she asks for the falcon for her son, Federigo begins weeping.

10 CRITICAL THINKING: EVALUATION

Note that the story views Federigo's act as a positive if rash one, and ask whether students agree. (Some may find it cruel and disloyal to the bird or showing too much disregard for Federigo's own needs.)

11 TEACHING IRONY

Elicit the irony of Monna's situation: She unknowingly eats the bird that she came to take alive.

12 CULTURAL BACKGROUND

Point out that courtesy was expected of the European nobility, at least in theory. In fact, the word *courtesy* originally referred to behavior expected of a knight or lady at *court.*

ART AND LITERATURE

Leonardo da Vinci (1452–1519) had a scientist's curiosity and an artist's eye for detail. He recorded in his many drawings all aspects of life, from religious themes to broad landscape vistas to intricate anatomical studies. Scientist and artist, Leonardo preferred the power of painting over science because an artist could portray the world in idealized, or imaginative, terms. His portraits, such as *Ginevra de'Benci,* combine matchless idealism with precise physical details.

■ Ask students what point in the story Leonardo's painting reminds them of most. (Students may choose the moment when Federigo takes Monna Giovanna to his garden.)

CRITICAL THINKING: GUIDED READING QUESTIONS

LITERAL

1a. After finding nothing else that will "do [her] honor," what does Federigo cook for Monna? (his falcon)

INFERENTIAL

1b. By killing his prized possession to do Monna honor, what positive qualities does Federigo display? (selflessness and generosity)

- Noting that Fortune has again worked against him, Federigo sadly explains what happened.
- At first critical that he killed such a bird for her meal, Monna then realizes the greatness of Federigo's soul.
- She leaves sadly, and a few days later her son dies.
- When her brothers urge her to remarry, the wealthy widow recalls Federigo's generosity and chooses him.

IN THE GLOSSARY

- deigned: condescended
- abate: lessen
- prudent: showing good judgment

13 TEACHING PERSONIFICATION

Point out that both here and in the queen's introduction, Fortune is personified, or given human qualities. The capital letter—as if *Fortune* were a name—is a traditional sign of personification.

14 TEACHING IRONY

Note that Federigo recognizes the irony of his situation and points out another: Monna never visited when he spent lavishly in the hopes of entertaining her but instead came when he was poor.

15 TEACHING THEME

Elicit that Monna's decision shows the rewards of selflessness and also points to another theme: Human beings can make choices that determine their fate instead of leaving it to chance.

16 TEACHING PLOT: RESOLUTION

Note that the tale has a traditional fairy-tale ending: It implies that they all lived happily ever after.

COLLABORATIVE LEARNING: ENRICHMENT ACTIVITY

Oral Report Have a group of students prepare an oral report on falconry. Each student can focus on a different area: the various breeds of falcons, how they were trained, how they were used in hunting and sport, and so on.

waited for Federigo's reply after his lamentation. And he said:

"Madonna, ever since it has pleased God that I should set my love upon you, I have felt that **13** Fortune has been contrary to me in many things, and have grieved for it. But they are all light in comparison with what she has done to me now, and I shall never be at peace with her again when I reflect that you came to my poor house, **14** which you never deigned to visit when it was rich, and asked me for a little gift, and Fortune has so acted that I cannot give it to you. Why this cannot be, I will briefly tell you.

"When I heard that you in your graciousness desired to dine with me and I thought of your excellence and your worthiness, I thought it right and fitting to honor you with the best food I could obtain; so, remembering the falcon you ask me for and its value, I thought it a meal worthy of you, and today you had it roasted on the dish and set forth as best I could. But now I see that you wanted the bird in another form, it is such a grief to me that I cannot serve you that I think I shall never be at peace again."

And after saying this, he showed her the feathers and the feet and the beak of the bird in proof. When the lady heard and saw all this, she first blamed him for having killed such a falcon to make a meal for a woman; and then she inwardly commended his greatness of soul, which no poverty could or would be able to abate. But, having lost all hope of obtaining the falcon, and thus perhaps the health of her son, she departed sadly and returned to the child. Now, either from disappointment at not having the falcon or because his sickness must inevitably have led to it, the child died not many days later, to the mother's extreme grief.

Although she spent some time in tears and bitterness, yet, since she had been left very rich and was still young, her brothers often urged her to marry again. She did not want to do so, **15** but as they kept on pressing her, she remembered the worthiness of Federigo and his last act of generosity, in killing such a falcon to do her honor.

"I will gladly submit to marriage when you please," she said to her brothers, "but if you want me to take a husband, I will take no man but Federigo degli[14] Alberighi."

At this her brothers laughed at her, saying:

"Why, what are you talking about, you fool? Why do you want a man who hasn't a penny in the world?"

But she replied:

"Brothers, I know it is as you say, but I would rather have a man who needs money than money which needs a man."

Seeing her determination, the brothers, who knew Federigo's good qualities, did as she wanted, and gave her with all her wealth to him, **16** in spite of his poverty. Federigo, finding that he had such a woman, whom he loved so much, with all her wealth to boot, as his wife, was more prudent with his money in the future, and ended his days happily with her.

---

14. **degli** [del'yē]: Italian for "of the"; formerly used in names as a sign of noble birth.

CRITICAL THINKING: GUIDED READING QUESTIONS

LITERAL

1a. Whom or what does Federigo blame for his inability to supply Monna with the one thing she wants, the falcon? (Fortune)

2a. Why does Monna decide to marry Federigo? (She recalls his worthiness and last act of generosity in killing his valued falcon to do her honor.)

INFERENTIAL

1b. In what way is Federigo himself also to blame for the misunderstanding? (He acts rashly in killing the bird and is overly concerned with impressing Monna.)

2b. In what way does Monna do what the queen, in her introduction, says ladies should do? (Monna rewards Federigo because she feels he deserves it instead of letting Fortune treat him capriciously.)

STUDY QUESTIONS

Recalling

1. Why does Federigo spend his money "without stint"? Where does he go after losing his wealth, and how does he occupy his time there?
2. Why does Monna Giovanna want Federigo's falcon?
3. Why does Federigo kill the falcon?
4. In what financial state is Monna left after the deaths of her husband and son? What does she remember about Federigo that prompts her to choose him as her new husband?

Interpreting

5. Explain in your own words the view of Fortune that the queen expresses in the opening paragraphs.
6. Based on her behavior and her final decision, what values would you say are most important to Monna?
7. Why is killing the falcon such a great sacrifice for Federigo?
8. Is Federigo in any way responsible for his eventual happiness? Explain.

Extending

9. What role do you think chance plays in the achievement of happiness? To what extent are we responsible for our own happiness?

LITERARY FOCUS

Stated and Unstated Themes

The **theme** of a story is the main idea that it conveys. All of a story's details point to the theme, which is usually an insight into life or human experience. Sometimes a theme is directly **stated** within the story, either by the narrator or another character. More often a theme is **unstated,** or implied, and we must infer the theme from the story details. Some literary works have more than one theme.

Thinking About Stated and Unstated Themes

1. The queen states one theme of "Federigo's Falcon" in the opening paragraphs. What lesson does she say her story will teach?

2. What unstated theme is conveyed in Federigo's experiences about a person's ability to control his or her fate?

LANGUAGE STUDY

The Romance Languages

Boccaccio was the first great prose writer to write in Italian. Italian belongs to a group of closely related European languages that come from Latin, the language of ancient Rome. For this reason, these languages are called **Romance languages.** Other Romance languages include Spanish, French, Portuguese, Romanian, and Catalan, a language spoken in parts of Spain and southern France and in the tiny European nation of Andorra.

1. Using a current almanac, identify four modern European nations where Italian is spoken. (Hint: Two of these nations are very small.)
2. Why do you think early novels were called *romances?* Use a dictionary to check the origin of the term.

COMPOSITION

Writing a Modern Version of a Story

■ Write an updated version of "Federigo's Falcon." In your frame story, make clear why ten modern people have left a particular city and are telling stories to pass the time. In your story within the frame story, use the basic plot and themes that Boccaccio uses, but substitute modern settings, names, and customs.

COMPARING STORIES

■ Why do you think Boccaccio spends more than a paragraph on the queen's explanation of where she heard the story of Federigo? Would a modern writer be likely to do such a thing? Base your answer on contemporary stories you have read, and explain.

COMPOSITION: GUIDELINES FOR EVALUATION

WRITING A MODERN VERSION OF A STORY

Objective

To update a story

Guidelines for Evaluation

■ suggested length: four to six pages

■ should include a frame story and a story within the frame
■ should use the basic plot and themes of "Federigo's Falcon" but should update the settings, names, and customs

Do you find Monna Giovanna and Federigo admirable people? Why or why not?

ANSWERS

STUDY QUESTIONS

1. He spends his money to win Monna's love. He goes to his farm, where he spends his time hawking.
2. Her son says it will help him recover from his illness.
3. He wants to serve a meal that will "do honor" to Monna, and he has nothing else to serve.
4. She is rich. She remembers his worthiness and his last act of generosity.
5. Fortune does not always justly reward the deserving.
6. Loyalty, fairness, generosity, and courtesy are important to Monna.
7. It is his only companion and means of happiness and his chief means of getting food.
8. Yes, his unselfish act prompts Monna to marry him.
9. Answers will vary. Students may feel that it is necessary to work for happiness but that chance may also play a part.

LITERARY FOCUS

1. People should "be givers of rewards when fitting, without allowing Fortune always to dispense them."
2. The values a person has and the choices a person makes often determine his or her fate.

LANGUAGE STUDY

1. Italy, San Marino, Vatican City, and parts of Switzerland
2. They evolved from stories of adventure written in Romance languages.

COMPARING STORIES

to make the story seem more authentic and believable; No, modern writers usually make their stories realistic by plunging into the action, providing vivid details, and presenting believable characters and dialogue.

LESSON PREVIEW

In this story from modern India, a schoolteacher, Sekhar, decides to tell nothing but the truth for a day, thus offending his wife and shocking a colleague. When asked to give his honest opinion of his headmaster's singing, he reluctantly tells him that he sings poorly. The headmaster thanks Sekhar for telling the truth but makes Sekhar grade overnight the test papers he had previously given him ten days to grade.

LITERARY SKILLS FOR THIS SELECTION

- theme
- character motivation

THEMES IN THIS SELECTION

- personal values: honesty and its consequences
- hypocrisy and self-deception

LESSON OBJECTIVES

1. to understand meanings and origins of words from place names
2. to analyze a story's theme
3. to evaluate a music performance

Teacher's Classroom Resources 1

- Teaching Notes 241
- Prereading Vocabulary 242
- Reading Guide 243
- Check Test 244
- Responding to World Cultures 245
- Language Study: Words from Place Names 246
- Writing Process Guides: Writing About Theme 247 Writing a Music Review 248
- Grammar in Literature: Creating Variety in Sentences 249
- Selection Test 250

IN THE CLASSROOM

TEACHING STUDENTS OF DIFFERENT ABILITIES

- **For less advanced students:** Have students read the first paragraph and predict the results of Sekhar's experiment. Have them complete the Reading Guide for this selection.

- **For more advanced students:** Have students read more stories by R. K. Narayan and compare and contrast his characters, settings, and themes.

R. K. Narayan (born 1906)

India

One of the best-known contemporary authors of India, R. K. Narayan [nä rī'än] writes fiction that is both strongly Indian in flavor and appealingly universal in its characters and themes. Born in the Indian city of Madras, Narayan grew up in Mysore, which inspired the fictional village of Malgudi that appears throughout his works. He published his first novel, *Swami and Friends,* in 1935, and his first story collection, *Malgudi Days,* six years later. His impressive body of fiction, as well as two essay collections and a memoir, has earned Narayan an international following. In the United States his tales often appear in *The New Yorker* magazine.

Some of Narayan's most acclaimed works include the novels *Waiting for the Mahatma* and *The Vendor of Sweets.* Narayan has also written prose adaptations of two Indian epics, the *Mahabharata* and the *Ramayana.*

Like many Indian authors, Narayan writes in English. "I am particularly fond of the language," he once commented. "English is a very adaptable language [that can] take on the tint of any country." Critics agree, pointing out that Narayan's English has a strong Indian touch.

140 *The Short Story*

India and Its Music

The vast nation of India has an ancient and varied musical tradition. In the classical music of southern India described in "Like the Sun," a melody pattern called a raga [rä'gə] provides the basic framework for creating a piece of music. In a raga the precise sequence of notes is not fixed. The word *raga* means "color" or "mood," and the performer improvises in a way similar to the improvisations of a jazz musician, following some basic musical rules in an attempt to convey an emotion. In capturing the particular mood of a raga, the performer actually becomes a composer.

Ragas may be played or sung. Some of the instruments most commonly heard are the sitar (a sort of lute), the tamboura (a stringed instrument that creates a steady drone), and the tabla (a pair of small drums). In "Like the Sun" the performance is vocal, with drum and violin.

See LITERATURE AND CULTURE SOURCEBOOK: India and the Middle East

DISCUSSING GEOGRAPHY AND CULTURE

Musical Entertainments

In this story an Indian teacher is invited to the home of his supervisor, who entertains him by singing to the accompaniment of a drum and violin. In America, particularly in the past, hosts often entertained guests with informal musical performances by family members, who usually sang or played the piano.

- Have students describe the type of live musical entertainment they would arrange for a group of guests.

R. K. Narayan

Like the Sun

1 Truth, Sekhar reflected, is like the sun. I suppose no human being can ever look it straight in the face without blinking or being dazed. He realized that, morning till night, the essence of human relationships consisted in tempering truth so that it might not shock. This day he set apart as a unique day—at least one day in the year we must give and take absolute Truth whatever may happen. Otherwise life is not worth living. The day ahead seemed to him full of possibilities. He told no one of his experiment. It was a quiet resolve, a secret pact between him and eternity.

The very first test came while his wife served him his morning meal. He showed hesitation over a tidbit, which she had thought was her culinary masterpiece. She asked, "Why, isn't it **2** good?" At other times he would have said, considering her feelings in the matter, "I feel full-up, that's all." But today he said, "It isn't good. I'm unable to swallow it." He saw her wince and said to himself, Can't be helped. Truth is like the sun.

His next trial was in the common room[1] when one of his colleagues came up and said, "Did you hear of the death of so and so? Don't you think it a pity?" "No," Sekhar answered. "He was such a fine man—" the other began. But Sekhar cut him short with: "Far from it. He always struck me as a mean and selfish brute."

3 During the last period when he was teaching geography for Third Form A,[2] Sekhar received a note from the headmaster: "Please see me before you go home." Sekhar said to himself: It must be about these horrible test papers. A hun-dred papers in the boys' scrawls; he had shirked this work for weeks, feeling all the time as if a sword were hanging over his head.

The bell rang and the boys burst out of the class.

Sekhar paused for a moment outside the headmaster's room to button up his coat; that was another subject the headmaster always sermonized about.

He stepped in with a very polite "Good evening, sir."

The headmaster looked up at him in a very friendly manner and asked, "Are you free this evening?"

Sekhar replied, "Just some outing which I have promised the children at home—"

"Well, you can take them out another day. Come home with me now."

"Oh . . . yes, sir, certainly . . ." And then he added timidly, "Anything special, sir?"

"Yes," replied the headmaster, smiling to himself. . . . "You didn't know my weakness for music?"

"Oh, yes, sir . . ."

"I've been learning and practicing secretly, and now I want you to hear me this evening. I've engaged a drummer and a violinist to accompany me—this is the first time I'm doing it full-**4** dress and I want your opinion. I know it will be valuable."

Sekhar's taste in music was well known. He was one of the most dreaded music critics in the town. But he never anticipated his musical inclinations would lead him to this trial. . . . "Rather a surprise for you, isn't it?" asked the headmaster. "I've spent a fortune on it behind closed doors. . . ." They started for the headmaster's house. "God hasn't given me a child, but at least let him not deny me the consolation of music,"

Like the Sun **141**

1. **common room:** faculty lounge or meeting room.
2. **Third Form A:** equivalent to a junior high school class.

CRITICAL THINKING: GUIDED READING QUESTIONS

LITERAL

1a. What does Sekhar recognize as "the essence of human relationships"? (It "consist[s] in tempering truth so that it might not shock.")

2a. What does Sekhar tell a colleague about a recently deceased acquaintance? ("He always struck me as a mean and selfish brute.")

INFERENTIAL

1b. If he already has this opinion, why do you think he conducts his experiment? (He probably wishes to see whether he himself can face truth and its harsh consequences.)

2b. Why is this honest opinion tactless and shocking? (People usually show respect for someone who just died.)

- The headmaster treats Sekhar as an honored guest and gives him ten days to grade the test papers that have been preying on Sekhar's mind.
- The headmaster's performance is awful.
- Sekhar asks whether he may give his opinion the next day, but the headmaster wants it then.
- After telling the truth, Sekhar worries about his career.
- At home his wife is still angry about his criticism of her breakfast.

IN THE GLOSSARY

- incessantly: continuously
- ingratiating: aiming to please
- increment: raise in salary

5 GRAMMAR IN LITERATURE

Note the use of a compound predicate to avoid short, choppy sentences. Have students identify the main verb in each part of the compound. (*sat, set, fussed*)

6 TEACHING FIGURATIVE LANGUAGE

Elicit that these comical similes help capture the sheer awfulness of the headmaster's performance.

7 TEACHING CHARACTER MOTIVATION

Note that Sekhar hopes to delay giving his opinion until his experiment with truth is over. Ask why he cares more about the headmaster's feelings than anyone else's so far. (Offending his superior at work could affect his career.)

8 TEACHING THEME

Point out that Sekhar learns first-hand the social dangers of total honesty.

9 TEACHING STUDENTS OF LIMITED ENGLISH PROFICIENCY

Help students with the figurative expressions "smooth sailing" ("free of problems or agitation") and "in store" ("awaiting one in the future").

---

the headmaster said, pathetically, as they walked. He incessantly chattered about music: how he began one day out of sheer boredom; how his teacher at first laughed at him, and then gave him hope; how his ambition in life was to forget himself in music.

5 At home the headmaster proved very ingratiating. He sat Sekhar on a red silk carpet, set before him several dishes of delicacies, and fussed over him as if he were a son-in-law of the house. He even said, "Well, you must listen with a free mind. Don't worry about these test papers." He added half humorously, "I will give you a week's time."

"Make it ten days, sir," Sekhar pleaded.

"All right, granted," the headmaster said generously. Sekhar felt really relieved now—he would attack them at the rate of ten a day and get rid of the nuisance.

The headmaster lighted incense sticks. "Just to create the right atmosphere," he explained. A drummer and a violinist, already seated on a Rangoon mat,[3] were waiting for him. The headmaster sat down between them like a professional at a concert, cleared his throat, and began an alapana,[4] and paused to ask, "Isn't it good, Kalyani?" Sekhar pretended not to have heard the question. The headmaster went on to sing a full song composed by Thyagaraja[5] and followed it with two more. All the time the headmaster **6** was singing, Sekhar went on commenting within himself, He croaks like a dozen frogs. He is bellowing like a buffalo. Now he sounds like loose window shutters in a storm.

The incense sticks burned low. Sekhar's head throbbed with the medley of sounds that had assailed his ear-drums for a couple of hours now.

---

3. **Rangoon** [rang goon'] **mat:** mat from Rangoon, now called Yangon, the capital of Myanmar, formerly Burma.
4. **alapana** [ä lä′pä nä]: in a performance of classical Indian music, the traditional slow start in which the scales are played or sung and the mood of the performance is established. (See the Geography and Culture feature that precedes the story.)
5. **Thyagaraja** [tī äg′ä rä′jä] (1764–1848): famous composer of classical Indian music; also spelled Tyagaraja.

142 *The Short Story*

He felt half stupefied. The headmaster had gone nearly hoarse, when he paused to ask, "Shall I go on?" Sekhar replied, "Please don't, sir, I think this will do. . . ." The headmaster looked stunned. His face was beaded with perspiration. Sekhar felt the greatest pity for him. But he felt he could not help it. No judge delivering a sentence felt more pained and helpless. Sekhar noticed that the headmaster's wife peeped in from the kitchen, with eager curiosity. The drummer and the violinist put away their burdens with an air of relief. The headmaster removed his spectacles, mopped his brow, and asked, "Now, come out with your opinion."

7 "Can't I give it tomorrow, sir?" Sekhar asked tentatively.

"No. I want it immediately—your frank opinion. Was it good?"

"No, sir . . ." Sekhar replied.

"Oh! . . . Is there any use continuing my lessons?"

"Absolutely none, sir . . ." Sekhar said with **8** his voice trembling. He felt very unhappy that he could not speak more soothingly. Truth, he reflected, required as much strength to give as to receive.

All the way home he felt worried. He felt that **9** his official life was not going to be smooth sailing hereafter. There were questions of increment and confirmation and so on, all depending upon the headmaster's goodwill. All kinds of worries seemed to be in store for him. . . . Did not Harishchandra[6] lose his throne, wife, child, because he would speak nothing less than the absolute Truth whatever happened?

At home his wife served him with a sullen face. He knew she was still angry with him for his remark of the morning. Two casualties for today, Sekhar said to himself. If I practice it for a week, I don't think I shall have a single friend left.

He received a call from the headmaster in his

---

6. **Harishchandra** [hä rish chän′drä]: legendary Hindu king whose extreme honesty led to misfortune.

CRITICAL THINKING: GUIDED READING QUESTIONS

LITERAL

1a. What does the headmaster say is his ambition in life? (He wishes "to forget himself in music.")

2a. What is Sekhar's reply when the headmaster asks, "Shall I go on?" ("Please don't, sir, I think this will do. . . .")

INFERENTIAL

1b. On the basis of the headmaster's remarks before the performance, how do you think he will feel if Sekhar criticizes his efforts? (He will be extremely disappointed.)

2b. Why does Sekhar tell him not to continue? (Sekhar finds the performance so awful that he cannot stand any more.)

classroom next day. He went up apprehensively.

10 "Your suggestion was useful. I have paid off the music master. No one would tell me the truth about my music all these days. Why such antics at my age! Thank you. By the way, what about those test papers?"

"You gave me ten days, sir, for correcting them."

"Oh, I've reconsidered it. I must positively have them here tomorrow. . . ." A hundred papers in a day! That meant all night's sitting up!
"Give me a couple of days, sir . . ."

11 "No. I must have them tomorrow morning. And remember, every paper must be thoroughly scrutinized."

"Yes, sir," Sekhar said, feeling that sitting up all night with a hundred test papers was a small price to pay for the luxury of practicing Truth.

Two vinas (stringed instruments), Indian.

- The next day the headmaster tells Sekhar he is glad someone told him the truth about his musical ability.
- He also asks to have the test papers the next day, saying he has reconsidered the ten days he'd given Sekhar to grade them.
- Sekhar feels that sitting up all night grading papers is a small price to pay for "the luxury of practicing Truth."

10 TEACHING THEME

Point out that the headmaster is being dishonest about his feelings, as his turnabout with the test papers shows. His behavior illustrates not a tactful "white lie" but a hypocrisy born of pride and self-delusion.

11 CRITICAL THINKING: EVALUATION

Ask students whether they think Sekhar gets what he deserves. (They may feel his harsh experiment hurt the feelings of others and that he deserves to suffer a bit himself.)

COLLABORATIVE LEARNING: ENRICHMENT ACTIVITY

Music Have groups of students research and report on folk or traditional music. Each group should focus on a different nation or culture—for example, India, China, the Middle East, West Africa, Brazil, Ireland, or Greece—and play recordings as part of their reports.

CRITICAL THINKING: GUIDED READING QUESTIONS

LITERAL

1a. About what has the headmaster changed his mind? (the ten days he gave Sekhar to grade the test papers)

INFERENTIAL

1b. Why does he now demand that Sekhar grade the papers overnight? (He is hurt and angry that Sekhar dashed his musical aspirations.)

ANSWERS

STUDY QUESTIONS

1. "tempering truth so it might not shock"; to tell the truth
2. "I'm unable to swallow it." She winces and later is sullen.
3. "God hasn't given me a child," so at least allow me "the consolation of music." He seats Sekhar on a silk carpet and gives him delicacies and extra time to grade papers.
4. It is no use. He thanks Sekhar but demands the graded papers the next day.
5. It can be harsh, unyielding, and hard to face. It can cause pain and embarrassment.
6. enthusiastic, vain, hypocritical, unfulfilled; He demands the papers right away.
7. probably not; One cannot always afford complete honesty.
8. Answers will vary; perhaps to test his principles or his courage in facing consequences

LANGUAGE STUDY

1. "type of cotton cloth"; from *Calicut,* former name of Indian city where first obtained
2. "fine wool"; from *Cashmere,* Asian region where goats produce fine wool
3. "lustrous fabric"; from *Damascus,* Syria, where made
4. "sturdy cotton cloth"; from *(serge) de Nîmes,* France, where first made
5. "hot spring"; from *Geysir,* a hot spring in Iceland
6. "car with hooded seat"; now, "luxurious car"; from hooded cloaks of *Limousin,* France
7. "purple-red dye or color"; from Battle of *Magenta,* Italy, fought in 1859, about when the dye was first made
8. "place drawing many visitors"; from *Mecca,* Saudi Arabia, to which Moslems make pilgrimages
9. "sheer cotton cloth"; from *Mosul,* Iraq, where first made
10. "mandarin orange"; from *Tangier,* Morocco, where obtained
11. "semipoisonous spider"; from epidemic of nervous disease around *Taranto,* Italy, wrongly blamed on the spider
12. "men's tailless evening jacket"; from *Tuxedo Park,* New York, where introduced

STUDY QUESTIONS

Recalling

1. What does Sekhar think is the essence of human relationships? For what special purpose does he set aside a "unique day"?
2. What does Sekhar tell his wife about her "culinary masterpiece"? How does she react?
3. What does the headmaster say that sounds pathetic to Sekhar as they start for the headmaster's house? What ingratiating things does the headmaster say and do when they reach his home?
4. What does Sekhar finally say about whether or not the headmaster should continue his music lessons? What does the headmaster tell Sekhar the next day?

Interpreting

5. Explain in your own words what Sekhar means when he compares truth to the sun. What do Sekhar's experiences prove about being totally honest?
6. What sort of person is the headmaster? How do we know that he is really angry at Sekhar at the end of the story?
7. Do you think Sekhar will continue his experiment beyond one day? What does the use of the word *luxury* in the last paragraph suggest about honesty?

Extending

8. Why do you think Sekhar conducts his experiment?

LANGUAGE STUDY

Words from Place Names

Like many Indian cities, Narayan's birthplace of

Madras is famous for its textiles. The fine, usually plaid, cotton cloth first made in the city is now known as *madras,* one of many English words that have their origins in place names.

Use a dictionary to determine the meanings and origins of the following English words, which all come from the names of places. Also indicate the geographical location of each place you identify. If you have an atlas, try to find the place on a map.

1. calico
2. cashmere
3. damask
4. denim
5. geyser
6. limousine
7. magenta
8. mecca
9. muslin
10. tangerine
11. tarantula
12. tuxedo

COMPOSITION

Writing About Theme

■ Write a brief composition about the theme of "Like the Sun." Clearly state the theme, the main insight into life that the story conveys. Then show how Narayan develops the theme through the characters, setting, plot, point of view, and tone. *For help with this assignment, refer to Lesson 6 in the Writing About Literature Handbook at the back of this book.*

Writing a Music Review

■ Write a review of a musical performance that you heard in concert, on television, or on the radio or a recording. The music may be vocal or instrumental. Begin by identifying the music, the composer, and the performer or performers. Then include a description of the performance, and state your opinions about it. Support your opinions with specific details.

COMPOSITION: GUIDELINES FOR EVALUATION

WRITING ABOUT THEME

Objective

To analyze a story's theme

Guidelines for Evaluation

■ suggested length: two to four paragraphs
■ should clearly state the theme
■ should show how characters, setting, plot, point of view, and tone support the theme

WRITING A MUSIC REVIEW

Objective

To evaluate a musical performance

Guidelines for Evaluation

■ suggested length: one to two pages
■ should identify the work, composer, and performer
■ should describe the performance
■ should express opinions about the performance and support them with details

Jan Neruda (1834–1891)

Czechoslovakia

Jan Neruda is the most prominent of the authors working in the nineteenth century to publish works that would ´ help revive and promote Czech. Neruda grew up in the city of Prague at a time when the Czech people lived under Austrian rule and when the authorities had for many decades suppressed the native Czech tongue. Neruda's desire to promote his native language spurred him to write for the *Czech National Journal.* He remained on the newspaper's staff until his death, contributing essays and reviews that made him famous throughout his homeland.

Neruda's reputation grew when he began publishing poetry and fiction. His stories display great imagination and a keen eye for detail. Among his most popular collections is *Tales of the Little Quarter,* set in the old part of Prague where he grew up. The collection is a classic in Czechoslovakia, and the people of Prague regard it as Londoners do the novels of Charles Dickens. Nor is Neruda without his admirers overseas: In the twentieth century the great Chilean poet Pablo Neruda (see p. 308) took his pen name in tribute to Jan Neruda.

GEOGRAPHY AND CULTURE

Bohemia and Prague's Little Quarter

A landlocked country in central Europe, Czechoslovakia became a unified and independent nation after World War I. The new nation joined the Czech-speaking regions of Bohemia and Moravia in the west with the Slovak-speaking region of Slovakia in the east. Though part of the Austro-Hungarian empire before World War I, Bohemia was for many centuries an independent kingdom. Prague, the capital of Czechoslovakia, is Bohemia's largest city.

Prague's Little Quarter is a picturesque district at the foot of Hradčany [hräd′chä nē] Palace, once the residence of Bohemia's kings. The Little Quarter is famous for its medieval palaces, its pleasant squares, and its quaint and narrow streets and alleys. In his *Tales of the Little Quarter,* however, Neruda focuses less on the area's architecture than on the people who inhabit it. "Hastrman" tells the story of one of this charming neighborhood's most memorable characters.

See *LITERATURE AND CULTURE SOURCEBOOK:*
Russia and Eastern Europe

Hastrman **145**

LESSON PREVIEW

In this Czech tale a man learns that family love is his most valued treasure. On learning that his treasured collection of gemstones has little value, Mr. Rybář fears his niece's family took him in because they thought he was rich. When his niece's husband says they are indeed rich to have him there, everything glitters for Mr. Rybář, and he thinks he sees the sea, which he loves.

LITERARY SKILLS FOR THIS SELECTION

- symbols
- setting
- point of view

THEMES IN THIS SELECTION

- personal values: family ties and shared experiences
- material vs. emotional riches

LESSON OBJECTIVES

1. to understand symbols
2. to create a story character's diary entry
3. to compare and contrast stories

Teacher's Classroom Resources 1

- Teaching Notes — 253
- Prereading Vocabulary — 254
- Reading Guide — 255
- Check Test — 256
- Responding to World Cultures — 257
- Literary Focus: Symbol — 258
- Writing Process Guides: Writing About a Symbol — 259
  Writing a Diary Entry — 260
- Grammar in Literature: Using Hyphens in Compound Adjectives — 261
- Selection Test — 262

IN THE CLASSROOM

TEACHING STUDENTS OF DIFFERENT ABILITIES

- **For less advanced students:** Have students list Mr. Rybář's actions and remarks and explain what each reveals about him. Also ask students to complete the Reading Guide.

- **For more advanced students:** Have students find out more about Neruda's role as a Czech nationalist and consider how Mr. Rybář's stones might be a symbol of Czech heritage.

DISCUSSING GEOGRAPHY AND CULTURE

Excavating the Past

Exploring the streets of old Prague is like excavating an ancient ruin: Each vista reveals new layers of history. Prague's Jewish cemetery, for instance, is composed of twelve superimposed layers of tombs. Prague's Romanesque and Gothic churches, Renaissance theaters, and Baroque palaces stand side by side in splendid harmony.

- Ask students to "excavate" their own town. What do the oldest buildings reveal about its history?

Castle in Prague, 1935, Oscar Kokoschka.

Jan Neruda

Hastrman[1]

Translated from the Czech by Edith Pargeter

He always walked with hat in hand, let the season threaten frost-stroke or heat-stroke; the greatest concession he ever made was to hold his low-crowned, rounded hat with the wide brim over his head like a parasol. His gray hair was smoothly combed to his skull, and drawn together behind in a queue[2] so firmly com-

---

1. **Hastrman** [häst′ər män]: water goblin of Czech legend, who wears knee-breeches, a green tail-coat, and his hair in a queue, or braid. Used in the story as a nickname.

2. **queue** [kū]: braid worn at the back of the head; an old-fashioned men's hair style at the time of the story.

146 *The Short Story*

---

pressed and bound that it did not even wag—this must have been one of the last queues in Prague, for there were then no more than two or three of them left.

His thin, slight little body was enveloped in a green frock-coat,[3] which had only short fronts, but descended behind in tails so long that they slapped Mr. Rybář[4] on his emaciated calves. A white waistcoat[5] covered his stooped breast, black trousers reached only to just below his knees, where two silver buckles gleamed, and below these were snow-white stockings down to the second pair of silver buckles on his large, shambling shoes. Whether these shoes were sometimes replaced by new ones I don't know, but they always looked as though the leather from them had been taken from the roof of a very old cab.

The withered, pointed face of Mr. Rybář was illuminated by an eternal smile. Walking through the streets, he presented an odd spectacle. At every twenty paces he would stop and look round to right and left. It was as though his thoughts were not within him, but walked respectfully a pace behind, and were always entertaining him with some flash of wit, so that Mr. Rybář had to smile and look round from time to time at the jokers. When he greeted anyone, he lifted only the forefinger of his right hand into the air, and gave a thin whistle. The same soft whistling was heard also whenever he began to speak, and he regularly began with "Zhaw!" which had an affirmative significance.

Mr. Rybář lived in Deep Street, just on the left beneath the prospect-tower on Petřín.[6] Even if he had almost reached his own home, if he caught sight of any strangers just turning to the right towards Hradčany,[7] he always went after them. When they stood on the prospect-tower and admired the beauty of our Prague, he stood beside them, lifted his finger, and whistled: "Zhaw, the sea!—Why don't we live by the sea!" Then he would follow them into the castle, and when the strangers admired the walls of St. Václav's chapel,[8] studded with semi-precious stones, he whistled again, and said: "You know what I think? Here in Bohemia a shepherd throws a stone after his herd, and the stone is often worth more than the whole herd!" He never made any other observations to them.

Because of his name, and his green coat,[9] and because of this cry of "The sea!" we called him "Hastrman." But, old and young, we all respected him. Mr. Rybář was a justiciary from somewhere by Turnov,[10] now retired on a pension. Here in Prague he lived with a young kinswoman of his, who was married to an official in a modest position and had already two or three children. It was rumored that Mr. Rybář was immensely rich, not so much in money, however, as in jewels. In his room he had, it was said, a tall black cupboard standing, and this cupboard was full of shallow, square black boxes, big ones, and the interior of every box was divided into squares with white pasteboard, and in each square, on a bed of cotton-wool, a jewel lay gleaming. There were people who had

---

3. **frock-coat:** knee-length, usually double-breasted men's coat fitted to the waist and popular in the nineteenth century.
4. **Rybář** [rē′bärzh]
5. **waistcoat** [wes′kət]: vest.
6. **prospect-tower on Petřín** [pet′ərzh in]: watchtower built in medieval times to protect the city.

7. **Hradčany** [hräd′chä nē]: former palace of the kings of Bohemia and the area around it. (See the Geography and Culture feature that precedes the story.)
8. **St. Václav's** [vät′slävz] **chapel:** small church located in Hradčany Palace and dedicated to Saint Václav (1361–1419), king and patron saint of Bohemia; known in English as Wenceslaus.
9. **Because of his name, and his green coat:** *Rybář* means "fisherman," and the *hastrman* of Czech legend traditionally wore a green coat (and a queue).
10. **justiciary** [jus tish′ē er′ē] **from somewhere by Turnov:** judge from somewhere near Turnov, northern Bohemian town noted for mining semiprecious stones.

Hastrman 147

CRITICAL THINKING: GUIDED READING QUESTIONS

LITERAL

1a. What does Mr. Rybář often exclaim to tourists viewing Prague from the tower? ("Zhaw, the sea!—Why don't we live by the sea!")

2a. In Saint Václav's chapel what does Mr. Rybář often say about Bohemian stones? ("Here in Bohemia a shepherd throws a stone after his herd, and the stone is often worth more than the whole herd!")

INFERENTIAL

→ **1b.** What does this comment suggest about his own life? (He is dissatisfied and would like to live elsewhere.)

→ **2b.** What does he mean? (He thinks Bohemia's semiprecious stones are very valuable.)

- Mr. Rybář collected the jewels himself on a Bohemian mountain near his former home.
- The narrator and other neighborhood children envy the Šajvls, the relatives with whom Mr. Rybář lives.
- The narrator is also impressed by Rybář's erudition (though Rybář calls Rousseau "Rosenau").
- One day everyone in the Little Quarter comes out to watch Mr. Rybář march down the street.

IN THE GLOSSARY

- constitutionals: walks taken for exercise
- potent: powerful; strong
- debauch: corrupt
- exalted: glorified
- frivolous: unimportant
- forfeit: give up; lose

8 TEACHING SYMBOLS

Point out that the jewels are native Bohemian stones that Mr. Rybář collected himself. These details help point to the symbolic significance of the stones.

9 CULTURAL BACKGROUND

Explain that sand was used to help scour the floor. The Šajvls do not really use sugar; the children's statement merely stresses their idea that the Šajvls are so rich they can be as extravagant as they like.

10 TEACHING POINT OF VIEW

Elicit that the narrator is a child at the time the events of the story take place.

11 TEACHING SETTING

Note that Prague's Little Quarter is portrayed as a warm, close, and gossipy community in which all the residents pay much attention to their neighbors' business.

---

8 seen them. They said he had found and collected them all himself on Mount Kozák.[11] We children used to tell one another, too, that when they 9 washed the floor at the Šajvls'[12] house—these young relatives of Mr. Rybář were called Šajvl—they scattered over it, in place of sand, fine-ground sugar. On Saturday, which was cleaning day, we always desperately envied the Šajvl children. Once I sat above the moat, to the left beyond the Bruska Gate, quite near to Mr. Rybář. He used to go there for an hour on every fine day, sit down comfortably in the grass, and smoke a short pipe. On that occasion two older students happened to come by. One of them spluttered, and said: "That one's smoking Mum's wadded jacket!" From that time forth I considered the smoking of Mum's wadded jacket as a luxury which only the wealthiest of people could allow themselves.

He walked, then, our Hastrman—but no, we won't call him that, since we're no longer children!—Mr. Rybář walked always along the Bruska ramparts.[13] If he met any of the canons,[14] who were also in the habit of taking their constitutionals there, he would stop and exchange a 10 few friendly words with them. Once—I loved to listen to what grown-up people said to one another—I heard him talking with two canons who were sitting on a bench there. He was standing. They talked about "France" and something called "liberty," strange words in themselves. Suddenly Mr. Rybář lifted his finger and whistled: "Zhaw, I hold with Rosenau! Rosenau says: 'Liberty is like those rich foods and potent wine on which strong natures that are used to them thrive and grow stronger, but which only

---

11. **Mount Kozák** [kŏ′zäk]: northern Bohemian mountain where many semiprecious stones are found.
12. **Šajvls'** [shä′yə vəlz]
13. **ramparts:** earth embankments built to protect a castle, a fort, etc.
14. **canons:** here, referring to members of the Roman Catholic clergy.

---

debauch, intoxicate and ruin feeble constitutions.'"

And then he waved his hat and went away.

The bigger canon, a fat man, asked then: "Who is this Rosenau he's always talking about?"

The smaller, but equally fat, canon replied: "A writer—most probably a writer."

But I remembered this sentence as the sum of the entire higher wisdom. Of Rosenau and of Mr. Rybář I entertained the same exalted impression. When as a growing boy I took up a variety of books into my own hands, I found that Mr. Rybář had indeed quoted very faithfully on this occasion. But with this variation: that the judgment he had quoted was written not by Rosenau, but by someone called Rousseau.[15] Evidently unkind chance had misled Mr. Rybář by throwing in his way some frivolous printer's error.

But he did not forfeit my respect on that account. A good, a very good man!

It was on a sunny August day, about three 11 o'clock in the afternoon. The people who were walking along Spur Street suddenly stood at gaze; those who were merely standing outside their houses called in haste to those inside; customers hurried out of the shops. All of them were gazing after Mr. Rybář as he marched away down the hill.

"He's going somewhere to show off his riches," said Mr. Herzl, the innkeeper at the Two Suns.

"I declare!" cried Mr. Vitouš,[16] the shopkeeper on the corner. "Things must be bad, he's taking them off to sell them!" I'm sorry to have to report that Mr. Vitouš did not enjoy a very good reputation among the neighbors. It was

---

15. **Rousseau:** Jean-Jacques Rousseau [zhän′ zhäk′ rōō sō′] (1712–1778), Swiss-born French philosopher and writer.
16. **Vitouš** [vi′toush]

CRITICAL THINKING: GUIDED READING QUESTIONS

LITERAL

1a. What is accurate and inaccurate in Mr. Rybář's remarks to the canons about liberty? (He quotes accurately but attributes the quote to Rosenau instead of Rousseau.)

2a. What does the innkeeper say as he and all the others go outside to watch Mr. Rybář? ("He's going somewhere to show off his riches.")

INFERENTIAL

1b. Since Rousseau is quite famous, what does this incident suggest about Mr. Rybář? (He is not really well read, although he is deeply interested in what he does read.)

2b. What can we infer has attracted the community's attention? (Mr. Rybář has taken his famous jewel collection with him on his walk.)

said of him that once already he'd been near to bankruptcy, and even today your good Little Quarter citizen looks upon a bankrupt as totally different from the rest of humanity.

But Mr. Rybář marched calmly on, a shade more quickly than on other days. Under his left arm he carried one of those square black boxes about which there existed so many legends. He clutched it firmly against his body, so that the hat he carried in the same hand was clamped against his thigh. In his right hand he carried a Spanish cane with a flat knob of ivory, which indicated that Mr. Rybář was going somewhere on a visit, for never at any other time did he carry a stick. When anyone greeted him he waved his stick, and whistled much more loudly than on other days.

He walked down Spur Street, crossed St. Nicholas's Square, and turned into the Žamberecký[17] house. There, on the second floor, lived a grammar school professor, Mr. Mühlwenzel, a mathematician and student of natural science, a man of unusually thorough education for those days. The visit did not last long.

The professor was in a good humor. His powerful, compact body had just enjoyed the refreshment of an afternoon nap. His long gray hair, encircling a bald crown, stood on end in all directions, in comfortable disorder. His blue, intelligent and always kindly eyes were gleaming. His cheeks, invariably ruddy, now glowed. Those broad, benevolent cheeks were rather strongly marked by small-pox, and provided the professor with a pretext for constant jokes. "That's the way of the world," he would say. "If a girl smiles, and she has one dimple in her cheek, they say 'How charming!' When I smile I have a hundred dimples, but all they say is what a fright I am!"

He waved Mr. Rybář to the sofa, and asked: "What can I do for you?"

_____
17. **Žamberecký** [zhäm′bər et′skē]

Mr. Rybář laid his box on the table and lifted the lid. A sparkle of variegated stones caught the light.

"I should—I only— These things—about what would their value be?" he stammered.

Then he sat down and leaned his chin on the knob of his cane.

The professor regarded the stones. Then he took out one dark one, weighed it in his hand, and examined it against the light. "That's moldavite,"[18] he said.

"What?"

"Moldavite."

"Zhaw, moldavite," whistled Mr. Rybář. In his face it could plainly be read that he now heard this word for the first time in his life.

"That would be a good item for our school collection, they're rather scarce now. You could sell it to us."

"Well, we'll see about that. About how much—"

"We could give you three zlatkas[19] for it, in twenties. What do you say?"

"Three zlatkas!" Mr. Rybář whistled thinly. His chin jerked upward, then fell back again onto the knob of his stick. "And the rest?" he whispered after a pause, from a throat suddenly constricted.

"Chalcedony, jasper, amethyst, smoke-quartz[20]—there's nothing of value here."

After some minutes Mr. Rybář was again seen at the corner of Spur Street. He marched slowly up the hill. For the first time his neighbors saw him with his hat upon his head. The broad brim was pulled low upon his forehead, the Spanish cane dragged its tip along the ground and rattled over the pavement. He took no notice of anyone, he didn't whistle even once. On this journey he did not even look round. Plainly today

_____
18. **moldavite** [mol′də vīt]: glass of meteoric origin.
19. **three zlatkas** [zlät′kəs]: small sum of money.
20. **Chalcedony** [kal sed′ən ē] . . . **smoke-quartz:** various semiprecious stones.

Hastrman **149**

PAGE SUMMARY: AT A GLANCE
- Mr. Rybář takes his jewel collection to Mr. Mühlwenzel, a schoolteacher and student of natural science.
- Mr. Mühlwenzel identifies the stones and explains that they are of little value.
- When Mr. Rybář leaves, he appears very different from his usually chipper self.

IN THE GLOSSARY
- benevolent: kindly
- pretext: excuse
- variegated: marked with different colors
- constricted: narrowed

12 CULTURAL BACKGROUND

Remind students that at the time of the story, Czechoslovakia was ruled by Austria (where German is spoken). Many ethnic Germans and Austrians lived in Prague: The name Mühlwenzel is of Germanic, not Czech, origin. You might mention that Franz Kafka and Rainer Maria Rilke, two very famous German-language writers, were both born in Prague.

13 GRAMMAR IN LITERATURE

Have students identify adjectives that help us picture Mr. Mühlwenzel. (*powerful, compact, bald, comfortable, kindly, ruddy,* and so on) Note that a comma separates two adjectives that independently describe the noun they precede, as in "powerful, compact body."

14 CRITICAL THINKING: LOGICAL REASONING

Elicit that the first-person narrator takes liberties in reporting events he is not likely to have witnessed or learned about in such detail. Such liberties may sometimes be taken when a first-person narrator is a minor character.

15 READING SKILL: CONTRAST

Elicit that after his visit Mr. Rybář walks differently and looks different from his usually chipper self.

CRITICAL THINKING: GUIDED READING QUESTIONS

LITERAL

1a. How does Mr. Rybář march as he goes to visit Mr. Mühlwenzel? (He walks calmly and a shade more quickly than usual.)

2a. What happens to Mr. Rybář's throat after Mr. Mühlwenzel offers only three zlatkas for the moldavite? (It constricts, and he talks in a whisper.)

INFERENTIAL

1b. What does his demeanor suggest about him? (He has a specific destination in mind and is excited about going there.)

2b. From the details what can you infer is Mr. Rybář's reaction to the news that his jewel collection is worth little? (He is deeply disappointed.)

- At home a grief-stricken Mr. Rybář begins casting his stones out the window.
- Mr. Šajvl interrupts to say he always knew the stones had little monetary value, but they still have value because Mr. Rybář collected them himself and can tell the Šajvl children all about them.
- When Mr. Rybář reveals his belief that the Šajvls took him in because they thought he was rich, Mr. Šajvl says they are indeed rich to have him there.
- Then everything glitters for Mr. Rybář, and he seems to see the sea at last.

IN THE GLOSSARY

- scintillated: flashed
- resplendent: gleaming
- distillation: concentration

16 READING SKILL: INFERENCE

Elicit that here Mr. Rybář's remark about having no sea clearly expresses deep dissatisfaction.

17 TEACHING SYMBOLS

Point out that Mr. Šajvl's remarks help explain the symbolic value of Mr. Rybář's stones: They represent (among other things) the love of beauty and of one's homeland and continuity with the past.

18 TEACHING THEME

Note that Mr. Šajvl's remarks here stress the spiritual and emotional enrichment a family gains in living with an elderly relative and being able to share in his or her experiences and memories.

19 TEACHING POINT OF VIEW

Elicit that the narrator, like Mr. Rybář, has been deeply moved by the story's conclusion.

COLLABORATIVE LEARNING: ENRICHMENT ACTIVITY

Oral Report Have a group of students prepare an oral report on the city of Prague. Each student should focus on a different aspect: its literature, music, landmarks, physical geography, political history, and so on.

---

not one of his thoughts was frolicking about outside him, they were all within him, deep within.

He did not go out of the house again that day, neither to the ramparts nor towards Bruska. And it was such a beautiful day!

It was almost midnight. The heaven was blue as at morning, the moon shone with its proudest, most magical radiance, the stars scintillated like white sparks. Petřín was covered with a resplendent silver mist, a flood of silver lay over the whole of Prague.

The smiling light flowed into Mr. Rybář's little room by both wide-open windows. At one of these stood Mr. Rybář, motionless as a statue. From below murmured the weirs of the Vltava,[21] in a long, steady thunder. Did the old man hear them?

16 Suddenly he shook himself. "The sea!—Why have we no sea?" he whispered, and his lips were trembling.

Perhaps his own grief surged in him like the waves of the sea.

"Well!—" He jerked himself away from the window and turned towards the room. On the floor lay the open boxes, and his gaze lit upon them. Slowly he took up the nearest of them and plucked out of it a handful of stones. "Pebbles—just pebbles!" and he flung them through the open window.

Down below there was a crash and a splintering of glass. Today Mr. Rybář hadn't even remembered that there was a greenhouse down there in the garden.

"Uncle, whatever are you doing?" cried a pleasant young voice outside, evidently from the next window.

---

21. **weirs** [wērz] **of the Vltava** [vul′tä vä]: river dams for adjusting water levels on the Vltava, a river that runs through Prague.

150   *The Short Story*

Mr. Rybář took an involuntary pace backwards.

The door creaked, and in came Mr. Šajvl. Perhaps it was the beauty of the night that had kept him so late at the window. Perhaps he had noticed in his old uncle signs of an unwonted disquiet, and heard from his little room the sounds of an activity which had lasted for some time. Perhaps, even, the old man's heavy sighs had flown in to him through the open window.

"Uncle, you surely don't want to throw out all those beautiful stones?"

The old man's body twitched. He whispered, staring intently towards Petřín: "They're of no value—mere pebbles!"

17 "I know they have no great value in money, I recognized that myself. But they have a value, all the same, for us and for you. You collected them all yourself, at the expense of a great deal of effort—Uncle, please leave them all for my children. They'll learn from them, you'll explain all about them, how you gathered them—"

"But perhaps you've been thinking," whispered the old man again, in a labored monotone, "that I was rich—and indeed, I thought—"

18 "Uncle," said Mr. Šajvl in a firm but very soft voice, and clasping the old man's hand, "do you think we're not rich in you? My children would have no grandfather, my wife would be fatherless, if we hadn't got you. Surely you see how happy we are around you, you are our blessing in the house—"

Suddenly the old man drew away and walked back to the same window at which he had been standing before. His mouth was shaking, he felt in his eyes an indescribable pressure. He gazed out, seeing nothing distinctly, for everything glittered like a distillation of diamonds, everything was surging into waves—up to his window—up to his eyes—the sea!—the sea!

19 I won't tell any more; I can't.

CRITICAL THINKING: GUIDED READING QUESTIONS

LITERAL

1a. What does Mr. Šajvl say he already recognized about his uncle's stones? (They have no great monetary value.)

2a. When Mr. Rybář walks to the window at the end, how does everything seem to him? ("Everything glittered like a distillation of diamonds, everything was surging up into waves. . . .")

INFERENTIAL

1b. Why is it significant that Mr. Šajvl already knew their true monetary value? (It shows that the Šajvls' decision to have their uncle live with them was not motivated by hopes of financial gain, as Mr. Rybář thought.)

2b. What changes in Mr. Rybář's outlook does seeing diamonds and the sea represent? (He has found emotional, if not material, wealth and happiness just living in Prague with the Šajvls.)

STUDY QUESTIONS

Recalling

1. Briefly describe Mr. Rybář's appearance and activities. Why do the narrator and the other residents of the Little Quarter call him "Hastrman"?
2. According to rumors, what does Mr. Rybář possess that makes him wealthy?
3. What does Mr. Rybář discover about his supposed wealth when he visits the teacher, Mr. Mühlwenzel? How does he look afterwards?
4. What does Mr. Rybář do that brings his nephew upstairs? What value does the nephew see in the stones, and what riches does he see in Mr. Rybář?
5. What does Mr. Rybář "see" after talking to his nephew?

Interpreting

6. What sort of person is Mr. Rybář? What do his constant remarks about not living near the sea suggest about him?
7. Explain Mr. Rybář's mistaken impression of his niece and nephew. Why, at the story's end, does he think he sees the sea?
8. Why, in the last line, is the narrator unable to tell any more?
9. What does the story suggest about family relationships?

Extending

10. What reasons do people have for keeping things that have little or no commercial value?

LITERARY FOCUS

Symbol

A **symbol** is a person, a place, an object, or an event that represents something beyond its literal meaning. In a story about a tiger, for example, the tiger exists literally as a wild animal. Since tigers are dangerous, however, the tiger may also symbolize danger or evil. On the other hand, tigers are also threatened by extinction, so a tiger could symbolize humanity's destruction of nature. To understand what a symbol represents you need to pay attention to details the author provides about it.

Symbols are usually important story elements that can help point to a story's theme. The use of symbols in a literary work is called **symbolism.**

Thinking About Symbols

1. What reasons might Mr. Rybář have for wanting to live by the sea? What abstract ideas might the sea represent to him? Does he literally see the sea at the end of the story, or does he see what it represents? Explain.
2. In the end, are Mr. Rybář's stones of any value? What might they symbolize? What theme does this symbol suggest for the story?

COMPOSITION

Writing About a Symbol

■ Write a composition about how the sea or Mr. Rybář's stones are used as symbols in the story. First write a general statement about what the symbol represents. Then trace the details the author provides about the symbol throughout the story. What does the narrator or Mr. Rybář say about the symbolic object, and what does the object reveal about Mr. Rybář? How does the object gather new meaning as the plot progresses? How did the symbolic object make the story's theme more memorable for you? *For help with this assignment, refer to Lesson 7 in the Writing About Literature Handbook at the back of this book.*

Writing a Diary Entry

■ Write the diary entry that Mr. Rybář might have written on the evening after the story ends. Describe the day's events, your feelings about them, and any new awarenesses that the day has brought.

COMPARING STORIES

Compare and contrast this story to other stories about personal values that you have read in this section or elsewhere. In which stories did you find the values and concerns of the characters or authors most relevant to your own life? Cite details from the story to explain your reasons.

Hastrman **151**

COMPOSITION: GUIDELINES FOR EVALUATION

WRITING ABOUT A SYMBOL

Objective

To analyze the meaning of a symbol

Guidelines for Evaluation

■ suggested length: three or four paragraphs
■ should state the meanings of the symbol and trace any changes in the meanings
■ should state Rybář's relationship to the symbol
■ should show how the symbol reinforces the theme

WRITING A DIARY ENTRY

Objective

To create a story character's diary entry

Guidelines for Evaluation

■ suggested length: three to five paragraphs
■ should use diary-entry form
■ should be written from the point of view of Rybář
■ should include details of the plot and Rybář's feelings and new awarenesses

ANSWERS

STUDY QUESTIONS

1. He is a thin, gray-haired man in outdated dress who walks about and talks to strangers. He resembles the legendary water goblin; his name means "fisherman"; he cries, "The sea!"
2. a jewel collection
3. It has little monetary value. He wears his hat low, drags his cane, and looks at no one.
4. He throws some stones out the window. Rybář collected the stones himself and can talk about them to the children; he is like a father or grandfather.
5. glittering diamonds and surging waves
6. He is eccentric, active, and crotchety but likable. He feels his life lacks something.
7. He thought they took him in because they believed he was rich, but they did so out of love. He has found the joy he associates with the sea and may have tears in his eyes.
8. Emotion overwhelms him.
9. They provide an emotional fulfillment more valuable than material things.
10. Answers will vary. Students may feel they evoke pleasant memories and establish continuity with the past.

LITERARY FOCUS

1. In a landlocked country the sea might have an exotic attraction. Possible answers: beauty, power, fullness; He sees that he has everything the sea represents to him.
2. Yes; Possible answers: family heritage, Czech heritage, shared experience, the past, beauty, anything whose emotional value is priceless; Family ties and shared experiences are priceless treasures.

COMPARING STORIES

Answers will vary. Students might find most relevant the generosity and love in "Hastrman" and "Federigo's Falcon."

PREVIEW: THE AUTHOR AND THE WORLD

LESSON PREVIEW

This contemporary Mexican fantasy concerns a village that stood outside time. When Matusalén's bell ringer and village priest discover that the bell controls time, they ring it often to increase productivity. Matusalén attracts geniuses from all eras. The bell ringing also accelerates aging, however, so the villagers do not live long. Eventually the village perishes.

LITERARY SKILLS FOR THIS SELECTION

- realistic fiction and fantasy
- allusion
- frame story

THEMES IN THIS SELECTION

- reality and fantasy: the nature of time and progress
- material versus spiritual growth

LESSON OBJECTIVES

1. to distinguish between realistic fiction and fantasy
2. to understand allusions
3. to analyze a setting's fantastic and realistic details
4. to recount a fantastic incident

Teacher's Classroom Resources 1

- Teaching Notes 265
- Prereading Vocabulary 266
- Reading Guide 267
- Check Test 268
- Responding to World Cultures 269
- Literary Focus: Realistic Fiction and Fantasy; Allusion 270
- Writing Process Guides: Writing About Fantasy and Reality in a Setting 271
  Writing a Fantasy 272
- Grammar in Literature: Using a Semicolon to Separate Main Clauses 273
- Selection Test 274

IN THE CLASSROOM

TEACHING STUDENTS OF DIFFERENT ABILITIES

- **For less advanced students:** Have students list the fantastic elements in the story. Have

---

them complete the Reading Guide.
- **For more advanced students:** Have students find out more about Magic Realism, discussed on page 585 of their text, and explain its influence on the story.

GEOGRAPHY AND CULTURE

Mexico and Its "Lost" Villages

Located just south of the United States, Mexico has a long history of village life that began well before the 1500s, when the Spanish conquered the land. The ancient peoples of Mexico started settling villages around 2000 B.C., and after A.D. 250 great civilizations began to flourish. Chief among these were the Mayas, Zapotecs, Toltecs, and Aztecs. All of these civilizations left magnificent ruins.

With the Spanish came Roman Catholic priests and other settlers who established new villages in isolated areas, some of which also fell to ruin with time. These mysterious traces of the past have given rise to Mexican legends about "lost" villages, and these legends probably helped inspire María's story.

The typical colonial Mexican village consisted of buildings grouped around a central square, or plaza, and surrounded by outlying farms. María's village retains elements of this structure but, as you will see, is not typical.

Gerardo María (born 1956)

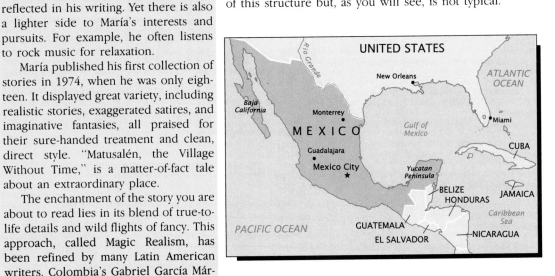

Mexico

The youngest author represented in this anthology of world authors, Gerardo María is part of a new generation of promising writers to emerge on the Latin American literary scene. María was born in Mexico City, the capital of Mexico. He is a serious student of sociology, economics, and political science, and these interests are often reflected in his writing. Yet there is also a lighter side to María's interests and pursuits. For example, he often listens to rock music for relaxation.

María published his first collection of stories in 1974, when he was only eighteen. It displayed great variety, including realistic stories, exaggerated satires, and imaginative fantasies, all praised for their sure-handed treatment and clean, direct style. "Matusalén, the Village Without Time," is a matter-of-fact tale about an extraordinary place.

The enchantment of the story you are about to read lies in its blend of true-to-life details and wild flights of fancy. This approach, called Magic Realism, has been refined by many Latin American writers. Colombia's Gabriel García Márquez, author of *One Hundred Years of Solitude,* is perhaps the most renowned master of Magic Realism.

152   *The Short Story*

See LITERATURE AND CULTURE SOURCEBOOK:
Latin America

DISCUSSING GEOGRAPHY AND CULTURE

Our Mexican Heritage

The histories of Mexico and the United States are closely interwoven. The two countries have been rivals and partners, enemies and friends. Portions of Texas, California, Arizona, and New Mexico were once part of Mexico and still bear the imprint of Mexican influence.
- Ask students to discuss Mexican influences on American culture. (Examples: adobe architecture; Mexican food, such as tacos and chili; towns planned around a central plaza)

Gerardo María

Matusalén,[1] the Village Without Time

Translated from the Spanish by Anne and Christopher Fremantle

1 "Where did you say it was?"

"Over there, beyond the mountains. It covered almost the whole valley."

"And what happened to that village? It must have been something very odd."

"There are many legends, and many old folks'
2 tales, but I'm more inclined to believe what my grandfather told me decades ago, because he was in charge of the belfry."

"Go on, Melitón, what did your grandfather say?"

"I don't remember too well anymore, but I'll try: Matusalén was a prosperous village from every point of view. It had been founded by Franciscan priests,[2] but the first municipal president claimed for himself the merit of having laid the first stone. He was a little fat man with a mustache bigger than his head and both his feet together. According to current gossip, this man was always quarreling with the little priest of the church, but, in fact, no one ever knew why. But one thing was sure—both of them, each on his own account, wished to remain in the village.

"Around the village were several farms and outlying buildings, which, as Matusalén prospered, had become incorporated in its domain. It really was a very rich place; the streets were paved and the drains worked everywhere. At night, gas lamps lit up the dark and dozens of night watchmen circulated in the avenues ac-
3 companying the strollers. Here was the first place in the world where cars and trucks were manufactured. The riches came from the mines, which were worked by the priests of the church, and with this money they attracted the wise men of that period in order that they should bring their wisdom to the valley. Here Einstein lived, Marx, Gutenberg, Lavoisier, Darwin,[3] and many others. High above the valley was a fairly big building where all these lived and worked, collaborating through their discoveries in the improvement of the village.

"The priest always wore a white tunic and preached, according to the people, beautifully.
4 He educated the crowds and fed them in a miraculous manner with a few loaves. They also said that he managed to transform the water in the rivers into wine, founding in this manner the first vinicultural[4] company in the country. He generally slept in the houses of his friends, and his chief passion was meditating in a garden behind the church which the natives of the place called the olive orchard. That priest, whose name was unknown, was the one who did most of the business together with a man named Peter, who was my grandfather.

---

1. **Matusalén** [mä tōō′ sä len′]: The village's name is Spanish for Methuselah, the biblical figure who, according to the Bible (Genesis 5:27), lived 969 years.
2. **Franciscan priests:** Roman Catholic priests belonging to the religious order founded by St. Francis of Assisi (1181?–1226).

3. **Einstein . . . Darwin:** Albert Einstein (1879–1955), German-born physicist who posed the theory of relativity; Karl Marx (1818–1883), German-born political economist who developed the ideas of modern socialism; Johann Gutenberg (1400?–1468), German inventor credited with building Europe's first printing press; Antoine Lavoisier (1743–1794), French scientist who helped establish the principles of modern chemistry; and Charles Darwin (1809–1882), English naturalist who posed the theory of evolution by natural selection.
4. **vinicultural:** here, relating to wine production.

Matusalén, the Village Without Time **153**

CRITICAL THINKING: GUIDED READING QUESTIONS

LITERAL

1a. According to Melitón, what sorts of stories exist about Matusalén? ("There are many legends, and many old folks' tales. . . .")

2a. What do the quarreling village priest and municipal president "each on his own account" want to do? (Each wants to remain in Matusalén.)

INFERENTIAL

1b. What do these details suggest about the version of Matusalén's story that Melitón recounts? (It may not be reliable; no one really knows the truth.)

2b. What does the phrase "each on his own account" suggest about these two men's motives? (Both may be more interested in personal goals than the welfare of the village.)

- Peter builds a tower to try to reach the sky and, when that fails, makes it a bell tower for signaling the time.
- Matusalén's great prosperity begins when Peter and the priest find that the bell's ringing controls the passage of time in the village.
- After reaping a year's harvest in a minute, they decide to go into big business.
- The frequent ringing causes villagers to age rapidly.

IN THE GLOSSARY

- furrows: plowed rows
- gospel: the account of Jesus' life in the New Testament
- transpired: happened

5 TEACHING ALLUSION

Note that Peter's actions are an allusion to the biblical story of the tower of Babel, with which people tried to reach the heavens.

6 CULTURAL BACKGROUND

Explain that Cortés conquered the Aztecs of Mexico between 1519 and 1521 and that Franciscan missionaries began arriving in Spain's New World colonies in 1522.

7 GRAMMAR IN LITERATURE

Point out the adverb clause that answers the question when: "before the village had become prosperous." Have students identify three more such clauses in this paragraph. ("When they arrived . . . belfry"; "When he realized . . . night"; and "after Peter . . . echo")

8 TEACHING FANTASY

Note that the fantastic idea that a bell's ringing can control time is central to the story's events and conflicts.

9 READING SKILL: PREDICTING OUTCOMES

Have students predict how Peter and the priest will solve the problem of rapid aging.

"Peter lived on the highest part of the hill, to **5** the north, and there he built a very high tower that he wanted to reach to the sky. As he did not succeed in this, he made of the tower a belfry that told the time. Hour after hour Peter climbed to the top to ring the bell, and as no one liked using watches, everyone followed the ringing from the belfry. Moreover, the rocks, the ears of corn, and the furrows preferred to give up counting time and to guide themselves by the ringing sounds. Peter had calculated that it took an hour to go up and to come down the mountain; therefore, what he did was to go down, turn around, go up, and ring the bell. But as he wished to be helpful, during his journey he thought about business problems and gave the solutions to the little priest in the white tunic. Those who knew him could not imagine him otherwise occupied than going up and down the hill."

"And how was it that they lost everything?"

"Wait a moment, I'm coming to that.

"For a while things went perfectly. With the ideas of the wise men, the business ventures of the priest, and the solutions of Peter, the village was going up and up. Economists came from all over to visit it, and could not explain either the advances or the riches. The cultural level of the people was so high that the shoemakers abandoned the tools of their calling and opened a school for postgraduates of every discipline; even men of letters came to learn from them. No one knew just why there had been such a rapid **6** development, as it was only twenty years before that priests had arrived to teach the gospel to the Indians of America. Even Cortés[5] himself took off his hat and made his soldiers pass by on the other side, without touching that place so sacred to him.

"But like the great enterprises that come to an end, the village of Matusalén had to disap-

---

5. **Cortés** [kôr tes′]: Hernando Cortés (1485–1547), Spanish soldier and explorer who conquered Mexico.

---

pear. This happened because of its own secret, which, according to my grandfather, was the fol-**7** lowing: On a certain day, before the village had become prosperous, the priest climbed up to sleep in the belfry. On the way he met Peter and the latter invited him to dine and to spend the night with him. The sun was already setting, and they hurried a bit in going up so that night should not overtake them. When they arrived at the belfry, they talked for hours and hours, and Peter forgot to ring the bell. When he realized and went out to look at the night, he found that no time had passed. The sun, the clouds, the first stars, everything was the same. The people down below were still working as though noth-**8** ing had happened. He told the news to the priest, who confirmed it: nothing had transpired, time had stood still. They decided to wait without ringing the bell, and they saw that still time did not pass. Only after Peter loosed the cords and the clear peal sounded, and was answered by the echo, did night fall. The two of them were struck dumb with admiration but said not a word.

"The following day the priest climbed up again and they experimented anew; the result was the same. Then they conceived the idea of hastening the tolling of the bell, and dawn broke; then they pealed the bell twelve times running and night fell without the people seeming to be affected; later on, they made it dawn and grow dusk, and then become afternoon and then morning, until they were convinced of the power of the belfry in the realm of time. My grandfather later told me that the control of time was possible only in the valley, because the mountains shut out the sound of the bell and it couldn't reach farther.

"For months they were trying out the functioning of the belfry, and one day they discovered that a year's harvests could be obtained in a few minutes. That's when they thought of start-**9** ing in big business. The only problem was that people got very old very quickly, like they them-

---

CRITICAL THINKING: GUIDED READING QUESTIONS

LITERAL

1a. Why does Peter build the tower, and for what does he then use it? (He hopes to reach the sky and, when that effort fails, turns the tower into a belfry for signaling the time.)

2a. In addition to the villagers, what things begin guiding themselves by Peter's bell ringing? (the rocks, ears of corn, and furrows)

INFERENTIAL

1b. What might these details suggest about Peter's ambitions or motives? (He wants to control fate or at least control others' lives and progress.)

2b. What does this control represent, and what may Peter himself symbolize? (It represents the control of nature; Peter may symbolize western or technological humanity.)

10 selves did, for which reason they took steps to make the bell rope with which the bell was rung much longer, and to leave the village so as not to hear it. Thus they avoided growing old and, carrying on the business, made big profits in a few days.

"The tourists never realized that every month the people of the village were different from the month before, because they changed and died very quickly on account of time running wildly on. Deeply impressed by the progress of the place, they didn't stop to look at the faces of the people. Apparently, the municipal president was aware of the secret and wished to participate in the fruits of the business, and as the others all vetoed this, he opted for buying various undertakings and leaving the village at the time the bell was rung: so he also could become rich."

11 "And how is it that you and your family didn't perish with the village?"

"Because Peter, my grandfather, told my father to go, and he would send us money from time to time.

"We frequently received news of the improvements and progress in Matusalén, and we just closed our eyes and kept our mouths shut, in order not to give away my grandfather. The real years in the rest of the world were passing, and Peter got old and died. He left us his great fortune, but we could never collect it, because when he died, the village died too. Many say that at the time of his death, everything flew into the air with a great explosion of his remorseful heart; others say that there was a massacre among those who were on the priest's side and those who sided with the municipal president; others say that the weight of progress made them sink into the earth; others say . . . say . . . and say . . . but nothing is for sure.

"The truth was, that at Peter's death, time was gently slowing down, in spite of the efforts that the priest made to get the bell working again. Little by little, everyone became aware

Detail. *Burro and Peddler,* 1947, Milton Avery.

that life was very slow and that the harvests occurred slowly, very slowly. The automobiles, which were tremendous there and which in good times developed very high speeds, after the tragedy, even though their speedometers marked 2,000 kilometers an hour, went slowly, very slowly. When, by chance and carelessness, a few objects fell to the ground, they, too, like everything else, fell slowly, very slowly. The people's hearts, it seemed, were not beating, but no—they were beating, but slowly, very slowly. Thus the inhabitants of the village began to die, until one fine day, with the total arrest of time, all the figures disappeared: the valley, and the church, and the belfry, and the wise men, and the cars, and the little priest with his white tunic, and everything."

"What a funny story, indeed."

"Yes, and the strangest thing is what happened to these men afterward. Have you ever felt a sudden chill, without any reason? Or have you thought that someone was staring at you in an empty stadium? Or have you ever thought that someone is walking beside you in the street **12** where there is no one at all? Those are the inhabitants of Matusalén, the village without time, who travel hither and thither throughout the world in search of the time which they never had in their valley."

Matusalén, the Village Without Time **155**

PAGE SUMMARY: AT A GLANCE

- Peter and the priest avoid aging rapidly by lengthening the rope so that they can ring the bell from outside Matusalén.
- Peter sends his family to safety, ages naturally, and dies, leaving a fortune that his family never inherits.
- Matusalén perishes as time slows and eventually stops.

IN THE GLOSSARY

- remorseful: feeling sorrow or guilt over past behavior

10 CRITICAL THINKING: EVALUATION

Have students evaluate Peter and the priest's method of solving the problem of rapid aging.

11 TEACHING REALISTIC FICTION AND FANTASY

Note that despite the fantastic details, the conversation in the frame story is realistic and matter of fact.

12 TEACHING THEME

Elicit that the ending suggests that rapid material progress does not make people happy.

COLLABORATIVE LEARNING: ENRICHMENT ACTIVITY

Time Line Have a group of students create a time line like the one on pages xxiv–xxv of their text but listing the historical figures, events, and technologies mentioned in the story; for example, "Mexico: Cortés conquers the Aztecs"; "Germany: First cars manufactured."

ART AND LITERATURE

The American artist Milton Avery (1893–1965) depicted recognizable subjects with bare traces of line and broad patches of flat color. With his signature pastel colors Avery turned landscapes into poetic compositions of color and shape. During a trip to Mexico, he painted *Burro and Peddler*.

- Ask students what sort of pace of life *Burro and Peddler* suggests. (slow) Ask when the pace of life in Matusalén reached this pace. (at the time of Peter's death)

CRITICAL THINKING: GUIDED READING QUESTIONS

LITERAL

1a. What do "many say" exploded when Peter died? ("his remorseful heart")

2a. What actually causes the demise of Matusalén, according to Melitón? (Everything begins slowing down until time is totally arrested and the village disappears.)

INFERENTIAL

1b. Why would Peter be remorseful? (He reaped benefits from actions that shortened the lives of other villagers.)

2b. What does the demise of Matusalén suggest about a materialistic civilization? (It eventually collapses or destroys itself; it is transient.)

Which fantastic elements did you find especially imaginative?

ANSWERS

STUDY QUESTIONS

1. It was very prosperous. The village attracted wise people.
2. They found that the bell controlled time. He did it to increase productivity, but everyone aged quickly and soon died.
3. It was destroyed by the explosion of Peter's heart, in the fighting between the priest's and the municipal president's followers, and because the "weight of progress" made it sink into the earth. Time gradually slowed until it stopped, and the village vanished.
4. traveling the world in search of the time they never had
5. its prosperity or culture; Time passes so quickly that no one lives long enough to enjoy the village's achievements.
6. greed and the desire for material progress; It suggests that material progress is transient.
7. Progress is illusive, and an excessive drive for material progress is destructive.
8. They should take life slowly and not devote too much time to material concerns.
9. Answers will vary. Students may focus on material advances or more spiritual fulfillment.

LITERARY FOCUS

Realistic Fiction and Fantasy

Fantastic details include the simultaneous arrival of famous people from different eras, the amazing progress in twenty years, and the simultaneous existence of Cortés and modern technology. Realistic details include the frame-story dialogue, Peter's and the priest's human flaws, and the physical descriptions of the village.

Allusion

The name stresses the significance of time in the story. Other allusions include Einstein and the other historical figures mentioned on page 153, Cortés, and the biblical allusions to Jesus' miracles and the tower of Babel.

STUDY QUESTIONS

Recalling

1. According to Melitón's recollection of his grandfather's stories, what was Matusalén's financial situation? What sort of people did the village attract?
2. What did Peter, Melitón's grandfather, discover that the bell controlled? For what reason did he ring it more quickly, and what then happened to everyone except Peter and the priest?
3. What three explanations do people give for the downfall of Matusalén? What does Melitón say is the true explanation?
4. According to the last paragraph, what are the inhabitants of Matusalén doing now?

Interpreting

5. What would you identify as the chief attraction of Matusalén? The chief problem?
6. What human drives or motives caused Peter to ring the bell more quickly? Why is it significant that Peter's family could not use his fortune?
7. What theme, or main insight, about progress does the story convey?
8. Through the lesson of Matusalén's downfall, what might the story be suggesting about the way individuals or societies should spend their time?

Extending

9. What is your own definition of progress? Discuss.

LITERARY FOCUS

Realistic Fiction and Fantasy

Although all fiction describes events that never actually occurred and details that may not exist, much fiction is **realistic;** that is, it presents events that seem as if they could have happened and details that seem true to life. **Fantasy,** in contrast, depicts fictional events that simply could not occur and details that do not exist in real life. "Matusalén, the Village Without Time" is a work of fantasy, for it is based on the idea that a village can exist outside of time as we know it in the real world. Many of its specific details are also **fantastic,** or part of the world of fantasy. For example, the existence of a bell that can control

the passage of time is impossible in the world as we know it.

Thinking About Realistic Fiction and Fantasy

■ List three additional events or details in the story that could not occur in the real world. Did anything about the story seem true to life? Explain.

Allusion

An **allusion** is a reference within a work of literature to a well-known character, place, or situation from another work of literature, music, or art or from history. Writers often make allusions to people and events in the Bible. For example, in choosing the name for his village, María makes an allusion to the biblical figure of Methuselah (Matusalén in Spanish), who is said to have lived for more than nine hundred years, longer than anyone else in the Bible.

Thinking About Allusion

■ Why do you think María calls his village Matusalén? Identify at least two more allusions in the story.

COMPOSITION

Writing About Fantasy and Reality in a Setting

■ Write a brief composition about the combination of realistic and fantastic details that María uses to describe his setting. First discuss the realistic details of the village of Matusalén, details that depict objects or practices that do occur in the real world. Then show how the *combination* of these details, especially given the time factors involved, makes the setting part of the world of fantasy. Also describe details that are fantastic in themselves.

Writing a Fantasy

■ Write a few paragraphs recounting an incident that could not happen in the real world. For example, you might write about a device that controls something that is impossible to control, as Matusalén's bell controlled time. Use your imagination, but also try to include some realistic details of setting to make the incident vivid and almost believable even though it could never actually happen.

COMPOSITION: GUIDELINES FOR EVALUATION

WRITING ABOUT FANTASY AND REALITY IN A SETTING

Objective

To analyze a setting's fantastic and realistic details

Guidelines for Evaluation

■ suggested length: three or four paragraphs
■ should discuss fantastic and realistic details
■ should explain why certain combinations of realistic details are fantastic

WRITING A FANTASY

Objective

To recount a fantastic incident

Guidelines for Evaluation

■ suggested length: one to two pages
■ should recount an incident that could not happen in the real world
■ should include realistic details of setting

PREVIEW: THE AUTHOR AND THE WORLD

Naguib Mahfouz

(born 1911)

Egypt

Naguib Mahfouz is definitely one of today's most well-known writers in the Arabic language. His name is pronounced as [nä jēb′ mä′fooz]. The youngest of four children, Mahfouz grew up in Cairo, Egypt, where most of his fiction is set. He studied philosophy and literature in college and after graduation took a civil-service job with the Egyptian government. He continued to work for the government despite his growing fame as an author, until he reached the retirement age of sixty.

Mahfouz began writing when he was twenty-five. A decade later he won acclaim throughout the Arabic world with his *Cairo Trilogy,* three novels that chronicle the experiences of three generations of a middle-class Cairo family. Over the years Mahfouz has written about forty novels and collections of stories, some of them set in Egypt at the time of the Pharaohs but most of them vividly depicting contemporary Egyptian life. Gradually his work gained an international reputation, and in 1988 he became the first Arabic-language author to be awarded the Nobel Prize for Literature.

GEOGRAPHY AND CULTURE

Cairo and the "Old Quarter"

Cairo is the capital of Egypt, an Arabic-speaking nation in northeastern Africa. Egypt's largest city, Cairo is strategically located on the banks of the Nile River just south of where the Nile empties into the Mediterranean Sea. Although its skyline is modern, Cairo is permeated with history. South of the city stand the ruins of Memphis, the capital of the Egyptian empire in the early days of the Pharaohs. Roman and Greek ruins are also scattered throughout the city. Cairo is divided into many different districts, or quarters. Naguib Mahfouz grew up in Cairo's Gamaliya, or "old quarter," a quaint medieval district in many of his tales. Here children explore the maze of crowded, narrow streets with the same curiosity and adventuresome spirit that children show throughout the world.

One place that piqued the children's interest was the Sufi [soo′fe] *takiya* [tä kĭ′yä], or religious retreat, described in the upcoming story. The Sufis are members of various Moslem religious groups.

See *LITERATURE AND CULTURE SOURCEBOOK: India and the Middle East*

A Tale of Our Quarter **157**

LESSON PREVIEW

In this tale by an Egyptian, the narrator ponders a cherished boyhood memory. Forbidden to enter a neighborhood religious retreat, he and other children taunt the dervishes and long for the mulberries in their garden. One day a dervish seems to toss the narrator a mulberry. Later the narrator is not sure the incident occurred, but the memory remains pure.

LITERARY SKILLS FOR THIS SELECTION

- first-person narrator
- atmosphere

THEMES IN THIS SELECTION

- reality and fantasy: memory and imagination
- tolerance and kindness

LESSON OBJECTIVES

1. to evaluate a first-person narrator
2. to analyze the effects of details of setting
3. to recount a childhood incident

Teacher's Classroom Resources 1

- Teaching Notes 277
- Prereading Vocabulary 278
- Reading Guide 279
- Check Test 280
- Responding to World Cultures 281
- Literary Focus: Evaluating a First-Person Narrator 282
- Writing Process Guides: Writing About Setting 283 Describing a Childhood Experience 284
- Grammar in Literature: Expanding Sentences with Words and Phrases 285
- Selection Test 286

IN THE CLASSROOM

TEACHING STUDENTS OF DIFFERENT ABILITIES

- **For less advanced students:** Have students identify the speakers of those lines of dialogue whose speakers are unidentified. Also have them complete the Reading Guide.

- **For more advanced students:** Have students research and report on Mahfouz's place in twentieth-century Arabic fiction.

DISCUSSING GEOGRAPHY AND CULTURE

Clothing and Culture

If you took a stroll through Cairo today, you would probably see old men wearing long cotton robes (galabiahs) and women shrouded in black gowns (milayahs). These clothes suit Cairo's desert climate and reflect Moslem beliefs regarding personal modesty.

- Discuss how religion, climate, and/or tradition determine the dress of some Americans. (Examples: the modest dress of the Amish and Hasidic Jews, Eskimo anoraks and mukluks; cowboy hats and boots)

La Palme ("The Palm"), 1912, Henri Matisse.

1 Naguib Mahfouz

A Tale of Our Quarter

Translated from the Arabic by Soad Sobhy, Essam Fattouh, and James Kenneson

2 I enjoy playing in the small square between the archway and the *takiya* where the Sufis live.[1] Like all the other children, I admire the mulberry trees in the *takiya* garden, the only bit of green in the whole neighborhood. Our tender hearts yearn for their dark berries. But it stands 3 like a fortress, this *takiya*, circled by its garden wall. Its stern gate is broken and always, like the windows, shut. Aloof isolation drenches the whole compound. Our hands stretch toward this wall—reaching for the moon.

Once in a while one of the longbeards appears in the garden in a bright, patterned skullcap and a huge rippling cape, and then we all

---

1. *takiya* [tä kĭ′yä] **where the Sufis** [sōō′fēz] **live:** religious retreat of the Sufis. (See the Geography and Culture feature that precedes the story.)

158 *The Short Story*

CRITICAL THINKING: GUIDED READING QUESTIONS

LITERAL

1a. What is special about the *takiya* garden? (It is "the only bit of green in the whole neighborhood.")

2a. What is always the case for the *takiya* gate and windows? (They are always shut.)

INFERENTIAL

1b. Why would the children find it attractive? (Gardens are usually pleasant, and the green spot is unlike anything else they know.)

2b. What effect would the shut gate and windows have on most children? (It would make them curious and interested in going inside.)

yell, "If God wills, you dervish,[2] you might get your wish."

But he just gazes at the grass and goes on, pausing, perhaps, beside the garden's small stream before vanishing behind the inner gate.

"Father, who are those men?"

"They are the men of God." And then in a very meaningful tone, "Damned be anyone who disturbs their peace."

5 But I still burn for those mulberries.

One day, tired of playing, I sit down to rest and immediately begin dozing. I wake to an empty square; even the sun has gone into hiding behind the ancient wall. The spring scene fades, heavy with the breath of sunset. I have to get away from the archway and back to our alley before it's pitch dark, so I jump up, ready to go. But then comes the uncanny feeling that I'm not alone, that I'm roaming in some pleasant magnetic field. When a warm breeze flows over me, I peer toward the *takiya*.

There, under the central mulberry tree, stands a man, a dervish unlike those I've seen before. He is great with age but extremely tall, his face a pool of glowing light. His cape is green, his long turban white. Everything about him is munificent beyond imagining. I look at him so intently that I become intoxicated, the sight of him filling the whole universe. It comes to me that he must be the owner and overseer of the place, and I see that he is loving, not like those others. I go up to the wall and say most respectfully, "I love mulberries."

Since he doesn't answer, doesn't even move, I assume he hasn't heard me, so I say it louder. "I love mulberries."

I believe that his single glance takes in everything and that his deep, melodious voice says, "My nightingale, *khoon deli khord wakuli hasel kared.*"

Then I think I see him tossing me a berry. I

bend down to pick it up. I find nothing. When I stand up again, the place is empty. Darkness veils the inner gate.

Of course I tell my father the whole thing.
6 He glares at me doubtfully. I tell it all over again. He says, "Your description doesn't fit anyone but the High Sheikh[3] himself, but he never leaves his retreat."

On all the names of God, I swear I'm telling the truth; I even repeat the words of the sheikh. My father says, "I wonder what this gibberish you've memorized could mean."

"I've heard it before in the chanting from the *takiya.*"

My father broods for a while before saying, "Don't tell a soul about this." He spreads his hands and recites the sura[4] of the Oneness of the Eternal.

I dash back across the square and wait about till all the other children are gone. I expect the sheikh to appear, but he doesn't. In my thin voice, I call out, "My nightingale, *khoon deli khord wakuli hasel kared.*"

No answer. I ache with expectation, but he takes no pity on my desire to see him. Mulling over the event much later, I wonder about its reality. Did I really see the sheikh or just pretend I did to get attention—and then end up believing my own fantasy? Did I merely see a drowsy mirage and then make the daydream real from stories about the High Sheikh I'd heard around the house? It seems it must have been something like that since the sheikh never appeared again and since everyone agreed that he never came outside.

7 That's how I created a myth and then destroyed it—except that this supposed vision of the sheikh burrowed deep down into my very marrow, a memory of great purity. And except that I'm still crazy about mulberries.

---

2. **dervish:** member of any Moslem sect known for forms of worship that include whirling.

---

3. **Sheikh** [shēk]: Moslem religious leader.
4. **sura:** chapter in the Koran, the sacred book of Moslems.

A Tale of Our Quarter **159**

PAGE SUMMARY: AT A GLANCE

- Often the children taunt the Sufis, but the narrator's father orders him not to.
- When the narrator sees a striking dervish in the garden, he respectfully tells him, "I love mulberries."
- The dervish chants mysterious words and seems to toss the narrator a mulberry.
- Later the narrator is not sure whether the incident happened, but it remains a memory of great purity, and he still loves mulberries.

IN THE GLOSSARY

- uncanny: eerie; strange
- munificent: lavish
- gibberish: nonsense language
- mirage: visual illusion
- marrow: innermost part

4 CULTURAL BACKGROUND

Explain that Sufis are members of various devout Moslem sects. Many are dervishes, who strive, through whirling, chanting, and the like, for mystical communion with God.

5 GRAMMAR IN LITERATURE

Note the use of present-tense verbs to capture the immediacy of the narrator's experiences. Have students cite examples. (*burn, sit, begin, wake,* and so on)

6 READING SKILL: CAUSE AND EFFECT

Elicit that the narrator's father is suspicious of his son's story because the High Sheikh, whom the narrator seems to be describing, never goes into the garden.

7 TEACHING FIRST-PERSON NARRATOR

Note the jumps in time in the last two paragraphs. In the final paragraph the narrator is no longer a child.

COLLABORATIVE LEARNING: ENRICHMENT ACTIVITY

Art Have a group of students create and compare different visual interpretations of incidents in the story.

CRITICAL THINKING: GUIDED READING QUESTIONS

LITERAL

1a. What does the narrator "see" about the mysterious dervish that makes him different from the other dervishes? (He is loving.)

2a. Why does the narrator think he may have imagined the incident? (He thinks he might have done so to get attention or because he has confused daydreams with reality.)

INFERENTIAL

1b. In what way do the dervish's actions show that he may be more loving than the other dervishes? (He seems to toss the narrator the mulberry that the narrator craves.)

2b. To the older narrator does it now really matter whether the incident was imaginary? Explain. (No, its strong effects on him make it important to him even if it never happened.)

Do you think the narrator really saw the High Sheikh? Explain.

ANSWERS

STUDY QUESTIONS

1. They are attracted by its garden and mulberries. "If God wills, you dervish, you might get your wish."
2. He is old, tall, and "munificent"; his face is a pool of glowing light, and he seems loving.
3. Did it really happen, did he invent it to get attention, or did he confuse a daydream with reality? It left a memory of great purity and has made him "crazy about" mulberries.
4. They are disrespectful and intolerant. He becomes respectful.
5. No; he re-creates the "myth" by writing this tale and shows that the "myth" continues to affect him.
6. It can be hard to distinguish, especially for a child, and the distinction may sometimes be unimportant.
7. We should respect and tolerate human differences. The mulberry might stand for the generosity we can offer one another despite our differences.
8. Answers will vary. Among the causes students might mention are a child's imagination, the power of suggestion, and optical illusions.

LITERARY FOCUS

He is not sure whether he really saw and heard the mysterious dervish, whether the dervish tossed him a mulberry, and whether the dervish was the High Sheikh. Young children often have trouble distinguishing between fantasy and reality and sometimes believe in the imaginary incidents they invent.

STUDY QUESTIONS

Recalling
1. What, in particular, attracts the narrator and the other children to the Sufi *takiya*? What do the children sometimes yell?
2. Briefly describe the unusual dervish who the narrator thinks may have tossed him a mulberry.
3. What does the narrator later ask himself about the incident? What effects has the incident had on him, according to the last paragraph?

Interpreting
4. What is the children's attitude toward the Sufis at the start of the story? How does the narrator's attitude change?
5. The narrator says, "That's how I created a myth and then destroyed it." Did he destroy the myth completely? Explain.
6. What does the story suggest about the line between reality and illusion or fantasy?
7. What lesson about human differences do you think the story conveys? In light of that lesson, what might the tossed mulberry symbolize, or represent?

Extending
8. Have you ever had an experience in which reality and illusion were confused? What factors do you think might cause such confusion?

LITERARY FOCUS

Evaluating a First-Person Narrator

When a story is told by a character who refers to himself or herself with the first-person pronoun *I*, we say that the story has a **first-person narrator.** In reading such a story, we need to consider how the narrator's personality and situation in life affect the view of events that he or she provides. For example, the narrator may be a foolish or inexperienced person whose view of the world is likely to be inaccurate or incomplete. The narrator may have such a strong stake in the events of the story that he or she distorts information.

Thinking About Evaluating a First-Person Narrator
■ What events does the first-person narrator of "A Tale of Our Quarter" have trouble understanding? How might his age affect his view of the events?

COMPOSITION

Writing About Setting
■ Write a brief composition about the garden setting in "A Tale of Our Quarter." First show how the details used to describe the setting help to convey a particular atmosphere, or mood. Then explain how this particular setting, with this particular atmosphere, is related to the author's purpose in writing the story. *For help with this assignment, refer to Lesson 4 in the Writing About Literature Handbook at the back of this book.*

Describing a Childhood Experience
■ Briefly describe a childhood experience that made a lasting impression on you. Discuss the thoughts and feelings you had at the time as well as your current thoughts and feelings about the incident. You might use the experience as the basis of a brief short story told by a first-person narrator.

COMPOSITION: GUIDELINES FOR EVALUATION

WRITING ABOUT SETTING

Objective
To analyze the effects of details of setting

Guidelines for Evaluation
■ suggested length: two or three paragraphs
■ should show how the details of setting help create a particular atmosphere
■ should explain how setting and atmosphere help support the author's purpose

DESCRIBING A CHILDHOOD EXPERIENCE

Objective
To recount a childhood incident

Guidelines for Evaluation
■ suggested length: one to two pages
■ should recount a memorable childhood experience
■ should be told in the first person
■ should contrast childhood thoughts and feelings with current ones

PREVIEW: THE AUTHOR AND THE WORLD

Don Quixote and Sancho Panza have famous adventures in this excerpt from the Spanish novel. After persuading Sancho to be his squire, Don Quixote goes in search of knightly adventure. He battles windmills, which he says are evil giants, and a barber whose bowl he claims is a helmet. The more realistic Sancho does not accept these fantastic claims.

LITERARY SKILLS FOR THIS SELECTION

- character foils
- tone
- symbols

THEMES IN THIS SELECTION

- reality and fantasy: imagination and living in the past
- romantic idealism vs. realism

LESSON OBJECTIVES

1. to examine character foils
2. to understand allusions that enter the language
3. to create a new episode

GEOGRAPHY AND CULTURE

Don Quixote and the Age of Chivalry

Miguel de Cervantes

(1547–1616)

Spain

Miguel de Cervantes [mē gel′ dā sər vän′täs], author of the first great novel of the Western world, was born near Madrid to a poor but noble Spanish family. His early years were adventurous. In 1571, when he was twenty-four, he was wounded in the Battle of Lepanto, a naval battle off the coast of Greece. On his journey back to Spain, he was captured by pirates. He spent the next five years as a slave in Africa before being ransomed and returning home.

Like other writers of his day, Cervantes wrote poetry and drama. Nonetheless, his reputation as Spain's greatest writer rests chiefly on *Don Quixote de la Mancha* [don′ kē hō′tā dā lä män′chä], his masterpiece in a then-new literary form, the novel. A **novel** is a book-length work of prose fiction. Part I of Cervantes' novel was published in 1605, and many subsequent editions were issued. Along with Part II, which appeared in 1615, it became the world's most frequently published novel. Yet the book did not make Cervantes wealthy. He died in poverty in 1616, the same year England lost its greatest writer, William Shakespeare.

Set in the southwestern European nation of Spain, Cervantes' novel depicts a gentleman named Don Quixote from a region of central Spain known as La Mancha. As the novel opens, Don Quixote has been avidly reading tales of knights-errant, warriors who traveled in search of adventure during Europe's Middle Ages (fifth to fifteenth centuries A.D.). These knights followed the code of chivalry, which stressed valor on the battlefield, courtesy off it, and loyalty at all times. A knight typically pledged his loyalty to a lady, as well as to his king or lord. At the knight's side would ride a loyal squire, or attendant and knight-in-training.

By Don Quixote's time the age of knights has passed, but he decides to become a knight anyway. He finds an old horse, which he names Rosinante [rō sē nän′tā], and dedicates his hoped-for battles to Dulcinea del Toboso [dōol sē nā′ä del tō bō′sō], a lady who exists chiefly in his imagination. The following excerpts tell some of his adventures.

See *LITERATURE AND CULTURE SOURCEBOOK: Spain*

Don Quixote **161**

Teacher's Classroom Resources 1

- Teaching Notes   289
- Reading Guide   290
- Check Test   291
- Responding to World Cultures   292
- Literary Focus: Character Foils   293
- Language Study: Allusions That Enter the Language   294
- Writing Process Guides: Writing About Character Foils   295 Writing a New Episode for a Story   296
- Grammar in Literature: Complete Subjects and Complete Predicates   297
- Selection Test   298

IN THE CLASSROOM

TEACHING STUDENTS OF DIFFERENT ABILITIES

- **For less advanced students:** Have students list Don Quixote's and Sancho Panza's contrasting opinions. Have them complete the Reading Guide.

- **For more advanced students:** Have students research and report on the tales of chivalry that inspired Don Quixote's quest for adventure.

DISCUSSING GEOGRAPHY AND CULTURE

Sports Rituals

Medieval knights proved their mettle by engaging in tournaments. Initially these contests were violent, but through the influence of chivalry, they became more ritualistic, following traditional procedures and patterns of behavior. By the sixteenth century they had evolved into elegant shows of horsemanship.

- Ask students to describe rituals that are associated with sports played in the United States. (Examples: cheerleading, football huddles, baseball signals)

Miguel de Cervantes

from **Don Quixote**[1]

Translated from the Spanish by George Kearns

Don Quixote and Sancho Set Out on Their Adventures

1   Don Quixote persuaded a laborer, a neighbor of his named Sancho Panza,[2] to join him on his adventures. This Sancho was a good man but not very bright. Don Quixote talked to him so much and made him so many promises that finally poor Sancho agreed to go along and serve him as squire. Don Quixote said that Sancho should be glad of the chance to serve him because upon one of their adventures they might easily conquer some island; and if that should happen, he would leave Sancho there as governor. In the light of this promise, and others like it, Sancho deserted his wife and children and became his neighbor's squire.

    Next, Don Quixote set about raising money. 2 Some things he sold, others he pawned—always making a bad bargain—until at last he had the sum he needed. Then he equipped himself with a shield, which he borrowed from a friend, and patched up his broken helmet as well as he could. Sancho, his squire, was informed of the day and hour on which they would set out so that he might prepare provisions for the journey. Don Quixote told him not to forget to bring saddlebags. Sancho agreed and added that he was going to bring along a very fine donkey, because he was not used to traveling on foot. The mention of the donkey made Don Quixote pause for a moment: he could not remember having heard of any instance in which a knight

---

1. **Don Quixote** [don′ kē hō′tē]
2. **Sancho Panza** [sän′chō pän′zä]

had been accompanied by a squire who rode on a donkey. But, in spite of this, he decided to let Sancho bring it and determined to provide him with a more noble mount as soon as he had a chance. After all, he was sure to meet with some discourteous knight whose horse he could take. He provided himself with shirts and everything else he could get his hands on. And when all these arrangements had been made, they set out upon their adventures: Sancho without saying goodbye to his wife and children, Don Quixote without bidding farewell to his housekeeper and niece. They left the town one evening without anyone seeing them and rode so far in the night that by morning they felt sure no one could ever find them.

    Sancho Panza sat upon his donkey like a patriarch; he had his saddlebags, his leather bottle, and great hopes of becoming governor of the island his master had promised him.

3   "Your Honor, knight errant," said Sancho, "don't forget about that island you've promised me. I shall be a good governor, even if it is a very large island!"

    Don Quixote replied: "Sancho Panza, my friend, you should know that the knights errant of old always appointed their squires to be governors of the islands or kingdoms they conquered. For my part, I shall honor this tradition. In fact, I shall improve upon it: some of those knights made their squires wait until they were very old. Then, after many hard days and worse 4 nights of service, they would give them the title of Count, or perhaps at the most Marquis, of some unimportant valley or province. But if you live—and if I live!—it may very well happen

---

CRITICAL THINKING: GUIDED READING QUESTIONS

LITERAL

1a. In selling and pawning goods to outfit himself, what sort of bargain does Don Quixote always make? (a bad one)

2a. With what promise does Don Quixote persuade Sancho to be his squire? (He will make Sancho governor of an island they will conquer.)

INFERENTIAL

1b. What does this detail reveal about Don Quixote? (He is foolish and easily duped.)

2b. In what way does Sancho at first seem similar to Don Quixote? (He also seems gullible.)

that we shall not have to wait six days until I conquer a kingdom of such importance that it has other kingdoms beneath it. And you shall be crowned the king of one of them. Do not say impossible! For such surprising and unbelievable adventures befall a knight errant that I may easily give you more than I promise!"

"In that case," answered Sancho Panza, "if I were to become King—through the miracle of which Your Honor speaks—then my wife would be Queen and my children Princes."

"Do you doubt it?" asked Don Quixote.

"Yes, I do doubt it," said Sancho. "I believe that even if God rained crowns on the Earth, none of them would fit my wife's head. She would be a poor queen, sir. Yet I believe that with God's help she might make a good countess."

"Leave it to Heaven, Sancho," answered Don Quixote. "God will know what is best for her. As for yourself, do not humble yourself to accept less than the governorship of a province."

5 "No, sir, I shall not," answered Sancho, "not with a master like yourself. I know you will give me whatever is good for me, and as much as I can handle."

The Adventure of the Windmills

Just then, as they rode across the plain, there appeared thirty or forty windmills. As soon as Don Quixote spied them, he said to his squire:

"Fortune has guided us better than we could have hoped for. Look there, friend Sancho Panza, and you will see more than thirty horrid giants! I shall do battle with them and kill them all. What we take from them will be the beginnings of our fortunes: for it is a good and holy fight in which I shall wipe from the face of the earth these evil creatures!"

6 "What giants?" asked Sancho Panza.

"Those giants right there!" answered his mas-

Don Quixote and Sancho Panza, Pablo Picasso (1881–1973).

ter. "The ones with the long arms. Some giants are said to have arms several miles long."

"But Your Honor," said Sancho, "what you are looking at are not giants. They are windmills, and what look like arms are merely sails[3] which turn in the wind."

"It is obvious that you know nothing about adventures," said Don Quixote. "If you are afraid, then fly and say your prayers. In the meantime I shall engage these giants in fierce and unequal battle."

Having said this, he dug his spurs into the sides of his horse Rosinante and dashed off, paying no attention to Sancho, who kept shouting

---

3. **sails:** arms of a windmill.

Don Quixote **163**

- When Don Quixote attacks the first windmill, one of its sails shatters his lance, lifts him and his horse into the air, and tosses them across the fields.
- Sancho forces him to recognize the windmills; then Don Quixote claims that an evil magician turned the giants into windmills.
- Don Quixote spies a man on horseback, who he claims is wearing the Helmet of Mambrino.
- Sancho perceives only a man riding a donkey and wearing something shiny on his head.

7 TEACHING POINT OF VIEW

Note that the omniscient narrator does not share Don Quixote's illusions but instead describes the real situation.

8 TEACHING ALLUSIONS

Ask what Don Quixote's allusion to the monster Briareus stresses about him. (He is romantic, fanciful, poetic, and well read.)

9 TEACHING SYMBOLS

Elicit that the battle with the windmills represents a conflict between illusion and reality in which reality must prevail.

10 TEACHING STUDENTS OF LIMITED ENGLISH PROFICIENCY

Point out that *Don Quixote* is famous for collecting Spanish sayings. Have any native Spanish speakers translate into Spanish both the italicized saying and the saying "Experience is the mother of science."

11 GRAMMAR IN LITERATURE

Note that Don Quixote's failure to use contractions gives his conversation an old-fashioned formality, in keeping with his attitudes. Ask where students would normally use contractions here. ("don't you" for "do you not" and "Isn't he" for "Is he not")

---

that the figures he was about to attack were windmills and not giants. But Don Quixote was so certain that they were giants that he did not hear Sancho's cries, nor, when he came near them, did he notice the true nature of his enemies. He cried out to them in a loud voice:

"Do not run away from me, you cowards, you hateful creatures! It is one lone knight who attacks you!"

7 Just then a small breeze came across the plain and caused the sails to start turning. When Don Quixote saw this, he cried:

"Though you have more arms than the famous giant Briareus,[4] you shall soon pay for **8** your evil deeds!"

Saying this, he dedicated himself to his lady, Dulcinea del Toboso,[5] that she might aid him in battle. Then he put up his shield, settled his lance in place, and set off on Rosinante at full **9** gallop. He attacked the first windmill he came to, thrusting his lance into one of its sails. But the wind turned the sail with such strength that it shattered his lance and lifted both horse and rider into the air, tossing Don Quixote across the fields.

As fast as his donkey could trot, Sancho Panza came to the aid of his injured master. But when he arrived at Don Quixote's side, he found that the knight could not get up: such was the shock Rosinante had given him when they fell.

"God help us!" cried Sancho. "Didn't I tell Your Honor to be careful about what you were doing? Didn't I tell you they were windmills? And how could anyone miss it unless he had windmills in his head!"

"Be quiet, friend Sancho," replied Don Quixote. "The affairs of war are subject to change. Moreover, I believe—and it is a fact—that the evil magician Frestón—the same one who has robbed me of my house and all my books—has

in fact changed those giants into windmills! He wants to rob me of the glory of conquering them. Yes, he hates me! But in the end, in the end, the power of his evil acts shall fall before the goodness of my sword!"

"God's will be done," said Sancho, and helped his master to get up and climb up on Rosinante, whose back was almost broken.

The Adventure of the Enchanted Helmet

Turning to the right, they set off on another road. They had not traveled far before Don Quixote spied a man on horseback. On his head, this man had something that shone like gold.

As soon as Don Quixote caught a glimpse of him, he turned to Sancho Panza and said: "It is **10** my opinion, Sancho, that all the old sayings have a good deal of truth in them. After all, they are drawn from Experience, which is the Mother of Science. I am thinking in particular of the saying that *When one door shuts, another door opens.* Look: here is another adventure—and a better one. Unless I am deceived, there comes towards us now a man wearing upon his head the Helmet of Mambrino.[6] As you know, I have sworn an oath about this very helmet."

"Look carefully before you speak, sir, and move carefully before you act," said Sancho. "If I were free to speak my mind, I could give you several reasons why you are mistaken."

"How can I be mistaken, faithless traitor?" **11** cried Don Quixote. "Tell me, do you or do you not see that knight who is riding towards us on a light gray horse? Is he not wearing upon his head a helmet of gold?"

"What I see," said Sancho, "or perhaps I should say what I *perceive*—is a man riding a gray donkey just like mine. And he has something shining on his head."

---

4. **Briareus** [brī ār'ē əs]: in Greek mythology, huge monster with a hundred arms and fifty heads.
5. **Dulcinea del Toboso** [dōōl sē nā'ä del tō bō'sō]

6. **Helmet of Mambrino** [mäm brē'nō]: helmet of pure gold that supposedly made Mambrino, a legendary pagan king, invulnerable.

CRITICAL THINKING: GUIDED READING QUESTIONS

LITERAL

1a. In admitting the existence of the windmills, what does Don Quixote believe has happened? (The evil magician Frestón has changed the giants into windmills.)

2a. When Don Quixote sees a man on horseback wearing a golden helmet, what does Sancho perceive? (a man riding a donkey and wearing something shiny on his head)

INFERENTIAL

1b. What does this belief show that Don Quixote will not give up entirely? (his illusions)

2b. What does this exchange stress about Sancho, in contrast to his master? (Sancho is more realistic, less imaginative, and more prosaic.)

"Well! It is the Helmet of Mambrino!" said Don Quixote. "Stand to one side and let me handle him alone. I shall save time by refusing to speak a single word—yet I shall bring this adventure to its end. And I shall soon have the helmet I have so long desired."

12 Now the truth of the matter about the helmet, the horse, and the horseman was this: There were two villages nearby. One of them was so small that it could afford neither a druggist's nor a barber shop. The other village, not far away, had both. The barber from the larger town took care of the smaller one, too. It happened that day that there was a sick man who had to be bled[7] and someone else who needed a shave. And so the barber was riding over to take care of them, and he was bringing along with him his brass bowl.

13 Now, just as the barber was riding along, it began to rain. He did not want to get his hat wet (it was probably a new one), and so he put the bowl over his head. Since the brass was polished, it could be seen from half a mile away. He was, as Sancho said, riding a gray donkey. And that is how Don Quixote came to believe that the barber was a knight on a gray horse and that he wore a golden helmet. Don Quixote found it easy to adapt everything he saw to his own fancies about chivalry.

When Don Quixote saw the poor rider approach, he did not bother to speak to him, but he spurred Rosinante into a full gallop. He lowered his lance, meaning to spear the poor barber on it. Without slowing down, he shouted out:

"Defend yourself, base creature! Or surrender freely the helmet which is rightly mine!"

The barber, who had no idea what was going on, saw this phantom descending upon him. All he could do to avoid the lance was to let himself fall down off his donkey. As soon as he touched the ground, he got up and ran across the fields like the wind. The brass bowl was left lying on the ground.

Don Quixote was overjoyed to see the bowl, and said that the pagan had acted wisely. He ordered Sancho to pick up the helmet.

"Lord!" said Sancho, holding it in his hands. "What a fine brass bowl! This is worth a real[8] if it's worth a penny."

He handed it to his master, who put it on his head and kept turning it around and around, looking for the visor. But there was no visor.

"The pagan for whom this helmet was made had an enormous head," said Don Quixote. "The worst of it is that part of it is missing."

When Sancho heard the brass bowl referred to as a helmet, he had to laugh. But he remembered how angry his master could get, and so he stopped.

"Why are you laughing, Sancho?" asked Don Quixote.

"I am laughing," Sancho said, "to think how big the head of the pagan who owned it must have been. In fact, it's exactly like the kind of bowl a barber uses."

14 "Sancho, do you know what I think?" said Don Quixote. "I think this famous and enchanted helmet had fallen into the hands of someone who did not know what it was. This person, when he saw it was made of pure gold, took part of it and melted it down for money. He turned the rest of it into what—as you say—looks like a barber's bowl. Never mind. The fact that it has undergone a transformation does not bother me, for I know what it really is. As soon as I arrive at a town where there is a blacksmith, I shall have it repaired. It shall be as fine a helmet as the one that Vulcan, god of blacksmiths, 15 gave to Mars, the god of War. In the meantime, I shall wear it as well as I can, for something is better than nothing. Moreover, it will protect my head from stones."

---

7. **sick man who had to be bled:** Until recent times, blood was drawn from patients as a supposed remedy for illness.

8. **real** [rā äl']: former Spanish coin.

Don Quixote **165**

CRITICAL THINKING: GUIDED READING QUESTIONS

LITERAL

1a. What does Don Quixote do to the barber he thinks a "base creature"? (He attacks him.)

2a. What does Sancho like about the brass bowl they acquire? (It is worth a fair amount of money.)

3a. What explanation does Sancho give for his laughter when Don Quixote calls the bowl a helmet? (He laughs at how big the owner's head was.)

INFERENTIAL

→ **1b.** What is our reaction to this attack, in contrast to the barber's? (We find it comical; the barber is puzzled and scared.)

→ **2b.** What does this reaction stress about him? (his pragmatism)

→ **3b.** Why does he not admit the real reason for his laughter? (He does not want to upset Don Quixote; he is being tactful.)

- The man is actually a traveling barber who put his brass barber's bowl on his head to protect his hat from the rain.
- When Don Quixote attacks, the frightened barber runs off, leaving the bowl behind.
- Don Quixote is upset that the "helmet" has no visor.
- He decides that someone who did not recognize the famous helmet melted down and sold some of the gold and used the rest for a barber's bowl.

IN THE GLOSSARY

- base: low; dishonorable
- pagan: person who worships many gods
- visor: front part of a helmet

12 TEACHING POINT OF VIEW

Note that the omniscient narrator again tells us the truth of the situation, providing information that even Sancho cannot know.

13 TEACHING TONE

Point out that the narrator's gently mocking tone extends to the barber, who allows himself to appear ridiculous merely to protect a new hat.

14 READING SKILL: COMPARISON

Elicit that Don Quixote once again admits the real situation—as he did with the windmills—and once again gives an explanation that shows a refusal to forgo all his fancies.

15 CRITICAL THINKING: EVALUATION

Note that "Something is better than nothing" is another famous saying from *Don Quixote*. Ask students whether they find the saying appropriate to Don Quixote's character. (Some may find it too practical for him and more suited to Sancho.)

COLLABORATIVE LEARNING: ENRICHMENT ACTIVITY

Dramatic Presentations Have groups of students perform scenes from *Man of la Mancha*, the musical based on *Don Quixote*.

Don Quixote **T-165**

Which passage or incident did you find the funniest? Why?

ANSWERS

STUDY QUESTIONS

1. He is a neighboring laborer. Sancho will be governor of an island they conquer.
2. He cannot recall any knights whose squires rode donkeys.
3. giants; windmills; One of the sails shatters his lance, raises him and his horse into the air, and tosses them across the fields.
4. the gold Helmet of Mambrino; something shiny on the man's head; his brass bowl, to protect his hat from the rain
5. Someone melted part of the gold down in order to sell it.
6. The tone is gently mocking.
7. an idealistic, romantic, poetic view versus a realistic, practical, prosaic one; The actual windmills represent reality, while Don Quixote's view of them represents illusion.
8. It is foolish but in some ways charming to live in the past.
9. Answers will vary. Students may feel that idealism can create an optimistic attitude or a blindly stubborn one.

LITERARY FOCUS

Don Quixote is impractical and idealistic, while Sancho is practical and realistic. The contrasting ways in which they view the windmills, barber, and barber's helmet all stress the difference in their approaches to life.

LANGUAGE STUDY

1. "idealistic and impractical"
2. fighting enemies that exist only in one's imagination

STUDY QUESTIONS

Recalling

1. What is Sancho Panza before he becomes Don Quixote's "squire"? What promise does Don Quixote make to persuade Sancho to join him?
2. Why does Sancho's mention of a donkey make Don Quixote hesitate?
3. What does Don Quixote say that the windmills are? What does Sancho say they are? What happens when Don Quixote tries to battle them?
4. What does Don Quixote decide that the barber is wearing on his head? What does Sancho say he "perceives"? What is the barber actually wearing, and for what reason?
5. What explanation does Don Quixote give when he puts on the headgear and discovers that part of it is "missing"?

Interpreting

6. Identify the narrator's tone, or attitude, toward his characters and their actions.
7. What two ways of looking at the world might Don Quixote and Sancho represent? What might the windmills symbolize?
8. Through the character of Don Quixote, what might Cervantes be suggesting about people who wish to live at a time previous to their own?

Extending

9. What do you think the dangers and benefits are of seeing the world in an idealized way?

LITERARY FOCUS

Character Foils

Every character in literature has certain personality traits or qualities that are revealed to us in the course of the literary work. Sometimes a writer creates characters who are **foils** for one another—two characters who have opposite personality traits and are best understood in contrast with one another. For example, one character may be kind, while the foil may be cruel. By showing us the two side by side in the same situations, the author stresses their differences and helps us recognize the contrasts between them.

Thinking About Character Foils

■ What are the chief personality traits of Don Quixote and Sancho Panza? Citing examples, show how we understand each character's personality better by contrasting it with that of the other character.

LANGUAGE STUDY

Allusions That Enter the Language

Writers frequently make **allusions,** or brief references, to famous works of literature. Sometimes allusions are made so often that they enter the language as words or expressions in their own right. An example is the adjective *quixotic* [kwik sot'ik]. So frequently were people describe as *quixotic,* or "like Don Quixote," that the allusion became a word in the English language.

1. What do you think the adjective *quixotic* now means?
2. The famous windmill episode in *Don Quixote* gave rise to another English expression, "tilting at windmills." Formerly *to tilt* meant specifically "to fight on horseback with lances or similar weapons, as knights did." What do you think we now mean when we say that a person is "tilting at windmills"?

COMPOSITION

Writing About Character Foils

■ Write a brief composition about the differences between Don Quixote and Sancho Panza. First show how the two characters are foils for each other, explaining how their different personality traits are revealed through contrasting behavior in the same situations. Then describe the contrasting abstract qualities or ways of looking at the world that each character might symbolize, or represent.

Writing a New Episode for a Story

■ Create a new adventure for Don Quixote and Sancho Panza. In your episode have both characters continue to act and react as they do in the adventures with the windmills and the golden helmet. You might recount how Don Quixote attempts to make Sancho Panza the governor of an island, as he had promised.

COMPOSITION: GUIDELINES FOR EVALUATION

WRITING ABOUT CHARACTER FOILS

Objective
To analyze the contrasts in character foils

Guidelines for Evaluation
■ suggested length: three or four paragraphs
■ should identify characters' contrasting personality traits and reactions to the same situations
■ should explain the contrasting world views that the characters symbolize

WRITING A NEW EPISODE FOR A STORY

Objective
To create a new episode featuring story characters

Guidelines for Evaluation
■ suggested length: two to three pages
■ should recount a fictional episode featuring Don Quixote and Sancho Panza
■ should reflect the characters' personalities
■ should employ a gently mocking tone

PREVIEW: THE AUTHOR AND THE WORLD

Thomas Wolfe

(1900–1938)

United States

A talented American writer known for his technique in long novels and in short stories, Wolfe was raised in North Carolina, where his father was a stonecutter and his mother ran a boardinghouse. After studying theater at the University of North Carolina, Wolfe was determined to become a playwright, but his efforts were largely unsuccessful. Finally he turned to fiction, achieving success in 1929 with his first novel, *Look Homeward, Angel.* This was followed by a second novel, *Of Time and the River,* and a short-story collection, *From Death to Morning,* both published in 1935. A man of great size and energy, Wolfe died unexpectedly of pneumonia at the age of thirty-eight. His lengthy manuscripts for additional works were extensively reshaped by the great editor Maxwell Perkins, who nurtured many other young talents of the day as well.

Wolfe's fiction is famous for its musical, poetic language and descriptive detail. Much of his work is also frankly autobiographical, in the tradition of such great American writers as Mark Twain and Herman Melville. "The Far and the Near" is a noted example of Wolfe's technique.

GEOGRAPHY AND CULTURE

America's Railroads

Before the automobile became central to life in the United States, railroads were among the nation's chief forms of transportation. Extensive rail lines crossed even rugged and isolated parts of the country, drawing the vast nation closer together.

American passengers first rode the rails in 1830, on a track that ran from Maryland to Ohio. Soon cities in South Carolina, New York, and Pennsylvania built their own private railroads. Some of the trains that traveled on these early tracks were pulled by horses. In 1869 the last spike was driven into the first transcontinental railroad, which ran from Sacramento, California to Omaha, Nebraska. American railroads reached the height of their glory in 1916, when more than 250,000 miles of track were in operation.

By the early twentieth century, during which "The Far and the Near" takes place, the railroads' wooden passenger cars and iron tracks were giving way to steel, making trains far more speedy and durable. Rapid express trains connected large cities, and traveling long distances by train was considered fashionable. Most trains of the era were still powered by steam, as is the one in the story.

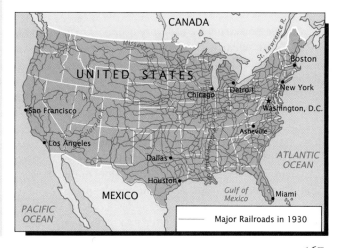

Major Railroads in 1930

The Far and the Near **167**

LESSON PREVIEW

In this tale by a noted American author, a man is disillusioned when he discovers the reality behind an idealized vision. Every day for over twenty years, a railroad engineer passes a little house and blows the train whistle as a woman and her daughter wave from the porch. The scene is a comfort, an unchanging tranquil oasis in his life. When at last he visits the cottage, however, he finds the woman hostile and suspicious, and he leaves with his vision shattered.

LITERARY SKILLS FOR THIS SELECTION

- style
- symbols

THEMES IN THIS SELECTION

- reality and fantasy: shattered illusions
- the importance of perspective

LESSON OBJECTIVES

1. to examine the significance of a story's title
2. to write a character's reaction to the events in a story

Teacher's Classroom Resources 1

- Teaching Notes   301
- Prereading Vocabulary   302
- Reading Guide   303
- Check Test   304
- Responding to World Cultures   305
- Writing Process Guides: Writing About a Story's Title   306
  Writing a Character's Reaction   307
- Grammar in Literature: Completing Sentences with Adverbs   308
- Selection Test   309

TEACHING STUDENTS OF DIFFERENT ABILITIES

- **For less advanced students:** Have students describe the kind of life the engineer leads and the reasons he finds the cottage vision so comforting. Also ask them to complete the Reading Guide.

- **For more advanced students:** Have students read additional fiction by Thomas Wolfe and write essays examining Wolfe's lyrical style.

DISCUSSING GEOGRAPHY AND CULTURE

The Decline of the Railroad

Automobiles are largely responsible for the decline of the American railroad industry since the 1920s. Los Angeles, for instance, had the most extensive intraurban rail system in the United States until the late 1940s, when the city's electric trains were supplanted by private automobiles and freeways.

- Ask students to discuss the importance of railroads to the economy and the environment.

Railroad in Spring, 1933, Charles Burchfield.

Thomas Wolfe

The Far and the Near

On the outskirts of a little town upon a rise of land that swept back from the railway there was a tidy little cottage of white boards, trimmed vividly with green blinds. To one side of the house there was a garden neatly patterned with plots of growing vegetables, and an arbor for the grapes which ripened late in August. Before the house there were three mighty oaks which sheltered it in their clean and massive shade in summer, and to the other side there was a border of gay flowers. The whole place had an air of tidiness, thrift, and modest comfort.

Every day, a few minutes after two o'clock in the afternoon, the limited express[1] between the two cities passed this spot. At that moment the great train, having halted for a breathing space at the town nearby, was beginning to lengthen evenly into its stroke, but it had not yet reached the full drive of its terrific speed. It swung into view deliberately, swept past with a powerful swaying motion of the engine, a low smooth rumble of its heavy cars upon pressed steel, and then it vanished in the cut. For a moment the

---

1. **limited express:** rapid train that connects two cities and makes only a few stops in between.

168 *The Short Story*

CRITICAL THINKING: GUIDED READING QUESTIONS

LITERAL

1a. What stands on either side of the little house? (On one side are a neatly patterned vegetable garden and a grape arbor; on the other side is a border of gay flowers.)

INFERENTIAL

1b. What do these details suggest about the inhabitants of the house? (They are productive and nurturing and are lovers of nature, beauty, and harmony.)

progress of the engine could be marked by heavy bellowing puffs of smoke that burst at spaced intervals above the edges of the meadow grass, and finally nothing could be heard but the 4 solid clacking tempo of the wheels receding into the drowsy stillness of the afternoon.

Every day for more than twenty years, as the train approached this house, the engineer had blown on the whistle, and every day, as soon as she heard this signal, a woman had appeared on the back porch of the little house and waved to him. At first she had a small child clinging to her skirts, and now this child had grown to full womanhood, and every day she, too, came with her mother to the porch and waved.

The engineer had grown old and gray in service. He had driven his great train, loaded with its weight of lives, across the land ten thousand times. His own children had grown up and married, and four times he had seen before him on the tracks the ghastly dot of tragedy converging like a cannon ball to its eclipse of horror at the boiler head[2]—a light spring wagon filled with children, with its clustered row of small stunned faces; a cheap automobile stalled upon the tracks, set with the wooden figures of people 5 paralyzed with fear; a battered hobo walking by the rail, too deaf and old to hear the whistle's warning; and a form flung past his window with a scream—all this the man had seen and known. He had known all the grief, the joy, the peril, and the labor such a man could know; he had 6 grown seamed and weathered in his loyal service, and now, schooled by the qualities of faith and courage and humbleness that attended his labor, he had grown old, and had the grandeur and the wisdom these men have.

But no matter what peril or tragedy he had known, the vision of the little house and the women waving to him with a brave free motion of the arm had become fixed in the mind of the 7 engineer as something beautiful and enduring, something beyond all change and ruin, and something that would always be the same, no matter what mishap, grief, or error might break the iron schedule of his days.

The sight of the little house and of these two women gave him the most extraordinary happiness he had ever known. He had seen them in a 8 thousand lights, a hundred weathers. He had seen them through the harsh bare light of wintry gray across the brown and frosted stubble of earth, and he had seen them again in the green luring sorcery of April.

He felt for them and for the little house in which they lived such tenderness as a man might feel for his own children, and at length the picture of their lives was carved so sharply in his heart that he felt that he knew their lives completely, to every hour and moment of the 9 day, and he resolved that one day, when his years of service should be ended, he would go and find these people and speak at last with them whose lives had been so wrought[3] into his own.

That day came. At last the engineer stepped from a train onto the station platform of the town where these two women lived. His years upon the rail had ended. He was a pensioned servant of his company, with no more work to do. The engineer walked slowly through the station and out into the streets of the town. Everything was as strange to him as if he had never seen this town before. As he walked on, his sense of bewilderment and confusion grew. Could this be the town he had passed ten thousand times? Were these the same houses he had seen so often from the high windows of his cab? It was all as unfamiliar, as disquieting as a city in a dream, and the perplexity of his spirit increased as he went on.

Presently the houses thinned into the strag-

---

2. **boiler head:** front section of a steam locomotive.

3. **wrought:** here, shaped; formed.

The Far and the Near 169

PAGE SUMMARY: AT A GLANCE

- For over twenty years the engineer has blown his whistle while passing the house, and a woman and her daughter have come outside and waved.
- The engineer has seen tragedies on the tracks, but the vision of the waving women has sustained him.
- When he retires, he decides to visit the house and the women whose lives helped shape his.
- He arrives in the town but finds it strange and puzzling.

IN THE GLOSSARY

- converging: coming together
- resolved: became determined
- disquieting: disturbing

4 TEACHING ONOMATOPOEIA

Note that *clacking* and several other words echo the sound of the train's wheels.

5 CULTURAL BACKGROUND

Explain that hobos often slept near railroad tracks and hopped aboard freight trains to travel without paying.

6 TEACHING STUDENTS OF LIMITED ENGLISH PROFICIENCY

Help students grasp less familiar meanings of familiar words such as *weathered,* meaning "worn down," and *attended,* meaning "accompanied."

7 TEACHING SYMBOLS

Elicit that the waving women are a symbol of hope and permanence in a changing, unhappy world.

8 TEACHING STYLE

Note the repetition of the clause "He had seen them" stresses the permanence the engineer associates with his vision. Have students cite an earlier example of similar repetition. ("Every day" in the first full paragraph of the first column)

9 READING SKILL: PREDICTING OUTCOMES

Have students predict the likely outcome of the engineer's visit.

CRITICAL THINKING: GUIDED READING QUESTIONS

LITERAL

1a. What has the engineer seen four times in front of him on the track? (He has seen people about to be struck by his train.)

2a. What has become fixed in the engineer's mind as something "beyond all change and ruin"? (the vision of the house and the waving women)

INFERENTIAL

1b. From this information what can you infer about the engineer's life? (It has been marked by guilt and grief.)

2b. How might the engineer's distance help foster this ideal vision? (It prevents him from knowing the women and allows him to idealize them.)

- The house and its surroundings seem like an unfamiliar landscape in an ugly dream, and the women turn out to be suspicious and unwelcoming.
- After an awkward visit, the engineer departs, feeling that a magic part of his life has been lost forever.

IN THE GLOSSARY

- meager: thin
- sallow: sickly yellow
- ghastly: terrible; horrible
- faltered: stumbled
- parlor: living room
- sullen: sulky; gloomy
- timorous: lacking courage

10 TEACHING STYLE

Note Wolfe's use of repetition and parallel structure to expand on his ideas and capture the intensity of the women's effect on the engineer.

11 TEACHING THEME

Point out the perplexity the engineer feels as he views the house and its surroundings from a new, more intimate perspective.

12 GRAMMAR IN LITERATURE

Have students identify adjectives that help capture the unpleasant appearance and attitude of the woman. (*harsh, pinched, meager, sallow, small, timid, uneasy*)

13 CRITICAL THINKING: EVALUATION

Ask students to evaluate the women's behavior toward the guest. How would they behave in the same situation?

COLLABORATIVE LEARNING: ENRICHMENT ACTIVITY

Panel Discussion Have students work together to plan a railroad trip around the United States. They should use maps and timetables in planning the journey.

---

gling outposts of the town, and the street faded into a country road—the one on which the women lived. And the man plodded on slowly in the heat and dust. At length he stood before the house he sought. He knew at once that he had found the proper place. He saw the lordly oaks before the house, the flower beds, the garden, and the arbor, and farther off, the glint of rails.

10 Yes, this was the house he sought, the place he had passed so many times, the destination he had longed for with such happiness. But now that he had found it, now that he was here, why did his hand falter on the gate; why had the town, the road, the earth, the very entrance to this place he loved turned unfamiliar as the land-

11 scape of some ugly dream? Why did he now feel this sense of confusion, doubt, and hopelessness?

At length he entered by the gate, walked slowly up the path and in a moment more had mounted three short steps that led up to the porch, and was knocking at the door. Presently he heard steps in the hall, the door was opened, and a woman stood facing him.

And instantly, with a sense of bitter loss and grief, he was sorry he had come. He knew at once that the woman who stood there looking at him with a mistrustful eye was the same woman who had waved to him so many thousand times.

12 But her face was harsh and pinched and meager; the flesh sagged wearily in sallow folds, and the small eyes peered at him with timid suspicion and uneasy doubt. All the brave freedom, the warmth, and the affection that he had read into her gesture vanished in the moment that he saw her and heard her unfriendly tongue.

And now his own voice sounded unreal and ghastly to him as he tried to explain his presence, to tell her who he was and the reason he had come. But he faltered on, fighting stubbornly against the horror of regret, confusion, disbelief that surged up in his spirit, drowning all his former joy and making his act of hope and tenderness seem shameful to him.

13 At length the woman invited him almost unwillingly into the house, and called her daughter in a harsh shrill voice. Then, for a brief agony of time, the man sat in an ugly little parlor, and he tried to talk while the two women stared at him with a dull, bewildered hostility, a sullen, timorous restraint.

And finally, stammering a crude farewell, he departed. He walked away down the path and then along the road toward town, and suddenly he knew that he was an old man. His heart, which had been brave and confident when he looked along the familiar vista of the rails, was now sick with doubt and horror as it saw the strange and unsuspected visage of an earth which had always been within a stone's throw of him, and which he had never seen or known. And he knew that all the magic of that bright lost way, the vista of that shining line, the imagined corner of that small good universe of hope's desire, was gone forever, could never be got back again.

CRITICAL THINKING: GUIDED READING QUESTIONS

LITERAL

1a. Into what sort of parlor does the woman reluctantly take the engineer? (It is an ugly parlor.)

2a. As a result of his visit, what happens to the engineer's vision? (He loses it.)

INFERENTIAL

1b. How does this description contrast with earlier details about the house? (From the train the house looked very pleasant.)

2b. What does the outcome suggest about our fantasies and ideals? (Often they cannot survive the harsh light of reality.)

STUDY QUESTIONS

Recalling

1. According to the first paragraph, what "air" does the little cottage have? What happens every day for more than twenty years as the engineer and his train pass the cottage?
2. According to the fifth paragraph, what "vision" counteracts each peril or tragedy that the engineer has known in his years of service?
3. When the engineer retires and at last visits the cottage, what sort of woman does he meet? In what manner does she invite him inside?
4. Summarize the engineer's thoughts and feelings as they are described in the final paragraph.

Interpreting

5. Over the years, what does the engineer, in his mind, or imagination, do to the little cottage and its inhabitants?
6. Why might the engineer place so much importance on his vision?
7. What does the story suggest about people's fantasies or visions of an ideal?

Extending

8. Do you think the engineer should have visited the cottage? In his place, would you have done so? Why or why not?

COMPOSITION

Writing About a Story's Title

■ Write a brief composition in which you explain the significance of the title of Wolfe's story. First state why you think Wolfe chose to call the story "The Far and the Near." Then support your statement with specific details from the story showing how the title is related to the plot, characters, settings, and theme.

Writing a Character's Reaction

■ Imagine that you are the woman in the cottage and that the engineer has just paid his visit. In a letter to a friend or a diary entry, or using any other suitable format, write your reaction to the engineer's visit. Describe your impressions of the engineer, and state your opinion about his behavior.

Why do you think the women always came out to wave to the engineer?

ANSWERS

STUDY QUESTIONS

1. It has an air of tidiness, thrift, and comfort. He blows the train whistle, and a woman and her daughter come out and wave.
2. the vision of the little house and the women waving with a "brave free motion"
3. She is mistrustful and harsh. She invites him in with timid suspicion and uneasy doubt.
4. He feels old, believes the magic world he saw from the train is gone forever, and is filled with doubt and horror.
5. He idealizes and romanticizes it.
6. The dull routine of his job, the tragedies he has witnessed, and the lack of comfort and security in his own life may prompt him to look elsewhere for signs of happiness, comfort, and security.
7. They may be spoiled if they are examined too closely; they may not survive the harshness of reality.
8. Answers will vary. Some students may feel that he is better off facing the truth; others, that his ideal vision was best left unexamined or that he should not have intruded on the women's privacy.

COMPOSITION: GUIDELINES FOR EVALUATION

WRITING ABOUT A STORY'S TITLE

Objective

To examine the significance of a story's title

Guidelines for Evaluation

■ suggested length: three or four paragraphs
■ should begin with a generalization about the significance of the story's title
■ should support the generalization by showing how the title is related to plot, characters, settings, and theme

WRITING A CHARACTER'S REACTION

Objective

To write a character's reaction to story events

Guidelines for Evaluation

■ suggested length: one to two pages
■ should be written in the first person and use letter, diary, or another suitable form
■ should express the woman's opinions of the engineer and his visit

In this ironic tale desire for wealth makes a young Parisian miss an opportunity for love. On his way to meet his fiancée, the rich Arabella, Max Péralbe is lured by spring fever into the Botanical Garden. He follows a lovely girl and fantasizes about marrying her. When she enters a shabby apartment building, Max rushes off, never learning that she is in fact wealthy and interested in meeting him. Meanwhile, Arabella has discovered his actions and ends their relationship.

LITERARY SKILLS FOR THIS SELECTION

- stream of consciousness
- tone
- irony

THEMES IN THIS SELECTION

- reality and fantasy: daydreams
- emotional vs. social fulfillment

LESSON OBJECTIVES

1. to examine stream-of-consciousness techniques
2. to interpret a foreign title
3. to write a stream-of-consciousness sequel

Teacher's Classroom Resources 1

- Teaching Notes — 311
- Prereading Vocabulary — 312
- Reading Guide — 313
- Check Test — 314
- Responding to World Cultures — 315
- Literary Focus: Stream of Consciousness — 316
- Language Study: Interpreting a Foreign Title — 317
- Writing Process Guide: Writing a Stream-of-Consciousness Sequel — 318
- Grammar in Literature: Commas and Nonessential Elements — 319
- Selection Test — 320

TEACHING STUDENTS OF DIFFERENT ABILITIES

- **For less advanced students:** Help students with the story's

Françoise Mallet-Joris

(born 1930)

Belgium/France

Belgian by birth but French by marriage, Françoise Mallet-Joris [frän swäz′ mäl ā′ zhô rēs′] has spent much of her adult life in Paris and the south of France. Her childhood was privileged, for her mother was a well-known playwright, and her father was Belgium's minister of justice. Yet as a youngster Mallet-Joris felt inhibited by her circumstances, "a prisoner in a big house that ran like clockwork." She took refuge in the family library, and by the age of twenty-one had published a volume of poetry and a best-selling novel, *The Illusionist.*

Over the years Mallet-Joris has produced several successful novels and collections of stories. Her writing, according to critic M. D. Evans, shows a fascination with human psychology and the masks people wear to face society and conceal their true identity. In addition, Mallet-Joris has worked for a Paris publishing house and served on the awards committee of the Prix Fémina, a prestigious French-language literary prize. She herself won the Prix Fémina for her 1958 novel *L'Empire Céleste.*

GEOGRAPHY AND CULTURE

Belgium and Paris, France

Belgium is a small nation on the western coast of Europe. More than half its population speaks Flemish, a version of Dutch sometimes classified as a separate language. The fact that about a third of all Belgians are Walloons, or speakers of French, reflects the influence of France to the country's south.

As a French-speaking Belgian interested in a literary career, Mallet-Joris naturally gravitated to Paris, the capital of France and international headquarters of the French-language publishing industry. With its fine theaters, ballet companies, and famous opera house, Paris is a great cultural mecca. It is also a beautiful city known for its wide, tree-lined boulevards, magnificent architecture, and many parks and public gardens, such as the Luxembourg Gardens. The city's Botanical Garden is the opening setting of "Air des Clochettes."

See LITERATURE AND CULTURE SOURCEBOOK: France

difficult vocabulary. Have them complete the Reading Guide.
- **For more advanced students:** Have students focus on Max's thoughts and consider whether Mallet-Joris has a keen understanding of human psychology.

DISCUSSING GEOGRAPHY AND CULTURE

Imagining a City

Even people who never forsake their armchairs can cherish images of Paris, for the writers who lived there have left eloquent records. The descriptions rendered by Charles Dickens, Ernest Hemingway, Honoré de Balzac, and Victor Hugo bring the city vividly to life.
- Ask students to name a city they have never been to but want to visit. How did they form a mental image of this place? (Students might mention stories, pictures, or films.)

Françoise Mallet-Joris

Air des Clochettes[1]

Translated from the French by Peter Green

1   No doubt Spring had had its eye on Max for some time: it sometimes rather enjoys leading ambitious young men a dance. At all events, when Max left the house, at about three o'clock, 2 with the firm intention of meeting Miss Arabella Graham for tea, Spring—which had been lying in wait for him at the corner of the street—pounced so abruptly, with such a wealth of bright sunlight and intoxicating scents, that Max could scarcely breathe.

As everyone willingly recognized, Max was a sensible young man. Even now, when he was sallying forth to meet a girl who, in all probability, would soon become his wife, his thoughts were of strictly prosaic matters. Did his blue suit look a little too worn? What make was Arabella's car? Would they marry on terms of separate maintenance? So it is not so much to him as to the insidious Spring weather that we should ascribe the birth of this exotic notion: *Suppose,* he told 3 himself, *I were to take a turn round the Botanical Garden while I'm waiting?* A fatal idea, since the Botanical Garden was Spring's quintessential domain; and indeed, no sooner had Max entered it than, by some magical metamorphosis, all his sensible ideas disappeared, like a lumbering herd of elephants in full retreat, leaving him alone and defenseless in this enchanted enclave.

The automatic sprinklers were revolving on the lawns, flinging out wide circles of glittering freshness. Small fair-haired children romped and tumbled and picked themselves up again with 4 short, shrill cries like bird-calls. Sitting there on a rustic bench, among all the mothers and nurses, this carefully dressed young man, with the solemn expression and stiff, rather awkward movements, might perhaps be considered a trifle ridiculous. But such a thought never entered his head. At the age of twenty-five, Max Péralbe,[2] shortly to become engaged to the wealthy Arabella Graham, and a future lawyer of note, was discovering his first Spring.

"Seven francs,[3] Monsieur,[4] if you please," murmured the woman chair-attendant.

"That's quite reasonable, Madame."

"Ah, Monsieur, don't I know it! I have to scrape a living from this job, and I'm a war-widow, too."

She moved off with some dignity, leaving Max reflecting, in a mood of absurd enthusiasm, how he loved war-widows in the Botanical Garden on a fine afternoon. It was at this precise moment that he noticed a gray skirt about ten yards away from him. It was a very simple skirt, made—as far as he could judge—of some ordinary, unremarkable material, and embroidered in white round the hemline with a pattern of small hoops like those bordering the lawns: in short, a skirt such as he must have seen a thousand times before.

Yet on this May afternoon the skirt, and its owner's slender, pliant waist, struck him with the force of a revelation. Never in his life had Max felt so young, so exhilarated, and so cheerfully irrational. It was all due to the Botanical

---

1. *Air des Clochettes* [är′ dä clŏ shet′]: title of a famous soprano aria from the opera *Lakmé* by French composer Léo Delibes (1836–1891). The aria is known in English as "The Bell Song."

2. **Péralbe** [pär älb′].
3. **francs:** French money.
4. **Monsieur** [mə syœ′]: French for "Sir" or "Mister."

CRITICAL THINKING: GUIDED READING QUESTIONS

LITERAL

1a. What three "prosaic matters" does Max consider? (Is his blue suit too worn? What is the make of Arabella's car? Will they marry "on terms of separate maintenance?")

2a. In the Botanical Garden what does Max discover for the first time? (He discovers spring.)

INFERENTIAL

→ **1b.** What do these thoughts show about his concerns and motives? (He is overly concerned with appearances and has social and financial motives for marrying Arabella.)

→ **2b.** What do his subsequent remarks and interests suggest that spring has done to him? (It has made him romantic and impractical.)

- When a small boy approaches the young woman in gray, Max is relieved to hear him address her as *Mademoiselle*.
- She responds in a sweet voice, and Max imagines conversing with her about the sycamore under which she sits.
- He half rises but does not approach, recalling his appointment at Mrs. Page's, where Arabella is to sing.
- Max's mother feels Arabella will be an eminently suitable wife.
- Until now Max has shared this opinion, rarely disagreeing with his mother.

IN THE GLOSSARY

- engendered: created
- diffident: shy
- benevolent: kindly

5 TEACHING CHARACTERIZATION

Elicit that until now Max has repressed all romantic longings and instead conformed to his mother's wishes. Then note that his mother cannot be entirely to blame for his past behavior, any more than spring is entirely to blame for today's rebellion.

6 TEACHING STUDENTS OF LIMITED ENGLISH PROFICIENCY

Note the use of *Mademoiselle* here and the French titles *Madame (Mme.)* and *Maître* in the next column. Ask nonnative students to provide similar titles in their own native tongue.

7 TEACHING STREAM OF CONSCIOUSNESS

Point out that in tracing Max's thoughts, the narrator tries to capture the leaps of the human mind from thought to thought.

8 READING SKILL: INFERENCE

Elicit that "above all" shows Max's mother to be more concerned with her own happiness than with her son's.

Garden, with its stretches of damp, green lawn, gleaming softly in the shade, and, above all, to this gray skirt and white blouse, bent so gracefully over what looked like a cheap paperback novel, under the shade of a majestic sycamore (*a variant of the maple; known also as the* 5 *false plane*). Max recalled, not for the first time, that he had done well in botany at school. (But then, what had he not done well in, with the ruthless discipline that his mother imposed on him?) But today, unprecedentedly, all these hard-won achievements seemed somehow a barren triumph. Had he not just discovered something his mother had never taught him—the joys of dreaming in the sunlight, in a garden, not too far from an attractive gray skirt?

Then he gave a tiny start. A child had just run up to the gray skirt, and a small, very grubby hand was tugging at her violently.

"Ma'mselle,[5] what are those things that spin round and round as they fall?" he asked. He was a nice little boy, rather pale, and not too well dressed. But Max paid no real attention to him: 6 he was so overwhelmed by the sense of relief that the word *Mademoiselle* had engendered in his own mind. So she wasn't married, then! And to complete the spell she now spoke, in an unforgettable voice, warm, disturbing, sweetly modulated. She said: "It's a seed, Emile, the seed of the plane-tree."

Max half rose from his park bench, a diffident yet (of course) attractive smile hovering on his lips. He would go over and correct this mistaken piece of information. Mademoiselle, he would say, that is not the plane-tree, but its pseudo-variant, the sycamore. She would be astonished 7 at his knowledgeability and they would thereupon launch into a long, passionate conversation about botany, with her raising her lovely eyes to his (what color were they? so far he hadn't got near enough to see) and then, sud-

denly, clasping her hand, he would say—he would say—well, what? Twice already, in fact, her eyes *had* looked up at Max, with a certain mild surprise; twice Max had half-risen and then sat down again. Half-risen, because Spring, mischievous yet benevolent, gave him an encouraging push from behind on each occasion; subsided, because his legs were promptly turned to water by an appalling realization, as potent in its way as the scent of trees and flowers all around him: Miss Arabella Graham was awaiting his arrival in Mrs. Page's drawing-room.[6] Miss Arabella Graham was going to sing.

8 In the opinion of Mme.[7] Péralbe, Max's mother, Miss Arabella Graham was the most eminently suitable fiancée, bride, and, above all, daughter-in-law that one could hope to find anywhere. Max had been of the same opinion; his views rarely differed from those expressed by his mother. Arabella would know exactly how to advance a rising young lawyer's interests; she would not only bring him a fortune, but help him to achieve a position in high society, get him into the fashionable swim. Max already visualized himself gliding along regally in his car, or receiving future clients in a luxurious suite of offices, while everywhere people whispered (how flattering to be thus recognized!): Look, there goes the famous Maître[8] Péralbe!

At least, this was the kind of picture he normally conjured up when he thought about his plans for the future. But by some incomprehensible trick of fate, these images, summoned up now as reserves against the too-seductive Spring, firmly refused to take shape in his mind. What he recalled instead, all too readily, were Arabella's extraordinary height (she stood a good half-head taller than he did), her outdoor,

---

5. **Ma'mselle** [mam zel′]: short for *Mademoiselle,* French for "Miss."

6. **drawing-room:** usually formal room for greeting and entertaining guests.
7. **Mme.:** abbreviation for *Madame,* French for "Mrs." or "Ma'am."
8. **Maître** [mã′trə]: French for "Master," used as a title of respect.

174 *The Short Story*

CRITICAL THINKING: GUIDED READING QUESTIONS

LITERAL

1a. What does the word *Mademoiselle* engender in Max's mind? (It engenders a sense of relief.)

2a. Whose opinions has Max usually shared? (his mother's)

INFERENTIAL

1b. Why is he relieved to learn that the girl in gray is unmarried? (He is attracted to her and hopeful of romance; for a moment he feared the boy was her son.)

2b. What does this detail reveal about Max? (He is a weak person.)

The Park, c. 1910, Gustav Klimt.

PAGE SUMMARY: AT A GLANCE

■ Now Max reconsiders Arabella, dwelling on her faults, such as her "frightful" singing voice.
■ He decides that he loathes the *"Air des clochettes,"* the aria she sings at the slightest opportunity.
■ Max rises when the girl in gray begins to leave, but a "guardian angel" who resembles his mother seems to whisper, "Don't follow *her!*"

IN THE GLOSSARY

■ loathe: hate
■ imperious: domineering

9 **READING SKILLS: CONTRAST; CAUSE AND EFFECT**

Elicit that Arabella's voice contrasts with the "sweetly modulated" voice of the woman in gray and that Max is no longer resigned to Arabella's voice because he mentally contrasts the two.

ART AND LITERATURE

The Austrian artist Gustav Klimt (1863–1918) combined decorative arabesques and colorful geometric designs to create melancholy portraits and moody, stylized landscapes. Because Austria sits at the threshold between Eastern and Western Europe, it was common for Austrian artists to blend a western figurative style with eastern pattern and decoration. In *The Park* Klimt's wall of towering, impenetrable trees borders on decorative abstraction, while the faintly shining light below creates a feeling of actual but ominous space.
■ Ask students what images of spring *The Park* conveys. (Possible answers: lush, verdant, budding, overgrown, blooming)

not to say military complexion (what Mme. Péralbe called a "good, healthy appearance"), and her frightful soprano voice—reedy, shrill, over-mannered—which issued so unexpectedly from that square, robust body, and which its owner was determined to make heard, at the slightest opportunity, singing the *"Air des clochettes"* from Delibes' *Lakmé.* For the first time he considered this voice, not with his customary feeling of resignation, but with something approaching active intolerance. "I loathe the *'Air des clochettes'!*" he told himself.

Then, for the third time, he rose to his feet— only to subside once more—as the unknown girl got up from her chair and walked off, with a light, graceful gait, holding the little boy by the hand. Max's private guardian angel (a guardian angel equipped in all likelihood with detachable lace collar, pince-nez[9], and gold watch-chain, and even, perhaps, displaying that faint mustache and Bourbon nose[10] which were the imperious Mme. Péralbe's most prominent features) now whispered in his ear: "Don't follow *her*! She's just an ordinary children's nurse—perhaps

---

9. **pince-nez** [pans′nā′]: small eyeglasses held on the nose by a spring.
10. **Bourbon nose:** large nose characteristic of the Bourbons, French royal family from 1589 to 1792 and 1814 to 1848.

Air des Clochettes **175**

CRITICAL THINKING: GUIDED READING QUESTIONS

LITERAL

1a. Whose prominent features does Max's "guardian angel" display? (those of his mother)

INFERENTIAL

1b. What does this detail suggest about the advice not to follow the girl in gray? (It is the advice of the practical, mercenary Mrs. Péralbe, which Max has internalized over the years.)

- Despite the practical advice of his "guardian angel," Max follows the woman in gray.
- When she stops for the boy to ride a merry-go-round, Max daydreams of becoming engaged to her and telling his mother that love is worth more than the world's riches.
- When the woman takes the boy to an open-air puppet theater, Max pictures himself as a rich and famous lawyer attending the Paris Opéra with his wife, the woman in gray.

IN THE GLOSSARY

- meritorious: deserving praise
- contralto: low female singing voice
- impeccable: faultless
- lethargic: sluggish

10 TEACHING STREAM OF CONSCIOUSNESS

Point out that Max's mind leaps between the present and the future he imagines. Have students identify the two locations in the park to which Max actually follows the woman in gray. (the merry-go-round and the open-air puppet theater)

11 CRITICAL THINKING: CLASSIFICATION

Have students classify Max's various daydreams as idealistic or materialistic. (For example, the remark he imagines telling his mother is idealistic.)

12 CULTURAL BACKGROUND

Explain that open-air puppet shows are simple, popular entertainments for children in Paris parks. In contrast, a première at the Paris Opéra is an elegant, costly entertainment of fashionable Paris society.

13 TEACHING TONE

Point out that the narrator mocks Max's absurdly unrealistic daydreams by dwelling on his trivial obsessions with status symbols.

---

even a typist, or a factory worker. *Not* the kind of woman that should attract the famous Maître Péralbe."

But Maître Péralbe, intoxicated with Spring, replied: "This girl's *really* twenty, and Arabella's been twenty for the last seven years. This girl has violet-colored eyes, the rarest shade in existence. If Arabella's eyes are of any particular color at all I can only say I've never noticed it. When Arabella walks, she looks as though she's marching behind a column of troops. But there are girls who walk on air, and I never knew it!" So he set off in pursuit of the gray skirt with its plain white hooped hemline.

The gray skirt stopped in front of a small merry-go-round, and the child rushed on to it. Max stood some ten yards off, watching her tenderly. **10** How pretty she was, sitting there on that little rustic bench! They had been engaged since the evening before. His jurisprudence all forgotten, Max was teaching Violet Eyes the names of flowers and trees. They were arguing (oh, very lovingly) about their plans for the future—plans which had nothing whatsoever in common with those he had conceived (so long ago, it seemed a century) regarding Arabella: schemes in which virtue and courage were the key qualities, schemes for a hard-working life crowned by **11** slow, meritorious success. Had he not told his mother the previous evening, when she ventured to criticize his plan to marry this young working-class girl: "Love is worth more than all the riches in the world."

Now they were at their wedding, a modest but poetical ceremony in some small, ivy-clad, suburban church, and it was his blushing bride who leaned on his arm, with her gray skirt and violet eyes and the dear contralto voice that never sang, never would sing the *"Air des clochettes."* Here they were in their small, comfortable apartment, with the curtains drawn and the lights switched on, and she—the impeccable young housewife personified—was setting a

steaming supper on the dazzlingly white tablecloth, sweet recompense after a hard day's work. And now, on this fine afternoon, it was their son riding on the merry-go-round, with such a dexterous mastery of the hand-rings, and very soon his father would go and make a fuss over him, while Violet Eyes looked tenderly on. . . .

Time passed as though in a dream; and as though in a dream he remembered Arabella, who was waiting for him to arrive at Mrs. Page's so that she could give her recital, and who would still be waiting a good many hours hence. No, he wouldn't waste any time, or keep her dangling; he's simply say: "Arabella, find yourself another man, and live for love." But she, in her despair, would commit suicide next day, in the most tactful possible manner, leaving her entire fortune to him in her will.

12 As they went into the little open-air puppet theater, with its musty damp-mushroom smell, they were an established, wealthy couple. Their son clapped his hands in delight. The velvet curtain raised clouds of dust. A gigantic crocodile was doing its best, in a surly, lethargic way, to devour the innocent puppet-hero. But what Max saw as he watched the stage was his first client, a murderer whom he defended with such dash and brilliance that from then on he was the one, the only attorney in Paris. With a languid gesture he waved away the crowds of journalists before returning to their apartment in the **13** Bois.[11] The car (a brand-new American model) was waiting to take him and his wife to some première. They said goodbye to their children (two or three of them now, dressed in the most fetching pajamas and romping about a spacious nursery) and finally arrived at the Opéra. The Republican Guards, sabers drawn, gave them a formal salute. Everyone recognized them: they

---

11. **Bois** [bwä]: short for Bois de Boulogne [boo lon'yə], former royal forest and now a fashionable residential area in western Paris.

176 *The Short Story*

CRITICAL THINKING: GUIDED READING QUESTIONS

LITERAL

1a. In contrasting Arabella and the girl in gray, on what specific things does Max focus? (He compares their respective ages, eyes, ways of moving, and voices.)

2a. As Max follows the woman to the open-air puppet show, what does he imagine they are attending as a married couple? (He imagines them attending the Paris Opéra.)

INFERENTIAL

1b. Considering these details, why is it illogical for him to leap ahead to loving and marrying the woman? (He seems to equate physical attraction with emotional fulfillment.)

2b. What does this daydream show about the values Max expressed a few paragraphs earlier? (He still cares about wealth and status.)

were the handsomest couple in Paris. A loud whisper ran through the foyer: "Look, there's Maître Péralbe and his wife—he's the one who defended that famous case, and inherited an enormous fortune—yes, some Englishwoman, she was in love with him—oh look, what a beautiful creature his wife is!"

There was clapping, applause. Why? Presumably the performance was over. Max drifted out with the other spectators, vaguely surprised at no longer seeing his wife in a gorgeous décolleté[12] dress, and at hearing little Emile exclaim, in his shrill little boy's voice: "It wasn't a real crocodile, was it?"

She was walking across the Botanical Garden now, through the main entrance, then into a dark and narrow street. Still wrapped in his dream, Max followed them. She did not turn round, but little Emile—doubtless unaware that this strange man had been his father for the last hour or so—showed ingenuous astonishment when he saw him still trailing along ten yards in the rear. Street succeeded street, each narrower than the last, each more proof against the magic power of the season. But Max failed to take the hint. They were going home together to their apartment. In a moment now—

Then, brutally torn out of his fantasy, he stopped at the same moment as she did, and watched her vanish into a red-brick apartment building, and stood there outside, dazed, irresolute. Their home? Here? In this hideous red-brick edifice, in this courtyard where no sunshine ever penetrated, among these humble streets—soiled and worn, as though by long over-use—with their dingy stores and screaming children? As though suddenly awakened from some *Arabian Nights*[13] fairy-tale, he stared

around him. What he saw, alas, stripped of the glamour which Spring had shed about him, was a scene all too similar to that which greeted his eyes every day, in the apartment he shared with his mother. "We must get out of this place," was her constant cry. "At all costs we must get out—"

He tried to recall his earlier rapture, the memory of two violet eyes that held the promise of happiness and tranquillity. Spring was working in him still. He conjured up that melodious voice, the dreams he had nursed of an obscure, hard-working life. His own talent and energy would suffice to let him scale the heights. But there was still that dark presence by his side; he heard his dangerous guardian angel whisper, insinuatingly: "What? Live for years in a house like *that*? Especially when one gesture, one decision will enable you to start from the top of the ladder instead of painfully scaling it rung by rung? Think: years of drudgery, and financial troubles, and domestic rows[14] blown up by your inability to make both ends meet. Years of wondering—as you wondered today—whether your blue suit isn't too shiny and worn. Years in which your wife gets old, and clients don't appear, and your stock of courage gets used up and cannot be redeemed . . ."

Spring was still struggling, but more weakly now: in these streets it was deprived of its natural allies, the trees and the sunlight. But with a last effort its voice still reached Max's ears, a long sighing murmur like the wind: "Come on, Max, show a little courage! Look round you again, more closely this time. Remember the tranquil light in those violet eyes of hers. There is more reality in these little concrete balconies and poky, shabby apartments than in the finest house on earth that has not been won by one's own efforts. . . ."

But Max did not hear; he was far too busy

---

12. **décolleté** [dā′kol tā′]: fashionably low cut.
13. **Arabian Nights:** another name for *The Thousand and One Nights,* famous collection of Arabian tales with strong elements of fantasy. (See Unit 2 of this book.)

14. **rows** [rouz]: quarrels; arguments.

Air des Clochettes **177**

PAGE SUMMARY: AT A GLANCE

■ When Max follows the woman to a hideous apartment building, his romantic impulses ebb.
■ The new scene very much resembles the apartment he shares with his mother, which she constantly cries they must escape "at all costs."
■ After the "guardian angel" points out the drudgery and financial woes of a life of poverty that would ensue if he married the woman in gray, Max no longer heeds the call of romance.

14 CULTURAL BACKGROUND

Explain that wealthy people from other nations have often settled in fashionable Paris. The Englishwoman mentioned here is Arabella, who in Max's daydream has left him her fortune. Her British background is indicated by her surname, Graham, and her English title, Miss, instead of *Mademoiselle.*

15 TEACHING SETTING AND ATMOSPHERE

Elicit that this change in setting is accompanied by a harsh change in atmosphere, as Max leaves the romantic park for a reality with which he is all too familiar.

16 GRAMMAR IN LITERATURE

Have students identify adjectives that vividly capture the harsh new atmosphere. (*hideous, humble, soiled, worn, dingy*)

17 READING SKILL: INFERENCE

Elicit that the "one gesture, one decision" refers to proposing to the wealthy Arabella, since marrying her will foster Max's career.

CRITICAL THINKING: GUIDED READING QUESTIONS

LITERAL

1a. When Max follows the woman in gray to the apartment building, to what is the new scene similar? (The apartment building resembles the one he shares with his mother.)

2a. What does the "guardian angel" say that Max will experience for years if he marries a poor woman? (He will experience drudgery, financial trouble, and domestic quarrels stemming from the inability to make ends meet.)

INFERENTIAL

1b. What does this detail reveal about the Péralbes' background? (They are rather poor.)

2b. How is this vision of the future different from Max's daydreams in the park? (It is harshly realistic.)

- Max rushes off to keep his appointment with Arabella.
- Ten minutes later the woman in gray drives off in a chauffeur-driven car.
- The chauffeur wonders why a rich woman chooses to visit a sick friend in a poor neighborhood and dress like a typist; the woman regrets that the nice young man who followed her never had the courage to speak to her.
- At Mrs. Page's Arabella tells Max's mother that she saw Max following a woman in the Botanical Garden and is thus ending their relationship.
- She then defiantly sings the *"Air des clochettes."*

IN THE GLOSSARY

- **poignant:** touching
- **filial:** befitting a son

18 READING SKILL: CONTRAST

Elicit that Max now takes a more sympathetic view of both Arabella and his mother.

19 TEACHING SYMBOLS

Point out that a large American car is a status symbol for both Max and his mother.

20 TEACHING POINT OF VIEW

Note that the narrator abandons Max's viewpoint in these final scenes and provides thoughts and experiences of several other characters.

21 TEACHING IRONY

Have students identify the many ironies of the story's ending. (The girl in gray is in fact rich, owns the kind of car that means so much to Max, and was interested in meeting him.)

COLLABORATIVE LEARNING: ENRICHMENT ACTIVITY

Music Have groups of students report on famous operas, including Delibes's *Lakmé.* Reports should include plot summaries as well as recordings of arias.

being sorry for himself. The wretched victim of Violet Eyes, he was ending his days in this frightful red-brick apartment house, an embittered failure, looking back with poignant regret to the brilliant life which his genius would inevitably have won him had he not, one spring day, in a fit of madness . . . Automatically he glanced at his watch. Five o'clock. Perhaps she was waiting for him still, the one who could, must, save him **18** from this dreadful fate. He pictured her stamping impatiently (no longer did he tell himself what a soldier-like charm those feet possessed). He imagined his mother, a dignified figure, with that air of a slumming duchess which American women always found so impressive, but nevertheless suffering dreadfully: twisting a fold of her old black satin dress between her fingers, suffering a thousand deaths at the thought that the whole scaffolding of small deceits and innocent lies and heroic self-assertion that she had so laboriously built up round the heiress might come crashing down.

"Your poor mother!" the guardian angel murmured, with unctuous hypocrisy. "Your poor widowed mother, who sacrificed so much in order to give you a decent upbringing! Think how hurt she'd be, how much she'd suffer if this **19** marriage didn't take place. Think how she's looking forward to riding in an American car. What's become of your filial devotion?" For a moment, leaning against the front window of the bakery, Max still hesitated. For a moment longer he glimpsed that gray skirt, those violet eyes, that light, buoyant step as she passed by him. Then, in a flash, the image faded, and Max, feeling as though he had suddenly recovered from a fit of insanity, flung himself into a taxi.

What on earth can have happened to me? he wondered, as he nervously begged the driver to hurry. *That was a close shave, and no mistake.*

20 Ten minutes later, a gray skirt appeared from the main entrance of a shabby red-brick apart-

178 *The Short Story*

ment house, and a pair of violet eyes glanced up and down the deserted street, with curiosity and, perhaps, some disappointment. A large American car was parked a short distance away. The gray skirt climbed into it.

"Take me home now, Albert," she said, in a soft, pleasant voice.

Albert obediently set the car in motion, his face, beneath the peaked and braided cap, a mask of sullen disapproval. He did not care for these lower-class districts. Two hours he had been kept hanging around, and not one suitable café in sight! What on earth had possessed Mademoiselle to come and visit this sick girl-friend of hers? To start with, one didn't have friends in this sort of area, it simply wasn't done. Mademoiselle simply didn't know how to behave. And **21** look at the way she dressed! You'd take her for a typist, despite all her money. God, if he, Albert, had his fingers on some of that . . . As he drove he, too, began to dream; so did Mademoiselle herself, ensconced in the back of the car. What a nice young man he'd been, she thought, the one who followed her. If only he'd had the courage to say something. . . . She sighed over this missed opportunity for at least five minutes before she forgot him.

Meanwhile at Mrs. Page's a lady was saying: "I ran across your son in the Botanical Garden, Madame Péralbe. Don't you think that's charming? Such a serious young man, and there he was daydreaming in the sunshine. . . ."

And Miss Arabella Graham went across to an imposing lady dressed in black satin, and murmured, through set, smiling lips: "Madame, your son is nothing but a lecher! He was following a girl in the street! I saw him. I never wish to set eyes on this—this person again. I have my dignity, Madame." And without listening to the dowager-like protestations that greeted this statement, she walked to the piano with her long, firm stride, while everyone applauded, and proceeded to render the *"Air des clochettes."*

CRITICAL THINKING: GUIDED READING QUESTIONS

LITERAL

1a. What is Mrs. Péralbe's marital and financial status? (She is a poor widow.)

2a. What sort of cap does Albert wear? (He wears a braided cap.)

3a. What does the woman regret about the "nice young man" who was following her? (She regrets that he never had the courage to speak to her.)

INFERENTIAL

1b. How does this detail make her more sympathetic? (It stresses her struggles and makes her desire for financial security more understandable.)

2b. Based on the details about Albert, what is his relationship to the woman in gray? (He is her chauffeur.)

3b. What do the ironies of the ending suggest about love? (It is often thwarted by fate and human error.)

STUDY QUESTIONS

Recalling

1. What kind of young man is Max ordinarily? What "magical metamorphosis" occurs in him?

2. Why do both Max and his mother consider Arabella a suitable fiancée for him?

3. What does Max recall about Arabella's appearance and voice? What does he notice about the appearance and voice of the girl in gray?

4. In his fantasies, what does Max tell his mother about love? What "brutally" tears Max from his fantasies? What does he do then?

5. At the end of the story, what do we discover about the financial situation of the girl in gray? What does Arabella say to Max's mother at the end of the story?

Interpreting

6. What do Max's fantasies and his final actions reveal about his values and his character?

7. What view of spring does the story convey?

8. What are the two central ironies of Max's situation at the end of the story? Does the story suggest that Max gets what he deserves? Cite details to support your conclusion.

Extending

9. If you were Max's friend, what advice would you give him?

LITERARY FOCUS

Stream of Consciousness

In providing a character's thoughts, Mallet-Joris is one of many modern writers who try to capture the way the human mind works. Human beings rarely think in straight-line, chronological (time) order or even in complete sentences. Most of what goes on in the mind is a series of thoughts and images that rapidly switch back and forth between the present, the past, and the future, as ideas remind us of other ideas. The technique of writing that imitates the way thoughts, feelings, and images flow through the human mind is called **stream of consciousness.**

When a story uses the stream-of-consciousness technique, many of its "events" occur not in the phys- ical world but rather in a character's mind. For example, we may be provided with a character's memories of past events and fantasies about the future. The sequence of these mental events is rarely chronological. Instead, the character's mind jumps back and forth in time.

Thinking About Stream of Consciousness

■ Identify two of Max's memories of past events involving Arabella and two of his fantasies about the future involving the girl in gray. Does the presentation of Max's thoughts realistically capture the way the human mind works? Cite details to support your opinion.

LANGUAGE STUDY

Interpreting a Foreign Title

If this story's translator had thought the title *"Air des Clochettes"* referred only to the aria Arabella often sings, he most likely would have substituted "The Bell Song," the name by which the aria is known in English-speaking countries. The fact that he retained the French title suggests that it has multiple meanings in French that cannot be translated. The French word *air* shares the many meanings that *air* has in English—"what we breathe," "aura," "song," and so on. *Des* is simply French for "of the." *Clochettes* means not only "small bells" but also "bellflowers," a group of pretty, usually violet-colored flowers that bloom mostly in spring.

■ Why do you think Mallet-Joris called her story *"Air des Clochettes"*? Which story details point to your conclusions?

COMPOSITION

Writing a Stream-of-Consciousness Sequel

■ Write a sequel to the story in which Arabella confronts Max or Max again meets the girl in gray. Use stream-of-consciousness techniques in providing the thoughts of at least one character. That is, make each thought lead to the next, and mix the present, past, and future as the character's mind moves from thought to thought.

Air des Clochettes **179**

READER'S RESPONSE

What is your opinion of Max Péralbe? Why?

ANSWERS

STUDY QUESTIONS

1. He is sensible. Spring makes him "cheerfully irrational."

2. She is rich and socially well placed.

3. She is tall, "military," and has a "frightful" soprano voice. She is pretty, slender, and has a warm contralto voice.

4. "Love is worth more than all the riches in the world." Seeing the woman enter a shabby building awakens Max to reality. He rushes to Arabella.

5. She is rich. She saw Max following a woman and never wants to see him again.

6. While he sees value in love and courage, he values status and wealth more.

7. Spring is mischievous, tempting, romantic, and impractical.

8. He thought he'd fled a poor woman, but she is rich; Arabella ends their relationship, while the woman in gray was interested in him. Yes, the story mocks Max and shows his cowardice and hypocrisy.

9. Answers will vary. Students may feel that Max should stop repressing his feelings and show more courage.

LITERARY FOCUS

Memories include Arabella's singing and his mother's views of her; fantasies about the future include the conversation about botany and the visit to the Opéra. Most students should find the presentation realistic.

LANGUAGE STUDY

The title stresses Arabella's unattractiveness, since various details indicate that she mangles the aria. Retaining the French wording also stresses the theme of spring fever, or an "aura of bellflowers"; all the details about botany and spring point to this interpretation.

COMPOSITION: GUIDELINES FOR EVALUATION

WRITING A STREAM-OF-CONSCIOUSNESS SEQUEL

Objective

To write a story sequel using stream-of-consciousness techniques

Guidelines for Evaluation

■ suggested length: two or three paragraphs

■ should reflect the story's plot, conflicts, and character portrayals

■ should use stream-of-consciousness techniques to capture a character's thoughts

This Japanese tale set in China concerns the power of art. Wang Shih-ku tells a friend how the art critic Yen-ko described the painting *Autumn Mountain* so glowingly that Wang Shih-ku felt he must see it. Years later the two saw the painting, but both felt that it was not the one Yen-ko had seen before. Since Wang Shih-ku still recalls the earlier work, he does not feel sorry even if it never existed.

LITERARY SKILLS FOR THIS SELECTION

- frame story
- character motivation

THEMES IN THIS SELECTION

- reality and fantasy: imagination and memory
- the nature and value of art

LESSON OBJECTIVES

1. to examine a frame story
2. to understand words from Japanese and Chinese
3. to write a description of a work of art
4. to compare and contrast stories

Teacher's Classroom Resources 1

- Teaching Notes 323
- Prereading Vocabulary 324
- Reading Guide 325
- Check Test 326
- Responding to World Cultures 327
- Literary Focus: Frame Story 328
- Language Study: Words from Japanese and Chinese 329
- Writing Process Guide: Describing a Work of Art 330
- Grammar in Literature: Subject-Verb Agreement with Intervening Expressions 331
- Selection Test 332

TEACHING STUDENTS OF DIFFERENT ABILITIES

- **For less advanced students:** Have students pronounce the character's names and then

Akutagawa Ryūnosuke

(1892–1927)

Japan

Akutagawa Ryūnosuke [ä′kōō tə gä wä rū′nō sū kě′] is one of the most widely translated writers of fiction in modern Japan. Born in the Japanese capital of Tokyo, Akutagawa* attended the Tokyo Imperial University, where he studied English literature and Oriental culture. While still at school, he and two friends started a literary magazine, which they called *Shin Shicho (New Thought)*. A story by Akutagawa in the first issue caught the attention of a celebrated Japanese novelist, Natsume Sōseki, who encouraged Akutagawa to become a writer.

In 1915 Akutagawa published one of his best-known stories, "Rashōmon," which later became the basis of an internationally famous film. His tales are noted for their careful craftsmanship and bizarre twists of plot. Many of the stories reflect Akutagawa's lifelong interest in Oriental history, and several are based on Japanese folk tales. One of Akutagawa's recurring concerns is the satisfaction people derive from art.

* his surname. In Japanese names the surname traditionally precedes the given name.

Japan, China, and Oriental Painting

Located in the western Pacific Ocean, Japan is an island nation off the eastern coast of continental Asia. China is just across the sea, on the Asian mainland, and Japanese students study the history and civilization of the neighboring land as part of their regular school curriculum. Akutagawa was a scholar of Chinese as well as Japanese culture, and his story "Autumn Mountain" is set in China. The story focuses on a mysterious painting by a Chinese master artist of the Mongol dynasty (1260–1368), a period of Chinese history known for its cultural achievements and opulence.

In both China and Japan painting has a long tradition that predates the Mongol dynasty by many centuries. Paintings are traditionally executed in watercolors, often with glue added to increase the colors' opacity, and many are painted on silk or paper scrolls. Over the centuries Oriental artists have enjoyed enormous respect, and the works of old masters have been studied and imitated by generations of later art students.

See LITERATURE AND CULTURE SOURCEBOOK: China and Japan

write a capsule description of each one. Then have them complete the Reading Guide.

- **For more advanced students:** Have students compare and evaluate the attitudes toward reality and illusion expressed in this story, "Hoodoo Valley," and "A Tale of Our Quarter."

East Meets West

Oriental art had a profound impact on nineteenth-century Western artists. Japanese woodcuts, for instance, greatly influenced the works of the French painter Edouard Manet, the Dutch artist Vincent van Gogh, and the American painter Mary Cassatt.

- Ask students to imagine that they are art students as they look at the examples of Oriental art on pages 183, 293, and 370. Which characteristics of these works, if any, would they use? Why?

Akutagawa Ryūnosuke

Autumn Mountain

Translated from the Japanese by Ivan Morris

"And speaking of Ta Chih,[1] have you ever seen his *Autumn Mountain* painting?"

One evening, Wang Shih-ku,[2] who was visiting his friend Yün Nan-tien,[3] asked this question.

"No, I have never seen it. And you?"

Ta Chih, together with Mei-tao-jen and Huang-hao-shan-chiao, had been one of the great painters of the Mongol dynasty.[4] As Yün Nan-tien replied, there passed before his eyes images of the artist's famous works, the *Sandy Shore* painting and the *Joyful Spring* picture scroll.

"Well, strange to say," said Wang Shih-ku, "I'm really not sure whether or not I have seen it. In fact . . ."

"You don't know whether you have seen it or you haven't?" said Yün Nan-tien, looking curiously at his guest. "Do you mean that you've seen an imitation?"

"No, not an imitation. I saw the original. And it is not I alone who have seen it. The great critics Yen-ko[5] and Lien-chou[6] both became involved with the *Autumn Mountain*." Wang Shih-ku sipped his tea and smiled thoughtfully. "Would it bore you to hear about it?"

"Quite the contrary," said Yün Nan-tien, bowing his head politely. He stirred the flame in the copper lamp.

At that time [began Wang Shih-ku] the old master Yüan Tsai[7] was still alive. One evening while he was discussing paintings with Yen-ko, he asked him whether he had ever seen Ta Chih's *Autumn Mountain*. As you know, Yen-ko made a veritable religion of Ta Chih's painting and was certainly not likely to have missed any of his works. But he had never set eyes on this *Autumn Mountain*.

"No, I haven't seen it," he answered shamefacedly, "and I've never even heard of its existence."

"In that case," said Yüan Tsai, "please don't miss the first opportunity you have of seeing it. As a work of art it's on an even higher level than his *Summer Mountain* or *Wandering Storm*. In fact, I'm not sure that it isn't the finest of all Ta Chih's paintings."

"Is it really such a masterpiece? Then I must do my best to see it. May I ask who owns this painting?"

"It's in the house of a Mr. Chang[8] in the County of Jun.[9] If you ever have occasion to visit the Chin-shan Temple, you should call on him and see the picture. Allow me to give you a letter of introduction."

As soon as Yen-ko received Yüan Tsai's letter, he made plans to set out for the County of Jun. A house which harbored so precious a painting as this would, he thought, be bound to have other great works of different periods. Yen-ko was quite giddy with anticipation as he started out.

When he reached the County of Jun, however, he was surprised to find that Mr. Chang's

---

1. **Ta Chih** [tä chē′ä]
2. **Wang Shih-ku** [wong tsū′kū]
3. **Yün Nan-tien** [yən nän′chen]
4. **Mongol dynasty** (1280–1368): era when China was ruled by the royal house established by Kublai Khan, leader of the central Asian people known as the Mongols. (See the Geography and Culture feature that precedes the story.)
5. **Yen-ko** [yen kō′]
6. **Lien-chou** [lin jōō′]

7. **Yüan Tsai** [yūn cha ē′]
8. **Chang** [chang]
9. **Jun** [jun]

Autumn Mountain **181**

CRITICAL THINKING: GUIDED READING QUESTIONS

LITERAL

1a. When Yün Nan-tien asks whether he has ever seen *Autumn Mountain*, what does Wang Shih-ku reply? ("Well, strange to say, I'm really not sure. . . .")

2a. Why is Yen-ko not likely to have missed any of Ta Chih's works? (He makes a "veritable religion" of Ta Chih's painting.)

INFERENTIAL

1b. What effect does this reply have on both Yün Nan-tien and the reader? (It is puzzling and makes Yün Nan-tien and us want to hear the story behind Wang Shih-ku's reply.)

2b. Given Yen-ko's interests, what does his lack of familiarity with *Autumn Mountain* stress about the painting? (It stresses its elusive, mysterious nature.)

PAGE SUMMARY: AT A GLANCE

- When Yen-ko arrives at Mr. Chang's imposing but dilapidated home, his host shows him *Autumn Mountain*.
- Yen-ko is astonished and calls it Ta Chih's finest work.
- The pronouncement seems to surprise Mr. Chang, and Yen-ko feels that his host's subsequent explanation for his reaction is intended to conceal his critical ignorance.
- After leaving, Yen-ko is haunted by the painting and longs to possess it.

IN THE GLOSSARY

- hamlets: small villages
- uncanny: eerie
- inveterate: habitual

5 TEACHING SETTING

Elicit that contrasting details, such as "imposing structure" and "dilapidated," imply that the once wealthy Changs have fallen on hard times.

6 CULTURAL BACKGROUND

Explain that in China and some other countries pale complexions and delicate hands signaled noble birth because they suggest that one does not engage in manual labor. Similarly, in China long fingernails were a sign of nobility.

7 READING SKILL: INFERENCE

Ask what is ambiguous about the wording of Mr. Chang's response. (It sounds as if there may be another *Autumn Mountain* or as if this is not the real one.)

8 TEACHING DESCRIPTION

Note that the details about the painting create a vivid description that helps us picture the scene the painting portrays.

9 CRITICAL THINKING: EVALUATION

Ask students whether they agree that Mr. Chang's explanation attempts to hide a deficiency in critical judgment. (Those who disagree may feel that he is speaking the truth or hiding something else.)

---

5 house, though imposing in structure, was dilapidated. Ivy was coiled about the walls, and in the garden grass and weeds grew rank. As the old man approached, chickens, ducks, and other barnyard fowl looked up, as if surprised to see any stranger enter here. For a moment he could not help doubting Yüan Tsai's words and wondering how a masterpiece of Ta Chih's could possibly have found its way into such a house. Upon a servant's answering his knock, he handed over the letter, explaining that he had come from far in the hope of seeing the *Autumn Mountain*.

He was led almost immediately into the great hall. Here again, though the divans and tables of red sandalwood stood in perfect order, a moldy smell hung over everything and an atmosphere of desolation had settled even on the tiles. The owner of the house, who now appeared, was an unhealthy-looking man; but he had a pleasant air **6** about him and his pale face and delicate hands bore signs of nobility. Yen-ko, after briefly introducing himself, lost no time in telling his host how grateful he would be if he might be shown the famous Ta Chih painting. There was an urgency in the master's words, as if he feared that were he not to see the great painting at once, it might somehow vanish like a mist.

Mr. Chang assented without hesitation and had the painting hung on the bare wall of the great hall.

7 "This," he said, "is the *Autumn Mountain* to which you refer."

At the first glance Yen-ko let out a gasp of admiration. The dominant color was a dark **8** green. From one end to the other a river ran its twisting course; bridges crossed the river at various places and along its banks were little hamlets. Dominating it all rose the main peak of the mountain range, before which floated peaceful wisps of autumn cloud. The mountain and its neighboring hills were fresh green, as if newly washed by rain, and there was an uncanny

beauty in the red leaves of the bushes and thickets scattered along their slopes. This was no ordinary painting, but one in which both design and color had reached an apex of perfection. It was a work of art instinct with the classical sense of beauty.

"Well, what do you think of it? Does it please you?" said Mr. Chang, peering at Yen-ko with a smile.

"Oh, it is truly of godlike quality!" cried Yen-ko, while he stared at the picture in awe. "Yüan Tsai's lavish praise was more than merited. Compared to this painting, everything I have seen until now seems second-rate."

"Really? You find it such a masterpiece?"

Yen-ko could not help turning a surprised look at his host. "Can you doubt it?"

"Oh no, it isn't that I have any doubts," said Mr. Chang, and he blushed with confusion like a schoolboy. Looking almost timidly at the painting, he continued: "The fact is that each time I look at this picture I have the feeling that I am dreaming, though my eyes are wide open. I cannot help feeling that it is I alone who see its beauty, which is somehow too intense for this world of ours. What you just said brought back these strange feelings."

But Yen-ko was not much impressed by his **9** host's evident attempt at self-vindication. His attention was absorbed by the painting, and Mr. Chang's speech seemed to him merely designed to hide a deficiency in critical judgment.

Soon after, Yen-ko left the desolate house.

As the weeks passed, the vivid image of the *Autumn Mountain* remained fresh in Yen-ko's mind [continued Wang Shih-ku after accepting another cup of tea]. Now that he had seen Ta Chih's masterpiece, he felt ready to give up anything whatsoever to possess it. Inveterate collector that he was, he knew that not one of the great works that hung in his own house—not

---

CRITICAL THINKING: GUIDED READING QUESTIONS

LITERAL

1a. When he first sees Mr. Chang's house, what does Yen-ko wonder? (He wonders how a masterpiece of Ta Chih's can have found its way into such a place.)

2a. What is Yen-ko's opinion of *Autumn Mountain*? (He considers it Ta Chih's finest work.)

INFERENTIAL

1b. What causes his doubts? (The home looks too decayed and impoverished to house a great painting.)

2b. Why do you think the painting produces such a powerful effect? (Answers will vary. Students may mention the rich colors, the lifelike details, the compelling design, or the beauty of the natural scene.)

Mt. Omei of Ssuch'uan, 1953, Chang Yuan.

Since ancient times Chinese painters, such as Chang Yuan, have followed specific rules of composition, using an exact vocabulary of brushstrokes and select pictorial themes. These themes were codified according to the ancient Chinese philosophy called the *Tao,* or "the Way." The purpose of the Tao was to help people discover in themselves the order and harmony that exists in nature. Although tightly structured, the best artists were never constricted by conventions. Instead, they used these conventions to find opportunities of expression. In this scroll the artist painted a timeless landscape. It looks naturalistic, yet it closely follows traditional ideals.

■ Ask students in what ways *Autumn Mountain* and *Mt. Omei* are similar, based on the descriptions on page 182. (Answers will vary; students may feel that these phrases describe each peak: "From one end to the other a river ran its twisting course"; the "mountains and its neighboring hills" seem "washed by rain.")

- Despite repeated overtures, Yen-ko is unable to persuade Mr. Chang to sell the painting.
- A year later Yen-ko returns to Mr. Chang's home, but Mr. Chang is away, and the servant will not admit Yen-ko.
- Almost fifty years later, when Wang Shih-ku visits the County of Jun, he decides to try to see the painting described so vividly by Yen-ko, which Wang can already see in his mind.

IN THE GLOSSARY

- transcendent: superior
- sojourning: living temporarily
- overtures: offers
- pallid: pale
- chagrin: deep disappointment

10 TEACHING STUDENTS OF LIMITED ENGLISH PROFICIENCY

You might have nonnative students identify the units of currency, weight, and measure used in the nations from which they came.

11 TEACHING CHARACTER MOTIVATION

Elicit that Yen-ko has a collector's desire to own what he loves, though in fact merely borrowing it should enable him to experience its joys.

12 TEACHING A FRAME STORY

Note that the frame story here interrupts Wang's narrative. When the narrative resumes, almost fifty years have passed.

13 TEACHING PLOT: RISING ACTION

Point out that Wang Shih-ku stops sipping his tea because the suspense in his story builds as the action rises to a climax.

14 CULTURAL BACKGROUND

Explain that with time all paintings suffer deterioration and that it is likely to be more rapid in a dilapidated home like Mr. Chang's than in a more sheltered site.

---

even Li Ying-chiu's *Floating Snowflakes*, for

10 which he had paid five hundred taels[10] of silver—could stand comparison with that transcendent *Autumn Mountain*.

While still sojourning in the County of Jun, he sent an agent to the Chang house to negotiate for the sale of the painting. Despite repeated overtures, he was unable to persuade Mr. Chang to enter into any arrangement. On each occasion that pallid gentleman would reply that while he deeply appreciated the master's admiration of the *Autumn Mountain* and while he would be quite willing to lend the painting, he must ask to be excused from actually parting with it.

11 These refusals only served to strengthen the impetuous Yen-ko's resolve. "One day," he promised himself, "that great picture will hang in my own hall." Confident of the eventual outcome, he finally resigned himself to returning home and temporarily abandoning the *Autumn Mountain*.

About a year later, in the course of a further visit to the County of Jun, he tried calling once more at the house of Mr. Chang. Nothing had changed: the ivy was still coiled in disorder about the walls and fences, and the garden was covered with weeds. But when the servant answered his knock, Yen-ko was told that Chang was not in residence. The old man asked if he might have another look at the *Autumn Mountain* despite the owner's absence, but his importunacy[11] was of no avail: the servant repeated that he had no authority to admit anyone until his master returned. As Yen-ko persisted, the man finally shut the door in his face. Overcome with chagrin, Yen-ko had to leave the house and the great painting that lay somewhere in one of the dilapidated rooms.

---

10. **taels** [tālz]: former Chinese coins, each weighing one tael, an Asian weight unit.
11. **importunacy** [im pôr′tōō nə sē]: the making of insistent demands.

184 *The Short Story*

---

12 Wang Shih-ku paused for a moment.

"All that I have related so far," he said, "I heard from the master Yen-ko himself."

"But tell me," said Yün Nan-tien, stroking his white beard, "did Yen-ko ever really see the *Autumn Mountain*?"

"He said that he saw it. Whether or not he did, I cannot know for certain. Let me tell you the sequel, and then you can judge for yourself."

13 Wang Shih-ku continued his story with a concentrated air, and now he was no longer sipping his tea.

When Yen-ko told me all this [said Wang Shih-ku] almost fifty years had passed since his visits to the County of Jun. The master Yüan Tsai was long since dead and Mr. Chang's large house had already passed into the hands of two successive generations of his family. There was no telling where the *Autumn Mountain* might be—

14 nor if the best parts of the scroll might not have suffered hopeless deterioration. In the course of our talk old Yen-ko described that mysterious painting so vividly that I was almost convinced I could see it before my eyes. It was not the details that had impressed the master but the indefinable beauty of the picture as a whole. Through the words of Yen-ko, that beauty had entered into my heart as well as his.

It happened that, about a month after my meeting with Yen-ko, I had myself to make a journey to the southern provinces, including the County of Jun. When I mentioned this to the old man, he suggested that I go and see if I could not find the *Autumn Mountain*. "If that painting ever comes to light again," he said, "it will indeed be a great day for the world of art."

Needless to say, by this time I also was anxious to see the painting, but my journey was crowded and it soon became clear that I would not find time to visit Mr. Chang's house. Meanwhile, however, I happened to hear a report that the *Autumn Mountain* had come into the hands

---

CRITICAL THINKING: GUIDED READING QUESTIONS

LITERAL

1a. Each time Yen-ko offers to buy *Autumn Mountain*, what does Mr. Chang say he is willing and not willing to do? (He is willing to lend but not sell it.)

2a. What effect do Yen-ko's descriptions of the painting have on Wang Shih-ku? (He is almost convinced that he has seen the painting; its beauty has entered his heart.)

INFERENTIAL

1b. What does this response suggest about Mr. Chang's attitude toward the painting and toward others? (He loves the painting too much to part with it, but he will generously let others share in its joys.)

2b. What does this effect suggest about reality and imagination? (If we imagine something vividly, the experience may seem the same as experiencing it in reality.)

of a certain nobleman by the name of Wang. Having learned of the painting, Mr. Wang had dispatched a messenger with greetings to Chang's grandson. The latter was said to have sent back with the messenger not only the ancient family documents and the great ceremonial caldron which had been in the family for countless generations, but also a painting which fitted the description of Ta Chih's *Autumn Mountain*. Delighted with these gifts, Mr. Wang had arranged a great banquet for Chang's grandson, at which he had placed the young man in the seat of honor and regaled him with the choicest delicacies, gay music, and lovely girls; in addition he had given him one thousand pieces of gold.

On hearing this report I almost leaped with **15** joy. Despite the vicissitudes of half a century, it seemed that the *Autumn Mountain* was still safe! Not only that, but it actually had come within my range. Taking along only the barest necessities, I set out at once to see the painting.

I still vividly remember the day. It was a clear, calm afternoon in early summer and the **16** peonies were proudly in bloom in Mr. Wang's garden. On meeting Mr. Wang, my face broke into a smile of delight even before I had completed my ceremonial bow. "To think that the *Autumn Mountain* is in this very house!" I cried. "Yen-ko spent all those years in vain attempts to see it again—and now I am to satisfy my own ambition without the slightest effort. . . ."

"You come at an auspicious time," replied Mr. Wang. "It happens that today I am expecting Yen-ko himself, as well as the great critic Lien-chou. Please come inside, and since you are the first to arrive you shall be the first to see the painting."

Mr. Wang at once gave instructions for the *Autumn Mountain* to be hung on the wall. And then it all leaped forth before my eyes: the little villages on the river, the flocks of white cloud floating over the valley, the green of the tower-ing mountain range which extended into the distance like a succession of folding-screens— the whole world, in fact, that Ta Chih had created, a world far more wonderful than our own. My heart seemed to beat faster as I gazed intently at the scroll on the wall.

17 These clouds and mists and hills and valleys were unmistakably the work of Ta Chih. Who but Ta Chih could carry the art of drawing to such perfection that every brush-stroke became a thing alive? Who but he could produce colors of such depth and richness, and at the same time hide all mechanical trace of brush and paint? And yet . . . and yet I felt at once that this was not the same painting that Yen-ko had seen once long ago. No, no, a magnificent painting it surely was, yet just as surely not the unique painting which he had described with such religious awe!

Mr. Wang and his entourage had gathered around me and were watching my expression, so I hastened to express my enthusiasm. Naturally I did not want him to doubt the authenticity of his picture, yet it was clear that my words of praise failed to satisfy him. Just then Yen-ko himself was announced—he who had first spoken to me of this *Autumn Mountain*. As the old man bowed to Mr. Wang, I could sense the excitement inside him, but no sooner had his eyes settled on the scroll than a cloud seemed to pass before his face.

"What do you think of it, Master?" asked Mr. Wang, who had been carefully observing him. "We have just heard the teacher Wang Shih-ku's enthusiastic praise, but . . ."

18 "Oh, you are, sir, a very fortunate man to have acquired this painting," answered Yen-ko promptly. "Its presence in your house will add luster to all your other treasures."

Yen-ko's courteous words only seemed to deepen Mr. Wang's anxiety; he, like me, must have heard in them a note of insincerity. I think we were all a bit relieved when Lien-chou, the famous critic, made his appearance at this

Autumn Mountain **185**

CRITICAL THINKING: GUIDED READING QUESTIONS

LITERAL

1a. What does Wang Shih-ku hear that Mr. Wang has obtained from Mr. Chang's grandson? (He has obtained ancient family documents, a ceremonial caldron, and a painting that fits the description of *Autumn Mountain*.)

2a. What makes Wang Shih-ku almost leap with joy? (He is overjoyed to hear that *Autumn Mountain* is safe and that he will be able to see it.)

INFERENTIAL

→ **1b.** What is unclear or ambiguous about the wording used to identify the painting? (It suggests that the painting may not be *Autumn Mountain*.)

→ **2b.** How do you think he feels after viewing the painting? (He is probably greatly disappointed.)

- Mr. Wang is relieved when Lien-chou pronounces the painting to be Ta Chih's greatest.
- Meanwhile, Yen-ko quietly indicates to Wang Shih-ku that the painting is not the same one Yen-ko saw years ago.
- Having concluded his narrative, Wang Shih-ku tells his friend Yün Nan-tien that he can still see the unique painting Yen-ko described.
- "So even if it never existed," Yün Nan-tien observes, "there is not really much cause for regret!"

IN THE GLOSSARY

- juncture: point in time
- hobgoblin: mischievous elf

19 TEACHING A FRAME STORY

Note that Wang Shih-ku's narrative ends here; the next section presents the final scene of the frame story.

20 TEACHING CHARACTER MOTIVATION

Ask students whether there could be reasons other than faulty memory for Yen-ko to have made a mistake about the painting. (Over the years he could have exaggerated the painting's merits because he regretted never having obtained it; in addition, when people build up something in their mind, they are often disappointed by the reality.)

21 TEACHING THEME

Ask what Yün Nan-tien's final remarks suggest about the purpose of art and the difference between reality and illusion. (The line between reality and illusion may not be important; what is important is that art gives joy.)

COLLABORATIVE LEARNING: ENRICHMENT ACTIVITY

Poetry Album Have a group of students write poems inspired by a scene similar to the one depicted in *Autumn Mountain* and then gather their efforts in an illustrated album.

---

juncture. After bowing to us, he turned to the scroll and stood looking at it silently, chewing his long mustaches.

"This, apparently, is the same painting that the master Yen-ko last saw half a century ago," Mr. Wang explained to him. "Now I would much like to hear your opinion of the work. Your candid opinion," Mr. Wang added, forcing a smile.

Lien-chou sighed and continued to look at the picture. Then he took a deep breath and, [20] turning to Mr. Wang, said: "This, sir, is probably Ta Chih's greatest work. Just see how the artist has shaded those clouds. What power there was in his brush! Note also the color of his trees. And then that distant peak which brings the whole composition to life." As he spoke, Lien-chou pointed to various outstanding features of the painting, and needless to say, a look of relief, then of delight, spread over Mr. Wang's face.

Meanwhile I secretly exchanged glances with Yen-ko. "Master," I whispered, "is that the real *Autumn Mountain*?" Almost imperceptibly the old man shook his head, and there was a twinkle in his eyes.

[19] "It's all like a dream," he murmured. "I really can't help wondering if that Mr. Chang wasn't some sort of hobgoblin."

"So that is the story of the *Autumn Mountain*," said Wang Shih-ku after a pause, and took a sip of his tea. "Later on it appears that Mr. Wang made all sorts of exhaustive inquiries. He visited Mr. Chang, but when he mentioned to him the *Autumn Mountain,* the young man denied all knowledge of any other version. So one cannot tell if that *Autumn Mountain* which Yen-ko saw all those years ago is not even now hidden away somewhere. Or perhaps the whole thing was just a case of faulty memory on an old man's part. It would seem unlikely, though, that Yen-ko's story about visiting Mr. Chang's house to see the *Autumn Mountain* was not based on solid fact."

"Well, in any case the image of that strange painting is no doubt engraved forever on Yen-ko's mind. And on yours too."

"Yes," said Wang Shih-ku, "I still see the dark green of the mountain rock, as Yen-ko described it all those years ago. I can see the red leaves of the bushes as if the painting were before my eyes this very moment."

[21] "So even if it never existed, there is not really much cause for regret!"

The two men laughed and clapped their hands with delight.

CRITICAL THINKING: GUIDED READING QUESTIONS

LITERAL

1a. In his final remark what does Yen-ko say Mr. Chang might have been? (He suggests that he might have been "some sort of hobgoblin.")

2a. What does Yün Nan-tien say is "no doubt engraved forever" on the minds of Yen-ko and Wang Shih-ku? (the image of the painting that Yen-ko described)

INFERENTIAL

1b. What do you think Yen-ko means? (Mr. Chang was somehow playing a trick on him.)

2b. Does the story suggest that Yen-ko ultimately regrets never having obtained possession of the painting? Explain. (No; Yün Nan-tien's final remarks suggest that both Yen-ko and Wang Shih-ku have experienced sufficient joy by seeing the painting in their imagination.)

STUDY QUESTIONS

Recalling

1. What does Wang Shih-ku say when his friend asks whether *he* has seen *Autumn Mountain*?
2. What was Yen-ko's first opinion of *Autumn Mountain*? What did the painting's owner ask? What was Yen-ko's impression of the owner?
3. What happened when Yen-ko tried to buy the painting?
4. About how many years passed before Yen-ko saw *Autumn Mountain* again, this time in Wang Shih-ku's company? What were the two men's reactions to the painting then?
5. In the end, what does Wang Shih-ku say that he still sees? What comment does his friend Yün Nan-tien make in response?

Interpreting

6. What attitude toward art do most of the characters in the story share? What does the story suggest about the role of art in human life?
7. Explain in your own words what Yün Nan-tien's comment at the end of the story means. What does his remark suggest about the line between reality and fantasy or illusion?
8. What do you think the explanation might be for the puzzling situation involving *Autumn Mountain*?

Extending

9. In your opinion, what makes some paintings great works of art? Can you describe specific works that illustrate your views?

LITERARY FOCUS

Frame Story

A **frame story** is a story in which one or more other stories unfold. While the frame story may be told from any point of view, a story within a frame story is almost always told by a first-person narrator. That narrator is usually introduced as a character in the frame story and then goes on to tell his or her own story. Sometimes the frame story appears only at the start and the end. At other times it pops up throughout, interrupting the story that it frames. In the latter case the interruptions can be a bit puzzling to read-

ers, although careful reading will usually make the distinctions clear.

Thinking About a Frame Story

1. Identify the portions of "Autumn Mountain" that are the frame story and the portions that are the story within the frame story. From what point of view is the frame story told? From what and whose point of view is the story within it told?
2. Why do you think Akutagawa chose to tell the story from shifting points of view?

LANGUAGE STUDY

Words from Japanese and Chinese

Although Japanese and Chinese belong to different language families, the two have borrowed many words from one another. Japanese and Chinese have also contributed several words to the English language. For example, our word *ketchup* (or *catsup*) comes from the Chinese *ke-tsiap* [ke′tsē äp], which originally meant "brine (or sauce) of fish."

Use a dictionary to determine the meaning and origin of these words from Japanese and Chinese.

1. bonsai	5. origami
2. chow mein	6. shanghai
3. gung-ho	7. tycoon
4. judo	8. typhoon

COMPOSITION

Describing a Work of Art

■ Write a brief description of a painting or other work of art. It may be a famous museum piece or something you saw at school or in someone's home. Describe not only the work itself but also your feelings about it, as the characters do in "Autumn Mountain."

COMPARING STORIES

■ Compare and contrast this story with other stories about reality and fantasy that you have read in this section or elsewhere. What similar or different views do the stories convey on the subject? Cite details to support your conclusions.

Autumn Mountain **187**

COMPOSITION: GUIDELINES FOR EVALUATION

WRITING A RESPONSE TO A STORY

Objective

To write a description of a work of art

Guidelines for Evaluation

■ suggested length: two to four paragraphs
■ should identify the work in some way (by title, artist, and/or location)
■ should describe it using vivid language
■ should state student's feelings about it

Do you think Yen-ko's *Autumn Mountain* ever existed? Explain.

ANSWERS

STUDY QUESTIONS

1. "I'm really not sure."
2. It was the "apex of perfection." "You find it such a masterpiece?" He lacked judgment.
3. The owner would only lend it.
4. fifty; They did not think it was the same one Yen-ko had seen.
5. the painting Yen-ko described; "So . . . there is not really much cause for regret!"
6. love; It brings satisfaction.
7. If Wang's imagination gives him pleasure, it doesn't matter whether the painting existed. It isn't always important.
8. Answers will vary. Yen-ko may have exaggerated; Mr. Chang may have switched paintings.
9. Answers will vary. Students may feel great art communicates in ways words cannot.

LITERARY FOCUS

1. The first, fourth, and sixth sections plus all bracketed remarks are the frame; the rest is the story within; third person; first person, from Wang Shih-ku's point of view.
2. probably to enhance the theme of different perspectives

LANGUAGE STUDY

1. "dwarfing and shaping plants"; from Japanese for "tray arrangement"
2. "fried noodle dish"; from Chinese for "fried noodles"
3. "eager"; from Chinese *kung ho*, "work together"
4. "means of unarmed self-defense"; from Japanese for "gentle art"
5. "art of folding paper into shapes"; from Japanese *ori*, "a folding," and *kami*, "paper"
6. "force someone underhandedly"; from kidnapping men to serve as sailors to Shanghai
7. "important businessman"; from Japanese *taikun*, "shogun," from Chinese for "great ruler"
8. "tropical storm"; from Chinese *tai fung*, "great wind"

COMPARING STORIES

Answers will vary. For example, in this story and "A Tale of Our Quarter," the narrators do not know what happened but are enriched by their experiences.

Autumn Mountain **T-187**

In this French tale of the Franco-Prussian War, an Alsatian boy learns the importance of his language. When Franz arrives at school, he finds that an order to teach only German in Alsace has come from the victorious Prussians, and today will be M. Hamel's last day as Franz's teacher. Franz understands M. Hamel's grammar lesson better than ever before. M. Hamel stresses the value of language to a conquered people and dismisses the class.

LITERARY SKILLS FOR THIS SELECTION

- point of view
- theme

THEMES IN THIS SELECTION

- cultures and conflicts: language, culture, and conquest
- appreciating what we take for granted

LESSON OBJECTIVES

1. to examine origins of names
2. to write a letter from the point of view of a character in the story

Teacher's Classroom Resources 1

- Teaching Notes   335
- Reading Guide   336
- Check Test   337
- Responding to World Cultures   338
- Language Study: Origins of Names 339
- Writing Process Guide: Writing a Letter from a Story Character 340
- Grammar in Literature: Combining Sentences by Using Adverb Clauses 341
- Selection Test   342

France

Alphonse Daudet

(1840–1897)

French author Alphonse Daudet [al fons' dō dā'] is famous for creating short stories and novels with a charming mixture of realism, humor, and sentiment. The son of a silk manufacturer, Daudet was born in Nîmes [nēm], France. He attended school in Lyon [lē ōN'] and began writing poetry and fiction when he was only fourteen. Three years later his parents lost all their money, and Daudet was forced to seek his fortune in Paris. He began contributing to the newspaper *Figaro* and also worked as secretary to the duke of Morny, a job that introduced Daudet to fashionable Paris life. Soon he fell in love with fellow writer Julia Allard, whom he married in 1867.

Four years later Daudet enlisted in the army to fight in the Franco-Prussian War. France's defeat had a profound impact on Daudet, as is clear in his *Contes du lundi* (*Monday Tales*), the story collection he published in 1873. In "The Last Lesson," one of his best-known stories, Daudet shows the change in France's fortunes through the eyes of a young boy from the border region of Alsace.

188   *The Short Story*

GEOGRAPHY AND CULTURE

The Region of Alsace

Located in northeastern France on the border with Germany, the region of Alsace [al sas'] has strong cultural ties to both nations. Inhabitants of Alsace speak dialects of German as well as French, and for several centuries the region of Alsace has alternately been a German and a French territory.

A long period of French rule ended in 1871 after the Franco-Prussian War. The war pitted France against Germany, which had only recently become a unified nation and was still often called Prussia, the name of the most powerful kingdom in the new nation. As the winner of the Franco-Prussian War, Germany—to France's great bitterness—annexed Alsace and the adjoining region of Lorraine [lə rān']. It is at this time that the events of "The Last Lesson" unfold. In the twentieth century the fate of Alsace and Lorraine changed again, and today the regions belong to France.

See LITERATURE AND CULTURE SOURCEBOOK: France

TEACHING STUDENTS OF DIFFERENT ABILITIES

- **For less advanced students:** For this brief, accessible story students might list the means by which M. Hamel stresses the value of language and culture. Also ask students to complete the Reading Guide.

- **For more advanced students:** Have students analyze the story's pro-French viewpoint and consider how the story might have differed if it had presented a pro-German view.

DISCUSSING GEOGRAPHY AND CULTURE

Looking at Borders

Alsace, the region in which this story is set, has been claimed by many peoples. Roman soldiers occupied it when Julius Caesar conquered Gaul in the first century B.C.; later it was part of the Holy Roman Empire for nearly eight hundred years. During both World Wars it was claimed by Germany.

- Ask students what the word *border* conjures up for them. What have they experienced when they have crossed borders between states or countries?

Alphonse Daudet

The Last Lesson

Translated anonymously from the French

I started for school very late that morning and was in great dread of a scolding, especially because M.[1] Hamel had said that he would question us on participles, and I did not know the first word about them. For a moment I thought of running away and spending the day out-of-doors. It was so warm, so bright! The birds were chirping at the edge of the woods; and in the open field back of the sawmill the Prussian soldiers[2] were drilling. It was all much more tempting than the rule for participles, but I had the strength to resist, and hurried off to school.

When I passed the town hall there was a crowd in front of the bulletin board. For the last two years all our bad news had come from there—the lost battles, the draft, the orders of the commanding officer—and I thought to myself, without stopping:

"What can be the matter now?"

Then, as I hurried by as fast as I could go, the blacksmith, Wachter, who was there with his apprentice reading the bulletin, called after me:

"Don't go so fast, boy; you'll get to your school in plenty of time!"

I thought he was making fun of me, and reached M. Hamel's little garden all out of breath.

Usually, when school began, there was a bustle, which could be heard out in the street, the opening and closing of desks, lessons repeated in unison, very loud, with our hands over our ears to understand better, and the teacher's great ruler rapping on the table. But now it was all so still! I had counted on the commotion to get to my desk without being seen; but, of course, that day everything had to be as quiet as Sunday morning. Through the window I saw my classmates, already in their places, and M. Hamel walking up and down with his terrible iron ruler under his arm. I had to open the door and go in before everybody. You can imagine how I blushed and how frightened I was.

But nothing happened. M. Hamel saw me and said very kindly:

"Go to your place quickly, little Franz. We were beginning without you."

I jumped over the bench and sat down at my desk. Not till then, when I had got a little over my fright, did I see that our teacher had on his beautiful green coat, his frilled shirt, and the little black silk cap, all embroidered, that he never wore except on inspection and prize days. Besides, the whole school seemed so strange and solemn. But the thing that surprised me most was to see, on the back benches that were always empty, the village people sitting quietly like ourselves; old Hauser, with his three-cornered hat, the former mayor, the former postmaster, and several others besides. Everybody looked sad; and Hauser had brought an old primer, thumbed at the edges, and he held it open on his knees with his great spectacles lying across the pages.

While I was wondering about it all, M. Hamel mounted his chair, and, in the same grave and gentle tone which he had used to me, said:

"My children, this is the last lesson I shall

---

1. **M.:** abbreviation of *Monsieur* [mə syœ′], French for "mister."
2. **Prussian soldiers:** soldiers from Prussia, largest and most powerful of the Germanic kingdoms that united as Germany early in 1871. (See the Geography and Culture feature that precedes the story.)

The Last Lesson **189**

CRITICAL THINKING: GUIDED READING QUESTIONS

LITERAL

1a. In the first paragraph, what does Franz think of doing instead of going to school? (He thinks of running off and spending the day outdoors.)

2a. What is unusual about the classroom today? (It is quiet, M. Hamel is dressed in fine clothes, and several villagers are sitting in on the class.)

INFERENTIAL

1b. Why does he think about doing this? (He fears a scolding for being ill prepared for the lesson on participles, and he finds the pleasant weather tempting.)

2b. Why do you think the villagers are there? (They are paying respect to M. Hamel, who is apparently giving his last lesson.)

- M. Hamel says he is leaving because the German government, having acquired Alsace, has ordered that only German be taught in its schools.
- Franz is now sorry for not having studied harder, and the schoolbooks that before seemed such a nuisance now suddenly seem like old friends.
- When Franz falters in recitation, M. Hamel speaks of the way in which all of them have procrastinated learning French.
- He comments on the beauty of the language, stresses the value of language to an enslaved people, and for handwriting practice has the students copy "France, Alsace, France, Alsace."

IN THE GLOSSARY

- reproach: blame

5 CRITICAL THINKING: LOGICAL REASONING

Ask why the German government would demand that only German be taught in the schools of the newly acquired Alsace and Lorraine. (to squelch pro-French feeling and assimilate the people into German culture)

6 TEACHING THEME

Elicit the theme implied here: We often fail to appreciate everyday experiences until we lose them.

7 TEACHING POINT OF VIEW

Note that the young narrator comes to several realizations that solve the "mysteries" of the story's opening paragraphs.

8 TEACHING STUDENTS OF LIMITED ENGLISH PROFICIENCY

You might ask nonnative students to describe their own feelings about their native tongue.

9 TEACHING THEME

Have students identify the stated theme concerning the value of language. ("when a people . . . prison")

---

5 give you. The order has come from Berlin[3] to teach only German in the schools of Alsace and Lorraine. The new master comes tomorrow. This is your last French lesson. I want you to be very attentive."

What a thunderclap these words were to me!

Oh, the wretches; that was what they had put up at the town hall!

My last French lesson! Why, I hardly knew how to write! I should never learn any more! I 6 must stop there, then! Oh, how sorry I was for not learning my lessons, for seeking birds' eggs, or going sliding on the Saar![4] My books that had seemed such a nuisance a while ago, so heavy to carry, my grammar,[5] and my history of the saints were old friends now that I couldn't give up. And M. Hamel, too; the idea that he was going away, that I should never see him again, made me forget all about his ruler and how cranky he was.

Poor man! It was in honor of this last lesson that he had put on his fine Sunday clothes, and 7 now I understood why the old men of the village were sitting there in the back of the room. It was because they were sorry, too, that they had not gone to school more. It was their way of thanking our master for his forty years of faithful service and of showing their respect for the country that was theirs no more.

While I was thinking of all this, I heard my name called. It was my turn to recite. What would I not have given to be able to say that dreadful rule for the participle all through, very loud and clear, and without one mistake? But I got mixed up on the first words and stood there, holding on to my desk, my heart beating, and not daring to look up. I heard M. Hamel say to me:

"I won't scold you, little Franz; you must feel bad enough. See how it is! Every day we have

said to ourselves: 'Bah! I've plenty of time. I'll learn it tomorrow.' And now you see where we've come out. Ah, that's the great trouble with Alsace; she puts off learning till tomorrow. Now those fellows out there will have the right to say to you: 'How is it; you pretend to be Frenchmen, and yet you can neither speak nor write your own language?' But you are not the worst, poor little Franz. We've all a great deal to reproach ourselves with.

"Your parents were not anxious enough to have you learn. They preferred to put you to work on a farm or at the mills, so as to have a little more money. And I? I've been to blame also. Have I not often sent you to water my flowers instead of learning your lessons? And when I wanted to go fishing, did I not just give you a holiday?"

8 Then, from one thing to another, M. Hamel went on to talk of the French language, saying that it was the most beautiful language in the world—the clearest, the most logical; that we 9 must guard it among us and never forget it, because when a people are enslaved, as long as they hold fast to their language it is as if they had the key to their prison. Then he opened a grammar and read us our lesson. I was amazed to see how well I understood it. All he said seemed so easy, so easy! I think, too, that I had never listened so carefully, and that he had never explained everything with so much patience. It seemed almost as if the poor man wanted to give us all he knew before going away, and to put it all into our heads at one stroke.

After the grammar, we had a lesson in writing. That day M. Hamel had new copies for us, written in a beautiful round hand:[6] France, Alsace, France, Alsace. They looked like little flags floating everywhere in the schoolroom, hung

---

3. **Berlin:** capital of Germany from 1871 to 1945.
4. **Saar** [sär]: river that flows through northeastern France.
5. **grammar:** book that teaches grammar and writing.

6. **new copies . . . round hand:** new material, written in a beautifully rounded handwriting, for the students to copy as part of penmanship practice.

190 *The Short Story*

CRITICAL THINKING: GUIDED READING QUESTIONS

LITERAL

1a. According to M. Hamel, what did the students and other Alsatians say to themselves every day? ("Bah! I've plenty of time. I'll learn it tomorrow.")

2a. What does M. Hamel have the students copy for their handwriting practice? ("France, Alsace, France, Alsace")

INFERENTIAL

1b. What does the remark suggest about the way people view time in general? (They often procrastinate, assuming that they will have time to do things in the future when in fact they might not.)

2b. Why does he give them these words to practice? (They stress his belief that Alsace should remain part of France, and they encourage the students' patriotic feelings for France.)

from the rod at the top of our desks. You ought to have seen how everyone set to work, and how quiet it was! The only sound was the scratching of the pens over the paper. Once some beetles flew in; but nobody paid any attention to them, not even the littlest ones, who worked right on tracing their fishhooks,[7] as if that was French, too. On the roof the pigeons cooed very low, and I thought to myself:

"Will they make them sing in German, even the pigeons?"

Whenever I looked up from my writing I saw M. Hamel sitting motionless in his chair and gazing first at one thing, then at another, as if he wanted to fix in his mind just how everything looked in that little schoolroom. Fancy! For forty years he had been there in the same place, with his garden outside the window and his class in front of him, just like that. Only the desks and benches had been worn smooth; the walnut trees in the garden were taller, and the hop vine that he had planted himself twined about the windows to the roof. How it must have broken his heart to leave it all, poor man; to hear his sister moving about in the room above, packing their trunks! For they must leave the country next day.

But he had the courage to hear every lesson to the very last. After the writing, we had a lesson in history, and then the babies chanted their ba, be, bi, bo, bu.[8] Down there at the back of the room old Hauser had put on his spectacles and, holding his primer in both hands, spelled the letters with them. You could see that he, too, was crying; his voice trembled with emotion, and it was so funny to hear him that we all wanted to laugh and cry. Ah, how well I remember it, that last lesson!

All at once the church clock struck twelve.

---

7. **tracing their fishhooks:** tracing fishhook shapes as part of their study of penmanship.

8. **ba, be, bi, bo, bu** [bä, bā, bē, bō, boō]: the sounds the young students use to practice their French vowels.

Prussian Guard Drum-Major, c. 1870, G. Oudry.

Then the Angelus.[9] At the same moment the trumpets of the Prussians, returning from drill, sounded under our windows. M. Hamel stood up, very pale, in his chair. I never saw him look so tall.

"My friends," said he, "I—I—" But something choked him. He could not go on.

Then he turned to the blackboard, took a piece of chalk, and, bearing down with all his might, he wrote as large as he could:

"Vive la France!"[10]

Then he stopped and leaned his head against the wall, and, without a word, he made a gesture to us with his hand:

"School is dismissed—you may go."

---

9. **Angelus** [an′jə ləs]: church bell rung at noon.
10. *Vive la France* [vēv′ lä fräns′]: Long live France!

The Last Lesson 191

CRITICAL THINKING: GUIDED READING QUESTIONS

LITERAL

1a. During handwriting practice what is the only sound in the classroom? (Only the scratching of pens over paper can be heard.)

2a. What happens when M. Hamel begins his final speech? (He chokes on his words and cannot go on.)

INFERENTIAL

1b. Why is it so unusually quiet? (The students are sad because M. Hamel is leaving and this is their last French lesson; also, they want to show respect for M. Hamel.)

2b. What do you think he planned to say, and why does he stop? (He probably planned to make a farewell speech; he stops because he is too close to tears to continue.)

What changes in behavior do you think Franz might now make?

ANSWERS

STUDY QUESTIONS

1. There is a great bustle. It is quiet, M. Hamel wears his best clothes, and villagers sit on the back benches.
2. This is the last French lesson, for tomorrow a new teacher will arrive and teach only in German. He is sorry for not having studied harder and no longer finds his books a nuisance.
3. As long as they "hold fast to their language," they have "the key to their prison."
4. "France, Alsace, France, Alsace"; *"Vive la France!"*
5. He is patriotic. They have come to show respect for M. Hamel and the French language.
6. An innocent young narrator wins the reader's sympathy. Since Franz observes but does not understand many events, his puzzlement creates a mystery readers want to solve.
7. People often fail to realize how precious time is until little is left; we fail to appreciate everyday experiences because they have grown routine.
8. Students learn better if they have an emotional stake and see relevance in what they learn. Answers will vary, but many should find the change realistic because being forced to give up one's language can shock one into changing.
9. Answers will vary. Among other things, language is a vital part of personal and cultural identity and gives people a sense of unity and pride.

LANGUAGE STUDY

Daudet makes the narrator a symbol of France and thus suggests that Alsace is truly French; by using the German *Franz* instead of *François*, he may want to imply (not necessarily accurately) that even Alsatians of German background considered themselves French; finally, he may want to suggest that Franz, along with every Alsatian, is a "free man."

STUDY QUESTIONS

Recalling

1. What usually happens in Franz's class when school begins? What is the classroom like now, and what surprising things does Franz see there?
2. What does M. Hamel announce at the start of the lesson? How do Franz's feelings toward schoolwork and schoolbooks suddenly change?
3. What does M. Hamel say about the importance of language to an "enslaved" people?
4. What words does M. Hamel have the students copy as part of their penmanship practice? What final words does he write on the board?

Interpreting

5. In one word, describe M. Hamel's feelings about being French. Why have Hauser and the other townspeople come to attend the lesson?
6. How does telling the story from young Franz's point of view affect the reader's reaction to the story? How does this point of view help build suspense at the start of the story?
7. What does the story suggest about the way human beings treat time and the way they perceive routine events?
8. What does the story suggest about how students can be motivated to learn? Do you find young Franz's change in attitude realistic? Explain.

Extending

9. History is full of instances in which victorious na-

tions outlawed or tried to suppress the language of a conquered people. Why do you think language can seem so important? How would you feel if you were forced to give up your language?

LANGUAGE STUDY

Origins of Names

Most names have meanings rooted in their histories. For example, the English names *Francis, Frank,* and *Frances* come from the Latin name *Francus. Francus* meant "a Frank" and hence "a free man," since the Franks were members of a ruling tribe in the region that was called Gaul in ancient times. Today we know that region as *France,* a name that also derives from the Franks who lived there.

■ The name *Franz* is a German form of *Francis* and has the same history. It is a common name in Alsace, where both French and German dialects are spoken. Why do you think Daudet chose the name *Franz* for his narrator?

COMPOSITION

Writing a Letter from a Story Character

■ Imagine that you are M. Hamel on the day story events take place. Write a letter to a friend in Paris or another French area not annexed by Germany. Describe events of the day and your feelings about them.

COMPOSITION: GUIDELINES FOR EVALUATION

WRITING A LETTER FROM A STORY CHARACTER

Objective

To write a letter from the point of view of a character in the story

Guidelines for Evaluation

■ suggested length: one or two pages

■ should use the tone and format of a friendly letter
■ should be written in the first person, from M. Hamel's point of view
■ should reflect M. Hamel's experiences and ideas as revealed in the story

PREVIEW: THE AUTHOR AND THE WORLD

Ernest Hemingway

(1899–1961)

United States

Hemingway is one of America's most famous stylists. He led an adventurous life that is often reflected in the exploits of his heroes. The typical Hemingway hero is a quietly courageous individual who displays "grace under pressure" and rarely expresses emotions. Rugged on the outside, sensitive underneath, the Hemingway hero has inspired scores of writers.

Hemingway was born in Oak Park, Illinois, and later worked as a reporter in Kansas City. He was wounded in Italy in World War I, an experience that left emotional as well as physical scars. War became a central topic of Hemingway's fiction, including his ground-breaking story collection *In Our Time* (1925).

A lifelong lover of adventure, Hemingway watched bullfights in Spain and hunted big game in Africa. When the Spanish Civil War broke out, he raised money for the Loyalist cause and became a war correspondent. His experiences in Spain inspired his novel *For Whom the Bell Tolls,* as well as the following story. In 1954, after publication of his novel *The Old Man and the Sea,* he was awarded the Nobel Prize.

GEOGRAPHY AND CULTURE

The Spanish Civil War

Located in the southwestern corner of continental Europe, Spain was the scene of a tragic civil war that lasted from 1936 to 1939. The Spanish Civil War pitted the Loyalist supporters of Spain's king and democratic government against the Fascists [fash'ists]. Led by General Francisco Franco, the Fascists favored a totalitarian government. Although the Loyalist cause drew many idealistic volunteers from abroad, in the end the Fascists proved victorious. Franco became Spain's dictator, and he remained in power until his death in 1975. After Franco's death, a democratic government was established with the help of Spain's king, Juan Carlos. (Like Queen Elizabeth in Great Britain, Juan Carlos now plays a largely ceremonial role in Spanish politics.)

The many wars fought in Europe in the first half of the twentieth century made millions of people homeless. Though the following story is set in northeastern Spain during the Spanish Civil War, the incident it recounts might have happened anywhere in war-torn Europe.

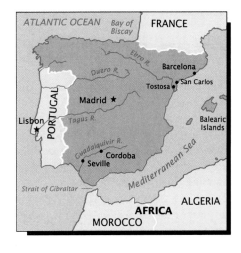

See LITERATURE AND CULTURE SOURCEBOOK: Spain

Old Man at the Bridge **193**

In this tale of the Spanish Civil War, an old man who wants to live in peace becomes a victim of war. After crossing a bridge to learn how far the enemy has advanced, the narrator meets an old man too tired to go any farther. The old man, "without politics," has fled artillery fire and is deeply concerned about the animals he had to leave behind. The narrator concludes that nothing can be done to help him.

LITERARY SKILLS FOR THIS SELECTION

- style and tone
- setting

THEMES IN THIS SELECTION

- cultures and conflicts: the tragedy of war
- the value of compassion

LESSON OBJECTIVES

1. to examine an author's style and tone
2. to rewrite a story using a different tone
3. to compare and contrast stories

Teacher's Classroom Resources 1

- Teaching Notes   345
- Reading Guide   346
- Check Test   347
- Responding to World Cultures   348
- Literary Focus: Style and Tone   349
- Writing Process Guide: Rewriting in a Different Tone   350
- Grammar in Literature: Compound Sentences   351
- Selection Test   352

IN THE CLASSROOM

TEACHING STUDENTS OF DIFFERENT ABILITIES

- **For less advanced students:** For this brief, simply worded story, students might list inferences they can make about the old man. Then have them complete the Reading Guide.

- **For more advanced students:** Have students research and report on Hemingway's influence on world literature or the influence of Modernism—discussed on page 585 of students' text—on Hemingway.

DISCUSSING GEOGRAPHY AND CULTURE

Volunteers and the Spanish Civil War

Many foreigners fought on the Loyalist side in the Spanish Civil War. About thirty-five thousand men volunteered to fight in the International Brigades; of them twenty-eight hundred were American. Many writers were drawn to the struggle, and some, including Hemingway and the British author George Orwell, wrote moving descriptions of it.

- Ask students under what circumstances—if any—they would volunteer to fight in a war.

Citizens of Madrid Fleeing the Suburbs, Robert Capa.

Ernest Hemingway

Old Man at the Bridge

An old man with steel rimmed spectacles and very dusty clothes sat by the side of the road. There was a pontoon bridge[1] across the river and carts, trucks, and men, women and children were crossing it. The mule-drawn carts staggered up the steep bank from the bridge with soldiers helping push against the spokes of the wheels. The trucks ground up and away heading out of it all and the peasants plodded along in the ankle deep dust. But the old man sat there without moving. He was too tired to go any farther.

It was my business to cross the bridge, explore the bridgehead beyond and find out to what point the enemy had advanced. I did this and returned over the bridge. There were not so many carts now and very few people on foot, but the old man was still there.

"Where do you come from?" I asked him.

"From San Carlos,"[2] he said, and smiled.

That was his native town and so it gave him pleasure to mention it and he smiled.

"I was taking care of animals," he explained.

---

1. **pontoon bridge:** temporary bridge supported by flat-bottomed boats, hollow cylinders, or other floating objects.

194 *The Short Story*

---

2. **San Carlos:** small city in northeastern Spain.

CRITICAL THINKING: GUIDED READING QUESTIONS

LITERAL

1a. What is the narrator's "business"? (It is to cross the bridge, explore the bridgehead beyond, and learn how far the enemy has advanced.)

INFERENTIAL

1b. What can we infer about the narrator's role in the war? (He is a scout for one of the armies, later revealed to be that of the Loyalists.)

"Oh," I said, not quite understanding.

"Yes," he said, "I stayed, you see, taking care of animals. I was the last one to leave the town of San Carlos."

He did not look like a shepherd nor a herdsman and I looked at his black dusty clothes and his gray dusty face and his steel rimmed spectacles and said, "What animals were they?"

"Various animals," he said, and shook his head. "I had to leave them."

3   I was watching the bridge and the African looking country of the Ebro Delta[3] and wondering how long now it would be before we would see the enemy, and listening all the while for the first noises that would signal that ever mysterious event called contact, and the old man still sat there.

"What animals were they?" I asked.

"There were three animals altogether," he explained. "There were two goats and a cat and then there were four pairs of pigeons."

"And you had to leave them?" I asked.

"Yes. Because of the artillery. The captain told me to go because of the artillery."

"And you have no family?" I asked, watching the far end of the bridge where a few last carts were hurrying down the slope of the bank.

"No," he said, "only the animals I stated. The cat, of course, will be all right. A cat can look out for itself, but I cannot think what will become of the others."

"What politics have you?" I asked.

"I am without politics," he said. "I am seventy-six years old. I have come twelve kilometers now and I think now I can go no further."

"This is not a good place to stop," I said. "If you can make it, there are trucks up the road where it forks for Tortosa."[4]

"I will wait a while," he said, "and then I will go. Where do the trucks go?"

"Towards Barcelona,"[5] I told him.

"I know no one in that direction," he said, "but thank you very much. Thank you again very much."

He looked at me very blankly and tiredly, then said, having to share his worry with some one, "The cat will be all right, I am sure. There is no need to be unquiet about the cat. But the others. Now what do you think about the others?"

"Why they'll probably come through it all right."

"You think so?"

"Why not," I said, watching the far bank where now there were no carts.

"But what will they do under the artillery when I was told to leave because of the artillery?"

"Did you leave the dove cage unlocked?" I asked.

"Yes."

"Then they'll fly."

"Yes, certainly they'll fly. But the others. It's better not to think about the others," he said.

5   "If you are rested I would go," I urged. "Get up and try to walk now."

"Thank you," he said and got to his feet, swayed from side to side and then sat down backwards in the dust.

"I was taking care of animals," he said dully, but no longer to me. "I was only taking care of animals."

There was nothing to do about him. It was 6 Easter Sunday and the Fascists[6] were advancing toward the Ebro. It was a gray overcast day with a low ceiling so their planes were not up. That and the fact that cats know how to look after themselves was all the good luck that old man would ever have.

---

5. **Barcelona** [bär′sə lōʹnə]: large city in northeastern Spain.

6. **Fascists** [fashʹists]: in the Spanish Civil War (1936–1939), forces supporting General Francisco Franco (1892–1975) and his totalitarian political ideology.

3. **Ebro Delta:** land at the mouth of the Ebro, a river that flows through northern Spain.

4. **Tortosa:** city on the Ebro River in northeastern Spain.

Old Man at the Bridge **195**

PAGE SUMMARY: AT A GLANCE

- The old man has no family and is "without politics."
- Forced to leave his animals behind, he hopes that his cat will take care of itself but is deeply concerned about his goats and birds.
- The narrator concludes that nothing can be done about the old man.

IN THE GLOSSARY

- artillery: mounted firearms capable of shooting projectiles

3 TEACHING STYLE

Point out that one aspect of Hemingway's style is his frequent use of simple statements strung together with the conjunction *and* to form long, rolling sentences.

4 CULTURAL BACKGROUND

Remind students that most Europeans have used the metric system for many decades. Twelve kilometers is about 7.5 miles.

5 READING SKILL: INFERENCE

Ask why the narrator urges the man to go. (That there is likely to be fighting nearby is suggested by the other refugees' flight and by the narrator's explorations across the bridge to see how far the enemy has advanced.)

6 TEACHING IRONY AND TONE

Elicit the sadness and irony of warfare on Easter Sunday, a holy day for Christians that is associated with peace. The matter-of-fact narrator again says nothing about the sadness or irony; he simply mentions a fact and forces us to make our own inferences.

COLLABORATIVE LEARNING: ENRICHMENT ACTIVITY

Literary Guide Have a group of students create a literary guide to Hemingway's world travels. Each student should contribute an article on a different place associated with Hemingway—Oak Park, upper Michigan, northern Italy, Paris, Spain, Africa, Key West, Cuba, and so on.

CRITICAL THINKING: GUIDED READING QUESTIONS

LITERAL

1a. When the narrator asks whether the old man has any family, what does he reply? ("No, only the animals I stated.")

2a. What are the old man's last remarks? ("I was taking care of animals. I was only taking care of animals.")

INFERENTIAL

→ **1b.** What can we infer from the old man's equating the animals with family? (He cares deeply about them.)

→ **2b.** By adding *only* in repeating his remark, what is the old man protesting? (being a victim of warfare when he did nothing to cause anyone to wish to harm him; warfare's unfairness to innocent civilians)

Do you agree that nothing could be done about the old man? Explain your opinion.

ANSWERS

STUDY QUESTIONS

1. He is scouting the land across the bridge to learn how far the enemy has advanced.
2. Artillery was shelling the town, but he stayed as long as he could to care for his animals. He has no politics.
3. Nothing can be done about him; the only luck he will ever have is that the weather has prevented war planes from flying on that day and his cat can look after itself.
4. He is simple, apolitical, and loyal to those he loves. They are its unfair victims.
5. It is destructive of nature and is itself unnatural.
6. His interest in the man and his efforts to comfort him suggest that he feels compassion and wishes he could help him.
7. Answers will vary. Students might feel that advanced communications technology has sharpened people's awareness of the brutality of warfare; moreover, civilian casualties, an incidental aspect of warfare in the past, have become a common feature of modern wars fought with weapons of mass destruction.

LITERARY FOCUS

The tone is matter-of-fact. "There was nothing to do about him." The sentence implies sorrow and regret. It stresses the ironic sadness of the facts that warfare shows no respect for a holy day, turns a usually joyous occasion into a tragic one, and contradicts religious teachings of peace.

COMPARING STORIES

Answers will vary. Students might compare Hemingway's style to Thomas Wolfe's in "The Far and the Near," noting that Wolfe uses more complex, poetic, and emotional language and often directly describes the feelings of the main characters.

STUDY QUESTIONS

Recalling

1. What task is the narrator performing when he encounters the old man?
2. Why was the old man forced to leave San Carlos, and why was he the last civilian to leave? What are his "politics"?
3. In the final paragraphs, what does the narrator conclude about the old man?

Interpreting

4. What sort of person is the old man? What does the story suggest about the effects of war on such people?
5. What does the story suggest about the relationship between war and nature?
6. Do you think the narrator wishes he could do something for the old man, or does he really not care about the old man's fate? Explain.

Extending

7. Do you think people today are more concerned about the effects of war than people were in the past? Explain your opinion.

LITERARY FOCUS

Style and Tone

Style refers to an author's characteristic way of writing. Important aspects of a prose writer's style include word choice, sentence structure, sentence length, and tone. **Tone** is the attitude that an author or narrator takes toward his or her subject. For example, the tone of a story may be formal or casual, matter-of-fact or emotional, witty, sarcastic, angry, or sad.

Ernest Hemingway is famous for a journalistic prose style characterized by simple yet precise word choice, simple but carefully constructed sentences, and a matter-of-fact tone. Notice, for example, the word choice and sentence patterns in the first paragraph of "Old Man at the Bridge." Except for the precise technical term "pontoon bridge," the language is quite simple. The sentences are also simply constructed, and many of the clauses are linked by the conjunction *and* to create a rolling effect. Hemingway then modifies this pattern in the last two sentences—simple, brief statements that put a rhythmical close to the paragraph. The brevity of the final sentences emphasizes their importance and stresses their content: The last paragraph comes to a stop just as the old man does.

The final sentence of the paragraph also helps illustrate Hemingway's matter-of-fact tone. The sentence expresses a mere fact. The narrator does not *say* that the situation is sad or that he feels sorry for the old man. It is up to the reader to *infer* the emotions of sympathy and sadness that underlie the narrator's words.

Thinking About Style and Tone

■ Consider how the story's last paragraph illustrates Hemingway's style. What tone does the narrator use? Which sentence is stressed by its brevity? What emotions underlie that sentence and the rest of the paragraph? How does the fact that it is Easter Sunday help us infer the underlying emotions?

COMPOSITION

Rewriting in a Different Tone

■ Imagine that you were trying to raise funds for refugees of the Spanish Civil War. Rewrite the incident recounted in "Old Man at the Bridge" using an emotional tone more suited to your purpose. Instead of having a soldier as first-person narrator, you might be a charity worker on the scene.

COMPARING STORIES

■ Choose another twentieth-century story you have read, and compare and contrast the author's style to Hemingway's. Be sure to cite specific examples in discussing diction, sentence structure, sentence length, and tone.

COMPOSITION: GUIDELINES FOR EVALUATION

REWRITING IN A DIFFERENT TONE

Objective
To rewrite a story using a different tone

Guidelines for Evaluation
■ suggested length: one to two pages

■ should recount the story's main incident from the first-person point of view of someone else on the scene, such as a charity worker
■ should use words and sentence structures that convey an emotional tone

PREVIEW: THE AUTHOR AND THE WORLD

Gabriel García Márquez
(born 1928)

Colombia

The Nobel Prize for Literature in 1982 went to Gabriel García Márquez [gä brē el′ gär sē′ä mär′kes], who is usually hailed as one of Latin America's greatest living authors. García Márquez* grew up in Aracataca, a small village in northern Colombia. He was raised by his maternal grandmother, who recounted magical tales that fascinated the young boy. Although a scholarship brought him a college education and the opportunity to study law, he soon returned to his interest in storytelling. He published stories in several Colombian newspapers and also worked as a journalist in the capital, Bogotá [bō gə tä′].

García Márquez won international fame with his novel *One Hundred Years of Solitude*. The novel takes place in an imaginary village clearly modeled on Aracataca. Though García Márquez now lives in Mexico City, he pays frequent visits to Colombia and continues to set most of his fiction there.

---

* In accordance with Spanish custom, the author's surname includes both his father's family name, García, and his mother's family name, Márquez.

GEOGRAPHY AND CULTURE

Colombia and Its Caribbean Coastline

Located in the northwestern corner of South America, the nation of Colombia borders both the Pacific Ocean and the Caribbean Sea. The nations of Panama, Venezuela, Brazil, Peru and Ecuador form parts of its boundaries. Its capital is Bogotá, which is located on a high plateau in the Andes Mountains. Named after the explorer Christopher Columbus, the country of Colombia is famous for its coffee and for the purity of the Spanish that is spoken there. Aracataca, García Márquez's childhood home, is on Colombia's Caribbean coastline, near the city of Cartagena [kär tä hä′nä].

The area around Aracataca has a hot and humid climate, particularly further inland away from the sea breezes. In the following story, two train passengers travel inland past the region's many banana plantations. They arrive in a small village on a stifling Tuesday afternoon, when most people are taking their afternoon rest, or siesta.

See *LITERATURE AND CULTURE SOURCEBOOK: Latin America*

Tuesday Siesta **197**

- Teaching Notes 355
- Prereading Vocabulary 356
- Reading Guide 357
- Check Test 358
- Responding to World Cultures 359
- Language Study: Words from Spanish 360
- Writing Process Guides: Writing About Tone 361 Writing an Epitaph 362
- Grammar in Literature: Adverb Clauses 363
- Selection Test 364

MOTIVATION: PRIOR KNOWLEDGE

Ask students to think of real or fictional people they admire and to explain the qualities in them they find admirable.

PAGE SUMMARY: AT A GLANCE

- On a hot day a mother and her twelve-year-old daughter, both dressed in poor mourning clothes, travel by train past endless banana plantations.
- After the two eat their simple lunch, the mother tells the daughter to put on her shoes and comb her hair.

IN THE GLOSSARY

- **symmetrical:** corresponding in size, shape, and position
- **cassock:** simple, ankle-length garment worn by clergymen
- **conscientious:** honest or painstaking
- **serenity:** peacefulness

1 TEACHING SETTING AND ATMOSPHERE

Note that details of the setting such as "interminable banana plantations" and "stifling blast" help create a harsh atmosphere.

2 CULTURAL BACKGROUND

Explain that in many countries, including the United States, trains have various grades of service, depending on the price travelers pay. Third-class seats are the cheapest.

3 TEACHING CHARACTERIZATION

Note that the mother's and daughter's clothing, along with details such as the third-class car and the plastic sack, show that they are poor.

4 GRAMMAR IN LITERATURE

Have students explain the sentence variety that helps make this paragraph interesting. (The first and third sentences are complex and begin with adverbial clauses; the second and fourth are simple and begin with their subject; the fifth is complex and begins with a prepositional phrase.)

Gabriel García Márquez

Tuesday Siesta

Translated from the Spanish by J. S. Bernstein

The train emerged from the quivering tunnel of sandy rocks, began to cross the symmetrical, **1** interminable banana plantations, and the air became humid and they couldn't feel the sea breeze any more. A stifling blast of smoke came in the car window. On the narrow road parallel to the railway there were oxcarts loaded with green bunches of bananas. Beyond the road, in uncultivated spaces set at odd intervals there were offices with electric fans, red-brick buildings, and residences with chairs and little white tables on the terraces among dusty palm trees and rosebushes. It was eleven in the morning, and the heat had not yet begun.

"You'd better close the window," the woman said. "Your hair will get full of soot."

The girl tried to, but the shade wouldn't move because of the rust.

2 They were the only passengers in the lone third-class car. Since the smoke of the locomotive kept coming through the window, the girl left her seat and put down the only things they had with them: a plastic sack with some things to eat and a bouquet of flowers wrapped in newspaper. She sat on the opposite seat, away **3** from the window, facing her mother. They were both in severe and poor mourning clothes.

The girl was twelve years old, and it was the first time she'd ever been on a train. The woman seemed too old to be her mother, because of the blue veins on her eyelids and her small, soft, and shapeless body, in a dress cut like a cassock. She was riding with her spinal column braced firmly against the back of the seat, and held a peeling patent-leather handbag in her lap with both hands. She bore the conscientious serenity of someone accustomed to poverty.

By twelve the heat had begun. The train stopped for ten minutes to take on water at a station where there was no town. Outside, in the mysterious silence of the plantations, the shadows seemed clean. But the still air inside the car smelled like untanned leather. The train did not pick up speed. It stopped at two identical towns with wooden houses painted bright colors. The woman's head nodded and she sank into sleep. The girl took off her shoes. Then she went to the washroom to put the bouquet of flowers in some water.

4 When she came back to her seat, her mother was waiting to eat. She gave her a piece of cheese, half a corn-meal pancake, and a cookie, and took an equal portion out of the plastic sack for herself. While they ate, the train crossed an iron bridge very slowly and passed a town just like the ones before, except that in this one there was a crowd in the plaza. A band was playing a lively tune under the oppressive sun. At the other side of town the plantations ended in a plain which was cracked from the drought.

The woman stopped eating.

"Put on your shoes," she said.

The girl looked outside. She saw nothing but the deserted plain, where the train began to pick up speed again, but she put the last piece of cookie into the sack and quickly put on her shoes. The woman gave her a comb.

"Comb your hair," she said.

The train whistle began to blow while the girl was combing her hair. The woman dried the

198   *The Short Story*

CRITICAL THINKING: GUIDED READING QUESTIONS

LITERAL

1a. What prevents the window from closing? (rust)

2a. After they pass the town with the band, what does the mother ask her daughter to do? (She asks her to put on her shoes and comb her hair.)

INFERENTIAL

1b. What does this detail stress about the third-class accommodations? (They are uncomfortable.)

2b. Why do you think the mother makes these requests? (They are approaching their destination.)

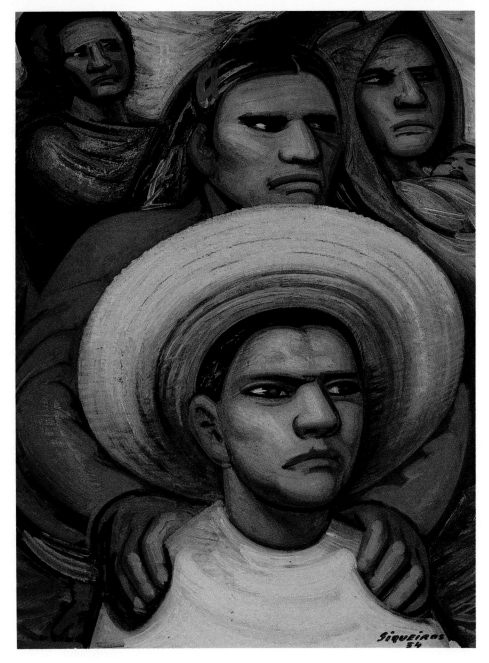

El Reto ("The Challenge"), 1954, David Alfaro Siqueiros.

The Mexican painter and muralist David Alfaro Siqueiros (1896–1974) devoted his art to the cause of the worker. He traveled throughout Latin America creating murals designed to encourage laborers' unity. Committed to socialist ideals, he often used his art to exhort the common people to fight for their rights. His style is simple, almost illustrative, yet the content carries great force. Siqueiros stiffly outlined his characters and modeled the color to add a sculptural dimension. For example, the staunch poses and unmoving eye of the characters in *El Reto* portray the resilience and determination of the common people.

■ Ask students in what way the quiet, determined expressions of Siqueiros' characters relate to the behavior of the mother. (Like them she is determined—not to let anyone or anything keep her from visiting her son's grave.)

- As the train nears a "larger but sadder" town, the woman tells her daughter to accept nothing to drink no matter how thirsty she is and above all not to cry.
- In the town everyone is escaping the August heat by taking a siesta.
- When the two arrive at the parish house and ask for the priest, a plump woman tells them to return after three o'clock, for the priest has just begun his nap.
- After the mother explains that their train leaves at three-thirty, the plump woman agrees to let them see the priest.

IN THE GLOSSARY

- permeated: spread throughout

5 TEACHING SETTING

Elicit the insight that this larger town may be "sadder" simply because it looks dingier or because more poverty and crime are often found in large towns and cities.

6 TEACHING ATMOSPHERE

Note that details such as "floating in the heat" and the description of the abandoned street contribute to a strong impression of the town's desolate, sleepy atmosphere.

7 TEACHING STUDENTS OF LIMITED ENGLISH PROFICIENCY

In conjunction with the Language Study, point out that *siesta, plaza,* and *patio* are all Spanish words that have entered English. Have native Spanish speakers name more examples of such words.

8 READING SKILL: PREDICTING OUTCOMES

Have students use the details provided so far to try to predict the reason the mother and daughter have come to the town.

9 TEACHING CHARACTERIZATION

Note that the woman's dignified, self-possessed behavior prompts good will and respect from others.

---

sweat from her neck and wiped the oil from her face with her fingers. When the girl stopped combing, the train was passing the outlying 5 houses of a town larger but sadder than the earlier ones.

"If you feel like doing anything, do it now," said the woman. "Later, don't take a drink anywhere even if you're dying of thirst. Above all, no crying."

The girl nodded her head. A dry, burning wind came in the window, together with the locomotive's whistle and the clatter of the old cars. The woman folded the plastic bag with the rest of the food and put it in the handbag. For a moment a complete picture of the town, on that bright August Tuesday, shone in the window. The girl wrapped the flowers in the soaking-wet newspapers, moved a little farther away from the window, and stared at her mother. She received a pleasant expression in return. The train began to whistle and slowed down. A moment later it stopped.

There was no one at the station. On the other side of the street, on the sidewalk shaded by the almond trees, only the pool hall was 6 open. The town was floating in the heat. The woman and the girl got off the train and crossed the abandoned station—the tiles split apart by the grass growing up between—and over to the shady side of the street.

It was almost two. At that hour, weighted 7 down by drowsiness, the town was taking a siesta. The stores, the town offices, the public school were closed at eleven, and didn't reopen until a little before four, when the train went back. Only the hotel across from the station, with its bar and pool hall, and the telegraph office at one side of the plaza stayed open. The houses, most of them built on the banana company's model, had their doors locked from inside and their blinds drawn. In some of them it was so hot that the residents ate lunch in the patio. Others leaned a chair against the wall, in

the shade of the almond trees, and took their siesta right out in the street.

Keeping to the protective shade of the almond trees, the woman and the girl entered the town without disturbing the siesta. They went directly to the parish house. The woman scratched the metal grating on the door with her fingernail, waited a moment, and scratched again. An electric fan was humming inside. They did not hear the steps. They hardly heard the slight creaking of a door, and immediately a cautious voice, right next to the metal grating: 8 "Who is it?" The woman tried to see through the grating.

"I need the priest," she said.

"He's sleeping now."

"It's an emergency," the woman insisted.

Her voice showed a calm determination.

The door was opened a little way, noiselessly, and a plump, older woman appeared, with very pale skin and hair the color of iron. Her eyes seemed too small behind her thick eyeglasses.

"Come in," she said, and opened the door all the way.

They entered a room permeated with an old smell of flowers. The woman of the house led them to a wooden bench and signaled them to sit down. The girl did so, but her mother remained standing, absent-mindedly, with both hands clutching the handbag. No noise could be heard above the electric fan.

The woman of the house reappeared at the door at the far end of the room. "He says you should come back after three," she said in a very low voice. "He just lay down five minutes ago."

"The train leaves at three-thirty," said the woman.

9 It was a brief and self-assured reply, but her voice remained pleasant, full of undertones. The woman of the house smiled for the first time.

"All right," she said.

When the far door closed again, the woman

CRITICAL THINKING: GUIDED READING QUESTIONS

LITERAL

1a. What does the mother tell her daughter "above all" not to do? (cry)

2a. When the mother says, "It's an emergency," what does her voice show? (calm determination)

INFERENTIAL

1b. What qualities does this demand suggest about the mother's values? (She values pride and dignity.)

2b. What does the mother's behavior here reveal about her? (She is persistent and dignified.)

sat down next to her daughter. The narrow waiting room was poor, neat, and clean. On the other side of the wooden railing which divided the room, there was a worktable, a plain one 10 with an oilcloth cover, and on top of the table a primitive typewriter next to a vase of flowers. The parish records were beyond. You could see that it was an office kept in order by a spinster.

The far door opened and this time the priest 11 appeared, cleaning his glasses with a handkerchief. Only when he put them on was it evident that he was the brother of the woman who had opened the door.

"How can I help you?" he asked.

"The keys to the cemetery," said the woman.

The girl was seated with the flowers in her lap and her feet crossed under the bench. The priest looked at her, then looked at the woman, and then through the wire mesh of the window at the bright, cloudless sky.

"In this heat," he said. "You could have waited until the sun went down."

The woman moved her head silently. The priest crossed to the other side of the railing, took out of the cabinet a notebook covered in oilcloth, a wooden penholder, and an inkwell, and sat down at the table. There was more than enough hair on his hands to account for what was missing on his head.

"Which grave are you going to visit?" he asked.

"Carlos Centeno's," said the woman.

"Who?"

"Carlos Centeno," the woman repeated.

The priest still did not understand.

12 "He's the thief who was killed here last week," said the woman in the same tone of voice. "I am his mother."

The priest scrutinized her. She stared at him with quiet self-control, and the Father blushed. He lowered his head and began to write. As he filled the page, he asked the woman to identify herself, and she replied unhesitatingly, with precise details, as if she were reading them. The 13 Father began to sweat. The girl unhooked the buckle of her left shoe, slipped her heel out of it, and rested it on the bench rail. She did the same with the right one.

It had all started the Monday of the previous week, at three in the morning, a few blocks from there. Rebecca, a lonely widow who lived in a house full of odds and ends, heard above the sound of the drizzling rain someone trying to force the front door from outside. She got up, rummaged around in her closet for an ancient revolver that no one had fired since the days of Colonel Aureliano Buendía,[1] and went into the living room without turning on the lights. Orienting herself not so much by the noise at the lock as by a terror developed in her by twenty-eight years of loneliness, she fixed in her imagination not only the spot where the door was but also the exact height of the lock. She clutched the weapon with both hands, closed her eyes, and squeezed the trigger. It was the first time in her life that she had fired a gun. Immediately after the explosion, she could hear nothing except the murmur of the drizzle on the galvanized roof. Then she heard a little metallic bump on the cement porch, and a very low voice, pleasant but terribly exhausted: "Ah, Mother." The man they found dead in front of the house in the morning, his nose blown to bits, wore a flannel shirt with colored stripes, everyday pants with a rope for a belt, and was barefoot. No one in town knew him.

"So his name was Carlos Centeno," murmured the Father when he finished writing. 14 "Centeno Ayala,"[2] said the woman. "He was my only boy."

---

1. **Aureliano Buendía** [ou′rä lyä′nō bwän dē′ä]
2. **Centeno Ayala** [sen tä′nō ä yä′lä]: In Spanish-speaking countries a person's full name customarily includes the father's family name followed by the mother's family name (although the mother's name is sometimes dropped). Carlos' full name was therefore Carlos Centeno Ayala.

Tuesday Siesta **201**

■ When the priest asks whether the mother tried to get Carlos on the right track, she says that Carlos was a good man who obeyed her order not to steal what people needed to eat.

■ On the other hand, when he was boxing, the mother felt her meals tasted of his beatings.

■ By the time she and her daughter are ready to leave, a crowd has gathered outside.

■ The mother does not accept the priest's suggestion to wait until sunset to visit the cemetery and politely refuses the sister's offer of a parasol.

IN THE GLOSSARY

■ inscrutable: mysterious

15 CRITICAL THINKING: EVALUATION

Have students discuss whether Carlos, an admitted thief, could have been a "good man."

16 TEACHING CHARACTER MOTIVATION

Note that Carlos turned to petty theft because boxing was too violent and painful and he apparently found no other way to support his family.

17 READING SKILL: INFERENCE

Discuss the fact that the sister offers a parasol for protection from the hot sun and that the priest advises waiting until sunset so that the two might avoid both the heat and the crowd.

18 TEACHING THEME

Note that the mother's walking to the cemetery in the hot sun shows that she is paying her respects proudly, even in the glaring light of public opinion.

COLLABORATIVE LEARNING: ENRICHMENT ACTIVITY

Literature Have a group of students prepare a booklet on the history of the Nobel Prize and its winners in literature, many of whom (including García Márquez) are represented in the students' textbook.

The priest went back to the cabinet. Two big rusty keys hung on the inside of the door; the girl imagined, as her mother had when she was a girl and as the priest himself must have imagined at some time, that they were Saint Peter's keys.[3] He took them down, put them on the open notebook on the railing, and pointed with his forefinger to a place on the page he had just written, looking at the woman.

"Sign here."

The woman scribbled her name, holding the handbag under her arm. The girl picked up the flowers, came to the railing shuffling her feet, and watched her mother attentively.

The priest sighed.

"Didn't you ever try to get him on the right track?"

The woman answered when she finished signing.

15 "He was a very good man."

The priest looked first at the woman and then at the girl, and realized with a kind of pious amazement that they were not about to cry. The woman continued in the same tone:

16 "I told him never to steal anything that anyone needed to eat, and he minded me. On the other hand, before, when he used to box, he used to spend three days in bed, exhausted from being punched."

"All his teeth had to be pulled out," interrupted the girl.

"That's right," the woman agreed. "Every mouthful I ate those days tasted of the beatings my son got on Saturday nights."

"God's will is inscrutable," said the Father.

But he said it without much conviction, partly because experience had made him a little skeptical and partly because of the heat. He suggested that they cover their heads to guard against sunstroke. Yawning, and now almost completely asleep, he gave them instructions about how to find Carlos Centeno's grave. When

---

3. **Saint Peter's keys:** the keys to the gates of heaven.

---

they came back, they didn't have to knock. They should put the key under the door; and in the same place, if they could, they should put an offering for the Church. The woman listened to his directions with great attention, but thanked him without smiling.

The Father had noticed that there was someone looking inside, his nose pressed against the metal grating, even before he opened the door to the street. Outside was a group of children. When the door was opened wide, the children scattered. Ordinarily, at that hour there was no one in the street. Now there were not only children. There were groups of people under the almond trees. The Father scanned the street swimming in the heat and then he understood. Softly, he closed the door again.

"Wait a moment," he said without looking at the woman.

His sister appeared at the far door with a black jacket over her nightshirt and her hair down over her shoulders. She looked silently at the Father.

"What was it?" he asked.

"The people have noticed," murmured his sister.

"You'd better go out by the door to the patio," said the Father.

"It's the same there," said his sister. "Everybody is at the windows."

The woman seemed not to have understood until then. She tried to look into the street through the metal grating. Then she took the bouquet of flowers from the girl and began to move toward the door. The girl followed her.

17 "Wait until the sun goes down," said the Father.

"You'll melt," said his sister, motionless at the back of the room. "Wait and I'll lend you a parasol."

"Thank you," replied the woman. "We're all right this way."

18 She took the girl by the hand and went into the street.

CRITICAL THINKING: GUIDED READING QUESTIONS

LITERAL

1a. By the time the mother and daughter are ready to leave, what is happening outside? (A crowd is gathering.)

2a. What offer from the priest's sister does the mother politely refuse? (a parasol)

INFERENTIAL

1b. Why has the crowd gathered? (The villagers are curious to see the family of the thief who was shot and killed the previous week.)

2b. What does her refusal stress about her attitude? (She is politely dignified and too proud to accept help on her pilgrimage to honor her son's memory.)

STUDY QUESTIONS

Recalling

1. Briefly describe the clothing and appearance of the mother and daughter. What instructions does the mother give the daughter before they leave the train?

2. What is the weather like when the mother and daughter arrive in the town? What is everyone in town doing?

3. How does the mother's voice sound as she insists on seeing the priest? What does she ask the priest for, and why?

4. How did Carlos Centeno Ayala die? What does his mother tell the priest about him?

5. What does the priest notice when he looks outside? What does the mother refuse at the story's end?

Interpreting

6. What atmosphere, or mood, does the setting create?

7. What sort of person is the mother? What attitude does she take toward the charity and sympathy offered by others?

8. What was the apparent motive for Carlos' crime? Does the story suggest that Carlos got what he deserved? Explain.

Extending

9. Is pride a vice or a virtue? Discuss.

LANGUAGE STUDY

Words from Spanish

The word *siesta,* which means "afternoon nap or rest," is one of many words that have come to English from Spanish. Several of these words trace back to Latin, the language from which Spanish evolved. For example, the Spanish word *siesta* goes back to the Latin expression *sexta hora,* meaning "sixth hour" or "noon," since noon was considered the sixth waking hour of the day.

Use a dictionary to help you determine the meanings and origins of the following words, some of which appear in the story. All of the words came to English from Spanish.

1. bonanza
2. guerrilla
3. mesa
4. mustang
5. patio
6. plaza
7. poncho
8. savvy
9. stampede

COMPOSITION

Writing About Tone

■ Write a brief composition about the narrator's tone in "Tuesday Siesta." Identify the tone, and then explain how the selection of details in the story helps to convey the tone. Finally, consider how the tone is related to the attitudes of the characters (especially the mother) and to the story's theme.

Writing an Epitaph

■ Carlos Centeno Ayala's gravestone is in need of an epitaph, which is a statement or a poem in memory of a person who has died. Write the epitaph for Carlos' gravestone, consulting story details as necessary to obtain appropriate information.

Tuesday Siesta **203**

COMPOSITION: GUIDELINES FOR EVALUATION

WRITING ABOUT TONE

Objective

To analyze a story's tone

Guidelines for Evaluation

■ suggested length: two or three paragraphs
■ should identify the story's tone
■ should show how story details convey tone
■ should explain how tone relates to the characters' attitudes and the story's theme

WRITING AN EPITAPH

Objective

To create an epitaph for a character in the story

Guidelines for Evaluation

■ suggested length: four to eight lines
■ should reflect Carlos' personality and life
■ may be written in prose or verse

Did you admire the mother in the story? Why or why not?

ANSWERS

STUDY QUESTIONS

1. They wear poor mourning clothes, the girl is twelve, and the mother looks older than her years; accept no drink and "above all, no crying."

2. It is hot; taking a siesta.

3. calm, self-assured, pleasant; She asks for the cemetery keys in order to visit her son's grave.

4. He was killed while trying to rob a home. He was a good man who never stole people's food and turned to theft only because boxing was so violent.

5. a crowd; to wait until sunset or carry a parasol

6. harshness and desolation

7. proud, dignified, principled; She refuses all offers.

8. to feed himself and his family; No, it suggests that his crime was minor and he was not evil.

9. Answers will vary. Some students might feel that a degree of pride is admirable but that too much promotes selfishness, vanity, or folly.

LANGUAGE STUDY

1. "rich vein of ore; any source of profit"; from Spanish for "fair weather; prosperity"

2. "irregular soldier in small-scale warfare"; from Spanish for "little war," from *guerra,* "war"

3. "small, high, steep plateau"; from Spanish for "table"

4. "wild horse of American Southwest"; from Spanish *mestengo,* from *mesteño,* "grazing, wild," from *mesta,* "group of grazing animals"

5. "courtyard; paved area adjoining a house"; from Spanish for "courtyard"

6. "public square; marketplace"; from Spanish, from Latin *platea,* "broad street"

7. "blanketlike cloak"; from American Spanish, from Aruacan *pontho*

8. slang, "shrewdness or know-how"; from Spanish *¿sabe (usted)?* "do you know?"

9. "sudden rush of animals; confused rush"; from American Spanish *estampida,* from Spanish *estampar,* "to stamp"

This contemporary tale from Germany concerns a man who makes his living by laughing. The narrator is a talented professional laugher, capable of producing "spontaneous" laughter in nightclubs and theaters. Nevertheless, he laughs only when paid to do so, for at heart he is serious and solemn and has never heard the sound of his own true laughter.

LITERARY SKILLS FOR THIS SELECTION

- single effect: irony
- point of view

THEMES IN THIS SELECTION

- cultures and conflicts: the artificiality of modern life
- the value of laughter

LESSON OBJECTIVES

1. to examine a story's single effect
2. to analyze and evaluate a story's irony
3. to create classified ads appropriate to a character in the story

Teacher's Classroom Resources 1

- Teaching Notes 367
- Prereading Vocabulary 368
- Reading Guide 369
- Check Test 370
- Responding to World Cultures 371
- Literary Focus: The Single Effect 372
- Writing Process Guides: Writing About Irony 373
  Writing Classified Ads 374
- Grammar in Literature: Using Colons 375
- Selection Test 376

TEACHING STUDENTS OF DIFFERENT ABILITIES

- **For less advanced students:** Have students take turns reading this brief story aloud; they should try to capture the tone they think appropriate to the narrator's statements. Have them complete the Reading Guide.

- **For more advanced students:** Have students learn more about Böll's work and consider how it exemplifies the recent trends in German literature discussed on page 566 of their text.

PREVIEW: THE AUTHOR AND THE WORLD

Heinrich Böll

(1917–1985)

Germany

One of the most prominent authors in Europe after the Second World War, Heinrich Böll [hĭn'rĭкн bœl'] grew up in Cologne [kə lōn'], Germany, and came of age during the dark days of Germany's rule by Nazi dictator Adolf Hitler. Unlike most of his schoolmates, Böll refused to join the militant Hitler Youth movement. Nevertheless, he was forced to serve in the German army when World War II broke out. After the war he returned to his native city and published two stories in a literary magazine. The stories won him a contract with a German publishing house, and by 1947 Böll had become a full-time writer.

Disillusioned by the postwar technological age, Böll satirized modern life in critically acclaimed novels, such as *The Clown, Group Portrait with Lady,* and *The Lost Honor of Katharina Blum.* He also wrote several volumes of short stories and is considered to be a master of that form. Throughout his work Böll proclaims the importance of the individual and the necessity of personal responsibility in a world that has become deaf to the voice of the common man. In 1972 Böll's achievements were honored with the Nobel Prize for Literature.

GEOGRAPHY AND CULTURE

West Germany and the Postwar Era

At the time that Böll wrote many of his most famous works, West Germany was one of the world's most highly industrialized nations. Formed in 1949 in the wake of World War II, West Germany rapidly rebuilt its ruined cities and industries. By the 1980s, it had become one of the leading economic powers of Western Europe. (This extraordinary recovery is known in German as the *Wirtschaftswunder,* or economic miracle.) Industry continues to be vital to the German economy, and German cars, appliances, pharmaceuticals, and textiles are renowned for their quality.

For Germans as well as residents of other industrialized nations, modernization has had both benefits and drawbacks. The way individuals deal with life in the technological age has become a vital subject for contemporary literature in many countries. It is the subject of "The Laugher," a brief, powerful tale that could be set in almost any industrialized nation.

See LITERATURE AND CULTURE SOURCEBOOK: Germany

Recent Developments in Germany

The country Heinrich Böll has described so vividly in his writing no longer exists. In 1990 East and West Germany reunited, and a once-divided Berlin again became the capital of the whole nation. In the preceding months the Berlin Wall, a symbol of totalitarian repression, was torn down by Germans euphoric at the prospect of freedom.

- Have students discuss their thoughts about the wave of freedom sweeping Eastern Europe.

Heinrich Böll

The Laugher

Translated from the German by Leila Vennewitz

When someone asks me what business I am in, I am seized with embarrassment: I blush and stammer, I who am otherwise known as a man of poise. I envy people who can say: I am a bricklayer. I envy barbers, bookkeepers and writers the simplicity of their avowal, for all these professions speak for themselves and need no lengthy explanation, while I am constrained to reply to such questions: I am a laugher. An admission of this kind demands another, since I have to answer the second question: "Is that how you make your living?" truthfully with "Yes." I actually do make a living at my laughing, and a good one too, for my laughing is—commercially speaking—much in demand. I am a good laugher, experienced, no one else laughs as well as I do, no one else has such command of the fine points of my art. For a long time, in order to avoid tiresome explanations, I called myself an actor, but my talents in the field of mime and elocution are so meager that I felt this designation to be too far from the truth: I love the truth, and the truth is: I am a laugher. I am neither a clown nor a comedian. I do not make people gay, I portray gaiety: I laugh like a Roman emperor, or like a sensitive schoolboy, I am as much at home in the laughter of the seventeenth century as in that of the nineteenth, and when occasion demands I laugh my way through all the centuries, all classes of society, all categories of age: it is simply a skill which I have acquired, like the skill of being able to repair shoes. In my breast I harbor the laughter of America, the laughter of Africa, white, red, yellow laughter—and for the right fee I let it peal out in accordance with the director's requirements.

I have become indispensable; I laugh on rec-

ords, I laugh on tape, and television directors treat me with respect. I laugh mournfully, moderately, hysterically; I laugh like a streetcar conductor or like a helper in the grocery business; laughter in the morning, laughter in the evening, nocturnal laughter and the laughter of twilight. In short: wherever and however laughter is required—I do it.

It need hardly be pointed out that a profession of this kind is tiring, especially as I have also—this is my specialty—mastered the art of infectious laughter; this has also made me indispensable to third- and fourth-rate comedians, who are scared—and with good reason—that their audiences will miss their punch lines, so I spend most evenings in night clubs as a kind of discreet claque,[1] my job being to laugh infectiously during the weaker parts of the program. It has to be carefully timed: my hearty, boisterous laughter must not come too soon, but neither must it come too late, it must come just at the right spot: at the pre-arranged moment I burst out laughing, the whole audience roars with me, and the joke is saved.

But as for me, I drag myself exhausted to the checkroom, put on my overcoat, happy that I can go off duty at last. At home I usually find telegrams waiting for me: "Urgently require your laughter. Recording Tuesday," and a few hours later I am sitting in an overheated express train bemoaning my fate.

I need scarcely say that when I am off duty or on vacation I have little inclination to laugh: the cowhand is glad when he can forget the

---

1. **claque** [klak]: group hired to applaud a performance.

The Laugher **205**

MOTIVATION: PRIOR KNOWLEDGE

Have students discuss the reasons people laugh and the effects of laughter on others.

PAGE SUMMARY: AT A GLANCE

- The narrator is a skilled, successful, and versatile professional laugher.
- He finds his job exhausting, and when off duty, he has little inclination to laugh.

IN THE GLOSSARY

- avowal: straight declaration
- mime: the art of acting out silently; pantomime
- elocution: public speaking
- nocturnal: happening at night
- infectious: spreading

1 TEACHING A SINGLE EFFECT: IRONY

Point out the irony of the narrator's situation: He claims to love truth but earns his living from false laughter.

2 CULTURAL BACKGROUND

Stress that the narrator's job is a product of advances in communications technology that have become part of everyday life in the contemporary industrial world.

3 TEACHING THEME

Elicit the insight that the story criticizes the artificiality of modern life, where joy must be falsely created. The story also emphasizes both the sadness and the absurdity of a world where false joy seems urgently needed.

4 GRAMMAR IN LITERATURE

Note that *infectious*, used five lines above, is here turned into an adverb of manner by adding the suffix -ly. Have students identify similarly formed adverbs earlier in the column. (*mournfully, moderately,* and *hysterically*)

5 TEACHING POINT OF VIEW

Note that although the first-person narrator recognizes some of the irony of his situation, he never sees its humorous side.

CRITICAL THINKING: GUIDED READING QUESTIONS

LITERAL

1a. Whom does the narrator envy? (bricklayers, bankers, bookkeepers, and writers)

2a. When does the narrator let his laughter "peal out in accordance with the director's requirements"? (when he receives the right fee)

3a. What do telegrams to the narrator typically say? ("Urgently require your laughter. Recording Tuesday.")

INFERENTIAL

1b. Why does he envy these people? (The usefulness of their jobs is readily apparent.)

2b. What criticism of the modern world does this detail suggest? (The world is an artificial and crassly commercial place where even joy is a commodity.)

3b. What makes this message funny? (The narrator's job is too trivial to be "urgently needed," but the wording suggests an emergency.)

PAGE SUMMARY: AT A GLANCE

- The narrator is a solemn person whose married life is quiet, since his wife has come to recognize his distaste for off-the-job laughter and noise.
- Though the narrator laughs in many ways, he has never heard his own laughter.

IN THE GLOSSARY

- profound: marked by intellectual depth or intensity of feeling
- taciturn: very quiet
- impassive: showing no emotion

6 TEACHING A SINGLE EFFECT: IRONY

Point out the irony of a solemn person who earns his living by laughing.

7 TEACHING POINT OF VIEW

Note that the entire story might be viewed as a dramatic monologue in which the first-person narrator speaks to readers about his job and his feelings about it.

COLLABORATIVE LEARNING: ENRICHMENT ACTIVITY

Résumés Have a group of students prepare résumés for the laugher and for other characters in the Short Story unit. Résumés should be in a standard form but need not be serious in tone.

ART AND LITERATURE

The contemporary Italian artist Francesco Clemente (born 1952) belongs to a generation of artists called Postmodernists, who borrow styles from various countries and eras but most notably from the first age of Modernism (from about 1880 through the Second World War). Clemente's work is considered neo-Expressionist because it derives from early Expressionist artists such as van Gogh and Munch, to whose style he adds his own overt emotional content. In this watercolor he portrays himself in an attitude that is self-assured, sober, and direct.

- Ask students which part of the laugher's life Clemente's self-portrait might represent. (the times when the laugher is not working and looks profoundly solemn)

I, 1982, Francesco Clemente.

cow, the bricklayer when he can forget the mortar, and carpenters usually have doors at home which don't work or drawers which are hard to open. Confectioners[2] like sour pickles, butchers like marzipan,[3] and the baker prefers sausage to bread; bullfighters raise pigeons for a hobby, boxers turn pale when their children have nosebleeds: I find all this quite natural, for I never **6** laugh off duty. I am a very solemn person, and people consider me—perhaps rightly so—a pessimist.

During the first years of our married life, my wife would often say to me: "Do laugh!" but since then she has come to realize that I cannot grant her this wish. I am happy when I am free

---

2. **Confectioners:** those who make candies, pastries, or other sweets.
3. **marzipan** [mär′zə pan′]: candy made of almond paste, sugar, and egg whites.

206 *The Short Story*

to relax my tense face muscles, my frayed spirit, in profound solemnity. Indeed, even other people's laughter gets on my nerves, since it reminds me too much of my profession. So our marriage is a quiet, peaceful one, because my wife has also forgotten how to laugh: now and again I catch her smiling, and I smile too. We converse in low tones, for I detest the noise of the night clubs, the noise that sometimes fills the recording studios. People who do not know me think I am taciturn. Perhaps I am, because I have to open my mouth so often to laugh.

I go through life with an impassive expression, from time to time permitting myself a gentle smile, and I often wonder whether I have ever laughed. I think not. My brothers and sisters have always known me for a serious boy.

7 So I laugh in many different ways, but my own laughter I have never heard.

CRITICAL THINKING: GUIDED READING QUESTIONS

LITERAL

1a. What does the narrator never hear? (He never hears the sound of his own laughter.)

INFERENTIAL

1b. What sort of laughter does he mean when he says, "My own laughter I have never heard"? (He is referring to spontaneous laughter that indicates real joy.)

STUDY QUESTIONS

1. What does the narrator do for a living? What is his specialty?
2. What does the narrator never do when he is off duty? To what other workers does he compare himself?
3. In the last four paragraphs, what does the narrator tell us about his personality? What does he say he has never heard?

Interpreting

4. Does the narrator have an ordinary job? How is his attitude toward his job typical of many workers' attitudes? Given the kind of job he has, what is ironic about its effects on him?
5. What tone does the narrator use? How does his tone help reflect his personality?
6. What aspects of the story seem deliberately exaggerated? What effect does this exaggeration have on readers?
7. What do you think the story's last sentence means? What meaning might it have for ordinary people in general?

Extending

8. Why is laughter important?

LITERARY FOCUS

The Single Effect

A century and a half ago American author Edgar Allan Poe defined the short story as a tale that can be read in a single sitting and that produces a **single effect** on its readers. In the case of Poe's own stories—eerie, macabre tales such as "The Fall of the House of Usher" and "The Cask of Amontillado"—the single effect is often horror.

If we apply Poe's definition to "The Laugher," we would probably say that the single effect of Böll's story is irony. Everything the narrator tells us points to the ironic contrast between his personality and his profession, and between what we expect his job and life to be like and what they really are like.

Thinking About the Single Effect

■ Find at least three statements in the story that emphasize the irony of the narrator's situation.

COMPOSITION

Writing About Irony

■ In a brief composition discuss the use of irony in "The Laugher." You may want to consider these questions as you write: Is Böll's use of irony primarily humorous or serious? How does his use of irony support the story's theme or themes? Be sure to cite story details to support your answers to these questions.

Writing Classified Ads

■ Imagine that the narrator is looking for a new job. Write an advertisement requesting a job that he might place in a newspaper's classified ads section. Mention talents identified in the story and the narrator's other qualifications and interests. Also write two or three help wanted ads that you think might interest the narrator. Each of these advertisements should be placed by a different kind of business or involve a different kind of work. Use your imagination.

The Laugher **207**

Did you find the laugher a comical or a sad person? Explain.

ANSWERS

STUDY QUESTIONS

1. He is a professional laugher; infectious laughter.
2. He never laughs. He compares himself with cowhands, bricklayers, carpenters, confectioners, butchers, bullfighters, and boxers, all of whom try to forget their jobs when they are off duty.
3. He is solemn and seems pessimistic and taciturn; his own laughter.
4. No. He finds it unpleasant and exhausting and does not want to think about it at home. It is ironic that he finds such an unusual and seemingly jolly job unpleasant and that he is unable to dismiss it.
5. The tone is sad and solemn. It reflects his mournful personality.
6. the narrator's solemnity, the suffering caused by the job, and his claim never to have laughed off the job; It makes his situation seem absurd and makes us uncertain whether we should laugh at him or pity him.
7. The narrator has heard only his false professional laughter, not his own spontaneous laughter. It might warn us of the dangers of losing touch with our sense of humor and with truly spontaneous and deeply felt joy.
8. Answers will vary. Among other things laughter can help us relax, gain a better perspective on problems, and face uncomfortable truths in a positive way; it can also bring people closer together.

LITERARY FOCUS

Ironic statements include the following: "For the right fee I let it peal out in accordance with the director's requirements"; "It need hardly be pointed out that a profession of this kind is tiring"; "When I am off duty or on vacation I have little inclination to laugh"; and "I am happy when I am free to relax . . . in profound solemnity."

COMPOSITION: GUIDELINES FOR EVALUATION

WRITING ABOUT IRONY

Objective

To analyze and evaluate a story's irony

Guidelines for Evaluation

■ suggested length: two or three paragraphs
■ should evaluate the effects of irony in the story
■ should relate irony to theme
■ should support general statements with details from the story

WRITING CLASSIFIED ADS

Objective

To create classified ads appropriate to the story's character

Guidelines for Evaluation

■ suggested length: three ads of five to eight lines
■ should use the format of help-wanted and situation-wanted ads
■ should reflect the narrator's talents and interests

LESSON PREVIEW

In this story of midcentury Algeria, a teacher tries to remain neutral in a politically explosive situation. When the local gendarme asks Daru to take to police headquarters an Arab convicted of killing a cousin, Daru tries to refuse, but to no avail. In vain he gives the Arab every opportunity to escape. When he finally gives him money and food and shows him the routes to prison and freedom, the Arab chooses prison. Meanwhile, at the school someone has scrawled on the board, "You handed over our brother. You will pay for this."

LITERARY SKILL FOR THIS SELECTION

■ elements of the short story

THEMES IN THIS SELECTION

■ cultures and conflicts: colonialism and rebellion
■ freedom and choice

LESSON OBJECTIVES

1. to examine the chief elements of a short story
2. to create a dialogue between story characters

Teacher's Classroom Resources 1

<table>
<tr><td>■ Teaching Notes</td><td>379</td></tr>
<tr><td>■ Prereading Vocabulary</td><td>380</td></tr>
<tr><td>■ Reading Guide</td><td>381</td></tr>
<tr><td>■ Check Test</td><td>382</td></tr>
<tr><td>■ Responding to World Cultures</td><td>383</td></tr>
<tr><td>■ Literary Focus: Elements of the Short Story</td><td>384</td></tr>
<tr><td>■ Writing Process Guide: Writing a Dialogue</td><td>385</td></tr>
<tr><td>■ Grammar in Literature: Compound Predicates</td><td>386</td></tr>
<tr><td>■ Selection Test</td><td>387</td></tr>
</table>

Albert Camus (1913–1960)

Algeria/France

One of our century's most influential authors, Albert Camus [äl bär′ ka moo′] was born and grew up in Algeria when it was still a colony of France. Though his family was extremely poor, he was able to work his way through the University of Algiers, where he studied philosophy, a subject that greatly influenced his work.

Camus held several jobs before winning fame as an author: actor, theater director, journalist, and schoolteacher in the northern Algerian city of Oran. During World War II he went to France and wrote for an underground newspaper that supported the Resistance movement against the Nazi occupation of France. At the same time he completed some of his most important works: his short novel *The Stranger* and his noted philosophical essay *The Myth of Sisyphus*.

After the war Camus's works were widely translated and soon won him international acclaim. In 1957, three years before he died in a car accident, he was awarded the Nobel Prize for Literature.

"The Guest," one of his later stories, is characteristic of Camus's fiction. Behind the exciting plot lies his ever-present philosophical question, "Why?"

GEOGRAPHY AND CULTURE

Algeria and Its Colonial Past

Located on the north coast of Africa, Algeria is a large nation stretching from the Mediterranean Sea in the north to the Sahara Desert in the south. Two chains of the Atlas Mountains run east to west through the country; the land between these mountain chains is mostly arid, dry plateau.

About three quarters of all Algerians are Arabs, and Arabic is the nation's official language. However, many people of European descent lived in Algeria when it was a French colony. Camus was of French and Spanish descent, and he wrote in French.

A colony of France since 1830, Algeria won its independence in 1962 after several years of guerrilla warfare. "The Guest," set in northern Algeria, takes place when Algeria was still a French colony but was experiencing the seeds of unrest.

See *LITERATURE AND CULTURE SOURCEBOOK: Africa*

IN THE CLASSROOM

TEACHING STUDENTS OF DIFFERENT ABILITIES

■ **For less advanced students:** Have students list the details that reveal Daru's attitudes toward society; then have them consider the themes developed by these details. Also have them complete the Reading Guide.

■ **For more advanced students:** Have students learn more about existentialism and its influence on Camus. Then have them consider how "The Guest" expresses existentialist ideas.

DISCUSSING GEOGRAPHY AND CULTURE

Living in a Foreign Country

During the years of French rule, ten percent of Algeria's inhabitants were European. Today the figure has shrunk to one percent. For Camus life in Algeria was both stimulating and frustrating: Though he lived, studied, and worked in the country for many years, he was always conscious of being an outsider.

■ Ask students what they think it would be like to study or work in a foreign country. What difficulties would they face?

Albert Camus

The Guest

Translated from the French by Justin O'Brien

The schoolmaster was watching the two men climb toward him. One was on horseback, the other on foot. They had not yet tackled the abrupt rise leading to the schoolhouse built on the hillside. They were toiling onward, making slow progress in the snow, among the stones, on the vast expanse of the high, deserted plateau. From time to time the horse stumbled. Without hearing anything yet, he could see the breath issuing from the horse's nostrils. One of the men, at least, knew the region. They were following the trail although it had disappeared days ago under a layer of dirty white snow. The schoolmaster calculated that it would take them half an hour to get onto the hill. It was cold; he went back into the school to get a sweater.

He crossed the empty, frigid classroom. On the blackboard the four rivers of France, drawn with four different colored chalks, had been flowing toward their estuaries for the past three days. Snow had suddenly fallen in mid-October after eight months of drought without the transition of rain, and the twenty pupils, more or less, who lived in the villages scattered over the plateau had stopped coming. With fair weather they would return. Daru now heated only the single room that was his lodging, adjoining the classroom and giving also onto the plateau to the east. Like the class windows, his window looked to the south too. On that side the school was a few kilometers from the point where the plateau began to slope toward the south. In clear weather could be seen the purple mass of the mountain range where the gap opened onto the desert.

Somewhat warmed, Daru returned to the window from which he had first seen the two men. They were no longer visible. Hence they must have tackled the rise. The sky was not so dark, for the snow had stopped falling during the night. The morning had opened with a dirty light which had scarcely become brighter as the ceiling of clouds lifted. At two in the afternoon it seemed as if the day were merely beginning. But still this was better than those three days when the thick snow was falling amidst unbroken darkness with little gusts of wind that rattled the double door of the classroom. Then Daru had spent long hours in his room, leaving it only to go to the shed and feed the chickens or get some coal. Fortunately the delivery truck from Tadjid,[1] the nearest village to the north, had brought his supplies two days before the blizzard. It would return in forty-eight hours.

Besides, he had enough to resist a siege, for the little room was cluttered with bags of wheat that the administration left as a stock to distribute to those of his pupils whose families had suffered from the drought. Actually they had all been victims because they were all poor. Every day Daru would distribute a ration to the children. They had missed it, he knew, during these bad days. Possibly one of the fathers or big brothers would come this afternoon and he could supply them with grain. It was just a matter of carrying them over to the next harvest. Now shiploads of wheat were arriving from France and the worst was over. But it would be hard to forget that poverty, that army of ragged ghosts wandering in the sunlight, the plateaus

---

1. **Tadjid** [tä jēd′]

The Guest **209**

MOTIVATION: PRIOR KNOWLEDGE

Have students write their own definitions of freedom. Then ask them to share their ideas with their classmates.

PAGE SUMMARY: AT A GLANCE

- From his isolated schoolhouse Daru watches as two men toil through the snow.
- A blizzard followed an eight-month drought that caused great suffering.
- Now the weather prevents Daru's pupils from coming to school and obtaining the food rations they need.

IN THE GLOSSARY

- siege: sustained attack in which supplies are cut off

1 TEACHING SETTING AND SYMBOLS

Note that the secluded schoolhouse represents the isolation that Daru has sought to achieve from the political struggles of his society.

2 CULTURAL BACKGROUND

Explain that when Algeria was a colony of France, French geography, history, and culture were taught in Algerian schools. The four rivers that Daru drew are probably the Loire, Seine, Rhône, and Garonne.

3 TEACHING POINT OF VIEW

Note that the story is told in the third person but is limited to Daru's thoughts and impressions. Though presented indirectly, the thoughts and opinions here are Daru's.

4 READING SKILL: INFERENCE

Elicit the fact that "these bad days" refers to an eight-month drought followed directly by a blizzard—with no interval of rain. Such harsh weather would cause great suffering among an already poor agricultural people.

CRITICAL THINKING: GUIDED READING QUESTIONS

LITERAL

1a. For how long has the map showing the rivers of France been on the blackboard? (three days)

2a. What does Daru think will be hard to forget? (the poverty and "army of ragged ghosts" that the drought has produced)

INFERENTIAL

1b. Why has it been there for so long? (A blizzard has prevented Daru's pupils from coming to school.)

2b. What do Daru's thoughts show about his feelings for others? (He is compassionate.)

- Having sufficient provisions, Daru is satisfied with his monk-like life at the school.
- Although he knows the region is cruel, he was born here and feels out of place everywhere else.
- The two approaching men turn out to be Balducci, the local gendarme, and an Arab prisoner.
- Because of the snow it has taken them an hour to travel a short distance, and now Daru gives them tea and heats up the stove to warm them.
- He suggests that the prisoner's hands be untied so that the man can drink his tea.

5 TEACHING SETTING

Point out that many of the details of the setting stress the physical harshness of the region. That human beings do not "help matters" alludes to the social and political turmoil also plaguing Algeria at the time the story takes place.

6 TEACHING STUDENTS OF LIMITED ENGLISH PROFICIENCY

Help students use footnote pronunciations and the Glossary pronunciation key to pronounce *gendarme*, originally a French word, and *djellaba*, of Arabic origin. Note that *djellaba* is a term for clothing, and ask nonnative students what terms for clothing from their own language are used in English.

7 CRITICAL THINKING: LOGICAL REASONING

Have students reason out the cause of Balducci's complaint. (Three kilometers is less than two miles, and in an hour two people on horseback would travel farther. The snow has apparently forced them off the horse and slowed their journey.)

8 TEACHING CHARACTERIZATION

Elicit the insight that the request to free the prisoner's hands shows compassion as well as the value Daru places on freedom.

burned to a cinder month after month, the earth shriveled up little by little, literally scorched, every stone bursting into dust under one's foot. The sheep had died then by thousands and even a few men, here and there, sometimes without anyone's knowing.

In contrast with such poverty, he who lived almost like a monk in his remote schoolhouse, nonetheless satisfied with the little he had and with the rough life, had felt like a lord with his whitewashed walls, his narrow couch, his unpainted shelves, his well, and his weekly provision of water and food. And suddenly this snow, without warning, without the foretaste of rain.

5 This is the way the region was, cruel to live in, even without men—who didn't help matters either. But Daru had been born here. Everywhere else, he felt exiled.

He stepped out onto the terrace in front of the schoolhouse. The two men were now halfway up the slope. He recognized the horseman **6** as Balducci, the old gendarme[2] he had known for a long time. Balducci was holding on the end of a rope an Arab who was walking behind him with hands bound and head lowered. The gendarme waved a greeting to which Daru did not reply, lost as he was in contemplation of the Arab dressed in a faded blue djellaba,[3] his feet in sandals but covered with socks of heavy raw wool, his head surmounted by a narrow, short chèche.[4] They were approaching. Balducci was holding back his horse in order not to hurt the Arab, and the group was advancing slowly.

7 Within earshot, Balducci shouted: "One hour to do the three kilometers from El Ameur!"[5] Daru did not answer. Short and square in his

---

2. **Balducci** [bäl dōō'chē], **the old gendarme** [zhän'därm]: A gendarme is a French police officer.
3. **djellaba** [jə lä'bə]: long robelike garment worn by men in North Africa.
4. *chèche* [shäsh'yä]: tall round cap commonly worn by men in North Africa.
5. **El Ameur** [äm ūr']: village in north-central Algeria.

thick sweater, he watched them climb. Not once had the Arab raised his head. "Hello," said Daru when they got up onto the terrace. "Come in and warm up." Balducci painfully got down from his horse without letting go the rope. From under his bristling mustache he smiled at the schoolmaster. His little dark eyes, deep-set under a tanned forehead, and his mouth surrounded with wrinkles made him look attentive and studious. Daru took the bridle, led the horse to the shed, and came back to the two men, who were now waiting for him in the school. He led them into his room. "I am going to heat up the classroom," he said. "We'll be more comfortable there." When he entered the room again, Balducci was on the couch. He had undone the rope tying him to the Arab, who had squatted near the stove. His hands still bound, the chèche pushed back on his head, he was looking toward the window. At first Daru noticed only his huge lips, fat, smooth, almost Negroid; yet his nose was straight, his eyes were dark and full of fever. The chèche revealed an obstinate forehead and, under the weathered skin now rather discolored by the cold, the whole face had a restless and rebellious look that struck Daru when the Arab, turning his face toward him, looked him straight in the eyes. "Go into the other room," said the schoolmaster, "and I'll make you some mint tea." "Thanks," Balducci said. "What a chore! How I long for retirement." And addressing his prisoner in Arabic: "Come on, you." The Arab got up and, slowly, holding his bound wrists in front of him, went into the classroom.

With the tea, Daru brought a chair. But Balducci was already enthroned on the nearest pupil's desk and the Arab had squatted against the teacher's platform facing the stove, which stood between the desk and the window. When **8** he held out the glass of tea to the prisoner, Daru hesitated at the sight of his bound hands. "He might perhaps be untied." "Sure," said Balducci. "That was for the trip." He started to get to his

---

CRITICAL THINKING: GUIDED READING QUESTIONS

LITERAL

1a. Where was Daru born, and how does he feel everywhere else? (He was born in this part of Algeria and feels like an exile everywhere else.)

2a. What strikes Daru about the Arab's "whole face"? (He is struck by its restless and rebellious look.)

INFERENTIAL

1b. What do the story's details suggest about Daru's social ties, even in this region? (His satisfaction with his monklike existence at the remote schoolhouse suggests that he is a social exile even here.)

2b. Does this look seem to frighten Daru? How do you know? (No, he invites the two men in and considerately asks that the prisoner's hands be untied.)

feet. But Daru, setting the glass on the floor, had knelt beside the Arab. Without saying anything, the Arab watched him with his feverish eyes. Once his hands were free, he rubbed his swollen wrists against each other, took the glass of tea, and sucked up the burning liquid in swift little sips.

"Good," said Daru. "And where are you headed?"

Balducci withdrew his mustache from the tea. "Here, son."

"Odd pupils! And you're spending the night?"

__9__ "No. I'm going back to El Ameur. And you will deliver this fellow to Tinguit. He is expected at police headquarters."

Balducci was looking at Daru with a friendly little smile.

"What's this story?" asked the schoolmaster. "Are you pulling my leg?"

"No, son. Those are the orders."

__10__ "The orders? I'm not . . ." Daru hesitated, not wanting to hurt the old Corsican.[6] "I mean, that's not my job."

"What! What's the meaning of that? In wartime people do all kinds of jobs."

"Then I'll wait for the declaration of war!" Balducci nodded.

"O.K. But the orders exist and they concern you too. Things are brewing, it appears. There is talk of a forthcoming revolt. We are mobilized, in a way."

Daru still had his obstinate look.

"Listen, son," Balducci said. "I like you and you must understand. There's only a dozen of us at El Ameur to patrol throughout the whole territory of a small department[7] and I must get back in a hurry. I was told to hand this guy over

---

6. **Corsican** [kôr′si kən]: native of the island of Corsica in the Mediterranean Sea. Though ruled by France, Corsica also has strong Italian influences: Balducci's name, for example, is Italian.
7. **department:** administrative district.

---

to you and return without delay. He couldn't be __11__ kept there. His village was beginning to stir; they wanted to take him back. You must take him to Tinguit tomorrow before the day is over. Twenty kilometers shouldn't faze a husky fellow like you. After that, all will be over. You'll come back to your pupils and your comfortable life."

Behind the wall the horse could be heard snorting and pawing the earth. Daru was looking out the window. Decidedly, the weather was clearing and the light was increasing over the snowy plateau. When all the snow was melted, the sun would take over again and once more would burn the fields of stone. For days, still, the unchanging sky would shed its dry light on the solitary expanse where nothing had any connection with man.

"After all," he said, turning around toward Balducci, "what did he do?" And, before the gendarme had opened his mouth, he asked: "Does he speak French?"

"No, not a word. We had been looking for him for a month, but they were hiding him. He killed his cousin."

"Is he against us?"

"I don't think so. But you can never be sure."

"Why did he kill?"

"A family squabble, I think. One owed the other grain, it seems. It's not at all clear. In short, he killed his cousin with a billhook.[8] You know, like a sheep, *kreezk*!"

Balducci made the gesture of drawing a blade across his throat and the Arab, his attention attracted, watched him with a sort of anxi- __12__ ety. Daru felt a sudden wrath against the man, against all men with their rotten spite, their tireless hates, their blood lust.

But the kettle was singing on the stove. He served Balducci more tea, hesitated, then served the Arab again, who, a second time, drank avidly.

---

8. **billhook:** hand-held cutting tool used for trimming trees and shrubs.

The Guest **211**

CRITICAL THINKING: GUIDED READING QUESTIONS

LITERAL

1a. What has Daru been ordered to do, and what does he say on hearing his "orders"? (He has been ordered to take the prisoner to police headquarters in Tinguit. He says, "That's not my job.")

2a. What does Balducci promise will happen after Daru performs his task? (He will return to his pupils and a comfortable life.)

INFERENTIAL

→ **1b.** Why does Daru refuse to become involved? (He is probably disgusted by the idea of helping to imprison someone.)

→ **2b.** Why might this promise prove invalid? (If rebellion is brewing and villagers are planning to free the prisoner, there is likely to be great local resentment against someone who helps the police transport the prisoner.)

- Daru says that he will fight if necessary but will not turn over the prisoner because he finds such an act disgusting.
- His remarks deeply insult Balducci, who nevertheless decides not to report his friend's treachery.
- Instead, before leaving, he simply makes Daru sign a paper showing that the prisoner has been left in Daru's care.

IN THE GLOSSARY

- denounce: condemn publicly
- peevishly: in an ill-tempered manner; irritably

13 GRAMMAR IN LITERATURE

Point out that Balducci's "we" has no expressed antecedent—that is, no noun to which the pronoun refers. Point out that Balducci uses the pronoun in a general way to mean "European colonials in Algeria," and have students find a similar example in the next column. ("If you want to drop *us*, go ahead.")

14 TEACHING STUDENTS OF LIMITED ENGLISH PROFICIENCY

Have students use context clues to determine the meanings of idioms such as "a little cracked" (here) and "we're all in the same boat" (above). ("a bit crazy" and "we all face the same problem")

15 CRITICAL THINKING: EVALUATION

Elicit the insight that Daru's disgust for "your fellow here" is disgust for the prisoner's crime. Daru is also disgusted by the idea of taking someone to prison, possibly to face a death sentence. On the other hand, Daru will fight if he must. Have students discuss and evaluate Daru's positions.

16 READING SKILL: INFERENCE

Ask what Balducci apparently means when he calls Daru a man. (He is someone with integrity, someone who keeps his word.)

His raised arms made the djellaba fall open and the schoolmaster saw his thin, muscular chest.

"Thanks, kid," Balducci said. "And now, I'm off."

He got up and went toward the Arab, taking a small rope from his pocket.

"What are you doing?" Daru asked dryly.

Balducci, disconcerted, showed him the rope.

"Don't bother."

The old gendarme hesitated. "It's up to you. Of course, you are armed?"

"I have my shotgun."

"Where?"

"In the trunk."

"You ought to have it near your bed."

"Why? I have nothing to fear."

13 "You're crazy, son. If there's an uprising, no one is safe, we're all in the same boat."

"I'll defend myself. I'll have time to see them coming."

Balducci began to laugh, then suddenly the mustache covered the white teeth.

"You'll have time? O.K. That's just what I was 14 saying. You have always been a little cracked. That's why I like you, my son was like that."

At the same time he took out his revolver and put it on the desk.

"Keep it; I don't need two weapons from here to El Ameur."

The revolver shone against the black paint of the table. When the gendarme turned toward him, the schoolmaster caught the smell of leather and horseflesh.

"Listen, Balducci," Daru said suddenly, 15 "every bit of this disgusts me, and first of all your fellow here. But I won't hand him over. Fight, yes, if I have to. But not that."

The old gendarme stood in front of him and looked at him severely.

"You're being a fool," he said slowly. "I don't like it either. You don't get used to putting a rope on a man even after years of it, and you're

even ashamed—yes, ashamed. But you can't let them have their way."

"I won't hand him over," Daru said again.

"It's an order, son, and I repeat it."

"That's right. Repeat to them what I've said to you: I won't hand him over."

Balducci made a visible effort to reflect. He looked at the Arab and at Daru. At last he decided.

"No, I won't tell them anything. If you want to drop us, go ahead; I'll not denounce you. I have an order to deliver the prisoner and I'm doing so. And now you'll just sign this paper for me."

"There's no need. I'll not deny that you left him with me."

16 "Don't be mean with me. I know you'll tell the truth. You're from hereabouts and you are a man. But you must sign, that's the rule."

Daru opened his drawer, took out a little square bottle of purple ink, the red wooden penholder with the "sergeant-major" pen he used for making models of penmanship, and signed. The gendarme carefully folded the paper and put it into his wallet. Then he moved toward the door.

"I'll see you off," Daru said.

"No," said Balducci. "There's no use being polite. You insulted me."

He looked at the Arab, motionless in the same spot, sniffed peevishly, and turned away toward the door. "Good-by, son," he said. The door shut behind him. Balducci appeared suddenly outside the window and then disappeared. His footsteps were muffled by the snow. The horse stirred on the other side of the wall and several chickens fluttered in fright. A moment later Balducci reappeared outside the window leading the horse by the bridle. He walked toward the little rise without turning around and disappeared from sight with the horse following him. A big stone could be heard bouncing down. Daru walked back toward the prisoner, who,

---

CRITICAL THINKING: GUIDED READING QUESTIONS

LITERAL

1a. What does Balducci decide to tell the authorities about Daru's refusal to obey orders? (He will not denounce Daru to the authorities.)

2a. According to the departing Balducci, why is there no need for Daru to be polite? (Daru has insulted Balducci.)

INFERENTIAL

1b. Why does Balducci decide not to denounce Daru? (Daru is an old friend who reminds Balducci of his son.)

2b. Why is he insulted? (Daru expresses disgust for actions that Balducci often performs as part of his job. In addition, Daru's refusal to obey orders shows disloyalty to colonial Europeans, the group to which Balducci feels both men belong.)

without stirring, never took his eyes off him. "Wait," the schoolmaster said in Arabic and went toward the bedroom. As he was going through the door, he had a second thought, went to the desk, took the revolver, and stuck it in his pocket. Then, without looking back, he went into his room.

For some time he lay on his couch watching the sky gradually close over, listening to the silence. **17** It was this silence that had seemed painful to him during the first days here, after the war. He had requested a post in the little town at the base of the foothills separating the upper plateaus from the desert. There, rocky walls, green and black to the north, pink and lavender to the south, marked the frontier of eternal summer. He had been named to a post farther north, on the plateau itself. In the beginning, the solitude and the silence had been hard for him on these wastelands peopled only by stones. Occasionally, furrows suggested cultivation, but they had been dug to uncover a certain kind of stone good for building. The only plowing here was to harvest rocks. Elsewhere a thin layer of soil accumulated in the hollows would be scraped out to enrich paltry village gardens. This is the way it was: bare rock covered three quarters of the region. Towns sprang up, flourished, then disappeared; men came by, loved one another or **18** fought bitterly, then died. No one in this desert, neither he nor his guest, mattered. And yet, outside this desert neither of them, Daru knew, could have really lived.

When he got up, no noise came from the **19** classroom. He was amazed at the unmixed joy he derived from the mere thought that the Arab might have fled and that he would be alone with no decision to make. But the prisoner was there. He had merely stretched out between the stove and the desk. With eyes open, he was staring at the ceiling. In that position, his thick lips were particularly noticeable, giving him a pouting look. "Come," said Daru. The Arab got up and

followed him. In the bedroom, the schoolmaster pointed to a chair near the table under the window. The Arab sat down without taking his eyes off Daru.

"Are you hungry?"

"Yes," the prisoner said.

Daru set the table for two. He took flour and oil, shaped a cake in a frying-pan, and lighted the little stove that functioned on bottled gas. While the cake was cooking, he went out to the shed **20** to get cheese, eggs, dates, and condensed milk. When the cake was done he set it on the window sill to cool, heated some condensed milk diluted with water, and beat up the eggs into an omelette. In one of his motions he knocked against the revolver stuck in his right pocket. He set the bowl down, went into the classroom, and put the revolver in his desk drawer. When he came back to the room, night was falling. He put on the light and served the Arab. "Eat," he said. The Arab took a piece of the cake, lifted it eagerly to his mouth, and stopped short.

"And you?" he asked.

"After you. I'll eat too."

The thick lips opened slightly. The Arab hesitated, then bit into the cake determinedly.

The meal over, the Arab looked at the **21** schoolmaster. "Are you the judge?"

"No, I'm simply keeping you until tomorrow."

"Why do you eat with me?"

"I'm hungry."

The Arab fell silent. Daru got up and went out. He brought back a folding bed from the shed, set it up between the table and the stove, perpendicular to his own bed. From a large suitcase which, upright in a corner, served as a shelf for papers, he took two blankets and arranged them on the camp bed. Then he stopped, felt useless, and sat down on his bed. There was nothing more to do or to get ready. He had to look at this man. He looked at him, therefore, trying to imagine his face bursting with rage. He

The Guest **213**

- Daru leaves the room and, on returning, is overjoyed when he thinks the prisoner has fled and left Daru with no decision to make.
- He then sees that the prisoner has merely lain down.
- He feeds the prisoner and sets up a folding bed for him.

IN THE GLOSSARY

- paltry: unimportant

17 CULTURAL BACKGROUND

Explain that the war mentioned here is World War II, in which many colonial Algerians—Camus included—helped fight the Nazis in Europe and North Africa.

18 TEACHING IRONY AND SETTING

Note the irony that Daru recognizes: The desert is hostile to human beings, yet both he and the prisoner would feel out of place anywhere else.

19 TEACHING CONFLICT

Make sure students understand the decision Daru hopes to avoid: whether or not he should follow orders and bring the Arab to prison and punishment.

20 GRAMMAR IN LITERATURE

Note the use of serial commas in "cheese, . . . condensed milk." Point out that this series of nouns forms a compound direct object. Then have students identify another use of serial commas in the paragraph. ("set it on the window . . . omelette," which forms a compound predicate)

21 TEACHING CHARACTERIZATION

Elicit the fact that the Arab's question shows his bewilderment. He has apparently been told he will face a judge, but he has little idea of courts of law and other trappings of the colonial legal system.

CRITICAL THINKING: GUIDED READING QUESTIONS

LITERAL

1a. What does Daru do with the revolver Balducci left him? (He takes it with him as a "second thought" when he leaves the schoolroom but then puts it in a desk drawer when he is cooking.)

2a. What questions does the prisoner ask Daru? ("Are you the judge?" and "Why do you eat with me?")

INFERENTIAL

1b. What do his actions show about his attitude toward the prisoner? (He is not afraid of the accused killer and soon abandons even his casual precautions.)

2b. Why might the prisoner be surprised that Daru shares a meal with him? (He is accustomed to harsh treatment by colonials and is surprised that one in a position of authority would share a meal with him, an Arab prisoner.)

- The Arab replies vaguely to Daru's questions about his crime and instead asks whether the gendarme will return; he then asks Daru to come with them.
- Both men sleep poorly at first, but then Daru hears his guest's regular breathing.
- Still awake himself, he later hears the Arab rise, and he remembers that he left the revolver in the desk drawer.

IN THE GLOSSARY

- **vulnerable:** able to be harmed
- **adversary:** enemy; opponent
- **fraternized:** socialized
- **musings:** thoughts

22 TEACHING CHARACTERIZATION

Ask why the prisoner may fail to understand this question. (Facing unusually complex circumstances, he is overwhelmed by fear and distress.)

23 TEACHING POINT OF VIEW

Note that the third-person limited point of view allows the narrator to focus on Daru's most private thoughts but still maintain a degree of distance.

24 TEACHING CHARACTER MOTIVATION

Elicit the idea that Daru's lack of fear of the prisoner comes in part from his recognition that he is physically stronger.

25 TEACHING THEME

Note that *brotherhood* relates to the bonds with society that Daru has all but broken, the bonds that both Balducci's request and the Arab's "Come with us" (in the first column) are meant to urge Daru to accept. Accepting these ties is especially hard under the circumstances because both Balducci (through his job) and the Arab have performed acts that Daru finds despicable.

26 TEACHING CONFLICT

Elicit the insight that Daru's inability to sleep stems from the troubling decision he must make about the fate of the prisoner.

---

couldn't do so. He could see nothing but the dark yet shining eyes and the animal mouth.

"Why did you kill him?" he asked in a voice whose hostile tone surprised him.

The Arab looked away.

"He ran away. I ran after him."

He raised his eyes to Daru again and they were full of a sort of woeful interrogation. "Now what will they do to me?"

"Are you afraid?"

He stiffened, turning his eyes away.

22 "Are you sorry?"

The Arab stared at him openmouthed. Obviously he did not understand. Daru's annoyance was growing. At the same time he felt awkward and self-conscious with his big body wedged between the two beds.

"Lie down there," he said impatiently. "That's your bed."

The Arab didn't move. He called to Daru: "Tell me!"

The schoolmaster looked at him.

"Is the gendarme coming back tomorrow?"

"I don't know."

"Are you coming with us?"

"I don't know. Why?"

The prisoner got up and stretched out on top of the blankets, his feet toward the window. The light from the electric bulb shone straight into his eyes and he closed them at once.

"Why?" Daru repeated, standing beside the bed.

The Arab opened his eyes under the blinding light and looked at him, trying not to blink.

"Come with us," he said.

23 In the middle of the night, Daru was still not asleep. He had gone to bed after undressing completely; he generally slept naked. But when he suddenly realized that he had nothing on, he hesitated. He felt vulnerable and the temptation came to him to put his clothes back on. Then he shrugged his shoulders; after all, he wasn't a

214 *The Short Story*

24 child and, if need be, he could break his adversary in two. From his bed he could observe him, lying on his back, still motionless with his eyes closed under the harsh light. When Daru turned out the light, the darkness seemed to coagulate all of a sudden. Little by little, the night came back to life in the window where the starless sky was stirring gently. The schoolmaster soon made out the body lying at his feet. The Arab still did not move, but his eyes seemed open. A faint wind was prowling around the schoolhouse. Perhaps it would drive away the clouds and the sun would reappear.

During the night the wind increased. The hens fluttered a little and then were silent. The Arab turned over on his side with his back to Daru, who thought he heard him moan. Then he listened for his guest's breathing, become heavier and more regular. He listened to that breath so close to him and mused without being able to go to sleep. In this room where he had been sleeping alone for a year, this presence bothered

25 him. But it bothered him also by imposing on him a sort of brotherhood he knew well but refused to accept in the present circumstances. Men who share the same rooms, soldiers or prisoners, develop a strange alliance as if, having cast off their armor with their clothing, they fraternized every evening, over and above their differences, in the ancient community of dream and fatigue. But Daru shook himself; he didn't like such musings, and it was essential to sleep.

26 A little later, however, when the Arab stirred slightly, the schoolmaster was still not asleep. When the prisoner made a second move, he stiffened, on the alert. The Arab was lifting himself slowly on his arms with almost the motion of a sleepwalker. Seated upright in bed, he waited motionless without turning his head toward Daru, as if he were listening attentively. Daru did not stir; it had just occurred to him that the revolver was still in the drawer of his desk. It was better to act at once. Yet he continued to

---

CRITICAL THINKING: GUIDED READING QUESTIONS

LITERAL

1a. What questions does Daru ask his "guest"? ("Why did you kill him?" "Are you afraid?" and "Are you sorry?")

2a. What final request does the Arab make before going to bed? (He says, "Come with us.")

INFERENTIAL

1b. Why do you think Daru asks these questions? (He is both fascinated and repelled by the man's outburst of murderous violence and wants to understand it better.)

2b. Why do you think he makes this request? (Daru has shown him kindness, and he probably thinks such a man will help or comfort him.)

observe the prisoner, who, with the same slithery motion, put his feet on the ground, waited again, then began to stand up slowly. Daru was about to call out to him when the Arab began to walk, in a quite natural but extraordinarily silent way. He was heading toward the door at the end of the room that opened into the shed. He lifted the latch with precaution and went out, pushing the door behind him but without shutting it. Daru had not stirred. "He is running away," he merely thought. "Good riddance!" Yet he listened attentively. The hens were not fluttering; __27__ the guest must be on the plateau. A faint sound of water reached him, and he didn't know what it was until the Arab again stood framed in the doorway, closed the door carefully, and came back to bed without a sound. Then Daru turned his back on him and fell asleep. Still later he __28__ seemed, from the depths of his sleep, to hear furtive steps around the schoolhouse. "I'm dreaming! I'm dreaming!" he repeated to himself. And he went on sleeping.

When he awoke, the sky was clear; the loose window let in a cold, pure air. The Arab was asleep, hunched up under the blankets now, his mouth open, utterly relaxed. But when Daru __29__ shook him, he started dreadfully, staring at Daru with wild eyes as if he had never seen him and such a frightened expression that the schoolmaster stepped back. "Don't be afraid. It's me. You must eat." The Arab nodded his head and said yes. Calm had returned to his face, but his expression was vacant and listless.

The coffee was ready. They drank it seated together on the folding bed as they munched their pieces of the cake. Then Daru led the Arab under the shed and showed him the faucet where he washed. He went back into the room, folded the blankets and the bed, made his own bed and put the room in order. Then he went through the classroom and out onto the terrace. The sun was already rising in the blue sky; a soft, bright light was bathing the deserted plateau.

On the ridge the snow was melting in spots. The stones were about to reappear. Crouched on the edge of the plateau, the schoolmaster looked at the deserted expanse. He thought of Balducci. He had hurt him, for he had sent him off in a way as if he didn't want to be associated with him. He could still hear the gendarme's farewell and, without knowing why, he felt strangely empty and vulnerable. At that moment, from the other side of the schoolhouse, the prisoner coughed. Daru listened to him almost despite himself and then, furious, threw a pebble that whistled through the air before sinking into the __30__ snow. That man's stupid crime revolted him, but to hand him over was contrary to honor. Merely thinking of it made him smart with humiliation. And he cursed at one and the same time his own people who had sent him this Arab and the Arab too who had dared to kill and not managed to get away. Daru got up, walked in a circle on the terrace, waited motionless, and then went back into the schoolhouse.

The Arab, leaning over the cement floor of the shed, was washing his teeth with two fingers. Daru looked at him and said: "Come." He went back into the room ahead of the prisoner. He slipped a hunting-jacket on over his sweater and put on walking-shoes. Standing, he waited until the Arab had put on his *chèche* and sandals. They went into the classroom and the schoolmaster pointed to the exit, saying: "Go ahead." The fellow didn't budge. "I'm coming," said Daru. The Arab went out. Daru went back into the room and made a package of pieces of rusk,[9] dates, and sugar. In the classroom, before going out, he hesitated a second in front of his desk, then crossed the threshold and locked the door. "That's the way," he said. He started toward the __31__ east, followed by the prisoner. But, a short distance from the schoolhouse, he thought he heard a slight sound behind them. He retraced

---

9. **rusk:** hard, dried bread.

The Guest **215**

CRITICAL THINKING: GUIDED READING QUESTIONS

LITERAL

1a. During the night what does Daru think when he hears the Arab going outside? ("He is running away! Good riddance!")

2a. How does Daru feel when he recalls Balducci's hurt farewell? (He feels "strangely empty and vulnerable.")

INFERENTIAL

1b. Why is he pleased to think that the Arab has run off? (It would solve his problem of having to decide the Arab's fate.)

2b. Why does he feel empty? (Balducci was one of his few social contacts, and Daru behaved as if he never wanted to see him again; breaking off this contact represents breaking off contact with the colonial society of which Balducci is a part.)

- After finding no one outside the school, Daru walks with the Arab for an hour, gives him food and money, and points out two routes: east to Tinguit and prison and south to the nomads and freedom.
- Heading back, Daru turns to see the Arab walking toward the prison.
- At the school someone has scrawled, "You handed over our brother. You will pay for this."
- Daru realizes that in this vast landscape he loves, he is now truly alone.

32 TEACHING PLOT: CLIMAX

Note that this scene is the climax, for here Daru makes his irrevocable decision about what to do with the Arab. Since his internal conflict is inextricably connected to his external one with society, his decision affects both.

33 TEACHING THEME AND SYMBOLS

Elicit the idea that the two routes represent society and its confinements versus freedom. By giving the Arab the choice to make, Daru himself chooses freedom—and cuts himself off from society.

34 CULTURAL BACKGROUND

Explain that the desert nomads' traditions of hospitality oblige them to shelter strangers.

35 TEACHING IRONY

Note that the ending is ironic: After Daru disobeys his own society's orders and gives the Arab food and money, we do not expect that he will be misunderstood by the rebels.

COLLABORATIVE LEARNING: ENRICHMENT ACTIVITY

Social Studies Have a group of students make an oral presentation on Algeria, with each student focusing on a different topic: peoples, climate, topography, colonial rule, the struggle for independence, and so on.

---

his steps and examined the surroundings of the house; there was no one there. The Arab watched him without seeming to understand. "Come on," said Daru.

They walked for an hour and rested beside a sharp peak of limestone. The snow was melting faster and faster and the sun was drinking up the puddles at once, rapidly cleaning the plateau, which gradually dried and vibrated like the air itself. When they resumed walking, the ground rang under their feet. From time to time a bird rent the space in front of them with a joyful cry. Daru breathed in deeply the fresh morning light. He felt a sort of rapture before the vast familiar expanse, now almost entirely yellow under its dome of blue sky. They walked an hour more, descending toward the south. They reached a level height made up of crumbly rocks. From there on, the plateau sloped down, eastward, toward a low plain where there were a few spindly trees and, to the south, toward outcroppings of rock that gave the landscape a chaotic look.

32 Daru surveyed the two directions. There was nothing but the sky on the horizon. Not a man could be seen. He turned toward the Arab, who was looking at him blankly. Daru held out the package to him. "Take it," he said. "There are dates, bread, and sugar. You can hold out for two days. Here are a thousand francs[10] too." The Arab took the package and the money but kept his full hands at chest level as if he didn't know what to do with what was being given him. **33** "Now look," the schoolmaster said as he pointed in the direction of the east, "there's the way to Tinguit. You have a two-hour walk. At Tinguit you'll find the administration and the police. They are expecting you." The Arab looked toward the east, still holding the package and the money against his chest. Daru took his elbow and turned him rather roughly toward the south. At the foot of the height on which they stood

---

10. **francs:** The franc, the chief monetary unit of France, was formerly used in Algeria.

---

could be seen a faint path. "That's the trail across the plateau. In a day's walk from here you'll find pasturelands and the first nomads. **34** They'll take you in and shelter you according to their law." The Arab had now turned toward Daru and a sort of panic was visible in his expression. "Listen," he said. Daru shook his head: "No, be quiet. Now I'm leaving you." He turned his back on him, took two long steps in the direction of the school, looked hesitantly at the motionless Arab, and started off again. For a few minutes he heard nothing but his own step resounding on the cold ground and did not turn his head. A moment later, however, he turned around. The Arab was still there on the edge of the hill, his arms hanging now, and he was looking at the schoolmaster. Daru felt something rise in his throat. But he swore with impatience, waved vaguely, and started off again. He had already gone some distance when he again stopped and looked. There was no longer anyone on the hill.

Daru hesitated. The sun was now rather high in the sky and was beginning to beat down on his head. The schoolmaster retraced his steps, at first somewhat uncertainly, then with decision. When he reached the little hill, he was bathed in sweat. He climbed it as fast as he could and stopped, out of breath, at the top. The rock-fields to the south stood out sharply against the blue sky, but on the plain to the east a steamy heat was already rising. And in that slight haze, Daru, with heavy heart, made out the Arab walking slowly on the road to prison.

A little later, standing before the window of the classroom, the schoolmaster was watching the clear light bathing the whole surface of the plateau, but he hardly saw it. Behind him on the blackboard, among the winding French rivers, sprawled the clumsily chalked-up words he had **35** just read: "You handed over our brother. You will pay for this." Daru looked at the sky, the plateau, and, beyond, the invisible lands stretching all the way to the sea. In this vast landscape he had loved so much, he was alone.

CRITICAL THINKING: GUIDED READING QUESTIONS

LITERAL

1a. What two routes does Daru show the Arab? (the route east to Tinguit and prison and the route south to freedom among the nomads, who will take him in)

2a. When he returns to the school, what does Daru find scrawled on the board? ("You handed over our brother. You will pay for this.")

INFERENTIAL

1b. By having the Arab choose prison, what is Camus suggesting about most people? (They are too weak and frightened to choose freedom and prefer the familiar authority of society, despite its confinements.)

2b. Who wrote this message, and why does it make Daru completely alone? (It was undoubtedly written by a native rebel. Daru has now antagonized both his own colonial society and the native society.)

Detail. *August Moon,* 1984, Paul Resika.

Paul Resika (born 1928) is an American painter of landscapes, seascapes, and, occasionally, portraits. He composes each picture with an eye for overall light, shadow, and color. Many of his paintings depict images of the New England shore. In each work he favors atmosphere and mood over detail. In this detail of *August Moon,* his brisk strokes of color suggest an evening seascape with a lone figure gazing at a luminous moon.

■ Ask students what aspect of Daru's personality the lone figure on the beach might represent (Daru's characteristic solitude or his inability to take sides)

READER'S RESPONSE

What do you think will happen to Daru?

ANSWERS

STUDY QUESTIONS

1. It stands alone on a plateau; a colonial policeman and an Arab prisoner in native dress.
2. to deliver the prisoner to the police; due to an impending uprising, no police can be spared.
3. It disgusts him, and he will not obey it. "If there's an uprising, no one is safe."
4. glad that the Arab may have escaped; thinks the man is running off; does nothing
5. going east to prison or south to the nomads and freedom; prison; the message "You handed over our brother. You will pay for this."
6. It criticizes Balducci's job and shows disloyalty to Daru's (and Balducci's) people.
7. He cannot understand Daru's motives. He is too scared and weak to choose the unfamiliar and has given in to despair.
8. It shows his refusal to interfere with another's freedom. He hopes to avoid taking sides.
9. He has tried to remain a bystander amid political upheaval, and although kind to the Arab, he abandons him. He has alienated all factions of society in his homeland.
10. Answers will vary.

LITERARY FOCUS

1. external conflict—with society; internal—deciding what to do with the prisoner
2. Despite his kindness to the prisoner, the rebels accuse him of betraying the man.
3. He believes strongly in individual freedom and though kind wants to avoid social ties.
4. barrenness and loneliness; a conflict between the natives and French colonial rule.
5. third-person limited; since we know only what Daru knows, we are as surprised as he is.
6. matter-of-fact; fatalistic view
7. Yes, Daru may represent uncommitted intellectuals; Balducci, the colonial presence; the prisoner, natives disrupted by colonial rule.
8. No one can escape society's struggles and still remain part of society.

T-218 The Short Story

STUDY QUESTIONS

Recalling

1. Briefly describe the school's surroundings and the two men who visit the schoolmaster.
2. What specific order is Daru, the schoolmaster, given? Why do the police need his help?
3. What does Daru tell Balducci about the order? What does Balducci answer when Daru says, "I have nothing to fear"?
4. How does Daru feel when he returns to the classroom after resting in his bedroom? What does Daru think and do when the prisoner gets up in the middle of the night?
5. What choice does Daru eventually give the prisoner? What choice does the prisoner make? What does Daru discover when he returns to the school?

Interpreting

6. Why is Balducci insulted by Daru's response to the order?
7. Why is the prisoner frightened by the choice that Daru gives him? Why do you think the prisoner chooses as he does?
8. Why is it significant that Daru never makes the decision himself, preferring to leave it up to the prisoner? What does Daru's behavior suggest about his attitude toward his society's political struggles?
9. In what sense is Daru responsible for the message he finds on the blackboard? Explain the significance of the story's last sentence.

Extending

10. Is it possible not to take sides in the political and social struggles of one's time? Explain.

LITERARY FOCUS

Elements of the Short Story

Every story weaves together a number of **elements**—plot, characters, setting, point of view, tone and style, and theme. In reading a story, we enter the world of its setting and are caught up in its characters

218 *The Short Story*

and plot. Our reactions to the story are governed by the point of view and tone of the narrator, the style in which the story is written, and any irony the story may employ. The story's theme is the product of all the other elements, including any symbols the story may contain.

Thinking About the Elements of the Short Story

1. **Plot:** The story events focus on an external conflict involving Daru and his society and a related internal conflict that Daru must resolve. What are these conflicts?
2. **Irony:** What is ironic about the outcome of Daru's decision?
3. **Character:** What do we learn about Daru from the way he treats the prisoner?
4. **Setting:** What atmosphere, or mood, pervades the Algerian landscape where the story is set? What social conflict stands in the background of the plot?
5. **Point of View:** From what point of view is the story told? How does this point of view help create the ironic ending?
6. **Tone and Style:** Identify the narrator's tone, or attitude toward story events and characters. What view of the world does the tone seem to convey?
7. **Symbol:** Could any of the characters be symbols of something more than themselves? Explain.
8. **Theme:** Based on your answers to the preceding questions, what would you identify as the story's theme, or main idea about life?

COMPOSITION

Writing a Dialogue

■ Imagine that Daru goes to Balducci to seek protection from the rebels who threaten Daru at the end of the story. Write the dialogue that might take place between Daru and Balducci. Answer these questions in your dialogue: (a) Does Daru have the right to ask for help? (b) What reasons might Balducci give for refusing? (c) Does Balducci finally help? Why or why not?

COMPOSITION: GUIDELINES FOR EVALUATION

WRITING A DIALOGUE

Objective

To create a dialogue between characters in a story

Guidelines for Evaluation

■ suggested length: one to two pages

■ should use the correct format and punctuation for dialogue
■ should reflect the story's events and Daru's and Balducci's personalities and attitudes
■ should address issues raised in the story

PREVIEW: THE AUTHOR AND THE WORLD

Grazia Deledda

(1875–1936)

Italy

Nobel Prize–winner Grazia Deledda [grät′sē ə dā lād′ə] is famous for her vivid and realistic portraits of life on the Italian island of Sardinia. A native of Sardinia, Deledda grew up in the small town of Nuoro [nōō ō′rō], where her father worked as a lawyer and served three times as mayor. Though her mother could neither read nor write, Deledda, with encouragement from her father, received a decent education and learned "proper" Italian at a local school. Deledda was still a student when she became interested in writing, and she was only seventeen when she published her first stories.

Fame came quickly as Deledda went on to produce several story collections and acclaimed novels such as *Flower of Sardinia* and *The Mother*. In 1926, ten years before her death, Deledda was awarded the Nobel Prize "for her idealistically inspired writings which with plastic clarity picture the life on her native island and with depth and sympathy deal with human problems in general." Many of her works explore in a vivid, naturalistic style the questions of temptation and sin.

GEOGRAPHY AND CULTURE

The Island of Sardinia

Sardinia is the second largest island in the Mediterranean Sea, which separates Europe and Africa. Located about 120 miles west of mainland Italy, Sardinia was claimed by Spain, Austria, and France before it became a permanent part of Italy in 1861, when Italy became a unified nation. Some inhabitants of the island speak a dialect of Italian called Sardinian—Grazia Deledda's mother spoke it, for example—and in the upcoming story the main character writes love poems in dialect to his wife. Nevertheless, Sardinians are taught "proper" Italian in school, as Deledda was.

Mountainous and largely deforested, Sardinia is subject to frequent droughts and violent winds, all of which make the landscape bleak and farming difficult. Thus Sardinia has historically been a poor and sparsely populated island. Most of its inhabitants scrape out a living by raising sheep and goats or by cultivating wheat, olives, and citrus fruits. Like many of the characters in Deledda's fiction, the main character of "The Shoes" is a victim of the island's poverty.

See *LITERATURE AND CULTURE SOURCEBOOK: Italy*

The Shoes **219**

LESSON PREVIEW

In this Sardinian tale fate fails to reward a poor but righteous man. Elia dreams of taking his wife on a holiday. Hearing that his rich uncle is dying, he sets off on foot, but his shoes fall apart and he steals a pair. Plagued by guilt, he goes back to return them. By the time he reaches his destination, the uncle has died, and since Elia failed to appear, he left his money to charity.

LITERARY SKILLS FOR THIS SELECTION

- total effect
- character motivation

THEMES IN THIS SELECTION

- cultures and conflicts: poverty and its problems
- romantic ideals versus reality

LESSON OBJECTIVES

1. to examine the total effect of a story
2. to understand words from Italian
3. to compare and contrast stories

Teacher's Classroom Resources 1

- Teaching Notes   389
- Prereading Vocabulary   390
- Reading Guide   391
- Check Test   392
- Responding to World Cultures   393
- Literary Focus: The Total Effect   394
- Language Study: Words from Italian   395
- Writing Process Guide: Writing About the Total Effect   396
- Grammar in Literature: Linking Verbs   397
- Selection Test   398

IN THE CLASSROOM

TEACHING STUDENTS OF DIFFERENT ABILITIES

- **For less advanced students:** Have students read the first page of the story and then try to predict the ending. Have them complete the Reading Guide.

- **For more advanced students:** Have students compare and contrast the views of fate expressed in this story and in "Federigo's Falcon," the other Italian tale in their text.

DISCUSSING GEOGRAPHY AND CULTURE

Dialects

Sardinian is one of many Italian dialects. From the northern regions around Venice to mountainous Calabria, in the toe of the boot, to the island of Sicily, Italians use distinct dialects. In fact, dialects may differ significantly between villages that are only a few miles apart.

- Ask students to offer their opinions of why dialects develop. (They might mention the influence of neighboring or immigrant peoples and relatively isolated environments.)

Grazia Deledda

The Shoes

Translated from the Italian by Alethea Graham

It often happened now that Elia Carái had nothing to do; for times were bad, folk hesitated about going to law, and even people like famous barristers and emeritus professors[1] and retired government official had to work as simple attorneys. But even when he had no cases, Elia used to go to the Law Courts all the same, settle down in the waiting-room, and there, leaning his note-book on his knee or on the wall, he would write poems in dialect to his wife. The storm raged around him. The crowd surged hither and thither; poor women, who had come about a matter of a few cents, shouted abuse at each other, as solemn and tragic as if they had the whole world to divide; swindlers, perfectly ready to swear they owed nothing to their own creditors, went by with their heads in the air and their chests thrust forward proudly; the solicitors,[2] poorer than their own clients, went round from one to the other wondering how they could manage to get hold of a sheet of stamped paper. Elia took it all very calmly. He wrote, in his old-fashioned verse, which he dedicated to his wife:

Su mundu lu connosco e áonzi cosa
Chi succedit succedere deviat.[3]

"I know what the world is like, and I know that everything that happens was destined to happen. I am a poet and a philosopher; nothing ever surprises me in this world. Life is a see-saw, one day up and the next day down, and the next day up again. Do not despair, my golden lily. Perhaps Uncle Agostino, who has driven his wife out of the house and disinherited her, will remember us one day. Then we will go to the seaside together, we will watch the boats in the distance, and hold hands like a honeymoon couple. And, after all, we too are happy now; peace and love reign in our dwellings, and thou, Cedar of Lebanon, *Venus hermosa,[4]* art my riches and my queen. . . ."

One winter morning, a carter slapped Elia heavily on the shoulder with a hand that felt like stone.

"Run, man! I've just been to Terranova[5] with a load of rubbish, and I saw the carrier,[6] your Uncle Agostino. He's dangerously ill. . . ."

Elia stood up calmly and smoothed his gray hair with his hand as a sign of grief.

"I will go and tell my wife the sad news at once."

His wife did not seem much disturbed by the sad news; she did not even get up from the doorstep where she was sitting, trying to get warm in the sun. She was respectably dressed, wore

---

1. **barristers and emeritus** [i mer'i təs] **professors:** trial lawyers and retired professors.
2. **solicitors:** lawyers who do lesser legal work, as opposed to trial lawyers.
3. **Su mundu . . . deviat** [sōō mōōn'dōō lōō kō nōs'kō e dōn'tsē kō'zä kē sōō che'dĕt sōō che'de rä dä'vē ät]: The next sentence translates these lines, which are in Sardinian dialect. (See the Geography and Culture feature that precedes the story.)

4. **Cedar of Lebanon,** *Venus hermosa* [ār mō'sä]: poetic compliments. The cedar trees of Lebanon are famous for their beautiful fragrance; *Venus hermosa*, or "beautiful Venus," compares his wife to the Roman goddess of love and beauty.
5. **Terranova** [ter ä nō'vä]: former name of Olbia, a town and port in northeastern Sardinia.
6. **carrier:** here, someone in the business of transporting goods.

220 *The Short Story*

CRITICAL THINKING: GUIDED READING QUESTIONS

LITERAL

1a. Since he has little work at the Law Courts, what does Elia spend most of his time doing? (He writes love poems to his wife.)

2a. In his poem what does Elia say about himself and the things in life that surprise him? ("I am a poet and a philosopher; nothing ever surprises me in this world.")

INFERENTIAL

1b. What do these actions reveal about his attitude toward his wife and toward life in general? (He loves his much and is a romantic, idealistic person.)

2b. Do you think these remarks are entirely accurate? Explain. (No, they seem exaggerated in order to strike a poetic pose. By writing love poems and dreaming of an inheritance, Elia reveals himself to be more naive and less cynical than these remarks suggest.)

A Pair of Boots, 1887, Vincent van Gogh.

PAGE SUMMARY: AT A GLANCE

- Elia's wife shows no excitement at his news.
- Her clothes and thin white hair, done in the latest fashion, only emphasize her poverty.

IN THE GLOSSARY

- anemic: pale
- inert: unmoving

5 READING SKILL: CONTRAST

Elicit the contrast between the wife's fashionable hair style and her worn and frayed clothes. The discrepancy underscores her poverty.

6 GRAMMAR IN LITERATURE

Point out that usual subject-verb order is reversed in this sentence: The first *noise* is the subject, but it comes after the verb, *came.* Have students identify the type of structure that opens the sentence. (a long prepositional phrase in which an adjective clause, *where . . . yard,* modifies the object of the preposition, *house*)

ART AND LITERATURE

The Dutch artist Vincent van Gogh (1853–1890), having failed as an art dealer and as a lay missionary to Belgian miners, depended on the support of his brother, Theo, a Parisian art dealer, during the last ten years of his life. Perhaps because of his own experiences, van Gogh believed that the best art expresses the tragedy that often stems from poverty. In this painting of worn boots—one upturned, one torn open with its laces untied— van Gogh tells a story of poverty, of endless trudging, of a man's exhaustion and fatigue. The boots evoke the artist's own struggle with poverty.

- Ask students which aspects of Elia's life seem appropriate to the boots and which seem inappropriate. (His poverty and his wife's appearance seem appropriate; his adoration of his wife and his hope for happier days seems inappropriate.)

5 shoes, and had her hair done in the latest fashion; but her worn, frayed frock, her old shoes, and thin hair framing her dead-white, anemic face like a halo, only served to show off her poverty more clearly. Her great eyes, which had once seemed so dark, were now a kind of golden hazel-color, and indifferent and staring, like the eyes of a hare.

6   From inside the house, where the two occupied one little ground-floor room giving on to the yard, came a noise like the noise of the Law Courts. It was the owners of the house quarreling, while in the tavern that belonged to them, men were playing *morra*[7] and laughing.

   Elia's wife behaved like her husband in the Law Courts—inert, and indifferent to what went

---

7. *morra:* popular Italian game in which one player guesses the number of fingers that another player holds up out of sight.

The Shoes   **221**

CRITICAL THINKING: GUIDED READING QUESTIONS

LITERAL

1a. How does Elia's wife behave amid the noise of her neighbors? (She is inert and indifferent to what goes on.)

INFERENTIAL

1b. What do the details suggest about the cause of her inertia and apathy? (She is unhappy with her impoverished life.)

- Elia says he has enough money for the trip to his uncle's and gives his wife a poem.
- In reality he has only three lire and must travel on foot, even though his shoes are full of holes.
- When the shoes give way, he is uncomfortable and ashamed to think that he must arrive at his uncle's looking like a beggar.
- He resolves to get another pair of shoes at all costs.
- At the inn where he stops, the sleeping patrons have removed their shoes for the night.

IN THE GLOSSARY

- provisions: supplies
- wayfarers: travelers

7 TEACHING CHARACTER MOTIVATION

Note that Elia's thoughts in the next column contradict or modify his thoughts here. While love for his wife may prompt him to accept her as she is, he does not really want her to stay sadly apathetic.

8 TEACHING THE TOTAL EFFECT

Point out that this view of fate shows more optimism than Elia showed earlier, and have students consider the theme of fate as suggested by the plot and the details of character and setting.

9 TEACHING STUDENTS OF LIMITED ENGLISH PROFICIENCY

In conjunction with the Language Study, note that the Italian word *lire* has entered English. Have nonnative students name monetary terms from their own native lands.

10 CRITICAL THINKING: EVALUATION

Have students evaluate Elia's reasoning here. Do you agree that it is so important for him to obtain another pair of shoes?

11 READING SKILL: PREDICTING OUTCOMES

Have students predict what Elia is likely to do. (take a pair of shoes from a sleeping patron)

---

7 on around her. He loved her and wanted her just like that.

"Do you know what I'm going to do?" he asked, stroking her hair and looking up at the sky. "I'm going."

"Where?"

"Where? But haven't you been listening? To Uncle Agostino's, of course. It's fine today," he added, without saying all that he was thinking; but his wife must have guessed because she looked down at his shoes, which were worn and full of holes, and asked:

"What about money for the journey?"

"I've got enough. Never you mind about me, **8** don't worry. In this world everything is bound to go all right in the end, if only you take things calmly and sensibly; the only thing that really matters is being fond of people and treating them kindly. I was just thinking about that sort of thing this morning; here . . . would you like to read it?"

He tore the sheet off his pad, and blushed as he shyly let it drop into her lap. It was all he left her in the way of provisions while he was away.

9 He set off on foot. He had only three lire[8] in the world, and he was much too wise to lose time by trying to borrow money for the journey.

He was, however, used to this sort of thing; he never expected anything to help him apart from his philosophic calm and his Uncle Agostino's will. He was an excellent walker, and thought far more about his shoes than about his feet; if matters went as well as he expected, then everything would be mended in due course.

Matters went well as far as Orosei.[9] The road was downhill all the way, smooth and straight, accompanied, preceded, and followed by the most beautiful scenery; the very sight of it made one forget all earthly cares and troubles. It was like traveling in an enchanted land; the sun, like

---

8. **lire** [lir′ā]: plural of lira, the Italian monetary unit.
9. **Orosei** [ôr ō zā′]: village in Eastern Sardinia.

222 *The Short Story*

---

a great diamond, shed its cold, pure luster around; the rocks and the grass were glistening. Then, as he went farther down, Elia felt the sun grow warmer and more golden, and at last, on the marble background of hills towards the sea, he saw, as in spring, pink almond-blossom in flower.

But the sun went down with cruel suddenness; after a short spell of twilight, the cold night fell, and Elia felt his feet were getting wet. His shoes had given way. This was obviously one of the things that were destined to happen, but all the same he did not accept it with his usual philosophical calm. He could not possibly mend **10** them or get someone to lend him a pair now. It was very uncomfortable walking with holes in one's shoes, and dreadfully lacking in dignity, moreover, to appear at one's uncle's house looking like a beggar. For the sake of the future, for his wife's health and well-being, he must get hold of a pair of shoes at all costs. The question was, how? Elia had not the slightest idea. And, meanwhile, he reached the village.

The streets were dark and swept by sea-wind; not a soul was astir. Only, on the piazza,[10] a tiny inn shed a hospitable light. Elia went in and asked for a night's lodging; he paid in advance and was given a bed in a dirty-looking room where two other wayfarers were asleep. One of them was snoring like Pluto.[11] Elia lay down with his clothes on, but he could not get **11** to sleep; he saw endless rows of shoes along all the streets in the world, among houses, and out in the fields; whenever there was a man, there was a pair of shoes. A great many pairs were hidden away in drawers and cupboards and all sorts of odd corners; others stood at the end of their master's bed, watching over his sleep; others were waiting outside doors, and there were still

---

10. **piazza** [pē ät′sə *or* pē az′ə]: public square typically found in Italian villages and cities.
11. **Pluto:** Roman god of the underworld, usually pictured as burly and muscular and often associated with death and thus sleep.

CRITICAL THINKING: GUIDED READING QUESTIONS

LITERAL

1a. Why does Elia travel on foot? (He has only three lire.)

2a. What does Elia feel he must obtain at all costs? (another pair of shoes)

INFERENTIAL

1b. Why would it be unwise to try borrowing money for the journey? (In such impoverished times it is unlikely that anyone will be able to lend him money, and he will only waste time by trying to get some.)

2b. What does Elia think will happen if he arrives at his uncle's house in shoes that have fallen apart? (Because he looks like a beggar, his uncle will be offended and will not make Elia his heir.)

others, like his own, that shared the poverty and despair of their wearers. . . .

The roaring of the wind outside, and the snoring of the man beside him, made an accompaniment to his obsession. The hours went by; a star rose in the heavens, delicately blue as if steeped in the waters of the sea, and stopped outside the rattling window-panes. Elia thought of his wife, and the poems he wrote for her, and the easy life they would both lead if only Uncle Agostino left them all his belongings. . . .

He got up and bent over, trembling, to take the snoring man's shoes. They were heavy; their worn nails felt cold against his hot fingers. He put them down, and groped about on the floor to find the other man's shoes, but he found nothing.

Then he heard a vague noise in the corridor, like the steps of unshod feet. He stopped there motionless, crouching down with his hands on the floor, and trembling like a frightened animal. He realized to the full the extent of his degradation; an instinctive sadness, like the sorrow of a heart in danger, weighed heavily upon him. But as soon as the noise had stopped, he went out to the door to see there was no one there; and by the light of a tiny lamp at the end of the passage he saw a cat rubbing itself against the wall with its tail in the air, and a pair of elastic-sided shoes by the door beside it, throwing a shadow on the floor like two great hooks.

He took them, hid them under his cloak, and went downstairs. A man was sleeping on a mat in the yard so as to watch over people's horses; the big gates were just closed with a latch. Elia managed to get away quietly, and found himself on the sea front, by the gray sea under the twinkling stars that seemed to wish to fall down from the sky, lower and lower. . . .

"It's odd, how everything in man and nature has a tendency to fall," mused Elia, walking quickly with the wind across the dark, hollow land, the dark mountains, and the gray sea.

After walking half an hour or so, he decided it was the moment to put on the stolen shoes. He sat down on a milestone, put on the shoes, and felt them critically. He was delighted; they were soft and roomy; but as he bent down over them he felt the sense of degradation suddenly overwhelm him again. . . .

"What if they follow me? A pretty figure I'll cut then. . . . Whatever will my wife say! 'While you're about it, Elia Carái, you might just as well steal a million lire as a pair of shoes!'"

Then: "A million lire! The question is where to find them, then I'd take them at once," he added, laughing at himself, stretching out his feet, and wriggling his toes about inside his shoes. It was an odd thing; but his feet burned and throbbed, and seemed to have a violent objection to being inside those shoes.

When he started walking back, with his own shoes under his arm so that he could put them on quickly and throw away the other pair if by any chance he was being followed, he found he could not walk anything like as quickly as before. His legs shook, and he stopped every now and then, seeming to hear steps coming up behind him.

Dawn rose from the pale sea behind a veil of mist, and terrified him, like a ghost. Now the people he had met on the road to Orosei could see him quite well, and when they reached the village and heard the story of the stolen shoes, they would be able to say: "Yes, I met a man who looked rather a suspicious character; he had a sort of parcel thing under his cloak."

As a matter of fact he did meet a peasant, walking quiet and dark through the dawn, with a knapsack and a stick; and Elia imagined he turned round to look at him and smiled.

Day was breaking, sad and gray; the clouds, like great, black, tangled skeins, ran from mountain to sea, from sea to mountain, clinging to cliffs and rocks that unraveled them a little. And the crows cawed as they passed over the windswept moorlands.

The quiet landscape of the day before

The Shoes 223

PAGE SUMMARY: AT A GLANCE

- Elia takes a pair of shoes from the inn, quietly leaves, and muses about his sinful act and its consequences.
- He finds that he cannot walk as quickly in the new shoes, and his feet feel as if they are burning and throbbing.
- After dawn he imagines people seeing him on the road and reporting him as a suspicious character.

IN THE GLOSSARY

- degradation: morally lowered state
- milestone: roadside stone that indicates the distance from a place
- skeins: bundles of yarn

12 TEACHING CHARACTER MOTIVATION

Note that again we are told that Elia is motivated by love for his wife, not selfishness.

13 CULTURAL BACKGROUND

Explain that in earlier times, European law stipulated severe punishments for even minor thefts. Thus Elia not only feels morally guilty about doing wrong, but he also fears legal consequences.

14 TEACHING CHARACTERIZATION

Have students trace Elia's changing attitudes in this and the next three paragraphs. (First he generalizes objectively about people's tendency to sin, next he feels degraded, then he fears capture, and finally he looks humorously at himself.) Note that ultimately guilt and fear prevail.

15 TEACHING THE TOTAL EFFECT

Point out that the details about the threatening weather mirror Elia's unhappiness and anxiety and add to his guilt and fear. Since the story is told in the third-person limited point of view, the impressions of the setting we get are Elia's.

CRITICAL THINKING: GUIDED READING QUESTIONS

LITERAL

1a. As Elia walks in the stolen shoes, what do his feet seem to do? (They burn and throb as if they have a violent objection to the shoes.)

2a. What does Elia imagine people on the road will say? ("Yes, I met a man who looked rather a suspicious character; he had a sort of parcel thing under his cloak.")

INFERENTIAL

1b. What causes his feet to feel this way? (Elia's feelings of guilt about taking the shoes)

2b. What fear prompts these imaginings? (Elia fears being caught with the stolen shoes.)

- Elia puts on his old shoes, leaves the others by the roadside, but still finds no peace.
- Finally, he walks all the way back to the inn and leaves the new shoes where he found them.
- When he arrives at his uncle's, he finds that his relative has died; he discovers that because he did not arrive in time, his uncle has left all his money to charity.
- Back at home Elia cannot tell his wife what really happened.

IN THE GLOSSARY

- diabolical: fiendish; cruel
- legacy: something left in a will
- sheepishly: with embarrassment

16 TEACHING CHARACTER MOTIVATION

Point out that again concern for the wife he loves impels Elia's actions.

17 TEACHING THE TOTAL EFFECT

Note that the weather now seems fine because Elia has eased his conscience and fears.

18 TEACHING THE TOTAL EFFECT

Elicit that Elia's character and actions and the ironic ending all help point to the story's themes: Romantic idealism does not reflect the real world, and fate is indifferent to human behavior.

19 CRITICAL THINKING: LOGICAL REASONING

Ask why Elia's question makes little sense. (Not only did his wife think he had already reached his uncle's, but she did not have money with which to pay for a reply.)

COLLABORATIVE LEARNING: ENRICHMENT ACTIVITY

Literature Have a group of students research nineteenth-century literary movements, and have them discuss how their ideas are reflected or refuted in this story. Each student should research a different movement—Romanticism, Realism, Naturalism, Regionalism, and so on.

---

seemed to have disappeared; now everything looked tortured and diabolical, and Elia thought he could hear voices in the distance, the voices of people following and mocking him.

At last he put on his old shoes again and left the others by the roadside; but still he found no peace. Fantastic happenings went on in his mind; one of the two poor travelers he had slept with was on the same road and picked up the shoes; then this man was followed and found out and pronounced guilty and let in for goodness knows how many awful punishments. . . . Or else the people he imagined were after him found the stolen shoes and went on tormenting him and tormenting him until finally in great 16 shame he confessed what he had done. What would his wife say? The idea grew in his childish mind, excited by exhaustion, cold, and hunger, and spread like the great clouds in the stormy winter sky. He wished he had never set out at all, and had not forsaken his usual peace and quiet merely to run after a shadow. His uncle's legacy would probably involve endless worries and complications; and meanwhile, he had completely disgraced himself.

He turned back, found the shoes where he had left them, and stood a long while looking at them sheepishly. He wondered what he had better do. If he hid them or buried them, it did not alter the fact that they had been stolen. He had stolen them; and the thought of that moment when he was on all-fours on the floor, trembling like a frightened animal, would cast its shadow over his whole existence.

He hid the stolen shoes under his cloak again and went back to the village, lingering on the way so as not to get there before evening. He had eaten nothing for twenty-four hours, and felt so weak that the wind made him sway like a blade of grass. He arrived at the inn in a dream, ready to confess what he had done; but every-

thing was quiet, no one mentioned the theft or bothered about him or his cloak in the least. He had supper and asked for a bed; he was given the same one as on the previous night. He put back the shoes where he had found them and then went to sleep. His sleep was heavy as death; he had to be woken up and told it was twelve o'clock. He bought a loaf of bread with the penny he had left, and went on his way again.

17 The weather was fine again now, and the moors, shut in between the dark mountains and the blue sea, had all the sorrowful enchantment of a primitive landscape; everything was green and strong, but, just as you see in certain human lives, it seemed as if no flowers could ever bloom there.

Elia was walking well, in spite of his old shoes; and because of them, he enjoyed the privilege of being treated everywhere as a tramp, and given milk and bread to eat.

When he arrived, he found his uncle had died a few hours previously. The maid looked at Elia rather suspiciously, and asked:

"Are you really his nephew? Then why didn't you come sooner?"

Elia didn't answer.

18 "The master was expecting you. He sent a wire to you three days ago. He always used to say you were his only relative, but that you'd forgotten all about him. So this morning, when he saw you hadn't come, he decided to leave everything to the sailors' orphans."

Elia went home and found his wife sitting in the sun, pale and indifferent to everything.

19 "Why on earth didn't you say I'd already gone, when the telegram came, my good woman?"

"But surely you'd have got there anyhow, wouldn't you? Why did you take such a long time?"

Elia did not answer.

CRITICAL THINKING: GUIDED READING QUESTIONS

LITERAL

1a. What does Elia finally do with the stolen shoes? (He walks all the way back to the inn and puts them back where he found them.)

2a. When Elia does not arrive, what does the uncle finally do with his money? (He leaves it to charity.)

INFERENTIAL

1b. How does he feel afterward? (He feels relieved and stronger.)

2b. Why does he do this? (He was offended that Elia seemed not to have enough respect to attend his deathbed.)

STUDY QUESTIONS

Recalling

1. According to the opening paragraph, why does Elia have so few cases? What does he usually do when he visits the Law Courts? What does he dream about doing with his uncle's money?
2. What news prompts Elia to visit his uncle? Why must he travel on foot? What are his reasons for wanting a new pair of shoes?
3. What causes Elia's delay in reaching his uncle's home? What does he discover when he gets there?

Interpreting

4. Identify Elia's motives for his three main actions in the story—his journey to his uncle's home, his temporary lapse of honesty, and his return of the shoes. Would you say that Elia is basically a man of integrity? Explain.
5. Is Elia a romantic person—that is, idealistic and impractical? Is the story's outcome romantic? What might the discrepancy suggest about romantic thinking?
6. What does the story's outcome suggest about the workings of fate? What does the story suggest about the effects of poverty on human behavior?

Extending

7. Do you think most people would have taken the shoes if they were in Elia's place? Would they have returned the shoes? Explain.

LITERARY FOCUS

The Total Effect

When we study literature, we sometimes look at individual story elements—plot, characters, settings, point of view, tone, style, theme, and, in some cases, symbols and irony. However, a good story is more than the sum of its elements. For a story to be successful, these elements must *interact,* or work together, to create a unified whole that produces a unique effect on the reader. The effect produced by the interaction of story elements is sometimes called the **total effect.**

Thinking About the Total Effect

1. Explain how the setting of "The Shoes" helps motivate the main character's behavior and determine the events of the plot.
2. What do the new shoes symbolize to Elia? What role do the shoes play in the conflicts within the story's plot?
3. What is ironic about the outcome of Elia's conflicts? How does irony point to the theme?
4. Identify the story's point of view and the narrator's tone. How does the tone reflect the story's theme?

LANGUAGE STUDY

Words from Italian

The word *piazza,* meaning "public square," is one of many English words that come from Italian. Many of the Italian words were in turn taken from Latin, the language from which Italian originates. For example, the Italian word *piazza* was derived from the Latin *platea,* meaning "broad street."

Use a dictionary to help you determine the meanings and origins of these English words from Italian.

1. ballot
2. confetti
3. fiasco
4. replica
5. soprano
6. trampoline
7. villa
8. zany
9. zucchini

COMPOSITION

Writing About the Total Effect

■ Write a composition about the total effect of "The Shoes." Begin by describing the story's impact on you. Then explain how the story's plot, characters, settings, point of view, tone, style, theme, symbols, and irony work together to create the total effect. *For help with the assignment refer to Lesson 10 in the Writing About Literature Handbook at the back of this book.*

COMPARING STORIES

Compare and contrast this story to other stories about cultures and conflicts that you have read in this section or elsewhere. How are the social conflicts of each story alike? How are they different? What is similar or different about their outcomes?

The Shoes **225**

ANSWERS

STUDY QUESTIONS

1. Times are bad, and people hesitate to go to court. He writes his wife love poems. He dreams of taking his wife on a romantic holiday.
2. His uncle is dying. He has just three lire. He is uncomfortable and ashamed.
3. He takes a pair of shoes and, guilty and scared, walks back to return them. The uncle died and, since Elia never came, left his money to charity.
4. His main motive is love for his wife; guilt and fear motivate his return of the shoes. Yes, his dishonesty is a brief lapse.
5. yes; no; It is frustrated by the real world.
6. Fate is unfair. It may lead to desperation or apathy.
7. Answers will vary. Students might feel that some people would have asked for help.

LITERARY FOCUS

1. The poverty of the time and place prompts Elia's actions.
2. at first, comfort and status; then, dishonesty and guilt; aid in resolving the external conflict of reaching the uncle but prompt an internal conflict.
3. He acts correctly but is not rewarded. Romantic acts go unrewarded, and fate is unfair.
4. third-person limited; matter-of-fact; it stresses that romanticism is not effective.

LANGUAGE STUDY

1. "written vote"; from Italian *balota,* "little ball," as balls were once used to cast votes
2. "small objects scattered at festivities"; from Italian for "candies"
3. "complete failure"; from Italian *(far) fiasco,* "to fail"
4. "copy"; from Italian for "repetition"
5. "highest female voice"; from Italian *sopra,* "above"
6. "canvas on which to jump"; from Italian *trampolino,* "springboard"
7. "rural estate"; from Italian, from Latin *villa,* "country house"
8. "silly"; from Italian *zanni,* "clown"
9. "summer squash"; from Italian for "gourds"

COMPOSITION: GUIDELINES FOR EVALUATION

WRITING ABOUT THE TOTAL EFFECT

Objective

To analyze a story's total effect

Guidelines for Evaluation

■ suggested length: five to eight paragraphs

■ should state the story's total effect on the student
■ should explain how elements of the story work together to re-create the total effect
■ should support general statements with details from the story

In many traditional cultures, such as those dating from early Africa, there is no form of writing. Cultural lore is maintained in the memory of the people and in art. The art of these cultures is highly representational, with a single image of a person or a crocodile, for example, standing for all persons or all crocodiles.

In the fabric depicted here different animals—a porcupine, an elephant, a peacock, a rooster, a lion, and a fish—are interspersed with decorative designs. Although in reality they are different sizes, all the animals on this fabric are depicted as if they were the same size. Accurate representation does not matter in traditional art; what matters, instead, is the power or characteristic associated with each creature. These characteristics, such as the crocodile's primordial strength, are encoded in the mythology of the culture. Each image relates to a story in the culture's lore. Such stories and myths form an encyclopedia that each person must know in order to preserve the culture.

■ Ask students whether they know of any stories that tell something about people or places in American culture. (Possible answers: George Washington cutting down the cherry tree, Abraham Lincoln learning to read by candlelight)

226   *The Short Story*   Fante chief's figurative cloth, Ghana.

The Tradition of Oral Storytelling

In the stories on the preceding pages, you have met characters from many different cultures and shared experiences that take place all over the globe. Storytelling is indeed a worldwide tradition that began centuries ago. The world's earliest stories were recounted orally and passed from generation to generation in what is often called the oral tradition. In certain areas of the world, oral storytelling remains an important part of the culture today.

Some of the most sophisticated examples of oral storytelling come from Africa, where storytellers traditionally hold a place of high honor in society. Among the Malinke (or Mandingo) tribe of West Africa, for example, storytellers known as *griots* served as tutors and advisers to royalty in the ancient African kingdoms of Ghana, Mali, and Songhay. The stories the *griots* told were much more than mere entertainment. Many helped explain the world or served as guidelines to human behavior. Others celebrated important heroes and great events in tribal history. With the conquest of Africa's ancient kingdoms by outsiders, *griots* or their counterparts elsewhere in Africa became one of the chief preservers of tribal history, customs, and traditions.

Throughout Africa oral storytellers continued to flourish over the centuries. Storytelling remained an important public event, often featured as part of traditional tribal ceremonies such as a marriage or the induction of a new tribal leader. The storytellers were usually gifted dramatic performers who acted out tales with different voices for different characters and often interspersed song and dance in the narrative. Their performances drew large crowds and frequently involved audience participation.

Although many African oral stories celebrate the noble deeds of high-born, larger-than-life characters, others focus more realistically on lowly but clever heroes and heroines who overcome a great obstacle or trick a powerful enemy. Also popular is the dilemma tale, in which the ending is left open and the audience must decide which of two choices a character made or should have made. For instance, in a Bura tale in which a man must choose between hurting his mother's feelings or his wife's, the story concludes, "Which would you choose?" These open-ended stories capture the audience with their engaging sophistication and puzzlelike ambiguity.

PRACTICING THE STORYTELLER'S ART

Perhaps no literary form comes more naturally than storytelling. Becoming an accomplished raconteur requires skill as well as imagination, however. Ask students to experiment with creating their own tales, according to the following guidelines.

Activities

1. Divide the class into groups of five or six students. Instruct each group to think of a modern American hero, either fictitious or real. Explain that the students in each group should work together to create an extemporaneous story that describes how their hero copes with a crisis. One student in each group should spin out the initial episodes of the tale, drop it after a minute or two, and let another student pick up the thread. Each student should contribute to the story; the last should bring it to a resolution. Then ask the class to discuss the effectiveness of the group-storytelling technique. Was it stimulating? Confusing? Did they find it difficult to remember the details of the story? What do their conclusions say about the art of oral storytelling?

2. Divide the class into pairs of students, and ask each pair to think of an idea for a modern American version of an African dilemma tale. One pair, for instance, might invent a story in which a young woman must decide whether to expose a crime being committed by her boss or to remain silent in order to protect her job. Have a member of each pair present the pair's story idea to the class, and have the class vote on the idea that seems the most plausible and the most effective.

A common belief of tribal cultures is that the power of certain objects is best maintained when the object is viewed by the public only on special occasions. (By contrast, Western art is always on view.) The ceremonial masks depicted here reflect simply stylized human facial features. The eyes either are closed or stare blankly, the hair and facial ornamentation are treated with distinctive patterns, and the shape of each mask is more geometric than normal.

A feeling of timelessness emanates from the masks, for mystery seems to lie within each one. This primordial mystery, which is also encoded in the tribes' myths, recalls the cultures' origins. Such traditional knowledge provides invaluable guidance for daily life.

■ Ask students whether they can name any emblems of our culture that are brought out occasionally. (Possible answers: the flag, which many households display on national holidays, pumpkins on Halloween, and so on) Why are these items not used daily? (Students should understand the nature of certain holidays and events and how their importance arises from their particularity.)

228 *Myths, Folk Tales, and Epics*

African ceremonial masks from the Ivory Coast, Ghana, and Sierra Leone.

MYTHS, FOLK TALES, AND EPICS

T*he folk stories my mother and elder sister told us had the immemorial quality of the sky and the forests and the rivers.*
—CHINUA ACHEBE
Nigeria

This excerpt recounts the well-known story of King Midas. When Bacchus offers Midas anything he desires, Midas asks to be able to turn whatever he touches into gold. At first entranced by the gift, Midas soon finds he can neither eat nor drink: All he touches turns to gold. He begs to have his power revoked, and Bacchus assents, instructing him to wash away his golden touch in a river.

LITERARY SKILLS FOR THIS SELECTION

- metamorphosis
- plot: foreshadowing

THEMES IN THIS SELECTION

- wealth and happiness
- consequences of greed

LESSON OBJECTIVES

1. to understand metamorphosis
2. to understand the meaning and origin of terms from Greek and Roman mythology
3. to write an updated version of the story of Midas

Teacher's Classroom Resources 2

- Teaching Notes 9
- Reading Guide 10
- Check Test 11
- Responding to World Cultures 12
- Literary Focus: Metamorphosis 13
- Language Study: Terms from Greek and Roman Mythology 14
- Writing Process Guide: Updating the Story of Midas 15
- Grammar in Literature: Predicate Adjectives, Predicate Nominatives 16
- Selection Test 17

TEACHING STUDENTS OF DIFFERENT ABILITIES

- **For less advanced students:** Discuss the meanings of *judicious*, *ruinous*, and *imbued*. Help students pronounce the names *Bacchus*, *Hesperides*, *Danae*, *Ceres*, and *Sardis*. Ask them to complete the Reading Guide for this selection.

Ovid (43 B.C.–A.D. 17)

Ancient Rome

Publius Ovidius Naso, better known as Ovid [ov′id], was born into a wealthy landowning family in Sulmona, Italy. He studied law and rhetoric before taking minor government positions in Rome. He soon discovered that his true interest was poetry, not politics, and turned his attention to writing. Ovid became renowned for his brilliant love poetry, particularly the *Art of Love,* a collection of poems giving advice about love, and the *Heroides,* a series of fictitious love letters from famous women in mythology.

Ovid considered the *Metamorphoses* [met′ə mor′fə sēz] his highest achievement. This great narrative poem is based on more than two hundred stories from ancient Greek and Roman mythology. Most of the stories involve a character who undergoes some type of **metamorphosis**, or transformation. The tales are told in chronological order, from the beginnings of time to the death of the Roman emperor Julius Caesar. Ovid describes the adventures of these gods and goddesses with biting wit and humor; he indulgently forgives their near-human frailties. Writers and artists from ancient times to the present have mined the rich subject matter of Ovid's tales.

Greek and Roman Mythology

The vast lands of ancient Greece encompassed parts of the Balkan peninsula, Asia Minor (an area that now includes Turkey), and many colonies on the Mediterranean Sea. The empire flourished from about 3000 B.C. to 146 B.C., when the weakened Greek cities fell to the Romans. The ancient city of Rome, legends say, was founded in 753 B.C. in what is now Italy and flourished until about A.D. 300.

Roman culture drew heavily on the learning and artistic achievements of the Greeks. For example, the Romans incorporated many Greek gods into their own mythology, though they gave them different names. The Greek god Zeus, for instance, became the Roman god Jupiter, and the Greek goddess Athena was transformed into the Roman goddess Minerva. The mythology of ancient Greece and Rome has strongly influenced Western culture. The following well-known Greek myth concerns Midas, the legendary king of Phrygia in Asia Minor. As the myth opens, a grateful Bacchus (the god of wine) rewards Midas for a favor he has done.

THE ROMAN EMPIRE IN 44 B.C.

Roman Roads

See *LITERATURE AND CULTURE SOURCEBOOK: Classical Greece and Rome*

- **For more advanced students:** Encourage students to find other versions of the story of Midas and to discuss ways in which the versions differ from the one in the *Metamorphoses.*

Modern Midases

This Roman myth describes the follies of Midas, a king who was consumed by greed. The myth of Midas may have been inspired by a king who is thought to have ruled Phrygia, an ancient country in Asia Minor.

- Each culture has its own Midases. Ask students to think of a famous person who seems to be possessed by greed. Then ask what elements of our culture support the desire for possessions. (advertising, an emphasis on competition)

Scythian gold helmet, fourth century B.C.

Ovid

from the **Metamorphoses**

Translated from the Latin by Rolfe Humphries

The Story of Midas

                                  Bacchus,
Happy and grateful, and meaning well, told Midas
To make his choice of anything he wanted.
And Midas, never too judicious, answered:
5 "Grant that whatever I touch may turn to gold!"
Bacchus agreed, gave him the ruinous gift,
Sorry the monarch had not chosen better.
So Midas went his cheerful way, rejoicing
In his own bad luck, and tried to test the promise
10 By touching this and that. It all was true,
He hardly dared believe it! From an oak tree
He broke a green twig loose: the twig was golden.
He picked a stone up from the ground; the stone
Paled with light golden color; he touched a clod,
15 The clod became a nugget. Awns[1] of grain
Were a golden harvest; if he picked an apple

---

1. **Awns:** bristles found on some cereal grasses.

Metamorphoses **231**

CRITICAL THINKING: GUIDED READING QUESTIONS

LITERAL

1a. How does Bacchus feel about Midas' choice of gifts? (He is sorry Midas hasn't chosen better.)

2a. What happens when Midas tests the gift? (Everything he touches turns to gold.)

INFERENTIAL

1b. What does Bacchus' sorrow over Midas' choice suggest about the gift? (It may bring pain rather than joy.)

2b. What might Midas touch that would be better left in its natural state? (Possible responses: a loved one, food, drink)

MOTIVATION: PRIOR KNOWLEDGE

Ask students to imagine what they would wish for if they were granted a wish. What undesirable consequences might result from this wish? Tell them that in this story a man gets more than he bargained for when his wish comes true.

PAGE SUMMARY: AT A GLANCE

- Bacchus offers to grant King Midas anything he wants.
- Bacchus regretfully grants Midas his request for the golden touch.
- Midas is enthralled as one thing after another turns to gold at his touch.

IN THE GLOSSARY

- judicious: showing good judgment
- ruinous: tending to bring disaster

1 TEACHING PLOT: FORESHADOWING

Call attention to the phrases "ruinous gift" and "rejoicing/In his own bad luck," and ask students to suggest what will happen. (something very unfortunate will result from the gift)

ART AND LITERATURE

The Scythians were a nomadic people who lived in the Steppes, the vast grasslands of Russia and Central Asia. They set up metal shops along the north coast of the Black Sea, where they traded with the Greeks. This golden helmet was found in a Scythian burial mound. In ancient times gold represented divine energy; because the head was considered the seat of life, radiance about the head represented divine power. Helmets like the one depicted were to be worn not in battle but in the afterlife.

- Ask students to identify naturalistic details in the Scythian helmet that might have been transformed by Midas' touch. (ram's horns, a flower like a sunflower, curling leaves)

- Everything Midas tries to eat or drink turns to gold.
- Midas begs the gods to forgive him and take back the gift.
- Bacchus agrees to take back the golden touch and tells Midas to wash the sin away in a river in the Lydian hills.
- Midas obeys, and his golden touch is transferred to the river, so that when the river floods, the surrounding fields are left a golden color.

IN THE GLOSSARY

- imbued: filled

2 TEACHING METAMORPHOSIS

Point out that in myths involving metamorphoses the ancients often tried to teach lessons about people's relationship to nature. Ask students what lesson Midas' inability to consume the transformed food and drink suggests here. (People should not tamper with nature.)

3 TEACHING THEME

Point out that Ovid makes clear his feelings toward Midas and his greed by using such phrases as "he is tortured, as he should be" and "hateful gold." Ask students what theme judgmental language like this suggests. (People should be punished for excessive greed; great wealth does not always bring happiness.)

4 TEACHING STUDENTS OF LIMITED ENGLISH PROFICIENCY

The word *owned* is used in an unusual way here to mean "admitted" or "confessed." Help students recognize that Bacchus forgives Midas because Midas confesses to having made a foolish and disastrous request.

COLLABORATIVE LEARNING: ENRICHMENT ACTIVITY

Drama Other stories, such as "The Fisherman and His Wife" and "Aladdin and the Wonderful Lamp," also tell about unfortunate wishes that come true. Have small groups of students create and present radio plays of stories with this theme. Students should divide the project into tasks, such as script writing, sound effects, and acting.

It seemed a gift from the Hesperides.[2]
He placed his fingers on the lofty pillars
And saw them gleam and shine. He bathed his hands
20   In water, and the stream was golden rain
Like that which came to Danae.[3] His mind
Could scarcely grasp his hopes—all things were golden,
Or would be, at his will! A happy man,
He watched his servants set a table before him
2 25 With bread and meat. He touched the gift of Ceres[4]
And found it stiff and hard; he tried to bite
The meat with hungry teeth, and where the teeth
Touched food they seemed to touch on golden ingots.[5]
He mingled water with the wine of Bacchus;
30   It was molten gold that trickled through his jaws.

Midas, astonished at his new misfortune,
Rich man and poor man, tries to flee his riches
Hating the favor he had lately prayed for.
No food relieves his hunger; his throat is dry
3 35 With burning thirst; he is tortured, as he should be,
By the hateful gold. Lifting his hands to Heaven,
He cries: "Forgive me, father! I have sinned.
Have mercy upon me, save me from this loss
That looks so much like gain!" The gods are kind,
4 40 And Bacchus, since he owned his fault, forgave him,
Took back the gift. "You need not be forever
Smeared with that foolish color: go to the stream
That flows by Sardis,[6] take your way upstream
Into the Lydian hills, until you find
45   The tumbling river's source. There duck your head
And body under the foaming white of the fountain,
And wash your sin away." The king obeyed him,
And the power of the golden touch imbued the water,
So that even now the fields grow hard and yellow
50   If that vein washes over them to flood
Their fields with the water of the touch of gold.

---

2. **Hesperides** [he sper'ə dēz']: nymphs (young goddesses) who, according to Greek mythology, guard a garden where golden apples grow.
3. **Danae** [dan'ā ē']: According to Greek mythology, the god Zeus took the form of a golden shower when he visited Danae, mother of the hero Perseus.
4. **gift of Ceres** [sir'ēz]: that is, grain. *Ceres* is the Roman name for the goddess of grain and agriculture.
5. **ingots:** chunks of cast metal.
6. **Sardis** [sär'dis]: capital of Lydia, an ancient region of Asia Minor that bordered the Aegean Sea.

232   *Myths, Folk Tales, and Epics*

CRITICAL THINKING: GUIDED READING QUESTIONS

LITERAL

1a. What problems does the golden touch create for Midas? (He is unable to eat or drink since everything he touches turns to gold.)

2a. Why does Bacchus forgive Midas and take back the gift? (because Midas willingly admits his mistake and begs for forgiveness)

INFERENTIAL

1b. What lesson do these problems teach Midas? (Possible responses: Greed often has unfortunate consequences; material wealth does not always lead to happiness; great riches cannot make up for many of life's simple pleasures.)

2b. What does Bacchus' forgiving of Midas suggest? (People can be forgiven for their mistakes if they show a willingness to learn from them and change.)

STUDY QUESTIONS

Recalling

1. What does Bacchus think of the gift that Midas requested?
2. What is Midas' reaction at first when he finds that everything he touches turns to gold?
3. What happens to make Midas realize that his gift is not as wonderful as he thought it was?
4. When Midas asks that his gift be withdrawn, what does Bacchus tell him to do?

Interpreting

5. What might Bacchus have predicted about Midas' reaction to the gift he requests?
6. What does Ovid mean when he refers to Midas as "rich man and poor man"?
7. What would probably have happened to Midas if Bacchus had not taken back the gift?

Extending

8. In your experience, does greed for material things affect people's lives the way it affected Midas' life? Do people who hunger for material things generally find them satisfying when they get them? Or do they find them more of a curse, as Midas did?

LITERARY FOCUS

Metamorphosis

A **metamorphosis,** in literature, is a character's change of shape or form. Greek and Roman myths include many stories in which humans change shape, often into things in nature. These stories reflect the great respect the ancients had for nature, often equating it with human nature or with goodness.

Metamorphosis has continued to be a common literary technique. You may remember it from stories about a prince being turned into a frog (and back again), or from "Cinderella," in which a poor girl is turned into a beautiful princess. In these stories, as in the tales from ancient cultures, metamorphosis is often used as a warning against certain kinds of behavior.

Thinking About Metamorphosis

1. What power does Midas request from Bacchus? What does Midas hope this power will do for him?
2. What kind of warning does the story of Midas give to readers?

LANGUAGE STUDY

Terms from Greek and Roman Mythology

Many English words and expressions come from the names of characters and places in Greek and Roman mythology. *Cereal,* for example, comes from *Ceres,* the Roman goddess of grain and agriculture. *Siren* comes from the name of a group of women whose singing voices were so appealing that any sailors who heard them were compelled to stop at their island.

Use a dictionary or encyclopedia to find out the meaning and mythological origins of these English words and expressions.

1. herculean
2. jovial
3. martial
4. mercurial
5. narcissistic
6. Olympian
7. Achilles' heel
8. Pandora's box

COMPOSITION

Updating the Story of Midas

■ Write a modern version of the story of Midas. The following questions will help you decide the kinds of changes you might make to update the story.
- What would you name your main character?
- What business would the character be in?
- What would your main character wish for?
- How would the wish be made to come true?
- What changes would take place in the character's life once the wish came true?
- How would the story end?

Metamorphoses **233**

READER'S RESPONSE

What gift might Midas ask for if he is given a second chance?

ANSWERS

STUDY QUESTIONS

1. He is sorry Midas has not made a wiser choice.
2. He is entranced.
3. When he touches his food and drink, they turn to gold.
4. He instructs him to bathe at the source of a certain river to wash away his sin.
5. He might have predicted exactly what happened, since he saw it was a "ruinous" gift.
6. Midas is materially rich but poor in spirit.
7. He would have starved.
8. Answers will vary. Many students might say that wealth is less satisfying than love or other intangible sources of happiness.

LITERARY FOCUS

1. He requests the power to turn everything he touches into gold; he hopes this will make him fabulously rich.
2. Wealth does not necessarily bring happiness.

LANGUAGE STUDY

1. "having extraordinary courage or power"; from the Greek hero Hercules, who performed difficult physical tasks
2. "good-humored"; from Jove, king of the Roman gods
3. "of or suitable to war"; from Mars, the Roman god of war
4. "quick or changeable"; from Mercury, the messenger of the Roman gods
5. "self-loving"; from Narcissus, the mythological Greek youth who fell in love with his own reflection
6. "magnificent, exalted"; from Olympus, the mountain where the Greek gods lived
7. "a weak spot"; from the Greek hero Achilles, whose entire body except for his heel was invulnerable
8. "a seemingly valuable gift that is really a curse"; from the Greek myth about Pandora, who loosed the world's evils by opening a box the gods had told her never to unseal

COMPOSITION: GUIDELINES FOR EVALUATION

UPDATING THE STORY OF MIDAS

Objective

To create a modern myth based on an ancient model

Guidelines for Evaluation

■ suggested length: one to two pages
■ should include variations on all important details from the original myth
■ should show evidence of consideration of the listed questions
■ should show awareness of the modern audience

LESSON PREVIEW

This myth explains why bats act as they do. At the beginning of time, God allows the bat to get feathers from birds to keep warm. The bat soon possesses beautiful plumage but angers the birds with his vanity. They complain to God, who asks the bat to show off his plumage. As he does, his feathers fall off. Ever since, the bat has flown alone and only at night so no one will see his ugliness.

LITERARY SKILL FOR THIS SELECTION

- myth

THEMES IN THIS SELECTION

- pride and vanity
- divine justice

LESSON OBJECTIVES

1. to understand the myth
2. to understand the meaning and origin of words from Mexico, South America, and the Caribbean
3. to write from another point of view

Teacher's Classroom Resources 2

- Teaching Notes   19
- Reading Guide   20
- Check Test   21
- Responding to World Cultures   22
- Literary Focus: Myth   23
- Language Study: Native Languages of Mexico, South America, and the Caribbean   24
- Writing Process Guide: Writing from Another Point of View   25
- Grammar in Literature: Using Infinitives   26
- Selection Test   27

IN THE CLASSROOM

TEACHING STUDENTS OF DIFFERENT ABILITIES

- **For less advanced students:** Ask students to watch for the explanation of why the bat acts as he does. Discuss the words *ethereal, plumage,* and *gyrations,* which appear in the Glossary. Have students complete the Reading Guide.

- **For more advanced students:** Invite students to find other myths from early Mexican cultures explaining why animals look or act as they do. Ask them to share the myths with the class.

Zapotec Mythology

Mexico

Although ancient Zapotec [zä′pə tek′] religion centered on various aspects of nature, no one knows exactly what their myths were like at the time Zapotec civilization reached its peak about 1,500 years ago because the myths were probably never written down. The ancient Zapotecs did have a hieroglyphic system of writing that has only been partially decoded by archaeologists. It is likely, though, that most ancient Zapotec hieroglyphs recorded battles or dynasties, not simple folk tales.

Like many ethnic groups in Mexico and in other parts of the world, the Zapotec people borrowed freely from other cultures when they created their myths. They borrowed from their neighbors and kin, the Mixtecs, and from Christian missionaries in the sixteenth and seventeenth centuries as well.

About the Reteller: Andrés Henestrosa (born 1908)

Andrés Henestrosa was born to a Zapotecan family in Mexico. He wrote for major Mexican newspapers and spent several years as a senator in the Mexican national assembly. He is probably best known for his retellings of stories from Zapotecan mythology.

Mexico and the Zapotecs

Oaxaca [wä hä′kä] is a state in southern Mexico, about halfway between Mexico City and the Guatemalan border. The Zapotec civilization originated in Oaxaca and reached its height between A.D. 300 and 600. The spiritual capital of the Zapotec empire was the ceremonial center of Monte Albán, just west of the modern city of Oaxaca. This splendid ruin contains temples, plazas, ball parks, and many large stone slabs carved with human figures that may represent vanquished warriors.

The Zapotec civilization was eventually absorbed by the Aztec empire. Today, many Zapotecs still live in the mountainous regions of Oaxaca. They raise corn and beans as their forefathers did and speak a language similar to that of their ancestors. The Zapotec culture has played an important role in Mexican history. One of Mexico's most revered presidents, Benito Juárez (1806–1872), was a Zapotec.

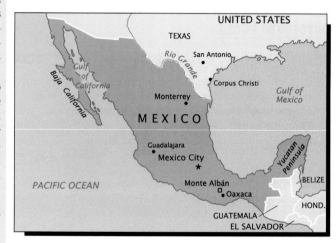

See LITERATURE AND CULTURE SOURCEBOOK: Latin America

DISCUSSING GEOGRAPHY AND CULTURE

A Medley of Cultures

The Zapotecs, like the Mayas, the Mixtecs, and the Otomis, are among dozens of Indian tribes who inhabit Mexico today. Each tribe speaks its own language, often in addition to Spanish, Mexico's official language.

- The United States is also a medley of cultures. Have students name different ethnic customs, languages, and holidays in their neighborhoods. What features of modern American culture do all these different groups share?

Zapotec clay urn of
maize god from Oaxaca,
c. fifth to eighth century.

Zapotec Traditional

The Bat

Retold by Andrés Henestrosa

Translated from the Spanish by Zoila Nelken

The butterflies we see today, ethereal, resting on the flowers, on the surface of the water and even on the tremulous air, are only the shadows of what the bat once was: the most beautiful bird in creation! However, there was a time when he was not.

When Light and Darkness began, the bat was just as we know him today, and was called *biguidibela* in Zapotec, from *beguidi* meaning butterfly, and *bela,* flesh: that is, a butterfly in the flesh, or bare-winged. Then the poor bat was the ugliest and the most unhappy of all creatures.

One day, tormented by the cold weather, he went up to Heaven and said to God, "I'm dying of cold; I need a few feathers." But God, although He never stops working, never revises the creatures He has finished, and so had not a single feather to offer the bat. He told the bat to go back to Earth and to beg a feather in His name from every bird. Thus God always gives more than is asked of Him.

The bat, back on Earth, sought out the birds of most colorful plumage. A green feather from the parrot's neck, a blue feather from the blue pigeon, a white feather from the dove, an iridescent feather from the humming-bird. All these and more the bat obtained. Proudly he would fly across the brow of the Morning, and all the other birds would pause in their flight to admire him. And a new glory spread over the Earth. . . . At dusk, flying with the West Wind, the bat colored the horizon. And once, coming from beyond the clouds, he left behind a rainbow as an echo of his flight.

Seated on a branch of a tree, the bat would spread out his wings coquettishly, and alternately shake them, first the right and then the left, in a flutter that thrilled the air. The birds began to feel envious, and to hate him as unanimously as they had once admired him.

One day, a flock of birds winged its way to Heaven, led by the humming-bird. God heard their complaint: the bat was mocking them; besides, each, with one feather less, was cold. And the birds themselves brought back the message from Heaven summoning the bat.

When he had entered the Lord's house, the bat was asked to repeat the gestures which had so offended his companions. And fluttering his wings he was left as naked as before, because for a whole day his feathers rained from Heaven, they say.

1 Ever since then the bat flies only alone and at night, and in swift gyrations, diving at imaginary feathers. He does not pause so no one will notice his ugliness.

The Bat **235**

CRITICAL THINKING: GUIDED READING QUESTIONS

LITERAL

1a. How does the bat look after he obtains feathers from different birds? (He is beautiful.)

2a. Why does the birds' initial admiration for the bat's beauty turn to envy and hatred? (The bat shows off too much.)

INFERENTIAL

1b. How do you think the bat feels about himself and his new beauty? (He probably feels proud and delighted.)

2b. How do you think the bat might have avoided bringing the bad feelings of the birds upon himself? (He might have treated his beauty with greater humility.)

MOTIVATION: PRIOR KNOWLEDGE

Ask students to explain how vain people sometimes act. Then ask them for their response to vanity in others. Tell them that this selection is about a vain animal who learns a lesson the hard way.

PAGE SUMMARY: AT A GLANCE

- The bat asks God for feathers and at His suggestion turns to the Earth's birds for plumage.
- The bat obtains feathers, becomes beautiful and vain, and makes the birds envious.
- When the birds complain to Him, God summons the bat and causes him to lose his feathers.

IN THE GLOSSARY

- ethereal: light and delicate
- plumage: coat of feathers
- gyrations: circular motions

1 TEACHING MYTHS

Explain that, as in many myths, the final words of this tale make clear its purpose and moral. Ask students what the purpose and moral of this myth are. (The purpose is to explain why the bat flies alone and at night; the moral is that excessive vanity can lead to a downfall.)

ART AND LITERATURE

This clay funerary urn represents a corn god, shown with ears of corn hanging from both sides of his breastplate. The grimacing creature on the headpiece represents a bat deity, who was a guardian of the corn god. The bat has two incisor teeth and is surrounded by a wreath of stylized flowers.

- Ask students to compare the featherless bat in the selection with the magical bat perched above the corn god. (The bat in the story is naked, ugly, and ashamed; the bat deity is opulently adorned and scowling.)

COLLABORATIVE LEARNING: ENRICHMENT ACTIVITY

Art Have students form groups to prepare a bulletin-board display of what the bat looked like as "the most beautiful bird in creation." Encourage students to make feathers like those of different birds and to arrange these around the bat.

Did the bat deserve what happened to him? Why or why not?

STUDY QUESTIONS

1. He was the ugliest and unhappiest of all creatures.
2. God told the bat to go to Earth and beg a feather in His name from every bird.
3. The bat was mocking them, and they were cold without the feathers they had given him.
4. They rained down from Heaven.
5. generosity (by allowing the bat to borrow his plumage from the birds) and fairness (by reversing His decision after the birds complain)
6. vanity
7. The story uses metamorphosis twice to warn about vanity. The bat's first metamorphosis makes him vain; the second is a punishment for his conceit.
8. pride and vanity
9. Answers will vary. Encourage students to cite specific examples from the media or personal experience to support their response.

LITERARY FOCUS

1. References to a time "When Light and Darkness began" and when creatures existed in other forms suggest that the story is ancient.
2. It attempts to explain why bats have no feathers and why they fly so quickly and erratically at night.

LANGUAGE STUDY

1. Nahuatl (a Mexican tribe); *chocolatl*
2. Spanish (West Indies); *barbacoa*
3. Araucan (a Chilean tribe); *pontho*
4. Taino (a West Indian tribe); *mahis*

STUDY QUESTIONS

Recalling

1. When Light and Darkness began, why was the bat a "poor" creature?
2. What did God tell the bat to do to relieve him of the cold?
3. What two complaints did the birds make to God about how His solution to the bat's problem had worked out?
4. What happened to the bat's feathers after God asked him to repeat the gestures the birds had found offensive?

Interpreting

5. What human virtues does the Zapotec god demonstrate?
6. Based on what happens in this story, what human failing would you say the Zapotecs probably disapproved of?
7. In what way does the story make use of metamorphosis to teach a lesson in human behavior?
8. What human qualities are attributed to the bat?

Extending

9. Do you think that people place too much emphasis on their appearance? Why or why not?

LITERARY FOCUS

Myth

A **myth** is an anonymous traditional story rooted in cultural folk beliefs that relies on the supernatural to explain the mysteries of the world. All mythologies revolve around ideas of creation, supernatural power, birth, and death.

Myths helped people understand how natural events and human actions happened. For example, in order to explain how the sun traveled across the sky, people created a myth about a sun god driving a mighty chariot.

Most myths include either supernatural characters—gods and goddesses—or human characters with one or more superhuman powers. Greek mythology, for example, collects stories told by the ancient Greeks about their gods, ancestors, and legendary heroes. Myths may also include animals and inanimate objects that think, behave, and speak like human beings.

Thinking About Myth

1. What parts of "The Bat" suggest that the story has been told for many generations?
2. What belief, custom, or aspect of nature does the story attempt to explain?

LANGUAGE STUDY

Native Languages of Mexico, South America, and the Caribbean

In "The Bat" Henestrosa explains that the Zapotec word for *bat—biguidibela—*is a combination of two words meaning "butterfly" and "flesh."

The English language includes several words that come from the languages spoken by Mexican, South American, and Caribbean peoples. Most of these words became Spanish words first, then came into English from Spanish. For example, *tomato* comes from the Aztec word *tomatl.*

Each of the words listed below originated in the native language of a Mexican, South American, or Caribbean tribe. Each word came into English through Spanish. Look up each word in a dictionary, and write the language and word it originally came from.

1. chocolate
2. barbecue
3. poncho
4. maize

COMPOSITION

Writing from Another Point of View

■ How might a bat explain the events that take place in the story? Imagine a bat telling its child about how the appearance of bats once underwent two drastic changes. First, think about how the events are told in the story. Then, think about how a bat might see the events differently from the way they appear in the story. Finally, plan and write a brief retelling of the story from the older bat's point of view.

COMPOSITION: GUIDELINES FOR EVALUATION

WRITING FROM ANOTHER POINT OF VIEW

Objective

To appreciate the impact of point of view

Guidelines for Evaluation

■ suggested length: two to four paragraphs
■ should be narrated by the older bat
■ should include details from "The Bat"
■ should show a change in emphasis, or in overall effect, based on the new point of view

GEOGRAPHY AND CULTURE

Aesop (c. 620–560 B.C.)

Ancient Greece

According to popular legend, Aesop [ē'səp] was a former slave who lived around 600 B.C. We know very little about Aesop's life and, indeed, many scholars doubt that he ever existed.

Fictitious or not, Aesop left an enduring legacy. His charming moral tales still entrance schoolchildren. Most of the fables were probably passed down by word of mouth for generations before being written down. Some, in fact, may go back to the *Panchatantra,* a collection of ancient Indian tales.

In time some of Aesop's fables were recorded, though some versions have been lost. The Greek philosopher Plato wrote that his mentor, Socrates, committed some of Aesop's tales to verse while he was in prison. The first person known to have collected Aesop's tales was Demetrius Phalereus, who lived during the fourth century B.C. During the first century A.D., the Roman poet Phaedrus rendered Aesop's fables into verse. Since then, many writers have embellished Aesop's tales, including the seventeenth-century French poet Jean de La Fontaine.

Ancient Greece: The Cradle of Western Civilization

Ancient Greece reached the height of its glory during the fifth century B.C. At that time the influence of the Greeks spread far beyond the southern portion of the Balkan peninsula, where most of modern Greece is located. Ancient Greek colonists settled in parts of modern Turkey, Bulgaria, Yugoslavia, and Albania, and Greek ports dotted the Mediterranean coastline.

Greece has always been an austere and rugged country. Its rocky coasts and isolated mountain valleys encouraged the development in ancient times of small, independent political units called city-states. Within these city-states—which included Athens, Corinth, and Sparta—both commerce and culture thrived, and the Greeks have left us a legacy of extraordinary works of art, literature, and philosophy. The Olympic games and other festivals helped to unite these city-states. Nonetheless, they often fell into bitter rivalries, fueled by the negative human traits that Aesop illustrates in his fables.

THE ANCIENT GREEK WORLD

See LITERATURE AND CULTURE SOURCEBOOK: Classical Greece and Rome

The Fox and the Grapes; The Goatherd . . . **237**

LESSON PREVIEW

In these fables Aesop exposes human foibles. In the first a fox tries in vain to reach a bunch of grapes. His conclusion that they are sour shows the tendency to disparage what cannot be had. In the second a goatherd gives some wild goats special treatment to coax them to join his flock. They leave because they realize he will treat them as badly as he treats the others once newer goats join the group.

LITERARY SKILLS FOR THESE SELECTIONS

- fable
- characterization

THEMES IN THESE SELECTIONS

The Fox and the Grapes

- rationalization for failure

The Goatherd . . .

- bribery

LESSON OBJECTIVES

1. to understand fable
2. to understand words from ancient Greek
3. to write a fable

Teacher's Classroom Resources 2

■ Teaching Notes	29
■ Reading Guide	30
■ Check Test	31
■ Responding to World Cultures	32
■ Literary Focus: The Fable	33
■ Language Study: Words from Greek	34
■ Writing Process Guide: Writing a Fable	35
■ Grammar in Literature: Using Participial Phrases	36
■ Selection Test	37

IN THE CLASSROOM

TEACHING STUDENTS OF DIFFERENT ABILITIES

- **For less advanced students:** Encourage students to pay close attention to the last sentence in each fable and to relate this sentence to the behavior of the animals and the events of the fable.

- **For more advanced students:** Ask students to suggest modern situations for which one or both of the morals of the fables might be applicable.

DISCUSSING GEOGRAPHY AND CULTURE

The Legacy of the Greeks

Ancient Greek culture has had a lasting impact on the culture of the United States. The style of many public buildings, with their use of marble, columns, elegant geometric patterns, and other classic motifs, recalls the ancient Greeks.

- Ask students to suggest specific buildings that show the influence of ancient Greece. (Examples: the Capitol, the U.S. Supreme Court, the Jefferson Memorial)

Ask students to recall the moral of Aesop's fable "The Tortoise and the Hare" and that of any other fables by Aesop they can think of. Guide them to see that fables are brief stories with moral lessons.

PAGE SUMMARY: AT A GLANCE

The Fox and the Grapes
- A fox rationalizes his failure to reach some grapes by saying that they are sour.

The Goatherd and the Wild Goats
- A goatherd tries to persuade some wild goats to join his flock by feeding them well while feeding his own goats poorly.
- The goats leave, noting that "if others came after us, you would prefer them to ourselves."

IN THE GLOSSARY
- quench: to satisfy
- mingled: joined
- enticing: tempting

1 TEACHING FABLES

Point out that here, as in many of Aesop's fables, the moral is directly stated. Ask students how the events of the fable lead to the moral. (The fox, unable to get the grapes, pretends they are not worth getting.) Have students note that in the next fable the moral is not stated directly.

2 TEACHING CHARACTERIZATION

Point out that fables often expose negative human characteristics. Ask students what negative words could describe the goatherd. (*calculating, unfair*)

ART AND LITERATURE

Before writing was invented, oral myths and fables formed a treasury of human knowledge. Such lore has been passed down through the ages in both literature and art. In this illustration the artist tries to capture the high point of the narrative: the frustrated fox leaping hopelessly for the grapes.
- Ask students to describe an illustration for "The Goatherd and the Wild Goats." (Students may describe the wild goats scampering away as the goatherd yells after them.)

The Fox and the Grapes, illustration from an early German edition of *Aesop's Fables.*

Aesop

The Fox and the Grapes

Translated from the Greek by Joseph Jacobs

One hot summer's day a Fox was strolling through an orchard till he came to a bunch of Grapes just ripening on a vine which had been trained over a lofty branch. "Just the thing to quench my thirst," quoth he. Drawing back a few paces, he took a run and a jump, and just missed the bunch. Turning round again with a One, Two, Three, he jumped up, but with no greater success. Again and again he tried after the tempting morsel, but at last had to give it up, and walked away with his nose in the air, saying: "I am sure they are sour."

¹ *It is easy to despise what you cannot get.*

238 *Myths, Folk Tales, and Epics*

Aesop

The Goatherd and the Wild Goats

Translated from the Greek by Will Nickless

A goatherd, driving his animals from their pasture at sunset, found that some wild goats had mingled with them, and shut them up together with his own goats for the night. In the morning it snowed very hard, so that he could not take the herd from the fold to their usual feeding-place. He gave his goats just enough food to keep them alive, but fed the strangers handsomely, in the hope of enticing them to stay with his flock.

When the thaw set in he led them all out to feed, and the wild goats scampered away as fast as they could to the mountains. The goatherd accused them of being very ungrateful for leaving him, when during the blizzard he had taken more care of them than he had of his own goats. One of the wild goats turned about and called back: "That is the very reason why we are leaving you. As you treated us much better than the goats you have had so long, it is clear that if others came after us, you would prefer them to ourselves."

CRITICAL THINKING: GUIDED READING QUESTIONS

LITERAL

1a. How does the fox act when he is unable to reach the grapes? (He acts as if he doesn't care about them anymore.)

2a. Compare the way the goatherd treats the wild goats with the way he treats the goats in his flock. (He feeds the wild goats well while giving his own goats barely enough to keep them alive.)

INFERENTIAL

1b. What opinion does Aesop seem to have of the fox? (Students will probably suggest that Aesop finds him slightly ridiculous in his inability to accept a small failure.)

2b. What opinion of the goatherd do you think Aesop wants us to have? (Students will probably suggest that Aesop wants us to disapprove of the goatherd's attempt to trick the wild goats and his poor treatment of his own goats.)

PREVIEW: THE AUTHOR AND THE WORLD

Jean de La Fontaine

(1621–1695)

France

One of the world's great writers of fables, Jean de La Fontaine [zhäɴ′də lä fōɴ ten′] grew up in a middle-class family; his father worked as an inspector of forests and waterways in the area of Château-Thierry. For many years he followed his father's profession but after 1659 began to devote himself full-time to literature, supported by a series of powerful patrons. His first major published work was an adaptation of a play by the Roman dramatist Terence. The publication in 1644 of *Tales and Novels in Verse,* which included many ironic and amusing fables, established his literary reputation. La Fontaine became a member of an important group of French writers that included the playwrights Molière [mōl yār′] and Racine [rä sēn′]. Subsequent volumes of fables and other writings, including opera librettos, plays, and poems, made La Fontaine one of the most popular writers of his age, but his reputation ultimately rests on his witty, insightful fables such as "The Fox and the Crow." Many of these fables are retellings of Aesop's original stories.

GEOGRAPHY AND CULTURE

The Palace of Versailles

La Fontaine was one of many French writers and artists who charmed Louis XIV's court at the magnificent palace of Versailles [vər sī′]. Louis XIV built the palace, located on a hill twelve miles southwest of Paris, in the middle of the seventeenth century. Constructed of pink and cream stone in the Baroque style, the palace is more than a quarter of a mile long and has more than 1,300 rooms. During Louis XIV's time it housed more than 5,000 noblemen, courtiers and servants. La Fontaine probably strolled through the palace's famous Hall of Mirrors and through its magnificent parks and gardens, which are laid out in graceful geometrical designs. The palace was the seat of French government for more than 100 years. It was sacked by French republicans during the Revolution of 1789–1799 and has since become a museum. Although the palace was a glittering and lively place in Louis XIV's time, it was also the scene of many intrigues and treacheries. "The Fox and the Crow," like La Fontaine's other fables, reflects the hypocrisy of court life in seventeenth-century France.

THE PALACE AND GARDENS OF VERSAILLES

1 Menagerie and Farm
2 Pheasantry
3 Basin of Neptune
4 Basin of Apollo
5 Garden of the Grand Trianon
6 Garden of the Petit Trianon
7 Tree Nursery

0   500 Meters

See LITERATURE AND CULTURE SOURCEBOOK:
France

The Fox and the Crow **239**

MOTIVATION: PRIOR KNOWLEDGE

Ask students to identify the difference between compliments and flattery. Compliments are good things said about someone, while flattery is praise that is excessive or untrue. Discuss with students why people sometimes use flattery.

PAGE SUMMARY: AT A GLANCE

- A fox wants a cheese that a crow is holding in his mouth.
- The fox flatters the crow and begs him to sing.
- The crow opens his mouth; the cheese falls to the waiting fox.

1 TEACHING FABLES

Point out that like most fables this one features animal characters and quickly establishes a basic situation in the first few lines. Ask students to predict what will happen in the fable, based on what they know about fables.

2 TEACHING DIALOGUE

Help students recognize that the fox's words show him to be a crafty flatterer intent on getting the cheese.

ART AND LITERATURE

In this illustration a "debonairly" perched crow holds a wheel of cheese in his beak as a pleasant-looking fox gazes up at him.
- Ask students to pinpoint the moment in the fable that this illustration depicts. (the moment before the crow sings and drops the cheese)

COLLABORATIVE LEARNING: ENRICHMENT ACTIVITY

Literature Modern authors have written memorable fables. Have small groups of students explore fables that have been written by such people as James Thurber and Arnold Lobel. Ask students to compare and contrast these fables with those of Aesop and La Fontaine and to share their conclusions with the class.

Jean de La Fontaine

The Fox and the Crow

Translated from the French by George Kearns

1 A crow, perched debonairly on a branch,
    Was holding a cheese he'd found—by chance.
    Along came a fox. He sniffed that cheese,
      And he spoke to its owner in words like these:

2 5 "Good morning, good morning, dear Brother Crow!
      My, you look fine! I've never seen you so—
    So—*handsome.* Yes! I mean every word of it!
      And your lovely voice! Won't you sing a bit?"
    The crow was enchanted—he could see no choice
10   But give the fox a sample of his voice.
    He opened his beak, and—cheese, good-bye!
      The fox grabbed it up without batting an eye.

    Said the fox: "As a payment for what you've lost
    I'll give you a lesson worth twice the cost:
15 *Flattery's a game for two, my dear,*
    One to talk—and another to hear."

The Fox and the Crow, illustration from an early German edition of *Aesop's Fables.*

240   *Myths, Folk Tales, and Epics*

CRITICAL THINKING: GUIDED READING QUESTIONS

LITERAL

1a. What is the crow's reaction when the fox tells him he has a lovely voice and asks him to sing? (He is enchanted.)

2a. What kind of behavior does the fox use to get the cheese? (He uses flattery.)

INFERENTIAL

1b. What does the crow's reaction to the fox's praises tell you about him? (He is gullible, foolish, and vain; a crow does *not* have a lovely voice.)

2b. La Fontaine's fables commented on French court life. Based on this fable, what do you think was one type of behavior common in the court? (People used flattery to achieve their ends.)

STUDY QUESTIONS

(Aesop and La Fontaine)

Recalling

1. What does the fox say when he gives up trying to get the grapes?
2. Why does the goatherd give the wild goats more food than he gives his flock?
3. How does the fox obtain the crow's cheese?

Interpreting

4. What does the phrase "with his nose in the air" imply about the fox's attitude at the end of "The Fox and the Grapes"?
5. Do you think that the wild goats are correct in their conclusion?
6. What can you infer about the characters of the fox and the crow through their behavior in "The Fox and the Crow"?

Extending

7. What other morals can you think of that illustrate human foibles?

LITERARY FOCUS

The Fable

A **fable** is a very brief story told to teach a lesson, often called a **moral.** Many fables feature animals as characters. Although fables are written to teach, the most memorable fables catch and hold our attention because they tell good stories as well.

Instead of explaining the point, a writer of fables dramatizes it. For example, in "The Fox and the Grapes," Aesop has the fox act out the story, trying and failing to get the juicy grapes and then consoling himself by saying they are probably sour anyway. The reader can almost see his shrug of disappointment.

The theme of a fable is usually stated explicitly, as in Aesop's "The Fox and the Grapes" and La Fontaine's "The Fox and the Crow," although it may also be indicated implicitly, as in Aesop's "The Goatherd and the Wild Goats."

Thinking About the Fable

1. In what ways did "The Fox and the Grapes" hold your attention?
2. State the moral that Aesop might have written for "The Goatherd and the Wild Goats."

3. What makes the crow a good choice for the fox's victim? What is it about the crow that makes his surrender to flattery amusing?

LANGUAGE STUDY

Words from Greek

Western culture is based on many ideas that had their origin in ancient Greece. Our language especially shows our debt to Greek civilization. The words *democracy, politics, philosophy, history,* and *school* are all derived from Greek, as are many other words that name important aspects of Western culture.

Look up each of the following words and write down the meaning of its root or roots in ancient Greek. To find the root, look for the etymology of each word, usually appearing in brackets either before or at the end of the definition. Word roots are listed separately in some dictionaries.

1. theater
2. dynamic
3. strategy
4. physics
5. academy
6. astronaut
7. biology
8. philanthropy

COMPOSITION

Writing a Fable

Starting with the words "Once upon a time there was . . . ," write a fable with animal characters illustrating one of the following morals or one of your own choice. You may state the moral or leave it unstated.

- Practice what you preach.
- Don't put off for tomorrow what you can do today.
- Beauty is in the eye of the beholder.
- All that glitters is not gold.

COMPARING FABLES

Aesop and La Fontaine, though they wrote centuries apart and lived in vastly different cultures, both found their favorite form in the simple beast-fable. They elaborated their tales in very different ways. Using the examples in this lesson (and perhaps other fables by Aesop and La Fontaine), compare these two authors' approach to the beast-fable. Pay particular attention to their style and use of language.

Aesop and La Fontaine Fables **241**

Which of the three fables' lessons do you think is most relevant to life today? Explain.

ANSWERS

STUDY QUESTIONS

1. "I am sure they are sour."
2. He hopes to entice them to stay with his flock.
3. He persuades the crow to sing so that the crow will drop the cheese.
4. He is conceited; since he cannot reach the grapes, he decides they are not good enough for him.
5. Answers may vary, but most students will probably say yes.
6. The fox is clever and subtle; the crow, foolish and vain.
7. Answers will vary. Students may suggest morals that treat greed, vanity, and foolishness.

LITERARY FOCUS

1. Answers will vary. Students may mention the suspense that occurs as the reader wonders whether the fox will get the grapes.
2. Answers will vary. Possible response: "Don't neglect what you have in hopes of getting something better."
3. The crow is dim-witted and susceptible to flattery; humor comes from our imagining such a bad singer falling prey to such obvious flattery.

LANGUAGE STUDY

1. "place for seeing"
2. "forceful; powerful"
3. "leadership of an army"
4. "nature"
5. "the grove of Academus where Plato taught, named after a pre-Grecian hero"
6. "sailor among the stars"
7. "study of life"
8. "love for humanity"

COMPARING FABLES

Point out that the works of Aesop and La Fontaine both expose human foibles. Aesop uses simple language and prose, however, while La Fontaine employs sophisticated language and poetic form.

COMPOSITION: GUIDELINES FOR EVALUATION

WRITING A FABLE

Objective

To dramatize a proverb using animal characters

Guidelines for Evaluation

- suggested length: one to two pages
- should use action and dialogue
- should use animals as characters
- should clearly illustrate the moral either explicitly or implicitly

LESSON PREVIEW

In this instructive tale, four youths set out to make their fortune. Three of them are educated but have no common sense; the fourth has common sense but no education. When they come across the bones of a lion, the educated youths decide to exercise their learning by bringing the lion back to life. The fourth youth realizes that a live lion will kill them. He climbs a tree to protect himself. The educated youths are killed, demonstrating the destructiveness of learning without common sense.

LITERARY SKILLS FOR THIS SELECTION

- verse proverb
- repetition

THEMES IN THIS SELECTION

- common sense
- the appropriate use of knowledge

LESSON OBJECTIVES

1. to understand fables
2. to recognize the origins of Indo-European languages
3. to write a fable

Teacher's Classroom Resources 2

- Teaching Notes   39
- Reading Guide   40
- Check Test   41
- Responding to World Cultures   42
- Language Study: The Indo-European Language Family   43
- Writing Process Guide: Writing a Fable   44
- Grammar in Literature: Inverted Subject-Verb Order   45
- Selection Test   46

GEOGRAPHY AND CULTURE

Panchatantra

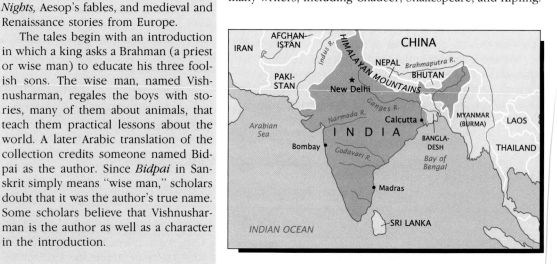

India

The *Panchatantra,* meaning "Five Books or Chapters," is a collection of Indian stories that is thought to date from A.D. 200–400, although some of the tales are even older. The anonymous author, or authors, wrote in Sanskrit, an ancient Indian language. The *Panchatantra* inspired many other storytellers: versions of the tales reappear in *The Thousand and One Nights,* Aesop's fables, and medieval and Renaissance stories from Europe.

The tales begin with an introduction in which a king asks a Brahman (a priest or wise man) to educate his three foolish sons. The wise man, named Vishnusharman, regales the boys with stories, many of them about animals, that teach them practical lessons about the world. A later Arabic translation of the collection credits someone named Bidpai as the author. Since *Bidpai* in Sanskrit simply means "wise man," scholars doubt that it was the author's true name. Some scholars believe that Vishnusharman is the author as well as a character in the introduction.

Ancient India and Its Storytelling Traditions

India, the second most populous country in the world, is located in south-central Asia. It occupies a roughly triangular peninsula that is separated from the rest of Asia by the Himalayan mountains and extends far into the Indian Ocean. Indian civilization dates back to at least 2500 B.C.

The literature of India is among the world's oldest. It consists of religious scriptures, epic poetry, drama, and stories, all of which have influenced other cultures for thousands of years. The easily memorized verse proverbs of the *Panchatantra* were written to entertain as well as to instruct. Illustrating simple lessons for practical living, this delightful collection of tales was so popular that it became one of the most widely translated books in medieval Europe. The *Panchatantra* was translated from the original Sanskrit into Persian and Arabic, and later into Greek, Hebrew, Latin, German, Italian, and English. Over two hundred versions exist in fifty languages. It has influenced many writers, including Chaucer, Shakespeare, and Kipling.

See LITERATURE AND CULTURE SOURCEBOOK:
India and the Middle East

242   *Myths, Folk Tales, and Epics*

IN THE CLASSROOM

TEACHING STUDENTS OF DIFFERENT ABILITIES

- **For less advanced students:** Students should be encouraged to consider the theme of the uselessness of education without common sense. Have them complete the Reading Guide.
- **For more advanced students:** Ask students to state the

lesson of the tale in their own words and suggest modern situations in which common sense should stop people from making use of knowledge gained through formal education.

DISCUSSING GEOGRAPHY AND CULTURE

Sanskrit and English: Distant Cousins

Sanskrit, the ancient language of the *Panchatantra,* is a member of the Indo-European family of languages. Many modern languages, including English, belong to this same family.

- Several English words bear a resemblance to their Sanskrit equivalents. The following Sanskrit words refer to family members. Ask students to suggest the corresponding English word for each: *matr* (mother), *duhitr* (daughter), *bhrātar* (brother).

Detail from an Indian painting. Ink, colors, gold and silver on paper. Mughal Period, c. 1585.

Indian Traditional

from the **Panchatantra**

Translated from the Sanskrit by Charles Lanman

The Lion-Makers

Even men of learning and noble birth are sometimes devoid of common-sense. For, true is the saying:

1
> Book-learning people rightly cherish;
> But gumption's[1] best of all to me.
> Bereft of gumption you shall perish,
> Like to the Lion-makers three.

"How was that?" said the Man-with-the-wheel.[2] And the Gold-magician narrated:

---
1. **gumption:** common sense; shrewdness.
2. **Man-with-the-wheel:** probably a potter, who uses a potter's wheel.

In a certain place there dwelled four brah-man[3] youths in the greatest friendship. Three of them had got to the further shore of the ocean of science but were devoid of common-sense; while the fourth had common-sense only, and no mind for science. Now once upon a time these friends took counsel together, and said, "Of what profit is science, if we cannot go with it to some foreign country and win the favor of

---
3. **brahman:** referring to the highest caste, or hereditary social class, into which Hindu society is traditionally divided. Caste members were restricted in their choice of occupation.

Panchatantra **243**

princes and make our fortune? Therefore to the Eastern Country let us go." And so it came to pass.

Now after they had gone a little way, the eldest spoke: "There is one among us, the fourth, who has no learning, but only common-sense; and a man can't get presents from kings by common-sense without learning. Not a whit will I give him of all that I gain; so let him go home." And the second said, "Ho there, Gumption! get you homeward, for you have no learning!" But the third made answer, "Alas, it is not fitting so to do: for we have played together since we were boys. So let him come along too. He's a noble fellow, and shall have a share in the riches that we win."

On then they went together, till in a jungle they saw the bones of a dead lion. Then spoke the first: "Ha! now we can put our book-learning to the test. Here lies some sort of a dead creature: by the power of our learning we'll bring it

to life. I'll put the bones together." And that then he did with zeal. The second added flesh, blood, and hide. But just as the third was breathing the breath of life into it, Gumption stopped him and said, "Hold: this is a lion that you are turning out. If you make him alive, he will kill every one of us." Thereupon made answer the other, "Fie, stupid! is learning to be fruitless in my hands?" "Well, then," said Gumption, "just wait a bit till I climb a tree."

Thereupon the lion was brought to life. But the instant this was done, he sprang up and killed the three. Afterwards Gumption climbed down and went home.

Therefore, concluded the Gold-magician, therefore I say:

3
> Book-learning people rightly cherish;
> But gumption's best of all to me.
> Bereft of gumption you shall perish,
> Like to the Lion-makers three.

Indian shield, painted leather with silver bosses, c. 1800.

244 *Myths, Folk Tales, and Epics*

CRITICAL THINKING: GUIDED READING QUESTIONS

LITERAL

1a. Why do the first two Brahmans want the uneducated Brahman to return home? (They think he will receive no presents because he has no learning.)

2a. What does the author say about the value of "book-learning"? (It is rightly cherished.)

INFERENTIAL

1b. What opinion do you think the author wants us to have of these two? (He wants us to recognize their foolish pride and selfishness.)

2b. Do you think the author really believes that people should live by common sense alone? Explain. (Since the author believes education is rightly cherished, he is probably exaggerating; he probably believes that people should combine common sense with education.)

STUDY QUESTIONS

Recalling

1. What accomplishment does the fourth youth lack, and what does he have in its place?
2. What do the four youths seek as they travel?
3. Explain what each of the three youths contributes to bringing the lion back to life.
4. What objection does the fourth youth have to bringing the lion back to life?

Interpreting

5. What does the fourth youth understand that the others do not?
6. For what reason do you think the three youths decided to bring the lion back to life?
7. What is the fable saying about the relationship of education and common sense?

Extending

8. How do you think the theme of "The Lion Makers" might be applied to debates about technology?

LANGUAGE STUDY

The Indo-European Language Family

The *Panchatantra* is written in Sanskrit, an ancient tongue that originated in India. Through studying Sanskrit, Greek, Latin, and other ancient languages, linguists have discovered that some languages came from the same mother tongue. The 3,000 to 4,000 languages spoken throughout the world today fall into roughly eighteen groups or families. Both English and Sanskrit, for example, belong to the Indo-European family, derived from a long dead language that was spoken somewhere in India or Europe thousands of years ago.

The chart at the bottom of this page shows the evolution of some languages in the Indo-European family. Study it and answer the following questions.

1. To what group of Indo-European languages do English, Norwegian, and German belong?
2. Which languages in the following pairs are most closely related?
   Modern Greek and Spanish
   Polish and Welsh
   French and Romanian
3. What common language formed the basis of French, Italian, and Portuguese?
4. Which languages in the following pairs are least closely related?
   Irish and Welsh
   Persian and Norse
   Slovak and Bulgarian

COMPOSITION

Writing a Fable

A fable is a very brief story told to teach a lesson. Try writing your own fable. You might start with a favorite proverb, such as "The early bird gets the worm," and invent a story to fit it. Or you might start by narrating an event you have observed or participated in, and find a theme that fits. Explain the lesson with a moral.

ANSWERS

STUDY QUESTIONS

1. He has "no mind for science," but he has common sense.
2. They seek to win the favor of princes and make their fortune.
3. The first assembles the bones; the second adds flesh, blood, and hide; the third gives the lion the breath of life.
4. He fears the lion will kill them.
5. He understands that this is not a dry, academic exercise and that lions are vicious animals.
6. to demonstrate their knowledge and their superiority
7. Education can be useless when not guided by common sense.
8. Answers will vary. Some students may say that the theme suggests that advances in technology—genetic engineering and improved computers, for example—can be harmful if not used with wisdom and common sense.

LANGUAGE STUDY

1. the Germanic group
2. French and Romanian
3. Latin
4. Persian and Norse

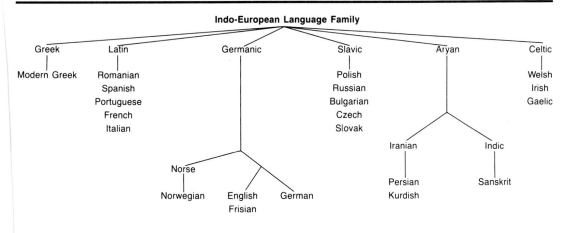

Indo-European Language Family

Panchatantra **245**

COMPOSITION: GUIDELINES FOR EVALUATION

WRITING A FABLE

Objective

To illustrate a practical truth about life or human nature through a fable

Guidelines for Evaluation

- suggested length: one to two pages
- should be realistic and believable
- should clearly relate the story and the moral
- should show some practical wisdom about life

This is the tale of Sindbad the Sailor's second voyage. Sindbad falls asleep on an uninhabited island, and his ship sails without him. He ties himself to a giant bird and lands in a snake-infested, diamond-filled valley. He takes many diamonds, ties himself to a sheep carcass, and is carried by a vulture to a mountaintop. He befriends some merchants, travels with them to exotic places, and returns home with riches and stories.

LITERARY SKILLS FOR THIS SELECTION

- legend
- characterization
- plot

THEMES IN THIS SELECTION

- heroism and adventure
- intelligence and bravery

LESSON OBJECTIVES

1. to understand legend
2. to recognize the meaning and origin of words from Arabic
3. to write a sequel to a legend

Teacher's Classroom Resources 2

- Teaching Notes   49
- Reading Guide   50
- Check Test   51
- Responding to World
  Cultures   52
- Literary Focus: Legend   53
- Language Study: Words
  from Arabic   54
- Writing Process Guide:
  Writing a Sequel to a
  Legend   55
- Grammar in Literature:
  Using Adverbs to
  Describe   56
- Selection Test   57

TEACHING STUDENTS OF DIFFERENT ABILITIES

- **For less advanced students:** Point out that the tale occurs in a world colored by imagination and exaggeration; its events should not be accepted as fact. Have students complete the Reading Guide.
- **For more advanced students:** Ask students to look for ways in which the tale blends reality

and fantasy and to discuss how true events may have been transformed over time by exaggeration and imagination to create the story.

The Thousand and One Nights (c. 1200)

Middle East

The Thousand and One Nights is one of the world's most famous collections of legends and folk tales. Also called *The Arabian Nights,* the collection was compiled in Arabic in the thirteenth century. Some of its tales, however, may have been borrowed from the oral traditions of other cultures of southwestern Asia, and several tales most likely date from an earlier time. For example, scholars believe that the earliest legends about Sindbad the Sailor—later made famous in *The Thousand and One Nights*—probably originated in the eighth or ninth century.

The title *The Thousand and One Nights* refers to the frame story that ties the tales together. This frame story introduces a woman named Scheherazade [shə her′ə zä′də], who has been condemned to death by a cruel king. The night before she is to die, she tells the king a tale but cleverly leaves it unfinished. The king then postpones her death sentence so he can hear the end of the story the next night. Scheherazade keeps up this ploy for a thousand and one nights, telling tale after tale until the king revokes her death sentence.

GEOGRAPHY AND CULTURE

Medieval Arabia and the City of Baghdad

Many of the tales in *The Thousand and One Nights* take place on or near Arabia, the large peninsula of southwestern Asia where Arabic is widely spoken. The tales about Sindbad the Sailor, for example, open in the city of Baghdad [bag′dad], the modern capital of the nation of Iraq. In Sindbad's day Baghdad was a thriving city whose merchants traded with kingdoms in many parts of the ancient world. To set out on a trading expedition, sailors traveled down the Tigris [tī′gris] River from Baghdad to Basra [bus′rə], the port where the Tigris and Euphrates [ū frā′tēz] rivers meet and flow into the Persian Gulf, a body of water east of the Arabian peninsula.

In *The Thousand and One Nights,* Sindbad the Sailor spins a lively tale about seven voyages he has made. He relates his adventures to a poor porter whose name is also Sindbad. In the upcoming selection Sindbad the Sailor has just described his first voyage to Sindbad the Porter.

MEDIEVAL ARABIA

See LITERATURE AND CULTURE SOURCEBOOK: India and the Middle East

DISCUSSING GEOGRAPHY AND CULTURE

Learning About Other Cultures

The traders who crossed medieval Arabia carried precious cargoes: tea and silks from the East, spices from India, ebony and ivory from Africa. They also carried news: stories of distant lands and of the exotic peoples who lived there.

- Ask students how they learn about different cultures today. (They may mention television, newspapers and magazines, movies, and books.)

Arabian and Persian Traditional

from **The Thousand and One Nights**

Retold from the Arabic by N. J. Dawood

The Second Voyage of Sindbad the Sailor

The day was drawing to its close, and Sindbad the Sailor invited Sindbad the Porter to join the guests in the evening meal. When the feast was finished he gave him a hundred pieces of gold, saying, "You have delighted us with your company today."

The porter thanked him for his generous gift and departed, marveling at all he had heard.

Next morning he went again to the house of the old sheikh,[1] who received him courteously and seated him by his side. Presently the other guests arrived, and when they had feasted and made merry, Sindbad the Sailor began:

1 For some time after my return from my first voyage I continued to lead a free and easy life, but I soon longed to travel again about the world and to visit distant cities and islands in quest of profit and adventure. So I bought a great quantity of goods, made preparations for a new voyage, and sailed down the river Tigris to Basra.[2] There I joined a band of merchants and embarked in a fine vessel that set sail the same day.

2 Helped by a favorable wind, we voyaged for many days from port to port and from island to island; and wherever we cast anchor we sold and bartered our goods, and haggled with officials and merchants. At last our ship reached the shores of an uninhabited island, rich in fruit and flowers, and echoing with the singing of birds and the murmur of crystal streams.

Here passengers and crew went ashore, and we all set off to enjoy the delights of the island. I strolled through the green meadows, leaving my companions far behind, and sat down in a shady thicket to eat a simple meal by a spring. Lulled by the soft and fragrant breeze that blew around me, I lay upon the grass and presently fell asleep.

I cannot tell how long I slept, but when I woke I saw none of my companions and feared **3** the ship had left. I ran in frantic haste toward the sea, and on reaching the shore saw the vessel, a white speck upon the vast blue ocean, dissolving into the far horizon.

Broken with terror and despair, I threw myself upon the sand, crying, "Now your end has come, Sindbad! The jar that drops a second time is sure to break!"[3] I repented my folly in venturing again upon the perils of the sea, and wished with all my heart that I had stayed safe at home. I wandered about aimlessly for some time, and then climbed into a tall tree. From the top I gazed in all directions, but could see nothing except the sky, the trees, the birds, the sands, and the boundless ocean. As I scanned the interior of the island more closely, however, I gradually became aware of a white object looming in the distance. At once I climbed down the tree and made my way toward it. Drawing near, I found to my astonishment it was a white dome of extraordinary size. Walking all around it, I

---

1. **sheikh** [shēk]: Moslem leader and holy man.
2. **Basra** [bus′rə]: port city in present-day Iraq. (See the Geography and Culture feature that precedes the selection.)

---

3. **The jar . . . break!:** Sindbad considers himself lucky to have escaped misfortune on his dangerous first voyage and uses this figurative saying to indicate that this time he does not expect to be as lucky.

The Thousand and One Nights **247**

CRITICAL THINKING: GUIDED READING QUESTIONS

LITERAL

1a. What does Sindbad do when he discovers the ship has left without him? (He throws himself upon the sand in terror and despair.)

2a. What does Sindbad say he sees from the top of a tall tree on the island? (He sees nothing but sky, trees, birds, sands, and boundless ocean.)

INFERENTIAL

1b. What does Sindbad reveal about himself by this reaction? (Students may say he shows that he recognizes the perils of travel and knows he is not invincible; they may also say he knows how to tell a good story and heighten interest.)

2b. Why do you think Sindbad as a storyteller emphasizes the desperate nature of his circumstances? (He is probably trying to make himself appear more heroic.)

PAGE SUMMARY: AT A GLANCE

- Sindbad discovers that the giant dome is a roc's egg.
- To escape from the island, he ties himself to one of the roc's talons and allows the giant bird to carry him away.
- He lands in a valley guarded by huge snakes and filled with diamonds.
- He sees a sheep carcass come tumbling down into the valley.

IN THE GLOSSARY

- talons: bird's claws

4 TEACHING DESCRIPTION

Encourage students to note how the storyteller heightens the drama by emphasizing details of the gigantic "dome." Ask students to describe the effect of such details. (It makes the reader highly curious about what the "dome" is.)

5 CULTURAL BACKGROUND

Point out that the roc might have been based on a real bird now extinct. Some scholars have suggested that the idea for the roc came from a gigantic Madagascan ostrich whose egg weighed many pounds.

6 TEACHING LEGENDS

Explain that legends often emphasize the extraordinary characteristics of their heroes. Ask students what heroic traits Sindbad displays here. (resourcefulness, courage, unwillingness to give in to fate)

7 GRAMMAR IN LITERATURE

Point out the author's use of adjectives to contrast the nature of the diamonds and the snakes. Words like *rarest* and *glittering* contrast with words like *deadly* and *dread*. Ask what impact these words have. (They make us admire the diamonds and fear and loathe the snakes.)

4 could see no door or entrance of any kind; and so smooth and slippery was its surface that any attempt to climb it would have been fruitless. I made a mark in the sand near its base, walked around it again, and found that its circumference measured more than fifty paces.

While I was doing this, the sun was suddenly hidden from my view as by a great cloud and the world grew dark around me. I lifted up my eyes toward the sky and was confounded to see a gigantic bird with enormous wings, which, as it flew through the air, screened the sun, hiding it from the island.

This strange sight instantly brought back to my mind a story I had heard in my youth from 5 pilgrims and adventurers: how in a far island dwelt a bird of monstrous size called the roc, which fed its young on elephants; and at once I realized that the white dome was none other than a roc's egg. In a twinkling, the bird alighted upon the egg, covered it completely with its wings, and stretched out its legs behind it on the ground. And in this posture it went to sleep.

6 Rising swiftly, I unwound my turban from my head, then doubled it and twisted it into a rope with which I tied myself securely to one of the great talons of the monster.

"It may be," I said to myself, "that this bird will carry me away to a civilized land; wherever I am set down, it will surely be better than an uninhabited island."

I lay awake all night, fearing to close my eyes lest the bird should fly away with me while I slept. At daybreak the roc rose from the egg and, spreading its wings, took to the air with a terrible cry. I clung fast to its talon as it winged its flight through the void and soared higher and higher until it almost touched the sky. After some time it began to drop and, floating swiftly downward, came to earth on the brow of a steep hill.

In great fear I hastened to untie my turban before the roc became aware of my presence. Scarcely had I released myself when the monster

248 *Myths, Folk Tales, and Epics*

darted off toward a great black object lying near, clutched it in its claws, and took wing again. As it rose in the air I saw that this was a serpent of immeasurable length; and with its prey the bird vanished from sight.

Now to find out where I was! I was looking out over an exceedingly deep and wide valley. On all sides there were rocky mountains whose towering summits no man could ever climb. I was stricken with fear and repented my rashness.

"If only I had stayed on that island!" I thought to myself. "There at least I lacked neither fruit nor water, while these barren rocks offer nothing to eat or drink. I have indeed come into worse misfortune."

7 On making my way down the hill I marveled to see that the ground was thickly covered with the rarest diamonds, so that the entire valley was bathed in a glorious light. But crawling among the glittering stones were deadly snakes and vipers, dread keepers of the fabulous treasure. Thicker and longer than giant palm trees, they could have swallowed whole elephants at one gulp. They were returning to their sunless dens, for by day they hid themselves from their enemies the rocs and the eagles, and moved about only at night.

Half crazed with terror, I roamed the valley all day searching for a shelter where I might pass the night. At dusk I crawled into a narrow-mouthed cave and blocked its entrance with a great stone. At daybreak I rolled back the stone and went out of my hiding place.

As I walked about I noticed a great piece of flesh come tumbling down into the valley from rock to rock. On examining it, I found it to be a whole sheep, skinned and drawn. I was deeply puzzled by the mystery, for there was not a soul in sight; but at that moment there flashed across my mind the memory of a story I had once heard from travelers who had visited the Diamond Mountains—how men obtained the diamonds from this remote and treacherous valley

CRITICAL THINKING: GUIDED READING QUESTIONS

LITERAL

1a. How does Sindbad feel when he first looks out over the "exceedingly deep and wide valley"? (He is stricken with fear and repentant of his rashness in leaving the island.)

2a. How does Sindbad describe the valley and its creatures? (The valley is covered with rare diamonds that bathe it in a "glorious light"; its snakes and vipers are "thicker and longer than giant palm trees" and big enough to swallow whole elephants.)

INFERENTIAL

1b. Why do you think Sindbad describes these feelings? (to heighten the suspense; He is now in worse danger than before.)

2b. In what way does this description enhance the adventure? (The valley provides an opportunity for great wealth while also presenting great danger.)

Detail. Illustration depicting Sindbad the Sailor from an early German edition of *The Thousand and One Nights*.

- Sindbad realizes that merchants throw sheep carcasses into the valley so that diamonds might become embedded in them; birds carry the carcasses out of the valley to the mountain, and the merchants then force the birds to drop the meat and retrieve the diamonds.
- Sindbad fills his clothing with as many diamonds as he can.
- He ties himself to a carcass and is lifted into the air by a vulture.

IN THE GLOSSARY

- carcasses: dead bodies of animals

8 READING SKILL: SEQUENCE OF EVENTS

Ask students to describe in their own words and in sequential order the way in which the merchants secure diamonds. (They throw sheep carcasses into the valley; diamonds become embedded in them; rocs and vultures pick up the carcasses and carry them to the mountaintops; the merchants shout at the birds, making them drop the meat and fly away; the merchants pick the diamonds out of the carcasses.)

ART AND LITERATURE

In this illustration Sindbad flies through a dark sky dangling from the talons of a great and magical bird. In traditional fashion the hero undergoes an extraordinary experience and survives through cunning and bravery.
- What characteristic quality of a hero does this illustration reinforce? (A hero performs an extraordinary task.)

8 by a strange device. Before sunrise they would throw whole carcasses of sheep from the top of the mountains, so that the gems on which they fell cut through the soft flesh and became embedded in it. At midday rocs and mighty vultures would swoop down upon the mutton and carry it away in their talons toward their nests in the mountain heights. Shouting loudly, the merchants would then rush at the birds and force them to drop the meat and fly away, after which all that remained was for them to look through the carcasses and pick out the diamonds.

As I recalled this story, a plan of escape formed in my mind. I selected a great quantity of substantial stones and hid them about me; I filled my pockets with them and pressed them into the folds of my belt and garments. Then I unrolled my turban, stuffed it with more diamonds, twisted it into a rope as I had done before and, lying under the carcass, tied it firmly to my chest. I had not remained long in that position when I suddenly felt myself lifted from the ground by a huge vulture whose talons had tightly closed upon the meat. The bird climbed

The Thousand and One Nights   **249**

CRITICAL THINKING: GUIDED READING QUESTIONS

LITERAL

1a. What does Sindbad do to escape from the valley? (He ties himself to a sheep carcass and lets himself be carried away by a vulture.)

INFERENTIAL

1b. What do Sindbad's actions show about him? (He continues to be resourceful and brave.)

- Sindbad is carried to a mountaintop by a vulture.
- After a merchant chases away the vulture, Sindbad unties himself from the carcass.
- Sindbad introduces himself to the merchant and gives him some diamonds.
- Sindbad is welcomed into the merchant's tent and soon travels with him and other merchants to exotic places.
- Sindbad returns home loaded with riches.

IN THE GLOSSARY

- innumerable: too many to count

9 TEACHING CHARACTERIZATION

Ask students what Sindbad's gift to the merchant reflects about him. (He is generous and believes that good will is as important as riches.)

10 TEACHING LEGENDS

Help students recognize that legends often include descriptions of wondrous settings and creatures. In this tale students have already seen the lush island with its roc and the deep, diamond-laden valley filled with snakes. On this island Sindbad finds additional settings and creatures considered amazing in his time.

11 TEACHING PLOT: RESOLUTION

Help students see that at the end of the story, Sindbad is much as he was at the beginning. He has returned home safely and settled into a free, easy life.

COLLABORATIVE LEARNING: ENRICHMENT ACTIVITY

Drama This tale lends itself to exciting dramatization. Have students divide the tasks needed to create a drama—writing a script, making costumes and props, performing music, creating sound effects, playing the roles—and work in small groups to carry them out. Have them perform the play for other classes.

higher and higher and finally alighted upon a mountaintop. As soon as it began to tear at the flesh there arose from the nearby rocks a hue and cry, at which the bird took fright and flew away. At once I freed myself and sprang to my feet.

A man came running to the spot and stopped in alarm as he saw me. Without uttering a word, he cautiously bent over the carcass to examine it, looking at me suspiciously all the while, but, finding no diamonds, he wrung his hands and started back in fear.

"Who are you?" he cried. "And what are you doing here?"

"Do not be alarmed, sir," I replied. "I am no thief but an honest man, a merchant by profession. My story is very strange, and the adventure that has brought me to these mountains is more extraordinary than all the marvels men have seen or heard. But first, please accept some of these diamonds, which I myself gathered in the fearful valley below."

9 I took some splendid jewels from my pocket and offered them to him, saying, "These will bring you all the riches you can desire."

The merchant was overjoyed at the unexpected gift; he thanked me warmly and called down blessings upon me. While we were talking, several other merchants came up from the mountainside. They crowded around us and listened in amazement to my story. Then they led me to their tent. They gave me food and drink, and I slept soundly for many hours. Early next day, we set out from our tent and, journeying over a vast range of mountains, came at last to 10 the seashore. After a short voyage we arrived at a pleasant, densely wooded island, covered with trees so huge that beneath only one of them a hundred men could shelter from the sun.

There I saw a gigantic beast called the karkadan, or rhinoceros, which grazes in the fields like a cow or buffalo. It is as big as a camel and has a single horn in the middle of its forehead. The rhinoceros attacks the elephant, im-

pales it upon its horn, and carries it aloft from place to place until its victim dies. Before long, however, the elephant's fat melts in the heat of the sun and, dripping down into the rhinoceros' eyes, blinds it, so that the beast blunders helplessly along and finally drops dead. Then the roc swoops down upon both animals and carries them off to its nest in the high mountains. I also saw many strange breeds in that island.

I sold several of my diamonds for a large sum and exchanged more for a vast quantity of merchandise. Then we set sail and traded from port to port and from island to island, at last arriving safely in Basra. After a few days I set out for Baghdad, the City of Peace.

Loaded with precious goods and the finest of my diamonds, I hastened to my old street and entered my own house, rejoicing to see my friends and kinfolk. I gave them gold and presents, and distributed a large sum among the poor of the city.

11 Soon I forgot the perils and hardships of my travels, and took again to extravagant living. I ate well, dressed well, and kept open house for innumerable gallants and merry companions.

From far and near, men came to hear me speak of my adventures and to learn from me the news of foreign lands. All were astounded at the dangers I had escaped and wished me joy of my return. Such was my second voyage.

Tomorrow, my friends, if Allah[4] wills, I shall relate to you the extraordinary tale of my third voyage.

The famous mariner stopped speaking, and the guests marveled at his story.

When the evening feast was over, Sindbad the Sailor gave Sindbad the Porter a hundred pieces of gold, which he took with thanks and blessings, and departed, lost in wonderment at all he had heard.

_____

4. **Allah:** the Supreme Being of the Moslem religion.

CRITICAL THINKING: GUIDED READING QUESTIONS

LITERAL

1a. What does Sindbad give the merchant? (He gives him diamonds.)

2a. What does Sindbad forget when he returns home and settles into "extravagant living," and why do people come from far and near to visit him? (He forgets the perils and hardships of travel and enjoys astounding people with his tales.)

INFERENTIAL

1b. Why does Sindbad's gift of diamonds change the merchant's attitude toward him? (The merchant sees that Sindbad is generous and is not intent on stealing the merchant's trade in diamonds.)

2b. Why do you think Sindbad will embark on still another adventure? (He forgets the bad and remembers only the good about his past adventures; he remains restless and adventurous.)

STUDY QUESTIONS

Recalling

1. For what reasons does Sindbad long to visit distant cities and islands?
2. Briefly describe the roc and its egg. By what means does Sindbad escape the roc's island?
3. In what manner do merchants obtain diamonds from the valley where Sindbad next lands?
4. How does Sindbad escape the valley? What does he bring with him?

Interpreting

5. Identify three personality traits that Sindbad displays, and cite details from the story that point to these traits.
6. What changing attitude toward fate or luck does Sindbad display in the course of the story?
7. Based on the story, what can you infer about Arabian attitudes toward travel and trade in Sindbad's day?
8. Why do you think tales of sailors' voyages were so fascinating in Sindbad's day?

Extending

9. What would you have done to obtain the diamonds from the dangerous valley?

LITERARY FOCUS

Legend

A **legend** is a story handed down from generation to generation among a particular people and believed to have a basis in fact, although that cannot always be confirmed. Most legends recount the adventures of a celebrated hero or heroine who may have been a historical figure. For example, several medieval European legends recount the deeds of King Arthur, a hero of the Celtic people of Britain.

A legend often gives people a positive image of their past and a vehicle for expressing their values in an exciting way. Often a legend magnifies the achievements of an actual person, turning him or her into a larger-than-life figure. The stories of the seven voyages of Sindbad are famous Arabic legends whose hero, a sailor, may very well have been a real person.

Thinking About the Legend

1. What makes Sindbad a larger-than-life hero?
2. What values does this legend express in exciting or heroic terms?

LANGUAGE STUDY

Words from Arabic

Arabic, the original language of *The Thousand and One Nights,* has contributed many words to English. For example, the English word *sheik,* which appears in the selection, comes from the Arabic *shaikh,* meaning "head of a village." The word literally means "old man" or "elder." Many other English words borrowed from Arabic reflect the great achievements of the Moslem world in science, mathematics, and navigation.

Use a dictionary to help you determine the meanings and origins of these English words.

1. admiral
2. alcove
3. algebra
4. caliber
5. cipher
6. henna
7. monsoon
8. tariff

COMPOSITION

Writing a Sequel to a Legend

■ Write your own sequel to Sindbad's second voyage. In your sequel have Sindbad the Sailor describe a new adventure to Sindbad the Porter. The adventure should involve sailing to a different place and perhaps meeting with another unusual creature.

COMPOSITION: GUIDELINES FOR EVALUATION

WRITING A SEQUEL TO A LEGEND

Objective

To explore the components of an adventure story

Guidelines for Evaluation

■ suggested length: one to two pages
■ should describe Sindbad sailing to a new land
■ should show Sindbad's bravery and cleverness
■ should include specific details and examples that describe Sindbad's new adventure

ANSWERS

STUDY QUESTIONS

1. He seeks profit and adventure.
2. The roc is a huge bird; its egg is an enormous white dome. He ties himself to one of the roc's talons and lets it carry him away.
3. They throw sheep carcasses into the valley so that they might become embedded with diamonds; rocs and vultures go after the meat and fly with it back to the mountains; the merchants force the birds to drop the meat and retrieve the diamonds.
4. He ties himself to the carcass of a sheep and is carried by a vulture to the mountaintop. He brings diamonds.
5. generosity (toward the porter); cleverness (in using his turban to escape); bravery (in the face of the creatures he meets)
6. At first he fears his luck has ended, but then he takes fate into his own hands.
7. Travel was admired and trade favored, for both could broaden horizons.
8. Few people traveled. Many longed to learn of new lands.
9. Answers will vary.

LITERARY FOCUS

1. He has extraordinary experiences and is clever and brave.
2. The legend emphasizes cleverness, courage, and generosity.

LANGUAGE STUDY

1. "commanding officer of a navy"; from *amîr a 'ālî,* "high leader"
2. "recessed section"; from *al-qubba,* "alcove"
3. "type of math"; from *al-jabr,* "reunion of broken parts"
4. "size of a bullet or shell"; from *galib,* "a mold"
5. "the symbol zero"; from *sifr, sefr,* "zero, nothing"
6. "a plant; its dye"; from *hinna,* name for the plant and dye
7. "seasonal wind of Indian Ocean and southern Asia"; from *mausim,* "time; season"
8. "system of taxes"; from *ta'rif,* "information"

In this entertaining folk tale only a commoner can solve riddles that a prince poses. She and the prince marry, but she stipulates that they must part should her wisdom surpass his. When it does, he asks her to leave, saying she may take whatever she wishes. She cleverly takes him, whom she loves dearly. Love having triumphed, the two return to the palace and live happily ever after.

LITERARY SKILLS FOR THIS SELECTION

- folk tale
- characterization

THEMES IN THIS SELECTION

- cleverness and ingenuity
- foolish pride
- the triumph of love

LESSON OBJECTIVES

1. to understand folk tales
2. to write about a folk tale's heroine
3. to retell a folk tale

Teacher's Classroom Resources 2

- Teaching Notes   59
- Reading Guide   60
- Check Test   61
- Responding to World
  Cultures   62
- Literary Focus:
  Folk Tale   63
- Writing Process Guides:
  Writing About a Folk
  Tale's Heroine   64
  Retelling a Folk Tale   65
- Grammar in Literature:
  Quotations Within
  Quotations   66
- Selection Test   67

IN THE CLASSROOM

TEACHING STUDENTS OF DIFFERENT ABILITIES

- **For less advanced students:** Encourage students to see that many of the statements made by the prince and the daughter make little sense at first but are explained as the tale unfolds. Ask them to complete the Reading Guide.
- **For more advanced students:** Explain that the tale includes the riddle of the Sphinx from

Kabyle Oral Tradition

Algeria/Tunisia

For centuries the Kabyles [kə bīlz′], a people of North Africa, told their stories, proverbs, and poems in the oral tradition reciting them aloud and passing them down by word of mouth from generation to generation. Kabyle storytellers traditionally begin with the sentence, "May my story be beautiful and unwind like a long thread."

Oral literature is preserved by memorization. Storytellers commit to memory the tales told by their elders and recount them to the next generation. Kabyle storytellers have also borrowed elements from the literature of other cultures with which they have come in contact. The upcoming Kabyle tale includes the riddle of the sphinx, which appears in Greek myths, and elements from the story of King Solomon, which appears in the Bible.

About the Reteller: Marguerite Amrouche (1913–1976)

Folklorist Marguerite Amrouche grew up in Tunisia and Algeria and later settled in France. In 1966 she published *Le grain magique,* which retold in French the Kabyle proverbs, tales, and songs she had learned from her mother Fadhma, a noted Kabyle storyteller.

The Kabyles of North Africa

The Kabyles are a people of northeastern Algeria, northwestern Tunisia, and some oases in the Sahara Desert. Like other peoples of North Africa, the Kabyles are Berbers, Moslems who speak one of the Berber languages. These languages are related both to ancient Egyptian and to the early Semitic languages from which Arabic and Hebrew descend. Many modern Kabyles are also fluent in Arabic and often speak French or Spanish.

Traditionally an agricultural people, the Kabyles raise sheep and goats and tend fig and olive groves. The Kabyles are also accomplished weavers, woodworkers and silversmiths. In early times Kabyle traders sold rugs and silver jewelry. They still gather weekly in open-air markets to sell or trade their wares. The heroine of the next story is the daughter of a poor supervisor at one such market.

See LITERATURE AND CULTURE SOURCEBOOK: Africa

Greek mythology and elements from the biblical story of Solomon. Ask students to find out how these items could have gotten into a Kabyle folk tale and to share their findings with the class.

DISCUSSING GEOGRAPHY AND CULTURE

Markets and Malls

Part of this tale is set in a market. In many places bazaars have changed little over the centuries: Vendors set up stalls displaying an array of goods.
- Three decades ago American merchants introduced a new kind of market: the shopping mall. Ask students how malls differ from traditional markets. How are they similar? (Malls differ in that they are permanent indoor structures; they are similar in that they bring many merchants together in one locale.)

Kabyle Traditional

The Story of the Chest

Retold by Marguerite Amrouche
Translated from the French by Charlotte H. Bruner

May my story be beautiful and unwind like a long thread . . .

Once there was a king—though there is no other king but God—and this king had a dearly beloved son who said to him, "King, my father, let me go to the market and see your subjects."

"Do what you please," the king replied to him.

1 So the prince went to market, and he said to all the men there, "You must not sell nor buy, you must not buy nor sell, until you can answer these riddles. Who is it who, in the morning, walks on four feet, at noon on two, and on three in the evening?[1] Second, what tree has twelve branches with thirty leaves to a branch?" No one knew what to answer. All were mute. The marketers dispersed. A week went by. The next market day brought back the king's son. He asked, "Have you found the answers to my riddles?"

Once again, all were silent, and they went away. He who went to buy, bought not. And he who went to sell, sold not. The market closed. But, among those assembled was the market supervisor. He was very poor and had two daughters—one very beautiful and the other, the younger, slight but keen of mind. In the evening when her father came home, the younger said to

him, "Father, for two market days you left home, but you returned empty-handed. Why?"

"My daughter," he replied, "the king's son came and told us not to buy or sell, and not to sell or buy until we would know the meaning of what he was going to say."

"And what did the prince ask you to guess?" replied the girl.

"He asked us, 'Who is it who in the morning walks on four feet, at noon on two, and on three in the evening? And, what tree has twelve branches with thirty leaves to a branch?'"

2 His daughter reflected a little before replying: "It's easy, father. He who walks in the morning on four feet, at noon, on two, and on three in the evening is Man. In the morning of his life, he crawls on all fours; later, he goes on two feet; and when he is old he leans on a cane. As for the tree, it is the year; the year has twelve months and each month has thirty days."

A week went by—in its course it brought another market day and with it the king's son. He asked, "And today have you figured it out?"

The supervisor spoke up. He said, "Yes, my lord. He who walks in the morning on four feet, on two at noon, and on three in the evening is Man. In the morning of his life, he crawls on all fours; older he goes on two feet; and when he is **3** old he leans on a cane. As for the tree, it is the year; the year has twelve months and each month has thirty days."

---

1. **Who is it . . . evening?:** This same riddle is asked by the sphinx of Greek mythology.

The Story of the Chest **253**

MOTIVATION: PRIOR KNOWLEDGE

Ask students what they hold dearest in the world and have them explain why they feel so strongly about it. Tell them that in this selection they will find out what one character holds dearest.

PAGE SUMMARY: AT A GLANCE

- A prince closes down the market until someone can answer two riddles.
- The market supervisor learns the answers to the riddles from his younger daughter and tells them to the prince.

1 CRITICAL THINKING: LOGICAL REASONING

Invite students to try to solve these two riddles, but don't give away the answers ("man" and "the year").

2 TEACHING FOLK TALES

Point out that this folk tale, like other true folk tales, features an everyday person—here the daughter of a poor market supervisor—as a main character.

3 CULTURAL BACKGROUND

Explain that the year referred to here was first used in ancient Egypt. It had twelve months of thirty days each and five extra days. Every fourth year had one extra day.

CRITICAL THINKING: GUIDED READING QUESTIONS

LITERAL

1a. What does the prince say will happen until his riddles are answered? (The market will be closed.)

2a. What does the market supervisor's daughter do when her father tells her the riddles? (She answers them easily.)

INFERENTIAL

1b. What does the prince's shutting down the market tell us about him? (He is arrogant, self-involved, and doesn't care about inconveniencing others.)

2b. What does this ability to answer the riddles tell us about the market supervisor's daughter? (She is highly clever and intelligent.)

- The prince goes to the supervisor's house, speaking all the time in riddles.
- The prince meets the supervisor's younger daughter, who greets him with riddles.
- After a family dinner the prince and the younger daughter explain each other's riddles.
- Over his father's objections the prince decides to marry the younger daughter.

IN THE GLOSSARY

- indignantly: with great anger

4 TEACHING CHARACTERIZATION

Ask students what we can learn about the prince from the detail of his speaking to the supervisor in riddles. (Some may think he is seeking others with a mind similar to his own. Others may feel he is showing off his cleverness.)

5 TEACHING FOLK TALES

Point out that folk tales were meant to entertain their audience and that paradoxical statements and riddles were often used to enhance the appeal of the stories.

6 TEACHING STUDENTS OF LIMITED ENGLISH PROFICIENCY

Some students may have difficulty with the idiomatic and figurative usages here. Help them understand such expressions as "head of the household," "heart of the house," "take flight," and "pillars of the house."

7 TEACHING FOLK TALES

Point out that the story follows the pattern of many folk tales in having a highborn person wishing to marry a commoner who is unique in some way. Ask students to think of other tales that follow this pattern. (Possible responses: "Rumpelstiltskin," "Cinderella," "Molly Whuppie")

"Open up the market!" commanded the king's son. Then evening fell; the prince approached the supervisor and said to him, "I want to go to your house." The supervisor replied, "Good, sir." And they went off together on foot.

4 The prince declared, "I have fled from God's paradise. I refused what God desired. The way is long; carry me or I shall carry you. Speak, or I shall speak." The supervisor kept still. They came to a river and the king's son said, "Make me cross the river or I shall make you cross it." The supervisor, who understood nothing of this, did not answer. They arrived at the house.

The younger daughter of the supervisor (she who was frail but intuitive), opened the door for them and said, "Welcome. My mother has gone out to see someone she has never seen. My brothers are fighting water with water. My sister finds herself between two walls."

The king's son came in. Looking at the most beautiful daughter, he said, "The plate is beautiful, but it has a crack in it."

Night found the whole family united. One had killed a chicken and one had prepared a holiday couscous.[2] When the meal was ready, the prince said, "Let me be the one to serve the chicken." He gave the head to the father, the wings to the daughters, the thighs to the two sons, the breast to the mother. He kept the feet for himself. Everyone ate and then got ready to 5 spend the evening. The king's son turned toward the lively daughter and told her, "In order for you to tell me 'My mother has gone to see someone she has never seen,' she would have to be a midwife. For you to say to me 'My brothers are fighting water with water,' they must have been watering the gardens. As for your sister 'between two walls,' she would be weaving with a wall behind her and a wall before her—the nature of the trade."

---

2. **couscous** [ko͞os′ko͞os]: North African dish of crushed grain. It is usually steamed and often served with meat such as chicken or lamb.

254 *Myths, Folk Tales, and Epics*

The girl replied, "When you started out, you told my father, 'I have fled from God's paradise.' That's the rain, which makes a paradise on earth—so you were afraid of getting wet. And when you said, 'I refused what God desired'—was it death you were refusing? God wants us all to die, but we don't want to. Finally you said to my father, 'The way is long; carry me or I shall carry you. Speak or I shall speak,' so that the journey would seem shorter. Just as you told him, when you found yourselves beside the river, 'Make me cross the river or I shall make you cross it,' you meant, 'Show me the ford or I shall seek it.' When you entered our house, you looked at my sister and said, 'The plate is beautiful, but it has a crack in it.' My sister is truly beautiful and virtuous too, but she is the daughter of a poor man. 6 And then you divided the chicken. You gave the head to my father because he is the head of the household. You gave the breast to my mother, for she is the heart of the house. To us, the girls, you gave the wings, because we won't stay home here; we'll take flight. You gave my brothers the thighs; they will be the support, the pillars of the house. And for yourself you took the claws[3] because you are the guest; your feet brought you here and your feet will take you away."

On the next day the prince went to find the king, his father, and said to him, "I wish to marry the market supervisor's daughter."

7 The king exclaimed indignantly, "How could you, the son of a king, marry the daughter of a supervisor? It would be shameful. We would become the laughing stock of our neighbors."

"If I don't marry her," said the prince, "I shall never marry at all."

The king, who had no other son, ended by conceding: "Marry her, then, my son, since you do love her."

---

3. **claws:** that is, the chicken's feet.

CRITICAL THINKING: GUIDED READING QUESTIONS

LITERAL

1a. What traits does the author say the younger daughter possesses? (She is frail but intuitive.)

2a. What do both the prince and the market supervisor's daughter do after the dinner? (They "translate" each other's riddles.)

INFERENTIAL

1b. Why does the younger daughter greet the prince by speaking to him in riddles? (She knows he asked the riddles in the marketplace and recognizes intuitively that he enjoys this kind of mental play.)

2b. Why does the prince want to marry the market supervisor's daughter? (They have much in common in the sense that they are both clever, and both enjoy talking in and figuring out riddles.)

The prince offered his fiancée gold and silver, silks and satins, and all kinds of marvels. But he also said to her gravely, "Remember this well. The day your wisdom surpasses my own, that day will we part."

She answered, "I will always do everything 8 that you wish." Nonetheless, before the wedding day, she sent for the carpenter and ordered a chest made the size for a man, with a cover to be pierced with small holes. For the chest she wove a satin lining. She put her trousseau in it and sent it to the home of her bridegroom.

The nuptials were followed by rejoicing which lasted seven days and seven nights. The king served a great feast. For many years after, the prince and princess lived happily at the court. And when the king died, his son succeeded him.

One day when the young king was dispensing justice, two women came before him with a child they were quarreling over. One said, "He's my son!" and the other claimed, "He's mine." They got to shouting and tearing each other's hair. The king was perplexed. The queen, curious, found out about it from a servant, who told her, "Two women are there with a child whom both are claiming. Each one had a baby, but one of the babies died. And the king hasn't been able to find out which is the mother of the living child." The queen thought it over for a moment. Then she replied, "Let the king simply say to the two women, 'I shall divide the child in two, and each of you may have half.' Then he will hear the true mother cry out, 'Lord, don't kill him, in God's name!'"[4]

The servant ran to tell the king the trick which would bring out the truth. The king turned toward his minister, saying, "Bring forth a blade so we can divide this child." "No, Lord," cried out one of the women; "he will die!" So

---

4. "Two women . . . in God's name": This story element is borrowed from the Bible, where wise King Solomon sits in judgment over a similar case and makes a similar ruling.

the king held out the child to her and said, "You are the mother, for you did not want him to die."

9 Then the king went off to find the queen. He told her, "Do you remember what we agreed to on our wedding day? I said to you, 'The day your wisdom surpasses my own, that day will we part.'"

She answered, "I do remember. But grant me just one favor. Let us eat together for the last time. Then I shall leave."

10 He consented, and added, "Choose whatever you wish in the palace and take it with you."

She herself prepared the meal. She gave the king a drug without his suspecting it. He ate, he drank, and suddenly he fell asleep. She lifted him up and put him in the chest and then carefully closed the lid over him. She called the servants and informed them that she was going to the country for a family visit. She directed them to move the chest cautiously. And she left the palace, never losing sight of the chest which followed.

Once she was back in her parents' home, she opened the chest. She took her husband tenderly in her arms and stretched him out on the bed. Seated at the head of the bed, she waited patiently for him to wake up. It was evening before the king opened his eyes, saying, "Where am I? And who brought me here?"

She answered, "I did."

Then he spoke again to her, "Why? How did I get here?"

11 And she answered him, smiling, "Remember when you told me, 'Look around you, and take whatever pleases you in the palace and bring it with you'? Nothing else in the palace could be as dear to me as you. So I took *you*. And I brought you here in a chest." Now they understood one another. They returned to the palace and lived happily there together until they died.

My story runs on like a brook; I have told it to the lords.

The Story of the Chest **255**

PAGE SUMMARY: AT A GLANCE

- The daughter marries the prince after agreeing that she will leave him if her wisdom ever exceeds his.
- The prince becomes king when his father dies.
- The two live together happily until the woman shows greater wisdom than the king in resolving a quarrel over a child.
- The king asks his wife to leave, telling her to take with her whatever pleases her.
- She drugs the king and takes him, since she holds him most dear.
- The king recognizes his wife's love, and the two live happily ever after.

IN THE GLOSSARY

- nuptials: wedding ceremony

8 TEACHING PLOT: FORESHADOWING

Point out that *nonetheless* suggests that the daughter suspects she may someday violate her promise. Ask students what she plans to do with the chest.

9 TEACHING CHARACTERIZATION

Ask students what the prince's words—the same words he spoke earlier—reflect about him. (They reflect his extreme pride in his own cleverness and supposed superiority.)

10 READING SKILL: PREDICTING OUTCOMES

Ask students what they think the daughter will take with her. (Students may suggest jewelry or other valuable objects.)

11 TEACHING PLOT: RESOLUTION

Remind students that folk tales were meant to entertain and delight their audience. Ask them what impact this resolution has. (The clever and happy ending opens the king's eyes and treats the wife justly.)

CRITICAL THINKING: GUIDED READING QUESTIONS

LITERAL

1a. What does the prince tell the daughter never to do? (He warns her to never let her wisdom surpass his own.)

2a. What does the queen take with her when she goes to her parents' home? (She takes her husband inside a chest.)

INFERENTIAL

1b. Why does the queen help resolve the quarrel over the child even though she is not supposed to show superior wisdom? (Students may say she is unable to hide her cleverness when something important is at stake.)

2b. Why does the king change his mind and let his queen return with him? (He recognizes how much she loves him, and it is this love that helps him overcome his need to feel superior.)

COLLABORATIVE LEARNING: ENRICHMENT ACTIVITY

Art Most students are probably not familiar with the arts and crafts of the Kabyles and other Berber peoples. Have them form groups to find pictures of Berber works to share with the class.

The Story of the Chest **T-255**

This story contains numerous riddles and puzzling statements. Which one did you find most intriguing? Why?

ANSWERS

STUDY QUESTIONS

1. "Who is it who, in the morning, walks on four feet, at noon on two, and on three in the evening?" "What tree has twelve branches with thirty leaves to a branch?"
2. The younger daughter of the market supervisor answers the riddles. The answer to the first is "man"; the answer to the second is "the year."
3. She speaks to him in riddles and answers all his riddles.
4. Since the king tells her she may take with her from the palace whatever pleases her, she drugs him, puts him in a chest, and takes him. When she explains that she holds him most dear, they return to the palace and live happily ever after.
5. She displays cleverness, loyalty, honesty, and a willingness to forgo pride for the sake of love.
6. He is tyrannical, proud, jealous, and insecure.
7. They can be equal, but their relationship should be based on love and mutual respect.
8. Answers will vary. Students might suggest riddles with multiple meanings or homonyms.

LITERARY FOCUS

It is a true folk tale because its heroine is an everyday figure and its chief purpose is to entertain or delight.

COMPARING FOLK LITERATURE

Answers will vary. Students will probably say that it most resembles a fable because its theme conveys a moral.

STUDY QUESTIONS

Recalling

1. What riddles does the prince ask at the market?
2. Who answers the riddles? What are the answers?
3. Summarize the behavior of the supervisor's daughter when the prince comes to visit.
4. Explain by what means the princess resolves the final predicament.

Interpreting

5. What chief personality traits does the supervisor's daughter display?
6. What character flaws does the prince display?
7. What message do you think the tale conveys about the relationships between men and women?

Extending

8. What other challenging riddles can you think of?

LITERARY FOCUS

Folk Tale

A **folk tale** is a traditional story composed by usually anonymous "common folk" and passed down by word of mouth before being written down. This broad definition includes myths, legends, and fables composed in the oral tradition; however, folklore specialists sometimes distinguish between true folk tales and these three other forms. True folk tales, according to this distinction, feature everyday people as their main characters rather than gods, goddesses, animals, or famous heroes and heroines. A similar distinction concerns purpose. The chief purpose of a myth is to explain, of a fable to instruct, and of a leg-

end to record important events. While a folk tale may also explain, instruct, or record information along the way, its chief purpose is usually to entertain or delight its audience.

Thinking About the Folk Tale

■ In what ways is "The Story of the Chest" a true folk tale?

COMPOSITION

Writing About a Folk Tale's Heroine

■ Write a brief composition about the supervisor's daughter in "The Story of the Chest." Discuss her personality traits and motivation. Use details from the story to illustrate the main points you make. Also consider her background and her situation at the end of the story.

Retelling a Folk Tale

■ In writing or in reading aloud to classmates, retell this folk tale for a contemporary American audience. Use the same basic plot elements and characters, with the same basic personalities and motivation. Adapt the setting details and characters' backgrounds and activities to reflect a modern American setting.

COMPARING FOLK LITERATURE

■ Compare this folk tale to the myths, legends, and fables you have read in this section. In your opinion, which of these three types of folk literature does "The Story of the Chest" most resemble? Why?

COMPOSITION: GUIDELINES FOR EVALUATION

WRITING ABOUT A FOLK TALE'S HEROINE

Objective

To write a sketch of the supervisor's daughter

Guidelines for Evaluation

■ suggested length: one to two pages
■ should discuss personality and motivation
■ should consider the daughter's background and her situation at the end of the story
■ should support the main points with details

RETELLING A FOLK TALE

Objective

To retell the story for a contemporary audience

Guidelines for Evaluation

■ suggested length: two to three pages
■ should include the same types of plot elements
■ should include similar kinds of characters
■ should adapt details of setting and character motivations to a modern American setting

PREVIEW: THE AUTHOR AND THE WORLD

Johann Wolfgang von Goethe (1749–1832)

Germany

Johann Wolfgang von Goethe [yō′ hän vôlf′gäng′ von gur′tə], was one of Germany's outstanding poets, dramatists, and novelists. The son of a wealthy lawyer, Goethe was born in the city of Frankfurt and practiced law there himself until 1774. In that year his novel about hopeless love, *The Sorrows of Young Werther,* became a best seller. It also won him the admiration of the duke of Weimar [vī′mär], who invited Goethe to move to that German city to study science and serve as his counselor. Later Goethe retired from politics, but he remained in Weimar to devote himself to his literary and scientific pursuits.

Goethe's interests were broad, encompassing folklore, natural science, philosophy, and Classical and Oriental literature. He also composed short stories, poetry, and plays, including his masterful drama *Faust.* Deeply interested in folk literature of the past, he based both *Faust* and the upcoming poem, "The Erl-King," on German folklore. Goethe's influence on European letters was enormous. One admirer, British author Sir Walter Scott (1771–1832), translated "The Erl-King" into English.

GEOGRAPHY AND CULTURE

Folk Tales from Germany's Black Forest

Germany's Black Forest (Schwarzwald) is a heavily wooded region in southwestern Germany, between the Rhine and Neckar rivers. Its ski resorts and hot springs attract many tourists, and it is famous for watches and cuckoo clocks.

In the early nineteenth century, more than two hundred of the folk tales from the Black Forest were collected by Jakob and Wilhelm Grimm. One of these tales, "The Erl-King," had already been made famous by Goethe. It is about an evil goblin who is said to inhabit the forests of Germany and the neighboring nation of Denmark. The goblin was known in Danish as *ellerkonge,* or "king of the elves." The Danish term was apparently mistranslated into German as *Erlkönig,* "king of the alders," a reference to the alder trees of the Black Forest. According to the legend, the Erl-King was visible only to the victims he enticed into his dark kingdom. The goblin thus became linked with the twisted, eerily human shapes that the alder trees seemed to assume at night.

See LITERATURE AND CULTURE SOURCEBOOK: Germany

The Erl-King **257**

In this eerie and ominous narrative poem a father and son are riding through the woods at night when the boy claims to see and hear the Erl-King. The father gives logical explanations for the boy's experiences. After the boy says that the Erl-King has seized him, the father draws him close and rushes home, only to find that the child is dead.

LITERARY SKILLS FOR THIS SELECTION

- narrative poem
- atmosphere
- dialogue

THEMES IN THIS SELECTION

- fatherly love
- power of evil

LESSON OBJECTIVES

1. to recognize words from Old English
2. to write about the author's purposes
3. to write a news article

Teacher's Classroom Resources 2

- Teaching Notes 69
- Reading Guide 70
- Check Test 71
- Responding to World Cultures 72
- Language Study: Words from Old English 73
- Writing Process Guides: Writing About the Author's Purposes 74
  Writing a News Article 75
- Grammar in Literature: Order of Subject and Predicate 76
- Selection Test 77

IN THE CLASSROOM

TEACHING STUDENTS OF DIFFERENT ABILITIES

- **For less advanced students:** The poem is largely dialogue. Encourage students to note carefully where quotation marks indicate a change in speaker. Help them understand words such as *dost, 'tis,* and *thro'.* Have them complete the Reading Guide.

- **For more advanced students:** Ask students to listen to Schubert's ballad "Erlkönig" and discuss how well the music conveys the poem's feeling.

DISCUSSING GEOGRAPHY AND CULTURE

Analyzing Fairy Tales

"The Erl-King" is one of many stories immortalized by the Grimm brothers. Translated into more than seventy languages, their fairy tales have been thrilling children for more than one hundred fifty years.

- Ask students to think of other Grimm fairy tales that they know, such as "Hansel and Gretel" and "Rapunzel." Do they depict a safe world? Are their endings always happy? Do the students think it is harmful for children to learn such frightening stories?

Johann Wolfgang von Goethe

The Erl-King[1]

Translated from the German by Sir Walter Scott

1   O who rides by night thro' the woodland so wild?
It is the fond father embracing his child;
And close the boy nestles within his loved arm.
To hold himself fast, and to keep himself warm.

5   "O father, see yonder! see yonder!" he says;
"My boy, upon what dost thou fearfully gaze?"
"O, 'tis the Erl-King with his crown and his shroud."
"No, my son, it is but a dark wreath of the cloud."

The Erl-King speaks

2   *"O come and go with me, thou loveliest child;*
10 *By many a gay sport shall thy time be beguiled;*
My mother keeps for thee full many a fair toy,
And many a fine flower shall she pluck for my boy."

"O father, my father, and did you not hear
The Erl-King whisper so low in my ear?"
3   15 "Be still, my heart's darling—my child, be at ease;
It was but the wild blast as it sung thro' the trees."

Erl-King

"O wilt thou go with me, thou loveliest boy?
My daughter shall tend thee with care and with joy;
She shall bear thee so lightly thro' wet and thro' wild,
20 *And press thee, and kiss thee, and sing to my child."*

4   "O father, my father, and saw you not plain
The Erl-King's pale daughter glide past thro' the rain?"
"O yes, my loved treasure, I knew it full soon;
It was the gray willow that danced to the moon."

---

1. **Erl-King:** in Germanic folk tales, king of the goblins who supposedly inhabited Germany's Black Forest. (See the Geography and Culture feature that precedes the selection.)

CRITICAL THINKING: GUIDED READING QUESTIONS

LITERAL

1a. What kind of atmosphere does the Erl-King try to convey with his words? (He tries to convey a warm, happy atmosphere.)

2a. What does the father do to comfort the boy when he claims to see and hear the Erl-King and his daughter? (He provides rational explanations for the boy's claims.)

INFERENTIAL

1b. Why do we disbelieve the Erl-King's words and suspect something evil? (The Erl-King lets himself be heard only by the boy; we know that the Erl-King is a goblin and is associated with evil; the poem's atmosphere conveys a feeling of dread.)

2b. Why doesn't the father seem to take his son's claims seriously? (He may think there are rational explanations for his son's fears and fantasies.)

Erl-King

25 "*O come and go with me, no longer delay,*
Or else, silly child, I will drag thee away."

5 "*O father! O father! now, now, keep your hold,*
The Erl-King has seized me—his grasp is so cold!"

Sore trembled the father; he spurr'd thro' the wild,
30 Clasping close to his bosom his shuddering child;

6 He reaches his dwelling in doubt and in dread,
But, clasp'd to his bosom, the infant was dead.

Frontispiece for sheet music for Franz Schubert's ballad "Erlkönig," Vienna, 1826.

The Erl-King **259**

PAGE SUMMARY: AT A GLANCE

- The Erl-King demands that the boy come away with him, and the child feels his cold grasp.
- Although the father rushes home, his son has died.

5 READING SKILL: INFERENCE

Point out that here for the first time the boy's words are printed in italics, just like the words of the Erl-King. Ask students what this suggests is happening. (The boy has been taken over by the Erl-King.)

6 TEACHING NARRATIVE POEMS

Remind students that this is a narrative poem and that narrative poems, like stories, have plots with resolutions. Here the story is resolved in a particularly grim and unhappy way.

COLLABORATIVE LEARNING: ENRICHMENT ACTIVITY

Music Goethe was a leading figure in German Romanticism, along with such composers as Beethoven, Brahms, Mendelssohn, Wagner, and Weber. Have students work together to prepare a brief festival exploring the music of the German Romantic era. Have each group member focus on a different composer and share what he or she has learned about the composers' works.

CRITICAL THINKING: GUIDED READING QUESTIONS

LITERAL

1a. What does the father do after the boy says that the Erl-King has seized him? (He trembles, rushes through the woods, and clasps the boy close to his chest.)

INFERENTIAL

1b. What do the father's actions suggest? (He now believes that his son actually saw the Erl-King and fears for the boy's life.)

How does this poem make you feel? Do you enjoy having this feeling? Explain.

ANSWERS

STUDY QUESTIONS

1. at night in a wild woodland
2. the Erl-King; It is a dark cloud, a wild blast of wind, or a gray willow dancing in the moonlight.
3. He will offer him gay sports; his mother will give him toys and flowers; his daughter will tend him carefully.
4. The boy is dead.
5. The eerie atmosphere enhances the supernatural events.
6. Words such as *fond*, *embracing*, *close*, *nestles*, *loved*, *fast*, and *warm* suggest that the father dearly loves his son.
7. Parents cannot always protect their children from evil.
8. Answers will vary. The boy could have imagined that the Erl-King was going to kidnap him and died of fright.
9. Answers will vary. Students may mention fairy tales, science fiction, or horror tales about evil creatures.

LANGUAGE STUDY

1. from "to make a nest"; *nestilian*
2. from *cyning*
3. from "garment or clothing"; *scrud*
4. from "a ring"; *writha*
5. from *dohtor*
6. from *welig*

STUDY QUESTIONS

Recalling

1. According to the opening line, where and when does the poem take place?
2. What does the young boy see and hear that his father does not see and hear? What explanations does the father provide?
3. Summarize the three arguments that the Erl-King gives the boy.
4. What does the father discover when he reaches his dwelling?

Interpreting

5. In what ways does the setting add to the poem's dramatic power?
6. Explain what the word choice in lines 2–4 tells about the father's feelings for his son.
7. What does the poem suggest about parent-child relationships?
8. Might there be a natural explanation for the events of this poem? Explain.

Extending

9. What stories still told to children are similar to the folk tale of the Erl-King?

LANGUAGE STUDY

Words from Old English

The German word *König* and the English word *king* look alike because they have similar origins. In fact, modern English has many similarities with German, since both languages have a common ancestry.

Modern English descends from **Old English,** the language spoken by the Germanic tribes who invaded England in the fifth century. These tribes—the Angles, the Saxons, and the Jutes—came to England from what today are northern Germany and Denmark. In fact, modern English, modern German, and modern Danish all have their origins in the Germanic languages of these earlier times.

Use a dictionary to determine which of the words from "The Erl-King" entered English during the Old English stage. Provide the Old English forms of these words. Also provide the Old English meanings when they differ from present-day meanings.

1. nestles   4. wreath
2. king   5. daughter
3. shroud   6. willow

COMPOSITION

Writing About the Author's Purposes

What do you feel were Goethe's chief purposes for composing "The Erl-King"? In a brief composition cite details from the poem to support each purpose you identify.

Writing a News Article

Retell the story of "The Erl-King" as it might appear in a newspaper or magazine article. Include an attention-grabbing headline. Like all good news articles, your article should provide information answering the questions *Who? What? When?* and *Where?* You may also want to speculate on the answers to *How?* and *Why?*

COMPOSITION: GUIDELINES FOR EVALUATION

WRITING ABOUT THE AUTHOR'S PURPOSES

Objective

To write about the author's purposes

Guidelines for Evaluation

- suggested length: one to two pages
- should discuss at least two of Goethe's purposes
- should cite specific details from the poem to support each purpose

WRITING A NEWS ARTICLE

Objective

To retell "The Erl-King" in the form of a news article

Guidelines for Evaluation

- suggested length: six to eight short paragraphs
- should be written in the form of a news article
- should include an attention-grabbing headline
- should tell *who, what, when,* and *where*
- may also tell *how* and *why*

PREVIEW: THE AUTHOR AND THE WORLD

Homer (c. 850 B.C.)

Ancient Greece

Homer, the first recognized poet of Western literature, is traditionally accepted as the author of the two great epics on which all Greek literature is founded: the *Iliad* [il′ē əd] and the *Odyssey* [od′ə sē]. Although some scholars doubt whether Homer ever existed, according to tradition, he was a poor, old, blind, and very wise poet who wandered from city to city singing his verse. He could neither read nor write; instead, he recited or sang his verses to the accompaniment of a small harplike instrument called a lyre.

By 400 B.C. Homer's epics had become classics studied by every Greek schoolchild. Homer's influence gradually spread throughout the world. Rome's greatest poet, Virgil, drew on Homer's epics in creating his own masterpiece, the *Aeneid.* Later, Greek scholars fleeing from the Ottoman Turks brought Homer's epics to Italy, where they had a profound impact on the development of Renaissance thought. Today Homer remains one of the most widely read authors in Western literature. In fact, much of the literary heritage of the Western world is rooted in Homer's epics.

GEOGRAPHY AND CULTURE

The Trojan War

The name of the *Iliad* comes from the word *Ilion,* another name for the city of Troy. Troy was located in Asia Minor, which includes present-day Turkey, across the Aegean [ə jē′ən] Sea from mainland Greece. Sometime around the early twelfth century B.C., the Greeks battled with Troy in the Trojan War. Homer's *Iliad,* which tells the story of the war, was composed three hundred and fifty years later.

According to Homer, the war began when Paris, a Trojan prince, abducted Helen, the queen of Sparta in Greece. For nine years the Greeks attacked Troy, and for nine years the Trojans successfully resisted them. Near the beginning of the *Iliad,* Agamemnon [ag′ə mem′non], leader of the Greek forces, angers Achilles [ə kil′ēz], the greatest of the Greek warriors. Achilles withdraws his powerful troops, the Myrmidons [mur′mə donz′], and sulks in his tent. Without Achilles' support, the Greeks are weakened and Hector—the greatest of Troy's warriors—ventures forth with a bold challenge. Hector has just voiced this challenge as the upcoming selection begins.

ANCIENT GREECE

See LITERATURE AND CULTURE SOURCEBOOK:
Classical Greece and Rome

Iliad 261

LESSON PREVIEW

This excerpt dramatically recounts the first battle between Troy's greatest fighter, Hector, and the huge young Greek, Ajax. Hector calls on the Greeks to elect a champion to fight him. Eventually nine warriors step forward. Ajax is chosen by lot, and the two battle fiercely, demonstrating the valor, strength, and ingenuity valued by their cultures. The combat ends in a draw as heralds from both sides intervene.

LITERARY SKILLS FOR THIS SELECTION

- epic
- characterization

THEMES IN THIS SELECTION

- strength and valor
- fair-mindedness
- pride and loyalty

LESSON OBJECTIVES

1. to understand the epic
2. to write about an epic
3. to write imaginary interviews

Teacher's Classroom Resources 2

■ Teaching Notes	79
■ Reading Guide	80
■ Check Test	81
■ Responding to World Cultures	82
■ Literary Focus: The Epic	83
■ Writing Process Guides: Writing About an Epic	84
Writing Imaginary Interviews	85
■ Grammar in Literature: Appositives and Appositive Phrases	86
■ Selection Test	87

IN THE CLASSROOM

TEACHING STUDENTS OF DIFFERENT ABILITIES

- **For less advanced students:** List all the names for the Greeks ("Achaeans," "Argives," "Danaans") to help students avoid confusion. Help students pronounce the characters' names. Ask them to complete the Reading Guide for this selection.

- **For more advanced students:** Ask students to compare and contrast the characters of Hector and Ajax as they read. What values do they share? In what ways are they different?

DISCUSSING GEOGRAPHY AND CULTURE

Heroes Great and Small

Ajax, a legendary warrior who is described by Homer in this selection, epitomizes the soldiers of ancient Greece: He is brave, strong, and loyal.

- Every culture has its own heroes. Some are famous military and political figures; others are ordinary people who have achieved exceptional accomplishments. Have students discuss some of the "local heroes" they know or have read about. What characteristics do they share?

Homer

from the **Iliad**

Translated from the Greek by Robert Fitzgerald

from Book VII

1

                                        A west wind rising
will cast a rippling roughness over water,
a shivering gloom on the clear sea. Just so
the seated mass of Trojans and Achaeans[1]
rippled along the plain.
                                        Hector[2] addressed them:

2

5   "Hear me, Trojans and Achaeans: listen
to what I am moved to say. The peace we swore to
Lord Zeus[3] throned on high would not confirm.
He has adversity for both in mind
until you take high Troy, or are defeated,
10   beated back to your deep-sea-going ships.

3

Knowing the bravest of Achaea's host
are here with you, my pride demands that I
engage some champion: let one come forward,
the best man of you all, to fight with Hector. . . ."

15   He finished, and the Achaeans all sat hushed,
ashamed not to respond, afraid to do so. . . .

Then Nestor[4] stood up, saying to the Argives:[5]

"Ah, what distress for our Achaean land!
How Peleus,[6] the old master of horse, would grieve,
20   that noble counselor of Myrmidons!
One day, questioning me in his own hall,
he took delight in learning of the Argives'
lineage and birth. If he should hear
how every man here quails before Hector now,
25   he'd lift his arms to the immortal gods
and pray to quit his body, to go down

---

1. **Achaeans** [ə kē′ənz]: another name for the Greeks (from *Achaea*, region of northeastern Greece).
2. **Hector:** son of King Priam of Troy and leader of the Trojan warriors.
3. **Zeus** [zo͞os]: king of the gods and son of the titan Cronus.
4. **Nestor:** king of Pylos; oldest and wisest of the Greeks at Troy.
5. **Argives:** another name for the Greeks.
6. **Peleus** [pēl′ūs]: father of Achilles and king of the Myrmidons, warriors from northern Greece.

CRITICAL THINKING: GUIDED READING QUESTIONS

LITERAL

1a. How do the Greeks respond to Hector's demand that one of them come forward to fight him? (No one comes forward.)

2a. What does Nestor say about old Peleus? (He says that Peleus delighted in his discovery of the Greeks' "lineage and birth"; if he discovered that no one came forward, he would grieve and pray for death.)

INFERENTIAL

1b. What does the Greeks' reluctance to fight tell you about Hector? (He is a formidable fighter.)

2b. To what values does Nestor appeal? (He appeals to the Greeks' pride in themselves and their nationality.)

into the house of Death! . . ."

So chided by the old man, volunteers
arose then, nine in all—first on his feet
30 being Lord Marshal Agamemnon,[7] second
Diomedes,[8] powerful son of Tydeus,
and, joining these, those two who were called Ajax,[9]
rugged impetuous men, and joining these
Idomeneus and that lord's right-hand man,
35 Meriones,[10] the peer of the battle-god
in butchery of war; along with these
Eurypylus, Euaemon's handsome son,
Thoas Andraemonides, and Odysseus.[11]
These were all willing to encounter Hector
40 in single combat. Then again they heard
from Nestor of Gerenia, charioteer:

"By lot now: whirl for the one who comes out first.
He is the one to make Achaeans proud,
and make himself, too, proud, if he survives
45 this bitter fight, no quarter asked or given."

At this each put his mark upon a stone
and dropped it in the helmet of Agamemnon.
Meanwhile the troops addressed the gods in prayer
with hands held up. You might have heard one say,
his eyes on heaven:

50   "Father Zeus, let Ajax's
pebble jump! Or make it Diomedes!
Make it the king himself of rich Mycenae!"

So they murmured. Then Lord Nestor gave
the helm a rolling shake and made that stone
55 which they desired leap out: Ajax's token.
A herald took it round amid the nine,
showing the fortunate mark, this way and that,
to all the Achaean champions; but none

---

7. **Agamemnon** [ag'ə mem'non]: king of Mycenae [mī sē'nē] and leader of the Greek warriors.
8. **Diomedes** [dī'ə mē'dēz]: king of Argos.
9. **those two who were called Ajax:** Ajax Telamonius (Ajax, son of Telamon), king of Salamis, and another Greek warrior also named Ajax.
10. **Idomeneus** [ī dom'ə nūs'] . . . **Meriones** [mer i'ə nēz']: king of Crete and his nephew.
11. **Odysseus** [ō dis'ē əs]: king of Ithaca; his further adventures are recounted in Homer's *Odyssey*.

Iliad 263

- Ajax expresses joy and self-confidence after having been selected to fight Hector.
- The soldiers pray that the battle will end in victory for Ajax or, failing that, in a draw.
- Ajax steps out, ready for battle.

IN THE GLOSSARY

- formidable: inspiring awe, impressive

7 TEACHING STUDENTS OF LIMITED ENGLISH PROFICIENCY

This selection contains many lengthy and convoluted sentences, such as this one. Help speakers of other languages to understand such sentences by having students read them aloud, paying close attention to internal punctuation. Then have the reader restate the passage in his or her own words.

8 TEACHING CHARACTERIZATION

Point out Ajax's air of self-confidence and fearlessness and his pride in his background. Point out further that Ajax is always described as a huge man; on this page he is described with the words *giant* and *huge;* he is said to "loom," and his legs move "in great strides."

9 READING SKILL: INFERENCE

Ask students what the soldier's prayer suggests about the way the Greeks perceived the gods. (Students should recognize that the Greeks believed the gods had human feelings and could favor one person over another.)

10 TEACHING EPIC SIMILES

Explain that Homer's epics contain many similes that differ from ordinary similes in the sense that they are more involved and ornate. An example is contained here, comparing Ajax with Ares, the Greek god of war.

could recognize it or acknowledge it.

7 60 Only when he had come at length to him
who made the sign and dropped it in the helmet,
Ajax, the giant, putting out his hand
for what the pausing herald placed upon it,
knew his mark. A thrill of joy ran through him.

65 Down at his feet he tossed the stone, and said:

"Oh, friends, the token's mine! And glad I am,
as I believe I can put Hector down.
Come, everyone, while I prepare to fight,
pray to Lord Zeus, the son of Cronus! Keep it
70 under your breath so Trojans will not hear—
or else be open about it; after all,

8 we have no fear of any. No man here
will drive me from the field against my will,
not by main force, not by a ruse. I hope
75 I was not born and bred on Salamis
to be a dunce in battle."

At this the soldiers
prayed to Zeus. You might have heard one say,
his eyes on heaven:

9 "Father Zeus, from Ida[12]
looking out for us all: greatest, most glorious:
80 let Ajax win the honor of victory!
Or if you care for Hector and are inclined
to favor him, then let both men be even
in staying power and honor!"

So they prayed,
while Ajax made his brazen helmet snug,
10 85 fitted his shield and sword strap. He stepped out
as formidable as gigantic Ares,[13]
wading into the ranks of men, when Zeus
drives them to battle in bloodletting fury.
Huge as that, the bastion of Achaeans
90 loomed and grinned, his face a cruel mask,
his legs moving in great strides. He shook
his long spear doubled by its pointing shadow,
and the Argives exulted. Now the Trojans
felt a painful trembling in the knees,

---

12. **Ida:** mountain near Troy.
13. **Ares** [ar′ēz]: god of war.

264 *Myths, Folk Tales, and Epics*

CRITICAL THINKING: GUIDED READING QUESTIONS

LITERAL

1a. What does Ajax say about his chances of victory? (He says that no one will drive him from the field, either by force or by trickery.)

2a. What do the Trojans feel as they see Ajax moving forward? (They feel a trembling in the knees.)

INFERENTIAL

1b. Why does Ajax say these things? (He really believes he can beat Hector, and he wants to make sure his fellow soldiers have the confidence he does.)

2b. What is it about Ajax that frightens them? (They are frightened by his huge size, his self-confidence, his "cruel mask" of a face, and his generally frightening appearance.)

Kalyx Krater, attributed to the Tyszkiewicz Painter, 490–480 B.C.

95 and even Hector's heart thumped in his chest—
but there could be no turning back; he could not
slip again into his throng of troops;
he was the challenger. Ajax came nearer,
carrying like a tower his body shield
100 of seven oxhides sheathed in bronze—a work
done for him by the leather-master Tychius
in Hyle:[14] Tychius made the glittering shield
with seven skins of oxhide and an eighth
of plated bronze. Holding this bulk before him,
105 Ajax Telamonius came on
toward Hector and stood before him. Now he spoke,
threatening him:

          "Before long, man to man,
Hector, you'll realize that we Danaans[15]
have our champions, too—I mean besides
110 the lionhearted breaker of men, Achilles.
He lies now by the beaked seagoing ships
in anger at Lord Marshal Agamemnon.
But here are those among us who can face you—

_____

14. **Hyle** [hī′lē]: city in central Greece.
15. **Danaans:** another name for the Greeks.

PAGE SUMMARY: AT A GLANCE

- Hector feels fear as Ajax approaches, carrying his huge body shield.
- Ajax asserts that Hector will soon recognize that the Greeks have other champions besides Achilles.

11 READING SKILL: CAUSE AND EFFECT

Ask students what effect Ajax has on Hector. (He feels fear but cannot retreat since he is the challenger.) Ask students what might cause Hector to be surprised by Ajax's apparent ferocity. (Ajax may not as yet have a reputation as a great warrior.)

12 TEACHING EPITHETS

Point out the epithet describing Achilles. Explain that Achilles is the main hero of the *Iliad* and became the prototype of the Greeks' ideas about manly valor and beauty. Achilles eventually routs the Trojans, killing many of them, including Hector.

ART AND LITERATURE

The period from the late seventh century B.C. to around 475 B.C. was the great age of Greek vase painting. This art form combined a craft industry with a growing tendency to portray Greek life. Common subjects in vase paintings were Greek mythology, legends, battles, and everyday life. This handled urn made of iron-rich clay shows two warriors engaged in battle.

- Ask students which characters from the selection might be subjects for a vase like the *Kalyx Krater.* (Hector and Ajax)

CRITICAL THINKING: GUIDED READING QUESTIONS

LITERAL

1a. Describe Ajax's shield. (It is made of seven oxhides sheathed in bronze.)

2a. What does Ajax tell Hector? (There are many Greeks capable of fighting him.)

INFERENTIAL

1b. Why does Ajax carry such a shield? (Its many layers can protect him from his enemies' heavy blows, and it makes him look formidable.)

2b. Why does Ajax say this to Hector? (He wants to make him recognize that he will be facing a strong adversary and that no victory against the Greeks will be easy.)

13 TEACHING DIALOGUE

Help students note that rather than using description here, the author uses Hector's own words to demonstrate the kind of man he is. Point out that Hector's response to Ajax shows great pride and confidence and suggests a man of great experience and strength.

14 TEACHING FIGURATIVE LANGUAGE

Explain that here and elsewhere the author uses figures of speech to maintain the elevated and dignified tone of the epic. Here war is likened to a dance. Elsewhere Ajax's face is likened to a "cruel mask," and death is likened to night.

15 TEACHING SUSPENSE

Point out that here and in the text that follows, the author describes the battle in great detail to build suspense. His description makes clear how evenly matched the men are and how difficult it will be to predict the winner.

16 CULTURAL BACKGROUND

Explain that the battling warriors epitomize the soldiers of ancient Greece. Here they display the characteristics admired by the Greeks: strength, valor, endurance, ingenuity, quickness, and determination.

plenty of us. Fight then, if you will!"
115 To this, great Hector in his shimmering helmet
answered:

13
"Son of the ancient line of Telamon,
Ajax, lordly over fighting men,
when you try me you try no callow boy
or woman innocent of war. I know
120 and know well how to fight and how to kill,
how to take blows upon the right or left
shifting my guard of tough oxhide in battle,
how to charge in a din of chariots,

14
or hand to hand with sword or pike to use
125 timing and footwork in the dance of war.
Seeing the man you are, I would not trick you
but let you have it with a straight shot,
if luck is with me."

15
Rifling his spear,
he hurled it and hit Ajax's wondrous shield
130 square on the outer and eighth plate of bronze.
The spearhead punched its way through this and through
six layers, but the seventh oxhide stopped it.
Now in his turn great Ajax made his cast
and hit the round shield braced on Hector's arm.
135 Piercing the bright shield, the whetted spearhead
cut its way into his figured cuirass,[16]
ripping his shirt along his flank; but he
had twisted and escaped the night of death.

16
Now both men disengaged their spears and fell
140 on one another like man-eating lions
or wild boars—no tame household creatures. Hector's
lancehead scored the tower shield—but failed
to pierce it, as the point was bent aside.
Then Ajax plunging forward, rammed his spear
145 into the round shield, and the point went through
to nick his furious adversary, making
a cut that welled dark blood below his ear.
But Hector did not slacken, even so.
He drew away and in one powerful hand
150 picked from the plain a boulder lying there,
black, rough and huge, and threw it,

---

16. **cuirass** [kwi ras']: breastplate used as body armor.

CRITICAL THINKING: GUIDED READING QUESTIONS

LITERAL

1a. What does Hector say to Ajax? (He says that he is an experienced fighter who can defend himself well and that he will not use any tricks against Ajax.)

2a. What methods do the two men use as they fight? (They use any method at hand. They hurl and ram spears, use hand-to-hand combat, and throw rocks.)

INFERENTIAL

1b. Why does Hector say these things to Ajax? (He wants to show that although he is to be feared, he will fight fairly.)

2b. What do these methods suggest about rules of warfare? (They suggest that there are no real rules and that ingenuity is important.)

hitting Ajax's gigantic sevenfold shield
square on the boss with a great clang of bronze.
Then Ajax lifted up a huger stone
155 and whirled, and put immeasurable force
behind it when he let it fly—as though
he flung a millstone[17]—crushing Hector's shield.
The impact caught his knees, so that he tumbled

17 backward behind the bashed-in shield. At once
160 Apollo[18] pulled him to his feet again,
and now with drawn swords toe to toe
they would have doubled strokes on one another,
had not those messengers of Zeus and men,
the heralds, intervened—one from the Trojans,
165 one from the Achaean side—for both
Idaeus[19] and Talthybius[20] kept their heads.
They held their staves out, parting the contenders,
and that experienced man, Idaeus, said:

18 "Enough, lads. No more fighting. The Lord Zeus,
170 assembler of bright cloud, cares for you both.
Both are great spearmen, and we all know it.
But now already night is coming on,
and we do well to heed the fall of night."

Said Ajax Telamonius in reply:

175 "Idaeus, call on Hector to say as much.
He was the one who dared our champions
to duel with him. Let him take the lead.

Whatever he likes, I am at his disposition."

Hector in his shimmering helmet answered:

180 "Ajax, a powerful great frame you had
as a gift from god, and a clear head; of all
Achaeans you are toughest with a spear.
And this being shown, let us break off our duel,
19 our bloodletting, for today. We'll meet again
185 another time—and fight until the unseen
power decides between these hosts of ours,
awarding one or the other victory."

---

17. **millstone:** heavy stone used to grind grain.
18. **Apollo** [ə pol′ō]: god of prophecy, healing, the arts, etc.; protector of Troy, which he helped build.
19. **Idaeus** [ī dē′əs]: chief herald of King Priam.
20. **Talthybius:** chief herald of Lord Agamemnon.

Iliad **267**

- Hector and Ajax continue their fierce battle.
- The heralds of the leaders of both sides call for an end to the battle because night is falling.
- Ajax calls on Hector to agree to end the fight.
- Hector agrees but predicts that he and Ajax will meet again.

IN THE GLOSSARY

- immeasurable: unable to be measured

17 TEACHING EPICS

Help students see that here, once again, a god is intervening in human affairs. Apollo helps Hector by pulling him to his feet after he has fallen.

18 CULTURAL BACKGROUND

Point out that it might seem strange to us that two men so engrossed in fighting could put an end to their hostilities so quickly. Much the same was done at the Olympic Games, however, which originated in Greece in the early eighth century B.C. Every four years athletes from all Greece's city-states—even those at war with each other—gathered to test their skills.

19 READING SKILL: INFERENCE

Ask students to identify the "unseen power" in lines 185–186 and explain why it will determine who wins any future battles. (The "unseen power" is the gods; the Greeks believed that the gods could determine the outcome of a battle by favoring one side.)

COLLABORATIVE LEARNING: ENRICHMENT ACTIVITY

Oratory The Greeks often used orations to celebrate the virtues of their heroes and leaders. Ask students to work together in small groups to prepare and deliver orations celebrating one of the heroes in the selection. Students should find additional information about the hero and focus on his achievements, values, and qualities.

CRITICAL THINKING: GUIDED READING QUESTIONS

LITERAL

1a. According to Idaeus, for whom does Zeus care? (He cares for both men.)

2a. What admiring things does Hector say as he addresses Ajax? (He says that Ajax has a powerful frame and clear head and that he is the toughest Greek with a spear.)

INFERENTIAL

1b. How does Zeus show that he cares for both men? (He does not allow either one to win.)

2b. What characteristics does Hector show with these words? (He shows that he is noble and generous in his recognition of the qualities of others.)

Which warrior did you want to win the battle? Explain.

ANSWERS

STUDY QUESTIONS

1. Hector asks the Greeks to find a champion to fight him. At first the Greeks are "ashamed not to respond, afraid to do so."
2. Stones are marked with each soldier's sign, and one is drawn from Agamemnon's helmet.
3. They ask that Zeus grant victory to Ajax or, if Zeus favors Hector, to let the battle end in a draw.
4. It ends in a draw after the heralds of Priam and Agamemnon intervene, saying that Zeus cares for both men, that both are great spearmen, and that night is falling.
5. at the beginning, by showing the Greeks' fearfulness in the face of Hector's challenge
6. They display bravery, strength, pride, honor, and loyalty.
7. They honor warfare as a means of testing bravery and skill and show respect and fair-mindedness toward opponents.
8. Answers will vary. Students might suggest that Homer's dramatic skills and ability to portray exciting adventures account for the *Iliad*'s continuing popularity.
9. Answers will vary. Students may suggest that his characters are both fearful and brave and both aggressive and fair-minded, just as people are today.

LITERARY FOCUS

1. Answers will vary. Students should see that they preserve values that are important to their civilization: pride, courage, strength, honor, and fair-mindedness.
2. Epithets include "deep-sea-going-ships," "Peleus, the old master of horse," "Diomedes, powerful son of Tydeus"; a simile appears in lines 85–88.

STUDY QUESTIONS

Recalling

1. What does Hector ask the Achaeans, or Greeks? What is the initial reaction to his request?
2. By what means do the Greeks select a leader to fight Hector?
3. Summarize the Greek soldiers' prayers before the battle between Ajax and Hector.
4. Briefly explain how the battle ends.

Interpreting

5. Where in this selection does Homer reveal human weaknesses in these warriors?
6. What noble qualities do Hector and Ajax display?
7. What attitude do the Greeks show toward warfare and their opponents?
8. What qualities do you think account for the *Iliad*'s continued appeal and enormous influence on other literature?

Extending

9. In what ways are Homer's characters much like people today?

LITERARY FOCUS

The Epic

An **epic** is a long narrative (storytelling) poem that recounts, in grave and stately language, the adventures of one or more heroes who usually embody their civilization's ideals. The heroes of epics appear to be larger than life and usually hold high positions in their societies. Often their actions are important to the history of their civilizations. Divine or supernatural forces protect and advise epic heroes and intervene in human affairs.

Early epics were told orally. Homer's epics, for example, were composed in the oral tradition and not written down until many centuries later. To help recite their material smoothly and meet a particular rhythmic pattern, epic poets often employed standard wordings called epithets. An **epithet** is a term or phrase that describes or identifies a person, place, or thing. It may be used along with or instead of the name of the person, place, or thing. Several of Homer's epithets refer to characters' backgrounds; for example, "the king of Salamis" (for Ajax) and "Hector, tamer of horses." Others are more descriptive, such as "rosy-fingered dawn" and "city of the topless towers" (for Troy). When referring to a character, setting, or thing that appeared often, the epic poet had on hand a stock of epithets to satisfy the rhythmic demands of a particular line.

Another device of Homer's epics is the Homeric simile, or epic simile. A **simile** is a figure of speech using *like* or *as* to compare seemingly unlike things, as in "Life is like a dance." A **Homeric simile,** or **epic simile,** is longer and more elaborate than a typical simile; for example:

> Conspicuous as the evening star that comes,
> amid the first of heaven, at fall of night,
> and stands most lovely in the west, so shone
> in sunlight the fine-pointed spear
> Achilles poised in his right hand.

Thinking About the Epic

1. Based on this selection from the *Iliad*, in what ways are the actions of the heroes important to their civilization?
2. Find at least three epithets and one Homeric simile in the selection.

COMPOSITION

Writing About an Epic

■ Based on this excerpt from the *Iliad*, what values can you conclude were important to the ancient Greeks? Answer this question in a brief composition that cites examples from the selection to support your main points.

Writing Imaginary Interviews

■ Imagine that you are a reporter covering the Trojan War by interviewing the participants. Report on the comments of two characters on the evening after the battle between Hector and Ajax. Then, report these characters' impressions of the day's events.

COMPOSITION: GUIDELINES FOR EVALUATION

WRITING ABOUT AN EPIC

Objective

To analyze values of ancient Greek culture

Guidelines for Evaluation

■ suggested length: one to two pages
■ should isolate the ideals or values important to the ancient Greeks
■ should cite examples from the selection to back up the main points

WRITING IMAGINARY INTERVIEWS

Objective

To provide an eyewitness point of view

Guidelines for Evaluation

■ suggested length: one to two pages
■ should be written from the point of view of a reporter present the evening after the battle
■ should contain the comments of any two characters in the epic

PREVIEW: THE AUTHOR AND THE WORLD

Virgil (70–19 B.C.)

Ancient Rome

Rome's greatest poet, Publius Vergilius Maro, known to us as Virgil [vur′jəl], was born in northern Italy near what is now the town of Mantua. Thanks to the patronage of a wealthy Roman statesman, he was able to devote himself fully to his studies in philosophy and rhetoric and to his literary pursuits. Although he spent most of his life in Rome, he never forgot his roots; his first important work, the *Bucolia,* praises the virtues of country life. He was already a famous poet by the time he wrote the *Aeneid* [i nē′id], a twelve-book epic that describes the wanderings of the hero Aeneas [i nē′əs] from the fall of Troy until the founding of Rome. In 19 B.C. Virgil set out on a voyage to Greece, intending to revise the masterpiece he had spent eleven years writing, but he became gravely ill. On his deathbed he gave orders that his epic be burned, but Emperor Augustus ordered the poem published. The emperor's instincts were sound: the *Aeneid* has had a profound influence on subsequent literature and culture. The upcoming selection, which recounts the episode of the Trojan Horse, is widely known.

GEOGRAPHY AND CULTURE

The Founding of Rome

The ancient city of Rome occupies both banks of the Tiber River near the western coast of Italy. As the capital of the Roman Republic and later of the Roman Empire, and as the seat of the Papacy, Rome has had great historical importance. The town emerged from obscurity in the eighth century B.C., when the Etruscans conquered it and created a city-state. Other groups also contributed to the founding of Rome, including the Sabines and the Latins, who bequeathed it their language. The Roman Republic was founded around 500 B.C.

Virgil drew upon the ancient legend of Troy to glorify Rome and the achievements of its new ruler, Augustus. According to the legend, the Trojan hero Aeneas escapes from Troy and visits Carthage in North Africa, where he falls in love with Queen Dido. He then travels to Italy, where he conquers the Latins and establishes a new nation. Aeneas' journey begins with the fall of Troy, caused by the stratagem of the Trojan Horse. The next selection begins as Aeneas tells Dido's court about the destruction of Troy.

THE VOYAGE OF AENEAS

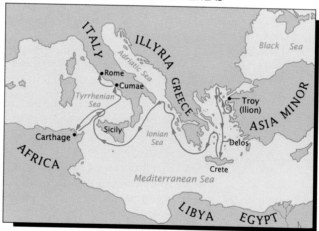

See *LITERATURE AND CULTURE SOURCEBOOK:
Classical Greece and Rome*

Aeneid **269**

The Trojan hero Aeneas sadly recalls Troy's fall. The Greeks place armed men inside a huge wooden horse and pretend to sail for home. The Trojans, excited by the "gift" and refusing to heed warnings, bring it inside their city. That night the Greek army returns, and the men within the horse leap out and open the gates. Troy is destroyed by its own citizens' foolishness.

LITERARY SKILLS FOR THIS SELECTION

- epic hero
- plot
- irony

THEMES IN THIS SELECTION

- deceptive appearances
- the power of destiny

LESSON OBJECTIVES

1. to understand the epic hero
2. to recognize meanings of roots from Latin
3. to create an epic hero

Teacher's Classroom Resources 2

- Teaching Notes 89
- Prereading Vocabulary 90
- Reading Guide 91
- Check Test 92
- Responding to World Cultures 93
- Literary Focus: The Epic Hero 94
- Language Study: Words from Latin 95
- Writing Process Guide: Creating an Epic Hero 96
- Grammar in Literature: Combining with Participles and Participial Phrases 97
- Selection Test 98

IN THE CLASSROOM

TEACHING STUDENTS OF DIFFERENT ABILITIES

- **For less advanced students:** Point out the main theme: Appearances are deceiving. Have students watch for a "gift" that is not what it seems. Help them pronounce difficult names. Have them complete the Reading Guide for this selection.
- **For more advanced students:** Have students read the episode of the Trojan horse in the *Odyssey* and compare and contrast the description of events in the two versions.

DISCUSSING GEOGRAPHY AND CULTURE

Colonies and Culture

The rulers of ancient Rome wielded great power over the lands they claimed. From the British Isles to North Africa, the Romans imposed not only their form of government but their language and culture.

- Like the colonies of Rome, the United States was once ruled by a great foreign power: Britain. Ask students to think of ways in which English culture helped to shape our own. (Students may mention language, food, clothing, and holidays.)

Ask students to describe an incident in which they ignored someone's advice, with unfortunate results. Ask whether, as a rule, they think advice should be heeded. Explain that in this selection the refusal to heed advice proves disastrous.

PAGE SUMMARY: AT A GLANCE

- Aeneas addresses Queen Dido.
- He expresses his great sadness over the fall of Troy.

1 TEACHING THE EPIC HERO

Explain that Aeneas is an epic hero whose courage, nobility, and intelligence are depicted throughout the *Aeneid* as he wanders in search of a new home. Here he is just at the beginning of his journey. He is preparing to tell about the fall of Troy, an event that prompted his search for a new homeland.

ART AND LITERATURE

The Frenchman Henri Motte (1846–1922) was a painter, architect, and writer. This print, taken from one of his paintings, is typical of the historical subject matter he favored. The image captures the mystery and majesty of the story of the Trojan Horse.

- Ask students to find lines in the selection that contain descriptions of the horse. (Students may cite lines 15–16, 60–62, and 84–85.) Does Motte's image match the descriptions? (Yes.)

The Trojan Horse, print after a painting by Henri Motte.

Virgil

from the **Aeneid**

Translated from the Latin by C. Day Lewis

from **Book II**

All fell silent now, and their faces were all attention
When from his place of honor Aeneas[1] began to speak:

O queen, the griefs you bid me reopen are inexpressible—
The tale of Troy, a rich and a most tragic empire
5 Erased by the Greeks; most piteous events I saw with my own
    eyes
And played no minor part in. What Myrmidon or Thessalian,[2]
What soldier of fell Ulysses[3] could talk about such events
And keep from tears? Besides, the dewy night drops fast

---

1. **Aeneas** [i nē′əs]: Trojan warrior who tells the story in the first person.
2. **Myrmidon** [mur′mə don′] **or Thessalian** [the sā′lē ən]: Greek soldiers from armies of Thessaly in northern Greece; the Myrmidons were led by Achilles [ə kil′ēz], greatest of the Greek warriors.
3. **Ulysses** [ū lis′ēz]: Latin form of Odysseus, Greek leader and hero of the Trojan War; described here as **fell**, cruel or savage.

270 *Myths, Folk Tales, and Epics*

CRITICAL THINKING: GUIDED READING QUESTIONS

LITERAL

1a. What feeling does Aeneas have as he recalls the fall of Troy? (grief)

INFERENTIAL

1b. Why does he feel such grief? (He is a Trojan who has lost his homeland and has personally seen his beloved city fall to the Greeks.)

From heaven, and the declining stars invite to sleep.
10 But if you want so much to know what happened to us
And hear in brief a recital of Troy's last agony,

2 Although the memory makes me shudder, and shrink from its
sadness,
I will attempt it.

Broken in war and foiled by fate,
With so many years[4] already slipping away, the Greek staff
15 Constructed a horse, employing the craft of the goddess
Athena[5]—

3 It was high as a hill, and its ribs were made from planks of
pinewood—
To pay for their safe return to Greece, they pretended: this
rumor
Got round. But, choosing warriors by lot, they secretly
Put them in on the blind side of the horse, until its vast
20 And cavernous belly was crammed with a party of armed men.

4 In sight of Troy there's an island, a well-known island, Tenedos—
Rich and powerful it was, while Priam's empire[6] stood;
Now, little but a bay, a roadstead unsafe for shipping.
Thither the Greeks sailed out, and hid on its desolate coast.
25 This was evacuation, we thought—they had sailed for Greece.

5 So all Troy threw off the chains of her long anguish.
We opened the gates, we enjoyed visiting the Greek camp,
Viewing the derelict positions on the abandoned beaches.
Here the Dolopes[7] camped; there, ferocious Achilles:
30 Here was beached their navy, and here the battle raged.
Some of us gaped at the gift—so deadly—the Greeks had left
for
Minerva,[8] and its stupendous bulk. Thymoetes[9] first,
Either from treachery or because Troy's fate now was sealed,
Urged that the horse be brought through the walls and placed
in our citadel.
35 But Capys[10] and all those of sounder views recommended

---

4. **so many years:** It is the tenth and last year of the Trojan War.
5. **Athena:** Greek goddess of wisdom and war.
6. **Priam's empire:** Troy, of which Priam was king.
7. **Dolopes** [dŏ′lə pēz]: Greeks from Dolopians, a region bordering Thessaly
on the southwest.
8. **Minerva:** Roman goddess of wisdom, identified with the Greek goddess
Athena.
9. **Thymoetes** [thī mē′tēz]: Trojan elder and adviser of Priam.
10. **Capys** [kap′is]: Trojan suspicious of the wooden horse; he later fled from
Troy with Aeneas.

Aeneid **271**

CRITICAL THINKING: GUIDED READING QUESTIONS

LITERAL

1a. How does Aeneas describe the memory of the fall of Troy? (He says that the memory makes him shudder and shrink from its sadness.)

2a. What was the condition of the Greek army before the construction of the horse? (They were "broken in war and foiled by fate.")

INFERENTIAL

1b. Given his feelings, why does Aeneas consent to recount the tale? (He does not want to offend the queen; he believes the story needs to be told.)

2b. What can we conclude about the effect of this "horse idea" on the fortunes of the Greeks? (Since Aeneas says that Troy fell to them, the horse must have reversed their fortunes and brought them victory.)

PAGE SUMMARY: AT A GLANCE

- Some Trojans recommend destroying the horse or boring holes in it to see what is inside.
- Laocoon, a Trojan priest, protests that the horse is a trick and pierces the horse's belly with a spear.
- The people, not heeding Laocoon's warning, cut through the walls of the city and start to drag the horse inside.

IN THE GLOSSARY

- guileless: candid
- concussion: the shock of a blow or collision
- hawsers: heavy ropes for moving or anchoring a ship

6 READING SKILL: CONTRAST

Ask students to contrast the two conflicting views of the horse. Which is based on logic and which on emotion? Why might emotion win out in this case? (Students should recognize that the idea of bringing the horse into the city is based on emotion. This view might win out because the Trojans desperately want to believe that the war is over and they are victorious.)

7 CRITICAL THINKING: EVALUATION

Have students evaluate Laocoon's argument. Is it convincing? Why or why not? What, if anything, could Laocoon have said to make his argument more convincing?

8 TEACHING THEME

Students should recognize that Aeneas believes the fall of Troy was part of destiny. His words in this powerful "if only" interjection reflect his regret, yet he recognizes the role of fate in what has occurred.

9 TEACHING IRONY

Help students recognize the use of dramatic irony here. The reader knows something the Trojans do not: that as they joyfully bring the horse into the city, they are really sealing their doom.

---

6 Hurling it into the sea or setting fire to it, as some
Booby-trap of the Greeks and not to be trusted—or else
Boring holes in its belly to see what might be inside it.
So the rank and file were violently torn between contraries.

40 Then out in front of them all, hundreds straggling behind him,
In a great temper Laocoon[11] came tearing down from the citadel,
Crying from far:

7   Citizens, are you all stark mad?
Do you really believe our foes are gone? Do you imagine
Any Greek gift is guileless? Is that your idea of Ulysses?
45 This thing of wood conceals Greek soldiers, or else it is
A mechanism designed against our walls—to pry into
Our homes and to bear down on the city; sure, some trick
Is there. No, you must never feel safe with the horse, Trojans.
Whatever it is, I distrust the Greeks, even when they are generous.

50 He spoke: he put forth his strength, and spun his huge great spear
At the flank of the monster, right into its belly's rounded frame.
The spear stuck quivering; the hollow womb of the creature
Grunted at the concussion and rumbled hollowly.

8 If destiny, if our own will had not been so contrary,
55 Laocoon would have made us rip open that cache of Greek troops—
There'd still be a Troy—O topless towers, you'd be standing now! . . .

"Bring the horse to Minerva's shrine! Pray for her goodwill!"
All of our people shouted.

9 We cut into our walls,[12] laid open the heart of the city.
60 Everyone set about the task: we inserted rollers
Under its hooves, put hawsers of hemp around its neck,
And strained. The disastrous engine[13] was jockeyed over our walls,

---

11. **Laocoon** [lā ok'ō on']: After warning the Trojans against the wooden horse, Laocoon, a Trojan priest, was killed, along with his two sons, by two enormous sea serpents.
12. **We . . . walls:** The Trojans had been convinced by Sinon [sī'nən], a pretended Greek deserter, that if they could succeed in getting the huge horse into their city, Troy would rule Europe.
13. **engine:** here, evil contrivance.

272 *Myths, Folk Tales, and Epics*

CRITICAL THINKING: GUIDED READING QUESTIONS

LITERAL

1a. What word is used to describe how "the rank and file were . . . torn between contraries"? (violently)

2a. What does Laocoon think the horse is? (a "thing of wood" made to conceal Greek soldiers or "a mechanism designed against our walls")

INFERENTIAL

1b. Why do the Trojans react this way? (They are in a state of excitement because most of them want to believe that the war is over.)

2b. Why don't the Trojans heed Laocoon's warning? (They prefer to believe that the war is over and the horse is just what it seems to be.)

An army in its womb. Boys and unmarried maidens
Escorted it, singing psalms, joyfully gripping the traces.
65 The menace mounts, comes trundling into the city center.

O, my country! O Ilium,[14] home of the gods! O Troy town,
Famous through war! Four times the monster stopped, just where the entrance
Was, and every time the accouterments[15] clanged in its belly.
Yet we persevered, with never a thought—we were madly blind—
70 Until we had lodged the ominous thing in our holy place.
Then, to cap all, Cassandra[16] opened her mouth for prophecy—
She whom her god had doomed to be never believed by the Trojans.
But we poor fools, whose very last day it was, festooned
The shrines of the gods with holiday foliage all over the city.

75 So now the sky rolled round, and night raced up from the ocean
Voluminously shrouding the earth and heaven's vault
And the villainous scheme of the Greeks. Not a sound from the Trojans, supine
Along the walls, tired out, in the embrace of sleep.
And now the main Greek army was moving from Tenedos
80 In fleet formation, under the favoring silences
Of a quiet moon, toward the coast they knew so well.

Their leading galley had signaled with flame: Sinon, protected
By fate's injustice, stealthily unlocked the wooden horse
And let the Greeks out from its belly. The horse disgorged, the men
85 Burst reveling forth from its hollow flank into the fresh air—
Thessander and Sthenelus in the lead, with Ulysses the terrible,
Sliding down a rope they had lowered—Acamas, Thoas,
Neoptolemus son of Peleus, Machaon and Menelaus,
And Epeus—the man who had actually built the clever contraption.

90 They broke out over a city drowned in drunken sleep;
They killed the sentries and then threw open the gates, admitting
Their main body, and joined in the prearranged plan of attack.

---

14. **Ilium** [il′ē əm]: another name for Troy.
15. **accouterments** [ə kōō′tər mənts]: arms and armor.
16. **Cassandra**: Trojan princess, sister of Hector; when she rejected the love of Apollo, he punished her by giving her the gift of prophecy along with the curse that she would never be believed.

Aeneid   273

PAGE SUMMARY: AT A GLANCE

- The horse enters the city amidst general rejoicing.
- Cassandra predicts disaster, but no one listens.
- The Greek ships return.
- As the Trojans sleep, the Greek Sinon unlocks the horse and lets the armed men out.
- The Greeks kill the sentries and open the gates to the main body of the Greek army.

IN THE GLOSSARY

- traces: straps or chains connecting an animal's harness to a vehicle being pulled
- supine: lying on one's back

10 CULTURAL BACKGROUND

Point out that here Aeneas indicates a deep love for and pride in his homeland. The Romans possessed a strong love for and sense of duty to the state. Virgil drew upon the ancient legend of Troy to glorify Rome and the achievements of its new ruler, Augustus Caesar.

11 TEACHING PLOT: CLIMAX

Help students recognize that the Greeks left a man behind, Sinon, to let the warriors out of the horse. His role is critical at this climactic moment.

12 TEACHING PLOT: RESOLUTION

Point out that the conflict between the Greeks and the Trojans is resolved in the fall of Troy. Ask how the Trojans themselves helped bring about this resolution. (They were blind to the possibility that the horse was a trick.)

COLLABORATIVE LEARNING: ENRICHMENT ACTIVITY

Maps Have students work in groups to make two maps of the Mediterranean regions mentioned in Virgil's *Aeneid*—one a historical map and the other representing the present day. Have students include the ancient cities of Athens, Sparta, Corinth, Troy, Rome, and Carthage on the historical map. For the present-day map, they will need to find out which of these ancient cities still exist.

CRITICAL THINKING: GUIDED READING QUESTIONS

LITERAL

1a. How does Aeneas describe Cassandra? ("she whom her god had doomed to be never believed by the Trojans")

2a. Briefly relate the Greeks' plan after the horse enters the city. (The Greek army would return; Sinon would let the men out of the horse; the men from the horse would kill the sentries and open the gates.)

INFERENTIAL

1b. What is ironic about the fact that Aeneas is able to describe her in this way? (If Aeneas had remembered the curse back in Troy, he might have had the good sense to heed her warnings.)

2b. What does this plan show about the Greeks? (They are clever and resourceful.)

If you were Aeneas, with whom would you be angrier—the Greeks for thinking up their trick or yourself for falling for it? Why?

ANSWERS

STUDY QUESTIONS

1. They pretend to sail away.
2. They suggest that the Trojans hurl it into the sea, set fire to it, or bore holes to see what might be inside.
3. They cut into the city walls, insert rollers into the horse's hooves, and pull it in with ropes tied around its neck.
4. It returns to Troy.
5. They kill the sentries and open the city gates to the army.
6. Answers will vary. Students might say the Trojans were anxious for an end to the conflict or were extremely curious about the horse.
7. He speaks of "griefs . . . inexpressible" and "piteous events"; the memory makes him shudder; he favors Capys' views and calls the Trojans "madly blind" and "poor fools"; he addresses his homeland with regret.
8. It is fated, thus inevitable.
9. Answers will vary. Students may suggest the idea that one can never be too careful, for appearances are deceiving.

LITERARY FOCUS

1. He will have to seek a new home for his people.
2. Answers will vary. Students may cite cunning, leadership, and perseverance.

LANGUAGE STUDY

1. *candidus*, "white, sincere"
2. *praesidere*, "to preside over"
3. from *legis*, "law," and *lator*, "proposer of"
4. *convenire*, "to convene"
5. *exequi* or *exsequi*, "to follow up"
6. *senex*, "old; aged"
7. *repraesentare*, "to present again"
8. *res*, "thing; affair," and *publica*, "public"
9. *populus*, "the people"
10. *taxare*, "to appraise"

STUDY QUESTIONS

Recalling

1. Besides building the great horse, what else do the Greeks do to trick the Trojans into letting down their guard?
2. What did Capys and others advise the Trojans to do with the horse?
3. Describe the process by which the Trojans bring the horse inside the city.
4. What does the Greek army do at nightfall?
5. What do the Greek soldiers, after release from the horse's belly, do first?

Interpreting

6. Which factors do you think best explain the success of the Trojan Horse strategy?
7. In what ways does Aeneas reveal his own feelings about the events he narrates?
8. What does Cassandra's prophesying suggest about the destruction of Troy?

Extending

9. What lessons illustrated by the Trojan Horse episode do you think would be useful today?

LITERARY FOCUS

The Epic Hero

The **epic hero** is a legendary, larger-than-life figure whose adventures form the core of the epic poem. An epic hero is a person of almost superhuman strength, intelligence, courage, and virtue who embodies the goals and virtues of an entire nation or culture. For example, Aeneas, the hero of the *Aeneid,* functions as an epic hero because he personifies his society's ideals of courage, nobility, and intelligence. Other national epic heroes include El Cid in Spain and the hero of the medieval *Song of Roland* in France. The stories of epic heroes often depict epic events, such as great battles, and epic heroes often

travel great distances to achieve their goals, as does Odysseus in the *Odyssey* and Aeneas in the *Aeneid.*

Thinking About the Epic Hero

1. What epic adventure will the epic hero Aeneas have to undertake as a result of the Trojan Horse?
2. List three other goals or virtues the Trojans admire, according to the story of the Trojan Horse.

LANGUAGE STUDY

Words from Latin

Though not a Romance language, English has a great many words borrowed from Latin, many of them indirectly through French or Spanish. Because the Romans established the basis for modern legal systems, many Latin words in English have to do with law and government.

Look up the following words in a dictionary and write their root meanings and the language they come from. Etymologies are usually found in brackets at the end of the definition; for example, "<L." means "comes from Latin."

1. candidate
2. president
3. legislature
4. convention
5. executive
6. senate
7. representative
8. republic
9. public
10. tax

COMPOSITION

Creating an Epic Hero

■ In a brief composition create an epic hero, a legendary, larger-than-life man or woman whose adventures can form the basis of an epic adventure. Begin by setting the hero within a culture and then enumerating the values the hero will embody for those people. As you write, include specific details and examples that clearly describe your hero's special qualities.

274 *Myths, Folk Tales, and Epics*

COMPOSITION: GUIDELINES FOR EVALUATION

CREATING AN EPIC HERO

Objective
To create an epic hero

Guidelines for Evaluation
■ suggested length: one to two pages
■ should create a larger-than-life character
■ should place the hero within a specific culture
■ should include details and examples that clearly demonstrate the hero's qualities

PREVIEW: THE AUTHOR AND THE WORLD

Dante Alighieri (1265–1321)

Italy

Dante's great masterpiece of medieval literature, the epic poem *The Divine Comedy,* has had a profound influence on Western literature. Yet Dante's life was full of misfortunes. Both his parents died before he was twenty. An ambitious and confident scholar, he educated himself through wide reading. In 1300 he was elected one of the six ruling officials of Florence, but soon after he was forced to banish his best friend, who later died in exile. Dante was exiled himself in 1302, when a rival party overthrew the Florentine government. He lived the rest of his life as the guest of wealthy patrons.

Dante's masterwork, *The Divine Comedy,* is divided into one part of thirty-four cantos—Hell *(Inferno)*—and two parts of thirty-three cantos each—Purgatory and Paradise. In the *Inferno* the damned souls occupy nine circles of increasing severity depending upon the nature of their sins. The poem can be read on two levels. On the literal level it tells the story of the state of souls after death, brought to that point by choices made during life. On an allegorical level its purpose is to turn the living to the path of salvation. Dante makes himself the central character, guided by Virgil.

GEOGRAPHY AND CULTURE

Medieval Florence

The city of Florence, located on the Arno River in the province of Tuscany in north-central Italy, was founded by the Romans. During its long history it became one of the great cities of Italy, rivaling Rome, Venice, and Naples as a center of wealth, culture, and political influence. By Dante's time Florence had become an independent city-state with its own government, army, and currency. Unfortunately, it was the scene of constant political strife. Rival parties fought each other for political control, dragging the city into a series of disastrous civil wars. Dante himself was exiled from Florence in 1302. He satirized many of the people who engaged in these vicious struggles in *The Divine Comedy,* relegating them to the fiercest realms of Hell.

Some of Italy's historical figures were treated more tenderly by Dante, however. In the following excerpt Dante meets a pair of unhappy lovers, Paolo and Francesca, in the second circle of Hell. Francesca had married a nobleman from Rimini in 1275 but later had fallen in love with her husband's younger brother, Paolo.

See *LITERATURE AND CULTURE SOURCEBOOK: Italy*

The Divine Comedy **275**

<table>
<tr><td valign="top">

Read aloud this quotation from Plato: "Punishment brings wisdom: it is the healing art of wickedness." Have students discuss the quotation, and guide them in a discussion of constructive and destructive forms of punishment. Explain that in this selection they will meet souls who are being punished for wrongdoing.

PAGE SUMMARY: AT A GLANCE

- Dante, guided by Virgil, comes to the second circle of Hell.
- Dante finds that this circle is a dark place where strong winds ceaselessly whirl the souls of those who have sinned in love.

IN THE GLOSSARY

- blaspheme: to curse

1 CULTURAL BACKGROUND

Explain that Dante is now in the second circle of Hell. Point out that this author wrote his masterpiece for common people to enjoy. He chose to write not in Latin, the language of the educated, but in Tuscan, the language of the ordinary people of his region. Inspired by Dante's verse, Renaissance thinkers also began to write in the languages of the common people.

2 READING SKILL: SUMMARY

Ask students to summarize what they know about the second circle of Hell up to this point. (They should mention that it is a place without light and filled with roaring winds in which the souls of those who have sinned in love are constantly whirled about as they shriek and blaspheme.)

3 TEACHING SIMILES

Help students recognize that here and in the preceding two tercets, Dante likens the uncontrollable up and down whirlings and the cries of the condemned souls to those of birds. The simile vividly portrays the hopelessness of the lovers' fate.

</td>
<td valign="top">

Dante

from **The Divine Comedy**

Translated by John Ciardi

from Canto V

1
I came to a place stripped bare of every light
  and roaring on the naked dark like seas
  wracked by a war of winds.[1] Their hellish flight

of storm and counterstorm through time foregone,
5 sweeps the souls of the damned before its charge.
  Whirling and battering it drives them on,

and when they pass the ruined gap of Hell
  through which we had come, their shrieks begin anew.
  There they blaspheme the power of God eternal.

2
10 And this, I learned, was the never ending flight
  of those who sinned in the flesh, the carnal and lusty
  who betrayed reason to their appetite.

As the wings of wintering starlings bear them on
  in their great wheeling flights, just so the blast
15 wherries these evil souls through time foregone.

Here, there, up, down, they whirl and, whirling, strain
  with never a hope of hope to comfort them,
  not of release, but even of less pain.

3
As cranes go over sounding their harsh cry,
20 leaving the long streak of their flight in air,
  so come these spirits, wailing as they fly.

And watching their shadows lashed by wind, I cried:
  "Master,[2] what souls are these the very air
  lashes with its black whips from side to side?"

---

1. **a place . . . of winds:** the second circle of Hell. The sinners in this circle are constantly whirled about by strong winds.
2. **Master:** the ghost of Virgil, the Roman poet, Dante's guide in Hell.

</td></tr>
</table>

CRITICAL THINKING: GUIDED READING QUESTIONS

LITERAL

1a. What constantly drives the movements of the condemned souls in the second circle? (strong winds)

2a. What do the souls do when they "pass the ruined gap of Hell"? (They shriek and blaspheme the power of God.)

INFERENTIAL

1b. In what way is being driven by winds like the sin of which the souls are guilty? (In life the souls were driven by the force of love.)

2b. Why do they do this? (They are in torment and resent God's power to cause their great suffering.)

Encounter of Dante and Beatrice, Venetian School, fourteenth century.

In 1273, when he was eight years old, Dante met Beatrice Portinari, who would become his lifelong symbol of love and inspiration. Beatrice married a nobleman in 1290 and died three years later. Dante married several years after her death but never wrote about his wife. Instead, he celebrated his ideal, Beatrice. Toward the end of the journey through Purgatory, Virgil must abandon Dante. Thereafter, it is Beatrice herself who becomes Dante's guide, leading him from Purgatory to Paradise. In this painting Dante and Beatrice stand on the flower-covered earth, illuminated by a radiant, benevolent night sky.

■ Ask students to compare the descriptions of Paolo and Francesca with the depictions of Dante and Beatrice. (Paolo and Francesca are swept through darkness by never-ending strong winds, tormented by painful thoughts, consumed by piteous sobs. Dante and Beatrice stand in a colorful, tranquil setting, smiling as they reach out to each other.)

- Virgil identifies some of the souls that Dante sees.
- Dante asks Virgil to let him speak to a pair who are being swept about together, and Virgil tells Dante to call to them in the name of love.

IN THE GLOSSARY

- corrupted: destroyed the morality of
- depravity: state of being corrupt

4 TEACHING STUDENTS OF LIMITED ENGLISH PROFICIENCY

Students for whom English is not the first language may have difficulty with the way in which sentences in this excerpt are presented. Encourage them to look for complete thoughts expressed in sentences and to read the selection one "sentence" at a time, formulating the meaning before moving on.

5 TEACHING ALLUSION

Point out that here and in the preceding five tercets Dante uses details of individuals' lives and allusions to well-known figures to demonstrate the kind of sin of love for which people are condemned to the second circle.

6 READING SKILL: PREDICTING OUTCOMES

Ask students what they think Dante will ask the two lovers. (Students might suggest that he will want to know the details of their sin.)

25 "The first of these whose history you would know,"
    he answered me, "was Empress of many tongues.[3]
    Mad sensuality corrupted her so

    that to hide the guilt of her debauchery
    she licensed all depravity alike,
30 and lust and law were one in her decree.

    She is Semiramis of whom the tale is told
    how she married Ninus and succeeded him
    to the throne of that wide land the Sultans hold.

    The other is Dido;[4] faithless to the ashes
35 of Sichaeus, she killed herself for love.
    The next whom the eternal tempest lashes

    is sense-drugged Cleopatra.[5] See Helen[6] there,
    from whom such ill arose. And great Achilles,[7]
    who fought at last with love in the house of prayer.

40 And Paris.[8] And Tristan."[9] As they whirled above
    he pointed out more than a thousand shades
    of those torn from the mortal life by love.

    I stood there while my Teacher one by one
    named the great knights and ladies of dim time;
45 and I was swept by pity and confusion.

    At last I spoke: "Poet, I should be glad
    to speak a word with those two swept together[10]
    so lightly on the wind and still so sad."

    And he to me: "Watch them. When next they pass,
50 call to them in the name of love that drives
    and damns them here. In that name they will pause."

---

3. **Empress of many tongues:** Semiramis [si mir′ə mis], a legendary queen who ruled Assyria after the death of her husband, Ninus [nī′nəs].
4. **Dido** [dī′dō]: queen of Carthage who betrayed her husband, Sichaeus [sə kē′əs], when she fell in love with Aeneas.
5. **Cleopatra:** the famous queen of Egypt who fell in love with Antony, Roman general and political leader.
6. **Helen:** wife of Menelaus; her abduction by Paris caused the Trojan War.
7. **Achilles** [ə kil′ēz]: the great Greek hero at Troy who, in one version of the legend, falls in love with Polyxena, a Trojan princess, and is killed by her brother.
8. **Paris:** the Trojan prince who loved Helen and killed Achilles.
9. **Tristan:** one of the knights of the Round Table. He and King Mark's fiancée, Isolde, fall in love when they drink a love potion.
10. **those two swept together:** Paolo [pä ō′lō] and Francesca [frän che′skä], killed in 1275. Dante knew Francesca's father.

278 *Myths, Folk Tales, and Epics*

CRITICAL THINKING: GUIDED READING QUESTIONS

LITERAL

1a. Whom does Virgil point out to Dante? (Semiramis, Dido, Cleopatra, Helen, Achilles, Paris, Tristan, and more than a thousand others)

2a. What feelings does Dante say he is swept by after Virgil identifies many of the souls? (pity and confusion)

INFERENTIAL

1b. Why does Dante use well-known figures as examples? (He assumes the reader knows their stories; his naming them helps readers understand the kinds of sins for which people are condemned.)

2b. Why might he feel this way? (Many of the souls are those of important people who have contributed to history and were respected in their time.)

Thus, as soon as the wind in its wild course
　　brought them around, I called: "O wearied souls!
　　if none forbid it, pause and speak to us."

7
55　As mating doves that love calls to their nest
　　guide through the air with motionless raised wings,
　　borne by the sweet desire that fills each breast—

Just so those spirits turned on the torn sky
　　from the band where Dido whirls across the air;
60　such was the power of pity in my cry.

8
"O living creature,[11] gracious, kind, and good,
　　going this pilgrimage through the sick night,
　　visiting us who stained the earth with blood,

were the King of Time[12] our friend, we would pray His peace
65　on you who have pitied us. As long as the wind
　　will let us pause, ask of us what you please.

The town where I was born[13] lies by the shore
　　where the Po[14] descends into its ocean rest
　　with its attendant streams in one long murmur.

9
70　Love, which in gentlest hearts will soonest bloom
　　seized my lover[15] with passion for that sweet body
　　from which I was torn unshriven[16] to my doom.

Love, which permits no loved one not to love,
　　took me so strongly with delight in him
75　that we are one in Hell, as we were above.

Love led us to one death. In the depths of Hell
　　Caïna waits[17] for him who took our lives."
　　This was the piteous tale they stopped to tell.

10
And when I had heard those world-offended lovers
80　I bowed my head. At last the Poet spoke:
　　"What painful thoughts are these your lowered brow
　　　covers?"

---

11. **O living creature:** Francesca speaks to Dante, who, guided by Virgil,
is visiting Hell while still living.
12. **the King of Time:** God.
13. **The town . . . born:** Rimini, an ancient Italian city on the Adriatic coast.
14. **Po:** river in northern Italy.
15. **my lover:** Paolo.
16. **unshriven:** without having confessed her sins and received absolution.
17. **Caïna** [kä ē′nə] **waits:** Caïna is a lower circle of Hell, where a place is
prepared for Giovanni Malatesta, who killed the two lovers. Giovanni was
still alive when Dante wrote this passage.

The Divine Comedy　**279**

PAGE SUMMARY: AT A GLANCE

- Dante calls out to Paolo and Francesca.
- The couple stops, and Francesca tells about how love overpowered the two and condemned them to Hell.
- Dante bows his head in thought.

7 TEACHING SIMILES

Point out that here Dante refers to birds—doves—to describe the lovers. Elsewhere he compares the souls to cranes and starlings. Ask why Dante uses so many similes involving birds. (Students may suggest that the movement and sound of the birds is like that of the souls and that the variety of types of birds allows different feelings and ideas to be presented.)

8 TEACHING CHARACTERIZATION

Point out that Francesca describes Dante as "gracious, kind, and good" and says that she would pray for Dante if she could. Ask students what this tells us about her. (She is gentle and sweet, not the kind of person one might expect to encounter in Hell.)

9 TEACHING ALLEGORY

Help students see that Paolo and Francesca are symbols for the strength of illicit passion and its unfortunate results. Despite the seeming innocence of Francesca's words and the apparent inevitability of the couple's love, the two still must suffer through eternity for their sin.

10 READING SKILL: PREDICTING OUTCOMES

Ask students to predict what Dante is thinking. (Students might suggest that Dante is wondering how this strong love began.)

CRITICAL THINKING: GUIDED READING QUESTIONS

LITERAL

1a. What does Francesca tell Dante he may do? (She says that he may ask what he pleases.)

2a. How does Francesca describe the love she experienced? (She calls it "love, which permits no loved one not to love.")

INFERENTIAL

1b. Why is Francesca willing to talk to Dante? (She is happy to see a living person; she is also happy to show by example how easy it is to sin and how difficult it is to avoid sin.)

2b. Why was Francesca unable to avoid her sin? (The love she experienced was too overpowering.)

- Dante asks the lovers how they were lured into committing their sin.
- Francesca explains that they first sinned after reading the romance of Lancelot.
- Dante falls to the floor in a faint, overcome by his feelings of sorrow and pity for the couple.

IN THE GLOSSARY

- dalliance: wasting of time

11 TEACHING IRONY

Help students note the irony Dante brings out here: A seemingly sweet and natural love can result in punishment.

12 TEACHING ALLEGORY

Francesca's recounting of the first kiss while she and Paolo were "alone with innocence" suggests the power of sin and the strength people must use to combat and defeat it. The couple becomes a symbol for the need to resist temptation and sin, lest they suffer through eternity.

13 TEACHING THEME

Help students recognize that while Dante regrets the situation of the lovers, he still, as author of *The Divine Comedy*, recognizes their behavior as sinful and thus deserving of punishment.

COLLABORATIVE LEARNING: ENRICHMENT ACTIVITY

Costume Design A play based on this episode of *The Divine Comedy* would require costumes from several periods. Have students work in groups to create sketches of costumes for the people who would appear in such a play: Dante, Virgil, Paolo, Francesca, Cleopatra, Helen, Achilles, and others. Students will need to research the types of dress that would be worn in the different periods during which these people lived.

11
When at length I answered, I began: "Alas!
What sweetest thoughts, what green and young desire
led these two lovers to this sorry pass."

85 Then turning to those spirits once again,
I said: "Francesca, what you suffer here
melts me to tears of pity and of pain.

But tell me: in the time of your sweet sighs
by what appearances found love the way
90 to lure you to his perilous paradise?"

And she: "The double grief of a lost bliss
is to recall its happy hour in pain.
Your Guide and Teacher[18] knows the truth of this.

But if there is indeed a soul in Hell
95 to ask of the beginning of our love
out of his pity, I will weep and tell:

On a day for dalliance we read the rhyme
of Lancelot,[19] how love had mastered him.
12
We were alone with innocence and dim time.

100 Pause after pause that high old story drew
our eyes together while we blushed and paled;
but it was one soft passage overthrew

our caution and our hearts. For when we read
how her fond smile[20] was kissed by such a lover,
105 he who is one with me[21] alive and dead

breathed on my lips the tremor of his kiss.
That book, and he who wrote it, was a pander.[22]
That day we read no further." As she said this,

the other spirit,[23] who stood by her, wept
13 110 so piteously, I felt my senses reel
and faint away with anguish. I was swept

by such a swoon as death is, and I fell,
as a corpse might fall, to the dead floor of Hell.

---

18. **Your Guide and Teacher:** Virgil.
19. **rhyme of Lancelot:** one of many medieval stories about the love of Sir Lancelot and Queen Guinevere, wife of King Arthur.
20. **her fond smile:** the smile of Guinevere.
21. **he . . . me:** Paolo, who share Francesca's torment in Hell as he shared her life on earth.
22. **pander:** go-between in a love affair.
23. **other spirit:** Paolo.

280 *Myths, Folk Tales, and Epics*

CRITICAL THINKING: GUIDED READING QUESTIONS

LITERAL

1a. What does Dante ask Francesca to tell him? (He asks what led her to commit her sin.)

2a. What does Dante do after hearing Francesca's story? (He swoons and falls to the floor.)

INFERENTIAL

1b. Why is Dante curious about what led the lovers to their sin? (Answers will vary. Students may say he is touched by their seeming innocence and wonders how they could have gotten into such a predicament.)

2b. Why does Dante have such an extreme reaction to the story? (Answers will vary. Students may say that although he recognizes the couple has sinned, he senses that the punishment is extreme.)

STUDY QUESTIONS

Recalling

1. Name several sights and sounds that greet Dante as he enters Hell.
2. What punishment do the souls in this circle of Hell suffer?
3. Which doomed souls does Virgil point out to Dante? To which of these does Dante speak?
4. As Francesca explains in lines 97–98, what were she and Paolo reading that led them astray?

Interpreting

5. What is Dante's attitude toward these sinners? Support your answer with examples from the poem.
6. What irony about love does the story of Paolo and Francesca illustrate?

Extending

7. What wrongdoings would you consider the most serious in today's world?

LITERARY FOCUS

Allegory

Allegory is a form of extended metaphor in which the events, objects, and persons in a narrative represent moral qualities or specific abstract ideas, such as love, fear, and virtue. In Dante's allegory every element corresponds first to a literal reality; the allegorical reality then expresses a separate, deeper significance.

For example, on the literal level Dante is the poet going on a journey, guided by Virgil, the poet of Rome. On the allegorical level, however, Dante represents the mortal soul experiencing after death the consequences of choices made in life. Although the poem is completely understandable on the literal level, Dante's purpose in writing it—to teach people the consequences of worldly actions in the hereafter—can best be appreciated through recognition of his masterful use of allegory.

A wide variety of literary works can be allegorical. George Lucas' movie *Star Wars,* for example, is a recent popular allegory in which Luke Skywalker, Darth Vader, and their respective allies represent the cosmic forces of good and evil.

Thinking About Allegory

1. Though they were real people who actually lived, Paolo and Francesca can be said to represent abstract ideas or ideals. What are these ideas?
2. What moral lesson do you think Dante is teaching in this section of his allegory?

COMPOSITION

Writing a Scene for *The Divine Comedy*

■ Imagine yourself on a tour of Heaven, guided by Virgil. There you encounter someone being rewarded for a virtuous life. Write a story narrating this encounter and describing the reward. Follow Dante's lead in describing the scenery of the place, in detailing the reward, and in narrating the events that led to it. Also, include your reaction to hearing the virtuous soul's story.

ANSWERS

STUDY QUESTIONS

1. Sights and sounds include "a place stripped bare of every light"; a roaring; shrieks; blaspheming; damned souls in "wheeling flights"; and wailing.
2. They are condemned to be carried along on an unceasing wind.
3. Virgil points out Semiramis, Dido, Cleopatra, Helen, Achilles, Paris, Tristan, Paolo, Francesca, and others; Dante speaks to Paolo and Francesca.
4. the romance of Lancelot
5. Dante's compassionate response—his "senses reel," and he faints—indicates that he feels sympathy rather than disapproval.
6. The sweetness of earthly love can end in painful punishment in Hell.
7. Answers will vary. Students will probably say that violent crimes are more serious than unintentional crimes prompted by love.

LITERARY FOCUS

1. Answers will vary. The couple may be said to represent the strength of love, which keeps true love alive even in torment.
2. Answers will vary. Students may suggest that Dante is saying that every wrongdoing has its punishment.

COMPOSITION: GUIDELINES FOR EVALUATION

WRITING A SCENE FOR *THE DIVINE COMEDY*

Objective

To write a scene in the style of Dante

Guidelines for Evaluation

- suggested length: one to two pages
- should use Heaven as a setting and should follow Dante's style in describing scenery and events
- should identify a soul's virtues and rewards
- should include the narrator's reactions

The mountain citadel of Machu Picchu was constructed in the fifteenth century by the Incas, who ruled Peru and the west coast of South America from the early fifteenth century until the Spanish conquest in the sixteenth century. Machu Picchu, abandoned soon after the Spanish took control, was not rediscovered until 1911, by the American explorer Hiram Bingham. The conquering Spaniards never found it, however.

Machu Picchu sits ten thousand feet high in the Peruvian Andes, on a granite saddle between two towering peaks. Incan artisans cut around two hundred habitable structures out of the granite, using no mortar; atop the stone they added sun-baked bricks and roof tiles.

Some scholars think that the central plaza, with radiating shrines along opposite sides, represented two moieties, or tribal divisions, that might have ruled Machu Picchu. Even today the actual purpose of this Inca fortress remains a mystery.

■ Ask students whether they can name another monument, mythic or otherwise, that rises toward the heavens. (Possible answers: the Egyptian Pyramids, the Tower of Babel, the Eiffel Tower, the Washington Monument)

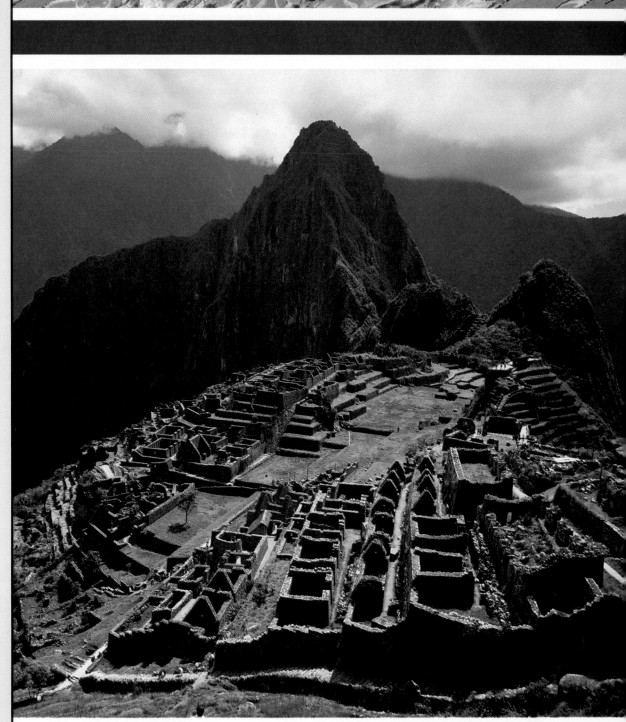

282 *Myths, Folk Tales, and Epics*

Machu Picchu, Peru, aerial view of the ruins.

MYTHS, FOLK TALES, AND EPICS

Saving the Past

The myths, folk tales, and epics you have just read provide us with a crucial link to the past. Through them we can understand how ancient peoples thought and felt. Ancient monuments—temples, pyramids, palaces, tombs—provide us with an even more tangible link to the past. Unfortunately, many of the world's most prized archaeological treasures are rapidly disintegrating. Natural forces, such as earthquakes, hasten their destruction. So do pollution, water seepage, and the shuffling feet and probing hands of millions of tourists.

One of the most famous ancient monuments, the Parthenon—a temple dedicated to the Greek goddess Athena built in Athens in the fifth century B.C.—is rapidly falling apart. Some of the damage was caused by a well-meaning architect who sought one hundred years ago to protect the Parthenon from the earthquakes that periodically rock southern Greece. He inserted iron bars into the temple's massive marble blocks. With time the bars rusted and expanded, cracking and staining the marble.

Archaeologists are now seeking to repair the Parthenon in a manner that won't damage it further. They are replacing the rusty iron bars with rods of titanium, a light, strong, rustproof metal used to make jet engines. They are also trying to develop a resin that they can paint onto the surface of the marble to protect it from corrosion.

In other parts of the world, the task is just as pressing. In Latin America, where many of the world's ancient civilizations arose, ruins are being destroyed by the twin scourges of nature and people. Pollution and rising ground water are destroying the Aztec Templo Mayor, located in the heart of Mexico City. Tree roots are ripping apart the magnificent Mayan temples at Copán in Honduras, and humidity and the thoughtless scribblings of tourists are ruining the magnificent Mayan frescoes of Bonampak in southern Mexico. On Latin America's Pacific coast rains wash away the giant adobe pyramids at Chan Chan near the Peruvian city of Trujillo.

These treasures urgently need protection, but the task is overwhelming. In Mexico alone there are more than eight thousand archaeological sites. Finding the millions of dollars necessary to repair ancient ruins is difficult in countries where many people lack basic necessities like food and housing. Yet if ancient treasures such as these are not restored, vital links with the past will be lost forever.

PRESERVING MEMORIES AND SKILLS

Great monuments are not the only objects worthy of preservation. Simple personal objects—a photograph, a trophy, or a diary, for example—can have great sentimental or even historical value. The past is also preserved in our minds and our hands—for example, in one's family heritage or in a skill learned from a parent or grandparent.

Activities

1. Divide the class into groups of six or seven students. Ask each group to explore ways in which families can preserve links with their past. For example, some students may tape conversations with elderly relatives, while others may construct family time capsules or draw family trees. Have individual students share their experiences with their group using these methods. Have the students, as a group, summarize their feelings about the preservation of a family heritage. Students may then display their family chronicles in the classroom for other groups to observe.

2. Divide the class into groups of three or four students. Have each group research the history of a particular colonial American or Native American craft that is still practiced today, such as the making of quilts, log cabins, adobe buildings, rugs, maple syrup, apple cider, or scrimshaw. After the students have finished their research, ask a leader from each group to explain to the rest of the class, step by step, how these items are made or produced. Then ask students whether any of them have learned a craft—such as embroidery, woodworking, or fly tying—from their parents or grandparents. Ask them what sorts of skills they think they might pass on to their own children or grandchildren.

The Mochica people flourished for several centuries along the north coast of Peru beginning around the first century. They developed stone carving and mined gold to make artworks and jewelry. These ear spools are a fine example of their artistry. Notice the twenty-four gold spheres around each earring—twice the number of months in a year. The design might seem accidental, but in early cultures elements such as number, pattern, form, rhythm, and shape were closely related to beliefs or mythology.

These ear spools depict the sun god, a half-man and half-bird creature that inhabits both the earth and the heavens. Typical of this style, the heads are depicted in profile, and the bodies are partly frontal, partly in profile.

■ The representation of a bird, or a bird with human attributes, is common to most world cultures. Ask students to name a similar representation in American culture. (Suggested answer: the American bald eagle)

284 *Poetry*

Gold ear spools inlaid with turquoise, Mochica, Peru.

Have a student read aloud the epigraph by Octavio Paz that appears on this page. Mention that Paz—winner of the 1990 Nobel Prize for Literature—is a Mexican poet whose work appears in the upcoming unit. Explain that Paz is using figurative language, language not meant to be taken literally, when he speaks of giving "eyes to mankind." Ask what Paz really means by this statement. (Poetry helps us all see the world more clearly and understand and appreciate it better.) Elicit that Paz's concise, figurative way of expressing this idea is more poetic, and also more powerful, than a direct statement would be. Then ask students whether they agree with Paz, and have them explain their opinions.

Note that from ancient to modern times, virtually every civilization has shown the need to express itself in poetry and song. The upcoming unit presents over forty poems by many of the world's greatest poets, both ancient and modern. The unit is divided into five thematic groupings:

- Poems About Love
- Poems About Nature
- Poems of Delight
- Poems of Sorrow
- Poems About Values and Ideals

Within these groups there is, nevertheless, great diversity of subject matter: The Poems About Love, for instance, treat not only romantic love but parental love, love of heritage, and love of homeland.

Point out that throughout the unit poems especially worthy of comparison are presented in pairs, with the study aids following each pair. When poems are so grouped, the study aids include a feature called Comparing Poems. To illustrate this arrangement, have students examine the first two paired poems, presented on pages 286–289.

POETRY

T*he mission of poetry is to give eyes to mankind....*
—OCTAVIO PAZ
Mexico

POEMS ABOUT LOVE

POEMS ABOUT NATURE

POEMS OF DELIGHT

POEMS OF SORROW

POEMS ABOUT VALUES AND IDEALS

Also note that the Poetry unit is the only unit in this anthology that does not include the Geography and Culture feature, since the content of a poem generally does not warrant the lengthier background that this feature provides. Instead, any necessary geographical or cultural information is included in footnotes or in the author biography that precedes each poem. Author biographies are, as usual, accompanied by a small world map that pinpoints the location of the author's homeland.

Finally, note that the unit includes three special features, on sonnets, haiku, and translation. You may wish to teach the Special Feature on Translation (pp. 340–343) in conjunction with the essay on Reading Literature in Translation (pp. xxvi–xxvii).

Tu Fu

(712–770) *China*

One of China's greatest poets, Tu Fu lived during the Tang dynasty (618–907), a period noted for its high cultural achievements, when poetry and art flourished. Through his mother Tu Fu was related to China's emperors; on his father's side he was descended from high-ranking officials at court. Politically ambitious himself, Tu Fu wrote many poems in praise of the emperor's greatness. The following poem, however, reflects a more personal side to royal authority.

Tu Fu

The Emperor

Translated from the Chinese by E. Powys Mathers

On a throne of new gold the Son of the Sky is sitting among his Mandarins.[1] He shines with jewels and is like a sun surrounded by stars.

The Mandarins speak gravely of grave things; but the Emperor's thought has flown out by the open window.

In her pavilion of porcelain the Empress is sitting among her women. She is like a bright flower among leaves.

She dreams that her beloved stays too long at council, and wearily she moves her fan.

A breathing of perfumed air kisses the face of the Emperor.

"My beloved moves her fan, and sends me a perfume from her lips."

Towards the pavilion of porcelain walks the Emperor, shining with his jewels; and leaves his grave Mandarins to look at each other in silence.

---

1. **the Son of the Sky . . . Mandarins:** the emperor of China is sitting among his high-ranking officials and advisers.

Detail from a Chinese painting, colors on silk, Ming dynasty (1368-1644).

TEACHING NARRATIVE POEMS

Have students identify the stanzas that correspond to the six elements of a typical plot—exposition and narrative hook (first and second stanzas), rising action (third through fifth), climax (sixth), falling action and resolution (seventh).

TEACHING SIMILES

Have students find the two similes used to describe the Emperor and Empress. ("He . . . is like a sun / surrounded by stars," ll. 2–3; "She is like a bright flower among leaves," l. 7.) In what way are these similes comparable? (They compare the couple to natural elements—sky and earth.)

CULTURAL BACKGROUND

The ancient Chinese believed that the imperial couple were divine manifestations of the yin and yang—the two opposing but complementary principles of the universe that embody female and male, dark and light, earth and sky. In his depiction of the love that unites the Emperor and Empress, Tu Fu draws on this cultural belief in the perfect harmony of the yin and yang.

COLLABORATIVE LEARNING: ENRICHMENT ACTIVITY

Social Studies Have students work in groups to find out more about the Tang dynasty. Assign each student an aspect of society to research—for example, the role of the imperial family, peasant life, art, music, or architecture.

ART AND LITERATURE

In the late Ming dynasty (1368–1644) Chinese painters called literati painted in a poetic, "spilled-ink" style. Most academic painters combined calligraphy—a pictographic form of writing—with painting and chose not to emphasize great detail. Figures depicted by literati generally contemplated something, as does the woman reading in this detail.
■ Ask students what simile in the third stanza might describe the woman depicted here. ("She is like a bright flower among leaves.")

The Emperor **T-287**

The sight of a woman distracts the speaker from a conversation about world affairs. Though he hears the men warn of war, he wishes he were young again and embracing the girl.

LITERARY SKILLS FOR THIS SELECTION

- lyric poetry
- speaker

THEMES IN THIS SELECTION

- love in relation to public matters
- youth and aging

LESSON OBJECTIVES

1. to recognize a lyric poem
2. to compare two poems

Teacher's Classroom Resources 2

Teaching Notes	123
Literary Focus: Types of Poetry	125
Selection Test	126

IN THE CLASSROOM

TEACHING STUDENTS OF DIFFERENT ABILITIES

- **For less advanced students:** Help students imagine the poem's setting (perhaps a party, where the speaker might see the girl in a crowd).
- **For more advanced students:** Have students provide an overview of world affairs at the time Yeats wrote this poem: 1938, just before the outbreak of World War II.

MOTIVATION: PRIOR KNOWLEDGE

Ask students to recall their feelings when they heard news of a world crisis. How might an older person's feelings differ?

TEACHING LYRIC POEMS

What intense emotion does this lyric poem convey? (nostalgia for youth and passion)

TEACHING THE SPEAKER

The speaker of a lyric poem may be someone other than the poet. Why might a reader reasonably assume, however, that the speaker in "Politics" is Yeats himself?

William Butler Yeats

(1865–1939) *Ireland*

Regarded as Ireland's greatest poet, William Butler Yeats [yāts] was born near Dublin when Ireland was still part of Great Britain. A supporter of Irish cultural independence, Yeats revived interest in ancient Irish myths and legends and helped found Dublin's Abbey Theatre. He was also Ireland's first writer to win the Nobel Prize. "Politics" was written late in Yeats's life, when Europeans turned their attention to the rise of fascism in Germany, Spain, and Italy and the possibility of a second world war.

Woman with Red Hair, 1917, Amedeo Modigliani.

288 *Poetry*

William Butler Yeats

Politics

In our time the destiny of man presents its meaning in political terms.

—THOMAS MANN[1]

How can I, that girl standing there,
My attention fix
On Roman[2] or on Russian
Or on Spanish politics?
5 Yet here's a traveled man that knows
What he talks about,
And there's a politician
That has read and thought,
And maybe what they say is true
10 Of war and war's alarms,
But O that I were young again
And held her in my arms!

---

1. **Thomas Mann** (1875–1955): German writer who left his homeland when the Nazis came to power in the 1930s. (See the Short Story unit.)
2. **Roman:** that is, Italian. Rome is the capital of Italy.

(Yeats was old when he wrote this poem and had been active in Irish politics.)

ART AND LITERATURE

The Italian artist Amedeo Modigliani (1884–1920) went to Paris in 1906 to become a sculptor but by 1915 had become a painter. Still, the hard lines and stony, gazing faces of his sitters, such as the *Woman with Red Hair,* retained the volume and weight of stone carving.

- Ask students what feelings this lyrical portrait conveys. (wistfulness, sadness, tranquillity)

STUDY QUESTIONS

The Emperor (Tu Fu)
Recalling
1. Where is the Emperor at the start of the poem? As his Mandarins speak "gravely of grave things," where do his thoughts stray?
2. Where is the Empress? As she fans herself, what does the perfume do, according to the poem?
3. What does the Emperor realize in the next-to-last sentence? What does he do?

Interpreting
4. What sort of matters are the Mandarins most likely discussing? In contrast, what matter is of most concern to the Emperor?
5. How do the Emperor and Empress feel about each other? Do the details suggest that their minds are closely attuned? Explain.
6. What do you think the poem suggests about the power of love?

Extending
7. Describe a situation in which, like the Emperor, you did not listen to others talk "gravely of grave things." What caused your thoughts to stray?

Politics (Yeats)
Recalling
1. What makes the speaker unable to fix his attention on Italian, Russian, or Spanish politics?
2. What does the speaker realize about the remarks of the traveled man and the politician?
3. What wish does the speaker express in the last two lines?

Interpreting
4. Why does the speaker sound regretful?
5. What does the poem suggest about a person's age and thoughts of love?
6. What response does the poem make to the Thomas Mann quotation, which focuses on the importance of politics?

Extending
7. Do people's concerns usually change as they grow older? Explain.

LITERARY FOCUS

Types of Poetry
Poetry is often divided into three categories. **Narrative poems** tell stories in verse. Some narrative poems concentrate on relating the main events of the plot; others provide extensive details of plot, setting, and character. **Lyric poems** express a speaker's personal thoughts and feelings. Most lyric poems are short and are marked by intense emotion and musical language. **Dramatic poems,** like plays, present characters speaking to themselves, to each other, or to the reader.

The three categories of poetry sometimes overlap, so identifying a particular poem by category will depend on what you feel is the poet's main purpose. When classifying a poem, ask yourself if the main purpose is to tell a story (narrative), to express private feelings (lyric), or to reveal character through speech (dramatic).

Thinking About Types of Poetry
■ Into which of the three categories would you place "Politics," and why?

Narrative Poetry
A **narrative poem** tells a story in verse. Like a prose story, it has one or more characters and a plot that centers around a conflict, or struggle. Because poetry is more concentrated than prose, a narrative poem may not follow the recognizable plot structure that we usually see in prose stories. The narrative poem may instead focus only on the most meaningful parts of the story and may make jumps of time, space, and logic that we would find difficult in prose fiction.

Thinking About Narrative Poetry
■ Retell the story presented in "The Emperor." Who is the main character, what conflict does he or she face, and how is it resolved?

COMPARING POEMS
■ What is similar about the conflict in Tu Fu's poem and the speaker's feelings in "Politics"? What is different about the Emperor's actions and decisions and those of the speaker in "Politics"?

The Emperor; Politics **289**

ANSWERS

STUDY QUESTIONS

The Emperor
1. He is on a gold throne among his Mandarins. They stray "out by the open window."
2. She is in a porcelain pavilion. It wafts through the air and "kisses" the Emperor's face.
3. The Empress has sent him "a perfume from her lips." He walks toward her pavilion.
4. political or military matters; his wife
5. They love each other. Her dreaming of his activities and his sensing of her perfume suggest that their minds are closely attuned.
6. Sometimes a steadying, sometimes a driving force in human behavior, love may overpower social concerns.
7. Answers will vary. Many students may mention a classroom situation. Causes may include spring fever, boredom, and so on.

Politics
1. a girl standing nearby
2. They may be true.
3. He wishes to be young again and hold the girl in his arms.
4. He cannot regain youth and youthful passion.
5. Thoughts of love can occur at any age.
6. Yeats seems to contradict Mann by implying that "the destiny of man" is linked not to politics but to the desire for love, a more potent force.
7. Answers will vary. Though many students may say that concerns change, some may note that certain concerns, such as the desire for love, seem never to change.

LITERARY FOCUS

Types of Poetry
"Politics" is a lyric poem: Its main purpose is to express the speaker's private feelings.

Narrative Poetry
The Emperor sits with counselors, who discuss grave matters; he thinks of his wife, who is longing for him. When she fans herself, her perfume reaches him, and he leaves his advisers to join her. The Emperor is the main character; he is torn between duty and love; he chooses love.

COMPARING POEMS
Both men are distracted from politics by thoughts of love. The Emperor can fulfill his wish for love, but Yeats's speaker can only wish that he were young enough to do so.

Sappho

(c. 612–580 B.C.) *Ancient Greece*

Sappho [saf′ō] lived in ancient times on one of the many Greek-speaking islands east of mainland Greece. Of noble birth herself, she gathered around her a group of young noblewomen whom she instructed in cultural and social values. Little else is known of her life, except that she had a daughter and three brothers whom she often addressed in her poems. Though only fragments of her work have survived, Sappho's intense, controlled verses have earned her a place as one of the world's greatest poets.

Girl with Pigeons, grave relief from Island of Paros, c. 455–450 B.C.

290   *Poetry*

Sappho

Fragment of a Lullaby

Translated from the Greek
by Mary Barnard

Sleep, darling

I have a small
daughter called
Cleis,[1] who is

5 like a golden
flower
    I wouldn't
take all Croesus'[2]
kingdom with love
10 thrown in, for her

———

1. **Cleis** [klā′ēs]
2. **Croesus'** [krē′səs]: referring to an ancient king famous for his great wealth.

Gabriela Mistral

(1889–1957) *Chile*

Gabriela Mistral [mēs träl'] was the first Latin American writer to be awarded the Nobel Prize for Literature (1945). Born Lucila Godoy Alcayaga in Vicuña, Chile, she worked as a schoolteacher and later represented her nation in educational conferences and diplomatic missions overseas. She took her pen name from the angel Gabriel and the cold "mistral" wind that periodically blows across southern France. Her four volumes of poetry reflect her religious faith and her love for nature and children.

Gabriela Mistral

Rocking

Translated from the Spanish
by Doris Dana

The sea rocks her thousands of waves.
The sea is divine.
Hearing the loving sea
I rock my son.

5 The wind wandering by night
rocks the wheat.
Hearing the loving wind
I rock my son.

God, the Father, soundlessly rocks
10 His thousands of worlds.
Feeling His hand in the shadow
I rock my son.

Rocking **291**

Of Sappho's and Mistral's poems, which would you pick to rock *you* to sleep? Why?

ANSWERS

STUDY QUESTIONS

Fragment of a Lullaby
1. "a golden flower"
2. "all Croesus' kingdom with love thrown in"
3. She is devoted to her; an infant: she is "small."
4. line 1; A lullaby is meant to ease someone into sleep.
5. Cleis is more precious than material wealth.
6. Possible answers: slow tempo, low volume, rocking rhythm, simple words

Rocking
1. She is rocking her son.
2. sea rocking waves, wind rocking wheat, God rocking worlds
3. Parental love imitates the patterns of nature.
4. Parental love imitates divine love.
5. Yes; it has parallel structure and shows a logical development of imagery.
6. Possible answers: waving branches, sound of crickets

LITERARY FOCUS

1. parental love
2. repetition, parallel structure of stanzas, simple language; musicality, loving words, repetition

LANGUAGE STUDY

1. "place of learning"; from the grove of Akademos
2. "huge"; from *Kolossos*, the name of a gigantic statue
3. "harsh"; relating to the law code attributed to Draco
4. "complex problem"; legendary knot of King Gordius
5. "place of learning"; name of grove where Aristotle taught
6. "foot race"; after the legendary Marathon-to-Athens run
7. "victory at great cost"; after victories by King Pyrrhus
8. "take final action"; after a river Caesar crossed
9. "severe"; after Sparta, a city-state known for its discipline
10. "relating to drama"; after Thespis, founder of Greek drama

COMPARING POEMS

Both lull a child. Sappho describes maternal love; Mistral connects parenthood, nature, and God.

STUDY QUESTIONS

Fragment of a Lullaby (Sappho)
Recalling
1. To what does the speaker compare her daughter?
2. What would the speaker not take in exchange for her daughter?

Interpreting
3. What is the speaker's attitude toward her daughter? About how old would you say the daughter is? Explain.
4. Which line reflects the specific purpose for which this lyric was composed or sung? Explain.
5. What do lines 7–10 suggest about the speaker's feelings for her daughter?

Extending
6. What poetic qualities do you think make a lullaby effective?

Rocking (Mistral)
Recalling
1. What is the speaker doing?
2. What three things does the speaker associate with her own actions?

Interpreting
3. What relationship does the poem suggest between parenthood and nature?
4. What relationship does the poem suggest between parenthood and one's religious faith?
5. Though the poem is simply worded, is it also carefully constructed? Cite details to support your answer.

Extending
6. What other images of nature do you think would convey the peace and serenity of a lullaby?

LITERARY FOCUS

Lyric Poetry
A **lyric poem** is a brief, often musical expression of the speaker's emotion. During the Lyric Age of ancient Greek literature (about 700 B.C. to 500 B.C.), poets sang of private feelings and accompanied themselves on stringed instruments called *lyres,* from which the word *lyric* comes. Although most poets no longer sing their poems, we still label as *lyric* any poem that is at heart an expression of feeling. We also use the term *lyrics* to apply to the words of songs.

Thinking About Lyric Poetry
1. What emotion lies at the heart of both Sappho's lyric and Mistral's poem?
2. What makes Mistral's poem musical? Would it make a good musical lullaby? Why or why not?

LANGUAGE STUDY

Terms from Ancient History
The name *Croesus,* the wealthy king referred to in Sappho's poem, is still used today in the common expression "as rich as Croesus." Many other English words and expressions have their origins in the people, places, and events of ancient history.

Use a dictionary to determine the meanings and origins of these words and expressions.

1. academy
2. colossal
3. Draconian
4. Gordian knot
5. lyceum
6. marathon
7. Pyrrhic victory
8. cross the Rubicon
9. Spartan
10. thespian

COMPOSITION

Writing a Lullaby
■ Write a brief lyric poem that could be used as a soothing lullaby. If you like, you may also set your poem to music.

COMPARING POEMS

■ What is similar about the speakers' situations in "Fragment of a Lullaby" and "Rocking"? What is different about the comparisons they make to express their feelings?

COMPOSITION: GUIDELINES FOR EVALUATION

WRITING A LULLABY

Objective
To write a lyric poem that could be used as a lullaby

Guidelines for Evaluation
■ suggested length: two to four stanzas
■ should show tender feelings
■ should have a soothing tone

Lady Ōtomo

(eighth century) *Japan*

Lady Ōtomo came from a family that was influential in both Japanese politics and literature. Her daughter, her nephew, and her brother Tabito were all noted poets; Tabito was also a governor and councilor of state. Lady Ōtomo spent much of her life traveling with her brother from place to place to assist in his official duties. Many of her poems describe her homesickness for family members; others are brief but intense romantic love poems.

Lady Ōtomo

My Heart, Thinking

Translated from the Japanese
by Arthur Waley

My heart, thinking
"How beautiful he is"
Is like a swift river
    which though one dams it
      and dams it
5 Will still break through.

Woodblock print
by Suzuki Harunobu (1725–1770).

LESSON PREVIEW

The speaker, thinking of her beloved's beauty, compares her heart to a dammed river that will break through any restraint.

LITERARY SKILLS FOR THIS SELECTION

- speaker
- simile

THEMES IN THIS SELECTION

- irrepressible love
- physical beauty

LESSON OBJECTIVES

1. to appreciate a poem's speaker
2. to write a poem with an invented speaker
3. to compare two poems

Teacher's Classroom Resources 2

- Teaching Notes   133
- Literary Focus: Speaker   134
- Writing Process Guide: Writing a Poem with an Invented Speaker   136
- Selection Test   137

IN THE CLASSROOM

TEACHING STUDENTS OF DIFFERENT ABILITIES

- **For less advanced students:** Encourage students to identify the essential way in which a river and a heart are different as well as the ways in which they may be seen as similar.
- **For more advanced students:** Have students create as many similes as they can that compare a strong emotion to a force of nature, such as "My anger whirls like a cyclone."

MOTIVATION: PRIOR KNOWLEDGE

Have students make associations between emotions such as sadness, joy, and fear and aspects of nature. For instance, they might compare fear with trembling leaves.

TEACHING THE SPEAKER

Ask students to describe the speaker's internal conflict. (Although she tries to "dam" up her love, it conquers her desire to control or hide her feelings.)

TEACHING FIGURES OF SPEECH

Point out that the simile in this poem achieves the opposite effect of personification: Instead of humanizing nature, it compares human emotions to natural forces.

ART AND LITERATURE

The Japanese woodblock artist Suzuki Harunobu specialized in portraying naturalistically drawn female figures often placed in architectural settings.

- Ask students what image in the print recalls the simile in the poem. (the river)

The speaker compares his beloved's face to the sun. Like the sunrise the first appearance of her face brings color to his world. He fears, however, the end of their love.

LITERARY SKILLS FOR THIS SELECTION

- speaker
- extended metaphor

THEMES IN THIS SELECTION

- the transience of love
- the emotional effects of love

LESSON OBJECTIVES

1. to appreciate a poem's speaker
2. to write about a poem's speaker
3. to write a poem with an invented speaker
4. to compare two poems

Teacher's Classroom Resources 2

- Teaching Notes   133
- Literary Focus:
  Speaker   134
- Writing Process Guides:
  Writing About a Poem's
  Speaker   135
  Writing a Poem with an
  Invented Speaker   136
- Selection Test   137

IN THE CLASSROOM

TEACHING STUDENTS OF DIFFERENT ABILITIES

- **For less advanced students:** Be sure students understand the implications of the central metaphor: Like the sun the beloved temporarily fills the speaker's world with light.
- **For more advanced students:** Encourage students to think of all the implications of the poem's title.

MOTIVATION: PRIOR KNOWLEDGE

Encourage students to think about the feelings that might accompany changes in a friendship or romantic relationship.

IN THE GLOSSARY

- slipshod: careless

Yevgeny Yevtushenko

(born 1933) *Soviet Union*

Yevgeny Yevtushenko [yev gen′ē̄ yev′tōō shen′kō] is among the most acclaimed poets of the contemporary Soviet Union. A graduate of the Gorki Literary Institute in Moscow, Yevtushenko won fame in his homeland when he published his poetry volume *Third Snow* in 1955. His reputation broadened as he began giving dramatic poetry recitals in Europe, Africa, and America. In much of his poetry—like his noted poems "Talk" and "Babi Yar"—he protested Soviet policies and practices. Yevtushenko is also known for his simple, moving love poems.

Yevgeny Yevtushenko

Colors

Translated from the Russian
by Robin Milner-Gulland and Peter Levi

When your face
appeared over my crumpled life
at first I understood
only the poverty of what I have.
5 Then its particular light
on woods, on rivers, on the sea,
became my beginning in the colored world
in which I had not yet had my beginning.
I am so frightened, I am so frightened,
10 of the unexpected sunrise finishing,
of revelations
and tears and the excitement finishing.
I don't fight it, my love is this fear,
I nourish it who can nourish nothing,
15 love's slipshod watchman.
Fear hems me in.
I am conscious that these minutes are short
and that the colors in my eyes will vanish
when your face sets.

TEACHING THE SPEAKER

Yevtushenko's speaker presents a personal view of the connection between love and fear. Point out that he sees his own life and the world as vivid realities ("revelations / and tears," ll. 11–12) and potentially harsh ones ("crumpled life," "colors . . . will vanish," ll. 2 and 18).

TEACHING EXTENDED METAPHORS

Have students identify the first instance of the beloved's face being compared to the sun. (ll. 1–2) What other lines in the poem extend this metaphor? (ll. 5–7, 10, and 17–19)

STUDY QUESTIONS

My Heart, Thinking (Ōtomo)
Recalling
1. What does the speaker say her heart is thinking?
2. With what does the speaker compare her heart?

Interpreting
3. Describe the speaker's feelings for the man to whom she refers.
4. What do lines 3–5 suggest about the speaker's ability or desire to control her feelings?

Extending
5. To what aspect of nature would you compare loving feelings? Uncontrollable feelings?

Colors (Yevtushenko)
Recalling
1. According to the opening lines, what did the speaker understand when his beloved's face first appeared? Then what happened?
2. What frightens the speaker? What does he nourish?
3. Of what is the speaker conscious in the last three lines?

Interpreting
4. To what aspect of nature is the speaker comparing his beloved? What does the comparison suggest that his beloved has done for his life?
5. Explain in your own words what the speaker fears and why he does not fight that fear.
6. What does the poem suggest about the ability of romantic love to endure?

Extending
7. How might romantic love change a person's life? How might romantic love evolve into something lasting?

LITERARY FOCUS

Speaker

Every poem has a **speaker,** the voice that addresses us in the poem. Sometimes the speaker is the poet, who may speak in order to share a current experience or a special memory. Sometimes poets invent speakers very different from themselves in order to explore new ways of looking at life. Such speakers may or may not share the poets' feelings. The speaker of a poem may even be an animal or an object that momentarily springs to life and tells us what the poet imagines such an animal or object would say.

One of the first things we should do when we read a poem is identify the speaker and decide what he, she, or it is like. Understanding who or what the speaker is can help us understand the poem's meaning more fully.

Thinking About the Speaker
■ What sort of person is the speaker in "My Heart, Thinking"? What sort of person is the speaker in "Colors"?

COMPOSITION

Writing About a Poem's Speaker
■ Write a brief composition about the speaker in "Colors." Citing examples from the poem, discuss the speaker's experiences and attitudes toward life and love. Also discuss the comparisons he makes to express his feelings.

Writing a Poem with an Invented Speaker
■ Write a brief poem in which the speaker is an animal, an object, or a person other than yourself. Express a strong emotion or opinion that you imagine this speaker would express. Remember that the emotion or opinion expressed by the speaker need not be the same as your own.

COMPARING POEMS

■ What is similar about the situations and attitudes of the speakers in "My Heart, Thinking" and "Colors"? What is different about their situations and attitudes? What sort of comparisons do both speakers make to express their feelings?

My Heart, Thinking; Colors **295**

COMPOSITION: GUIDELINES FOR EVALUATION

WRITING ABOUT A POEM'S SPEAKER

Objective

To analyze a speaker's experiences and attitudes

Guidelines for Evaluation
■ suggested length: two or three paragraphs
■ should describe the speaker's attitude toward love
■ should interpret who the speaker is

WRITING A POEM WITH AN INVENTED SPEAKER

Objective

To write a poem from a different point of view

Guidelines for Evaluation
■ suggested length: six or more lines
■ should express a strong emotion or opinion
■ should use a voice other than the student's

Léopold S. Senghor

(born 1906) *Senegal*

Poet and statesman Léopold Sédar Senghor grew up in the West African nation of Senegal [sen′ə gôl′]. Before Senegal achieved its independence from France, Senghor represented his homeland in the French Assembly. Later he became Senegal's president, working for unity as his nation made the transition from colonial to independent rule. Many of Senghor's poems were written for musical accompaniment. Virtually all of his verse, like the speaker of the upcoming poem, is "steeped . . . in the presence of Africa."

Léopold S. Senghor

And We Shall Be Steeped

Translated from the French by John Reed and Clive Wake

For khalam[1]

And we shall be steeped my dear in the presence of Africa.
Furniture from Guinea and Congo,[2] heavy and polished, somber and serene.
On the walls, pure primordial[3] masks distant and yet present.
Stools of honor for hereditary guests, for the Princes of the High Lands.
5 Wild perfumes, thick mats of silence
Cushions of shade and leisure, the noise of a wellspring of peace.
Classic words. In a distance, antiphonal[4] singing like Sudanese cloths[5]
And then, friendly lamp, your kindness to soothe this obsessive presence
White black and red, oh red as the African soil.

---

1. **khalam** [кнä′läm]: four-stringed African guitar.
2. **Guinea** [gin′ē] **and Congo:** African nations that are the sites of great kingdoms of the past.
3. **primordial** [prī môr′dē əl]: existing from the beginning; ancient.
4. **antiphonal** [an tif′ən əl]: alternately sung and chanted.
5. **Sudanese cloths:** fine, hand-woven, traditional fabrics from Sudan, historical region and present-day nation in northern Africa.

296 *Poetry*

A Baule mask, Ivory Coast.

STUDY QUESTIONS

Recalling

1. In what will the speaker and his "dear" be steeped?
2. List three items that convey the presence of Africa in the poem. To what "noise" does the speaker refer in line 6?
3. What colors does the speaker say are part of Africa's "obsessive presence"?

Interpreting

4. What feelings does the speaker have toward his African heritage?
5. What do the words "primordial," "hereditary," and "classic" stress about African culture?
6. Remembering that the poet was part of his country's move to independence, what do you think the colors in the last line represent? What might the poem suggest in the contrast between the "wellspring of peace" and the red African soil?

Extending

7. What do people gain from having a strong awareness of their ethnic heritage?

LANGUAGE STUDY

Words for Musical Instruments

Different cultures have their own musical instruments on which their music is traditionally played. Senghor, for example, specifies that his poem should be sung or recited to the accompaniment of a *khalam,* or four-stringed African guitar. Ancient Greeks accompanied their lyric poems on a small harplike instrument called a *lyra,* what we now call a *lyre.*

The following musical instruments come from around the world, and their names have become part of the English language. Use a dictionary to help you describe each instrument and identify the language or languages from which its name was borrowed.

1. balalaika
2. bouzouki
3. castanets
4. koto
5. maraca
6. marimba
7. sitar
8. ukulele
9. viola

COMPOSITION

Writing About a Lyric Poem

■ In discussing this poem and others in Senghor's volume *Nocturnes,* one critic called them "love poems in which the poet expresses his dual love, first for Africa and then for the human race." Write a brief composition in which you apply this statement to "And We Shall Be Steeped." Support your ideas with examples.

Writing About Homeland or Heritage

■ Write a brief poem or personal essay that expresses your feelings about your homeland or your heritage. Like Senghor, include specific examples of cultural achievements or similar details that evoke strong feelings. If you write a poem, you may also specify the musical instrument that you would want to accompany a musical rendition of your poem.

Of all the images in Senghor's poem, which best evokes "the presence of Africa" in your mind? Why?

ANSWERS

STUDY QUESTIONS

1. "the presence of Africa"
2. Possible answers: furniture, masks, stools, perfumes, mats, cushions, classic words, singing; "a wellspring of peace"
3. white, black, and red
4. love and pride
5. It is ancient, full of tradition, and enduring.
6. Possible answers: white colonists, black natives, and the blood shed between them; Traditional African culture can form the basis of peace once the struggle for independence ends.
7. They gain pride, a sense of belonging, a spirit of community, and an appreciation of the past.

LANGUAGE STUDY

1. "three-stringed Russian guitar"
2. "Greek mandolin"
3. "wooden percussion instrument manipulated with the fingers"; from Spanish and Latin words for "chestnuts"
4. "Japanese zither"
5. "gourd-shaped rattle"; from Portuguese and native Brazilian words
6. "instrument like a xylophone with resonators beneath the bars"; from Mbundu, an African language
7. "Indian stringed instrument"
8. "small Hawaiian guitar"
9. "stringed instrument larger than a violin"; from Italian

And We Shall Be Steeped **297**

COMPOSITION: GUIDELINES FOR EVALUATION

WRITING ABOUT A LYRIC POEM

Objective

To apply a critical statement to a poem

Guidelines for Evaluation

■ suggested length: two or three paragraphs
■ should match ideas in the statement with ideas in the poem
■ should use specific examples as support

WRITING ABOUT HOMELAND OR HERITAGE

Objective

To write a poem or essay about one's heritage

Guidelines for Evaluation

■ suggested length: eight to twenty lines or three or four paragraphs
■ should express the writer's personal feelings

Anna Akhmatova

(1888–1966) *Soviet Union*

Anna Akhmatova [äкн mä′tō və] achieved great success with her poetry and was an inspiration to Soviet poets who followed her. Born Anna Gorenko in Odessa, Russia, Akhmatova assumed her grandmother's name when she began publishing poetry in her early twenties. After several early volumes Akhmatova published nothing for twenty years. At the start of World War II, she resumed writing and regained her popularity with poems about life, love, and politics. In the following poem she gives her personal response to the biblical story of Lot's wife (Genesis 19:1–26).

Anna Akhmatova

Lot's Wife

Translated from the Russian by Richard Wilbur

The just man[1] followed then his angel guide
Where he strode on the black highway, hulking and bright;
But a wild grief in his wife's bosom cried,
Look back, it is not too late for a last sight

5 *Of the red towers of your native Sodom, the square
Where once you sang, the gardens you shall mourn,
And the tall house with empty windows where
You loved your husband and your babes were born.*

She turned, and looking on the bitter view
10 Her eyes were welded shut by mortal pain;
Into transparent salt her body grew,[2]
And her quick feet were rooted in the plain.

Who would waste tears upon her? Is she not
The least of our losses, this unhappy wife?
15 Yet in my heart she will not be forgot
Who, for a single glance, gave up her life.

---

1. **The just man:** Lot. In the Bible angels warned Lot to remove his family from the sinful city of Sodom and not to look back as God destroyed it.
2. **Into...salt her body grew:** According to the Bible, Lot's wife was changed into a pillar of salt when she disobediently looked back at Sodom.

298 *Poetry*

TEACHING RHYME AND STANZA FORM

Have the poem read aloud so that students can hear the rhymes that form an *abab-cdcd-efef-ghgh* pattern. Point out that most of the stanzas are self-contained units of thought held together by the rhyme scheme. (The one exception, l. 4, seems to create a bridge to the second stanza.)

TEACHING ASSONANCE

As the poem is read aloud, point out the repetition of certain vowel sounds, especially the long *i* in lines 2 and 3. Help students see that such echoes help tie the poem together.

STUDY QUESTIONS

Recalling

1. Summarize the thought that possesses Lot's wife in lines 4–8.
2. What happens to Lot's wife when she looks back at Sodom?
3. According to the last line, what was the reason Lot's wife gave up her life?

Interpreting

4. Though Sodom is famous for being a wicked city, how does Lot's wife think of it? Why does she look back?
5. Is Lot's wife destroyed by something besides God's punishment? What does the phrase "mortal pain" suggest?
6. What other human experiences might be associated with the feelings expressed by Lot's wife?
7. How does the speaker or narrator view Lot's wife's experiences? Would you classify this as a lyric or narrative poem? Explain your answer.

Extending

8. Can grief be a destructive experience? Discuss.

LITERARY FOCUS

Rhyme and Rhyme Scheme

Words **rhyme** when they repeat the same stressed vowel sounds and any sounds that come after the stressed vowel sounds. For example, the words *guide* and *cried* rhyme, as do *tea* and *key, elect* and *checked,* and *region* and *legion.* Poems often use **end rhymes,** rhymed words which occur at the ends of lines. The pattern of rhymes formed by end rhymes is called the **rhyme scheme** of the poem. To show a poem's rhyme scheme, we assign a different letter of the alphabet to each new rhyming sound. The rhyme scheme of the first four lines of "Lot's Wife" is *abab:*

The just man followed then his angel **guide**	a
Where he strode on the black highway, hulking and **bright;**	b
But a wild grief in his wife's bosom **cried,**	a
Look back, it is not too late for a last **sight**	b

In translating a rhymed poem, translators often have difficulty in maintaining the rhyme scheme and still retaining the original meaning. Richard Wilbur, one of America's finest translators and a talented poet in his own right, has done a masterful job of translating Akhmatova's poem.

Thinking About Rhyme Scheme

■ Examine the rest of the end rhymes in Wilbur's translation. Then, on a separate sheet of paper, indicate the poem's complete rhyme scheme.

Stanza Form

A **stanza** is a group of lines forming a unit in a poem. For example, "Lot's Wife" has four stanzas. Common types of stanzas include the **couplet,** or two-line stanza; the **quatrain,** or four-line stanza; the **sestet,** or six-line stanza; and the **octave,** or eight-line stanza. The four stanzas in "Lot's Wife" are all quatrains.

Though most poems have spaces between stanzas, some do not. In such cases you can usually identify each stanza by each new group of end rhymes. Even if "Lot's Wife" had no spaces between stanzas, the end rhymes *abab* would mark the first stanza, *cdcd* would mark the next, and so on.

The division of stanzas within a poem is usually based not only on rhyme but also on content. In other words, like a new paragraph in prose, a new stanza usually introduces a new idea or thought.

Thinking About Stanza Form

■ Examine the four quatrains of "Lot's Wife." What would you identify as the main idea of each?

COMPOSITION

Reacting to a Poem

■ Were you moved by "Lot's Wife"? Did it provide you with an effective or interesting new perspective on the biblical story? Describe your reactions in a brief composition. Include specific details from the poem to support the general statements that you make about it.

Writing a Diary Entry

■ Imagine that you are Lot on the day the events of the poem take place. Write a diary entry in which you describe what happened and express your feelings about the events.

Lot's Wife **299**

ANSWERS

STUDY QUESTIONS

1. She wants "a last sight" of Sodom.
2. Her eyes are welded shut; her body is turned to salt; her feet are rooted to the ground.
3. She gave up her life "for a single glance."
4. It is home, where she enjoyed life and loved her family. She grieves for the place where she was happy.
5. She is also destroyed by the very human pain of seeing her home and way of life ended. This is her "mortal pain."
6. Possible answers: emigration, divorce, loss of a loved one, or loss of one's home through natural disaster or war
7. The speaker is moved by her unforgettable, tragic fate. The poem is primarily narrative, but it also contains lyric elements. It tells a story, but it also expresses the speaker's feelings.
8. Answers will vary. Grief is a necessary step in overcoming a loss; it becomes destructive when it prevents a person from getting on with life.

LITERARY FOCUS

Rhyme and Rhyme Scheme
abab cdcd efef ghgh

Stanza Form

First stanza—Lot and his wife leave Sodom, but her grief cries for her to look back; second stanza—she recalls her former happiness; third stanza—she looks back and is destroyed; fourth stanza—the speaker reacts to her fate.

COMPOSITION: GUIDELINES FOR EVALUATION

REACTING TO A POEM

Objective

To describe personal reactions to a poem

Guidelines for Evaluation

■ suggested length: two or three paragraphs
■ should explain the writer's response to the poem
■ should analyze specific reasons for the response
■ should identify insights gained

WRITING A DIARY ENTRY

Objective

To write an imaginary diary entry

Guidelines for Evaluation

■ suggested length: 150–300 words
■ should assume Lot's point of view
■ should express Lot's feelings about the events

Petrarch

(1304–1374) *Italy*

Francesco Petrarca, better known as Petrarch [pēˈträrk], is often called the founder of the Renaissance, the rebirth of European art, literature, and learning after the Middle Ages. The son of an exile from Florence, Italy, Petrarch spent his early years in France and later traveled throughout Europe as a diplomat. A scholar of ancient Greek and Latin, he wrote some of his earliest works in those languages. His Italian poems, which include Sonnet 3 below, are dominated by the figure of Laura, the object and image of Petrarch's poetic, ideal love.

Petrarch

Sonnet 3

Translated from the Italian by Anthony Mortimer

It was that very day on which the sun
in awe of his creator dimmed the ray,
when I was captured, with my guard astray,
for your fine eyes, my lady, bound me then.

5　It hardly seemed the time for me to plan
defense against Love's stroke; I went my way
secure, unwary; so upon that day
of general sorrow all my pains began.

Love found me with no armor for the fight,
10　my eyes an open highway to the heart,
eyes that are now a vent for tears to flow.

And yet he[1] played no honorable part,
wounding me with his shaft in such a state;
he saw you armed and dared not lift the bow.[2]

---

1. **he:** referring here to Love, who is often portrayed as an archer whose arrows pierce the heart and cause humans to fall in love.
2. **dared not lift the bow:** that is, dared not shoot his arrows at you as he did at me.

300　*Poetry*

William Shakespeare

(1564–1616) *England*

Usually named as England's greatest writer, William Shakespeare is best known for his brilliant plays. However, even if he had never written a play, Shakespeare would have been famous for his lyric and narrative poetry. Shakespeare first won attention as a poet with *Venus and Adonis,* a long narrative poem published in 1593. Over the next years he produced a series of lyric poems now considered the finest sonnets in the English language. In these he wrote about friendship, time, and, as exemplified in Sonnet 29, about love.

William Shakespeare

Sonnet 29

When, in disgrace[1] with Fortune and men's eyes,
I all alone beweep my outcast state,
And trouble deaf heaven with my bootless[2] cries,
And look upon myself and curse my fate,
5 Wishing me like to one more rich in hope,
Featured like him, like him with friends possessed,
Desiring this man's art[3] and that man's scope,[4]
With what I most enjoy contented least;
Yet in these thoughts myself almost despising,
10 Haply[5] I think on thee, and then my state,
Like to the lark at break of day arising
From sullen earth, sings hymns at heaven's gate;
    For thy sweet love remembered such wealth brings,
    That then I scorn to change my state with kings.

---

1. **disgrace:** disfavor.
2. **bootless:** useless; futile.
3. **art:** here, skill.
4. **scope:** mental power.
5. **Haply:** by chance.

Portrait of a Youth, c. 1485, Filippino Lippi.

Sonnet 29 **301**

LESSON PREVIEW

When the speaker is forsaken by fortune and society and is jealous of others, he thinks of his beloved, and his mood brightens.

LITERARY SKILLS FOR THIS SELECTION

- slant rhyme
- Shakespearean sonnet

THEMES IN THIS SELECTION

- the restorative power of love
- depression versus love

LESSON OBJECTIVES

1. to analyze a poem's rhymes
2. to recognize the structure of sonnets
3. to contrast Shakespearean and Modern English
4. to write about a sonnet
5. to write letters
6. to compare two poems

Teacher's Classroom Resources 2

- Teaching Notes   151
- Reading Guide   152
- Literary Focus: Slant Rhyme; The Shakespearean Sonnet   153
- Language Study: Shakespearean English   154
- Writing Process Guides: Writing About a Sonnet   155
  Writing Letters Requesting and Giving Advice   156
- Selection Test   157

IN THE CLASSROOM

TEACHING STUDENTS OF DIFFERENT ABILITIES

- **For less advanced students:** Point out that the poem is a single sentence; note its punctuation and structure.

- **For more advanced students:** Have students search anthologies for sonnets by other poets.

MOTIVATION: PRIOR KNOWLEDGE

Ask volunteers what they do to break out of a gloomy mood.

TEACHING SLANT RHYME

Some slant rhymes in Shakespeare's sonnets result from changes in the pronunciation of English. Have students identify the slant rhyme here. (*possessed/least*)

TEACHING THE SHAKESPEAREAN SONNET

Ask where the mood shifts. (In the third quatrain the mood shifts from despair to cheerfulness.)

GRAMMAR IN LITERATURE

Point out that sentence structure and punctuation help organize the sonnet. Before the first semicolon is a list of things the speaker does in his gloomy state; before the next semicolon lines 9–12 signal his brightening mood; and lines 13–14 explain the change.

ART AND LITERATURE

With the invention of linear perspective, Italian Renaissance painters like Filippino Lippi (1457–1504) created naturalistic art.

- Ask which lines best fit the youth's mood. (ll. 1–8 or 9–12)

Sonnet 29 **T-301**

Which of these sonnets strikes you as more forcefully and convincingly imagined? Why?

ANSWERS

STUDY QUESTIONS

Sonnet 3

1. He was captured and bound by his lady's eyes. His guard was astray; he had no defense against Love's stroke.
2. He was without armor for the fight. She was armed.
3. a martial image; a battle for which he was unprepared
4. His eyes were the opening through which his lady reached his heart and won the battle. Now they are the outlet of tears, a sign of his sorrow.
5. Love brings him pain because his love is unrequited.
6. Answers will vary. Students may say that only the hardhearted can truly defend against falling in love. People may be afraid of being hurt or losing the loved one.

Sonnet 29

1. He is without luck and friends; no one hears his prayers; he curses his fate and envies others.
2. He remembers his beloved friend. He compares his feelings to the lark at daybreak.
3. remembering his friend's love and the "wealth" it brings
4. The speaker's despair changes to cheerfulness. Remembering his friend's love causes the change.
5. The phrase refers to luck or fate and society's views or opinions. It relates directly to "kings," who presumably occupy the highest position fate or society allows.
6. He values love more than anything else. Worldly success becomes less important.
7. Answers will vary. Students may say that people do yield to such emotions but can overcome them by positive thinking, talking with others, keeping busy, and so on.

STUDY QUESTIONS

Sonnet 3 (Petrarch)

Recalling

1. What happened to the speaker on the day the sun dimmed its ray? What allowed this to happen?
2. According to the last six lines, in what state did Love find the speaker? In what state did Love find the speaker's lady?

Interpreting

3. What image is conveyed in words like "captured," "defense," "armor," and "armed"? What does the speaker think love is like?
4. Contrast the two roles the speaker's eyes played. What do his eyes reveal about him now?
5. To the speaker, what does love bring? Why does he feel this way?

Extending

6. Do you think it is possible for people to defend themselves against falling in love? Why might someone want to do this?

Sonnet 29 (Shakespeare)

Recalling

1. Summarize the speaker's complaints in lines 1–8.
2. What does the speaker remember in line 10? To what does he then compare his feelings?
3. In the last two lines, what makes the speaker scorn the idea of changing places with kings?

Interpreting

4. What change in attitude occurs in this poem? What causes the change?
5. What does the speaker mean by the phrase "Fortune and men's eyes"? How does the remark in the last two lines relate back to this idea?
6. In the end, what does the speaker value the most? What becomes less important?

Extending

7. Do you think people often give in to feeling lonely and discouraged? How can people overcome such emotions?

LITERARY FOCUS

Slant Rhyme

Words **rhyme** when they repeat the same stressed vowel sounds and any sounds that come after the

stressed vowel sounds: *beak* and *seek, bat* and *sat.* When these sounds are similar, but not identical, the rhyme that is produced is called **slant rhyme** (or **approximate rhyme, near rhyme,** or **off rhyme**). In some slant rhymes the words have the same stressed vowel sounds but different consonant sounds after the vowels: *beat* and *seek.* In other slant rhymes the words have different stressed vowel sounds but the same consonant sounds after the vowels: *bat* and *sit.* Slant rhymes in which vowel sounds are repeated employ what is known as **assonance;** slant rhymes in which final consonant sounds are repeated employ **consonance.**

When translating a poem from one language into another, translators must sometimes resort to slant rhymes to maintain the rhyme scheme of the original. For example, in Petrarch's original Italian, the end rhymes in lines 1 and 4 rhyme exactly, but in Mortimer's translation they are slant rhymes: *sun* and *then.*

Thinking About Slant Rhyme

■ What other end rhymes in Mortimer's translation are slant rhymes? Where does Shakespeare use slant rhyme in his sonnet?

The Petrarchan Sonnet

A **sonnet** is a fourteen-line poem that usually follows a strict pattern of stanza divisions and end rhymes. Most sonnets are lyric poems. The world's first sonnets were composed in Italy and were meant to be sung to musical accompaniment. In fact, the word *sonnet* comes from the Italian word *sonnetto,* which means "little song." The strict pattern of the **Italian** or **Petrarchan** [pi trär′kən] **sonnet** was developed in the thirteenth century and was named for Petrarch, the most famous practitioner of the form.

The Petrarchan sonnet is divided into two stanzas, an eight-line stanza called an **octave** and a six-line stanza called a **sestet.** The octave generally has the rhyme scheme *abbaabba;* the sestet usually rhymes *cdecde, cdedce,* or *cdccdc.* In most cases the structure of the sonnet is reflected in the content of the poem. Usually the octave presents a situation, an idea, or a question, and the sestet then provides a resolution, a comment, or an answer.

Thinking About the Petrarchan Sonnet

■ Keeping in mind that Mortimer's translation uses several slant rhymes, identify the rhyme scheme of Petrarch's sonnet. How does the poem's content reflect the octave-sestet structure?

COMPOSITION: GUIDELINES FOR EVALUATION

WRITING ABOUT A SONNET

Objective

To analyze the structure and content of a sonnet

Guidelines for Evaluation

■ suggested length: three or four paragraphs
■ should identify stanzas and rhyme scheme
■ should show how the form influences the content

WRITING LETTERS REQUESTING AND GIVING ADVICE

Objective

To write two letters between friends

Guidelines for Evaluation

■ suggested length: 200–400 words each
■ in asking for and giving advice, should reflect each speaker's situation

The Shakespearean Sonnet

The popularity of Petrarch's sonnets spurred many poets in England to imitate the form. Because of the nature of the English language, however, these poets found it difficult to maintain the *abbaabba* rhyme scheme found in the first stanza or octave of the Petrarchan sonnet. Instead, many English poets modified the form to suit their language. Their modified form is now called the **English** or **Shakespearean sonnet,** named for William Shakespeare, who made this type of sonnet famous.

The Shakespearean sonnet consists of three **quatrains,** or four-line stanzas, followed by a **rhymed couplet,** or pair of rhyming lines. The usual rhyme scheme is *abab cdcd efef gg.* Again, the divisions in the sonnet usually give structure to its content. The quatrains often present a series of problems or arguments, and the couplet usually presents a solution or draws a conclusion about the subject. In Shakespeare's sonnets the final couplet often provides a direct and memorable statement of the poem's central idea.

Thinking About the Shakespearean Sonnet

■ How does the content of Sonnet 29 reflect its form or structure? In what way does the final couplet draw a conclusion or resolve the ideas expressed in the rest of the poem?

LANGUAGE STUDY

Shakespearean English

Although Shakespeare wrote in English, the language he used was much different from what we use today. One difference is in the use of prepositions. For example, Shakespeare often used *on* where we would say *of* or *about,* and he sometimes used *like* to where we would just say *like.* Also, some words that Shakespeare used are rarely or never used today. For example, we no longer say *haply* to mean "by chance."

■ Find four lines or phrases in Sonnet 29 that illustrate differences between Shakespeare's English and our present-day language, focusing especially on prepositions and pronouns. Then explain the wording that might be used in updated versions of these lines.

COMPOSITION

Writing About a Sonnet

■ Choosing either Petrarch's Sonnet 3 or Shakespeare's Sonnet 29, write a brief composition about the sonnet's structure. Discuss the stanza divisions, the rhyme schemes they use, and the ideas they contain. Show how the form of the sonnet structures its content.

Writing Letters Requesting and Giving Advice

■ Imagine that the speaker of Petrarch's Sonnet 3 and the speaker of Shakespeare's Sonnet 29 are friends living today. Seeking advice about his love life, the speaker of Sonnet 3 writes a letter to the speaker of Sonnet 29, who responds in a letter which gives advice. Write the letters that the two friends might write. Use modern-day language, but assume that each speaker's situation and feelings are the same as those described in the poems.

COMPARING POEMS

■ What is the difference between the views of love presented in the two sonnets? Which view do you find more realistic, or true to life? Why?

Sonnet 3; Sonnet 29   **303**

Antonio Machado

(1875–1939) *Spain*

Antonio Machado [mä chä′dō] came from a family of intellectuals who inspired his lifelong love of literature and learning. As a young man in Madrid, Spain's capital, Machado worked for a publishing company, wrote articles for a local newspaper, and was even briefly employed as an actor. His career as a poet began in 1903 with the publication of his poetry volume *Solidades.* Most of Machado's verse shows his deep love for the Spanish landscape, both urban and rural.

Antonio Machado

Winter Sun

Translated from the Spanish by Richard L. Predmore

It is noon. A park.
Winter. White paths;
symmetrical little mounds
and skeletal branches.

5   Under the hothouse roof,
orange trees in pots,
and in its barrel, painted
green, the palm tree.

A little old man says
10 to his old cape:
"The sunshine, this beautiful
sunshine! . . ." The children play.

The water in the fountain
glides, runs and dreams
15 licking, almost silent,
the greenish stone.

Detail. *La Pie* ("The Magpie"), c. 1869, Claude Monet.

304 *Poetry*

Victor Hugo

(1802–1885) *France*

Victor Hugo [hū′gō] was one of nineteenth-century France's most gifted writers. At fifteen he won praise for his poetry from the Académie Française, an influential organization of French writers and scholars; at seventeen he wrote and published a literary magazine with his older brothers. In the United States Hugo is probably best known for his classic novels *The Hunchback of Notre Dame* and *Les Misérables,* recently made into a popular musical. In France he is revered as a poet, "the greatest painter and musician of the French language."

Victor Hugo

June Nights

Translated from the French by George Kearns

In summer, when the daylight's gone, the fields,
Covered with blossoms, scent the air for miles around.
We sleep, but in a half sleep of transparent dreams,
Eyes shut, ears half opened to the summer's sound.

5 Pure are the stars, then; and the dark is sweet:
A faint half daylight stains the eternal dome,
And gentle dawn, waiting for her hour to come,
All night below the sky's edge seems to roam.

LESSON PREVIEW

On June nights flowers scent the air. Even in sleep we are half-aware of the summer. Though it is night, a half light stains the starlit sky as dawn waits just below the horizon.

LITERARY SKILLS FOR THIS SELECTION

- imagery and mood
- rhyme

THEMES IN THIS SELECTION

- the gentle comforts of nature
- nature's purity

LESSON OBJECTIVES

1. to recognize a poem's imagery and mood
2. to write an essay about a poem's imagery
3. to write a poem or paragraph using vivid imagery
4. to compare two poems

Teacher's Classroom Resources 2

- Teaching Notes   159
- Literary Focus: Imagery and Mood   160
- Writing Process Guides: Writing About Imagery   161
  Writing with Imagery   162
- Selection Test   163

IN THE CLASSROOM

TEACHING STUDENTS OF DIFFERENT ABILITIES

- **For less advanced students:** Help students appreciate the imagery in lines 6–8. Remind them that in the Northern Hemisphere nights are shortest in June, especially in northern Europe, where "faint half daylight" lingers on the horizon.

- **For more advanced students:** Explain that repeated words in short poems are significant. Have students explain why Hugo repeats *half* three times. (The word emphasizes the mood of dreamy semiconsciousness felt on June nights.)

MOTIVATION: PRIOR KNOWLEDGE

Have students recall a natural setting in which they felt at peace with themselves and the world.

TEACHING IMAGERY, MOOD, AND PERSONIFICATION

Point out the personification of dawn (ll. 7–8). Then have students describe the mental picture and the feelings the imagery in these lines evokes. (a picture of a gentle woman bringing light; feelings of maternal love)

TEACHING RHYME

Have students find the rhymes in the second and fourth lines of each stanza. Explain that rhymes are often used as a sound effect to reinforce a poem's mood. In this translation the dominant *n* and *m* sounds add to the poem's dreamy, peaceful mood.

June Nights **T-305**

ANSWERS

STUDY QUESTIONS

Winter Sun
1. It is winter at noon.
2. They are skeletal; orange trees and a palm.
3. "The sunshine, this beautiful / sunshine!"
4. It "glides," "runs," "dreams," and licks the greenish stone.
5. cold, deathlike feelings; feelings of warmth and rejuvenation
6. Outside it is cold and forbidding; he may be cheered by the sun's warmth and vitality.
7. Possible answers: eternal summer or the coming spring
8. Even in winter we can find unexpected warmth and delight.
9. They may do so to celebrate light and warmth, which are absent in winter.

June Nights
1. It is June at night.
2. "in a half sleep of transparent dreams,/Eyes shut, ears half opened to the summer's sound"
3. *sweet, pure, gentle*
4. "a faint half daylight"; dawn
5. from the pleasant scent of blossoms and the strain of faint daylight; No, the night is starlit, and sunlight lingers.
6. The people's "half sleep" mirrors nature's "half daylight."
7. delight in the sweetness of gentle summer nights; They should appreciate nature.
8. They may enjoy the sensations that come from being close to nature.

LITERARY FOCUS

"Winter Sun"—white paths, symmetric mounds, skeletal branches, a green barrel; "June Nights"—fields in blossom, stars, faint daylight, sky's edge; other senses—blossoms in fields scenting the air, summer's sound; the mood—peacefulness, quiet joy

COMPARING POEMS

"Winter Sun"—at noon in winter in a park, probably in a city; "June Nights"—on a summer night, probably in a rural area. Both suggest that nature is a source of delight and comfort.

STUDY QUESTIONS

Winter Sun (Machado)
Recalling
1. At what time of year is the park described? At what time of day?
2. How do the tree branches outside look? What kinds of trees are growing inside?
3. What does the little old man exclaim?
4. What does the water in the fountain do?

Interpreting
5. What feelings do the words "skeletal branches" convey? What feelings do the words "orange trees" and "palm tree" convey?
6. Why is the little old man so excited about the sunshine?
7. In the speaker's imagination, what do you think the water in the fountain "dreams" of?
8. What view of winter does the poem convey?

Extending
9. Why do you think many cultures hold festivals of light in winter?

June Nights (Hugo)
Recalling
1. At what time of year are the fields described? At what time of day?
2. How do the speaker and his companions sleep?
3. What adjectives are used to describe the dark, the stars, and the dawn?
4. What "stains the eternal dome"? What seems to roam all night below the sky's edge?

Interpreting
5. Why is the dark "sweet"? Is it a very dark night? Explain.
6. How does the human world mirror the natural world in the poem?
7. What feelings about summer does the poem express? What attitude toward nature does it suggest that people should take?

Extending
8. Why do people enjoy camping and sleeping outdoors on summer nights?

LITERARY FOCUS

Imagery and Mood

Images are concrete details that appeal to the senses. Although the word *image* most often suggests a visual picture, an image may appeal to our sense of hearing, taste, smell, or touch as well as our sense of sight. For example, in describing a crab apple tree, you might mention not only its green apples and drooping shape but also the rustling of its leaves, the sour taste of the apples, their fruity scent, and their firm surfaces. A poem's **imagery** is its collection of such images.

As we read a poem, its images remind us of our own sensory experiences and make the poem more vivid and real for us. Imagery also appeals to our emotions. Often a poem's images work together to convey a particular emotional quality, or **mood.** For example, the mood of one poem may be sad, while the mood of another may be cheerful.

Thinking About Imagery and Mood
■ List at least four images from "Winter Sun" and four from "June Nights." Which images in "June Nights" appeal to senses other than sight? What mood does the imagery in each poem help convey?

COMPOSITION

Writing About Imagery
■ Write a brief composition about the imagery in either "Winter Sun" or "June Nights." Identify the poem's images and the sense or senses to which each image appeals. Also explain how the images work together to create a particular mood and convey the poem's main ideas about nature.

Writing with Imagery
■ Write a poem or a paragraph describing a winter or summer scene. Use vivid images that appeal to different senses. Also try to choose images that help convey the mood of the scene.

COMPARING POEMS

■ What is different about the settings (time and place) of the two scenes described in the poems? What is similar about the view of nature in each poem?

COMPOSITION: GUIDELINES FOR EVALUATION

WRITING ABOUT IMAGERY

Objective

To analyze how imagery creates mood and conveys ideas

Guidelines for Evaluation
■ suggested length: two or three paragraphs
■ should list the senses to which the images appeal
■ should relate the imagery to the poem's mood and main ideas

WRITING WITH IMAGERY

Objective

To use imagery effectively in a poem or paragraph

Guidelines for Evaluation
■ suggested length: one paragraph or five to ten lines
■ should contain vivid images that appeal to several senses
■ should convey a definite mood

Nelly Sachs

(1891–1970) *Germany*

Nobel Prize–winning poet Nelly Sachs grew up in Berlin, Germany, and by the 1920s was publishing poems in Berlin's newspapers. The daughter of a German Jewish inventor, Sachs found her life in jeopardy when the Nazis came to power in the 1930s. She was able to escape Nazi Germany with the help of another Nobel Prize winner, Sweden's Selma Lagerlöf (see Unit 1), with whom Sachs had maintained correspondence for many years. Sachs spent the rest of her life in Sweden, where she continued to produce her acclaimed German-language verse.

Nelly Sachs

The Swan

Translated from the German by Michael Roloff

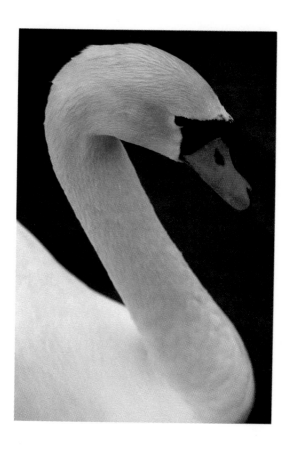

Nothing
above the waters
and at once on the flick of an eye
is suspended
5 swanlike geometry
rooted in water
vining up
and bowed again
Swallowing dust
10 and measuring the universe
with air—

The Swan **307**

The speaker sees nothing upon the water until a swan appears suddenly. It swims "rooted in water," its shape stretching upward like a vine. The swan seems to swallow dust and measure the universe with air.

LITERARY SKILLS FOR THIS SELECTION

- implied metaphor
- imagery

THEMES IN THIS SELECTION

- the beauty of nature
- natural truth

LESSON OBJECTIVES

1. to understand an implied metaphor in a poem
2. to compare two poems

Teacher's Classroom Resources 2

■ Teaching Notes	165
■ Selection Test	167

IN THE CLASSROOM

TEACHING STUDENTS OF DIFFERENT ABILITIES

- **For less advanced students:** To prepare students for the unusual image in lines 10–11, discuss the etymology of *geometry* (from Greek, "measurement of the earth"). Suggest that poetry, like geometry, is a way of looking closely at the world to discover basic truths.
- **For more advanced students:** Explain that symbolic meaning has long been attached to many animals and that swans traditionally represent purity, innocence, and ideal beauty. Ask what Sachs's swan symbolizes. (the beauty or perfection of nature)

MOTIVATION: PRIOR KNOWLEDGE

On the chalkboard list various animals and have students name the virtues or vices they associate with each.

TEACHING IMPLIED METAPHORS

Explain that implied metaphors are often expressed with unexpected verbs. Note the use of *rooted* and *vining* here.

TEACHING IMAGERY

The meaning of lines 10–11 in the context of geometry will become startlingly evident if students have a clear mental image of the floating swan. On the board draw a swan like the one pictured on this page, along with its upside-down reflection. Then have students look up the meaning of *calipers*. Help them see how the floating swan's mirrored neck resembles wide-open calipers "measuring the universe / with air."

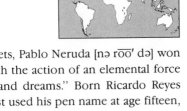

Pablo Neruda

(1904–1973) *Chile*

One of South America's greatest poets, Pablo Neruda [nə rōō′ də] won his Nobel Prize "for poetry that with the action of an elemental force brings alive a continent's destiny and dreams." Born Ricardo Reyes Basoalto in Parral, Chile, Neruda first used his pen name at age fifteen, when he published some poems in a magazine. He went on to produce twenty volumes of poetry and also served as a diplomat for the Chilean government. Many of Neruda's poems are strongly political; others, like "The Horses," show his close relationship with nature.

Pablo Neruda

The Horses

Translated from the Spanish by George Kearns

From my window I saw the horses.

It was in Berlin, one winter. The light
was without light, there was no sky in the sky.

The air was white like fresh bread.

5 From my window I saw a kind of circus-ring,
a ring bitten in snow by the teeth of winter.

Suddenly, led out by a man,
ten horses walked out into the snow.

They scarcely shook or moved as they came out,
10 like fire, but to my eyes they filled the world,
which had been empty before. Perfect, flaming,
they were like ten gods with great, clean hooves,
their manes were like a dream of salt-spumed waves.

Their rumps were round as worlds or oranges.

15 Their color was honey, amber, fire.

Their necks were like towers
carved out of stone in pride.

308 *Poetry*

Blaues Pferd I, 1911, Franz Marc.

And energy, like a prisoner,
looked out from their furious eyes.

20 And there in the silence, in the middle of the day,
one dirty, disorganized winter,
those intense horses became blood,
became rhythm, became the vibrant treasure of life.

I looked at them, looked, and revived!
25 I hadn't known it, but this was the fountain,
the golden dance, the sky, the fire that lived in beauty!

I have forgotten that dark winter in Berlin.

I shall never forget the light from those horses.

The Horses **309**

ANSWERS

STUDY QUESTIONS

The Swan
1. "nothing"; "swanlike geometry"
2. "rooted in water/vining up/and bowed again"; dust; the universe
3. mathematical perfection, beauty, and harmony
4. Its startling beauty can appear suddenly.
5. The bottom is "rooted in water"; the neck is "vining up"; the head is "bowed again." The swan belongs to both the everyday and the ideal worlds.
6. Answers will vary. Students may note that art can convey the simple, basic truths of nature.

The Horses
1. "without light"; They "filled the world,/which had been empty before."
2. "energy, like a prisoner"; "blood," "rhythm," and "the vibrant treasure of life"
3. Berlin's dark winter; the light from the horses
4. Before they arrive, the scene is bleak and barren; they impart it with life and energy. They revive the speaker's spirits and make an unforgettable impression. The mood of bleakness gives way to ecstasy.
5. their beauty and energy; Possible answer: the human desire to be strong and vital
6. optimistic; "Light" can transform a person's life.
7. Possible answers: lions, bears, peacocks, thunder, rainbows, floods. Answers will vary; lions inspire feelings of majesty or strength; thunder suggests heavenly force.

LITERARY FOCUS

Figurative Language: Simile and Metaphor
1. The horses "came out,/like fire" and "were like ten gods." The similes reveal the horses' energy and splendor and link them to a divine reality.
2. Similes—"air was white like fresh bread"; "manes were like a dream of salt-spumed

STUDY QUESTIONS

The Swan (Sachs)
Recalling
1. What is above the waters in line 1? In line 5?
2. How is the swan described in lines 6–8? What does the swan swallow? What does it measure?

Interpreting
3. What does the phrase "swanlike geometry" imply about the swan's appearance?
4. What does the suddenness of the swan's appearance suggest about nature?
5. Which images suggest a contrast between the bottom and the top of the swan? What do you think the poet wants to imply by the contrast?

Extending
6. Why do you think people—especially artists—continue to marvel at the simple facts of nature?

The Horses (Neruda)
Recalling
1. Before the horses appeared, what was the light like? According to lines 10–11, how did the horses change the world?
2. What looked out from the horses' eyes? What did the horses become in lines 22–23?
3. What has the speaker now forgotten? What will he never forget?

Interpreting
4. Contrast the horses with the scene before their arrival. What effect do the horses have on the speaker? On the mood of the poem?
5. What does the speaker especially admire about the horses? What aspects of human behavior might the horses represent?
6. Do the last two lines suggest an optimistic or a pessimistic outlook on life? Explain.

Extending
7. Describe some creatures or natural events that you have found memorable. What feelings did they inspire?

LITERARY FOCUS

Figurative Language: Simile and Metaphor
Language used for descriptive effect and not meant to be taken literally is known as **figurative language.**

Instances of such language, called **figures of speech,** usually contain vivid images that help us see things in new, unusual ways. Two of the most common figures of speech are simile and metaphor.

A **simile** compares two seemingly unlike things by using a word of comparison such as *like* or *as.* When Neruda says the horses' necks "were like towers carved out of stone" (lines 16–17), he uses a simile. A **metaphor** compares two seemingly unlike things without using words such as *like* or *as.* If Neruda had written, "Their necks were towers carved out of stone," he would have been using metaphor.

Both similes and metaphors draw attention to qualities that two otherwise unlike things have in common. Horses' necks and stone towers are unlike in many ways, but if we picture a stone tower, we see something tall, slender, and strong—the same qualities Neruda wants us to see when we imagine the necks of the horses.

Thinking About Simile and Metaphor
1. What two similes occur in lines 9–12 of "The Horses"? What qualities does each simile help us recognize in the horses?
2. Find at least three more similes and metaphors in Neruda's poem.

Implied Metaphor
An **implied metaphor** is a metaphor in which the connection between two unlike things is suggested rather than directly expressed in the form "A is B." For example, when Neruda describes "a ring bitten in snow by the teeth of winter," he uses an implied metaphor. He never says directly that winter is the mouth of a beast with sharp teeth. Instead he *implies* the comparison by his use of the words "bitten" and "teeth."

Thinking About Implied Metaphor
■ What comparison is being suggested in the implied metaphor in lines 6–7 of "The Swan"? Which words suggest the comparison?

COMPARING POEMS
■ What is similar about the attitudes toward nature shown in "The Swan" and "The Horses"? How do the qualities of the animals differ, and what do the differences suggest about what each poem's speaker admires in nature?

---

waves"; "rumps were round as worlds or oranges"; "necks were like towers"; "energy, like a prisoner,/looked out"; metaphors—"color was honey, amber, fire"; "horses became blood,/became rhythm, became the vibrant treasure of life"; "this was the fountain,/the golden dance, the sky, the fire that lived in beauty!"

Implied Metaphor
A swan and a plant are being compared; *rooted* and *vining.*

COMPARING POEMS
Both express wonder at nature's beauty. The swan is calm and serene; the horses, vibrant and exciting. The differences suggest that the speaker of "The Swan"

admires nature's soothing stillness; the speaker of "The Horses" admires nature's power.

Oswald Mbuyiseni Mtshali

(born 1940) *South Africa*

Oswald Mbuyiseni Mtshali [m bōō'yə sān'ē   m tə shäl' ē] is among the most widely read of black South African poets writing in English. Born in rural Natal, a province in eastern South Africa, Mtshali now lives in Soweto, the large black township near the city of Johannesburg. He worked as a chauffeur, a messenger, and a delivery man before publishing his best-selling first book of poetry, *Sounds of a Cowhide Drum,* in 1971. Mtshali's poems explore the experiences of black South Africans and depict both urban and rural life.

Oswald Mbuyiseni Mtshali

Sunset

The sun spun like
a tossed coin.
It whirled on the azure sky,
it clattered into the horizon,

5 it clicked in the slot,
and neon-lights popped
and blinked "Time expired,"
as on a parking meter.

From the Plains I, 1953, Georgia O'Keeffe.

LESSON PREVIEW

At sunset the sun spins, whirls, and clatters like a tossed coin. It clicks into a parking meter, and neon lights blink, "Time expired."

LITERARY SKILLS FOR THIS SELECTION

- extended simile
- onomatopoeia

THEMES IN THIS SELECTION

- nature's beauty in an urban setting
- nature and artifice

LESSON OBJECTIVES

1. to analyze a poem's extended simile
2. to write an essay about a poem's extended simile
3. to write a poem or paragraph using an extended simile
4. to compare two poems

Teacher's Classroom Resources 2

- Teaching Notes 169
- Literary Focus: Extended Simile and Extended Metaphor 170
- Writing Process Guides: Writing About an Extended Simile or Metaphor 171
  Creating an Extended Simile or Metaphor 172
- Selection Test 173

IN THE CLASSROOM

TEACHING STUDENTS OF DIFFERENT ABILITIES

- **For less advanced students:** Help students find and hear the many long-*i* and *k* sounds that contribute to the poem's tonal unity and exuberant mood.

- **For more advanced students:** Point out that the image in line 6 might refer to city lights coming on at dusk as well as to the sunset's colors.

MOTIVATION: PRIOR KNOWLEDGE

Ask students to recall a spectacular sunset.

TEACHING EXTENDED SIMILES

Point out that each action of the sun/coin is part of an overall downward progression—from sky to horizon to "slot."

TEACHING ONOMATOPOEIA

Point out that *whirled, clattered, clicked, popped,* and *blinked* complement the poem's images by creating a rich aural texture.

ART AND LITERATURE

The American painter Georgia O'Keeffe (1887–1986) turned natural subjects into flat shapes and patterns of color. The hard edges and angles in this painting abstract the changing light in a way that is almost machinelike.

- Have students find words and phrases that mechanize the sun. ("spun like a tossed coin," *clattered, clicked, blinked*)

One rooster needs others to weave a morning. Together their shouts weave "sun-threads" into a cloth, which grows into a tent. This tent of morning light soars free as a balloon.

LITERARY SKILLS FOR THIS SELECTION

- extended metaphor
- poetic syntax

THEMES IN THIS SELECTION

- nature's unity
- motion and change

LESSON OBJECTIVES

1. to analyze a poem's extended metaphor
2. to write an essay about a poem's extended metaphor
3. to write a poem or paragraph using an extended metaphor
4. to compare two poems

Teacher's Classroom Resources 2

- Teaching Notes   169
- Literary Focus: Extended Simile and Extended Metaphor   170
- Writing Process Guides: Writing About an Extended Simile or Metaphor   171
  Creating an Extended Simile or Metaphor   172
- Selection Test   173

IN THE CLASSROOM

TEACHING STUDENTS OF DIFFERENT ABILITIES

- **For less advanced students:** Having this poem read aloud two or more times will help students decode the complicated syntax and appreciate the main ideas.
- **For more advanced students:** Point out that this poem is composed of two long "sentences." Challenge students to distill the poem into a brief statement, such as "One rooster needs the call of other roosters to weave the morning into a tent of light that soars free like a balloon."

João Cabral de Melo Neto
(born 1920) *Brazil*

João [zhōō ouɴ'] Cabral de Melo Neto is a highly regarded poet from the South American nation of Brazil. Born in Recife, a city in northeastern Brazil, Cabral published his first volume of poetry, *Stone of the Sleep,* in 1942. Five years later, he joined his nation's diplomatic service and was sent to Barcelona, Spain, where he lived for several years. Cabral's musical poems are written in Portuguese, Brazil's chief language. Many describe the landscape and people of northeastern Brazil, where he grew up.

João Cabral de Melo Neto

Weaving the Morning

Translated from the Portuguese by Galway Kinnell

One rooster does not weave a morning,
he will always need the other roosters,
one to pick up the shout that he
and toss it to another, another rooster
5 to pick up the shout like a rooster before him
and toss it to another, and other roosters
with many other roosters to criss-cross
the sun-threads of their rooster-shouts
so that the morning, starting from a frail cobweb,
10 may go on being woven, among all the roosters.

And growing larger, becoming cloth,
pitching itself a tent where they all may enter,
inter-unfurling itself for them all, in the tent
(the morning) which soars free of ties and ropes—
15 the morning, tent of a weave so light
that, woven, it lifts itself through itself: balloon light.

MOTIVATION: PRIOR KNOWLEDGE

Have students describe the smells, sights, and especially the sounds they associate with sunrise.

TEACHING EXTENDED METAPHORS

Help students understand that an extended metaphor starts with a central comparison (roosters as weavers of morning) that is logically expanded with related comparisons (sunlight as threads, the morning as a tent).

TEACHING POETIC SYNTAX

Help students realize how appropriate Cabral's syntax is for the action and mood of this poem. His elaborate sentence structure relies on conjunctions (*and* appears five times) and commas, one of which connects independent clauses. The poet's syntax mimics the chain reaction of the roosters' shouts as dawn spreads from a glimmer to a blanket of light that encompasses the whole sky.

A Benin brass rooster.

COLLABORATIVE LEARNING: ENRICHMENT ACTIVITY

Choral Reading Ask a group of students to present a choral reading of "Weaving the Morning." Students may mix individual and group vocalizations to create the weaving effect.

ART AND LITERATURE

The Benin people of the southwest coast of Africa learned to cast bronze and brass in the late thirteenth century. They used the lost-wax process, in which clay forms are covered in beeswax and then covered again with clay so that when fired and hardened, the wax melts away and molten metal can be poured inside. Works such as this cast and carved rooster decorated portable altars that the Benin used in ritual ceremonies.

In 1472 Portuguese explorers discovered the city of Benin. It was a kingdom in the jungle—a city of smooth clay walls, wooden pillars covered with metal plaques, and houses with small turrets at their corners on which were perched bronze birds.

■ Ask students to find phrases in the poem that recall details found in the sculpture. ("criss-cross / the sun-threads," "a . . . cobweb . . . woven," "a weave . . . woven")

What emotions do you think these two poets wanted you to feel during and after reading their poems?

ANSWERS

STUDY QUESTIONS

Sunset
1. It spins, whirls, clatters, and clicks.
2. They pop and blink, "Time expired."
3. They are the lights and colors in the sky that appear at sunset. They mean that daylight has ended.
4. a coin clinking into a slot, neon lights, a parking meter
5. Nature's cycles are apparent in urban settings but are often described with urban metaphors.
6. Answers will vary. Students may feel that city dwellers value nature more than people in rural areas because they experience less of it.

Weaving the Morning
1. He cannot weave a morning by himself but needs other roosters to pick up the shout, toss it to yet another rooster, and crisscross the "sun-threads."
2. cloth; a tent that in turn becomes a balloon of light
3. crowing at dawn
4. feeling fresh, free, and hopeful as the new day begins
5. Possible answer: working with one another to enhance one's sense of community
6. Possible answers: bees, ants, birds, and wolves

LITERARY FOCUS

1. *spun, tossed, whirled, clattered,* and *clicked;* a coin's clicking into the slot of a parking meter. The popping up of a "time expired" sign is compared to the setting of the sun.
2. roosters as weavers of morning; crisscrossing the "sun-threads" to create a cobweb that becomes cloth and finally a tent that soars free like a balloon

COMPARING POEMS

"Sunset" describes an urban evening; "Weaving," a rural dawn. Both compare natural events to human creations, but in "Sunset" the images are more modern, urban, and mechanical.

STUDY QUESTIONS

Sunset (Mtshali)
Recalling
1. According to the poem, what four things does the setting sun do?
2. What do the "neon lights" do?

Interpreting
3. Why do the "neon lights" come on as the sun clicks "in the slot"? How do the words "Time expired" relate to the subject of the poem?
4. What images in the poem suggest an urban setting?
5. What does the poem suggest about the role of nature in urban life?

Extending
6. Do people in cities appreciate nature as much as they should? Do people in rural areas appreciate cities as much as they should? Discuss.

Weaving the Morning (Cabral de Melo Neto)
Recalling
1. According to the first ten lines, what can one rooster not do alone? For what specific activities does he need the other roosters?
2. What does the "frail cobweb" of morning become in line 11? In lines 12–16?

Interpreting
3. To what activity of roosters in rural areas does this poem refer?
4. What feelings about morning do the details in lines 14–16 help convey?
5. What kind of human activity might the details about the roosters be intended to inspire?

Extending
6. What are some other creatures of nature whose behavior suggests the importance of teamwork?

LITERARY FOCUS

Extended Simile and Extended Metaphor

An **extended simile** or **extended metaphor** is a figure of speech carried through several lines of a poem or even sustained through an entire poem. In "Sunset," for exam-

---

ple, the simile that compares the sun to a coin is extended throughout the poem.

An extended metaphor or simile allows the poet to investigate in depth the similarities between the unlike things that are being compared. It often gives us a rich, rounded, and fresh perspective on the subject being described and stretches our imaginations, challenging us to recognize and accept the many connections the poet has made.

Thinking About Extended Simile or Metaphor
1. In Mtshali's extended simile, what verbs appropriate for a coin's activities are applied to the sun's activities? To what final activity of the coin is the sun's final activity compared? What result of the coin's final activity is compared to what result of the sunset?
2. What implied metaphor in line 1 of "Weaving the Morning" is extended throughout the poem? Identify three steps or stages in the process to which the roosters' activities are compared.

COMPOSITION

Writing About an Extended Simile or Metaphor
■ Write a brief composition about the extended simile in "Sunset" or the extended metaphor in "Weaving the Morning." First identify the basic simile or metaphor and the two unlike things being compared. Then show how specific details of the poem extend the simile or metaphor.

Creating an Extended Simile or Metaphor
■ Write a poem or a paragraph in which a simile or metaphor is extended over several lines. Begin with a basic simile or metaphor; for example, "A person's life is like the seasons of the year" or "Travel is a dancing lesson." Then extend the comparison by drawing parallels between specific parts, stages, or aspects of the compared items.

COMPARING POEMS

■ What is different about the settings depicted in "Sunset" and "Weaving the Morning"? What is similar and different about the images to which each poem compares events of nature?

COMPOSITION: GUIDELINES FOR EVALUATION

WRITING ABOUT AN EXTENDED SIMILE OR METAPHOR

Objective
To analyze the details of an extended simile or metaphor

Guidelines for Evaluation
■ suggested length: one or two paragraphs
■ should identify the things being compared
■ should tell how details extend the figure of speech

CREATING AN EXTENDED SIMILE OR METAPHOR

Objective
To create an extended simile or metaphor

Guidelines for Evaluation
■ suggested length: five to ten lines of poetry or one paragraph
■ should logically extend the figure of speech

Chaim Nachman Bialik

(1873–1934) *Russia/Israel*

Though he died before Israel became a nation, Chaim Nachman Bialik [кнä′yim näкн′mən byä′lik] is revered as one of Israel's greatest poets. The son of a pious Jewish scholar, Bialik grew up in Russia and attended a Hebrew seminary there. In 1904 he paid his first visit to the area that is now Israel but was then known as Palestine; he settled there permanently two decades later. Over the years Bialik produced poems, essays, and stories, all in the modern Hebrew language. Today he is best remembered for his poetry.

Chaim Nachman Bialik

Summer Is Dying

Translated from the Hebrew by L. V. Snowman

Summer is dying, woven in fine gold,
   Couched on a purple bed
Of falling garden leaves and twilight clouds
   That lave[1] their hearts in red.

5 The garden is deserted, save where a youth
   Saunters, or a maiden walks,
Casting an eye and a sigh after the flight
   Of the last and lingering storks.

The heart is orphaned. Soon a rainy day
10   Will softly tap the pane.
*"Look to your boots, patch up your coats,
   go fetch*
   The potatoes in again."

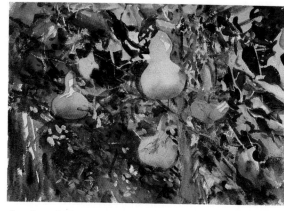

Gourds, c. 1905-1908, John Singer Sargent.

---

1. **lave** [lāv]: wash.

LESSON PREVIEW

Wind, water, and stone are connected, each affecting the others but remaining separate. Ultimately each disappears.

LITERARY SKILLS FOR THIS SELECTION

- personification
- repetition

THEMES IN THIS SELECTION

- the interconnectedness of nature
- permanence amid change

LESSON OBJECTIVES

1. to appreciate the effect of personification in a poem
2. to write about a cycle in a poem or paragraph
3. to compare two poems

Teacher's Classroom Resources 2

- Teaching Notes 175
- Literary Focus: Personification 176
- Writing Process Guide: Writing About a Cycle 178
- Selection Test 179

IN THE CLASSROOM

TEACHING STUDENTS OF DIFFERENT ABILITIES

- **For less advanced students:** Organize a choral reading of the poem, treating the final line of each stanza as a refrain.
- **For more advanced students:** Help students see that in the first two stanzas each object mentioned in the title acts upon both of the others.

MOTIVATION: PRIOR KNOWLEDGE

Ask students to identify some processes in nature that involve the transformation or interconnection of separate elements, such as the formation of rain, a thunderstorm, a rainbow, or sedimentary rock.

TEACHING PERSONIFICATION

By adding sound to his description of natural processes in the third stanza, Paz implies human parallels: "Wind sings," "water murmurs," and "stone is quiet." Likewise, people interact and blend within society while retaining separate identities until they "pass and disappear."

TEACHING REPETITION

Help students realize that Paz's repetitions give the poem an incantatory tone. His use of a refrain (ll. 4, 8, 12, and 16) emphasizes the theme of permanence within the ceaseless changes of nature's cycles.

ART AND LITERATURE

Georgia O'Keeffe (1887–1986) frequently painted the arid American Southwest, capturing its dramatic vistas, such as this rocky precipice.
- Ask students what natural elements sculpted the stone in both the poem and the painting. (the water and the wind)

Octavio Paz

(born 1914) *Mexico*

One of modern Mexico's most distinguished men of letters, Octavio Paz [päs] grew up outside Mexico City and published his first volume of poetry, *Luna silvestre* ("Forest Moon"), before he was twenty. As a diplomat he traveled widely in Europe and Asia, where he was influenced by the ancient poetry of India and Japan. A prolific author, Paz has published major works of literary criticism as well as poetry and fiction. Many of his poems reflect his interest in his nation's history and his fascination with the Mexican landscape. In 1990 Paz was awarded the Nobel Prize for Literature.

Octavio Paz

Wind and Water and Stone

Translated from the Spanish by Mark Strand

For Roger Caillois[1]

The water hollowed the stone,
the wind dispersed the water,
the stone stopped the wind.
Water and wind and stone.

5 The wind sculpted the stone,
the stone is a cup of water,
the water runs off and is wind.
Stone and wind and water.

The wind sings in its turnings,
10 the water murmurs as it goes,
the motionless stone is quiet.
Wind and water and stone.

One is the other, and is neither:
among their empty names
15 they pass and disappear,
water and stone and wind.

From the White Place, 1940, Georgia O'Keeffe.

---

1. **Roger Caillois** [rō zhä′ kī wä′]: (1913–1978) French writer who theorized that writing was inspired by marks on stones.

STUDY QUESTIONS

Summer Is Dying (Bialik)

Recalling

1. On what is the dying summer "couched"?
2. Where does the youth or maiden walk? On what does the maiden cast an eye?
3. How is the heart described in the last stanza? What does the rainy day say?

Interpreting

4. What mood do the images in the first two stanzas help create?
5. Why are the last two lines in italics? What impact did the poet want them to have?
6. What overall view of autumn does the poem present?

Extending

7. What are some of the things, both joyful and sad, that you associate with autumn?

Wind and Water and Stone (Paz)

Recalling

1. What does the water do in stanza 1? What does the wind do? The stone?
2. What does the wind do in stanza 2? What does the stone become? What happens to the water?
3. In stanza 3, how is the stone different from the wind and water? What happens to the water and stone and wind in the last stanza?

Interpreting

4. How does the stone become a cup of water? How does the water become wind?
5. What does the poem suggest about how the elements of nature are related?
6. What aspect of human life might the poet be reminding us of in stanza 4?

Extending

7. What aspects of nature have reminded you of the interconnectedness of things?

LITERARY FOCUS

Personification

Personification is a figure of speech in which an animal, object, or idea is given human qualities. The thing that is personified might speak, feel emotions, perform human activities, and even assume a human appearance.

Sometimes personification lasts for several lines or even a whole poem. For example, an entire poem may describe a cat in human terms, discussing different aspects of the cat's "personality" and behavior. At other times personification may be as fleeting as a single image. For example, we use personification when we say that winter is cruel or love is blind. Poets often use personification to make their images more vivid or to add a more emotional level to the objects and ideas they describe.

Thinking About Personification

■ What examples of personification occur in the first stanza of Bialik's poem and the third stanza of Paz's poem? How does each example add an emotional level to what is being described? Find three more examples of personification in the poems.

LANGUAGE STUDY

Words from Hebrew

Hebrew, the language of most of the Old Testament, or Jewish Bible, has contributed several words to English. A few more have come from modern Hebrew, the version of the language spoken in Israel today.

Use a dictionary to determine the meanings and origins of the following English words.

1. amen	5. kibbutz	9. sabra
2. cherub	6. manna	10. schwa
3. hallelujah	7. maven	11. seraph
4. jubilee	8. sabbatical	12. shibboleth

COMPOSITION

Writing About a Cycle

■ Using Paz's poem as a model, create your own poem or prose description of three interconnected things in which A does something to B, B does something to C, and C does something to A. Use personification to make your images come alive.

COMPARING POEMS

■ What do the two poems both convey about nature's cycles? Which poem is more emotional? Support your answer with details from the poem.

Summer Is Dying; Wind and Water and Stone **317**

COMPOSITION: GUIDELINES FOR EVALUATION

WRITING ABOUT A CYCLE

Objective

To create a poem or paragraph describing a cycle

Guidelines for Evaluation

- suggested length: one paragraph or one or two stanzas
- should describe how three things are interconnected
- should use personification

READER'S RESPONSE

What sounds did you particularly enjoy in these two poems?

ANSWERS

STUDY QUESTIONS

Summer Is Dying

1. "a purple bed"
2. in a deserted garden; the last storks
3. It is "orphaned." "Look to your boots, patch up your coats, go fetch/The potatoes in again."
4. a sad, lonely, nostalgic mood
5. to emphasize the shift from nature's romance to practical human affairs; Readers feel connected to summer's end.
6. Autumn is a sad time of quiet beauty and practical urgency.
7. Possible answers: colorful or falling leaves, cool weather

Wind and Water and Stone

1. It hollows stone. It disperses water. It stops the wind.
2. It sculpts stone; a cup of water; It runs off and becomes wind.
3. It is quiet and motionless. They pass and disappear.
4. Wind sculpts the stone, which holds water. It evaporates.
5. All are interconnected.
6. transience, death
7. Possible answer: the food chain

LITERARY FOCUS

Bialik's "Summer is dying" emphasizes sadness. Paz's singing wind and murmuring water add spirituality. "Summer Is Dying"— "The heart is orphaned"; the day taps on the window and gives instructions; "Wind and Water"— the wind sculpts the stone.

LANGUAGE STUDY

1. "exclamation of assent"; "truly"
2. "a kind of angel"
3. "praise the Lord"
4. "celebration"; from *yobel,* "a ram's-horn trumpet"
5. "collective farm"; from modern Hebrew
6. "divine aid"; from Exodus 16
7. "an expert"; from late Hebrew
8. "period of absence"; "to rest"
9. "native Israeli"; "cactus fruit"
10. "unstressed vowel sound"; "mark of unstressed vowel"
11. "a kind of angel"; "to burn"
12. "test word or password"; "stream," as a test word

COMPARING POEMS

Death is inevitable; Bialik's, with details of summer dying.

LESSON PREVIEW

"Autumn"—A crow on a withered branch is equated with autumn nightfall. "Winter"—Snow covers a scene. "After a Long Winter"—Two people with spring blossoms in their hands collide after a long winter of neglect. "Heat"—In summer a horse and rider wade through a river rather than take the bridge.

LITERARY SKILLS FOR THIS SELECTION

- haiku
- implied metaphor

THEMES IN THIS SELECTION

- seasonal change in nature
- austerity versus abundance

LESSON OBJECTIVES

1. to appreciate the haiku form
2. to write a haiku
3. to compare haiku

Teacher's Classroom Resources 2

■ Teaching Notes	181
■ Literary Focus: The Haiku	182
■ Writing Process Guide: Writing a Haiku	183
■ Selection Test	184

IN THE CLASSROOM

TEACHING STUDENTS OF DIFFERENT ABILITIES

- **For less advanced students:** Point out that dashes may signify the traditional shift in mood or imagery between the second and third lines of a haiku—as in "Autumn" and "Winter."
- **For more advanced students:** Encourage students to publish their haiku in a class literary magazine.

MOTIVATION: PRIOR KNOWLEDGE

Have students associate a mood with one of the four seasons and brainstorm to generate images that capture or evoke this mood and season.

IN THE GLOSSARY

- collide: crash into something

TEACHING HAIKU

Point out that a season is almost

Four Japanese Haiku Poets

Japan

Bashō (1644–1694) is generally regarded as the greatest of Japan's classical haiku poets. Widely respected in his own lifetime, Bashō started a school of haiku poetry in the city of Edo, now Tokyo, Japan's capital. Among his ten star pupils—sometimes known as the Ten Philosophers—was **Jōso** (1661–1704). **Chiyo** (1703–1775), born a few decades later, is considered the most important of the many woman poets who wrote during this classical age of haiku poetry. Representing Japan's more recent haiku composers is **Shiki** (1867–1902), who published haiku in his monthly magazine *Hototogisu* ("The Cuckoo").

Bashō, Jōsō, Chiyo, Shiki

Four Japanese Haiku

Translated from the Japanese
by Harold G. Henderson and David Ray

Autumn

On a withered branch
   a crow has settled—
     autumn nightfall.

—*Bashō, tr. Henderson*

Winter

Mountains and plains,
   all are captured by the snow—
     nothing remains.

—*Jōsō, tr. Henderson*

After a Long Winter

After a long winter, giving
   each other nothing, we collide
     with blossoms in our hands.

—*Chiyo, tr. Ray*

Heat

The summer river:
   although there is a bridge, my horse
     goes through the water.

—*Shiki, tr. Henderson*

318   *Poetry*

---

always mentioned or implied in haiku and the poems rarely bear titles. Ask students to locate words or phrases in each haiku that identify the season that is implied. (In Jōsō's haiku *snow* implies winter.)

TEACHING IMPLIED METAPHORS

Explain that the juxtapositions so characteristic of haiku often create implied metaphors. What meta-

phors are implied in Bashō's poem? (The black crow is compared to night, passing time to an aging tree, and autumn to a withered branch on that tree.)

TEACHING TRANSLATION

Increase students' appreciation of foreign literary forms by explaining that internal rhymes are common in haiku because almost every Japanese syllable ends with a

vowel sound. Point out that Henderson's translation of Jōsō's poem tries to capture some of the natural musicality of Japanese by rhyming *mountains, plains,* and *remains.* You might also mention that Japanese words are more often polysyllabic than English words. Accordingly, translators usually must use more words when rendering the originally terse haiku into English.

Spring Landscape with Blossoming Cherry Tree and Waterfall, lid from a Japanese writing box.

Four Japanese Haiku   **319**

Art Students might look in books of Japanese art to find suitable illustrations for the haiku. Students can then display their choices to the rest of the class, provide brief information on the artists or styles, and discuss the ways in which the paintings capture the poems' imagery and moods.

ART AND LITERATURE

Most Japanese writers were artists as well as calligraphers and used their pictographic skills to create paintings of subjects from nature. They kept their writing tools in exquisitely crafted wood boxes whose lids bore carved, lacquered scenes such as this landscape. Some artists were also poets and included lines of poetry or haiku in their paintings.
■ Suggest that some students use the spring landscape on this box cover as inspiration for the haiku they will write for the Composition assignment (p. 320).

Which haiku had the most meaning for you? What deeper meaning did it suggest?

ANSWERS

STUDY QUESTIONS

1. a withered branch
2. nothing
3. blossoms
4. It wades across the river.
5. They suggest the decay and increasing darkness of autumn. They create a sad mood, as do *captured* and *nothing* in Jōsō's poem.
6. The change from winter to spring parallels the human change from a chilled relationship to a renewal of love or friendship.
7. Summer is represented. Crossing the river rather than the bridge is a way of cooling off. The choice also suggests the taking of a natural rather than an artificial path through life.
8. Answers will vary but should evoke specific seasons.

LITERARY FOCUS

Bashō's poem suggests that people find autumn a time of decay and gloom. Jōsō's might refer to death or the ideal "emptiness" achieved through meditation.

COMPARING POEMS

Answers will vary. Students should focus on the haiku's central image, such as the crow settling on the withered branch in Bashō's poem or the all-encompassing snow in Jōsō's.

STUDY QUESTIONS

Recalling

1. On what kind of branch does the crow settle in "Autumn"?
2. In "Winter," what remains after mountains and plains are "captured" by the snow?
3. In Chiyo's haiku, what do the speaker and her companion have in their hands when they collide "after a long winter"?
4. In "Heat," what does the speaker's horse do "although there is a bridge"?

Interpreting

5. In Bashō's haiku, why are the words "withered" and "nightfall" especially appropriate? What mood do they help create? Which words in Jōsō's haiku help achieve a similar mood?
6. What seasonal change is represented in Chiyo's haiku? Does her poem also depict a changing human relationship? Explain.
7. What season is represented in Shiki's haiku? Why does the horse (or its rider) do what it does?

Extending

8. What images would you use to represent the four seasons?

LITERARY FOCUS

The Haiku

A **haiku** is a three-line poem, usually about nature, but often with a suggestion of a deeper meaning. The form of the traditional haiku, as established by Bashō and other early haiku composers, requires seventeen syllables—five in the first line, seven in the second, and five in the third. In the original Japanese the four haiku presented here follow this traditional form.

The haiku is native to Japan, although poets from many other nations have also experimented with the form. Most haiku use vivid but fleeting images to sketch a scene or an incident that usually involves the world of nature but also says something about human experience. For example, a haiku may comment on the human response to nature or use images from nature to express ideas about people.

Thinking About the Haiku

■ What does Bashō's haiku suggest about the human response to autumn? To what human experience might Jōsō's haiku refer?

COMPOSITION

Writing a Haiku

■ Write your own haiku in which you sketch a scene or an incident from nature and perhaps touch on a deeper meaning. Use vivid images, and make your haiku three lines long. If possible, use the traditional seventeen-syllable form.

COMPARING POEMS

■ In which of the four haiku did you find the imagery the most vivid? Why?

COMPOSITION: GUIDELINES FOR EVALUATION

WRITING A HAIKU

Objective

To create an original poem based on models

Guidelines for Evaluation

■ suggested length: three lines
■ should use vivid images to depict a scene from nature
■ may convey a deeper meaning about life
■ may follow the seventeen-syllable haiku form

Gabon Pygmy Traditional

Gabon

The Pygmies of the West African nation of Gabon are mostly members of the Babinga tribe. Like most tribal peoples, they have centuries-old traditions of poetry and song. The lyrics of "All That Dances," a traditional song of the Gabon Pygmies, were recorded by scholar C. M. Bowra. Bowra reports that the song was part of the repertoire of Mba Sholé [m′bä shō′lā], a tribal entertainer noted for his "remarkable gifts for dancing and singing and miming."

Gabon Pygmy Traditional

All That Dances

Retold by Mba Sholé and C. M. Bowra

The fish does . . . *hip!*
The bird does . . . *viss!*
The monkey does . . . *gnan!*

I throw myself to the left,
5 I turn myself to the right,
I act the fish,
Which darts in the water, which darts,
Which twists about, which leaps—
All lives, all dances, and all is loud.

10 The fish does . . . *hip!*
The bird does . . . *viss!*
The monkey does . . . *gnan!*

The bird flies away,
It flies, flies, flies,
15 Goes, returns, passes,
Climbs, soars, and drops.
I act the bird—
All lives, all dances, and all is loud.

All That Dances **321**

LESSON PREVIEW

The singer observes the fish, the bird, and the monkey and mimics their movements in a dance of his own. "All lives, all dances, and all is loud," he concludes.

LITERARY SKILLS FOR THIS SELECTION

- onomatopoeia
- repetition
- poetic structure

THEMES IN THIS SELECTION

- delight in nature's creatures
- nature's vital rhythms

LESSON OBJECTIVES

1. to appreciate the use of onomatopoeia and repetition in a song
2. to write a children's song

Teacher's Classroom Resources 2

- Teaching Notes 185
- Literary Focus: Onomatopoeia; Repetition 186
- Writing Process Guide: Writing a Children's Song 187
- Selection Test 188

IN THE CLASSROOM

TEACHING STUDENTS OF DIFFERENT ABILITIES

- For less advanced students: Have a group of students choreograph the poem with simple percussion accompaniment and perform it for the class. The remainder of the class could participate by reciting the refrain.
- **For more advanced students:** Have students research the important role of dance and

song in Pygmy culture and prepare written or oral reports. One excellent resource is Joseph Campbell's *Historical Atlas of World Mythology,* Vol. 1, Part 1.

MOTIVATION: PRIOR KNOWLEDGE

Ask students to describe some animal movements that seem dancelike.

TEACHING ONOMATOPOEIA

Have the class brainstorm to generate a list of common English words that mimic animal sounds, such as *hiss* and *neigh.* Point out that such onomatopoeic words are usually identified in dictionary etymologies as "echoic."

TEACHING REPETITION

Help students appreciate the effectiveness of repetition in any song that is meant to be danced. They should recognize the correlation between the repeated words and refrains (ll. 1–3, 10–12, and 19–21) and the repeated movements that constitute a series of dance steps.

Ask students to describe the logical organization that gives this poem its structure. (Each animal mentioned in the refrain is described in turn in its own stanza.) Point out that the choice of the three animals is significant within this poetic structure: As representatives of the "all" that lives and dances, they symbolize the life-giving elements of water, air, and earth.

CULTURAL BACKGROUND

Called "singers and dancers of God," Pygmies traditionally live in the dense jungle, which they believe is a manifestation of divine providence. In *The Forest People*, Colin M. Turnbull quotes one tribal member: "The forest is a father and mother to us, and like a father and mother it gives us everything we need—food, clothing, shelter, warmth . . . and affection."

ART AND LITERATURE

The Douala people lived along the coastline and mangrove swamps of Cameroon in west equatorial Africa. They were known for their complex woodcarvings, which they pieced together from wood stalks and branches and then decorated. This elaborate prow sculpture would have been attached to a long canoe that could hold up to one hundred people. The Douala's carvings often honored their rulers in a symbolic fashion, with animals such as snakes, lizards, crocodiles, and chamelions serving as emblems of royal power.

■ Help students identify some of the figures in the sculpture. (humans, snakes, a crocodile) In what way do these figures reflect the action in the poem? (The human figures perform with the animals.)

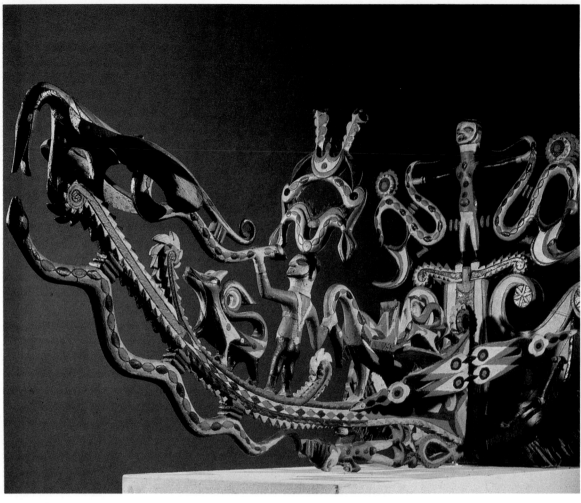

Carved and painted prow from Douala, Cameroun, nineteenth century.

The fish does . . . *hip!*
20 The bird does . . . *viss!*
The monkey does . . . *gnan!*

The monkey from branch to branch,
Runs, bounds, and leaps,
With his wife, with his brat,
25 His mouth full, his tail in the air,
There is the monkey! There is the monkey!—
All lives, all dances, and all is loud.

322 *Poetry*

STUDY QUESTIONS

Recalling

1. According to stanzas 1, 3, and 5, what does the fish do? The bird? The monkey?
2. What does the speaker or performer act like in stanza 2? Stanza 4? According to stanzas 2, 4, and 6, what lives, dances, and is loud?

Interpreting

3. What does the song suggest about the place of music and dance in the world? What does it suggest about the feelings that music and dance inspire in people?
4. What does the song suggest about nature and the relationships of its creatures?
5. Explain what the performer is doing as he sings the song. What specific instructional purposes might the song serve for young children?

Extending

6. What childhood song or game does this song bring to mind? Why?

LITERARY FOCUS

Onomatopoeia

Onomatopoeia [on′ə mat′ə pē′ə] is the use of a word whose sound mimics or suggests its meaning. For example, the word *chirp* actually sounds like what it names—a noise made by birds. Onomatopoeia usually reinforces the meaning or mood of a poem or song and adds to its musical qualities.

Thinking About Onomatopoeia

■ What three words in "All That Dances" are examples of onomatopoeia? How does the use of these words contribute to the song's effectiveness?

Repetition

Repetition—the repeated use of sounds, words, phrases, lines, or even stanzas—also adds to a poem's or song's musical qualities. In addition, repetition usually emphasizes the importance of whatever is repeated and helps tie a work together into a unified whole. A line or a stanza repeated in a poem or a song is called a **refrain.**

Thinking About Repetition

■ How many times is the word *all* used in "All That Dances"? Which of the song's lines or stanzas are refrains? What main ideas does the repetition help stress?

COMPOSITION

Writing a Children's Song

■ Write a funny song that could be used to help teach small children about the world around them. Use onomatopoeia and repetition to make your song more musical and appealing.

What animals would you choose to illustrate the point that the singer makes in the last line?

ANSWERS

STUDY QUESTIONS

1. The fish does *"hip!"*; the bird does *"viss!"*; the monkey does *"gnan!"*
2. He acts like the fish in the second stanza and like the bird in the fourth stanza; "all" lives, dances, and is loud.
3. They have a natural place in the world. They inspire joy and delight in people.
4. It suggests the energy and vitality of all life and the unity of all creatures.
5. He is mimicking the animals' movements. The song might teach children the differences between animals and that they should find joy in music, dance, and nature.
6. Answers will vary. Students might mention "Old MacDonald Had a Farm" because of the repetition and the onomatopoetic words.

LITERARY FOCUS

Onomatopoeia
Hip, viss, and *gnan* are onomatopoetic. They enhance the joyful mood and musical sound and suggest the movements of the animals and the human dancers.

Repetition
"All" is repeated nine times. The first stanza and line 9 become refrains. The repetitions emphasize the joy that all creatures take in dance and song, as well as the unity of all creatures in nature.

COMPOSITION: GUIDELINES FOR EVALUATION

WRITING A CHILDREN'S SONG

Objective

To create a song based on a model

Guidelines for Evaluation

- suggested length: three or more stanzas
- should be humorous and educational to children
- should use onomatopoeia and repetition in an appealing and musical way

At dawn, when people begin their "ardent toil," the cry "Buy bread" is heard. In the "cruel heat" of noon, the cry "Buy fruit" fills the street. At twilight lovers appear on rooftops as the cry "Buy flowers" floats down the street.

LITERARY SKILLS FOR THIS SELECTION

- alliteration and assonance
- parallelism
- imagery

THEMES IN THIS SELECTION

- delight in the rhythms of urban life
- the passage of time

LESSON OBJECTIVES

1. to recognize alliteration and assonance and appreciate their effects in a poem
2. to recognize parallelism and appreciate its effect
3. to write about the use of poetic devices in a poem

Teacher's Classroom Resources 2

- Teaching Notes   189
- Literary Focus: Alliteration and Assonance; Parallelism   191
- Writing Process Guide: Writing About Poetry   192
- Selection Test   193

IN THE CLASSROOM

TEACHING STUDENTS OF DIFFERENT ABILITIES

- **For less advanced students:** Have students preview the footnotes, as well as the Glossary words *falters, implacable,* and *languid.* Remind them that the poem is set in urban India.
- **For more advanced students:** Have students read and bring to class other poems by Indian poets who write in English, such as Meena Alexander, Aga Shahid Ali, Jayanta Mahapatra, G. S. Sharat Chandra, and R. Parthasarathy.

Sarojini Naidu

(1879–1949) *India*

Sarojini Naidu [sä′rō jē′nē nī′d̄oo], an important poet of modern India, was also an active campaigner for Indian independence and women's rights. Born to a wealthy Indian family, Naidu attended college in England and, on her return, joined Mahatma Gandhi's nonviolent struggle for India's freedom from British rule. After independence was achieved, she became the first woman to serve as a state governor in India. Like many Indians, Naidu wrote in English. Her poetry, which she began publishing in 1905, earned her the nickname "the Nightingale of India."

Fish Seller and Sweet Meat Maker and Seller with Their Wares, c. 1870, Shiva Dayal Lal.

324   *Poetry*

ART AND LITERATURE

The career of Shiva Dayal Lal (c. 1820–1880) coincided with the British rule of India, from about 1820 until 1947. Lal's English patrons requested portraits of Indian daily life, such as this depiction of meat and fish vendors. Yet his use of stylized figures and foods, his shallow depth of field, and the vivid colors recall the Indian preference for the general over the specific.

- Using the poem as a model, ask students at what time of day the vendors in this painting might be selling their wares. (in the morning, before the noon meal)

Sarojini Naidu

Street Cries

When dawn's first cymbals beat upon the sky,
Rousing the world to labor's various cry,
To tend the flock, to bind the mellowing grain,
From ardent toil to forge a little gain,
5   And fasting men go forth on hurrying feet,
Buy bread, buy bread, rings down the eager street.

When the earth falters and the waters swoon
With the implacable radiance of noon,
And in dim shelters koels[1] hush their notes,
10   And the faint, thirsting blood in languid throats
Craves liquid succor[2] from the cruel heat,
Buy fruit, buy fruit, steals down the panting street.

When twilight twinkling o'er the gay bazaars,[3]
Unfurls a sudden canopy of stars,
15   When lutes are strung and fragrant torches lit
On white roof-terraces where lovers sit
Drinking together of life's poignant sweet,
Buy flowers, buy flowers, floats down the singing street.

---

1. **koels** [kō'əlz]: birds related to the cuckoo.
2. **succor** [suk'ər]: relief.
3. **bazaars** [bə zärz']: outdoor marketplaces.

To start the barley harvest, Juan blows on a bull's horn. Seven families leave for the fields and cut the barley with sickles. One reaper, Tomasa, holds sheaves in her arms and seems a part of the landscape. At noon the men and women stop to drink "sun-juice" from clay jars.

LITERARY SKILLS FOR THIS SELECTION

- alliteration and assonance
- implied metaphor
- personification

THEMES IN THIS SELECTION

- delight in nature's bounties
- the value of community

LESSON OBJECTIVES

1. to recognize alliteration and assonance and appreciate their effects in a poem
2. to recognize implied metaphors and personification and appreciate their effects

Teacher's Classroom Resources 2

- Teaching Notes   189
- Responding to World Cultures   190
- Literary Focus: Alliteration and Assonance   191
- Selection Test   193

TEACHING STUDENTS OF DIFFERENT ABILITIES

- **For less advanced students:** Have students discuss the colors mentioned in the poem and the feelings these colors convey. (warmth, excitement, happiness) Ask how the families in the poem seem to feel about their work. (joyful, satisfied)
- **For more advanced students:** Help students recognize the close relationship between the mood of the poem (joy) and its theme (nature's abundance and the value of community).

MOTIVATION: PRIOR KNOWLEDGE

Ask students to recall (or imagine) tending a vegetable garden. Have them describe the feelings they had (or might have) watching plants grow and bear fruit.

Jorge Carrera Andrade

(1903–1978) *Ecuador*

A leading poet of the South American nation of Ecuador, Jorge Carrera Andrade [hôr′hā kä rā′rä än drä′thā] was born in Quito [kē′tō], Ecuador's capital. At college in Europe, he edited a literary review and studied law as well as literature. After graduation he joined his nation's diplomatic service and traveled all over the world. Nevertheless, Carrera Andrade's best-known poems are strongly Ecuadorean in flavor. Most, like "Reaping the Barley," paint vivid portraits of Ecuador's landscape and people.

Jorge Carrera Andrade

Reaping the Barley

Translated from the Spanish by Muna Lee de Muñoz Marín

On a bull's hollow horn
Juan blew the message that the barley was ready.

In their clay huts
the seven families
5 poured the sun-juice
into brown jars.

The hill squatted in the field
wrapped in a plaid poncho.

Red, green, yellow dresses
10 began to climb the road.

Amid a riot of colors
the glowing barley sheaves went down with a swish,
decimated by the sickles.

326   *Poetry*

- decimated: destroyed

Sheaves of Wheat, 1890, Vincent van Gogh.

Tomasa weighed the ripeness of the sky
15 in the scales of her sunflower arms.

The slow swing of the field
molded the shape of her waist.

Men and women of the seven families,
seated in the tender noon-day gold,
20 drank sun-juice
from the clay jars.

Reaping the Barley **327**

ANSWERS

STUDY QUESTIONS

Street Cries
1. dawn; "Buy bread."
2. noon; "Buy fruit."
3. twilight; "Buy flowers."
4. People want daily bread in the morning, thirst-quenching fruit at midday, flowers for loved ones in the evening.
5. bustling (first stanza), exhausted (second), serene (third); *rousing* and *eager* (first stanza); *falters, swoon, thirsting,* and *panting* (second); *unfurls* and *singing* (third)
6. its bustle, variety, and vibrant life; She seems to feel that everyday life is a struggle but that it has its pleasant rewards.
7. Possible answers: the sound of traffic, the colors of spring

Reaping the Barley
1. The barley is ready.
2. They climb the road. They are cut with a swish of the sickles.
3. They drink "sun-juice" from clay jars.
4. the barley harvest; Examples: "sun-juice," "a riot of colors," "glowing barley sheaves," "the ripeness of the sky"
5. women and girls; Possible answers: holding sheaves, stretching her arms, or offering a prayer of thanksgiving
6. They are all in close affinity.
7. Possible answers: holidays, annual fairs, sports victories

LITERARY FOCUS

Alliteration and Assonance
1. *f* and *b* sounds, *eager street;* They enhance the subject of the poem, which is sound.
2. *h* and *b* sounds, short *o* and short and long *e* sounds; They suggest the sound of the horn.

Parallelism
Each stanza follows an overall "when . . . then" syntactic pattern and concludes with a vendor's cry that moves down the street. In each case the line begins with a repetition of "Buy" and ends with "down the . . . street." The parallelism emphasizes the unchanging general pattern of daily life, as well as the shifting activities and moods within it.

STUDY QUESTIONS

Street Cries (Naidu)
Recalling
1. At what time of day do the first street cries ring out? What specific cry fills the street?
2. At what time of day do the next street cries ring out? What specific cry fills the street?
3. At what time of day do the last street cries ring out? What specific cry fills the street?

Interpreting
4. Why are the street vendors' different cries appropriate for the different times of day?
5. What does the speaker like about the town she describes? What feelings does she seem to have about everyday life?
6. What different moods do the images in each stanza help convey? What examples of personification contribute to the moods?

Extending
7. What sounds and sights would you include in a poem about your town or neighborhood?

Reaping the Barley (Carrera Andrade)
Recalling
1. What message does Juan blow?
2. What do "red, green, yellow dresses" soon do? What happens to the barley sheaves?
3. What do the men and women of the seven families do in the "tender noon-day gold"?

Interpreting
4. What are the seven families celebrating? What images help capture their joyous mood?
5. Who are the "red, green, yellow dresses"? What might Tomasa be doing in lines 14–15?
6. What does the poem suggest about the relationships that families of farm workers have with nature and one another?

Extending
7. What seasonal events, tasks, or achievements might town dwellers celebrate together?

LITERARY FOCUS

Alliteration and Assonance
Alliteration is the repetition of consonant sounds within a short space. Usually alliteration occurs at the

beginnings of words, but it may also occur within words. Notice the repetition of consonant sounds in the sentence "The *calico* *cat* atta*ck*ed the *c*ouch." **Assonance** refers to the repetition of vowel sounds, as in the phrase "*coo*l b*lue* m*oo*n." Both alliteration and assonance add to a poem's musical qualities by creating echoes among its sounds. When these devices are used, a translator will usually try to retain them in any translation.

Thinking About Alliteration and Assonance
1. What examples of alliteration and assonance occur in lines 5–6 of "Street Cries"? Why is the use of such musical devices especially appropriate for this poem?
2. What examples of alliteration and assonance occur in lines 1–2 of "Reaping the Barley"? Why is the use of these musical devices especially appropriate in these lines?

Parallelism
Parallelism is the placement of related ideas in parallel, or similar, structures. For example, Julius Caesar's famous statement "I came, I saw, I conquered" is an example of parallelism because, as translated into English, it is composed of three parallel clauses consisting of the pronoun *I* and a past-tense verb. Parallelism gives extra emphasis to the ideas arranged in parallel structures and helps tie a work together.

Thinking About Parallelism
■ Explain how the three stanzas of "Street Cries" employ parallelism. What are the specific parallels in lines 6, 12, and 18? What related ideas does the parallelism emphasize?

COMPOSITION

Writing About Poetry
■ Write a composition showing how Naidu uses poetic techniques to convey her ideas in "Street Cries." First identify the central ideas of the poem. Then explain how imagery and figurative language, sound devices such as rhyme and alliteration, parallelism, and stanza form all help to convey or emphasize these ideas. *For help with this assignment, refer to Lesson 9 in the Writing About Literature Handbook at the back of this book.*

COMPOSITION: GUIDELINES FOR EVALUATION

WRITING ABOUT POETRY

Objective
To analyze the use of poetic devices in a poem

Guidelines for Evaluation
■ suggested length: three paragraphs

■ should identify the main ideas in the poem
■ should describe the use of imagery, figurative language, sound devices, parallelism, and stanza form
■ should explain how these elements help convey the poem's main ideas

Nguyen Trai

(1380–1442) *Vietnam*

Nguyen Trai [ngī en′ trī′] is considered among the most notable classical poets of the southeast Asian nation of Vietnam. Born at a time when Vietnam was still dominated by neighboring China, Nguyen Trai helped repel a Chinese invasion and was instrumental in rebuilding his war-torn land. A scholar as well as a soldier and politician, he produced the first major treatment of the geography of Vietnam and pioneered literature composed in the native Vietnamese language. His poetry, written late in life, helped establish the principles of Vietnamese verse.

Nguyen Trai

The Bamboo Hut

Translated from the Vietnamese by Nguyen Ngoc Bich
with Burton Raffel and W. S. Merwin

A bamboo hut and a plum tree bower—
That's where I spend my days, far from the world's talk.
For meals, only some pickled cabbage,
But I've never cared for the life of damask[1] and silk.
5 There's a pool of water for watching the moon,
And land to plow into flower beds.
Sometimes I feel inspired on snowy nights—
That's when I write my best poems, and sing.

---

1. **damask** [dam′əsk]: thick reversible fabric made of threads woven into elaborate patterns.

The Bamboo Hut **329**

Emily Dickinson

(1830–1886) *United States*

Now widely regarded as one of America's greatest poets, Emily Dickinson published only seven poems in her own lifetime. Instead she led a shy and retiring life in Amherst, Massachusetts, her home town. Despite her isolation, she had a probing, highly original mind and a vivid imagination—evident in the bundles of poems she left behind, many of them written on scraps of paper neatly tied with ribbons. Her poems explore such topics as nature, faith, death, and the importance of being a self-reliant individual.

Emily Dickinson

How Happy Is the Little Stone

How happy is the little Stone
That rambles in the Road alone,
And doesn't care about Careers
And Exigencies never fears—
5   Whose Coat of elemental Brown
A passing Universe put on,
And independent as the Sun
Associates or glows alone,
Fulfilling absolute Decree
10 In casual simplicity—

The Trail to Champney Falls, 1983, Robert Jordan.

330   *Poetry*

STUDY QUESTIONS

The Bamboo Hut (Nguyen Trai)
Recalling
1. Where does the speaker spend his days? What is he far from? What has he never cared for?
2. What happens sometimes on snowy nights?

Interpreting
3. What does the speaker mean by the "life of damask and silk"?
4. What things does the poem suggest are needed for human happiness? What things does it suggest are not necessary?
5. What does the poem suggest are the sources of poetic creativity?

Extending
6. Do you agree with the speaker's ideas about what makes for a happy life? Why or why not?

How Happy Is the Little Stone (Dickinson)
Recalling
1. Where does the happy little stone ramble? What does it not care about?
2. What puts on the stone's "Coat of elemental Brown"? Like the "independent" sun, what does the stone do?

Interpreting
3. What sort of person does the stone represent?
4. What does the poem suggest are the sources of human happiness? What cares or fears does it suggest can lead to unhappiness?
5. Does the speaker consider herself to be like the stone? Explain.

Extending
6. Do isolation and independence bring happiness to most people? Discuss your opinions.

LITERARY FOCUS

Rhythm and Meter

In poetry **rhythm** refers to the pattern of beats created by the syllables and stresses of the words in each line. In some poems the pattern of beats is regular and predictable. These poems are said to have regular **meter**. For example, the following lines from Sarojini Naidu's poem "Street Cries" have a regular meter in which unstressed syllables, which are marked ‿ , alternate with stressed syllables, which are marked ´ :

When twi / light twink / ling o'er / the gay / bazaars,
Unfurls / a sud / den can / opy / of stars,

A unit of meter made up of one unstressed syllable followed by one stressed syllable is called an **iamb.** How many iambs can you count in each of the lines of poetry above? A poem that has five iambs per line is said to be written in **iambic pentameter** [pen tam'ə tər], one of the most common meters in English poetry.

Most Western poetry written before 1900 is **metrical** verse, or poetry using regular meter. Traditional Oriental poetry, on the other hand, is usually **syllabic** rather than metrical. That is, it is written in a pattern based on the number of syllables rather than the sequence of stressed and unstressed syllables. Poems that have been translated from one language to another often do not follow the original metrical or syllabic pattern of their original language.

Thinking About Rhythm and Meter
■ Copy Dickinson's poem on a separate sheet, and mark the stressed and unstressed syllables. Does the meter of the poem use iambs? Is the poem written in iambic pentameter? Explain.

COMPOSITION

Reacting to a Poem
■ Imagine that you are writing a letter to Nguyen Trai or Emily Dickinson. In the letter give your personal response and express your opinion of the ideas in the poem you have read. Citing details from the poem, discuss in particular its ideas about happiness. Then state whether you agree or disagree with the ideas, and explain why.

COMPARING POEMS
■ What is similar about the views of happiness expressed in the two poems? Which poem places more emphasis on nature's role in human happiness? Cite details to support your answer.

The Bamboo Hut; How Happy Is the Little Stone **331**

COMPOSITION: GUIDELINES FOR EVALUATION

REACTING TO A POEM

Objective
To write a letter of opinion

Guidelines for Evaluation
■ suggested length: one to two pages
■ should be in the form of a friendly letter addressed to one of the poets
■ should give a personal response, discuss the ideas in the poem about happiness, and cite details from the poem
■ should state and support an opinion about the ideas in the poem

ANSWERS

STUDY QUESTIONS

The Bamboo Hut
1. in a bamboo hut and a plum-tree bower; the world's talk; "the life of damask and silk"
2. He writes poems and sings.
3. a life of luxury and riches
4. closeness to nature, a simple life, an independent spirit; society and wealth
5. nature, a simple life, and contemplative isolation
6. Answers will vary. Some may say closeness to nature brings happiness, but rejecting society is ill-advised.

How Happy Is the Little Stone
1. "in the Road alone"; "Careers"
2. "A passing Universe"; "Associates or glows alone,/Fulfilling absolute Decree/In casual simplicity"
3. an independent, untroubled, self-fulfilled person with few social ties and a simple life
4. solitude, independence, simplicity, and affinity with the natural and the spiritual; concern about one's job, fear of the unexpected, bonds that sap independence, and not fulfilling one's inner nature
5. to some extent, though the stone symbolizes an ideal
6. Answers will vary. Some may say that too much solitude may cause callousness; too much independence, selfishness.

LITERARY FOCUS

How happy is the little Stone
That rambles in the Road alone,
and doesn't care about Careers
And Exigencies never fears—
Whose Coat of elemental Brown
A passing Universe put on,
And independent as the Sun
Associates or glows alone,
Fulfilling absolute Decree
In casual simplicity—

No; The poem is written in iambic tetrameter (lines of four iambs).

COMPARING POEMS

Both associate happiness with isolation, simplicity, independence, and affinity with nature and spirituality. "The Bamboo Hut" emphasizes nature's role more.

The Bamboo Hut; How Happy Is the Little Stone **T-331**

Vicente Aleixandre

(1898–1984) *Spain*

Vicente Aleixandre [bē then′tā ä′leks än′drä] grew up in the Spanish city of Málaga and later moved to Madrid, where he attended high school and college. There he studied law and business management and, after graduation, found work writing articles for a business magazine. In 1922 he began to suffer from the first of the many illnesses that made him a partial invalid for most of his life. Confined to his home, he started writing the poetry that eventually made him famous. In 1977 Aleixandre's literary achievements were honored with the Nobel Prize.

Vicente Aleixandre

On the Way to School

Translated from the Spanish by Stephen Kessler

I rode my bicycle to school.
Along a peaceful street that ran through the center of the noble,
    mysterious city.
I rode by, surrounded by lights, and the carriages made no
    noise.
They passed, majestic, pulled by distinguished bays or
    chestnuts[1] that moved with a proud bearing.
5 How they lifted their hooves as they went along, like
    gentlemen, precise,
not disdaining the world, but studying it
from the sovereign grace of their manes!
And inside, what? Old ladies, scarcely a little more than lace,
silent ornaments, stuck-up hairstyles, ancient velvet:
10 a pure silence passing, pulled by the heavy shining animals.

I rode my bicycle, I almost had wings, I was inspired.
And there were wide sidewalks along that sunny street.
In the sunlight, some sudden butterfly hovered over the
    carriages and then, along the sidewalks,
over the slow strollers made of smoke.

---

1. **bays or chestnuts:** reddish-brown horses.

Kids on Bikes, 1950, David Park.

15 But they were mothers taking their littlest children for a walk.
    And fathers who, in their offices of glass and dreams . . .
    I looked as I went by.
    I sailed through the sweet smoke, and the butterfly was no
        stranger.
    Pale in the iridescent winter afternoon,
20 she spread herself out in the slow street as over a sheltered,
        sleepy valley.
    And I saw her swept up sometimes to hang suspended
    over what could as well have been the pleasant bank of a river.
    Ah, nothing was terrible.
    The street had a slight grade and up I went, driven on.
25 A wind swept the hats of the old ladies.
    It wasn't hurt by the peaceful canes of the gentlemen.
    And it lit up like an imaginary rose, a little like a kiss, on the
        cheeks of the children.
    The trees in a row were a motionless vapor, gently
    suspended under the blue. And by now nearly up in the air,
30 I hurried past on my bicycle and smiled . . .
    and I remember perfectly
    how I folded my wings mysteriously on the very threshold of
        the school.

On the Way to School **333**

- iridescent: rainbow-colored
- vapor: something cloudy or not solid
- threshold: doorstep

TEACHING IMAGERY AND MOOD

Have students find the images in the poem that suggest a dream-like feeling of floating, such as "I almost had wings" (l. 11), "hovered over the carriages" (l. 13), "strollers made of smoke" (l. 14), "swept up . . . to hang suspended" (l. 21), "a motionless vapor, gently/suspended under the blue" (ll. 28–29), "nearly up in the air" (l. 29). What feelings does this imagery convey? (Possible answers: fantasy, freedom, happiness, exaltation, exhilaration, transcendence)

TEACHING SYMBOLISM

Explain that the butterfly is traditionally a symbol for the soul. Then ask why this symbol is particularly appropriate in this poem. (It helps render in a concrete way the speaker's transcendent, spiritual experience.)

COLLABORATIVE LEARNING: ENRICHMENT ACTIVITY

Illustration Have students work together to create a collage or mural that evokes the images and feelings of the speaker on his bicycle ride.

ART AND LITERATURE

The figurative artist David Park (1911–1960) used a thick, painterly style called impasto. He has situated figures in a field of color with very little foreshortening.

- Ask students to explain how each boy in the painting suggests a different aspect of the boy riding his bike in the poem. (The boy in the background suggests the concentration of the poem's bicyclist and the uphill grade of the street. The boy in the foreground suggests the speaker's reflectiveness and his stillness at the end of the ride.)

What lines do you think best capture the feeling of riding a bicycle? Explain.

STUDY QUESTIONS

1. "peaceful street"; "noble, mysterious city"
2. wings; the butterfly
3. old ladies in carriages, mothers walking with children, and fathers in offices
4. "how I folded my wings mysteriously on the very threshold of the school"
5. Possible answers: free, exhilarated, happy, exalted, and transcendent
6. No; line 23 suggests that the speaker has experienced terrible things since his boyhood.
7. The speaker compares himself to a butterfly; "the butterfly was no stranger" (l. 18), "nearly up in the air" (l. 29), and "I folded my wings mysteriously" (l. 32).
8. He feels nostalgia for that lost world.
9. Possible answers: waking up on Christmas morning, dressing up on Halloween, and playing games; Answers will vary; many students will say that they would not feel the same way now.

LITERARY FOCUS

The break in line 21 enhances the feeling of floating by making the phrase "hang suspended" itself hang suspended above the next line. The shortness of line 23 adds emphasis to the poignant declaration and suggests that the speaker does not want to think about his current feelings. In a poem about feelings of expansiveness and freedom, Aleixandre appropriately uses free-verse lines of differing lengths that exhibit freedom from traditional poetic conventions.

STUDY QUESTIONS

Recalling

1. What adjectives describe the street and city where the speaker rode his bicycle to school?
2. What does the speaker say he "almost had" when he rode? What was no stranger to him?
3. List three groups of people that the speaker passed on his ride.
4. What does the speaker "remember perfectly"?

Interpreting

5. How did the speaker feel during his bicycle rides?
6. Does the speaker seem as happy now as he was then? What does line 23 imply about how his world has changed?
7. What metaphor is implied in line 11? Which details later in the poem extend this metaphor?
8. What feeling does the speaker now have toward his bicycle rides to school and the world he knew then?

Extending

9. What childhood experiences do you remember with fondness? Do you think you would enjoy them as much today as you did then? Explain.

LITERARY FOCUS

Free Verse

Free verse is poetry that does not follow a regular, predictable pattern of rhythm, line length, or rhyme. Free verse is a relatively recent form of poetry. Before the twentieth century most poets wrote in regular metrical or syllabic verse, which follows fixed patterns. Toward the end of the nineteenth century, however, a few poets broke with long-established poetic traditions and began writing poems in free verse. Their experiments prompted many poets in our own century to use free verse when it suited their purposes.

Usually, when a poet chooses to use free verse, there is some relationship between the form of the poem and its meaning. Since the lines of free verse can be of any length, the poet must consider several factors in determining where to end lines: how the lines look on the page, how they sound when they are read, and especially how the breaks at the ends of the lines affect the meaning and flow of the poem. The poet using free verse must therefore be sensitive to the natural rhythms and pauses of a language; if the poem is being translated, the translator must display a similar sensitivity.

Thinking About Free Verse

■ In "On the Way to School," why do you think line 21 breaks where it does? Why is line 23 so short? Why is free verse especially appropriate for the poem as a whole, given its subject matter?

COMPOSITION

Writing About Free Verse

■ Write a brief composition about the use of free verse in "On the Way to School." First discuss the poem as a whole and the suitability of free verse to the poem's overall content. Then examine specific lines of the poem, explaining how line lengths and the places where the lines break reflect or enhance the content of the lines.

Writing Free Verse

■ Using free verse, write a poem about an outdoor activity or sport that you enjoy performing or watching. Pay particular attention to your line breaks and the way they affect the meaning and flow of the poem.

COMPOSITION: GUIDELINES FOR EVALUATION

WRITING ABOUT FREE VERSE

Objective

To analyze and evaluate the relationship between the form of a poem and its content

Guidelines for Evaluation

■ suggested length: one or two paragraphs
■ should make a general statement about how the form of the poem suits its content
■ should provide details about specific lines

WRITING FREE VERSE

Objective

To write a poem in free verse

Guidelines for Evaluation

■ suggested length: five to ten lines
■ should describe an outdoor activity or sport
■ should not have a predictable rhythm or rhyme
■ should have lines of varying lengths

Rainer Maria Rilke

(1875–1926) *Austria*

The great German-language poet Rainer Maria Rilke [rī′nər mə rē′ə ril′kə] was born in Prague, Czechoslovakia, when it was still part of the Austro-Hungarian Empire. A man who always seemed to be searching for a home, Rilke traveled all over Europe. One of his most beloved places was Paris, France, where he worked as secretary to the famous sculptor Auguste Rodin [ō gōōst′ rō dan′]. Rodin's techniques influenced Rilke's early poetry, in which he captured the essence of an object or person in concrete terms. He called these "thing-poems."

Rainer Maria Rilke

Spanish Dancer

Translated from the German by Stephen Mitchell

As on all its sides a kitchen-match darts white
flickering tongues before it bursts into flame:
with the audience around her, quickened, hot,
her dance begins to flicker in the dark room.

5 And all at once it is completely fire.

One upward glance and she ignites her hair
and, whirling faster and faster, fans her dress
into passionate flames, till it becomes a furnace
from which, like startled rattlesnakes, the long
10 naked arms uncoil, aroused and clicking.

And then: as if the fire were too tight
around her body, she takes and flings it out
haughtily, with an imperious gesture,
and watches: it lies raging on the floor,
15 still blazing up, and the flames refuse to die—.
Till, moving with total confidence and a sweet
exultant smile, she looks up finally
and stamps it out with powerful small feet.

Detail. *Ballet Espagnol,* 1862, Edouard Manet.

Spanish Dancer **335**

Did Rilke succeed in capturing the essence of the dancer? Which details seem exactly right?

ANSWERS

STUDY QUESTIONS

1. a kitchen match; It becomes fire.
2. It ignites her hair. It fans her dress into passionate flames.
3. She throws it onto the floor and stamps it out.
4. flamenco; castanets
5. passion, haughtiness, and exultation; a magnetic, spellbinding effect
6. The dance is compared to fire. The dance flickers like a match and then bursts into flame (ll. 1–5); the dancer's movements spread the fire over her body (ll. 6–10); the dancer throws the fire onto the floor (ll. 11–15); and the dancer extinguishes the fire by stamping it out (ll. 16–18).
7. an intense, exciting mood
8. Answers will vary. Students may mention appearance, skill, style, voice, and rapport with the audience.

LANGUAGE STUDY

1. "kind of metal"; from *kobold,* "goblin that haunts mines"
2. "prepared meats, salads, and so on, or store where they are sold"; from *delikatessen,* "delicacies"
3. "sign or spell that brings bad luck"; from *hexe,* "witch"
4. "gathering to drink coffee and chat"; from *kaffee,* "coffee," and *klatsch,* "gossip"
5. "to export or import illegally in secret"; from *smuggeln,* "to smuggle"
6. "device for taking in air while underwater"; from *schnörkel,* "spiral"
7. "kind of dance"; from *walzen,* "to roll or dance"
8. "longing to wander or travel"; from *wandern,* "to wander," and *lust,* "desire"

STUDY QUESTIONS

Recalling

1. What does the dance begin to flicker like in lines 1–5? What happens "all at once"?
2. According to lines 6–10, what does one upward glance do to the dancer's hair? What does her whirling do to her dress?
3. Summarize what the dancer seems to do to the fire in lines 11–18.

Interpreting

4. What variety of dance does this poem portray? What is the "clicking" sound in line 10?
5. What personality traits does the dancer display? What effect does she have on her audience?
6. What extended metaphor runs through the poem? Identify at least three steps or stages in the metaphor.
7. What mood do the extended metaphor and the poem's other details help achieve?

Extending

8. In your opinion, what makes a performer exciting? What makes a performance memorable?

LANGUAGE STUDY

Words from German

The German language, in which Rilke wrote, has contributed many words to English. Some of these words were borrowed in Europe; others were brought to North America by German-speaking immigrants and were borrowed by English speakers here.

Use a dictionary to help you determine the meanings and origins of the following English words, which all came to English from German.

1. cobalt
2. delicatessen
3. hex
4. kaffeeklatsch
5. smuggle
6. snorkel
7. waltz
8. wanderlust

COMPOSITION

Writing About Imagery and Figurative Language

■ Write a brief essay about the imagery and figurative language in "Spanish Dancer." Citing specific details, show how the images and figurative language help us to picture the dancer and allow us to feel as if we are witnessing the performance. Also discuss how the images and figurative language work together to achieve a particular mood.

Describing a Person's or an Object's Movements

■ Write a poem or a paragraph describing a person or an object engaged in a particular activity that involves movement. For example, you might describe a person throwing a bowling ball or an airplane zooming through the sky. Use images and figurative language to help readers get a vivid sense of the movement you are describing.

COMPOSITION: GUIDELINES FOR EVALUATION

WRITING ABOUT IMAGERY AND FIGURATIVE LANGUAGE

Objective

To analyze and evaluate the effects of the imagery and figurative language in a poem

Guidelines for Evaluation

■ suggested length: two or three paragraphs
■ should relate the imagery and language to the mood

DESCRIBING A PERSON'S OR AN OBJECT'S MOVEMENTS

Objective

To write a vivid description of a person or object in motion

Guidelines for Evaluation

■ suggested length: one paragraph or five to ten lines
■ should use vivid imagery and figurative language

Li Po

(701–762) *China*

For many centuries Li Po [lē′ bō′] has been one of China's most highly regarded poets. In his lifetime he served briefly as an official poet at the Chinese emperor's court, and later he wrote verse for Prince Lin, one of the emperor's sons. The political intrigues of the day were not to Li Po's liking, however, and he spent most of his life wandering across China, visiting friends and writing poetry as the impulse took him. Many of Li Po's poems explore the topics of nature, friendship, solitude, and the passage of time.

Li Po

Taking Leave of a Friend

Translated from the Chinese by Ezra Pound

Blue mountains to the north of the walls,
White river winding about them;
Here we must make separation
And go out through a thousand miles
    of dead grass.

5 Mind like a floating wide cloud,
Sunset like the parting of old acquaintances
Who bow over their clasped hands at a distance.
Our horses neigh to each other
        as we are departing.

Detail from an eight-panel Chinese screen, 1773.

Taking Leave of a Friend **337**

LESSON PREVIEW

Two friends are about to part. The sunset seems to mirror the sad parting while the friends' horses neigh to each other.

LITERARY SKILLS FOR THIS SELECTION

- tone
- imagery

THEMES IN THIS SELECTION

- sorrow at separation from friends
- harmony between humanity and nature

LESSON OBJECTIVES

1. to recognize the tone of a poem and the images that contribute to it
2. to write a poem about an emotional incident
3. to compare two poems

Teacher's Classroom Resources 2

■ Teaching Notes	213
■ Literary Focus: Tone	214
■ Writing Process Guide: Writing About an Emotional Incident	215
■ Selection Test	216

IN THE CLASSROOM

TEACHING STUDENTS OF DIFFERENT ABILITIES

- **For less advanced students:** Point out that lines 1–2 and 5–7 are elliptical: They lack the parts of speech that would make them complete sentences. Have students supply the appropriate verbs and articles.
- **For more advanced students:** Have students revise the images and tone of the poem to suit a new title: "Seeing a Friend After a Long Absence."

MOTIVATION: PRIOR KNOWLEDGE

Have students recall scenes from movies that portray a parting. Discuss the various emotions that such scenes elicit (sadness, grief, hope, humor).

TEACHING TONE

Point out how imagery can indicate tone. Here the speaker's sad tone is evident in "a thousand miles/of dead grass" and in the human silence implied in "Our horses neigh to each other/ as we are departing."

ART AND LITERATURE

Wood and fabric screens have long been used in China as room dividers. Many depicted stories, as does this intricately carved and painted screen from 1773.

- Ask students what the three characters on the screen might be saying and in what tone. (They may be saying farewell in a solemn, subdued tone.)

Taking Leave of a Friend **T-337**

Czeslaw Milosz

(born 1911) *Poland/United States*

Among the finest poets from the Eastern European nation of Poland, Nobel Prize–winner Czeslaw Milosz [ches′wäf me̅′wôsh] spent his youth traveling in Eastern Europe with his engineer father. During World War II he wrote anti-Nazi poems for an underground journal in Warsaw, Poland's capital. Later Milosz served as a diplomat, but then he grew disillusioned with Poland's Communist government and sought political asylum in the West. His poetry finds inspiration in the landscapes of his childhood and often treats the topics of exile, loss, and separation.

Czeslaw Milosz

Encounter

Translated from the Polish by Czeslaw Milosz and Lillian Vallee

We were riding through frozen fields in a wagon at dawn.
A red wing rose in the darkness.

And suddenly a hare ran across the road.
One of us pointed to it with his hand.

5 That was long ago. Today neither of them is alive,
Not the hare, nor the man who made the gesture.

O my love, where are they, where are they going
The flash of a hand, streak of movement, rustle of pebbles.
I ask not out of sorrow, but in wonder.

STUDY QUESTIONS

Taking Leave of a Friend (Li Po)
Recalling
1. Where must the speaker take leave of his friend? According to lines 1–4, through what must they go out?
2. What is the sunset like? What do the horses do?

Interpreting
3. How does the speaker feel about taking leave of his friend?
4. Why does the sunset seem the way it does to the speaker?
5. What do the simile in lines 6–7 and the remark about the horses reveal about the way people sometimes view nature?

Extending
6. Have modern improvements in communications and transportation made partings from friends easier to bear than they were in Li Po's day? Why or why not?

Encounter (Milosz)
Recalling
1. What happened when the speaker and his companions were riding through the frozen fields?
2. What has since happened to the hare and the man who made the gesture?
3. What does the speaker ask in the last three lines? What does he say causes him to ask these questions?

Interpreting
4. How do the images in lines 2–4 contrast with the "frozen fields" in line 1?
5. To whom or what do the images in line 8 refer? Why do the images arouse the speaker's sense of wonder?
6. What "encounters" occur in the poem? What larger questions about existence is the speaker actually posing?

Extending
7. Why do seemingly insignificant incidents in our lives sometimes take on great importance?

LITERARY FOCUS

Tone

The **tone** of a poem is the attitude the speaker or narrator takes toward the poem's subject matter. Just as our tone of voice often reveals our feelings, written words can also express emotions and attitudes. For example, the tone of a poem may be angry, joyous, sad, amused, puzzled, casual, solemn, or matter-of-fact. The tone may even combine different emotions or may change in the course of a work.

In poetry, as in any piece of writing, tone is conveyed chiefly by the writer's word choices and sentence structures. For example, to achieve a happy tone, a writer can use words that create pleasant images and combine them in musical sentences that have a lighthearted effect. Although some of a poem's music may be lost in translation, a good translator tries to use images and figurative language that capture the tone of the original work.

Thinking About Tone
1. What is the speaker's tone in "Taking Leave of a Friend"? Which image in the first stanza most strongly conveys this tone?
2. What changes in tone occur in "Encounter"?

COMPOSITION

Writing About an Emotional Incident
■ Write a brief poem about a departure or an encounter to which you had a strong emotional response. For example, you might describe a sad departure, a joyous reunion, or an accidental encounter with someone or something you like or dislike very much. Write in a tone that suits your emotions, and use images and figurative language to help convey your tone.

COMPARING POEMS

■ What is similar about the incidents described in the two poems? What is different about the feelings and attitudes that the incidents prompt in the poems' speakers?

COMPOSITION: GUIDELINES FOR EVALUATION

WRITING ABOUT AN EMOTIONAL INCIDENT

Objective
To write a poem describing an emotional incident

Guidelines for Evaluation
■ suggested length: ten lines
■ should describe an emotional departure or reunion
■ should use images and figurative language to convey an appropriate tone

---

Which poem was it easier for you to identify with? Why?

ANSWERS

STUDY QUESTIONS

Taking Leave of a Friend
1. "north of the walls," where a white river winds through blue mountains; a "thousand miles/ of dead grass"
2. "the parting of old acquaintances"; They "neigh to each other."
3. He feels sad.
4. It mirrors his sense of loss.
5. People sometimes attribute human emotions and concerns to events in nature.
6. Answers will vary. Students may feel that some partings remain difficult.

Encounter
1. "A red wing rose," "a hare ran across the road," and one of the speaker's companions pointed to it.
2. They have died.
3. He asks where they are and where they are going; wonder.
4. They suggest motion and life, whereas the frozen fields suggest immobility and death.
5. to the hare and the man who pointed; He realizes that life's experiences are fleeting.
6. The riders encounter the red wing and the hare; the speaker encounters his memory of the incident and his own questions about life and death.
7. Possible answer: We fail to grasp their importance until much later, when our perspective is different.

LITERARY FOCUS

1. The tone is sad. The image of "a thousand miles / of dead grass" conveys it most strongly.
2. Lines 1–4 have an unemotional tone. Lines 5–6 suggest something disturbing. Line 7 introduces strong emotion and bewilderment.

COMPARING POEMS

Both poems involve the parting of companions—one by distance, the other by death. In Li Po's poem the parting prompts sorrow; in Milosz's it prompts bewildering questions about the meaning of life.

LESSON PREVIEW

The original Spanish version and three English translations of a poem comparing the sound of a guitar to weeping are given. The guitar begins at dawn and cannot be stopped. It cries for faraway and tragic things. The instrument is like a heart wounded by five swords.

LITERARY SKILLS FOR THIS SELECTION

- translation and word choice
- imagery and mood
- metaphor

THEMES IN THIS SELECTION

- the power of music to express human sorrow
- the connection between art and nature

LESSON OBJECTIVES

1. to analyze word choices in three translations of a poem
2. to write a comparison of the three translations
3. to write a poem about music

Teacher's Classroom Resources 2

- Teaching Notes   217
- Literary Focus: Translation and Word Choice   218
- Writing Process Guides: Comparing and Contrasting Translations   219
  Writing About Music   220
- Selection Test   221

IN THE CLASSROOM

TEACHING STUDENTS OF DIFFERENT ABILITIES

- **For less advanced students:** Have students, especially those unfamiliar with Spanish, find words in the original version that closely resemble English words, such as *guitarra* (l. 2), *imposible* (l. 8), *monótona* (l. 10), *agua* (l. 11), *arena* (l. 18), *camelias* (l. 19), and *primer* (l. 22). Then have them find the English counterparts of these words in each of the translations.
- **For more advanced students:** Have students work in groups to research and find additional English translations of one or two other poems in this an-

thology—Petrarch's Sonnet 3 or Heinrich Heine's "The Lorelei," for example. Then ask students to compare the translations.

MOTIVATION: PRIOR KNOWLEDGE

Have students bring to class and introduce recordings of music that they consider mournful. You might then play a recording of Spanish guitar music.

Federico García Lorca

(1899–1936) *Spain*

Federico García Lorca [gär sē′ə lôr′kə], one of modern Spain's greatest poets, grew up on his family's farm outside the city of Granada, Spain. There he developed a love of music from his mother, a noted pianist, and his godfather, Spanish composer Manuel de Falla. He began publishing his poetry in 1921. He also won fame as the author of several plays, including *Blood Wedding* and *The House of Bernardo Alba*. Music is both a topic and a tool of much of García Lorca's poetry. His noted poem "The Guitar" is presented here in three different translations so that you may compare and contrast the translators' efforts.

Federico García Lorca

La Guitarra

Empieza el llanto
de la guitarra.
Se rompen las copas
de la madrugada.
5 Empieza el llanto
de la guitarra.
Es inútil callarla.
Es imposible
callarla.
10 Llora monótona
como llora el agua,
como llora el viento
sobre la nevada.

Es imposible
15 callarla.
Llora por cosas
lejanas.
Arena del Sur caliente
que pide camelias blancas.
20 Llora flecha sin blanco,
la tarde sin mañana,
y el primer pájaro muerto
sobre la rama.
¡Oh guitarra!
25 Corazón malherido
por cinco espadas.

The Guitar

Translated from the Spanish
by Robert Bly

The crying of the guitar
starts.
The goblets
of the dawn break.
5 The crying of the guitar
starts.
No use to stop it.
It is impossible
to stop it.
10 It cries repeating itself
as the water cries,
as the wind cries
over the snow.
It is impossible
15 to stop it.
It is crying for things
far off.
The warm sand of the South
that asks for white camellias.
20 For the arrow with nothing to hit,
the evening with no dawn coming,
and the first bird of all dead
on the branch.
Guitar!
25 Heart wounded, gravely,
by five swords.

Guitar, 1912-1913, Pablo Picasso.

IN THE GLOSSARY

- goblets: drinking glasses
- camellias: roselike flowers

TEACHING STUDENTS OF LIMITED ENGLISH PROFICIENCY

Have students bring favorite poems to class that reflect their cultural background. Whenever possible, have students read foreign-language poems in both the original version and an English translation.

CULTURAL BACKGROUND

Strongly influenced by the Spanish artist Salvador Dali and the film maker Luis Buñuel, García Lorca became closely associated with the modern literary and artistic movement called surrealism. Surrealism typically employs seemingly irrational images to express the unconscious mind and inner states of reality. Images such as "goblets/of the dawn" (ll. 3–4) and "the evening with no dawn coming" (l. 21) in Bly's translation attempt to evoke such inner landscapes.

TEACHING TRANSLATION

Explain that the act of translating is not only a means of gaining access to ideas written in a foreign language but also a means of scrutinizing a foreign writer's style and craft. Accordingly, many American poets translate the works of foreign poets to increase their own poetic skills. Robert Bly, who translated this version, is a celebrated American poet noted for his use of "deep images"—archetypal imagery that reveals the inner reality of human experience, often in surreal ways. He credits García Lorca and other Spanish surrealists as important influences on his own work.

ART AND LITERATURE

The Spanish artist Pablo Picasso (1881–1973) was a major force in twentieth-century painting and sculpture. One of his startlingly modern innovations was to piece works together. Instead of carving a shape from wood or stone, Picasso often assembled his sculptures from fragments or disparate, nontraditional elements, as in his tin and wire *Guitar.*

- Ask students to explain how Picasso's sculpting a guitar from pieces of tin and wire might resemble the process of translating a poem from one language to another. (As a translator would, Picasso has given an idea—the guitar—a somewhat different expression, in tin and wire.)

TEACHING TRANSLATION

Explain that translation involves not only diction—such as the choice of *cry, weep,* or *mourn* for the Spanish word *llora*—but also syntax, or word order. Have students compare the word order of lines 12–13 and line 19 in these two translations to see how word order can vary.

TEACHING IMAGERY AND MOOD

Ask students to list the images of faraway things in lines 19–24 (ll. 18–23 in Bly's translation). Why are these images particularly mournful? (They are so distant as to be unattainable: The sands, arrow, evening, and bird will never attain or possess the camellias, target, morning, or branch.)

TEACHING METAPHORS

Ask students to identify the powerful metaphor in the last three lines of the poem. (The guitar is compared to a heart wounded by five swords.) How does this metaphor reinforce the poet's earlier claim that it is impossible to stop, still, or hush the guitar? (A beating heart, like a guitar, is impossible to stop without killing its "music.")

COLLABORATIVE LEARNING: ENRICHMENT ACTIVITY

Music or Choral Reading Ask a group of students to prepare and present musical renditions or choral readings of "The Guitar." Students' performances should include word or line repetition in different voices, tones, and rhythms and may incorporate lines from all three translations and the original Spanish. Students might set the poem to their own music or incorporate suitable songs, such as George Harrison's "While My Guitar Gently Weeps."

The Guitar

Translated from the Spanish
by Elizabeth du Gué Trapier

Now begins the cry
Of the guitar,
Breaking the vaults
Of dawn.
5 Now begins the cry
Of the guitar.
Useless
To still it.
Impossible
10 To still it.
It weeps monotonously
As weeps the water,
As weeps the wind
Over snow.
15 Impossible
To still it.
It weeps
For distant things,
Warm southern sands
20 Desiring white camellias.
It mourns the arrow without a target,
The evening without morning.
And the first bird dead
Upon a branch.
25 O guitar!
A wounded heart,
Wounded by five swords.

The Guitar

Translated from the Spanish
by J. L. Gili and Stephen Spender

The lament
of the guitar begins.
The glasses of the dawn
are broken.
5 The lament
of the guitar begins.
It is useless
to hush it.
It is impossible
10 to hush it.
Monotonously weeping
as the water weeps,
as the wind weeps
over the snowfall.
15 It is impossible
to hush it.
Weeping for things
far away.
Sands of the warm South
20 seeking white camellias.
It weeps, like an arrow without a target,
evening without morning,
and the first bird dead
upon the branch.
25 Oh guitar!
Heart pierced through
with five swords.

STUDY QUESTIONS

Recalling

1. According to the opening lines of the Bly translation, what is it impossible to do?
2. In lines 11–14 of the Gué Trapier translation, how does the guitar weep? What three things does it mourn?
3. In the last two lines of the Gili-Spender translation, how is the guitar described?

Interpreting

4. How would you describe the music that the guitar seems to be playing in all three translations? In the last two lines, what are the "five swords" that wound or pierce the guitar?
5. What extra dimensions does the guitar take on when it is compared to wind and water? When its sounds are compared to crying or weeping?
6. Does the speaker enjoy the sound of the guitar? Why is it impossible to "stop," "still," or "hush" its crying?

Extending

7. What changes would you make in the poem if you were describing an *electric* guitar?

LITERARY FOCUS

Translation and Word Choice

Because poets choose and arrange their words carefully to capture particular images, sounds, moods, and tones, poetry is the most difficult form of literature to translate. A translation that is too literal may convey the word-for-word details of the original but lose the subtleties of sound, mood, and tone that are part of the poem's essential spirit. On the other hand, a looser translation may evoke the spirit of the poem but neglect its details.

An important factor in translating a poem is **word choice,** or **diction,** the selection of words to convey meaning, suggest attitude, and create images. The translator must choose words that retain the mood and tone as well as the meaning of the original. In choosing among synonyms, he or she must therefore pay attention to each synonym's **connotations**—the emotional associations that the word conveys beyond its literal meaning—and also to its sound.

To illustrate the differences that can exist among translations, three translations of "The Guitar" are presented on the preceding pages. Although the original Spanish poem is free verse—poetry without a regular pattern of rhythm, rhyme, and line length—it does use rhythm, line lengths, and word repetition to capture the sound of a guitar being strummed. In addition, it has a strong mood and tone. All three translations attempt to capture García Lorca's sound, mood, and tone while also being faithful to the meaning of his original wording.

Thinking About Translation and Word Choice

1. In the first three lines of each translation, what different words are used to describe the sound of the guitar? Which synonym most clearly establishes the mood of the poem? Explain.
2. In the next eight lines, do you find the word "hush" as effective as its synonyms in the other two translations? Why or why not?
3. Which of the three translations do you think most effectively captures the sound of a guitar being strummed? Cite details to support your opinion.
4. In the last three lines of each translation, which wording creates the most powerful image? Does the image suit the action to which it refers? Explain.

COMPOSITION

Comparing and Contrasting Translations

■ Write a composition in which you compare and contrast the three translations of "The Guitar." Begin by stating which translation you find most effective. Then support your opinion by citing examples of word choice and other details from the translations. If you know Spanish, you may also bring into your discussion the word choices of the original Spanish version of the poem.

Writing About Music

■ Listen to a work of classical music, jazz, or any other music with no lyrics. Then write a poem about the feelings and images that the music creates in your mind. Try to capture the mood of the music, as "The Guitar" does.

The Guitar **343**

ANSWERS

STUDY QUESTIONS

1. It is impossible to stop the guitar from crying.
2. "monotonously," like water or wind over snow; the "arrow without a target," the "evening without morning," and the "first bird dead/Upon a branch"
3. as a heart "pierced through/with five swords"
4. Possible answers: sad, mournful, yearning for the unattainable; the guitarist's fingers, the five senses through which all the sadness of human experience is perceived, or five strings
5. It becomes like a natural, elemental force. It is like a sensitive person.
6. Answers will vary. The guitar's sound is emotionally painful but also beautiful. It is unstoppable because it expresses the inevitable sadness of the human heart.
7. Answers will vary. Students should consider the louder and often less melancholy sound of electric guitars.

LITERARY FOCUS

1. *Cry, crying,* and *lament* describe the sound. *Lament* most clearly establishes the mournful mood, although *cry* conveys anguish and power.
2. Answers will vary. *Hush* suggests scolding a child and may therefore seem less appropriate. *Stop* loses the idea of sound. *Still* comes closest to the sound of the original Spanish word, *callarla.*
3. Answers will vary. Students should support their opinions by citing passages that they think suggest strumming.
4. Answers will vary. *Wounded,* a more exact translation of *malherido* than *pierced through,* seems preferable if the "five swords" are interpreted as the guitarist's fingers. *Pierced through,* however, creates a more violent, intense image. The image is appropriate because the sound of the guitar is painful to the listener.

COMPOSITION: GUIDELINES FOR EVALUATION

COMPARING AND CONTRASTING TRANSLATIONS

Objective

To compare alternate translations of a poem

Guidelines for Evaluation

■ suggested length: two or three paragraphs
■ should name the most effective translation
■ should cite supporting details from each translation

WRITING ABOUT MUSIC

Objective

To write a poem that captures the mood of a piece of music

Guidelines for Evaluation

■ suggested length: five to ten lines
■ should use images and figurative language
■ may be written in formal or free verse

George Seferis

(1900–1971) *Greece*

Greece's first writer to win the Nobel Prize, George Seferis [sə fer'is] was born Georgios Sepheriades to Greek parents in Smyrna, now part of Turkey. In his youth he experienced great homesickness, first when his family fled to Athens, Greece, to escape the devastation of World War I and then when he left Athens to study in Paris and London. Seferis later traveled the world as a Greek diplomat and served as Greece's ambassador to the United Nations. His poetry, which he began writing as a teen-ager, is marked by a sense of loneliness and loss.

Le Coeur, 1947, Henri Matisse.

George Seferis

I Am Sorry

Translated from the Greek by Rex Warner

I am sorry to have allowed a broad river to pass
    between my fingers
Without drinking a single drop.
Now I sink into the stone.
A small pine on the red soil
5 Is all the companionship I have.
What I loved has disappeared with the houses
Which were new last summer
And fell to pieces before the autumn wind.

344   Poetry

Jorge Luis Borges

(1899–1986) *Argentina*

Jorge Luis Borges [hôr′hā l͞oo ēs′ bôr′hās] grew up in Buenos Aires, capital of the South American nation of Argentina. In addition to Spanish, he spoke English in childhood, since one of his grandmothers was English; later, while living in Switzerland, he became fluent in French and German. Borges served as director of the National Library in Argentina and as a college professor both at home and abroad. A lifelong student of philosophy, he produced influential literary criticism as well as fiction and poetry.

Jorge Luis Borges

Afterglow

Translated from the Spanish by Norman Thomas di Giovanni

Sunset is always disturbing
whether theatrical or muted,
but still more disturbing
is that last desperate glow
5 that turns the plain to rust
when on the horizon nothing is left
of the pomp and clamor of the setting sun.
How hard holding on to that light, so tautly drawn and different,
that hallucination which the human fear of the dark
10 imposes on space
and which ceases at once
the moment we realize its falsity,
the way a dream is broken
the moment the sleeper knows he is dreaming.

Afterglow **345**

LESSON PREVIEW

The speaker finds the afterglow even more disturbing than sunset. That "different" light is illusive, ceasing as soon as we realize its falsity.

LITERARY SKILLS FOR THIS SELECTION

- symbolism
- simile

THEMES IN THIS SELECTION

- sorrow over the passage of time
- fear of mortality

LESSON OBJECTIVES

1. to understand the meaning of symbolism in a poem
2. to write a description of an unreal experience
3. to compare two poems

Teacher's Classroom Resources 2

- Teaching Notes   223
- Writing Process Guide: Writing About an Unreal Experience   226
- Selection Test   227

IN THE CLASSROOM

TEACHING STUDENTS OF DIFFERENT ABILITIES

- **For less advanced students:** Borges' sight began to fail in the 1950s, and by 1970 he was almost totally blind. Discuss what this information adds to lines 4 and 9 and to the poem's equation of light with life.
- **For more advanced students:** Help students appreciate Borges' unexpected tone: Whereas most people find the afterglow comforting and beautiful, Borges finds it "disturbing" and "desperate."

MOTIVATION: PRIOR KNOWLEDGE

Ask students to recall a particularly memorable sunset and explain how it made them feel.

IN THE GLOSSARY

- hallucination: illusion

TEACHING SYMBOLISM

Explain that poets may use interrelated symbols to give their poems deeper meaning. Students may recognize the sunset as a universal symbol for death and other endings. Ask them to explain by extension the symbolic meanings of the afterglow and "the dark" in line 9. (Possible answers: the unknown, the soul's afterlife, the end of existence)

TEACHING SIMILES

Point out that "the way" in line 13 means "in the same way that." Have students identify the simile it creates. (The ceasing of the light/hallucination is compared to the breaking of a dream.)

Afterglow **T-345**

Which poem seems more mysterious?

STUDY QUESTIONS

I Am Sorry
1. He has allowed a broad river to pass between his fingers.
2. "a small pine on the red soil"
3. "What I loved"
4. love or life itself; something the speaker loved
5. lonely, depressed, stultified
6. He may have failed to seize an opportunity. Lines 1–2 indicate that he blames himself for having allowed it to pass.
7. Most students will probably consider it universal.

Afterglow
1. sunset; the "last desperate glow"
2. "that hallucination which the human fear of the dark/imposes on space"
3. It ceases "the moment we realize its falsity."
4. a sunset and its afterglow
5. fear of the dark and regret of the day's end; They cause us to try to hold on to this illusory light.
6. death of the body; finitude of the soul or fame; the end of any experience
7. Many students will have experienced strong emotions that affected their senses.

LANGUAGE STUDY

1. "science of sound transmission"; from *akouein*, "to hear"
2. "science of the human species"; from *anthropos*, "human being," and *logos*, "thought"
3. "historical record"; from *chronos*, "time"
4. "short-lived"; from *epi-*, "upon," and *hemera*, "day"
5. "tube that reflects glass bits in symmetrical designs"; from *kalos*, "beautiful," *eidos*, "form," and *skopein*, "to look"
6. "showy display"; from *pempein*, "to send"
7. "relating to the theater"; from *theasthai*, "to view"
8. "relating to heat"; from *therme*, "heat"

COMPARING POEMS

Both are regretful and sad, but "I Am Sorry" is more realistic and "Afterglow" more fantastic. The use of *I* in "I Am Sorry" makes it more personal.

STUDY QUESTIONS

I Am Sorry (Seferis)
Recalling
1. According to the opening lines, why is the speaker sorry?
2. What is the only companionship that the speaker says he now has?
3. What has disappeared "with the houses / Which were new last summer"?

Interpreting
4. What might the "broad river" represent? What does line 6 suggest that it represents?
5. What do lines 3–5 suggest is the speaker's present condition?
6. What do you think actually happened in the speaker's life to cause such feelings? Does he blame himself for the loss? Explain.

Extending
7. Is regret a common human emotion? Discuss.

Afterglow (Borges)
Recalling
1. According to the opening lines, what is always disturbing? What is even more disturbing?
2. In lines 9–10, what is the afterglow called?
3. What happens to the afterglow, according to lines 11–14?

Interpreting
4. Explain in your own words the literal visual experience that this poem describes.
5. According to the speaker, what feelings do people have as the sun goes down? How do their emotions influence what they see?
6. What disturbing things might the sunset and its afterglow represent to the speaker?

Extending
7. Do you think people's emotions influence what they see and hear? Explain.

LANGUAGE STUDY

Words from Greek
The modern Greek in which George Seferis wrote is a direct descendant of the Greek spoken in ancient times. Over the centuries English has borrowed many words from Greek. Some came directly from Greek; many came via Latin, French, and other languages that had incorporated Greek words.

Use a dictionary to help you determine the meanings and origins of these English words from Greek. Some of the words appear in "Afterglow."

1. acoustics
2. anthropology
3. chronicle
4. ephemeral
5. kaleidoscope
6. pomp
7. theatrical
8. thermal

COMPOSITION

Writing About Imagery and Figurative Language
■ Write a brief composition about the imagery and figurative language in "I Am Sorry." First discuss the images that the poet uses and explain how they figuratively express the feelings and experiences of the speaker; then show how the images might all be part of a particular scene or setting that we can picture as we read the poem.

Writing About an Unreal Experience
■ Write a poem or a brief prose description of an experience similar to the one described in Borges' poem. For example, you might describe a mirage, a dream, or an experience of *déjà vu*. Use imagery and comparisons to help readers understand details of the experience and your feelings at the time.

COMPARING POEMS

■ Compare and contrast the tones of these two poems. Which poem would you say is more personal? Why do you think so?

COMPOSITION: GUIDELINES FOR EVALUATION

WRITING ABOUT IMAGERY AND FIGURATIVE LANGUAGE

Objective
To analyze and evaluate figurative language in a poem

Guidelines for Evaluation
■ suggested length: two or three paragraphs
■ should describe the images and the scene created
■ should relate the language to the speaker's emotions

WRITING ABOUT AN UNREAL EXPERIENCE

Objective
To write a poem or prose description about an unreal experience

Guidelines for Evaluation
■ suggested length: five to ten lines or one or two paragraphs
■ should use vivid imagery and comparisons

Heinrich Heine

(1797–1856) *Germany*

Heinrich Heine [hīn′rikн hī′nə] was one of Germany's greatest poets. Born in the city of Düsseldorf, Heine was encouraged by his family to study law, but he was always more interested in history and literature. His best-known poems, including "The Lorelei," were set to music and traveled all over the world as songs. According to German legend, the Lorelei [lôr′ə lī′] was a siren, or beautiful female spirit, who sat on a cliff overlooking Germany's Rhine River and sang an enticing song that lured sailors to their deaths in the rocky waters nearby.

Heinrich Heine

The Lorelei

Translated from the German by Aaron Kramer

I cannot explain the sadness
That's fallen on my breast.
An old, old fable haunts me,
And will not let me rest.

5 The air grows cool in the twilight,
And softly the Rhine flows on;
The peak of a mountain sparkles
Beneath the setting sun.

More lovely than a vision,
10 A girl sits high up there;
Her golden jewelry glistens,
She combs her golden hair.

With a comb of gold she combs it,
And sings an evensong;[1]
15 The wonderful melody reaches
A boat, as it sails along.

---

1. **evensong:** here, evening song.

The Lorelei **347**

TEACHING ALLITERATION AND ASSONANCE

Ask volunteers to find examples of these two sound devices in the ballad, such as the *k* sounds (l. 7) and the long *o* sounds (ll. 11–13). Point out especially the long *i* sounds in lines 18–20, which prepare the ear for the final resounding rhyme *cry/Lorelei*.

TEACHING LINE ENDINGS

Point out that the translator consistently ends the first and third lines of each stanza with an unstressed syllable (called a feminine ending) and the second and fourth lines with a stressed syllable (a masculine ending). Explain that this alternating pattern makes the poem's rhythm flow lightly and then pause emphatically at the rhymes.

COLLABORATIVE LEARNING: ENRICHMENT ACTIVITY

Folklore As a group, students might research the legend of the Lorelei and other myths and legends rooted in geography—the Sirens of Greek mythology, Scylla and Charybdis, and so on.

The boatman hears, with an anguish
More wild than was ever known;
He's blind to the rocks around him;
His eyes are for her alone.

—At last the waves devoured
The boat, and the boatman's cry;
And this she did with her singing,
The golden Lorelei.

STUDY QUESTIONS

Recalling

1. In the opening stanza, what does the narrator say about the effects the fable of the Lorelei has had on him?
2. What details of time and place are provided in the second stanza?
3. Briefly describe the girl and her actions in the third and fourth stanzas.
4. According to the last two stanzas, what happens to the boatman when he hears the girl's song?

Interpreting

5. In what sense is the ending of the poem ironic?
6. What details contribute to the fairy-tale qualities of the poem?
7. What view of beauty does the poem provide?
8. What aspects of human experience might the Lorelei represent, especially to a poet?

Extending

9. What are some legends or fairy tales that you find especially memorable? Why?

LITERARY FOCUS

The Ballad

A poem that tells a story is called a **narrative poem.** A **ballad** is a short, musical narrative poem that usually follows a set pattern of rhythm and rhyme. **Folk ballads,** or **popular ballads,** were anonymously composed and passed on by word of mouth from generation to generation before being written down. Most folk ballads recount dramatic episodes in simple language and were com-posed for musical accompaniment. Many use the so-called **ballad stanza,** a four-line stanza, or quatrain, in which the first and third lines have four stressed syllables, the second and fourth lines have three stressed syllables, and only the second and fourth lines rhyme. Professional writers imitating the style of folk ballads produce what are known as **literary ballads.** "The Lorelei" is a literary bal-lad based on an old German legend.

Thinking About the Ballad

■ In what ways does Heine's literary ballad imitate a folk ballad? Does this translation use the rhyme scheme typical of the ballad stanza? Does it use the meter, or fixed pattern of rhythm, typical of the ballad stanza? Explain.

COMPOSITION

Writing About Poetry

■ Write a composition in which you show how poetic techniques are used to create dramatic effects in "The Lorelei." In particular consider the use of imagery, figurative language, word repetition, stanza form, and sound devices such as rhyme, assonance, alliteration, and rhythm. Tell how such devices convey the speaker's tone and create the poem's mood.

Writing a Newspaper Account

■ Retell the story of "The Lorelei" as it might appear in a newspaper article today. Begin with an attention-grabbing headline. Then provide information that answers the questions Who? What? When? Where? Why? and How?, as good newspaper articles do. Use details from the poem and invent additional facts to answer these questions.

The Lorelei 349

What reason do you imagine the Lorelei had for luring sail-ors to their death?

ANSWERS

STUDY QUESTIONS

1. It has made him sad, haunted, and restless.
2. It is twilight along the Rhine; a mountain peak is nearby.
3. She is beautiful, wears golden jewelry, combs her golden hair with a golden comb, and sings a wonderful song.
4. He becomes anguished and, blind to the rocks around him, is devoured by the waves.
5. It is ironic that something wondrously beautiful causes destruction.
6. the repetition of *old*, the word *fable*, the speaker's being haunted, the twilight setting, the repetition of *golden*, the magical song
7. It has a mysterious and alluring power that can be destructive.
8. Possible answers: artistic beauty, intellectualism, or ide-alism that lures people away from practical matters in the real world; the destructiveness of blind fascination or ob-session
9. Answers will vary. Students may cite especially frightening stories or those with happy re-versals of fortune.

LITERARY FOCUS

"The Lorelei" is like a folk ballad in recounting a dramatic episode in simple, musical language. The translation uses the typical *abcb* rhyme scheme of ballads, but it does not use the alternating four-beat-three-beat meter between lines. Each line has three feet (with an extra syllable on the odd lines).

COMPOSITION: GUIDELINES FOR EVALUATION

WRITING ABOUT POETRY

Objective

To analyze techniques that create the tone and mood

Guidelines for Evaluation

■ suggested length: two or three paragraphs
■ should provide examples of poetic techniques used in the poem
■ should relate poetic techniques to the tone and mood of the poem

WRITING A NEWSPAPER ACCOUNT

Objective

To write an article based on a narrative poem

Guidelines for Evaluation

■ suggested length: three or four paragraphs
■ should begin with an attention-getting headline
■ should answer the questions Who? What? When? Where? Why? and How?
■ should be based on details in the poem

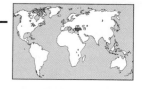

LESSON PREVIEW

The speaker marvels at the size and wonder of the world. Though he has never traveled, he has friends everywhere—people he has never met but who share his beliefs and his willingness to fight and die for freedom. Without this struggle love and the earth's beauty and diversity are not enough for the speaker.

LITERARY SKILLS FOR THIS SELECTION

- theme
- free verse

THEMES IN THIS SELECTION

- struggling to realize an ideal
- the power of community

LESSON OBJECTIVES

1. to recognize a poem's theme
2. to determine the meaning and origin of words from Turkish
3. to write a poem expressing personal convictions

Teacher's Classroom Resources 2

- Teaching Notes   235
- Reading Guide   236
- Literary Focus: Theme   237
- Language Study: Words from Turkish   238
- Writing Process Guide: Writing About Personal Convictions   239
- Selection Test   240

IN THE CLASSROOM

TEACHING STUDENTS OF DIFFERENT ABILITIES

- **For less advanced students:** Have students complete the Reading Guide to reinforce their understanding of the poem.
- **For more advanced students:** Hikmet was imprisoned for his Marxist beliefs. Have students research the lives of other authors who wrote while suffering imprisonment, exile, or other forms of oppression. Ovid, Sir Walter Raleigh, John Bunyan, Dostoevski, Anne Frank, and Aleksandr Solzhenitsyn are just a few examples.

Nazim Hikmet

(1902–1963) *Turkey*

Modern Turkey's best-known poet, Nazim Hikmet [nä zim′ hik met′] began publishing his verse when he was sixteen. After attending school in the European part of Turkey, Hikmet worked as a teacher in the Asian part of Turkey, now called Anatolia. His early poems show his deep admiration for Anatolia's peasants. Always politically active, Hikmet made forceful attacks on Turkish government policies that led to his arrest in 1938. He spent over ten years in prison and wrote some of his finest verse, including the following poem, during that time.

Nazim Hikmet

The World, My Friends, My Enemies, You, and the Earth

Translated from the Turkish by Randy Blasing and Mutlu Konuk

I'm wonderfully happy I came into the world,
I love its earth, its light, its struggle, and its bread.
Even though I know its dimensions from pole to pole to the
    centimeter,
and while I'm not unaware that it's a mere toy next to the sun,
5 the world for me is unbelievably big.
I would have liked to go around the world
and see the fish, the fruits, and the stars that I haven't seen.
However,
I made my European trip only in books and pictures.
10 In all my life I never got one letter
              with its blue stamp canceled in Asia.
Me and our corner grocer,
we're both mightily unknown in America.

MOTIVATION: PRIOR KNOWLEDGE

Have volunteers enumerate beliefs and convictions that they believe they share with others around the world.

IN THE GLOSSARY

- dimensions: measurable extent

TEACHING THEME

To prepare students for the Literary Focus about theme, draw two columns on the board, and label them "Things I Love About the Earth" and "Things I Love About Life's Struggle." Have the poem read aloud two or more times, and after each reading ask students to list details and ideas from the poem under the relevant heading. The lists should help students grasp Hikmet's central theme: Love and the world's beauty, although powerful nourishment for the soul, cannot sustain us unless they are balanced by life's struggles.

Nevertheless,

15 from China to Spain, from the Cape of Good Hope[1] to Alaska,
in every nautical mile, in every kilometer, I have friends and
enemies.
Such friends that we haven't met even once—
we can die for the same bread, the same freedom, the same
dream.
And such enemies that they're thirsty for my blood,
20   I am thirsty for their blood.
My strength
is that I'm not alone in this big world.
The world and its people are no secret in my heart,
                     no mystery in my science.
25 Calmly and openly
               I took my place
                            in the great struggle.
And without it,
               you and the earth
30   are not enough for me.
And yet you are astonishingly beautiful,
               the earth is warm and beautiful.

---

1. **Cape of Good Hope:** southern tip of Africa.

World Map, 1543, Battista Agnese.

Remind students that free verse often uses repetition in place of a regular rhythm. Have students find examples of repeated words (such as *world* in ll. 5–6 and *beautiful* in ll. 31–32), repeated phrases ("thirsty for . . . blood," in ll. 19–20), and repeated syntactic patterns (such as those in ll. 2, 15, 16, 18, and 23–24). Point out Hikmet's use of staggered line placement (especially in ll. 25–32), and explain that this stylistic device helps control the rhythm in free verse. Here the staggered lines add weight and emphasis to each phrase by making the reader pause briefly at the end of each line.

ART AND LITERATURE

In the mid-sixteenth century the workshop of Battista Agnese produced over sixty atlases and maps, such as the one shown here. During this time cartographers began to correct charts for the curvature of the earth, adding latitude and longitude lines to their plans, as can be seen in this world map.
■ Have sudents find on the map the places the poet says he wants to visit. (China, Spain, the Cape of Good Hope—but not Alaska, which had not yet been discovered)

What was your reaction to the sound of this poem? Did it sound like poetry to you? Why or why not?

STUDY QUESTIONS

1. earth, light, struggle, and bread; travel the world and see fish, fruit, and stars
2. all over the world; They would die for the same bread, freedom, and dream.
3. He is not alone in the world. He has taken his place in it, and without it his beloved and the earth are insufficient.
4. optimism
5. He struggles to free the world from hunger and oppression; those sharing in the struggle; those who withhold bread and freedom.
6. It expresses love for the world, for the struggle to make it better, and for the "you" addressed in line 29.
7. Answers will vary, but most students will probably agree that biographical knowledge adds to one's appreciation of a writer's work.

LITERARY FOCUS

The world is a wonderful place for those who embrace life and share in the struggle to rid it of hunger and oppression. The title stresses the all-embracing attitude expressed in the poem.

LANGUAGE STUDY

1. "nonsense"; from *bosh*, "empty"
2. "long-sleeved robe"; from *qaftān*, "dress"
3. "brimless, conical hat"; through French from *fes*, after the Moroccan city Fes
4. "kind of wild dog"; from Turkish *chaqāl*, from Persian *shagāl* and Sanskrit *sṛgāla*
5. "newsstand"; from Turkish *köşk* and Persian *kūshk*, "pavilion"
6. "fate, destiny"; from Turkish *qismet* and Arabic *qismah*, "portion; lot; fate"
7. "kind of frozen dessert"; through Turkish *sharbat*, from Arabic *sharbah*, "drink"
8. "headdress wound from a long cloth"; from Turkish *tülbend*, from Persian *dülband*, "sash"
9. "food made from milk fermented by bacteria"; from Turkish *yōghurt*

STUDY QUESTIONS

Recalling

1. According to the first seven lines, what does the speaker love about the world? What would he have liked to do and see?
2. Where does the speaker have friends and enemies whom he has never met? What do the speaker and his friends have in common?
3. What does the speaker say is his strength? What does he say about the "great struggle"?

Interpreting

4. What attitude toward the world does the poem convey?
5. What might the speaker mean by the "great struggle"? What sort of people does he feel are his friends? His enemies?
6. Is this in any way a love poem? Explain.

Extending

7. Many literary works have come from writers who were living in prison or under oppression when they wrote. Do you think that knowing this background about a writer influences a reader's reaction to a poem or story, and if so, how?

LITERARY FOCUS

Theme

A **theme** is the main idea or insight found in a poem or other literary work. The theme is usually expressed as a general message about life or human behavior. For example, in a poem about how the auk, a type of bird, came to be extinct, the theme might be "The destruction of nature is tragic" or "We need to protect nature." It is not something as specific as "Hunting made the auk extinct."

A poem's theme may be stated directly in the poem or implied by the details of the poem. Among the details that can point to a poem's theme are the title, the imagery and figurative language, the mood of the poem, and the speaker's tone.

Thinking About Theme

■ In a single sentence, state what you feel is the theme of Hikmet's poem. How does the title help point to this theme?

LANGUAGE STUDY

Words from Turkish

Turkish, the language in which Hikmet wrote, has contributed a number of words to English. Some of these words were in turn borrowed from other languages of southwestern Asia, including Arabic and Persian. For example, our word *coffee* comes from the Turkish *qahwe*, which came from the Arabic *qahwa*, originally meaning "wine."

Use a dictionary to help you determine the meanings and origins of these English words.

1. bosh
2. caftan
3. fez
4. jackal
5. kiosk
6. kismet
7. sherbet
8. turban
9. yogurt

COMPOSITION

Writing About Personal Convictions

■ Write a poem expressing your own ideas and convictions about the world, as Hikmet does in "The World, My Friends, My Enemies, You, and the Earth." You might begin with the same first line that Hikmet uses but then continue with your own ideas and details. As you write, keep in mind the theme you want to convey in your poem.

COMPOSITION: GUIDELINES FOR EVALUATION

WRITING ABOUT PERSONAL CONVICTIONS

Objective

To write a poem expressing personal convictions

Guidelines for Evaluation

■ suggested length: eight or more lines
■ should express the writer's own beliefs
■ should convey a theme about the world

C. P. Cavafy

(1863–1933) *Greece*

Though he visited Greece only twice in his life, Constantine P. Cavafy [kä vä′fē] is considered the leading Greek poet of the early twentieth century. Born in Alexandria, Egypt, to a Greek family, Cavafy lived in England and Constantinople before settling back in Alexandria. He began writing poetry early in life but, rarely satisfied with his efforts, did not publish anything until he was forty-one. Many of Cavafy's poems explore Greek history and mythology. Many, like the poem below, show his interest in using the past to illuminate the present and the future.

C. P. Cavafy

Che Fece . . . Il Gran Rifiuto[1]

Translated from the Greek by Rae Dalven

To certain people there comes a day
when they must say the great Yes or the great No.
He who has the Yes ready within him
reveals himself at once, and saying it he crosses over

5 to the path of honor and his own conviction.
He who refuses does not repent. Should he be asked again,
he would say No again. And yet that No—
the right No—crushes him for the rest of his life.

---

1. ***Che Fece . . . Il Gran Rifiuto*** [kā′ fā′ chā ēl grän′ rē fū′ tō]: Italian for "who made . . . the Great Refusal," famous quotation from Dante's *Divine Comedy* (see the Myths, Folk Tales, and Epics unit). The line refers to a pope who resigned from office, thereby shirking his responsibility.

To certain people there comes a time when they must make an ultimate answer of Yes or No. The person saying Yes will find honor and conviction; the person saying No will keep on saying it, though he or she is crushed by the denial.

LITERARY SKILL FOR THIS SELECTION

- allusion

THEMES IN THIS SELECTION

- the values in embracing or withdrawing from life
- the effects of important decisions

LESSON OBJECTIVES

1. to appreciate how allusion adds meaning to a poem
2. to compare two poems

Teacher's Classroom Resources 2

■ Teaching Notes	241
■ Selection Test	242

IN THE CLASSROOM

TEACHING STUDENTS OF DIFFERENT ABILITIES

- **For less advanced students:** Have students preview the footnote to help them understand the literary and historical context of the poem's title and subject. Focus on the consequences of each answer, Yes and No.
- **For more advanced students:** Have students read lines 1–69 from Canto III of Dante's *Inferno,* from which Cavafy took his title. Ask them to discuss Dante's reasons for saying that people like the one who made the great refusal are hateful to both God and His enemies.

. . . .

MOTIVATION: PRIOR KNOWLEDGE

Discuss students' attitudes toward people who refuse to get involved in such things as sports, social events, or community concerns.

TEACHING ALLUSION

Point out that Cavafy's poem is almost entirely devoid of concrete imagery. Instead, it relies on its allusion to line 60 of Canto III of Dante's *Inferno* to supply both an intellectual context for its theme and an evocative setting— the shores of the River Acheron, where the souls of the dead wait to be ferried across by Charon. Discuss how this knowledge adds to the meaning of "crosses over" in line 4 and "does not repent" in line 6. (Those who say Yes are compared to the souls of the dead crossing the Acheron, but they pass into honor rather than damnation; those who say No are incapable of repentance because they have damned themselves.)

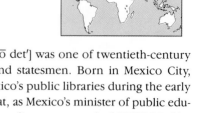

Jaime Torres Bodet

(1902–1974) *Mexico*

Jaime Torres Bodet [hī′mä tō′res bō det′] was one of twentieth-century Mexico's most respected poets and statesmen. Born in Mexico City, Torres Bodet was in charge of Mexico's public libraries during the early 1920s. Later he served as a diplomat, as Mexico's minister of public education and foreign minister, and as director-general of UNESCO (the United Nations Educational, Scientific, and Cultural Organization). Throughout his illustrious career as a public servant, he also wrote over forty books, including novels, memoirs, essays, and poetry collections.

Jaime Torres Bodet

The Window

Translated from the Spanish by George Kearns

You closed the window. And it was the world,
the world that wanted to enter, all at once,
the world that gave that great shout,
that great, deep, rough cry
5 you did not want to hear—and now
will never call to you again as it called today,
asking your mercy!

The whole of life was in that cry:
the wind, the sea, the land
10 with its poles and its tropics,
the unreachable skies,
the ripened grain in the resounding wheat field,
the thick heat above the wine presses,
dawn on the mountains, shadowy woods,

15 parched lips stuck together longing for
cool water condensed in pools,
and all pleasures, all sufferings,
all loves, all hates,
were in this day, anxiously
20 asking your mercy . . .

But you were afraid of life.
And you remained alone,
behind the closed and silent window,
not understanding that the world calls
     to a man
25 only once that way, and with that kind
     of cry,
with that great, rough, hoarse cry!

Che Fece . . . Il Gran Rifiuto (Cavafy)

Recalling

1. According to the first stanza, what decision faces certain people?
2. What happens to the person who has the "Yes ready within him"?
3. What happens to the person who says "the right No"?

Interpreting

4. How important is the choice facing "certain people" in this poem? Why?
5. What does the phrase "ready within him" suggest about the kind of person who says Yes? What do lines 6–7 suggest about the kind of person who says No?
6. Why is the refusal called "the right No"?
7. Who might the "certain people" of line 1 be?

Extending

8. What does the "great Yes" or the "great No" mean to you? How do you know whether the answer is "ready within" you?

The Window (Torres Bodet)

Recalling

1. According to lines 1–7, what wanted to enter the window? What will never happen again?
2. According to line 8, what was in the world's cry? What was the cry asking?
3. List four details used to describe the positive and negative elements in life.
4. What was the person behind the window like? What did he or she not understand?

Interpreting

5. What attitude toward the world does the speaker convey?
6. What might the word "mercy" mean? Why would the world be asking for "mercy"?
7. What kind of behavior does the poem criticize?
8. What central message does this poem have for readers?

Extending

9. Do you agree that the world calls to a person only once, that if a person closes "the window" it will never call again? Explain your opinion.

LITERARY FOCUS

Symbolism

A **symbol** is a person, a place, an object, or an experience that represents something beyond its literal meaning. For example, in a poem about climbing mountains, the mountain may exist literally as something the poem's speaker climbs. If the mountain also represents something else, however, such as nature or life's hardships, it is a symbol. Most symbols represent an abstract idea or a range of related ideas. When a poem uses symbols, the symbols are usually important clues to the theme of the poem. The use of symbols in a literary work is called **symbolism.**

Thinking About Symbolism

■ What does opening the window symbolize, or represent, in Torres Bodet's poem? What does remaining behind the closed window symbolize? What is the theme conveyed in this symbolism?

COMPOSITION

Writing About Poetry

■ Write a brief composition about the meaning of "The Window." First state what you think is the main theme of the poem. Then show how the details of the poem point to the theme. Among the details and techniques you may wish to consider are the title, images, and symbols of the poem; its use of repetition and sound devices; and the tone of the speaker. *For help with this assignment, refer to Lesson 9 in the Writing About Literature Handbook at the back of this book.*

Writing with Symbolism

■ Write a poem or a short prose piece in which a person, a place, an object, or an experience is used as a symbol. Do not state directly what the symbol represents. Instead, make its meaning clear from the other details you provide.

COMPARING POEMS

■ What is similar about the choices faced in these two poems? In which poem is the speaker more certain about the correct choice to make? Explain.

These poems express similar ideas but in different ways. Which did you enjoy more? Why?

ANSWERS

STUDY QUESTIONS

Che Fece . . . Il Gran Rifiuto
1. to "say the great Yes or the great No"
2. That person reveals himself at once and crosses over to the path of honor and conviction.
3. He is crushed for life.
4. It is crucial, affecting one's entire life.
5. He is prepared to seize life. He is certain that he is right to say No.
6. The person may be sure that saying No is the right choice.
7. Possible answer: They might be people who are confronted with ethical, political, or spiritual dilemmas.
8. Answers will vary. Readiness involves maturity, responsibility, and awareness of self.

The Window
1. The world wanted to enter the window. It will never call again.
2. the whole of life; mercy
3. positive—grain, dawn, woods, all pleasures, and loves; negative—lips, all sufferings, and hates
4. He or she was afraid of life and did not understand that the world calls only once.
5. an all-embracing attitude
6. Possible answers: concern, compassion; For all its failings and imperfections, the world cries out for the passionate participation and love of all beings.
7. Possible answers: timidity, indifference
8. Do not cut yourself off from the world, but embrace it in its entirety.
9. Answers will vary.

LITERARY FOCUS

Opening the window symbolizes the embracing of life. Remaining behind the closed window symbolizes fear and the denial of life. It is best to embrace life.

COMPARING POEMS

Both involve making crucial choices in life. Torres Bodet's speaker seems more certain; Cavafy's speaker suggests that No might be right for some.

COMPOSITION: GUIDELINES FOR EVALUATION

WRITING ABOUT POETRY

Objective

To analyze the theme of a poem

Guidelines for Evaluation

- suggested length: three or four paragraphs
- should state the theme
- should analyze how the theme is revealed
- should cite details from the poem to support the analysis

WRITING WITH SYMBOLISM

Objective

To use symbolism in a poem or short prose piece

Guidelines for Evaluation

- suggested length: two or three stanzas or paragraphs
- should use a person, place, object, or experience as a symbol
- should express the symbol's meaning indirectly

A "swagman," or hobo, camps by a waterhole and sings as his food cooks. When a sheep comes to drink, the hobo stows it in his food bag. Then a rancher and law officers arrive to arrest the hobo for poaching; rather than go to jail, the hobo jumps into the waterhole and drowns. His ghost can still be heard there singing his song.

LITERARY SKILLS FOR THIS SELECTION

- folk song and refrain
- theme
- rhyme scheme

THEMES IN THIS SELECTION

- freedom as an ideal
- individual versus society

LESSON OBJECTIVES

1. to recognize the effect of a refrain on a folk song
2. to appreciate the use of dialect in literature
3. to write the lyrics to a song

Teacher's Classroom Resources 2

- Teaching Notes   247
- Responding to World Cultures   248
- Literary Focus: Folk Song and Refrain   249
- Language Study: Dialect and Slang   250
- Writing Process Guide: Writing Song Lyrics   251
- Selection Test   252

TEACHING STUDENTS OF DIFFERENT ABILITIES

- **For less advanced students:** Bring to class some examples of the "Buzz Words" column from *Newsweek* magazine, and discuss the importance of slang in imparting a cultural identity to various ethnic groups. Then have students preview the footnoted examples of Australian dialect and slang. If possible, play a recording of this song for the class.

- **For more advanced students:** Have students research other versions of "Waltzing Matilda" as well as Australia's official national anthem.

MOTIVATION: PRIOR KNOWLEDGE

Discuss some popular American folk songs (such as "This Land Is Your Land"), eliciting the values they represent.

A. B. ("Banjo") Paterson

(1864–1941) *Australia*

Tradition has it that Australian poet A. B. Paterson, better known as "Banjo" Paterson, wrote the lyrics to "Waltzing Matilda" in 1895 while visiting his fiancée on her family's sheep ranch in the Australian outback, the remote and sparsely settled part of Australia. Many scholars, insisting that versions of the song were sung in Australia well before 1895, dispute this tradition. Despite the controversy, no one denies the enduring popularity of the song, which most Australians regard as an unofficial national anthem.

A. B. ("Banjo") Paterson

Waltzing Matilda[1]

Australian Traditional

Once a jolly swagman[2] camped by a billabong[3]
Under the shade of a coolibah tree,[4]
And he sang as he watched and waited till his billy[5] boiled,
"You'll come a-waltzing, Matilda with me!"
5   Waltzing Matilda, waltzing Matilda,
    You'll come a-waltzing, Matilda, with me!
    And he sang as he watched and waited till his billy boiled,
    "You'll come a-waltzing, Matilda, with me!"

Down came a jumbuck[6] to drink at the billabong,
10 Up jumped the swagman and grabbed him with glee,
And he sang as he stowed that jumbuck in his tucker-bag,[7]
"You'll come a-waltzing, Matilda, with me!"
    Waltzing Matilda, waltzing Matilda,

---

1. **Waltzing Matilda:** traveling from town to town and carrying one's matilda, the bundle of worldly goods carried by a hobo.
2. **swagman:** person who travels around seeking odd jobs; hobo.
3. **billabong:** waterhole or small lake.
4. **coolibah tree:** gum tree; eucalyptus.
5. **billy:** tin can holding food or liquid.
6. **jumbuck:** sheep.
7. **tucker-bag:** sack for carrying food.

356 *Poetry*

You'll come a-waltzing, Matilda, with me!
15 And he sang as he stowed that jumbuck in his tucker-bag,
"You'll come a-waltzing, Matilda, with me!"

Up rode the squatter[8] mounted on his thoroughbred,
Up rode the troopers, one, two, three.
"Where's that jolly jumbuck you've got in your tucker-bag?
20 You'll come a-waltzing, Matilda, with me!"
    Waltzing Matilda, waltzing Matilda,
    You'll come a-waltzing, Matilda, with me!
    "Where's that jolly jumbuck you've got in your tucker-bag?
    You'll come a-waltzing, Matilda, with me!"

25 Up jumped the swagman and sprang into the billabong.
"You'll never take me alive!" said he.
And his ghost may be heard as you pass by that billabong,
"You'll come a-waltzing, Matilda, with me!"
    Waltzing Matilda, waltzing Matilda,
30 You'll come a-waltzing, Matilda, with me!
    And his ghost may be heard as you pass by that billabong,
    "You'll come a-waltzing, Matilda, with me!"

---

8. **squatter:** sheep rancher; large landowner.

Waltzing Matilda **357**

TEACHING FOLK SONGS AND REFRAINS

Explain that refrains in folk songs often use slight changes in each repetition to help move the story along. Have students examine the last two lines of each stanza and identify both the speaker and the person or thing being addressed as Matilda. (ll. 7–8: The swagman addresses his knapsack; ll. 15–16: the swagman addresses the sheep; ll. 23–24: the rancher addresses the swagman; ll. 31–32: the ghost addresses the passerby.)

TEACHING THEME

To help students infer the song's theme, ask them why they suppose Australian soldiers customarily sing this song when they march off to war. (Like the swagman soldiers are willing to die in the defense of freedom.)

TEACHING RHYME SCHEME

Ask students to recall "The Lorelei" (p. 347), and then point out that the first four lines of each stanza in this poem follow the rhyme scheme—*abcb*—found in that ballad. This rhyme scheme is appropriate for this poem because it evokes the folk tradition and narrative style associated with such earlier ballads.

COLLABORATIVE LEARNING: ENRICHMENT ACTIVITY

Music As a group students might create a book of folk songs from around the world. Each student should contribute—in the original language, in English translation, or both—the lyrics to one or more songs from a different culture. Student singers and musicians might perform some of the songs for their classmates.

What did you expect to happen when the sheep rancher arrived with the troopers? Were you surprised by the ending?

STUDY QUESTIONS

1. by a waterhole under the shade of a tree
2. to drink; He puts it in his food bag.
3. The squatter, or rancher, and three troopers arrive and ask, "Where's that jolly jumback you've got in your tucker-bag?/You'll come a-waltzing, Matilda, with me."
4. "You'll never take me alive"; his ghost can be heard singing in the billabong.
5. The squatter is a wealthy landowner, representing legally established society; the swagman is a poor drifter, representing the independent, self-sufficient free spirit.
6. The swagman had stolen a sheep. They were probably going to arrest him.
7. He is basically sympathetic; he is happy, bold, and proud.
8. to avoid arrest; his freedom
9. The song helped soldiers identify with home and their national spirit; it affirmed a willingness to die for freedom and provided an inspiring marching rhythm.

LITERARY FOCUS

first stanza—a happy tone, since the swagman is carefree; second stanza—a gleeful tone, since the swagman has caught some food; third stanza—menacing, since the swagman is being threatened with arrest; fourth stanza—sad but triumphant, since the swagman continues his happy song from the grave; the rhythmic and memorable refrain holds the song together

LANGUAGE STUDY

Examples: line 1—Once a jolly hobo camped by a waterhole; line 3—And he sang as he watched and waited till his tin of food boiled; line 9—Down came a sheep to drink at the waterhole; line 11—And he sang as he stowed that sheep in his food bag. The song loses its distinctive rhythm and cultural spirit in standard English.

STUDY QUESTIONS

Recalling

1. Where does the jolly swagman camp?
2. Why does the jumbuck, or sheep, appear? What does the swagman do to the sheep?
3. Who rides up to question the swagman? What do they say to him?
4. What does the swagman exclaim as he springs into the billabong, or waterhole? Since then, who can be heard singing in the billabong?

Interpreting

5. How is the squatter, or ranch owner, different from the swagman? What does each represent?
6. Why did the rancher and the troopers approach the swagman? What do you think they were going to do?
7. Is the swagman basically a sympathetic character or a villain? What personality traits does he display?
8. Why did the swagman jump into the waterhole? What do you think he was unwilling to lose?

Extending

9. Australian soldiers marched to two world wars singing this song, and other troops had their own national favorites. Why do you think this song and others like it held such appeal?

LITERARY FOCUS

Folk Song and Refrain

A **folk song** is a traditional song anonymously composed by common folk and passed from singer to singer before being written down. As a result of this process, several versions of the same folk song often evolved over time. Most folk songs use simple language to tell a story or express emotion. They usually contain **refrains,** lines or stanzas repeated at regular intervals.

Scholars dispute whether "Waltzing Matilda" is a true folk song or a composition by A. B. ("Banjo") Paterson in the style of a folk song. Whatever the case, it does display characteristics of folk songs. For one thing, it exists in several versions, each slightly different from the rest. For another, the song includes a memorable refrain.

Thinking About Folk Song and Refrain

■ If you were singing "Waltzing Matilda," what tone would you use for line 4 and the rest of the refrain in stanza 1? How would your tone change for the refrain in each of the next stanzas, and why? How does the refrain help the song as a whole?

LANGUAGE STUDY

Dialect and Slang

A **dialect** is a variation of language spoken by a particular group, often in a particular region. The variations are found in sounds, forms, and meanings that differ from the standard form of the language. Dialects often contain **slang,** or extremely and distinctively nonstandard words and expressions. Slang develops from people's attempts to find fresh and colorful ways of expressing themselves and describing the changing world around them.

Much of the color and appeal of "Waltzing Matilda" comes from its use of dialect and slang. The phrase *waltzing Matilda* is itself a slang expression that means "traveling from place to place with one's bundle of goods." It means the same as the expression *carrying the swag,* a *swag* being a rolled blanket and pack of belongings. The word *tuckerbag* in the poem is a clue to *tucker,* an Australian slang word for "food." The dialect of the poem even hints at the country's history. During Australia's gold rush, cans of French meat labeled *bouilli* [bwē′yē] (French for "boiled beef") were often imported and used by prospectors. This probably gave rise to the use of the word *billy.*

■ Select four lines from "Waltzing Matilda" that use Australian dialect. Rewrite the lines using words and phrases from standard English. Read both versions of each line out loud. Do you think this folk song could be translated effectively into standard English? Why or why not?

COMPOSITION

Writing Song Lyrics

■ Write the lyrics to a short song, either in the style of a folk song or in any style you wish. Use the lyrics to tell a story or to express a strong feeling. You may want to match your lyrics to the music of a popular tune.

COMPOSITION: GUIDELINES FOR EVALUATION

WRITING SONG LYRICS

Objective

To write song lyrics

Guidelines for Evaluation

■ suggested length: two or three verses and a refrain
■ should tell a story or express a strong feeling
■ should match the melody of a popular tune

Horace

(65–8 B.C.) *Ancient Rome*

Quintus Horatius Flaccus, better known as Horace, was one of ancient Rome's brightest poetic stars. Born in Venusia in southeast Italy, Horace was educated in Rome and in Athens. He found support as a poet from Octavian, later Emperor Augustus, and, in turn, he wrote patriotic political verse for the ruling government. Much of his elegant writing, including his famous *Odes* and *Epodes,* was patterned on earlier Greek models. In his other poetry, he often relates subtle impressions and sophisticated advice about love, friendship, and the conduct of life.

Horace

Ode: Better to Live, Licinius[1]

Translated from the Latin by Joseph P. Clancy

Better to live, Licinius, not always
rushing into deep water, and not, when fear
of storms makes you shiver, pushing too close to the
    dangerous coast.

A man who prizes golden moderation
5 stays safely clear of the filth of a run-down
building, stays prudently out of a palace others will envy.

The giant pine is more often troubled by the
wind, and the tallest towers collapse with a
heavier fall, and bolts of lightning strike the tops of the
    mountains.

10 Hopeful in the bad times, fearful in the good times,
that is the man who has readied his heart for
the turn of the dice. Jupiter[2] brings back foul winters; he also

---

1. **Licinius** [li sin′yəs]: Lucius Licinius, Roman political leader (c. 23 B.C.)
who plotted against Emperor Augustus. Horace was a friend of his family.
2. **Jupiter:** chief god of Roman mythology.

Ode: Better to Live, Licinius **359**

LESSON PREVIEW

Addressing a risk-taking leader, the speaker advises moderation: Neither rush into deep water nor hug the dangerous coast. A person should be ready for the twists of fate and remember that good luck follows bad. In a time of trouble, the poet counsels stoutheartedness; in good times, caution and self-restraint.

LITERARY SKILLS FOR THIS SELECTION

- the ode
- stanza form

THEMES IN THIS SELECTION

- moderation as an ideal
- the perils of ambition

LESSON OBJECTIVES

1. to understand the conventions of an ode
2. to understand the meanings and origins of words relating to the Muses
3. to write an imagined response to a poem

Teacher's Classroom Resources 2

- Teaching Notes   253
- Responding to World Cultures   254
- Literary Focus: The Ode   255
- Language Study: Words from the Greek Muses   256
- Writing Process Guide: Responding to a Poem   257
- Selection Test   258

IN THE CLASSROOM

TEACHING STUDENTS OF DIFFERENT ABILITIES

- **For less advanced students:** Focus students' attention on each stanza's contrasting images and phrases and the way in which they are used to argue for a balance between extremes.

- **For more advanced students:** Have students read the chapter on Horace in *The Roman Way* by Edith Hamilton to learn more about his life, works, and influence on western literature.

MOTIVATION: PRIOR KNOWLEDGE

Have students look up the term *golden mean* in a dictionary (which should credit Horace in its etymology), and ask them to ex-

plain why they agree or disagree with the idea of "moderation in all things."

IN THE GLOSSARY

- moderation: state of avoiding extremes

TEACHING ANTITHESIS

Explain that antithesis is the use of parallel phrases to emphasize

contrasting ideas, and point out line 10 as an example. Have students find other instances of antithesis in the poem, and ask them to explain how the device helps Horace make his point about moderation. (Other examples can be found in ll. 1–3 and 5–6; moreover, each stanza contains contrasting ideas that strike a balance between extremes.)

Ode: Better to Live, Licinius **T-359**

Greek two-handled drinking cup showing Apollo crowned with myrtle, fifth century.

takes them away. No, if things are bad now, they
will not remain that way: sometimes Apollo[3]
15 wakes the silent Muse with his lyre[4] and is not always an archer.

When troubles come, show that you have a stout heart
and a stern face: but see that you have the good sense
to take in sail[5] when it swells in a wind that's a little too kind.

---

3. **Apollo** [ə pol′ ō]: god of music and archery, among other things; his arrows often brought misfortune to humans.
4. **wakes . . . with his lyre:** composes music; wakes the goddess in charge of music with his lyre, a harplike musical instrument.
5. **take in sail:** that is, lower a boat's sail to protect it from strong winds.

STUDY QUESTIONS

Recalling

1. According to the first two stanzas, how is it better to live? What two places does a person who prizes "golden moderation" avoid?
2. What happens to the giant pine, the tallest towers, and the tops of mountains?
3. According to stanzas 4 and 5, who is "Hopeful in the bad times, fearful in the good times"? What is true of bad times?
4. What does the last stanza recommend for times of trouble? For times that are "a little too kind"?

Interpreting

5. What comparison is made in stanza 1? How is this metaphor extended later in the poem?
6. Why is a life of wealth and power to be avoided? What happens to a boat when its sail swells too much in the wind?
7. What view of fate is suggested in this poem?
8. According to the speaker, how should people conduct their lives?

Extending

9. What proverbs or other sayings give advice similar to that given in this ode?

LITERARY FOCUS

The Ode

Along with the Greek poet Pindar (522?–443 B.C.), Horace was the most famous ancient writer of odes. An **ode** is a lyric poem that is serious and dignified in subject, tone, and style. Many odes celebrate an event or honor a person. Others offer advice or private thoughts on a serious subject. A **Horatian ode,** as established by Horace, is one that follows a regular stanza pattern.

Almost all odes are poems of address, in which the speaker speaks directly to someone or something. For example, Horace's ode directly addresses Lucius Licinius, a Roman political leader who plotted against Emperor Augustus and was executed for treason. Though Horace was a friend of Licinius' family, he did not write this ode as some sort of private letter to Licinius. Rather, the ode uses the device of **apostrophe,** a figure of speech in which an object, an animal, or an absent person is addressed directly, as if the object, animal, or person were actually listening.

Thinking About the Ode

■ Why would Horace choose to address Licinius in this ode? How would the poem and its serious message have been affected if apostrophe had not been used?

LANGUAGE STUDY

Words from the Greek Muses

In Greek (and later Roman) mythology, there were nine Muses who were the goddesses of the arts and sciences, including literature, history, and music. In fact, the English word *music* comes via Latin from the Greek *mousikē technē,* which originally meant "an art of the Muses." Use a dictionary to help you answer these questions about other English terms related to the Muses.

1. What English word meaning "place for exhibiting artistic, historic, and scientific objects" is derived from the Greek *mouseion,* "place for the Muses"?
2. What are the pronunciations, meanings, and origins of these English words: *calliope, cliometrics, terpsichorean*?
3. Why was a famous theater named the *Thalia*?
4. What is meant by the phrase "a poet's *muse*"?

COMPOSITION

Responding to a Poem

■ Imagine that Licinius saw Horace's ode while in prison awaiting execution for treason. In a poem or short piece of prose, write a possible response by Licinius to Horace's ode. Use figurative language, including apostrophe, as Horace does, to express ideas about human behavior.

Do you think Horace gave Licinius sound advice? Why or why not?

ANSWERS

STUDY QUESTIONS

1. neither "always rushing into deep water" nor always hugging the coast; a run-down building and a tempting palace
2. They are more likely to be troubled by wind, to fall, and to be struck by lightning, respectively.
3. the man who has readied his heart for the turn of the dice; They lead to good times.
4. stoutheartedness and a stern face; good sense
5. A person is compared to a ship. The metaphor returns in the last line when the poet advises Licinius to "take in sail."
6. Wealth brings envy, and power is subject to collapse. The boat capsizes.
7. It is uncontrollable but cyclical.
8. with moderation and adaptability to life's changes
9. Possible answers: Steer a middle course. Save for a rainy day. Forewarned is forearmed. Better to bend than to break. Loss and gain are brothers twain.

LITERARY FOCUS

Licinius' ambition and downfall provide Horace with proof that moderation is the best course. Without the direct, concrete form of address made possible by apostrophe, the poem would have lost vividness and risked preachiness.

LANGUAGE STUDY

1. museum
2. [kə lī'ə pē' *or* kal'ē op'], "kind of organ with steam whistles"; from *Calliope,* "the beautiful voiced," Muse of eloquence and epic poetry [klī'ō met'riks], "use of statistical methods to analyze historical data"; from *Clio,* "the celebrator," Muse of history, plus *metron,* "measure" [turp'si kə rē'ən *or* turp'si kôr'ē ən], "related to dancing"; from *Terpsichore* "the delighter in the dance," Muse of dancing
3. *Thalia* is the Muse of comedy.
4. the source of inspiration

COMPOSITION: GUIDELINES FOR EVALUATION

RESPONDING TO A POEM

Objective

To write a poem or prose piece in response to advice given in a poem

Guidelines for Evaluation

- suggested length: three stanzas or paragraphs
- should express ideas about human behavior
- should reflect Licinius' point of view
- should use apostrophe and figurative language

The speaker cultivates white roses the year round for the friend who helps him and for the brute who assails his heart.

LITERARY SKILLS FOR THIS SELECTION

- imagery
- symbolism

THEMES IN THIS SELECTION

- the ideal of brotherly love
- treating enemies as friends

LESSON OBJECTIVES

1. to recognize symbolism
2. to write about symbolism
3. to write a letter using symbolism

Teacher's Classroom Resources 2

- Teaching Notes   259
- Writing Process Guides:
  Writing About a
  Symbol   260
  Writing a Letter with
  Symbols   261
- Selection Test   262

TEACHING STUDENTS OF DIFFERENT ABILITIES

- **For less advanced students:** Make sure students understand what grubs and thistles are (l. 7). Then focus on the connotations of these and other details in the poem, such as "white," "roses," "January," and "July."
- **For more advanced students:** Have students research the traditional symbolism of flowers and find examples of their use in art and literature.

MOTIVATION: PRIOR KNOWLEDGE

Have students explain the sayings "turn the other cheek" and "an eye for an eye," and discuss the possible consequences of each attitude in various situations.

IN THE GLOSSARY

- nurture: nourish

José Martí

(1853–1895) *Cuba*

José Martí [hō sā′ mär tē′] was a famous poet, journalist, and patriot. Born on the Caribbean island of Cuba, Martí spent his life struggling for Cuba's independence from Spain and died on the battlefield just seven years before Cuba gained its freedom. In addition to poetry, Martí published influential essays and newspaper articles that championed the cause of Latin American independence. His famous long work *Versos sencillos* expresses his idealistic belief in artistic freedom and brotherly love.

José Martí

from **Versos Sencillos**[1]

Translated from the Spanish by Elinor Randall

XXXIX

I cultivate white roses
In January as in July
For the honest friend who freely
Offers me his hand.

5 And for the brute who tears from me
The heart with which I live,
I nurture neither grubs nor thistles,
But cultivate white roses.

---

1. **Versos sencillos** [vär′sōs sen sēl′yōs]: Spanish for "Simple Verses."

362   *Poetry*

TEACHING IMAGERY

Ask students to note the striking image of the brute tearing out the speaker's heart. How does it add power to the speaker's convictions about his enemies? (It vividly suggests the strength of will needed to treat an enemy as a friend.)

TEACHING SYMBOLISM

Explain that a white rose is a traditional symbol of innocent love and spiritual unfolding. Ask students to explain why this rose is appropriate for this poem. (The speaker's love is ideal and spiritual.)

STUDY QUESTIONS

Recalling

1. When does the speaker cultivate white roses? Whom does he cultivate them for in stanza 1?
2. Whom does the speaker cultivate white roses for in the second stanza? What does he say he does *not* nurture for this person?

Interpreting

3. What are the speaker's feelings for his "honest friend"?
4. What does the image of nurturing grubs and thistles represent? How is this symbolism related to the symbol of the white roses?
5. What range of related ideas or values might the white roses symbolize?
6. What message is conveyed in these two stanzas about the way we should treat people?

Extending

7. Do you agree with the speaker's attitude in these stanzas? Do you think it wise? Discuss.

COMPOSITION

Writing About a Symbol

■ Write a brief composition about the symbol of the white roses in Martí's stanzas. First explain the range of related ideas or values that the roses might represent, and show how these meanings are suggested by the other details of the stanzas, including the other symbols. Consider also what the roses might represent if the speaker is the poet himself. What might he cultivate for his friends? Then explain how the symbolism helps express the theme, or main insight, of the stanzas.

Writing a Letter with Symbols

■ Write a letter in which you express your ideas on how to behave thoughtfully and tactfully. For example, you might offer advice on how to treat a friend or an enemy or on how to act while participating in a particular game or sport. Instead of stating your ideas directly, convey your ideas in figurative terms by using symbols, as Martí does.

READER'S RESPONSE

This is one of Martí's "Simple Verses." Do you think his message in this poem is really simple? Why or why not?

ANSWERS

STUDY QUESTIONS

1. He cultivates white roses in January as well as in July for the honest friend who freely offers his hand.
2. He cultivates them for the brute who tears out his heart. He nurtures "neither grubs nor thistles."
3. good will and generosity
4. It represents ill will, grudges, anger, and so on. The image represents the destructive elements in a garden, which are the opposite of the white rose—a beautiful, desirable element.
5. good will, kindness, generosity, peace, purity of thought, spiritual love, forgiveness, and so on
6. We should treat enemies with the same good will and generosity that we show our friends.
7. Answers will vary. Most students will likely recognize the practical difficulty of living by Martí's ideal, but many will admire it as a goal, however difficult.

Versos Sencillos **363**

COMPOSITION: GUIDELINES FOR EVALUATION

WRITING ABOUT A SYMBOL

Objective

To analyze the use of symbolism in a poem

Guidelines for Evaluation

■ suggested length: three or four paragraphs
■ should identify the ideas symbolized by the white rose and other images
■ should explain how the symbolism expresses the poem's theme

WRITING A LETTER WITH SYMBOLS

Objective

To write a letter about thoughtful behavior

Guidelines for Evaluation

■ suggested length: two or three paragraphs
■ should express the writer's advice on how to behave thoughtfully and tactfully
■ should convey the ideas through the use of symbols

Alexander Pushkin

(1799–1837) *Russia*

The great Russian author Alexander Pushkin was born into an aristocratic but poor family. He worked in the civil service until he was exiled to southern Russia as a result of several revolutionary poems. He was later pardoned but continued to live under the czar's close scrutiny. In his lifetime Pushkin produced some of Russia's finest lyric poems, as well as plays, stories, and his masterpiece, the "verse novel" *Eugene Onegin*. "Message to Siberia" may have been prompted by his friendship with rebels exiled after a conspiracy against the czar in 1825.

Alexander Pushkin

Message to Siberia[1]

Translated from the Russian by Max Eastman

Deep in the Siberian mine,
Keep your patience proud;
The bitter toil shall not be lost,
The rebel thought unbowed.

5 The sister of misfortune, Hope,
In the under-darkness dumb
Speaks joyful courage to your heart:
The day desired will come.

And love and friendship pour to you
10 Across the darkened doors,
Even as round your galley-beds[2]
My free music pours.

The heavy-hanging chains will fall,
The walls will crumble at a word;
15 And Freedom greet you in the light,
And brothers give you back the sword.

---

1. **Siberia:** cold, remote area of northern Asia; Russia's place of exile and punishment for political crimes.
2. **galley-beds:** narrow prison beds. A *galley slave,* now used to refer to any drudge or prisoner, was originally a slave forced to row an ancient ship called a galley.

364 *Poetry*

TEACHING IMAGERY

Ask students to find images of darkness in the poem. ("under-darkness dumb" and "darkened doors" in ll. 6 and 10) What ideas does the poet associate with "the light" in line 15? (emerging from the mine into daylight; attaining freedom; the fulfillment of patience and hope; the validity of the prisoners' "rebel thought")

TEACHING STANZA FORM

The poem uses the ballad stanza (p. 349): alternating four-beat-three-beat lines rhyming *abcb*. In the last stanza, however, each line has four feet. This change in meter (like a shift from a minor to a major key in music) gives the stanza a fuller sound and brings the poem to an emphatic close.

Joseph Brodsky

(born 1940) *Soviet Union/United States*

Winner of the 1987 Nobel Prize for Literature, Joseph Brodsky grew up in Leningrad, working in a factory and educating himself. Always rebellious, Brodsky found solace in reading and writing poetry. His work came to international attention in 1964, when Soviet police arrested him for "social parasitism" and he was sentenced to a labor camp. In 1972 Brodsky was exiled and settled in the United States. Much of his poetry, including "The Monument," is sometimes angry, sometimes ironic, cultural criticism.

Joseph Brodsky

The Monument

Translated from the Russian by W. S. Merwin

Let us set up a monument
in the city, at the end of the long avenue,
or at the center of the big square,
a monument
5 that will stand out against any background
because it will be
quite well built and very realistic.
Let us set up a monument
that will not disturb anybody.

10 We will plant flowers
around the pedestal
and with the permission of the city fathers
we will lay out a little garden
where our children
15 will blink
at the great orange sun
and take the figure perched above them
for a well-known thinker
a composer
20 or a general.

The Monument **365**

The speaker proposes setting up a well-built, realistic, but inoffensive monument. Children will assume that it represents someone important. Adults will revere it in ignorance, for it actually represents a great lie.

LITERARY SKILLS FOR THIS SELECTION

- irony
- repetition

THEMES IN THIS SELECTION

- the value of truth and freedom
- propaganda and totalitarianism

LESSON OBJECTIVES

1. to write an analysis of poetic techniques
2. to write a political poem
3. to compare two poems

Teacher's Classroom Resources 2

- Teaching Notes   263
- Responding to World Cultures   264
- Writing Process Guides: Writing About Poetry   265 Writing a Political Poem   266
- Selection Test   267

IN THE CLASSROOM

TEACHING STUDENTS OF DIFFERENT ABILITIES

- **For less advanced students:** Focus students' attention on lines 9, 17–20, 21, and 25, which convey the speaker's irony and prepare for the biting criticism at the end.
- **For more advanced students:** Have students use periodicals to research the recent fate of monumental statues of Lenin,

Marx, Stalin, and other icons of the totalitarian Communist states that have recently been swept away by democratic revolutions.

MOTIVATION: PRIOR KNOWLEDGE

Have students discuss the various reasons that governments have for erecting statues and monuments.

CULTURAL BACKGROUND

Brodsky refers ironically to one of the many monumental statues erected by the Soviet government in order to glorify the Bolshevik revolution and idealize the virtue and industry of the workers and peasants within the one-party state. The government-approved style for such public art "that will not disturb anybody" is known as Socialist Realism.

- pedestal: base for a statue
- silhouette: outline
- rendezvous: arranged meetings

TEACHING IRONY

Explain that irony often uses words of praise to imply actual blame (ll. 5–7, 13–20, and 21–29). In Brodsky's poem the irony of the first thirty-six lines is somewhat veiled until the poem's final two words. Ask students to describe the irony in this poem. (It is ironic that a public monument, which normally commemorates abiding cultural values, should represent a lie.)

TEACHING REPETITION

Ask students to tell what changes in tone they detect each time the line "Let us set up a monument" is repeated. (The refrain subtly increases in sarcasm.)

COLLABORATIVE LEARNING: ENRICHMENT ACTIVITY

Social Studies Working in groups, students might report on recent changes in the totalitarian regimes that prevailed in Eastern Europe during the postwar era. Each student should report on a different country and the political changes it has undergone in the late 1980s and early 1990s. Students might present their findings on time lines or in oral reports.

ART AND LITERATURE

The Italian Renaissance sculptor Andrea Verrocchio (1435–1488) was perhaps the greatest sculptor of his day. Verocchio, whose name literally means "true eye," counted Leonardo da Vinci among his pupils. His commissioned bronze monument of the Venetian general Bartolomeo Colleoni combines drama, realistic motion, and self-assured power with a degree of skill in a way that was scarcely seen before his day.

- Ask students what aspect of a totalitarian regime might be represented by Verrocchio's statue. (naked, brutal power, as suggested by the general's aggressive pose and cruel, determined face)

I guarantee that flowers will appear
every morning
on the pedestal.
Let us set up a monument
25 that will not disturb anybody.
Even taxi drivers
will admire its majestic silhouette.
The garden will be a place
for rendezvous.
30 Let us set up a monument,
we will pass under it
       hurrying on our way to work,
foreigners will have their pictures taken
       standing under it,
35 we will splash it at night with the glare
       of floodlights.

Let us set up a monument to The Lie.

Monument to Bartolomeo Colleoni, Andrea del Verrocchio.

366 *Poetry*

STUDY QUESTIONS

Message to Siberia (Pushkin)
Recalling
1. In stanza 1, what does the speaker tell those "Deep in the Siberian mine"?
2. Whose "sister" is Hope? What pours across "darkened doors"?
3. What does the speaker predict in stanza 4?

Interpreting
4. Describe the people to whom this poem is addressed.
5. What does the figurative language in the last stanza actually mean?
6. What chief message does this poem have for the people to whom it is addressed? What does it say to a more universal audience?

Extending
7. What role can poetry and other literature play in comforting and encouraging others?

The Monument (Brodsky)
Recalling
1. In lines 1–9, where does the speaker suggest setting up a monument? Whom will it disturb?
2. In lines 10–20, what will the "city fathers" allow? What will "our children" think?
3. In lines 21–35, what does the speaker say people will do?

Interpreting
4. Why is it significant that the monument "will not disturb anybody"? What sort of monument do you think the speaker is suggesting?

5. Will the monument actually portray a well-known thinker, composer, or general? Explain.
6. What do the details in lines 21–34 suggest about human behavior?
7. How does the last line affect your reading of the rest of the poem? What do you think "The Lie" is?

Extending
8. What role can writers play in effecting political change? Do you think the pen is mightier than the sword?

COMPOSITION

Writing About Poetry
■ Write a composition showing how Pushkin's or Brodsky's poem uses techniques of poetry to express its meaning. If you treat "The Monument," elements you might discuss include speaker, tone, repetition, imagery, symbolism, and apostrophe. If you treat "Message to Siberia," you might discuss speaker, tone, rhyme, meter, apostrophe, personification, and other figurative language. *For help with the assignment, refer to Lesson 9 in the Writing About Literature Handbook at the back of this book.*

Writing a Political Poem
■ Write a poem that praises or criticizes a political situation somewhere in the world today.

COMPARING POEMS
■ What do Pushkin's and Brodsky's poems have in common in terms of their subject matter and sympathies? How are the tones of the two poems different?

Are the messages of these two poems relevant for Americans? Why or why not?

ANSWERS

STUDY QUESTIONS

Message to Siberia
1. "Keep your patience proud;/ The bitter toil shall not be lost,/ The rebel thought unbowed."
2. misfortune's; love, friendship
3. The chains will fall, the walls will crumble, and freedom will greet those now imprisoned.
4. They are exiles who are toiling in darkness but are nonetheless proud and courageous.
5. The freed prisoners will be able to fight for their cause again.
6. They should not give up hope. People should maintain hope and courage when persecuted for their beliefs.
7. It can comfort and inspire unhappy, oppressed people; it can connect people who are physically separated.

The Monument
1. at the end of a long avenue or in a big square; no one
2. a little garden; The figure is a thinker, composer, or general.
3. put flowers on the pedestal, admire the monument, meet at it, walk under it, and have their pictures taken under it
4. A monument that does not disturb anybody cannot be meaningful; a mindlessly patriotic monument with no real significance or value
5. No, by realistically and grandly portraying no one in particular, the monument can represent anyone important.
6. People are unthinking conformists willing to believe any lie presented with sufficient pomp.
7. It ironically undermines the positive statements about the monument; any political propaganda that distorts reality by idealizing meaningless values or oppressive ideologies
8. Many students will feel that writers can play a very influential role and that written truths will eventually overcome brute force.

COMPARING POEMS

Both are political and criticize political oppression. Pushkin's is uplifting; Brodsky's, ironic and bitter.

COMPOSITION: GUIDELINES FOR EVALUATION

WRITING ABOUT POETRY

Objective
To analyze how a writer uses poetic techniques

Guidelines for Evaluation
■ suggested length: four to six paragraphs
■ should identify the speaker, tone, imagery, and other techniques used in the poem
■ should explain how these techniques help express the theme

WRITING A POLITICAL POEM

Objective
To praise or criticize a political situation

Guidelines for Evaluation
■ suggested length: twelve to twenty-four lines
■ should relate to a present-day political situation
■ Should identify positive or negative aspects of the situation

The *Rothschild Miscellany* is a collection of over forty religious and secular illuminated manuscripts. These are handmade, hand-copied books with colorful illustrations that "illuminate" the text. This particular image is from a Book of Psalms. The Hebrew word shown in the rectangle, pronounced äsh rā′, means "happy is [he]." This early Renaissance pastoral image depicts King David seated with his harp amidst creatures of the wilderness.

The painting is characteristically Italian because of its realistic depiction of space. Linear perspective was developed in Italy not long before this manuscript painting was executed.

In the Renaissance the actual world was taken to be an imperfect reflection of the heavenly world. During the Middle Ages and the early Renaissance the subject matter of art was inspired by stories in the Bible.

- Ask students what mood or tone is captured by this painting. (peace, serenity, joy) Does this mood or tone seem appropriate for a biblical text? Why? (It does because peace and serenity may be seen as spiritual goals.) In general, how might an illuminated manuscript enhance the spiritual impact of the Bible or another religious text? (It can make the content and, particularly, the mood of the text seem more immediate and powerful.)

368 *Poetry*

Initial word panel of the Book of Psalms featuring King David playing his harp. Detail from a *Rothschild Miscellany* illuminated manuscript, northern Italian, 1470–1480.

POETRY

EXPLORING THE PSALMS

The psalms, which number one hundred fifty in most canons, were probably intended to be chanted or sung. Like other lyric poems the psalms express a broad range of emotions: joy, fear, anger, awe, vengefulness, sorrow, and resignation.

Activities

1. Divide students into groups of six or seven. Ask each group to jot down a list of examples of some of the poetic devices that are used in the King James Version of Psalm 23. One group could look for examples of figurative language (such as the Lord as a shepherd); another group could concentrate on imagery (such as "green pastures" and "still waters"); while another could find examples of sound devices (such as the grave repetition of "he maketh me," "he leadeth me," and "he restoreth my soul"). Then ask each group to present its findings to the class.

2. Divide the class into groups of three or four students, and ask each group to explore the literary qualities of other psalms, such as those numbered 121, 148, and 150 in the King James Version. Alternatively, ask each group to compare a passage in the Bible with a poem or song inspired by that passage. Students could compare, for instance, Anna Akhmatova's "Lot's Wife" with the Old Testament verses (Genesis 19:1–26) that inspired the poem. Then ask each group to share a few examples of their findings with the class.

The Bible's Influence on World Literature

The poetry of the world has been enormously influenced by the poetry in the Bible, the most widely read work of literature in the Western world. The Bible is a collection of books, produced over many centuries, that incorporates the sacred writings of both Judaism and Christianity. The Jewish Bible, which is the Old Testament of the Christian Bible, was composed mainly in ancient Hebrew with a few sections in Aramaic. It contains world-renowned poetry, including the Book of Psalms, the Book of Job, and the Song of Solomon.

The Bible is the world's most widely translated work of literature. One of the earliest translations of the Jewish Bible was a Greek version known as the Septuagint, written in the third century B.C. The Vulgate, an important early Christian translation into Latin, was completed by Saint Jerome about A.D. 405. In the sixteenth century Protestant reformer Martin Luther produced a famous German translation of the Bible. Probably the best-known English translation is the King James Version of the early seventeenth century. This work, produced by a group of scholars and translators, had an enormous influence on the history of English and American literature. Its lofty language, masterful style, and powerful rhythms affected generations of writers, including John Milton, William Blake, John Keats, Ralph Waldo Emerson, Walt Whitman, and Emily Dickinson.

Attributed mainly to David, king of the Jews about 1000 B.C., the Book of Psalms contains some of the world's finest examples of lyric poetry, such as the King James translation of Psalm 23, which appears below.

Psalm 23

The Lord is my shepherd; I shall not want.

He maketh me to lie down in green pastures: he leadeth me beside the still waters.

He restoreth my soul: he leadeth me in the paths of righteousness for his name's sake.

Yea, though I walk through the valley of the shadow of death, I will fear no evil: for thou art with me; thy rod and thy staff they comfort me.

Thou preparest a table before me in the presence of mine enemies: thou anointest my head with oil; my cup runneth over.

Surely goodness and mercy shall follow me all the days of my life: and I will dwell in the house of the Lord forever.

The tiger is one of the twelve animals of the Chinese zodiac. The embroidered dragonlike tiger with wings represented here adds the element of flight to one of the most powerful images in Chinese mythology. The grimace on the tiger's face signifies a deity that can both give life and take it away—an all-powerful figure that one must submit to and pass through in order to discover one's inner, or true, self.

To the Chinese there is a beneficial side to this fierce figure, for majesty, justice, and a high sense of morality are associated with the winged tiger.

- All cultures have symbols that are intended to evoke cultural pride, such as the American bald eagle. Ask students to name other images that stand for loyalty or pride. (Possible answers: the flag, a school's or a team's colors, a ring, a soldier's uniform)

370 *Nonfiction*

Embroidered silk banner showing a winged tiger, Chinese, nineteenth century.

NONFICTION

I *f one but tell a thing well, it moves on with undying voice.*
—PINDAR
Ancient Greece

LESSON PREVIEW

This autobiographical selection relates an Indian's first experience with Anglo-Indian schooling. The account contrasts the two cultures and shows the reactions of the author, Santha, and her sister, Premila, to the condescending treatment they receive. When Premila's teacher orders the Indian children to sit apart during a test because "Indians cheat," Premila angrily leaves, and she and Santha return home.

LITERARY SKILLS FOR THIS SELECTION

- autobiography
- purpose

THEMES IN THIS SELECTION

- cultural misconceptions
- growth and learning

LESSON OBJECTIVES

1. to recognize purpose in autobiography
2. to determine the meaning of words with Indian origins
3. to write an autobiographical narrative

Teacher's Classroom Resources 3

- Teaching Notes 9
- Prereading Vocabulary 10
- Reading Guide 11
- Check Test 12
- Responding to World Cultures 13
- Literary Focus: Purpose in Autobiography 14
- Language Study: Words from Indian Languages 15
- Writing Process Guide: Writing an Autobiographical Incident 16
- Grammar in Literature: Sensory Details 17
- Selection Test 18

Santha Rama Rau

(born 1923)

India

Born in Madras, India, Santha Rama Rau spent a childhood enriched by cultural diversity. Her family was obliged to accompany her father on the frequent travels dictated by his job as a high-ranking civil servant in India's British colonial administration. By the time she arrived in the United States as a freshman at Wellesley College in Massachusetts, Rau had lived in many parts of India, as well as England and South Africa.

Mining the rich experience of her youth, she produced her first book, *Home to India* (1945), an autobiography that achieved both critical and popular success. Her subsequent world travels led to several other volumes of autobiography, travel writing, and fiction. In 1960 she dramatized E. M. Forster's celebrated novel *A Passage to India* for an acclaimed presentation on the London stage.

Her abiding theme of the interaction of people from widely differing cultures has been well served by autobiography. The upcoming selection is drawn from a collection of autobiographical sketches entitled *Gifts of Passage*.

372 *Nonfiction*

GEOGRAPHY AND CULTURE

India's British Colonial Legacy

The English gained their first important foothold in India in 1661, when Portugal ceded the territory around Bombay to England. For almost three centuries, until India gained independence in 1947, England consolidated and governed the vast country, which is about one third the size of the continental United States. Over the centuries the centers of colonial administration grew into the major cities of India: Bombay, Calcutta, Madras, and Delhi, which became the capital in 1912. Before independence many Indians, like Santha Rama Rau's father, were educated in England and served as high-ranking administrators in the colonial government.

The fact that Rau herself writes in English reflects one of the most notable legacies of India's colonial past: In this populous country with its many distinct regional languages, English has become the common second language of a large majority of Indians.

MAJOR LANGUAGES OF INDIA

See LITERATURE AND CULTURE SOURCEBOOK: India and the Middle East

IN THE CLASSROOM

TEACHING STUDENTS OF DIFFERENT ABILITIES

- **For less advanced students:** Pronounce and explain difficult Indian words. Ask students to complete the Reading Guide.

- **For more advanced students:** Ask students to pay attention to differing cultural characteristics that are implied through characterization and the use of details.

DISCUSSING GEOGRAPHY AND CULTURE

Exploring the Meaning of Names

In this story an incident involving names serves as a metaphor for the power of British colonialism in India. Indians' last names often reflect their native region, class, and religion. For instance, "Rau" refers to an ancient Maharashtrian royal office. Our own last names tell much about our immigrant past.

- Ask students to discuss their surnames. Were they ever Anglicized or shortened? Did they allude to a trade (for example, smith or miller)?

Santha Rama Rau

By Any Other Name

1   At the Anglo-Indian[1] day school in Zorinabad[2] to which my sister and I were sent when she was eight and I was five and a half, they changed our names. On the first day of school, a hot, windless morning of a north Indian September, we stood in the headmistress's study and she said, "Now you're the *new* girls. What are your names?"

My sister answered for us. "I am Premila, and she"—nodding in my direction—"is Santha."

The headmistress had been in India, I suppose, fifteen years or so, but she still smiled her helpless inability to cope with Indian names. Her rimless half-glasses glittered, and the precarious bun on the top of her head trembled as she shook her head. "Oh, my dears, those are much too hard for me. Suppose we give you pretty English names. Wouldn't that be more jolly? Let's see, now—Pamela for you, I think." She shrugged in a baffled way at my sister. "That's as close as I can get. And for *you*," she said to me, "how about Cynthia? Isn't that nice?"

My sister was always less easily intimidated than I was, and while she kept a stubborn silence, I said, "Thank you," in a very tiny voice.

We had been sent to that school because my father, among his responsibilities as an officer of the civil service, had a tour of duty to perform in the villages around that steamy little provincial town, where he had his headquarters at that time. He used to make his shorter inspection tours on horseback, and a week before, in the stale heat of a typically postmonsoon[3] day, we

had waved good-by to him and a little procession—an assistant, a secretary, two bearers, and the man to look after the bedding rolls and luggage: They rode away through our large garden, still bright green from the rains, and we turned

2 back into the twilight of the house and the sound of fans whispering in every room.

Up to then, my mother had refused to send Premila to school in the British-run establishments of that time, because, she used to say, "you can bury a dog's tail for seven years and it still comes out curly, and you can take a Britisher away from his home for a lifetime and he

3 still remains insular." The examinations and degrees from entirely Indian schools were not, in those days, considered valid. In my case, the question had never come up, and probably never would have come up if Mother's extraordinary good health had not broken down. For the first time in my life, she was not able to continue the lessons she had been giving us every morning. So our Hindi[4] books were put away, the stories of the Lord Krishna[5] as a little boy were left in mid-air, and we were sent to the Anglo-Indian school.

That first day at school is still, when I think of it, a remarkable one. At that age, if one's name is changed, one develops a curious form of dual personality. I remember having a certain detached and disbelieving concern in the actions of "Cynthia," but certainly no responsibility. Accordingly, I followed the thin, erect back of the headmistress down the veranda to my classroom feeling, at most, a passing interest in what

---

1. **Anglo-Indian:** English Indian; referring to people of English descent living in India. (See the Geography and Culture feature that precedes the story.)
2. **Zorinabad** [zō rēn′ä bäd]
3. **postmonsoon:** referring to the dry period following the seasonal rains in India.

4. **Hindi** [hin′dē]: language of northern India and India's most widely spoken native language.
5. **Lord Krishna** [krish′nə]: eighth incarnation, or earthly form, taken by Vishnu, an important Hindu god.

By Any Other Name   **373**

CRITICAL THINKING: GUIDED READING QUESTIONS

LITERAL

1a. What does the headmistress do when the sisters tell her their names? (She gives them similar-sounding English ones.)

2a. What quality of the British does the mother single out in her objection to English schooling? (insularity)

INFERENTIAL

1b. What attitude is she revealing in doing this? (a lack of respect for Indians and a conviction about the superiority of things English)

2b. Why does she object to this quality? (It would result in snobbishness and a lack of understanding of other cultures.)

- Santha's class includes only four other Indian children, one of whom is a small girl who dresses in a mixed English and Indian style.
- When asked her name, a resentful Santha says, "I don't know."
- Santha pays little attention to the lesson, since she is already largely familiar with its content.
- Premila and Santha share an Indian lunch, but Premila instructs Santha to sit with her classmates.
- The small Indian girl in Santha's class refuses Santha's offer of Indian food and eats her sandwiches instead.

IN THE GLOSSARY

- incomprehensible: unable to be understood

4 READING SKILL: CONTRAST

Ask students to contrast the Indian and British verandas. What do their differences suggest about the two cultures? (The Indians build and paint in harmony with the climate. The British cling almost fanatically to their own traditions, despite the discomfort it causes.)

5 TEACHING DESCRIPTION

Draw students' attention to the carefully detailed description of the Indian girl. Ask them how the details reflect the difficulties of Indian assimilation into British culture. (Her mixed mode of dress suggests an uneasy compromise, and her sad solemnity shows the price of this compromise.)

6 CULTURAL BACKGROUND

Ask any Indian students you may have in class (or any foreign students who may be familiar with Indian food) to describe in more detail the Indian food items discussed in this passage and any others with which they are familiar.

7 TEACHING CHARACTERIZATION

Ask students what Premila's actions reveal about her character. (She wishes to conform to the class's expectations.)

was going to happen to me in this strange, new atmosphere of School.

The building was Indian in design, with wide verandas opening onto a central courtyard, but **4** Indian verandas are usually whitewashed, with stone floors. These, in the tradition of British schools, were painted dark brown and had matting on the floors. It gave a feeling of extra intensity to the heat.

I suppose there were about a dozen Indian children in the school—which contained perhaps forty children in all—and four of them were in my class. They were all sitting at the back of the room, and I went to join them. I sat **5** next to a small, solemn girl who didn't smile at me. She had long, glossy-black braids and wore a cotton dress, but she still kept on her Indian jewelry—a gold chain around her neck, thin gold bracelets, and tiny ruby studs in her ears. Like most Indian children, she had a rim of black kohl[6] around her eyes. The cotton dress should have looked strange, but all I could think of was that I should ask my mother if I couldn't wear a dress to school, too, instead of my Indian clothes.

I can't remember too much about the proceedings in class that day, except for the beginning. The teacher pointed to me and asked me to stand up. "Now, dear, tell the class your name."

I said nothing.

"Come along," she said, frowning slightly. "What's your name, dear?"

"I don't know," I said, finally.

The English children in the front of the class—there were about eight or ten of them—giggled and twisted around in their chairs to look at me. I sat down quickly and opened my eyes very wide, hoping in that way to dry them off. The little girl with the braids put out her hand and very lightly touched my arm. She still didn't smile.

---

6. **kohl** [kōl]: powder used in Asia as a cosmetic, especially to darken the eyelids.

Most of that morning I was rather bored. I looked briefly at the children's drawings pinned to the wall, and then concentrated on a lizard clinging to the ledge of the high, barred window behind the teacher's head. Occasionally it would shoot out its long yellow tongue for a fly, and then it would rest, with its eyes closed and its belly palpitating, as though it were swallowing several times quickly. The lessons were mostly concerned with reading and writing and simple numbers—things that my mother had already taught me—and I paid very little attention. The teacher wrote on the easel blackboard words like "bat" and "cat," which seemed babyish to me; only "apple" was new and incomprehensible.

When it was time for the lunch recess, I followed the girl with braids out onto the veranda. There the children from the other classes were assembled. I saw Premila at once and ran over to her, as she had charge of our lunchbox. The children were all opening packages and sitting down to eat sandwiches. Premila and I were the **6** only ones who had Indian food—thin wheat chapatties,[7] some vegetable curry, and a bottle of buttermilk. Premila thrust half of it into my hand and whispered fiercely that I should go **7** and sit with my class, because that was what the others seemed to be doing.

The enormous black eyes of the little Indian girl from my class looked at my food longingly, so I offered her some. But she only shook her head and plowed her way solemnly through her sandwiches.

I was very sleepy after lunch, because at home we always took a siesta.[8] It was usually a pleasant time of day, with the bedroom darkened against the harsh afternoon sun, the drifting off into sleep with the sound of Mother's voice reading a story in one's mind, and, finally,

---

7. **chapatties** [chä pät'ēz]: fried, unleavened cake used as a bread.
8. **siesta** [sē es'tə]: a brief nap or rest usually taken after lunch or in the early afternoon.

CRITICAL THINKING: GUIDED READING QUESTIONS

LITERAL

1a. What does Santha do when the children laugh at her? (She opens her eyes wide to dry them.)

2a. What does the other Indian girl do when Santha offers her some food? (She refuses it and eats her own sandwiches.)

INFERENTIAL

1b. What does this action show about her feelings? (She is hurt enough to cry but does not wish to show it.)

2b. Why does she do this? (Although she would like the Indian food, she feels she must conform to the British ways.)

Indian fabric, cotton painted with gold and silver, design of Gopis in a garden, seventeenth century.

8 GRAMMAR IN LITERATURE

Point out how the vivid adjectives *shrill* and *fussy* not only describe the quality of the ayah's voice but also reveal character in a highly economical way.

ART AND LITERATURE

Traditional Indian art draws on images of daily life to reflect a higher or supreme reality. According to mythology, the *gopis* were milkmaids who fell in love with Krishna, a deity who in his earthly manifestation arose from the same caste of herders as the *gopis* to become a god.

The center tree in the tapestry rises and opens into a sunlike image; its perfect alignment amidst the schematically drawn *gopis* alludes to the fact that these are not real trees or maidens but earthly reflections of a Hindu ideal.

■ Ask students whether Santha would have been more likely to learn about this artwork in her Anglo-Indian school or at home. (She would have learned about it at home, where she learned stories of Lord Krishna.)

8 the shrill, fussy voice of the ayah[9] waking one for tea.

At school, we rested for a short time on low, folding cots on the veranda, and then we were expected to play games. During the hot part of the afternoon we played indoors, and after the shadows had begun to lengthen and the slight breeze of the evening had come up we moved outside to the wide courtyard.

9. **ayah** [ī′ä]: children's nanny or maid in India.

By Any Other Name **375**

CRITICAL THINKING: GUIDED READING QUESTIONS

LITERAL

1a. What are the children expected to do after resting? (They are expected to play games.)

INFERENTIAL

1b. What does the use of the word *expected* suggest about how Santha views such play? (It is another required activity, and Santha derives no pleasure from it.)

- Santha allows the English children to win at games and is puzzled when they do not reciprocate.
- Premila reprimands Santha for running to the ayah at the end of the school day.
- At home Premila tells their mother about upcoming tests and asks to take sandwiches for lunch.
- Santha spends the evening playing joyfully with the cook's son.
- On the day of Premila's first test, the older sister appears abruptly in Santha's classroom.

IN THE GLOSSARY

- sedately: calmly

9 TEACHING PURPOSE

Explain that in writing an autobiography the author's purpose may be to express a general truth about life. Ask what general truth about life can be found in the passage about competitive games. (Misunderstanding and intolerance can grow out of differences between cultures.)

10 TEACHING STUDENTS OF LIMITED ENGLISH PROFICIENCY

Explain that "donkey's years" is slang for "a very long time." Point out that slang expressions are constantly coming in and out of vogue. Discuss modern slang expressions whose meaning is comparable to "donkey's years."

11 TEACHING DESCRIPTION

Direct attention to the use of descriptive details regarding the physical environment (tepid water, lime trees, the smell of jasmine). What feeling toward India is being expressed indirectly? (a positive feeling for the beauty, sensuousness, and mystery of the land)

12 CRITICAL THINKING: EVALUATION

Ask students to evaluate how Santha is getting along with the children at her new school. (While she has made friends among the Indians, Santha is not allowed to have close associations with the English or Anglo-Indian children.)

I had never really grasped the system of competitive games. At home, whenever we played tag or guessing games, I was always allowed to "win"—"because," Mother used to tell Premila, "she is the youngest, and we have to allow for that." I had often heard her say it, and it seemed quite reasonable to me, but the result was that I had no clear idea of what "winning" meant.

When we played twos-and-threes that afternoon at school, in accordance with my training, I let one of the small English boys catch me, but was naturally rather puzzled when the other children did not return the courtesy. I ran about for what seemed like hours without ever catching anyone, until it was time for school to close.

9 Much later I learned that my attitude was called "not being a good sport," and I stopped allowing myself to be caught, but it was not for years that I really learned the spirit of the thing.

When I saw our car come up to the school gate, I broke away from my classmates and rushed toward it yelling, "Ayah! Ayah!" It seemed like an eternity since I had seen her that morning—a wizened, affectionate figure in her white cotton sari[10] giving me dozens of urgent and useless instructions on how to be a good girl at school. Premila followed more sedately, and she told me on the way home never to do that again in front of the other children.

When we got home we went straight to Mother's high, white room to have tea with her, and I immediately climbed onto the bed and bounced gently up and down on the springs. Mother asked how we had liked our first day in school. I was so pleased to be home and to have left that peculiar Cynthia behind that I had nothing whatever to say about school, except to ask what "apple" meant. But Premila told Mother about the classes, and added that in her class they had weekly tests to see if they had learned their lessons well.

I asked, "What's a test?"

10 Premila said, "You're too small to have them. You won't have them in your class for donkey's years."[11] She had learned the expression that day and was using it for the first time. We all laughed enormously at her wit. She also told Mother, in an aside, that we should take sandwiches to school the next day. Not, she said, that *she* minded. But they would be simpler for me to handle.

That whole lovely evening I didn't think about school at all. I sprinted barefoot across the lawns with my favorite playmate, the cook's son, to the stream at the end of the garden. We quarreled in our usual way, waded in the tepid water under the lime trees, and waited for the night to bring out the smell of the jasmine.[12] I listened with fascination to his stories of ghosts and demons, until I was too frightened to cross the garden alone in the semidarkness. The ayah found me, shouted at the cook's son, scolded me, hurried me in to supper—it was an entirely usual, wonderful evening.

It was a week later, the day of Premila's first test, that our lives changed rather abruptly. I was sitting at the back of my class, in my usual inattentive way, only half listening to the teacher. I had started a rather guarded friendship with the girl with the braids, whose name turned out to be Nalini (Nancy, in school). The three other Indian children were already fast friends. Even at that age it was apparent to all of us that friendship with the English or Anglo-Indian children was out of the question. Occasionally, during the class, my new friend and I would draw pictures and show them to each other secretly.

The door opened sharply and Premila marched in. At first, the teacher smiled at her in a kindly and encouraging way and said, "Now, you're little Cynthia's sister?"

Premila didn't even look at her. She stood

---

10. **sari** [sär′ē]: traditional Hindu female's garment worn wrapped around the body and draped over a shoulder.

11. **donkey's years:** slang for "a very long time."

12. **jasmine** [jaz′min]: fragrant flowering shrub.

376 *Nonfiction*

CRITICAL THINKING: GUIDED READING QUESTIONS

LITERAL

1a. What does Premila tell Santha never to do again in front of the other children? (Premila instructs Santha never to run to the car joyfully yelling, "Ayah! Ayah!")

2a. What is apparent to the Indian children regarding friendships with the English or Anglo-Indian children? (They would be "out of the question.")

INFERENTIAL

1b. Why does Premila reprimand Santha? (She desperately wants to fit in and is embarrassed by Santha's actions.)

2b. Why is this thought to be the case? (Cultural differences and English snobbishness and intolerance prohibit such friendships.)

with her feet planted firmly apart and her shoulders rigid, and addressed herself directly to me. "Get up," she said. "We're going home."

I didn't know what had happened, but I was aware that it was a crisis of some sort. I rose obediently and started to walk toward my sister.

"Bring your pencils and your notebook," she said.

I went back for them, and together we left the room. The teacher started to say something just as Premila closed the door, but we didn't wait to hear what it was.

In complete silence we left the school grounds and started to walk home. Then I asked Premila what the matter was. All she would say was "We're going home for good."

It was a very tiring walk for a child of five and a half, and I dragged along behind Premila with my pencils growing sticky in my hand. I can still remember looking at the dusty hedges, and the tangles of thorns in the ditches by the side of the road, smelling the faint fragrance from the eucalyptus trees and wondering whether we would ever reach home. Occasionally a horse-drawn tonga[13] passed us, and the women, in their pink or green silks, stared at Premila and me trudging along on the side of the road. A few coolies[14] and a line of women carrying baskets of vegetables on their heads smiled at us. But it was nearing the hottest time of day, and the road was almost deserted. I walked more and more slowly, and shouted to Premila, from time to time, "Wait for me!" with increas-

---

13. **tonga** [tän′gə]: two-wheeled horse-drawn carriage.
14. **coolies**: manual laborers.

ing peevishness. She spoke to me only once, and that was to tell me to carry my notebook on my head, because of the sun.

When we got to our house the ayah was just taking a tray of lunch into Mother's room. She immediately started a long, worried questioning about what are you children doing back here at this hour of the day.

Mother looked very startled and very concerned, and asked Premila what had happened.

Premila said, "We had our test today, and She made me and the other Indians sit at the back of the room, with a desk between each one."

Mother said, "Why was that, darling?"

"She said it was because Indians cheat," Premila added. "So I don't think we should go back to that school."

Mother looked very distant, and was silent a long time. At last she said, "Of course not, darling." She sounded displeased.

We all shared the curry she was having for lunch, and afterward I was sent off to the beautifully familiar bedroom for my siesta. I could hear Mother and Premila talking through the open door.

Mother said, "Do you suppose she understood all that?"

Premila said, "I shouldn't think so. She's a baby."

Mother said, "Well, I hope it won't bother her."

Of course, they were both wrong. I understood it perfectly, and I remember it all very clearly. But I put it happily away, because it had all happened to a girl called Cynthia, and I never was really particularly interested in her.

PAGE SUMMARY: AT A GLANCE

- Premila boldly removes Santha from her class, and the girls go home.
- Premila informs their mother that the teacher claimed that Indians cheat on tests.
- Unbeknownst to Premila and their mother, Santha understands what occurred but is indifferent because of her detachment from the girl called Cynthia.

IN THE GLOSSARY

- trudging: walking laboriously

13 TEACHING CHARACTERIZATION

Ask students what Premila's behavior here reveals about her. (She can be assertive and rebellious and is very proud.)

14 CULTURAL BACKGROUND

Point out that the word *coolie*, which in English now refers to "an unskilled laborer who works for little pay," probably came originally from the Hindi *koli*, which was the name of a low-ranking tribe or caste in Gujarat, a state in western India.

15 READING SKILL: INFERENCE

Ask students what they can infer about the teacher and the school from the teacher's comment about Indians cheating. (She is prejudiced and insensitive; the school routinely treats Indians as second-class citizens.)

16 TEACHING AUTOBIOGRAPHY

Explain that autobiographies often detail the growth of the author's personal identity. Ask what the author might be suggesting by distancing her own identity from that of Cynthia. (Santha has defined herself as an Indian and has embraced her culture. By viewing Cynthia as a foreigner, Santha demonstrates her resistance to assimilation.)

COLLABORATIVE LEARNING: ENRICHMENT ACTIVITY

Social Studies Have a group of students research the history of India's struggle for independence from Great Britain and report their findings to the class.

CRITICAL THINKING: GUIDED READING QUESTIONS

LITERAL

1a. What does Premila answer when Santha asks what is wrong? ("We're going home for good.")

2a. How does the mother sound when she agrees not to send the girls back to school? (displeased)

INFERENTIAL

1b. Why doesn't Premila tell Santha why they are going home? (She wishes to protect Santha and thinks she would not understand.)

2b. Why might she sound this way? (She is probably angry at the teacher's prejudice.)

Do you think Premila was justified in taking herself and Santha
out of school? Why or why not?

ANSWERS

STUDY QUESTIONS

1. The girls' mother had fallen ill and could no longer tutor them; also, Indian degrees were not considered valid.
2. She looks at it longingly but refuses it.
3. to bring Santha home with her; The Indian children were forced to sit apart because the teacher said that Indians cheat.
4. She understood them but was not troubled since they happened to Cynthia.
5. Premila tells Santha to sit with her class at lunch, repeats an expression she learned at school, and suggests that they take sandwiches to school.
6. The English are more competitive.
7. It suggests that names are important because they help define cultural and personal identity.
8. Answers will vary. Some will agree with the mother; others will not. The mother might have spoken to the school officials about the teacher.

LITERARY FOCUS

Answers will vary. Students might say that when people from different cultures come into close contact, there are inevitable strains and conflicts, and there must be respect and tolerance in order for them to get along.

LANGUAGE STUDY

1. "long women's garment"; from Hindi
2. "patterned cotton cloth"; from Hindi
3. "spiritual guide"; from Hindi
4. "ferretlike, snake-killing animal"; from Marathi
5. "ornamental bracelet"; from Hindi
6. "spicy powder or sauce"; from Tamil
7. "dull yellow-brown"; from Hindi, from Persian
8. "small boat"; from Bengali and Hindi

STUDY QUESTIONS

Recalling

1. Explain why the girls were sent by their parents to the Anglo-Indian school.
2. When the author offers Nalini some of her Indian food on the first day of school, how does Nalini react?
3. On the day of the test, why does Premila suddenly burst into the author's classroom? What does she later explain at home about her reason?
4. At the end of this account, what does the author report about her own reaction to the events at school?

Interpreting

5. What evidence can you find in the selection that up to the day of the test Premila is more eager than her younger sister to fit in at the school?
6. What contrast between different viewpoints does the author suggest in her comments about the competitive games at school?
7. In her title the author alludes to a passage from William Shakespeare's play *Romeo and Juliet* (Act II, Scene 2, lines 43–44): "That which we call a rose / By any other name would smell as sweet." How does this allusion relate to the main idea of the story?

Extending

8. Would you have handled the incident as Santha's mother did? If so, why? If not, what would you have done differently?

LITERARY FOCUS

Purpose in Autobiography

An **autobiography** is the story of a person's life written by that person. In an autobiography the author relates events from memory and interprets those events with insights provided by time. Rau's purpose for writing her autobiography went beyond simply recording facts and experiences about her life. The **purpose** of Rau's autobiography is the central idea—

a general truth about life—that she wanted to convey to her readers.

Thinking About the Purpose in Autobiography

■ State in a sentence or two Rau's chief purpose in writing "By Any Other Name." Before you write, think about how Premila and Santha are treated in the school. What do you think both girls learn from this experience?

LANGUAGE STUDY

Words from Indian Languages

During the long English presence in India, many words from Indian languages became part of the English language. These words come from Hindi, the most widely spoken of India's native languages, as well as from Tamil (spoken in the region around the city of Madras), Marathi (spoken in the region around Bombay), and other languages.

Use a dictionary to help you determine the meanings and origins of these English words, some of which appear in the selection. Each word is from one of the native languages of India.

1. sari	5. bangle
2. chintz	6. curry
3. guru	7. khaki
4. mongoose	8. dinghy

COMPOSITION

Writing an Autobiographical Incident

■ In a preface to her autobiography, Rau wrote that she hoped to describe the "illuminating moments" of her life. Recall an incident in your life that had a powerful impact on you. Write an autobiographical account of this incident. Begin by describing the incident in detail. Then explain why you think it was an "illuminating moment" by telling what you learned from the incident. Did you immediately realize its lesson, or did the realization come later? If you would rather not write about yourself, write a fictitious autobiographical account.

COMPOSITION: GUIDELINES FOR EVALUATION

WRITING AN AUTOBIOGRAPHICAL NARRATIVE

Objective

To write about an incident that had a powerful impact on the writer

Guidelines for Evaluation

■ suggested length: three or four paragraphs

■ should describe the incident in detail
■ should show what the writer learned from the incident
■ should state when the writer realized why the incident was illuminating

PREVIEW: THE AUTHOR AND THE WORLD

GEOGRAPHY AND CULTURE

Camara Laye

(1928–1980)

Guinea

Camara Laye [kä mä rä′ lī′] grew up in Kouroussa [kōō rōō′sä], in Guinea, where his father and grandfather were skilled metalworkers. Laye attended schools in Conakry, the capital of Guinea, and then in Paris, where he studied mechanical engineering. While he was working in France as an automobile mechanic, he completed his first book, *The Dark Child* (1954), an autobiographical account of his childhood and youth, from which the upcoming selection is taken. In his book Laye paints a picture of a traditional African village in which family ties are strong and reverence for the land is paramount.

In 1956, after Laye had published his novel *The Radiance of the King,* he returned to his homeland, serving in various government posts before going into voluntary exile in the neighboring West African country of Senegal. There he completed *A Dream of Africa,* a sequel to his autobiographical memoirs. Laye's books have been widely admired for their ingenious use of allegory and their sensitive insight into political and social change in modern Africa.

Guinea's Economy and Culture

Guinea is located on the west coast of Africa. A colony of France from the late nineteenth century, Guinea became independent in 1958. The country has a warm, tropical climate and a rainy season that lasts for nearly six months.

The country's rich popular culture thrives on music, oral folk tales, drama, and history as recited by storytellers called *griots.* With about eighty percent of the population employed in agriculture, Guinea is one of the least industrially developed countries in the world. Yet the nation has vast potential: It has, for example, nearly one third of the known reserves of bauxite, a material used to make aluminum. Another important natural resource is gold, which washes up from the banks of the Niger River in the uplands of the interior. "The Snake and the Goldsmith" discusses the renown enjoyed by the narrator's father for his skill as a goldsmith.

See *LITERATURE AND CULTURE SOURCEBOOK:* Africa

The Snake and the Goldsmith **379**

LESSON PREVIEW

In this autobiographical account the author describes with affection and wonder his boyhood in Guinea. He tells of his father, a goldsmith who attributes his skill and renown to the influence of a guiding spirit that takes the form of a snake. The boy comes to share in the belief of his father, developing great respect for family, tradition, and craftsmanship.

LITERARY SKILLS FOR THIS SELECTION

- description
- character
- theme

THEMES IN THIS SELECTION

- family and tradition
- craftsmanship
- the supernatural

LESSON OBJECTIVES

1. to understand the meaning and origin of words from African languages
2. to write about autobiography

Teacher's Classroom Resources 3

■ Teaching Notes	21
■ Prereading Vocabulary	22
■ Reading Guide	23
■ Check Test	24
■ Responding to World Cultures	25
■ Language Study: Words from African Languages	26
■ Writing Process Guide: Writing About Autobiography	27
■ Grammar in Literature: Spatial Order	28
■ Selection Test	29

TEACHING STUDENTS OF DIFFERENT ABILITIES

- **For less advanced students:** Point out that the selection is nonfiction: an account of events that really occurred, fantastic as they may seem. Ask students to complete the Reading Guide.

- **For more advanced students:** Ask students to focus on the author's attitude and the values he is endorsing. Then ask them to decide whether they agree with the author and to explain their answer.

DISCUSSING GEOGRAPHY AND CULTURE

Skills and Crafts

Craftspeople occupy an important niche in Guinean society. These talented men and women—musicians, praise singers, smiths, leatherworkers, tattooers, and woodworkers—marry within their own caste and pass on their skills to their children.

- Even in our industrialized society, skills are often passed down from one generation to the next. Ask students to name a skill they have learned from their parents. (Possible answers: fishing, knitting)

Gold rings of the Mawerehene, Ashanti, Ghana.

Camara Laye

The Snake and the Goldsmith

Translated from the French by James Kirkup, Ernest Jones, and Elaine Gottlieb

1

I was a little boy playing around my father's hut. How old would I have been at that time? I cannot remember exactly. I must still have been very young: five, maybe six years old. My mother was in the workshop with my father, and I could just hear their familiar voices above the noise of the anvil and the conversation of the customers.

Suddenly I stopped playing, my whole attention fixed on a snake that was creeping around the hut. After a moment I went over to him. I had taken in my hand a reed that was lying in the yard—there were always some lying around; they used to get broken off the fence of plaited reeds that marked the boundary of our concession[1]—and I thrust it into his mouth. The snake did not try to get away: he was beginning to enjoy our little game; he was slowly swallowing the reed; he was devouring it, I thought, as if it were some delicious prey, his eyes glittering with voluptuous bliss; and inch by inch his head was drawing nearer to my hand. At last the reed was almost entirely swallowed, and the snake's jaws were terribly close to my fingers.

I was laughing. I had not the slightest fear, and I feel sure that the snake would not have hesitated much longer before burying his fangs

---

1. **concession:** within an African village, the land granted to, or owned by, one family.

in my fingers if, at that moment, Damany, one of the apprentices, had not come out of the workshop. He called my father, and almost at once I felt myself lifted off my feet: I was safe in the arms of one of my father's friends.

Around me there was a great commotion. My mother was shouting hardest of all, and she gave me a few sharp slaps. I wept, more upset by the sudden uproar than by the blows. A little later, when I was somewhat calmer and the shouting had ceased, my mother solemnly warned me never to play that game again. I promised, although the game still didn't seem dangerous to me.

My father's hut was near the workshop, and I often played beneath the veranda that ran around the outside. It was his private hut, and like all our huts built of mud bricks that had been pounded and molded with water; it was round, and proudly helmeted with thatch. It was entered by a rectangular doorway. Inside, a tiny window let in a thin shaft of daylight. On the right was the bed, made of beaten earth like the bricks, and spread with a simple wicker-work mat on which lay a pillow stuffed with kapok.[2] At the rear, right under the window where the light was strongest, were the tool-boxes. On the left were the *boubous*[3] and the prayer-rugs. At the head of the bed, hanging over the pillow and watching over my father's slumber, stood a row of pots that contained extracts from plants and the bark of trees. These pots all had metal lids and were profusely and curiously garlanded with chaplets of cowrie shells;[4] it did not take me long to discover that they were the most important things in the hut; they contained

---

2. **kapok** [kā′pok]: silklike fiber from a tropical tree called the ceiba, used as stuffing for mattresses, pillows, and life preservers.
3. *boubous* [boo′booz]: Long robes worn by Moslem men when praying, at which time they also kneel on a prayer-rug. Many Guineans are Moslems.
4. **chaplets of cowrie shells**: strings of the brightly colored shells of cowries, warm-water mollusks found in Africa and Southern Asia.

magic charms—those mysterious liquids that keep the evil spirits at bay, and, if smeared on the body, make it invulnerable to every kind of black magic. My father, before going to bed, never failed to smear his body with a little of each liquid, first one, then another, for each charm had its own particular property: but exactly *what* property I did not know: I had left my father's house too soon.

From the veranda under which I played I could keep an eye on the workshop opposite, and the adults for their part could keep an eye on me. This workshop was the main building in our concession, and my father was generally to be found there, looking after the work, forging the most important items himself, or repairing delicate mechanisms; there he received his friends and customers, and the place resounded with noise from morning to night. Moreover, everyone who entered or left our concession had to cross the workshop. There was a perpetual coming and going, though no one seemed to be in any particular hurry; each had his bit of gossip; each lingered at the forge to watch. Sometimes I came near the door, but I rarely went in; everyone there frightened me, and I would run away as soon as anyone tried to touch me. It was not until very much later that I got into the habit of crouching in a corner of the workshop to watch the fire blazing in the forge.

My private domain at that time was the veranda that encircled my father's hut, my mother's hut, and the orange tree that grew in the middle of the concession.

As soon as you crossed the workshop and went through the door at the back, you would see the orange tree. Compared with the giants of our native forests, the tree was not very big, but its mass of glossy leaves cast a dense shade that kept the heat at bay. When it was in flower a heady perfume pervaded the entire concession. When the fruit first appeared we were only allowed to look: we had to wait patiently until it was ripe. Then my father, who as head of the

The Snake and the Goldsmith **381**

PAGE SUMMARY: AT A GLANCE

- An apprentice rescues Camara from the snake, and the boy is reprimanded by his mother.
- The father's hut contains, among other things, liquid magic charms, which he applies to his body for protection.
- The father's workshop is visited frequently by friends and customers.
- There is an orange tree at the center of the concession.

IN THE GLOSSARY

- commotion: bustle; confusion
- profusely: abundantly
- encircled: surrounded

3 TEACHING DESCRIPTION

Point out that the passage that begins here is one of many descriptions of places within Camara's village. Have students note that the author's skillful inclusion of details allows the reader to picture the places described.

4 CULTURAL BACKGROUND

Many residents of West Africa, including the father in this selection, adhere to religious beliefs that others often consider mutually exclusive. Thus, for example, the father is a believer in both Islam and African tribal religions that stress belief in magic charms and a multitude of good and evil spirits.

5 TEACHING STUDENTS OF LIMITED ENGLISH PROFICIENCY

Point out that although the style of the selection as a whole is not difficult, some sentences are long enough to present challenges. Have students pay close attention to punctuation, such as the semicolon here, which allows the sentence to be separated into easily comprehensible parts.

6 TEACHING IRONY

Have students note the irony in the fact that the boy is afraid of people who would not harm him while he showed no fear of a dangerous snake.

CRITICAL THINKING: GUIDED READING QUESTIONS

LITERAL

1a. What are the most important things in the father's hut? (pots containing liquid magic charms)

2a. What habit does Camara develop later in his childhood? (He would crouch in a corner of his father's workshop.)

INFERENTIAL

1b. What does this tell you about the father? (He has a strong belief in the supernatural.)

2b. Why would he do this? (He could then watch what was going on without having to interact with anyone.)

- The father's generosity in giving food to visitors and neighbors displeases his wife.
- Trains pass close by, their sparks threatening the concession with fire.
- Camara's mother, who ordinarily beats snakes to death, warns Camara not to kill a certain snake because it is his father's guiding spirit.
- The snake apparently goes to visit the father.

IN THE GLOSSARY

- lavish: extravagant
- temperate: moderate
- immunity: protection from harm

7 TEACHING CHARACTERIZATION

Ask students to summarize the character of the father as it has been developed up to this point. (He believes in the supernatural, is a skillful craftsman, and is sociable, generous, and temperate.)

8 READING SKILL: CONTRAST

Have students note the contrasting ways in which women and men kill snakes. What does this suggest? (The women are more emotional in their method and not as powerful as the men.)

9 CULTURAL BACKGROUND

In many animistic religions, such as that of the people described in this story, everything in nature has a spirit. The spirit of some things—such as this snake—is thought to play a crucial role in guiding the behavior of, and providing insight to, humans who are spiritually tied to them.

10 TEACHING IMAGERY

Point out that the concrete details about the snake help paint a picture in the reader's mind. Phrases such as "black and brilliant" and "glittered in the harsh light of the sun" are especially vivid.

family—and a very large family it was—governed the concession, gave the order to pick the fruit. The men who did the picking brought their baskets one by one to my father, who portioned them out among the people who lived in the concession and among his neighbors and customers. After that we were permitted to help ourselves from the baskets and we were allowed as much as we liked! My father was open-handed; in fact, a lavish giver. Any visitor, no matter who he was, shared our meals; since I could never keep up with the speed at which such guests ate I might have remained forever hungry if my mother had not taken the precaution of putting my share aside.

"Sit here," she would say, "and eat, for your father's mad."

She did not look upon such guests with a kindly eye. There were too many for her liking, all bent on filling their bellies at her expense. _7_ My father, for his part, ate very little; he was an extremely temperate man.

We lived beside a railroad. The trains skirted the reed fence of the concession so closely that sparks thrown off from the locomotive set fire to it every now and then, which had to be quickly extinguished so that the whole concession would not go up in smoke. These alarms, frightening yet exciting, made me aware of the passing trains. And even where there were no trains—for in those days the railroad was dependent on a most irregular water traffic—much of my time was spent watching the iron rails. They glistened cruelly in a light which nothing in that place could relieve. Baking since dawn, the roadbed was so hot that oil which dropped from the locomotives evaporated immediately, leaving no trace. Was it the oven-like heat or the smell of oil—for the smell remained in spite of everything—which attracted the snakes? I do not know. But often I came upon them crawling in that hot roadbed. It would have been fatal if they had gotten into the concession.

Ever since the day when I had been forbid-

den by my mother to play with snakes I ran to her as soon as I saw one.

"There's a snake!" I would cry.

"What? Another?"

And she would come running to see what sort of snake it was. If it was just a snake like any other snake—actually they were all quite different—_8_ she would immediately beat it to death; and, like all the women of our country, she would work herself into a frenzy, beating the snake to a pulp. The men contented themselves with a single hard blow, neatly struck.

One day, however, I noticed a little black snake with a strikingly marked body. He was proceeding slowly in the direction of the workshop. I ran to warn my mother, as usual. But as soon as she saw the black snake she said to me gravely:

"My son, this one must not be killed: he is not like other snakes, and he will not harm you; you must never interfere with him."

Everyone in our concession knew that this snake must not be killed—everyone except myself, and, I suppose, my little playmates, who were still ignorant children.

_9_ "This snake," my mother added, "is your father's guiding spirit."

I gazed dumbfounded at the little snake. He was proceeding calmly toward the workshop, gracefully, very sure of himself, and almost as if _10_ conscious of his immunity; his body, black and brilliant, glittered in the harsh light of the sun. When he reached the workshop, I noticed for the first time a small hole in the wall, cut out level with the ground. The snake disappeared through this hole.

"Look," said my mother, "the snake is going to pay your father a visit."

Although I was familiar with the supernatural, this sight filled me with such astonishment that I was struck dumb. What business would a snake have with my father? And why this particular snake? No one was to kill him because he was my father's guiding spirit! At any rate, that

---

CRITICAL THINKING: GUIDED READING QUESTIONS

LITERAL

1a. What words and phrases does the author use to describe the father in regard to sharing food? (_openhanded_; "a lavish giver")

2a. What does the mother say the little black snake is? (It is the father's guiding spirit.)

INFERENTIAL

1b. What evidence suggests that the father is not necessarily typical of the people of the village? (Some of the guests eat greedily; the mother characterizes the father as "mad.")

2b. What does this tell you about the mother? (She also believes in the supernatural.)

was the explanation my mother had given me. But what exactly *was* a "guiding spirit"? What were these guiding spirits that I encountered almost everywhere, forbidding one thing, commanding another to be done? I could not understand it at all, though their presences surrounded me as I grew to manhood. There were good spirits, and there were evil ones; and more evil than good ones, it seemed. And how was I to know that this snake was harmless? He was a snake like the others: black, to be sure, with extraordinary markings—but for all that a snake. I was completely perplexed, but I did not question my mother: I had decided that I must ask my father about it, as if this were a mystery to be discussed only between men, a mystery in which women had no part. I decided to wait until evening to speak to him.

Immediately after the evening meal, when the palavers[5] were over, my father bade his friends farewell and sat under the veranda of his hut; I seated myself near him. I began questioning him in a dilatory manner, as all children do, regarding every subject under the sun. Actually I was no more talkative than on other evenings. Only this evening I withheld what troubled me, waiting for the opportunity when—my face betraying nothing—I might ask the question which had worried me so deeply from the moment when I first saw the black snake going toward the workshop. Finally, unable to restrain myself any longer, I asked:

"My father, what is that little snake that comes to visit you?"

"What snake do you mean?"

"Why, the little black snake that my mother forbids us to kill."

"Ah!" he said.

He gazed at me for a long while. He seemed to be considering whether to answer or not. Perhaps he was thinking about how old I was, per-haps he was wondering if it was not a little too soon to confide such a secret to a twelve-year-old boy. Then suddenly he made up his mind.

11 "That snake," he said, "is the guiding spirit of our race. Can you understand that?"

"Yes," I answered, although I did not understand very well.

"That snake," he went on, "has always been with us; he has always made himself known to one of us. In our time, it is to me that he has made himself known."

"Yes," I said.

12 And I said it with all my heart, for it seemed obvious to me that the snake could have made himself known to no one but my father. Was not my father the head man in our concession? Was it not my father who had authority over all the blacksmiths in our district? Was he not the most skilled? Was he not, after all, my father?

"How did he make himself known?" I asked.

13 "First of all, he made himself known in the semblance of a dream. He appeared to me several times in sleep and told me the day on which he would appear to me in reality: he gave me the precise time and place. But when I really saw him for the first time, I was filled with fear. I took him for a snake like any other snake, and I had to keep myself under control or I would have tried to kill him. When he saw that I did not receive him kindly, he turned away and departed the way he had come. And there I stood, watching him depart, wondering all the time if I should not simply have killed him there and then; but a power greater than I stayed my hand and prevented me from pursuing him. I stood watching him disappear. And even then, at that very moment, I could easily have overtaken him; a few swift strides would have been enough; but I was struck motionless by a kind of paralysis. Such was my first encounter with the little black snake."

He was silent a moment, then went on:

"The following night, I saw the snake again in my dream. 'I came as I foretold,' he said, 'but

---

5. **palavers** [pə lav′ərz]: here, discussions or informal conferences.

The Snake and the Goldsmith **383**

CRITICAL THINKING: GUIDED READING QUESTIONS

LITERAL

1a. Why does Camara not question his mother further about the snake? (He feels it is "a mystery to be discussed only between men.")

2a. What was the father "filled with" when he first saw the snake? (He was "filled with fear.")

INFERENTIAL

→ **1b.** What does this suggest about the role of women in Laye's culture? (They hold a secondary role to men in religious matters.)

→ **2b.** What might this suggest? (He did not completely trust the dream or fully believe that the snake was a guiding spirit.)

- After a second dream in which the snake appeared, the father received him kindly.
- The father attributes his fame to the snake, which gives him foreknowledge.
- He fears that the guiding spirit will not visit Camara because the boy spends little time at home and will leave to go to school.

IN THE GLOSSARY

- transmitted: sent; communicated

14 GRAMMAR IN LITERATURE

Point out that *thou* is the archaic second-person singular (familiar) form of *you*, its objective form is *thee*, and its possessive forms are *thy* and *thine*. Explain that these forms are used to give the snake's words spiritual or religious significance.

15 TEACHING CHARACTERIZATION

Point out that here the father indicates that he attributes his skills to the snake-spirit. Ask students why he says this and how they react to it. (Some will accept it at face value; some may see it as an inability to come to terms with innate skills; some may see it as falsely modest or dishonesty.)

16 TEACHING CHARACTER MOTIVATION

Point out that the father tells the boy about the guiding spirit because Camara is his oldest son and he has nothing to hide from him. Ask what other motivation he implies for doing so. (Camara must behave in certain ways if the spirit is to approach him. The father wants the boy to share his beliefs and follow in his footsteps.)

17 TEACHING THEME

Ask students to examine this passage and any others up to this point in order to state the principal themes of the selection. (respect for tradition, culture, and family)

---

¹⁴ thou didst not receive me kindly; nay, rather I did perceive that thou didst intend to receive me unkindly: I did read it thus in thine eyes. Wherefore dost thou reject me? Lo, I am the guiding spirit of thy race, and it is even as the guiding spirit of thy race that I make myself known to thee, as to the most worthy. Therefore forbear to look with fear upon me, and beware that thou dost not reject me, for behold, I bring thee good fortune.' After that, I received the snake kindly when he made himself known to me a second time; I received him without fear, I received him with loving kindness, and he brought me nothing but good."

My father again was silent for a moment, then he said:

¹⁵ "You can see for yourself that I am not more gifted than other men, that I have nothing which other men have not also, and even that I have less than others, since I give everything away, and would even give away the last thing I had, the shirt on my back. Nevertheless I am better known. My name is on everyone's tongue, and it is I who have authority over all the blacksmiths in the five cantons.⁶ If these things are so, it is by virtue of this snake alone, who is the guiding spirit of our race. It is to this snake that I owe everything; it is he who gives me warning of all that is to happen. Thus I am never surprised, when I awake, to see this or that person waiting for me outside my workshop: I already know that he will be there. No more am I surprised when this or that motorcycle or bicycle breaks down, or when an accident happens to a clock: because I have had foreknowledge of what would come to pass. Everything is transmitted to me in the course of the night, together with an account of all the work I shall have to perform, so that from the start, without having to cast about in my mind, I know how to repair

---

6. **cantons:** small political divisions of a country or territory.

384 Nonfiction

---

whatever is brought to me. These things have established my renown as a craftsman. But all this—let it never be forgotten—I owe to the snake, I owe it to the guiding spirit of our race."

He was silent; and then I understood why, when my father came back from a walk he would enter the workshop and say to the apprentices: "During my absence, this or that person has been here, he was dressed in such and such a way, he came from such and such a place and he brought with him such and such a piece of work to be done." And all marveled at this curious knowledge. When I raised my eyes, I saw that my father was watching me.

¹⁶ "I have told you all these things, little one, because you are my son, the eldest of my sons, and because I have nothing to hide from you. There is a certain form of behavior to observe, and certain ways of acting in order that the guiding spirit of our race may approach you also. I, your father, was observing that form of behavior which persuades our guiding spirit to visit us. ¹⁷ Oh, perhaps not consciously: but nevertheless it is true that if you desire the guiding spirit of our race to visit you one day, if you desire to inherit it in your turn, you will have to conduct yourself in the selfsame manner; from now on, it will be necessary for you to be more and more in my company."

He gazed at me with burning eyes, then suddenly he heaved a sigh.

"I fear, I very much fear, little one, that you are not often enough in my company. You are all day at school, and one day you will depart from that school for a greater one. You will leave me, little one. . . ."

And again he heaved a sigh. I saw that his heart was heavy within him. The hurricane-lamp hanging on the veranda cast a harsh glare on his face. He suddenly seemed to me an old man.

"Father!" I cried.

"Son . . ." he whispered.

And I was no longer sure whether I ought to

CRITICAL THINKING: GUIDED READING QUESTIONS

LITERAL

1a. What does Camara's father say he owes the snake? (He owes him everything—his skill, popularity, leadership, and foreknowledge.)

2a. What does the father say he fears? (He fears Camara's absence and eventual departure.)

INFERENTIAL

1b. What might be some explanations for these things other than the supernatural? (Students might say that the confidence the father derives from his belief in a guiding spirit might have resulted in his superior qualities.)

2b. Why does he fear this? (Personal love of his son and fear that the tradition will be ended cause this fear.)

18 continue to attend school or whether I ought to remain in the workshop: I felt unutterably confused.

"Go now," said my father.

I went to my mother's hut. The night was full of sparkling stars; an owl was hooting nearby. Ah! what was the right path for me? Did I know **19** yet where that path lay? My perplexity was boundless as the sky, and mine was a sky, alas, without any stars. . . . I entered my mother's hut, which at that time was mine also, and went to bed at once. But sleep did not come and I tossed restlessly on my bed.

"What's the matter with you?" asked my mother.

"Nothing."

No. I couldn't find anything to say.

"Why don't you go to sleep?" my mother continued.

"I don't know."

"Go to sleep!" she said.

"Yes," I said.

Ornament from African ceremonial state sword, cast gold, early twentieth century.

The Snake and the Goldsmith   **385**

PAGE SUMMARY: AT A GLANCE

- Camara is confused about whether to attend school or remain in his father's workshop.
- He is unable to sleep, despite his mother's pleas that he do so.

IN THE GLOSSARY

- perplexity: state of confusion

18 TEACHING CONFLICT

The concept of conflict, which is usually applied to works of fiction, can also play an important role in nonfiction. Ask students to state Camara's internal conflict as expressed in this passage. (He wants to go to school, but doing so means leaving family and tradition behind.)

19 TEACHING SIMILES AND METAPHORS

Explain that in both simile and metaphor seemingly unlike things are compared or equated. A simile uses the word *like* or *as;* a metaphor does not. Point out that the first part of the sentence uses the word *as:* "My perplexity was boundless as the sky." The second part does not: " . . . and mine was a sky, alas, without any stars." Ask students to identify the effect of the figure of speech. (It emphasizes the extent of the boy's confusion.)

ART AND LITERATURE

This African snake ornament combines repose and force in its seemingly tranquil pose. A tiny, as yet unconsumed frog is captured in the coiled snake's mouth. The snake is a symbol of solemn, earthly might. Many early societies integrated snake deities into their mythologies.

- After students read the selection, ask them whether they think Camara's father might make such a golden ornament in honor of his guiding spirit. Why or why not? (He would because he believes that both the snake and gold have special magical qualities.)

CRITICAL THINKING: GUIDED READING QUESTIONS

LITERAL

1a. What does Camara say when his mother asks what is the matter? ("Nothing.")

INFERENTIAL

1b. Why does he say this? (He might think that his mother would not understand, or he might feel that he must resolve his own problems.)

PAGE SUMMARY: AT A GLANCE

- Camara falls asleep weeping.
- He frequently watches the snake go to his father, who strokes it, evoking an answering tremor in the snake.
- Women sometimes come with gold for the father to transform into trinkets for them.
- The women make use of praise-singing go-betweens to increase their chances of being served.

IN THE GLOSSARY

- divined: discovered supernaturally
- monotony: tiresome sameness

20 TEACHING DESCRIPTION

Draw attention to the portrayal of the snake's appearance and strange encounter with the father. Ask students what details increase the sense of the uncanniness of the situation. (the father's immediate awareness of the snake, the snake's direct approach, the father's stroking of it, and its quivering response)

21 TEACHING WORD CHOICE

Call attention to the choice of words in the phrases "appealing caress" and "answering tremor." Ask them what *appealing* conveys in this case. (The father is seeking or pleading for the answering response of the snake.)

22 GRAMMAR IN LITERATURE

Point out the use of italics for emphasis. Ask what effect the emphasized word has here. (It points out that to Camara the father's working in gold is a truly special occasion.)

23 READING SKILL: PREDICTING OUTCOMES

Ask students to predict whether the women's use of a praise singer will really cause the father to serve her before others. (In view of the father's modesty, most students will not expect him to be so vain as to yield to such flattery.)

"Sleep . . . Nothing can resist sleep," she said sadly.

Why did she, too, appear so sad? Had she divined my distress? Anything that concerned me she sensed very deeply. I was trying to sleep, but I shut my eyes and lay still in vain: the image of my father under the hurricane-lamp would not leave me: my father who had suddenly seemed so old and who was so young, so lively—younger and livelier than the rest of us, a man no one could outrun, who was swifter of limb than any of us. . . . "Father! . . . Father! . . ." I kept repeating. "What must I do if I am to do the right thing?" And I wept silently and fell asleep still weeping.

After that we never mentioned the little black snake again: my father had spoken to me about him for the first and last time. But from that time on, as soon as I saw the little snake, I **20** would run and sit in the workshop. I would watch him glide through the little hole in the wall. As if informed of his presence, my father at that very instant would turn his eyes to the hole and smile. The snake would go straight to him, opening his jaws. When he was within reach my father would stroke him and the snake would accept the caress with a quivering of his whole body. I never saw the little snake attempt to do the slightest harm to my father. That caress and the answering tremor—but I ought to say: that **21** appealing caress and that answering tremor—threw me each time into an inexpressible confusion. I imagined I know not what mysterious conversations: the hand inquired and the tremor replied. . . .

Yes. It was like a conversation. Would I too converse that way some day? No. I would continue to attend school. Yet I should have liked so much to place my hand, my own hand, on that snake, and to understand and listen to that tremor too; but I did not know whether the snake would have accepted my hand, and I felt now that he would have nothing to tell me. I was afraid that he would never have anything to tell me.

386 *Nonfiction*

When my father felt that he had stroked the snake enough he left him alone. Then the snake coiled himself under the edge of one of the sheepskins on which my father, facing his anvil, was seated.

2

Of all the different kinds of work my father engaged in, none fascinated me so much as his skill with gold. No other occupation was so noble, no other needed such a delicate touch. **22** And then, every time he worked in gold it was like a festival—indeed it *was* a festival—that broke the monotony of ordinary working days.

So, if a woman, accompanied by a go-between, crossed the threshold of the workshop, I followed her in at once. I knew what she wanted: she had brought some gold, and had come to ask my father to transform it into a trinket. She had collected it in the placers of Siguiri[7] where, crouching over the river for months on end, she had patiently extracted grains of gold from the mud.

These women never came alone. They knew my father had other things to do than make trinkets. And even when he had the time, they knew they were not the first to ask a favor of him, and that, consequently, they would not be served before others.

Generally they required the trinket for a certain date, for the festival of Ramadan[8] or the Tabaski[9] or some other family ceremony or dance.

23 Therefore, to enhance their chances of being served quickly and to more easily persuade my father to interrupt the work before him, they used to request the services of an official praise-singer, a go-between, arranging in advance the

---

7. **placers of Siguiri:** [sē gē'rē]: places near Siguiri where gold has washed up from the Niger [nī'jər] River. Siguiri is a town in Guinea and is noted for its gold deposits.
8. **Ramadan** [räm'ə dän']: holy month in which Moslems fast daily from sunrise to sunset.
9. **Tabaski** [tä bäs'kē]: holiday in Guinea.

CRITICAL THINKING: GUIDED READING QUESTIONS

LITERAL

1a. To what does Camara compare the interaction between his father and the snake? (It is like a conversation.)

2a. What is Camara afraid of in regard to the snake? (The snake will never have anything to tell him.)

INFERENTIAL

1b. In what sense does it seem like one? (There is communication in terms of an appeal and a response.)

2b. Why does he feel this way? (Since he will go to school instead of staying with his father, Camara does not feel he will ever get to know the snake.)

fee they were to pay him for his good offices.

The go-between installed himself in the workshop, tuned up his *cora,* which is our harp, and began to sing my father's praises. This was 24 always a great event for me. I heard recalled the lofty deeds of my father's ancestors and their names from the earliest times. As the couplets[10] were reeled off it was like watching the growth of a great genealogical tree that spread its branches far and wide and flourished its boughs and twigs before my mind's eye. The harp played an accompaniment to this vast utterance of names, expanding it with notes that were now soft, now shrill.

25 I could sense my father's vanity being inflamed, and I already knew that after having sipped this milk-and-honey he would lend a favorable ear to the woman's request. But I was not alone in my knowledge. The woman also had seen my father's eyes gleaming with contented pride. She held out her grains of gold as if the whole matter were settled. My father took up his scales and weighed the gold.

"What sort of trinket do you want?" he would ask.

"I want . . ."

And then the woman would not know any longer exactly what she wanted because desire kept making her change her mind, and because she would have liked all the trinkets at once. But it would have taken a pile of gold much larger than she had brought to satisfy her whim, and from then on her chief purpose in life was to get hold of it as soon as she could.

"When do you want it?"

Always the answer was that the trinket was needed for an occasion in the near future.

"So! You are in that much of a hurry? Where do you think I shall find the time?"

"I am in a great hurry, I assure you."

"I have never seen a woman eager to deck herself out who wasn't in a great hurry! Good! I

_____
10. **couplets:** two-line, usually rhyming stanzas of a poem or a song.

shall arrange my time to suit you. Are you satisfied?"

He would take the clay pot that was kept specially for smelting gold, and would pour the grains into it. He would then cover the gold with powdered charcoal, a charcoal he prepared by using plant juices of exceptional purity. Finally, he would place a large lump of the same kind of charcoal over the pot.

As soon as she saw that the work had been duly undertaken, the woman, now quite satisfied, would return to her household tasks, leaving her go-between to carry on with the praise-singing which had already proved so advantageous.

At a sign from my father the apprentices began working two sheepskin bellows. The skins were on the floor, on opposite sides of the forge, connected to it by earthen pipes. While the work was in progress the apprentices sat in front of the bellows with crossed legs. That is, the younger of the two sat, for the elder was sometimes allowed to assist. But the younger—this time it was Sidafa—was only permitted to work the bellows and watch while waiting his turn for 26 promotion to less rudimentary tasks. First one and then the other worked hard at the bellows: the flame in the forge rose higher and became a living thing, a genie implacable and full of life.

Then my father lifted the clay pot with his long tongs and placed it on the flame.

Immediately all activity in the workshop almost came to a halt. During the whole time that the gold was being smelted, neither copper nor aluminum could be worked nearby, lest some particle of these base metals[11] fall into the container which held the gold. Only steel could be worked on such occasions, but the men, whose task that was, hurried to finish what they were doing, or left it abruptly to join the apprentices gathered around the forge. There were so many, and they crowded so around my father, that I, the smallest person present, had to come near

_____
11. **base metals:** here, metals of lesser value than gold.

The Snake and the Goldsmith **387**

CRITICAL THINKING: GUIDED READING QUESTIONS

LITERAL

1a. What does the father ask when the woman says that the trinket is needed soon? (He asks her where she thinks he will find the time.)

2a. What is the practical reason for the laborers to stop working with other metals while the father smelts the gold? (Doing so prevents particles from the base metals falling into the gold.)

INFERENTIAL

1b. What evidence suggests that he does not ask the question sincerely? (He always asks the question, even though by that point he has already been flattered into accepting the gold.)

2b. Why do they really stop? (They stop to observe the father working with the gold.)

- The father invokes genies to aid in his smelting of gold.
- All are excited as the gold melts and is poured into a hollow brick.
- Before the father hammers the gold, he strokes the snake.

IN THE GLOSSARY

- incantations: words spoken to cast spells
- espousal: advocacy of a cause
- besought: pleaded for
- protracted: extended in time

27 CULTURAL BACKGROUND

Point out that in many cultures gold symbolizes lofty concepts. Because it does not tarnish, it often stands for purity, eternity, and otherworldliness and is seen as a source of creative power. Thus, it is highly valued, and as illustrated in this passage, people working with it are often seen as engaged in a magical process.

28 TEACHING STUDENTS OF LIMITED ENGLISH PROFICIENCY

Alert students that in this case dashes set off a complete thought, one containing a subject and a predicate.

29 TEACHING IMAGERY

In this passage vividly presented sensory details are used to produce an arresting description of a process. Ask students which senses are appealed to in this case. (sight, sound, smell, and touch)

30 READING SKILL: COMPARISON

Explain that the author has made use of subtle points of similarity between the snake and the characteristics of the gold, thus tying them effectively together into something of a symbolic whole. Ask students to compare the snake and the gold, examining the selection to find similarities or connections between the two. (Both are handled reverentially by the father; both are believed to have magical qualities; the molten gold moves in a flowing way and hisses.)

the forge in order not to lose track of what was going on.

If he felt he had inadequate working space, my father had the apprentices stand well away from him. He merely raised his hand in a simple gesture; at that particular moment he never uttered a word, and no one else would—no one was allowed to utter a word. Even the go-between's voice was no longer raised in song. The silence was broken only by the panting of the bellows and the faint hissing of the gold. But if my father never actually spoke, I know that he was forming words in his mind. I could tell from his lips, which kept moving, while, bending over the pot, he stirred the gold and charcoal with a bit of wood that kept bursting into flame and had constantly to be replaced by a fresh one.

What words did my father utter? I do not know. At least I am not certain what they were. No one ever told me. But could they have been anything but incantations? On these occasions was he not invoking the genies of fire and gold, of fire and wind, of wind blown by the blast-pipes of the forge, of fire born of wind, of gold married to fire? Was it not their assistance, their friendship, their espousal that he besought? Yes. Almost certainly he was invoking these genies, all of whom are equally indispensable for smelting gold.

27 The operation going on before my eyes was certainly the smelting of gold, yet something more than that: a magical operation that the guiding spirits could regard with favor or disfavor. That is why, all around my father, there was absolute silence and anxious expectancy. Though only a child, I knew there could be no craft greater than the goldsmith's. I expected a ceremony; I had come to be present at a ceremony; and it actually was one, though very protracted. I was still too young to understand why, but I had an inkling as I watched the almost religious concentration of those who followed the mixing process in the clay pot.

When finally the gold began to melt I could

have shouted aloud—and perhaps we all would have if we had not been forbidden to make a
28 sound. I trembled, and so did everyone else watching my father stir the mixture—it was still a heavy paste—in which the charcoal was gradually consumed. The next stage followed swiftly. The gold now had the fluidity of water. The genies had smiled on the operation!

"Bring me the brick!" my father would order, thus lifting the ban that until then had silenced us.

The brick, which an apprentice would place beside the fire, was hollowed out, generously
29 greased with Galam butter.[12] My father would take the pot off the fire and tilt it carefully, while I would watch the gold flow into the brick, flow like liquid fire. True, it was only a very sparse trickle of fire, but how vivid, how brilliant! As the gold flowed into the brick, the grease sputtered and flamed and emitted a thick smoke that caught in the throat and stung the eyes, leaving us all weeping and coughing.

But there were times when it seemed to me that my father ought to turn this task over to one of his assistants. They were experienced, had assisted him hundreds of times, and could certainly have performed the work well. But my father's lips moved and those inaudible, secret words, those incantations he addressed to one we could not see or hear, was the essential part. Calling on the genies of fire, of wind, of gold and exorcising the evil spirits—this was a knowledge he alone possessed.

By now the gold had been cooled in the hollow of the brick, and my father began to hammer and stretch it. This was the moment when
30 his work as a goldsmith really began. I noticed that before embarking on it he never failed to stroke the little snake stealthily as it lay coiled up under the sheepskin. I can only assume that

---

12. **Galam butter:** solid oil or fat of vegetable origin, named for a former French district on the Senegal River in western Africa.

CRITICAL THINKING: GUIDED READING QUESTIONS

LITERAL

1a. What are the people watching the father not permitted to do? (No one may speak.)

2a. Why does the father not allow the apprentices to pour the gold into the brick? (They do not know the incantations.)

INFERENTIAL

1b. Why does this rule exist? (The process is a difficult and sacred one.)

2b. Why does the father not teach the incantations to the apprentices? (The father may feel that only one who knows the guiding spirit should know the incantations.)

this was his way of gathering strength for what remained to be done, the most trying part of his task.

31   But was it not extraordinary and miraculous that on these occasions the little black snake was always coiled under the sheepskin? He was not always there. He did not visit my father every day. But he was always present whenever there was gold to be worked. His presence was no surprise to *me*. After that evening when my father had spoken of the guiding spirit of his race I was no longer astonished. The snake was there intentionally. He knew what the future held. Did he tell my father? I think that he most certainly did. Did he tell him everything? I have another reason for believing firmly that he did.

The craftsman who works in gold must first of all purify himself. That is, he must wash himself all over and, of course, abstain from all sexual commerce during the whole time. Great respecter of ceremony as he was, it would have been impossible for my father to ignore these rules. Now, I never saw him make these preparations. I saw him address himself to his work without any apparent preliminaries. From that moment it was obvious that, forewarned in a dream by his black guiding spirit of the task which awaited him in the morning, my father must have prepared for it as soon as he arose, entering his workshop in a state of purity, his body smeared with the secret potions hidden in his numerous pots of magical substances; or perhaps he always came into his workshop in a state of ritual purity. I am not trying to make him out a better man than he was—he was a man and had his share of human frailties—but he was always uncompromising in his respect for ritual observance.

The woman for whom the trinket was being made, and who had come often to see how the work was progressing, would arrive for the final time, not wanting to miss a moment of this spectacle—as marvelous to her as to us—when the gold wire, which my father had succeeded in drawing out from the mass of molten gold and charcoal, was transformed into a trinket.

There she would be. Her eyes would devour the fragile gold wire, following it in its tranquil and regular spiral around the little slab of metal which supported it. My father would catch a glimpse of her and I would see him slowly beginning to smile. Her avid attention delighted him.

"Are you trembling?" he would ask.

"Am I trembling?"

And we would all burst out laughing at her.

32   For she would be trembling! She would be trembling with covetousness for the spiral pyramid in which my father would be inserting, among the convolutions, tiny grains of gold. When he had finally finished by crowning the pyramid with a heavier grain, she would dance in delight.

No one—no one at all—would be more enchanted than she as my father slowly turned the trinket back and forth between his fingers to display its perfection. Not even the praise-singer, whose business it was to register excitement, would be more excited than she. Throughout this metamorphosis he did not stop speaking faster and ever faster, increasing his tempo, accelerating his praises and flatteries as the trinket took shape, shouting to the skies my father's skill.

33   For the praise-singer took a curious part—I should say rather that it was direct and effective—in the work. He was drunk with the joy of creation. He shouted aloud in joy. He plucked his *cora* like a man inspired. He sweated as if he were the trinket-maker, as if he were my father, as if the trinket were his creation. He was no longer a hired censer-bearer,[13] a man whose services anyone could rent. He was a man who created his song out of some deep inner necessity. And when my father, after having soldered the

---

13. **censer-bearer:** person who carries the receptacle in which incense is burned at a religious ceremony; used figuratively here.

The Snake and the Goldsmith   **389**

PAGE SUMMARY: AT A GLANCE

- The snake is always present when gold is worked.
- The father is always purified before working with gold, either because he is forewarned by the snake or because he always comes to the workshop in a state of ritual purity.
- The gold is drawn to form a spiral pyramidal trinket, and the woman for whom the trinket is being made trembles with covetousness.
- The praise singer speaks more and more during the last phase, apparently sincerely excited by the process.

IN THE GLOSSARY

- covetousness: greed

31 **CRITICAL THINKING: EVALUATION**

Ask students to evaluate the author's argument that the snake's presence during the working of the gold is proof of its magical role in the process. (Some students may find the argument convincing. Others may bring up the possibility that the father may have some nonmagical way of attracting the snake.)

32 **TEACHING STUDENTS OF LIMITED ENGLISH PROFICIENCY**

This passage is one of relatively few that are likely to present difficulties for students whose vocabulary is limited. Explain, or have other students explain, the meanings of words such as *covetousness*, *spiral*, *pyramid*, and *convolutions*.

33 **TEACHING THEME**

Ask students how the praise singer's reaction helps to illustrate some of the themes of the selection. (The members of a culture are bound together, sharing in the experience of life and in the joy and magic of creation and self-expression.)

CRITICAL THINKING: GUIDED READING QUESTIONS

LITERAL

1a. What possibility other than that his father was forewarned by the snake does Camara give for the fact that his father is always purified on the days he works with gold? (Perhaps he always came into his workshop in a state of ritual purity.)

2a. Out of what inward state does the author say the praise singer finally creates his song? ("some deep inner necessity")

INFERENTIAL

→ **1b.** What does this second explanation suggest about Camara? (He might not fully believe in the supernatural.)

→ **2b.** What does this mean? (The performance is sincere, the singer having been overwhelmed by what he has seen and what he feels.)

- After protective preparations the singer chants the *douga*, and the father dances to it.
- The father and the singer are congratulated by all, and the latter is given gifts.
- The mother is angry with the father for endangering his health and for keeping some gold.

IN THE GLOSSARY

- provocative: tending to stir up emotion

34 TEACHING STUDENTS OF LIMITED ENGLISH PROFICIENCY

If your class includes foreign-born students, ask them about folk dances or folk songs performed in their native culture to express strong feelings or to honor important occasions. If they know the foreign words used in such performances, ask them to translate them for the class.

35 READING SKILL: CONTRAST

Ask students to contrast the mother's reaction to what has occurred with the reactions of the other people. (She is angry, belittling, worried; they are in awe, delighted, full of praise.)

36 TEACHING CHARACTERIZATION

Ask students what this passage reveals about the mother. (She believes in complete honesty. She is also a bit hypocritical in objecting to her husband's keeping some gold while not objecting to weavers' keeping some of her cloth.)

COLLABORATIVE LEARNING: ENRICHMENT ACTIVITY

Art Ask a group of students to research African metalwork, especially the making of gold jewelry and ritual objects. Have them divide the topic into convenient parts (for example, the processes, designs, and uses involved).

---

large grain of gold that crowned the summit, held out his work to be admired, the praise-singer would no longer be able to contain himself. He would begin to intone the *douga,* the great chant which is sung only for celebrated men and which is danced for them alone.

But the *douga* is a formidable chant, a provocative chant, a chant which the praise-singer dared not sing, and which the man for whom it is sung dared not dance before certain precautions had been taken. My father had taken them as soon as he woke, since he had been warned in a dream. The praise-singer had taken them when he concluded his arrangements with the woman. Like my father he had smeared his body with magic substances and had made himself invulnerable to the evil genies whom the *douga* inevitably set free; these potions made him invulnerable also to rival praise-singers, perhaps jealous of him, who awaited only this song and the exaltation and loss of control which attended it, in order to begin casting their spells.

At the first notes of the *douga* my father would arise and emit a cry in which happiness and triumph were equally mingled; and brand- 34 ishing in his right hand the hammer that was the symbol of his profession and in his left a ram's horn filled with magic substances, he would dance the glorious dance.

No sooner had he finished than workmen and apprentices, friends and customers in their turn, not forgetting the woman for whom the trinket had been created, would flock around him, congratulating him, showering praises on him and complimenting the praise-singer at the same time. The latter found himself laden with gifts—almost his only means of support, for the praise-singer leads a wandering life after the fashion of the troubadours[14] of old. Aglow with dancing and the praises he had received, my fa-

---

14. **troubadours** [trōo′bə dôrz′]: poet-musicians who roamed southern France during the Middle Ages.

390 *Nonfiction*

---

ther would offer everyone cola nuts,[15] that small change of Guinean courtesy.

Now all that remained to be done was to redden the trinket in a little water to which chlorine and sea salt had been added. I was at liberty to leave. The festival was over! But often as I came out of the workshop my mother would be in the court, pounding millet[16] or rice, and she would call to me:

"Where have you been?" although she knew perfectly well where I had been.

"In the workshop."

"Of course. Your father was smelting gold. Gold! Always gold!"

And she would beat the millet or rice furiously with her pestle.

35 "Your father is ruining his health!"

"He danced the *douga.*"

"The *douga*! The *douga* won't keep him from ruining his eyes. As for you, you would be better off playing in the courtyard instead of breathing dust and smoke in the workshop."

My mother did not like my father to work in gold. She knew how dangerous it was: a trinket-maker empties his lungs blowing on the blowpipe and his eyes suffer from the fire. Perhaps they suffer even more from the microscopic precision which the work requires. And even if there had been no such objections involved, my mother would scarcely have relished this work. 36 She was suspicious of it, for gold cannot be smelted without the use of other metals, and my mother thought it was not entirely honest to put aside for one's own use the gold which the alloy had displaced. However, this was a custom generally known, and one which she herself had accepted when she took cotton to be woven and received back only a piece of cotton cloth half the weight of the original bundle.

---

15. **cola nuts:** nuts of an African tree.
16. **millet:** cereal grass, here pounded with a club-shaped tool called a pestle so that the millet can be used for food.

CRITICAL THINKING: GUIDED READING QUESTIONS

LITERAL

1a. When does the praise singer take the precautions for the *douga*? (He takes the precautions when he concludes his arrangements with the woman.)

2a. What does the mother say after Camara tells her the father danced the *douga*? ("The *douga*! The *douga* won't keep him from ruining his eyes.")

INFERENTIAL

1b. What does this suggest? (He knew he would chant the *douga* before the trinket was even made. This means he had confidence in the father's skill.)

2b. What does this suggest about the mother's attitude toward the *douga*? (She does not regard it with as much importance as the others do.)

STUDY QUESTIONS

Recalling

1. What does the writer's mother tell him after he reports seeing the little black snake with the extraordinary markings?
2. According to the writer's father, how did his behavior change the second time the snake appeared to him? What was the snake's reaction to this change in behavior?
3. Who would accompany the women who brought gold to Laye's father to be smelted into trinkets, and why?
4. What reason does the author give for calling the smelting of gold a "magical operation"?
5. Why did the author's mother not approve of his father's smelting gold?

Interpreting

6. What internal conflicts do you think the narrator experiences after the conversation with his father about the little black snake?
7. What details in the selection suggest that the process of smelting the gold resembles a festival or a symbolic ritual?
8. What qualities about his father do you think the writer admires most?

Extending

9. What might be some important lessons for modern life that you could draw from this account of the author's childhood?

LANGUAGE STUDY

Words from African Languages

Laye uses a number of words in his writing that either are derived from African languages or have an African origin. For example, the word *cola* comes from a word in the African language Malinké for the brownish seed of a tropical tree. The word *palavers,* meaning "lengthy discussions," comes from Portuguese; originally, however, it referred to long talks between native Africans and European traders, explorers, or colonial officials.

Use a dictionary to find the origins of these English words; then write the definition of each word.

1. banjo
2. chimpanzee
3. gumbo
4. mamba
5. marimba
6. okra

COMPOSITION

Writing About Autobiography

■ In the course of his autobiographical account, the narrator presents memorable portraits of both his father and himself as a twelve-year-old child. In a brief essay analyze the narrator's emotions about his father. Begin by deciding what the narrator admires about his father. Then describe the narrator's internal conflicts. Finally, evaluate the effectiveness of the writer's use of techniques such as dialogue and anecdote in his portrayal of his relationship with his father.

READER'S RESPONSE

What do you think the father's reaction will be when Camara tells him he will leave to go to school? What do you think the mother's reaction will be?

ANSWERS

STUDY QUESTIONS

1. The snake is the father's guiding spirit and must not be killed.
2. He received it kindly the second time. The snake has since brought nothing but good.
3. Praise singers would accompany the women to flatter the father so that he would do the work immediately.
4. Guiding spirits could regard it favorably or unfavorably.
5. The work is dangerous, and she thinks it is dishonest of him to keep some of the gold.
6. He is unsure whether to go to school or be more in his father's company and whether the snake will accept him.
7. Possible answers: the behavior of the praise singer and the bystanders, the invocation of genies, the ritual purification, and the singing and dancing of the *douga*
8. Possible answers: generosity, skill, temperance, authority, and respect for ritual
9. Possible answers: respect for family and tradition, feeling of oneness with nature and others, pride in craftsmanship

LANGUAGE STUDY

1. probably from Bantu (akin to Kimbundu); "stringed instrument"
2. from Bantu (Kongo); "small ape"
3. from Bantu (akin to Mbundu); "thick soup"
4. from Zulu; "poisonous snake"
5. from Bantu (Mbundu); "African musical instrument"
6. from West African (akin to Twi); "vegetable"

The Snake and the Goldsmith **391**

COMPOSITION: GUIDELINES FOR EVALUATION

WRITING ABOUT AUTOBIOGRAPHY

Objective

To write an essay evaluating the narrator's relationship with his father

Guidelines for Evaluation

■ suggested length: four or five paragraphs

■ should state the qualities the narrator admires in his father
■ should comment on the narrator's internal conflicts
■ should evaluate the writer's use of dialogue and anecdote

Colette (1873–1954)

France

Sidonie-Gabrielle Colette [kô let'] was born and brought up in a small village in the Burgundy region of France. Around the turn of the century, she and her first husband moved to Paris and collaborated on a series of novels. These books, published under the pen name "Willy" and tracing the fortunes of a young heroine whose name is Claudine, enjoyed considerable popularity.

After her divorce Colette continued to write. Before World War I her books contained lyrical impressions of the French countryside, amusing dialogues between various animals, and reminiscences of her personal experiences. Between the two world wars she published a series of novels that were highly acclaimed for their insight into women's emotions. She also wrote several books of autobiographical memoirs centering on her early years and her mother's remarkable personality. Some of her most famous works include *La Maison de Claudine (Claudine's House)*, *Sido*, *La Chatte (The Cat)*, *Duo* and *Gigi*. *Gigi* was made into a popular musical film. At her death in 1954, she was given a state funeral, an unprecedented honor for a French woman writer at that time.

GEOGRAPHY AND CULTURE

The French Countryside

Although France is a highly industrialized modern nation, the life of the French people is still vividly expressed in its particular regions and small villages. Each region, for example, boasts its distinctive accent, architecture, agricultural produce, cuisine, crafts, history, and small-town folkways.

Some of these regions include Normandy and Brittany in the northwest, the home of sailors and explorers; Alsace and Lorraine in the east, where German influence is considerable; and the Auvergne in south central France, a mountainous, rugged region. Other areas in the French countryside include the Loire Valley, whose gently rolling hills by the banks of the Loire River are dotted with magnificent castles; and Provence in the south, which is home to many French painters. Colette grew up in Burgundy, in the central southeastern region, famous for its beautiful countryside. The following selection evokes the village life of her childhood.

See LITERATURE AND CULTURE SOURCEBOOK: France

DISCUSSING GEOGRAPHY AND CULTURE

The Region of Burgundy

Famous for its forests, its Romanesque churches, and its vineyards, Burgundy is also renowned for its cuisine. Dijon, the region's ancient capital and still its most important city, is celebrated for its mustard. Visitors to the region can also feast on local trout, ham, goat cheese, snails, and wild mushrooms.

- Ask students to identify some of the foods and other products associated with their state or region.

Colette

Two Memories of Sido

Translated from the French by Enid McCleod and Una Vincenzo Troubridge

The Time Came . . .

The time came when all her strength left her. She was amazed beyond measure and would not believe it. Whenever I arrived from Paris to see her, as soon as we were alone in the afternoon in her little house, she had always some sin to confess to me. On one occasion she turned up the hem of her dress, rolled her stocking down over her shin, and displayed a purple bruise, the skin nearly broken.

"Just look at that!"

"What on earth have you done to yourself this time, Mother?"

She opened wide eyes, full of innocence and embarrassment.

"You wouldn't believe it, but I fell downstairs!"

"How do you mean—'fell'?"

"Just what I said. I fell, for no reason. I was going downstairs and I fell. I can't understand it."

"Were you going down too quickly?"

"Too quickly? What do you call too quickly? I was going down quickly. Have I time to go downstairs majestically like the Sun King?[1] And if that were all . . . But look at this!"

On her pretty arm, still so young above the faded hand, was a scald forming a large blister.

"Oh goodness! Whatever's that!"

"My footwarmer."

"The old copper footwarmer? The one that holds five quarts?"

"That's the one. Can I trust anything, when that footwarmer has known me for forty years? I can't imagine what possessed it, it was boiling fast, I went to take it off the fire, and crack, something gave in my wrist. I was lucky to get nothing worse than the blister. But what a thing to happen! After that I let the cupboard alone. . . ."

She broke off, blushing furiously.

"What cupboard?" I demanded severely.

My mother fenced, tossing her head as though I were trying to put her on a lead.

"Oh, nothing! No cupboard at all!"

"Mother! I shall get cross!"

"Since I've said, 'I let the cupboard alone,' can't you do the same for my sake? The cupboard hasn't moved from its place, has it? So, shut up about it!"

The cupboard was a massive object of old walnut, almost as broad as it was high, with no carving save the circular hole made by a Prussian[2] bullet that had entered by the right-hand door and passed out through the back panel.

"Do you want it moved from the landing, Mother?"

An expression like that of a young she-cat, false and glittery, appeared on her wrinkled face.

"I? No, it seems to me all right there—let it stay where it is!"

All the same, my doctor brother and I agreed that we must be on the watch. He saw my

---

1. **Sun King:** Because of the magnificence of his reign, France's King Louis XIV, who ruled from 1643 to 1715, is known as the Sun King. The Palace of Versailles, built during his reign, is renowned for its splendor.

2. **Prussian:** referring to Prussia, most powerful of the former kingdoms that united as Germany while fighting France in the Franco-Prussian War (1870–1871). The bullet hole was most likely made at that time.

Two Memories of Sido   **393**

- Colette and her brother try to look after Sido.
- Sido resists her declining health, continuing to do heavy chores.
- Sido's end is felt to be near when she does not rise to do her morning chores.
- During one of her periods of relatively good health, Sido falls while attempting to move the cupboard.

IN THE GLOSSARY

- elasticity: ability to adapt; flexibility
- adversaries: enemies
- undaunted: not discouraged
- respites: intervals of relief

5 TEACHING STUDENTS OF LIMITED ENGLISH PROFICIENCY

This lengthy sentence, with its intricate clauses and wide temporal scope, may present difficulties for some students. Help them to break it down into more manageable parts.

6 TEACHING CHARACTER MOTIVATION

Ask students what may be motivating Sido to do work early, before help arrives. (She wishes to remain active and maintain her independence.)

7 CULTURAL BACKGROUND

Point out that a typical French farmhouse of this period—the early twentieth century—would be without electricity, making most chores more difficult to perform. The beauty of life under such difficult circumstances, however, was celebrated in many works of art and literature of the period.

8 TEACHING DESCRIPTION

Point out the beautiful use of details in this descriptive passage, which lends vividness to the account of Sido's outlook, surroundings, and activities.

---

mother every day, since she had followed him and lived in the same village, and he looked after her with a passionate devotion which he hid.

5 She fought against all her ills with amazing elasticity, forgot them, baffled them, inflicted on them signal if temporary defeats, recovered, during entire days, her vanished strength; and the sound of her battles, whenever I spent a few days with her, could be heard all over the house till I was irresistibly reminded of a terrier tackling a rat.

At five o'clock in the morning I would be awakened by the clank of a full bucket being set down in the kitchen sink immediately opposite my room.

6 "What are you doing with that bucket, Mother? Couldn't you wait until Josephine arrives?"

And out I hurried. But the fire was already blazing, fed with dry wood. The milk was boiling on the blue-tiled charcoal stove. Nearby, a bar of chocolate was melting in a little water for my breakfast, and, seated squarely in her cane armchair, my mother was grinding the fragrant coffee which she roasted herself. The morning hours were always kind to her. She wore their rosy colors in her cheeks. Flushed with a brief return to health, she would gaze at the rising sun, while the church bell rang for early Mass, and rejoice at having tasted, while we still slept, so many forbidden fruits.

7 The forbidden fruits were the overheavy bucket drawn up from the well, the firewood split with a billhook[3] on an oaken block, the spade, the mattock,[4] and above all the double steps propped against the gable window of the woodhouse. There were the climbing vine whose shoots she trained up to the gable windows of the attic, the flowery spikes of the too-tall lilacs, the dizzy cat that had to be rescued from the ridge of the roof. All the accomplices

---

3. **billhook:** cutting tool with a curved tip, usually used for pruning trees and shrubs.
4. **mattock:** gardening tool resembling a pickax, used for loosening soil and cutting roots.

---

of her old existence as a plump and sturdy little woman, all the minor rustic divinities who once obeyed her and made her so proud of doing without servants, now assumed the appearance and position of adversaries. But they reckoned without that love of combat which my mother was to keep till the end of her life. At seventy-one, dawn still found her undaunted, if not always undamaged.

8 Burned by the fire, cut with the pruning knife, soaked by melting snow or spilled water, she had always managed to enjoy her best moments of independence before the earliest risers had opened their shutters. She was able to tell us of the cats' awakening, of what was going on in the nests, of news gleaned, together with the morning's milk and the warm loaf, from the milkmaid and the baker's girl, the record in fact of the birth of a new day.

It was not until one morning when I found the kitchen unwarmed, and the blue enamel saucepan hanging on the wall, that I felt my mother's end to be near. Her illness knew many respites, during which the fire flared up again on the hearth, and the smell of fresh bread and melting chocolate stole under the door together with the cat's impatient paw. These respites were periods of unexpected alarms. My mother and the big walnut cupboard were discovered together in a heap at the foot of the stairs, she having determined to transport it in secret from the upper landing to the ground floor. Whereupon my elder brother insisted that my mother should keep still and that an old servant should sleep in the little house. But how could an old servant prevail against a vital energy so youthful and mischievous that it contrived to tempt and lead astray a body already half-fettered by death? My brother, returning before sunrise from attending a distant patient, one day caught my mother red-handed in the most wanton of crimes. Dressed in her nightgown, but wearing heavy gardening sabots,[5] her little gray septuagenarian's plait of hair turning up like a scorpi-

---

5. **sabots** [sa bō′]: wooden shoes.

CRITICAL THINKING: GUIDED READING QUESTIONS

LITERAL

1a. What collective term is used to describe the bucket, firewood, and other objects used in Sido's labor? ("forbidden fruits")

2a. When does Colette feel her mother's end to be near? (when Sido fails to do her morning chores)

INFERENTIAL

1b. Why is this term used? (Sido treasures these tasks, and they tempt her even though she knows she should not be doing them.)

2b. Why does she feel this way? (Almost nothing but death could stop Sido from doing her work.)

Madame Roulin Rocking the Cradle, Vincent van Gogh (1853–1890).

ART AND LITERATURE

The Dutchman Vincent van Gogh depicted simple, almost primitive images drawn from life—still lifes, portraits, landscape paintings, scenes of everyday life.

In *Madame Roulin Rocking the Cradle,* van Gogh depicts a postman's wife. Her strong, crossed hands combined with her determined gaze convey a pensive feeling. The hovering, undulating flowers against the dark background enhance the mood of thoughtful introspection.

■ Ask students which character from the selection van Gogh's portrait might depict. Why? (Sido; Like her the woman in the portrait seems determined and independent.)

- Sido is caught sawing logs on a freezing morning.
- A year before her death Sido explains in a letter that she will not visit Colette and her husband because she wishes to watch a pink cactus bloom.
- Colette describes the strength she derived from her relationship with her mother.

9 CRITICAL THINKING: EVALUATION

Ask students to evaluate Sido's reason for refusing the invitation. Is her motive a good one? (Some students may feel that Sido's motive is sound since she is near death and wants to get as much enjoyment out of life and nature as she can. Others may feel that her reason is too trivial.)

10 TEACHING REPETITION

Draw attention to the repeated phrase "I am the daughter of the/a woman who . . ." This repetition lends powerful cadence, increases the feeling of unity, and helps to underscore the deep emotion and pride the author feels for her mother.

11 TEACHING THEME

Ask students to state the theme of the selection, as implied by this concluding passage. (Independence, generosity, love, and a regard for nature and beauty are priceless assets for the spirit, especially in adversity.)

COLLABORATIVE LEARNING: ENRICHMENT ACTIVITY

Art Ask a group of students to research and compare the works of artists such as Corot, Monet, Seurat, Pissarro, van Gogh, and Cézanne, all of whom painted landscapes of the French countryside. The students should prepare an in-class presentation.

ART AND LITERATURE

The careful arrangement of pots and auriculas in this detail by the English painter John Morley suggests a nurturing quality on the part of their caretaker.
- Ask students what aspect of Sido's life this painting suggests. (her love of nature)

Detail. *Auriculas in a Basket,* John Morley.

on's tail on the nape of her neck, one foot firmly planted on the crosspiece of the beech trestle, her back bent in the attitude of the expert jobber,[6] my mother, rejuvenated by an indescribable expression of guilty enjoyment, in defiance of all her promises and of the freezing morning dew, was sawing logs in her own yard.

"Sir, you ask me . . ."

Sir,

You ask me to come and spend a week with you, which means I would be near my daughter, whom I adore. You who live with her know how rarely I see her, how much her presence delights me, and I'm touched that you should ask me to come and see her. All the same I'm not going to accept your kind invitation, for the time being at any rate. The reason is that my pink cactus is probably going to flower. It's a very rare plant I've been given, and I'm told that in our climate it flowers only once every four years. Now, I am already a very old woman, and if I went away

6. **jobber:** person who does odd jobs; handyman.

396 *Nonfiction*

when my pink cactus is about to flower, I am certain I shouldn't see it flower again.

So I beg you, sir, to accept my sincere thanks and my regrets, together with my kind regards.

This note, signed *"Sidonie Colette, née[7] Landoy,"* was written by my mother to one of my husbands, the second. A year later she died, at the age of seventy-seven.

Whenever I feel myself inferior to everything about me, threatened by my own mediocrity, frightened by the discovery that a muscle is losing its strength, a desire its power, or a pain the keen edge of its bite, I can still hold up my head and say to myself: "I am the daughter of the woman who wrote that letter—that letter and so many more that I have kept. This one tells me in ten lines that at the age of seventy-six she was planning journeys and undertaking them, but that waiting for the possible bursting into bloom of a tropical flower held everything up and silenced even her heart, made for love. I am the daughter of a woman who, in a mean, close-fisted, confined little place, opened her village home to stray cats, tramps, and pregnant servant girls. I am the daughter of a woman who many a time, when she was in despair at not having enough money for others, ran through the wind-whipped snow to cry from door to door, at the houses of the rich, that a child had just been born in a poverty-stricken home to parents whose feeble, empty hands had no swaddling clothes[8] for it. Let me not forget that I am the daughter of a woman who bent her head, trembling, between the blades of a cactus, her wrinkled face full of ecstasy over the promise of a flower, a woman who herself never ceased to flower, untiringly, during three quarters of a century."

7. *née* [nā]: French for "born"; used to indicate a woman's maiden name.
8. **swaddling clothes:** long, narrow bands of cloth in which newborn infants were formerly wrapped.

CRITICAL THINKING: GUIDED READING QUESTIONS

LITERAL

1a. What sort of feeling does Sido's facial expression reveal when she is discovered sawing logs? (guilty enjoyment)

2a. What reason does Sido give for not going away when her pink cactus is about to bloom? (She is certain she will not see it bloom again.)

INFERENTIAL

1b. Why is she experiencing this feeling? (She enjoys remaining active but feels guilty about defying her children.)

2b. Why does she believe this to be the case? (She is old and unwell and does not expect to live another four years, the interval between bloomings.)

STUDY QUESTIONS

Recalling

1. When Colette arrived to visit her mother, what mishaps did Sido report to her?
2. What was Sido's happiest and most active part of the day? What would she do then?
3. What was "the most wanton of crimes" at which the writer's brother caught Sido "red-handed"?
4. Why did Sido refuse Colette's second husband's invitation to pay a visit?

Interpreting

5. In what ways does Sido use humor when she explains her various mishaps to her daughter? What do these humorous touches suggest about Sido's personality?
6. What evidence can you find in this biography that Sido loved nature?
7. What lesson about life does Colette draw from the letter Sido wrote to Colette's second husband?

Extending

8. What do you hope you will be like when you reach your seventies? What qualities do you feel are important to have at that time of life?

LITERARY FOCUS

Biography

A **biography** is an account of a person's life written by someone other than the subject. Biographies can be short sketches, as in this selection about Colette's mother, or book-length works. One of the most useful tools a writer can use in a short biography is the **anecdote,** a brief account of something the subject said or did. A well-chosen anecdote vividly reveals important traits of the subject's personality.

Thinking About Biography

■ What does the anecdote about Colette's brother finding Sido sawing logs reveal about Sido's personality?

LANGUAGE STUDY

French Expressions

The French word *née,* which occurs in the selection, is often used in English newspaper wedding announcements to indicate a woman's maiden name. English speakers use numerous French expressions, both in writing and conversation.

Use a dictionary to determine the meanings of these originally French terms.

1. apropos
2. bon voyage
3. esprit de corps
4. faux pas
5. laissez faire
6. tête-à-tête

COMPOSITION

Writing a Biography

■ Choose someone whom you admire or who has strongly influenced your life, and write a biographical sketch of the person. First identify your subject's outstanding personality traits. Then select two or three anecdotes that will serve to reveal these traits vividly to your readers.

Do you think Sido should have spent her later years more prudently? Why or why not?

ANSWERS

STUDY QUESTIONS

1. She bruised her shin falling downstairs and scalded her arm on a foot warmer.
2. early morning; She would light the fire, make breakfast, gaze at the rising sun, draw water from the well, split firewood, garden, observe birds' nests and cats, and learn the news of the village.
3. sawing logs
4. She wanted to see her pink cactus bloom.
5. She compares herself negatively with Louis XIV and personifies the foot warmer. She is strong, independent, intelligent, and unlikely to pity herself.
6. Her pleasure in the rising sun, cats, birds' nests, gardening, vines, and the pink cactus attests to her love of nature.
7. Independence, love, generosity, and regard for nature and beauty are priceless assets for the human spirit, especially in adversity.
8. Possible answers: healthy, independent, and generous; self-reliance and a sense of humor

LITERARY FOCUS

It is evidence of Sido's determination not to give in to age or weakness, her independence, and her joy in working.

LANGUAGE STUDY

1. "relevant"; ap′rə pō′
2. "(have a) pleasant trip"; bän′ voi äzh′
3. "group morale"; es prē′ də kôr′
4. "breach of courtesy"; fō′ pä′
5. "lenient policy"; les′a fãr′
6. "intimate conversation"; tāt′ ə tāt′

COMPOSITION: GUIDELINES FOR EVALUATION

WRITING A BIOGRAPHY

Objective

To write a biographical sketch

Guidelines for Evaluation

■ suggested length: three or four paragraphs
■ should identify the subject's main personality traits
■ should make use of anecdotes to reveal these traits

LESSON PREVIEW

This selection comprises a set of aphorisms that offer concise observations on human behavior and values. They constitute part of an overall philosophy of life, Confucianism, that has had a profound impact for most of the last two thousand years of Chinese history. The sayings are somewhat pedantic in tone but are illuminated with striking insight and occasional subtle wit.

LITERARY SKILLS FOR THIS SELECTION

- sayings
- simile

THEMES IN THIS SELECTION

- moral virtue
- social behavior

LESSON OBJECTIVES

1. to understand sayings
2. to compare and contrast the sayings and maxims of Confucius and La Rochefoucauld

Teacher's Classroom Resources 3

- Teaching Notes — 41
- Reading Guide — 42
- Check Test — 43
- Responding to World Cultures — 44
- Literary Focus: Sayings and Maxims — 45
- Writing Process Guide: Comparing and Contrasting the Sayings and Maxims — 46
- Grammar in Literature: Writing Concisely — 47
- Selection Test — 48

IN THE CLASSROOM

TEACHING STUDENTS OF DIFFERENT ABILITIES

- **For less advanced students:** Although many of the sayings' basic concepts will seem familiar to students, their concentrated mode of expression may present difficulties. Thus, have students read each saying several times and then paraphrase it. Ask them to complete the Reading Guide.

Confucius

(c. 551–479 B.C.)

China

The teachings of Confucius [kən fū′ shəs] rank among the world's great achievements in political and ethical philosophy. Born in what is now Shandong [shän′doong′] Province in China, Confucius was really named Kong Qiu; the name Confucius comes from a Latin adaptation of a Chinese title meaning "Great Master Kong."

During Confucius' lifetime China was still divided among numerous warring states, and social upheaval threatened to destroy the traditional values of Chinese civilization. Confucius sought to become an adviser to a powerful ruler in order to put his philosophical system into practice, but he was forced to settle for a series of minor official appointments.

After his death his followers started to spread and publish his ethical precepts, as expressed in his *Sayings* or *Analects*. These were eventually developed into the philosophy of Confucianism, which over the last two thousand years has become the most important single influence on Chinese life in all its aspects, including education, government, and the relationship of the individual to society.

398 *Nonfiction*

Ancient Chinese Civilization

The vast nation of China has a history that dates back thousands of years. From about 1750 to 1027 B.C., the Shang dynasty ruled over the region of China that includes Beijing, the modern capital. The first strong central government of imperial China evolved under the Qin [ching] dynasty in the early third century B.C., when much of China's Great Wall was built to keep out invaders. Shortly afterward, the Han rulers expanded the Chinese Empire into central Asia.

It was during the Han dynasty, from 202 B.C. until A.D. 220, that Confucianism began to influence Chinese life. The Han dynasty was a time of great political, cultural, and technological growth. Han emperors promoted scholarly research, and new inventions made learning easier. In the upcoming sayings Confucius emphasizes the virtues of moderation, goodness, and justice in shaping excellence in moral character.

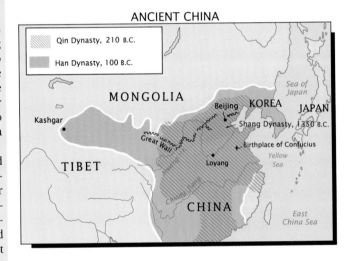

ANCIENT CHINA

Qin Dynasty, 210 B.C.

Han Dynasty, 100 B.C.

See LITERATURE AND CULTURE SOURCEBOOK: China and Japan

- **For more advanced students:** Ask students to give examples of situations in which each of the sayings applies and examples of situations in which each is limited.

DISCUSSING GEOGRAPHY AND CULTURE

Great Innovations

The Han dynasty was a time of innovation in China. During this period paper was invented, calendars and astronomical instruments were improved, and the classic texts of Chinese medicine were written.

- The twentieth century has also been a time of dazzling innovation. Ask students to describe some of the outstanding scientific advances of our time. (Examples: computers, spacecraft, nuclear weapons, genetic engineering)

Confucius

Sayings
from **The Analects**

Translated from the Chinese by James Legge

The cautious seldom err.

With coarse rice to eat, with water to drink, and my bended arm for a pillow—I have still joy in the midst of these things. Riches and honors acquired by unrighteousness are to me as a floating cloud.

To go beyond is as wrong as to fall short.

He who speaks without modesty will find it difficult to make his words good.

Recompense injury with justice, and recompense kindness with kindness.

What the superior man seeks is in himself. What the mean man seeks is in others.

What you do not want done to yourself, do not do to others.

To be able to practice five things everywhere under heaven constitutes perfect virtue: gravity, generosity of soul, sincerity, earnestness, and kindness.

Confucius, woodblock print.

Sayings from The Analects **399**

LESSON PREVIEW

The aphorisms in this selection, taken from the author's collection entitled *Maxims*, offer pithy insights into human social behavior and vanity. Their style is elegant and economical; their tone, intelligent and witty. They reflect directly the vices and foibles of seventeenth-century France but are also painfully applicable to our own time.

LITERARY SKILLS FOR THIS SELECTION

- maxims
- analogy

THEMES IN THIS SELECTION

- the vices of selfishness and vanity
- the virtues of restraint, wisdom, and self-control

LESSON OBJECTIVES

1. to understand maxims
2. to compare and contrast the sayings and maxims of Confucius and La Rochefoucauld

Teacher's Classroom Resources 3

- Teaching Notes — 41
- Reading Guide — 42
- Check Test — 43
- Responding to World Cultures — 44
- Literary Focus: Sayings and Maxims — 45
- Writing Process Guide: Comparing and Contrasting the Sayings and Maxims — 46
- Grammar in Literature: Writing Concisely — 47
- Selection Test — 48

IN THE CLASSROOM

TEACHING STUDENTS OF DIFFERENT ABILITIES

- **For less advanced students:** Help students understand the sophisticated points the author makes. Give examples illustrating each maxim. Ask students to complete the Reading Guide for this selection.

- **For more advanced students:** Ask students to identify the specific virtue or vice that the author is treating in each maxim and to identify the corresponding vice or virtue that is contrasted with it implicitly.

François de La Rochefoucauld

(1613–1680)

France

French writer François de La Rochefoucauld [frän swä′ də lä rōsh f‾oo kō′] elevated the use of the aphorism (a brief and wise statement about an aspect of life) into a high art. Born into a French noble family, he became a duke on the death of his father and spent an adventurous youth in soldiering and politics, supporting the opposition to Cardinal Richelieu [rish′ ə l‾oo′]. His memoirs, published in 1662, recount the intrigues of the nobles who plotted against Richelieu.

Wounded three times in battles against the aggrandizing Spanish crown and heavily in debt, La Rouchefoucald retired from politics to devote himself to intellectual pursuits. One brilliant result of this introspective period is his *Maxims* (1665), a collection of witty, elegant epigrams that cast a merciless light on the foibles of human behavior. The polished style and predominantly pessimistic philosophy of the *Maxims* had a considerable influence on French literature in the seventeenth and eighteenth centuries.

400 *Nonfiction*

GEOGRAPHY AND CULTURE

France in the Age of Louis XIV

In the seventeenth century France was dominated by the personality of Louis XIV, often called the "Sun King." The identification of the king with the state was so close that historians often refer to this period in France as "the Century of Louis XIV." Part of this identification was due to his remarkably long reign—from 1643 to 1715—and part to his influence on every aspect of French life. For example, the king waged a succession of foreign wars that resulted in economic difficulties at home. He also had a splendid palace built for his court at Versailles [vər sī′].

Louis XIV encouraged culture by patronizing many of the leading painters, writers, and musicians of his day, including Molière [mōl yār′], who wrote comic plays, and Racine [rä sēn′], who wrote tragedies. Other notable writers of the period included Jean de La Fontaine [zhän′ də lä fōn ten′], the celebrated author of animal fables, and François de La Rochefoucauld, many of whose maxims may have been inspired by the hypocrisy of court life.

FRANCE IN 1648

IRELAND
ENGLAND
London ★
UNITED NETH.
SPAN. NETH.
English Channel
Rhine R.
Paris
Versailles ●★
Seine R.
FRANCHE-COMTÉ
ATLANTIC OCEAN
Loire R.
KINGDOM of FRANCE
SWITZ.
SAVOY
Bay of Biscay
Rhône R.
Avignon ●
Marseilles ●
KINGDOM of SPAIN
Mediterranean Sea

See LITERATURE AND CULTURE SOURCEBOOK:
France

DISCUSSING GEOGRAPHY AND CULTURE

Learning a Foreign Language

By the end of Louis XIV's reign, French had become the language of choice among diplomats and aristocrats in continental Europe—and even as far away as Russia. The first official dictionary of the French language was completed by the Académie Française in 1694.

- Ask students which foreign language they are studying or would like to study. Which foreign language do they feel is most likely to be useful in their career?

Detail. *The Thinker,* Auguste Rodin (1840–1917).

François de La Rochefoucauld

from Maxims

Translated from the French by Louis Kronenberger

Self-love is the greatest of all flatterers.

We all have strength enough to endure the misfortunes of others.

With nothing are we so generous as advice.

1 Nature creates ability; luck endows it with opportunities.

True eloquence means saying all that is necessary and only what is necessary.

The vast pleasure we get from talking about ourselves should warn us that we are giving almost no pleasure to those who are listening.

We can easily forgive those faults in our friends which do not affect us personally.

2 Wisdom is to the mind what health is to the body.

If we cannot find peace inside ourselves, it is useless to look for it elsewhere.

We are never so unhappy as we imagine, nor so happy as we had longed to be.

How can we expect someone else to keep our secret if we cannot keep it ourselves?

Maxims **401**

CRITICAL THINKING: GUIDED READING QUESTIONS

LITERAL

1a. What does the author say we have the strength to endure? (the misfortunes of others)

2a. What faults in our friends can we easily forgive? (those that do not affect us personally)

INFERENTIAL

1b. What is he really saying about us? (We are much more sensitive to our own pain than to the pain of others.)

2b. What vice is this maxim criticizing? (self-centeredness; If something does not affect us personally, we are not concerned about it.)

Is it comforting or disturbing to think that observations made on human behavior so many years ago continue to be so apt? Why?

ANSWERS

STUDY QUESTIONS

Sayings from The Analects
1. He considers them to be like a floating cloud.
2. gravity (seriousness), generosity of soul, sincerity, earnestness, and kindness
3. "To go beyond . . ." and "He who speaks without modesty . . ."
4. "What you do not want done . . ."
5. Answers will vary. Possible answers include sayings about materialism, conservation, and greed.

STUDY QUESTIONS

from Maxims
1. self-love
2. "saying all that is necessary and only what is necessary"
3. wisdom
4. "Self-love is . . ." and "The vast pleasure we get . . ."
5. Answers will vary. Some students will argue that they would have valued his candor and insight; others will admit that they might have been put off by these same qualities.

LITERARY FOCUS

Possible answers: the golden rule, the importance of self-knowledge and self-control, the belief that true satisfaction comes from within, and the destructive effects of vanity and selfishness

STUDY QUESTIONS (*Confucius*)

Recalling
1. What does the writer say his attitude is toward unrighteous riches and honors?
2. According to these sayings, what five qualities constitute perfect virtue?

Interpreting
3. Which sayings emphasize the values of moderation and modesty in human conduct?
4. Which saying comes closest to expressing what you understand to be the meaning of "the golden rule"?

Extending
5. Write two sayings in the style of Confucius to guide people in today's world.

STUDY QUESTIONS (*La Rochefoucauld*)

Recalling
1. According to the writer, what human tendency is the greatest flatterer?
2. How does the writer define *eloquence*?
3. What mental quality does the writer compare to bodily health?

Interpreting
4. Cite two maxims that would support the view that La Rochefoucauld considered vanity as one of the most widespread and troublesome flaws in human character.

Extending
5. Would you like to have had La Rochefoucauld as a friend? Explain why or why not.

LITERARY FOCUS

Sayings and Maxims

A **saying** or **maxim** is a concise, pointed statement that expresses a wise observation about life or human behavior. Sayings and maxims can also be called *aphorisms, adages,* or *epigrams.* To be effective, these brief statements must contain a widely acknowledged general truth. Writers of memorable maxims avoid the overworked language of clichés by expressing their observations with wit and penetrating insight.

Thinking About the Sayings and Maxims
- What general truths do you see expressed in these sayings and maxims?

COMPOSITION

Comparing and Contrasting the Sayings and Maxims
- In a brief essay compare and contrast the sayings and maxims of Confucius and La Rochefoucauld. First decide which aspects of human conduct or character each of the two authors addresses in his maxims. Then evaluate the writers' philosophies of human behavior. Finally, comment on the style of each author in the sayings and maxims.

COMPOSITION: GUIDELINES FOR EVALUATION

COMPARING AND CONTRASTING THE SAYINGS AND MAXIMS

Objective
To compare and contrast the sayings and maxims of the two authors

Guidelines for Evaluation
- suggested length: three or four paragraphs
- should identify the aspects of human behavior addressed in the sayings and maxims
- should evaluate each author's philosophy
- should comment on each author's style

GEOGRAPHY AND CULTURE

Isaac Bashevis Singer

(born 1904)

Poland/United States

The author Isaac Bashevis Singer attained eminence by writing in Yiddish, a language rarely spoken in the contemporary world. The son of a rabbi (a Jewish scholar, teacher, and spiritual leader), he was born in Radzymin, a small village in Poland near Warsaw. Soon after, the family moved to Warsaw, where Singer grew up in the Jewish community around Krochmalna Street, the setting for "Shosha."

His father's interest in European folklore helped to kindle Singer's interest in writing. He emigrated to the United States in 1935 and began to write for the *Jewish Daily Forward* in Brooklyn, New York. *Satan in Goray,* published the same year, is regarded by many as his masterpiece. Widespread acclaim followed the translation of his works into English from Yiddish, the Germanic vernacular language used by Eastern European Jews.

Singer's short stories and novels have established him as a master storyteller, worthy of the Nobel Prize, which he won in 1978. The upcoming selection is from *A Day of Pleasure* (1969), a book of memoirs of his childhood in Warsaw.

Poland and Its Jewish Community

Poland is a large nation in central Europe that borders on the Baltic Sea. Its land neighbors are the Soviet Union, Germany, and Czechoslovakia. Poland's capital is Warsaw, a city of approximately one and a half million people that is located in the eastern central part of the country and divided by the Vistula River. Other important cities are Gdańsk [gə dänsk′], on the northern coast, and Kraków [kra′kou′], in the south.

Before the Holocaust in World War II, Poland was home to a large Jewish community, centered in Warsaw. Many of these Jews belonged to the Hasidic movement in Judaism, whose religious zeal is expressed in spiritualism, religious storytelling, and a philosophy of joy. In "Shosha" Isaac Bashevis Singer recalls growing up as the son of a Hasidic rabbi in the Jewish community in Warsaw before World War I.

See *LITERATURE AND CULTURE SOURCEBOOK: Russia and Eastern Europe.*

Shosha **403**

In this narrative essay the author tells of his childhood in the Jewish community in Warsaw. He relates the touching story of his relationship with Shosha, a girl with whom he trades fanciful tales. When he returns to Warsaw as an adult, he meets Shosha's daughter and gains a sense of the mysterious relationship linking past and present.

LITERARY SKILLS FOR THIS SELECTION

- narrative essay
- theme
- symbol

THEMES IN THIS SELECTION

- past and present
- childhood and adulthood

LESSON OBJECTIVES

1. to understand narrative essays
2. to determine the meaning and origin of words from Yiddish
3. to write a narrative essay

Teacher's Classroom Resources 3

- Teaching Notes — 51
- Reading Guide — 52
- Check Test — 53
- Responding to World Cultures — 54
- Literary Focus: Narrative Essay — 55
- Language Study: Words from Yiddish — 56
- Writing Process Guide: Writing a Narrative Essay — 57
- Grammar in Literature: Combining Sentences Through Coordination — 58
- Selection Test — 59

IN THE CLASSROOM

TEACHING STUDENTS OF DIFFERENT ABILITIES

- **For less advanced students:** Point out the underlying similarities between Singer's childhood world of fantasy and that of the students. Ask students to complete the Reading Guide.

- **For more advanced students:** Ask students to focus on the aspects of the author's inner and outward worlds that remain basically the same and those that change with time.

DISCUSSING GEOGRAPHY AND CULTURE

Vanished Places

Warsaw's Jewish quarter, which Singer has described so vividly in "Shosha" and many other tales, no longer exists. It was destroyed by the Nazis in 1943.

- Ask students to imagine a situation in which a place they once cherished was destroyed in a catastrophe or somehow changed beyond recognition. How would they feel if they revisited the site years later?

The Jewish section of Warsaw during World War II.

Isaac Bashevis Singer

Shosha

Translated from the Yiddish

1   In the days when we used to live at 10 Krochmalna Street, I mostly stayed home at night. Our courtyard was dark and the small kerosene lamps in the hallway gave more smoke than light. The stories my parents told about devils, demons, and werewolves made me afraid to go out, so I would remain indoors and read.

In those days, we had a neighbor called Basha, who had three daughters: Shosha, who was nine; Ippa, five; and Teibele,[1] two. Basha owned a store that stayed open until late in the evening.

2   In the summertime the nights are short, but in winter they are very long. The only place I could go at night was Shosha's apartment, but to

—————
1. **Teibele** [tĭ′bə lə]: diminutive, or familiar form, of *Teibel,* a Yiddish female's name.

404   *Nonfiction*

CRITICAL THINKING: GUIDED READING QUESTIONS

LITERAL

1a. What is the only place to which the young Singer can go at night? (Shosha's apartment)

INFERENTIAL

1b. Why is this so? (He fears the night, and she lives close by.)

get there I had to pass through a dark corridor. It took only a minute, yet that minute was filled with terror. Luckily, Shosha would almost always hear me coming, running and breathing heavily, and would quickly open the door. At the sight of her, I lost all fear. Shosha, though she was a year older than I, was more childish. She was fair, with blond braids and blue eyes. We were drawn to each other because we loved to tell each other stories, and we also loved to play together.

The moment I entered the apartment, Shosha took out "the things." Her toys consisted of articles discarded by grown-ups: buttons from old coats, a teakettle handle, a wooden spool with no thread left, tinfoil from a package of tea, and other such objects. With my colored pencils, I often drew people and animals for Shosha. Shosha and her sister Ippa admired my artwork.

3 There was a tile stove in Shosha's apartment behind which there lived a cricket. It chirped the nights through all winter long. I imagined that the cricket was telling a story that would never end. But who can understand the language of crickets? Shosha believed that a house imp[2] also made its home behind the stove. A house imp never does anyone any harm. Sometimes it even helps the household. Just the same, one is afraid of it.

4 Shosha's house imp liked to play little tricks. When Shosha took off her shoes and stockings before she went to sleep and placed them near her bed, she'd find them on the table in the morning. The house imp had put them there. Several times when Shosha went to bed with her hair unbraided, the house imp braided it while she was asleep. Once when Shosha was playing at casting goat shadows on the wall with her fingers, the shadow goat jumped off the wall and butted her on the forehead. This, too, was a trick of the house imp. Another time Shosha's mother sent her to the baker to buy fresh rolls and gave

_____
2. **imp:** here, a mischievous spirit.

her a silver gulden[3] to pay for them. Shosha lost the gulden in the gutter and came home frightened and crying. Suddenly she felt a coin in her hand. The house imp tweaked her left braid and whispered into her ear: "Shlemiel."[4]

I had heard these stories many times, but they never failed to make me shiver with excitement. I myself liked to invent things. I told the girls that my father had a treasure that was hidden in a cave in the forest. I boasted that my grandfather was the King of Bilgoray.[5] I assured Shosha that I knew a magic word that could destroy the world if spoken. "Please, Itchele,[6] please don't say it," she would beg me.

5 The trip home was even more frightening than getting to Shosha's. My fear grew with the stories we told each other. It seemed to me that the dark hall was full of evil spirits. I had once read a story about a boy who had been forced by the demons to marry one of their she-devils. I was afraid that it might happen to me. According to the story, the couple lived somewhere in the desert near Mount Seir.[7] Their children were half human and half demon. As I ran through the dark corridor, I kept repeating words that would guard me against the creatures of the night:

"Thou shalt not permit a witch to live—
A witch to live thou shalt not permit."

6 When we moved to 12 Krochmalna Street, there was no question of visiting Shosha at night. Also, it was not fitting for a Hasidic[8] boy, a student of the Talmud,[9] to play with girls. I missed

_____
3. **gulden** [gool'dən]: coin formerly used in central Europe; also called a *guilder.*
4. **Shlemiel** [shlə mēl']: Yiddish for "unlucky fool."
5. **Bilgoray** [byel gô rī']: town in eastern Poland.
6. **Itchele** [ich'ə lə]: diminutive of *Itzak,* the Yiddish form of *Isaac,* the author's name.
7. **Mount Seir** [sē'ər]: biblical name of Mount Hor, site of the ancient city of Petra in what today is the nation of Jordan.
8. **Hasidic** [hä sid'ik]: referring to a Jewish sect devoted to strict observance of ritual law.
9. **Talmud** [täl'mood]: the written body of Jewish civil and religious law.

Shosha **405**

PAGE SUMMARY: AT A GLANCE

- To visit Shosha, Itchele must walk down a dark corridor, which frightens him.
- He and Shosha love to tell stories and play together.
- A chirping cricket lives behind the stove, which the children think also shelters a house imp.
- Various stories about the house imp, a treasure, a magic word, and demons are told.
- After Itchele moves away, he stops visiting Shosha.

IN THE GLOSSARY

- tweaked: pulled sharply

3 TEACHING SYMBOLS

Explain that a symbol is anything that stands for something other than what it is. Ask students what the cricket and its never-ending "story" symbolize. (continuity, art)

4 TEACHING CHARACTERIZATION

In this passage the author relates Shosha's fanciful accounts of the house imp. Ask students what Shosha's stories show about her character. (She is playful and imaginative.)

5 READING SKILL: CAUSE AND EFFECT

Ask students to state the reason that the trip home was even more frightening for Itchele. (The stories the children told made him more fearful.)

6 CULTURAL BACKGROUND

Point out that like many Hasidic Jews today, those of Singer's time believed in very separate roles for males and females. It was very important for boys to study the Talmud (the body of writing constituting Jewish civil and religious law). Playing with girls would have been considered a frivolous activity for a boy. Also, any physical contact between boys and girls would have been frowned upon.

CRITICAL THINKING: GUIDED READING QUESTIONS

LITERAL

1a. What are Shosha's toys? (old buttons, a kettle handle, an empty spool, and tinfoil scraps)

2a. After telling how Shosha's stories made him shiver with excitement, what does Singer say he himself liked to do? (He liked to invent things.)

INFERENTIAL

1b. Why do you think she and Itchele treasure objects that adults consider useless? (They have no other toys, and their rich imagination lends these articles special meaning.)

2b. What does this tell you about how he viewed Shosha's stories? (He did not really believe them.)

- Shosha becomes an image of the past for Singer, and he dreams about her.
- He goes on to become a writer, marries, has a son, and plans to move to the United States.
- Before he leaves, he visits his old neighborhood, finding it very much the same.
- He goes to Shosha's apartment and finds her daughter, Basha, who knows of Itchele's stories and questions Singer about them.

IN THE GLOSSARY

- emigrate: move out of a country

7 TEACHING SYMBOLS

Point out that Shosha herself has now become a symbol of the past for Singer. Having left her behind, he has begun to see her as standing for the entire lost world of childhood.

8 TEACHING THEME

Ask students how the theme of the cyclical nature of life is illustrated in this passage. (Singer returns to Warsaw; he retells ancient stories but this time in writing; he has a child of his own.)

9 READING SKILL: PREDICTING OUTCOMES

Have students attempt to predict whether Singer will find Shosha. (Many students will probably guess, incorrectly, that there will be no trace of Shosha or her family.)

10 TEACHING THEME

Point out that the theme of the cycle of time and the relationship between past and present is suggested in a startling and highly dramatic way in this passage, as the little girl Shosha seems to reappear.

Shosha. I hoped we'd meet on the street sometime, but months and years passed and we did not see each other.

7   In time Shosha became for me an image of the past. I often thought about her during the day and dreamed about her at night. In my dreams Shosha was as beautiful as a princess. Several times I dreamed that she had married the house imp and lived with him in a dark cellar. He brought her food but never let her go out. I saw her sitting on a chair, to which she had been tied with rope, while the house imp fed her jam with a tiny spoon. He had the head of a dog and the wings of a bat.

8   After the First World War, I left my family in Bilgoray and returned to Warsaw. I began to write and my stories appeared in newspapers and magazines. I also wrote a novel called *Satan in Goray* in which I described the devils and demons of olden times. I was married and had a son. I applied for a passport and a visa to emigrate to the United States, and one day they arrived. I was about to leave Warsaw forever.

A few days before I left, my feet led me to Krochmalna Street. I hadn't been there for years and I wanted once again to see the street where I grew up.

Few changes had taken place, though the buildings were older and even shabbier. I peered into some courtyards: huge trash cans; barefoot, half-naked children. The boys played tag, hide-and-seek, cops-and-robbers, just as we had twenty-five years ago. The girls occupied

9 themselves with hopscotch. Suddenly it occurred to me that I might be able to find Shosha. I made my way to the building where we used to live. God in heaven, everything was the same— the peeling walls, the refuse. I reached the corridor that led to Shosha's apartment, and it was just as dark as in the old days. I lit a match and found the door. As I did so, I realized how foolish I was being. Shosha would be over thirty now. It was most unlikely that the family would

406   *Nonfiction*

---

still be living in the same place. And even if her parents were still alive and living there, Shosha would surely have married and moved away. But some power I cannot explain forced me to knock on the door.

There was no reply. I drew the latch (as I had sometimes done in the old days) and the door opened. I entered a kitchen that looked exactly like Basha's kitchen of twenty-five years before. I recognized the mortar and pestle,[10] the table, the chairs. Was I dreaming? Could it be true?

10   Then I noticed a girl of about eight or nine. My God, it was Shosha! The same fair face, the same blond hair braided with red ribbons, the same longish neck. The girl stared at me in surprise, but she didn't seem alarmed.

"Who are you looking for?" she asked, and it was Shosha's voice.

"What is your name?" I said.

"Me? Basha."

"And your mother's name?"

"Shosha," the girl replied.

"Where is your mother?"

"In the store."

"I once lived here," I explained. "I used to play with your mother when she was a little girl."

Basha looked at me with large eyes and inquired, "Are you Itchele?"

"How do you know about Itchele?" I said. A lump stuck in my throat. I could barely speak.

"My mother told me about him."

"Yes, I am Itchele."

"My mother told me everything. Your father had a cave in the forest full of gold and diamonds. You knew a word that could set the whole world on fire. Do you still know it?"

"No, not anymore."

"What happened to the gold in the cave?"

"Somebody stole it," I said.

---

10. **mortar and pestle:** utensils once widely used for breaking down grains and spices for use in cooking.

CRITICAL THINKING: GUIDED READING QUESTIONS

LITERAL

1a. What prompts Singer to return to Krochmalya Street? (He says that his "feet led" him there because he wanted to see his old street before leaving Warsaw.)

2a. What does Singer observe about the corridor leading to Shosha's apartment? (It is as dark as it was before.)

INFERENTIAL

1b. What may his almost involuntary return to the street suggest? (His past remains a vital, compelling part of his life.)

2b. What formerly important quality of the corridor does he not mention, and what might this mean? (its scariness; He has matured.)

The Jewish section of Warsaw during World War II.

11 "And is your grandfather still a king?"

"No, Basha, he is not a king anymore."

For a while we were both silent. Then I asked, "Did your mother tell you about the house imp?"

"Yes, we used to have a house imp, but he's gone."

"What happened to him?"

"I don't know."

"And the cricket?"

"The cricket is still here, but it chirps mostly at night."

I went down to the candy store—the one where Shosha and I used to buy candy—and bought cookies, chocolate, and halvah.[11] Then I went back upstairs and gave them to Basha.

"Would you like to hear a story?" I asked her.

"Yes, very much."

12 I told Basha a story about a beautiful blond girl whom a demon had carried away to the desert, to Mount Seir, and had forced to marry

---

11. **halvah** [häl vä′]: crumbly sweet made from honey and sesame seeds.

him, and about the children that were born of the marriage, who were half human, half demon.

Basha's eyes grew pensive. "And she stayed there?"

"No, Basha, a saintly man called Rabbi Leib learned about her misfortune. He traveled to the desert and rescued her."

"How?"

"An angel helped him."

"And what happened to her children?"

"The children became completely human and went with their mother. The angel carried them to safety on his wings."

"And the demon?"

"He remained in the desert."

"And he never married again?"

"Yes, Basha, he did. He married a she-demon, one of his own kind."

13 We were both silent again, and suddenly I heard the familiar chirping of a cricket. Could it be the cricket of my childhood? Certainly not. Perhaps her great-great-great-granddaughter. But she was telling the same story, as ancient as time, as puzzling as the world, and as long as the dark winter nights of Warsaw.

Shosha **407**

PAGE SUMMARY: AT A GLANCE

- Basha continues to question Singer about the stories.
- She tells him that the imp is gone, but the cricket remains.
- He tells her a story about a girl who is carried off by a demon and later saved.
- Singer hears the cricket, which seems to tell the same ancient story.

IN THE GLOSSARY

- pensive: thoughtful

11 TEACHING THEME

Ask students what Singer's responses illustrate about the theme of childhood and adulthood. (Growing up forces us to abandon the magical aspects of childhood.)

12 GRAMMAR IN LITERATURE

Direct attention to the use of *whom,* which here precedes the subject and verb of the clause in which it appears. Ask students what case it is in and why it must be used instead of *who.* (It is in the objective case and is the object of the verb *had carried.*)

13 TEACHING SYMBOLS

Ask students what the cricket, which has brought the story full circle, symbolizes in this passage. (It symbolizes that which is unchanging in the face of change.)

COLLABORATIVE LEARNING: ENRICHMENT ACTIVITY

Writing a Short Story Have a group of students plan and write a short story as a sequel to this selection. They should focus on Shosha's return to the apartment and Basha's recounting of what has occurred. Have them draw up an outline before writing the story.

CRITICAL THINKING: GUIDED READING QUESTIONS

LITERAL

1a. Who is the protagonist of the story Singer tells Basha? ("a beautiful blond girl whom a demon had carried away . . .")

INFERENTIAL

1b. Why does Singer use this protagonist? (He uses her so that Basha can identify with her, since both Basha and the protagonist are beautiful blond little girls.)

What positive effects might have resulted from Singer's childhood involvement with sometimes frightening imaginary figures? What negative effects?

ANSWERS

STUDY QUESTIONS

1. the movement of her shoes, the braiding of her hair, the movement of a shadow, and the return of a lost coin
2. He repeats a phrase regarding witches.
3. He has not been to that street for years and wants to see the place where he grew up. Shosha's daughter looks exactly like her mother.
4. The imp is gone. The house looks the same, and there is still a cricket.
5. Possible answers: surprise, affection, nostalgia, and regret
6. He has had to abandon his childhood fantasies.
7. Answers will vary. Students may suggest that we are all bound up with the past.
8. Answers will vary. Some students may suggest that the past is comforting when compared with the present.

LITERARY FOCUS

1. Answers will vary. Students may say that the past and present are closely related.
2. Answers will vary. Students may refer to his comments on his childhood fear of the dark hall, his later belief that Shosha is an image of the past, or his adult feelings about the apartment and Basha.

LANGUAGE STUDY

1. "doughnut-shaped roll"; from Yiddish *beygel*, from German *beugel*
2. "onlooker who gives unwanted advice"; from Yiddish *kibitzen*, from German *kiebitzen*
3. "baked, filled piece of dough"; from Yiddish *knish*, from Russian *knish*
4. "carry with effort; an ineffectual person"; from Yiddish *shleppen*, from German *schleppen*
5. "eat a snack; a snack"; from Yiddish *nashen*, from German *naschen*
6. "foolish person who habitually fails or is victimized"; from Yiddish *shlumiel*, from Hebrew proper name *Shelumiel*

STUDY QUESTIONS

Recalling

1. What events convince Shosha that a house imp lives behind the stove?
2. What does Singer do to quiet his fear as he walks through the dark hall between their apartments?
3. What causes Singer to look for Shosha years later? What is surprising about the person he meets instead?
4. What has changed in Shosha's apartment? What has remained the same?

Interpreting

5. What emotions does the adult Singer feel when he meets Basha?
6. What do you think Singer means when he tells Basha that he no longer knows the magic word that could destroy the world?
7. What do you think Singer is saying about the relationship of the present to the past?

Extending

8. Why does the idea of reentering the past appeal so much to people?

LITERARY FOCUS

Narrative Essay

A **narrative essay** is a nonfiction work that tells a true story, usually presenting events in chronological order. The chronological organization of a narrative essay is similar to the plot line of a story. Writers of narrative essays thus build reader interest much as short story writers do. In addition, writers of narrative essays use skillfully chosen details to draw their readers into the experience being narrated.

Narrative essays often go beyond the objective reporting of facts. Writers of narrative essays often offer their personal comments and reflections on the events they relate. Just as a short story has a theme, a narrative essay relates an experience for a particular purpose: to illustrate an idea or to find within the incident some truth about life in general.

Thinking About the Narrative Essay

1. What truth about life in general does Singer convey in this narrative essay?
2. What personal comments does he offer on the events he describes?

LANGUAGE STUDY

Words from Yiddish

Yiddish is the Germanic vernacular language used by eastern European Jews. Although many of Singer's works have been translated from Yiddish into English, some familiar Yiddish words have been left untranslated because they have entered the English language—for example, the word *schlemiel* in the selection, which is Yiddish for a foolish or clownish person. Many Yiddish words are derived from German, Russian, Hebrew, and Romanian.

Use a dictionary to find the origins and meanings of the following words from Yiddish.

1. bagel
2. kibitzer
3. knish
4. schlep
5. nosh
6. schlemiel

COMPOSITION

Writing a Narrative Essay

■ Write a brief narrative essay about an actual event in which you participated. First select an interesting event and decide on a purpose for your essay. Then use chronological order to structure your account and build suspense. In addition, choose details that give readers an eyewitness view of the event.

COMPOSITION: GUIDELINES FOR EVALUATION

WRITING A NARRATIVE ESSAY

Objective

To write a narrative essay about an actual event in which the writer participated

Guidelines for Evaluation

■ suggested length: four or five paragraphs
■ should use chronological order
■ should include vivid details

GEOGRAPHY AND CULTURE

Aleksandr Solzhenitsyn

(born 1918)

Soviet Union

The name Aleksandr Solzhenitsyn [sŏl′zhə nēt′sin] looms large not only in twentieth-century literature but in the modern political sphere as well. Born one year after the outbreak of the Russian Revolution, Solzhenitsyn was caught up in the early idealism of the revolution. He grew disillusioned, however, as the totalitarian regime of Joseph Stalin consolidated power in the 1930s. During World War II Solzhenitsyn served in the Soviet army, but in 1945 he was arrested and sentenced to eight years in prison for criticizing Stalin.

In 1962 he presented a vivid, chilling account of life in a Soviet prison camp in his first novel, *One Day in the Life of Ivan Denisovich.* Two subsequent novels, *The First Circle* (1968) and *Cancer Ward* (1969), bore witness to the author's political and personal courage. In 1970 he was awarded the Nobel Prize but declined to accept it in person, fearing he would be denied reentry to the Soviet Union. In 1973 Solzhenitsyn was deported and stripped of his Soviet citizenship. He settled in the United States, where he continues to write.

The Soviet Union's Cultural Diversity

The Soviet Union is a vast nation made up of diverse republics that span parts of two continents, Europe and Asia. A wide array of landscapes, ethnic groups, and geographical regions contributes to the nation's rich cultural heritage. The most populous group, and the dominant group politically, is the Russians. Other important groups have given their names to many of the federated republics within the Soviet Union. For example, Georgia, Armenia, and Azerbaijan [äz′ər bī jän′] are three republics in the Caucasus Mountain region between the Black Sea and the Caspian Sea. It was in this region that Solzhenitsyn was born.

Customs and life styles vary sharply throughout this huge land. For instance, in Soviet Central Asia, the inhabitants of Turkmenistan [turk′men i stan′], Uzbekistan [ooz bek′i stan′], and Kazakhstan [kä′zäk stän′], lead a largely nomadic existence. By contrast, the Soviet capital, Moscow, is a large industrial and commercial center where eight million people share a pace of life and a cultural sophistication that is closer to urban life in the West.

See LITERATURE AND CULTURE SOURCEBOOK: Russia and Eastern Europe.

Three Prose Poems **409**

Three prose poems celebrate, in a tone of wondrous appreciation, the beauty of nature and the sense of being alive and free. The first is concerned with a blossoming apple tree; the second, with a duckling; the third, with a storm in the mountains.

LITERARY SKILLS FOR THIS SELECTION

- sensory language
- prose poems
- description

THEMES IN THIS SELECTION

- the beauty of nature
- appreciation of freedom
- the wonder of life

LESSON OBJECTIVES

1. to recognize sensory language
2. to write a prose poem

Teacher's Classroom Resources 3

■ Teaching Notes	61
■ Reading Guide	62
■ Check Test	63
■ Responding to World Cultures	64
■ Literary Focus: Sensory Language	65
■ Writing Process Guide: Writing a Prose Poem	66
■ Grammar in Literature: Prepositional Phrases	67
■ Selection Test	68

TEACHING STUDENTS OF DIFFERENT ABILITIES

- **For less advanced students:** Explain to students that the material in this selection celebrates special moments in nature rather than telling a story. Then have them complete the Reading Guide.

- **For more advanced students:** Ask students to find illustrations that depict a celebration of nature or life, and have them describe the way in which the pictures do this. Also ask them to describe the feelings that such pictures evoke. As they read, have them note which of these same feelings are evoked by the prose poems.

DISCUSSING GEOGRAPHY AND CULTURE

A Sense of Place

Russian writers often have a strong sense of place. Leo Tolstoy immortalized Russia's birch forests in winter; Anton Chekhov, its blossoming cherry orchards. Boris Pasternak captured the bleakness of Siberia; Mikhail Bulgakov, the wan cheer of Moscow's parks.

- Ask students to think of a place that has strong emotional significance for them. Have volunteers describe their special place.

Apple Blossoms, c. 1864–1874, John William Hill.

Aleksandr Solzhenitsyn

Three Prose Poems

Translated from the Russian by Michael Glenny

Freedom to Breathe

1 A shower fell in the night and now dark clouds drift across the sky, occasionally sprinkling a fine film of rain.

2 I stand under an apple tree in blossom and I breathe. Not only the apple tree but the grass round it glistens with moisture; words cannot describe the sweet fragrance that pervades the air. I inhale as deeply as I can, and the aroma invades my whole being; I breathe with my eyes open, I breathe with my eyes closed—I cannot say which gives me the greater pleasure.

This, I believe, is the single most precious freedom that prison takes away from us: the freedom to breathe freely, as I now can. No food on earth, no wine, not even a woman's kiss is sweeter to me than this air steeped in the fragrance of flowers, of moisture and freshness.

No matter that this is only a tiny garden, hemmed in by five-story houses like cages in a zoo. I cease to hear the motorcycles backfiring, radios whining, the burble of loudspeakers. As long as there is fresh air to breathe under an apple tree after a shower, we may survive a little longer.

The Duckling

A little yellow duckling, flopping comically on its white belly in the wet grass and scarcely

410 *Nonfiction*

able to stand on its thin, feeble legs, runs in front of me and quacks: "Where's my mommy? Where's my family?"

He has no mommy, because he has been fostered by a hen: duck eggs were put in her nest, she sat on them and hatched them with her own. To shelter them from the bad weather, their home—an upturned basket without a bottom—has been moved into a shed and covered with sacking. They are all in there, but this one is lost. Come on then, little thing, let me take you in my hand.

3 What keeps it alive? It weighs nothing; its little black eyes are like beads, its feet are like sparrows' feet, the slightest squeeze and it would be no more. Yet it is warm with life. Its little beak is pale pink and slightly splayed, like a manicured fingernail. Its feet are already webbed, there is yellow among its feathers, and its downy wings are starting to protrude. Its personality already sets it apart from its foster brothers.

And we men will soon be flying to Venus; if we all pooled our efforts, we could plow up the whole world in twenty minutes.

Yet, with all our atomic might, we shall

Overhanging Cloud in July, 1947–1959, Charles Burchfield.

4 never—never!—be able to make this feeble speck of a yellow duckling in a test tube; even if we were given the feathers and bones, we could never put such a creature together.

A Storm in the Mountains

It caught us one pitch-black night at the foot of the pass. We crawled out of our tents and ran for shelter as it came towards us over the ridge.

Everything was black—no peaks, no valleys, no horizon to be seen, only the searing flashes of lightning separating darkness from light, and the gigantic peaks of Belaya-Kaya and Djugutur-lyuchat[1] looming up out of the night. The huge black pine trees around us seemed as high as the mountains themselves. For a split second we felt ourselves on terra firma;[2] then once more everything would be plunged into darkness and chaos.

5 The lightning moved on, brilliant light alternating with pitch blackness, flashing white, then pink, then violet, the mountains and pines always springing back in the same place, their hugeness filling us with awe; yet when they disappeared we could not believe that they had ever existed.

The voice of the thunder filled the gorge, drowning the ceaseless roar of the rivers. Like the arrows of Sabaoth,[3] the lightning flashes rained down on the peaks, then split up into serpentine streams as though bursting into spray against the rock face, or striking and then shattering like a living thing.

As for us, we forgot to be afraid of the lightning, the thunder, and the downpour, just as a droplet in the ocean has no fear of a hurricane. Insignificant yet grateful, we became part of this world—a primal world in creation before our eyes.

---

1. **Belaya-Kaya** [bye li′ə kī′ə] **and Djuguturlyuchat** [djōō gōō tōōr lyōō′chət]: Russian mountains.
2. **terra firma** [ter′ə fur′mə]: Latin expression for "solid earth."
3. **Sabaoth** [sab′ē äth′]: biblical word for "armies."

Three Prose Poems **411**

CRITICAL THINKING: GUIDED READING QUESTIONS

LITERAL

1a. What animal hatched the duckling? (a hen)

2a. What does the author claim to have become a part of during the storm? ("a primal world in creation")

INFERENTIAL

1b. Why might this have been necessary? (Perhaps the mother duck died or abandoned her eggs.)

2b. To what might this phrase refer? (the world as being constantly renewed, as symbolized by the lightning, which seems to call the mountains and trees into being)

Do you think that the author's ideas would have been better expressed in the form of verse? Why or why not?

STUDY QUESTIONS

1. under a blossoming apple tree; He can see the tree, grass, and five-story houses; he can hear motorcycles, radios, and loudspeakers.
2. It was hatched by a hen. He picks it up.
3. lightning and thunder
4. Freedom is precious and makes life bearable.
5. Life is full of awesome mystery and beauty.
6. Answers will vary. Possible answers include adjectives such as *awed, humbled, exhilarated,* and *amazed.*
7. Answers will vary. Possible answers include a feeling of peace, a sense of harmony, and a greater appreciation of beauty.

LITERARY FOCUS

touch ("weighs nothing," "the slightest squeeze," "warm with life") and sight ("little black eyes," "feet are like sparrows' feet," "little beak is pale pink and slightly splayed," etc.)

STUDY QUESTIONS

Recalling

1. Where is the author standing in "Freedom to Breathe"? What can he see and hear?
2. Why does the little yellow duckling in "The Duckling" have no mommy? What does the writer do when he realizes the duckling is lost?
3. What two aspects of the storm does the author describe in paragraphs 3 and 4 of "A Storm in the Mountains"?

Interpreting

4. What do you think the author wants his readers to understand about freedom in "Freedom to Breathe"?
5. What is the author's main idea in "The Duckling"?
6. Which single adjective would you use to describe the writer's feelings about nature in "A Storm in the Mountains"? Explain your answer.

Extending

7. What do you think we can experience from close contact with animals and nature that we may miss in our interactions with humans?

LITERARY FOCUS

Sensory Language

Sensory language is descriptive language that appeals to one or more of the five senses: sight, hearing, smell, taste, and touch. Writers use sensory language to make people, places, objects, and experiences especially vivid to their readers. Although this type of language is often associated with poetry, writers of prose also use sensory language for vivid effects. Solzhenitsyn uses sensory language in his three prose poems to evoke more fully the emotions he describes.

Thinking About Sensory Language

■ Which senses does Solzhenitsyn appeal to in his description of the small bird in the third paragraph of "The Duckling"? Give specific examples of sensory language from the selection to support your answer.

COMPOSITION

Writing a Prose Poem

■ Choose a single setting that stands out in your mind, and write your own brief prose poem to describe the scene. First make a list of details of sight, hearing, smell, taste, and touch that you think will give your readers an eyewitness view of the setting. Then use sensory, poetic language to convey each of these details in prose. Be sure that all your details contribute to a single, vivid, overall impression or mood.

412　*Nonfiction*

COMPOSITION: GUIDELINES FOR EVALUATION

WRITING A PROSE POEM

Objective
To describe a single setting in a prose poem

Guidelines for Evaluation
■ suggested length: one or two paragraphs
■ should include vivid details
■ should use sensory language
■ should create a single, overall impression

Juan Ramón Jiménez

(1881–1958)

Spain

Poet Juan Ramón Jiménez [hwän rä môn′ hē mä′neth] was born in the town of Moguer in the southern region of Spain that is known as Andalusia. After he completed his studies at the University of Seville, Jiménez started to write poetry. Soon after moving to Madrid, he came under the influence of the Spanish Symbolists. His first books of poetry, *Violet Souls* and *Water Lilies,* appeared in 1900. Over the next decade his poetry grew richer, developing its characteristic delicacy of feeling, technical innovation, and gentle lyricism. In 1914 he published his masterpiece, *Platero and I.* The blend of fantasy and realism in these charming prose poems has endeared them to children and adults.

During his long career Jiménez continued to write poetry, critical essays, and nonfiction while he worked as an editor for literary journals in Spain. In 1936, following the outbreak of the Spanish Civil War, he and his wife settled permanently in Puerto Rico. Jiménez, widely acclaimed as one of the most sensitive, original voices in modern Spanish literature, was awarded the Nobel Prize for Literature in 1956.

GEOGRAPHY AND CULTURE

Spain and Andalusia

Like its neighbor, France, Spain is notable for its varied regions, each with its own distinctive geography, history, culture, and folk traditions. The region of Andalusia, where Juan Ramón Jimenéz was born, is in the south. Famous for its mild climate, beautiful mountains, and bullfighting tradition, Andalusia is largely rural.

The regional capital is the city of Seville. Other important centers are the seaport of Cádiz and the cities of Granada and Córdoba, which preserve stunningly beautiful examples of architecture in the Arab style. The most famous of these is the Alhambra, a Moorish palace near Granada that was built in the thirteenth and fourteenth centuries.

In the selections from *Platero and I* that follow, Jimenéz vividly conveys impressions of rural life in this region of bright colors, majestic landscapes, and fragrant orange trees.

See LITERATURE AND CULTURE SOURCEBOOK:
Spain

Platero and I **413**

LESSON PREVIEW

This selection contains four prose poems about the experiences of a man traveling with his donkey in Spain. The first describes the animal itself; the second, poor children at play; the third, an eclipse of the sun; the fourth, fear on a moonlit night. The works are delicately crafted, lyrical, and filled with insights into nature and human feeling.

LITERARY SKILLS FOR THIS SELECTION

- simile
- symbol

THEMES IN THIS SELECTION

- hope and fear
- the power of nature

LESSON OBJECTIVES

1. to write about nonfiction
2. to write a prose poem
3. to compare essays

Teacher's Classroom Resources 3

■ Teaching Notes	71
■ Reading Guide	72
■ Check Test	73
■ Responding to World Cultures	74
■ Writing Process Guides: Writing About Nonfiction	75
Writing a Prose Poem	76
■ Grammar in Literature: Compatibility of Tenses	77
■ Selection Test	78

IN THE CLASSROOM

TEACHING STUDENTS OF DIFFERENT ABILITIES

- **For less advanced students:** Although the selection seems quite accessible, you should help students look for the truths that lie beneath the deceptively simple surface of the material. Ask students to complete the Reading Guide for this selection.
- **For more advanced students:** Encourage students to read other selections from *Platero and I* and report on their specific subject matter and themes.

DISCUSSING GEOGRAPHY AND CULTURE

Migrations

Andalusia is one of Spain's poorest regions. Those who cannot find work on its haciendas—which produce wheat, grapes, and olives—flock to nearby towns or to the industrial cities of the north. In the United States people also move from one region to another: Today the West is gaining in population, while many eastern cities are shrinking.

- Ask students to discuss the reasons that Americans move from region to region.

MOTIVATION: PRIOR KNOWLEDGE

Ask students to think about the kind of animal they might select as a pet or companion and why. Have them explain what they would hope to gain by having such an animal. Point out that this selection is about experiences a man has while traveling with his donkey.

PAGE SUMMARY: AT A GLANCE

- The author describes the appearance, habits, and disposition of his donkey, Platero.
- People admire the strong and sturdy donkey.

IN THE GLOSSARY

- scarabs: gems cut in the shape of beetles

1 TEACHING SIMILES

Direct students' attention to the use of simile, or the comparison of dissimilar things—in this case, eyes and crystals—through use of *like* or *as*. Such similes are used frequently in prose poems. Ask the students to find another example of this figure of speech in the next paragraph. ("a gay little trot that is like laughter")

2 CULTURAL BACKGROUND

Explain that the author conveys impressions of rural life in the region of Andalusia in the south of Spain. This region is rich in bright colors, beautiful landscapes, and fragrant orange trees. In this passage the bright colors of Andalusia are reflected in the vivid descriptions of the food.

ART AND LITERATURE

Despite his tragically brief career, Mexican painter Abraham Angel (1905–1924) earned a reputation for imbuing his simple paintings with an ennobling quality. Here he paints a lone peasant and mule moving with an almost regal bearing through a quiet Mexican town.

- Ask students what sentence in "Platero" seems to describe the little mule in the painting. ("Steel and moon silver at the same time.")

The Little Mule, 1923, Abraham Angel.

Juan Ramón Jiménez

from **Platero and I**

Translated from the Spanish by Eloïse Roach

Platero

Platero is a small donkey, a soft, hairy donkey: so soft to the touch that he might be said to be made of cotton, with no bones. Only the jet mirrors of his eyes are hard like two black crystal scarabs.

I turn him loose, and he goes to the meadow, and, with his nose, he gently caresses the little flowers of rose and blue and gold. . . . I call him softly, "Platero?" and he comes to me at a gay little trot that is like laughter of a vague, idyllic, tinkling sound.

He eats whatever I give him. He likes mandarin oranges, amber-hued muscatel grapes, purple figs tipped with crystalline drops of honey.

He is as loving and tender as a child, but strong and sturdy as a rock. When on Sundays I ride him through the lanes in the outskirts of the town, slow-moving countrymen, dressed in their Sunday clean, watch him awhile, speculatively:

"He is like steel," they say.

Steel, yes. Steel and moon silver at the same time.

Twilight Games

At dusk, when, stiff with cold, Platero and I enter the purple darkness of the miserable

414   *Nonfiction*

CRITICAL THINKING: GUIDED READING QUESTIONS

LITERAL

1a. In what way is Platero like a child? (He is loving and tender.)

2a. To what two metals is Platero compared? (steel and "moon silver")

INFERENTIAL

1b. What does this description tell you about the author's feelings for the donkey? (He is very fond of Platero.)

2b. What do these metals seem to symbolize? (The steel might symbolize strength; the silver, ethereal grace and beauty.)

bystreet that fronts the dry river bed, the children of the poor are playing at make-believe, frightening one another, playing beggars. One throws a sack over his head, another says he is blind, another limps. . . .

Later, with that fickleness of childhood, since they at least wear shoes and clothes, and since their mothers—though only they know how—have fed them, they become princes and princesses.

3
"My father has a silver clock."

"Mine has a horse."

"Mine a gun."

Clock to rouse him at daybreak; gun that cannot kill hunger; horse to take him to misery. . . .

Then the children join hands, dancing in a circle. In the darkness a little girl with fragile voice like a thread of liquid crystal in the shadow sings proudly like a princess:

> I am the young widow
> Of great Count Oré. . . .

Aye, aye! Sing, dream, children of the poor! Soon, at the awakening of your youth, spring, like a beggar disguised as winter, will frighten you.

"Let us go, Platero."

Eclipse

We unwittingly put our hands in our pockets, and on our brows we felt the fine touch of a cool shadow, as when entering a thick pine forest. The chickens began going up their perch, one by one. All around, the countryside darkened its greenness, as if the purple veil of the main altar were spread over it. The distant sea was visible as a white vision, and a few stars shone palely. How the whiteness of the roofs took on a changed whiteness! Those of us who were on the roofs called to each other more or less wittily, small dark creatures in the confining silence of the eclipse.

We tried looking at the sun through all sorts of things: opera glasses, telescopes, bottles, smoked glass; and from all angles: the dormer window,[1] the ladder in the yard, the granary window; through the scarlet and blue panes of the skylight. . . .

On hiding, the sun, which a moment before made everything twice, thrice, a hundred times greater and better with its complexities of light 4 and gold, now leaves all things, without the long transition of twilight, lonely and poverty-stricken as though one had exchanged gold for silver first and then silver for copper. The town resembles a musty and valueless copper cent. How gloomy and unimportant the streets, the squares, the tower, the mountain roads.

Down in the yard Platero appears less real, different and diminished, a different donkey. . . .

Fear

5
Large, round, pure, the moon comes with us. In the sleepy meadows we see shadowy forms like black goats among the blackberry bushes. At our passing, someone hides noiselessly. A huge almond tree, snowy with blooms and moonlight, its top enveloped in a white cloud, shadows the 6 road shot with March stars. A penetrating smell of oranges. Dampness and silence. The witches' glen. . . .

"Platero, it is . . . cold!"

Platero—I do not know whether spurred on by his fear or by mine—trots, enters the creek bed, steps on the moon and breaks it into pieces. It is as if a swarm of clear crystal roses were entangled at his feet, trying to hold him. . . .

And Platero trots uphill, shortening his croup[2] as if someone were after him, already sensing the soft warmth—which seems unattainable—of the approaching town.

---

1. **dormer window:** window in an upright projection that juts out from a sloping roof.
2. **croup** [kro͞op]: back part of a donkey, a horse, etc.

Platero and I **415**

CRITICAL THINKING: GUIDED READING QUESTIONS

LITERAL

1a. How does Platero appear during the eclipse? (He seems "less real, different and diminished.")

2a. As Platero trots uphill on the moonlit night, what does the "soft warmth" of the approaching town seem? ("unattainable")

INFERENTIAL

1b. What idea about nature might this suggest? (All creatures seem insignificant when confronted with the power of nature.)

2b. Why does it seem unattainable? (Their fear makes the author and his donkey feel that they will never be safe and warm again.)

- The author sees poor children at play and reflects on their harsh lives.
- An eclipse makes the town look gloomy and unimportant to him.
- He feels cold and afraid as he travels on a moonlit night.
- Platero crosses the creek and trots toward the town.

IN THE GLOSSARY

- transition: passage or change
- entangled: caught in a tangle

3 READING SKILL: CONTRAST

Have students contrast the children's and the author's ideas about the clock, horse, and gun. (The children see them as beautiful, useful sources of pride and pleasure. The author sees them as symbols of hopelessness and toil.)

4 TEACHING SYMBOLS

Direct students' attention to the references to the three metals as double symbols, standing for both the diminution of light and worth.

5 TEACHING FIGURES OF SPEECH

Point out that in this passage the author uses personification (describing the moon) and simile (comparing shadowy forms with black goats). Ask students to describe the effect of these two figures of speech. (They intensify the fearful, gloomy mood of the poem.)

6 GRAMMAR IN LITERATURE

Point out that the author purposely uses incomplete sentences to obtain an effect. What effect is created? (one of tension, mystery)

COLLABORATIVE LEARNING: ENRICHMENT ACTIVITY

Travel Brochure Have a research group create an Andalusian travel brochure featuring history, architecture, art, literature, music, and food. Assign each student a city, such as Seville, Córdoba, Granada, Cádiz, or Málaga. Students should collect maps and photographs to illustrate the brochure.

Do experiences such as those in "Twilight Games," "Eclipse," and "Fear" generally heighten or decrease the sense of the value of human life? Explain.

ANSWERS

STUDY QUESTIONS

1. a creature made of "cotton, with no bones"; eyes are hard, "like two black crystal scarabs"; trot is like "tinkling" laughter; and so on
2. At first they pretend to be beggars and then princes and princesses.
3. gold, silver, and copper
4. He enters the creek bed and trots uphill toward town.
5. The donkey is loving and tender yet strong and sturdy.
6. They will be exposed to harsher realities.
7. Possible answer: the dangers of death, separation, and loneliness
8. They are like prose in the dialogue and in the sequence of sentences and paragraphs, but they are like poetry in their use of figurative language and sensory images and in their conciseness.

COMPARING ESSAYS

The objective of the essay is to compare and contrast the Solzhenitsyn and Jiménez selections. The essay should be three or four paragraphs long. Students should comment on the authors' use of sensory language and compare and contrast the authors' purposes.

STUDY QUESTIONS

Recalling

1. Find at least three comparisons that the writer uses in "Platero" for the appearance and behavior of the donkey.
2. When the children play in "Twilight Games," what do they pretend to be?
3. What three metals does the narrator compare the sun's light to in "Eclipse"?
4. What does Platero do in reaction to his fear—or the narrator's fear—in the last section, "Fear"?

Interpreting

5. What apparently opposite qualities does the donkey possess in "Platero"?
6. Explain in your own words the narrator's prediction about the children's lives at the end of "Twilight Games."
7. What symbolic interpretation of the darkness and cold do the details in "Fear" suggest to you?

Extending

8. In what ways are these essays both similar to and different from poetry?

COMPOSITION

Writing About Nonfiction

- In a brief essay discuss Jiménez's purpose in writing *Platero and I.* First explain what you think is the purpose of the essays, the effect that Jimé-nez wanted them to have. Then cite with examples the particular techniques that he uses to accomplish that purpose. You may want to consider the following: (a) narration, (b) description, (c) figurative language, and (d) tone. *For help with this assignment, refer to Lesson 8 in the Writing About Literature Handbook at the back of this book.*

Writing a Prose Poem

- In the manner of Jiménez, write a poetic essay that describes an object and hints at emotions that the object awakens. To do so, describe an object in prose, but choose words and images carefully to reveal the feelings associated with the object. You may choose any object for the description, but you may want to consider one of the following: (a) a hamburger, (b) a catcher's mitt (or other piece of sports equipment), (c) a lawnmower, (d) a favorite item of clothing, or (e) a caterpillar.

COMPARING ESSAYS

- Write a short composition comparing and contrasting "Three Prose Poems" by Aleksandr Solzhenitsyn with the selections from *Platero and I* by Juan Ramón Jiménez. In your paper comment on how each author uses sensory language. Also compare and contrast the purposes of both authors in these selections.

COMPOSITION: GUIDELINES FOR EVALUATION

WRITING ABOUT NONFICTION

Objective

To discuss the author's purpose

Guidelines for Evaluation

- suggested length: three or four paragraphs
- should explain the purpose of the essays
- should cite examples of techniques used
- should consider elements such as narration, description, figurative language, and tone

WRITING A PROSE POEM

Objective

To write a poetic essay in the manner of Jiménez

Guidelines for Evaluation

- suggested length: three or four paragraphs
- should describe an object and hint at emotions called forth by it
- should use words and images to reveal associated feelings

Camilo José Cela

(born 1916)

Spain

Camilo José Cela, [kä mē′lō hō sā′ sā′lä], who won the Nobel Prize for Literature in 1989, was born in the small village of Iria-Flavia in the northern region of Galicia [gə lish′ə] in Spain. The son of a Spanish father and an English mother, Cela studied at the University of Madrid and fought with Nationalist troops on the side of General Francisco Franco during the Spanish Civil War (1936–1939).

Cela gained wide recognition in Spain with the publication of his powerful first novel, *Pascual Duarte's Family* (1942). This novel foreshadowed some of Cela's preoccupations in his later fiction, such as oppression and poverty. His novel *The Hive* (1951), boldly experimental in style and structure, presents a panoramic view of postwar Madrid.

Cela has also written several travel books. His keen powers of observation and skill with vivid descriptive language are especially clear in these works, drawn from his walking tours through Spain and Latin American countries. The upcoming selection is part of his celebrated account of a walking tour through the Spanish countryside, entitled *Journey to the Alcarria* (1948).

GEOGRAPHY AND CULTURE

Spain and the Alcarria

The Alcarria is a largely rural region of Spain northeast of the capital city, Madrid, in the territory traditionally called New Castile. The landscape is high, rocky, and dry, for the province of New Castile is located in the southern part of a vast plateau whose average height is 2,000 feet. Bounded on all sides by mountain ranges, the region of the Alcarria is chiefly agricultural; it is famous for its honey, wheat, tomatoes, and olives. The castles and ruined palaces that dot the countryside bear witness to Spain's past glories. Most of these beautiful castles, called *alcázars,* date back to the Middle Ages.

When he planned his walking tour through the Alcarria [äl cä′rē ä], Cela was living in Madrid. As "Traveling in the Alcarria" opens, the author—who refers to himself as "the traveler"—is about to enter the small town of Fuentes de la Alcarria.

See *LITERATURE AND CULTURE SOURCEBOOK: Spain*

Traveling in the Alcarria **417**

Set in a rural region northeast of Madrid, this selection records the author's perceptive observations of landscape and architecture as he proceeds on a walking tour. It also moves beyond the realm of typical travel writing in its sensitive portrayal of two of the local people to whom the author speaks: a young woman in mourning and an old farmer.

LITERARY SKILLS FOR THIS SELECTION

- figurative language
- description
- purpose

THEMES IN THIS SELECTION

- impressions on a journey
- beauty and sorrow

LESSON OBJECTIVES

1. to recognize figurative language
2. to analyze style

Teacher's Classroom Resources 3

■ Teaching Notes	81
■ Reading Guide	82
■ Check Test	83
■ Responding to World Cultures	84
■ Literary Focus: Figurative Language	85
■ Writing Process Guide: Analyzing Style	86
■ Grammar in Literature: Writing with Vivid Adjectives	87
■ Selection Test	88

TEACHING STUDENTS OF DIFFERENT ABILITIES

- **For less advanced students:** Encourage students to focus on the writer's insights into the influence of geography on human behavior. Have students complete the Reading Guide for this selection.

- **For more advanced students:** Ask students to think about the ways in which the qualities of climate and terrain in a place such as the Alcarria may affect character and temperament.

Spain's Medieval Castles

Castile's castles were built during the fourteenth and fifteenth centuries, when Spain's eight-hundred-year battle against the Moors (Moslems) was ending. Often built atop high hills, the fortified castles protected the lands that Spain's Catholic rulers had reconquered from the Moors. Today some of these ancient castles have been turned into hotels called *paradores*.

- Ask students to discuss the past and present uses of a historical building they know about.

Camilo José Cela

Traveling in the Alcarria

Translated from the Spanish by Frances M. López-Morillas

1 Fuentes de la Alcarria[1] is at the right of the road. The little oak wood has become thicker. The countryside has a strong deep smell, and bees are sucking in the thorn bushes with their masses of tiny white flowers. Two rabbits, crouched back with their ears twitching, stare at the traveler for an instant and then run away quickly to hide behind some rocks. An eagle is flying in circles overhead, not far away. A woman riding on a donkey meets and passes the traveler. He speaks to her, and the woman nei- 2 ther looks at him nor answers. She is a young woman, pale and beautiful, dressed in mourning, with a kerchief on her head and with great deep dark eyes. The traveler turns around. The woman is absolutely motionless, letting the pace of the strong, sturdy donkey carry her along. One would think she was a dead woman without mourners, going alone to the cemetery to be buried.

The traveler takes an extra swallow of wine for comfort, and goes to sit at the foot of a tree near the walls of the palace of Ibarra, which is beside the highway. The palace of Ibarra is a huge place half in ruins, with an abandoned garden which is full of enchantment; it is like an exhausted dancer, gentle and ill, breathing the health-giving air of the countryfolk. The garden is choked with undergrowth. A goat tied with a rope is dozing and chewing, stretched out in the sun, and a hairy little donkey is frisking about, 3 kicking at the air like a mad creature. A tall, slim Japanese pine rises out of the brambles; it has a graceful and aristocratic air and seems like an

old ruined nobleman, formerly proud but today the debtor of those who used to serve him.

A league[2] farther on, the wood comes to an end and there is cultivated land again. A few puddles are visible in the fields. An old man complains to the traveler.

"Don't you believe that's a good thing. It's rained too much. The Alcarria needs its water, you know, but not too much and not too little."

The traveler thinks to himself that a man who talks like that runs the risk of always being right.

---

2. **league:** measure of distance equaling about three miles.

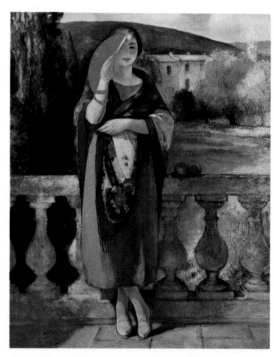

Jeune fille à l'éventail, 1920, Henri Lebasque.

---

1. **Fuentes de la Alcarria** [fwen′tes dä lä äl kär′ē ä]: town in the Alcarria region of Spain. (See the Geography and Culture feature that precedes the selection.)

418 *Nonfiction*

CRITICAL THINKING: GUIDED READING QUESTIONS

LITERAL

1a. What does the woman do when the author speaks to her? (She neither looks at him nor answers.)

INFERENTIAL

1b. Why does she act this way? (She is in deep sorrow and is not aware of the world around her.)

STUDY QUESTIONS

Recalling

1. As the traveler approaches Fuentes de la Alcarria, whom does he meet?
2. After this meeting where does the traveler go?
3. What complaint does the old man make to the traveler?

Interpreting

4. In what way does the sight of the young woman on the donkey sharply contrast with the description of Fuentes de la Alcarria at the beginning of the essay?
5. In your opinion what mood is created by the description of the palace of Ibarra?
6. What does the last sentence of the essay imply about the traveler's impression of the old man?

Extending

7. Imagine that you, like Camilo José Cela, were planning a walking tour to collect material for a travel book. Where would you go, and why? What kind of material would you find especially interesting?

LITERARY FOCUS

Figurative Language

Figurative language is language used for descriptive effect, often to imply ideas indirectly. Figurative language appears often in poetry, but prose writers also use figures of speech to shake up our imaginations and to help us see the world in new ways. Common figures of speech include similes and metaphors, which are used to compare seemingly unlike things. A **simile** uses a word such as *like* or *as* to make the comparison. A **metaphor** directly compares or equates two things.

Thinking About Figurative Language

■ Identify two similes that describe the palace of Ibarra. What mood do they help to create?

COMPOSITION

Analyzing Style

■ In a brief composition analyze Cela's style, or choice and arrangement of words. Pay special attention to his use of figurative language, and comment on how the author's style may relate to his purpose.

READER'S RESPONSE

Are the experiences related by the author the sort you would enjoy having on a trip? Why or why not?

ANSWERS

STUDY QUESTIONS

1. a young woman in mourning on a donkey
2. He goes to sit at the foot of a tree near the walls of the palace of Ibarra.
3. He complains that it has rained too much.
4. The countryside is vibrant with life; she is motionless, like "a dead woman without mourners."
5. Students will most likely describe the mood as sad.
6. The traveler reacts in a light-hearted manner to what he sees as the man's simple, homespun wisdom.
7. Answers will vary. Some students might mention exotic destinations, while others might argue that a walking tour in their own region would be most interesting.

LITERARY FOCUS

The garden of the palace is described as an "exhausted dancer"; one of its trees is likened to a "ruined nobleman." The mood is melancholy.

COMPOSITION: GUIDELINES FOR EVALUATION

ANALYZING STYLE

Objective

To analyze the author's style

Guidelines for Evaluation

■ suggested length: three or four paragraphs
■ should identify examples of figurative language
■ should comment on the relationship between the author's style and purpose

In this descriptive essay the author recounts several experiences she had in Africa that helped her realize that natural objects are most beautiful in their proper setting. She tells of shooting an iguana for its beautiful skin only to discover that its beauty faded with the creature's life. Anecdotes about a bracelet and a fish illustrate variations on the same lesson.

LITERARY SKILLS FOR THIS SELECTION

- descriptive essay
- theme
- symbol

THEMES IN THIS SELECTION

- beauty and its natural setting
- the wonders of nature
- the value of life

LESSON OBJECTIVES

1. to understand descriptive essays
2. to write a descriptive essay

Teacher's Classroom Resources 3

- Teaching Notes   91
- Reading Guide   92
- Check Test   93
- Responding to World Cultures   94
- Literary Focus: Descriptive Essay   95
- Writing Process Guide: Writing a Descriptive Essay   96
- Grammar in Literature: Participles Used as Adjectives   97
- Selection Test   98

TEACHING STUDENTS OF DIFFERENT ABILITIES

- **For less advanced students:** To help students recognize the connection between the selection's three anecdotes, emphasize the theme they have in common. Ask students to complete the Reading Guide.
- **For more advanced students:** Encourage students to analyze the changes in outlook the author undergoes as a result of the experiences she describes.

Isak Dinesen (1885–1962)

Denmark/Kenya

Isak Dinesen [ē'säk dē'nə sən] studied to become a painter but gained fame as one of the century's best novelists. She was born Karen Dinesen in Ringsted, Denmark. In 1914 she married a distant cousin, the Swedish Baron Blixen, and traveled with him to settle in the part of British East Africa that is now Kenya. For seven years she and her husband owned and managed a large coffee plantation in the hills. After their divorce in 1921, Dinesen continued to run the plantation until it failed ten years later.

During this period she began to write, in both English and Danish, to occupy herself during the long rainy seasons. Although she published under a variety of pseudonyms, her best-known pen name was Isak Dinesen. She has been widely praised for her collections of short stories, including *Seven Gothic Tales* (1934) and *Winter's Tales* (1943). In 1931 Dinesen returned to live and write in Denmark. In addition to her fiction, she published two volumes of memoirs. The upcoming selection is drawn from *Out of Africa* (1937), a book that was recently the basis for a highly acclaimed film about Dinesen's life in Africa.

420   *Nonfiction*

Kenya: Preserve of Natural Beauty

Until it gained independence in 1963, Kenya had been a British colony, part of the region of British East Africa for almost seventy years. The tremendously varied terrain of Kenya, which straddles the equator, includes vast plains, tropical beaches and swamps along the coast, and well-watered highlands. Isak Dinesen's coffee plantation was located in the Ngong [nə gong'] Hills, near the capital city of Nairobi.

Together with its southern neighbor, Tanzania, Kenya boasts one of the last great concentrations of wildlife in the world. The spectacular animals, including elephants, zebras, giraffes, lions, leopards, and rhinoceroses, are not only a major tourist attraction but the focus of international concern as well, since many species are threatened by extinction. In "The Iguana" Dinesen bears eloquent witness to the beauty of nature in her adopted country.

See LITERATURE AND CULTURE SOURCEBOOK: Africa

Parks and Preservation

Kenya, which attracts more tourists than any other African country, has more than twenty-four thousand square miles set aside as wildlife sanctuaries. These reserves, like our national parks, provide tourists with a sense of what Kenya was like before the human population altered the landscape.

- Ask students to describe a national or state park they have visited. Why are these large park systems important?

T-420   Nonfiction

Isak Dinesen

The Iguana

In the Reserve[1] I have sometimes come upon the Iguana, the big lizards, as they were sunning themselves upon a flat stone in a river-bed. They are not pretty in shape, but nothing can be imagined more beautiful than their coloring. They shine like a heap of precious stones or like a pane cut out of an old church window. When, as you approach, they swish away, there is a flash of azure, green and purple over the stones, the color seems to be standing behind them in the air, like a comet's luminous tail.

Once I shot an Iguana. I thought that I should be able to make some pretty things from his skin. A strange thing happened then, that I have never afterwards forgotten. As I went up to him, where he was lying dead upon his stone, and actually while I was walking the few steps, he faded and grew pale, all color died out of him as in one long sigh, and by the time that I touched him he was gray and dull like a lump of concrete. It was the live impetuous blood pulsating within the animal, which had radiated out all that glow and splendor. Now that the flame was put out, and the soul had flown, the Iguana was as dead as a sandbag.

Often since I have, in some sort, shot an Iguana, and I have remembered the one of the Reserve. Up at Meru[2] I saw a young native girl with a bracelet on, a leather strap two inches wide, and embroidered all over with very small turquoise-colored beads which varied a little in color and played in green, light blue and ultramarine. It was an extraordinarily live thing; it seemed to draw breath on her arm, so that I wanted it for myself, and made Farah[3] buy it from her. No sooner had it come upon my own arm than it gave up the ghost.[4] It was nothing now, a small, cheap, purchased article of finery. It had been the play of colors, the duet between the turquoise and the "nègre"—that quick, sweet, brownish black, like peat and black pottery, of the native's skin—that had created the life of the bracelet.

In the Zoological Museum of Pietermaritzburg,[5] I have seen, in a stuffed deep-water fish in a showcase, the same combination of coloring, which there had survived death; it made me wonder what life can well be like, on the bottom of the sea, to send up something so live and airy. I stood in Meru and looked at my pale hand and at the dead bracelet; it was as if an injustice had been done to a noble thing, as if truth had been suppressed. So sad did it seem that I remembered the saying of the hero in a book that I had read as a child: "I have conquered them all, but I am standing amongst graves."

In a foreign country and with foreign species of life one should take measures to find out whether things will be keeping their value when dead. To the settlers of East Africa I give the advice: "For the sake of your own eyes and heart, shoot not the Iguana."

---

1. **Reserve:** game sanctuary in the Ngong [n gong'] Hills of Kenya. (See the Geography and Culture feature that precedes the selection.)
2. **Meru** [mä´roo]: mountain in what is now Tanzania.
3. **Farah:** the author's servant.
4. **gave up the ghost:** expression meaning here, "lost its life and beauty."
5. **Pietermaritzburg** [pē´tər mer´its burg']: city in South Africa.

The Iguana 421

Do you think we have the right to kill animals for food and clothing? Why or why not?

STUDY QUESTIONS

1. a heap of precious stones; a pane from a church window
2. She thought she could make pretty things from its skin.
3. It seemed to lose its color and die.
4. a colorful stuffed fish; She wonders what life could be like at the bottom of the sea.
5. Both show a failure to see that many beautiful things are better left in their natural environment.
6. Like them it illustrates the vanity of ownership.
7. Beauty should be left unmolested; killing things destroys their value.
8. Answers will vary. Students should understand that much of the beauty of natural objects derives from their proper setting.

LITERARY FOCUS

1. the iguana grows pale (sight); the iguana's color as it dies is like "one long sigh" (sight and hearing); dead, the iguana is "gray and dull like a lump of concrete" (touch and sight); alive, its blood was "pulsating" (touch and sight); its death "put out [the flame]" (sight)
2. Her chief purpose was to point out that people, in their quest to acquire beautiful things, can lose sight of the natural beauty that exists in harmony with the environment.

STUDY QUESTIONS

Recalling

1. To what does the writer compare the beautiful iguanas in the first paragraph of the essay?
2. In the second paragraph what reason does the author give for shooting the iguana?
3. What happened to the embroidered bracelet when the author put it on?
4. What does the writer report having seen in the Zoological Museum of Pietermaritzburg? What thought does this sight prompt in her?

Interpreting

5. In what way is the incident of shooting the iguana similar to the incident involving the bracelet?
6. Discuss how the quotation Dinesen cites at the end of the fourth paragraph relates to the incidents she describes in her essay.
7. What does the author mean in the last line of the essay when she advises East African settlers to "shoot not the Iguana"?

Extending

8. Explain why you think objects in nature often lose their beauty when they are removed from their proper setting.

LITERARY FOCUS

Descriptive Essay

A **descriptive essay** re-creates a person, an object, a place, or a scene in the reader's imagination.

Good descriptive writing creates a strong impression of its subject for a particular *purpose,* which is to illustrate vividly a general idea or an observation about life.

A descriptive essay leads the reader to such observations by presenting specific details and concrete language that add up to an overall idea about life. **Concrete language** is another name for sensory language, or words that appeal to our senses of sight, hearing, taste, smell, and touch.

Thinking About the Descriptive Essay

1. Identify at least three uses of concrete language in the second paragraph of the essay. To which senses do your examples of concrete language appeal?
2. State in a sentence or two what you believe to be Dinesen's chief purpose in writing "The Iguana."

COMPOSITION

Writing a Descriptive Essay

■ Dinesen combines three distinct examples in her descriptive essay to produce a unified effect: the iguana, the bracelet, and the fish. Write a short descriptive essay in which you combine at least two examples of scenes, objects, places, or people. First identify the elements for your description and decide on a purpose. Then use concrete language to create a vivid, overall impression in your reader's imagination.

COMPOSITION: GUIDELINES FOR EVALUATION

WRITING A DESCRIPTIVE ESSAY

Objective

To write a descriptive essay that combines examples of scenes, objects, places, or people

Guidelines for Evaluation

- suggested length: three or four paragraphs
- should present at least two scenes, objects, places, or people
- should use vivid, concrete language

PREVIEW: THE AUTHOR AND THE WORLD

Thucydides

(c. 460–400 B.C.)

Ancient Greece

One of the greatest historians of the Western world was also one of the first — Thucydides [thoo sid′ə dēz′]. However, little is known about his life; even his dates of birth and death must be inferred by modern historians from references in his *History of the Peloponnesian War*. He was probably born in or near Athens to a wealthy, upper-class family. In 424 B.C. he was appointed general in command of the Athenian fleet off the Thracian coast. When he failed to prevent a major defeat, the Spartan capture of Amphipolis, he was sent into exile.

He devoted the next quarter of a century to the composition of his life's work, the *History of the Peloponnesian War*. In his attempt to present the most accurate account possible, he interviewed participants and eyewitnesses on both sides, sifted through statements others had made, and presented his results in concise, chronological order. He often reported the words of especially significant political speeches, as in the upcoming selection. Thucydides is celebrated as the first historian to apply truly rigorous standards of accuracy to his work.

GEOGRAPHY AND CULTURE

Athens and the Peloponnesian War

In ancient times Greece was not a single, unified country but rather a collection of city-states, each with its own government and sphere of influence. The most powerful and brilliant city-state in the fifth century B.C. was Athens, whose enduring achievements in democratic government, philosophy, and literature owe much to the brilliant leadership of Pericles [per′ə klēz′] (c. 495–429 B.C.). The undisputed leader of Athens, he was elected over fifteen times to the office of general. Under his rule the Athenians built up a great empire throughout Greece and the Aegean Islands.

When the Peloponnesian War erupted in 431 B.C. between Athens and Sparta, Pericles was called upon as head of state to honor the dead by delivering the funeral oration you are about to read. The struggle ended with the defeat of Athens in 404 B.C. and the eclipse of the Athenian civilization.

AREA OF THE PELOPONNESIAN WAR

See *LITERATURE AND CULTURE SOURCEBOOK:*
Ancient Greece and Rome

Pericles' Funeral Oration **423**

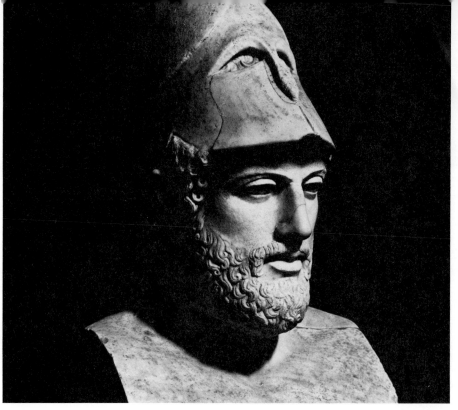

Pericles, c. 450 B.C., possibly by Kresilas.

Thucydides

Pericles' Funeral Oration

Translated from the Greek by Alfred Zimmern and Richard Crawley

1   In the same winter, following the law of their fathers, the Athenians[1] held the first public funeral of those who had fallen in the war. The ceremony is as follows. The bones of the dead are exposed on a covered platform for three days, during which anyone may place his personal offerings at their side. On the third day they are laid in ten coffins of cypress[2] wood, one 2 for each tribe, every man's bones in the coffin of his tribe; these are put on carriages and driven to the grave. One empty bed covered with a winding sheet[3] is also borne for the missing whose bodies were not recovered for burning. All who so desire, whether citizens or strangers, may join in the procession, and the womenfolk of the dead are at the graveside bewailing them. The interment takes place in the State burial ground, which is situated in the most beautiful suburb of the city. All Athenians who have died

---

1. **Athenians** [ə thē'nē ənz]: residents of Athens. (See the Geography and Culture feature that precedes the selection.)
2. **cypress** [sī'prəs]: tree common to swampy areas; its fragrant wood is a traditional symbol of mourning.

3. **winding sheet:** burial garment; shroud.

424   *Nonfiction*

in war lie buried there, except those who fell at Marathon;[4] their valor was adjudged so conspicuous that the funeral was held on the field of battle. When the coffins have been laid in the earth some speaker elected by the city for his wisdom and public estimation delivers an appropriate eulogy; after this the gathering disperses. This is the customary ceremonial, and it was adhered to throughout the war whenever occasion arose. It was at the funeral of this first group of fallen that Pericles, the son of Xanthippus,[5] was elected to speak. When the moment came, he stepped forward from the graveside on to a high platform made for the occasion, so that his voice might carry as far as possible over the crowd, and spoke as follows:

[3] "Most of those who have stood in this place before me have commended the institution of this closing address. It is good, they have felt, that solemn words should be spoken over our [4] fallen soldiers. I do not share this feeling. Acts deserve acts, not words, in their honor, and to me a burial at the State's charges, such as you see before you, would have appeared sufficient. Our sense of the deserts[6] of a number of our fellow-citizens should not depend upon the felicity[7] of one man's speech. Moreover, it is very hard for a speaker to be appropriate when many of his hearers will scarce believe that he is truthful. For those who have known and loved the dead may think his words scant justice to the memories they would hear honored; while those who do not know will occasionally, from jealousy, suspect me of overstatement when they hear of any feat beyond their own powers. For it is only human for men not to bear praise of others beyond the point at which they still feel that they can rival their exploits. Transgress that

---

4. **Marathon:** plain northeast of Athens where, in 490 B.C., an Athenian army defeated a far larger invading force of Persians.
5. **Xanthippus** [zan tip′əs]
6. **deserts:** rewards or punishments that one deserves.
7. **felicity:** here, the quality of speaking appropriately and pleasingly.

boundary and they are jealous and distrustful. But since the wisdom of our ancestors enacted this law I too must submit and try to suit as best I can the wishes and feelings of every member of this gathering.

"My first words shall be for our ancestors; for it is both just to them and seemly that on an occasion such as this our tribute of memory should be paid them. For, dwelling always in this country, generation after generation in unchanging and unbroken succession, they have handed it down to us free by their exertions. So they are worthy of our praises; and still more so are our fathers. For they enlarged the ancestral patrimony[8] by the Empire which we hold today and delivered it, not without labor, into the hands of our own generation; while it is we ourselves, those of us who are now in middle life, who consolidated our power throughout the greater part of the Empire and secured the city's complete independence both in war and peace. Of the battles which we and our fathers fought, whether in the winning of our power abroad or in bravely withstanding the warfare of foreigner or Greek at home, I do not wish to say more: they are too familiar to you all. I wish rather to set forth the spirit in which we faced them, and the constitution and manners with which we rose to greatness, and to pass from them to the dead; for I think it not unfitting that these things should be called to mind in today's solemnity, and expedient too that the whole gathering of citizens and strangers should listen to them.

"For our government is not copied from those of our neighbors: we are an example to [5] them rather than they to us. Our constitution is named a democracy, because it is in the hands not of the few but of the many. But our laws secure equal justice for all in their private disputes, and our public opinion welcomes and honors talent in every branch of achievement, not for any sectional reason but on grounds of

---

8. **enlarged the ancestral patrimony:** increased the lands that we now inherit.

CRITICAL THINKING: GUIDED READING QUESTIONS

LITERAL

1a. What group of people does Pericles discuss in what he calls his first words? (ancestors)

2a. What does Pericles talk about next? (the government)

INFERENTIAL

1b. Why is this group worthy of honor on this funeral occasion? (They created what those who have been killed died to protect.)

2b. Why does he do this? (The government is one of the things for which the dead fought.)

- Pericles praises the friendly and law-abiding nature of the Athenians.
- He praises Athens for its wealth and its "recreations for the spirit."
- He contrasts the military attitudes of the Athenians with those of the Spartans.
- He praises the Athenian love of beauty, wisdom, reflectiveness, and commitment to public duty.

IN THE GLOSSARY

- churlishness: surliness
- ordinances: laws
- deportations: ejections of foreigners
- vainglory: great vanity
- foredoomed: condemned in advance

6 GRAMMAR IN LITERATURE

Explain this correct use of who rather than the objective whom by pointing out that the object of to is the entire clause "who so notes them"; the nominative who is used because it is the subject of the clause. Point out the error below in an analogous clause in which whomsoever is used instead of the correct whosoever. Give examples of the correct use of whom and whomsoever.

7 READING SKILL: CONTRAST

Ask students to contrast the Athenians with their opponents. (The Athenians are democratic, open, friendly, and relaxed about military preparedness; their opponents, undemocratic, xenophobic, secretive, and laborious in pursuit of courage and military preparedness.)

8 TEACHING ARGUMENT

Explain that Pericles' speech is an argument, a kind of writing in which reason is used to influence ideas or actions. Ask students what opinion Pericles is advancing in this paragraph and how he supports it. (Native, un-self-conscious courage is superior to state-enforced courage, since it makes for a more pleasant peacetime life and does not limit bravery when it is needed.)

excellence alone. And as we give free play to all in our public life, so we carry the same spirit into our daily relations with one another. We have no black looks or angry words for our neighbor if he enjoys himself in his own way, and we abstain from the little acts of churlishness which, though they leave no mark, yet cause annoyance to who so notes them. Open and friendly in our private intercourse, in our public acts we keep strictly within the control of law. We acknowledge the restraint of reverence; we are obedient to whomsoever is set in authority, and to the laws, more especially to those which offer protection to the oppressed and those unwritten ordinances whose transgression brings admitted shame.

"Yet ours is no work-a-day city only. No other provides so many recreations for the spirit—contests and sacrifices all the year round, and beauty in our public buildings to cheer the heart and delight the eye day by day. Moreover, the city is so large and powerful that all the wealth of all the world flows into her, so that our own Attic[9] products seem no more homelike to us than the fruits of the labors of other nations.

"Our military training too is different from our opponents'. The gates of our city are flung open to the world. We practice no periodical deportations, nor do we prevent our visitors from observing or discovering what an enemy might usefully apply to his own purposes. For our trust is not in the devices of material equipment, but in our own good spirits for battle.

"So too with education. They toil from early boyhood in a laborious pursuit after courage, while we, free to live and wander as we please, march out nonetheless to face the self-same dangers. Here is the proof of my words. When the Spartans[10] advance into our country, they do

not come alone but with all their allies; but when we invade our neighbors we have little difficulty as a rule, even on foreign soil, in defeating men who are fighting for their own homes. Moreover, no enemy has ever met us in full strength, for we have our navy to attend to, and our soldiers are sent on service to many scattered possessions; but if they chance to encounter some portion of our forces and defeat a few of us, they boast that they have driven back our whole army, or, if they are defeated, that the victors were in full strength. Indeed, if we choose to face danger with an easy mind rather than after a rigorous training, and to trust rather in native manliness than in state-made courage, the advantage lies with us; for we are spared all the weariness of practicing for future hardships, and when we find ourselves amongst them we are as brave as our plodding rivals. Here as elsewhere, then, the city sets an example which is deserving of admiration.

"We are lovers of beauty without extravagance, and lovers of wisdom without unmanliness. Wealth to us is not mere material for vainglory but an opportunity for achievement; and poverty we think it no disgrace to acknowledge but a real degradation to make no effort to overcome. Our citizens attend both to public and private duties, and do not allow absorption in their own various affairs to interfere with their knowledge of the city's. We differ from other states in regarding the man who holds aloof from public life not as "quiet" but as useless; we decide or debate, carefully and in person, all matters of policy, holding not that words and deeds go ill together, but that acts are foredoomed to failure when undertaken undiscussed. For we are noted for being at once most adventurous in action and most reflective beforehand. Other men are bold in ignorance, while reflection will stop their onset. But the bravest are surely those who have the clearest vision of what is before them, glory and danger alike, and yet notwithstanding go out to meet it.

---

9. **Attic:** referring to Attica, the area of Greece where Athens was located.
10. **Spartans:** inhabitants of Sparta, the militaristic city-state with whom the Athenians have been battling.

426 *Nonfiction*

CRITICAL THINKING: GUIDED READING QUESTIONS

LITERAL

1a. What do the enemies say when they are defeated by a small force of Athenians? (The victors were in full strength.)

2a. In what terms does Pericles describe wealth? (It is not mere material for vainglory but an opportunity for achievement.)

INFERENTIAL

1b. Why do they say this? (They wish to save face.)

2b. What does this mean? (Wealth means nothing as an end in itself; it should be a means of promoting human achievement.)

In doing good, too, we are the exact opposite of the rest of mankind. We secure our friends not by accepting favors but by doing them. And so we are naturally more firm in our attachments: for we are anxious, as creditors, to cement by kind offices[11] our relation towards our friends. If they do not respond with the same warmth it is because they feel that their services will not be given spontaneously but only as the repayment of a debt. We are alone among mankind in doing men benefits, not on calculations of self-interest, but in the fearless confidence of freedom.

"In a word I claim that our city as a whole is an education to Greece, and that her members yield to none, man by man, for independence of spirit, manysidedness of attainment, and complete self-reliance in limbs and brain.

"That this is no vainglorious phrase but actual fact the supremacy which our manners have won us itself bears testimony. No other city of the present day goes out to her ordeal greater than ever men dreamed; no other is so powerful that the invader feels no bitterness when he suffers at her hands, and her subjects no shame at the indignity of their dependence. Great indeed are the symbols and witnesses of our supremacy, at which posterity, as all mankind today, will be astonished. We need no Homer[12] or other man of words to praise us; for such give pleasure for a moment, but the truth will put to shame their imaginings of our deeds. For our pioneers have forced a way into every sea and every land, establishing among all mankind, in punishment or beneficence, eternal memorials of their settlement.

"Such then is the city for whom, lest they should lose her, the men whom we celebrate died a soldier's death: and it is but natural that all of us, who survive them, should wish to spend ourselves in her service. That, indeed, is why I have spent many words upon the city. I wished to show that we have more at stake than men who have no such inheritance, and to support my praise of the dead by making clear to you what they have done. For if I have chanted the glories of the city it was these men and their like who set hand to array her. With them, as with few among Greeks, words cannot magnify the deeds that they have done. Such an end as we have here seems indeed to show us what a good life is, from its first signs of power to its final consummation. For even where life's previous record showed faults and failures it is just to weigh the last brave hour of devotion against them all. There they wiped out evil with good and did the city more service as soldiers than they did her harm in private life. There no hearts grew faint because they loved riches more than honor; none shirked the issue in the poor man's dreams of wealth. All these they put aside to strike a blow for the city. Counting the quest to avenge her honor as the most glorious of all ventures, and leaving Hope, the uncertain goddess, to send them what she would, they faced the foe as they drew near him in the strength of their own manhood; and when the shock of battle came, they chose rather to suffer the uttermost than to win life by weakness. So their memory has escaped the reproaches of men's lips, but they bore instead on their bodies the marks of men's hands, and in a moment of time, at the climax of their lives, were rapt away from a world filled, for their dying eyes, not with terror but with glory.

"Such were the men who lie here and such the city that inspired them. We survivors may pray to be spared their bitter hour but must disdain to meet the foe with a spirit less triumphant. Fix your eyes on the greatness of Athens as you have it before you day by day, fall in love with her, and when you feel her great, remember that this greatness was won by men with

---

11. **offices:** here, services.
12. **Homer** (c. 850 B.C.): great Greek epic poet. (See "Myths, Folk Tales, and Epics" in this book.)

Pericles' Funeral Oration **427**

9 READING SKILL: CAUSE AND EFFECT

Ask students to state the cause and effect in this passage. (The cause is that the Athenians secure friends not by accepting favors but by doing them; the effect is that they are more firm in their attachments.)

10 TEACHING SPEECHES

Point out this sentence as a capsule of Pericles' overall argument. Explain that such summations are rhetorically effective in lengthy speeches.

11 TEACHING TONE

Explain that tone is the attitude taken by an author or speaker toward the subject of a work and that it often conveys an emotion. Ask students to characterize Pericles' tone at this point. (prideful, confident)

12 TEACHING THEME

The principal theme of the speech, which is tied to its purpose, is most clearly set forth here. Ask students to restate it. (Patriotic citizens of a great city should be willing to sacrifice anything for the good of the place.)

13 TEACHING PERSONIFICATION

Remind students that personification is a figure of speech in which an animal, object, or idea is given human form or characteristics. Ask students to identify the personification in this passage. (Hope is personified as a goddess.)

CRITICAL THINKING: GUIDED READING QUESTIONS

LITERAL

1a. According to Pericles, in what way is Athens "alone among mankind"? (It is animated by its confidence in freedom rather than by self-interest.)

2a. What does Pericles say about the ability of words to magnify the deeds of the fallen? (It is impossible for them to do so.)

INFERENTIAL

→ **1b.** What motivates the confidence of the Athenians? (generosity, enlightenment, their past successes, and so on.)

→ **2b.** What does he mean by this? (Their sacrifice was so notable that it would be impossible to overpraise it.)

- Pericles claims that praise for the fallen is undying.
- He comforts the mourning parents and tells them to "keep a brave heart in the hope of other children"; for those beyond childbearing age, he advises them to find comfort in the glory of the dead.
- He tells the children and brothers of the dead that their achievements will never be deemed as great as those of the fallen.
- He counsels the widows not to "lower the nature that is within" them.

IN THE GLOSSARY

- prescribes: directs

14 TEACHING METAPHORS

Direct attention to the use of the word sepulcher as a figure of speech; here it is used as a metaphor in which the minds of men, containing the memories of great deeds, become the "grandest of all sepulchers," spanning "the whole earth."

15 TEACHING STUDENTS OF LIMITED ENGLISH PROFICIENCY

Long sentences like this might confuse students. Have them read such sentences aloud and paraphrase them before continuing.

16 READING SKILL: INFERENCE

Ask students to use Pericles' words to infer the role of women in Greek society. (It was considered a virtue for widows to remain faithful to the memory of their deceased husbands.)

COLLABORATIVE LEARNING: ENRICHMENT ACTIVITY

Social Studies Have a group of students prepare a report on various aspects of the life and role of Pericles in the golden age of Athens. They should include photographs of art and architecture of the period.

courage, with knowledge of their duty, and with a sense of honor in action, who, if they failed in any ordeal, disdained to deprive the city of their services, but sacrificed their lives as the best offerings on her behalf. So they gave their bodies to the commonwealth and received, each for his own memory, praise that will never die, and

14 with it the grandest of all sepulchers, not that in which their mortal bones are laid, but a home in the minds of men, where their glory remains fresh to stir to speech or action as the occasion comes by. For the whole earth is the sepulcher of famous men; and their story is not graven only on stone over their native earth, but lives on far away, without visible symbol, woven into the stuff of other men's lives. For you now it remains to rival what they have done and, knowing the secret of happiness to be freedom and the secret of freedom a brave heart, not idly to

15 stand aside from the enemy's onset. For it is not the poor and luckless, as having no hope of prosperity, who have most cause to reckon death as little loss, but those for whom fortune may yet keep reversal in store and who would feel the change most if trouble befell them. Moreover, weakly to decline the trial is more painful to a man of spirit than death coming sudden and unperceived in the hour of strength and enthusiasm.

"Therefore I do not mourn with the parents of the dead who are here with us. I will rather comfort them. For they know that they have been born into a world of manifold chances and that he is to be accounted happy to whom the best lot falls—the best sorrow, such as is yours today, or the best death, such as fell to these, for whom life and happiness were cut to the selfsame measure. I know it is not easy to give you comfort. I know how often in the joy of others you will have reminders of what was once your own, and how men feel sorrow, not for the loss of what they have never tasted, but when something that has grown dear to them has been snatched away. But you must keep a brave heart

in the hope of other children, those who are still of age to bear them. For the newcomers will help you to forget the gap in your own circle, and will help the city to fill up the ranks of its workers and its soldiers. For no man is fitted to give fair and honest advice in council if he has not, like his fellows, a family at stake in the hour of the city's danger. To you who are past the age of vigor I would say: count the long years of happiness so much gain to set off against the brief space that yet remains, and let your burden be lightened by the glory of the dead. For the love of honor alone is not staled by age, and it is by honor, not, as some say, by gold, that the helpless end of life is cheered.

"I turn to those amongst you who are children or brothers of the fallen, for whom I foresee a mighty contest with the memory of the dead. Their praise is in all men's mouths, and hardly, even for supremest heroism, you will be adjudged to have achieved, not the same but a little less than they. For the living have the jealousy of rivals to contend with, but the dead are honored with unchallenged admiration.

16 "If I must also speak a word to those who are now in widowhood on the powers and duties of women, I will cast all my advice into one brief sentence. Great will be your glory if you do not lower the nature that is within you—hers greatest of all whose praise or blame is least bruited[13] on the lips of men.

"I have spoken such words as I had to say according as the law prescribes, and the graveside offerings to the dead have been duly made. Henceforward the city will take charge of their children till manhood: such is the crown and benefit she holds out to the dead and to their kin for the trials they have undergone for her. For where the prize is highest, there, too, are the best citizens to contend for it.

"And now, when you have finished your lamentation, let each of you depart."

---

13. **bruited** [br$\overline{oo}$t′id]: talked about; rumored.

CRITICAL THINKING: GUIDED READING QUESTIONS

LITERAL

1a. Into what does Pericles say the story of the fallen men is woven? (It is woven "into the stuff of other men's lives.")

2a. What does he foresee for the children and brothers of the fallen? (a contest with the memory of the dead)

INFERENTIAL

1b. In what sense does he mean this? (The living, owing their prosperity and freedom to the bravery of the dead, must preserve the fruits of victory with a like courage.)

2b. Why does he tell them this? (to warn and enlighten them, so that they do not become bitter)

STUDY QUESTIONS

Recalling

1. Why does Pericles disapprove of the custom of giving a solemn public speech to honor the Athenian war dead? Give two of his reasons.
2. According to Pericles, how do the Athenians and Spartans contrast in their military training?
3. What is the Athenian attitude toward wealth and poverty? Toward participation in public life?
4. According to the speaker, why do the fallen soldiers possess the grandest of all sepulchers?
5. What advice does Pericles offer the widows in his audience?

Interpreting

6. Ancient Greek culture often promoted the ideal of the "golden mean," referring to moderation and balance in all aspects of life. From what Pericles says about Athenian qualities, how might the Athenian life style be regarded as an example of the "golden mean"?
7. Explain why you think Pericles devotes so much space in his speech to describing the virtues of the city of Athens and of the Athenians.
8. From Pericles' comments on the women and children in the audience, what can you infer about family life in ancient Athens?

Extending

9. How would you compare Pericles' description of Athenian democracy with American democratic government today? Explain your answer.

LITERARY FOCUS

Speech

A **speech** is a formal address delivered by a speaker to an audience, usually on an occasion that marks a significant event in the life of the community. A speech may have various purposes: for example, to inform, to describe, to entertain, or to persuade. Although one of Pericles' purposes in his speech is to pay tribute to the war dead and to console the survi-

vors, it is clear that he also wants to persuade his audience of the importance of certain values.

Thinking About the Speech

■ State in a sentence or two Pericles' persuasive purpose in the funeral oration. What values does he hope to promote in his listeners when he urges them to fix their eyes on the greatness of Athens and to fall in love with her?

LANGUAGE STUDY

Words from Greek

Many words in English are derived from Greek. Two examples from Pericles' speech are the words *eulogy* and *symbol*. Each word consists of a Greek prefix and a Greek root. Study the following chart.

Prefix	Root
eu- ("good," "well")	log ("word")
sym-, syn- ("with")	bol, bal ("to throw")

A *eulogy* is a speech of praise; a *symbol* is something "thrown together," or something that stands for something else.

Use a dictionary to identify the Greek prefixes and roots in the following words. Then write the meanings of the words.

1. ballistics
2. dialogue
3. embolism
4. euphemism
5. euphoria
6. logistical
7. sympathy
8. synergy

COMPOSITION

Writing a Speech

■ Write a public reply to Pericles' speech that you might deliver at an Athenian assembly. First decide on how you evaluate Pericles' persuasive arguments. Do you agree or disagree with his points? Begin your speech by referring to specific points that Pericles made, and then go on to comment on his views about them. Try to persuade the Athenians to reward or blame Pericles.

COMPOSITION: GUIDELINES FOR EVALUATION

WRITING A SPEECH

Objective

To write a persuasive speech in response to the oration and to recommend that Pericles be rewarded or blamed

Guidelines for Evaluation

■ suggested length: four or five paragraphs

■ should evaluate and respond to Pericles' major points
■ should use persuasive arguments appropriate to the audience and purpose

READER'S RESPONSE

In what ways do you think this is an effective speech? In what ways could it be improved?

ANSWERS

STUDY QUESTIONS

1. "Acts deserve acts, not words"; the merit of the dead should not depend on a speech.
2. The Spartans toil in pursuit of courage; the Athenians face danger when it arises.
3. Wealth is an opportunity for achievement, and poverty is not degradation if there is an effort to overcome it. Participation is everyone's duty.
4. They live in men's minds everywhere.
5. to act uprightly so as not to be talked about
6. Athenians pursued recreation as well as work and loved beauty "without extravagance" and wisdom "without unmanliness."
7. He wants to inspire pride, patriotism, and self-sacrifice in his audience.
8. Families mourned the loss of loved ones, and the city-state took financial responsibility for the children of the fallen soldiers. The role of women in the society seems to have been limited.
9. Answers will vary. Some may say, for example, that interest in public affairs was greater in Athens than it is in America.

LITERARY FOCUS

Pericles' goal seems to be to instill his audience with pride and the desire to make acts of sacrifice for the good of the city.

LANGUAGE STUDY

1. *bal,* "throw"; "study of projectile motion"
2. *dia,* "through," and *logos,* "word"; "conversation"
3. *em,* "in," and *bal,* "throw"; "blockage in a blood vessel"
4. *eu,* "good; well," and *phem,* "say"; "substitution of a mild expression for a harsher one"
5. *eu,* "good; well," and *phore,* "bearer"; "feeling of well-being"
6. *logos,* "word"; "dealing with the movement of military material"
7. *sym,* "with," and *pathos,* "suffering"; "compassion"
8. *syn,* "with," and *erg,* "work"; "combined action"

This expository essay reveals the paradoxes of change in the Ivory Coast. In a concerned but ironic tone the author describes the establishment of an ultramodern capital at Yamoussoukro, a primitive village. There the president has built a vast palace with an artificial lake that contains crocodiles. The crocodiles, which are fed live offerings, symbolize the president's power.

LITERARY SKILLS FOR THIS SELECTION

- expository essay
- symbol
- tone

THEMES IN THIS SELECTION

- paradoxes of change
- cultures and conflicts

LESSON OBJECTIVES

1. to understand the expository essay
2. to write about an expository essay

Teacher's Classroom Resources 3

- Teaching Notes 113
- Prereading Vocabulary 114
- Reading Guide 115
- Check Test 116
- Responding to World Cultures 117
- Literary Focus: Expository Essay 118
- Writing Process Guide: Writing About an Expository Essay 119
- Grammar in Literature: Complex and Compound-Complex Sentences 120
- Selection Test 121

TEACHING STUDENTS OF DIFFERENT ABILITIES

- **For less advanced students:** Help students understand the culturally rich but materially limited life of a premodern society so that they can better grasp the paradoxes of modernization. Ask them to complete the Reading Guide.

V. S. Naipaul (born 1932)

Trinidad/England

V. S. Naipaul [nī′ pəl] received his education at Oxford University in England, but his writing is rooted in the Third World cultures that blend so vibrantly in his native Trinidad, an island in the Caribbean Sea near the coast of South America. Of Indian descent, Naipaul became immersed in the cultures of both Asia and the West Indies.

After completing his studies at Oxford, he worked as a writer for the British Broadcasting Corporation in London for several years. In the late 1950s he published his first novel, *The Mystic Masseur,* and his first collection of stories, *Miguel Street,* which were based on childhood memories of Trinidad. In 1961 Naipaul achieved international acclaim with his novel *A House for Mr. Biswas,* an epic account of a Trinidadian family.

Since then Naipaul has lived and worked in England, although he has roamed the world in search of material for his writing. A master of fiction and nonfiction travel writing, Naipaul has been lauded for his keen perception and ironic style. In the upcoming selection, drawn from his book *Finding the Center* (1984), he records his impressions of a visit to the Ivory Coast.

GEOGRAPHY AND CULTURE

The Ivory Coast and Yamoussoukro

The Ivory Coast (Côte d'Ivoire) is a nation in West Africa, about twice the size of the state of Georgia in the United States. The country's name derives from the 1400s, when French sailors began to trade for ivory there. The French acquired the territory as a colony in 1893. It became independent in 1960 under President Houphouet-Boigny [$\overline{oo}$ fwet′ bwän yē′], who has ruled the country ever since.

The former capital, Abidjan [ab′i jän′], referred to in the selection, has become one of West Africa's most important ports. Since 1983, however, a new capital has been designated at the inland town of Yamoussoukro [yä m$\overline{oo}$′s$\overline{oo}$ krō′], the site of the president's birth.

The mainstay of the economy is agriculture, especially the growing of coffee and cacao beans, although there are also substantial mineral deposits and important industries in timber and textiles. As the following selection hints, tne development of the Ivory Coast since independence has been largely carried out by foreign experts.

See LITERATURE AND CULTURE SOURCEBOOK: Africa

- **For more advanced students:** Ask students to think of the selection by Camara Laye and compare the kind of society depicted there with the emerging one detailed here.

DISCUSSING GEOGRAPHY AND CULTURE

Changes in Urban Landscapes

The most prosperous country in tropical Africa, the Ivory Coast has become increasingly urban: More than 42 percent of the population live in cities. This trend toward urban development is changing the country's landscape and way of life.

- Ask students to describe ways in which urban development—construction of a mall on the site of a former dairy farm, for instance—has changed their local landscape and way of life.

Ornament from African ceremonial state sword, cast gold, early twentieth century.

V. S. Naipaul

The Crocodiles of Yamoussoukro[1]

1. Yamoussoukro, a place deep in the wet forests of the Ivory Coast, is one of the wonders of black Africa. It used to be a village, and perhaps then it was like some other West African bush[2] villages, where grass huts perish after two years. But Yamoussoukro was also the seat of a regional tribal chief; and during the half a century or so of direct French rule in the interior, the authority of the chieftaincy—moral, or spiritual, or magical authority—was not forgotten.

The very old man who is still chief received a French education. He became what the French called a "colonial" doctor—not the finished French product, but a doctor nonetheless. Later he became a politician, a protest leader. With independence in 1960—the bush returned with alterations to its people—he began to rule the Ivory Coast. And he has ruled ever since.

2. He has ruled well. He has used the French as technicians, advisers, administrators; and, with no ready-made mineral wealth, with the resources only of tropical forests and fields, he has made his country rich. So rich that the Ivory Coast imports labor from its more depressed or chaotic African neighbors. Labor immigration, as much as natural increase, has raised the population from three million in 1960 to nine million today. Abidjan,[3] the capital, begun unpromisingly on the black mud of a fetid lagoon, has become one of the biggest ports in West Africa. And one hundred and fifty miles inland, at the end of an auto-route that would not disgrace France itself, the president's ancestral village of Yamoussoukro has been transformed.

The ancestral village has in fact vanished from public sight. The entire village—huts (if they still survive), common ground, the semisacred palaver tree[4]—has been incorporated into the grounds of a new presidential palace. And all is hidden by a high palace wall that must be many miles long.

Down one side of the palace there is an artificial lake, and in this lake turtles and man-eating

3. crocodiles have been introduced. There are totemic, emblematic creatures, and they belong to the president. There were no crocodiles in Yamoussoukro before. No one knows precisely what they mean. But to all Africans they speak at once of danger and of the president's, the chief's, magically granted knowledge of his

---

1. **Yamoussoukro** [yä mōō′sōō krō′]
2. **bush:** referring to shrubby or tropical forest land that has not been cleared for wide-scale settlement.

3. **Abidjan** [äb′i jän′]
4. **palaver** [pə lav′ər] **tree:** tree where villagers gather and converse.

The Crocodiles of Yamoussoukro **431**

- The surrounding forest has been replaced by ordered plantations.
- The president wishes Yamoussoukro to become a great city and has created a golf course that he wishes his people to use.
- The ritual of feeding the crocodiles and the anxieties it awakens regarding the nature and future of Africa are described.

IN THE GLOSSARY

- emanating: issuing from
- prefiguration: something that foreshadows
- frivolities: objects of little importance
- protracted: extended in time
- induces: brings about

4 CULTURAL BACKGROUND

Explain that in most preindustrial cultures land is considered sacred and cannot be owned by individuals; it is used by the entire community.

5 TEACHING STUDENTS OF LIMITED ENGLISH PROFICIENCY

Ask students who come from a developing country to describe the conditions of life there and the difficulties of modernization.

6 TEACHING TONE

Have students describe the tone taken toward such aspects of the president's plans. (skeptical, ironic, and pessimistic)

7 READING SKILL: CONTRAST

Elicit the stark contrast between this ritual and the quest for modernization. (The ritual suggests cruelty, connectedness to the past, superstition, and tyranny; modernization suggests efficiency, modernity, westernization, progress, and enlightenment.)

COLLABORATIVE LEARNING: ENRICHMENT ACTIVITY

Social Studies Ask a group of students to research the Ivory Coast and prepare a report on its history, including photographs of the new capital.

---

power as something more than human, something emanating from the earth itself.

The power and wisdom of the chief have caused the forest around Yamoussoukro to disappear. Where once were African fields, unused common land, and wild trees there are now ordered, mechanized plantations. For square mile upon square mile mangoes, avocados, or pineapples grow in straight lines, the straight lines that are beautiful to people to whom Nature is usually formless, unfriendly bush. Land in this part of Africa, it is said, belongs to the user; there can be no title[5] in bush. And until they were given to the state some years ago, these plantations around Yamoussoukro were the president's personal estates.

The president's ideas have always been big, and his plans for Yamoussoukro are very big. He would like it to be one of the great cities of Africa and the world. The land has been leveled, and avenues as wide as runways outline the metropolis that is to be. Extravagant and sometimes brilliant modern buildings have been set down in the stripped wilderness and await full use.

To attract visitors, there is a great golf course, beautifully landscaped and so far steadfastly maintained against the fast-growing bush. It is the president's idea, though he doesn't play golf himself. The golf idea came to him when he was old, and now in his benign, guiding way he would like all his people, all the sixty or so tribes of the Ivory Coast, to take up golf. To house the visitors, there is a twelve-story Hotel President, one of the French Sofitel hotel chain. The hotel brochure is printed in France; its silvery gray cover looks princely. "Find the traces of the native village of President Houphouët-Boigny,"[6] the brochure says, "and discover the ultra-modern prefiguration of the Africa of tomorrow."

The two ideas go together. The ultra-modern

---

5. **there can be no title:** that is, no one can claim ownership of the land simply by virtue of possessing a deed to it.
6. **Houphouët-Boigny** [$\overline{oo}$ fwet′ bwän yē′]

---

dream also serves old Africa. It is pharaonic:[7] it has a touch of the antique world. Away from the stupendous modern frivolities of the golf course and the golf club and the swimming pool of the Hotel President there is the presidential palace with its artificial lake. Outside the blank walls that hide the president's ancestral village and the palaver tree from the common view, the president's totemic crocodiles are fed with fresh meat every day. People can go and watch. But distances in Yamoussoukro are so great, and the scarred, empty spaces so forbidding, that only people with cars can easily go; and they tend to be visitors, tourists.

The feeding ritual takes place in the afternoon, in bright light. There are the cars, the tourists in bright clothes, the cameras. But the crocodiles are sacred. A live offering—a chicken—has to be made to them; it is part of the ritual. This element of sacrifice, this protracted display of power and cruelty, is as unsettling as it is meant to be, and it seems to bring night and the forest close again to the dream of Yamoussoukro.

To the man from outside, whatever his political or religious faith, Africa can often seem to be in a state of becoming. It is always on the point of being made something else. So it arouses hope, ambition, frustration, irritation. And even the success of the Ivory Coast induces a kind of anxiety. Will it last? Will the Africans be able to take over from the French and the Israelis and the others who have built it all for them and still effectively run it?

And then at a place like Yamoussoukro, where the anxiety becomes most acute, it also begins to feel unreal. You get a glimpse of an African Africa, an Africa which—whatever the accidents of history, whatever the current manifestations of earthly glory—has always been in its own eyes complete, achieved, bursting with its own powers.

---

7. **pharaonic** [fãr′ā on′ik]: resembling the Pharaohs, powerful rulers of ancient Egypt.

CRITICAL THINKING: GUIDED READING QUESTIONS

LITERAL

1a. What is hidden from view by the blank walls of the presidential palace? (the president's ancestral village and the palaver tree)

2a. To outsiders, in what sort of state does Africa seem to be? (It is "in a state of becoming.")

INFERENTIAL

1b. What does this suggest about the president? (He wants to maintain the old ways, but he does not want his people to be attached to the past.)

2b. What does it mean to be a developing country? (The country is developing and modernizing in the Western sense.)

Recalling

1. Name three ways in which the ancestral village of Yamoussoukro has changed under the president's rule since 1960.
2. What are the president's ambitions for Yamoussoukro?
3. What does the author say happens at the "feeding ritual" of the crocodiles?
4. What "anxiety" about the future of the Ivory Coast does the author refer to in the concluding paragraphs of the essay?

Interpreting

5. Naipaul's description of the crocodiles strongly hints that they are symbolic. What might the crocodiles symbolize, in your opinion?
6. Explain how the president's special crocodiles, on the one hand, and his dreams about golf, on the other, suggest two sharply contrasting images of modern life in the Ivory Coast.
7. From the last two paragraphs of the essay, what is one conclusion that you can draw concerning Naipaul's ideas about cultural change in modern Africa?

Extending

8. Modern life is marked by rapid changes. Why do people both fear and welcome change?

LITERARY FOCUS

Expository Essay

An **expository essay** explains a term, process, or idea to the reader. The writer of an expository essay often indicates the essay's purpose by means of a **thesis statement,** which directly tells the reader what the essay will explain. This statement usually occurs toward the beginning of the essay; the body of the essay develops this statement with explanations and examples; the conclusion of the essay may re-state the thesis in different words.

Sometimes, as in Naipaul's essay, the main idea of an expository essay is not stated directly but rather hinted at through the writer's tone and the choice of facts and details. In such a case the essay has an **implied thesis.**

Thinking About the Expository Essay

■ What generalization about social change do you think Naipaul wants his readers to understand in this essay about Yamoussoukro and the Ivory Coast?

COMPOSITION

Writing About an Expository Essay

■ In a short essay analyze V. S. Naipaul's purpose in his expository essay. What truth about social change does he set out to explain in "The Crocodiles of Yamoussoukro"? What specific facts, examples, details, incidents, and ideas does he use to achieve his purpose? At the end of your paper, indicate whether you think Naipaul has accomplished his purpose successfully. *For help with this assignment, refer to Lesson 8 in the Writing About Literature Handbook at the back of this book.*

COMPOSITION: GUIDELINES FOR EVALUATION

WRITING ABOUT AN EXPOSITORY ESSAY

Objective

To write an essay analyzing Naipaul's purpose

Guidelines for Evaluation

■ suggested length: three or four paragraphs
■ should identify Naipaul's purpose as making a commentary on social change
■ should state details used to achieve the purpose
■ should evaluate the author's success

This thirteenth century manuscript illumination was painted in Flanders for a missal, or prayer book, that was used by monks in a Benedictine abbey. It shows the Italian explorer Marco Polo arriving at the court of Kublai Khan, a Mongolian ruler of China. Before Marco Polo's trip to China, most Europeans had no knowledge of Chinese culture or even knew what the Chinese people looked like. In fact, all the figures in this painting by a Flemish artist look European. The only distinguishing characteristic of Kublai Khan is his cone-shaped hat and crown.

■ Have students contrast this cultural document with others that are the product of modern technology, such as the camera. (This image is not as accurate or informational.) Ask them how modern technology has affected our knowledge of the world. (Technologies such as photography and telecommunication have made knowledge of remote cultures of the world accessible to us.)

Marco Polo arriving in the court of Kublai Khan, thirteenth century.

International Travel Writing

As your readings in this section have clearly illustrated, nonfiction comes in many forms and is written for many different purposes. One of the oldest and most enduringly popular forms of nonfiction is the accounts and descriptions that travelers provide of their journeys. Often the traveler describes a foreign land with which few readers at home are familiar—as V. S. Naipaul does on the preceding pages in his essay about the Ivory Coast. Sometimes the traveler brings to light undiscovered corners of his own country—as Camilo José Cela does in his journey through the Alcarria. In any case, good travel writing is sprinkled with fascinating information and vivid descriptions that allow readers to feel like travelers themselves and to see the world from their armchairs.

One of history's most famous and influential pieces of travel literature was written by Marco Polo, who lived in the Italian city of Venice and journeyed to China in the late thirteenth century. At the time Europe was just emerging from the darkness of the Middle Ages, and Europeans knew little of distant lands. China's Mongol Empire, on the other hand, was at its peak of power and opulence. The descriptions that Marco Polo's *Travels* provided of the magnificent achievements of Mongol ruler Kublai Khan made for fascinating reading among Europeans back at home. Moreover, the *Travels* helped change the course of history, for the book inspired an interest in trade with the Orient that helped to lead Europe out of the Middle Ages and into a new era of exploration and commerce.

In our own century China once again became a nation largely unknown to outsiders when its Communist government imposed repressive travel restrictions. The easing of tensions that began in the late 1970s opened China's doors to Western travelers eager to experience what to them had again become a largely unknown land. A recent travel book about China, *Riding the Iron Rooster* by the American writer Paul Theroux, describes a train journey the author made across China in the mid-1980s. From the opening paragraph Theroux establishes a sense of discovery for readers: "The bigness of China makes you wonder. . . . It is more like a whole world than a mere country." He goes on to capture the landscape, life styles, and people of China with compelling narrative prose and a keen eye for descriptive detail, hallmarks of fine travel writing.

DEVELOPING A SENSE OF PLACE

Great travel writers are consummate observers: They capture and reflect the essence of a place. Some of the best travel writers—D. H. Lawrence, Evelyn Waugh, and Mary McCarthy—were novelists. Fine travel books have also been written by scholars and adventurers, including T. E. Lawrence, commonly known as Lawrence of Arabia; the British explorer Sir Richard Francis Burton; and Freya Stark, one of the first European women to travel extensively in the Middle East.

Activities

1. Divide the class into groups of six or seven students, and ask each group to create an issue of a travel magazine. Assign students in each group roles as editor, photo editor, designer, and writers. Each group should come up with a title and design for its magazine, ideas for three or four feature articles, and suitable artwork and photographs, including a cover image. Students may wish to look at magazines such as *Travel and Leisure, The Traveller,* or *Geo* for ideas. Have each group present its sample issue to the class, and have the class vote on the magazines with the best concept, design, and article ideas.

2. Divide the class into pairs in such a way that each member knows a particular local or distant place well. Have each pair compose a brief literary travel essay about the place. Student A should interview Student B, asking for a detailed description of the place, facts about its history, and the student's memories and feelings about it. If Student A is also familiar with the place, the students should reverse roles. Each team should then write a personal, firsthand account of the place. Ask students to look at some of the literary travel pieces in this book, such as those by Camilo José Cela and V. S. Naipaul, for ideas regarding style and structure. When the essays are complete, have volunteers read them to the class.

The Italian Antonio Canaletto painted numerous views of Venice during his lifetime. Here we see a panorama that includes the Zecca Mint with the towering campanile, or bell tower, behind it; the columns of Saint Theodore and Saint Mark (with the lion on top) standing in front of the *piazetta,* or small plaza; and to the right, the orangy Ducal Palace rising above the Venetian harbor, where the gondoliers slowly wend their way. Although naturalistic in appearance, Canaletto's scenes display the theatrical eye of a stage director. Each one portrays an aspect of the fabled city of canals with drama, grandness, and idealism.

- Ask students what dramatic elements they can find in this painting. (the lighting; the swirling clouds; the energetic poses of the gondoliers, especially as they try to avoid hitting other boats; the grand, impressive buildings)

436 *Drama*

The View of Ducal Palace and the Piazzeta San Marco, Antonio Canaletto (1697–1768).

DRAMA

T*he purpose of playing... is to hold, as 'twere, the mirror up to nature.*
—WILLIAM SHAKESPEARE
England

To prepare students for the plays in this unit, have volunteers discuss their own experiences attending live theater or watching a stage play on television. What did they like and dislike about the production? In what ways did the play seem to capture real life, and in what ways did it seem to differ from reality?

Discuss the differences between reading a book and seeing a story dramatized as a stage play, film, or television program. Elicit the response that drama, though it shares certain elements with other forms of literature, is unique because it must present its story almost entirely through action and speech.

Explain that drama is one of the oldest forms of literature and that most early dramas were written in verse. This is true not only of Western drama, such as the tragedies and comedies of ancient Greece and the works of England's great playwright William Shakespeare, but also of the No dramas of medieval Japan. Note that the unit contains an example of a classic Japanese No play by Seami; a short folk drama by Nigeria's James Ene Henshaw; and a full-length European classic, *Cyrano de Bergerac*, by the French playwright Edmond Rostand.

Remind students that the experience of reading a play is very different from that of watching a performance. To help students visualize the way in which the plays in this unit would come to life, have students read portions of each play aloud or even act out the plays in their entirety. Encourage students in the "audience" to play their parts as fully as those performing the roles.

LESSON PREVIEW

In this engaging one-act play an elderly man outwits his greedy, disrespectful grandsons. The grandsons treat Okorie shabbily until he tells them that he has uncovered a cache of jewels. By threatening disinheritance Okorie manipulates them into giving him an honorable burial; but when the will is read, the grandsons learn that they are bankrupt and homeless. The play emphasizes that those who refuse to honor their elders will reap their just reward.

LITERARY SKILLS FOR THIS SELECTION

- dialogue
- staging
- plot

THEMES IN THIS SELECTION

- lack of respect for elders
- tradition versus modernity
- greed and hypocrisy

LESSON OBJECTIVES

1. to understand the concepts of dialogue and staging
2. to write an offstage scene

Teacher's Classroom Resources 3

- Teaching Notes 129
- Prereading Vocabulary 130
- Reading Guide 131
- Check Test 132
- Responding to World Cultures 133
- Literary Focus: Dialogue; Staging 134
- Writing Process Guide: Writing an Offstage Scene 135
- Grammar in Literature: Linking Verbs 136
- Selection Test 137

IN THE CLASSROOM

TEACHING STUDENTS OF DIFFERENT ABILITIES

- **For less advanced students:** Help students pronounce the characters' names. Ask them to complete the Reading Guide.
- **For more advanced students:** Ask students to list those values identified in the play with traditional Nigerian life and those identified with contemporary life. Then ask students to discuss problems that are likely to arise as these sets of values come into conflict.

James Ene Henshaw

(born 1924)

Nigeria

James Ene Henshaw is well known in Nigeria as a dramatist writing in English. Born in 1924 into an aristocratic family and the youngest of nine children, Henshaw was raised by a brother after his father's death. After graduating from a local high school in 1943, he traveled to Ireland to study medicine at the National University in Dublin. He qualified as a physician in 1949 and in 1955 returned to his homeland to practice medicine. Since then Henshaw has held various important positions as a public health professional for the Nigerian government.

Henshaw's work as a dramatist came second to his career as a physician. He won recognition in 1952, when *The Jewels of the Shrine* took first prize as the best one-act play in the All-Nigeria Festival of the Arts. In 1956 Henshaw became the first Nigerian dramatist to have a full-length work published abroad. His first book, containing *The Jewels of the Shrine,* was reprinted nine times by 1970. His popular plays, written in simple language, are read and performed all over West Africa.

GEOGRAPHY AND CULTURE

Nigerian Rural Village Life

Located on the southern coast of West Africa, Nigeria is the most populous country in Africa. It is home to more than two hundred ethnic groups, each with its own language and customs, though only ten of them account for about ninety percent of the country's population. Nigeria was under British rule for nearly a century before it won independence in 1960, and English is its official language.

English is spoken mainly in the cities, however, and daily life in rural farming villages such as that depicted in *The Jewels of the Shrine* has not changed much over the past few centuries. Still, as the attitudes of urban society slowly influence rural villages, traditional values, such as respect for the elderly, are challenged. In addition, health conditions in rural areas are poor, and life expectancy is relatively low. In the early 1980s, well after Henshaw wrote this play, the average person in Nigeria could expect to live only forty-nine years. Therefore, the play's Grandfather Okorie, at age eighty, is indeed an elderly man.

See LITERATURE AND CULTURE SOURCEBOOK: Africa

DISCUSSING GEOGRAPHY AND CULTURE

Rural Homes

Three-fourths of Nigeria's population live in rural areas. Many rural Nigerians build houses of mud bricks and decorate the outside with geometric designs. The houses are usually clustered in walled compounds, where parents, grandparents, and children live together.

- Ask students to discuss the advantages of an extended family. (Examples include the availability of family members to care for the young and the elderly and the keeping of traditions.)

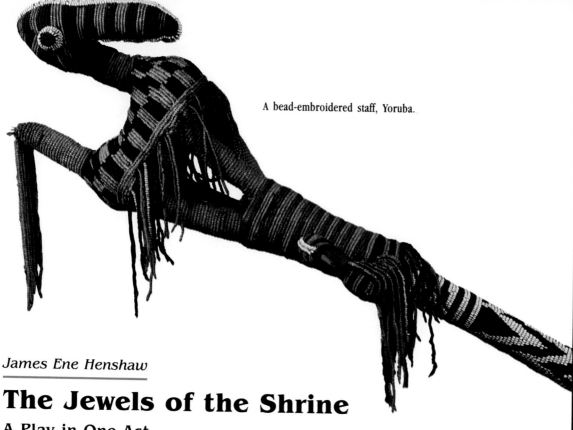

A bead-embroidered staff, Yoruba.

James Ene Henshaw

The Jewels of the Shrine

A Play in One Act

CHARACTERS

OKORIE [ō kou′rē]: an old man

AROB [ä′rōb]

OJIMA [ō′jē mä] } Okorie's grandsons

BASSI [bä′sē]: a woman

A STRANGER

1 *An imaginary village close to a town in Nigeria. All the scenes of this play take place in Okorie's mud-walled house. The time is the present.*

SCENE 1

[*The hall in* OKORIE's *house. There are three doors. One leads directly into* OKORIE's *room. The two others are on either side of the hall. Of these, one leads to his grandsons' apartment, whilst the other acts as a general exit.*

The chief items of furniture consist of a wide bamboo bed, on which is spread a mat; a wooden chair; a low table; and a few odds and ends, including three hoes.

OKORIE, *an old man of about eighty years of age, with scanty gray hair and dressed in the way his village folk do, is sitting at the edge of the bed. He holds a stout, rough walking-stick,*

The Jewels of the Shrine **439**

MOTIVATION: PRIOR KNOWLEDGE

Ask students to discuss how the elderly are viewed and treated in modern society. Have them consider such questions as how the emphasis on youthfulness has affected the way the elderly are perceived and how they themselves think the elderly should be treated. Explain that in the play they are about to read, a grandfather is mistreated by his grandsons.

PAGE SUMMARY: AT A GLANCE

■ The play's setting, a village in Nigeria, and its main character, the eighty-year-old Okorie, are introduced.

1 TEACHING SETTING

Point out that the time and place of the play are established: an imaginary village close to a town in Nigeria in the present. All of the action of the play takes place in Okorie's mud-walled house.

ART AND LITERATURE

The Yoruba people of western Nigeria created an art form using the colorful beads made from cowrie shells that European traders brought to Nigeria as barter. Varying in color and luminosity, the beads were thought by the Yoruba to represent the transmission of heavenly light through earthly matter. This bead-covered staff, made for a tribal leader, has a single bird at the top to symbolize heavenly ascent. The staff itself represents authority.

■ Ask students which of the play's characters might be most familiar with the traditions associated with this staff. (Okorie, the "old man")

PAGE SUMMARY: AT A GLANCE

- Okorie and a Stranger commiserate about changes brought about by modern life.
- Okorie bemoans the fact that his grandsons show no respect for him.
- The Stranger leaves.
- Bassi enters, and Okorie tells her that the Stranger's visit has renewed his hope.

2 TEACHING THEME

Point out that the play opens with an intimation of its theme, the conflict between generations and the younger generation's lack of respect for the older generation.

3 CULTURAL BACKGROUND

Explain that in traditional Nigerian societies people lived within extended families. When brothers and sisters grew up and married, they remained close to one another, helping each other. Elders were respected for their wisdom, and when they died, family members often pooled their resources to pay for elaborate funerals.

4 TEACHING CHARACTERIZATION

Make sure that students understand that Bassi is not Okorie's granddaughter. She is a friend and calls him Grandfather out of respect.

5 CULTURAL BACKGROUND

Explain that in many African societies people have faced conflicts between traditional ways and the ways of the modern world. One conflict has come in the form of religion. Many Nigerians have accepted Christianity but do not feel entirely comfortable with it. Often they mix elements from traditional religion with Christian worship.

---

and a horn filled with palm wine.[1]

On the wooden chair near the bed sits a STRANGER, *a man of about forty-five years of age. He too occasionally sips wine from a calabash cup.*[2] *It is evening. The room is rather dark, and a cloth-in-oil lantern hangs from a hook on the wall.*]

2 OKORIE. Believe me, Stranger, in my days things were different. It was a happy thing to become an old man, because young people were taught to respect elderly men.

STRANGER. [*Sipping his wine.*] Here in the village you should be happier. In the town where I come from, a boy of ten riding a hired bicycle will knock down a man of fifty years without any feeling of pity.

OKORIE. Bicycle. That is why I have not been to town for ten years. Town people seem to enjoy rushing about doing nothing. It kills them.

STRANGER. You are lucky that you have your grandchildren to help you. Many people in town have no one to help them.

OKORIE. Look at me, Stranger, and tell me if these shabby clothes, and this dirty beard, show that I **3** have good grandchildren. Believe me, Stranger, in my younger days things were different. Old men were happy. When they died they were buried with honor. But in my case, Stranger, my old age has been unhappy. And my only fear now is that when I die my grandsons will not accord me the honor due to my age. It will be a disgrace to me.

STRANGER. I will now go on my way, Okorie. May God help you.

OKORIE. I need help, Stranger, for although I have two grandsons I am lonely and unhappy because they do not love or care for me. They

---

1. **palm wine:** drink made from the fruit of various palm trees.
2. **calabash cup:** drinking vessel made from the hard shell of the calabash gourd.

440 *Drama*

---

tell me that I am from an older world. Farewell, Stranger. If you call again and I am alive, I will welcome you back. [*Exit* STRANGER.]

4 [BASSI, *a beautiful woman of about thirty years, enters.*]

BASSI. Who was that man, Grandfather?

OKORIE. He was a stranger.

BASSI. I do not trust strangers. They may appear honest when the lights are on. But as soon as there is darkness, they creep back as thieves.

[OKORIE *smiles and drinks his wine.*]

BASSI. [*Pointing to him.*] What has happened, Grandfather? When I left you this afternoon, you were old, your mind was worried, and your eyes were swollen. Where now are the care, the sorrow, the tears in your eyes? You never smiled before, but now—

OKORIE. The stranger has brought happiness back into my life. He has given me hope again.

BASSI. But don't they preach in town that it is only God who gives hope? Every other thing gives despair.

OKORIE. Perhaps that stranger was God. Don't the preachers say that God moves like a stranger?

BASSI. God moves in strange ways.

OKORIE. Yes, I believe it, because since that **5** stranger came, I have felt younger again. You know, woman, when I worshipped at our forefathers' shrine I was happy. I knew what it was all about. It was my life. Then the preachers came, and I abandoned the beliefs of our fathers. The old ways did not leave me; the new ways did not wholly accept me. I was therefore unhappy. But soon I felt the wings of God carrying me high. And with my loving and helpful son, I thought that my old age would be as happy as that of my father before me. But death played me a trick. My son died and I was left to the mercy of his

---

CRITICAL THINKING: GUIDED READING QUESTIONS

LITERAL

1a. Why does Okorie say that he has not been to town for ten years? ("Town people seem to enjoy rushing about doing nothing. It kills them.")

2a. What does Okorie say about the behavior of his grandsons toward him? (They do not respect or care for him.)

INFERENTIAL

1b. What do his statements about town life suggest about his feelings toward modernization? (He believes that modernization has had more negative than positive effects.)

2b. What do you suspect that Okorie's grandsons are like? (They are probably selfish and disrespectful.)

two sons. Once more unhappiness gripped my **6** life. With all their education my grandsons lacked one thing—respect for age. But today the stranger who came here has once more brought happiness to me. Let me tell you this—

BASSI. It is enough, Grandfather. Long talks make you tired. Come, your food is now ready.

OKORIE. [*Happily.*] Woman, I cannot eat. When happiness fills your heart, you cannot eat.

[*Two voices are heard outside, laughing and swearing.*]

BASSI. Your grandchildren are coming back.

OKORIE. Don't call them my grandchildren. I am alone in this world.

7 [*Door flings open. Two young men, about eighteen and twenty, enter the room. They are in shirt and trousers.*]

AROB. By our forefathers, Grandfather, you are still awake!

BASSI. Why should he not keep awake if he likes?

8 **AROB.** But Grandfather usually goes to bed before the earliest chicken thinks of it.

OJIMA. Our good grandfather might be thinking of his youthful days when all young men were fond of farming and all young women loved the kitchen.

BASSI. Shame on both of you for talking to an old man like that. When you grow old, your own children will laugh and jeer at you. Come, Grandfather, and take your food.

[OKORIE *stands up with difficulty and limps with the aid of his stick through the exit followed by* BASSI, *who casts a reproachful look on the two men before she leaves.*]

AROB. I wonder what Grandfather and the woman were talking about.

OJIMA. It must be the usual thing. We are bad boys. We have no regard for the memory of our father, and so on.

AROB. Our father left his responsibility to us. Nature had arranged that he should bury Grandfather before thinking of himself.

OJIMA. But would Grandfather listen to Nature when it comes to the matter of death? Everybody in his generation, including all his wives, have died. But Grandfather has made a bet with death. And it seems that he will win.

OKORIE. [*Calling from off stage.*] Bassi! Bassi! Where is that woman?

OJIMA. The old man is coming. Let us hide ourselves. [*Both rush under the bed.*]

OKORIE. [*Comes in, limping on his stick as usual.*] Bassi, where are you? Haven't I told that girl never . . .

An Ife head, Yoruba, fourteenth or fifteenth century.

The Jewels of the Shrine **441**

CRITICAL THINKING: GUIDED READING QUESTIONS

LITERAL

1a. What does Ojima say men and women did during Okorie's youthful days? (Men farmed, and women "loved the kitchen.")

2a. What does Ojima say about Okorie and death? (He says that Okorie does not listen to Nature; he has made a bet with death, and it seems he will win.)

INFERENTIAL

→ **1b.** What can you infer from these remarks about what life is like for the men and women of the grandsons' generation? (They have broader interests and greater opportunities.)

→ **2b.** From his remarks what can you infer that Ojima wishes would happen to his grandfather? (He wishes he would die.)

PAGE SUMMARY: AT A GLANCE

■ Okorie's grandsons, Arob and Ojima, arrive and talk rudely to their grandfather.
■ Okorie leaves, and Arob and Ojima complain about having to care for him.
■ They hide under the bed when they hear Okorie returning.

IN THE GLOSSARY

■ jeer: to shout at derisively
■ reproachful: full of blame

6 TEACHING CONFLICT

Point out that one of the play's main conflicts is between the younger and the older generations. The educated younger generation mocks the older generation, which has no formal education and clings to traditional values.

7 TEACHING STAGING

Have students compare the way the grandsons and Okorie are dressed. (Okorie wears traditional clothing; the grandsons, shirts and trousers.) Ask what the costuming shows about the difference in values between the men. (Okorie's values are traditional; his grandsons', modern.)

8 TEACHING DIALOGUE

Ask students what attitudes the grandsons demonstrate through their words. (They are disrespectful and cruel toward Okorie personally as well as toward his traditional way of life.)

ART AND LITERATURE

Members of the Ife tribe of Nigeria were the first Africans to create naturalistic art. Influenced by Asians and Near Eastern travelers, the Ife used clay and cast bronze to make works such as this crowned head of a man. The faces of these life-sized heads were incised with vertical ridges. Small holes about the mouth and chin may have held coral beads. The Ife created these sculptures to represent all men rather than any one man in particular.

■ Ask students whether this sculpture represents the modern or the traditional world. (the traditional) Might it be a part of Okorie's treasure? Why or why not? (Yes, because it is a part of the ancient tradition Okorie adheres to.)

- Okorie asks Bassi whether she can keep a secret and has Bassi check the room to make sure no one is listening.
- Okorie discloses that his father offered costly jewels to the village Shrine to protect the village from a great fever.

9 READING SKILL: INFERENCE

Ask students to infer why Okorie refers to his grandsons as "two people." (Students might suggest that since they treat Okorie so poorly, he feels they are strangers to him.)

10 TEACHING DIALOGUE

Point out that the dialogue reveals Okorie's continuing concern that he have an honorable burial. Explain that much of the action hinges on this concern.

11 TEACHING SUSPENSE

Encourage students to recognize the element of suspense here. If Bassi looks under the bed, she will find the two grandsons, who are hiding there, overhearing everything.

12 TEACHING PERSONIFICATION

Point out that Okorie is a skillful storyteller. He uses personification to help his story come alive. For example, the statement "Death roamed through all the other villages" creates a vivid image of a brooding figure stalking the villages and leaving the dead in his wake.

BASSI. [*Entering.*] Don't shout so. It's not good for you.

9 OKORIE. Where are the two people?

BASSI. You mean your grandsons?

OKORIE. My, my, well, call them what you like.

BASSI. They are not here. They must have gone into their room.

OKORIE. Bassi, I have a secret for you. [*He narrows his eyes.*] A big secret. [*His hands tremble.*] Can you keep a secret?

BASSI. Of course I can.

OKORIE. [*Rubbing his forehead.*] You can, what can you? What did I say?

BASSI. [*Holding him and leading him to sit on the bed.*] You are excited. You know that whenever you are excited you begin to forget things.

OKORIE. That is not my fault. It is old age. Well, but what was I saying?

BASSI. You asked me if I could keep a secret.

OKORIE. Yes, yes, a great secret. You know, Bassi, I have been an unhappy man.

BASSI. I have heard it all before.

OKORIE. Listen, woman. My dear son died and left me to the mercy of his two sons. They are the worst grandsons in the land. They have sold all that their father left. They do not care for me.
10 Now when I die what will they do to me? Don't you think that they will abandon me in disgrace? An old man has a right to be properly cared for. And when he dies he has a right to a good burial. But my grandchildren do not think of these things.

BASSI. See how you tremble, Grandfather! I have told you not to think of such things.

OKORIE. Why should I not? But sh! . . . I hear a voice.

442 *Drama*

BASSI. It's only your ears deceiving you, Grandfather.

OKORIE. It is not my ears, woman. I know when old age hums in my ears and tired nerves ring bells in my head, but I know also when I hear a human voice.

BASSI. Go on, Grandfather, there is no one.

OKORIE. Now, listen. You saw the stranger that came here. He gave me hope. But wait, look around, Bassi. Make sure that no one is listening to us.

BASSI. No one, Grandfather.

OKORIE. Open the door and look.

BASSI. [*Opens the exit door.*] No one.

OKORIE. Look into that corner.

BASSI. [*Looks.*] There is no one.

11 OKORIE. Look under the bed.

BASSI. [*Irritably.*] I won't, Grandfather. There is no need, I have told you that there is nobody in the house.

OKORIE. [*Pitiably.*] I have forgotten what I was talking about.

BASSI. [*Calmly.*] You have a secret from the stranger.

OKORIE. Yes, the stranger told me something. Have you ever heard of the "Jewels of the Shrine"?

BASSI. Real jewels?

OKORIE. Yes. Among the beads which my father got from the early white men were real jewels.
12 When war broke out, and a great fever invaded all our lands, my father made a sacrifice in the village Shrine. He promised that if this village were spared he would offer his costly jewels to the Shrine. Death roamed through all the other villages, but not one person in this village died of the fever. My father kept his promise. In a big

---

CRITICAL THINKING: GUIDED READING QUESTIONS

LITERAL

1a. What does Okorie have Bassi do before he begins telling her his secret? (He has her promise not to tell the secret and look around the room to make sure no one else can hear them.)

2a. What does Bassi say happens whenever Okorie gets excited? (He begins to forget things.)

INFERENTIAL

1b. What does this suggest about his secret? (It is of great importance.)

2b. What does this suggest? (His advanced years are affecting his mental abilities.)

ceremony, the jewels were placed on our Shrine. But it was not for long. Some said they were stolen. But the stranger who came here knew where they were. He said that they were buried somewhere near the big oak-tree in our farm. I must go out and dig for them. They can be sold for fifty pounds³ these days.

BASSI. But, Grandfather, it will kill you to go out in this cold and darkness. You must get someone to do it for you. You cannot lift a hoe.

OKORIE. [*Infuriated.*] So, you believe I am too old to lift a hoe. You, you, oh, I . . .

BASSI. [*Coaxing him.*] There now, young man, no temper. If you wish, I myself will dig up the whole farm for you.

OKORIE. Every bit of it?

BASSI. Yes.

OKORIE. And hand over to me all that you will find?

BASSI. Yes.

OKORIE. And you will not tell my grandsons?

BASSI. No, Grandfather, I will not.

OKORIE. Swear, woman, swear by our Fathers' Shrine.

BASSI. I swear.

OKORIE. [*Relaxing.*] Now life is becoming worthwhile. Tell no one about it, woman. Begin digging tomorrow morning. Dig inch by inch until you bring out the jewels of our Forefathers' Shrine.

BASSI. I am tired, Grandfather, I must sleep now. Good night.

OKORIE. [*With feeling.*] Good night. God and our Fathers' Spirits keep you. When dangerous bats alight on the roofs of wicked men, let them not

3. **fifty pounds:** formerly, units of money in Nigeria.

trouble you in your sleep. When far-seeing owls hoot the menace of future days, let their evil prophecies keep off your path. [BASSI *leaves.*]

OKORIE. [*Standing up and trembling, moves to a corner and brings out a small hoe; and struggling with his senile joints he tries to imitate a young man digging.*] Oh, who said I was old? After all, I am only eighty years. And I feel younger than most young men. Let me see how I can dig. [*He tries to dig again.*] Ah! I feel aches all over my hip. Maybe the soil here is too hard. [*He listens.*] How I keep on thinking that I hear people whispering in this room! I must rest now.

[*Carrying the hoe with him, he goes into his room.* AROB *and* OJIMA *crawl out from under the bed.*]

AROB. [*Stretching his hip.*] My hip, oh my hip!

OJIMA. My legs!

AROB. So there is a treasure in our farm; we must waste no time. We must begin digging soon.

OJIMA. Soon? We must begin tonight; now. The old man has taken one hoe. [*Pointing to the corner.*] There are two over there. [*They fetch two hoes from among the heap of things in a corner of the room.*] If we can only get the jewels we can go and live in town and let the old man manage as he can. Let's move now.

[*As they are about to go out, each holding a hoe,* OKORIE *comes out with his own hoe. For a moment the three stare at each other in silence and surprise.*]

AROB. Now, Grandfather, where are you going with a hoe at this time of night?

OJIMA. [*Impudently.*] Yes, Grandfather, what is the idea?

OKORIE. I should ask you; this is my house. Why are you creeping about like thieves?

The Jewels of the Shrine 443

PAGE SUMMARY: AT A GLANCE

■ Okorie reveals that the Stranger told him the jewels from the Shrine are now buried on the family's farm.
■ Bassi agrees to dig up the jewels the next morning and goes to bed.
■ Okorie picks up a hoe and goes to his room.
■ The grandsons crawl out from under the bed and agree to dig for the jewels that night.
■ Okorie and the grandsons run into each other as they are all about to go digging.

IN THE GLOSSARY

■ alight: to land

13 **TEACHING PLOT: RISING ACTION**

Point out that an important complication has been added to the plot: Okorie, currently impoverished, appears to have great wealth within his grasp.

14 **TEACHING CHARACTERIZATION**

Ask students what Bassi's words reflect about her. (Students should see that she is generous and caring toward Okorie: She treats him with the respect that is part of the traditional way of life.)

15 **TEACHING STUDENTS OF LIMITED ENGLISH PROFICIENCY**

Students with limited English proficiency may have difficulty with the saying here and the one that begins in the previous column. Help them paraphrase the sayings to make them more understandable. (Possible paraphrasings: When bad things seem about to happen to bad people, do not be worried; when there are prophecies of bad things, I hope the prophecies have nothing to do with you.)

16 **TEACHING DIALOGUE**

Ask students what the dialogue reveals about the grandsons' characters. (Students should see that just as the grandfather has said, the grandsons care nothing about him; they are greedy and grasping, here even stooping to stealing his treasure.)

CRITICAL THINKING: GUIDED READING QUESTIONS

LITERAL

1a. What does Bassi say when Okorie states his intention to dig for the jewels? (". . . It will kill you to go out in this cold and darkness. You must get someone to do it for you.")

2a. By what title does Bassi address Okorie? (Grandfather)

INFERENTIAL

1b. What does this suggest about Bassi's feelings for Okorie? (She truly cares about him and does not want him to get hurt.)

2b. Why is this ironic? (Although Bassi is not a blood relation, she treats Okorie with more kindness and respect than his own grandchildren.)

17 TEACHING CHARACTERIZATION

Ask what new information Okorie reveals about the grandsons. (Students should recognize that the grandsons are lazy and unwilling to do traditional forms of work, such as farming.)

18 TEACHING STAGING

Point out that the sight of the men on tiptoes sneaking out with their hoes has a humorous effect.

ART AND LITERATURE

Hammered copper, beads, and seashells cover this carved wood stool-throne from Cameroon. Crocodile figures, which reflect the tribal leader's earthly power, form an interconnective support structure around the base. Such stools symbolize royal authority, because only the leader of the tribe could use such a throne; others sit on the ground around him.

- Ask students to identify the quality of the past that this throne might represent for Okorie. (respect for authority and traditional values)

Stool-throne carved with crocodiles, emblems of royalty, and overlaid with sheet copper and beads, Cameroon.

AROB. All right, Grandfather, we are going back 18 to bed.

OKORIE. What are you doing with hoes? You were never fond of farming.

OJIMA. We intend to go to the farm early in the morning.

17 OKORIE. But the harvest is over. When everybody in the village was digging out the crops, you were going around the town with your hands in your pockets. Now you say you are going to the farm.

OJIMA. Digging is good for the health, Grandfather.

OKORIE. [*Re-entering his room.*] Good night.

AROB and OJIMA. Good night, Grandfather.

[*They return to their room. After a short time* AROB *and* OJIMA *come out, each holding a hoe,*

444 *Drama*

and tip-toe out through the exit. Then, gently, OKORIE *too comes out on his toes, and placing his hoe on the shoulder, warily leaves the hall.*]

SCENE 2

[*The same, the following morning.*]

BASSI. [*Knocking at* OKORIE'*s door. She is holding a hoe.*] Grandfather, wake up. I am going to the farm.

OKORIE. [*Opening the door.*] Good morning. Where are you going so early in the morning?

BASSI. I am going to dig up the farm. You remember the treasure, don't you?

CRITICAL THINKING: GUIDED READING QUESTIONS

LITERAL

1a. What does Okorie say when Ojima tells him he and Arob intend to go to the farm early in the morning? (He says that the harvest is over and they did nothing to help when everyone was harvesting the crops.)

INFERENTIAL

1b. What does this suggest? (Okorie does not believe his grandsons. He knows that they are going after the treasure.)

OKORIE. Do you expect to find a treasure whilst you sleep at night? You should have dug at night, woman. Treasures are never found in the day.

BASSI. But you told me to dig in the morning, Father.

OKORIE. My grandsons were in this room somewhere. They heard what I told you about the Jewels of the Shrine.

BASSI. They could not have heard us. I looked everywhere. The stranger must have told them.

OKORIE. [*Rubbing his forehead.*] What stranger?

BASSI. The stranger who told you about the treasure in the farm.

OKORIE. So it was a stranger who told me! Oh yes, a stranger! [*He begins to dream.*] Ah, I remember him now. He was a great man. His face shone like the sun. It was like the face of God.

BASSI. You are dreaming, Grandfather. Wake up! I must go to the farm quickly.

OKORIE. Yes, woman, I remember the jewels in the farm. But you are too late.

BASSI. [*Excitedly.*] Late? Have your grandsons discovered the treasure?

OKORIE. They have not, but I have discovered it myself.

BASSI. [*Amazed.*] You?

[OKORIE *nods his head with a smile on his face.*]

19 BASSI. Do you mean to say that you are now a rich man?

OKORIE. By our Fathers' Shrine, I am.

BASSI. So you went and worked at night. You should not have done it, even to forestall your grandchildren.

OKORIE. My grandsons would never have found it.

BASSI. But you said that they heard us talking of the treasure.

20 OKORIE. You see, I suspected that my grandsons were in this room. So I told you that the treasure was in the farm but in actual fact it was in the little garden behind this house, where the village Shrine used to be. My grandsons traveled half a mile last night to the farm for nothing.

BASSI. Then I am glad I did not waste my time.

OKORIE. [*With delight.*] How my grandsons must have toiled in the night! [*He is overcome with laughter.*] My grandsons, they thought I would die in disgrace, a pauper, unheard of. No, not **21** now. [*Then boldly.*] But those wicked children must change, or when I die I shall not leave a penny for them.

BASSI. Oh, Grandfather, to think you are a rich man!

OKORIE. I shall send you to buy me new clothes. My grandsons will not know me again. Ha—ha—ha—ha! [OKORIE *and* BASSI *leave.*]

[AROB *and* OJIMA *crawl out from under the bed, where for a second time they have hidden. They look rough, their feet dirty with sand and leaves. Each comes out with his hoe.*]

AROB. So the old man fooled us.

22 OJIMA. Well, he is now a rich man, and we must treat him with care.

AROB. We have no choice. He says that unless we change, he will not leave a penny to us.

[*A knock at the door.*]

AROB *and* OJIMA. Come in.

OKORIE. [*Comes in, and seeing them so rough and dirty, bursts out laughing. The others look surprised.*] Look how dirty you are, with hoes and all. "Gentlemen" like you should not touch

The Jewels of the Shrine **445**

CRITICAL THINKING: GUIDED READING QUESTIONS

LITERAL

1a. How does Okorie behave when he thinks about his grandsons' wasting their time digging for the treasure? (He laughs with delight.)

2a. What does Okorie say his grandsons must do in order for him to leave them part of his wealth? (They must change.)

INFERENTIAL

1b. What does this laughter suggest about his feelings toward his grandsons? (His feelings of disgust and anger are deep.)

2b. Do you think Okorie suspects that the grandsons can hear him when he makes his comment? (Most students will probably think Okorie suspects they are within earshot, since he makes his intentions so clear and since he suspected they were under the bed when he misled them earlier.)

- Okorie reveals that he saw his grandsons under the bed and knows that they know about his new wealth.
- The grandsons claim they like Okorie, but Okorie laughs at them.
- The grandsons decide to show Okorie they like him by seeing to all his needs.

23 TEACHING PLOT: RISING ACTION

Point out that an important element of the plot is added here as Okorie tells his grandsons that he knows they have overheard him saying that he is now a wealthy man.

24 READING SKILL: INFERENCE

Ask students to infer why Okorie refers to his grandsons as "gentlemen." Students should recognize that the grandsons think themselves too good for the old ways of life. By calling them "gentlemen," Okorie scorns their modern values and their disregard for tradition.

25 TEACHING CHARACTER MOTIVATION

Ask students what motivates the grandsons to want to scratch Okorie's back and fan him. (Students should recognize that greed is the only motivating factor.)

26 TEACHING TONE

Explain that tone is the attitude an author takes toward his or her subject. Ask students to identify the tone of this passage. (Students should recognize the lighthearted and humorous tone conveyed by the greedy grandsons as they furiously try to please their grandfather.)

hoes. You should wear whites gloves and live in towns. But see, you look like two pigs. Ha—ha—ha—ha—ha! oh what grandsons! How stupid they look! Ha—ha—ha! [AROB *and* OJIMA *are*
23 *dumbfounded.*] I saw both of you a short while ago under the bed. I hope you now know that I have got the Jewels of the Shrine.

AROB. We, too, have something to tell you, Grandfather.

24 OKORIE. Yes, yes, "gentlemen." Come, tell me. [*He begins to move away.*] You must hurry up. I am going to town to buy myself some new clothes and a pair of shoes.

AROB. New clothes?

OJIMA. And shoes?

OKORIE. Yes, Grandsons, it is never too late to wear new clothes.

AROB. Let us go and buy them for you. It is too hard for you to—

OKORIE. If God does not think that I am yet old enough to be in the grave, I do not think I am too old to go to the market in town. I need some clothes and a comb to comb my beard. I am happy, Grandchildren, very happy.

[AROB *and* OJIMA *are dumbfounded.*]

OKORIE. Now, "gentlemen," why don't you get drunk and shout at me as before? [*Growing bolder.*] Why not laugh at me as if I were nobody? You young puppies, I am now somebody, somebody. What is somebody? [*Rubbing his forehead as usual.*]

AROB. [*To* OJIMA.] He has forgotten again.

OKORIE. Who has forgotten what?

OJIMA. You have forgotten nothing. You are a good man, Grandfather, and we like you.

OKORIE. [*Shouting excitedly.*] Bassi! Bassi! Bassi! Where is that silly woman? Bassi, come and hear

446 *Drama*

this. My grandchildren like me, I am now a good man. Ha—ha—ha—ha! [*He limps into his room.*]

[AROB *and* OJIMA *look at each other. It is obvious to them that the old man has all the cards now.*]

AROB. What has come over the old man?

OJIMA. Have you not heard that when people have money, it scratches them on the brain? That is what has happened to our grandfather now.

25 AROB. He does not believe that we like him. How can we convince him?

OJIMA. You know what he likes most; someone to scratch his back. When he comes out, you will scratch his back, and I will use his big fan to fan at him.

AROB. Great idea. [OKORIE *coughs from the room.*] He is coming now.

OKORIE. [*Comes in.*] I am so tired.

AROB. You said you were going to the market, Grandfather.

OKORIE. You do well to remind me. I have sent Bassi to buy the things I want.

26 OJIMA. Grandfather, you look really tired. Lie down here. [OKORIE *lies down and uncovers his back.*] Grandfather, from now on, I shall give you all your breakfast and your midday meals.

AROB. [*Jealously.*] By our Forefathers' Shrine, Grandfather, I shall take care of your dinner and supply you with wine and clothing.

OKORIE. God bless you, little sons. That is how it should have been all the time. An old man has a right to live comfortably in his last days.

OJIMA. Grandfather, it is a very long time since we scratched your back.

CRITICAL THINKING: GUIDED READING QUESTIONS

LITERAL

1a. What does Okorie tell his grandsons he is going to buy for himself? (clothes, shoes, and a comb)

2a. How does Okorie react when his grandsons insist that they like him? (He laughs at them.)

INFERENTIAL

1b. Why are the grandsons surprised when their grandfather says he is going to buy these things? (They think of him as a useless old man who does not need anything.)

2b. Why does Okorie laugh at his grandsons? (He sees that their change of heart is motivated by their interest in his wealth.)

AROB. Yes, it is a long time. We have not done it since we were infants. We want to do it now. It will remind us of our younger days when it was a pleasure to scratch your back.

OKORIE. Scratch my back? Ha—ha—ha—ha. Oh **27** go on, go on; by our Fathers' Shrine you are now good men. I wonder what has happened to you.

OJIMA. It's you, Grandfather. You are such a nice man. As a younger man you must have looked very well. But in your old age you look simply wonderful.

28 AROB. That is right, Grandfather, and let us tell you again. Do not waste a penny of yours any more. We will keep you happy and satisfied to the last hour of your life.

[OKORIE *appears pleased.* AROB *now begins to pick at, and scratch,* OKORIE's *back.* OJIMA *kneels near the bed and begins to fan the old man. After a while, a slow snore is heard. Then, as* AROB *warms up to his task,* OKORIE *jumps up.*]

OKORIE. Oh, that one hurts. Gently, children, gently. [*He relaxes and soon begins to snore again.* OJIMA *and* AROB *gradually stand up.*]

AROB. The old fogy is asleep.

OJIMA. That was clever of us. I am sure he be-**29** lieves us now. [*They leave.* OKORIE *opens an eye and peeps at them. Then he smiles and closes it again.*]

[BASSI *enters, bringing some new clothes, a pair of shoes, a comb and brush, a tin of face powder, etc. She pushes* OKORIE.]

BASSI. Wake up, Grandfather.

OKORIE. [*Opening his eyes.*] Who told you that I was asleep? Oh! you have brought the things. It is so long since I had a change of clothes. Go on, woman, and call those grandsons of mine. They must help me to put on my new clothes and shoes.

[BASSI *leaves.* OKORIE *begins to comb his hair and beard, which have not been touched for a long time.* BASSI *re-enters with* AROB *and* OJIMA. *Helped by his grandsons and* BASSI, OKORIE *puts on his new clothes and shoes. He then sits on the bed and poses majestically, like a Chief.*]

SCENE 3

[*The same, a few months later.* OKORIE *is lying* **30** *on the bed. He is well dressed and looks happy, but it is easily seen that he is nearing his end. There is a knock at the door.* OKORIE *turns and looks at the door, but cannot speak loudly. Another knock; the door opens, and the* STRANGER *enters.*]

OKORIE. Welcome back, Stranger. You have come in time. Sit down. I will tell you of my Will.

[*Door opens slowly.* BASSI *walks in.*]

BASSI. [*To* STRANGER.] How is he?

STRANGER. Just holding on.

BASSI. Did he say anything?

STRANGER. He says that he wants to tell me about his Will. Call his grandsons. [BASSI *leaves.*]

OKORIE. Stranger.

STRANGER. Yes, Grandfather.

OKORIE. Do you remember what I told you about my fears in life?

STRANGER. You were afraid your last days would be miserable, and that you would not have a decent burial.

OKORIE. Now, Stranger, all that is past. Don't you see how happy I am? I have been very well cared for since I saw you last. My grandchildren have

The Jewels of the Shrine **447**

CRITICAL THINKING: GUIDED READING QUESTIONS

LITERAL

1a. What do the grandsons say to flatter Okorie? (They say he is a nice man who must have looked good as a youth since he looks so wonderful now.)

2a. What does Okorie do after his hair and beard are combed and he has put on his new clothes? (He "poses majestically, like a Chief.")

INFERENTIAL

1b. What does this kind of flattery suggest about the grandsons' ideas about Okorie? (They think he is simple-minded enough to believe that they really have changed and now are truly concerned about him.)

2b. What does this behavior suggest he is feeling about what is taking place? (He is pleased with the success of his plans and with the way he has manipulated his grandsons' behavior toward him.)

- Okorie introduces the Stranger to his grandsons, who feign sadness at their grandfather's imminent death.
- Okorie tells his grandsons that his Will is buried in a small box with all his wealth; it is to be read by the Stranger two weeks after Okorie's death.
- Okorie instructs his grandsons to make his burial the best they can.

IN THE GLOSSARY

- compensated: repaid
- atone: to make amends
- destitute: impoverished

31 CRITICAL THINKING: EVALUATION

Ask students to evaluate Okorie's sincerity in forgiving his grandsons. Does he mean what he says? Why or why not? (Most students will probably say that Okorie is not sincere since he knows his grandsons are just being nice to him out of greed.)

32 TEACHING PLOT: RISING ACTION

Point out that the play approaches its climax as Okorie demands that his grandsons give him a grand burial.

33 CULTURAL BACKGROUND

Explain that Okorie's treatment of Bassi would not be considered cruel or unfair within their traditional society. Wealth is passed down through the males of the family, and a woman comes under the protection of her husband's family when she marries.

done everything for me, and I am sure they will bury me with great ceremony and rejoicing. I want you to be here when I am making my Will. Bend to my ears, I will whisper something to you. [STRANGER *bends for a moment.* OKORIE *whispers. Then he says aloud.*] Is that clear, Stranger?

STRANGER. It is clear.

OKORIE. Will you remember?

STRANGER. I will.

OKORIE. Do you promise?

STRANGER. I promise.

OKORIE. [*Relaxing on his pillow.*] There now. My end will be more cheerful than I ever expected.

[*A knock.*]

STRANGER. Come in.

[AROB, OJIMA, *and* BASSI *enter. The two men appear as sad as possible. They are surprised to meet the* STRANGER, *and stare at him for a moment.*]

OKORIE. [*With effort.*] This man may be a stranger to you, but not to me. He is my friend. Arob, look how sad you are! Ojima, how tight your lips are with sorrow! Barely a short while ago, you would not have cared whether I lived or died.

AROB. Don't speak like that, Grandfather.

OKORIE. Why should I not? Remember, these are my last words on earth.

OJIMA. You torture us, Grandfather.

31 OKORIE. Since my son, your father, died, you have tortured me. But now you have changed, and it is good to forgive you both.

STRANGER. You wanted to make a Will.

OKORIE. Will? Yes, Will. Where is Bassi? Has that woman run away already?

448 *Drama*

BASSI. [*Standing above the bed.*] No, Grandfather, I am here.

OKORIE. Now there is my family complete.

STRANGER. The Will, Grandfather, the Will.

OKORIE. Oh, the Will; the Will is made.

AROB. Made? Where is it?

OKORIE. It is written out on paper.

AROB }
OJIMA } [*Together.*] Written?
                     What?

OKORIE. [*Coolly.*] Yes, someone wrote it for me soon after I had discovered the treasure.

AROB. Where is it, Grandfather?

OJIMA. Are you going to show us, Grandfather?

OKORIE. Yes, I will. Why not? But not now, not until I am dead.

AROB and OJIMA. What?

OKORIE. Listen here. The Will is in a small box buried somewhere. The box also contains all my **32** wealth. These are my wishes. Make my burial the best you can. Spend as much as is required, for you will be compensated. Do not forget that I am the oldest man in this village. An old man has a right to be decently buried. Remember, it was only after I had discovered the Jewels of the Shrine that you began to take good care of me. You should, by carrying out all my last wishes, atone for all those years when you left me poor, destitute, and miserable.

[*To the* STRANGER, *in broken phrases.*] Two weeks after my death, Stranger, you will come and unearth the box of my treasure. Open it in the presence of my grandsons. Read out the division of the property and share it among them. **33** Bassi, you have nothing. You have a good husband and a family. No reward or treasure is greater than a good marriage and a happy home. Stranger, I have told you where the box containing the Will is buried. That is all. May God—

CRITICAL THINKING: GUIDED READING QUESTIONS

LITERAL

1a. What does Okorie say the grandsons have done since their father died? (They have tortured him, but now they have changed.)

2a. According to Okorie, when will the terms of the Will be revealed? (two weeks after his death)

INFERENTIAL

1b. Do you think Okorie really believes the grandsons have changed? Explain. (No, he is probably saying this to trick his grandsons.)

2b. What might be a reason for waiting so long to reveal the terms of the Will? (There is probably something in the Will that the grandsons will not like; if they know the terms right away, they might not give Okorie the kind of burial he wants.)

AROB and OJIMA. [*Rushing to him.*] Grandfather, Grandfather—

STRANGER. Leave him in peace.

34 [BASSI, *giving out a scream, rushes from the room.*]

STRANGER. I must go now. Don't forget his Will. Unless you bury him with great honor, you may not touch his property. [*He leaves.*]

SCENE 4

[*All in this scene are dressed in black.* AROB, OJIMA, *and* BASSI *are sitting around the table. There is one extra chair. The bed is still there, but the mat is taken off, leaving it bare. The hoe with which* GRANDFATHER *dug out the treasure is lying on the bed as a sort of memorial.*]

AROB. Thank God, today is here at last. When I get my own share, I will go and live in town.

OJIMA. If only that foolish stranger would turn up! Why a stranger should come into this house and—

BASSI. Remember, he was your grandfather's friend.

35 OJIMA. At last, poor Grandfather is gone. I wonder if he knew that we only played up just to get something from his Will.

AROB. Well, it didn't matter to him. He believed us, and that is why he has left his property to us. A few months ago, he would rather have thrown it all into the sea.

OJIMA. Who could have thought, considering the way we treated him, that the old man had such a kindly heart!

[*There is a knock. All stand.* STRANGER *enters*

A beaded headdress.

The Jewels of the Shrine **449**

PAGE SUMMARY: AT A GLANCE

- Okorie dies.
- Two weeks later Arob, Ojima, and Bassi wait for the Stranger to arrive and read the Will.

34 **TEACHING STAGING**

Ask students what this stage direction reveals about Bassi. (By having Bassi scream and rush from the room, the playwright conveys how upset she is by Okorie's death.)

35 **TEACHING DRAMATIC IRONY**

Point out that dramatic irony occurs when a character acts without knowing important pieces of information that the audience knows. Here the grandsons think they have tricked Okorie into leaving them his treasure. What information does the audience know that they do not? (Okorie was not asleep when they called him an old fogy and said that they were clever in making him believe them; Okorie whispered something to the Stranger regarding his Will.)

ART AND LITERATURE

This beaded Yoruba headdress was worn by the tribal leader during ritual ceremonies, such as marriages or funerals. The bird at the top—like the one atop the beaded staff on p. 439—symbolizes the leader's connection with the heavens. The surrounding figures represent the tribe's ancestors.

- Ask students which characters besides Okorie might be likely to appreciate this headdress. (the Stranger and Bassi)

CRITICAL THINKING: GUIDED READING QUESTIONS

LITERAL

1a. What do Ojima and Bassi say about the Stranger? (Ojima calls him "that foolish stranger" and expresses annoyance that he has been allowed in the house; Bassi points out that he was Okorie's friend.)

INFERENTIAL

→ **1b.** What do these references to the Stranger show about how Ojima and Bassi still feel toward Okorie? (Ojima still has no respect for his grandfather, while Bassi retains her good feelings toward him.)

PAGE SUMMARY: AT A GLANCE

- The Stranger arrives carrying the box with the Will.
- The grandsons begin quarreling about who took better care of Okorie and thus deserves his treasure.
- The grandsons reveal that their grandfather has had a fine burial, and Bassi indicates that the two have sold almost everything in order to pay for it.
- The Stranger opens the box, revealing only a piece of paper.

IN THE GLOSSARY

- querulously: in a complaining or fault-finding way

36 TEACHING DIALOGUE

Ask students what new things we now learn about the grandsons through their words. (Students should recognize that the grandsons are quarrelsome even between themselves and that their greed overwhelms their behavior.)

37 CULTURAL BACKGROUND

Point out that some of the masks we associate with African art are used in burial ceremonies. The dancers who wear these masks and the drummers who accompany them at ceremonies such as burials are usually hired.

38 TEACHING PLOT: RISING ACTION

Be sure students recognize that as the play approaches its climax, we learn one last important piece of information: The grandsons have impoverished themselves in order to give Okorie the kind of burial he wanted.

from GRANDFATHER's *room. He is grim, dressed in black, and carries a small wooden box under his arm.*]

AROB. Stranger, how did you come out from Grandfather's room?

STRANGER. Let us not waste time on questions. This box was buried in the floor of your grandfather's room. [*He places the box on the table;* AROB *and* OJIMA *crowd together. Sternly.*] Give me room, please. Your grandfather always wanted you to crowd around him. But no one would, until he was about to die. Step back, please. [*Both* AROB *and* OJIMA *step back.* OJIMA *accidentally steps on* AROB.]

AROB. [*To* OJIMA.] Don't you step on me!

OJIMA. [*Querulously.*] Don't you shout at me!

[STRANGER *looks at both.*]

36 AROB. When I sat day and night watching Grandfather in his illness, you were away in town, dancing and getting drunk. Now you want to be the first to grab at everything.

OJIMA. You liar! It was I who took care of him.

AROB. You only took care of him when you knew that he had come to some wealth.

BASSI. Why can't both of you—

AROB. [*Very sharply.*] Keep out of this, woman. That pretender [*Pointing to* OJIMA.] wants to bring trouble today.

OJIMA. I, a pretender? What of you, who began to scratch the old man's back simply to get his money?

AROB. How dare you insult me like that! [*He throws out a blow.* OJIMA *parries. They fight and roll on the floor. The* STRANGER *looks on.*]

BASSI. Stranger, stop them.

STRANGER. [*Calmly looking at them.*] Don't interfere, woman. The mills of God, the preachers tell us, grind slowly.

450 *Drama*

BASSI. I don't know anything about the mills of God. Stop them, or they will kill themselves.

STRANGER. [*Clapping his hands.*] Are you ready to proceed with your grandfather's Will, or should I wait till you are ready? [*They stop fighting, and stand up, panting.*] Before I open this box, I want to know if all your grandfather's wishes have been kept. Was he buried with honor?

AROB. Yes, the greatest burial any old man has had in this village.

OJIMA. You may well answer, but I spent more money than you did.

37 AROB. No, you did not. I called the drummers and the dancers.

OJIMA. I arranged for the shooting of guns.

AROB. I paid for the wine for the visitors and the mourners.

OJIMA. I—

STRANGER. Please, brothers, wait. I ask you again, was the old man respectably buried?

38 BASSI. I can swear to that. His grandsons have sold practically all they have in order to give him a grand burial.

STRANGER. That is good. I shall now open the box. [*There is silence. He opens the box and brings out a piece of paper.*]

AROB. [*In alarm.*] Where are the jewels, the money, the treasure?

STRANGER. Sh!—Listen. This is the Will. Perhaps it will tell us where to find everything. Listen to this.

AROB. But you cannot read. Give it to me.

OJIMA. Give it to me.

STRANGER. I can read. I am a school-teacher.

AROB. Did you write this Will for Grandfather?

CRITICAL THINKING: GUIDED READING QUESTIONS

LITERAL

1a. What do Ojima and Arob begin doing after the Stranger arrives? (They begin arguing and fighting.)

2a. What does the Stranger say when Bassi asks him to stop the grandsons from fighting? (He instructs her not to interfere, saying, "The mills of God . . . grind slowly.")

INFERENTIAL

1b. Why do you think they now begin fighting with each other? (They are both greedy, and each is probably concerned with getting the larger share of his grandfather's bequest.)

2b. What do you think he means when he says, "The mills of God . . . grind slowly"? (He probably means that it has taken a long time, but the grandsons are behaving according to their true nature and are about to be treated as they deserve.)

STRANGER. Questions are useless at this time. I did not.

AROB. Stop talking, man. Read it.

STRANGER. [*Reading.*] Now, my grandsons, now that I have been respectably and honorably buried, as all grandsons should do to their grandfathers, I can tell you a few things.

39   First of all, I have discovered no treasure at all. There was never anything like the "Jewels of the Shrine." [AROB *makes a sound as if something had caught him in the throat.* OJIMA *sneezes violently.*] There was no treasure hidden in the farm or anywhere else. I have had nothing in life, so I can only leave you nothing. The house which you now live in was my own. But I sold it some months ago and got a little money for what I needed. That money was my "Jewels of the Shrine." The house belongs now to the stranger who is reading this Will to you. He shall take possession of this house two days after the Will has been read. Hurry up, therefore, and pack out of this house. You young puppies, do you think I never knew that you had no love for me, and that you were only playing up in order to get the money which you believed I had acquired?

When I was a child, one of my first duties was to respect people who were older than myself. But you have thrown away our traditional love and respect for the elderly person. I shall
40 make you pay for it. Shame on you, young men, who believe that because you can read and write, you need not respect old age as your forefathers did! Shame on healthy young men like you, who leave the land to go to waste because they will not dirty their hands with work!

OJIMA. [*Furiously.*] Stop it, Stranger, stop it, or I will kill you! I am undone. I have not got a penny left. I have used all I had to feed him and to bury him. But now I have not even got a roof to stay under. You confounded Stranger, how dare you buy this house?

STRANGER. Do you insult me in my own house?

41 **AROB.** [*Miserably.*] The old cheat! He cheated us to the last. To think that I scratched his back only to be treated like this! We are now poorer than he had ever been.

OJIMA. It is a pity. It is a pity.

STRANGER. What is a pity?

OJIMA. It is a pity we cannot dig him up again.

[*Suddenly a hoarse, unearthly laugh is heard from somewhere. Everybody looks in a different direction. They listen. And then again—*]

VOICE. Ha—ha—ha—ha!

[*They all look up.*]

VOICE. Ha—ha—ha—ha!

[*The voice is unmistakably* GRANDFATHER OKORIE's *voice. Seized with terror, everybody except* BASSI *runs in confusion out of the room, stumbling over the table, box, and everything. As they run away, the voice continues.*]

Ha—ha—ha—ha!

[BASSI, *though frightened, boldly stands her ground. She is very curious to know whether someone has been playing them a trick.*]

VOICE. [*Louder.*] Ha—ha—ha—ha!

[BASSI *too is terrorized, and runs in alarm off the stage.*]

VOICE. [*Continues.*] Ha—ha—ha—ha!!!

The Jewels of the Shrine **451**

PAGE SUMMARY: AT A GLANCE

■ The Stranger reads the Will, revealing that there were no "Jewels of the Shrine," that Okorie sold his house to the Stranger, and that there is no inheritance for the grandsons.
■ The impoverished grandsons bewail their fate.
■ An unearthly laugh is heard clearly belonging to Okorie is heard, frightening everyone away.

IN THE GLOSSARY

■ acquired: got by one's own efforts

39 TEACHING PLOT: CLIMAX

Point out that the play reaches its climax with the reading of the Will, which reveals how Okorie has hoaxed his grandsons.

40 TEACHING THEME

Point out that here the author states his theme: Those who abandon the traditions of their ancestors, especially the traditions of respecting and caring for the elderly and the land, will reap their just reward.

41 CRITICAL THINKING: EVALUATION

Have students evaluate Okorie's behavior. Is his revenge on his grandsons just, or is it excessive? Divide students into two groups with opposing views, and have the groups briefly debate the issue.

COLLABORATIVE LEARNING: ENRICHMENT ACTIVITY

Social Studies Have students form groups, each to research one facet of Nigerian life. Students might explore such areas as customs, music, languages, foods, clothing, art, or types of homes. Have each group present an oral report with accompanying visual or audio material.

CRITICAL THINKING: GUIDED READING QUESTIONS

LITERAL

1a. What does the Will reveal about the "Jewels of the Shrine"? (There never were any such jewels; Okorie made them up.)

2a. How does the play end? (It ends with the sound of Okorie's laughter.)

INFERENTIAL

1b. What does the elaborateness of the hoax show about Okorie? (He was more clever than he appeared, and his disgust with his grandsons and their disregard for tradition was very great.)

2b. Why is the laughter a good ending to the play? (It reinforces the idea that Okorie enjoyed his final days by outwitting his disrespectful grandsons.)

Does the play have a satisfying ending? Why or why not?

ANSWERS

STUDY QUESTIONS

1. They are going to the farm to dig up the jewels they think are buried there.
2. Okorie knew they were in the room, the jewels were buried behind the house, and Okorie has already dug them up.
3. He asks whether Arob and Ojima have buried their grandfather with honor.
4. The story of the jewels was a lie, the house has been sold to the Stranger, and Okorie knew all along that the grandsons' "respect" was insincere.
5. He limps and walks with a stick, forgets what he is talking about, tires easily, and talks "in broken phrases" just before he dies.
6. Their behavior toward him changes only after they believe he is rich.
7. It emphasizes the cleverness of Okorie's victory and stresses that those who try to achieve wealth through insincerity and disrespect are doomed to failure.
8. Possible responses: love and respect of one's family; a sense of accomplishment in one's achievements; freedom from having to earn a living

LITERARY FOCUS

Dialogue

1. He often forgets what he just said and needs reminding.
2. She knows him well, has patience, and cares enough about him to dig up the jewels for him.
3. He asks her whether she can keep a secret; he says that he thinks he hears voices; he tells her to look around the room for listeners; he makes her swear not to tell his grandsons.

Staging

1. His garments might be shabby; he might be without shoes.
2. Their clothing might be dirty and stained with sweat.
3. The sparse furnishings suggest a lack of wealth; the hoes suggest a rural setting.

STUDY QUESTIONS

Recalling

1. Where are Arob and Ojima headed with their hoes at the end of Scene 1?
2. In Scene 2 what surprising information do Arob and Ojima overhear when they hide under the bed for the second time?
3. In Scene 4 what does the Stranger ask before he opens the box to read Okorie's will?
4. What do the grandsons learn when they finally hear the will?

Interpreting

5. In what specific ways does Okorie's behavior show that he is an old man?
6. Why does Okorie doubt the sincerity of his grandsons when they suddenly begin to treat him with love and respect?
7. How does the laughter at the end reinforce the play's theme?

Extending

8. In *The Jewels of the Shrine* old age is portrayed as a difficult time of life. What might make old age a time of delight and satisfaction for many people in modern American society?

LITERARY FOCUS

Dialogue

Dramatic **dialogue** is the conversation exchanged by the characters in a play. Because a play consists largely of people talking to one another, dialogue is a playwright's most important means of establishing characters and advancing the action.

For example, at the beginning of the play, Okorie talks with the Stranger about what it means to be elderly. We can see that Okorie is old by the way he looks close up, but when we hear him complain of his grandsons' disrespect, we know how disappointed and upset he feels. This knowledge helps the audience to understand Okorie's motives for what follows.

Thinking About Dialogue

Reread the passage of dialogue between Okorie and Bassi in Scene 1 beginning with Bassi's line "Don't shout so. It's not good for you" and ending with Okorie's observation "Now life is becoming worthwhile." Answer the following questions:

1. How can we tell from the way Okorie speaks that he is an old man?
2. What do we learn about Bassi's attitude toward the old man from what she says to him in this passage?
3. How do Okorie's remarks to Bassi indicate that he wants to keep his story about the jewels a secret?

Staging

Reading the script of a play is a little like following the score of a symphony: We must imagine hearing the music as we read. Just as an orchestra makes music out of a composer's notes, **staging**—scenery, lighting, costumes, and acting—brings a playwright's words to vivid life for an audience. Therefore, as we read any play, we can add tremendously to our pleasure by imagining how it might come to life on the stage.

Thinking About Staging

Costuming and stage set and prop design are especially important in the staging of *The Jewels of the Shrine*. Appropriate costumes and a set that effectively depicts Okorie's mud-walled house can help audiences to understand the play's social setting. Suggest some ideas for the costuming and set design for a production of the play. Consider the following questions:

1. How could Okorie's clothing in Scene 1 suggest that his grandsons neglect him?
2. How would the grandsons' clothing in Scene 2 show where they had been during the night?
3. How do details of the set design and props specified in the stage directions at the beginning of Scene 1 suggest the play's social setting?

COMPOSITION

Writing an Offstage Scene

■ Imagine that Bassi goes home after seeing the events of Scene 4 and hearing Okorie's terrifying disembodied laughter. Write a short scene using dramatic dialogue in which Bassi tells her husband what she saw and heard. Then have the grandsons enter to ask Bassi if they can stay with her. Think carefully about what she would say to them so that her comments are consistent with her character.

COMPOSITION: GUIDELINES FOR EVALUATION

WRITING AN OFFSTAGE SCENE

Objective

To use dialogue to continue a story

Guidelines for Evaluation

■ suggested length: two to three pages
■ should show knowledge of the play's events
■ should show understanding of the characters and their different points of view
■ should use the format for dramatic dialogue

PREVIEW: THE AUTHOR AND THE WORLD

GEOGRAPHY AND CULTURE

Seami Motokiyo (1363–1443)

Japan

Seami Motokiyo [ze ä′mē mō tō′kē yō] was one of the greatest dramatists of Japan. Together with his father, also an actor and playwright, Seami* established the traditions of the Japanese No theater. Besides acting and teaching he wrote about two hundred plays for this theater, many of which are still performed today. When he was a boy in his father's theater troupe, Seami gained the support of the shogun Ashikaga Yoshimitsu, the military ruler of Japan. The shogun's sponsorship allowed him to create No drama, a highly refined poetic dance-drama. This form has become Japan's classical theater.

Seami wrote manuals developing the standards for No drama. He had pupils and had hoped to pass on his art to his son, Motomasa, who showed great promise. But Motomasa died before his father, and Seami himself lost the favor of the shoguns who succeeded his patron, Ashikaga. Exiled at the age of seventy-two, he was pardoned shortly before his death. His plays and manuals on the training of actors have had a profound influence on Japanese culture.

---

* his surname. In Japanese names the surname traditionally precedes the given name.

Japan's Former Feudal Society

The country of Japan consists mainly of four large islands, close together, located in the western Pacific Ocean off the east coast of Asia. The isolation of Japan's island geography made possible the strict control that Japan's rulers imposed on the country between 1603 and 1867. Japan developed its own highly feudal society independent of European feudalism (the medieval political, economic, and social system in which loyalty and homage were paid to overlords).

Until 1868, when the emperor reassumed power, shoguns (military dictators) ruled Japan and were supported by lesser lords. Samurai (knights) provided manpower for the shoguns' armies. An aristocratic warrior class, samurai followed a strict code of honor and conduct that emphasized unwavering loyalty to their lords and the shogun. In Seami's play *The Dwarf Trees* Tsuneyo is a poor samurai, and the wandering priest is the lord himself in disguise. The play turns on Tsuneyo's loyalty to his lord, that critically important value in Japanese feudal society.

See LITERATURE AND CULTURE SOURCEBOOK: China and Japan

The Dwarf Trees **453**

LESSON PREVIEW

In this No drama a poor man's noble behavior is rewarded. Disguised as a priest, the ruler of Japan seeks shelter at the home of Tsuneyo, an impoverished nobleman. Tsuneyo and his wife share their meager meal, and Tsuneyo chops down his treasured dwarf trees to build a fire. When the ruler returns to the throne, he summons an army, and Tsuneyo heeds the call. The ruler then rewards Tsuneyo for his generosity and loyalty.

LITERARY SKILLS FOR THIS SELECTION

- the Japanese No play
- irony

THEMES IN THIS SELECTION

- generosity and loyalty
- appearance versus reality

LESSON OBJECTIVES

1. to examine the elements and devices of a No play
2. to understand words from Japanese
3. to write a haiku

Teacher's Classroom Resources 3

- Teaching Notes — 139
- Prereading Vocabulary — 140
- Reading Guide — 141
- Check Test — 142
- Responding to World Cultures — 143
- Literary Focus: The Japanese No Play — 144
- Language Study: English Words Borrowed from Japanese — 145
- Writing Process Guide: Writing a Haiku — 146
- Grammar in Literature: Subject-Verb Agreement in Inverted Sentences — 147
- Selection Test — 148

IN THE CLASSROOM

TEACHING STUDENTS OF DIFFERENT ABILITIES

- **For less advanced students:** Preview the Glossary words and footnotes. Ask students to complete the Reading Guide.

- **For more advanced students:** Have students research and report on the influence of No drama and other Asian literary forms on twentieth-century Western writers, such as Ezra Pound and Amy Lowell.

DISCUSSING GEOGRAPHY AND CULTURE

Comparing the Dress of Medieval Knights

The dress of the samurai was both practical and symbolic. Samurai wore armor made of laced reeds and chain-mail sleeves, two decorated swords, and a steel helmet with horns, which symbolized strength and invincibility.

- Ask students to compare the dress of the samurai with that of medieval European knights. (The latter wore metal armor over a chain-mail shirt, a visored helmet, and a sword, dagger, and mace.)

Seami Motokiyo

The Dwarf Trees

Translated from the Japanese by Arthur Waley

CHARACTERS

1 THE PRIEST: Lord Tokiyori[1] disguised

TSUNEYO GENZAYEMON:[2] a former retainer of Tokiyori

TSUNEYO'S WIFE

TOKIYORI'S MINISTER, and FOLLOWERS

CHORUS

---

2 PRIEST. No whence nor whither know I, only onward,
   Onward my way.

I am a holy man of no fixed abode. I have been traveling through the land of Shinano,[3] but the snow lies thick. I had best go up to Kamakura[4] now and wait there. When Spring comes I will set out upon my pilgrimage.

[*He walks round the stage singing his song of travel.*]

Land of Shinano, Peak of Asama,[5]
Thy red smoke rising far and near! Yet cold
Blows the great wind whose breath
From Greatwell Hill is fetched.
On to the Village of Friends—but friendless I,

---

1. **Lord Tokiyori** [tö kē′yō rē]: member of the Hōjō family, regents who served as Japan's rulers in the thirteenth century. According to tradition, after ruling from 1246 to 1256, Hōjō Tokiyori disguised himself as a priest and traveled the countryside to learn the needs of the people.
2. **Tsuneyo Genzayemon** [tsōō nā′yō gen zī′e mŏn′]
3. **Shinano** [shē nā′nō]: former Japanese province located on the island of Honshu.
4. **Kamakura** [kä mä′kōō rä]: Honshu city from which the Hōjō family ruled.
5. **Peak of Asama** [ə sä′mə]: Mount Asama, an active volcano in central Honshu.

454 *Drama*

Whose self is cast aside, go up the path
Of Parting Hill, that from the temporal world
Yet further parts me. Down the river, down
Runs my swift raft plank-nosed to Plank-nose Inn,
And to the Ford of Sano[6] I am come.

3 I have traveled so fast that I am come to the Ford of Sano in the country of Kotsuke.[7] *Ara!*[8] It is snowing again. I must seek shelter here. [*Goes to the wing and knocks.*] Is there anyone in this house?

TSUNEYO'S WIFE. [*Raising the curtain that divides the hashigakari[9] from the stage.*] Who is there?

PRIEST. I am a pilgrim; pray lodge me here to-night.

4 WIFE. That is a small thing to ask. But since the master is away, you cannot lodge in this house.

PRIEST. Then I will wait here till he comes back.

WIFE. That must be as you please. I will go to the corner and watch for him. When he comes I will tell him you are here.

[*Enter* TSUNEYO *from the wing, making the gesture of one who shakes snow from his clothes.*]

TSUNEYO. Ah! How the snow falls! Long ago when I was in the World I loved to see it:

---

6. **Ford of Sano** [sä′nō]: town where one can cross the Shinano River by ferry. The Shinano River is the longest river on the island of Honshu.
7. **Kotsuke** [kō′tsōō ke]: another former Japanese province on the island of Honshu.
8. *Ara* [a rä′]: Japanese exclamation similar in meaning to "Oh!" or "Alas!"
9. *hashigakari* [hä shē′gä kä rē]: a runway that leads from the actors' dressing room to the stage.

CRITICAL THINKING: GUIDED READING QUESTIONS

LITERAL

1a. According to the legend explained in the footnote, why does Lord Tokiyori, ruler of Japan, disguise himself as a wandering priest? (He does so to learn his people's needs.)

2a. What does the "priest" ask Tsuneyo's wife? (He asks to be lodged for the night.)

INFERENTIAL

1b. What does this motivation reveal about his concerns as Japan's ruler? (He cares more about ruling wisely and helping his subjects than he does about the trappings of wealth and power, which he is willing to give up temporarily.)

2b. Why must he seek shelter? (He must escape the snow and cold.)

"Hither and thither the snow blew like feathers plucked from a goose;
Long, long I watched it fall, till it dressed me in a white coat."

5 So I sang; and the snow that falls now is the same that I saw then. But I indeed am frost-white that watch it!

Oh how shall this thin dress of Kefu-cloth
Chase from my bones the winter of today,
Oh pitiless day of snow!

[*He sees his* WIFE *standing waiting.*]

What is this! How comes it that you are waiting here in this great storm of snow?

WIFE. A pilgrim came this way and begged for a night's lodging. And when I told him you were not in the house, he asked if he might wait till you returned. That is why I am here.

TSUNEYO. Where is this pilgrim now?

WIFE. There he stands!

PRIEST. I am he. Though the day is not far spent, how can I find my way in this great storm of snow? Pray give me shelter for the night.

TSUNEYO. That is a small thing to ask; but I have no lodging fit for you; I cannot receive you.

PRIEST. No, no. I do not care how poor the lodging may be. Pray let me stay here for one night.

TSUNEYO. I would gladly ask you to stay, but there is scarce space for us two that are husband and wife. How can we give you lodging? At the village of Yamamoto yonder, ten furlongs[10] further, you will find a good inn. You had best be on your way before the daylight goes.

PRIEST. So you are resolved to turn me away?

6 TSUNEYO. I am sorry for it, but I cannot give you lodging.

_____
10. **furlongs:** short distances. One furlong equals one eighth of a mile.

PRIEST. [*Turning away.*] Much good I got by waiting for such a fellow! I will go my way. [*He goes.*]

7 WIFE. Alas, it is because in a former life we neglected the ordinances[11] that we are now come to ruin. And surely it will bring us ill-fortune in our next life, if we give no welcome to such a one as this! If it is by any means possible for him to shelter here, please let him stay.

TSUNEYO. If you are of that mind, why did you not speak before? [*Looking after the* PRIEST.] No, he cannot have gone far in this great snowstorm. I will go after him and stop him. Hie, traveler, hie! We will give you lodging. Hie! The snow is falling so thick that he cannot hear me. What a sad plight he is in. Old-fallen snow covers the way he came and snow new-fallen hides the path where he should go. Look, look! He is standing still. He is shaking the snow from his clothes; shaking, shaking. It is like that old song:

"At Sano Ferry
No shelter found we
To rest our horses,
Shake our jackets,
In the snowy twilight."

That song was made at Sano Ferry,
At the headland of Miwa on the Yamato Way.[12]

8 CHORUS. But now at Sano on the Eastern Way
Would you wander weary in the snow of twilight?
Though mean the lodging,
Rest with us, oh rest till day!

[*The* PRIEST *goes with them into the hut.*]

TSUNEYO. [*To his* WIFE.] Listen. We have given him lodging, but have not laid the least thing before

_____
11. **ordinances:** that is, Buddhist ordinances, or rules, which teach hospitality to priests, among other things.
12. **headland of Miwa on the Yamato Way:** headland at the town of Miwa on the route to Yamato, another former Japanese province on Honshu. A headland is a stretch of land that juts out into the water.

The Dwarf Trees **455**

PAGE SUMMARY: AT A GLANCE

■ Since his home is small, Tsuneyo reluctantly refuses to lodge the traveler and recommends that he seek shelter at a nearby inn.
■ Then Tsuneyo's wife, citing Buddhist rules of hospitality, persuades her husband to lodge the traveler.

IN THE GLOSSARY

■ resolved: determined
■ hie: hurry

5 **READING SKILL: CONTRAST**

Ask students to contrast Tsuneyo's feelings about snow when he was "in the World" as a wealthy landowner with his feelings about it now. (Students should recognize that he enjoyed the snow when he was rich, but now, poor and ill-clad, he finds the same snow "pitiless.")

6 **TEACHING CHARACTERIZATION**

Point out that Tsuneyo turns down the priest's request even though he regrets doing so. Ask what this shows about his character. (He is a kind man but ashamed of his poverty.)

7 **CULTURAL BACKGROUND**

Explain that as Buddhists, Tsuneyo and his wife believe in reincarnation—the soul's return, after death, in a new bodily form. According to their beliefs, the suffering one experiences in one's present life stems from irreverent behavior in a former life.

8 **TEACHING THE NO PLAY**

Point out that some portions of the play are in verse (as in the chorus' speech here), while other portions are in prose. The same is true of many classic European dramas, including the plays of William Shakespeare.

CRITICAL THINKING: GUIDED READING QUESTIONS

LITERAL

1a. What is Tsuneyo's initial reason for refusing to lodge the traveler? (His home is barely large enough for his wife and himself.)

2a. Who persuades Tsuneyo to change his mind about lodging the traveler? (Tsuneyo's wife)

INFERENTIAL

1b. What does the information about Tsuneyo's home and dress reveal about his financial status? (He is now quite poor.)

2b. By changing his mind when his wife cites Buddhist teachings, what traits does Tsuneyo display? (He is not stubborn and tries to behave piously.)

PAGE SUMMARY: AT A GLANCE

- Tsuneyo and his wife offer the traveler boiled millet, the food of the poorest peasants—and the only food they have.
- Regretting his lack of fuel for a fire to warm his guest, Tsuneyo offers to burn his three treasured dwarf trees, but the visitor protests.

IN THE GLOSSARY

- recollection: remembrance

9 READING SKILL: INFERENCE

Ask students to infer why the wife thinks that the priest might not want to eat the millet. (Since millet is the food of the poor, the wife probably thinks that the priest may consider eating such food to be beneath his dignity.)

10 TEACHING CHARACTERIZATION

Ask what the disguised ruler's acceptance of the millet shows about his character. (He displays humility as well as courtesy by accepting with such seeming pleasure his hosts' poor dinner fare.)

11 CULTURAL BACKGROUND

Explain that gardening is a time-honored tradition in Japan. Japanese gardeners—now imitated the world over—cultivate many dwarf plants, or plants of a smaller-than-usual size. In the Japanese art form called *bonsai,* large trees and shrubs are patiently pruned and nurtured to create miniature specimens suitable for shallow pots.

12 TEACHING STUDENTS OF LIMITED ENGLISH PROFICIENCY

Have students note that Tsuneyo and his wife here and at the beginning of the next page recite alternating lines of a continuous speech. One of the lines recited before the next speaker takes over ("For snow falls . . . ") has no end punctuation. Have two students take the roles of Tsuneyo and his wife and recite the lines aloud so that the class may get a feel for the sound of the dialogue.

him. Is there nothing we can give?

9 WIFE. It happens that we have a little boiled millet;[13] we can give him that if he will take it.

TSUNEYO. I will tell him. [*To the* PRIEST.] I have given you lodging, but I have not yet laid anything before you. It happens that we have a little boiled millet. It is coarse food, but pray eat it if you can.

10 PRIEST. Why, that's a famous[14] dish! Please give it me.

TSUNEYO. [*To* WIFE.] He says he will take some; make haste and give it to him.

WIFE. I will do so.

TSUNEYO. Long ago when I was in the World I knew nothing of this stuff called millet but what I read of it in poems and songs. But now it is the prop of my life.

Truly Rosei's dream of fifty years' glory[15]
That he dreamed at Kántán[16] on lent pillow propped
Was dreamed while millet cooked, as yonder dish now.
Oh if I might but sleep as he slept, and see in my dream
Times that have passed away, then should I have comfort;
But now through battered walls——

───────────

13. **millet:** cereal grass that is ground for food in Asia. At the time of the play, millet was the food of the poorest peasants.
14. **famous:** here, wonderful; fine.
15. **Rosei's** [rō sāz′] **dream of fifty years' glory:** Chinese legend of Rosei, who travels to the city to become a public servant. Along the way he meets an old man who offers him food and lodging. While his host prepares a meal of millet, Rosei falls asleep. In his dream he rises to power but is unhappy until he returns to his birthplace. When he awakes, he decides to abandon his plans and return home.
16. **Kántán** [kän′ tän′]: the ancient Chinese village where Rosei stops to rest and has his legendary dream.

456 *Drama*

CHORUS. Cold wind from the woods
Blows sleep away and the dreams of recollection.

[*While the* CHORUS *sings these words an* ATTENDANT *brings onto the stage the three dwarf trees.*]

TSUNEYO. How cold it is! And as the night passes, each hour the frost grows keener. If I had but fuel to light a fire with that you might sit by it and warm yourself! Ah! I have thought of something. I have some dwarf trees. I will cut them down and make a fire of them.

11 PRIEST. Have you indeed dwarf trees?

TSUNEYO. Yes, when I was in the World I had a fine show of them; but when my trouble came I had no more heart for tree-fancying, and gave them away. But three of them, I kept—plum, cherry and pine. Look, there they are, covered with snow. They are precious to me; yet for this night's entertainment I will gladly set light to them.

PRIEST. No, no, that must not be. I thank you for your kindness, but it is likely that one day you will go back to the World again and need them for your pleasure. Indeed it is not to be thought of.

12 TSUNEYO. My life is like a tree the earth has covered;
I shoot no blossoms upward to the world.

WIFE. And should we burn for you
These shrubs, these profitless toys,

TSUNEYO. Think them the fagots of our Master's servitude.[17]

WIFE. For snow falls upon them, as it fell——

───────────

17. **fagots . . . servitude:** the firewood that Gautama Buddha carried after he renounced his high rank and worked as a servant in Asia's Himalaya Mountains. Gautama Buddha is the historic founder of Buddhism.

CRITICAL THINKING: GUIDED READING QUESTIONS

LITERAL

1a. What did Tsuneyo know about millet when he was "in the World"? (He knew nothing except what he read in poems and songs.)

2a. What does Tsuneyo offer to burn for firewood? (He offers his three treasured dwarf trees.)

INFERENTIAL

1b. From details in the play, what can you infer that Tsuneyo means by "in the World"? (He was wealthy and part of fashionable or influential society.)

2b. What qualities does Tsuneyo display in making this offer? (generosity, unselfishness, and hospitality)

Detail from a No robe, Japanese, seventeenth century.

PAGE SUMMARY: AT A GLANCE

■ Tsuneyo and his wife override the visitor's protests, although Tsuneyo deeply regrets having to kill his beautiful trees.

13 TEACHING THE NO PLAY

Note that in addition to narrating certain events, the chorus sometimes speaks directly for the characters. In viewing the play, the audience must use pronouns and other context clues to determine which choral lines are characters' speech and which are narration, since clues such as stage directions and quotation marks are absent. We do the same when we listen to a folk ballad or any song that contains dialogue but does not identify the speaker.

ART AND LITERATURE

No costumes, such as the robe shown here, were often designed to evoke tranquillity. This silk robe embroidered with blossoms, butterflies, leaves, and rhythmically curving grass suggests nature's replenishment and the airy, meditative warmth of the springtime sun.

■ Ask students which words from the chorus' speech on page 457 might describe this robe. ("bare boughs blossoming"; "earliest of Spring")

TSUNEYO. When he to hermits of the cold
  Himalayan Hills was carrier of wood.

WIFE. So let it be.

13 **CHORUS.** [*Speaking for* TSUNEYO.] "Shall I from
  one who has cast life aside,
  Dear life itself, withhold these trivial trees?"

[TSUNEYO *goes and stands by the dwarf trees.*]

Then he brushed the snow from off them, and
  when he looked,

"I cannot, cannot," he cried, "O beautiful
  trees,
Must I begin?
You, plum-tree, among bare boughs blossom-
  ing
Hard by the window, still on northward face
Snow-sealed, yet first to scent
Cold air with flowers, earliest of Spring;
'You first shall fall.'
You by whose boughs on mountain hedge en-
  twined
Dull country folk have paused and caught
  their breath,

The Dwarf Trees **457**

CRITICAL THINKING: GUIDED READING QUESTIONS

LITERAL

1a. What question does the chorus, speaking for Tsuneyo, ask? ("Shall I from one who has cast life aside, / Dear life itself, withhold these trivial trees?")

INFERENTIAL

1b. Who has "cast life aside," and why do his actions make the trees seem "trivial"? (The priest, or the person Tsuneyo thinks is a priest, has "cast life aside" by giving up material comforts and possessions in favor of an ascetic life; he makes Tsuneyo feel vain and materialistic for valuing possessions.)

- Tsuneyo sadly cuts down his trees to use for firewood.
- When the priest asks him his clan, Tsuneyo explains that he is Lord of Sano, sunk to desperate circumstances because relatives usurped his lands. Furthermore, since Japan's ruler is away on a pilgrimage, he is unable to present his claims at court.
- Tsuneyo expresses his readiness to fight and die for his ruler, but he fears he will "die useless."
- After responding reassuringly, the priest announces his departure.

IN THE GLOSSARY

- quaking: shaking
- beacon: guiding light
- usurped: took unjustly
- mischance: bad luck
- gird: fasten with a belt

14 CRITICAL THINKING: EVALUATION

Have students evaluate Tsuneyo's strong feelings for his dwarf trees. Is his great sadness at cutting them down justified? Why or why not? (Students should recognize that the trees are symbols of his former wealth and prestige. As such they have great meaning for him.)

15 TEACHING CHARACTER MOTIVATION

Ask students what motivates Tsuneyo to at first refuse to give his clan name. (He feels shame and despair about his impoverished situation.)

16 TEACHING IRONY

Point out that this question helps achieve dramatic irony, since we know that the priest is really the *Shikken*, but Tsuneyo does not know this.

17 READING SKILL: PREDICTING OUTCOMES

Have students predict whether these heartening words will prove valid. (They probably will, since they are spoken by someone in a position to reward Tsuneyo.)

Hewn down for firewood. Little had I thought
My hand so pitiless!"

[*He cuts down the plum-tree.*]

14 "You, cherry (for each Spring your blossom comes
Behind the rest), I thought a lonely tree
And reared you tenderly, but now
I, I am lonely left, and you, cut down,
Shall flower but with flame."

TSUNEYO. You now, O pine, whose branches I had thought
One day when you were old to lop and trim,
Standing you in the field, a football-post,[18]
Such use shall never know.
Tree, whom the winds have ever wreathed
With quaking mists, now shimmering in the flame
Shall burn and burn.
Now like a beacon, sentinels at night
Kindle by palace gate to guard a king,
Your fire burns brightly.
Come, warm yourself.

PRIEST. Now we have a good fire and can forget the cold.

TSUNEYO. It is because you lodged with us that we too have a fire to sit by.

PRIEST. There is something I must ask you: I would gladly know to what clan my host belongs.

15 TSUNEYO. I am not of such birth; I have no clan-name.

PRIEST. Say what you will, I cannot think you a commoner. The times may change; what harm will you get by telling me your clan?

TSUNEYO. Indeed I have no reason to conceal it. Know then that Tsuneyo Genzayemon, Lord of Sano, is sunk to this!

---

18. **football-post:** referring to an old Japanese ball game.

458 *Drama*

PRIEST. How came it, sir, that you fell to such misery?

TSUNEYO. Thus it was: kinsmen usurped my lands, and so I became what I am.

16 PRIEST. Why do you not go up to the Capital and lay your case before the *Shikken*'s[19] court?

TSUNEYO. By further mischance it happens that Lord Saimyōji[20] himself is absent upon pilgrimage. And yet not all is lost; for on the wall a tall spear still hangs, and armor with it; while in the stall a steed is tied. And if at any time there came from the City news of peril to our master—

Then, broken though it be I would gird this armor on,
And rusty though it be I would hold this tall spear,
And lean-ribbed though he be I would mount my horse and ride
Neck by neck with the swiftest,
To write my name on the roll.
And when the fight began
Though the foe were many, yet would I be the first
To cleave their ranks, to choose an adversary
To fight with him and die.

[*He covers his face with his hands; his voice sinks again.*]

But now, another fate, worn out with hunger
To die useless. Oh despair, despair!

17 PRIEST. Take courage; you shall not end so. If I live, I will come to you again. Now I go.

TSUNEYO and WIFE. We cannot let you go. At first we were ashamed that you should see the mis-

---

19. *Shikken*'s [shĕk′kenz]: that is, Hōjō Tokiyori's. Rather than claiming the emperor's throne directly or even taking the title of *shogun* ("military ruler"), members of the Hōjō family took the title of *shikken,* which means "regent" or "acting ruler."
20. **Lord Saimyōji** [sī mē ō′jē]: another name for Lord Tokiyori.

CRITICAL THINKING: GUIDED READING QUESTIONS

LITERAL

1a. How did Tsuneyo rear his cherry tree, and what were his plans for the pine? (He reared the cherry tenderly; he planned to "lop and trim" the pine, making it into a "football-post" when it was old.)

2a. What does Tsuneyo promise to do upon receiving news of peril to his ruler? (He plans to don his rusty armor and help his ruler fight.)

INFERENTIAL

1b. What chief emotion accompanies his cutting down of the trees? (sadness; grief)

2b. What chief quality does this promise reveal? (loyalty) ery of our dwelling; but now we ask you to stay with us awhile.

PRIEST. Were I to follow my desire, think you I would soon go forth into the snow?

TSUNEYO and **WIFE.** After a day of snow even the clear sky is cold, and tonight—

PRIEST. Where shall I lodge?

WIFE. Stay with us this one day.

PRIEST. Though my longing bides with you—

TSUNEYO and **WIFE.** You leave us?

PRIEST. Farewell, Tsuneyo!

BOTH. Come back to us again.

18 **CHORUS.** [*Speaking for* PRIEST.] "And should you one day come up to the City, seek for me there. A humble priest can give you no public further-ance, yet can he find ways to bring you into the presence of Authority. Do not give up your suit."[21] He said no more. He went his way—he sad to leave them and they to lose him from their sight.

[*Interval of six months.*]

TSUNEYO. [*Standing outside his hut and seeming to watch travelers on the road.*] Hie, you travel-
19 ers! Is it true that the levies[22] are marching to Kamakura? They are marching in great force, you say? So it is true. Barons and knights from the Eight Counties of the East all riding to Kamakura! A fine sight it will be. Tasseled breast-plates of beaten silver; swords and daggers fret-ted with gold. On horses fat with fodder they ride; even the grooms of the relay-horses are magnificently appareled. And along with them [*Miming the action of leading a horse.*] goes

---

21. **suit:** here, cause; case; plea in court.
22. **levies** [lev′ēz]: troops enlisted for military service; enlisted armies.

Tsuneyo, with horse, armor and sword that scarce seem worthy of such names. They may laugh, yet I am not, I think, a worse man than they; and had I but a steed to match my heart, then valiantly—[*Making the gesture of cracking a whip.*]—you laggard!

CHORUS. The horse is old, palsied as a willow-bough; it cannot hasten. It is lean and twisted.
20 Not whip or spur can move it. It sticks like a coach in a bog. He follows far behind the rest.

PRIEST. [*Again ruler of Japan, seated on a throne.*] Are you there?

MINISTER. I stand before you.

PRIEST. Have the levies of all the lands arrived?

MINISTER. They are all come.

21 **PRIEST.** Among them should be a knight in bro-ken armor, carrying a rusty sword, and leading his own lean horse. Find him, and bring him to me.

MINISTER. I tremble and obey. [*Going to* TSUNEYO.] I must speak with you.

TSUNEYO. What is it?

MINISTER. You are to appear immediately before my lord.

TSUNEYO. Is it I whom you are bidding appear before his lordship?

MINISTER. Yes, you indeed.

TSUNEYO. How can it be I? You have mistaken me for some other.

MINISTER. Oh no, it is you. I was told to fetch the most ill-conditioned of all the soldiers; and I am sure you are he. Come at once.

TSUNEYO. The most ill-conditioned of all the sol-diers?

MINISTER. Yes, truly.

TSUNEYO. Then I am surely he.
Tell your Lord that I obey.

The Dwarf Trees **459**

PAGE SUMMARY: AT A GLANCE

- The priest tells Tsuneyo not to give up his suit of armor.
- Six months after the visitor leaves, Tsuneyo learns that an army is being raised.
- On his broken-down horse he joins the forces, as he pledged he would do.
- The *Shikken*, having aban-doned his disguise and re-turned to the throne, asks a minister to find among the arriv-ing warriors a knight in broken armor leading a lean horse.
- The minister locates and fetches Tsuneyo.

IN THE GLOSSARY

- **bides:** waits; stays
- **appareled:** dressed
- **laggard:** one who lags behind

18 **TEACHING IRONY AND THEME**

Elicit that these words, spoken for the priest, are ironic, as he is not really a "humble priest" but the *Shikken*, and no man is in a better position to give Tsuneyo "public furtherance." The ironic situation stresses the theme of appearance versus reality, since the priest is not what he seems. It also helps convey the impor-tance of generosity, another of the play's themes.

19 **CULTURAL BACKGROUND**

Point out that in both feudal Japan and feudal Europe, armies were supplied by loyal lords, who pledged in advance a certain number of warriors. Today gov-ernment levies require payment in money, not personnel.

20 **TEACHING STUDENTS OF LIMITED ENGLISH PROFICIENCY**

Have students indicate the mul-tiple meanings of the word *coach*. ("enclosed carriage of a horse-drawn vehicle; to train or instruct") Then use context clues to deter-mine which one applies. (the first)

21 **READING SKILL: PREDICTING OUTCOMES**

Have students predict the *Shik-ken*'s intentions. (He plans to reward Tsuneyo for his generosity and loyalty.)

CRITICAL THINKING: GUIDED READING QUESTIONS

LITERAL

1a. What does the chorus, speaking for the priest, tell Tsuneyo not to give up? (his suit, or plea in court)

2a. What sort of horse does Tsuneyo ride? (He rides an old, palsied, slow, lean, and twisted horse.)

INFERENTIAL

1b. Why do you think the priest encourages Tsuneyo to bring to court the case of his usurped lands? (When he returns to the throne, the priest—really Japan's ruler—intends to help Tsuneyo.)

2b. What does his willingness to fight on such a horse stress about Tsuneyo? (It stresses his loyalty and valiance.)

- At first Tsuneyo thinks he has been summoned to be executed as a traitor.
- Then the *Shikken* reveals himself to be the priest Tsuneyo helped and explains that he summoned the warriors to see whether Tsuneyo would keep his promise.
- To reward Tsuneyo, the *Shikken* not only restores his lawful estate in Sano but also grants him three new fiefdoms.
- When the warriors disperse, Tsuneyo travels home on a splendid steed.

IN THE GLOSSARY

- perpetual: eternal; endless

22 TEACHING IRONY

Point out that Tsuneyo's words are ironic since we know he is being summoned for reward, not punishment.

23 TEACHING THE NO PLAY

Note that these two lines are actually third-person narration, in which the actor playing Tsuneyo is speaking as a leading voice of the chorus. Have students identify two similar cases in the next column. ("Then Tsuneyo took the deeds"; "And among them Tsuneyo—")

24 TEACHING THEME

Elicit the observation that the *Shikken*'s reward points to the value of generosity and loyalty, an important theme of the play.

COLLABORATIVE LEARNING: ENRICHMENT ACTIVITY

Drama Have a group of students prepare an oral report on the theatrical arts in Japan, with different students focusing on different aspects of the topic—No drama; Kabuki; Bunraku, or puppet theater; modern drama; and so on.

MINISTER. I will do so.

22 TSUNEYO. I understand; too well I understand. Some enemy of mine has called me traitor, and it is to execution that I am summoned before the throne. Well, there is no help for it. Bring me into the Presence.

CHORUS. He was led to where on a great dais
    All the warriors of this levy were assembled
    Like a bright bevy of stars.
    Row on row they were ranged,
    Samurai[23] and soldiers;
    Swift scornful glances, fingers pointed
    And the noise of laughter met his entering.

23 TSUNEYO. Stuck through his tattered, his old side-sewn sash,
    His rusty sword sags and trails—yet he undaunted,
    "My Lord, I have come."

[*He bows before the throne.*]

PRIEST. Ha! He has come, Tsuneyo of Sano! Have you forgotten the priest whom once you sheltered from the snowstorm? You have been true to the words that you spoke that night at Sano:

    "If at any time there came news from the City
        of peril to our master
    Then broken though it be, I would gird this
        armor on,
    And rusty though it be, I would hold this tall
        spear,
    And bony though he be, I would mount my
        horse and ride
    Neck by neck with the swiftest."

These were not vain words; you have come valiantly. But know that this levy of men was made to this purpose: to test the issue of your words whether they were spoken false or true; and to hear the suits of all those that have obeyed my

summons, that if any among them have suffered injury, his wrongs may be righted.

And first in the case of Tsuneyo, I make judgment. To him shall be returned his lawful estate, thirty parishes[24] in the land of Sano.

24 But above all else one thing shall never be forgotten, that in the great snowstorm he cut down his trees, his treasure, and burned them for firewood. And now in gratitude for the three trees of that time—plum, cherry and pine—we grant to him three fiefs,[25] Plumfield in Kaga, Cherrywell in Etchū and Pine-branch in Kotsuke.

He shall hold them as a perpetual inheritance for himself and for his heirs; in testimony whereof we give this title-deed, by our own hand signed and sealed, together with the safe possession of his former lands.

TSUNEYO. Then Tsuneyo took the deeds.

CHORUS. He took the deeds, thrice bowing his head.

[*Speaking for* TSUNEYO.]

    "Look, all you barons! [TSUNEYO *holds up the documents.*]
    Look upon this sight
    And scorn to envy turn!"
    Then the levies of all the lands
    Took leave of their lord
    And went their homeward way.

TSUNEYO. And among them Tsuneyo—

CHORUS. Among them Tsuneyo,
    Joy breaking on his brow,
    Rides now on splendid steed
    To the Boat-bridge of Sano,[26] to his lands once torn
    Pitiless from him as the torrent tears
    That Bridge of Boats at Sano now his own.

---

23. **Samurai** [sam′ə rī′]: members of the hereditary Japanese warrior class.

---

24. **parishes:** here, small land divisions.
25. **fiefs** [fēfs]: lands granted by a lord or ruler in return for service.
26. **Boat-bridge of Sano:** that is, Sano Ferry.

460 *Drama*

CRITICAL THINKING: GUIDED READING QUESTIONS

LITERAL

1a. Why has the *Shikken* summoned the army? (He wants to test the loyal words that Tsuneyo spoke earlier and to right any wrongs that the *Shikken*'s loyal followers may have suffered during the ruler's absence.)

2a. On what sort of horse does Tsuneyo ride home? (He rides home on a splendid steed.)

INFERENTIAL

1b. What do these motives reveal about the kind of ruler he is? (He is a just ruler who recognizes and rewards loyalty.)

2b. What does the change of horse stress? (Tsuneyo's wealth and position in society have been restored.)

The Old Plum, panel four of sliding door, 1647, attributed to Kano Sansetsu.

The Dwarf Trees **461**

What concerns of the play do you find relevant today? Why?

ANSWERS

STUDY QUESTIONS

1. He is seeking shelter for the night. The wife says she cannot give him shelter until Tsuneyo returns; at first Tsuneyo refuses because his poverty shames him, but later his wife convinces him to change his mind.
2. He cuts down his precious dwarf trees for firewood.
3. Kinsmen usurped his lands.
4. He promises to answer the call to defend his lord.
5. The priest is really the *Shikken*, or regent, and he restores Tsuneyo's lands and gives him three new fiefdoms.
6. His wife's reminder about Buddhist laws restores his sense of honor and hospitality.
7. They are valuable and a reminder of his former life.
8. A generous person need not be ashamed of his or her poverty, and loyalty is worthy of recognition.
9. Answers will vary. Possible answers include "What goes around comes around" and "Do unto others as you would have them do unto you."

LITERARY FOCUS

The audience would be helped by the following:
1. the priest's descriptions of the snow and Tsuneyo's pantomime of brushing it off
2. a woman's costume, a female mask, and the actor's high-pitched voice
3. Tsuneyo's descriptions and pantomime involving the fire

LANGUAGE STUDY

1. "loose, sashed robe"; from word for "clothes"
2. "small charcoal stove"; from *hi*, "fire," and *bachi*, "bowl"
3. "means of unarmed self-defense"; from *ju*, "soft," and *jitsu*, "skill"
4. "means of unarmed self-defense"; from *ju*, "soft," and *do*, "art"
5. "means of unarmed self-defense"; from *kara*, "empty," and *te*, "hand"
6. "dwarfing woody plants by pruning; plants so dwarfed"; from word for "tray arrangement," as such plants are usually set in shallow pots

STUDY QUESTIONS

Recalling

1. What does the Priest want? How do Tsuneyo and his wife respond at first and then later on?
2. What personal sacrifice does Tsuneyo make for the Priest's warmth?
3. How did Tsuneyo, Lord of Sano, become so poor?
4. What promise about his actions in the future does Tsuneyo make to the Priest?
5. What are we shown about the Priest after the interval of six months, and what does Tsuneyo receive from him?

Interpreting

6. What factors contribute to Tsuneyo's changing his mind about giving the Priest shelter?
7. Why do you think the three dwarf trees are precious to Tsuneyo?
8. Tsuneyo has learned two lessons by the end of the play. Explain them in your own words.

Extending

9. *The Dwarf Trees* emphasizes the importance of loyalty and generosity. What modern-day proverbs reinforce the play's messages?

LITERARY FOCUS

The Japanese No Play

On the stage the Japanese No play is quite different from Western drama. A No play performance combines poetry, ritual dance, music, symbolic settings and props, and elaborate masks and costumes.

No plays are acted even today on a plain stage of polished wood. In place of changing scenery there are a stylized pine tree painted on the back wall, pillars supporting a temple roof, and a forty-foot runway approaching the rear of the stage. Two or three actors play the main parts, supported by four musicians (three drums and a flute) and a chorus of eight to ten singers. The chorus often sings the lines of the main character while he mimes or dances the action.

The word *No* means "talent" or "skill," and the acting indeed requires great skill, acquired over many years of training. A No actor must be an accomplished singer, dancer, and mime. Performing in traditional wooden masks and elaborate, colorful costumes, male actors play the parts of gods, ghosts, demons, warriors, and women. The highly stylized

acting is not meant to be realistic. It consists of singing, symbolic gestures, and slow dance movements.

No plays typically center on an encounter with a mysterious person. The encounter, usually involving a test, is followed by a revelation, or new awareness. In *The Dwarf Trees*, for example, Tsuneyo's hospitality and loyalty are rewarded by his master, the shogun, who turns out to have been the priest whom Tsuneyo sheltered.

Thinking About the No Play

Since No plays are symbolic rather than realistic, the audience must imagine what they cannot see. Explain how the play's poetry, props, costumes, and pantomime would help the audience to visualize the following:

1. the snowfall at the beginning
2. the role of the Wife
3. the fire fed by the three dwarf trees

LANGUAGE STUDY

English Words Borrowed from Japanese

American English has been enriched by many words borrowed from other languages, including Japanese. Look up each of the following words in a dictionary and write down its definition. Include etymologies, information about the origin and history of words, wherever they are given.

1. kimono
2. hibachi
3. jujitsu
4. judo
5. karate
6. bonsai

COMPOSITION

Writing a Haiku

■ The Japanese verse form of the haiku has become popular in the West. A **haiku** (see page 320) is a seventeen-syllable, three-line poem focused on a single image, often drawn from nature. The first line has five syllables, the second seven, and the third five.

Try writing your own haiku. Prepare by looking closely at some aspect of nature that interests you, such as the sound of raindrops or the image of a falling leaf. Then use words that will convey the sound or image to a reader in three short lines. Your haiku does not have to rhyme or have exactly seventeen syllables.

COMPOSITION: GUIDELINES FOR EVALUATION

WRITING A HAIKU

Objective

To write a haiku

Guidelines for Evaluation

■ suggested length: three lines
■ should reflect haiku form
■ should make an observation about nature
■ should focus on a single, possibly symbolic image

PREVIEW: THE AUTHOR AND THE WORLD

Edmond Rostand

(1869–1918)

France

The son of a distinguished French journalist, economist, and poet, Edmond Rostand [ed môn′ rôs tän′] grew up in Marseilles [mär sā′], a city in southern France. Although Rostand studied law in Paris, he abandoned his legal career to write for the stage and won quick success with a series of popular dramas based on historical subjects. Several of his plays starred the legendary French actress Sarah Bernhardt (1844–1923).

Rostand's career was crowned by *Cyrano de Bergerac* [sē′rə nō′ də bur′zhə rak′], a colorful and witty drama loosely based on the life of a seventeenth-century French poet and playwright. Rostand called this play a **heroic comedy**—that is, a comedy focusing on the exploits of a larger-than-life hero. First produced in 1897, *Cyrano de Bergerac* became an overnight sensation in Paris, and its popularity spread rapidly throughout the world. Frequently performed on stage, it has also been the basis of several films and most recently was adapted in a modern setting as the film *Roxanne*.

GEOGRAPHY AND CULTURE

France in the Seventeenth Century

The real Cyrano de Bergerac (1619–1655) was a poet, playwright, philosopher, and soldier noted for his dashing swordsmanship. He lived in a golden age of French history, when the king's chief minister, Cardinal Richelieu [rish′ ə lōō′], expanded both the territories of France and the power of the crown. The ornate French court set the style for the rest of the country in an era often called the Age of Elegance. With the support of France's kings, intellectual life flourished, as did literature and all the arts. The true gentleman of the day was expected to be both a man of action and a man of culture; to excel in both swordplay and wordplay; to fight bravely, compose music, and create poetry with equal brilliance and ease.

As *Cyrano de Bergerac* begins, we enter that glittering but fiercely competitive world. The play opens in an elegant seventeenth-century Paris theater just as a performance is about to start.

FRANCE IN 1648

See *LITERATURE AND CULTURE SOURCEBOOK: France*

Cyrano de Bergerac **463**

In this witty and engaging five-act period play set in the 1600s, flamboyant characters appear in exciting and colorful situations. Cyrano de Bergerac stands at the center of the play, and his words and actions ask the audience to consider questions of love, individualism, idealism, beauty, and the value of language and poetry. Cyrano is a dashing swordsman who defies conventions and fights bravely to defend his honor and his friends. He is also a poet as skilled with language as he is with his sword. Nonetheless, Cyrano is a man self-condemned by his own feelings of ugliness. Thus, he feels hopelessly disabled in matters of love, and only in his final hour does he realize the love that might have been his.

To assist you in teaching the play, this Teacher's Edition treats each of the play's five acts as a separate lesson. The annotations for each act begin with a Preview and listings of literary skills, themes, and objectives for that act, as well as suggestions for teaching students of different abilities.

TEACHER'S CLASSROOM RESOURCES

You will find listings of Teacher's Classroom Resources for each of the play's five acts on TAE pages 464 and 465.

DISCUSSING GEOGRAPHY AND CULTURE

Drama and Artistic Freedom

Drama flowered in seventeenth-century France, thanks largely to the efforts of Cardinal Richelieu. The cardinal's predecessors had banned theatrical performances, and actors could not be baptized, married, or given a Christian burial. Under Richelieu's auspices, however, troupes gained royal favor, and acting became a legitimate profession.

■ Ask students to discuss today's attitudes toward actors.

ACT I
- Teaching Notes 151–154
- Prereading Vocabulary 155
- Reading Guide 156
- Check Test 157
- Responding to World Cultures 158
- Selection Test 159

ACT II
- Teaching Notes 151–154
- Prereading Vocabulary 161
- Reading Guide 162
- Check Test 163
- Literary Focus: Dramatic Irony 164
- Selection Test 165

ACT III
- Teaching Notes 151–154
- Prereading Vocabulary 167
- Reading Guide 168
- Check Test 169
- Literary Focus: Staging and Character 170
- Selection Test 171

ACT IV
- Teaching Notes 151–154
- Prereading Vocabulary 173
- Reading Guide 174
- Check Test 175
- Literary Focus: Dramatic Plot 176
- Selection Test 177

ACT V
- Teaching Notes 151–154
- Reading Guide 179
- Check Test 180
- Literary Focus: The Total Effect 181
- Language Study: English Words Borrowed from French 182
- Writing Process Guides: Writing About Character 183
  Writing a Speech for a Character 184
- Grammar in Literature: Using Phrases as Adjectives 185
- Selection Test 186

Cyrano.   Roxane.   Christian.

Edmond Rostand

Cyrano de Bergerac

Translated by Lowell Bair

CHARACTERS

CYRANO DE BERGERAC [sē′rə nō′ də bur′zhə rak′]: soldier, philosopher, and poet; famous for his wit, great courage, and large nose

CHRISTIAN DE NEUVILLETTE [krēs′tē an′ də nu′vē yet′]: handsome young soldier; inept at expressing himself

MAGDELEINE ROBIN [mad′lin rō ban′], known as ROXANE [roks an′]: beautiful, rich, and cultured cousin of Cyrano; loved by both Cyrano and Christian

Friends of Cyrano

LIGNIÈRE [lē nyār′]: mischievous poet

RAGUENEAU [ra′gə nō′]: poet and pastrycook

LISE [lēz]: wife of Ragueneau

LE BRET [lə brā′]: officer in Cyrano's regiment

CARBON DE CASTEL-JALOUX [kär bôn′ də kas tel′ zha loo′]: captain of Cyrano's regiment

Opponents of Cyrano

COUNT DE GUICHE [də gēsh′]: ambitious nobleman and military commander; in love with Roxane

VISCOUNT DE VALVERT [vī′kount də val vār′]: follower of de Guiche; wooer of Roxane

MONTFLEURY [mon′flu rē′]: fat, untalented actor

464 *Drama*

Other named characters *(in order of their appearance)*

CUIGY [kwē zhē′]: officer in Cyrano's regiment
BRISSAILLE [brē sī′]: officer in Cyrano's regiment
BELLEROSE [bel rōz′]: theater manager
THE DUENNA [dwā′nə]: Roxane's chaperone, or companion
BERTRANDOU [bār′tron dōō′]: fife-player
SISTER MARTHE [mär′tə]: nun of the Ladies of the Cross Convent
MOTHER MARGUERITE DE JESUS [mär′gə rēt′ də zhā′zōō]: Mother Superior of the Convent
SISTER CLAIRE: nun of the Convent

Others *(in order of their appearance)*

A DOORKEEPER	A PICKPOCKET	THE CADETS OF GASCOYNE
SEVERAL CAVALIERS	A MEDDLER	TWO MUSICIANS
SEVERAL PAGES	ACTORS	A CAPUCHIN [kap′yə shin] PRIEST
A REFRESHMENT GIRL	ACTRESSES	A SPANISH OFFICER
SEVERAL MARQUISES [mär kē′]	PASTRYCOOKS	SEVERAL NUNS
A CROWD OF THEATER-GOERS	A MUSKETEER	
A LAMPLIGHTER	SEVERAL POETS	

Cyrano de Bergerac **465**

ACT I

The auditorium of the Hôtel de Bourgogne [ō tel′ də bōōr gō′nyə] in Paris in 1640.

[It resembles an indoor tennis court, decorated and fitted out for theatrical performances. As the curtain rises, the auditorium is in semidarkness and still empty. The chandeliers have been lowered to the floor and are waiting to be lighted. A tumult of voices is heard from outside the door; then a CAVALIER *enters abruptly, followed by an angry* DOORKEEPER.*]*

THE DOORKEEPER. [*Pursuing him.*] Stop! You haven't paid your fifteen sols.[1]

THE CAVALIER. I don't have to pay!

THE DOORKEEPER. Why not?

THE CAVALIER. I'm a light-horseman[2] of the King's Household.

THE DOORKEEPER. [*To another* CAVALIER *who has just entered.*] And you?

SECOND CAVALIER. I don't have to pay either.

THE DOORKEEPER. But . . .

SECOND CAVALIER. I'm a musketeer.[3]

FIRST CAVALIER. [*To the second.*] The play doesn't begin till two o'clock and the floor is empty. Let's have a little fencing practice. [*They fence with the foils they have brought.*]

[*A* BAND OF PAGES *enters.*]

THE DOORKEEPER. [*Sternly, to the* PAGES.] Behave yourselves, boys! No pranks!

FIRST PAGE. [*With wounded dignity.*] Oh, sir, how can you even suspect such a thing? [*With animation, to the* SECOND PAGE, *as soon as the* DOORKEEPER *has turned his back.*] Do you have your string?

SECOND PAGE. Yes, and my fishhook.

FIRST PAGE. Good. We'll fish for wigs when we're up there.

A VOICE FROM THE UPPER GALLERY. Light the chandeliers!

A PAGE. [*On the floor.*] Ah, here's the refreshment girl!

THE REFRESHMENT GIRL. [*Appearing behind the refreshment table.*] Oranges, milk, raspberry syrup, cider. . . .

[*Commotion at the door.*]

A MARQUIS.[4] [*Seeing that the theater is half empty.*] What's this? We've arrived like tradesmen, without disturbing people, without stepping on their feet? What a shameful way to make an entrance! [*Finds himself in front of some other noblemen who have entered shortly before.*] Cuigy![5] Brissaille![6] [*They embrace enthusiastically.*]

CUIGY. Ah, the faithful are here! Yes, it's true: we've come before the candles. . . .

THE MARQUIS. No, don't talk about it! I'm so annoyed. . . .

ANOTHER MARQUIS. Cheer up, Marquis, here comes the lighter!

THE CROWD. [*Greeting the entrance of the* LIGHTER.] Ah! . . .

[LIGNIÈRE[7] *and* CHRISTIAN DE NEUVILLETTE[8] *enter,*

---

1. **sols:** The sol, or sou, is a French coin no longer in use. It was worth about one cent.
2. **light-horseman:** cavalry soldier who carries light arms.
3. **musketeer:** soldier armed with a musket.

466 *Drama*

---

4. **Marquis** [mär kē′]: nobleman who ranks below a duke and above a count.
5. **Cuigy** [kwē zhē′]
6. **Brissaille** [brē sī′]
7. **Lignière** [lē nyär′]
8. **Christian de Neuvillette** [krēs′tē an′ də nu′vē yet′]

arm in arm. LIGNIÈRE *is rather disheveled.* CHRISTIAN *is elegantly dressed, but in a somewhat outmoded style. He seems preoccupied, and looks up at the boxes.*]

2 CUIGY. Lignière!

LIGNIÈRE. [*To* CHRISTIAN.] Shall I introduce you? [CHRISTIAN *nods.*] Baron de Neuvillette. [*They bow.*]

THE CROWD. [*Acclaiming the raising of the first lighted chandelier.*] Ah!

CUIGY. [*To* BRISSAILLE, *looking at* CHRISTIAN.] He has a charming face!

LIGNIÈRE. [*Introducing them to* CHRISTIAN.] Messieurs[9] de Cuigy, de Brissaille. . . .

CHRISTIAN. [*Bowing.*] Delighted to meet you, gentlemen.

LIGNIÈRE. [*To* CUIGY.] Monsieur de Neuvillette has just arrived from Touraine.[10]

CHRISTIAN. Yes, I've been in Paris only three weeks. I'm entering the Guards tomorrow, as a Cadet.[11]

CUIGY. [*To* CHRISTIAN, *pointing to the auditorium, which is beginning to fill.*] People are arriving.

CHRISTIAN. Yes, in droves!

FIRST MARQUIS. All of fashionable society is here! Look, our lady intellectuals are taking their places.

3 LIGNIÈRE. [*Taking* CHRISTIAN *aside.*] My friend, I came with you to help you, but since the lady isn't here—

CHRISTIAN. [*Imploringly.*] No, stay! You know everyone at court and in the city: you'll be able

---

9. **Messieurs** [mā syu′]: sirs or gentlemen; plural for *Monsieur* [mə syu′], which means "Mister."
10. **Touraine** [tōō ren′]: region of central France.
11. **Cadet:** nobleman who served as a common soldier to gain experience and eventually earn a commission as an officer.

---

to tell me the name of the lady for whom I'm dying of love. I'm afraid she may be coquettish **4** and refined. I don't dare to speak to her, because I have no wit. I don't know how to use the elegant language that's in style nowadays. I'm only a soldier, a shy soldier. . . . She always sits in that box—there, on the right. It's still empty. . . .

LIGNIÈRE. Aha! I'll stay a little longer, since you insist.

VOICES FROM THE CROWD. [*Greeting the entrance of a plump, jolly-looking little man.*] Ah, Ragueneau![12]

LIGNIÈRE. [*To* CHRISTIAN.] There's Ragueneau, the great baker.

RAGUENEAU. [*Dressed like a pastry cook in his Sunday best, hurrying toward* LIGNIÈRE.] Sir, have you seen Monsieur de Cyrano?

LIGNIÈRE. [*Introducing* RAGUENEAU *to* CHRISTIAN.] This is Ragueneau, the pastry cook of actors and poets!

RAGUENEAU. [*Embarrassed.*] You honor me too highly.

LIGNIÈRE. Not at all! You're a patron of the arts!

5 RAGUENEAU. Poets do come to my shop . . .

LIGNIÈRE. To buy on credit. And you yourself are a talented poet.

RAGUENEAU. So I've been told.

LIGNIÈRE. You're madly in love with poetry!

RAGUENEAU. It's true that for an ode . . .

LIGNIÈRE. You give a tart.

RAGUENEAU. Only a little one, if it's a short ode.

LIGNIÈRE. You love the theater, too, don't you?

RAGUENEAU. I adore it.

---

12. **Ragueneau** [ra′gə nō′]

Cyrano de Bergerac, Act I **467**

CRITICAL THINKING: GUIDED READING QUESTIONS

LITERAL

1a. Why has Lignière come to the play? (He has come to help Christian identify a lady.)

2a. How does Ragueneau help poets? (He lets them buy pastry on credit and trades pastries for poems.)

INFERENTIAL

→ **1b.** What does the fact that Christian does not even know the name of this lady indicate about the conventions of love in his society? (Since he knows her only by sight, the implication is that love affairs of the day were based largely on appearances.)

→ **2b.** What can you infer about poets from this? (Poets were usually poor and needed financial help to survive.)

- Cyrano dislikes the lead actor, Montfleury.
- Le Bret, Ragueneau, and Cuigy discuss Cyrano's extraordinary character and unusual nose.
- Roxane enters and is admired by the crowd.

IN THE GLOSSARY

- **impetuous:** rash; impulsive
- **spawned:** brought into existence; produced

6 READING SKILL: PREDICTING OUTCOMES

Ask students what could happen when Montfleury appears on stage. (Based on Ragueneau's words, students may predict that Cyrano will somehow make him leave.)

7 GRAMMAR IN LITERATURE

Point out the way in which a series of simple nouns prepares the audience for an unconventional character. Students should see that these nouns (without modifiers) help to characterize Cyrano as a man of many talents.

8 TEACHING THEME

Point out that one of the play's main themes—the effects of Cyrano's physical disfigurement—is introduced comically.

9 TEACHING FIGURATIVE LANGUAGE

Point out that Roxane is described with a simile and metaphor: "like a peach," "smiling with strawberry lips." Ask students to identify the kind of heroine such figurative language leads the audience to expect. (a beautiful, conventionally romantic heroine)

LIGNIÈRE. You pay for your theater tickets with pastry! Tell me, just between ourselves, how much did you pay this time?

RAGUENEAU. Four custard tarts and fifteen cream puffs. [*Looks all around.*] Monsieur de Cyrano isn't here? I'm surprised.

LIGNIÈRE. Why?

RAGUENEAU. Montfleury[13] is in the play!

6 **LIGNIÈRE.** Yes, that walking barrel will play the part of Phaedo[14] today. But what does it matter to Cyrano?

RAGUENEAU. Haven't you heard? He took a dislike to Montfleury and ordered him not to appear on the stage for a month.

LIGNIÈRE. Well, what of it?

RAGUENEAU. Ah, that's what I've come to see!

FIRST MARQUIS. Who is this Cyrano?

CUIGY. He's a Cadet in the Guards. [*Points to a gentleman who is walking back and forth as though looking for someone.*] But his friend Le Bret[15] can tell you. . . . [*Calls him.*] Le Bret! [LE BRET *comes over to them.*] You're looking for Bergerac?

LE BRET. Yes, and I'm worried. . . .

CUIGY. He's an extraordinary man, isn't he?

LE BRET. [*Affectionately.*] The most delightful man under the sun!

7 **RAGUENEAU.** A poet!

CUIGY. A swordsman!

BRISSAILLE. A scientist!

LE BRET. A musician!

LIGNIÈRE. And what an uncommon appearance!

---

13. **Montfleury** [mŌN′flu rē′]: seventeenth-century French actor.
14. **Phaedo** [fā dō′]
15. **Le Bret** [lə brā′]

468   *Drama*

RAGUENEAU. Odd, impetuous, brash, and outlandish as he is, proudest of all the thin-skinned swaggerers lovingly spawned by Gascony,[16] I think he would have given the late Jacques Callot[17] a wild swashbuckler[18] to place among his portraits. With his triple-plumed hat, his billowing doublet,[19] and his cape majestically held out behind by a sword, he carries his nose above a
8 punchinello ruff,[20] a nose that . . . Ah, gentlemen, what a nose! Those who see it pass by can't help exclaiming, "No, it can't be true!" Then they smile and say, "He'll soon take it off." But Monsieur de Bergerac never takes it off.

LE BRET. [*Nodding.*] He keeps it on—and runs his sword through anyone who looks at it too closely.

FIRST MARQUIS. [*Shrugging.*] He won't come.

RAGUENEAU. He will! I'll bet you a chicken à la Ragueneau!

FIRST MARQUIS. [*Laughing.*] I'll take that bet!

[*Murmurs of admiration from the crowd:* ROXANE[21] *has just appeared in her box. She sits at the front of it, her* DUENNA[22] *sits at the rear.* CHRISTIAN, *occupied in paying the* REFRESHMENT GIRL, *has not yet seen her.*]

9 **SECOND MARQUIS.** [*With little cries.*] Gentlemen, she's terrifyingly lovely!

FIRST MARQUIS. Skin like a peach, smiling with strawberry lips!

---

16. **Gascony:** a region of southwestern France; Gascons were famous for their boastfulness.
17. **Jacques Callot** [zhäk kä lō′]: French artist (1592–1635) who was famous for his portraits of colorful figures, especially from the theater.
18. **swashbuckler:** flamboyant soldier or adventurer.
19. **doublet:** close-fitting, waist-length jacket.
20. **punchinello** [pun′chə nel′ō] **ruff:** A punchinello is a grotesque, humpbacked character in an Italian puppet show; his costume includes a ruff, or large frilled collar like those worn by clowns today.
21. **Roxane** [roks an′]
22. **Duenna** [dwā′nə]: older woman serving as a chaperone and companion to a young woman.

CRITICAL THINKING: GUIDED READING QUESTIONS

LITERAL

1a. What four occupations do Cyrano's friends attribute to him? (poet, swordsman, scientist, and musician)

2a. What does Le Bret say Cyrano does to anyone who looks at his nose too closely? (He runs his sword through him.)

INFERENTIAL

1b. What does this suggest about Cyrano's character? (He is a well-educated, cultured person with diverse abilities.)

2b. What can you infer about Cyrano's attitude toward his nose? (He is sensitive about it and aggressively defends his pride.)

SECOND MARQUIS. And so fresh and cool that anyone coming near her might catch a cold in his heart!

CHRISTIAN. [*Looks up, sees* ROXANE, *and clutches* LIGNIÈRE's *arm*.] There she is!

LIGNIÈRE. [*Looking*.] Ah, so she's the one?

CHRISTIAN. Yes. Quickly, tell me who she is! I'm afraid.

10 LIGNIÈRE. Magdeleine Robin,[23] known as Roxane. Sharp-witted, an intellectual . . .

CHRISTIAN. Alas!

LIGNIÈRE. . . . free, an orphan, a cousin of Cyrano, whom we were just discussing. . . .

[*At this point a very elegant gentleman, wearing the Cordon Bleu[24] around his neck, enters* ROXANE's *box and stands talking with her for a few moments*.]

CHRISTIAN. [*Starting*.] Who is that man?

11 LIGNIÈRE. [*Winking*.] That, my friend, is Count de Guiche.[25] He's in love with her, but he's married to Cardinal Richelieu's[26] niece. He wants to arrange a marriage between Roxane and Viscount[27] de Valvert,[28] a sad specimen of a man whom he can count on to be obliging. She's opposed to it, but De Guiche is powerful: he can persecute an untitled girl like her. Incidentally, I've written a song exposing his crafty scheme. He must hate me for it! The ending is positively vicious. Listen, I'll sing it for you. . . . [*He rises to his feet ready to sing*.]

---

23. **Magdeleine Robin** [mad′lin rō ban′]
24. **Cordon Bleu** [kôr dôn′ blu′]: blue ribon worn as decoration by members of the order of the Holy Ghost, the highest order of French knighthood at the time.
25. **Count de Guiche** [də gēsh′]
26. **Cardinal Richelieu's** [rish′ə lōō′]: Cardinal Richelieu, born Armand Jean du Plessis (1585–1642), was a cardinal of the Roman Catholic Church, chief minister of King Louis XIII, and the most powerful man in France in the mid-1600s.
27. **Viscount** [vī′kount]: nobleman below the rank of count.
28. **de Valvert** [də val vār′]

CHRISTIAN. No. I'm leaving now.

LIGNIÈRE. Where are you going?

12 CHRISTIAN. I'm going to pay a visit to Viscount de Valvert!

LIGNIÈRE. Don't do anything rash: there's a good chance he'd kill you. [*Discreetly calls his attention to* ROXANE.] Stay. You're being watched.

CHRISTIAN. It's true! [*He stands staring at her*.]

LIGNIÈRE. *I'm* the one who's leaving. I'm thirsty and I have an appointment. [*He leaves*.]

LE BRET. [*With relief, coming back to* RAGUENEAU *after having searched everywhere*.] No sign of Cyrano.

RAGUENEAU. [*Incredulously*.] It doesn't seem possible.

THE CROWD. Begin the play! Begin!

A MARQUIS. [*Watching* DE GUICHE *come down from* ROXANE's *box and walk across the floor, surrounded by obsequious noblemen, one of whom is* VISCOUNT DE VALVERT.] De Guiche has his own little court!

DE GUICHE. I'm going to sit on the stage. Are you coming with me? [*He walks toward the stage, followed by all the* MARQUISES *and other noblemen, then looks back and calls*.] Come, Valvert!

[CHRISTIAN *has been observing and listening to them. He starts when he hears* VALVERT's *name*.]

13 CHRISTIAN. Valvert! I'll throw my glove in his face this instant! [*Reaches for his gloves and encounters the hand of a thief picking his pocket. Turns around*.] What . . .

THE THIEF. Oh, no!

CHRISTIAN. [*Holding him*.] I was reaching for a glove!

THE THIEF. [*With a pitiful smile*.] You found a

Cyrano de Bergerac, Act I **469**

CRITICAL THINKING: GUIDED READING QUESTIONS

LITERAL

1a. What information does Lignière offer about Count de Guiche? (He is elegant, powerful, and married; he is in love with Roxane and wants to marry her to his friend Valvert, who will "be obliging.")

2a. What does Ligniere say just after he warns Christian not to be rash about Valvert? ("Stay. You're being watched.")

INFERENTIAL

1b. What can you conclude about his character from this information? (He is an unscrupulous and manipulative aristocrat.)

2b. What can you infer about Roxane's feelings for Christian from her gaze? (She is interested in him.)

- The thief says that one hundred men will attack Lignière.
- Christian leaves to warn Lignière, and the stage play begins.
- As Montfleury recites his lines, Cyrano's voice is heard ordering him offstage.

14 READING SKILL: INFERENCE

Ask students who might have ordered the men to attack Lignière. (Students should recall that Lignière wrote a vicious song about De Guiche; De Guiche has probably ordered the attack.)

15 TEACHING CHARACTERIZATION

Ask students what Christian's words and actions suggest about his character. (They should see that Christian is loyal, devoted to his friends, and willing to sacrifice his own desires for an innocent man's safety.)

16 CULTURAL BACKGROUND

Point out that stage directions specify costumes, cast, and staging of the play within a play. Explain that the ridiculousness of the production parodies the pretentious theater of the early 1600s, which often featured pastoral dramas in which shepherds and shepherdesses played key roles.

17 CRITICAL THINKING: EVALUATION

Ask students to identify this voice and to explain how they know it. Then have them evaluate the strength of Cyrano's "entrance." (Most students will find the entrance dramatic, effective, and suitable for a character known for his flair.)

---

hand instead. [*Lowering his voice and speaking rapidly.*] Let me go and I'll tell you a secret.

CHRISTIAN. [*Still holding him.*] What is it?

THE THIEF. Lignière, who just left you . . .

CHRISTIAN. [*Without letting go of him.*] Yes? Go on.

14 THE THIEF. He's about to meet his death. He wrote a song that offended a certain very powerful person, and tonight a hundred men—I know, because I'm to join them soon—have been posted . . .

CHRISTIAN. A hundred! By whom?

THE THIEF. Sorry, I can't tell you that.

CHRISTIAN. [*Shrugging.*] Oh, come, come!

THE THIEF. [*With great dignity.*] It's a professional secret!

CHRISTIAN. Where are the men posted?

THE THIEF. At the Porte de Nesle,[29] on his way. Warn him!

15 CHRISTIAN. Yes, I'll go! Oh, the vile cowards! A hundred men against one! [*Looks at* ROXANE *with love.*] How can I bear to leave her? [*At* VALVERT *with fury.*] And him! But I must save Lignière!

[*He runs out.* DE GUICHE, VALVERT, *the* MARQUIS, *and the other noblemen have disappeared behind the curtain to take their places on the benches on the stage. The floor, the gallery, and the boxes are now completely filled.*]

THE CROWD. Begin the play!

A SPECTATOR. Silence!

[*Three more raps from the stage. The curtain opens. Tableau.[30] The* MARQUISES *are seated on either side of the stage in insolent poses. The*

---

29. **Porte de Nesle** [pôrt′ de nes′əl]
30. **Tableau** [tab lō′]: picturesque and motionless scene.

470 *Drama*

---

backdrop represents a bluish pastoral[31] scene. Four small crystal chandeliers light the stage. The violins are playing softly.]

LE BRET. [*To* RAGUENEAU, *in a low voice.*] Will Montfleury soon be on the stage?

RAGUENEAU. [*Also in a low voice.*] He'll be the first to appear.

LE BRET. Cyrano isn't here.

16 [*A bagpipe melody is heard, then the enormously fat* MONTFLEURY *appears on the stage, wearing a shepherd's costume, a hat adorned with roses tilted over one ear, blowing into a beribboned bagpipe.*]

THE CROWD. [*Applauding.*] Montfleury!—Bravo!—Montfleury!

MONTFLEURY. [*After bowing, playing the part of Phaedo.*]
"Happy is he who shuns the pomp of courts
In solitary exile, self-imposed;
And who, when gentle breezes . . ."

17 A VOICE. [*From the middle of the floor.*] Haven't I ordered you off the stage for a month, you wretched scoundrel?

[*Astonishment in the audience. Everyone looks around. Murmurs.*]

VARIOUS VOICES. Oh!—What!—Who? [*Those in the boxes stand up to see.*]

CUIGY. He's here!

LE BRET. [*Terrified.*] Cyrano!

THE VOICE. Off the stage this instant, king of buffoons!

THE WHOLE AUDIENCE. [*Indignantly.*] Oh!

MONTFLEURY. But . . .

THE VOICE. You refuse?

---

31. **pastoral:** referring to shepherds and other rural subjects.

CRITICAL THINKING: GUIDED READING QUESTIONS

LITERAL

1a. Describe Montfleury's appearance onstage. (He is dressed somewhat ridiculously in "a shepherd's costume, a hat adorned with roses tilted over one ear, [and is] blowing into a beribboned bagpipe.")

INFERENTIAL

1b. What do you think the playwright intends us to think of Montfleury? (He is ridiculous and deserves reproach.)

PAGE SUMMARY: AT A GLANCE

■ Cyrano continues to heckle Montfleury.
■ Montfleury begins to speak his lines but seems less sure of himself as the heckling continues.
■ Cyrano stands threateningly on a chair, thus creating a sensation.

18 TEACHING IRONY

Point out the contrast between Montfleury's lines ("Happy is he . . .") and his actual feelings of embarrassment and fear.

19 TEACHING STAGING

Note that this is the audience's first sight of Cyrano. Students should recognize that Cyrano's air of aggressive confidence and control fulfills the audience's expectations of him.

VARIOUS VOICES. [*From the floor and the boxes.*] Sh!—Enough!—Go on, Montfleury!—Don't be afraid!

MONTFLEURY. [*In a faltering voice.*] "Happy is he who shuns the pomp of . . ."

THE VOICE. [*More threateningly.*] Well, prince of louts, must I give your shoulders a taste of wood?

[*An arm holding a cane rises above the heads of the audience.*]

18 MONTFLEURY. [*In an increasingly feeble voice.*] "Happy is he who . . ."

[*The arm waves the cane.*]

THE VOICE. Off the stage!

THE CROWD. Oh!

MONTFLEURY. [*Choking.*] "Happy is he who shuns . . ."

19 CYRANO. [*Standing up on a chair with his arms folded, his hat cocked, his mustache bristling, and his nose pointing aggressively.*] I'm about to lose my temper! [*His appearance creates a sensation.*]

MONTFLEURY. [*To the* MARQUISES.] Protect me, gentlemen!

A MARQUIS. [*Nonchalantly.*] Go on with your acting.

Cyrano de Bergerac, Act I   **471**

CRITICAL THINKING: GUIDED READING QUESTIONS

LITERAL

1a. In what way does Cyrano reveal himself to the audience? (He stands on a chair, takes an aggressive stance, and tells Montfleury that he is losing his temper.)

INFERENTIAL

1b. In what way does Cyrano's entrance fulfill the audience's expectations of him? (We expect to see a character with nerve and flair who keeps his word; his appearance confirms these characteristics. He is the play's hero, and his highly dramatic first appearance draws all attention to him.)

- The crowd protests Cyrano's conduct.
- Cyrano invites audience members to challenge him individually, but no one steps forward.
- Cyrano intimidates Montfleury into leaving the stage on a count of three.

IN THE GLOSSARY

- callow: immature; inexperienced
- deplorable: extremely bad
- ponderously: heavily and clumsily

20 TEACHING STUDENTS OF LIMITED ENGLISH PROFICIENCY

Help students understand the playwright's use of idioms and figurative language in the following colorful remarks: "I'll tan your cheeks" ("strike you on the bottom") and "my cane will rumple your ribbons" ("strike you in ways that will make a mess of you and your clothes").

21 GRAMMAR IN LITERATURE

Point out that this series of adjectives echoes the series of nouns on page 468. Both series quickly and dramatically suggest various opinions of Cyrano's.

22 TEACHING CHARACTERIZATION

Ask students what Cyrano reveals about himself in challenging the crowd. (Cyrano's bravery and daring are informed by insight and wit: He knows that no one is likely to step forward.)

23 TEACHING CHARACTERIZATION

Point out that Cyrano's succinct critique of Montfleury's acting suggests that the hero is a man of artistic discrimination.

---

20 CYRANO. If you do, you fat oaf, I'll tan your cheeks!

THE MARQUIS. Enough!

CYRANO. [*To all the* MARQUIS.] I advise you all to sit quietly in your seats. Otherwise my cane will rumple your ribbons!

THE CROWD. [*Retreating.*] Make room!—Step back!

CYRANO. [*To* MONTFLEURY.] Off the stage! [*The crowd closes in with an angry murmur. He quickly turns around.*] Is there something you want to say to me? Speak up!

21 A LADY. [*In the boxes.*] This is incredible!

A NOBLEMAN. Scandalous!

A BURGHER. Exasperating!

A PAGE. Hilarious!

THE CROWD. Montfleury!—Cyrano!

CYRANO. Silence!

THE CROWD. [*Uproariously.*] Hee-haw!—Baa!—Woof, woof!—Cock-a-doodle-doo!

CYRANO. Quiet, or I'll . . .

A PAGE. Meow!

22 CYRANO. I order you to be silent! And I issue a collective challenge! Come, I'll write down your names. Step forward, young heroes! You'll all have a turn, I'll give each of you a number. Now, who wants to be at the top of the list? You, sir? No? You? No? [*Silence.*] No names? No hands? . . . Then I'll get on with my business. [*He turns back toward the stage, where* MONTFLEURY *has been waiting in great anxiety.*] I want to see the theater cured of this boil. Otherwise . . . [*Puts his hand to his sword.*] . . . I'll lance it!

MONTFLEURY. I . . .

CYRANO. [*Descends from his chair, sits down in the middle of the circle that has formed around*

472 *Drama*

---

him, and settles himself as though at home.] I'm going to clap my hands three times. By the third clap, you will be gone.

THE CROWD. [*Amused.*] Ah!

CYRANO. [*Clapping his hands.*] One!

MONTFLEURY. I . . .

A VOICE. [*From the boxes.*] Stay!

THE CROWD. He'll stay—He'll go!

MONTFLEURY. Gentlemen, I believe . . .

CYRANO. Two!

MONTFLEURY. I'm sure it would be better . . .

CYRANO. Three!

[MONTFLEURY *suddenly disappears. Storm of laughter, hisses, and boos.*]

THE CROWD. Boo!—Boo!—Coward!—Come back!

CYRANO. [*Leans back in his chair, beaming, and crosses his legs.*] Let him come back if he dares!

A YOUNG MAN. [*To* CYRANO.] Tell me, sir, what reason do you have to hate Montfleury?

23 CYRANO. [*Graciously, still seated.*] I have two reasons, my callow young friend, either of which would be sufficient. The first is that he's a deplorable actor who brays like an ass and wrestles ponderously with lines that ought to soar lightly from his lips. The second—is my secret.

BELLEROSE.[32] What about the money that will have to be refunded?

CYRANO. [*Turning his chair toward the stage.*] Now there's the first sensible thing that's yet been said! Far be it from me to impose hardship on practitioners of the Thespian[33] art. [*Stands*

---

32. **Bellerose** [bel rōz′]: seventeenth-century French actor.
33. **Thespian:** having to do with drama.

CRITICAL THINKING: GUIDED READING QUESTIONS

LITERAL

1a. What does Cyrano say to bring the crowd to order? (He challenges any "young heroes" to step forward and fight him.)

2a. What are Cyrano's two reasons for hating Montfleury? ("He's a deplorable actor"; "The second—is my secret.")

INFERENTIAL

1b. What does Cyrano suspect their response will be to his challenge? (Most people are brave in a mob, but few will act bravely alone.)

2b. What can you infer about Cyrano's character from his explanation? (He is a man of artistic taste; he is discreet and does not readily divulge personal information.)

24 *up and throws a bag onto the stage.*] Here, take this purse and be quiet.

THE CROWD. [*Astonished.*] Ah!—Oh!

AN ACTOR. [*Quickly picking up the purse and weighing it in his hand.*] At this price, sir, I'll be glad to have you come and stop our performance every day!

THE CROWD. Boo! Boo!

BELLEROSE. Please clear the hall!

[*The spectators begin leaving while* CYRANO *watches with satisfaction, but they soon stop when they hear the following scene. The ladies in the boxes, who have already stood up and put on their cloaks, stop to listen, and finally sit down again.*]

LE BRET. [*To* CYRANO.] This is madness!

A MEDDLER. [*Who has approached* CYRANO.] What a scandal! Montfleury, the great actor! Don't you know he's protected by the Duke de Candale?[34] Do you have a patron?[35]

CYRANO. No!

25 THE MEDDLER. What? You have no great lord whose name protects . . .

CYRANO. I don't rely on some remote patron for protection. [*Puts his hand to his sword.*] My protector is always near at hand.

THE MEDDLER. Are you going to leave the city?

CYRANO. That depends.

THE MEDDLER. But the Duke de Candale has a long arm!

CYRANO. Not as long as mine . . . [*Pointing to his sword.*] . . . when I give it this extension!

THE MEDDLER. But surely you wouldn't dare . . .

---

34. **Duke de Candale** [kan dal´]
35. **patron:** wealthy person who supports an artist.

CYRANO. I would.

THE MEDDLER. But . . .

CYRANO. Go now.

THE MEDDLER. But . . .

26 CYRANO. Go! Or tell me why you're looking at my nose.

THE MEDDLER. [*Petrified.*] I . . .

CYRANO. [*Moving toward him.*] Do you find it surprising?

THE MEDDLER. [*Stepping back.*] You're mistaken, my lord . . .

CYRANO. Is it limp and dangling, like an elephant's trunk?

THE MEDDLER. [*Stepping back again.*] I didn't . . .

CYRANO. Or hooked like an owl's beak?

THE MEDDLER. I . . .

CYRANO. Do you see a wart at the end of it?

THE MEDDLER. I . . .

CYRANO. Or a fly walking on it? What's unusual about it?

THE MEDDLER. Nothing, I . . .

CYRANO. Then why that disdainful expression? Do you find it, perhaps, a little too large?

THE MEDDLER. [*Stammering.*] Oh, no, it's quite small . . . very small . . . diminutive. . . .

CYRANO. What! How dare you accuse me of anything so ridiculous? A small nose? *My* nose? You've gone too far!

THE MEDDLER. Please, sir, I . . .

CYRANO. My nose is *enormous,* you snub-nosed, flat-faced wretch! I carry it with pride, because a big nose is a sign of affability, kindness, courtesy, wit, generosity, and courage. I have all those qualities, but you can never hope to have

Cyrano de Bergerac, Act I **473**

PAGE SUMMARY: AT A GLANCE

■ Cyrano offers to refund the audience for the interrupted performance.
■ As people leave the theater, a meddler warns Cyrano that Montfleury is protected by a powerful patron.
■ When the meddler stares at Cyrano's nose, Cyrano challenges him to comment on it.

IN THE GLOSSARY

■ diminutive: tiny

24 TEACHING CHARACTERIZATION

Point out that here Cyrano makes the first of many grand gestures: He provides enough money to pay the actors and refund the audience. Help students recognize that Cyrano is motivated by a sense of fairness: The actors should not have to suffer for his victory over Montfleury.

25 TEACHING THEME

Help students recognize that this exchange reflects a major theme in the play: Cyrano's individualism and independence are at odds with society's conventions.

26 TEACHING DIALOGUE

Point to the way in which Cyrano shows both his oversensitivity about his nose and his method of facing this disfigurement: He takes the offensive and, if possible, turns the insult back to the offending person.

CRITICAL THINKING: GUIDED READING QUESTIONS

LITERAL

1a. What does the actor say when he picks up the purse Cyrano has thrown? ("At this price, sir, I'll be glad to have you come and stop our performance every day!")

2a. What does the meddler tell Cyrano about Montfleury? (Montfleury is protected by the Duke de Candale, who "has a long arm.")

INFERENTIAL

1b. What can you gather about the amount of money Cyrano gave away? (It is more than is needed to cover the refund; Cyrano made the gesture as grand and as extravagant as he could.)

2b. What does this information tell you about Cyrano's risk in interfering with Montfleury? (His risk appears much greater once we become aware of the identity of Montfleury's powerful patron.)

- Valvert tries to silence Cyrano with a tepid insult.
- Cyrano counters with an elaborate speech suggesting more interesting insults about his nose.
- Valvert insults Cyrano's dress.
- Cyrano replies that morals, deeds, and wit are more important than appearance.

IN THE GLOSSARY

- vivacity: liveliness
- fatuous: foolish
- amputated: cut off
- tankard: large mug with a lid
- grandiloquent: using flowery but empty language
- rustic: a person from the country, often considered unsophisticated
- impeccable: without fault or flaw; perfect

27 **TEACHING CONFLICT**

Help students recognize that De Guiche's hostility toward Cyrano is a major source of the play's external conflict. The incident illustrates De Guiche's treatment of Cyrano: He manipulates other people or events but never confronts Cyrano directly.

28 **TEACHING STYLE: EXAGGERATION**

Point out that Cyrano's exuberant burst of language uses exaggeration to make his nose ridiculous rather than pitiable. Cyrano demonstrates both his facility with language and his humor.

29 **TEACHING THEME**

Note that Valvert's criticism of Cyrano's appearance reveals the values of the era's fashionable class: A person's appearance supersedes his qualities of mind or heart.

---

any of them, since the ignoble face that my hand is about to meet above your collar has no more glory, nobility, poetry, quaintness, vivacity, or grandeur—no more *nose,* in short— [*Slaps him. The* MEDDLER *cries out in pain.*]

THE MEDDLER. [*Running away.*] Help! Guards!

27 DE GUICHE. [*Who has come down from the seats on the stage, with the* MARQUIS.] He's beginning to be annoying!

VALVERT. [*Shrugging.*] He likes to bluster.

DE GUICHE. Isn't anyone going to silence him?

VALVERT. Yes, *I* will! Just watch his face when he hears what I have to say to him! [*Walks up to* CYRANO, *who observes him, and stands in front of him with a fatuous expression.*] You have a nose that . . . Your nose is . . . um . . . very big.

CYRANO. [*Gravely.*] Yes, very.

VALVERT. [*Laughing.*] Ha!

CYRANO. [*With perfect calm.*] Is that all?

VALVERT. Well . . .

28 CYRANO. I'm afraid your speech was a little short, young man. You could have said . . . oh, all sorts of things, varying your tone to fit your words. Let me give you a few examples.

In an aggressive tone: "If I had a nose like that, I'd have it amputated!"

Friendly: "The end of it must get wet when you drink from a cup. Why don't you use a tankard?"

Descriptive: "It's a rock, a peak, a cape! No, more than a cape: a peninsula!"

Gracious: "What a kind man you are! You love birds so much that you've given them a perch to roost on."

Solicitous: "Be careful when you walk: with all that weight on your head, you could easily lose your balance and fall."

Thoughtful: "You ought to put an awning over it, to keep its color from fading in the sun."

Flippant: "That tusk must be convenient to hang your hat on."

474 *Drama*

Grandiloquent: "No wind but the mighty Arctic blast, majestic nose, could ever give you a cold from one end to the other!"

Dramatic: "When it bleeds, it must be like the Red Sea!"[36]

Admiring: "What a sign for a perfume shop!"

Rustic: "That don't look like no nose to me. It's either a big cucumber or a little watermelon."

Military: "The enemy is charging! Aim your cannon!"

There, now you have an inkling of what you might have said to me if you were witty and a man of letters. Unfortunately you're totally witless and a man of very few letters: only the four that spell the word "fool."

DE GUICHE. [*Trying to lead away the outraged* VALVERT.] Come, never mind.

29 VALVERT. [*Choking with anger.*] Such arrogance from an uncouth barbarian who . . . who . . . isn't even wearing gloves! Who appears in public without ribbons, or tassels, or braid!

CYRANO. I have a different idea of elegance. I don't dress like a fop,[37] it's true, but my moral grooming is impeccable. I never appear in public with a soiled conscience, a tarnished honor, threadbare scruples, or an insult that I haven't washed away. I'm always immaculately clean, adorned with independence and frankness. I may not cut a stylish figure, but I hold my soul erect. I wear my deeds as ribbons, my wit is sharper than the finest mustache, and when I walk among men I make truths ring like spurs.

VALVERT. [*Exasperated.*] Buffoon!

CYRANO. [*Crying out as if in pain.*] Oh! I have a cramp in my sword.

VALVERT. [*Drawing his own.*] So be it!

---

36. **Red Sea:** sea in the Near East that is colored by a reddish algae at certain periods of the year.
37. **fop:** man who is overly concerned with his appearance; a dandy.

CRITICAL THINKING: GUIDED READING QUESTIONS

LITERAL

1a. What does Valvert reply when De Guiche says that Cyrano is annoying? ("He likes to bluster.")

2a. What does Cyrano say when Valvert calls him a buffoon? ("I have a cramp in my sword.")

INFERENTIAL

1b. Do you think this comment reflects something that is true about Cyrano? Explain. (No, Cyrano is not blustering: He backs up his extravagant talk with action.)

2b. What does he mean by this? What does his fanciful way of expressing himself tell you about him? (It means that he wants to fight in response to Valvert's insult. Cyrano's fanciful way of speaking suggests that he is imaginative and witty.)

CYRANO. I'll give you a charming little thrust.

30 VALVERT. [*Contemptuously.*] Poet!

CYRANO. Yes, sir, I *am* a poet, as I'll demonstrate by composing an impromptu[38] ballade while I fence with you.

VALVERT. A ballade?

CYRANO. You don't know what that is? Allow me to explain.

VALVERT. But . . .

CYRANO. [*As though reciting a lesson.*] The ballade consists of three eight-line stanzas . . .

VALVERT. [*Stamping his foot.*] Oh!

CYRANO. [*Continuing.*] . . . with a four-line refrain at the end.

VALVERT. You . . .

CYRANO. I'm going to compose one as I fight with you, and when I come to the last line, I'll draw blood.

VALVERT. No!

CYRANO. No? Wait and see.

THE CROWD. [*Greatly excited.*] Make room!—This will be worth seeing!—Step back!—Quiet!

CYRANO. [*Closing his eyes for a moment.*] Wait, I'm thinking of how to begin. . . . There, I have it. [*His actions match his words throughout the ballade.*]
I take off my hat and discard it,
I slowly abandon my cloak,
I draw my sword out of its scabbard,
Preparing to put it to use.
For the moment, I stand here before you,
Elegant, calm, and serene,
But I warn you, my impudent scoundrel,
When I end the refrain, I draw blood.

[*They begin fencing.*]

---

38. **impromptu:** spontaneous, without preparation.

You should have avoided this battle.
Now, where shall I skewer you, goose?
In the side, 'neath the sleeve of your doublet?
In the heart, 'neath the ribbon you wear?
No, I've carefully thought and reflected,
And finally made up my mind;
The paunch: that's where I've decided,
When I end the refrain, to draw blood.
I see you give ground when I press you;
Your face is as white as a sheet;
Is "coward" a name that would suit you?
I dexterously parry the point[39]
That you hoped to thrust into my entrails;
Your efforts are doomed to be vain.
Prepare yourself now to be punctured:
When I end the refrain, I draw blood.

[*Announces solemnly.*]

31
Refrain:
Pray God to forgive your transgressions!
The close of our combat draws near;
A coupé,[40] then a feint,[41] then the finish!
[*He lunges.* VALVERT *staggers.* CYRANO *bows.*]
When I end the refrain, I draw blood.

[*Cheers. Applause from the boxes. Flowers and handkerchiefs are thrown down. Officers surround and congratulate* CYRANO. RAGUENEAU *dances with delight.* LE BRET *is both happy and appalled.* VALVERT'*s friends lead him away, holding him up.*]

32 THE CROWD. [*In a long cry.*] Ah! . . .

A LIGHT-HORSEMAN. Magnificent!

A WOMAN. Charming!

RAGUENEAU. Phenomenal!

A MARQUIS. Unheard of!

LE BRET. Foolhardy!

---

39. **parry the point:** prevent an opponent from striking with his sword.
40. **coupé** [k$\overline{oo}$ pā′]: forceful stroke.
41. **feint** [fānt]: movement meant to deceive.

Cyrano de Bergerac, Act I **475**

CRITICAL THINKING: GUIDED READING QUESTIONS

LITERAL

1a. What word does Valvert use to insult Cyrano before their fight? (He contemptuously calls him "poet.")

2a. What does Cyrano do while carrying on his fight with Valvert? (He spontaneously composes a ballade.)

INFERENTIAL

1b. What do you gather are Cyrano's and Valvert's contrasting attitudes toward poets? (Valvert finds poets unattractive and despicable, whereas Cyrano believes that writing poetry is a delightful and worthy talent.)

2b. What is his motivation for doing this? (Cyrano wants to teach Valvert a lesson for insulting him and the art of poetry. He proves that being a poet does not make one a coward or a buffoon.)

- Cyrano reveals that the money he threw on the stage was his entire month's allotment: He is now penniless.
- The young woman selling refreshments offers him food, but he takes only a little.
- Le Bret warns Cyrano that his actions have made him new enemies.

IN THE GLOSSARY

- bravado: pretended bravery, especially when it is boastful

33 READING SKILL: CAUSE AND EFFECT

Ask students why Cyrano changes his tone once the doorkeeper is out of earshot. (Students should recognize that Cyrano is proud and does not want the doorkeeper to know he has no money.)

34 TEACHING CHARACTERIZATION

Ask students what Cyrano's gesture of giving away his entire month's allotment shows about him. (They should see that Cyrano loves flamboyant acts.)

35 TEACHING CHARACTER MOTIVATION

Point out that Cyrano's behavior is motivated by tact and consideration. Help students see that Cyrano takes very little of the woman's food because she is poor, but he refuses in such a flattering way that she goes away feeling appreciated.

THE CROWD. [*Swarming around* CYRANO.] Congratulations!—My compliments!—Bravo!

A WOMAN'S VOICE. He's a hero!

LE BRET. [*To* CYRANO, *taking his arm.*] I'd like to have a talk with you.

CYRANO. Wait till this crowd thins out a little. [*To* BELLEROSE.] May I stay?

BELLEROSE. [*Respectfully.*] Of course, sir! [*Changing his tone, to the* DOORKEEPER *and the man who is preparing to put out the candles.*] Sweep out the theater and lock the door, but leave the candles burning. We'll come back after dinner to rehearse the new farce we're going to present tomorrow. [*Goes out.*]

33 THE DOORKEEPER. [*To* CYRANO.] Aren't you going to dine, sir?

CYRANO. No. [*The* DOORKEEPER *withdraws.*]

LE BRET. [*To* CYRANO.] Why not?

CYRANO. [*Proudly.*] Because . . . [*Changing his tone, seeing that the* DOORKEEPER *is out of earshot.*] Because I have no money.

LE BRET. [*Making the gesture of throwing a bag.*] What! That bag of money . . .

34 CYRANO. Alas, my month's allotment lived only for a day!

LE BRET. And for the rest of the month . . .

CYRANO. I have nothing left.

LE BRET. What foolishness to throw it all away!

CYRANO. Yes, but what a gesture!

THE REFRESHMENT GIRL. [*Coughing from behind her little counter.*] Ahem! . . . [CYRANO *and* LE BRET *turn around. She comes forward timidly.*] Sir, I . . . I can't bear to think of you going hungry. [*Points to the refreshment table.*] I have plenty of food here. . . . Take whatever you like!

476 *Drama*

---

35 CYRANO. [*Gallantly taking off his hat.*] My dear child, my Gascon pride forbids me to accept the slightest morsel from your fingers, but since I fear a refusal would offend you, I will accept . . . [*Goes to the refreshment table and chooses.*] Oh, very little! One of these grapes . . . [*She tries to give him the whole cluster; he picks off a single grape.*] Only one! . . . This glass of water . . . [*She tries to pour him a glass of wine; he stops her.*] And half a macaroon. [*Breaks one and gives her back the other half.*]

LE BRET. But that's ridiculous!

THE REFRESHMENT GIRL. Oh, please take something else!

CYRANO. I will. Your lovely hand. [*She holds out her hand to him and he kisses it as if she were a princess.*]

THE REFRESHMENT GIRL. Thank you, sir. [*Bows.*] Good-by. [*Leaves.*]

CYRANO. [*To* LE BRET.] You wanted to have a talk with me? I'm ready to listen. [*Sets the macaroon down on the refreshment table in front of him.*] My dinner! . . . [*Sets down the glass of water.*] My drink! . . . [*And finally the grape.*] My dessert! [*Sits down.*] There, I'm ready to begin. I have an excellent appetite this evening. [*Eating.*] What was it you wanted to tell me?

LE BRET. That you're going to have some badly distorted ideas if you listen only to those fools who like to give themselves such warlike airs. Talk with a few sensible people and you'll be better informed of the effect produced by your act of bravado.

CYRANO. [*Finishing his macaroon.*] It was enormous.

LE BRET. You've made too many enemies!

CYRANO. About how many would you say I made today?

CRITICAL THINKING: GUIDED READING QUESTIONS

LITERAL

1a. About what two things does Le Bret scold Cyrano? (He tells him that it is foolish to throw away a whole month's pay and that he should be careful about making too many powerful enemies.)

2a. What does Cyrano take from the woman selling refreshments? (one grape, a glass of water, and half a macaroon)

INFERENTIAL

1b. Do you think Le Bret is right? Explain. (Possible responses: Cyrano should have kept some of the money, since he will have nothing to live on; he should not make powerful enemies because he cannot always avoid retribution.)

2b. Why do you think Cyrano takes such a small amount of food? (He has sympathy for the young woman and does not want to take away her livelihood.)

LE BRET. There's Montfleury, then the burgher[42] you kicked, De Guiche, Valvert, of course, Baro,[43] the Academy[44] . . .

CYRANO. Stop! That's already enough to delight me!

LE BRET. I don't understand the way you live. Where will it lead you? What are you trying to accomplish?

CYRANO. I was once confused and bewildered by all the complicated courses of action that were open to me. Finally I chose . . .

LE BRET. What did you choose?

CYRANO. The simplest course of all. I decided to be admirable in everything!

LE BRET. If you say so. . . . But let me ask you something else. What's the real reason for your hatred of Montfleury? You can tell *me* the truth.

CYRANO. [*Standing up.*] That bloated old sot, I've hated him since the day when I saw him look at . . . It was like watching a slimy slug crawling on a flower!

LE BRET. [*Astonished.*] What's this? Do I understand you rightly? Is it possible that . . .

[36] **CYRANO.** [*With a bitter laugh.*] That I'm in love? [*Changing to a grave tone.*] Yes, it's true.

LE BRET. May I ask with whom? You've never told me . . .

[37] **CYRANO.** With whom I'm in love? Come now, think a moment: this nose of mine, which precedes me by a quarter of an hour wherever I go, forbids me ever to dream of being loved by even an ugly woman. Whom else would I love but the

most beautiful woman in the world?

LE BRET. The most beautiful . . .

CYRANO. Of course! The most beautiful of all women! The most captivating, the most intelligent . . . [*Dejectedly.*] . . . the blondest. . . .

LE BRET. Tell me: who is she?

[38] **CYRANO.** Anyone who has seen her smile has known perfection. She creates grace without movement, and makes all divinity fit into her slightest gesture. And neither Venus[45] in her shell, nor Diana[46] striding in the great, blossoming forest, can compare to her when she goes through the streets of Paris in her sedan chair![47]

LE BRET. Now I believe I know! It *is* becoming clear!

CYRANO. It's perfectly transparent.

LE BRET. Your cousin, Magdeleine Robin?

CYRANO. Yes—Roxane.

LE BRET. Then you ought to be overjoyed! You love her? Tell her so! You've covered yourself with glory in her eyes today!

[39] **CYRANO.** Look at me and tell me what hope this protuberance might leave me! I have no illusions. Sometimes, in the blue shadows of evening, I give way to tender feelings. I go into a garden, smelling the fragrance of spring with my poor monstrous nose, and watch a man and a woman strolling together in the moonlight. I think how much I, too, would like to be walking arm in arm with a woman, under the moon. I let myself be carried away, I forget myself—and then I suddenly see the shadow of my profile on the garden wall.

---

42. **burgher:** person who lives in a town.
43. **Baro** [ba rō′]: Balthazar Baro (1600–1650), author of *La Clorise,* the play that Cyrano interrupted.
44. **Academy:** The French Academy, founded in 1635, is made up of France's forty most distinguished writers.

---

45. **Venus:** Roman goddess of love and beauty.
46. **Diana:** Roman goddess of the moon and hunting.
47. **sedan chair:** enclosed chair carried on poles.

Cyrano de Bergerac, Act I **477**

CRITICAL THINKING: GUIDED READING QUESTIONS

LITERAL

1a. What does Cyrano tell Le Bret about a decision that ended his confusion? (He decided "to be admirable in everything.")

2a. What reason does Cyrano give for not telling Roxane of his love? (He says that no woman could ever love him because of his nose.)

INFERENTIAL

1b. Do you think Cyrano lives up to this motto? (Opinions will vary, but most students will admit that he has displayed many talents and an unusual degree of integrity.)

2b. What does this tell you about Cyrano's opinion of romance and women? (About romance Cyrano is completely without confidence; he seems to think that women admire only the superficial and are incapable of appreciating deeper qualities.)

- Le Bret encourages Cyrano to think of his good qualities and repeats that Cyrano should tell Roxane of his love.
- Roxane's duenna tells Cyrano that Roxane wants to see him; a meeting is arranged at Ragueneau's bakery.
- Cyrano becomes deliriously happy at the thought of the forthcoming meeting.

IN THE GLOSSARY

- sullied: dirtied; dishonored

40 **TEACHING THEME**

Point out that Le Bret's speech emphasizes one of the major themes of the play: the relative values of inner and outer beauty.

41 **TEACHING CHARACTERIZATION**

Ask students what important aspect of Cyrano's character is revealed by his response to Le Bret. (Students should note that Cyrano is a proud man who fears ridicule more than anything else.)

42 **CULTURAL BACKGROUND**

Be sure that students understand the role of the duenna. Unmarried ladies of Cyrano's period were not supposed to be alone with a man; they had to have a companion, usually an elderly woman, as a chaperon. The duenna often acted as a confidant and go-between, setting up meetings and carrying messages.

43 **TEACHING DIALOGUE**

Point out the way in which the duenna's discreet wording here promotes ambiguity. Remind students that Cyrano is in love. Then ask them what Cyrano thinks "things to tell you" means. (He thinks it is a reference to confessions of love for him.)

LE BRET. [*Deeply moved.*] My friend . . .

CYRANO. My friend, I have bad moments now and then, feeling myself so ugly, all alone. . . .

LE BRET. [*With concern, taking his hand.*] Do you weep?

CYRANO. Oh, no, never! No, it would be grotesque if a tear ran down this nose! As long as it's in my power to prevent it, I'll never let the divine beauty of tears be sullied by such gross ugliness.

40 LE BRET. But you're overlooking your courage, your wit! . . . Take that girl who offered to give you dinner just now, for example: you could see for yourself that she was far from detesting you!

CYRANO. [*Struck by this realization.*] Yes, it's true!

LE BRET. Well, then? You see? And Roxane herself was pale as she watched your duel. . . .

CYRANO. Pale?

41 LE BRET. You've already made a deep impression on her heart and her mind. Don't be timid: speak to her, tell her, so that . . .

CYRANO. So that she'll laugh in my face? No! That's the one thing in the world that I fear!

THE DOORKEEPER. [*Bringing in* ROXANE's DUENNA.] Sir, this lady would like to speak to you.

42 CYRANO. [*Seeing the* DUENNA.] Her duenna!

THE DUENNA. [*With a deep bow.*] My lady wishes me to ask her valiant cousin where she can see him in private.

43 CYRANO. [*Thunderstruck.*] See me?

THE DUENNA. [*With another bow.*] Yes. She has things to tell you.

CYRANO. Things to . . .

THE DUENNA. [*Bowing again.*] To tell you.

CYRANO. [*Unsteady on his feet.*] My—

478 *Drama*

THE DUENNA. She will go to early Mass at the Saint-Roch[48] church tomorrow morning.

CYRANO. [*Clutching* LE BRET *to steady himself.*] Ah—

THE DUENNA. When she leaves the church, where can she go to talk with you?

CYRANO. [*Agitated.*] Where? . . . I . . . Where . . .

THE DUENNA. Well?

CYRANO. I'm trying to think!

THE DUENNA. Tell me.

CYRANO. At . . . at Ragueneau's shop . . . Ragueneau, the pastry cook. . . .

THE DUENNA. [*Withdrawing.*] Very well. At seven o'clock.

CYRANO. I'll be there.

[*The* DUENNA *leaves.*]

CYRANO. [*Falling into* LE BRET's *arms.*] Me! She wants to see *me*!

LE BRET. I see your sadness has vanished!

CYRANO. Ah, for whatever reason, she knows I exist!

LE BRET. Please be calm.

CYRANO. No! I'm going to be frenzied and turbulent! I need a whole army to vanquish! I have ten hearts, twenty arms! It's no longer enough for me to cut down dwarfs . . . [*Shouts at the top of his lungs.*] . . . I need giants!

[*For some time now, the* ACTORS *and* ACTRESSES *have been moving on the stage: the rehearsal is beginning.*]

A VOICE. [*From the stage.*] Quiet! We're rehearsing!

---

48. **Saint-Roch** [san rōsh′]

CRITICAL THINKING: GUIDED READING QUESTIONS

LITERAL

1a. Why does Le Bret encourage Cyrano to tell Roxane of his love? (He says that Cyrano has wonderful qualities to offer and that Roxane has already shown concern for him.)

2a. What does the duenna tell Cyrano? (She says that Roxane wants to see him.)

INFERENTIAL

1b. Do you think Le Bret is correct in encouraging Cyrano? (Possible response: Yes, if he does not make his feelings known, he will never know whether she might return his love.)

2b. Why does Cyrano's mood change after speaking with the duenna? (He thinks that Roxane may tell him that she loves him.)

PAGE SUMMARY: AT A GLANCE

■ Cyrano learns that Lignière is being pursued by one hundred men.
■ Cyrano resolves to fight the men himself.

44 TEACHING CHARACTERIZATION

Ask students what Cyrano's decision to fight the hundred men reveals about him. (Students should see that Cyrano is brave and loyal to his friends yet often acts heedlessly.)

CYRANO. [*Laughing.*] And we're leaving!

[*He goes upstage. Through the entrance of the theater come* CUIGY, BRISSAILLE, *and several* OFFICERS *holding up* LIGNIÈRE.]

CUIGY. Cyrano!

CYRANO. What is it?

CUIGY. We've brought a friend—

CYRANO. [*Recognizing him.*] Lignière! . . . What's happened to you?

CUIGY. He wants to see you.

BRISSAILLE. He can't go home.

CYRANO. Why not?

LIGNIÈRE. [*Holding up a rumpled piece of paper.*] This note warns me . . . hundred men against me . . . because of . . . of a song . . . great danger . . . Porte de Nesle . . . on my way home. . . . Will you let me . . . let me sleep under your roof tonight?

CYRANO. A hundred men, you say? You'll sleep at home tonight!

LIGNIÈRE. [*Alarmed.*] But . . .

44 CYRANO. [*In a thunderous voice.*] Take that lantern . . . [LIGNIÈRE *quickly obeys.*] . . . and walk! I'll cover you! [*To the* OFFICERS.] And you, follow at a distance: you'll be witnesses!

Cyrano de Bergerac, Act I **479**

CRITICAL THINKING: GUIDED READING QUESTIONS

LITERAL

1a. What does Lignière ask Cyrano? (He asks him whether he can stay the night at Cyrano's house because a hundred men are lying in wait for him.)

INFERENTIAL

1b. Why might Cyrano seem so excited at the prospect of defending Lignière? (The odds against him probably appeal to his theatrical flair. He also despises injustice. Exalted by the prospect of meeting Roxane, he had asked to have "giants" to battle; battling Lignière's one hundred opponents will be roughly equivalent to battling giants.)

- Cyrano sets off for the confrontation.
- Cyrano claims that Lignière's opponents are dispatching one hundred men for the fight because Lignière is a friend of his.

IN THE GLOSSARY

- nebulous: not clear; hazy

45 TEACHING FIGURATIVE LANGUAGE

Help students recognize the theatrical quality of Cyrano's bravado. Cyrano seems to envision all of Paris as a stage for his brave deeds.

COLLABORATIVE LEARNING: ENRICHMENT ACTIVITY

History The French Age of Elegance forms the backdrop for *Cyrano de Bergerac.* Have students work in groups to find out more about this period. They might look into such topics as Richelieu, France's role in the Thirty Years' War and the Peace of Westphalia, and the founding of the French Academy. Encourage the groups to share their findings with the class.

READER'S RESPONSE

What do you admire most about Cyrano so far? What do you admire least about him?

ANSWERS

STUDY QUESTIONS

1. He has come to see Roxane. He is afraid to speak to her since he is not witty.
2. He is "odd, impetuous, brash, and outlandish" and has a very large nose.
3. Cyrano orders him offstage. He throws a bag of money onstage to pay the players and reimburse the audience.
4. Possible answers: "That tusk must be convenient to hang your hat on"; "When it bleeds, it must be like the Red Sea!"; "What a sign for a perfume shop!"
5. He loves Roxane. She says Roxane wants to meet him.
6. He asks Cyrano whether he can spend the night at Cyrano's house to hide from some enemies. Cyrano vows to help him fight the enemies.

CUIGY. But a hundred men! . . .

CYRANO. I need at least that many this evening!

[*The* ACTORS *and* ACTRESSES, *in their various costumes, have come down from the stage and approached the group.*]

AN ACTRESS. [*To the others.*] But why should there be a hundred men against one poor poet?

CYRANO. Let's go! [*To the* OFFICERS.] Gentlemen, when you see me charge, don't come to my assistance, no matter how great the danger!

ANOTHER ACTRESS. [*Leaping down from the stage.*] I want to go and watch!

CYRANO. Bravo! Officers, ladies in costume, and twenty paces in front . . . [*He takes up the station he has described.*] . . . I will walk alone, under the plume that glory herself has placed on my hat, with twice the pride of Scipio,[49] and a nose three times as long! . . . Remember, now:

---

49. **Scipio** [sip'ē ō] (234–183 B.C.): Roman general.

---

no one is allowed to lift a finger to help me! . . . All ready? One, two, three! Doorkeeper, open the door! [*The* DOORKEEPER *opens both halves of the door, giving a glimpse of picturesque old Paris in the moonlight.*] Ah, Paris lies before us, dim and nebulous in the shadows, with moonlight flowing down the slopes of her roofs! An exquisite setting for the scene about to be performed! There, beneath the mist, the Seine[50] quivers like a mysterious magic mirror. . . . And you will see what you will see!

ALL. To the Porte de Nesle!

CYRANO. [*Standing on the threshold.*] To the Porte de Nesle! [*Turns to the* ACTRESS.] You asked, mademoiselle, why a hundred men had been sent to attack one poet. [*Calmly, drawing his sword.*] I'll tell you: it's because that poet is known to be a friend of mine. [*He goes out. The procession moves forward into the night, to the sound of the violins, and in the dim glow of the candles.*]

---

50. **Seine** [sen]: river that flows through Paris.

STUDY QUESTIONS

Recalling

1. Why has Christian come to the play? What concern does he express to Lignière?
2. Prior to his entry on stage, what do we learn of Cyrano's appearance and personality from the descriptions by his friends?
3. Briefly retell what happens when Montfleury tries to begin the play. How does Cyrano appease the audience?
4. List three of the comments Cyrano makes up about his nose. Describe his duel with Valvert.
5. What does Cyrano confide to Le Bret after the crowd leaves? How does the duenna's visit change his mood?

6. What favor does Lignière ask of Cyrano, and how does Cyrano respond?

Interpreting

7. What does the fact that Cyrano gives away his money to refund the tickets show about him?
8. In his verbal battles in Act I, what skills and qualities does Cyrano display?
9. What does Cyrano's eagerness to take on the enemies of Lignière reveal about him?
10. What does Cyrano mean when he says, "I may not cut a stylish figure, but I hold my soul erect"? List two actions that illustrate this statement.

Extending

11. Do you think pride like Cyrano's is foolish, or do you find it admirable? Why?

---

7. He is fearless, honest, and proud and loves to make grand gestures.
8. wit, poetic ability, integrity, and love of a challenge
9. He is courageous and confident but somewhat foolhardy.
10. He never compromises his ideals, honor, or integrity. He refunds the audience and volunteers to help Lignière.

11. Answers will vary. Students may say that he is foolish because he makes enemies and gives away money or that he is admirable because of his integrity.

ACT II

The large workroom of the pastry shop of RAGUENEAU. *The next morning.*

[*The street, seen through the panes of the door in the background, is gray in the first glow of dawn. Copper pots and pans are gleaming. Spits are turning. The morning rush has begun. Fat* COOKS *and small* KITCHEN BOYS *are jostling one another. Some tables are covered with cakes and dishes. Others, surrounded by chairs, are awaiting eaters and drinkers. A smaller one in a corner is laden with papers.* RAGUENEAU *is seated at it, writing, as the curtain rises.*]

RAGUENEAU. The silver of dawn is already gleaming on the copper pots! Silence the god who sings within you, Ragueneau! The hour of the lute will come—it is now the hour of the oven! [*Stands up and speaks to a* COOK.] There's something lacking in this sauce.

THE COOK. What shall I do to it?

RAGUENEAU. Make it a little more lyrical.

AN APPRENTICE. [*Bringing a tray covered with a cloth.*] I've baked this in your honor, sir. I hope it will please you. [*He uncovers the tray, revealing a large pastry lyre.*[1]]

RAGUENEAU. [*Enraptured.*] A lyre!

THE APPRENTICE. Made of pastry dough.

RAGUENEAU. [*Deeply moved.*] With candied fruit!

THE APPRENTICE. And I made the strings of sugar.

RAGUENEAU. [*Giving him some money.*] Here, go and drink to my health! [*Sees* LISE[2] *coming in.*] My wife! Quickly, go about your business—and hide that money! [*To* LISE, *pointing to the lyre with embarrassment.*] Isn't it beautiful?

---

1. **lyre** [līr]: stringed musical instrument, used to accompany singing or poetry.
2. **Lise** [lēz]

LISE. It's ridiculous! [*She puts a pile of paper bags on the counter.*]

RAGUENEAU. You've brought some paper bags? Good, thank you. [*Looks at them more closely.*] Oh, no! My treasured books! My friends' poetry! Desecrated, dismembered, to make bags for pastry! How can you treat poetry with such disrespect?

LISE. I'll treat poetry however I please!

RAGUENEAU. I shudder to think of what you might do with prose!

[CYRANO *enters abruptly.*]

CYRANO. What time is it?

RAGUENEAU. [*Bowing to him.*] Six o'clock.

CYRANO. [*With great emotion.*] One more hour! [*He begins pacing the floor.*]

RAGUENEAU. [*Following him.*] Congratulations!

CYRANO. For what?

RAGUENEAU. I saw your duel!

CYRANO. Which one?

RAGUENEAU. At the Hôtel de Bourgogne!

CYRANO. [*Disdainfully.*] Oh, that one. . . .

RAGUENEAU. [*Admiringly.*] A duel in verse!

LISE. He talks about nothing else!

CYRANO. I'm glad to hear it.

RAGUENEAU. [*Lunging with a spit that he has picked up.*] "When I end the refrain, I draw blood!" . . . Magnificent! [*With growing enthusiasm.*] "When I end the refrain . . ."

CYRANO. What time is it, Ragueneau?

RAGUENEAU. [*Looking at the clock while holding the position of the lunge he has just made.*] Five

Cyrano de Bergerac, Act II **481**

- Cyrano tells Ragueneau that he plans to meet someone and asks to be left alone during the meeting.
- Cyrano fears that he will be unable to speak of his love to Roxane and begins to write a love letter.
- Ragueneau's poets arrive and describe eight men they saw who had been felled at the Porte de Nesle.

2 TEACHING COMEDY

Explain that Cyrano's joke refers to the folk belief that if you tell a lie, your nose will twitch. Point out that his joke about this sensitive subject shows a new-found ease since he has come to believe that Roxane loves him.

3 TEACHING CHARACTERIZATION

Ask students what Cyrano's comment to himself suggests about his character. (Cyrano is brave in everything but affairs of the heart; only when it comes to his love for Roxane does he falter.)

4 TEACHING METAPHORS

Ask students what the humorous metaphors "eagle of pastry cooks" and "a fragrant nest" suggest about the poets' real interests. (Their main interest is in Ragueneau's cooking, not in his poetry.)

5 TEACHING DRAMATIC IRONY

Point out that this incident is an example of dramatic irony: The audience is aware that Cyrano has routed the assassins, but the poets are not. What does the use of dramatic irony add to the scene? (interest and humor, because only the audience is able to understand Cyrano's comments)

---

past six. "... I draw blood!" [*Stands up straight.*] Ah, what a ballade!

LISE. [*To* CYRANO, *who has absentmindedly shaken her hand while passing by her counter.*] Your hand is wounded!

CYRANO. It's nothing, just a small gash.

RAGUENEAU. Have you been doing something dangerous?

CYRANO. No, I've been in no danger.

2 LISE. [*Shaking her finger at him.*] I believe you're telling a lie!

CYRANO. Why? Was my nose twitching? If so, it must have been an enormous lie! [*Changing his tone.*] I'm waiting for someone here. If I don't wait in vain, I want you to leave us alone together.

RAGUENEAU. I can't do that: my poets will soon be here.

LISE. [*Sarcastically.*] For their first meal!

CYRANO. You will take them away when I give you a signal. . . . What time is it?

RAGUENEAU. Ten past six.

CYRANO. [*Nervously sitting down at* RAGUENEAU'*s table and taking a sheet of paper.*] May I have a pen?

RAGUENEAU. [*Giving him the pen he has been carrying behind his ear.*] Here, take my swan's feather! [*A* MUSKETEER *with a superb mustache enters.*]

THE MUSKETEER. [*In a stentorian[3] voice.*] Greetings! [LISE *hurries toward him.*]

CYRANO. [*Looking around.*] Who's that?

RAGUENEAU. A friend of my wife's. A mighty warrior—according to what he says! He . . .

---

3. **stentorian** [sten tôr′ē ən]: loud. Stentor was a legendary Greek herald with a voice as loud as fifty men.

482 *Drama*

---

3 CYRANO. [*Taking his pen again and waving* RAGUENEAU *away.*] Never mind. [*To himself.*] Coward! You don't have the courage to say one word to her! [*To* RAGUENEAU.] What time is it?

RAGUENEAU. Quarter past six.

CYRANO. [*To himself.*] I'm afraid to speak a single one of all the words I have in here. [*Strikes his chest.*] But writing is a different matter. . . . [*Takes his pen again.*] I'll now put down on paper the love letter that I've already written within myself a hundred times. I have only to look into my soul and copy the words inscribed in it. [*He begins writing. Through the glass of the door, thin figures are seen moving hesitantly.*]

LISE. [*Entering, to* RAGUENEAU.] Here come your mud-spattered poets!

FIRST POET. [*Entering, to* RAGUENEAU.] Colleague!

4 SECOND POET. Eagle of pastry cooks! [*Sniffs.*] What a fragrant nest you have!

THIRD POET. O culinary[4] god!

RAGUENEAU. [*Surrounded, embraced, shaken.*] They always make me feel at ease as soon as they come in!

5 FIRST POET. We were delayed by a crowd gathered at the Porte de Nesle.

SECOND POET. Eight bandits had been felled by swordplay and lay bleeding on the pavement!

CYRANO. [*Briefly looking up.*] Eight? I thought there were only seven. [*Resumes writing his letter.*] "I love you. . . ." [*He is heard murmuring from time to time.*]

FIRST POET. We were told that one man had routed a whole band of assassins!

SECOND POET. There were pikes and clubs strewn all over the ground!

---

4. **culinary** [kū′lə ner′ē]: pertaining to cooking.

CRITICAL THINKING: GUIDED READING QUESTIONS

LITERAL

1a. What does Lise reply when Ragueneau says that his poets will be there soon? ("For their first meal!")

2a. What is Cyrano's explanation for the ease with which he writes a love letter to Roxane? (He has already composed the letter in his soul; he has only to look inside and "copy the words inscribed" there.)

INFERENTIAL

1b. What is Lise's understanding of the reason for the poets' friendly behavior toward Ragueneau? (She sees that they are friendly toward him only so that they can get a free meal.)

2b. What does this explanation suggest about the nature and duration of his love for Roxane? (He has loved her a long time, and though his love clamors strongly for expression, he has always been afraid to let it be known for fear of rejection.)

CYRANO. [Writing.] "Your eyes . . ."

FIRST POET. The man who could do a thing like that . . .

CYRANO. [Writing.] "Your lips . . ."

FIRST POET. . . . must have been some sort of ferocious giant!

CYRANO. [Writing.] ". . . and I become faint with fear each time I see you."

SECOND POET. [Snatching a cake.] What have you been writing, Ragueneau?

6 CYRANO. [Writing.] "Your faithful worshiper . . ." [He stops as he is about to sign his name, stands up, and puts the letter in his doublet.] No need to sign it, since I'll give it to her myself.

RAGUENEAU. [To the SECOND POET.] I've written a recipe in verse.

THIRD POET. [Sitting down next to a tray of cream puffs.] Let's hear it!

RAGUENEAU. [Clears his throat, straightens his hat, strikes a pose, and prepares to recite.] A recipe in verse . . .

"How to Make Almond Tarts"
Beat some eggs till they are foamy;
Mix with tangy citron juice;
Then fold in sweet milk of almonds.
Line your pans with pastry dough,
Slowly pour your foam to fill them;
Let them bake till golden brown.
Now remove them from the oven:
Luscious, dainty almond tarts!

7 THE POETS. [With their mouths full.] Exquisite! Delightful!

CYRANO. [From the door in the background, motioning RAGUENEAU to take the POETS away.] Psst! . . .

RAGUENEAU. [Showing the POETS the door on the right.] Come this way, gentlemen, we'll be much more comfortable . . . [They all go out behind RAGUENEAU, in procession, after having snatched up several trays of pastry.]

CYRANO. I'll give her my letter if I feel that there's the slightest hope! [ROXANE appears behind the glass of the door, followed by the DUENNA. CYRANO throws open the door.] Come in! [Takes the DUENNA aside.] May I have a word with you?

THE DUENNA. Have several, if you like.

CYRANO. Are you fond of pastry?

THE DUENNA. I'm sinfully fond of it!

8 CYRANO. [Quickly taking some of the paper bags on the counter.] Good. Here are two sonnets by Monsieur Benserade[5] . . .

THE DUENNA. [Disappointed.] Oh. . . .

CYRANO. . . . which I will fill with custard tarts for you. [The DUENNA's face brightens.]

THE DUENNA. Ah!

CYRANO. Do you like cream puffs?

THE DUENNA. [With dignity.] I hold them in high regard.

CYRANO. Here are six of them for you, in a poem by Saint-Amant. And in this verse by Chapelain[6] I'll place a piece of butter cake. You really like pastry, do you?

THE DUENNA. I adore it!

CYRANO. [Loading her arms with filled bags.] Then I'm sure you'll enjoy going out and eating all this in the street.

THE DUENNA. But . . .

CYRANO. [Pushing her outside.] And please don't

---

5. **Benserade** [bon′sə rod′]: Isaac de Benserade (1613–1691), French poet and playwright.
6. **Saint-Amant** [san′ta mon′]. . . **Chapelain** [shap lan′]: Marc-Antoine de Gerard, Sieur de Saint-Amant (1594–1661) and Jean Chapelain (1595–1674) were both French poets and original members of the Academy.

Cyrano de Bergerac, Act II **483**

PAGE SUMMARY: AT A GLANCE

- The poets continue to discuss the Port de Nesle incident.
- Cyrano finishes his letter but does not sign it.
- Ragueneau recites a poetic recipe.
- Roxane and her duenna arrive, and Cyrano bribes the duenna to leave them alone.

6 TEACHING PLOT: FORESHADOWING

Point out that Cyrano's decision not to sign his love letter foreshadows the use of the letter later in the act.

7 TEACHING CHARACTERIZATION

Encourage students to note the playwright's characterization of poets: Even they are not exempt from the hypocrisy and servility Cyrano so dislikes in the fashionable classes. They flatter Ragueneau, touching upon his greatest desire—to be a poet—in order to be able to eat his delicious pastries without paying for them.

8 READING SKILL: COMPARISON AND CONTRAST

Ask students to contrast the duenna's attitude toward poetry with that of Cyrano. (Students should see that the duenna has very practical values; she prefers food for her stomach to poetry for her mind. This contrasts with Cyrano's impractical, idealistic attitudes, which frequently get him in trouble.)

CRITICAL THINKING: GUIDED READING QUESTIONS

LITERAL

1a. What do the poets assume about the man who routed a whole band of assassins the night before? (He must have been some sort of ferocious giant.)

2a. What makes the duenna's face brighten? (the addition of custard tarts to sonnets)

INFERENTIAL

1b. In what way does this assumption contrast with Cyrano's feelings as he writes the love letter? (Writing words of love to Roxane, he is at his most benign and even feels frightened about giving the letter to her.)

2b. Why does Cyrano bribe the duenna with pastry and push her outside? (He wants to be alone with Roxane.)

Cyrano de Bergerac, Act II **T-483**

- Roxane and Cyrano talk nostalgically about their childhood.
- She asks him about his exploits the night before.
- Roxane speaks of someone she loves who also loves her, and Cyrano responds hopefully to her words.

9 TEACHING CHARACTERIZATION

Encourage students to note how Roxane skillfully begins their talk by flattering Cyrano and painting herself as vulnerable. She deftly controls and manipulates the conversation.

10 TEACHING IMAGERY AND MOOD

Point out the gentle, carefree mood created by the charming images Cyrano and Roxane recall from their childhood. Explain that the mood of this quiet moment contrasts with the turbulence to come.

11 TEACHING DRAMATIC IRONY

Help students recognize that Cyrano's building excitement at Roxane's forthcoming declaration creates dramatic irony because the audience suspects that Roxane does not love Cyrano. Recall with students that in Act I Roxane gave Christian reason to believe she was in love with *him*.

---

come back until you've finished. [*He closes the door and approaches* ROXANE.] May this day be blessed above all others: the day when you ceased to forget my existence and came here to tell me . . . to tell me? . . .

9 ROXANE. First let me thank you for humbling that arrogant fop with your sword yesterday, because he's the man whom a certain great lord, infatuated with me . . .

CYRANO. De Guiche?

ROXANE. [*Lowering her eyes.*] . . . was trying to impose on me as . . . as a husband. . . .

CYRANO. A husband only for the sake of form? [*Bows.*] I'm happy to know that I fought not for my ugly nose, but for your beautiful eyes.

ROXANE. And then, I wanted to tell you . . . But before I make my confession, give me time to see you again as I did in the past, when I thought of you almost as my brother. We used to play together in the park, beside the lake. . . .

CYRANO. Yes. . . . You came to Bergerac every summer.

10 ROXANE. You used a reed for a sword in those days!

CYRANO. And you used corn silk to make hair for your dolls.

ROXANE. We played all sorts of games.

CYRANO. And ate blackberries before they were ripe.

ROXANE. You always did whatever I wanted! Was I pretty then?

CYRANO. You weren't ugly.

ROXANE. Sometimes you came to me with your hand bleeding from some accident and I acted as if I were your mother, trying to make my voice stern. [*Takes his hand.*] "What's this?" I'd say. "Have you hurt yourself again?" [*Looks at his*

484 *Drama*

hand.] Oh! No! Let me see! You're still hurting yourself, at your age! How did you do it this time?

CYRANO. I was playing again—at the Porte de Nesle.

ROXANE. [*Sits down and wets her handkerchief in a glass of water.*] Give me that hand!

CYRANO. [*Also sits down.*] You still mother me!

ROXANE. While I wash away this blood, I want you to describe what happened. How many were there against you?

CYRANO. Oh, not quite a hundred.

ROXANE. Tell me about it!

CYRANO. No, never mind. Tell me what you couldn't bring yourself to say just now.

ROXANE. [*Without letting go of his hand.*] Yes, I can say it now that the past has returned to encourage me. Here it is. I'm in love with someone.

CYRANO. Ah! . . .

11 ROXANE. Someone who doesn't know.

CYRANO. Ah! . . .

ROXANE. But he *will* know soon.

CYRANO. Ah! . . .

ROXANE. He's a poor man who till now has loved me timidly, from a distance, without daring to say anything.

CYRANO. Ah! . . .

ROXANE. Let me keep your hand, it feels feverish. . . . But I've seen a confession of love trembling on his lips.

CYRANO. Ah! . . .

ROXANE. [*Bandaging his hand with her handkerchief.*] And it so happens, cousin, that he's a member of your regiment.

CRITICAL THINKING: GUIDED READING QUESTIONS

LITERAL

1a. What does Roxane talk about before she begins her confession of love? (She thanks Cyrano for confronting Valvert, she recalls their childhood together, and she asks Cyrano to tell her how he received his wound.)

2a. Why does Roxane say she wants to continue holding Cyrano's hand? (She says that it feels feverish.)

INFERENTIAL

1b. Why do you think she brings up these matters? (It is possible that she wants to ease, soften, or delay the uncomfortable confession she is about to make.)

2b. Why might his hand feel feverish? (He is growing excited because Roxane's hints suggest that she loves him.)

PAGE SUMMARY: AT A GLANCE
■ Roxane confesses that she loves Christian.
■ Cyrano is heartbroken.

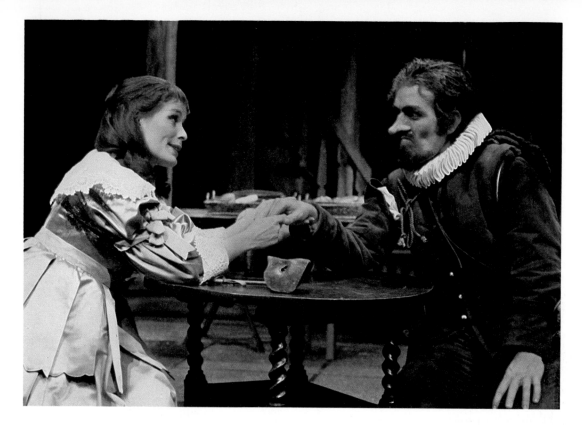

CYRANO. Ah! . . .

12 ROXANE. His face shines with wit and intelligence. He's proud, noble, young, fearless, handsome. . . .

CYRANO. [*Standing up, with a stricken expression.*] Handsome!

ROXANE. What is it? What's the matter?

13 CYRANO. Nothing. . . . It's . . . it's . . . [*Shows her his hand, with a smile.*] It's only a twinge of pain from this little scratch.

ROXANE. Well, I love him, even though I've never seen him anywhere but in the theater.

CYRANO. You've never spoken to each other?

ROXANE. Only with our eyes.

CYRANO. Then how do you know he loves you?

ROXANE. . . . Talkative acquaintances have told me. . . .

14 CYRANO. You say he's a Cadet?

ROXANE. Yes, in the Guards.

CYRANO. His name?

ROXANE. Baron Christian de Neuvillette.

CYRANO. Neuvillette? There's no Cadet by that name.

ROXANE. There is now. He began serving only this morning, under Captain Carbon de Castel-Jaloux.[7]

---

7. **Carbon de Castel-Jaloux** [kär bôn′ də kas tel′ zha loo′]

Cyrano de Bergerac, Act II **485**

---

12 TEACHING CHARACTERIZATION

Point out the way in which the single word *handsome* is a death knell for Cyrano's hopes. Help students see that the descriptions of fine inner qualities could apply to Cyrano; only by the description of the outer quality of handsomeness does Cyrano recognize that Roxane has been talking about another man.

13 READING SKILL: INFERENCE

Ask students why Cyrano attributes his sudden expression of dismay to physical pain. (Students should recognize that he is hiding great emotional pain.)

14 CULTURAL BACKGROUND

Explain that during this period the Guards formed the French Army's best organized and most famous regiment. The army and the church were the two most acceptable professions for young men of good family, and many sons of noble families began their military career in the Guards.

CRITICAL THINKING: GUIDED READING QUESTIONS

LITERAL

1a. What word does Roxane say just before Cyrano realizes that she loves another man? (She says that the man she loves is "handsome.")

INFERENTIAL

1b. What does his reaction to this word show about Cyrano's self-image? (He knows that he could never be considered handsome. He is realistic about his appearance yet is pained by it. That the woman he adores loves a *handsome* man makes his own love seem hopeless.)

- Roxane tells Cyrano that she is worried that Christian may get into duels and asks Cyrano to protect him; Cyrano agrees.
- Roxane leaves, and Ragueneau and his friends return, along with Cyrano's captain, Carbon de Castel-Jaloux.

15 TEACHING THEME

Point out that Cyrano's observation underscores the idea that a person's inner and outer qualities do not always correspond. In contrast, Roxane insists that Christian's external beauty reflects a beautiful mind.

16 READING SKILL: INFERENCE

Ask students to identify the kind of person they think Roxane is, based on her comment and behavior here. (She is quick to anger when contradicted and used to having her own way.)

17 TEACHING PLOT: RISING ACTION

Emphasize the importance of Cyrano's promise: It sets in motion an unusual alliance.

18 TEACHING DIALOGUE

Point out the way Roxane's words convey her self-centeredness. Realizing she has monopolized the talk, she makes a gesture toward Cyrano yet immediately says, "Tell him to write to me."

19 TEACHING IRONY

Help students see that Cyrano assumes Roxane will think his comment refers to another act of *physical* courage. Then ask what the comment really means. (The courage he showed in the fight pales beside that required to hide his present disappointment.)

CYRANO. You've lost your heart so quickly! But, my poor girl . . .

THE DUENNA. [*Opening the door in the background.*] I've eaten all the pastry, Monsieur de Bergerac!

15 CYRANO. Then read the poetry on the bags! [*The* DUENNA *disappears.*] My poor girl, you're so fond of fine words and gracious wit—what if he should prove to be an uncultured savage?

ROXANE. Impossible. He has the hair of one of d'Urfés[8] heroes!

CYRANO. His speech may be as crude as his hair is elegant.

ROXANE. No, there's delicacy in everything he says. I feel it!

16 CYRANO. Yes, all words are delicate when they come from lips adorned with a shapely mustache. . . . But what if he's a fool?

ROXANE. [*Stamping her foot.*] Then I'll die! There, are you satisfied?

CYRANO. [*After a time.*] You brought me here to tell me this? I confess I don't quite understand why.

ROXANE. It's because someone terrified me yesterday by telling me that most of you in your company are Gascons, and . . .

CYRANO. And that we always provoke a duel with any newcomer who gains the favor of being admitted among us without being a Gascon? Is that what you were told?

ROXANE. Yes. You can imagine how I trembled for him when I heard it! But when I saw you yesterday, great and invincible, punishing that scoundrel and holding all those brutes at bay, I said to myself, "Everyone fears him. If he were willing to . . ."

---

8. **D'Urfé's** [dur fāz′]: Honoré d'Urfé (1567–1625), French novelist whose heroes were models of chivalry.

486 *Drama*

17 CYRANO. Very well, I'll protect your little baron.

ROXANE. Oh, I knew you would! I've always had such tender affection for you. . . .

CYRANO. Yes, yes.

ROXANE. You'll be his friend?

CYRANO. I will.

ROXANE. And he'll never have a duel?

CYRANO. No. I promise.

18 ROXANE. I knew I was right to like you so much! And now I must go. But you haven't told me about your battle last night. It must have been incredible! . . . Tell him to write to me. [*Throws him a kiss.*] Oh, I love you!

CYRANO. Yes, yes.

ROXANE. A hundred men against you? Well, goodby. You're my best friend!

CYRANO. Yes, yes.

ROXANE. Tell him to write! . . . A hundred men! You'll tell me about it some other time; I can't stay now. A hundred men! What courage!

19 CYRANO. [*Bowing to her.*] Oh, I've done better since then.

[*She leaves. He remains motionless, looking down at the floor. A silence, then the door opens and* RAGUENEAU *puts in his head.*]

RAGUENEAU. May we come back in?

CYRANO. [*Without moving.*] Yes.

[RAGUENEAU *signals to his friends and they come in. At the same time* CARBON DE CASTEL-JALOUX, *dressed as a Captain of the Guards, appears at the door in the background and makes broad gestures when he sees* CYRANO.]

CARBON. Here he is!

CYRANO. [*Looking up.*] Captain!

CRITICAL THINKING: GUIDED READING QUESTIONS

LITERAL

1a. What does Roxane say when Cyrano suggests Christian may be an "uncultured savage"? ("Impossible. He has the hair of one of d'Urfé's heroes!")

2a. What words of affection does Roxane address to Cyrano after he has promised to protect Christian? ("I've always had such tender affection for you. . . ."; "I knew I was right to like you so much!"; "Oh, I love you!"; "You're my best friend!")

INFERENTIAL

1b. What does her response suggest about how she judges people? (She is impressed by superficial qualities and assumes that surface beauty reflects inner beauty.)

2b. How do you think these comments make him feel? (Although her words are exactly what he wants to hear, he painfully recognizes that she means them only superficially.)

CARBON. [*Exultant.*] Our hero! We know all about it! Thirty of my Cadets are here!

CYRANO. [*Stepping back.*] But . . .

CARBON. [*Rubbing his hands together.*] Here they come!

A CADET. [*Entering.*] Bravo!

SEVERAL CADETS. [*Entering.*] Let's all embrace him!

LE BRET. [*Entering and hurrying to* CYRANO.] Everyone wants to see you! There's a wild crowd led by those who were with you last night. . . .

A BURGHER. [*Entering, followed by a group.*] Sir, all the fashionable people in Paris are coming here!

[*Outside, the street is filled with people. Sedan chairs and carriages are stopping.*]

LE BRET. [*Softly, smiling at* CYRANO.] Have you seen Roxane?

CYRANO. [*Sharply.*] Quiet!

THE CROWD. [*Shouting from outside.*] Cyrano!

[*A throng bursts into the shop. Jostling. Cheers.*]

RAGUENEAU. [*Standing on a table.*] They're invading my shop! They're breaking everything! It's magnificent!

20 PEOPLE. [*Around* CYRANO.] My friend!—My friend!

CYRANO. I didn't have so many friends yesterday!

LE BRET. [*Delighted.*] What a triumph!

MARQUIS. Sir, I'd like to introduce you to some ladies who are outside in my carriage.

CYRANO. [*Coldly.*] And who will introduce me to *you?*

21 LE BRET. [*Surprised.*] What's the matter with you?

CYRANO. Quiet! Enough!

[*Movement, then the disorder of the crowd begins to subside.* DE GUICHE *enters, escorted by* OFFICERS, *then* CUIGY, BRISSAILLE, *and the* OFFICERS *who left with* CYRANO *at the end of Act I.* CUIGY *hurries to* CYRANO.]

CUIGY. [*To* CYRANO.] Monsieur de Guiche . . . [*Murmurs. Everyone stands aside.*] . . . has come with a message from Marshal de Gassion![9]

DE GUICHE. [*Bowing to* CYRANO.] The Marshal has just learned of your latest exploit and wishes me to express his admiration to you.

THE CROWD. Bravo!

LE BRET. [*Aside, to* CYRANO, *who appears to be distracted.*] Aren't you going to . . .

CYRANO. Quiet!

LE BRET. You seem to be suffering!

22 CYRANO. [*Starting, then quickly drawing himself erect.*] In front of all these people? [*His mustache bristles; he throws out his chest.*] I, suffering? You'll see!

DE GUICHE. [*To whom* CUIGY *has been whispering.*] Your career is already rich in noble exploits. You serve with those wild Gascons, don't you?

CYRANO. Yes, I'm a Cadet in the Guards.

A CADET. [*With fierce pride.*] He's one of us!

DE GUICHE. [*Looking at the Gascons grouped behind* CYRANO.] Ah! Then all these haughty-looking gentlemen are the famous . . .

CARBON. Cyrano!

CYRANO. Yes, Captain?

---

9. **Marshal de Gassion** [mär shal' də gas yōn']

Cyrano de Bergerac, Act II **487**

PAGE SUMMARY: AT A GLANCE

- The captain of the Guards and several Cadets arrive and praise Cyrano's exploit of the night before.
- Le Bret enters and says that a crowd is on its way to praise Cyrano.
- Le Bret notices Cyrano's pain, but Cyrano is too proud to let anyone else see his suffering.

IN THE GLOSSARY

- exultant: rejoicing; triumphant

20 TEACHING THEME

Point out that Cyrano shows his innate integrity by refusing to be flattered by the adulation of the fashionable world, which he knows to be fickle.

21 TEACHING PLOT: CONFLICT

Help students recognize the conflict implicit in the contrast between Le Bret's and Cyrano's personalities. Le Bret is a loving and admiring friend whose tolerance and practicality conflict with Cyrano's uncompromising idealism.

22 READING SKILL: INFERENCE

Ask students what Cyrano's response to Le Bret's concerned comment reflects about him. (Students should see that he is too proud to allow anyone to know that he is suffering; rather than express his hurt, he masks his pain with anger and bitterness.)

CRITICAL THINKING: GUIDED READING QUESTIONS

LITERAL

1a. What does Le Bret say after Cyrano comments that he didn't have so many friends yesterday? ("What a triumph!")

2a. What does Le Bret notice about Cyrano's feelings? (Cyrano seems to be suffering.)

INFERENTIAL

1b. Why is this triumph particularly ironic for Cyrano at this time? (He has just had the greatest defeat he can imagine: He has learned that Roxane does not love him.)

2b. What does this observation tell you about Le Bret's relationship with Cyrano? (He knows Cyrano well enough to be able to recognize Cyrano's true feelings.)

- De Guiche arrives and offers Cyrano his patronage; Cyrano refuses.
- De Guiche admits to having hired the men Cyrano defeated.
- Cyrano insults him, and he threatens Cyrano.

IN THE GLOSSARY

- peremptory: not permitting argument or delay; commanding

23 CULTURAL BACKGROUND

Point out that at the time of the play, the French court was complex and competitive, with courtiers vying for the king's favor. Powerful people acted as patrons, using their influence at court to protect and advance their protégés, who often included poets and artists.

24 TEACHING THEME

Point out that the importance of language, a major preoccupation of Cyrano's day, is underscored here. Cyrano nearly succumbs to the temptation of having De Guiche help him promote his writing.

25 TEACHING STUDENTS OF LIMITED ENGLISH PROFICIENCY

Help students understand these colorful circumlocutions by having them visualize the images and put them in different words. Be sure students realize that the word *game* means "animals hunted for food."

26 TEACHING ALLUSION

Point out the way in which De Guiche's allusion to *Don Quixote* (excerpts on pp. 162–165) underlines Cyrano's idealism. Explain that whereas Don Quixote was devoted to the chivalric code, Cyrano believes in his own integrity and independence.

CARBON. Since all the men of my company are here, please introduce them to the Count.

CYRANO. [*Taking two steps toward* DE GUICHE *and pointing to the* CADETS.]

> These are the stouthearted Gascon Cadets
> Of Carbon de Castel-Jaloux;
> They fight over trifles and shamelessly lie;
> These are the stouthearted Gascon Cadets!
> Their knowledge of heraldry can't be surpassed;
> No plowman can claim nobler birth;
> These are the stouthearted Gascon Cadets
> Of Carbon de Castel-Jaloux.

DE GUICHE. [*Casually seated in an armchair that* RAGUENEAU *has quickly brought for him.*] Poets are a fashionable luxury these days. Would you like to become one of my followers?

CYRANO. No, sir, I prefer to follow no one.

DE GUICHE. My uncle, Cardinal Richelieu, was amused by your dashing combat yesterday. I'm willing to help you with him, if you like.

LE BRET. [*Dazzled.*] Ah!

DE GUICHE. You've written a play, I believe. . . .

LE BRET. [*Aside, to* CYRANO.] Your *Agrippine*[10] will soon be performed, my friend!

DE GUICHE. Take it to him.

CYRANO. [*Tempted and rather pleased.*] Really, I . . .

DE GUICHE. He knows a great deal about the theater. He'll rewrite a few lines. . . .

CYRANO. [*Whose face has immediately darkened.*] Impossible, sir; my blood curdles at the thought of having a single comma changed.

DE GUICHE. But when a piece of writing pleases him, he pays very well for it.

---

10. **Agrippine** [a grə pēn']: *La Mort d'Agrippine (The Death of Agrippine)* was a play written by the real Cyrano.

488 Drama

CYRANO. He couldn't pay as well as I do. When I write something that I like, I reward the author by reciting it to myself.

DE GUICHE. You're a proud man.

CYRANO. Have you noticed that?

[*A* CADET *enters, holding his sword aloft to display the hats that are spitted on it. They are all shabby and misshapen, with bedraggled plumes.*]

THE CADET. Look, Cyrano, at the strange feathered game we took in the street this morning! The men you routed seem to have run away too fast for their hats to follow them!

CUIGY. The man who hired those cowardly brutes must be in a rage today!

BRISSAILLE. Do you know who did it?

DE GUICHE. I did. [*The laughter ceases.*] I hired them for a task that one doesn't do oneself: punishing a drunken rhymester.

[*Uncomfortable silence.* CYRANO *takes the sword on which the hats are spitted and lowers it in a gesture of homage to* DE GUICHE, *making them all slide off onto the floor at his feet.*]

CYRANO. Sir, would you like to take these back to your friends?

DE GUICHE. [*In a peremptory tone, standing up.*] Bring my sedan chair immediately. I'm leaving. [*With a smile, having regained his self-control.*] Have you read *Don Quixote?*[11]

CYRANO. Yes, I have, and I take off my hat to you in the name of that scatterbrained hero.

DE GUICHE. You would do well to meditate on the chapter concerning windmills.

---

11. **Don Quixote** [don' kē hō'tā]: tragicomical novel by the Spanish writer Miguel de Cervantes (1547–1616). Don Quixote, an idealistic knight, mistakes windmills for giants and is knocked from his horse during a charge against them.

CRITICAL THINKING: GUIDED READING QUESTIONS

LITERAL

1a. Who "fight[s] over trifles and shamelessly lie[s]?" (the Gascon Cadets)

2a. Why does Cyrano decide not to have his play shown to Cardinal Richelieu? (De Guiche indicates that Richelieu would rewrite it before helping Cyrano get it performed.)

INFERENTIAL

1b. What does Cyrano's introduction of the Gascon Cadets suggest about them? (They are swaggering and fun loving.)

2b. Why doesn't Cyrano want "a single comma changed"? (He is very independent and strongly believes in his own talent. If his play is ever performed, he wants the production to be entirely his own.)

CYRANO. [*Bowing.*] Chapter Thirteen.

DE GUICHE. When one attacks them, their great arms often hurl one down into the mud!

CYRANO. Or up into the stars!

[DE GUICHE *leaves. The* CROWD *leaves.*]

CYRANO. [*Mockingly bowing to those who are leaving without daring to bid him good-by.*] Gentlemen. . . . Gentlemen. . . . Gentlemen. . . .

LE BRET. [*Coming back from the door and throwing up his arms in despair.*] This time you've outdone yourself! You shatter every opportunity that comes your way! You'll have to admit that you go too far!

CYRANO. Yes, I go too far.

LE BRET. [*Triumphantly.*] You *do* admit it!

CYRANO. But for the sake of principle, and to set an example, too, I feel that it's good to go too far in that direction.

LE BRET. If you would only soften your haughty spirit a little, fortune and glory would . . .

CYRANO. But what would I have to do? Cover myself with the protection of some powerful patron? Imitate the ivy that licks the bark of a tall tree while entwining itself around its trunk, and make my way upward by guile, rather than climbing by my own strength? No, thank you. Dedicate poems to financiers, as so many others do? Change myself into a buffoon in the hope of seeing a minister give me a condescending smile? No, thank you. Swallow insults every day? Crawl till the skin of my belly is rubbed raw? Dirty my knees and make my spine as limber as an eel's? No, thank you. Develop the art of sitting on both sides of a fence at once? Pay for an ounce of favor with a ton of flattery? No, thank you. Be always scheming and afraid of schemes? Like paying visits better than writing poetry? Make humble requests? Seek introductions to useful people? No, thank you! No! No! I prefer to lead a different kind of life. I sing, dream, laugh, and go where I please, alone and free. My eyes see clearly and my voice is strong. I'm quarrelsome or benign as it suits my pleasure, always ready to fight a duel or write a poem at the drop of a hat. I dream of flying to the moon but give no thought to fame or fortune. I write only what comes out of myself, and I make it my modest rule to be satisfied with whatever flowers, fruit, or even leaves I gather, as long as they're from my own garden. I scorn to be like parasitic ivy, even though I'm not an oak. I may not rise very high, but I'll climb alone!

LE BRET. Be alone if you like, but why have everyone against you? How did you acquire that appalling mania for making enemies wherever you go?

CYRANO. Let's call it my vice. It pleases me to displease. I love to be hated.

LE BRET. [*After a silence, passing his arm under* CYRANO'*s.*] Proclaim your pride and bitterness loudly to the world, but to me speak softly and tell me simply that she doesn't love you.

CYRANO. [*Sharply.*] Stop! Enough!

[CHRISTIAN *has entered some time earlier and mingled with the* CADETS, *who have not spoken to him. He has finally sat down alone at a small table where* LISE *is now serving him.*]

A CADET. [*Seated at a table upstage, with a glass in his hand.*] Cyrano! [CYRANO *looks around.*] Will you tell us your story now?

CYRANO. Not now. A little later. [*He and* LE BRET *walk upstage, arm in arm, talking quietly together.*]

THE CADET. [*Standing up and coming downstage.*] The story of Cyrano's combat will be the best lesson [*Stops at* CHRISTIAN'*s table.*] . . . for this timid apprentice.

Cyrano de Bergerac, Act II **489**

PAGE SUMMARY: AT A GLANCE

- Le Bret again scolds Cyrano for his inability to compromise.
- Cyrano proclaims his independence and individuality.
- Le Bret guesses that Cyrano has been disappointed by Roxane.
- Christian sits with the Cadets.

IN THE GLOSSARY

- parasitic: living at the expense of another person or thing

27 CRITICAL THINKING: EVALUATION

Ask students which man's point of view they agree with and why. (Many students will support Cyrano because of their respect for individuality and idealism; others will be more practical and recognize the hazards Cyrano creates for himself.)

28 GRAMMAR IN LITERATURE

Point out Cyrano's use of parallel structure for rhetorical effect: He begins each response to his own question with a strong action verb. Ask what impact the repetition of this structure has on the speech. (It adds a powerful rhythmic quality.)

29 TEACHING THEME

Help students see that in his burst of eloquent language Cyrano enunciates a major theme of the play: A high moral price must be paid by an individual who seeks fame and fortune on the world's terms.

30 TEACHING FIGURATIVE LANGUAGE

Ask students what Cyrano's metaphors from the natural world convey about his ideals. (Students should see that Cyrano is contrasting his life of idealism and independence with the life of compromise and flattery.)

CRITICAL THINKING: GUIDED READING QUESTIONS

LITERAL

1a. What does De Guiche tell Cyrano that windmills can do, and what does Cyrano answer? (He says they can "hurl one down into the mud." Cyrano rejoins, "Or up into the stars!")

2a. According to Le Bret, for what does Cyrano have an "appalling mania"? (making enemies)

INFERENTIAL

1b. What do you think their comments mean? (De Guiche threatens Cyrano by indicating that if he sticks to his principles too strongly and insults people, he will be destroyed. Cyrano argues that adherence to principles can elevate one spiritually.)

2b. Does Cyrano really try to make enemies? Explain. (No, he doesn't actively try to make enemies; making enemies is an outgrowth of his adherence to his ideals.)

- The Cadets warn Christian never to mention Cyrano's nose.
- Cyrano begins to recount his exploits from the night before.
- Christian, determined to prove his courage, tries to provoke Cyrano by interrupting the story with comments that contain references to noses.

IN THE GLOSSARY

- banteringly: in a teasing or joking way
- scrupulously: with strict attention to what is right; carefully
- allusion: a casual or indirect reference

31 TEACHING STYLE: EXAGGERATION

Point out the way in which the Cadets use exaggeration to impress their lesson on Christian. Ask students why even taking out a handkerchief might anger Cyrano. (A handkerchief is associated with noses.)

32 TEACHING PLOT: RISING ACTION

Underscore that Carbon's advice to Christian on how to prove his courage provides important motivation for what follows.

33 TEACHING CONFLICT

Note the way in which dialogue and stage directions show Cyrano's inner conflict: He allows no one to insult his nose, yet he cannot fight with Christian because he promised Roxane he would protect him.

CHRISTIAN. [*Looking up.*] Apprentice?

ANOTHER CADET. Yes, you sickly northerner.

CHRISTIAN. Sickly?

FIRST CADET. [*Banteringly.*] Monsieur de Neuvillette, it's time for you to learn something. There's a certain object that we all avoid naming as scrupulously as we would refrain from mentioning rope in the house of a man whose father had been hanged.

CHRISTIAN. What is it?

SECOND CADET. [*With majestic authority.*] Look at me! [*Puts his finger to his nose three times, mysteriously.*] Do you understand?

CHRISTIAN. I think so. You must mean . . .

THIRD CADET. Sh! You must never speak that word! [*Points to* CYRANO, *who is still talking upstage with* LE BRET.] If you do, you'll have *him* to deal with!

FOURTH CADET. [*In a hollow tone, standing up after having crawled under the table.*] The slightest allusion to that protuberance brings an untimely death!

31 FIFTH CADET. [*Putting his hand on* CHRISTIAN'S *shoulder.*] One word is enough! Even a gesture! If you take out your handkerchief, you've taken out your shroud! [*Silence. The* CADETS *are all around* CHRISTIAN, *looking at him. He stands up and goes to* CARBON DE CASTEL-JALOUX.]

CHRISTIAN. Captain!

CARBON. [*Turning around and looking him up and down.*] Yes?

32 CHRISTIAN. What should one do when southerners become too boastful?

CARBON. Prove to them that a northerner can be courageous. [*Turns his back on* CHRISTIAN.]

CHRISTIAN. Thank you.

490 *Drama*

FIRST CADET. [*To* CYRANO.] Now tell us your story!

ALL. Your story!

CYRANO. [*Comes toward them.*] My story? . . . [*They all draw up their stools and group themselves around him, straining their necks forward.* CHRISTIAN *has straddled a chair.*] Well, I was walking alone to meet them. The moon was gleaming like a big silver watch in the sky when suddenly some heavenly hand slipped it into a pocket of clouds. The sky was black as pitch and there were no lights in the street. I couldn't see . . .

CHRISTIAN. Beyond the end of your nose.

[*Silence. The* CADETS *all stand up slowly, looking at* CYRANO *in terror. He has stopped short, dumbfounded. Several moments of tense waiting go by before he finally speaks.*]

CYRANO. Who is this man?

A CADET. [*In a low voice.*] He came to us only this morning.

CYRANO. [*Taking a step toward* CHRISTIAN.] This morning?

CARBON. [*In a low voice.*] His name is Baron de Neuvil—

33 CYRANO. [*Quickly, stopping.*] Oh! [*His face takes on an expression of shock, then anger, and he makes a movement as though to attack* CHRISTIAN.] I . . . [*He controls himself and speaks dully.*] Very well. . . . As I was saying . . . [*With a burst of rage in his voice.*] Mordious! [*Continues in a natural tone.*] It was so dark that I couldn't see anything. [*The* CADETS *are amazed. They sit down again, staring at him.*] I walked on, thinking that for the sake of a poor drunkard I was about to anger some powerful nobleman who would surely . . .

CHRISTIAN. Resent your nosiness. [*The* CADETS *all stand up again.* CHRISTIAN *tilts his chair.*]

CRITICAL THINKING: GUIDED READING QUESTIONS

LITERAL

1a. What do the Cadets warn Christian never to do? (mention Cyrano's nose)

2a. How does Cyrano react when he discovers that the man who is insulting his nose is Christian? (He is angry but remembers his promise to Roxane and gains control of his feelings.)

INFERENTIAL

1b. Why does Christian purposely use the word *nose* in front of Cyrano? (He realizes that he can prove his courage by doing exactly what he has been warned not to do—insult Cyrano's nose.)

2b. How do you think Cyrano would have reacted if anyone else but Christian had insulted his nose? (He would have punished any other offender memorably.)

34 CYRANO. [*Choking.*] . . . who would surely bear a grudge against me, and that I was rashly putting . . .

CHRISTIAN. Your nose into . . .

CYRANO. . . . myself into a bad situation, because that nobleman might . . .

35 CHRISTIAN. Look down his nose at you.

CYRANO. [*Wiping sweat from his forehead.*] . . . be able to make things a bit difficult for me. But I said to myself, "Come, Gascon, do what has to be done. Onward, Cyrano!" A moment later, someone . . .

CHRISTIAN. Nosed you out in the darkness.

CYRANO. . . . lunged at me with his sword. I parried the thrust and suddenly found myself . . .

CHRISTIAN. Nose to nose . . .

CYRANO. [*Rushing toward him.*] No! By all the saints in heaven, I'll . . . [*The Gascons crowd forward to see better, but as soon as he is in front of* CHRISTIAN *he again controls himself and continues his story.*] I found myself facing a hundred shouting brutes, all smelling . . .

CHRISTIAN. With their noses, of course.

CYRANO. [*Smiling wanly.*] . . . of onions and cheap wine. I plunged into the midst of them . . .

CHRISTIAN. Nose first!

CYRANO. . . . and immediately cut down two of them. As I was attacking a third, I saw a sword . . .

CHRISTIAN. Right under your nose!

36 CYRANO. [*Bellowing.*] Out! All of you! Get out!

[*The* CADETS *all hurry toward the doors.*]

FIRST CADET. The tiger has finally awakened!

CYRANO. Leave me alone with this man!

37 SECOND CADET. He'll soon be turned into mincemeat!

THIRD CADET. It makes me tremble just to think of what's going to happen to him!

FOURTH CADET. [*Closing the door on the right as he goes out.*] It will be something horrifying!

[CHRISTIAN *and* CYRANO *are left standing face to face. They look at each other for a moment.*]

CYRANO. Embrace me!

CHRISTIAN. Sir . . .

38 CYRANO. You're a brave man.

CHRISTIAN. Perhaps, but . . .

CYRANO. Very brave. I'm glad to know that.

CHRISTIAN. Would you mind telling me . . .

CYRANO. Embrace me. I'm her brother.

CHRISTIAN. Whose brother?

CYRANO. *Hers!*

CHRISTIAN. Hers?

CYRANO. Roxane's!

CHRISTIAN. [*Hurrying toward him.*] Oh! You? Her brother?

CYRANO. Yes, or almost. A brotherly cousin.

CHRISTIAN. And she's told you . . .

CYRANO. Everything!

CHRISTIAN. Does she love me?

CYRANO. Perhaps!

CHRISTIAN. [*Taking his hands.*] How happy I am to know you!

CYRANO. That's a rather sudden change of feeling.

CHRISTIAN. Forgive me. . . .

Cyrano de Bergerac, Act II **491**

PAGE SUMMARY: AT A GLANCE

- Cyrano's story and Christian's insults continue.
- Furious, Cyrano asks to be left alone with Christian.
- The Cadets leave.
- Cyrano confesses his relationship with Roxane, and he and Christian embrace.

IN THE GLOSSARY

- parried: turned aside; fought off
- wanly: weakly; faintly

34 TEACHING CHARACTERIZATION

Point out Christian's cleverness in this continuing verbal duet. Ask students whether Christian's previous evaluation of his own wit was accurate. (Students may recognize that he can be clever with men but lacks wit with women.)

35 TEACHING STUDENTS OF LIMITED ENGLISH PROFICIENCY

Help students with a limited English background to define the idioms "putting your nose into," "look down his nose," "nosed you out," "nose to nose," and "right under your nose."

36 TEACHING FIGURATIVE LANGUAGE

Ask students why the metaphor comparing Cyrano to a sleeping tiger is apt. (Cyrano is known for his fierceness toward anyone who insults his nose.)

37 TEACHING DRAMATIC IRONY

Point out the dramatic irony in this scene: Unlike the Cadets the audience knows that Cyrano cannot duel with Christian because of his promise to Roxane.

38 TEACHING CHARACTERIZATION

Ask students why Cyrano is glad to know that Christian is brave. Students should see that it is because he would hate to think that Roxane loves a coward.

CRITICAL THINKING: GUIDED READING QUESTIONS

LITERAL

1a. What doubts does Cyrano express about becoming involved in the fight with De Guiche's assassins? (He says that perhaps he is rash, and De Guiche could make things difficult for him.)

2a. How does Cyrano answer when Christian asks whether Roxane loves him? ("Perhaps.")

INFERENTIAL

1b. What do these doubts show about Cyrano's practical judgment? (Perhaps it is keener than he sometimes lets on. Whenever Le Bret expresses similar concerns, Cyrano argues, but apparently he sometimes has the same doubts.)

2b. Why does he give this answer when Roxane has said that she loves Christian? (He respects Roxane's confidences. Also, he is indulging himself by toying with Christian.)

- Christian and Cyrano exchange compliments.
- Cyrano tells Christian that Roxane expects a letter from him.
- Christian expresses his despair, saying that he is too much of a fool to write a letter to Roxane.

39 TEACHING CHARACTERIZATION

Ask students what this exchange of compliments suggests about the two men. (Students should see that it shows Cyrano's noble nature—he is able to admire his rival and concede his handsomeness—and that Christian is secure enough to apologize for his insults.)

40 TEACHING DIALOGUE

Underscore Cyrano's point that Christian's insults were clever despite his claim to be a fool.

39 CYRANO. [*Looks at him and puts his hands on his shoulders.*] It's true: you *are* a handsome devil!

CHRISTIAN. If you only knew, sir, how much I admire you!

CYRANO. But all those "noses" you gave me. . . .

CHRISTIAN. I take them all back!

CYRANO. Roxane expects to receive a letter from you this evening.

CHRISTIAN. Oh, no!

CYRANO. What? . . .

CHRISTIAN. If I write to her, she'll never want to see me again.

CYRANO. Why?

40 CHRISTIAN. Because I'm such a fool that I could die of shame!

CYRANO. No, you're not, since you've said it yourself. Besides, you didn't attack me like a fool.

CHRISTIAN. Words come easily to anyone when

492 *Drama*

CRITICAL THINKING: GUIDED READING QUESTIONS

LITERAL

1a. What does Cyrano reply when Christian claims to be a fool? ("No, you're not, since you've said it yourself.")

INFERENTIAL

1b. What do you think he means by this? (He means that those who are truly foolish never acknowledge it.)

he wants to pick a quarrel. I may have a certain quick, soldierly wit, but with women I'm always at a loss for anything to say. Their eyes show interest when I pass by, but . . .

CYRANO. Aren't their hearts also interested when you stop?

CHRISTIAN. No! It's all too clear to me that I'm one of those men who don't know how to speak of love.

CYRANO. I have the feeling that if my features had been shaped more harmoniously, I would have been one of those men who *do* know how to speak of love.

41 CHRISTIAN. Ah, if only I could express myself gracefully!

CYRANO. If only I had a handsome face!

CHRISTIAN. Roxane is so elegant and refined—I'm sure to disillusion her!

CYRANO. [*Looking at* CHRISTIAN.] If I had such an interpreter to speak for my soul . . .

CHRISTIAN. [*Despairingly.*] I need eloquence, and I have none!

42 CYRANO. [*Abruptly.*] I'll lend you mine! Lend me your conquering physical charm, and together we'll form a romantic hero!

CHRISTIAN. What do you mean?

CYRANO. Do you feel capable of repeating what I tell you every day?

CHRISTIAN. Are you suggesting . . .

CYRANO. Roxane won't be disillusioned! Together, we can win her heart! Will you let my soul pass from my leather jerkin[12] and lodge beneath your embroidered doublet?

CHRISTIAN. But Cyrano . . .

---

12. **jerkin:** short, close-fitting coat or jacket, often sleeve-less, worn in the 1500s and 1600s.

CYRANO. Are you willing?

43 CHRISTIAN. You frighten me! Your eyes are shining. . . .

CYRANO. Will you do it?

CHRISTIAN. Would it please you so much?

CYRANO. [*Ardently.*] It would . . . [*Restrains himself and adopts a more detached tone.*] It would amuse me! It's an experiment that would tempt any poet. Shall we complete each other? We'll walk together: you in the light, I in the shadows. I'll make you eloquent, you'll make me handsome.

CHRISTIAN. But I must write her a letter without delay! I'll never be able to . . .

CYRANO. [*Taking out the letter he has written.*] Here's your letter!

CHRISTIAN. What . . .

CYRANO. It lacks only the name and address. You can send it as it is. Don't worry, it's well written.

CHRISTIAN. Had you already . . .

44 CYRANO. I always have a letter in my pocket, written to some imaginary lady, because I'm one of those men whose only sweethearts are dreams breathed into the bubble of a name. You can change my fantasy to reality. You'll see that in this letter my feelings are all the better expressed for being insincere! Here, take it.

CHRISTIAN. Won't some things in it have to be changed? How can it fit Roxane?

CYRANO. You can count on vanity to make her think it was written for her!

CHRISTIAN. Ah, my friend! . . . [*He throws himself into* CYRANO's *arms. They stand embracing each other.*]

A CADET. [*Pushing the door ajar.*] Nothing. . . . A deathly silence. . . . I'm afraid to look. . . . [*Puts his head through the doorway.*] What!

Cyrano de Bergerac, Act II **493**

PAGE SUMMARY: AT A GLANCE

- Cyrano proposes that he and Christian combine their assets—Christian's handsomeness and Cyrano's wit—to win Roxane.
- Cyrano gives Christian the unsigned letter he had written to Roxane.

41 TEACHING CONFLICT

Point out that this exchange shows the internal conflict of each man. Cyrano's conflict pits his love for Roxane against his feelings of physical inadequacy; Christian's conflict pits his love for Roxane against his lack of eloquence.

42 TEACHING PLOT: RISING ACTION

Be sure that students recognize that the idea Cyrano proposes here is central to the plot. Point out, too, that the joining of Cyrano's soul with Christian's handsomeness further develops the theme of inner versus outer beauty.

43 READING SKILL: CONCLUSION

Ask students to name the man for whom the alliance seems more important. (Most students will see from the ardor of Cyrano's response that the alliance is more important to him, for he cannot express his love without Christian's handsome exterior.)

44 TEACHING IRONY

Note the irony of Cyrano's comments: He paints himself as a lover of imaginary women, yet the opposite is true. The superficial infatuation he describes seems more like Christian and Roxane's love.

CRITICAL THINKING: GUIDED READING QUESTIONS

LITERAL

1a. What does Cyrano reply when Christian asks, "Would it please you so much?" (He says that it would amuse him as an experiment.)

INFERENTIAL

1b. Why do you think he replies so carelessly when moments before he was intensely interested? (He restrains himself so Christian will not guess his real reason for wanting a partnership: He wants to be able to express his love without being ridiculed.)

- The Cadets return to find Cyrano embracing Christian.
- Lise's musketeer assumes Cyrano now allows people to talk about his nose and insults him.
- Cyrano slaps the musketeer.

45 TEACHING CHARACTER FOILS

Point out that the musketeer, Lise, and Ragueneau form a comic version of the Christian-Roxane-Cyrano triangle. It is especially appropriate that the handsome musketeer receives the punishment Christian was spared.

COLLABORATIVE LEARNING: ENRICHMENT ACTIVITY

Geography Paris is the backdrop for much of the play's action. In 1640 the city was still surrounded by walls (though the population had begun to move beyond them). Have students work in groups to find maps of seventeenth-century Paris. Ask them to locate the Porte de Nesle (site of Cyrano's battle), as well as the Porte Saint-Denis, the Porte Sainte-Honoré, Notre Dame, the Marais quarter, and the Seine River.

READER'S RESPONSE

Would you rather have a love like Christian's or like Cyrano's? Explain your answer.

ANSWERS

STUDY QUESTIONS

1. She tells him she loves Christian, whom he promises to protect.
2. De Guiche offers his patronage; Cyrano refuses it.
3. He taunts Cyrano with puns about his nose.
4. Cyrano will provide Christian with eloquent and witty words; Christian will deliver them.
5. Disguising his disappointment after learning she loves Christian requires greater courage than does fighting.
6. Answers will vary. Students may note that she is manipulative. She charms Cyrano to get what she wants. She seems not to deserve his love, since she seems to be a shallow person: Her love for Christian is based only on his good looks.
7. De Guiche thinks everyone can be bought. Cyrano values art and integrity above advancement.

ALL THE CADETS. [*Entering and seeing* CYRANO *and* CHRISTIAN *embracing each other*.] Oh!—Ah!

A CADET. I can't believe my eyes! [*Consternation*.]

THE MUSKETEER. [*Jeeringly*.] Well, look at that!

CARBON. Our demon has become as gentle as a lamb! When he's struck on one nostril, he turns the other!

45 THE MUSKETEER. He lets people talk about his nose now? [*Calls out to* LISE, *with a triumphant expression*.] Lise! Watch this! [*Approaches* CYRANO *and insolently stares at his nose*.] What's that long thing on your face, sir? It reminds me of something, but I can't recall what it is.

CYRANO. Then let me help you by jarring your memory! [*Slaps him. The* CADETS *are delighted to see* CYRANO *behaving like himself again. They caper joyfully.*]

STUDY QUESTIONS

Recalling

1. Briefly relate Cyrano's conversation with Roxane at the beginning of Act II. What news does she give him, and what promise does he make to her?
2. Describe De Guiche's offer to Cyrano. What is Cyrano's response?
3. What does Christian do to prove himself to the Cadets?
4. Relate the terms of the private agreement between Cyrano and Christian concerning Roxane.

Interpreting

5. In referring to his triumph over a hundred men, Cyrano tells Roxane, "Oh, I've done better since then." What does he mean?
6. What is your impression of Roxane from her conversation with Cyrano? How does she treat her cousin? Do you think she deserves his love? Explain.
7. What does his offer to Cyrano reveal about De Guiche's attitude toward other people? What does Cyrano's refusal reveal about *his* attitude toward himself and his art?
8. Why do you think Cyrano makes his agreement with Christian? What might he hope to gain?

Extending

9. Do you think the agreement between Cyrano and Christian is practical? What problems do you foresee in it?

LITERARY FOCUS

Dramatic Irony

Dramatic irony is a form of irony that occurs when a character acts without knowing an important piece of information that the audience knows—for example, if the audience knows that a character is in danger, but the character does not know. Dramatic irony can occur in both fiction and drama, but this technique is an especially effective way of building tension in drama.

Thinking About Dramatic Irony

1. Explain the dramatic irony in the scene between Cyrano and Roxane in the pastry shop. What piece of information does the audience know that a character on stage lacks? How does dramatic irony add to the tension in this scene?
2. In what way is Christian's attempt to provoke Cyrano in front of the Cadets another instance of dramatic irony?

494 *Drama*

---

8. He loves Roxane and sees a chance to express his feelings to her, though indirectly.
9. Answers will vary. Students will probably say it is impractical: Both risk rejection if found out, and neither will know whether Roxane might have loved him for himself.

LITERARY FOCUS

1. The audience knows that Cyrano loves Roxane and hopes she loves him. Dramatic irony creates tension and helps the audience share Cyrano's hope and disappointment.
2. The audience knows Cyrano has promised to protect Christian and, therefore, will not fight.

ACT III

A little square in the Marais[1] quarter of Paris. A few weeks later.

[ROXANE's *house and the wall of its garden are seen, overflowing with foliage. Above the door, a window and a balcony garlanded with quivering, drooping jasmine. As the curtain rises, the* DUENNA *is seated on the bench. Beside her stands* RAGUENEAU, *dressed in livery.[2] He is finishing a story and wiping his eyes.*]

RAGUENEAU. . . . and then she ran off with a musketeer! Alone and ruined, I felt I had nothing to live for, so I tried to hang myself, but Monsieur de Bergerac came in and cut me down. Then he offered me this position as his cousin's steward.

THE DUENNA. But how did you come to be ruined?

RAGUENEAU. Lise liked warriors and I liked poets. Mars ate everything that Apollo left.[3] At that rate, it didn't take long!

THE DUENNA. [*Standing up and calling toward the open window.*] Roxane, are you ready? We're late!

ROXANE'S VOICE. [*From the window.*] I'm just putting on my cloak!

THE DUENNA. [*To* RAGUENEAU, *pointing to the door opposite.*] That's where we're going, to Clomire's.[4] She holds regular discussion meetings in her house. A discourse on the Tender Passion[5] will be read today.

CYRANO'S VOICE. [*Singing offstage.*] La-la-la.

THE DUENNA. [*Surprised.*] Is someone coming to play for us?

CYRANO. [*Entering, followed by two* PAGES *carrying lutes.*] Those are thirty-second notes, you fool!

ROXANE. [*Appearing on the balcony.*] Ah, it's you!

CYRANO. [*Singing his words to the melody.*] I've come to salute your lilies, and pay my respects to your roses!

ROXANE. I'm coming down! [*Leaves the balcony.*]

THE DUENNA. [*Pointing to the* PAGES.] Where did these two virtuosi[6] come from?

CYRANO. I won them from d'Assoucy[7] on a bet. We were arguing about a point of grammar when suddenly he pointed to these lute-playing louts, who always accompany him wherever he goes, and said to me, "I'll bet you a day of music!" He lost, and therefore ordered them to follow me and bear harmonious witness to everything I do until tomorrow. It was charming at first, but it has already begun to pall. [*To the* PAGES.] Go and serenade Montfleury and tell him I sent you! [*The* PAGES *go upstage to leave.* CYRANO *turns back to the* DUENNA.] I've come to ask Roxane, as I do every day . . . [*To the* PAGES, *as they are leaving.*] Play a long time—and off-key! [*To the* DUENNA.] . . . whether her soulmate is still a model of perfection.

ROXANE. [*Coming out of the house.*] Oh, he's so handsome! And such a brilliant mind! I can't tell you how much I love him!

---

1. **Marais** [ma rā′]
2. **livery:** uniform.
3. **Mars . . . Apollo left:** The soldiers (represented by Mars, the god of war) ate all the pastries left by the poets (represented by Apollo, the god of poetry).
4. **Clomire's** [klō mērz′]
5. **Tender Passion:** that is, a lecture on love.

6. **virtuosi** [vur′chōō ō′sē]: those with great skill in a fine art, especially music.
7. **d'Assoucy** [da sōō sē′]: probably a reference to Charles d'Assouci (1605–1677), who was a comic poet and contemporary of the real Cyrano de Bergerac.

Cyrano de Bergerac, Act III **495**

- Roxane praises Christian's facility with language and recalls lines from the letters she thinks he has written.
- De Guiche arrives, and Cyrano hides at the duenna's request.
- De Guiche announces that he is going away to war.

IN THE GLOSSARY

- declaiming: reciting or speaking in a dramatic or artificial way

2 TEACHING PLOT: RISING ACTION

Ask students what Roxane's comment reveals about Christian's performance. Students should see that although he was coached by Cyrano, he has not performed flawlessly.

3 TEACHING STUDENTS OF LIMITED ENGLISH PROFICIENCY

Some students may have difficulty understanding the flowery and seemingly paradoxical statements in Cyrano's letters (and, later, in his flowery speech to Roxane). Help students rephrase such statements as "The more you take of my heart, the more I have."

4 TEACHING IRONY

Have students note this example of irony: Roxane blunders into the truth and startles Cyrano with her comment. In fact, this scene contains a double irony, as he is indeed jealous—but not of the writing, which is his own.

5 TEACHING DRAMATIC IRONY

Ask students to identify the dramatic irony here. (They should see that Roxane does not know that the fluency she praises is Cyrano's, but the audience and Cyrano do.)

CYRANO. [*Smiling.*] You feel that Christian has a brilliant mind?

ROXANE. Even more brilliant than yours!

CYRANO. I won't contest that.

2 ROXANE. I don't believe there's anyone in the world who can match him in saying those sweet nothings that mean everything. Sometimes he seems distracted and his inspiration falters, then all at once he says exquisite things to me!

CYRANO. [*Incredulously.*] Really?

ROXANE. Just like a man! Because he's handsome, you think he has to be dull-witted!

CYRANO. Does he speak well about matters of the heart?

ROXANE. Not well—superbly!

CYRANO. And how does he write?

3 ROXANE. Even better than he speaks! Just listen to this! [*Declaiming.*] "The more you take of my heart, the more I have!" [*Triumphantly.*] There, what do you think of that?

CYRANO. [*Unenthusiastically.*] Oh . . .

ROXANE. And this: "Since I need a heart with which to suffer, if you keep mine, send me yours!"

CYRANO. First he has too much heart, then not enough. He can't seem to make up his mind.

4 ROXANE. [*Stamping her foot.*] You're exasperating! You only talk like that because you're jealous . . .

CYRANO. [*Starting.*] What?

ROXANE. . . . of the way he writes! Listen to this and tell me if you think anything could be more tender: "Believe me when I say that my heart cries out to you, and that if kisses could be sent in writing, you would read this letter with your lips."

496 *Drama*

CYRANO. [*Smiling with satisfaction in spite of himself.*] Well, those lines are . . . [*Catches himself and continues in a disdainful tone.*] . . . rather affected.

ROXANE. And listen to this. . . .

5 CYRANO. [*Delighted.*] You know all his letters by heart?

ROXANE. Every one of them!

CYRANO. [*Twisting his mustache.*] That's quite flattering.

ROXANE. He's a master of eloquence!

CYRANO. [*Modestly.*] Let's not exaggerate. . . .

ROXANE. [*Peremptorily.*] A master!

CYRANO. [*Bowing.*] Very well, then, a master!

THE DUENNA. [*Hurrying downstage, after having gone upstage earlier.*] Monsieur de Guiche is coming! [*To* CYRANO, *pushing him toward the house.*] Go inside! It will be better for him not to find you here; it might put him on the scent. . . .

ROXANE. [*To* CYRANO.] Yes, on the scent of my precious secret! He's in love with me and he's powerful—he mustn't know! He might strike a cruel blow at my love for Christian!

CYRANO. [*Entering the house.*] I'll do as you wish.

[DE GUICHE *appears.*]

ROXANE. [*To* DE GUICHE, *with a curtsey.*] We were about to leave. . . .

DE GUICHE. I've come to say good-by.

ROXANE. You're going away?

DE GUICHE. Yes. To war.

ROXANE. Ah!

DE GUICHE. I'm leaving tonight.

ROXANE. Ah!

CRITICAL THINKING: GUIDED READING QUESTIONS

LITERAL

1a. What does Roxane tell Cyrano about Christian's delivery of "sweet nothings"? (No one can match him, yet sometimes he falters and then goes on to say exquisite things.)

2a. What questions does Cyrano ask Roxane about Christian? ("You feel that Christian has a brilliant mind?"; "Does he speak well about matters of the heart?"; "And how does he write?")

INFERENTIAL

1b. Why do you think Christian falters and then recovers? (He probably forgets the words Cyrano told him to use.)

2b. Why does Cyrano ask Roxane such details about Christian? (He wants to observe the impact of his own words; he wants to see how well Christian is conveying his words.)

6 DE GUICHE. I have my orders. We're besieging Arras.[8]

ROXANE. Ah! A siege?

DE GUICHE. Yes. . . . My departure seems to leave you cold.

ROXANE. [*Politely.*] Not at all.

DE GUICHE. For my part, I'm heartbroken. Will I ever see you again? If so, when? . . . Do you know that I've been made a colonel?

ROXANE. [*With indifference.*] Congratulations.

7 DE GUICHE. And I'm in command of the Guards.

ROXANE. [*Startled.*] The Guards?

DE GUICHE. Yes, the regiment in which your boastful cousin serves. I'll find a way to take revenge on him when we're at Arras.

ROXANE. [*Choking.*] What! The Guards are being sent there?

DE GUICHE. [*Laughing.*] Of course: that's my regiment!

ROXANE. [*Aside.*] Christian! . . .

DE GUICHE. What's the matter?

8 ROXANE. [*Overwhelmed with emotion.*] I'm in despair at . . . at what you've told me. . . . When a woman cares for a man and learns that he's going to war . . .

DE GUICHE. [*Surprised and delighted.*] Why did you wait for the day of my departure to say such a tender thing to me for the first time?

ROXANE. [*Changing her tone and fanning herself.*] So you're going to take revenge on my cousin?

DE GUICHE. Do you see him?

---

8. **Arras** [ä rä′]: city that was in the Spanish Netherlands and is now in France.

ROXANE. Very seldom.

DE GUICHE. He's seen everywhere with one of the Cadets . . . [*Tries to think of the name.*] . . . a young man named Neu . . . Neuvillen . . . Neuviller . . .

ROXANE. Tall?

DE GUICHE. Yes, with blond hair.

ROXANE. Reddish blond.

DE GUICHE. And handsome.

ROXANE. Not very.

DE GUICHE. But stupid.

ROXANE. He looks like it. [*Changing her tone.*] Are you planning to take revenge on Cyrano by exposing him to the fire of the enemy? If so, you'll get little satisfaction from it, because he loves danger! I know how you could really make him suffer!

DE GUICHE. How?

9 ROXANE. Leave him behind with his dear Cadets when the regiment goes off to fight. Make him sit idly in Paris through the whole war! He'll eat his heart out at not being in action, his friends will angrily chew their fingernails, and you'll be avenged.

DE GUICHE. [*Drawing closer.*] Then you do love me a little! [*She smiles.*] I like to think that your sharing my rancor is a sign of love, Roxane!

ROXANE. It is.

DE GUICHE. [*Showing her several sealed envelopes.*] I have orders that will be delivered to each company without delay, except . . . [*Separates one of them from the others.*] . . . for this one, addressed to the Cadets! [*Puts it in his pocket.*] I'll keep it. [*Laughing.*] Ha, ha, Cyrano! We'll see how your warlike temperament takes to this! . . . Tell me, Roxane, do you sometimes play tricks on people yourself?

Cyrano de Bergerac, Act III **497**

CRITICAL THINKING: GUIDED READING QUESTIONS

LITERAL

1a. What feeling does Roxane pretend to have for De Guiche? (She lets him believe she loves him.)

2a. What trick does Roxane play on De Guiche? (She tells him that if he truly wants to punish Cyrano, he should deny him the adventure of war and keep the Cadets at home.)

INFERENTIAL

1b. Why do you think De Guiche is so eager to believe that Roxane loves him? (He loves her, and since he doesn't know about Christian, he has no way of knowing that she is talking about someone else.)

2b. Do you think this will be a real punishment for Cyrano? (Most students will probably say yes, because it seems fitting that Cyrano would desire the action of a war.)

- De Guiche tries to talk Roxane into a romantic meeting that evening.
- He persists in interpreting her comments about Christian as declarations of love for himself.

10 TEACHING CHARACTERIZATION

Help students recognize Roxane's cleverness here. (Students should see that rather than lying, she tells the truth in a way that reveals nothing.)

11 CULTURAL BACKGROUND

Explain that the Capuchins were a branch of the Franciscan order of monks noted for their strict rules of conduct. *Capuchins* means "hooded ones" in Italian, and the Capuchins were easily recognized both by their hoods and by their beards.

12 TEACHING DRAMATIC IRONY

Point out that Roxane's answer is an honest one, but it creates dramatic irony because De Guiche is led to believe she's talking about him, even though she and the audience know that she is referring to Christian.

---

10 ROXANE. [*Looking at him.*] Yes, sometimes.

DE GUICHE. [*Close to her.*] You drive me mad! I intended to leave tonight, but how can I part from you when you've just revealed such feel-
11 ings to me? Listen. . . . Near here, on the Rue d'Orléans,[9] there's a monastery founded by the Capuchins.[10] Laymen aren't allowed to enter it, but I'll see to it that the good monks make an exception in my case. Everyone will believe I've left Paris. I'll then come to you, masked. Let me delay my departure one day!

ROXANE. [*Anxiously.*] But if it becomes known, your glory will be . . .

---

9. **Rue d'Orléans** [rōō′ dôr′lā ōn′]
10. **Capuchins** [kap′yə shinz]: monks who belong to a branch of the Franciscan order.

DE GUICHE. Never mind! Let me do it!

ROXANE. No!

DE GUICHE. Let me!

ROXANE. [*Tenderly.*] I must refuse.

DE GUICHE. Ah!

ROXANE. Go! [*Aside.*] And Christian will stay. [*To* DE GUICHE.] I want you to be heroic . . . Antoine!

12 DE GUICHE. What heavenly words! Do you love . . .

ROXANE. Yes, I love the man for whom I fear.

DE GUICHE. [*Overjoyed.*] I'm going now! [*Kisses her hand.*] Are you satisfied?

ROXANE. Yes, Antoine. [*He leaves.*]

498 *Drama*

CRITICAL THINKING: GUIDED READING QUESTIONS

LITERAL

1a. What do the stage directions say about the way in which Roxane refuses to accept a visit from De Guiche that evening? (She is to act "tenderly.")

INFERENTIAL

1b. Why do you suppose she suddenly speaks tenderly to De Guiche, a man she hates and fears? (Answers will vary. Some students will say she is trying to control and manipulate him; others may say she is thinking of Christian.)

THE DUENNA. [*Bowing comically to him behind his back.*] Yes, Antoine!

ROXANE. [*To the* DUENNA.] Don't say a word about what I've done. Cyrano would never forgive me if he knew I'd robbed him of his war! [*Calls toward the house.*] Cousin! If Christian comes, as I presume he will, tell him to wait for me.

CYRANO. [*Quickly, as she is about to disappear.*] One moment! [*She turns back toward him.*] You always have a subject on which you question him; what will it be this time?

ROXANE. This time . . .

CYRANO. [*Eagerly.*] Yes?

ROXANE. You won't tell him?

CYRANO. I'll be as silent as a tomb.

ROXANE. Well, this time I'm not going to question him about anything! I'll say to him, "Give free rein to your mind! Improvise! Speak to me of love in your magnificent way!"

CYRANO. [*Smiling.*] Good.

ROXANE. Sh!

CYRANO. Sh!

ROXANE. Not a word! [*Goes inside and closes the door behind her.*]

CYRANO. [*Bowing to her, after the door is closed.*] I thank you.

[*The door opens again and* ROXANE's *head appears.*]

ROXANE. If he knew, he might prepare a speech in advance!

BOTH TOGETHER. Sh! [*The door closes.*]

CYRANO. [*Calling.*] Christian! [CHRISTIAN *appears.*] I know what we need to know. Prepare your memory: here's a chance to cover yourself with glory! Why are you looking so unhappy? Come,

there's no time to lose! We'll hurry to your house and I'll tell you . . .

CHRISTIAN. No!

CYRANO. What?

CHRISTIAN. No! I'm going to wait for Roxane here.

CYRANO. Have you lost your reason? Come with me, you must learn . . .

CHRISTIAN. No, I tell you! I'm tired of borrowing my letters and speeches, of always playing a part and trembling lest I forget my lines! It was necessary at the beginning and I'm grateful to you for your help, but now that I feel she really loves me, I'm no longer afraid. I'm going to speak for myself.

CYRANO. [*Ironically.*] Do you believe that's a good idea?

CHRISTIAN. What makes you think I can't do it? After all, I'm not so stupid! You'll see! Your lessons haven't been wasted on me, my friend: I'm sure I can speak without your guidance now. And in any case I'll certainly know how to take her in my arms! Here she comes! No, Cyrano, don't leave me!

CYRANO. [*Bowing to him.*] Speak for yourself, sir. [*Disappears behind the garden wall.*]

ROXANE. [*She sees* CHRISTIAN.] Ah, it's you! [*Goes to him.*] Dusk is gathering. Wait. . . . The air is pleasant and no one is passing by. Let's sit down. Talk to me. I'm listening.

[CHRISTIAN *sits down beside her on the bench. There is a silence.*]

CHRISTIAN. I love you.

ROXANE. [*Closing her eyes.*] Yes, speak to me of love.

CHRISTIAN. I love you.

Cyrano de Bergerac, Act III **499**

PAGE SUMMARY: AT A GLANCE

■ Cyrano reappears and elicits the topic Roxane will ask Christian to discuss that evening: love.
■ Christian arrives and tells Cyrano that he no longer wants to borrow words from him.
■ Christian begins to speak to Roxane.

13 READING SKILL: CONCLUSION

Ask students what they learn from Cyrano's words about how the partnership between Cyrano and Christian works. (Each day Cyrano finds out the subject on which Roxane will question Christian. He then invents a response, which he gives to Christian to convey to Roxane.)

14 TEACHING CHARACTERIZATION

Point out that Christian shows himself to be an essentially honest man. Feeling sure of Roxane's love, he now wishes to appear before her without pretense.

15 TEACHING DIALOGUE

Bring to students' attention the way in which Cyrano's refusal to stay when Christian asks him to reveals his quick temper. Students should also see that by refusing to stay, Cyrano hopes to show Christian what Roxane loves—Cyrano's own eloquent words.

16 READING SKILL: PREDICTING OUTCOMES

Ask students to predict what will happen now that Christian no longer has Cyrano's eloquence to draw on. (They will probably predict that Christian will falter.)

CRITICAL THINKING: GUIDED READING QUESTIONS

LITERAL

1a. What information does Cyrano find out from Roxane? (He finds out the topic on which she will ask Christian to converse that evening.)

2a. What does Cyrano say when Christian tells him that he wants to speak for himself? ("Do you believe that's a good idea?")

INFERENTIAL

1b. Why is this necessary information? (Since Cyrano can't be there to speak for Christian, he must learn the topic in advance in order to coach Christian.)

2b. Why do you think Cyrano says this? (By now Cyrano has a good idea of Christian's limitation. Also, Cyrano is certain that no one else can match his eloquence.)

■ Christian declares his love.
■ Roxane demands more eloquence, becomes annoyed, and leaves.
■ Cyrano suggests they stand together under Roxane's balcony; Cyrano will again provide Christian with eloquent language.

17 TEACHING THEME

Point out the way in which one of the play's themes—the value of language and poetry—is underscored here. Because Christian cannot speak eloquently of his love, Roxane does not take his feelings seriously.

18 TEACHING STYLE: HUMOR

Help students see the way the small variations on the words "I love you" add humor to the scene and illustrate the idea that sincerity is not always enough to influence people.

19 CRITICAL THINKING: LOGICAL REASONING

Ask students whether in real life either eloquence or good looks guarantees a good long-term relationship. Encourage students to suggest what a modern Roxane might look for in a potential mate.

20 TEACHING PLOT: CONFLICT

Encourage students to note that Christian's rejection of Cyrano's help and recent skepticism about its value annoy Cyrano; nonetheless, Cyrano's powerful love for Roxane causes him to help Christian once more.

ROXANE. That's the theme—now elaborate on it.

CHRISTIAN. I love . . .

ROXANE. Develop your theme!

CHRISTIAN. I love you so much!

ROXANE. Go on.

CHRISTIAN. I . . . I'd be so happy if you loved me! Tell me that you do, Roxane!

ROXANE. [*Pouting.*] You're giving me water when I expected cream! Tell me how you love me.

CHRISTIAN. I love you . . . very much!

17 ROXANE. Surely you can express your feelings better than that!

CHRISTIAN. [*Who has moved closer to her and is now devouring her neck with his eyes.*] Your neck! I'd like to kiss it. . . .

ROXANE. Christian!

18 CHRISTIAN. I love you!

ROXANE. [*Starting to stand up.*] Again!

CHRISTIAN. [*Quickly, holding her back.*] No, I don't love you!

ROXANE. [*Sitting down again.*] At least that's a change.

CHRISTIAN. I adore you!

ROXANE. [*Standing up and moving away.*] Oh!

CHRISTIAN. Yes. . . . I'm becoming foolish!

19 ROXANE. [*Curtly.*] And it displeases me! As it would displease me if you became ugly.

CHRISTIAN. But . . .

ROXANE. Try to bring back your vanished eloquence!

CHRISTIAN. I . . .

500 *Drama*

ROXANE. I know: you love me. Good-by. [*Goes toward the house.*]

CHRISTIAN. Wait! Let me tell you . . .

ROXANE. [*Opening the door.*] That you adore me? I already know that. No, no! Go away!

CHRISTIAN. But I . . . [*She closes the door in his face.*]

CYRANO. [*Who has returned a short time earlier without being seen.*] Congratulations on your success.

CHRISTIAN. Help me!

CYRANO. No.

CHRISTIAN. If I don't win her back immediately, I'll die!

CYRANO. How do you expect me to teach you immediately . . .

CHRISTIAN. [*Gripping his arm.*] Oh! Look! [*A light has appeared in the balcony window.*]

CYRANO. [*With deep emotion.*] Her window!

CHRISTIAN. [*Shouting.*] I'll die!

CYRANO. Lower your voice!

CHRISTIAN. [*Softly.*] I'll die. . . .

CYRANO. It's dark now.

CHRISTIAN. What of it?

20 CYRANO. The damage can be repaired. You don't deserve . . . Stand here, in front of the balcony, you wretched fool! I'll be under it, telling you what to say.

CHRISTIAN. But . . .

CYRANO. Quiet! [*The* PAGES *appear in the background.*] Sh! [*Signals them to speak softly.*]

FIRST PAGE. [*In an undertone.*] We've been serenading Montfleury!

CYRANO. [*Quickly, also in an undertone.*] I want

CRITICAL THINKING: GUIDED READING QUESTIONS

LITERAL

1a. What happens when Christian tries to speak to Roxane on his own? (He merely repeats, "I love you"; Roxane becomes annoyed at his speech and sends him away.)

2a. How does Cyrano react when Christian asks for help after his failure? (First he refuses; then he relents.)

INFERENTIAL

1b. Do you think this inability to speak in beautiful language means Christian does not love Roxane deeply? (No, his love is sincere and deeply felt, but he lacks the imagination to express it.)

2b. What do you think Cyrano feels when Christian asks for help? (He pities Christian but is also excited at the idea of once again playing a part in the wooing of Roxane.)

21 you to stand watch, one at that corner, the other at that one. If you see anyone coming, begin playing your lutes.

SECOND PAGE. What shall we play?

CYRANO. A happy melody for a woman, a sad one for a man. [*The* PAGES *disappear, one toward each street corner.* CYRANO *speaks to* CHRISTIAN.] Call her!

CHRISTIAN. Roxane!

CYRANO. [*Picking up pebbles and throwing them against the window.*] Just a moment. First, a few pebbles. . . .

ROXANE. [*Partially opening her window.*] Who's there?

CHRISTIAN. It's I.

ROXANE. Who?

CHRISTIAN. Christian.

ROXANE. [*With disdain.*] Oh, it's you.

CHRISTIAN. I'd like to speak to you.

CYRANO. [*Under the balcony, to* CHRISTIAN.] That's good. Keep your voice down.

ROXANE. No! You speak too awkwardly. Go away.

CHRISTIAN. Please. . . .

ROXANE. No! You've stopped loving me!

CHRISTIAN. [*Repeating what* CYRANO *tells him.*] Impossible! . . . I could no more . . . stop loving you . . . than I could stop . . . the rising of the sun!

ROXANE. [*Pausing just as she was about to close the window.*] Ah! That's better!

CHRISTIAN. [*Still repeating* CYRANO's *words.*] My cruel love . . . has never ceased to grow . . . in my tormented soul . . . since the day . . . when it was born there.

ROXANE. [*Leaning forward with her elbows on the railing of the balcony.*] Very good! . . . But why do you speak so haltingly? Has your imagination gone lame?

CYRANO. [*Pulling* CHRISTIAN *under the balcony and taking his place.*] Sh! This is becoming too difficult!

ROXANE. Your words are hesitant tonight. Why?

22 CYRANO. [*Speaking softly, like* CHRISTIAN.] Because of the darkness, they must grope their way to your ears.

ROXANE. *My* words have no such difficulty.

CYRANO. They go straight to my heart, a goal too large to miss, whereas your ears are small. And your words travel swiftly because they fall, while mine must slowly climb.

ROXANE. But they seem to be climbing better now.

23 CYRANO. They've finally become accustomed to that exercise.

ROXANE. It's true that I'm speaking from high above you.

CYRANO. Yes, and it would kill me if you let a harsh word fall on my heart from that height!

ROXANE. [*Making a movement.*] I'll come down to you!

CYRANO. [*Urgently.*] No!

24 ROXANE. [*Pointing to the bench below the balcony.*] Then climb up on that bench.

CYRANO. [*Stepping back into the shadows.*] No!

ROXANE. Why not?

CYRANO. [*Increasingly overcome by emotion.*] I want to go on taking advantage of this opportunity . . . this chance for us to talk quietly . . .without seeing each other.

ROXANE. Why should we talk without seeing each other?

Cyrano de Bergerac, Act III **501**

PAGE SUMMARY: AT A GLANCE

- Cyrano arranges for the pages to warn him if anyone nears.
- He and Christian stand under Roxane's balcony; Cyrano whispers eloquent phrases that Christian repeats to her.
- Cyrano begins speaking in his own voice.

21 **TEACHING PLOT: FORESHADOWING**

Point out that Cyrano's act of setting up a musical signal with the pages creates the expectation of an imminent arrival. Help students recognize the way in which this plot device adds tension.

22 **TEACHING FIGURATIVE LANGUAGE**

Encourage students to recognize Cyrano's new inventiveness in explaining the irregular sound of his words: He turns to metaphor to explain why her speeches are more audible than his.

23 **TEACHING STUDENTS OF LIMITED ENGLISH PROFICIENCY**

Students may have difficulty understanding that the word *they* here refers to "words." They may also have difficulty with the flowery and metaphorical nature of the entire interchange of words. Help them paraphrase the conversation to increase their understanding.

24 **TEACHING SUSPENSE**

Make sure students recognize that Cyrano must remain hidden so that he can make his declaration of love without being recognized. Roxane's reasonable request increases the tension of the scene.

CRITICAL THINKING: GUIDED READING QUESTIONS

LITERAL

1a. How does Roxane interpret Christian's sudden inability to speak fluently of his love? (She says he doesn't love her anymore.)

2a. What does Cyrano do when Roxane complains that Christian's words are halting? (He pushes Christian out of the way, takes his place, and begins to speak to Roxane himself.)

INFERENTIAL

1b. What does this show about Roxane's character? (She is frivolous and superficial; ill-expressed feelings bore her.)

2b. Why is this an extremely important event for Cyrano? (It is the first time he is able to speak directly to Roxane of his love.)

25 TEACHING PLOT: RISING ACTION

Point out that the dramatic intensity of this scene rests in the double meaning of Cyrano's words. Encourage students to recognize that several times Cyrano seems on the brink of revealing himself but always turns to some other thought just before doing so.

26 TEACHING CHARACTERIZATION

Help students see that here another side of Cyrano is revealed: He is a man who can be less than smooth and fluent in expressing his most deeply held feelings.

27 TEACHING FIGURATIVE LANGUAGE

Point out the way in which Cyrano contrasts the "little flowers of eloquence" with the utterance of true passion. Help students see that Cyrano does not abandon eloquence for passion; his revealed passions make him *more* eloquent.

28 TEACHING MOOD

Point out how Cyrano's language soars when freed from the constraints of artifice and cleverness. The playful verbal fencing of past encounters gives way to a sense of urgency.

CYRANO. I find it delightful. We're almost invisible to each other. You see the blackness of a long cloak, I see the whiteness of a summer dress. I'm only a shadow, you're only a spot of brightness. You can't know what these moments mean to me! I may sometimes have been eloquent in the past . . .

ROXANE. You have!

CYRANO. . . . but until now my words have never come from my true heart.

ROXANE. Why?

25 CYRANO. Because . . . till now I always spoke through . . .

ROXANE. Through what?

CYRANO. The intoxication that seizes anyone who stands before your gaze! . . . But tonight it seems to me that I'm speaking to you for the first time.

ROXANE. Perhaps it's true—even your voice is different.

26 CYRANO. [*Impetuously moving closer.*] Yes, quite different, because in the protecting darkness I dare at last to be myself, I dare . . . [*Pauses, then continues distractedly.*] What was I saying? I don't know. . . . All this . . . Excuse my agitation! All this is so enchanting . . . so new to me!

ROXANE. So new?

CYRANO. [*Deeply stirred, trying to cover up what he has admitted.*] Yes, it's new to me to be sincere . . . without fear of being laughed at. . . .

ROXANE. Laughed at for what?

27 CYRANO. For . . . for an outburst of feeling! My heart always timidly hides itself behind my mind. I set out to bring down stars from the sky, then, for fear of ridicule, I stop and pick little flowers of eloquence.

ROXANE. Those little flowers have their charm.

502 *Drama*

CYRANO. Yes, but let's scorn them tonight!

ROXANE. You've never talked to me like this before.

CYRANO. One look at the starry sky above us is enough to make me want to throw off all artificiality. If the expression of feeling is refined too much, the feeling itself is lost.

ROXANE. But it seems to me that elegant language . . .

CYRANO. It has no place in true love! It's only a game, and those who love will suffer if they play it too long. For most of them there comes a time—and I pity those for whom it doesn't come!—when they feel a noble love inside themselves that's saddened by every grandiloquent word they say.

ROXANE. Well, if that time has come for us, what words will you say to me?

28 CYRANO. All those that enter my mind of their own accord. I'll give them to you as they come, without arranging them in bouquets: I love you, I'm overwhelmed, I love you to the point of madness! Your name is in my heart like a bell shaken by my constant trembling, ringing day and night: Roxane, Roxane, Roxane! Loving everything about you, I forget nothing. I remember the day last year, the twelfth of May, when you wore your hair in a different style. Just as a man who has looked at the sun too long sees red circles everywhere, when I've gazed on the bright glory of your hair my dazzled eyes see golden spots on everything!

ROXANE. [*In a tremulous voice.*] Yes, that's really love. . . .

CYRANO. The feeling that holds me in its merciless grip could be nothing else but love! It has all the terrible jealousy and somber violence of love, and all the unselfishness, too. How gladly I would give my happiness for the sake of yours, even without your knowledge, asking only to

---

CRITICAL THINKING: GUIDED READING QUESTIONS

LITERAL

1a. What does Cyrano say is new about his speeches? (It is new to him to be sincere without fear of being laughed at.)

INFERENTIAL

1b. What does he mean by this? (Before he was afraid Roxane would find him ridiculous; now he knows she won't laugh at him because she thinks that he is Christian.)

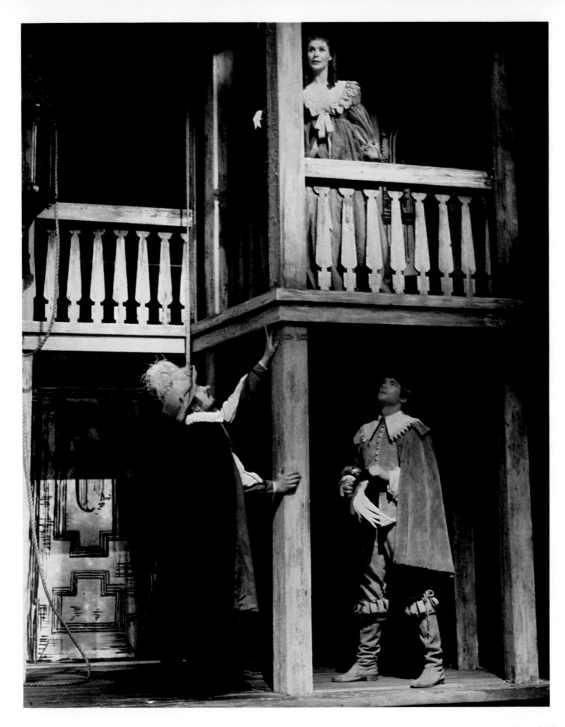

Cyrano de Bergerac, Act III **503**

- Cyrano proclaims his joy at speaking directly to Roxane.
- Roxane professes passionate love for him.
- Christian urges Cyrano to ask for a kiss; Cyrano refuses and then changes his mind.
- A Capuchin enters, looking for Roxane; Cyrano misdirects him.

29 TEACHING DRAMATIC IRONY

Point out that as Cyrano reaches his most eloquent pitch, the irony of his situation also reaches a peak. Cyrano says "*you* listen to *me*," but Roxane continues to think she is listening to Christian.

30 TEACHING STAGING

Point out that Cyrano's speech can be staged in such a way that the audience may almost forget that Christian is present. Here Cyrano seems to have forgotten Christian's presence until Christian demands a kiss from Roxane.

31 TEACHING CONFLICT

Underscore the way in which the conflict over Roxane's love surfaces at this point. Christian wants Roxane's kiss, but Cyrano is unwilling to let him have it.

32 READING SKILL: PARAPHRASING

Ask students to paraphrase Cyrano's words. (A kiss should be an expression of true, deeply felt emotion, deeper than banter and heartfelt as tears.)

---

hear from a distance, now and then, the laughter born of my sacrifice! Are you beginning to understand now? Do you feel my soul rising to you in the darkness? Ah, it's all too beautiful, too **29** sweet, this evening! I say all these things and you listen to me—*you* listen to *me*! It's more than my poor heart can bear! Even in my most daring dreams I never hoped for so much! I could die happily at this moment! It's because of my words that you're trembling—for you *are* trembling, like one of the leaves in the dark foliage above me: I've felt the beloved tremor of your hand descending along the jasmine branches! [*Fervently kisses the end of a drooping branch.*]

ROXANE. Yes, I'm trembling, and I'm weeping, and I love you, and I'm yours!

CYRANO. Then let death come, now that I've aroused such feelings in you! I ask only one thing . . .

30 CHRISTIAN. [*From under the balcony.*] A kiss!

ROXANE. [*Quickly drawing back.*] What?

CYRANO. Oh!

ROXANE. You ask . . .

31 CYRANO. Yes, I . . . [*To* CHRISTIAN, *in an undertone.*] You're going too fast!

CHRISTIAN. She's in a willing mood—I must take advantage of it!

CYRANO. [*To* ROXANE.] Yes, I . . . asked for a kiss, but I now realize that I was much too bold.

ROXANE. [*A little disappointed.*] You don't insist?

CYRANO. Yes, I insist . . . but not insistently! I've offended your modesty. . . . Don't give me that kiss!

CHRISTIAN. [*To* CYRANO, *tugging at his cloak.*] Why do you say that?

CYRANO. Quiet, Christian!

504 *Drama*

ROXANE. [*Leaning forward.*] What are you saying?

CYRANO. I was scolding myself for having gone too far. I just said to myself, "Quiet, Christian!" [*The lutes begin playing.*] Wait! Someone's coming! [ROXANE *closes the window.*] A sad tune and a happy one, both at the same time? What do they mean? Is it a man or a woman? . . . Ah! [*A* CAPUCHIN *enters; holding a lantern in his hand, he goes from house to house, looking at the doors.*]

CYRANO. [*To the* CAPUCHIN.] What are you doing?

THE CAPUCHIN. I'm looking for the house of Madame . . . Magdeleine Robin.

CYRANO. [*To the* CAPUCHIN, *showing him an uphill street.*] It's that way. Straight ahead.

THE CAPUCHIN. Thank you. [*He leaves.*]

CHRISTIAN. You must get that kiss for me!

CYRANO. No!

CHRISTIAN. Sooner or later . . .

CYRANO. Yes, it's true. Sooner or later there will be an ecstatic moment when your mouths are drawn together. [*To himself.*] I prefer it to be because of . . .

[*Sound of the window being opened again.* CHRISTIAN *hides under the balcony.*]

ROXANE. [*Coming out onto the balcony.*] Are you still there? We were talking about . . . about a . . .

32 CYRANO. A kiss. The word is so sweet! Why should you be afraid to say it? Don't be alarmed; you've already given up your bantering tone and gradually drifted from smiles to sighs, and then from sighs to tears! Let yourself drift a little further.

ROXANE. Stop!

CYRANO. After all, what is a kiss? A vow made at

CRITICAL THINKING: GUIDED READING QUESTIONS

LITERAL

1a. What is Roxane's reaction to Cyrano when he speaks from the heart? (Moved, she trembles, weeps, and confesses her love.)

INFERENTIAL

1b. Why do you think this speech affects her differently from the ones Cyrano has been making through Christian? (Cyrano is carried away by his love and expresses his feeling in a deeper, more genuine way.)

33 closer range, a more precise promise, a confession that contains its own proof, a seal placed on a pact that has already been signed; a fleeting moment filled with the hush of eternity, a communion that has the fragrance of a flower, a way of living by the beat of another heart.

ROXANE. Come to me! Come and give me that matchless flower . . .

CYRANO. [*Pushing* CHRISTIAN *toward the balcony.*] Climb up to her!

ROXANE. . . . that communion . . .

CYRANO. Climb!

ROXANE. . . . that hush of eternity . . .

CYRANO. Climb!

34 CHRISTIAN. [*Hesitating.*] But now it seems to me that it's wrong!

CYRANO. [*Pushing him.*] Climb, you fool!

[CHRISTIAN *stands on the bench, then climbs up onto the balcony.*]

CHRISTIAN. Ah, Roxane! [*Takes her in his arms and kisses her.*]

35 CYRANO. What a strange pang in my heart! I must content myself with very little, but I still have a few small crumbs. Yes, I feel something of that kiss in my heart, because Roxane is kissing not only Christian's lips, but also the words I spoke to her! [*The lutes begin playing again.*] A sad tune and a happy one: the Capuchin! [*Takes a few rapid steps, pretending to have just arrived, and calls out loudly.*] Roxane!

ROXANE. Who is it!

CYRANO. It's I. I was passing by. . . . Is Christian still here?

CHRISTIAN. [*Surprised.*] Cyrano!

ROXANE. Good evening, cousin.

CYRANO. Good evening, cousin.

ROXANE. I'm coming down! [*She disappears into the house. The* CAPUCHIN *enters in the background.*]

CHRISTIAN. [*Seeing him.*] No! Not again! [*Follows* ROXANE.]

THE CAPUCHIN. *This* is Magdeleine Robin's house!

CYRANO. You said "Rolin" before.

THE CAPUCHIN. No, I said "Robin!" R-O-B-I-N!

ROXANE. [*Appearing in the doorway of the house, followed by* RAGUENEAU, *who carries a lantern, and* CHRISTIAN.] Who's this?

THE CAPUCHIN. I have a letter for you.

CHRISTIAN. A letter?

THE CAPUCHIN. [*To* ROXANE.] It surely concerns some holy matter. It's from a worthy lord who . . .

ROXANE. [*To* CHRISTIAN.] It's from De Guiche!

CHRISTIAN. How dare he . . .

ROXANE. He won't bother me much longer! [*Opening the letter.*] I love you, and if . . . [*By the light of* RAGUENEAU's *lantern, she read the letter to herself in a low voice.*] "The drums are beating and my regiment is preparing to leave. Everyone believes that I have already gone, but I am staying, in disobedience to your orders. I am in a monastery. This letter is to inform you that I will soon come to visit you. The monk who will deliver it to you is as simpleminded as a goat, so **36** there is no danger of his guessing my plan. Your lips have smiled at me too much today; I must see them again. I hope that you have already forgiven my boldness, and I remain your . . ." And so on. [*To the* CAPUCHIN.] Father, you must hear what's in this letter. Listen. [*The others gather around her and she pretends to read aloud.*] "You must bow to the Cardinal's will, however difficult it may be for you. This letter will be delivered into your charming hands by a saintly,

Cyrano de Bergerac, Act III **505**

- Christian and Roxane kiss, and Cyrano feels that part of the kiss belongs to him.
- The Capuchin returns, and Cyrano calls to Roxane.
- The Capuchin gives her a letter from De Guiche.
- The letter states that De Guiche will visit her that night.

33 TEACHING FIGURATIVE LANGUAGE

Point out the series of metaphors Cyrano uses to describe a kiss. Cyrano compares this physical act with six ideas, each intangible and suggestive of the emotional underpinnings of a kiss.

34 READING SKILL: INFERENCE

Ask students why Christian suddenly feels that the kiss is wrong. (Some students may think that he recognizes that Cyrano deserves the kiss; others may feel that Christian wants to protect Roxane's honor.)

35 TEACHING CONFLICT

Help students recognize that Cyrano is both proud and disturbed by the kiss—proud and happy because his words elicited the kiss, yet disturbed and sad because he must be content with mere "crumbs" of Roxane's love.

36 TEACHING A SUBPLOT

Be sure students recognize that De Guiche's love for Roxane is an important subplot throughout most of the play. Point out that Roxane's use of the letter now links the subplot directly to the events of the main plot: the romance between Roxane and Christian.

CRITICAL THINKING: GUIDED READING QUESTIONS

LITERAL

1a. When do Christian and Roxane kiss? (after Cyrano persuades Roxane and pushes Christian up the balcony)

2a. How does De Guiche refer to the Capuchin in his letter? (He says he is "as simpleminded as a goat.")

INFERENTIAL

1b. Why does Cyrano arrange this kiss when earlier he tried to stop Christian and Roxane from kissing? (He knows that the kiss is inevitable. If he arranges it, he proves the power of his words to move her.)

2b. Why does De Guiche rely on a simpleminded man to deliver his message? (He needs someone who will not guess his true intent.)

PAGE SUMMARY: AT A GLANCE

- Roxane pretends that the letter orders her to marry Christian.
- De Guiche enters; Cyrano delays him by pretending to have fallen from the moon.

IN THE GLOSSARY

- tremolo: a wavering or trembling sound
- mystified: puzzled; bewildered

37 TEACHING CHARACTERIZATION

Ask students what Roxane's use of the letter shows about her character. (Students should see that she has the ability to think quickly and manipulate others.)

38 TEACHING STYLE: HUMOR

Point out the humor of this brief exchange. Help students recognize that Rostand's humor points up the hypocrisy of Cyrano's age: Monks would bend their scruples for money.

39 TEACHING STAGING

Make sure students understand that by this point the audience is willing to suspend its disbelief and accept the idea that Cyrano successfully disguises himself by wrapping himself in his cloak and using his Gascon accent.

40 TEACHING THEME

Help students see that the play celebrates Cyrano's creativity and his facility with language. Here he uses both to try to delay De Guiche. His zany talk is typical of his unfettered imagination.

37 intelligent, and discreet Capuchin. You will inform him that we wish him to give you the blessing of holy matrimony . . ." [*Turns the page.*] ". . . in your house, and without delay. Christian must secretly become your husband. I have already sent him to you. I know that you dislike him, but you must accept the Cardinal's decision, and you may rest assured that heaven will bless you for your resignation. With the respect that I have always borne for you, I remain your humble and devoted . . ." And so on. [*Loudly, with despair.*] Oh! This is horrible!

THE CAPUCHIN. [*Turning the light of his lantern on* CYRANO.] Are you the . . .

CHRISTIAN. No, *I* am!

THE CAPUCHIN. [*Turns the light on* CHRISTIAN, *then, seeing how handsome he is, appears to become suspicious.*] But . . .

38 ROXANE. [*Quickly, pretending to read again.*] "P.S. You will make a gift of a thousand francs[11] to the monastery."

THE CAPUCHIN. A worthy, worthy lord! [*To* ROXANE.] Resign yourself!

ROXANE. [*In a tone of martyrdom.*] I am resigned. [*While* RAGUENEAU *opens the door for the* CAPUCHIN, *whom* CHRISTIAN *has invited to enter, she speaks softly to* CYRANO.] De Guiche will soon be here. Delay him, don't let him come in until . . .

CYRANO. I understand. [*To the* CAPUCHIN.] How long will you need for the wedding ceremony?

THE CAPUCHIN. About a quarter of an hour.

CYRANO. [*Pushing them all toward the house.*] Hurry! I'll stay here.

ROXANE. [*To* CHRISTIAN.] Come! [*They go inside.*]

---

11. **francs:** The franc is the French monetary unit; it is worth about twenty cents.

506 *Drama*

CYRANO. How can I make De Guiche waste a quarter of an hour? [*Leaps onto the bench and climbs up the wall, toward the balcony.*] Up we go! . . . I have my plan! [*The lutes begin playing a mournful melody.*] Aha! A man is coming! [*The tremolo becomes sinister.*] No doubt of it this time! [*He is now on the balcony. He pushes his hat down over his eyes, takes off his sword, wraps his cloak around himself, leans forward, and looks down.*] No, it's not too high. . . . [*He sits on the railing, takes one of the long tree branches that overhang the garden wall, pulls it toward him, and holds it with both hands, ready to swing down.*] I am going to trouble this peaceful atmosphere a little!

DE GUICHE. [*Entering masked, groping in the darkness.*] What's happened to that Capuchin?

39 CYRANO. My voice! What if he recognizes it? [*Lets go of the branch with one hand and makes the motion of turning an invisible key.*] There! I've unlocked my Gascon accent!

DE GUICHE. [*Looking at the house.*] Yes, this is it. I can hardly see where I'm going. This mask is so annoying! [*He walks toward the door.* CYRANO *leaps from the balcony, holding the branch, which bends and sets him down between* DE GUICHE *and the door. He pretends to fall heavily, as if from a great height, and lies motionless on the ground, as though dazed.* DE GUICHE *jumps back.*] What! . . . What's this? . . . [*He looks up, but the branch has already sprung back into place. Seeing nothing but the sky, he is mystified.*] Where did this man fall from?

40 CYRANO. [*Sitting up, and speaking with a Gascon accent.*] From the moon!

DE GUICHE. Did you say . . .

CYRANO. [*Dreamily.*] What time is it?

DE GUICHE. He's lost his reason!

CYRANO. What time is it? What country is this? What day? What season?

CRITICAL THINKING: GUIDED READING QUESTIONS

LITERAL

1a. What job is Cyrano given during the wedding ceremony? (He is asked to intercept De Guiche and keep him occupied until the ceremony is over.)

INFERENTIAL

1b. How do you think Cyrano feels about this? (He seems comfortable with the job and throws himself into it once De Guiche arrives.)

DE GUICHE. But . . .

CYRANO. I'm still dazed.

DE GUICHE. Sir . . .

CYRANO. I fell from the moon like a cannonball!

DE GUICHE. [Impatiently.] Look, sir . . .

CYRANO. [Loudly and emphatically, standing up.] I fell from the moon!

DE GUICHE. [Stepping back.] Very well, then, you fell from the moon! [Aside.] He may be a maniac!

CYRANO. A hundred years ago, or perhaps a minute ago—I have no idea how long my fall lasted—I was on that yellow sphere!

41 DE GUICHE. [Shrugging.] Yes, of course. Let me pass.

CYRANO. [Stepping in front of him.] Where am I? Be frank, don't hide anything from me! What is this place where I've just fallen like a meteorite?

DE GUICHE. Enough of this!

CYRANO. As I was falling, I wasn't able to choose my destination, and I don't know where I've landed. Has the weight of my posterior brought me back to earth, or to another moon?

42 DE GUICHE. [Trying to get past him.] A lady is expecting me. . . .

CYRANO. Ah, then I'm in Paris!

DE GUICHE. [Smiling in spite of himself.] This lunatic is rather amusing!

CYRANO. You're smiling?

DE GUICHE. Yes, but I still want you to let me pass!

43 CYRANO. [Beaming.] I've fallen back into Paris! [Thoroughly at ease, smiling, brushing himself off, bowing.] Excuse me; I've just come by the latest whirlwind and I have ether all over me. Such a journey! My eyes are full of stardust. I

still have a little planet fur on my spurs. [Picks something off his sleeve.] A comet hair on my doublet! [Pretends to blow it away.]

DE GUICHE. [Beside himself with exasperation.] Sir! . . . [Just as DE GUICHE is about to pass, CYRANO stops him by putting out his leg, as though to show him something on it.]

CYRANO. The Great Bear bit me as I passed. Look, you can see the tooth marks on my leg. Then, when I swerved to avoid Orion's Sword, I fell into the Scales.[12] The pointer still marks my weight. [Prevents DE GUICHE from passing and takes hold of his doublet.] If you were to squeeze my nose, sir, milk would spurt from it.

DE GUICHE. Milk?

CYRANO. From the Milky Way!

DE GUICHE. Sir, I've been very patient with you. Now will you please . . .

CYRANO. I understand. I'll be glad to oblige you.

DE GUICHE. At last!

CYRANO. You want me to tell you what the moon is like and whether anyone lives there, isn't that right?

DE GUICHE. No! No! I want to . . .

CYRANO. Yes, of course—you want to know how I got to the moon. I did it by a method that I invented myself.

DE GUICHE. [Discouraged.] He's raving mad!

CYRANO. I didn't imitate anything that had been done before! [DE GUICHE succeeds in getting past him. He walks toward ROXANE's door while CY-**44**RANO follows him, ready to take hold of him.] I invented six ways.

DE GUICHE. [Stopping and turning around.] Six?

_____

12. **Great Bear, Orion's Sword, Scales:** constellations in the zodiac.

Cyrano de Bergerac, Act III **507**

PAGE SUMMARY: AT A GLANCE

- Cyrano delays De Guiche with stories of his space travels.
- De Guiche attempts to get past him.

IN THE GLOSSARY

- meteorite: a body from space that has fallen to Earth
- posterior: the buttocks
- ether: a supposed substance once thought to fill outer space

41 TEACHING STAGING

Help students see that this scene, one of the most famous in the play, draws much of its power from the fact that the audience is aware of what is going on off-stage. Each time De Guiche tries to pass Cyrano, the comic tension increases.

42 TEACHING STYLE: HUMOR

Help students understand the humor in Cyrano's reply, which suggests that romantic assignations are a common Paris cliché.

43 TEACHING IMAGERY

Point out the vivid images Cyrano uses—"whirlwind," "ether," "stardust"—to make his incredible story compelling.

44 TEACHING THEME

Call attention to the power of Cyrano's imagination and language in capturing De Guiche's interest quite against his will.

CRITICAL THINKING: GUIDED READING QUESTIONS

LITERAL

1a. What does De Guiche think of the man who says he fell from the moon? (He thinks he is crazy. At first he wants to get rid of him, but then he becomes intrigued.)

2a. What does Cyrano say that finally halts De Guiche? (He says that he invented six ways to get to the moon.)

INFERENTIAL

1b. Why does Cyrano pretend to be crazy? (Craziness allows him to take quick and extreme actions and also disguise his identity.)

2b. What can you infer about De Guiche from his stopping? (He has a curious and slightly gullible nature.)

IN THE GLOSSARY

- volubly: talkatively

45 GRAMMAR IN LITERATURE

Point out the repetition of the auxiliary verb phrase "could have" in describing possible modes of space travel. Ask students to identify the impact of this repetition. (It makes readers wonder what method Cyrano will finally claim to have used.)

46 TEACHING CHARACTERIZATION

Help students see how Cyrano shows his cleverness: He had said there were six ways to get to the moon, but, seeing that the time is not yet up, he comes up with a seventh.

47 TEACHING DIALOGUE

Note how the dialogue shows Cyrano's dislike for De Guiche: Cyrano abruptly switches from foolishness to the brutal truth as soon as it is safe to do so.

48 TEACHING PLOT: RISING ACTION

Be sure students recognize the marriage of Christian and Roxane as an important plot development. Students should also see that since the relationship is not a traditional romance but part of a triangle, the marriage is not the climax of the play.

---

45 CYRANO. [*Volubly.*] I could have clothed my naked body with crystal bottles full of dew and exposed myself to the morning sun; then, as the sun drew up the dew, I would have been drawn up with it!

DE GUICHE. [*Surprised, and taking a step toward* CYRANO.] Yes, that's one way!

CYRANO. [*Stepping back to lead him away from the door.*] And I could have rarefied[13] the air in a cedar chest by means of twenty burning-mirrors[14] suitably arranged, thus producing a great rush of wind that would have sent me on my way!

DE GUICHE. [*Taking another step toward him.*] Two!

CYRANO. [*Still moving back.*] Or, with my mechanical skill and my knowledge of pyrotechnics,[15] I could have constructed a large steel grasshopper propelled by successive explosions of gunpowder.

DE GUICHE. [*Following him without realizing it, and counting on his fingers.*] Three!

CYRANO. Since smoke tends to rise, I could have blown enough of it into a globe to carry me away!

DE GUICHE. [*Increasingly surprised, and still following him.*] Four!

CYRANO. Since the new moon likes to suck up the marrow of cattle, I could have coated my body with it!

DE GUICHE. [*Fascinated.*] Five!

CYRANO. [*Who, while speaking, has led him to the other side of the square, near a bench.*] Fi-

---

13. **rarefied:** made thinner, like the hot air in a balloon. The real Cyrano de Bergerac wrote a work of science fiction proposing these various methods of space travel.
14. **burning-mirrors:** curved mirrors used for producing great heat by focusing the sun's rays.
15. **pyrotechnics** [pī'rə tek'niks]: art of making and using fireworks.

---

nally, I could have sat on a sheet of iron and thrown a magnet into the air. It's a very good method: the iron follows the magnet in its flight, then you quickly throw the magnet again, and keep repeating the process until you've reached the moon!

46 DE GUICHE. Six! . . . But which of those six excellent methods did you choose?

CYRANO. A seventh!

DE GUICHE. Amazing! Tell me about it.

CYRANO. Try to guess.

DE GUICHE. This rascal is becoming interesting!

CYRANO. [*Making a sound of waves, with broad, mysterious gestures.*] Hoo! . . . Hoo! . . .

DE GUICHE. What's that?

CYRANO. Can't you guess?

DE GUICHE. No!

CYRANO. The tide! . . . After taking a dip in the sea, I lay on the beach at the hour when the moon was exerting the pull that causes the tides, and I was lifted into the air—head first, of course, since it was my hair that held the most moisture. I was rising straight up, slowly and effortlessly, like an angel, when suddenly I felt a shock! Then . . .

DE GUICHE. [*Sitting down on the bench, seized with curiosity.*] Yes? Then what?

47 CYRANO. Then . . . [*Resumes his natural voice.*] The quarter of an hour has passed, so I won't keep you any longer. The wedding is over.

DE GUICHE. [*Leaping to his feet.*] I must be losing my mind! That voice! . . . And that nose! . . . Cyrano!

48 CYRANO. [*Bowing.*] At your service. They've just been married.

DE GUICHE. Who? [*He turns around. Tableau.* ROXANE *and* CHRISTIAN *are holding hands. The*

CRITICAL THINKING: GUIDED READING QUESTIONS

LITERAL

1a. What methods does Cyrano name for getting to the moon? (clothing himself with crystals, producing a wind, building a large grasshopper, filling a glove with smoke, coating himself with marrow, throwing magnets and iron into the air, and letting the moon pull him)

INFERENTIAL

1b. What do these ideas tell us about Cyrano? (He has an acquaintance with scientific concepts as well as a creative imagination.)

CAPUCHIN *follows them, smiling.* RAGUENEAU *is also holding a candelabrum. The* DUENNA *brings up the rear. To* ROXANE.] You! [*With amazement, recognizing* CHRISTIAN.] And he? . . . [*Bowing to* ROXANE *with admiration.*] I congratulate you on your cleverness! [*To* CYRANO.] And to you, the great inventor, my compliments! Your story would have stopped a saint at the gates of

⁴⁹ heaven! Write down the details to it, because you really could use them in a book!

CYRANO. [*Bowing.*] I promise to follow your advice.

THE CAPUCHIN. [*Showing the couple to* DE GUICHE.] Here's the handsome couple you've united, my son!

DE GUICHE. [*Giving him an icy look.*] Yes. [*To* ROXANE.] And now you must tell your husband good-by, madame.

ROXANE. Why?

DE GUICHE. [*To* CHRISTIAN.] The regiment is about to leave. Join it!

ROXANE. To go to war?

DE GUICHE. Of course!

ROXANE. But the Cadets aren't going!

DE GUICHE. Yes, they are. [*Takes the envelope from his pocket.*] Here's the order. [*To* CHRISTIAN.] Deliver it at once, Baron.

ROXANE. [*Throwing herself in* CHRISTIAN's *arms.*] Christian!

⁵⁰ CHRISTIAN. It's hard to leave her. . . . You can't know. . . .

CYRANO. [*Trying to lead him away.*] I do know. . . .

[*Drums are heard beating in the distance.*]

DE GUICHE. [*Who has gone upstage.*] The regiment! It's leaving!

ROXANE. [*To* CYRANO, *clutching* CHRISTIAN, *whom he is still trying to lead away.*] I trust you to look after him! Promise me that nothing will endanger his life!

CYRANO. I'll do my best, but I can't promise anything.

ROXANE. [*Still holding* CHRISTIAN *back.*] Promise me that you'll make him be very careful!

CYRANO. I'll try, but . . .

ROXANE. [*Still holding* CHRISTIAN.] Promise me that he'll never be cold during that terrible siege!

CYRANO. I'll do whatever I can, but . . .

⁵¹ ROXANE. [*Still holding* CHRISTIAN.] Promise me that he'll write often!

CYRANO. [*Stopping.*] Ah! That's one thing I can promise you!

Cyrano de Bergerac, Act III **509**

PAGE SUMMARY: AT A GLANCE

- De Guiche realizes Roxane and Christian have gotten married.
- He announces that the Cadets will go to war after all.
- A distraught Roxane pleads with Cyrano to look after Christian; Cyrano agrees to do what he can.

IN THE GLOSSARY

- candelabrum: a large candlestick with holders for several candles

49 CULTURAL BACKGROUND

Explain that the actual Bergerac did write a fantasy about a trip to the moon, *Le voyage dans la lune*, after his return from Arras. He also wrote another fantasy, maxims, a study of physics, and two plays.

50 TEACHING DRAMATIC IRONY

Point out the irony of Christian's remark: As the audience well knows, Cyrano does indeed know how hard it is to leave Roxane.

51 TEACHING DRAMATIC IRONY

Help students understand the dramatic irony here: Cyrano can promise Christian will write because (as the audience knows) Cyrano welcomes the opportunity to continue expressing *his* love.

COLLABORATIVE LEARNING: ENRICHMENT ACTIVITY

Humanities The role of Cyrano has been played by many well-known actors, including Constant Coquelin (the first Cyrano), José Ferrer, Walter Hampden, Ralph Richardson, Gino Cervi, Jean Piat, Christopher Plummer, and Gérard Depardieu. Have students work in groups to research different productions of the play.

CRITICAL THINKING: GUIDED READING QUESTIONS

LITERAL

1a. What does De Guiche tell Roxane after the Capuchin announces her marriage? (She must now say good-by to her husband.)

2a. What does Roxane ask Cyrano to do to protect Christian? (She asks him to make sure nothing endangers Christian's life, to make sure Christian is careful, and to make sure Christian doesn't get cold.)

INFERENTIAL

→ **1b.** Why does De Guiche change his mind about sending the Cadets to war? (He recognizes the trick that Roxane has played on him and decides to deny her her happiness.)

→ **2b.** What do Roxane's requests suggest about her ideas about Cyrano? (Students may suggest that she sees him as strong and powerful; they may also suggest that she sees him as less important than Christian.)

Is Roxane wrong to want both physical and spiritual beauty in the man she loves? Explain your answer.

ANSWERS

STUDY QUESTIONS

1. His eloquence in speaking is matched only by his writing; she has memorized all of his letters.

2. Christian insists on speaking to Roxane for himself; Roxane responds to his awkwardness with scorn and sends him away; Christian turns to Cyrano for help.

3. Cyrano says that he has never spoken to her from his heart, and he is overwhelmed by his love. She responds with an intense admission of love.

4. She pretends that the letter she has received contains an order from Cardinal Richelieu that she marry Christian.

5. He disguises himself and pretends to be a madman who has fallen from the moon; De Guiche orders Christian and Cyrano to join their regiment at Arras.

6. He might be happy that Roxane is responding to his words but sad that she does not realize they are his.

7. The richness and passion of Cyrano's spirit in his speech to Roxane allows him to triumph over the realities of his appearance; the ingenuity of the story allows him to captivate De Guiche and prevent him from seeing what is happening between Roxane and Christian.

8. He is selfless toward Roxane, for whose happiness he would sacrifice his own; he has turned her into an ideal to love; he insists on following his own course, no matter what enemies he makes.

9. Answers will vary. Students may say that Cyrano's superior skill at expressing his love verbally is not in itself evidence that his love is deeper than Christian's.

LITERARY FOCUS

Sample responses follow.
1. Cyrano would stand below the balcony wearing a cloak and holding a plumed hat. Looking up at Roxane, he would be

---

STUDY QUESTIONS

Recalling

1. In the beginning of Act III, what does Roxane tell Cyrano about Christian and his letters?

2. Explain the circumstances that lead to Cyrano's speech under the balcony to Roxane.

3. During the balcony speech what does Cyrano tell Roxane about his feelings for her? Describe Roxane's response to him.

4. Explain how Roxane arranges for her marriage to Christian.

5. What does Cyrano do to delay De Guiche, and what does De Guiche do to retaliate?

Interpreting

6. Describe Cyrano's mixed feelings when he speaks to Roxane unseen. Why might he be both happy and sad?

7. Explain how Cyrano's speech to Roxane and his deception of De Guiche each represents a triumph of the imagination over physical reality.

8. An idealist is someone who follows his or her beliefs beyond the point of practicality and who acts as if the world were better than it really is. From what you have seen of Cyrano so far, show how he is an idealist.

Extending

9. Do you think a love like Cyrano's is actually greater than a love like Christian's? Why or why not?

LITERARY FOCUS

Staging and Character

Because plays are written to be performed by actors for an audience, acting is a vital part of any dramatic work. Actors greatly increase the impact of a play by creating living, breathing people from the playwright's words. In addition, actors can emphasize certain aspects of the characters, presenting the audience with a particular interpretation not simply of their characters but of the play as a whole.

The role of Cyrano is a favorite one for actors because it is so colorful and lends itself to different interpretations. Some actors have played Cyrano as a big-voiced swashbuckler; others, as a soft-spoken poet. Some actors have emphasized Cyrano's wit; others, his pride; still others, his bittersweet love of Roxane. In order to appreciate the play fully, we should imagine what dimensions an actor's performance might add to Cyrano's words.

Thinking About Staging and Character

Look again at the balcony scene in Act III of this play, and decide how you would direct the actor playing the role of Cyrano. You might want to keep the following questions in mind:

1. How far would Cyrano be from Roxane? Would he look at Roxane throughout his speech to her?

2. Would Cyrano speak softly or in full voice? Would he grow louder or softer during his speech to Roxane?

---

able to see her back and part of her face. As he begins to speak, he might kneel and put one hand on his chest and hold his hat with the other. He would vacillate between profound joy and melancholy. He would watch Roxane to see how his words affected her and might show the greatest emotion when repeating her name.

2. His voice would probably be tremulous and soft at first and would grow louder and become filled with conviction.

ACT IV

The post occupied by CARBON DE CASTEL-JALOUX's *company in the siege of Arras. About a month later.*

[*In the background, an embankment crosses the entire stage. Beyond is a plain covered with siegeworks. Far off in the distance, the walls and rooftops of Arras are silhouetted against the sky. Tents, scattered weapons, drums, etc. Daybreak is near. Yellowish glow in the east. Sentries at intervals. Campfires. Wrapped in their cloaks, the* GASCON CADETS *are asleep.* CARBON *and* LE BRET *are awake. They are both pale and gaunt.* CHRISTIAN, *sleeping like the others, is in the foreground, with the light of a campfire on his face. Silence.*]

LE BRET. It's horrible!

CARBON. Yes. Not one scrap of food left.

[*A few shots are heard in the distance.*]

CARBON. Those shots! They'll wake my children! [*To the* CADETS, *who have begun to raise their heads.*] Go back to sleep! [*The* CADETS *settle down again, then there are more shots, from closer range.*]

A CADET. [*Stirring.*] What, again?

CARBON. It's nothing, only Cyrano coming back. [*The heads that have been raised are lowered again.*]

THE SENTRY ON THE PARAPET. Halt! Who goes there?

CYRANO. [*Appearing on the parapet.*] Bergerac, you idiot! [*Comes down from the parapet.* LE BRET *anxiously goes forward to meet him.*]

LE BRET. Thank God you're back!

CYRANO. [*Motioning him not to awaken anyone.*] Sh!

LE BRET. Are you wounded?

1 CYRANO. You know very well that they make it a habit to miss me every morning!

LE BRET. Don't you think it's going a little too far to risk your life every day to send a letter?

CYRANO. [*Stopping in front of* CHRISTIAN.] I promised he would write often! [*Looks at him.*] He's asleep. His face is pale. If poor Roxane knew he was dying of hunger . . . But he's still handsome!

LE BRET. You ought to bring us some food.

CYRANO. I have to travel light to get through! . . . But you can expect a change by this evening. If I saw what I think I saw, the French will soon either eat or die.

LE BRET. Tell me about it!

CYRANO. No, I'm not sure. . . . You'll see!

2 CARBON. We're the besiegers, and yet we're starving! It's shameful!

LE BRET. Unfortunately, nothing could be more complicated than this siege. We're besieging Arras, we ourselves are caught in a trap, the Cardinal Prince of Spain is besieging us. . . .

LE BRET. Excuse me if I don't laugh.

CYRANO. You're excused.

LE BRET. To think that every day you risk a life like yours to carry . . . [*Sees* CYRANO *walking toward a tent.*] Where are you going?

CYRANO. I'm going to write another one. [*Lifts the flap of the tent and disappears. Reveille[1] is heard.*]

CARBON. [*With a sigh.*] Reveille, alas! [*The* CADETS *stir in their cloaks and stretch.*] Their delicious

---

1. **reveille** [rev'ə lē]: signal on bugle or drum to waken soldiers.

Cyrano de Bergerac, Act IV **511**

- The Cadets complain about their hunger.
- Cyrano tries to distract them with nostalgic images and melodies of Gascony.

IN THE GLOSSARY

- martial: relating to war

3 TEACHING CONFLICT

Ask students what serious external conflicts the Cadets face. (battle and starvation)

4 TEACHING CHARACTERIZATION

Ask students to identify the way in which Cyrano remains true to his character, even in war. (He remains flippant, quick witted, and jocular even in this tragic situation.)

5 TEACHING THEME

Help students see that Cyrano's nobility and idealism remain intact even under the harsh conditions of war.

6 TEACHING CHARACTERIZATION

Point out the bravado in Cyrano's speech about death and what it reveals about his character: Ever the showman, Cyrano hopes that his death will be filled with drama and high style.

7 TEACHING FIGURATIVE LANGUAGE

Call attention to the way Cyrano turns to poetic similes and lyrical descriptions to distract the Cadets.

sleep has ended, and I know only too well what their first words will be!

A CADET. [*Sitting up.*] I'm hungry!

3 ANOTHER. I'm starving!

ALL. Oh! . . .

CARBON. On your feet, all of you!

FIRST CADET. [*Looking at himself in a piece of polished armor.*] My tongue is yellow—living on air has given me indigestion!

SECOND CADET. We must have food!

CARBON. [*Calling softly into the tent where CYRANO has gone.*] Cyrano!

OTHER CADETS. We're dying!

CARBON. [*Still softly, standing at the doorway of the tent.*] I need your help! You always know how to answer them—come and cheer them up!

SECOND CADET. [*Hurrying to the* FIRST CADET, *who is chewing something.*] What are you eating?

FIRST CADET. Ammunition wadding cooked in axle grease, using a steel helmet as a pot. There's not much game in this country!

CYRANO. [*Calmly coming out of the tent with a quill pen behind his ear and a book in his hand.*] What's the trouble? [*Silence. He speaks to the* FIRST CADET.] Why are you standing so stiffly?

FIRST CADET. I have to.

CYRANO. Why?

FIRST CADET. My stomach is so empty that if I bend at the waist I'll break in half!

4 CYRANO. Be glad you've lost weight: it may save your life.

FIRST CADET. How?

CYRANO. By making you a smaller target for the enemy!

5 THIRD CADET. Why is it that *you* never complain about hunger?

CYRANO. Because there's one thing I'm not hungry enough to swallow: my pride.

FIRST CADET. [*Shrugging.*] You're never at a loss for a clever remark.

6 CYRANO. Yes, and I hope that when death comes to me it will find me fighting in a good cause and making a clever remark! I want to be struck down by the only noble weapon, the sword, wielded by an adversary worthy of me, and to die not in a sickbed but on the field of glory, with sharp steel in my heart and a flash of wit on my lips!

ALL THE CADETS. [*Shouting.*] I'm hungry!

CYRANO. [*Folding his arms.*] Can't you think of anything but food? . . . Come here, Bertrandou.[2] You're a fifer[3] now, but you were once a shepherd; take out your fife and play some of the old 7 Gascon music for the gluttons! Let them hear those soft, haunting melodies in which each note is like a little sister, melodies that hold the sound of loved voices and have the slowness of smoke rising from the chimneys of our home villages, melodies that speak to us in our mother tongue! [BERTRANDOU *begins playing melodies from the south of France.*] Listen, Gascons. . . . He's no longer playing the martial fife: it's now the flute of our forests! It's not a call to battle, but the slow piping of our goatherds! Listen. . . . It's our valleys, our moors, our woodlands; it's a dark-haired little cowherd wearing a red beret; it's the sweetness of evenings on the banks of the Dordogne[4]. . . . Listen, Gascons: it's all of Gascony!

[*The* CADETS *have all sat down and dreamily*

---

2. **Bertrandou** [bār'tron doō']
3. **fifer:** one who plays a fife, an instrument like a flute that often accompanies a military drum.
4. **Dordogne** [dôr dō'nyə]: river in region of same name.

CRITICAL THINKING: GUIDED READING QUESTIONS

LITERAL

1a. What kind of help does Carbon ask of Cyrano? (He asks Cyrano to answer the Cadets' complaints about hunger and to cheer them up.)

2a. How does Cyrano behave despite his own discomfort? (He jokes and talks with bravado about facing death.)

INFERENTIAL

1b. What does this reveal about Cyrano's place in the regiment? (Though not commander, he is the Cadets' natural leader.)

2b. What does this reveal about Cyrano's general attitude toward life? (He does not let misfortune daunt his optimism.)

bowed their heads. Now and then one of them furtively wipes away a tear with his sleeve or his cloak.]

CARBON. [*Softly, to* CYRANO.] You're making them weep!

CYRANO. Yes, from homesickness! It's a nobler pain than hunger. I'm glad that their suffering has shifted from their bellies to their hearts.

CARBON. You'll weaken them by stirring up such feelings!

CYRANO. [*Motioning the drummer to approach.*] Not at all! The courage in their blood is easily awakened. It takes only . . . [*He makes a gesture and the drummer beats a roll.*]

ALL THE CADETS. [*Leaping to their feet and rushing for their weapons.*] What?—Where?—What is it?

CYRANO. [*Smiling.*] You see? It takes only a drumbeat! Farewell dreams, regrets . . .

8 A CADET. Oh! Here comes Monsieur de Guiche! [*The* CADETS *all murmur irritably.*]

CYRANO. [*Smiling.*] That's a flattering greeting!

THE CADET. He annoys us!

SECOND CADET. He's coming to strut in front of us with his big lace collar over his armor!

SECOND CADET. He's not a soldier, he's a courtier!

CARBON. He's still a Gascon.

LE BRET. He looks pale.

THIRD CADET. He's hungry, like the rest of us poor devils, but since his armor has gilded studs, his stomach cramps glitter in the sunlight!

CYRANO. [*Urgently.*] We mustn't let him see us looking miserable! Take out your cards, your pipes, your dice. . . . [*They all quickly begin playing cards and dice on drums, stools, and*

their cloaks spread out on the ground, and they light their long pipes.] As for me, I'm going to read Descartes.[5]

[*He walks slowly back and forth, reading from a small book that he has taken from his pocket. Tableau.* DE GUICHE *enters. The* CADETS *all seem happily absorbed in what they are doing.* DE GUICHE *is very pale. He walks toward* CARBON.]

DE GUICHE. [*To* CARBON.] Ah! Good morning! [*Aside, with satisfaction, after they have observed each other a moment.*] He looks green around the gills!

CARBON. [*Aside, also with satisfaction.*] His eyes are sunken, and big as saucers!

DE GUICHE. [*Looking at the* CADETS.] So here are the grumblers! . . . Yes, gentlemen, it's been reported to me from all sides that you jeer at me, that you rustic barons have nothing but contempt for your colonel. [*Silence. The* CADETS *continue their games and smoking.*] Am I going to have you punished by your captain? No.

CARBON. Let me point out to you that I'm free to do as I see fit, and I don't choose to punish my 9 men. I've paid for my company; it's my own. I obey only battle orders.

DE GUICHE. That will do! [*To the* CADETS.] I can afford to despise your mockery, because my 10 conduct under fire is well known. Only yesterday, at Bapaume, I furiously drove back Count de Bucquoi.[6] Bringing my men down upon his like an avalanche, I charged three times!

CYRANO. [*Without looking up from his book.*] And don't forget your white scarf.

DE GUICHE. [*Surprised and pleased.*] Ah, you know about that? . . . Yes, as I was rallying my

---

5. **Descartes** [dā kärt′]: René Descartes (1596–1650), French philosopher and mathematician.
6. **Bapaume** [bä pōm′], **de Bucquoi** [də bū kwä′]

Cyrano de Bergerac, Act IV **513**

PAGE SUMMARY: AT A GLANCE

- Cyrano's remembrances of Gascony cause some Cadets to weep.
- To the Cadets' disdain De Guiche arrives; the Cadets try to hide their misery.
- De Guiche chastises them for grumbling and brags of his exploits; Cyrano subtly challenges him.

8 TEACHING CHARACTERIZATION

Point out that until now De Guiche has been seen only through the eyes of those who have a personal reason to dislike him. Now the more objective Cadets confirm his character as pretentious and vain.

9 CULTURAL BACKGROUND

Explain that as late as the American Revolution, free companies formed a large part of any army. Soldiers enlisted under a well-known leader, who then offered his services to a general. The captain of a free company paid his own men, and they were responsible only to him; they could not be disciplined even by the commander-in-chief.

10 TEACHING DIALOGUE

Ask what this exchange implies about De Guiche. Students should see that De Guiche is a braggart (and that Cyrano hints that he is lying). They should also note that De Guiche appears rather defensive despite his pretense of not caring about the Cadets' opinion.

CRITICAL THINKING: GUIDED READING QUESTIONS

LITERAL

1a. What does Cyrano tell the Cadets to do when they see De Guiche coming? (He tells them to get out their cards, pipes, and dice.)

2a. What comment does Cyrano make after De Guiche brags about his conduct under fire? (He says, "And don't forget your white scarf.")

INFERENTIAL

1b. Why is it important to him that De Guiche not see the Cadets looking miserable? (De Guiche has contempt for the Cadets; Cyrano's pride forbids their exposing any vulnerability to him.)

2b. What does this comment tell you? (It suggests that Cyrano knows that De Guiche's behavior has been less valiant than De Guiche claims.)

- De Guiche says he dropped his scarf in order to slip by the Spaniards unnoticed and then return for an attack.
- He says that the scarf lies behind enemy lines; Cyrano hands it to him.
- De Guiche reveals that the enemy is about to attack the Gascon Cadets.

11 CULTURAL BACKGROUND

Explain that military strategy dictates killing or capturing officers first in order to leave troops leaderless and ineffective. De Guiche realizes this and in a cowardly way disposes of his emblem of rank.

12 TEACHING THEME

Note that Cyrano articulates his own ideas of honor and courage: He will not save his skin at the expense of ideals. Help students see that De Guiche serves throughout most of the play as a foil for Cyrano's idealism.

13 TEACHING CHARACTERIZATION

Ask students what Cyrano's possession of the white scarf shows about his character. (He takes many risks.)

14 TEACHING PLOT: RISING ACTION

Be sure students recognize that De Guiche reveals two important pieces of information: (1) food is on the way; (2) the Cadets are vulnerable to attack because half the army has gone for supplies.

---

11 men for the third charge, I was caught in a rush of fugitives and swept along toward the enemy. I was in danger of being captured or shot when I had the good sense to take off the scarf that showed my rank and drop it on the ground. I was thus able to slip away from the Spaniards without attracting attention, then come back to them, followed by all my men, and beat them! . . . Well, what do you think of that?

[*The* CADETS *do not seem to have been listening, but they now stop puffing on their pipes and suspend the movements of their card and dice games; they are waiting.*]

CYRANO. I think that Henry the Fourth[7] would never have given up his white plume, even when surrounded by the enemy.

[*Silent joy among the* CADETS. *They resume laying down their cards, rolling their dice, and smoking their pipes.*]

DE GUICHE. But my trick succeeded! [*The* CADETS *again become motionless, waiting.*]

12 CYRANO. Perhaps, but I don't believe in declining the honor of being a target. [*The* CADETS *resume their activities with growing satisfaction.*] You and I, sir, have different ideas of courage. If I had been there when you dropped the scarf, I would have picked it up and put it on.

DE GUICHE. That's nothing but Gascon bragging!

CYRANO. Bragging? Lend me the scarf and accept my offer to wear it while I lead an assault today.

DE GUICHE. And that's a Gascon offer! You know very well that my scarf remained on the river bank, in a place that's now under heavy enemy fire, so that no one can go and bring it back.

---

7. **Henry the Fourth** (1553–1610): king of France from 1589 to 1610, who often led his army in battle. Before a battle he told his soldiers, "If you lose your banners, rally around my white plume; you will always find it on the path of honor and glory."

---

13 CYRANO. [*Taking the white scarf from his pocket and holding it out to* DE GUICHE.] Here it is.

[*Silence. The* CADETS *stifle their laughter behind their cards and dice cups.* DE GUICHE *turns around and looks at them. They immediately take on serious expressions and resume their games. One of them casually whistles a melody played earlier by the fifer.*]

DE GUICHE. [*Taking the scarf.*] Thank you. Now that I have this piece of white cloth, I can use it for a signal that I was hesitating to make. [*Climbs to the top of the embankment and waves the scarf several times.*]

ALL THE CADETS. What! . . .

THE SENTINEL ON THE PARAPET. I see a man down there, running away!

DE GUICHE. [*Returning.*] He's a false Spanish spy. He's very useful to me. He reports to the enemy whatever I tell him, which makes it possible for us to influence their decisions. Now, what was I saying? . . . Ah, yes, I was about to tell you some 14 news. Last night, in a supreme effort to get food for us, the Marshal quietly left for Dourlens,[8] where our supplies are. He'll arrive there by traveling across the fields, but in order to come back safely he took so many troops with him that we're now extremely vulnerable to an enemy attack: half the army is absent!

CARBON. If the Spaniards knew that . . . But they don't, do they?

DE GUICHE. Yes, they know. And they're going to attack.

CARBON. Ah!

DE GUICHE. My false spy came to warn me. He said, "I can make the attack come at any place you like, by reporting that it's your most weakly

---

8. **Dourlens** [dōōr lon′]

CRITICAL THINKING: GUIDED READING QUESTIONS

LITERAL

1a. Of what does De Guiche accuse Cyrano when he offers to wear the white scarf in battle? (He accuses him of bragging.)

2a. What do the Cadets do when Cyrano produces the white scarf? (They stifle their laughter and resume their games; one resumes a melody that was played earlier.)

INFERENTIAL

1b. How does Cyrano's return of the white scarf refute that charge? (In order to get it, Cyrano must have had to brave heavy enemy fire, thus proving he wouldn't be afraid to risk his life in battle.)

2b. How do you think the Cadets' behavior makes De Guiche feel? (It probably angers or humiliates him.)

defended point. Just tell me where." I answered, "Very well, leave the camp and watch our lines. I'll signal to you from the place I've chosen."

CARBON. [*To the* CADETS.] Gentlemen, prepare yourselves. [*They all stand up. Sounds of swords and sword belts being buckled on.*]

DE GUICHE. The attack will begin in an hour.

FIRST CADET. Oh. . . . In that case . . . [*They all sit down again and resume their games.*]

DE GUICHE. [*To* CARBON.] The most important thing is to gain time. The Marshal will soon be on his way back.

CARBON. And how shall we gain time?

DE GUICHE. You will be so kind as to fight till the last of you is killed.

15 CYRANO. Ah, so that's your revenge?

DE GUICHE. I won't pretend that if I liked you I would have chosen you and your men, but since you're known to be incomparably brave, I'm serving my king by serving my rancor.

CYRANO. [*Bowing.*] Allow me to be grateful to you, sir.

16 DE GUICHE. [*Returning his bow.*] I know that you like to fight against odds of a hundred to one. I'm sure this is an opportunity you wouldn't have wanted to miss. [*Goes upstage with* CARBON. *Preparations to meet the attack are being made.* CYRANO *goes to* CHRISTIAN, *who is standing motionless, with his arms folded.*]

CYRANO. [*Putting his hand on* CHRISTIAN's *shoulder.*] Christian?

CHRISTIAN. [*Shaking his head.*] Roxane. . . .

CYRANO. Yes, I know. . . .

CHRISTIAN. I wish I could at least pour out my heart to her in one last letter.

CYRANO. I thought something might happen today, so . . . [*Takes a letter from his doublet.*] . : . I wrote your farewell.

CHRISTIAN. Let me see!

CYRANO. Do you want . . .

CHRISTIAN. [*Taking the letter.*] Of course! [*Opens it and begins reading it, then stops.*] What's this?

CYRANO. Where?

CHRISTIAN. Here—this little stain.

17 CYRANO. [*Quickly takes the letter back and looks at it with an innocent expression.*] A stain?

CHRISTIAN. It was made by a tear!

CYRANO. Yes. . . . A poet is sometimes caught up in his own game; that's what makes it so fascinating. This letter, you understand . . . It was so moving that I made myself weep while I was writing it.

CHRISTIAN. Weep?

CYRANO. Yes, because . . . Dying is no great matter. What's unbearable is the thought of never seeing her again. And it's true: I'll never see her . . . [CHRISTIAN *looks at him.*] . . . we'll never . . . [*Quickly.*] . . . you'll never . . .

CHRISTIAN. [*Snatching the letter from him.*] Give me that letter!

18 [*A distant clamor is heard from the edge of the camp.*]

CARBON. What is it?

THE SENTRY. [*Now on the parapet.*] A carriage! [*Everyone rushes to look.*]

VOICES. What!—It seems to have come from the direction of the enemy!—Shoot!—No! Didn't you hear what the driver shouted?—He said, "King's service!" [*Everyone is now on the parapet, looking down. The sound of jingling bells is coming closer.*]

Cyrano de Bergerac, Act IV **515**

- De Guiche reveals that he has arranged to have the enemy attack the Cadets.
- Facing death, Christian wants to write to Roxane.
- Cyrano has already written to her and produces a tear-stained letter.
- A carriage approaches.

15 TEACHING CONFLICT

Remind students that De Guiche and Cyrano have represented sharply different values and have been enemies throughout the play. Point out that here the conflict between De Guiche and Cyrano is acknowledged openly as De Guiche prepares to take his final revenge.

16 TEACHING TONE

Remind students that in Act I Cyrano protected the poet Lignière by fighting off a force of one hundred men who had been hired by De Guiche. Ask students to characterize De Guiche's tone in this speech. (It is bitter and sarcastic.)

17 READING SKILL: INFERENCE

Ask students what the tear stain on the letter reveals about Cyrano. (It reveals the depth of Cyrano's love and suffering.)

18 CRITICAL THINKING: LOGICAL REASONING

Ask students what might have occurred if this exchange were not interrupted. (Christian might have tried to elicit Cyrano's true feelings.)

CRITICAL THINKING: GUIDED READING QUESTIONS

LITERAL

1a. What words of Cyrano's alert Christian to Cyrano's true feelings for Roxane? ("What's unbearable is the thought of never seeing her again. And it's true: I'll never see her . . .")

INFERENTIAL

→ **1b.** What does Cyrano's momentary slip reveal to Christian? (Cyrano also loves Roxane.)

- Roxane arrives and describes how her carriage traveled through enemy lines.
- De Guiche, Cyrano, Le Bret, Christian, and Carbon insist that she leave immediately.

IN THE GLOSSARY

- rabble: a mass of people, usually regarded as being of a low class
- stupefaction: astonishment; bewilderment

19 TEACHING PLOT: RISING ACTION

Point out the way in which Roxane's arrival heightens the scene's tension: The Cadets await attack, Christian is on the verge of discovering Cyrano's secret, and now Roxane herself arrives.

20 TEACHING THEME

Roxane's comment shows her wit and suggests one of the play's themes: Genuine love can lead a character to grow.

21 TEACHING STAGING

Call students' attention to the way the stage direction reveals Cyrano's reaction to Roxane's arrival: His uncharacteristic paralysis and inability to speak tell how deeply affected he is.

22 TEACHING CHARACTERIZATION

Ask students what Roxane's behavior, as she traveled through Spanish lines, reveals about her personality. (She is conscious of her beauty and not above using it to get what she wants; she is brave.)

DE GUICHE. [*Shouting into the wings.*] King's service! . . . Line up, you rabble! Don't you know how to receive a carriage in the king's service?

[*The carriage enters at a rapid trot. It is covered with mud and dust. The curtains are drawn. Two* FOOTMEN *behind. It stops abruptly.*]

CARBON. [*Shouting.*] Beat the general salute! [*Ruffle of drums. All the* CADETS *take off their hats.*]

DE GUICHE. Lower the step! [*Two men rush forward. The carriage door opens.*]

19 ROXANE. [*Alighting from the carriage.*] Good morning! [*The men have bowed low; hearing the sound of a woman's voice, they all straighten up at once. Stupefaction.*]

DE GUICHE. King's service? You?

20 ROXANE. I'm in the service of the greatest of all kings: love!

CYRANO. Oh!

CHRISTIAN. [*Hurrying to her.*] You! Why?

ROXANE. This siege had lasted too long!

CHRISTIAN. Why . . .

ROXANE. I'll tell you!

21 CYRANO. [*Who, at the sound of her voice, has remained rooted to the spot, not daring to turn his eyes toward her.*] I can't look at her. . . .

DE GUICHE. You can't stay here!

ROXANE. [*Gaily.*] Yes I can! [*Laughs.*] They shot at my carriage! [*Proudly.*] We met a patrol! . . . It looks as if it had been made from a pumpkin, like the carriage in the fairy tale, doesn't it? And my footmen look as if they had once been rats. [*Throws a kiss to* CHRISTIAN.] Good morning! [*Looks at everyone.*] You don't seem very cheerful! . . . [*Notices* CYRANO.] Cousin! Delighted to see you!

516 *Drama*

CYRANO. [*Approaching.*] And I'm amazed! How . . .

ROXANE. How did I find the army? It was quite simple: I went where I saw that the countryside had been laid waste. Oh, such horrors! I would never have believed them if I hadn't seen them! Gentlemen, if that's how you serve your king, I much prefer to serve mine!

CYRANO. This is insane! How did you get here?

ROXANE. I went through the Spanish lines.

DE GUICHE. How were you able to pass?

22 ROXANE. I simply rolled along in my carriage. Whenever a Spanish officer gave me a suspicious look, I smiled at him sweetly from the window, and since, with all due deference to the French, Spaniards are the most gallant gentlemen in the world, I was always allowed to continue on my way.

CHRISTIAN. But . . .

ROXANE. What's the matter?

DE GUICHE. You must leave here!

ROXANE. Leave?

CYRANO. Yes, and quickly!

LE BRET. Immediately!

CHRISTIAN. Yes!

ROXANE. But why?

CHRISTIAN. [*Embarrassed.*] Because . . .

CYRANO. [*Embarrassed.*] In three-quarters of an hour . . .

DE GUICHE. [*Embarrassed.*] Or maybe an hour . . .

CARBON. [*Embarrassed.*] You'd better . . .

LE BRET. [*Embarrassed.*] You might . . .

ROXANE. I'm staying. There's going to be a battle, isn't there?

CRITICAL THINKING: GUIDED READING QUESTIONS

LITERAL

1a. According to Roxane, how was she able to find the army? (She says she followed the devastation of the countryside.)

2a. What do the Cadets tell Roxane she must do, and how do they tell her? (They say she must leave. They speak in an embarrassed way.)

INFERENTIAL

1b. What does this tell you about the kind of war the Cadets are fighting? (It is a hard-fought, destructive war.)

2b. Why are they embarrassed by their request? (They are reluctant to speak of the danger they are about to face.)

ALL. Oh, no!

ROXANE. He's my husband! [*Throws herself into* CHRISTIAN's *arms.*] Let them kill me with you!

CHRISTIAN. Such a look in your eyes!

ROXANE. Do I have to tell you why?

23 **DE GUICHE.** [*Desperately.*] This is a terribly dangerous post!

ROXANE. [*Turning around.*] Dangerous?

CYRANO. He knows what he's saying: he gave it to us!

ROXANE. [*To* DE GUICHE.] Ah, so you wanted to make me a widow!

DE GUICHE. Oh! I swear to you that . . .

ROXANE. No! I don't care what happens to me now! I'm staying! Besides, it's amusing.

24 **CYRANO.** What? You're both an intellectual and a heroine?

ROXANE. I'm your cousin, Monsieur de Bergerac. [*Looks at* DE GUICHE.] Don't you think it's time for you to leave? The fighting may begin. . . .

DE GUICHE. This is too much! I'm going to inspect my cannons, and then I'll come back. . . . You still have time: change your mind!

ROXANE. Never! [DE GUICHE *leaves.*]

CHRISTIAN. [*Beseechingly.*] Roxane! . . .

ROXANE. No!

FIRST CADET. [*To the others.*] She's staying!

ALL. [*Jostling one another as they hurry to make themselves more presentable.*] A comb!—Soap!—Give me a needle, I have to sew up a hole!—A ribbon!—Your mirror!—My cuffs!—Your mustache curler!—A razor!

A CADET. [*To the others.*] Now that I've seen her face, I could die without regret if I only had a little food in my stomach!

CARBON. [*Indignantly, having overheard.*] Shame! Speaking of food when an exquisite lady . . .

ROXANE. But I'm hungry too! It must be the cool air. I'd like some pâté, cold chicken, and wine. Would you please bring it to me?

[*Consternation.*]

A CADET. Bring it to you?

ANOTHER. Where can we get it?

ROXANE. [*Calmly.*] In my carriage.

ALL. What!

ROXANE. But the food will have to be carved and served. Look at my coachman a little more closely, gentlemen, and you'll recognize a valuable man. If you like, each sauce will be reheated.

THE CADETS. [*Rushing toward the carriage.*] It's Ragueneau! [*Loud cheers.*]

ROXANE. [*Watching them.*] Poor men! . . .

THE CADETS. Bravo! Bravo!

25 **RAGUENEAU.** The Spaniards were so busy feasting their eyes that they didn't eye the feast! [*Applause.*]

CYRANO. [*Softly, to* CHRISTIAN.] Christian!

RAGUENEAU. Distracted by Beauty, they overlooked . . . [*Picks up a roast suckling pig on a tray and holds it aloft.*] . . . the Beast! [*Applause. The tray is passed from hand to hand.*]

CYRANO. [*Softly, to* CHRISTIAN.] Please let me have a word with you.

26 **RAGUENEAU.** The sight they saw was so pleasant that they failed to notice . . . [*Picks up another tray.*] . . . this pheasant! [*More enthusiasm. The tray is seized by a dozen eager hands.*]

CYRANO. [*Softly, to* CHRISTIAN.] I want to talk to you! I must talk to you before you talk to her!

RAGUENEAU. [*More and more exuberant.*] The handle of my whip is a sausage!

Cyrano de Bergerac, Act IV **517**

CRITICAL THINKING: GUIDED READING QUESTIONS

LITERAL

1a. What do the Cadets begin to do as soon as it is clear that Roxane is staying? (They begin to tidy themselves up, making themselves presentable.)

2a. How does Ragueneau explain the way he and Roxane got so much food past the Spaniards? (He says that the Spaniards were so dazzled by Roxane's beauty they didn't investigate the carriage.)

INFERENTIAL

1b. What do these actions tell you about the effect of Roxane's presence on the Cadets? (She raises morale, helping to restore the Cadets' pride in themselves.)

2b. What does the fact that Roxane succeeded in getting food to the Cadets tell you about her? (She is intelligent, brave, resourceful, and not as frivolous as she pretends.)

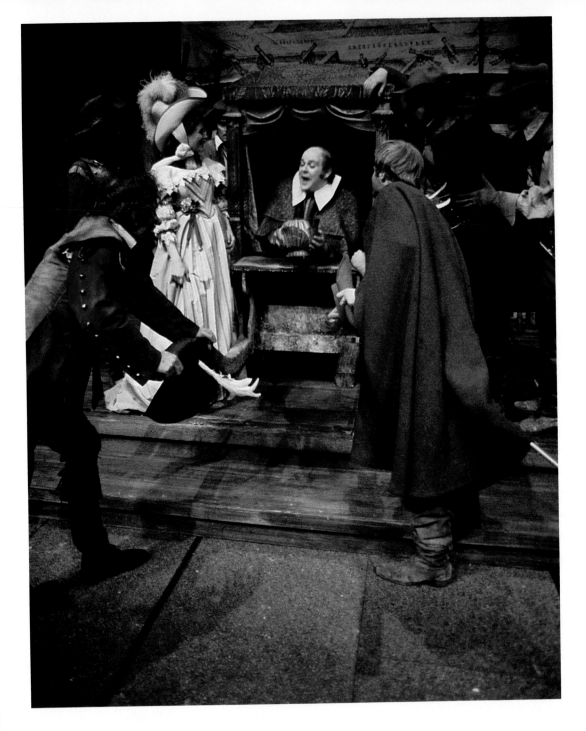

518   *Drama*

ROXANE. [*Pouring wine and handing out food.*] Since we're the ones who are going to be killed, we don't care about the rest of the army! Everything for the Gascons! And if De Guiche comes, he's not invited! [*Going from one to another.*] There's plenty of time. . . . Don't eat so fast! . . . Why are you weeping?

FIRST CADET. It's too good!

LE BRET. [*Who has gone upstage to pass a loaf of bread, at the end of a lance, to the* SENTRY *on the parapet.*] Here comes De Guiche!

CYRANO. Quickly! Hide the food, the bottles, the baskets, everything! And act as if nothing had happened! [*To* RAGUENEAU.] Hurry back to your driver's seat! . . . Is everything out of sight?

[*In the twinkling of an eye, everything is hidden in the tents or under cloaks and hats.* DE GUICHE *enters rapidly, then suddenly stops, sniffing. Silence.*]

DE GUICHE. Something smells good here.

27 A CADET. [*Casually singing.*] Tra-la-la . . .

DE GUICHE. [*Looking at him.*] What's the matter with you? Your face is red.

THE CADET. It's nothing. We'll soon be fighting, and the thought of it has made the blood rush to my head.

SECOND CADET. Poom-poom-poom . . .

DE GUICHE. [*Turning around.*] What's that?

SECOND CADET. Nothing. Just a song, a little song. . . .

DE GUICHE. You're in a gay mood!

SECOND CADET. It's because danger is approaching!

DE GUICHE. [*To* ROXANE.] Well, what have you decided?

ROXANE. I'm staying!

DE GUICHE. You must leave!

ROXANE. No!

DE GUICHE. In that case, I'll need a musket.

CARBON. What do you mean?

28 DE GUICHE. I'm staying too.

CYRANO. Sir, you've finally shown pure courage!

FIRST CADET. Are you really a Gascon, in spite of your lace?

ROXANE. What! . . .

DE GUICHE. I won't leave a woman in danger.

SECOND CADET. [*To the first.*] I think we can give him something to eat! [*The food reappears as though by magic.*]

DE GUICHE. [*His face lighting up.*] Food!

THIRD CADET. It's coming out from under every cloak!

29 DE GUICHE. [*Haughtily, controlling himself.*] Do you think I'm going to eat your leavings?

CYRANO. [*Bowing.*] You're making progress!

DE GUICHE. [*Proudly.*] An empty belly won't stop me from fighting!

FIRST CADET. [*Enthusiastically.*] Spoken like a Gascon!

DE GUICHE. [*Laughing.*] I *am* a Gascon!

FIRST CADET. It's true! He's really one of us!

CARBON. [*Reappearing on the parapet, after having disappeared behind the embankment a few moments earlier.*] I've stationed my pikemen.[9] They're ready to fight to the end! [*Points to a row of pikes showing above the parapet.*]

_____

9. **pikemen:** soldiers armed with pikes, or long wooden shafts with pointed tips of iron or steel. Pikes were used in repelling attacks on forts and other walled structures.

Cyrano de Bergerac, Act IV **519**

PAGE SUMMARY: AT A GLANCE

■ The Cadets begin to eat but hide the food when De Guiche approaches.
■ Roxane tells him that she has decided to stay.
■ He says he will stay to protect her; the Cadets accept him.

27 TEACHING DRAMATIC IRONY

This exchange is both humorous and suggestive of the deeper seriousness of the soldiers' situation. An audience may well laugh at De Guiche's ignorance at the same time as they identify with his hunger.

28 TEACHING CHARACTERIZATION

Invite students to note that De Guiche puts aside personal safety to defend Roxane. His character begins to change in this scene.

29 TEACHING THEME

Help students recognize how this exchange shows De Guiche to be a proud man willing to make sacrifices for an ideal and Cyrano to be generous enough to compliment a rival.

CRITICAL THINKING: GUIDED READING QUESTIONS

LITERAL

1a. How do the Cadets act toward De Guiche when he first arrives? (They sing and act as if they are in a gay mood.)

2a. How does De Guiche behave toward Roxane and in relation to the food? (He refuses to leave the battle scene because he wants to protect her; he refuses food out of pride, though he is starving.)

INFERENTIAL

1b. Why do the Cadets act this way? (They want to taunt De Guiche.)

2b. Why do these actions cause the Cadets and Cyrano to have more respect for De Guiche? (His sudden carelessness about his own well-being in order to protect Roxane and his pride appeal to the brave, idealistic Gascon Cadets.)

- Roxane goes off with De Guiche to inspect the troops.
- Cyrano confesses to Christian that he has written to Roxane more often than Christian knows.
- Roxane returns and reveals that she loves Christian more deeply than before because of his letters.

IN THE GLOSSARY

- infested: spread over; overrun

30 TEACHING CONFLICT

Point out that Cyrano's revelation shows one of his major conflicts: his need to conceal from Christian his own love for Roxane.

31 TEACHING CHARACTERIZATION

Ask students what Cyrano's revelation about the frequency of his letters tells about him. (His love for Roxane is overwhelming and compelling.)

32 TEACHING DIALOGUE

Have students note how this dialogue reveals that Christian expects to hear how Roxane loves him and cannot stay away. He hardly considers the letters, most of which he had nothing to do with.

33 TEACHING FIGURATIVE LANGUAGE

Help students recognize how a simile ("Each page was like a petal fallen from your soul") and a metaphor ("felt the flame . . .") suggest the powerful effect of Cyrano's letters.

DE GUICHE. [*To* ROXANE, *bowing*.] Will you accept my hand and go with me to inspect them?

[*She takes his hand and they go upstage toward the embankment. The others follow them, taking off their hats.*]

CHRISTIAN. [*Hurrying to* CYRANO.] Tell me what you have to say, quickly! What's your secret?

CYRANO. If Roxane should . . .

CHRISTIAN. Yes?

CYRANO. If she should speak to you about the letters . . .

CHRISTIAN. Go on!

30 CYRANO. Don't make the mistake of being surprised if . . .

CHRISTIAN. If what?

CYRANO. You've . . . you've written to her more often than you think.

CHRISTIAN. I have?

CYRANO. Yes. I made myself the interpreter of your passion. I sometimes wrote to her without telling you so.

CHRISTIAN. Oh!

CYRANO. It's quite simple!

CHRISTIAN. But we're blockaded! How did you send those letters?

CYRANO. I was able to get through the enemy lines before dawn.

31 CHRISTIAN. [*Folding his arms*.] And I suppose that was quite simple too? . . . How often have I been writing? Twice a week? Three times? Four?

CYRANO. More than that.

CHRISTIAN. Every day?

CYRANO. Yes, every day . . . twice.

CHRISTIAN. [*Violently*.] And you were carried

520 *Drama*

away by the letters you wrote! So much so that you defied death . . .

CYRANO. [*Seeing* ROXANE *returning*.] Quiet! Not in front of her! [*He quickly goes into his tent*.]

32 ROXANE. [*Hurrying to* CHRISTIAN.] And now, Christian! . . .

CHRISTIAN. [*Taking her hands*.] And now, Roxane, tell me why you traveled such appalling roads, infested with lawless soldiers, in order to join me here.

ROXANE. Because of your letters!

CHRISTIAN. What?

ROXANE. It's your fault if I'm in danger: your letters made me lose my reason! You've written so many of them in the last month, each more beautiful than the one before!

CHRISTIAN. Do you mean to say that because of a few love letters . . .

ROXANE. Yes! You can't know. . . . I've adored you since the evening when, under my window, you began to reveal your soul to me in a voice I'd never heard you use before, and when I read your letters it was like hearing that same voice.

CHRISTIAN. But . . .

33 ROXANE. I read your letters over and over, until I began to feel faint! I knew I belonged to you totally! Each page was like a petal fallen from your soul. In every word I felt the flame of a powerful, sincere love. . . .

CHRISTIAN. Powerful and sincere? Did you really feel that in my letters, Roxane?

ROXANE. Oh, yes!

CHRISTIAN. And so you came. . . .

ROXANE. I've come to ask you to forgive me—and now is the time to ask forgiveness, since we may be about to die!—for having insulted you,

---

CRITICAL THINKING: GUIDED READING QUESTIONS

LITERAL

1a. What does Cyrano want to discuss with Christian before he sees Roxane? (He wants to warn Christian that he has written to Roxane more often than Christian realizes.)

2a. What does Roxane say about her new appreciation for Christian? (Receiving so many letters has made her love him more deeply.)

INFERENTIAL

1b. Why do you suppose Cyrano kept this information from Christian in the first place? (He didn't want to reveal his ardor, because Christian might have guessed his love for Roxane.)

2b. Why do you think the letters inspired a deepening of her feelings? (The depth of the feelings expressed in the letters combined with her knowledge of the dangers of war have deepened her own feelings.)

in my frivolity, by first loving you only because you were handsome.

CHRISTIAN. [*In consternation.*] Oh, Roxane!

34 ROXANE. Later, when I became a little less frivolous, I was like a bird hopping before taking flight, held back by your handsome face and drawn forward by your soul. I then loved you for both of them together.

CHRISTIAN. And now?

ROXANE. Your true self has prevailed over your outer appearance. I now love you for your soul alone.

CHRISTIAN. [*Stepping back.*] Oh, Roxane!

ROXANE. I know how painful it is for a noble heart to be loved because of an accident of nature that will soon pass away. But you can be happy now: your thoughts outshine your face. Your handsomeness was what first attracted me, but now that my eyes are open I no longer see it!

CHRISTIAN. Oh! . . .

35 ROXANE. Do you still doubt your victory?

CHRISTIAN. I don't want it! I want to be loved simply for . . .

ROXANE. For what women have always loved in you till now? Let me love you in a better way!

CHRISTIAN. No! It was better before!

ROXANE. You don't know what you're saying! It's better now! I didn't really love you before. It's what makes you yourself that I now love. If you were less handsome . . .

CHRISTIAN. Enough!

ROXANE. I'd still love you. If you suddenly became ugly . . .

CHRISTIAN. Oh, don't say that!

ROXANE. I *will* say it!

CHRISTIAN. Even if I were ugly? . . .

ROXANE. Yes, even if you were ugly! I swear I'd still love you! Now are you happy?

CHRISTIAN. [*Choking.*] Yes. . . .

ROXANE. What's the matter?

CHRISTIAN. [*Gently pushing her away.*] Nothing. I must go and say a few words to someone. It will take only a minute.

ROXANE. But . . .

CHRISTIAN. [*Pointing to a group of* CADETS *in the background.*] My love has taken you away from those poor men. Go and smile at them a little, since they're about to die.

ROXANE. [*Deeply moved.*] Dear Christian! . . . [*She goes to the* CADETS, *who eagerly but respectfully crowd around her.*]

CHRISTIAN. [*Calling outside* CYRANO's *tent.*] Cyrano?

CYRANO. [*Coming out of the tent, armed for battle.*] Yes? Oh! How pale you are!

CHRISTIAN. She doesn't love me any more!

CYRANO. What!

36 CHRISTIAN. It's you she loves!

CYRANO. No!

CHRISTIAN. She loves only my soul now!

CYRANO. No!

CHRISTIAN. Yes! That means it's you she loves—and you love her too!

CYRANO. I?

CHRISTIAN. I know it's true.

37 CYRANO. Yes, it's true.

CHRISTIAN. You love her with all your heart.

CYRANO. More than that.

CHRISTIAN. Tell her so!

Cyrano de Bergerac, Act IV **521**

PAGE SUMMARY: AT A GLANCE

- Roxane tells Christian she now loves him for his inner qualities, not for his looks.
- Broken-hearted, Christian tells Cyrano that it is Cyrano Roxane really loves.
- He forces Cyrano to admit his love for her.

IN THE GLOSSARY

- frivolity: silliness; playfulness

34 TEACHING DRAMATIC IRONY

Help students recognize that the power of this scene derives from its dramatic irony: To the audience and Christian, Roxane's words mean more than she knows. If she loves Christian's "soul," then she loves Cyrano.

35 TEACHING CONFLICT

Point out Christian's internal conflict: He still wants Roxane's love but now knows who deserves it.

36 TEACHING THEME

Have students note the way in which Christian shows that nobility of character requires self-sacrifice. He tells Cyrano that Roxane loves him, and he urges his friend to confess his own love to her.

37 TEACHING PLOT: RISING ACTION

Ensure that students are aware of the way the plot quickens and, with Cyrano's revelation to Christian of his love for Roxane, seems to be moving toward a climax.

CRITICAL THINKING: GUIDED READING QUESTIONS

LITERAL

1a. What does Christian say when Roxane asks him whether he still doubts his victory? ("I don't want it! I want to be loved simply for . . .")

2a. What does Cyrano say to Christian when he first enters the tent? ("How pale you are!")

INFERENTIAL

1b. Why does Christian not want such a victory in love? (The victory doesn't belong to him. He now sees that she loves Cyrano, not him.)

2b. What does Christian's paleness tell you about his state of mind? (He is stunned and heartbroken.)

- Cyrano still doubts Roxane could love an ugly man.
- Christian convinces Cyrano to tell Roxane the truth and let her choose between them.
- Roxane tells Cyrano she would love Christian even if he were disfigured.

38 CRITICAL THINKING: EVALUATION

Ask students to evaluate Cyrano's remarks. Is he right, or would Roxane really be able to love an ugly man? (Many students will think Roxane has had a true conversion and could love an ugly man with a beautiful soul. Others will think she is fooling herself and cherishes the handsome exterior.)

39 TEACHING THEME

Point out that here Cyrano and Christian raise the question that underlies the entire play: Which is more important in winning love, inner or outward beauty?

40 TEACHING PLOT: RISING ACTION

Be sure students recognize that as Christian demands that Roxane be told the truth and be allowed to make a choice, the plot is moving swiftly toward a climax.

41 TEACHING THEME

Call students' attention to the way Roxane echoes the rivals' recent questions to one another. She confirms that inner beauty is more important than outward beauty.

CYRANO. No!

CHRISTIAN. Why not?

CYRANO. Look at my face!

CHRISTIAN. She would still love me if I were ugly!

CYRANO. She told you that?

CHRISTIAN. Yes!

38 CYRANO. I'm glad she said it, but don't believe such nonsense! Yes, I'm very glad she had that thought. . . . But don't take her at her word! Don't become ugly—she would never forgive me!

CHRISTIAN. We'll see!

CYRANO. No, no!

CHRISTIAN. Let her choose! I want you to tell her everything!

CYRANO. No! I couldn't bear that torture!

39 CHRISTIAN. Do you expect me to kill your happiness because I'm handsome? That would be too unjust!

CYRANO. And do you expect me to kill yours because I happen to have been born with a gift for expressing . . . what you may feel?

CHRISTIAN. Tell her everything!

CYRANO. It's cruel of you to persist in tempting me!

CHRISTIAN. I'm tired of being my own rival!

CYRANO. Christian!

CHRISTIAN. Our wedding took place in secret, without witnesses. The marriage can be broken—if we survive!

CYRANO. You still persist! . . .

40 CHRISTIAN. I want to be loved for myself or not at all! We'll see what she decides. I'm going to walk to the end of the camp, then come back. Talk to

522 *Drama*

---

her while I'm gone, and tell her she must choose one of us.

CYRANO. It will be you!

CHRISTIAN. I hope so! [*Calls.*] Roxane!

CYRANO. No! No!

ROXANE. [*Hurrying toward them.*] Yes?

CHRISTIAN. Cyrano has something important to tell you.

[CHRISTIAN *leaves.*]

ROXANE. Something important?

CYRANO. [*Frantically.*] He's leaving! . . . [*To* ROXANE.] No, it's really nothing. . . . You must know how he is: he often sees importance where none exists!

ROXANE. [*Anxiously.*] Does he doubt what I told him? Yes, he does! I could see he doubted it!

CYRANO. [*Taking her hand.*] But was it really the truth?

ROXANE. Yes. I'd love him even if he were . . . [*Hesitates.*]

CYRANO. [*Smiling sadly.*] The word embarrasses you in front of me?

ROXANE. No, I . . .

CYRANO. It won't hurt me! You'd love him even if he were ugly?

ROXANE. Yes! [*Several musket shots are heard offstage.*] The shooting seems to have begun.

41 CYRANO. [*Ardently.*] Even if he were hideous?

ROXANE. Yes!

CYRANO. Disfigured?

ROXANE. Yes!

CYRANO. Grotesque?

ROXANE. Nothing could make him seem grotesque to me!

CRITICAL THINKING: GUIDED READING QUESTIONS

LITERAL

1a. What does Cyrano say when Christian first tells him to let Roxane choose? ("No! I couldn't bear that torture!")

2a. What do Christian and Cyrano say about obstructing each other's chances? (Christian says he will not spoil Cyrano's happiness just because he is handsome; Cyrano says he will not spoil Christian's just because he can express himself well.)

INFERENTIAL

1b. Why does Cyrano still think that revealing his love to Roxane would be "torture"? (He is still afraid that she will find his love ridiculous because of his ugliness.)

2b. What do these arguments tell you about Christian's feelings at this point? About Cyrano's? (Christian wants to win Roxane's love fairly; Cyrano seems unwilling to abandon his idealism and risk facing rejection.)

CYRANO. You'd still love him?

ROXANE. Yes! Maybe even more!

42 **CYRANO.** [*Aside, losing his head.*] Perhaps it's true! Can it be that happiness is here, within my grasp? [*To* ROXANE.] I . . . Roxane . . . Listen to me. . . .

LE BRET. [*Entering rapidly and calling softly.*] Cyrano!

CYRANO. [*Turning around.*] Yes?

LE BRET. Sh! [*Whispers something to* CYRANO, *who lets go of* ROXANE's *hand with a cry.*]

CYRANO. Oh!

ROXANE. What's the matter?

CYRANO. [*To himself, dazed.*] It's all over now. [*More shots are heard.*]

ROXANE. What is it? Those shots . . . [*Takes a few steps and looks offstage.*]

CYRANO. It's all over. Now I can never tell her!

ROXANE. What's happened?

CYRANO. [*Stopping her as she is about to rush forward.*] Nothing!

[*Some* CADETS *have entered, hiding the burden they are carrying. They group themselves to prevent* ROXANE *from approaching.*]

ROXANE. Those men . . .

CYRANO. [*Leading her away.*] Come away from them!

ROXANE. But what were you about to tell me?

43 **CYRANO.** Tell you? Oh, nothing. . . . Nothing, I swear! [*Solemnly.*] I swear that Christian's mind and soul were . . . [*Catches himself in alarm.*] . . . are the greatest . . .

ROXANE. *Were?* [*She screams, runs to the group of* CADETS, *and pushes them aside.*]

CYRANO. It's all over.

ROXANE. [*Seeing* CHRISTIAN *lying wrapped in his cloak.*] Christian!

LE BRET. [*To* CYRANO.] The first shot fired by the enemy!

44 [ROXANE *throws herself onto* CHRISTIAN. *More shots. Clatter of weapons. Voices. Drums.*]

CARBON. [*Holding his drawn sword.*] Here comes the attack! Get ready! [*Followed by the* CADETS, *he climbs over the parapet.*]

ROXANE. Christian!

CARBON'S VOICE. [*From the other side of the embankment.*] Hurry!

ROXANE. Christian!

CARBON. Fall in!

ROXANE. Christian!

CHRISTIAN. [*In a dying voice.*] Roxane . . .

45 **CYRANO.** [*Speaking rapidly and softly in* CHRISTIAN's *ear while* ROXANE, *distraught, tears a strip of cloth from her dress and dips it in the water to wash his wound.*] I told her everything. It's still you she loves! [CHRISTIAN *closes his eyes.*]

ROXANE. Yes, my love? [*To* CYRANO.] He's not dead, is he?

CARBON. Bite open your charges!

ROXANE. I feel his cheek turning cold against mine!

CARBON. Ready! Aim!

ROXANE. Here's a letter he was carrying! [*Opens it.*] For me!

CYRANO. [*Aside.*] *My* letter!

CARBON. Fire! [*Shots. Cries. Sounds of battle.*]

CYRANO. [*Trying to draw his hand away from* ROXANE, *who clutches it, kneeling.*] Roxane! The attack has begun!

ROXANE. [*Holding him back.*] Stay a little longer.

Cyrano de Bergerac, Act IV **523**

---

46 TEACHING REPETITION

Point out that by repeating, "Yes, Roxane," Cyrano spares Roxane the pain of disillusionment. Help students see that the more he repeats the phrase, the more the audience remembers that Christian was none of these things and Cyrano is all of them.

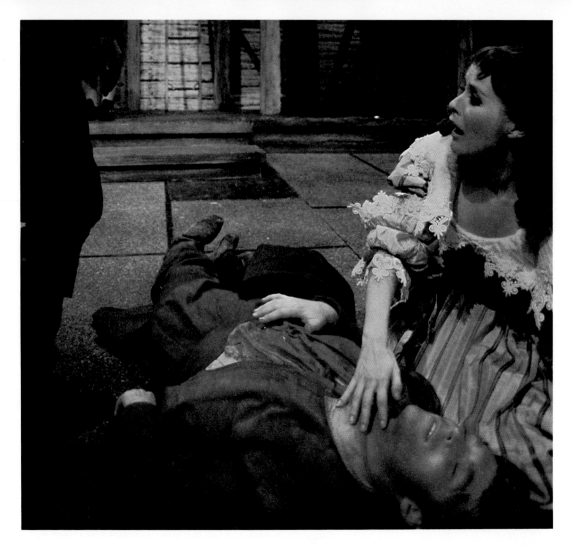

He's dead. You were the only one who knew him. [*She weeps gently.*] He was a great and wonderful man, wasn't he?

46 **CYRANO.** [*Standing, bareheaded.*] Yes, Roxane.

ROXANE. A brilliant, captivating poet!

CYRANO. Yes, Roxane.

ROXANE. A magnificent mind!

CYRANO. Yes, Roxane.

ROXANE. A vast heart whose depths remained hidden from the world! A noble and charming soul!

CYRANO. [*Firmly.*] Yes, Roxane!

ROXANE. [*Throwing herself onto* CHRISTIAN'S *body.*] He's dead!

CYRANO. [*Aside, drawing his sword.*] And now I too must die, since, without knowing it, she's mourning for me in him!

524 *Drama*

CRITICAL THINKING: GUIDED READING QUESTIONS

LITERAL

1a. What assessment of Christian does Roxane make? (She pays tribute to his powers of intellect, language, and feeling.)

INFERENTIAL

1b. Why does Cyrano assent to this evaluation when he knows it's not true? (He wants to reassure Roxane in her grief.)

[*Trumpets in the distance.* DE GUICHE *reappears on the parapet, bareheaded, with a wound on his forehead.*]

DE GUICHE. [*In a thunderous voice.*] That's the signal! A fanfare! The French are on their way back to camp with provisions! Hold fast a little longer!

ROXANE. There's blood on his letter, and tears!

47 A VOICE. [*Shouting from the other side of the embankment.*] Surrender!

CADETS' VOICES. No!

RAGUENEAU. [*Who has climbed up on his carriage to watch the battle beyond the embankment.*] They're coming closer!

CYRANO. [*To* DE GUICHE, *pointing to* ROXANE.] Take her away! I'm going to charge!

ROXANE. [*Feebly, kissing the letter.*] His blood! His tears!

RAGUENEAU. [*Leaping down from the carriage and running toward her.*] She's fainted!

DE GUICHE. [*On the parapet, shouting fiercely to the* CADETS.] Hold fast!

A VOICE. [*From beyond the embankment.*] Lay down your arms!

CADETS' VOICES. No!

48 CYRANO. [*To* DE GUICHE.] You've proved your valor, sir. [*Points to* ROXANE.] Flee now, and save her!

DE GUICHE. [*Hurrying to* ROXANE *and picking her up in his arms.*] I'll do it, for her sake. But we can win if you gain time!

CYRANO. We will! [*Watches* ROXANE, *unconscious, being carried away by* DE GUICHE *and* RAGUENEAU.] Good-by, Roxane!

[*Tumult. Shouts.* CADETS *reappear, wounded, and fall onstage.* CYRANO, *rushing toward the*

battle, is stopped on the parapet by CARBON, covered with blood.*]

CARBON. We're giving ground! I've been wounded twice!

CYRANO. [*Shouting to the* CADETS *in their native Gascon tongue. To* CARBON, *holding him up.*] Don't give up hope! I have two deaths to avenge: Christian's and that of my happiness! [*They go downstage.* CYRANO *brandishes the lance and fastens* ROXANE's *handkerchief to it.*] Float proudly, little lace banner bearing her monogram! [*Plants it on the parapet and again shouts. The fifer plays. Some of the wounded men stand up. Other* CADETS *come down the embankment and group themselves around* CYRANO *and the little flag. The carriage is filled and covered with men. Bristling with muskets, it is transformed. A* CADET *appears on the parapet, moving backward, still fighting.*]

THE CADET. [*Shouting.*] They're coming up the embankment! [*He falls dead.*]

CYRANO. We'll give them a salute! [*In an instant the parapet is crowned by a formidable line of enemy soldiers. Large Imperial banners are raised.*]

CYRANO. Fire! [*General volley.*]

A VOICE. [*Shouting from the enemy ranks.*] Fire! [*Murderous counterfire.* CADETS *fall on all sides.*]

A SPANISH OFFICER. Who are these men who have such scorn for death?

CYRANO. [*Reciting, facing the enemy fire.*]
These are the stouthearted Gascon Cadets
Of Carbon de Castel-Jaloux;
They fight over trifles and shamelessly lie. . . .

[*He rushes forward, followed by the few survivors.*]
These are the stouthearted Gascon . . .

[*The rest is lost in the tumult of battle.*]

Cyrano de Bergerac, Act IV **525**

PAGE SUMMARY: AT A GLANCE

- The Spaniards attack.
- Roxane faints, and Cyrano sends De Guiche off with her in order to save her.
- Many Cadets are killed, and Cyrano leads a suicidal charge.

47 TEACHING CHARACTERIZATION

Help students see that the Gascon Cadets are characterized as proud, valorous, and unwilling to surrender, even with the odds overwhelmingly against them.

48 TEACHING DIALOGUE

Ask students what Cyrano's comments and directive reveal about his new feelings toward De Guiche. (He sees his old enemy as brave and trustworthy.)

49 TEACHING STAGING

Point out the dramatic effect and symbolic impact of Cyrano's using Roxane's lace handkerchief to inspire him in battle. The handkerchief is a symbol of what he is fighting for: the idealism of his love, unsullied by selfishness or compromise.

COLLABORATIVE LEARNING: ENRICHMENT ACTIVITY

History War plays a central role in Act IV. Have students work in small groups to find out about the weapons and tactics that were used in the wars of Cyrano's time and to determine what life must have been like for the common soldier.

CRITICAL THINKING: GUIDED READING QUESTIONS

LITERAL

1a. What does Cyrano tell the Cadets he has to avenge? (two deaths: Christian's and that of his happiness)

2a. How does Act IV end? (Many Cadets are dead, and Cyrano is advancing on the enemy with the few survivors while reciting his tribute to the Cadets.)

INFERENTIAL

1b. What does he mean by saying that he must avenge himself for the death of his happiness? (His chance to declare his love to Roxane ended with Christian's death.)

2b. What effect does this ending create? (The act ends on a note of uncertainty. Disaster seems at hand; it is unclear how Cyrano will fare.)

ANSWERS

STUDY QUESTIONS

1. He takes a letter through enemy lines to be sent to Roxane.
2. She says she was moved to come by his letters. She says that at first she loved him for his handsomeness but because of the letters she now loves him for his soul.
3. He feels shattered, because he realizes she loves Cyrano. He asks Cyrano to tell Roxane the truth and let her choose between them.
4. Christian dies; He says Roxane knows the truth and still loves Christian.
5. her new bravery and her deep feelings for Christian; She fails to see how disturbed Christian is.
6. He realizes that Roxane truly loves Cyrano even though she does not know it and that Cyrano loves Roxane. We see a new depth of character and integrity.
7. He learns that Christian has been mortally wounded, and he cannot tell her in good conscience as Christian dies. He wants Christian to die happy.
8. Answers will vary. Some students may feel she is in love with the beauty of Cyrano's heart and soul. Others may feel that she loves the combination of Christian's handsomeness and Cyrano's beautiful soul.
9. Answers will vary. Students may say that she may have been unable to overcome her shock and grief and thus unable to respond favorably to Cyrano, that she may have refused to believe Cyrano, or she may have been unable to love anything but the ideal combination of Christian and Cyrano.
10. Answers will vary. Some students may say that his idealism and sense of fair play will prevent him from doing so. Others may feel that the strength of his feeling makes an admission inevitable.

STUDY QUESTIONS

Recalling

1. What mission does Cyrano undertake each morning at Arras?
2. How does Roxane explain the reason for her visit to the camp to Christian? According to her, how and why has her love for him changed?
3. How does Christian feel about Roxane's declaration? What does he ask Cyrano to do?
4. What event prevents Cyrano from fulfilling Christian's request? What does Cyrano tell Christian about Roxane's love?

Interpreting

5. What new dimensions does Roxane reveal in her conversation with Christian? What does she fail to see?
6. What discoveries about Roxane and Cyrano does Christian make in this act? What new sides to his character do we see?
7. Why does Cyrano not tell Roxane the truth about the letters? Why does he not tell Christian the truth about Roxane?
8. Do you agree with Christian when he says that it is really Cyrano whom Roxane loves? Explain.

Extending

9. How do you think Roxane would have responded if Cyrano had been able to tell her the truth about the letters and his feelings for her?

10. Do you think Cyrano will reveal his feelings to Roxane? Why or why not?

LITERARY FOCUS

Dramatic Plot

A play follows a **plot structure** that is similar in many ways to the plot structure of a story. In fact, since drama is an older form of literature than fiction, most of our ideas about plot originally come from ancient writers' observations about drama. The plot structure of a play, however, is usually defined more sharply than that of a story or novel. Because the audience at a play does not have the luxury of re-reading what they have just seen, every speech and event must clearly advance the action and develop the characters.

In a well-made play the exposition establishes the play's overall setting and introduces the main characters. Conflict appears very early in a drama; the rising action complicates this conflict, and the climax points toward the final outcome of this conflict. The falling action grows logically from the climax, and the resolution provides a satisfying conclusion to the play.

Thinking About Dramatic Plot

■ In the first four acts of *Cyrano de Bergerac,* identify the exposition, the major conflicts, the rising action, and the climax.

526 *Drama*

LITERARY FOCUS

Exposition—Act I introduces characters and conflicts.
Conflicts—Christian's love for Roxane and his fear that she will not love him because of his lack of eloquence; Cyrano's love for Roxane and his fear that she will not love him because of his physical ugliness
Rising action—In Act II Roxane reveals that she loves Christian; Christian and Cyrano decide to work together to create one "romantic hero" to woo Roxane. In Act III Cyrano woos Roxane alone; Christian marries her; both are sent to war.
Climax—In Act IV Cyrano is about to reveal his love when his lips are sealed by the news that Christian has been mortally wounded.

ACT V

The park of the convent occupied by the Ladies of the Cross,[1] in Paris. Fifteen years later, in 1655.

[*Magnificent shady foliage. To the left is the house, whose front steps lead up to a broad landing with several doors opening onto it. An enormous tree stands alone in the middle of the stage in a small oval-shaped open space. To the right is a semicircular stone bench among large box shrubs. It is autumn. The foliage above the green lawn has turned red. Dead leaves are falling and are strewn over the whole stage; they crackle underfoot along the lanes and half cover the bench. Between the bench on the right and the tree stands a large embroidery frame with a small chair in front of it. As the curtain rises,* NUNS *are coming and going in the park. Some are seated on the bench, around an older* NUN.]

SISTER MARTHE.[2] [*To* MOTHER MARGUERITE.[3]] Sister Claire has stopped in front of the mirror twice, to see how her headdress looks.

MOTHER MARGUERITE. [*Sternly.*] I'll tell Monsieur Cyrano this evening.

---

1. **Ladies of the Cross:** religious order.

2. **Marthe** [mär′tə]
3. **Marguerite** [mär′gə rēt′]

Cyrano de Bergerac, Act V **527**

- Roxane has been in the convent for fourteen years, and Cyrano has visited her faithfully.
- De Guiche, now a duke, is visiting her.
- Roxane reveals that she still mourns Christian.

IN THE GLOSSARY

- coquettish: flirtatious

2 TEACHING DIALOGUE

Point out the way in which the casual conversation in the act's opening lines brings the audience up to date on events that have occurred since the last act. The conversation also demonstrates Cyrano's continued devotion to Roxane.

3 CULTURAL BACKGROUND

Explain that in the seventeenth century gentlewomen often retired to convents when they suffered a special grief or fell into disgrace.

4 TEACHING CHARACTERIZATION

Ask students what these lines of dialogue indicate about Cyrano's character fifteen years later. (His idealism still keeps him poor, and his pride still prevents him from accepting help.)

5 TEACHING CHARACTERIZATION

Note that these lines indicate that De Guiche has become a worldly success and has visited Roxane occasionally during the past fifteen years.

6 TEACHING PLOT: FORESHADOWING

Point out that Roxane's comments suggest that an important event may soon occur: Roxane may soon discover that the man she loves is indeed still alive.

SISTER CLAIRE. [*Alarmed.*] No! He'll make fun of us!

SISTER MARTHE. He'll say that nuns are very coquettish!

MOTHER MARGUERITE. [*Smiling.*] And very good.

2 SISTER CLAIRE. He's been coming every Saturday for the past ten years, hasn't he, Mother Marguerite de Jésus?

MOTHER MARGUERITE. Longer than that! Ever since his cousin came to us fourteen years ago, mingling her black mourning veil with our linen hoods, like a raven among a flock of white doves.

3 SISTER MARTHE. In all the time since she first took a room in this cloister, no one but Monsieur Cyrano has ever been able to distract her from the grief that afflicts her night and day.

ALL THE NUNS. He's so amusing!—His visits are delightful!—He teases us!—Such a nice man!—We all like him!—He always appreciates the pastry we make for him!

MOTHER MARGUERITE. Well, the last time he came, he hadn't eaten anything for two days.

SISTER MARTHE. Oh, Mother!

4 MOTHER MARGUERITE. He's poor.

SISTER MARTHE. Who told you so?

MOTHER MARGUERITE. Monsieur Le Bret.

SISTER MARTHE. Doesn't anyone help him?

MOTHER MARGUERITE. No. It would only make him angry if anyone tried. [ROXANE *appears, walking slowly along a lane in the background. She is dressed in black, with a widow's cap and long veils.* DE GUICHE, *who has aged gracefully, walks beside her.* MOTHER MARGUERITE *stands up.*] Come, we must go inside. Madame Magdeleine is strolling in the park with a visitor.

SISTER MARTHE. This is the first time he's come to see her for months!

528 *Drama*

---

5 OTHER NUNS. He's very busy—The court—The army. . . .

SISTER CLAIRE. Worldly concerns!

[*The* NUNS *leave.* DE GUICHE *and* ROXANE *come downstage in silence and stop near the embroidery frame. Several moments pass.*]

THE DUKE. [*Formerly* DE GUICHE.] And so you remain here, letting your blond beauty go to waste, still in mourning?

ROXANE. Still in mourning.

THE DUKE. And still faithful?

ROXANE. Still faithful.

THE DUKE. [*After a moment of silence.*] Have you forgiven me?

ROXANE. [*Simply, looking at the cross of the convent.*] Of course, since I'm here. [*Another silence.*]

THE DUKE. Was he really such a . . .

ROXANE. He showed his true nature only to those who knew him well.

THE DUKE. His true nature? . . . Yes, perhaps I didn't know him well enough. . . . Do you still carry his last letter over your heart?

ROXANE. Yes, like a holy relic.

THE DUKE. You love him even in death?

6 ROXANE. Sometimes it seems to me that he's not really dead. I feel that our hearts are together, and that his love floats around me, very much alive!

THE DUKE. [*After another silence.*] Does Cyrano come to see you?

ROXANE. Yes, often. My old friend gives me all the news; he replaces the gazettes[4] for me. He visits

---

4. **gazettes:** newspapers.

CRITICAL THINKING: GUIDED READING QUESTIONS

LITERAL

1a. What information do the nuns give about Cyrano? (Cyrano visits Roxane weekly, is liked by the nuns, is very poor, and allows no one to help him.)

2a. What does Roxane say she sometimes senses that makes her feel that Christian is not really dead? (Their "hearts are together," and Christian's love "floats" around her, "very much alive.")

INFERENTIAL

1b. What can you infer about the changes, or lack of them, in Cyrano's life? (Cyrano's life has changed little: He loves Roxane and is still witty, idealistic, poor, and proud.)

2b. Why might Roxane sometimes feel as if Christian is alive? (The "soul" of the Christian she knew—Cyrano—is still present in her life.)

me regularly. If the weather is good, his chair is always brought out and placed under this tree. I embroider while I wait for him. When the clock strikes the hour of his arrival, I don't even turn around to look for him, because I know I'll hear his cane coming down the steps immediately after the last stroke. He sits down and laughs at my eternal tapestry. Then he begins telling me about the week's happenings, and . . . [LE BRET *appears on the steps.*] Ah! Here's Le Bret! [LE BRET *comes down.*] How is our friend doing?

LE BRET. Badly.

THE DUKE. Oh!

ROXANE. [*To the* DUKE.] He's exaggerating!

LE BRET. Cyrano is living in isolation and poverty, just as I predicted! His writings constantly make new enemies for him! He attacks false noblemen, false saints, false heroes, plagiarists—everyone!

ROXANE. But his sword fills everyone with terror. No one will ever get the best of him.

THE DUKE. [*Shaking his head.*] Who knows?

LE BRET. I'm not afraid of his meeting a violent death. Loneliness, hunger, the cold of winter creeping into his dark room—those are the assassins that will end his life! He tightens his belt one more notch every day, his poor nose has turned as pale as ivory, he has only one threadbare black coat. . . .

THE DUKE. It's certainly true that he hasn't scaled the heights of worldly success, but don't feel too sorry for him. He lives without compromise, free in both his thoughts and his acts.

LE BRET. [*Still smiling bitterly.*] Sir, you . . .

THE DUKE. [*Loftily.*] Yes, I know: I have everything and he has nothing. But I'd be honored to shake his hand. [*Bows to* ROXANE.] I must go. Good-by.

ROXANE. I'll accompany you to the door. [*The*

DUKE *bows to* LE BRET *and walks toward the steps with* ROXANE.]

THE DUKE. [*Stopping as they are climbing the steps.*] Yes, sometimes I envy him. When a man has been too successful in life, even though he hasn't done anything really wrong, he still has all sorts of reasons for feeling a little disgusted with himself. Their combined weight isn't enough to form a burden of remorse, but he can never escape a kind of vague uneasiness. As he continues to climb toward even greater success, he hears dead illusions and old regrets rustling under his mantle, like the fallen leaves swept along by the train of your black dress when you mount these steps.

ROXANE. [*Ironically.*] You're in a thoughtful mood today.

THE DUKE. Yes, I'm afraid so. [*Abruptly, just as he is about to leave.*] Monsieur Le Bret! [*To* ROXANE.] Will you excuse me? I want to have a word with him. [*Goes to* LE BRET *and speaks in a low voice.*] It's true that no one would dare to attack our friend openly, but it's also true that he's hated by many people. Only yesterday, during a card game at court, someone said to me, "That Cyrano may have a fatal accident someday."

LE BRET. Oh?

THE DUKE. Yes. Tell him not to go out very often, and to be careful.

LE BRET. [*Throwing up his arms.*] Careful! . . . He'll soon be here; I'll warn him. But . . .

ROXANE. [*Who has remained on the steps, to a* NUN *coming toward her.*] What is it?

THE NUN. Ragueneau would like to see you, madame.

ROXANE. Bring him in. [*To the* DUKE *and* LE BRET.] He's come to complain about his poverty. Since the day when he set out to be a writer, he's been a singer . . .

LE BRET. A bathhouse attendant . . .

Cyrano de Bergerac, Act V **529**

CRITICAL THINKING: GUIDED READING QUESTIONS

- Ragueneau enters, and Roxane leaves to see De Guiche off.
- Ragueneau tells Le Bret that Cyrano has been attacked and injured.
- Le Bret and Ragueneau go off to help the supposedly bedridden Cyrano.
- Roxane returns and notes that Cyrano is late for the first time in all the years he has been visiting her.
- Cyrano appears.

IN THE GLOSSARY

- lackey: a servant
- colonnade: a row of columns

11 TEACHING DIALOGUE

Point out the way the words of an eyewitness are used to convey an important event in the plot: Cyrano has been attacked.

12 TEACHING FIGURATIVE LANGUAGE

Help students recognize the way in which Roxane uses personification to convey her state of mind: Her sorrow is "smiling," offended by April but charmed by September.

13 TEACHING CHARACTERIZATION

Ask students what Roxane's monologue reflects about her feelings toward Cyrano. (Students should see that his visits are important to her, but she is a bit smug and insensitive, accepting them as her due and never wondering how he benefits from them.)

14 TEACHING STAGING

Point out the way in which the dead leaf's interruption of Roxane's sewing and her distracted speech subtly foreshadow the possibility that she may soon be touched by difficulty or even death.

ROXANE. A hairdresser . . .

LE BRET. A lute teacher . . .

ROXANE. What can he have become now?

RAGUENEAU. [*Entering rapidly.*] Ah, madame! [*Sees* LE BRET.] Sir!

ROXANE. [*Smiling.*] Tell Le Bret your troubles. I'll be back soon.

RAGUENEAU. But madame . . . [ROXANE *ignores him and leaves with the* DUKE. RAGUENEAU *goes to* LE BRET.]

RAGUENEAU. Since you're here, I'd rather she didn't know. . . . As I was approaching our friend's house this afternoon, on my way to visit 11 him, I saw him come out. I hurried to catch up with him. I can't say for certain that it wasn't an accident, but when he was about to turn the corner a lackey dropped a piece of firewood on him from an upstairs window.

LE BRET. The cowards! . . . Cyrano! . . .

RAGUENEAU. I ran to him. . . .

LE BRET. It's horrible!

RAGUENEAU. Our friend, sir, our poet, was lying on the ground with a big hole in his head!

LE BRET. Is he dead?

RAGUENEAU. No, but . . . I carried him back into his house, to his room, rather. Oh, that room! What a wretched little closet!

LE BRET. Is he in pain?

RAGUENEAU. No, sir, he's unconscious.

LE BRET. Did you bring a doctor?

RAGUENEAU. Yes, I found one who was willing to come out of charity.

LE BRET. Poor Cyrano! . . . We mustn't tell Roxane all at once. . . . What did the doctor say?

RAGUENEAU. I don't remember very clearly, something about fever. . . . Oh, if you'd seen him lying there, with his head wrapped in bandages! . . . Come with me quickly! There's no one with him now, and he may die if he tries to get up!

LE BRET. [*Leading him to the right.*] Let's go this way, through the chapel. It's shorter. [ROXANE *appears on the steps and sees* LE BRET *hurrying along the colonnade that leads to the side door of the chapel.*]

ROXANE. Monsieur Le Bret! [LE BRET *and* RAGUENEAU *leave without answering.*] Le Bret runs away when I call him? Poor Ragueneau must really be in trouble this time! [*She comes down* 12 *the steps.*] What a beautiful autumn day! Even my sorrow is smiling. It's offended by April, but gives in to the gentler charm of September. [*She sits down in front of her embroidery frame. Two* NUNS *come out of the house, carrying a large armchair, and set it down under a tree.*] 13 Ah, here's the chair for my old friend! He'll soon be here. [*She begins working. The clock strikes.*] There, it's time. I'll take out my skeins.[5] . . . This is surprising: the clock has finished striking and he's not here yet. Is he going to be late for the first time? The Sister at the door must be— Where's my thimble? There, I see it—must be trying to persuade him to repent of his sins. [*Several moments pass.*] Still persuading him! 14 He'll surely be here before long. . . . A dead leaf. . . . [*She brushes aside the leaf that has fallen onto the embroidery frame.*] Nothing could— My scissors . . . in my bag!—prevent him from coming!

A NUN. [*Appearing on the steps.*] Monsieur de Bergerac is here.

ROXANE. [*Without turning around.*] I knew it! [*She continues her work.* CYRANO *appears. He is very pale, and his hat is pulled down over his eyes. The* NUN *who has accompanied him leaves.*]

---

5. **skeins** [skānz]: thread or yarn wound in a coil.

CRITICAL THINKING: GUIDED READING QUESTIONS

LITERAL

1a. What does Roxane say and do when Cyrano arrives? (She says "I knew it!" but does not even turn to look at him.)

INFERENTIAL

1b. What do Roxane's words and actions suggest about her feelings toward Cyrano? (She takes him for granted and assumes he will always visit her on schedule regardless of what is happening in his own life.)

He slowly comes down the steps, leaning on his cane and making an obvious effort to stay on his feet. ROXANE *is still working.*] Oh, these faded colors! . . . How will I ever match them? [*To* CYRANO, *in a tone of friendly rebuke.*] Late, for the first time in fourteen years!

[CYRANO *has succeeded in reaching his chair and sitting down in it. When he speaks, his cheerful voice contrasts with his face.*]

CYRANO. Yes, it's scandalous! I can't tell you how annoyed I am. I was delayed by . . .

ROXANE. By what?

CYRANO. By an untimely visit.

ROXANE. [*Distractedly, still working.*] A friend of yours?

CYRANO. An old acquaintance. We've met on the battlefield, among other places. I knew we'd meet again some day, but this wasn't the time for it.

ROXANE. You sent him away?

CYRANO. Yes, I said to him, "Excuse me, but this is Saturday, the day when I always keep a certain appointment. Nothing can make me miss it. Come back in an hour."

ROXANE. [*Lightly.*] Well, I'm afraid he'll have to wait for you, because I won't let you leave before nightfall.

CYRANO. [*Gently.*] I may have to leave a little sooner than that. [*He closes his eyes and remains silent.* SISTER MARTHE *walks across the park, from the chapel to the steps.* ROXANE *sees her and nods to her.*]

ROXANE. [*To* CYRANO.] Aren't you going to tease Sister Marthe today?

CYRANO. [*Quickly, opening his eyes.*] Yes, of course! [*In a comically gruff voice.*] Sister Marthe! Come here! [*She comes to him.*] When you have such lovely eyes, why do you keep them cast down?

SISTER MARTHE. [*Looking up with a smile.*] I . . . [*Sees his face and makes a gesture of astonishment.*] Oh!

CYRANO. [*In an undertone, pointing to* ROXANE.] Sh! It's nothing. . . .

ROXANE. [*Who has heard them whispering.*] She's trying to convert you!

SISTER MARTHE. I'm doing no such thing!

CYRANO. Now that I think of it, you never preach to me! It's amazing! [*With mock ferocity.*] I'll show you that you're not the only one who can be amazing! Just listen to this! I'm going to . . . [*Seems to be trying to think of a good way to tease her.*] Ah! I've got it! I'm going to allow you to pray for me tonight in the chapel!

ROXANE. Oh! Oh!

CYRANO. [*Laughing.*] Sister Marthe is dumbfounded!

SISTER MARTHE. [*Gently.*] I haven't waited for your permission. [*She goes into the house.*]

CYRANO. [*Turning back to* ROXANE, *who is leaning over her work.*] May the devil take me if I ever see that tapestry finished!

ROXANE. I was expecting some such remark. [*A breeze makes some leaves fall.*]

CYRANO. The leaves . . .

ROXANE. [*Raising her head and looking into the distance.*] They're Titian red.[6] . . . Look at them falling.

CYRANO. How well they fall! Such beauty in that short drop from branch to earth! They give their fall the grace of flight.

_____
6. **Titian** [tē′shən] **red:** a particular shade of red used by Titian (1490?–1576), an Italian painter.

Cyrano de Bergerac, Act V **531**

15
16
17

PAGE SUMMARY: AT A GLANCE

- Cyrano visits Roxane, and they spar verbally.
- She fails to notice his wound.

15 READING SKILL: INFERENCE

Ask students to interpret what Cyrano is saying figuratively. (Possible answer: I've come close to death in battle and at other times. I always knew I'd have to die sometime, but I wish death had come at a time other than the time of our visit.)

16 TEACHING CHARACTERIZATION

Ask students why Cyrano puts on a "comically gruff" voice when he is really suffering. (He is trying to shield Roxane and to serve her by entertaining her to the end.)

17 TEACHING DRAMATIC IRONY

Point out the dramatic irony in Cyrano's remarks. Cyrano pretends that granting Sister Marthe permission to pray for him is lighthearted teasing; actually he and the audience know that he is dying.

CRITICAL THINKING: GUIDED READING QUESTIONS

LITERAL

1a. What does Cyrano say when Roxane tells him she won't let him leave before nightfall? ("I may have to leave a little sooner than that.")

2a. What does Cyrano admire about the autumn leaves? (He admires the way they fall so gracefully.)

INFERENTIAL

1b. Why might Cyrano have to leave early? (He's afraid he will die before then; his parting may not be a voluntary leave-taking but death.)

2b. Why do you think Cyrano expresses such an interest in the leaves? (He knows he is dying and identifies himself with the dying leaves; he is also expressing sadness at having to leave the beauty of the earth.)

- Cyrano tells Roxane news of the fashionable world.
- Cyrano faints and then revives.
- Cyrano asks to see Christian's last letter and begins reading it aloud.

18 TEACHING STUDENTS OF LIMITED ENGLISH PROFICIENCY

Students with limited English may have difficulty with this figurative language. Help them understand that Cyrano personifies the king's illness in order to make fun of the petty concerns of the court. Assist them in rephrasing Cyrano's remarks so that they can better understand them.

19 CULTURAL BACKGROUND

You may wish to explain that Madame Montglat was a widow notorious for her many love affairs. Olympe Mancini was the beautiful daughter of a future French prime minister; at one time Louis XIV considered marrying her.

20 TEACHING PLOT: FALLING ACTION

Help students recognize that Cyrano's fainting shows the extent of his weakness and the nearness of death. The plot is now moving quickly toward its resolution.

21 TEACHING STAGING

Note the eerie appropriateness and pathos of the letter's message. Help students recognize that Cyrano's reading it aloud gives it dramatic focus and weight.

22 READING SKILL: PREDICTING OUTCOMES

Ask students what they think is about to happen. Most students will suspect that Roxane is about to realize that Cyrano is the author of the letter and that he has loved her for many years.

ROXANE. Can it be that you're melancholy—you?

CYRANO. [*Catching himself.*] Not at all!

ROXANE. Then forget about the falling leaves and tell me the latest news. Aren't you still my gazette?

CYRANO. I'll begin this very moment.

ROXANE. Good.

18 CYRANO. [*More and more pale, struggling against his pain.*] Last Saturday, the nineteenth, after eating eight helpings of preserved fruit, the King took to his bed with a fever; his illness was convicted of high treason and executed by his physician, and since then the royal pulse has returned to normal.

ROXANE. That will do, Monsieur de Bergerac!

CYRANO. [*Whose face is increasingly twisted by pain.*] On Tuesday, the whole court went to 19 Fontainebleau.[7] On Wednesday, Madame Montglat[8] said no to Count de Fiesque.[9] On Thursday, Olympe[10] Mancini was the Queen of France—or almost! On Friday, the twenty-fifth, Madame Montglat said yes to Count de Fiesque. And today, Saturday the twenty-sixth . . . [*He closes his eyes and his head falls. Silence. Surprised at no longer hearing him speak,* ROXANE *turns and looks at him, then stands up in alarm.*]

20 ROXANE. Has he fainted? [*Hurries to him with a cry.*] Cyrano!

CYRANO. [*Vaguely, opening his eyes.*] What is it? . . . What . . . [*Seeing her leaning over him, he quickly puts his hand to his hat to make sure it is still pulled down, and draws away from her in his chair.*] No! It's nothing, believe me! Go back to your chair.

---

7. **Fontainebleau** [fŏn′tạn blō′]: town near Paris and site of the royal palace.
8. **Madame Montglat** [mŏn glä′]
9. **Count de Fiesque** [də fē esk′]
10. **Olympe** [ō lĕmp′]

532 *Drama*

ROXANE. But you . . .

CYRANO. It's only my old wound from Arras. Sometimes it . . . You know. . . .

ROXANE. My poor friend!

CYRANO. It's really nothing. It will soon go away. [*Smiles with an effort.*] There, it's gone.

ROXANE. [*Standing beside him.*] Each of us has his wound. Mine is old but still unhealed, here . . . [*Puts her hand to her bosom.*] . . . under the yellowed paper of a letter still stained with tears and blood! [*Twilight is beginning to fall.*]

CYRANO. His letter! . . . Didn't you once tell me that you might let me read it some day?

ROXANE. You want to read . . . his letter?

CYRANO. Yes, I do. Now.

ROXANE. [*Removing the little bag that hangs from around her neck.*] Here!

CYRANO. [*Taking it.*] May I open it?

ROXANE. Yes, read it. [*She goes back to the embroidery frame and begins putting away her thread.*]

CYRANO. [*Reading.*] "Farewell, Roxane! Death is near. . . ."

21 ROXANE. [*Stopping in surprise.*] You're reading it aloud?

CYRANO. [*Reading.*] "I believe this will be my last day, my beloved. My soul is still heavy with unexpressed love, and I must die! Never again will my eyes delight . . ."

ROXANE. How well you read his letter!

CYRANO. [*Continuing.*] ". . . will my eyes delight in kissing each of your graceful gestures. I remember one of them, a way of putting your hand to your forehead, and I want to cry out . . ."

22 ROXANE. [*Troubled.*] How well you read . . . that letter! [*The twilight is turning to darkness.*]

CRITICAL THINKING: GUIDED READING QUESTIONS

LITERAL

1a. As her "gazette" what kind of news does Cyrano bring Roxane? (He tells her about the happenings at court and in the fashionable world.)

2a. What does Cyrano do with Christian's letter? (He begins to read it aloud.)

INFERENTIAL

1b. What attitude toward the fashionable world does he project in the way he tells the news? (He is joking and scornful.)

2b. Why do you think Cyrano reads the letter aloud? (Though he still doesn't want Roxane to realize that he loves her, he wants to express his love to her before he dies.)

PAGE SUMMARY: AT A GLANCE

- As Cyrano reads the letter, Roxane recalls a voice speaking words of love to her once before: Cyrano's voice.

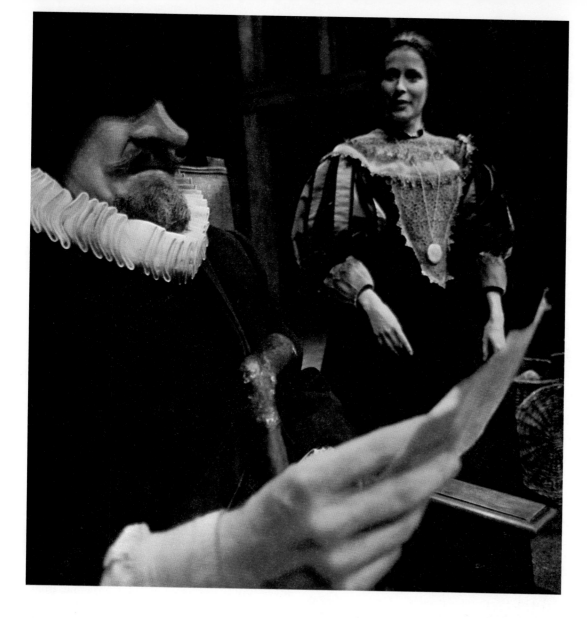

23 GRAMMAR IN LITERATURE

Point out the author's repetition of the possessive *my* followed by a noun of endearment, and ask what impact the repetition of this possessive-noun sequence has. (It makes the depth of Cyrano's feelings clear and adds to the pathos of the letter and the scene: Ironically, Roxane has never been his.)

24 TEACHING STAGING

Point out the way the interlacing words of Cyrano and Roxane heighten the drama of the scene and suggest an imminent revelation.

CYRANO. "... to cry out, 'Good-by!' ..."

ROXANE. You read it ...

23 CYRANO. "... my dearest, my darling, my treasure ..."

ROXANE. [*Thoughtfully.*] ... in a voice that ...

24 CYRANO. "... my love!"

ROXANE. ... that ... [*She starts.*] A voice that I'm not hearing for the first time! [*She slowly approaches him without his seeing her, stands behind his chair, silently bends down, and looks at the letter. The darkness is deepening.*]

Cyrano de Bergerac, Act V **533**

CRITICAL THINKING: GUIDED READING QUESTIONS

LITERAL

1a. What does Roxane say about the way Cyrano reads the letter? ("You read it ... in a voice that ... that ... A voice that I'm not hearing for the first time!")

INFERENTIAL

1b. What do her words and actions show about her realization? (It is slowly dawning on her that Cyrano spoke to her from under the balcony the night she was so moved by Christian's sincere words of love and that he was the real author of Christian's letters.)

■ Roxane guesses that Cyrano wrote the letters and spoke to her from under the balcony.
■ Le Bret and Ragueneau enter, revealing that Cyrano is near death.
■ Cyrano announces his impending death and says that he is a failure in everything, even the way in which he dies.

25 READING SKILL: CAUSE AND EFFECT

Ask students why Roxane recognizes Cyrano as the author of the letter. (She realizes that because it is dark, Cyrano is unable to see well enough to read. She then realizes that he must be speaking the words of the letter from memory.)

26 TEACHING CHARACTERIZATION

Point out the way in which Roxane's words sum up Cyrano's behavior: He has been selfless in love, always thinking of her happiness and well-being before his own.

27 TEACHING IRONY

Ensure that students understand the irony of this scene: After years of wanting to speak his love without disguise, Cyrano tries to deny his feelings.

28 TEACHING CHARACTERIZATION

Help students see that Cyrano chooses to die as he lived: with courage in his heart and with wit on his lips. Students should recognize that his ability to detach himself and treat his own murder as a newspaper story, as though it happened to someone else, is typical of his style.

CYRANO. "My heart has never left you for a moment, and in the next world my love for you will still be as boundless, as . . ."

25 ROXANE. [Putting her hand on his shoulder.] How can you read now? It's dark. [He starts, turns around, sees her standing close to him, makes a gesture of alarm, and bows his head. A long silence. Then, in the shadowy darkness, she clasps her hands and speaks slowly.] And for fourteen years you played the part of an old friend who came to be amusing!

CYRANO. Roxane!

ROXANE. It was you.

CYRANO. No, Roxane, no!

ROXANE. I should have guessed it each time I heard you say my name!

CYRANO. No! It wasn't . . .

ROXANE. It was you!

CYRANO. I swear . . .

26 ROXANE. I see the whole selfless imposture now! The letters . . . It was you.

CYRANO. No!

ROXANE. The wild, endearing words . . . It was you.

CYRANO. No!

ROXANE. The voice in the night . . . It was you.

CYRANO. I swear it wasn't!

27 ROXANE. The soul . . . It was yours!

CYRANO. I didn't love you!

ROXANE. You did love me!

CYRANO. [Desperately.] It was Christian!

ROXANE. You loved me!

CYRANO. No, no, my love, I didn't love you!

534 Drama

ROXANE. Ah, how many things have died, and how many have now been born! Why were you silent for fourteen years, knowing that he hadn't written that letter, and that the tears on it were yours?

CYRANO. [Handing her the letter.] The blood was his.

ROXANE. And why have you let that sublime silence be broken this evening?

CYRANO. Why? . . .

[LE BRET and RAGUENEAU enter, running.]

LE BRET. What foolhardiness! I knew we'd find him here!

CYRANO. [Smiling, and sitting more erect.] You were right. Here I am.

LE BRET. [To ROXANE.] He's killed himself by leaving his bed!

ROXANE. [To CYRANO.] Your faintness a little while ago . . . Was it . . .

28 CYRANO. That reminds me: I didn't finish my gazette! Today, Saturday the twenty-sixth, an hour before dinner time, Monsieur de Bergerac was murdered. [He takes off his hat, showing the bandages around his head.]

ROXANE. What is he saying? . . . Cyrano! . . . Those bandages! . . . What have they done to you? Why?

CYRANO. "To be struck down by the only noble weapon, the sword, wielded by an adversary worthy of me . . ." Yes, I once said that. Fate is a great jester! I've been struck down, but from behind, in an ambush, by a lackey wielding a log! I've been consistent to the end. I've failed in everything, even in my death.

RAGUENEAU. Oh, sir! . . .

CYRANO. Don't weep so loudly, Ragueneau.

CRITICAL THINKING: GUIDED READING QUESTIONS

LITERAL

1a. What does Cyrano say when Roxane confronts him with her knowledge that he wrote the letters? (He denies that it is true.)

INFERENTIAL

1b. Why does Cyrano reject his last chance to confess his love to Roxane? (He is faithful to his original honorable intentions toward Roxane and doesn't want to cause her pain by degrading her memories of her great love; he is also faithful and loyal to Christian.)

[*Takes his hand.*] Tell me, brother poet, what are you doing these days?

RAGUENEAU. [*Through his tears.*] I'm the candle-snuffer in a theater . . . Molière's[11] company. . . .

CYRANO. Molière!

RAGUENEAU. Yes, but I'm leaving him tomorrow. I'm outraged! Yesterday they played his *Scapin,* and I saw that he'd taken a scene from you!

LE BRET. A whole scene!

CYRANO. Be calm. He was right to take it. [*To* RAGUENEAU.] How did the audience react to the scene?

RAGUENEAU. [*Sobbing.*] Oh, sir, they laughed and laughed!

CYRANO. Yes, my life has been that of a man who provides words and ideas for others, spurs them to action, and is then forgotten. [*To* ROXANE.] Do you remember the evening when Christian spoke to you below your balcony? Well, that evening was the essence of my life: while I remained below, in the shadows, others climbed up to receive the kiss of glory. But now, on the threshold of my grave, I acknowledge the justice of it all—Molière is a genius and Christian was handsome! [*The chapel bell has begun ringing; the* NUNS *are now seen walking along the lane in the background, on their way to Vespers.*[12]] Let them go to their prayers, since their bell is ringing.

ROXANE. [*Looking up and calling.*] Sister! Sister!

CYRANO. [*Holding her back.*] No, no, don't go to bring anyone! You'd find me gone when you returned. [*The* NUNS *have entered the chapel, and the organ is heard.*] I needed a little harmony, and there it is.

---

11. **Molière's** [mōl yārz′]: Molière (1622–1673) was a famous French dramatist, actor, and director.
12. **Vespers:** church service held in the evening.

ROXANE. I love you! You must live!

CYRANO. No. In the fairy tale, when Beauty said, "I love you" to the prince, his ugliness melted away like snow in the warmth of the sun, but as you can see, those words have no such magic effect on me.

ROXANE. Your life has been unhappy because of me! Me!

CYRANO. No, Roxane, quite the contrary. Feminine sweetness was unknown to me. My mother made it clear that she didn't find me pleasant to look at. I had no sister. Later, I dreaded the thought of seeing mockery in the eyes of a mistress. Thanks to you, I've at least had a woman's friendship, a gracious presence to soften the harsh loneliness of my life.

LE BRET. [*Pointing to the moonlight shining through the branches.*] Your other friend has come to visit you.

CYRANO. [*Smiling at the moon.*] Yes, I see her.

ROXANE. I've loved only one man, and I've lost him twice!

CYRANO. Le Bret, I'll soon be soaring up to the moon, this time without having to invent a machine. . . . "Philosopher, scientist, poet, swordsman, musician, aerial traveler, maker of sharp retorts, and lover (not to his advantage!), here lies Savinien[13] de Cyrano de Bergerac, who was everything, and who was nothing." [*Half raising himself from his chair.*] Excuse me, I must go now: a moonbeam has come to take me away, and I can't keep it waiting! [*He falls back into his chair.* ROXANE's *weeping recalls him to reality. He looks at her and strokes her veils.*] I don't want you to mourn any less for that good, charming, handsome Christian; my only hope is that when the great cold has seeped into my

---

13. **Savinien** [sa vē nyan′]: Cyrano's first name.

Cyrano de Bergerac, Act V **535**

PAGE SUMMARY: AT A GLANCE

■ Cyrano reviews his life; he says that his role has always been to support others.
■ Roxane declares her love.
■ Cyrano thanks Roxane for the gracious presence she has been in his life; he thinks of his imminent death.

29 CULTURAL BACKGROUND

You might wish to tell students that Molière's play *Les Fourberies de Scapin* (which was first staged in 1671, not 1655) did indeed contain a scene taken almost without change from a play by the actual Cyrano (titled *Pedant joué*).

30 TEACHING THEME

Point out that as Cyrano reviews his life, he finds that its essence has consisted of being in the shadows while others collected prizes. This recognition underscores one of the play's main themes: Sacrifice is often necessary to support one's ideals.

31 TEACHING PLOT: RESOLUTION

The plot's resolution occurs when Roxane realizes that she loves Cyrano. This resolution is both satisfying and tragic, since it is too late for the two of them to enjoy their love.

32 TEACHING CONFLICT

Note that Cyrano confesses his vulnerability concerning his physical disfigurement. He reveals the origin of his major conflict: His ugliness was rejected even by his mother.

CRITICAL THINKING: GUIDED READING QUESTIONS

LITERAL

1a. How does Cyrano compare Roxane and himself to Beauty and the Beast? (He says that when Beauty said she loved the Beast, he turned into a handsome prince; but when Roxane says she loves him, he stays the same.)

INFERENTIAL

1b. What does his reference to this story tell you about his feelings about his appearance? (Despite Roxane's confession of love, he still feels that his ugliness is a barrier to love.)

bones, you'll give a double meaning to those black veils, and mourn for me a little when you mourn for him.

ROXANE. I swear to you that . . . [CYRANO *is shaken by a great tremor, and abruptly stands up.*]

CYRANO. No! Not there! Not in a chair! [*The others move toward him.*] Stand back! I want no support from anyone! [*Leans against the tree.*] Only from this tree! [*Silence.*] He's coming. I already feel stone boots . . . lead gloves. . . . [*Stiffens himself.*] Yes, he's coming, but I'll meet him on my feet . . . [*Draws his sword.*] . . . sword in hand!

LE BRET. Cyrano!

ROXANE. [*Half fainting.*] Cyrano! [*They all draw back in terror.*]

CYRANO. I believe I see . . . yes, I see him, with his noseless face, daring to look at my nose! [*Raises his sword.*] What's that you say? It's useless? Of course, but I've never needed hope of victory to make me fight! The noblest battles are always fought in vain! . . . You there, all of you, who are you? Your numbers seem endless. . . . Ah, I recognize you now: my old enemies! Lies!

My greetings to you! [*Thrusts his sword into the empty air.*] And here's Compromise! And Prejudice! And Cowardice! [*Thrusts again.*] What's that? Come to terms with you? Never! Never! . . . Ah, there you are, Stupidity! . . . I know I can't defeat you all, I know that in the end you'll overwhelm me, but I'll still fight you as long as there's a breath in my body! [*Swings his sword in great arcs, then stops, panting.*] Yes, you've robbed me of everything: the laurels of glory, the roses of love! But there's one thing you can't take away from me. When I go to meet God this evening, and doff my hat before the holy gates, my salute will sweep the blue threshold of heaven, because I'll still have one thing intact, without a stain, something that I'll take with me in spite of you! [*Springs forward with his sword raised.*] You ask what it is? I'll tell you! It's . . . [*His sword drops from his hand; he staggers and falls into the arms of* LE BRET *and* RAGUENEAU.]

ROXANE. [*Bending down and kissing him on the forehead.*] What is it?

CYRANO. [*Opening his eyes and smiling at her.*] My white plume.

Cyrano de Bergerac, Act V **537**

CRITICAL THINKING: GUIDED READING QUESTIONS

LITERAL

1a. What images does Cyrano use to tell how his body feels as death draws closer? (He says he feels "stone boots" and "lead gloves.")

2a. What enemies does Cyrano name? (lies, compromise, prejudice, cowardice, and stupidity)

INFERENTIAL

1b. What sensations do you think Cyrano is describing by these images? (His limbs probably seem to grow heavier as he grows weaker and less able to support himself.)

2b. What does Cyrano mean when he says that he cannot defeat these enemies but will continue to fight? (He is dying and so will not know victory in the material world, where his enemies rule. But he can choose to fight and so win a spiritual victory.)

Do you think the ending of *Cyrano de Bergerac* is triumphant or tragic? Explain.

ANSWERS

STUDY QUESTIONS

1. Roxane has been living at the convent, mourning Christian's death, for fifteen years. Cyrano, poor, lives according to his principles.
2. He is near death from a head wound. He wears his hat low and speaks cheerfully.
3. He pretends to read Christian's last letter but is actually reciting it. Roxane recognizes his voice as the one she heard under the balcony; she tells Cyrano that she loves him.
4. lies, compromise, prejudice, cowardice, stupidity; "I'll still have one thing intact. . . . My white plume."
5. He knows he is dying.
6. She thought it was Christian who spoke to her from under the balcony and wrote her the eloquent letters, and she mourned his death; she realizes it was Cyrano, and she will lose her love again. Answers will vary; students should state their opinion.
7. He makes a grand gesture in visiting Roxane, hiding his wound, and treating death like a dueling opponent. He means that he dies with his ideals intact.
8. He did many things without earning distinction or achieving material success. Students will probably feel that a brilliant reputation and the admiration of friends are far from "nothing."
9. Cyrano may strike some students as extravagant and artificial, but some may say that aspects of his personality make them think of idealists and individualists they know.

LITERARY FOCUS

1. The falling action—Roxane's retreat to a convent and Cyrano's decline into poverty—reinforces the idea that after the play's climax (Christian's death) the protagonists' important choices in life are behind them. Students may say that the ending is satisfying because Cyrano is at last revealed as the author of the letters, and Roxane at last declares her love for him.

STUDY QUESTIONS

Recalling

1. According to the nuns, what has happened since Christian's death? What do they and Le Bret reveal about Cyrano's circumstances?
2. Describe Cyrano's condition when he arrives at the convent. How does he disguise it from Roxane?
3. How does Cyrano finally reveal his feelings to Roxane? How does she respond?
4. What "old enemies" does Cyrano see in his dying vision? What are his last words?

Interpreting

5. Why do you think Cyrano finally reveals his love to Roxane?
6. What does Roxane mean when she says that she has lost the man she loved twice? Do you agree?
7. Show that Cyrano meets his death in a style that is consistent with his life. What do his very last words mean?
8. Cyrano says of himself that he "was everything and was nothing." Why would he make such a comment about his life? Do you agree with him?

Extending

9. Cyrano is a very colorful character. Do you think that he is too flamboyant for real life, or do you believe that people like Cyrano actually exist?

LITERARY FOCUS

The Total Effect

In staging a play a director tries to present the audience with an integrated view of the entire work. *Cyrano de Bergerac* presents a fascinating challenge to any director, because it is full of contrasting emotions and effects that move audiences both to laughter and to tears. Anyone who directs this rich work must be aware of the impact of each of the various elements in the play—its plot, characters, setting, symbols, irony, and themes—on the work as a whole.

Thinking About Plot, Character, and Setting

1. Explain how the falling action and resolution of the play follow logically from the play's major conflict and its climax. Did you find the ending a satisfying conclusion to the play? Why or why not?
2. Romantic heroes are colorful characters, more

dashing and flamboyant than the people around them. In addition, they are usually attractive and inspire great love. Using examples from the play, explain why Cyrano could be regarded as a romantic hero. In what ways is he an *unusual* romantic hero?

3. Identify the setting of each act of *Cyrano de Bergerac*. Briefly explain how the action of each act is appropriate to the setting in which it occurs.

Thinking About Symbol

4. The image of the white plume appears several times in the play—for example, in the exchange between Cyrano and De Guiche in Act IV (page 514). What might the white plume symbolize in this exchange? What does it come to symbolize at the end of the play?

Thinking About Irony

5. Since irony often involves a gap between appearance and reality, why is it fitting that Cyrano's life should be so full of irony?

Thinking About Theme

6. What does the play say about the relationship between physical and spiritual beauty? Is one more "real" than the other? Explain.
7. According to the play, why should we admire an idealist like Cyrano? Does the play suggest that idealists are ultimately defeated by the real world?
8. What are the good and bad sides to individualism like Cyrano's, according to the play?
9. What is the value of poetry and beautiful language, according to the play? Do you think the play places too high a value on language? Why?

LANGUAGE STUDY

English Words Borrowed from French

William the Conqueror invaded England in 1066 from Normandy, a province on the northern coast of France. The Norman Conquest made French the official language of the ruling class of England, and a tremendous number of French words came into the English language. The English word *language* itself comes from the French word *langage,* meaning "speech." In most cases the spellings and pronunciations of the French loan-words gradually changed as they entered the English language.

2. He proves his dash in his treatment of Montfleury and his battle with Valvert; he proves his courage in his fight with the hundred men and his restraint with Roxane; he shows his eloquence in his speeches and letters. He is unusual in being ugly and not living to enjoy the love he ultimately wins.

3. *Act I*—the theater establishes Cyrano's flamboyance; *Act II*—a pastry shop is the backdrop for light, comic counterpoint; *Act III*—evening under Roxane's balcony is a romantic backdrop for declarations of love; *Act IV*—in the battlefield the struggle for survival meshes with the struggle to live up to personal ambitions and ideals; *Act V*—the convent on a fall afternoon is

tranquil and serious, providing the backdrop for Cyrano's death.

4. *Act IV*—It symbolizes personal courage, a sense of honor that will not admit defeat; *Act V*—it refers to personal style (his *panache*), love for the grand gesture, and individualism as well as pride and commitment to ideals.

All of the following words, taken from the English version of *Cyrano de Bergerac,* were originally French words and have since become part of our language. Using a dictionary, write the original French word and note any changes in spelling.

1. cadet
2. stage
3. secret
4. fool
5. courage
6. brilliant
7. danger
8. tremble
9. flower
10. plume

In English we also use many French words *without* changing their French spellings and pronunciations—for example, *tableau* and *gazette.* Another French word used by speakers of English is *panache* [pə nash′], which is actually the last word that Cyrano speaks in the original French text of *Cyrano de Bergerac.* Look up the various meanings of *panache,* and explain why the word is a fitting one for Cyrano.

COMPOSITION

Writing About Character

■ Of all of Cyrano's speeches, choose the one that you think best sums up his character. Identify the speech, noting where it occurs in the play, to whom it is addressed, and why Cyrano speaks it. Then explain what it reveals about Cyrano and why you think it represents his character so well. You should take into account both what Cyrano says in the speech and the style in which he says it. Use quotations from the speech to support your opinion.

Writing a Speech for a Character

■ Look again at Cyrano's "nose" speech to Valvert in Act I, and add new descriptions to it. Follow the form that Cyrano uses — for example, "Dramatic: 'When it bleeds, it must be like the Red Sea!'" Try to match Cyrano's humor.

5. Ironic events mirror the irony that Cyrano's physical ugliness masks the beauty of his soul.
6. Spiritual beauty endures; physical beauty does not. Spiritual beauty is more real because it is lasting and gives life meaning.
7. He has courage, and his virtue is uncompromised. The play suggests that idealism can never be defeated by "reality."
8. *good*—It makes him an inspiring example of possibilities of the human spirit; *bad*—it shows how it can make someone difficult and unreasonable.
9. The play shows poetry as the expression of the soul. Some students may say that the play values language above real feeling.

LANGUAGE STUDY

1. *capdet* (Gascon dialect of French)
2. *estage* (Old French)
3. *secret* (Old French)
4. *fol* (Old French)
5. *corage* (Old French)
6. *brillant* (French)
7. *danger* (Old French)
8. *trembler* (Old French)
9. *flour* (Old French)
10. *plume* (Middle French) "a plume, especially for a helmet; dash, swagger, verve"; The word fits Cyrano because of his love of showmanship and dash, no matter what the realities of life around him.

COMPOSITION: GUIDELINES FOR EVALUATION

WRITING ABOUT CHARACTER

Objective

To show how character is revealed through speech

Guidelines for Evaluation

■ suggested length: three to four paragraphs
■ should cite one of Cyrano's speeches
■ should name characteristics it reveals
■ should use quotations to support ideas

WRITING A SPEECH FOR A CHARACTER

Objective

To add to a humorous speech

Guidelines for Evaluation

■ suggested length: two to three paragraphs
■ should create new descriptions within the established format
■ should be in a humorous and witty style
■ should use Cyrano's nose as the target of humor

Technology provides tools that enable us to enrich our lives. With the invention of alphabetic writing by the Greeks around the eighth century B.C., language was made visible and preservable. In about the 1400s the printing press and engraving made thoughts and images far more exactly replicable, so that how-to manuals and practical science could proliferate. In the nineteenth century photography freeze-framed reality. Now in the twentieth century we can catalog on film human events as they occur: Sound, sight, and motion can be recorded with precision and detail. Much of the world's culture is now brought to us on film.

In this picture film makers replicate ancient Rome. The remote past, once described in myth and retold in history books, can now be scrutinized, reshaped, and re-presented as if it were alive in front of us.

■ Ask whether any students take photographs or make videotapes. Ask them what the function of such pictures is. (Possible answer: to create personal histories and mythologies)

Marlon Brando waiting for a cue in the filming of Metro-Goldwyn-Mayer's *Julius Caesar,* 1954.

540 *Drama*

From Literature into Film

Twentieth-century technology allows film makers to take us to real settings anywhere in the world or to create highly imaginative settings that could never exist in the world as we know it. The camera can zoom in on the smallest details of a scene and help us appreciate the finest points of an acting performance. Despite these attributes of films, most films still begin with the written word. The written version of a film is a special kind of play script called a *screenplay.*

Adapting a stage play for the screen is far easier than adapting a novel. A play is already in dramatic form, presenting characterization and plot events through characters' speech and actions. In addition, it already unfolds in a length of time suitable for the audience to see in a single sitting. A novel, on the other hand, usually contains long narrative sections in which the narrator speaks directly to readers— summarizing, describing, explaining, interpreting, and so on. A novel may also present characters' unspoken thoughts. Finally, it may contain hundreds of characters and events and take days or even weeks to read. To turn a novel into a film, the narration must be transformed into dramatic material—action or speech—or into background material that the camera can photograph. Similarly, characters' thoughts must somehow be translated into speech or action. Finally, the novel may need to be condensed or simplified so that audiences can see it in a few hours' time.

Over the decades film makers have produced film versions of many classics of world literature. In 1950, for example, *Cyrano de Bergerac* was adapted into an Academy Award–winning film. The plays of England's William Shakespeare, such as *Romeo and Juliet* and *Julius Caesar,* and dramas by Russia's Anton Chekhov and Norway's Henrik Ibsen have had many successful film versions. Famous novels that have been adapted for the screen include *The Count of Monte Cristo* by France's Alexandre Dumas, *War and Peace* by Russia's Leo Tolstoy, and *A Tale of Two Cities* by England's Charles Dickens. Indeed, in parts of the world as far apart as Japan, India, and Brazil, film making is an extremely popular art form, and film makers have brought some of the most important works of literature in their cultures to the screen.

CREATING A SCREENPLAY

The writer of a screenplay must harmonize many elements, including dialogue, action, description, sound effects, special effects, and camera angles. At the opening of a scene, the writer of a screenplay briefly describes the setting and the initial placement of the characters. Then, as the dialogue progresses, the writer adds brief instructions regarding actors' movements, camera angles (such as zooming in for closeups or pulling back for panoramic views), sound effects, special effects, and the like. When screenplays are published, these instructions often appear in italics to set them apart from the dialogue.

Activities

1. Divide the class into groups of four or five students. The students in each group should work together to write a screenplay for a scene from *Cyrano de Bergerac.* They might choose the scene in Act II in which Cyrano and Roxane meet at Ragueneau's pastry shop or the scene in Act III in which Cyrano distracts De Guiche so that Roxane can marry Christian. One member of each group should assume the role of chief scriptwriter. Each of the other students should be responsible for developing a specific aspect of the screenplay: camera angles, sound effects, special effects, and instructions to the actors, for instance. Under the chief scriptwriter's supervision, the group should mold these instructions into a cohesive script. When the screenplays are complete, have the groups exchange scripts, and have each group evaluate the script that it has been given. Is it clear? Complete? Imaginative?

2. Divide the class into groups of five or six students. Ask each group to write a screenplay for a scene from one of the short stories in this book, such as "A Piece of String," "Tuesday Siesta," "The Quarry," or "Air des Clochettes." Each student should take charge of a specific aspect of the directions, as described in the first activity. Point out that each group will also need to supplement the dialogue in passages of the story in which the characters' speech is described rather than quoted directly or in which characters' thoughts are implied but not expressed. When the screenplays are complete, have the groups exchange them for evaluation.

A major goal of the *Macmillan Literature Series* is to enrich students' experience of literature in as many ways as possible. Our primary goal is to encourage students to become active, independent thinkers who integrate new knowledge with old and apply what they have learned to each new work they read. The resources on the following pages are designed to help students develop and refine the skills that mature readers use constantly as they interact with literature.

These pages also contain historical, linguistic, literary, and other cultural information that students can use to enhance their experience of the literature and their understanding of the nationalities represented in this anthology. Students will be able to refer to these pages throughout the term, not simply in connection with a single literary work. In short, students can use the resources in this section to create links between the various works in this book and, more important, to relate the literature they read to the rich and diverse world they inhabit.

This resource section contains the following special features:

- The **Literature and Culture Sourcebook** provides historical, literary, and cultural information about ten regions of the world.
- The **Guide to Literary Movements** outlines thirteen major movements in world literature, from the Classical Age to the late twentieth century.
- The **Author Time Line** places the authors in this anthology in chronological perspective.
- The **Winners of Nobel Prize for Literature** lists in chronological order all Nobel Prize winners for Literature from 1901 to 1990.
- The **Writing About Literature Handbook** includes ten lessons using a writing-process approach to the development of compositions on literary topics.
- The **Literary Terms Handbook** defines and illustrates the literary terms taught in this book.

STUDENT'S RESOURCES 542

LITERATURE AND CULTURE SOURCEBOOK

Classical Greece and Rome 544

Italy 548

France 552

Spain 556

Latin America 560

Germany 564

Russia and Eastern Europe 568

China and Japan 572

Africa 576

India and the Middle East 580

GUIDE TO LITERARY MOVEMENTS
. . . . 584

AUTHOR TIME LINE
. . . . 586

WINNERS OF NOBEL PRIZE FOR LITERATURE
. . . . 590

WRITING ABOUT LITERATURE HANDBOOK 592

Lesson 1: Writing a Response to Literature 592
Lesson 2: Writing About Plot 594
Lesson 3: Writing About Character 596
Lesson 4: Writing About Setting 598
Lesson 5: Writing About Point of View 600
Lesson 6: Writing About Theme 602
Lesson 7: Writing About a Symbol 604
Lesson 8: Writing About Nonfiction 606
Lesson 9: Writing About Poetry 608
Lesson 10: Writing About the Total Effect 610

LITERARY TERMS HANDBOOK 612

Glossary 621
Index of Skills 633
Index of Fine Art 637
Index of Authors and Titles 641

SUMMARY: GREECE

This essay is intended to give students a brief overview of some of the outstanding characteristics of Classical Greek and Roman cultures.

- Greek civilization flowered from the eighth to the fourth centuries B.C. and peaked in the fifth century B.C., the Golden Age.
- Greek culture has had a profound impact on Western art, politics, and philosophy.
- The arts thrived in the democratic climate of Athens, the greatest of Greece's city-states.
- The Parthenon is perhaps the most perfect embodiment of the Greek ideal of beauty.
- The spirit of ancient Greece survives in the Olympic Games, which are still held today.

STUDY QUESTIONS: GREECE

1. **Review:** Ask students to describe some of the accomplishments of the Greek Golden Age. (Possible answers: Socrates and Plato formulated their philosophies; Sophocles and Euripides wrote their great tragedies; the Parthenon was constructed.)
2. **Discussion:** Ask students to contrast the modern Olympic Games with those held in Classical Greece. (Possible answers: The modern Olympics are held in both summer and winter; the ancient Greek Olympics were held only in summer. Today winning athletes are awarded bronze, silver, and gold medals rather than the traditional palm branch and crown of laurels.)
3. **Thinking About Art:** Tell students that in ancient times the Parthenon was painted brilliant hues of red, blue, and gold. Ask them to imagine that the city of Athens is planning to restore the building's original colors. Would they support the plan, or would they prefer the pure white temple we see today? Ask them to explain their choice.

CLASSICAL GREECE

Of all the world's civilizations, that of the Greeks was the most short-lived. During its prime, its influence was small, confined mostly to the southern Balkan peninsula, where modern Greece is located, and the islands and coasts of the Aegean Sea. Nonetheless, the brief flowering of Greek culture between the eighth and fourth centuries B.C. had a prodigious impact on the world. Western ideas of democracy and freedom are rooted in the philosophies of ancient Greece. Western ideals of beauty, order, and harmony are grounded in Greek art and literature.

Athens was the queen of Greek democratic city-states. Governed by a council of four hundred men, Athens guaranteed broad rights to many of its citizens. In this climate of democracy, the arts flourished. During the fifth century B.C. Athenian culture reached its apex. Socrates

Built between 448 and 432 B.C. atop the Acropolis in Athens, the Parthenon was dedicated to Athena, the ancient Greek goddess of wisdom and warfare.

and his pupil, Plato, developed their ideas about eternal truths and human goodness. Sophocles and Euripides wrote their tragic dramas, whose emotional depth still stirs modern audiences. The Parthenon, perhaps the most perfect expression of the Greek ideal of beauty, was built atop a rocky hill in Athens. The Parthenon symbolized democracy because it was built with money from the people.

The spirit of ancient Greece survives in the Olympic Games. Begun in the early eighth century B.C., the games were held in midsummer at Olympia in the western Peloponnesus. Every four years athletes from all Greece's city-states—even those at war with each other—gathered to test their skills. The winners were given a palm branch and a crown of laurel leaves: In the games, as in art, the Greeks cherished simplicity above all things.

This Greek vase, made in the six century B.C., depicts a group of women who are filling jars with water from a well.

IN THIS BOOK

The following Classical Greek selections can be found in this book:

Aesop, "The Fox and the Grapes," p. 238
Aesop, "The Goatherd and the Wild Goats," p. 238
Homer, from the *Iliad,* p. 262
Sappho, "Fragment of a Lullaby," p. 290
Thucydides, "Pericles' Funeral Oration," p. 424

FURTHER INVESTIGATION: GREECE

Encourage students to pursue their individual interests in various aspects of Classical Greek culture. Some suggestions appear below.

- **Art:** the lives and works of the Greek sculptors Phidias and Praxiteles
- **Architecture:** the styles and functions of the buildings located on the Acropolis, including the Parthenon, the Erechtheum, and the Propylaea
- **Drama:** reviews of modern films, plays, or operas that are based on characters from Greek dramas, such as *Medea, Iphigenia at Aulis,* or *Antigone*
- **Mythology and Folklore:** the Greek myths of Narcissus, Sisyphus, and Orpheus and Eurydice and their relevance, if any, to modern life
- **Politics:** the rivalry between the city-states of Athens and Sparta

ROME

Even before Greek civilization began to decline, another great culture began to develop on the banks of the Tiber River on the Italian peninsula. The Romans were farmers and warriors who were deeply conservative and wary of foreign interference. Their state, which began with the founding of Rome in the eighth century B.C., gradually expanded over a period of 900 years until it encompassed Greece, Asia Minor, Egypt and the northern coast of Africa, and much of Western Europe. The Romans left a deep mark on Western civilization. Our public buildings and statues and the structure and laws of our government have been influenced by Roman ideas. Roman philosophers helped to inspire the great cultural awakening of the Renaissance, and Roman orators helped to shape modern prose.

The Romans borrowed many ideas from their predecessors, the Etruscans, who had established a network of cities in the northern Italian peninsula in the sixth century B.C. The Etruscans were not only traders, farmers, and herders; they were also ambitious city planners and builders. From the Etruscans the Romans learned to construct buildings with arches and vaults. The Etruscans, who were enamored of Greek culture, identified the Greek gods with their own and passed them on to the Romans: The Greek god Zeus became the Roman god Jupiter, Athena became Minerva, and Poseidon became Neptune. The Etruscans also helped to pass on Greek ideas about freedom and human dignity that were to have a lasting impact on Western thought. Their successors, the Romans, possessed a strong sense of duty to the state and a gift for organization on a scale more vast than any the world had ever seen. Roman culture is often criticized for merely imitat-

The anonymous artist who sculpted this statue of Augustus Caesar sometime around 20 B.C. depicted the great emperor in a serene and idealized manner.

ing Greek models, but the Romans fashioned brilliant works by blending Greek traditions with their own practical spirit.

The Romans left a legacy of great accomplishments. They built great roads, bridges, and aqueducts, some of which still stand today. They created the first public hospitals. Their great triumphal arches and massive public buildings—notably the great Colosseum and the Pantheon in Rome—inspired generations of architects in Europe and the New World. The concept of justice, on which Western law is based, was developed in Roman tribunals. The triumphs of Roman civilization are celebrated by the great poet Virgil, who wrote during the reign of Augustus Caesar, the first Roman emperor.

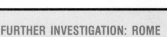

Designed to hold up to 50,000 spectators, the vast Colosseum in Rome, dedicated in A.D. 80, was the site of lavish events.

IN THIS BOOK

The following Classical Roman selections can be found in this book:

Ovid, from the
  Metamorphoses, p. 231
Virgil, from the
  Aeneid, p. 270
Horace, "Ode: Better to
  Live, Licinius," p. 359

Classical Greece and Rome **545**

- The civilization of ancient Rome began in the eighth century B.C. and endured more than nine centuries.
- Western architecture, laws, and literature have been shaped by Roman ideas.
- Many Roman ideas are rooted in the culture of the Etruscans, an earlier Mediterranean people who transmitted to the Romans the aesthetics and ideals of the ancient Greeks.
- The Romans were great engineers and architects. Some of their most impressive monuments, such as the Colosseum and the Pantheon in Rome, still stand.
- Western concepts of justice developed in Roman courts.
- Virgil, the great epic poet, praised the accomplishments of the early Roman Empire.

STUDY QUESTIONS: ROME

1. **Review:** Which Greek ideas did the Etruscans pass on to the Romans? (Greek notions of freedom and democracy, as well as Greek mythology)
2. **Discussion:** Explain to students that in Roman times the art of oration, or public speaking, was highly prized. Ask students whether we place a high value on oration today. Students may wish to give examples in regard to modern politicians or the influence of television and advertising on styles of public speaking.
3. **Thinking About Art:** Ask students to look at the portrait of the Roman woman on page 547. What can they infer about her position in society? (Possible answer: Students may say that the woman appears to be cultured and aristocratic.)

FURTHER INVESTIGATION: ROME

Encourage students to pursue their individual interests in various aspects of Classical Roman culture. Some suggestions appear below.

- **Art:** the most famous ancient Roman paintings, the murals in the Villa of the Mysteries just outside Pompeii
- **Architecture:** the design of Roman houses, such as those at Herculaneum and Pompeii
- **Politics and Society:** the roles of women and slaves in Roman society
- **Science and Technology:** the impact of the following innovations on Roman society: concrete, blown glass, public water and sewer systems, and a vast network of public roads

This outline can be used in the following ways.

- **With less advanced students:** Point out the total time span covered in the outline. Then, beginning at the top of the chart, point out the period covered in each section in order to emphasize the chronology. Also point out the famous authors listed in the outline, particularly those whose work appears in this anthology.
- **With more advanced students:** Suggest that students compare the outlines of literature in this Literature and Culture Sourcebook with the Guide to Literary Movements (pp. 584– 585). They will discover that literary trends often cut across cultural boundaries—that many cultures had, for instance, a Romantic or a Modernist period. You might also ask students to report on an author who appears in the outline but is not featured in this anthology.

THE AUTHORS IN THIS BOOK

Here are additional notes on the Classical Greek and Roman authors whose work appears in this anthology.

Greece

- **Aesop:** While Aesop's fables were possibly invented during the Lyric Age, they are linked to older oral traditions.
- **Homer:** Homer's epics, which celebrate heroism and moral greatness, set the standard for the genre for many centuries.
- **Sappho:** Sappho's emotional, elegantly wrought verses were without peer in the Lyric movement.
- **Thucydides:** One of the finest ancient historians, Thucydides sought to maintain high standards of veracity in accordance with the rational spirit of the Golden Age.

Rome

- **Virgil:** The *Aeneid*, Virgil's best-known epic, celebrated the birth of Rome and the accomplishments of the Augustan empire.
- **Horace:** A close friend of Augustus Caesar, Horace paid tribute to the empire and its ruler in many of his odes.
- **Ovid:** The verses of Ovid, an educated nobleman, reflected the intellectual caliber of early imperial Rome.

AN OUTLINE OF CLASSICAL GREEK AND ROMAN LITERATURE

GREECE

PERIOD	MAJOR WRITERS AND MAJOR WORKS	
Epic Age (900–700 B.C.) Noble families ruled and wandering bards sang heroic verses at the courts. Two great epics, the *Iliad* and the *Odyssey*, recounted tales of the Trojan War.	Homer Hesiod	Iliad Odyssey Works and Days
Lyric Age (700–500 B.C.) In Athens democracy was born. Poets broke away from objective styles and wrote of deep personal experiences.	Alcaeus Sappho Pindar	Lyric poetry Lyric poetry Odes
Golden Age (500–400 B.C.) In the arts, the city-state of Athens dominated the scene. Three masters of tragedy wrote their finest plays, and a fourth dramatist, Aristophanes, satirized Athenian society. Plato conveyed his philosophy in lively dialogues, and historians wrote vivid accounts of war.	Aeschylus Sophocles Euripides Aristophanes Plato Herodotus Thucydides	Oresteia trilogy Oedipus the King Antigone Medea The Frogs The Republic The Symposium History History of the Peloponnesian War

ROME

PERIOD	MAJOR WRITERS AND MAJOR WORKS	
Late Republic (250–27 B.C.) Roman territory expanded under Julius Caesar and other rulers. Roman philosophers were split between those who favored morality and patriotism and those who favored pleasure for its own sake.	Plautus Terence Cicero Lucretius Catullus	Comedies Comedies Orations On the Nature of Things Poetry
Early Empire (27 B.C.–A.D. 180) The reign of Augustus Caesar ushered in a period of peace and prosperity, and the arts reached a new sophistication. Virgil praised the empire, but later historians, such as Tacitus, were more critical.	Virgil Horace Seneca Ovid Tacitus	Aeneid Odes Philosophical discourses Metamorphoses Germania

Classical Greek

Ἄνδρα μοι ἔννεπε, μοῦσα, πολύτροπον, ὃς μάλα πολλὰ
πλάγχθη, ἐπεὶ Τροίης ἱερὸν πτολίεθρον ἔπερσεν·

—Homer, the *Odyssey,* Book I

A Translation

Sing in me, Muse, and through me tell the story
of that man skilled in all ways of contending,
the wanderer, harried for years on end,
after he plundered the stronghold
on the proud height of Troy.

—translated by Robert Fitzgerald

Latin

Tu regere imperio populos, Romane, memento
(hae tibi erunt artes), pacique imponere morem,
parcere subiectis et debellare superbos.

—Virgil, the *Aeneid,* Book VI

A Translation

Roman, remember by your strength to rule
Earth's peoples—for your arts are to be these:
To pacify, to impose the rule of law,
To spare the conquered, battle down the proud.

—translated by Robert Fitzgerald

Made in the fourth century B.C., this Roman coin dates from the Republican period, when trade began to expand.

This fresco from Pompeii, painted sometime around the first century B.C., shows the elaborate hair style typical of Roman women.

COLLABORATIVE RESEARCH

1. As a group, research and report on the topic "Classical Culture Today." The purpose of your report is to answer the question "How are the Greek and Roman cultures still alive in our modern world?" Assign each member of the group one element of modern culture to investigate—for example, politics, painting, music, science, literature, movies, and advertising.

2. As a group, research and report on the topic "Saving the Past." The purpose of your report is to answer the question "What is happening to the art and architecture of the past, and what can be done about it?" Assign each member of the group one aspect of the topic, such as the effects of air pollution, methods of restoration, and current conservation projects.

Classical Greece and Rome **547**

THE ORIGINAL LANGUAGE

You might want to use the following pronunciations to give students an idea of the sound of Classical Greek and Latin.

Classical Greek

Ἄνδρα μοι ἔννεπε, μοῦσα,
än'drä moi e'ne pe mōō'sä

πολύτροπον,   ὃς   μάλα
pô loe'trō pôn hōs mä'lä

πολλὰ / πλάγχθη, ἐπεὶ
pô lä' pläng'tä e pä'

Τροίης ἱερὸν
troi'äs   hĕ e rōn'

πτολίεθρον ἔπερσεν·
ptō lĕ'e trōn e'per sen

Latin

The stresses in the following pronunciation are not those used in prose but reflect the meter in which the *Aeneid* is written.

Tu regere imperio
tōō' re ge rim'pe ri ō'

populos,   Romane,
pô pōō lōs' rō mä'ne

memento / (hae tibi erunt
me men'tō hī' ti be roont'

artes), pacique imponere
är täs' pä kē'kwim pō'ne re

morem, / parcere subiectis
mō'rem pär'ke re soob'yek tēs'

et debellare   superbos.
et dä'bel lä're soo pär'bōs

GUIDELINES FOR COLLABORATIVE RESEARCH ACTIVITIES

1. For information about Classical Greek and Roman cultures, students might consult *The Story of Civilization* by Will and Ariel Durant or the *Atlas of the Greek World,* published by Facts on File. These and similar sources should help students find modern ideas that were influenced by Classical ideals.

2. Students might consult a periodicals or newspaper index for articles about art conservation, architectural restoration, and names of specific monuments. They may find, for instance, that air pollutants were so badly damaging the sculptures of the Erechtheum, a temple near the Parthenon, that several of them have been removed and placed in nitrogen-filled cases in a museum. In addition, they might call a city or county historical society to find out about local restoration projects.

SUMMARY

This essay is intended to give students a brief overview of some of the outstanding characteristics of Italian civilization.

- Unified in 1870, Italy is one of the newest nations in Western Europe.
- Since World War II Italy has made great economic strides and has set trends in the arts.
- Many modern Italian writers, film directors, and fashion designers have won international acclaim.
- Italy has exerted a powerful cultural influence on the West since the beginning of the Renaissance, in the fourteenth century.
- Dante, who wrote in the vernacular rather than Latin, helped to forge a new national culture.
- The artist Leonardo da Vinci embodies the achievements of the Renaissance.
- Italian music, epitomized by the Baroque compositions of Vivaldi and the operas of Verdi, continues to thrive.
- Contemporary Italian writers have experimented with a variety of themes and styles.

STUDY QUESTIONS

1. **Review:** Ask students to name the language in which Dante wrote. (Italian, the language of the common people, not Latin, the language of the clergy and scholars) Why was Dante's choice of language important? (He elevated the status of the Italian language and made literature more accessible.)

2. **Discussion:** In English the term *Renaissance man* denotes a cultivated person who is skilled in many scientific and artistic disciplines, as Leonardo da Vinci was. Ask students to discuss whether they would like to become Renaissance men. Does our system of higher education enable students to excel in many disciplines? (Students might say that although it is admirable to aspire to be a Renaissance man, our system of higher education often channels students into specialized fields of expertise.)

3. **Thinking About Art:** Point out that in Italy craftsmanship—as evidenced by the violin and

ITALY

Made by Nicolò Amati in the seventeenth century, this violin testifies to the superb craftsmanship typical of Italian artists.

One of western Europe's newest nations, Italy occupies a boot-shaped peninsula that juts into the Mediterranean Sea. Its rugged terrain—the towering Alps dominate the north, and the Appenine range runs the length of the country—was one of the many factors that prevented its unification. Italy did not become a completely unified nation until 1870.

Over the past century, however, Italy has been transformed from a poor agricultural country to a highly industrialized nation. Devastated during World War II, Italy has bounced back to become one of Europe's major economic powers. Italian cars, textiles, leather goods, and furniture are renowned. Italian arts—particularly cinema, literature, and fashion—set trends throughout the world.

Italy has been a driving cultural force since the Renaissance, which began in the fourteenth century. At

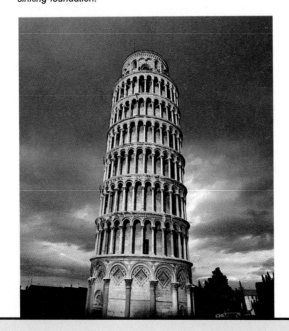

Located in the region of Tuscany, the tower of Pisa, a graceful example of Romanesque architecture, tilts perilously on a slowly sinking foundation.

that time the Italian peninsula was dotted with powerful city-states. These states—which included Florence, Siena, Pisa, Genoa, and Venice—were like quarrelsome families, each controlling commerce, law, and politics within its domain. The states fell within various regions—Tuscany, Lombardy, Piedmont—each with its own language and culture.

During the late Middle Ages and the Renaissance, the power of the individual city-states began to break down, and something resembling a national culture began to develop. Dante Alighieri, the author of the fourteenth-century masterpiece *The Divine Comedy,* helped to forge this national culture. He chose to write not in Latin, the language of the educated classes, but in Tuscan, the language of the ordinary people in his region. Inspired by Dante's verse, Renaissance thinkers began to write in the languages of the common people.

The artists of the Italian Renaissance have left a magnificent legacy. The Basilica of St. Peter's in Rome and the soaring Duomo in Florence testify to the genius of its architects. Michelangelo's frescoes in the Sistine Chapel in Rome, Leonardo da Vinci's *The Last Supper,* and Raphael's *The School of Athens* remind us of the brilliance of its painters. Their ideas

the majolica ware that are illustrated on these pages—is held in high esteem. Do students think that craftsmanship is valued in the United States? Ask them to support their conclusions with examples. (Students might say that although craftsmanship is valued, manufactured objects have largely replaced those that have traditionally been made by hand.)

St. Mark's Square in Venice, depicted here in an eighteenth-century painting by Canaletto, is one of the most picturesque spots in Italy.

about composition and perspective have had a profound influence on Western art.

No single person embodies the achievements of the Renaissance better than Leonardo da Vinci. A master painter and draftsman, da Vinci was also an architect, sculptor, and engineer. His insatiable curiosity about how the world works led him to study the flight of birds, the flow of water in a stream, the delicate structure of plants, and the anatomy of the human body. Like the Renaissance scientist Galileo, whose discoveries in astronomy changed forever many basic concepts of the universe, da Vinci believed in the power of human beings to understand and master their environment.

The spirit of the Renaissance also remains alive in the lyrical clarity of Italian music. The music of Baroque

This exceptional piece of sixteenth-century majolica pottery contains a portrait of a girl who shows us her aristocratic profile.

composer Antonio Vivaldi (best known for his concerto *The Four Seasons*) and of the Romantic opera composer Giuseppe Verdi (known for *La Traviata* and *Aïda*) seems as fresh today as it was when first heard. Italy is still the spiritual home of opera, and some of the world's most acclaimed opera singers are Italian. Chief among them is tenor Luciano Pavarotti.

Since World War II, the most significant cultural contributions in Italy have been in the areas of literature and film. Directors Roberto Rossellini and Vittorio de Sica created realistic films of Italian life in the tumultuous years after the war. One of Rossellini's students, Federico Fellini, has made daring, often surrealistic films that poke fun at Italian customs and institutions.

Italian writers are a lively and varied lot. In the years surrounding World War II, Elio Vittorini and Carlo Levi wrote vivid novels about Italy's dark years under Fascism. Vittorini set many of his works in his native Sicily, an island off Italy's west coast. Levi described his life in exile in southern Italy, a region poetically known as the Mezzogiorno, which means "midday." Novelist Natalia Ginzburg, who comes from the Sicilian city of Palermo, describes the joys and sorrows of the Italian family. In 1981, Umberto Eco, a professor who specializes in semiotics, the study of signs and symbols, published *The Name of the Rose.* The novel became an international best seller, bringing Italian culture once again into the limelight.

IN THIS BOOK

The following Italian selections can be found in this book:

Giovanni Boccaccio, "Federigo's Falcon," p. 135
Grazia Deledda, "The Shoes," p. 220
Dante Alighieri, from *The Divine Comedy,* p. 276
Petrarch, Sonnet 3 ("It Was That Very Day on Which the Sun"), p. 300

Italy **549**

MODERN ITALIAN CULTURE

Ask whether any students in the class are of Italian heritage. If some are, ask them to describe to the class what they know about Italian culture. Students could bring in photographs, recordings of Italian opera or folk music, family mementos or other objects, or samples of Italian cuisine.

FURTHER INVESTIGATION

Encourage students to pursue their individual interests in various aspects of Italian culture. Some suggestions appear below.

- **Art:** the life and works of the painter Giotto, Leonardo da Vinci, or Giorgio de Chirico
- **Architecture:** the life and works of the Renaissance architect Filippo Brunelleschi or the Baroque architect Giovanni Lorenzo Bernini
- **Mythology and Folklore:** Italian folk tales, as compiled by the novelist Italo Calvino, possibly in comparison with the Grimm fairy tales
- **Politics:** the rivalries between the Italian city-states of Florence and Siena
- **Religion:** the history of Vatican City, an independent state within the city of Rome

This outline can be used in the following ways.

- **With less advanced students:** Point out the total time span covered in the outline. Then, beginning at the top of the chart, point out the period covered in each section in order to emphasize the chronology. Also point out the famous authors listed in the outline, particularly those whose work appears in this anthology.

- **With more advanced students:** Suggest that students compare the outline of literature in this Literature and Culture Sourcebook with the Guide to Literary Movements (pp. 584–585). They will discover that literary trends often cut across cultural boundaries—that many cultures had, for instance, a Romantic or a Modernist period. You might also ask students to report on an author who appears in the outline but is not featured in this anthology.

THE AUTHORS IN THIS BOOK

Here are additional notes about the Italian authors whose work appears in this anthology.

- **Dante:** By choosing to write in Italian, Dante opened the doors to the secular and humanistic ideals of the Renaissance.
- **Petrarch:** Sometimes called the first modern poet, Petrarch rejected medieval literary conventions in favor of highly personal verse.
- **Boccaccio:** Boccaccio's daring experiments with prose exemplify the liberal intellectual climate of the Renaissance.
- **Deledda:** Deledda's clear and evocative prose is typical of twentieth-century Italian Realism.

AN OUTLINE OF ITALIAN LITERATURE

PERIOD	MAJOR WRITERS AND MAJOR WORKS	
Medieval (1150–1325) Italian replaced Latin as the language of everyday speech and writing. Poets celebrated God and courtly love, and Dante's epic traced the soul's spiritual journey.	Sicilian School St. Francis of Assisi Dante	
Renaissance (1325–1550) Inspired by Classical Greek and Roman culture, artists developed a humanistic outlook. Writers described contemporary life and politics with a clear and objective eye.	Petrarch Giovanni Boccaccio Niccolò Machiavelli Ludovico Ariosto	Poetry Decameron The Prince Orlando Furioso
Baroque to Romantic (1550–1880) Carefree improvisational comedy enjoyed a revival, and playwrights drew sharp-edged portraits of everyday life. A young poet wrote meditative verses about love and solitude.	Carlo Goldoni Alessandro Manzoni Giacomo Leopardi	The Mistress of the Inn The Betrothed Poetry
Realism (1880–1940) Novelists described the details of modern experience with psychological insight and sly wit. Pirandello, a dramatist, invented new forms to express the uncertainties of modern life.	Giovanni Verga Luigi Pirandello Italo Svevo	The House by the Medlar Tree Six Characters in Search of an Author The Confessions of Zeno
Recent Trends (1940–present) Novelists observed the double tragedies of Fascism and war with depth and acuity. A poet writes elegant and restrained verse, and a woman dedicates her life to portraying the Italian family. Two writers, Eco and Calvino, invent dizzyingly original forms to express their ideas about time and imagination.	Elio Vittorini Carlo Levi Italo Calvino Primo Levi Eugenio Montale Natalia Ginzburg Umberto Eco	Conversation in Sicily Christ Stopped at Eboli Invisible Cities The Periodic Table Poetry Family The Name of the Rose

Italian

Nel mezzo del cammin de nostra vita
mi ritrovai per una selva oscura,
ché la diritta via era smarrita.

—Dante, *La Divina Commedia,*
Inferno

A Translation

Midway in our life's journey, I went astray
from the straight road and woke to find myself
alone in a dark wood.

—*The Divine Comedy,* Inferno,
translated by John Ciardi

This sensitive drawing attests to Leonardo da Vinci's skill as a draftsman. A brilliant painter, da Vinci was also an amateur architect.

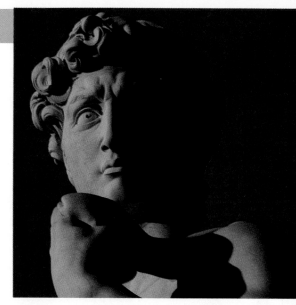

Michelangelo's colossal statue of David, completed in 1504, is a masterpiece of Renaissance sculpture. It was fashioned from a single block of marble.

COLLABORATIVE RESEARCH

1. As a group, research and report on the topic "Tourism in Italy." The purpose of your report is to answer the question "What aspects of history, culture, and contemporary life make Italy a center of world tourism?" Assign each member of the group one aspect of the topic—for example, cities such as Milan, Venice, Florence, Rome, and Naples; smaller towns such as Siena, Assisi, Pisa, Padua, and Orvieto; the Italian countryside; and resorts such as the Italian Riviera.

2. As a group, research and report on the topic "Italy and the United States Today." The purpose of your report is to answer the question "What are the most important influences of Italian culture on American life?" Assign each member of the group one aspect of the topic—for example, sports, decorative arts, fashion, food, films, architecture, sculpture, and classical and popular music.

Italy **551**

You might want to use the following pronunciations to give students an idea of the sound of Italian.

Nel mezzo del cammin de
nel met′sō del kä mēn′ dā

nostra vita / mi ritrovai
nōs′trä vē′tä mē rē trō vī′

per una selva oscura, /
pâr ōō′nä sel′vä ōs kōō′rä

ché la diritta via era
kā lä dē rē′tä vē′ä ā′rä

smarrita.
smä rē′ tä

GUIDELINES FOR COLLABORATIVE RESEARCH ACTIVITIES

1. Students might look for guidebooks on Italy in a bookstore or library, search newspaper and magazine indexes for articles about Italian tourism, get brochures from a travel agency, or interview friends or relatives who have toured Italy on vacation.

2. Students might search for information about people of Italian heritage in the United States, consulting encyclopedias, magazines, and nonfiction books for younger readers, such as *The Italian Americans* by J. Philip di Franco. If their community has a large Italian American population, they may wish to call a local Italian-language institute or Italian American society.

STUDY QUESTIONS

1. **Review:** Ask students to name some of the American writers who settled in Paris early in the twentieth century. (Ernest Hemingway, F. Scott Fitzgerald, and Gertrude Stein) What attracted them to the city? (They were attracted to the lively artistic climate of the city.)

2. **Discussion:** Discuss with students the meaning of the word *expatriate.* Point out that some expatriates are involuntary exiles; generally, they are forced to leave their country because of political differences with their government. Other expatriates leave their homeland voluntarily and settle in their adopted country for some years or, occasionally, for the rest of their life. You might explain that the United States is the home to many expatriate writers, including Czeslaw Milosz and Joseph Brodsky. Conversely, many American writers have chosen to live abroad, including Henry James and T. S. Eliot (in England), Ezra Pound (in Italy), and Gertrude Stein (in France). Ask students whether they can imagine living abroad for an extended period at any point in their life. In which country would they choose to live? Why?

3. **Thinking About Art:** Point out that I. M. Pei's additions to the Louvre, which were completed in 1989, provoked great controversy, for their style differs

FRANCE

The landscapes of France, the largest country in Western Europe, have inspired generations of artists. Its sunny coasts, gentle plains, and rugged mountains are familiar to us through the paintings of nineteenth-century Impressionists. Camille Pissarro immortalized its forests and rivers. Claude Monet preserved its misty harbors, flowering pastures, and haystacks.

The name of France is synonymous with elegance. French architects, painters, and writers have often been without peer. France has set widely imitated standards in fashion, design, and cuisine.

French sophistication springs from a love of beauty and order. The French language is logical, musical, and elegant. Paris, renowned for its romantic setting on the Seine River, is also one of the world's most carefully planned capitals. Its cathedrals, particularly the Gothic Notre Dame, are monuments to the union of mind and spirit. French philosophers, including Voltaire and Jean-Jacques Rousseau, meticulously analyzed the ideas of nature, reason, and freedom. Their writings laid the intellectual groundwork for the French

Baring harmless teeth, this charming dog by the artist Emile Gallé (1846–1904) is made of faience, a type of glazed earthenware.

and American Revolutions in the late eighteenth century.

French artistic achievement — and monarchical France's political power — reached its height during the reign of Louis XIV, the "Sun King" (1643–1715). Louis XIV established a splendid court at Versailles near

The magnificent palace of Versailles is a superb example of French baroque architecture. Surrounded by vast formal gardens, the palace contains hundreds of elegant, sumptuously decorated rooms.

Paris. There he cultivated musicians such as Jean-Baptiste Lully, one of the creators of French opera, and playwrights such as Molière, whose comedies have never been surpassed.

A later French artistic movement, Impressionism, also has its roots in the French love of logic and simplicity. Painters such as Monet sought to capture brief moments in time and reduce them to their simplest elements: light and color. They painted their landscapes with strokes of pure pigment. Later artists, including Edgar Degas and Paul Cézanne, built on these new ideas.

By the early twentieth century Paris had become the artistic capital of Europe. Painters, writers, and musicians mingled and inspired one another. André Gide and Marcel Proust wrote dense, memory-filled novels whose complex structures mirrored the chaos of everyday life. Painters such as Georges Braque tried to evoke the complexities of the modern world by breaking their pictures into multiple planes. This approach, called Cubism, influenced Surrealist writers such as André Breton, who drew on dreams and other messages from the unconscious for his strange and jarring verse. Musicians such as Eric Satie, inspired by the surrealists, wrote spare and haunting melodies.

552 *Literature and Culture Sourcebook*

radically from that of the original buildings. Ask students to look at the photograph of Pei's pyramidal entrance to the museum (p. 553). Does it harmonize with the old structure? Does it seem as "French" as the original Louvre?

The stately rooms of the Louvre in Paris, built in the seventeenth century, house many fine works of art. The glass pyramid is part of a new addition by architect I. M. Pei.

This artistic ferment attracted many artists from other countries, including many Americans. Ernest Hemingway, F. Scott Fitzgerald, and Gertrude Stein migrated to Paris and wrote some of their best work there.

The events surrounding World War II forced French artists to examine their consciences. Writing took on a philosophical bent. Novelists and essayists such as Albert Camus and Jean-Paul Sartre studied the questions of isolation, freedom, and individual responsibility. Their works reflect the logic and purity that have dominated French thought through the centuries.

IN THIS BOOK

The following French selections can be found in this book:

Guy de Maupassant, "The Piece of String," p. 12
Françoise Mallet-Joris, "Air des Clochettes," p. 173
Alphonse Daudet, "The Last Lesson," p. 189
Albert Camus, "The Guest," p. 209
Jean de La Fontaine, "The Fox and the Crow," p. 240
Victor Hugo, "June Nights," p. 305
Colette, "Two Memories of Sido," p. 393
François de La Rochefoucauld, from *Maxims,* p. 401
Edmond Rostand, *Cyrano de Bergerac,* p. 464

A jewel of Gothic architecture, the cathedral of Notre Dame in Paris was completed in the thirteenth century. It is famous for its stained-glass windows.

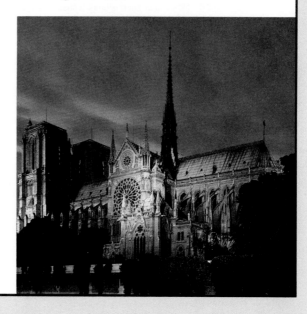

MODERN FRENCH CULTURE

Ask whether any students in the class are of French heritage. If some are, ask them to describe to the class what they know about French culture. Students could bring in photographs, including pictures from French fashion magazines; recordings by widely known French singers, such as Edith Piaf; weavings or other objects; or samples of French cuisine.

FURTHER INVESTIGATION

Encourage students to pursue their individual interests in various aspects of French culture. Some suggestions appear below.

- **Art:** the lives and works of the painters Edgar Dégas and Paul Gauguin or the sculptor Auguste Rodin
- **Architecture:** the Gothic cathedrals of Chartres and Reims and the manner in which they were built; Students may wish to refer to David McCaulay's book *Cathedral.*
- **Dance:** the evolution of ballet in eighteenth-century France, focusing on the achievements of Pierre Beauchamps, who developed the five classical ballet positions, and Marie Salle, France's first female choreographer
- **Drama:** the play *No Exit* by Jean-Paul Sartre
- **Politics:** the history of the Dreyfus affair, particularly the role played by the author Emile Zola, who wrote "I Accuse," the famous letter defending Dreyfus, a Jewish officer in the French Army who was convicted of treason in 1894
- **Science and Technology:** the lives and discoveries of Louis Pasteur and Pierre and Marie Curie

This outline can be used in the following ways.

- **With less advanced students:** Point out the total time span covered in the outline. Then, beginning at the top of the chart, point out the period covered in each section in order to emphasize the chronology. Also point out the famous authors listed in the outline, particularly those whose work appears in this anthology.
- **With more advanced students:** Suggest that students compare the outlines of literature in this Literature and Culture Sourcebook with the Guide to Literary Movements (pp. 584–585). They will discover that literary trends often cut across cultural boundaries—that many cultures had, for instance, a Romantic or a Modernist period. You might also ask students to report on an author who appears in the outline but is not featured in this anthology.

THE AUTHORS IN THIS BOOK

Here are additional notes on the French authors whose work appears in this anthology.

- **La Rochefoucauld:** His mordant observations of court life made La Rochefoucauld a leading author of the Golden Age.
- **La Fontaine:** Trenchant and ironic, La Fontaine's fables highlight the extravagances of Louis XIV's court.
- **Hugo:** His poems and epic novels placed Hugo at the head of the nineteenth-century Romantic movement.
- **Daudet:** By seeking to portray his characters with gentleness and humor, Daudet brought a sense of grace to nineteenth-century Realism.
- **Maupassant:** Writing in the spare, direct style typical of the Naturalists, Maupassant sympathetically explored the frailties of his characters.
- **Rostand:** One of the most popular French playwrights at the turn of this century, Rostand was commended for his wit and style.
- **Colette:** Lauded for her sensitive portrayals of women and nature, Colette earned a respected place among twentieth-century Realists.
- **Camus:** An Existentialist, Camus dramatized his views in pure and understated prose.
- **Mallet-Joris:** Her preoccupations with psychology and social roles place Mallet-Joris in the modern Realist school.

AN OUTLINE OF FRENCH LITERATURE

PERIOD	MAJOR WRITERS AND MAJOR WORKS	
Medieval (850–1400) Wandering bards entertained audiences with heroic and lyric poetry.	Oral Tradition	Romance of the Rose Song of Roland Lyric poetry
Renaissance (1400–1600) Humanistic literature flowered, inspired by Greek, Latin, and Italian models and patronized by courts.	François Villon François Rabelais Pierre de Ronsard Michel de Montaigne	Lyric poetry Gargantua and Pantragruel Lyric poetry Essays
The Golden Age (1600–1700) Literature emphasized rationalism, order, and polished style. Louis XIV had a long rule.	Pierre Corneille Jean de La Fontaine Molière Blaise Pascal Jean Racine René Descartes	The Cid Fables The Misanthrope Tartuffe Thoughts Phaedra Discourse on Method
The Enlightenment (1700–1800) There was great social and political change. Literature was dominated by philosophy and social criticism.	Montesquieu Voltaire Jean-Jacques Rousseau Denis Diderot Pierre de Beaumarchais	Persian Letters Candide Confessions Emile Encyclopedia The Marriage of Figaro
Romanticism (1800–1850) This was an age of self-expression in lyric poetry and the novel.	Chateaubriand Stendhal Alfred de Vigny Alexandre Dumas Victor Hugo	Atala The Red and the Black Lyric poetry The Three Musketeers The Hunchback of Notre Dame
Realism, Naturalism, and Symbolism (1850–1900) Novels and short stories focused on the realistic details of everyday life. Poets rejected realism in favor of suggestive, highly musical verse.	Honoré de Balzac Charles Baudelaire Gustave Flaubert Alphonse Daudet Emile Zola Stéphane Mallarmé Paul Verlaine Guy de Maupassant Arthur Rimbaud	The Human Comedy Flowers of Evil Madame Bovary Short stories Germinal The Afternoon of a Faun Songs Without Words Short stories Illuminations
Modern (1900–present) New movements such as surrealism and existentialism are explored in many literary genres, including poetry, drama, and the novel.	André Gide Marcel Proust Paul Valéry Guillaume Apollinaire André Breton Jean-Paul Sartre Albert Camus Marguerite Duras Alain Robbe-Grillet	The Immoralist Remembrance of Things Past Lyric poetry Alcools Surrealist Manifesto Poetry No Exit The Stranger The Plague The Lover The Erasers

554   *Literature and Culture Sourcebook*

French

De ce terrible paysage,
Tel que jamais mortel n'en vit,
Ce matin encore l'image,
Vague et lointaine, me ravit.

—Charles Baudelaire, "Rêve Parisien"

A Translation

That marvellous landscape of my dream—
Which no eye knows, nor ever will—
At moments, wide awake, I seem
To grasp, and it excites me still.

—"Parisian Dream,"
translated by Edna St. Vincent Millay

COLLABORATIVE RESEARCH

1. As a group, research and report on the topic "France and America Today." The purpose of your report is to answer the question "What are the most important influences of French culture on American life?" Assign each member of the group one aspect of the topic to investigate—for example, films, fashion, decorative arts, food, technology and communications, literature, music, and painting.

2. As a group, research and report on the topic "French Painting and French Society." The purpose of your report is to answer the question "What can French paintings tell us about French culture and society?" Have each group member find a copy of a painting by one of the following French artists: Auguste Renoir, Edouard Manet, and Georges Seurat. Show the class a copy of the painting, and explain what it shows about French society, manners, customs, or class differences.

Camille Pissarro's Boulevard des Italiens, Morning, Sunlight *(1897), like many impressionist paintings, is suffused with pure light.*

France **555**

THE ORIGINAL LANGUAGE

You might want to use the following pronunciations to give students an idea of the sound of French.

De ce terrible paysage, /
də sə te rēb′lə pā ē säzh′

Tel que jamais mortel n'en
tel kə zhä mā′ môr tel′ näɴ

vit, / Ce matin encore
vē sə mä taɴ′ äɴ côr′

l'image, / Vague et lointaine,
lē mäzh′ väg ā lwaɴ ten′

me ravit.
mə rä vē′

GUIDELINES FOR COLLABORATIVE RESEARCH ACTIVITIES

1. Students might look up books and encyclopedia articles on French culture; visit film and record libraries, museums, and stores selling French products; or leaf through French magazines and cookbooks.
2. To research the links between the art of France and its mores and customs, students might look for general art books, such as Janson's *History of Art for Young People*. Biographies of specific artists may also be useful.

SPAIN

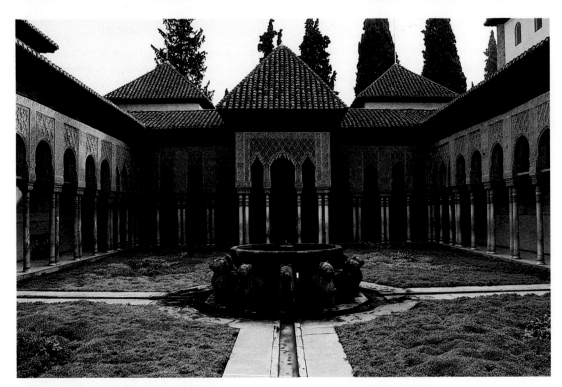

Flanked by lions, this fountain in a courtyard of the Alhambra provides a cool and tranquil focal point in an austere, harmonious setting.

Spain occupies most of the Iberian Peninsula in southwestern Europe. The Pyrenees Mountains isolate Spain from its northern neighbor, France, and the Atlantic Ocean and the Mediterranean Sea lap against its borders. This isolation—and Spain's proximity to Africa, less than twenty-five miles across the Strait of Gibraltar—have had a profound effect on Spanish history and culture.

Spain's rich artistic tradition has been shaped by its conquerors. Greeks settled on the Mediterranean coast in ancient times, and the Celts, an early people who also migrated to Ireland and western France, ventured across the Pyrenees and settled in the northern region now called Galicia. Roman soldiers marched across the Iberian plains in the third century A.D. and dominated the peninsula for the next two centuries. The Moors, who were Moslems, invaded Iberia from Africa in the eighth century, but the newly Christianized Iberian kings gradually reconquered their lost territories and finally expelled the Moslems in 1492, the same year Columbus landed in the New World.

Travelers can still see monuments to Spain's varied past. Roman aqueducts cross the dusty plains of Castile. Moorish mosques and palaces (called *alcázars*) stand in many towns in southern Spain. Perhaps the most famous *alcázar* is the Alhambra in the city of Granada. Built in the thirteenth and fourteenth centuries, the Alhambra is constructed around a series of courtyards.

556 *Literature and Culture Sourcebook*

Its myriad rooms are faced with tiles decorated with exquisite geometric and floral designs, for Moslems are forbidden by religious teachings to create representations of living beings.

By the sixteenth century, Spain had become a world power, claiming territories in Italy, the east Atlantic, and the New World. At the same time Spanish arts and letters flowered. During the Golden Age of the sixteenth and seventeenth centuries, El Greco painted his intensely religious scenes, and Diego Velázquez depicted the people of the Spanish court with humor, compassion, and psychological insight. Miguel de Cervantes published his masterpiece, *Don Quixote,* and Lope de Vega wrote plays that gave depth and dignity to peasants and kings alike.

Pablo Picasso (1881–1973), in his whimsical The Bull, *recalls the prehistoric cave paintings at Altamira in northern Spain.*

Much of Spain's recent history is familiar to us through its painting. Francisco de Goya captured the frivolities of the Spanish court and the horrors of the Napoleonic invasion in the early nineteenth century. Pablo Picasso created the most famous image of Spain's Civil War (1936–1939) with his somber canvas *Guernica.*

The Spanish people, now united by a democratic government, are renowned for their regional traditions

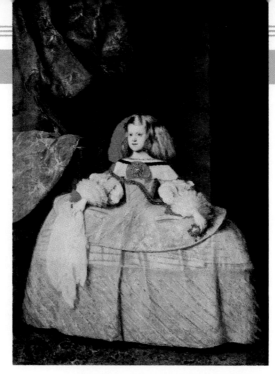

Golden Age painter Diego Velázquez (1599–1660) captured the opulence of court life in his portrait of a youthful Austrian princess.

and their vivacious spirit. The Gypsies who migrated to southern Spain are credited with the invention of flamenco, the flamboyant dance performed to the accompaniment of guitars and castanets. The Basques and Catalans of northern Spain are renowned for their industriousness, their tongue-twisting languages, and their sophisticated cuisine. Natives of Galicia still spin lively tales that are descended from the myths told by their Celtic ancestors—a reminder that in Spain the past is always very much alive.

IN THIS BOOK

The following Spanish selections can be found in this book:

Miguel de Cervantes, from *Don Quixote,* p. 162
Antonio Machado, "Winter Sun," p. 304
Vicente Aleixandre, "On the Way to School," p. 332
Federico García Lorca, "The Guitar," p. 340
Juan Ramón Jiménez, from *Platero and I,* p. 414
Camilo José Cela, "Traveling in the Alcarria," p. 418

Spain **557**

This outline can be used in the following ways.

- **With less advanced students:** Point out the total time span covered in the outline. Then, beginning at the top of the chart, point out the period covered in each section in order to emphasize the chronology. Also point out the famous authors listed in the outline, particularly those whose work appears in this anthology.

- **With more advanced students:** Suggest that students compare the outlines of literature in this Literature and Culture Sourcebook with the Guide to Literary Movements (pp. 584–585). They will discover that literary trends often cut across cultural boundaries—that many cultures had, for instance, a Romantic or a Modernist period. You might also ask students to report on an author who appears in the outline but is not featured in this anthology.

THE AUTHORS IN THIS BOOK

Here are additional notes on the Spanish authors whose work appears in this anthology.

- **Cervantes:** One of the shining figures of the Golden Age, Cervantes is sometimes called the first novelist in the West.
- **Machado:** Machado's limpid, melancholy verses made him one of Spain's most celebrated Modernist poets.
- **Jiménez:** Linked early in his career with the Modernists, Jiménez later developed an austere and mystical poetic style.
- **Aleixandre:** By turns Surrealistic and Romantic, Aleixandre's verses broke new ground in the Modernist movement.
- **García Lorca:** His passionate verses made him the most popular poet of his generation.
- **Cela:** A political conservative turned liberal, Cela has experimented with a wide range of literary styles.

AN OUTLINE OF SPANISH LITERATURE

PERIOD	MAJOR WRITERS AND MAJOR WORKS	
Medieval (1100–1400) Lyric poetry and epic poems prevailed. Alfonso X sponsored early Castilian prose.	Anonymous Juan Ruíz	Song of My Cid Poetry
The Golden Age (1500–1680) This was the richest period in Spanish literature, influenced by the ideas of the Italian Renaissance. Pastoral and picturesque novels became popular, and Spanish theater thrived.	Saint Teresa of Avila Anonymous Miguel de Cervantes Lope de Vega Tirso de Molina Luis de Góngora Pedro Calderón de la Barca Francisco de Quevedo	Mystical prose Lazarillo de Tormes Don Quixote Fuenteovejuna The Trickster of Seville Lyric poetry Life Is a Dream Life of a Scoundrel
Neoclassicism (1680–1800) The philosophy of the Enlightenment inspired some writers. Others were influenced by Greek and Roman classics.	José Cadalso Gaspar Melchor de 　Jovellanos Juan Meléndez Valdés	Cartas marruecas Poetry, essays Poetry
Romanticism and Realism (1880–1895) Romantic poets wrote sensitive verses about love and loneliness. Novelists drew realistic portraits of Spain's history and regional traditions.	Gustavo Adolfo Bécquer Pedro Antonio de Alarcón Benito Pérez Galdós Vicente Blasco Ibáñez	Poetry The Three-Cornered Hat Fortunata and Jacinta The Four Horsemen of 　the Apocalypse
Generation of '98 (1895–1925) Spain's defeat in the Spanish-American war of 1898 forced writers to re-examine the Spanish character.	Miguel de Unamuno José Ortega y Gasset	Mist Abel Sánchez Meditations on Quixote
Modernism (1900–1950) Nicaragua's Rubén Darío and the French Surrealists inspired a generation of Spanish poets who wrote introspective, anguished, and passionate verse.	Antonio Machado Juan Ramón Jiménez Vicente Aleixandre Federico García Lorca	Poetry Platero and I Poetry The House of Bernardo 　Alba The Gypsy Ballads Blood Wedding

Spanish

Y en diciendo esto, y encomendándose de todo corazón a su señora Dulcinea, pidiéndole que en tal trance le socorriese, bien cubierto de su rodela, con la lanza en el ristre, arremetió a todo galope de Rocinante y embistió con el primero molino que estaba delante; y dándole una lanzada en el aspa, la volvió el viento con tanta furia, que hizo la lanza pedazos, llevándose tras sí al caballo y al caballero, que fue rodando muy maltrecho por el campo.

—Miguel de Cervantes, *Don Quixote*

A Translation

Saying this, he dedicated himself to his lady, Dulcinea del Toboso, that she might aid him in battle. Then he put up his shield, settled his lance in place, and set off on Rosinante at full gallop. He attacked the first windmill he came to, thrusting his lance into one of its sails. But the wind turned the sail with such strength that it shattered his lance and lifted both horse and rider into the air, tossing Don Quixote across the fields.

—translated by George Kearns

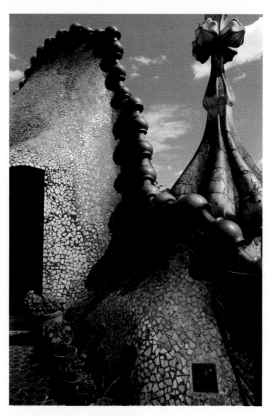

A fanciful house in Barcelona designed by architect Antonio Gaudí (1852–1926) has few straight lines; rather, it is composed of fluid organic shapes.

COLLABORATIVE RESEARCH

1. As a group, research and help your class to compare and contrast the art of Pablo Picasso, Juan Gris, Joan Miró, and Salvador Dali. Assign each member of the group one artist and the following topics to investigate: the style or styles of painting the artist is known for, the ideas the artist has sought to convey, and several of the artist's most famous paintings. Prepare a chart that summarizes each researcher's findings.

2. Form a group to prepare a poster highlighting the local heritage of different regions in Spain. Assign each member of the group one region—for example, Catalonia, Andalusia, the Basque provinces, Galicia, and Castile. Students should investigate the food, music, festivals, and unique cultural traditions of the region. As a group, decide the best way to organize the poster and present each person's findings.

Spain **559**

THE ORIGINAL LANGUAGE

You might want to use the following pronunciations of the first two lines of the excerpt to give students an idea of the sound of Spanish.

Y en diciendo esto, y
ē en dē thyen'dō es'tō ē

encomendándose de todo
eng kō'men dän'dō sā dā tō'thō

corazón a su señora
kō rä thôn' ä sōō sā nyō'rä

Dulcinea, ...
dool'thē nā'ä

GUIDELINES FOR COLLABORATIVE RESEARCH ACTIVITIES

1. Students might consult biographies and critical studies of Spanish artists. One useful book is Piero Ventura's *Great Painters*. They might also wish to see whether they may interview a curator of a local museum or gallery that exhibits paintings by these artists.
2. Information about Spain's regions can be found in the Time-Life *Encyclopedia of Spain,* travel guides, Spanish Tourist Board brochures, and local Spanish clubs. Students should also look for Basque and Catalan clubs if they live near a large Spanish population.

SUMMARY

This essay is intended to give students a brief overview of some of the outstanding characteristics of Latin American culture.

- Latin America is home to a diverse population whose predominant languages are Spanish, Portuguese, and French.
- Three great civilizations were born in Latin America: the Mayan, Aztec, and Inca.
- Spanish conquistadors overthrew the Aztec and Inca empires in the sixteenth century.
- Following the conquest Latin America was dominated by Spain and Portugal for three hundred years.
- By the early nineteenth century most Latin American countries had won their independence.
- In the twentieth century an era of bold experimentation in the arts began.

STUDY QUESTIONS

1. **Review:** Ask students to name the two native Latin American civilizations that were discovered by the Spaniards in the sixteenth century. (the Aztec and the Inca) Where were they located, and what was their fate? (The Aztec Empire of Mexico was conquered by Cortés; the Incas of the Andean highlands were conquered by Pizarro.)

2. **Discussion:** Explain that some native peoples of Latin America had their own literary traditions. The Aztecs and Mayas recorded their poetry and history in books made of pounded tree bark. During the conquest Spanish priests burned thousands of these books; today only a few remain. Ask students to discuss what they think would happen if all the books that are now in our libraries were destroyed.

3. **Thinking About Art:** Direct students' attention to the Chac Mool that appears in the photograph of Chichén Itzá. Ask students to develop a story about the Chac Mool that is both realistic and fantastic, in the manner of the Magic Realism found, for example, in the writings of Gerardo María (p. 152). Students might describe what the Chac Mool looks like and explain where he lives, what he eats, and why he is so vigilant.

LATIN AMERICA

South of the United States lies a vast territory known as Latin America. This territory stretches from the deserts and plains of northern Mexico to the southernmost tip of the continent of South America. It also includes most of the sickle-shaped chain of islands in the Caribbean Sea known as the West Indies. Most of the people in Latin America speak Spanish, but some speak Portuguese or French. All these languages come from Latin, hence the region's name.

Latin America has given the world many things. Corn, beans, potatoes, chocolate, and rubber originated in Latin America. Latin rhythms have influenced musicians throughout the world. The hot colors and bold compositions of Latin American painters have inspired countless artists. The continent has some of the world's most vibrant cities, including Rio de Janeiro in Brazil and Buenos Aires, the capital of Argentina. Nowhere is Latin America's influence more strongly felt than the United States, where more than seven percent of the population is Hispanic.

The earliest inhabitants of Latin America are thought to have crossed over from Siberia on a land bridge some twenty thousand years ago. By the ninth century, a great culture thrived in the Yucatán Peninsula in what is now southern Mexico and Guatemala. The Maya Indians who lived there built great temples, developed a highly accurate calendar based on the solar year, and invented a sophisticated system of hieroglyphic writing that, though partially deciphered, still evades archaeologists.

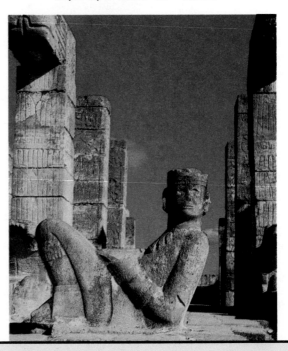

Ever vigilant, this reclining figure, called a Chac Mool, watches over the ruins of the Mayan city of Chichén Itzá in Mexico.

When Spanish and Portuguese conquistadors reached the New World in the early sixteenth century, they discovered two advanced civilizations. Hernán Cortés discovered the flourishing Aztec Empire in central Mexico and admired the brilliantly painted pyramids of its capital, which was built on an island in the middle of a lake. Another Spaniard, Francisco Pizarro, marched into the Peruvian city of Cuzco, capital of the Inca Empire. There he found temples made of perfectly cut stones and sacred gardens with life-sized plants and animals made of hammered silver and gold.

The Aztec and Inca Empires were soon conquered, but native cultures still thrive in Latin America. In Mexico Indians still speak the languages of the Aztec, Zapotec, and Mayan civilizations, and tourists from all over the world come to admire their ruined temples. In the highlands of Ecuador, Peru, and Bolivia, many Indians still speak Quechua, the language of the Incas. The magnificent stonework of the Inca ruins in Cuzco and Machu Picchu awes visitors to this day.

Indian tribes also inhabit the jungles of the Amazon basin, a vast lowland area drained by the world's largest river. The basin occupies the northern third of Brazil and parts of Colombia and Venezuela. Portuguese explorers colonized Brazil, and Spanish-speaking immigrants settled parts of Venezuela and Colombia. In many isolated areas of the Amazonian interior, however, Indian languages and customs still predominate.

In the early nineteenth century region after re -

This precious mask from the Chimú culture of Peru (900–1470) once graced a nobleman's tomb; it is now in the Gold Museum in Lima.

gion in Latin America rose in rebellion against colonial rule. Military leaders such as Venezuela's Simón Bolívar and Argentina's José de San Martín led liberation movements across the continent, and by 1825 most of the modern-day nations of Latin America had won their independence from Portugal and Spain.

With independence came a great cultural flowering. Over the past one hundred fifty years Latin American artists have created powerful new forms to express their Hispanic and Indian heritage. The murals of Mexican painters Diego Rivera and José Orozco, the music of Brazilian composer Heitor Villa-Lobos and Mexican composer Carlos Chávez, and the dreamlike portraits of Colombian Fernando Botero celebrate this dual heritage. Likewise, the daring experiments by Latin American writers such as Argentina's Jorge Luis Borges and Julio Cortázar, Colombia's Gabriel García Márquez, and Peru's Mario Vargas Llosa are also based on the complex interweavings of Spanish and Indian, modern and colonial, and agricultural and urban strains.

IN THIS BOOK

The following Latin American selections can be found in this book:

Manuel Rojas, "The Glass of Milk," p. 57
Gerardo María, "Matusalén, the Village Without Time," p. 153

Gabriel García Márquez, "Tuesday Siesta," p. 198
Zapotec Traditional (retold by Andrés Henestrosa), "The Bat," p. 235
Gabriela Mistral, "Rocking," p. 291
Pablo Neruda, "The Horses," p. 308
João Cabral de Melo Neto, "Weaving the Morning," p. 312
Octavio Paz, "Wind and Water and Stone," p. 316
Jorge Carrera Andrade, "Reaping the Barley," p. 326
Jorge Luis Borges, "Afterglow," p. 345
Jaime Torres Bodet, "The Window," p. 354
José Martí, from *Versos Sencillos,* p. 362

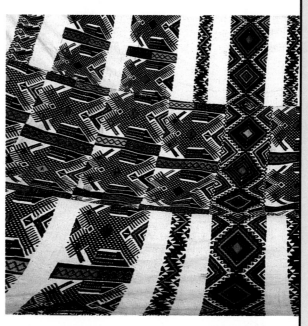

Traditional arts and crafts are still very much alive in many parts of Latin America, as this weaving from Guatemala attests.

Latin America **561**

OUTLINE OF LITERATURE

This outline can be used in the following ways.

- **With less advanced students:** Point out the total time span covered in the outline. Then, beginning at the top of the chart, point out the period covered in each section in order to emphasize the chronology. Also point out the famous authors listed in the outline, particularly those whose work appears in this anthology.

- **With more advanced students:** Suggest that students compare the outlines of literature in this Literature and Culture Sourcebook with the Guide to Literary Movements (pp. 584–585). They will discover that literary trends often cut across cultural boundaries—that many cultures had, for instance, a Romantic or a Modernist period. You might also ask students to report on an author who appears in the outline but is not featured in this anthology.

THE AUTHORS IN THIS BOOK

Here are additional notes on the Latin American authors whose work appears in this anthology.

- **Zapotec Traditional:** The anonymous composer of this tale belonged to the Zapotec tribe, whose descendants still inhabit southern Mexico.
- **Martí:** An accomplished Modernist poet, Martí also wrote political verses exhorting his fellow Cubans to fight for their independence.
- **Mistral:** Mistral's delicately lyrical poems about nature and motherhood won her international acclaim.
- **Rojas:** His stark, insistent language and sensitivity to the life of ordinary people identify Rojas with the Latin Realist school.
- **Borges:** Initially influenced by the Modernists, Borges wrote poetry, essays, criticism, and short stories in a variety of styles.
- **Torres Bodet:** Like Neruda, Torres Bodet was both a statesman and a master of modern verse.
- **Carrera Andrade:** In his gently lyrical poems Carrera Andrade evokes the austere landscapes of Ecuador.
- **Neruda:** By turns lyrical, Surrealistic, and dogmatic, Neruda's verses betray the eclecticism

typical of many modern Latin American writers.
- **Paz:** A master poet and essayist, Paz writes with a versatility that is typical of many modern Latin writers.
- **Cabral:** Rhythmic and lyrical, Cabral's verses recall the bleak landscapes of northeast Brazil.

- **García Márquez:** The consummate author of the school of Magic Realism, García Márquez also writes historical fiction.
- **Naipaul:** The grandson of an East Indian who migrated to Trinidad, Naipaul is praised for his refined prose style and his incisive analyses of the Third World.

- **María:** This young Mexican author writes realistic stories that show his strong political beliefs and also fantastic tales typical of the Magic Realists.

PERIOD	MAJOR WRITERS AND MAJOR WORKS	
Renaissance and Baroque (1600–1700) Writers chronicled the tumultuous years following the conquest, and a Mexican nun wrote simple verses of sacred and profane love.	Garcilaso de la Vega (Peru)	Royal Commentaries
	Sor Juana Inés de la Cruz (Mexico)	First Dream
Romanticism (1800–1880) Authors idealized the romantic Indian past and the people of the new Latin American nations.	José Hernández (Argentina)	Martín Fierro
Modernism (1880–1910) Poets rejected sentimentality and wrote clean, pure verse that often reflected a sophisticated knowledge of art and culture.	José Martí (Cuba)	Simple Verses
	Rubén Darío (Nicaragua)	Blue / Profane Prose
Realism and Lyricism (1910–1950) Novelists created sympathetic portraits of peasants, Indians, the urban poor, and people displaced by war. Lyricists, many of them women, wrote verses about love, motherhood, and social concerns.	Mariano Azuela (Mexico)	The Underdogs
	Rómulo Gallegos (Venezuela)	Doña Bárbara
	Manuel Rojas (Chile)	Son of a Thief
	Gabriela Mistral (Chile)	Desolation
Recent Trends (1950–present) Essayists and poets such as Paz explore universal themes such as solitude and identity. Others, like Neruda, celebrate the vitality of life in all its forms, from everyday objects to the struggles of the poor and romantic love. Novelists and short-story writers such as Borges and García Márquez explore new forms that allow them to express their ideas about dream and reality and about myth and history.	Octavio Paz (Mexico)	Labyrinth of Solitude
	Pablo Neruda (Chile)	The Heights of Machu Picchu
	Gabriel García Márquez (Colombia)	One Hundred Years of Solitude / No One Writes to the Colonel
	Jorge Luis Borges (Argentina)	Labyrinths
	Jorge Amado (Brazil)	Gabriela, Clove and Cinnamon
	Mario Vargas Llosa (Peru)	Aunt Julia and the Scriptwriter
	Julio Cortázar (Argentina)	Hopscotch

Spanish

Muchos años después, frente al pelotón de fusilamiento, el coronel Aureliano Buendía había de recordar aquella tarde remota en que su padre lo llevó a conocer el hielo.

—Gabriel García Márquez, *Cien Años de Soledad*

A Translation

Many years later, as he faced the firing squad, Colonel Aureliano Buendía was to remember that distant afternoon when his father took him to discover ice.

—*One Hundred Years of Solitude*, translated by Gregory Rabassa

COLLABORATIVE RESEARCH

1. As a group, research and report on the topic "The Conquest of Latin America." The purpose of your report is to answer the question "How did the conquest change the lives of Indians in Latin America?" Assign each group member one aspect of Indian life to examine: health, religion, social organization, language, art, music, or cuisine. If you like, enact a brief historical drama about the encounter between the Spanish conquistador Hernán Cortés and the Aztec emperor Montezuma, or between the Spanish conquistador Francisco Pizarro and the Inca leader Atahualpa.

2. As a group, research and report on the topic "Native Products of Latin America." The purpose of your report is to answer the question "Which common foods and products came from Latin America, and how were they important to their own Latin American cultures?" Assign each group member one of these products: potatoes, corn, chocolate, hot chilies, quinine, and rubber. Show photographs or pictures of the regions and cultures associated with these products.

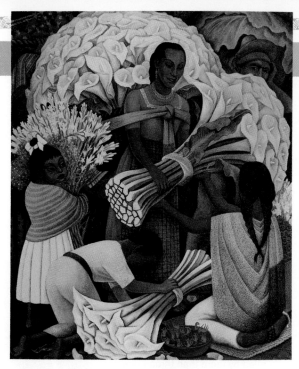

The Mexican people are sensitively portrayed in many paintings by Diego Rivera, including this one, entitled Flower Vendor *(1948).*

Born on the arid coast of Peru, the Nazca culture, which thrived from 100 B.C. to A.D. 200, left behind many treasures, including this vessel.

Latin America **563**

You might want to use the following pronunciations to give students an idea of the sound of Spanish.

Muchos años después,
mo͞o'chōs ä'nyōs des pwes'

frente al pelotón de
fren'tā äl pä'lō tōn' dā

fusilamiento, el
fo͞o'sē lä myen'tō el

coronel Aureliano
kō'rō nel' ou'rä lyä'nō

Buendía había de
bwen dē'ä ä bē'ä dā

recordar aquella tarde
rä'kôr där' ä kā'yä tär'dā

remota en que su padre
rä mō'tä en kā so͞o pä'drä

lo llevó a conocer el
lō yä bō' ä kō'nō ser' el

hielo.
yä'lō

GUIDELINES FOR COLLABORATIVE RESEARCH ACTIVITIES

1. Students might search for accounts of the conquest of the Aztec and Inca empires, such as the books by Albert Marrin, and for biographies of Cortés, Pizarro, Montezuma, and Atahualpa.

2. Students might consult general reference sources—the Time-Life *Encyclopedia of Mexico*, for example—for information on Latin American agriculture and forestry. They could research and report on specific subjects, such as the destruction of the rain forests, or specific products, such as quinine.

SUMMARY

This essay is intended to give students a brief overview of some of the outstanding characteristics of German culture.

- Germany is one of the most powerful and influential European nations.
- German borders and political allegiances have shifted continually over the years.
- Differences in language and dialect have also divided the German people.
- A national culture began to develop in the sixteenth century.
- German composers such as Bach, Beethoven, and Wagner have made great contributions to classical music.
- German philosophers such as Kant, Hegel, and Nietzsche broke new intellectual ground.
- Modern physics has been shaped by German scientists such as Planck and Einstein.
- The twentieth century has produced many fine German writers, among them Brecht, Grass, and Böll.

STUDY QUESTIONS

1. **Review:** What impact did Martin Luther have on German culture? (His translation of the Bible helped standardize the German language.)
2. **Discussion:** Ask students whether they play a musical instrument. How many of them are familiar with the music of Bach, Beethoven, or Brahms? Do they think that it is useful for them to learn about classical music even if they are primarily interested in, say, folk music or jazz? Why or why not?
3. **Thinking About Art:** Ask students to look at the photograph of the Neuschwanstein castle on the next page and to think of ideas for folk tales that are set in or around the castle. They might wish to model their stories after a Grimm fairy tale that they know.

GERMANY

One of the most powerful and influential European countries historically, Germany as a whole is nonetheless difficult to define. Its borders and its political allegiances have shifted constantly over the centuries, and the German language only loosely unites its many regions. The impact of German culture, however, is clear. The world would be much poorer without the contributions of German philosophers, scientists, writers, and musicians.

Germany is a hilly and heavily forested country that is divided by many beautiful rivers, among them the Danube, the Elbe, and the Rhine. Fierce tribes of Germanic peoples settled in these river valleys some 3,000 years ago, pushing out the Celts. For centuries Germany was nothing more than a loose confederation. (For a time during the seventeenth century, it was ruled by more than three hundred princes.) Even language divided the German people. During the Middle Ages the educated elite spoke Latin. Peasants in the south of Germany spoke a language called High German, and those in the north spoke Low German. In addition, various ethnic groups, such as the Bavarians, spoke their own dialects.

During the sixteenth century all this began to change. The monk Martin Luther, hoping to popularize his ideas about church reform, translated the Bible into clear, readable German. Printed on mechanical presses, which had only recently been invented, the German Bibles were widely read and did much to help to standardize the German spoken by the common people.

German instruments are renowned for their high quality, as this mid-eighteenth century clavicytherium, a type of harpsichord, shows.

Today, most of the country's citizens speak High German, though dialects still thrive.

If Luther transformed the German language, his contemporary, Albrecht Dürer, revolutionized German painting. The son of a goldsmith, Dürer traveled to Italy and was strongly influenced by the Italian Renaissance. His portraits and engravings show his intense interest in classical ideas.

The great era of German music was ushered in with the birth of Johann Sebastian Bach in 1685, roughly one hundred fifty years after Dürer's death. An accomplished organist, Bach perfected the art of polyphony, the interweaving of several melodies in the same composition. One century later Ludwig van Beethoven made extraordinary contributions to the musical forms of the symphony, sonata, and quartet. In the late nineteenth century the composer Richard Wagner synthesized music and drama in his operas, which were based on medieval German legends. His bold experiments with harmony laid the groundwork for much modern music.

Germany has also produced some of the world's great philosophers. In the eighteenth and nineteenth centuries Immanuel Kant, Georg Wilhelm Friedrich Hegel, and Friedrich Nietzsche broke new ground in the perennial debates about the nature of freedom and morality and the struggle between the mind and the heart.

German philosophy had a direct impact on German science. At the turn of the twentieth century, physicist Max Planck transformed the standard thinking

564 *Literature and Culture Sourcebook*

The dark cross timbers and leaded-glass windows of this house, located in the Rhine Valley, are typical of German architecture.

about the structure of the atom. In 1916 physicist Albert Einstein announced his brilliant general theory of relativity. Einstein also made critical discoveries about the relationship between mass and energy and the physical composition of light. Like many German intellectuals he fled his native country during the years of Nazi rule; he became a U.S. citizen in 1940.

Made for the German count Heinrich von Brühl, these eighteenth-century fruit stands are an exquisite example of Meissen porcelain.

The Neuschwanstein castle in Bavaria, a forested region in southern Germany, could have been lifted from a Grimm fairy tale.

In the twentieth century a current of pessimism and despair ran through much German thought. Playwright Bertolt Brecht savagely attacked middle-class values in *The Threepenny Opera* and other plays. Artist Georg Grosz and novelist Günter Grass satirized German life. Not all writings were negative, however. Novelist Heinrich Böll, though critical of many aspects of his native country, developed a profoundly moral and spiritual vision of modern humanity.

IN THIS BOOK

The following German selections can be found in this book:

Thomas Mann, "The Infant Prodigy," p. 113
Heinrich Böll, "The Laugher," p. 205
Johann Wolfgang von Goethe, "The Erl-King," p. 258
Nelly Sachs, "The Swan," p. 307
Heinrich Heine, "The Lorelei," p. 347

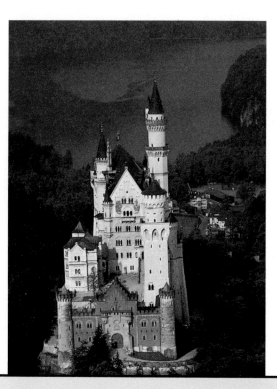

MODERN GERMAN CULTURE

Ask whether any students in the class are of German heritage. If some are, ask them to describe to the class what they know about German culture. Students might bring in photographs, recordings of German music, regional costumes or other objects, or samples of German cuisine.

FURTHER INVESTIGATION

Encourage students to pursue their individual interests in various aspects of German culture. Some suggestions appear below.
- **Art:** the life and work of the Renaissance artist Albrecht Dürer or the Surrealist painter Max Ernst
- **Architecture:** the Bauhaus movement of the early twentieth century, which had a strong impact on modern design
- **Music:** the life of the composer Ludwig van Beethoven, particularly during his later years, when he composed some of his best works despite his total deafness
- **Science and Technology:** the life of the physicist Albert Einstein and the role that he played as an adviser to the United States during World War II

This outline can be used in the following ways.

- **With less advanced students:** Point out the total time span covered in the outline. Then, beginning at the top of the chart, point out the period covered in each section in order to emphasize the chronology. Also point out the famous authors listed in the outline, particularly those whose work appears in this anthology.
- **With more advanced students:** Suggest that students compare the outlines of literature in this Literature and Culture Sourcebook with the Guide to Literary Movements (pp. 584–585). They will discover that literary trends often cut across cultural boundaries— that many cultures had, for instance, a Romantic or a Modernist period. You might also ask students to report on an author who appears in the outline but is not featured in this anthology.

THE AUTHORS IN THIS BOOK

Here are additional notes on the German authors whose work appears in this anthology.

- **Goethe:** Goethe's interest in mysticism and folklore shaped his Romantic sensibility.
- **Heine:** A leading German Romantic poet of the nineteenth century, Heine wrote many verses that were set to music by Schubert and Schumann.
- **Mann:** The foremost German Modernist, Mann explored the connections between an individual's psychological struggles and changing social values.
- **Sachs:** One of the leading lyric poets of the twentieth century, Nelly Sachs describes the beauties of nature and the lives of the Jewish people.
- **Böll:** Böll's realistic tales of postwar Germany are infused with a strong moral tone.

AN OUTLINE OF GERMAN LITERATURE

PERIOD	MAJOR WRITERS AND MAJOR WORKS	
Medieval (900–1350) Epic and lyric poetry flourished. *Spielmänner*, or wandering minstrels, recited popular legends, and poets entertained courts with tales of love and adventure.	Oral Tradition	Song of Hildebrand
	Oral Tradition	Nibelungenlied
	Gottfried von Strassburg	Tristan
	Wolfram von Eschenbach	Parzival
	Walther von de Vogelweide	Lyric poetry
Reformation and Baroque (1500–1700) Luther's vigorous translations of the Bible gave written German new power. Sachs perfected the art of epic verse, and Lessing wrote pioneering dramas about the family and everyday life.	Martin Luther	Translations of religious works
	Hans Sachs	Lyric poems
	Gotthold Ephraim Lessing	Emilia Galotti
Romanticism (1750–1830) This was the golden age of the novel, drama, and lyric poetry. Writers emphasized the importance of emotions, as well as intellect, and praised nature and freedom. Romantic authors developed an intense interest in history and folklore.	Johann Wolfgang von Goethe	The Sorrows of Young Werther
		Faust
	Friedrich Schiller	Wallenstein
		The Maid of Orleans
	Novalis	Lyric poetry
	Heinrich von Kleist	The Prince of Homburg
	Joseph von Eichendorff	Lyric poetry
	Jakob and Wilhelm Grimm	Fairy tales
	Heinrich Heine	Lyric poetry
Modernism (1900–1945) Some writers used symbol and myth to explore the human mental and spiritual state. Others emphasized the absurdity and futility of modern life.	Thomas Mann	The Magic Mountain
	Hermann Hesse	Steppenwolf
	Franz Kafka	The Trial
	Bertolt Brecht	The Threepenny Opera
Recent Trends (1945–present) Writers examine the moral dilemmas of the postwar years; authors resort to satire, comedy, and the grotesque to describe the human condition.	Nelly Sachs	Lyric poetry
	Heinrich Böll	Group Portrait with Lady
	Günter Grass	The Tin Drum
		The Flounder

German

Drum hab' ich mich der Magie ergeben . . .
Daß ich erkenne, was die Welt
Im Innersten zusammenhält,
Schau' alle Wirkenskraft und Samen,
Und tu' nicht mehr in Worten kramen.

—Goethe, *Faust*

A Translation

Therefore I have turned to magic . . .
that I might gain the sight
of the world's inmost fabric,
of its essential will and fount
and need no longer rummage in words.

—translated by Peter Salm

COLLABORATIVE RESEARCH

1. As a group, research and report on the topic "German Myth and Folklore in World Art." The purpose of your report is to answer the question "How have German myths, legends, and folk tales inspired and influenced writers, artists, and musicians from diverse cultures?" Assign each member of the group one aspect of the topic—for example, Germanic mythology, epics, legends, folk tales, and fairy tales.

2. As a group, research and report on the topic "Tourism in Modern Germany." The purpose of your report is to answer the question "What does Germany offer today's tourists?" Imagine that each member of your group is a tour guide from a particular German region. Choose regions that have many tourist attractions, such as Bavaria, the Rhine Valley, the Black Forest, Franconia, Westphalia, Saxony, and Thuringia. Present a brief talk to the class about your region.

This portrait by Gabriele Münter (1877–1962), entitled Reflection, *is typical of the German expressionist school, which strove to express intense human feeling.*

Germany **567**

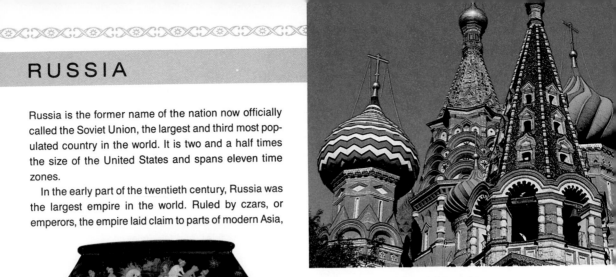

Crowned with onion-shaped domes, the Cathedral of St. Basil on Moscow's Red Square is typical of sixteenth-century Russian religious architecture.

SUMMARY: RUSSIA

This essay is intended to give students a brief overview of some of the outstanding characteristics of Russian and Eastern European cultures.

- The Soviet Union is the largest and third most populated country in the world and is home to more than one hundred ethnic groups.
- The Russian Empire reached its peak of power and influence in the early years of the twentieth century.
- Most of the images we associate with Russian culture come from the Slavic peoples, who form the bulk of the population in the western Soviet Union.

STUDY QUESTIONS: RUSSIA

1. **Review:** Ask students to name some of the images we associate with Slavic culture. (Moscow's domed churches, Ukrainian embroidery and folk dances, Cossack horsemen)
2. **Discussion:** In the Soviet Union today the ethnic groups that inhabit certain republics are demanding more autonomy, and some republics are threatening to secede from the Soviet Union altogether. Ask students to imagine a situation in which a modern-day state or region wanted to separate from the United States. Do students think it would be a good idea or a bad one? Why?
3. **Thinking About Art:** Direct students' attention to the painting by Chagall entitled *Green Violinist* (p. 571). Ask them to compile a list of adjectives that best describe the mood of the painting. Does Chagall seem nostalgic for his lost childhood? (Possible answers: Students may say that the mood is wistful, dreamlike, bittersweet, gay, playful, or nostalgic and that the artist seems to miss the innocence, simplicity, and fantasy of his youth.)

MODERN RUSSIAN CULTURE

Ask whether any students in the class are of Russian heritage. If some are, ask them to describe to the class what they know about Russian culture. Students might bring in photographs; recordings of Russian choral, folk,

RUSSIA

Russia is the former name of the nation now officially called the Soviet Union, the largest and third most populated country in the world. It is two and a half times the size of the United States and spans eleven time zones.

In the early part of the twentieth century, Russia was the largest empire in the world. Ruled by czars, or emperors, the empire laid claim to parts of modern Asia,

Painted with scenes from a Russian folk tale, this lacquered chest was made in 1985. It is from Palekh, a town in the western Soviet Union.

the Middle East, and Eastern Europe. After the Revolution of 1917, the Soviet Union's Communist leaders divided the country into fifteen diverse republics.

The Soviet Union is home to more than one hundred ethnic groups, many of whom speak their own languages. Slavs inhabit many of the republics near Moscow, in the western part of the country. Four thousand miles east of Moscow, in Siberia, Asian peoples related to the native peoples of Alaska fish in the Bering Sea. To the south Moslem peoples live in the deserts and mountains near the borders with China, Afghanistan, and Iran.

Most of the images we associate with Russia come from the Slavic cultures. The onion-shaped domes of

Crowned with onion-shaped domes, the Cathedral of St. Basil on Moscow's Red Square is typical of sixteenth-century Russian religious architecture.

Moscow's churches, the brightly colored embroidery and folk dances of the Ukraine, and the proud Cossack horsemen are all familiar icons of Russian culture. Some traditions from czarist Russia also remain. Russian ballet, which reached its apex during the waning years of the empire, is still renowned. The leading modern company, the Bolshoi, excels in the performance of nineteenth-century classics such as *Swan Lake*.

If one art form could be said to convey the Russian character best, it would be music. Russian choirs are matchless. Some of the world's most accomplished nineteenth- and early-twentieth-century composers were Russian. A symphony by Peter Ilich Tchaikovsky or a piano concerto by Sergei Rachmaninoff reveals as much about the Russian character as a novel by Leo Tolstoy or Feodor Dostoevski.

IN THIS BOOK

The following selections can be found in this book:

Anton Chekhov, "The Beggar," p. 24
Yevgeny Yevtushenko, "Colors," p. 294
Anna Akhmatova, "Lot's Wife," p. 298
Chaim Nachman Bialik, "Summer Is Dying," p. 315
Alexander Pushkin, "Message to Siberia," p. 364
Joseph Brodsky, "The Monument," p. 365
Aleksandr Solzhenitsyn, "Prose Poems," p. 410

or classical music; traditional costumes or other objects; or samples of Russian cuisine.

FURTHER INVESTIGATION: RUSSIA

Encourage students to pursue their individual interests in various aspects of Russian culture. Some suggestions appear below.

- **Art:** the history of icon painting, which reached its peak in

Moscow in the fourteenth and fifteenth centuries
- **Architecture:** the wooden churches of northern Russia, which were constructed during the seventeenth and eighteenth centuries
- **Dance:** the life of dancer and choreographer Vaslav Nijinsky, considered by many the finest male dancer of the twentieth century

- **Music:** the life and works of Romantic composer Peter Ilich Tchaikovsky
- **Politics:** the accomplishments of the Romanov czar Peter the Great, who was so eager to learn about Western ways that he traveled incognito throughout Europe

EASTERN EUROPE

Hemmed in by the powerful nations of Western Europe and the massive Russian Empire, the small nations of Eastern Europe have been the site of many political and economic battles. During the course of these struggles, the countries of Eastern Europe have changed names and boundaries and have sometimes disappeared altogether. During the late eighteenth century, for instance, Poland was partitioned among three vying powers and for several years ceased to exist.

Peoples from many corners of the world have sought territory in Eastern Europe. Ancient Celts and Romans —and, later, Austrians and Germans—marched into Eastern Europe from the west. Greeks and Turks invaded from the south. Mongols, Slavs, and Russians swept in from the north. Gypsies who left India around the tenth century settled on the Hungarian plains.

All these invaders left their mark. Romanians, for instance, speak a language derived from that of their Roman conquerors. In Yugoslavia evidence of the tug of war between east and west shows up in the scripts used by different ethnic groups. The Croatians, a Slavic people from Yugoslavia, write in the Roman alphabet; their Slavic compatriots, the Serbs, write in the Cyrillic alphabet used in the Soviet Union.

If Eastern Europe has been a political battleground, it has also been a cultural crossroads. Many of the region's most accomplished artists have managed to combine the best of several worlds. Frédéric Chopin, the nineteenth-century Polish composer, wrote pieces inspired by the folk music of his native country that also reflect the sophistication he acquired during his years in Paris. The music of Hungarian Franz Liszt, a contemporary of Chopin's, derives its strength from the same blend of east and west. Twentieth-century Romanian sculptor Constantin Brancusi chose simple subjects inspired by folk carvings—a bird, a hand—and executed them in sleek marble or brass in his Paris studio.

In the Ukraine, a region of fertile plains in the western Soviet Union, Easter is commemorated with hand-painted wooden eggs.

IN THIS BOOK

The following Eastern European selections can be found in this book:

Jan Neruda, "Hastrman," p. 146
Czeslaw Milosz, "Encounter," p. 338
Isaac Bashevis Singer, "Shosha," p. 404

OUTLINE OF LITERATURE

This outline can be used in the following ways.

- **With less advanced students:** Point out the total time span covered in the outline. Then, beginning at the top of the chart, point out the period covered in each section in order to emphasize the chronology. Also point out the famous authors listed in the outline, particularly those whose work appears in this anthology.

- **With more advanced students:** Suggest that students compare the outlines of literature in this Literature and Culture Sourcebook with the Guide to Literary Movements (pp. 584–585). They will discover that literary trends often cut across cultural boundaries—that many cultures had, for instance, a Romantic or a Modernist period. You might also ask students to report on an author who appears in the outline but is not featured in this anthology.

THE AUTHORS IN THIS BOOK

Here are additional notes on the Russian and Eastern European authors whose work appears in this anthology.

Russia

- **Pushkin:** The preeminent Romantic writer of his day, Pushkin was inspired by Russian history and folklore.
- **Chekhov:** A sympathetic observer of everyday life, Chekhov expanded the limits of nineteenth-century Realism.
- **Akhmatova:** The clear musicality of her verses established her as a leading Russian lyric poet of the postrevolutionary period.
- **Solzhenitsyn:** His descriptions of Soviet labor camps and the excesses of Stalinism made him a leading modern Realist.
- **Yevtushenko:** By turns personal and political, Yevtushenko's carefully wrought poems have revived modern Russian lyric poetry.
- **Brodsky:** Sharp and ironic, Brodsky's poems frequently explore contemporary issues, such as exile and alienation.

Eastern Europe

- **Neruda:** Closely observed and sharply drawn, Neruda's tales are gems of early Czech Realism.

- **Singer:** The foremost living Yiddish author, Singer is also one of the finest modern short story writers.
- **Milosz:** The verses of Poland's finest modern poet focus on metaphysical themes.

RUSSIA

PERIOD	MAJOR WRITERS AND MAJOR WORKS	
Romanticism (1800–1850) Under the influence of European ideas, a literature of international importance began to emerge.	Alexander Pushkin	Lyric poetry
		Eugene Onegin
	Mikhail Lermontov	A Hero of Our Time
Realism (1850–1917) Novelists and playwrights drew inspiration from close observation of psychological and moral behavior.	Nikolai Gogol	Dead Souls
	Ivan Turgenev	Fathers and Sons
	Feodor Dostoevski	Crime and Punishment
		The Brothers Karamazov
	Leo Tolstoy	War and Peace
		Anna Karenina
	Anton Chekhov	The Cherry Orchard
	Maxim Gorki	The Lower Depths
Postrevolutionary Period (1917–present) Writers struggle to define themselves in the face of Soviet repression. A powerful literature of dissent begins to emerge.	Boris Pasternak	Doctor Zhivago
	Aleksandr Solzhenitsyn	The Gulag Archipelago
	Yevgeny Yevtushenko	Poetry
	Joseph Brodsky	Poetry

EASTERN EUROPE

PERIOD	MAJOR WRITERS AND MAJOR WORKS	
Romanticism and Realism (1800–1917) Writers embarked on a search for national identity and explored social and moral problems.	Adam Mickiewicz (Poland)	Poetry
	Karel Hynek Mácha (Czechoslovakia)	Poetry
	Jan Neruda (Czechoslovakia)	Short stories
Modernism and Futurism (1918–1939) During a brief period of freedom between the wars, Czech and Polish writers experimented with new literary forms and viewpoints.	Karel Čapek (Czechoslovakia)	The White Plague
	Maria Dabrowska (Poland)	Nights and Days
Recent Trends (1940–present) Writers meditate on the anguish of war, the perils of totalitarianism, and their yearnings for freedom.	Ivo Andrić (Yugoslavia)	The Bridge on the Drina
	Isaac Bashevis Singer (Poland)	Short stories
	Czeslaw Milosz (Poland)	Poetry
	Milan Kundera (Czechoslovakia)	The Unbearable Lightness of Being
	Václav Havel (Czechoslovakia)	The Garden Party

570 *Literature and Culture Sourcebook*

Russian

Все счастливые семьи похожи
друг на друга, каждая
несчастливая семья несчастлива
по-своему.

—Leo Tolstoy, *Anna Karenina*

A Translation

Happy families are all alike; every unhappy family
is unhappy in its own way.

—translated by Constance Garnett

COLLABORATIVE RESEARCH

1. As a group, research and report on the topic "Folk
Cultures Among the Slavic People." Russia, Poland, and
other countries in Eastern Europe have long traditions
of popular folk cultures. Your purpose is to investigate
and report on traditional costumes, dances, songs and
music, crafts, and decorative arts. Assign individuals

*Encrusted with diamonds and rubies, this
Fabergé egg contains a replica of the coach
that carried Czar Nicholas II to his coronation
in 1894.*

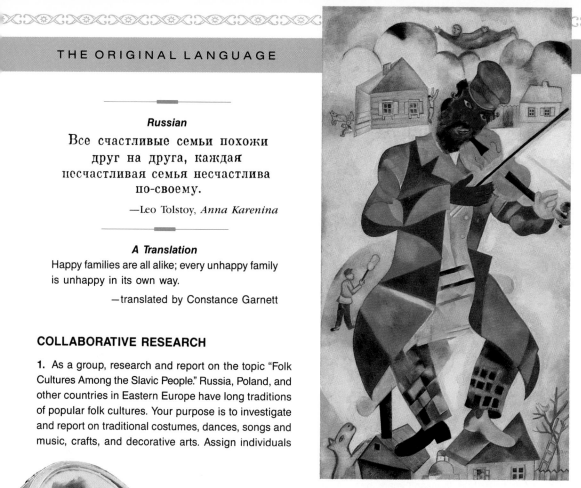

*Like many paintings by Marc Chagall, this
one, entitled* Green Violinist *(1923–1924),
draws on scenes from the artist's childhood in
rural Russia.*

or pairs to report on these arts or on the folk cultures
of each of the Slavic countries.

2. As a group, research and report on the topic "Russians and Eastern Europeans in America Today." Immigrants from these countries have been coming to the
United States for many years, bringing with them their
languages, their customs, and their cultures. Your purpose is to investigate and report on these immigrant
groups, focusing on their contributions to American history and culture. Assign individuals or pairs to report
on each of the national or ethnic groups.

Russia and Eastern Europe **571**

CHINA

SUMMARY: CHINA

This essay is intended to give students a brief overview of some of the outstanding characteristics of Chinese and Japanese cultures.

- China is roughly the same size as the United States but is far more densely populated.
- Tea, silk, gunpowder, opera, books, and movable type originated in China.
- The written Chinese language helps to bind together the country's many ethnic groups.
- Chinese civilization evolved for many centuries in relative isolation.
- Two philosophies—Taoism and Confucianism—had a great influence on the development of Chinese culture.

STUDY QUESTIONS: CHINA

1. **Review:** Why was the Great Wall constructed? (to protect the western portion of the Chinese Empire from invaders)
2. **Discussion:** Ask students to imagine a time in the future in which American culture is as old as Chinese culture is today. Ask students whether they think that Americans living twenty-five hundred years from now will still find the works of Benjamin Franklin and Abraham Lincoln relevant, as the modern Chinese find *The Analects* of Confucius.
3. **Thinking About Art:** Explain to students that many art objects function as symbols. The lions that guard the Forbidden City in Beijing, for instance, symbolized the power of the Chinese emperors. Ask students to think of modern symbols that convey the power of our own government. (Students may mention the eagle, which symbolizes freedom and strength, and the flag, which symbolizes pride and unity.)

MODERN CHINESE CULTURE

Ask whether any students in the class are of Chinese heritage. If some are, ask them to describe to the class what they know of Chinese culture. Students could bring in photographs, recordings of Chinese music, traditional costumes or other objects, or samples of Chinese cuisine.

A ribbon of earth and stone, the Great Wall meanders over the landscape west of Beijing; in stretches, its height exceeds thirty feet.

Occupying an area roughly as large as the United States in east Asia, China is far more densely populated: For every American, there are five Chinese. China's contributions to the world have been vast. Tea, silk, and gunpowder originated in China, and the Chinese created opera and invented paper books printed with movable type centuries before the Europeans. Chinese literature, which extends back three thousand years, has deeply influenced writers in all Asian countries.

The Chinese people are a fascinating mix of cultures. About 90 percent of the population is Han Chinese; most of them speak the Mandarin dialect. In addition, more than 50 other ethnic groups live in China. China's written language helps to bind its people together. If a resident of Beijing (China's capital) meets a resident of Shanghai (one of China's largest cities), they won't be able to talk to each other because each one speaks a different dialect. If they write down their conversation, however, they both can understand it, because words with the same meaning in different Chinese dialects are written with the same set of characters.

For centuries Chinese emperors sought to isolate themselves from the rest of Asia. In the third century B.C. the emperor Shih Huang-ti built vast stretches of a great wall that extends for more than two thousand miles along what was then the empire's western border. (The Great Wall, one of China's architectural wonders, can still be seen today.) Thus protected from marauding tribes, Chinese civilization evolved for centuries in peaceful isolation.

Two schools of thought influenced the development of Chinese culture in the imperial period. Confucius, who lived in the sixth century B.C., developed a philosophy based on the importance of ethical living and respect for the family. Lao-Tze, his contemporary, stressed the importance of simplicity, spontaneity, and a mystical union with nature. The influence of Taoism, as Lao-Tze's philosophy is called, can be seen in the elegant economy of Chinese poetry, music, and painting. The legacy of Confucius lives on in the Chinese respect for families and moral values, despite the attempts by the Communist government since 1949 to discredit Confucian ideals, as well as other ancient traditions.

IN THIS BOOK

The following Chinese selections can be found in this book:

Tu Peng-cheng, "Lingkuan Gorge," p. 73
Tu Fu, "The Emperor," p. 286
Li Po, "Taking Leave of a Friend," p. 337
Confucius, Sayings from *The Analects,* p. 399

Snarling lions guard the sacred precincts of the Forbidden City in Beijing. The sculptures date from the Ming dynasty (1368–1644).

FURTHER INVESTIGATION: CHINA

Encourage students to pursue their individual interests in various aspects of Chinese culture. Some suggestions appear below.

- **Archaeology:** the recent discovery of thousands of terracotta figures buried near the city of Xian in Shensi Province; The lifelike figures are thought to represent the armies of emperors of the Han and Ch'in dynasties.
- **Drama:** the comparison of Chinese and American drama outlined in *Salesman in Beijing,* a recent book by the playwright Arthur Miller, who directed a Chinese version of his play *Death of a Salesman* in Beijing in 1983
- **Politics:** the curbing of intellectual and artistic freedom during the Cultural Revolution in the late 1960s
- **Science:** the medical technique of acupuncture, which was developed in China nearly three thousand years ago

JAPAN

The island nation of Japan is an extraordinary blend of ancient and modern. Less than a century ago Japan was a feudal, rural society with few links to other nations. Today Japan is an urban, highly industrialized country with the second largest economy in the world. Trade has released a flood of Western ideas and practices into this complex country, which has prided itself on its ethnic and linguistic purity. Today many Japanese are as likely to be fond of steaks, baseball, and comic books as they are of rice, sumo wrestling, and haiku. Underneath, however, Japan is still a conservative country, and family ties and traditional culture are deeply honored.

Just as Japan has borrowed from Western cultures in the twentieth century, it borrowed from Chinese and Korean cultures earlier in its history. Until the second or third century A.D. the Japanese had no written language. At that time Japanese scribes began to use written Chinese characters to record Japanese laws and literature. Gradually, the Chinese characters were adapted to fit the peculiarities of Japanese speech until Japan had its own written language. In the middle of the sixth century, Buddhism was introduced into Japan by way of Korea. Buddhism soon became the main religion of Japan's upper classes and exerted a strong influence on the development of Japanese painting, sculpture, architecture, and music.

Dancers from the ancient Japanese city of Kyoto perform the "Miyako Odori," or Cherry Blossom Dance; they are dressed in traditional silk kimonos.

In the thirteenth century a Buddhist sect, Zen, was introduced to Japan from China. Zen monks, who rejected ritual and analytical thought in favor of meditation, had a deep impact on Japanese art. Zen ideas helped to shape the Japanese arts of landscape gardening, the tea ceremony, and classic Nō drama.

Many of the ancient arts and beliefs of Japan still thrive today. Japanese homes often have Buddhist and Shinto shrines (Shinto is a very ancient native Japanese religion). Japanese poets still experiment with the forms of traditional poetry, such as haiku, and gardens are laid out in the austere, symbolic Zen style. People still practice the ancient art of flower arranging, and masked Nō actors continue to enthrall modern audiences.

Exquisitely carved, this ivory sculpture by the artist Okinomo exemplifies the elegant economy of Japanese art.

IN THIS BOOK

The following Japanese selections can be found in this book:

Akutagawa Ryūnosuke, "Autumn Mountain," p. 181
Lady Ōtomo, "My Heart, Thinking," p. 293
Bashō, "Autumn," p. 318
Jōsō, "Winter," p. 318
Chiyo, "After a Long Winter," p. 318
Shiki, "Heat," p. 318
Seami Motokiyo, *The Dwarf Trees,* p. 454

China and Japan **573**

AN OUTLINE OF CHINESE AND JAPANESE LITERATURE

This outline can be used in the following ways.

- **With less advanced students:** Point out the total time span covered in the outline. Then, beginning at the top of the chart, point out the period covered in each section in order to emphasize the chronology. Also point out the famous authors listed in the outline, particularly those whose work appears in this anthology.

- **With more advanced students:** Suggest that students compare the outlines of literature in this Literature and Culture Sourcebook with the Guide to Literary Movements (pp. 584–585). They will discover that literary trends often cut across cultural boundaries—that many cultures had, for instance, a Romantic or a Modernist period. You might also ask students to report on an author who appears in the outline but is not featured in this anthology.

THE AUTHORS IN THIS BOOK

Here are additional notes on the Chinese and Japanese authors whose work appears in this anthology.

China

- **Confucius:** One of the most influential thinkers of the Classical Period, Confucius himself wrote little; his teachings were recorded by his students.
- **Li Po:** A master of the less formal verse forms developed during the T'ang dynasty, Li Po was one of the leading lyric poets of his time.
- **Tu Fu:** Often called the greatest lyric poet of the T'ang era, Tu Fu was a keen observer of social and political life.
- **Tu Peng-cheng:** Tu's preoccupation with patriotic themes is typical of many modern Chinese realists.

Japan

- **Lady Ōtomo:** Lady Ōtomo's refined verses describing love and court life were typical of early lyric poetry in the Classical Period.
- **Seami Motokiyo:** Written in supple verse, Seami's plays expanded the aesthetic possibilities of Nō drama.
- **Bashō:** A masterful teacher and poet, Basho is generally regarded as the finest writer of classical haiku.

CHINA

PERIOD	MAJOR WRITERS AND MAJOR WORKS	
Classical Age (1500–250 B.C.) During the Chou dynasty Confucian moralism and Taoist mysticism took root.	Oral Tradition Confucius Lao-Tze Ch'ü Yüan	The Five Classics Analects Tao Te Ching Poetry
Middle Epoch (250 B.C.–A.D. 600) Court poetry flowered under the Han rulers.	Pan Chao Fu Yi	Poetry Poetry
Renaissance (600–1000) Chinese poets of the T'ang era reached sublime heights.	Li Po Tu Fu Po Chü-i	Poetry Poetry Poetry
Age of Reason (1000–1900) In the Sung era novels and plays thrived.	Yen Shu Ts'ao Chan	Poetry Dream of the Red Chamber
Recent Trends (1900–present) With the overthrow of the Manchu dynasty, writers forged a new national language.	Lu Hsün Mao Tun	The True Story of Ah Q Midnight

JAPAN

PERIOD	MAJOR WRITERS AND MAJOR WORKS	
Classical (A.D. 750–1200) During the Heian period courtly literature and prose flowered.	Various Poets Lady Murasaki Shikibu	Manyōshū The Tale of Genji
Medieval (1200–1600) As the samurai came to power during the Kamakura period, epic war stories appeared. No drama reached its zenith during the Muromachi period.	Anonymous Kannami Kiyotsugu Seami Motokiyo	The Tale of Heike No plays No plays
Renaissance (1600–1870) Poets of the Tokugawa period perfected haiku, and Kabuki theater thrived.	Matsuo Bashō Chikamatsu Monzaemon	Poetry Plays
Modern (1870–present) As Japan gradually opens its doors to the West, the realistic novel comes of age.	Akutagawa Ryūnosuke Kawabata Yasunari Mishima Yukio	Short stories Snow Country The Temple of the Golden Pavilion

- **Jōsō:** One of Bashō's most accomplished students, Jōsō wedded the temporal and the eternal in his poems.
- **Chiyo:** Considered to be one of the finest haiku poets of the eighteenth century, Chiyo captured her surroundings in delicate and evocative verse.
- **Shiki:** During the late nineteenth century Shiki wrote vigorous and unsentimental haiku that rivaled the best classical poems.
- **Akutagawa Ryūnosuke:** A preoccupation with the macabre and sharp psychological insight characterize Akutagawa's tales.

Chinese

低頭思故鄉！
舉頭望明月，
疑是地上霜。
牀前明月光，

—Li Po, "On a Quiet Night"

A Translation

I saw the moonlight before my couch,
And wondered if it were not the frost
   on the ground.
I raised my head and looked out on the
   mountain moon;
I bowed my head and thought of my
   far-off home.

—translated by Shigeyoshi Obata

Japanese

閑さや岩にしみ入蟬の声

—Haiku, Bashō

A Translation

In this hush profound,
   Into the very rocks it seeps—
      The cicada sound.

—translated by Dorothy Britton

This nineteenth-century Chinese platter, decorated with enamel and gilt, was probably made for export.

COLLABORATIVE RESEARCH

1. As a group, research and report on the topic "China's Relations with the United States, Past and Present." Your purpose is to trace and report on Chinese culture as it has affected American life. Assign individuals or pairs to work on various aspects of the topic, such as foods and cooking, philosophy and religion, literature, immigration, tourism, and present-day political relations.

2. As a group, research and report on the topic "Fascinating Facts About Japanese Culture." Your purpose is to investigate aspects of Japanese culture. Assign people to work on such topics as Zen Buddhism, samurai and shoguns, the No drama, Japanese music, Japanese foods, and the rock garden.

China and Japan **575**

THE ORIGINAL LANGUAGE

You might want to use the following pronunciations to give students an idea of the sound of Chinese and Japanese.

Chinese

牀 前 明 月
chwäng' chen ming yōō'e

光 疑 是 地 上
gwäng' ē' shu dē' shang

霜 舉 頭 望 明
shwäng' ju'e tō' wang ming'

月 低 頭 思 故
yōō'e dē' tō' su' gōō

鄉
shi ang'

Japanese

閑
shē zū kä'

さ
sä

や
yä'

岩
ē wä'

に
nē

し
shē

み
mē

入
ē'rū

蟬
se mē

の
nō

声
kō'e

SUMMARY

This essay is intended to give students a brief overview of some of the outstanding characteristics of African culture.

- The second largest continent in the world, Africa is the home of many ancient civilizations.
- European traders came to Africa in the fifteenth century.
- Merchants sought gold, ivory, diamonds, ebony, leather, cloth—and slaves.
- By the early twentieth century European powers had claimed almost every corner of the continent.
- Today Africa consists of more than fifty independent nations.
- In modern Africa more than eight hundred languages are spoken.
- Africa has a venerable oral tradition, and storytelling is an art.

STUDY QUESTIONS

1. **Review:** Ask students to name some of the languages spoken in Africa today. (Possible answers: the Bantu group, including Swahili; Arabic; English; French; Portuguese)

2. **Discussion:** Explain to students that many Egyptian antiquities have been sold to museums and private collections in England, the United States, and other foreign countries. The Egyptian government is trying to limit further exports of antiquities. Ask students whether they believe that African countries have a right to block such exports or whether they think that objects belonging to ancient cultures should be bought and sold freely.

3. **Thinking About Art:** Ask students to look at the photograph on the following page showing the juxtaposition of architectural styles in an African city. Which building do students find more appealing, the traditional mud home or the skyscraper? Why?

AFRICA

Staring down an unseen enemy, this lion is from the Royal Palace of Benin, a country in West Africa formerly known as Dahomey.

Africa is the second largest continent in the world. Divided almost equally in two by the equator, it contains the world's largest desert (the Sahara) and the world's longest river (the Nile). Geologically speaking, it is ancient: The crystalline rocks that form its great plateaus are some of the oldest in the world. Anthropologically, it is ancient, too, for the civilizations that thrived along its rivers and oases have venerable histories.

The oldest African civilization for which we have accurate records is the Egyptian, which was born on the banks of the Nile more than five thousand years ago. From its magnificent remains—pyramids, temples, hieroglyphic inscriptions—we can piece together much

Made by the Ashanti people of Ghana, this wood and silver stool was both functional and symbolic, for it was thought to enshrine its owner's soul.

576 *Literature and Culture Sourcebook*

of its history. Far less is known about the kingdoms of black Africa that prospered in the first millennium A.D., partly because most of them had no written language.

The early black African kingdoms of Ghana, Ethiopia, Mali, and Nigeria prospered from trade. Gold dust, ivory, ebony, kola nuts, ostrich feathers, and leather were carried to ports on the Atlantic and Mediterranean coasts. Over the centuries traders from Mesopotamia, Greece, and Rome came to barter for African goods.

Then, in the fifteenth century, the modern Europeans began to arrive. Portuguese merchants established outposts along Africa's coasts, and French, British, and Dutch traders soon followed. More African goods—including cloth, palm oil, and diamonds—were loaded onto European ships. So were slaves. Between the fifteenth and nineteenth centuries, more than ten million black slaves were shipped to the New World.

The slave trade ended in the middle of the nineteenth century, but colonization continued. By the outbreak of World War I in 1914, every inch of Africa, except for Liberia and the empire of Ethiopia, was claimed by a European power. The French dominated the northwest; the English, the present-day nations of Egypt, Sudan, Nigeria, Kenya, Zimbabwe, and South Africa, among others. The Portuguese controlled Angola and Mozambique, and the Belgians and Germans claimed areas in central Africa drained by the Congo River.

Spare and graceful, this modern wooden sculpture of a bird was created by an artist from the Ivory Coast in West Africa.

After World War II profound political changes shook the continent. Territory after territory demanded an end to colonial rule. Today Africa is composed of more than fifty independent nations, though clear traces of its colonial past remain. Many African authors, for instance, continue to write in the languages brought by the Europeans, particularly Portuguese, English, and French.

Modern Africa is a brilliant patchwork of cultures. Between eight hundred and one thousand languages are spoken. Different ethnic groups abound. The north is dominated by the Arabic-speaking Moslems who began to migrate to the continent in the seventh century A.D. Bantu-speaking tribes occupy central Africa south of the Sahara. Pygmies armed with Stone Age weapons hunt in the jungles of the Congo, and Swahili-speaking peoples inhabit the coasts by the Indian Ocean.

Out of this dense mix of cultures has come beautiful art. The magnificent mosques of North Africa show the impact of Moslem cultures. The subtle syncopations of African music have had a profound effect on American jazz. The clean lines of African sculpture exerted a strong influence on European artists in the early twentieth century.

In Niamey, capital of the West African nation of Niger, ancient and modern exist side by side; adobe huts and high rises form the skyline.

Africans have a deep reverence for the spoken word. In many traditional African cultures stories about creation, the gods, mythical heroes, animals, and ordinary men and women have been handed down for centuries. Children are taught the rules of society through proverbs and riddles. Some modern African writers have sought to preserve this rich heritage by recording ancient tales. Other writers attempt to incorporate the lively lilt of their native tongue into their adopted colonial language.

IN THIS BOOK

The following African selections can be found in this book:

Barbara Kimenye, "The Winner," p. 3
Chinua Achebe, "Dead Men's Path," p. 40
Tayeb Salih, "A Handful of Dates," p. 78
Alan Paton, "The Quarry," p. 97
Kabyle Traditional (retold by Marguerite Amrouche), "The Story of the Chest," p. 253
Léopold S. Senghor, "And We Shall Be Steeped," p. 296
Oswald Mbuyiseni Mtshali, "Sunset," p. 311
Gabon Pygmy Traditional, "All That Dances," p. 321
Camara Laye, "The Snake and the Goldsmith," p. 380
Isak Dinesen, "The Iguana," p. 421
James Ene Henshaw, *The Jewels of the Shrine,* p. 439

Africa **577**

Ask whether any of the students in the class are of African heritage. If some are, ask them to describe to the class what they know about African culture. Students might bring in photographs, recordings of African music, weavings, jewelry, costumes, or traditional objects, such as musical instruments, wood carvings, or carved gourds.

FURTHER INVESTIGATION

Encourage students to pursue their individual interests in various aspects of African culture. Some suggestions appear below.

- **Art:** the art of mask making in Africa and the role of masked dancers in entertaining, healing, settling disputes, and foretelling the future
- **Architecture:** the adobe architecture of the Moslem tribes of West Africa; The women of these tribes often decorate buildings with brilliant abstract paintings.
- **Drama:** the comic play *The Lion and the Jewel* by Wole Soyinka of Nigeria, one of modern Africa's most acclaimed playwrights
- **Mythology and Folklore:** the riddles told by many West African peoples, such as the poetic Yoruba riddle "We tie a horse in the house, but its mane flies above the roof" (The riddle refers to fire and smoke.)
- **Music:** the music of the "talking drums" of Nigeria, which imitate the tones of the human voice
- **Politics and Society:** the lives of children in Africa: their life expectancy, the quality of their education, the countries in which they fare the worst and the best

This outline can be used in the following ways.

- **With less advanced students:** Point out the total time span covered in the outline. Then, beginning at the top of the chart, point out the period covered in each section in order to emphasize the chronology. Also point out the famous authors listed in the outline, particularly those whose work appears in this anthology.

- **With more advanced students:** Suggest that students compare the outlines of literature in this Literature and Culture Sourcebook with the Guide to Literary Movements (pp. 584–585). They will discover that literary trends often cut across cultural boundaries—that many cultures had, for instance, a Romantic or a Modernist period. You might also ask students to report on an author who appears in the outline but is not featured in this anthology.

THE AUTHORS IN THIS BOOK

Here are additional notes on the African authors whose work appears in this anthology.

- **Kabyle Traditional:** This tale is part of the oral tradition of the Berber tribes of North Africa, whose culture extends back more than four thousand years.
- **Gabon Pygmy Traditional:** This is a traditional song sung by the Pygmies, nomadic peoples who inhabit forested areas in and around the Congo Valley.
- **Dinesen:** Writing was in Dinesen's family background. Her father, who lived for many years with a Pawnee Indian tribe in Minnesota, wrote several novels.
- **Senghor:** Written in French, Senghor's verses extol the beauty of precolonial Africa.
- **Henshaw:** Henshaw's plays, written in English, describe the contradictions of modern West African society.
- **Laye:** Written in French, Laye's novels and memoirs capture the innocence and the cruelty of colonial West African life.
- **Paton:** One of the most lauded modern South African writers, Paton fought tirelessly for social change.

AN OUTLINE OF AFRICAN LITERATURE

PERIOD	MAJOR WRITERS AND MAJOR WORKS	
Traditional (to 1780) Storytellers spun out tales and chanted songs of praise; eighteenth-century Swahili poets wrote epic verse in Arabic script.	Anonymous	Epic poetry (Swahili)
Colonial (1780–1950) Slaves and missionaries wrote their stories, and early twentieth-century black writers longed for freedom.	Olaudah Equiano (West Africa)	Autobiography (English)
	Joseph E. Casely-Hayford (Ethiopia)	Ethiopia Unbound (English)
Négritude Movement (1950–1965) French-speaking writers from West Africa searched for their roots, rejecting colonial rule.	Léopold S. Senghor (Senegal)	Poetry (French)
	Camara Laye (Guinea)	The Dark Child (French) The Radiance of the King (French)
Recent Trends (1965–present) Authors from young independent nations explore the conflicts of a new black Africa and the struggles between tradition and modernization. In South Africa writers of all colors describe the tragedies of apartheid.	Antonio Agostinho Neto (Angola)	Poetry (Portuguese)
	Alan Paton (South Africa)	Cry, the Beloved Country (English)
	Chinua Achebe (Nigeria)	Things Fall Apart (English)
	Wole Soyinka (Nigeria)	The Lion and the Jewel (English)
	Ngugi Wa Thiong'o (Kenya)	A Grain of Wheat (English)
	Alex La Guma (South Africa)	A Walk in the Night (English)
	Ezekiel Mphahlele (South Africa)	Chirundu (English)

- **Salih:** Salih's straightforward and unsentimental tales describe Moslem social values in his native Sudan.
- **Achebe:** One of English-speaking West Africa's most celebrated authors, Achebe has published poetry and several novels.

- **Mtshali:** One of the most widely read modern South African poets, Mtshali writes engagingly direct and vivid verse.
- **Kimenye:** Kimenye's sharply observed tales of Kenyan village life were shaped by her journalistic training.

Swahili

Aliondoka Sungura kuenda kutafuta chakula
mwituni, akaona mbuyu mkubwa sana, akatazama juu, akaona mzinga wa asali ya nyuki.
Akarudi mjini kuenda kutafuta wenziwe wa kuja
kula naye.

> —Zanzibar Traditional,
> "The Hare and the Lion"

A Translation

The hare arose and went to look for food in the
forest, and saw a very large calabash tree; and
he looked up and saw a hive of honey, and he
returned to the town to look for companions to
come and eat with him.

> —translated by Edward Steere

Barely six inches high, this sculpture,
also a stool, was made in the nineteenth century by the Ngindo people
of Tanzania.

COLLABORATIVE RESEARCH

1. As a group, research and report on the topic "African Storytelling." The purpose of your report is to answer
the question "What can African stories tell us about
African culture and society?" Ask each member of the
group to find a traditional story or poem from an African country. Ideally, the stories should be from different African tribes, such as the Yoruba, the Ibo, the Zulu,
the Xhosa, and the Kikuyu. Read your story, or selections from it, to the class. Explain which region of Africa
the story comes from, and explain what you think the
story says about the beliefs and customs of the tribe
that created it.

2. As a group, research and report on the topic "African Arts." The purpose of your report is to answer the
question "How have African arts influenced art in other
countries?" Assign each member of the group one
African art form to investigate, such as dance, music,
sculpture, fashion, and architecture. Try to bring in an
example of your art form to share with the class: Play
a recording of an African song, or find a picture of African clothing. Explain how these art forms have affected
art in the United States or in other countries.

You may want to use the following pronunciations to give students an idea of the sound of
Swahili.

Aliondoka   Sungura
ä lē ōn dō'kä   sōon gōo'rä

kuenda   kutafuta
kōo en'dä   kōo'tä fōo'tä

chakula   mwituni,
chä kōo'lä   mwē tōo'nē

akaona   mbuyu   mkubwa
ä kä ō'nä   m bōo'yōo   m kōo'bwä

sana,   akatazama   juu,
sä'nä   ä kä tä zä'mä   jōo'ōo

akaona   mzinga   wa asali
ä kä ō'nä   m zing'ä   wä ä sä'lē

ya nyuki.   Akarudi
yä nŭ'kē   ä kä rōo'dē

mjini   kuenda
m jē'nē   kōo en'dä

kutafuta   wenziwe   wa
kōo'tä fōo'tä   wen zē'wä   wä

kuja   kula   naye.
kōo'jä   kōo'lä   nä'yä

GUIDES FOR COLLABORATIVE RESEARCH ACTIVITIES

1. Students may wish to investigate Yoruba "talking drum"
stories, Zulu or Yoruba praise-
name poems, Bantu or Ibo
trickster tales, or Senegalese
or Ghanaian dilemma tales.

2. Students may wish to investigate the influence of African
sculpture on artists such
as Gauguin, Picasso, and
Braque; the influence of African storytelling on writers
such as the American author
Langston Hughes and the
Cuban poet Nicolas Guillen;
or the influence of traditional
African clothing on contemporary American fashion
designers.

SUMMARY: INDIA

This essay is intended to give students a brief overview of some of the outstanding characteristics of Indian and Middle Eastern culture.

- The world's largest democracy, India is also one of the most populous of nations.
- India became a nation in 1947, in part through the efforts of Mohandas Gandhi.
- England dominated India for nearly two hundred years.
- India is the birthplace of two great religions: Hinduism and Buddhism.
- In 1947 two Moslem regions seceded from India; they are now the nations of Pakistan and Bangladesh.
- Many Americans are familiar with India through its music, popularized by the sitar player Ravi Shankar.

STUDY QUESTIONS: INDIA

1. **Review:** Which nation dominated India for nearly two centuries? (Great Britain) What are some of the legacies of colonial rule? (India's laws, bureaucracies, roads, and railways were shaped by British rule, and many modern Indians write and speak English.)
2. **Discussion:** Explain to students that Mohandas Gandhi's philosophy of nonviolence influenced the civil rights movement in the United States in the 1960s. Ask students whether they think it is always possible to resolve conflicts peacefully. Why or why not?
3. **Thinking About Art:** Ask students to look at the photograph of the Taj Majal. Do they think it is a beautiful building? If so, why? (Students might mention its harmonious proportions and its mirrorlike pool, which create a sense of serenity, and its pristine white surface, which reflects the changing colors of the sky.) Ask students whether they think that people from different cultures have similar notions of beauty.

MODERN INDIAN CULTURE

Ask whether any students in the class are of Indian heritage. If some are, ask them to describe to the class what they know about Indian culture. Students could bring in photographs, re-

INDIA

India is one of the most populated countries in the world: One billion people are expected to crowd against its borders by the end of the century. India is also the world's largest democracy. Aside from occasional flare-ups of old ethnic and factional conflicts, its diverse peoples manage to live together in remarkable harmony.

The modern nation of India was founded in 1947, in part because of the efforts of one extraordinary man. Mohandas Gandhi, known as "Mahatma," a frail, soft-spoken lawyer, labored for years to improve the lot of India's poor. His philosophy of nonviolence, inspired by the writings of Russian novelist Leo Tolstoy, helped to galvanize the Indian people in their struggle against British rule.

Prior to independence India had been dominated by England for nearly two hundred years. English merchants founded the British East India Company in 1600, and a brisk trade between the two countries ensued. The colonial era left deep marks on both countries. A sizable East Indian population lives in Great Britain today, and Britons are still fond of Indian curry and strong East Indian tea. Indian laws, government bureaucracies, roads, and railways bear the stamp of British rule, and many Indian intellectuals choose to write in English.

Two of the world's great religions, Hinduism and Buddhism, were born in India, and many others flourish there. The two major areas at the time of independence that were inhabited mostly by Moslems split off from India later in 1947 and are now two separate countries, Pakistan and Bangladesh. Christians and Sikhs are two other influential religious minorities.

Indian culture has left its imprint on many parts of the world. The great traditional Indian texts—written in San-

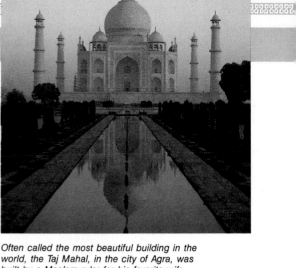

Often called the most beautiful building in the world, the Taj Mahal, in the city of Agra, was built by a Moslem ruler for his favorite wife.

skrit, Hindi, and Arabic—are known and quoted by millions of people. Indian architecture, which thrived during the period of Moslem rule from the fifteenth to the seventeenth centuries, has bestowed on us such masterpieces as the Taj Mahal. Sitar player Ravi Shankar and other musicians have popularized the subtle intricacies of Indian music, bringing what was once an exotic and distant culture into the homes of many Americans.

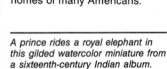

A prince rides a royal elephant in this gilded watercolor miniature from a sixteenth-century Indian album.

IN THIS BOOK

The following Indian selections can be found in this book:

Rumer Godden, "You Need to Go Upstairs," p. 19
Rabindranath Tagore, "The Kabuliwallah," p. 49
R. K. Narayan, "Like the Sun," p. 141
Indian Traditional, from the *Panchatantra*, p. 243
Sarojini Naidu, "Street Cries," p. 325
Santha Rama Rau, "By Any Other Name," p. 373

580 *Literature and Culture Sourcebook*

cordings of Indian music, regional costumes or other objects, or samples of Indian cuisine.

FURTHER INVESTIGATION: INDIA

Encourage students to pursue their individual interests in various aspects of Indian culture. Some suggestions appear below.

- **Art:** the art of the miniature, which was perfected by Mogul artists in the sixteenth and seventeenth centuries, or twentieth-century Indian painters and their work, including masters such as Jamini, Roy, M. F. Husain, and Bhupen Khakhar
- **Dance:** the meaning of hand gestures in Indian dance; In the dance form of northern India known as Kathak, for instance, hand gestures symbolize the names of Hindu gods, objects such as trees and

birds, and specific verbs and adjectives.
- **Music:** Indian folk songs, including the folk epics of Kashmir, harvest songs from the Punjab, and songs to bring rain, ward off disease, and celebrate birth
- **Politics:** the lives of Mohandas Gandhi and Jawaharlal Nehru, two men who helped secure Indian independence

THE MIDDLE EAST

The Middle East is a region of extremes. More a political than a geographical entity, it spans a vast area: from Egypt in the west to Pakistan in the east, and from Turkey in the north to the Arabian peninsula in the south. Within its boundaries are some of the world's hottest deserts (such as the Dasht-e Kavir in central Iran, where temperatures often exceed 130 degrees Fahrenheit) and some of the world's highest mountains (the Himalayas extend into Pakistan). Many of its people live in poverty, but the oil-rich nations of the Persian Gulf are among the wealthiest in the world. Its diverse cultures, which have made great contributions to Western civilization, have clashed throughout its history, often with tragic results.

Civilized life may have begun in the Middle East some six thousand years ago, in what is now Iraq, in the fertile lowlands between the Tigris and Euphrates rivers known in ancient times as Mesopotamia. One thousand years later another extraordinary civilization, the Egyptian, took root on the irrigated lowlands of the Nile.

Today the majority of the inhabitants of the Middle East are Arabs who practice the Islamic religion and speak one of many Arabic dialects. In medieval times Arabic doctors, astronomers, and mathematicians made important contributions to learning. Arab scholars also helped to preserve many of the writings of the ancient Greeks, which otherwise would have been lost forever.

Many other peoples inhabit the varied landscapes of

Designed by Russian artist Marc Chagall, this window at the Hadassah Hospital in Jerusalem represents one of the tribes of Israel.

the Middle East. Jews from many corners of the globe helped to found the modern state of Israel, one of the Middle East's youngest nations, in 1948. In some countries of the Middle East, non-Arabic languages predominate. About three quarters of Israel's residents speak Hebrew. Turkish is spoken in Turkey, Pushtu in Afghanistan, and Farsi in Iran.

Three of the world's great religions were born in the Middle East. Judaism appeared first, followed by Christianity and later by Islam. Every year millions of pilgrims flock to the region's holy cities, such as Jerusalem, which attracts worshipers from all three religions. Jews pray at the Western (Wailing) Wall, Christians worship at the Church of the Holy Sepulcher, and Moslems visit the Dome of the Rock.

IN THIS BOOK

The following Middle Eastern selections can be found in this book:

Naguib Mahfouz, "A Tale of Our Quarter," p. 158
Arabian and Persian Traditional, from *The Thousand and One Nights,* p. 247
Chaim Nachman Bialik, "Summer Is Dying," p. 315
Nazim Hikmet, "The World, My Friends, My Enemies, You, and the Earth," p. 350

Rising majestically above the desert near Cairo, Egypt, the pyramids of Giza, built after 2000 B.C., may have symbolized stability.

MODERN MIDDLE EASTERN CULTURE

Ask whether any students in the class are of Middle Eastern heritage. If some are, ask them to describe to the class what they know about the culture of a Middle Eastern country. Students could bring in photographs, recordings of Middle Eastern music, regional costumes or other objects, or samples of Middle Eastern cuisine.

FURTHER INVESTIGATION: THE MIDDLE EAST

Encourage students to pursue their individual interests in various aspects of Middle Eastern culture. Some suggestions appear below.
- **Art:** the carpets of Iran (formerly Persia), Turkey, and Afghanistan and the materials, dyes, patterns, and techniques used in creating them; Some carpets, for instance, have as many as twenty-four hundred knots per square inch.
- **Archaeology:** the ancient city of Babylon, which was located in present-day Iraq and was, at its height, in the seventh and sixth centuries B.C., the largest city in the world; The ruins of Babylon are located in Iraq.
- **Religion:** the history of the Jewish calendar and an explanation of the major Jewish holidays
- **Science:** the development of map making by ancient Arabic cartographers

OUTLINE OF LITERATURE

This outline can be used in the following ways.

- **With less advanced students:** Point out the total time span covered in the outline. Then, beginning at the top of the chart, point out the period covered in each section in order to emphasize the chronology. Also point out the famous authors listed in the outline, particularly those whose work appears in this anthology.
- **With more advanced students:** Suggest that students compare the outlines of literature in this Literature and Culture Sourcebook with the Guide to Literary Movements (pp. 584–585). They will discover that literary trends often cut across cultural boundaries—that many cultures had, for instance, a Romantic or a Modernist period. You might also ask students to report on an author who appears in the outline but is not featured in this anthology.

THE AUTHORS IN THIS BOOK

Here are additional notes on the authors whose work appears in this anthology.

India
- **Indian Traditional:** The *Panchatantra,* from which this tale is taken, influenced many other storytellers, including Aesop.
- **Tagore:** A poet, novelist, and translator, Tagore was also an accomplished composer.
- **Naidu:** A leading modern lyric poet, Naidu published many acclaimed collections of verse, including *The Golden Threshold* and *The Bird of Time.*
- **Narayan:** Narayan's expertly crafted tales about the imaginary Indian town of Malgudi won him a loyal readership in the West.
- **Godden:** Godden's novel *Black Narcissus,* about a group of nuns who establish a convent in the mountains of northern India, was made into a successful feature film.
- **Rau:** A native of south India, Rau is one of her country's most celebrated contemporary authors.

The Middle East
- **The Thousand and One Nights:** Compiled in Arabic in the early Middle Ages, it is one of the world's most renowned collections of folk tales.

- **Bialik:** Born in Russia just over a century ago, Bialik was one of the most acclaimed Hebrew poets of his day.
- **Hikmet:** The verses of Turkey's best-known twentieth-century poet were often shaped by his strong political values.
- **Mahfouz:** One of the first authors to write novels in Arabic, Mahfouz was influenced by Dickens, Proust, and Hemingway.

INDIA

PERIOD	MAJOR WRITERS AND MAJOR WORKS	
Vedic (1500–300 B.C.) Aryan tribes invaded India from southwest Asia; scribes recorded sacred hymns, myths, and commentaries about Hindu ritual.	Oral Tradition Oral Tradition	Rig Veda (Sanskrit) Brāhmanas (Sanskrit)
Classical (300 B.C.–A.D. 1100) This was the great age of the heroic epic.	Oral Tradition Vālmīki Oral Tradition	Mahābhārata (Sanskrit) Rāmāyana (Sanskrit) Panchatantra (Sanskrit)
Medieval and Postclassical (1100–1900) Indian vernacular languages flourished with elaborate adaptations of Sanskrit classics.	Kamban Tulsīdās	Rāmāyana (Tamil) Rāmcaritmānas (Hindi)
Modern (1900–present) Literature in the Indian vernacular languages and in English responded to Western influences and styles and developed distinctive Indian themes.	Sarojini Naidu Rabindranath Tagore R. K. Narayan Santha Rama Rau Ruth Prawer Jhabvala Anita Desai	Poetry (English) Poetry (Bengali and English) The Man-Eater of Malgudi (English) Gifts of Passage (English) Heat and Dust (English) Clear Light of Day (English)

THE MIDDLE EAST

PERIOD	MAJOR WRITERS AND MAJOR WORKS	
Ancient (4000 B.C.–A.D. 600) Writings focused on law and on religious views of divine revelation and the afterlife.	Hammurabi	Book of the Dead (Egyptian) Legal Code (Babylonian) The Bible (Hebrew, Aramaic, and Greek) The Talmud (Hebrew)
Medieval (600–1500) Religious themes continued. Secular forms—lyric poetry, epics, and tales of adventure—also thrived.	Mohammed Oral Tradition Firdausī Omar Khayyám Moses Maimonides	The Koran (Arabic) The Thousand and One Nights (Arabic) Shāh-Nāmeh (Farsi) The Rubáiyát (Persian) Guide for the Perplexed (Arabic)
Modern (1900–present) Distinct national literatures with predominantly realistic subjects and themes arose.	Chaim Nachman Bialik Nazim Hikmet Naguib Mahfouz Aharon Appelfeld Abraham B. Yehoshua	The Scroll of Fire (Hebrew) The Epic of Sheik Bedreddin (Turkish) Cairo Trilogy (Arabic) The Age of Wonders (Hebrew) A Late Divorce (Hebrew)

582 *Literature and Culture Sourcebook*

THE ORIGINAL LANGUAGE

Sanskrit

यावत् स्थास्यन्ति गिरयः सरितश्च महीतले
तावद्रामायणकथा लोकेषु प्रचरिष्यति

—Vālmīki, *Rāmāyaṇa*, Book I

A Transliteration

yāvat sthāsyanti girayaḥ saritaś ca mahītale
tāvad rāmāyaṇakathā lokeṣu pracariṣyati

A Translation

As long as the mountains and rivers shall endure upon the earth, so long will the story of the *Ramayana* be told among men.

—translated by Robert P. Goldman

Made in the thirteenth century, this partially glazed earthenware tile from Iran is carved in the shape of an elaborate eight-pointed star.

Knotted from strands of silk, wool and cotton, this Turkish carpet, which dates from the late sixteenth century, was made by the Bursa tribe.

COLLABORATIVE RESEARCH

1. As a group, research and report on the topic "Ancient and Modern in India." The purpose of your report is to answer the question "What are the ways in which ancient traditions and modern concepts or technologies are combined in Indian life today?" Assign each member of the group one aspect of the topic, such as politics, the caste system, the film industry, marriage, advertising and communications, music, fashion, decorative arts, and literature.

2. As a group, research and report on the topic "Archaeology and Ancient Civilizations in the Middle East." The purpose of your report is to answer the question "What new light have archaeological discoveries shed on the ancient civilizations of the Middle East?" Assign each member of the group one country or aspect of the topic, such as Troy (Turkey), Jericho (Israel), and the Pyramids (Egypt).

India and the Middle East **583**

THE ORIGINAL LANGUAGE

You might want to use the transliteration on the pupil page to give students an idea of the sound of Sanskrit.

GUIDELINES FOR COLLABORATIVE RESEARCH ACTIVITIES

1. Students may find special reference books for younger readers helpful, particularly James Traub's *India: The Challenge of Change.*

2. Students might search in newspaper and magazine indexes for articles about discoveries at Troy, Qumran (the site of the discovery of the Dead Sea Scrolls), and the Pyramids. They might find, for instance, that excavations at Troy seem to indicate that Troy was attacked and burned around 1250 B.C., close to the date traditionally given for the Trojan War. This lends some credence to the Homeric epics, although some scholars point out that there is no proof that the Greeks were the attackers.

This guide provides, in chronological order, brief descriptions of major literary movements in world literature. Each entry defines the time period during which the movement flourished, summarizes the principal ideas and characteristics of the movement, and names well-known writers and works associated with the movement. Encourage students to use this guide to consider whether and to what degree a particular author displays characteristics and ideas typical of his or her time or whether an author shows the influence of a past literary movement. Students may also use this guide to compare works by different authors within the same movement or to contrast works by authors associated with different movements.

Note that students' chronological perspective on world literature may be further enhanced by their examination of the World Events Time Line (pp. xxiv–xxv), the outlines of regional or national literatures that appear throughout the Literature and Culture Sourcebook (pp. 544–583), and the Author Time Line (pp. 586–588).

GUIDE TO LITERARY MOVEMENTS

CLASSICAL LITERATURE In Western literature *Classical* refers to the characteristics of Greek and Roman literature created between approximately 750 B.C. and A.D. 200. These qualities include order, simplicity, balance, proportion, and formal elegance. The Classical principles of poetry discussed by the philosopher Aristotle in his *Poetics* exerted an enormous influence on later Western literature. Among the literary types that flourished in this period are the epic poem, tragedy, comedy, and the ode. Major works of Classical literature include Homer's *Iliad* and *Odyssey,* Sophocles' *Oedipus the King,* and the odes of Pindar and Horace.

Many literatures of the world enjoyed their own classical periods. The Classical Age of Sanskrit writing in India, the period of the *Mahābhārata* and the *Panchatantra,* covered approximately 300 B.C. to A.D. 1100. The Classic Period of Arabic literature ran from approximately the sixth century to the tenth century. The Classical Age of Chinese literature is generally considered to be approximately 1500 B.C. to 250 B.C. The Classic Period of Japanese literature was approximately the ninth to the twelfth centuries, a time that saw an enormous amount of subtle and delicate poetry, as well as prose romances, including the masterful *Tale of Genji* by Lady Murasaki. Throughout Africa rich and varied oral traditions, active for thousands of years, produced myths, epic songs, and folk tales that have served later African writers as "classical" sources.

MEDIEVAL LITERATURE *Medieval* refers to the characteristics of the drama, poetry, and prose of the Middle Ages, from approximately the sixth through the fifteenth centuries. Medieval drama focuses on religious and moral themes, while the poetry and prose of medieval romance includes the legends of King Arthur and adventurous tales of love and chivalry. Medieval masterpieces include the anonymous play *Everyman,* Dante's *Divine Comedy,* Chaucer's *Cantebury Tales,* and Omar Khayyám's *Rubáiyát.*

RENAISSANCE LITERATURE *Renaissance* literally means "rebirth" and refers to the renewed appreciation for Classical ideas and ideals in the fourteenth, fifteenth, and sixteenth centuries. Beginning in Italy, the Renaissance spread across Europe as a reaction against the feudalism of the Middle Ages. Renaissance writers and artists emphasize the value, the abilities, and the beauty of the human individual. Major Renaissance writers include Petrach and Boccaccio in Italy, Cervantes and

Lope de Vega in Spain, Villon and Ronsard in France, and Shakespeare in England.

NEOCLASSICISM *Neoclassicism* literally means "new classicism" and refers to an attempt during the seventeenth and eighteenth centuries to imitate Classical style and form. Neoclassical writers emphasize emotional restraint, structural balance, and formal elegance. In England, Neoclassical writers include Dryden, Pope, and Swift. Neoclassical qualities are also found in the works of the French writers Molière, Corneille, Racine, and La Fontaine.

THE ENLIGHTENMENT The period of the Enlightenment, also known as the Age of Reason, flourished during the eighteenth century in Europe and the United States. Enlightenment literature abandons the idealism of the past and emphasizes human logic and reason. It places great value on learning and on practical solutions in social and political matters. The writings of Diderot and Voltaire in France, Locke in England, and Franklin in America reflect the ideas of this movement.

ROMANTICISM As a literary movement Romanticism began in England and Germany and spread through Europe and the United States from the late eighteenth century through the mid-nineteenth century. Romantic writers rejected Neoclassical values, such as order and logic, in favor of faith in the individual human experience. Romantics demonstrated love of nature, focus on the self, fascination with the supernatural, yearning for the exotic, deep-rooted idealism, and passionate love of country. Major Romantic writers include Wordsworth, Coleridge, Byron, Shelley, Keats, and Scott in England; Goethe, Schiller, and Heine in Germany; Pushkin in Russia; Hugo in France; Pérez Galdós in Spain; Manzoni and Leopardi in Italy; and Hawthorne, Melville, Poe, Whitman, and Dickinson in the United States.

AESTHETICISM This movement, emphasizing "art for art's sake," took place during the nineteenth century in Europe. Aestheticism celebrates beauty without any moral or social or religious implications. Aestheticism revived interest in Classical mythology and medieval romance and chivalry. The best writers associated with this movement took inspiration from it and then grew away from it: Goethe in Germany, Flaubert in France, and Wordsworth in England.

SYMBOLISM Often considered an extension of Romanticism in France in the nineteenth century, Symbolism was influenced by the writing of the American Edgar Allan Poe. Symbolist writers emphasize mood and the music of poetry; they use symbols to express emotions and ideas. Baudelaire's *Flowers of Evil* and Rimbaud's *Illuminations* are two of the finest examples of Symbolism. Symbolism had a powerful effect on modern poets, especially on Yeats in Ireland, the Imagists in England and America, Valéry in France, and Rilke in Austria.

IMAGISM As a literary movement Imagism flourished in England and the United States only from 1912 to about 1917, although many later writers used Imagist techniques. In direct imitation of Japanese verse, Imagism emphasizes brevity, clarity, precision, and devotion to a single image to convey a complex of emotions. Those writers most closely associated with the movement were Ezra Pound, H.D. (Hilda Doolittle), and William Carlos Williams.

REALISM Realism overlapped Romanticism in the nineteenth century in Europe and the United States and then became the dominant attitude of fiction writers and dramatists. Concerned with presenting life as it is lived by ordinary people, Realist writers present events in common language, often in "slice of life" stories. Examples of Realist literature include Balzac's *Human Comedy* and Flaubert's *Madame Bovary* in France, Dickens' *David Copperfield* in England, Tolstoy's *War and Peace* in Russia, Ibsen's *Master Builder* in Norway, and Azuela's *Underdogs* in Mexico.

NATURALISM The major ideas of Naturalism were formulated by Emile Zola in France in the late nineteenth century. Naturalist writers believe that heredity and environment—nature and society—determine the human experience. Sometimes considered an extreme form of Realism, Naturalism concerns itself with the harsh and brutal aspects of life, usually showing human beings as subject to chance and unable to control their own lives. Writers associated with Naturalist ideas are, in addition to Zola, Maupassant in France, Chekhov and Gorki in Russia, and Crane and Dreiser in the United States.

MODERNISM The word *Modernism* refers to many separate literary movements that flourished throughout Europe and the Americas from the late nineteenth century to the mid-twentieth century. These movements include Symbolism, Imagism, Expressionism, Dadaism, Surrealism, and Futurism. Modernist writers broke many literary traditions, writing about new subjects in new styles. At first considered experimental or obscure, the best Modernist writers have come to be accepted as pioneers of the imagination who explored fresh ways of reaching the minds and hearts of twentieth-century readers. Modernist writers include Joyce in Ireland, Kafka in Czechoslovakia, Mann and Brecht in Germany, Pound and Eliot in the United States and Europe, Woolf in England, Proust in France, García Lorca in Spain, Darío in Nicaragua, and Martí in Cuba.

MAGIC REALISM Magic Realism is a Latin American literary approach of the mid-twentieth century. Magic Realist works combine realistic, believable details of ordinary life with an element of fantasy. The best-known work of Magic Realism is Gabriel García Márquez' novel *One Hundred Years of Solitude*.

This listing places the authors represented in this anthology on a time line according to their year of birth. Students might consult this listing to see where a particular author stands in the overall chronology of world literature or for a quick overview of the time periods and authors represented in the anthology.

Note that students' chronological perspective on world literature will also be enhanced by their examination of the World Events Time Line (pp. xxiv–xxv), the outlines of national or regional literatures that appear throughout the Literature and Culture Sourcebook (pp. 544–583), and the Guide to Literary Movements (pp. 584–585).

This Author Time Line presents authors chronologically, grouped into periods or centuries according to the year of their birth.

AUTHOR	AUTHOR'S DATES	TITLE OF SELECTION
ANCIENT PERIOD		
Homer	c. 850 B.C.	*from the* Iliad (p. 262)
Aesop	c. 620–560 B.C.	The Fox and the Grapes (p. 238)
		The Goatherd and the Wild Goats (p. 238)
Sappho	c. 612–580 B.C.	Fragment of a Lullaby (p. 290)
Confucius	c. 551–479 B.C.	Sayings *from* The Analects (p. 399)
Thucydides	c. 460–400 B.C.	Pericles' Funeral Oration (p. 424)
Virgil	70–19 B.C.	*from the* Aeneid (p. 270)
Horace	65–8 B.C.	Ode: Better to Live, Licinius (p. 359)
Ovid	43 B.C.–A.D. 17	*from the* Metamorphoses (p. 231)
Indian Traditional	c. 200–400	*from the* Panchatantra (p. 243)
MEDIEVAL PERIOD		
Li Po	701–762	Taking Leave of a Friend (p. 337)
Tu Fu	712–770	The Emperor (p. 286)
Lady Ōtomo	8th century	My Heart, Thinking (p. 293)
Arabian and Persian Traditional	c. 1200	*from* The Thousand and One Nights (p. 247)
Dante Alighieri	1265–1321	*from* The Divine Comedy (p. 276)
RENAISSANCE		
Petrarch	1304–1374	Sonnet 3 (It Was That Very Day on Which the Sun) (p. 300)
Giovanni Boccaccio	1313–1375	Federigo's Falcon (p. 135)
Seami Motokiyo	1363–1443	The Dwarf Trees (p. 454)
Nguyen Trai	1380–1442	The Bamboo Hut (p. 329)
Miguel de Cervantes	1547–1616	*from* Don Quixote (p. 162)
William Shakespeare	1564–1616	Sonnet 29 (When, in Disgrace with Fortune and Men's Eyes) (p. 301)
SEVENTEENTH CENTURY		
François de La Rochefoucauld	1613–1680	*from* Maxims (p. 401)
Jean de La Fontaine	1621–1695	The Fox and the Crow (p. 240)
Bashō	1644–1694	Autumn (p. 318)
Jōsō	1661–1704	Winter (p. 318)

586 *Author Time Line*

AUTHOR	AUTHOR'S DATES	TITLE OF SELECTION

EIGHTEENTH CENTURY

Chiyo	1703–1775	After a Long Winter (p. 318)
Johann Wolfgang von Goethe	1749–1832	The Erl-King (p. 258)
Heinrich Heine	1797–1856	The Lorelei (p. 347)
Alexander Pushkin	1799–1837	Message to Siberia (p. 364)

NINETEENTH CENTURY

Victor Hugo	1802–1885	June Nights (p. 305)
Emily Dickinson	1830–1886	How Happy Is the Little Stone (p. 330)
Bjørnstjerne Bjørnson	1832–1910	The Father (p. 45)
Jan Neruda	1834–1891	Hastrman (p. 146)
Alphonse Daudet	1840–1897	The Last Lesson (p. 189)
Guy de Maupassant	1850–1893	The Piece of String (p. 12)
José Martí	1853–1895	from Versos Sencillos (p. 362)
Selma Lagerlöf	1858–1940	The Rat Trap (p. 64)
Anton Chekhov	1860–1904	The Beggar (p. 24)
Rabindranath Tagore	1861–1941	The Kabuliwallah (p. 49)
C. P. Cavafy	1863–1933	Che Fece . . . Il Gran Rifiuto (p. 353)
A. B. ("Banjo") Paterson	1864–1941	Waltzing Matilda (p. 356)
William Butler Yeats	1865–1939	Politics (p. 288)
Shiki	1867–1902	Heat (p. 318)
Edmond Rostand	1869–1918	Cyrano de Bergerac (p. 464)
Chaim Nachman Bialik	1873–1934	Summer Is Dying (p. 315)
Colette	1873–1954	Two Memories of Sido (p. 393)
Rainer Maria Rilke	1875–1926	Spanish Dancer (p. 335)
Grazia Deledda	1875–1936	The Shoes (p. 220)
Antonio Machado	1875–1939	Winter Sun (p. 304)
Thomas Mann	1875–1955	The Infant Prodigy (p. 113)
Sarojini Naidu	1879–1949	Street Cries (p. 325)
Juan Ramón Jiménez	1881–1958	from Platero and I (p. 414)
Isak Dinesen	1885–1962	The Iguana (p. 421)
Katherine Mansfield	1888–1923	The Doll's House (p. 105)
Anna Akhmatova	1888–1966	Lot's Wife (p. 298)
Gabriela Mistral	1889–1957	Rocking (p. 291)
Nelly Sachs	1891–1970	The Swan (p. 307)
Akutagawa Ryūnosuke	1892–1927	Autumn Mountain (p. 181)
Manuel Rojas	1896–1973	The Glass of Milk (p. 57)
Vicente Aleixandre	1898–1984	On the Way to School (p. 332)
Federico García Lorca	1899–1936	The Guitar (p. 340)
Ernest Hemingway	1899–1961	Old Man at the Bridge (p. 194)
Jorge Luis Borges	1899–1986	Afterglow (p. 345)

Author Time Line **587**

AUTHOR	AUTHOR'S DATES	TITLE OF SELECTION

TWENTIETH CENTURY

AUTHOR	AUTHOR'S DATES	TITLE OF SELECTION
Thomas Wolfe	1900–1938	The Far and the Near (p. 168)
George Seferis	1900–1971	I Am Sorry (p. 344)
Sean O'Faolain	born 1900	The Trout (p. 92)
Nazim Hikmet	1902–1963	The World, My Friends, My Enemies, You, and the Earth (p. 350)
Jaime Torres Bodet	1902–1974	The Window (p. 354)
Jorge Carrera Andrade	1903–1978	Reaping the Barley (p. 326)
Alan Paton	1903–1988	The Quarry (p. 97)
Pablo Neruda	1904–1973	The Horses (p. 308)
Åsta Holth	born 1904	Salt (p. 130)
Isaac Bashevis Singer	born 1904	Shosha (p. 404)
R. K. Narayan	born 1906	Like the Sun (p. 141)
Léopold S. Senghor	born 1906	And We Shall Be Steeped (p. 296)
Rumer Godden	born 1907	You Need to Go Upstairs (p. 19)
Gabrielle Roy	1909–1983	Hoodoo Valley (p. 121)
Naguib Mahfouz	born 1911	A Tale of Our Quarter (p. 158)
Czeslaw Milosz	born 1911	Encounter (p. 338)
Albert Camus	1913–1960	The Guest (p. 209)
Octavio Paz	born 1914	Wind and Water and Stone (p. 316)
N. V. M. Gonzalez	born 1915	On the Ferry (p. 84)
Camilo José Cela	born 1916	Traveling in the Alcarria (p. 418)
Heinrich Böll	1917–1985	The Laugher (p. 205)
Aleksandr Solzhenitsyn	born 1918	Three Prose Poems (p. 410)
João Cabral de Melo Neto	born 1920	Weaving the Morning (p. 312)
Tu Peng-cheng	born 1921	Lingkuan Gorge (p. 73)
Santha Rama Rau	born 1923	By Any Other Name (p. 373)
James Ene Henshaw	born 1924	The Jewels of the Shrine (p. 439)
Camara Laye	1928–1980	The Snake and the Goldsmith (p. 380)
Stan Barstow	born 1928	The Actor (p. 30)
Gabriel García Márquez	born 1928	Tuesday Siesta (p. 198)
Tayeb Salih	born 1929	A Handful of Dates (p. 78)
Chinua Achebe	born 1930	Dead Men's Path (p. 40)
Françoise Mallet-Joris	born 1930	Air des Clochettes (p. 173)
V. S. Naipaul	born 1932	The Crocodiles of Yamoussoukro (p. 431)
Yevgeny Yevtushenko	born 1933	Colors (p. 294)
Joseph Brodsky	born 1940	The Monument (p. 365)
Barbara Kimenye	born 1940	The Winner (p. 3)
Oswald Mbuyiseni Mtshali	born 1940	Sunset (p. 311)
Gerardo María	born 1956	Matusalén, the Village Without Time (p. 153)

RETELLINGS OF TRADITIONAL FOLK LITERATURE

AUTHOR	TITLE OF SELECTION
Gabon Pygmy Traditional	All That Dances (p. 321)
Kabyle Traditional	The Story of the Chest (p. 253)
Zapotec Traditional	The Bat (p. 235)

588 *Author Time Line*

NOBEL PRIZE MEDAL

This chronological listing identifies the winners of the Nobel Prize for Literature and indicates each winner's nationality. In having students examine the list, point out that the prize has been awarded since the beginning of the century and is the best-known award in world literature.

Note that all names preceded by a blue asterisk are authors represented in this anthology. These authors are also identified in the Table of Contents (pp. v–xiii), where the label "Nobel Prize" appears in blue print after each winner's name.

WINNERS OF NOBEL PRIZE FOR LITERATURE

1901	René Sully-Prudhomme	France
1902	Theodor Mommsen	Germany
*1903	Bjørnstjerne Bjørnson	Norway
1904	José Echegaray	Spain
	Frédéric Mistral	France
1905	Henryk Sienkiewicz	Poland
1906	Giosuè Carducci	Italy
1907	Rudyard Kipling	England
1908	Rudolf Eucken	Germany
*1909	Selma Lagerlöf	Sweden
1910	Paul Heyse	Germany
1911	Maurice Maeterlinck	Belgium
1912	Gerhart Hauptmann	Germany
*1913	Rabindranath Tagore	India
1914	Not awarded	
1915	Romain Rolland	France
1916	Verner von Heidenstam	Sweden
1917	Karl Gjellerup	Denmark
	Henrik Pontoppidan	Denmark
1918	Not awarded	
1919	Carl Spitteler	Switzerland
1920	Knut Hamsun	Norway
1921	Anatole France	France
1922	Jacinto Benavente y Martínez	Spain
*1923	William Butler Yeats	Ireland
1924	Wladyslaw Reymont	Poland
1925	George Bernard Shaw	England
*1926	Grazia Deledda	Italy
1927	Henri Bergson	France
1928	Sigrid Undset	Norway
*1929	Thomas Mann	Germany
1930	Sinclair Lewis	United States
1931	Erik A. Karlfeldt	Sweden
1932	John Galsworthy	England
1933	Ivan A. Bunin	Russia
1934	Luigi Pirandello	Italy
1935	Not awarded	
1936	Eugene O'Neill	United States
1937	Roger Martin du Gard	France
1938	Pearl S. Buck	United States
1939	Frans Eemil Sillanpää	Finland
1940	Not awarded	
1941	Not awarded	
1942	Not awarded	

*Author represented in this text.

Year	Winner	Country
1943	Not awarded	
1944	Johannes V. Jensen	Denmark
*1945	Gabriela Mistral	Chile
1946	Hermann Hesse	Switzerland
1947	André Gide	France
1948	T. S. Eliot	England
1949	William Faulkner	United States
1950	Bertrand Russell	England
1951	Pär Lagerkvist	Sweden
1952	François Mauriac	France
1953	Winston Churchill	England
*1954	Ernest Hemingway	United States
1955	Halldór Kiljan Laxness	Iceland
*1956	Juan Ramón Jiménez	Spain
*1957	Albert Camus	France
1958	Boris Pasternak	Soviet Union (Declined)
1959	Salvatore Quasimodo	Italy
1960	Saint-John Perse	France
1961	Ivo Andrić	Yugoslavia
1962	John Steinbeck	United States
*1963	George Seferis	Greece
1964	Jean-Paul Sartre	France (Declined)
1965	Mikhail Sholokhov	Soviet Union
1966	S. Y. Agnon	Israel
*	Nelly Sachs	Germany
1967	Miguel Angel Asturias	Guatemala
1968	Yasunari Kawabata	Japan
1969	Samuel Beckett	France
*1970	Aleksandr Solzhenitsyn	Soviet Union
*1971	Pablo Neruda	Chile
*1972	Heinrich Böll	Germany
1973	Patrick White	Australia
1974	Eyvind Johnson	Sweden
	Harry Martinson	Sweden
1975	Eugenio Montale	Italy
1976	Saul Bellow	United States
*1977	Vicente Aleixandre	Spain
*1978	Isaac Bashevis Singer	United States
1979	Odysseus Elytis	Greece
*1980	Czeslaw Milosz	United States
1981	Elias Canetti	Bulgaria
*1982	Gabriel García Márquez	Colombia
1983	William Golding	England
1984	Jaroslav Siefert	Czechoslovakia
1985	Claude Simon	France
1986	Wole Soyinka	Nigeria
*1987	Joseph Brodsky	United States
*1988	Naguib Mahfouz	Egypt
*1989	Camilo José Cela	Spain
*1990	Octavio Paz	Mexico

*Author represented in this text.

The Writing About Literature Handbook guides students through the kinds of writing assignments they are most likely to encounter in literature classes. Ten lessons show them how to write analyses of literary works, including a personal response to a work. The handbook follows a writing-process approach to the various assignments, beginning with prewriting and continuing through writing and revising. Clearly sequenced instructions with specific examples reinforce students' familiarity with the writing process. Lessons conclude with specific assignments and cross-references to appropriate Composition assignments throughout *World Literature*.

WRITING A RESPONSE TO LITERATURE

Focusing on the task of responding in general to a work of literature, this first lesson introduces students to a writing-process approach to writing about literature. Since the lesson uses examples from the story "The Winner," you may want to assign that story before you teach this lesson. The lesson concludes with open-ended assignments in which students apply what they have learned.

WRITING ABOUT LITERATURE HANDBOOK

LESSON 1: *Writing a Response to Literature*

This first lesson will deal with the most general points you should observe in writing literary analysis. The following lessons will deal with writing specific kinds of literary analysis in response to common essay questions.

PREWRITING

Before you begin to write apply these hints.

1. Read the question or assignment. Then reread it. As you reread the assignment, underline or copy the key words, which tell you specifically what is expected of you in your written answer.

   Example: Write an evaluation of a short story. First decide whether or not you like the story. Then explain your response, considering the following questions: Does the story arouse your interest at the beginning? What questions does it raise that you want to see answered? Does it sustain your interest and lead toward a logical solution? Support your opinions with specific examples.

2. Paraphrase the assignment to assure yourself that you know exactly what is expected of you.

   Example: Tell what you thought about a short story. Begin by saying whether or not you liked the story. Then give reasons for your opinion. Concentrate on whether the story grabbed your interest, held your interest, and ultimately satisfied you. Give examples to back up your generalizations.

3. Sketch diagrams or charts, or prepare an outline that will help you organize your thoughts as you reread the literature with the essay question in mind. For example, the following chart will help you think about the preceding assignment.

EVALUATION OF A STORY		
SELECTION: _____		
LIKED _____ DID NOT LIKE _____		
QUESTION	ANSWER	EXAMPLE
DID THE STORY AROUSE YOUR INTEREST?		
WHAT QUESTIONS DID THE STORY RAISE?		
DID THE STORY SUSTAIN YOUR INTEREST?		
DID THE ENDING SEEM LOGICAL?		

WRITING AN ESSAY PARAGRAPH BY PARAGRAPH

1. Begin with an introductory paragraph that contains a thesis statement. A **thesis statement** addresses itself to the question that is directly asked or implied in the assignment. It suggests an answer to the question—an answer that the rest of your essay will discuss. The thesis statement is a summary of the topic sentences that the reader will find in the body of the essay.

   Example: "The Winner" by Barbara Kimenye offers an enjoyable reading experience from the beginning, when it arouses readers' interest and gently brings up a variety of social issues and questions for consideration, through its rising action, when the complications continue to intrigue readers, and to its ending, when the readers cannot help but be impressed with the satisfying conclusion.

The thesis statement may at times be longer than a single sentence. The introductory paragraph can be made up of the thesis statement and any other sentences that you might need to clarify it.

2. Write the body of your essay, perhaps two to three paragraphs. In each paragraph develop further one of the ideas from your thesis statement. Each of these paragraphs should provide proof that your thesis statement is valid. Each of these paragraphs should have its own **topic sentence**, which will state the main idea of that particular paragraph. For example, the paragraph that comes after the introductory paragraph with the thesis statement about "The Winner" might begin with the following topic sentence:

Example: The story arouses readers' interest from the very beginning.

Each subsequent sentence in the paragraph must support the topic sentence of that paragraph. The supporting sentences should be examples, quotations, or incidents that come from the literature you are writing about.

3. Tie or hook your paragraphs together with transitions such as *however, in addition, similarly, next,* and *because.* For example, the paragraph that might follow the paragraph begun in the previous step could begin as follows:

Example: After readers find that they are hooked on the story, they realize they have questions about the plot and the characters.

4. Conclude your essay with a summary paragraph. Restate—in different words—the thesis statement from your introductory paragraph.

Example: From beginning to end, "The Winner" offers readers a thoroughly involving vicarious experience.

WRITING A ONE-PARAGRAPH ANSWER

All the preceding advice on structure applies as well to answers that are only one paragraph long. If you are limited to one paragraph, begin with a strong topic sentence. Each of your following sentences should develop and provide evidence for one aspect of the topic sentence.

REVISING AND EDITING

Once you have finished the first draft, you must take time to polish it into an improved second draft.

1. Read your writing aloud.
2. Use the following checklist to revise your writing. If you can answer "yes" to each question on the list, you will submit an essay that your audience will find interesting and logical.

I. Organization
   a. Does your thesis statement relate directly to the assignment?
   b. Are the ideas mentioned in the thesis statement then taken up in the following paragraphs with a topic sentence for each?
   c. Is there effective, clear movement from paragraph to paragraph by means of transitions?
   d. Does the final paragraph offer a restatement of the thesis statement along with additional insights?
II. Content
   a. Does the essay adequately answer the question posed in the assignment?
   b. Is each idea adequately developed with supporting details from the literature?
III. Grammar, Usage, Mechanics
   a. Is each sentence complete (no fragments, no run-ons)?
   b. Have you avoided errors in the use of verbs, pronouns, and modifiers?
   c. Have you correctly capitalized and punctuated all sentences?
   d. Are all words spelled correctly?
IV. Word Choice, Style
   a. Have you used words that are appropriate for your audience and your purpose?
   b. Have you avoided slang and clichés?
   c. Have you eliminated wordiness?
   d. Have you varied sentence length and structure while checking for parallelism?

ASSIGNMENTS

1. Use the preceding checklist to evaluate and revise an essay that you have written.

2. Select another story that you have read in this book. Then use the advice in this lesson to write an evaluation of the story.

Writing About Literature Handbook **593**

LESSON 2: *Writing About Plot*

When you write about **plot** (the sequence of events or actions in a story), you may have to evaluate the story line by explaining how the problems and the conflicts lead up to the climax and resolution of the story. You have to demonstrate how the ending makes sense in light of what has come before, and you have to give one or more specific examples to prove your point.

▬ CONCEPTS TO REMEMBER

In order to think clearly about a story's ending, you must know how all the parts of a story work together. Here are statements about each part:

Exposition—"Background" information that may tell you how and why the characters arrived at this particular place and time. Many stories have very brief or no exposition.

Narrative hook—The point at which the author snares your attention. This may be the point at which the reader begins to say, "I want to know what's going to happen next—and why!"

Rising action—The buildup of events and the presentation of the problems and conflicts faced by the characters.

Climax—The turning point of the story; the point of greatest emotional involvement. This is the point when you know whether the main character will be successful or not.

Falling action—The point at which the reader learns of the character's reaction to the climax. This section of the story may be very short.

Resolution—The end of the falling action; the final tying together of the story.

▬ TYPICAL ESSAY QUESTION

When you are asked to write about the plot of a story, you are often answering an essay question such as the following:

Show how the events and conflicts prepare the reader for the climax and the resolution of the selection. Indicate if you are satisfied with the climax and the resolution or why you would have preferred different developments.

▬ PREWRITING

Think of the overall structure of the work. "Map" the plot of the selection. For "The Winner" (page 3) your map might look like this:

PLOT STRUCTURE

SELECTION: "The Winner"

CLIMAX: Pius learns that he has won less money but Sarah doesn't seem to mind and stays on.

Sarah arrives and is welcomed by Pius' friends.

The exhausted Pius is rescued by his friends and taken to their home.

Salongo sees Sarah's plans to "snare" Pius and warns him.

RISING ACTION

FALLING ACTION:
The pair discuss marriage. Pius visits Salongo, gives him a donation, and invites him to the wedding.

EXPOSITION:
Pius wins football pool; news spreads.

NARRATIVE HOOK:
Sarah takes over as mistress of the house and spokesperson for Pius.

RESOLUTION:
Salongo accepts the marriage and sends Sarah a gift.

WRITING PARAGRAPH BY PARAGRAPH

1. In your first paragraph write a thesis statement of one or two sentences in which you paraphrase the main idea of the essay question.

   Example: Many of the events and conflicts in "The Winner" prepare the reader for the climax and resolution, the point when the reader is made aware of the fact that Pius now has won less money, of his decision to marry Sarah, and of Salongo's grudging approval of the match.

2. In the next paragraph discuss the exposition and the narrative hook. What does the author tell you in the exposition that helps you understand the way a character acts later in the plot? What happens at the narrative hook that sets the stage for what comes later?

3. In the next paragraph discuss the conflicts in the rising action and the climax, explaining how the climax follows from preceding events.

4. In the next paragraph explain why the falling action and the resolution are necessary. What remaining questions about the characters are answered during the falling action? How does the main character feel after the climax? Explain whether the resolution makes sense.

5. In your concluding paragraph reemphasize your thesis statement from the introductory paragraph, but use different words to state it. Are you satisfied with the climax and the resolution? If not, why do you think they should have been different?

REVISING AND EDITING

See Lesson 1 for detailed reminders about improving your writing.

ASSIGNMENTS

1. Use the "map" of "The Winner" to write about its plot and its ending. Show how the events and conflicts in the rising action prepare the reader for the climax and the resolution. Indicate if you are satisfied with them or why you would have preferred different developments.

2. Do the assignment called "Writing About Plot" for "The Piece of String" (page 17), or select another story you have read in this book, and answer the following: Show how the events and conflicts prepare the reader for the climax and resolution. Look for clues, known as **foreshadowing,** that help the reader anticipate what is to come. Indicate whether you are satisfied with the climax and resolution or why you would have preferred different developments.

This lesson guides students through the process of writing a comparison of two fictional characters. The lesson reinforces the textbook's instruction on characterization, character motivation, flat and round characters, static and dynamic characters, and character foils. You may want to teach this lesson in conjunction with the second section in the Short Story unit, Stories About Human Relationships, in which several Literary Focus features highlight aspects of character. Since the lesson uses examples from "The Father" and "The Kabuliwallah," you may want to assign those stories before you teach this lesson. Under Assignments on the following page, you will find a cross-reference to a Composition assignment in this textbook that focuses on comparing characters.

LESSON 3: *Writing About Character*

We can gain insight into a character by looking at him or her in relation to another character. Sometimes we look at two characters from the same work of literature in order to learn more about each. Sometimes, though, a character in one work will remind us of a character in another selection. In either case—whether we are working with one selection or two—we can compare and contrast characters, examining the similarities and differences in the ways they act and react to conflicts, in how they think, in what they value, in how they change, and so on.

CONCEPTS TO REMEMBER

1. **To compare** in this lesson means "to examine two or more things, ideas, people, and so on, for the purpose of noting similarities." **To contrast** means "to examine two or more items for the purpose of noting differences."
2. A character may be **flat** or **round**. A flat character's personality is dominated by a single trait; a round character possesses many different traits, some of which may even seem to be contradictory.
3. A character may be **static** or **dynamic**. A static character does not change from the beginning of the work of literature to the end. A dynamic character changes in some way during the course of the work. This change may be a positive one (for example, toward maturity) or a negative one (for example, the worsening of a flaw).

TYPICAL ESSAY QUESTION

When you are asked to compare and contrast characters in a story, you will often have to answer an essay assignment such as the following one:

Compare and contrast two characters within a piece of literature or in two different pieces of literature. Identify a number of points of comparison and contrast, and for each point explain how the characters are similar or different.

PREWRITING

1. Select two characters, and ask yourself questions about them as a brainstorming technique for developing points of comparison and contrast. Here are just a few suggestions regarding the kinds of questions you can ask about each of the two characters.

   a. What are each character's key traits? (Examining the character's actions, comments, thoughts, and feelings will help you determine key traits.)
   b. What is each character's underlying motivation (the basic reason that he or she acts in a particular way) or goal?
   c. Does each character remain the same from the beginning to the end, or does he or she change? In what way?

2. Prepare a chart on which to record your answers to the questions in Prewriting Step 1. The chart on the opposite page details the similarities and differences between Thord in "The Father" (page 45) and the title character in "The Kabuliwallah" (page 49). The plus or minus indicates whether the two characters are similar (+) or different (−) in respect to the particular characteristic under discussion.

WRITING PARAGRAPH BY PARAGRAPH

1. Begin your introductory paragraph with a thesis statement. The thesis statement (which, at times, may be longer than one sentence) should address the main points of the essay question and should clearly indicate whether you intend to compare and contrast two characters from the same work or two characters from different works. Be sure to state in a general way how the characters are alike and how they are different.

   Example: Thord in "The Father" and the title character in "The Kabuliwallah" are devoted fathers who want the best for their children. Each father has a dream for his child. In both cases the outcome of the dream is determined by outside circumstances. The outcomes change the two men, but each changes in a different way.

2. Use one of the following options for organizing the body of the essay:

SIMILARITIES AND DIFFERENCES IN CHARACTERS
SELECTIONS: "The Father" and "The Kabuliwallah"

	1ST CHARACTER (Thord)	2ND CHARACTER (The Kabuliwallah)		
KEY TRAITS	*Fatherly devotion:* Rich and powerful, he demands the best for his only son.	*Fatherly devotion:* A poor man, he works hard far from home to provide for his daughter, his only child.	⊕	–
	Arrogance and selfishness: He ignores those less fortunate as well as the spiritual meaning of religious rituals.	*Humility and generosity:* He cherishes the handprint of his child and shares his goods and affection.	+	–
GOALS	*Dream:* He wants his son to lead the community in wealth, power, and position.	*Dream:* He misses his daughter terribly and dreams of the day when he can see her once again.	+	⊖
	Result: The father's dream evaporates after his son dies in a terrible and inexplicable accident.	*Result:* His dream is realized when Mini's father gives him money to return home to his daughter.	+	⊖
CHANGES	*Major change:* After his son dies, Thord becomes richer in spirit as he learns to think of and care about others.	*Subtle change:* The Kabuliwallah realizes that his daughter, like Mini, has grown up and may no longer know him.	+	⊖

Option A

Introductory paragraph
Next paragraph: Describe one character.
Next paragraph: Describe the other character.
Next paragraph: Discuss similarities and differences based on two preceding paragraphs.
Concluding paragraph

Option B

Introductory paragraph
Next paragraph: Note the similarities between the two characters.
Next paragraph: Note the differences between the two characters.
Concluding paragraph

Option C

Introductory paragraph
Next paragraph: Note similarities and differences in the characters' key traits.
Next paragraph: Note similarities and differences in the characters' goals.
Next paragraph: Note similarities and differences in the characters' changes.
Concluding paragraph

3. In the concluding paragraph use different words to remind readers of your thesis. Focus on whether the two characters are more alike or more different. You might end by noting whether one character seemed more admirable or appealing on the basis of the traits and experiences you have already discussed.

REVISING AND EDITING

See Lesson 1 for detailed reminders about improving your writing.

ASSIGNMENTS

1. Use the chart for "The Father" and "The Kabuliwallah" to compare and contrast Thord and the Kabuliwallah.

2. Do the assignment called "Writing About Character" for "The Rat Trap" (page 71). Or select two other stories that you have read in this book and answer the following: Compare and contrast two characters from the stories you have selected by showing how they are alike and how they are different with respect to their key traits, their motivation or goal, and the ways they change.

Writing About Literature Handbook **597**

LESSON 4: *Writing About Setting*

As you read a story and note its setting, you should ask yourself why the author chose to create or use that setting and why he or she dropped characters and events into that time and place. Keep in mind that **setting** includes time, place, weather, seasons, physical props, and the characters' clothing, as well as the wider culture in which the conflicts and action occur. If setting is effective, it is impossible to consider these particular characters and these particular events existing elsewhere. That is to say, the theme of a story may be universal, but its time and place may still be very specific.

Setting may become clear in the beginning of a story, or it may emerge as the story unfolds. Sometimes, if the author wants to focus on character or plot, setting serves only as a backdrop for action. It will simply be the place or situation in which events occur. At other times setting may take on much more importance, representing something abstract or symbolic.

CONCEPTS TO REMEMBER

1. An author always has a purpose in telling a story. The **purpose** is the theme, or general idea about life, that the author wants to communicate.

2. The author's choice of setting can reveal that purpose by

   a. creating a mood or atmosphere
   b. illuminating the characters
   c. unifying or organizing the plot
   d. pointing beyond itself to a deeper symbolic meaning

   Sometimes the author uses the setting in only one of the preceding ways; sometimes the author uses the setting in all four ways.

TYPICAL ESSAY QUESTION

When you are asked to write about the setting of a piece of literature, you are often answering a question such as the following:

Select a piece of literature that you have read. How does the choice of setting reveal the author's purpose?

598 *Writing About Literature Handbook*

PREWRITING

1. Fill in a chart on which you can record your thoughts about the ways in which setting reveals the author's purpose. The recommended chart has a left column that contains questions to help you think about what the setting adds to the story. In the middle column you should write your answers to those questions, and in the right column you should provide details to support your answers. For the short story "Hoodoo Valley" (page 121) the chart might look like the one on the opposite page.

2. The chart should help you learn more about the mood, characters, plot, and theme of the story. With these insights you should now be able to state the author's overall purpose in writing.

   Example: The author's purpose in "Hoodoo Valley" is to show the persistence of a group of immigrants to Canada in their search for the remembered beauties of their homeland.

WRITING PARAGRAPH BY PARAGRAPH

1. Begin your introductory paragraph with a thesis statement that addresses the main ideas of the essay question. In this case, your thesis statement should note the author's purpose and indicate the ways in which the setting makes that purpose clear.

   Example: Gabrielle Roy uses the immense, flat Canadian prairies as the setting or locale that the Russian immigrants steadfastly reject as a place to live. In sharp contrast is Hoodoo Valley, a setting that they can accept as a comforting reminder of their homeland. The author accomplishes her purpose with the setting because it enables her to create a certain mood, unify the plot, illuminate the characters in the story, and underline the theme.

2. In each of the following paragraphs, write about one of the ways in which the setting reveals the author's purpose. That is, use the Prewriting chart to show how the setting affects the mood, characters, plot, and meaning of the story.

SETTING REVEALS PURPOSE
SELECTION: "Hoodoo Valley"

QUESTION	ANSWER	SUPPORTING DETAIL
SETTING AND MOOD WHAT IS THE PERVASIVE MOOD OF THE STORY?	The mood is one of sadness and disappointment but with an undercurrent of persistence and strength.	"From the very start the plain had set about rebuffing them..." "Their leaders ...went out every day with...McPherson the settlement agent."
SETTING AND PLOT IS THE SETTING SIGNIFICANT AT EACH POINT IN THE PLOT?	The plot revolves completely around the setting, which is the central issue of the story.	The exposition describes the plains and the Dukhobors' despairing attitude toward it. At the narrative hook, the Dukhobors are in search of a new prospect — a stretch of grassy plain. In the rising action they keep riding through the vast landscape until McPherson thinks they are lost. At the climax they see Hoodoo Valley, at its peak. In the falling action they are captivated and, at the resolution, decide to settle there.
SETTING AND CHARACTERS WHAT PHYSICAL OR PSYCHOLOGICAL STRENGTHS OR WEAKNESSES ARE REVEALED AS CHARACTERS INTERACT WITH SETTING?	Most of the Dukhobor men are passive. Among the women, the older ones especially, are fighters, notably babushka, who urges the leaders to keep looking for a good place to settle.	"But...husbands...had all the leisure they needed for sighing and lamenting." "A very angry babushka scolded.... There's no such thing as a country where we can be of one mind unless we try, each one of us, to make it so."
SETTING AND THEME WHAT DOES THE SETTING SAY ABOUT LIFE?	The persistence of the Dukhobors and their faith seem to be rewarded with the discovery of Hoodoo Valley.	The three Dukkhobors say, "...if the three of us, by God's grace, can again see in this place the mountains and river of our sweet homeland, why should it be any different for our wives...?"

3. In the concluding paragraph restate your thesis statement in different words.

▬▬ REVISING AND EDITING
See Lesson 1 for detailed reminders about improving your writing.

▬▬ ASSIGNMENTS
1. Use the chart for "Hoodoo Valley" to write about how setting reveals purpose.

2. Do the assignment called "Writing About Setting" for "Salt" (page 133) or for "A Tale of Our Quarter" (page 160). Or select another story you have read in this book, and answer the following: What is the author's purpose in telling this story? How does the choice of setting reveal the author's purpose? In answering, consider how the setting creates mood, illuminates characters, unifies or organizes the plot, and has a more significant meaning than its literal meaning.

LESSON 5: *Writing About Point of View*

Point of view is the relationship between the narrator, or storyteller, and the story. One point of view is not inherently better or worse than another, but for any given work of literature one particular point of view may be a more effective choice. Every aspect of a story is affected by the choice of the point of view. Most obviously, the decision about point of view determines what information the reader receives and how that information is presented.

After you ask yourself, "Who is telling the story?" and "What does this narrator tell me, and not tell me, about the characters and events?" your next question should be "Why did the author select this particular point of view?"

▆▆ CONCEPTS TO REMEMBER

1. The narrator of a story may know everything about the characters and events in a story—or may not. It is important for you not only to determine what the narrator tells you but also to think about what the narrator does *not* tell you.

2. The author may choose to tell the story with a narrator who uses a **first-person point of view.** This narrator uses "I" and other first-person pronouns. The important thing about a first-person narrator is that he or she cannot directly know what is going on in anyone else's mind or anywhere else.

   Strengths of first-person narrator: The narrator's comments are immediate, vivid, personal, involving.
   Limitations of first-person narrator: (1) The narrator may not be aware of the significance of events and implications of actions. (2) The narrator may be untrustworthy.
   Effect of first-person narrator on reader: The reader becomes very involved and must constantly question the narrator's truthfulness.

3. The author may choose to tell the story from the **limited third-person point of view.** In this case the narrator focuses on a particular character and tells us about events as they relate to this character. This narrator will report the *actions and words* of all characters but will reveal the *thoughts and feelings* of only the focal character.

   Strengths of limited third-person narrator: The reader has fewer unanswered questions than with a first-person narrator.
   Limitations of a limited third-person narrator: The narrator cannot tell us everything we may want to know.
   Effect of limited third-person narrator on reader: The reader will feel more secure than with a first-person narrator but will still have questions—especially about characters whose thoughts are not revealed by the narrator.

4. The author may choose to tell the story from an **omniscient point of view.** In this case the narrator knows about everything that is happening and knows what all the characters are thinking and feeling.

   Strengths of omniscient narrator: The narrator can tell us everything that is happening and, therefore, can answer all our questions.
   Limitations of omniscient narrator: (1) Narration is not as intimate as with the first-person or limited third-person narrator. (2) There is less chance for suspense when the narrator seems to know everything that is happening.
   Effect of omniscient narrator on reader: The reader may trust the narrator.

▆▆ TYPICAL ESSAY QUESTION

When you are asked to write about the point of view of a story, you are often answering a question like this one:

Select a piece of literature that you have read. Why is the point of view chosen by the author effective? What are the strengths and limitations of the point of view? How does the point of view affect the reader's response?

▆▆ PREWRITING

1. Determine the point of view by asking the following questions:

a. Does the narrator use first-person pronouns (e.g., *I, me, mine*) or third-person pronouns (e.g., *she, her, hers*)?

b. Does the narrator know about only the events that he or she witnesses, or does the narrator seem to know about everything?

2. Prepare a chart that focuses on the strengths and limitations of the particular point of view represented in the story you have selected (see Concepts to Remember). Consider also how the point of view in this story affects your response to the story. For "A Handful of Dates" (page 78), a story told from the first-person point of view, your chart might look like the one below.

▌ WRITING PARAGRAPH BY PARAGRAPH

1. Begin the introductory statement with a thesis statement. The thesis statement should restate the main ideas of the essay question. Identify the type of narrator, state whether the choice of narrator has advantages or limitations, and indicate whether the selection of the point of view and narrator is a key to the story's impact on the reader.

Example: Tayeb Salih's choice of a first-person narrator, a young boy, has several advantages. Specifically, the first-person narrator helps sharpen the characterization of the grandfather, provides opportunities for fore-

shadowing, and heightens suspense as to the outcome of the story.

2. In each of the following paragraphs select one of the characteristics (strengths and limitations) of this point of view, and give examples of it from the story.

3. In the final paragraph tell how the point of view affected your response to the story.

▌ REVISING AND EDITING

See Lesson 1 for detailed reminders about improving your writing.

▌ ASSIGNMENTS

1. Use the chart for "A Handful of Dates" to write about point of view. Why is the point of view effective? That is, what are the strengths and limitations of the first-person point of view in this story? How does the point of view affect your response to the story?

2. Do the assignment "Writing About Point of View" for "The Trout" (page 95) or for "The Quarry" (page 103). Or select another story you have read in this book, and answer these questions: What is the point of view in this selection? Why is it effective? What are the strengths and limitations of this point of view? How does the point of view affect the reader's response?

POINT OF VIEW: STRENGTHS, LIMITATIONS, EFFECT ON READER		
SELECTION: "A Handful of Dates"		
POINT OF VIEW: First person		
STRENGTHS	**LIMITATIONS**	**EFFECT ON READER**
Intimacy: We see the grandfather through the boy's eyes; the boy also sees Masood in a warm and sympathetic light. *Suspense:* We gain insights only as the narrator does. The grandson can drop hints (foreshadowing) without realizing he is doing so. *Vividness:* We learn many details about the events because the narrator was actually there.	The first-person narrator cannot see into his grandfather's mind, but this "limitation" actually builds suspense as to the story's outcome. The grandson is a very good observer. However, he is young and inexperienced. Once again, this "limitation" helps to heighten suspense.	Despite the narrator's youth, we feel that he is fair and that his judgment is good. Overall, we concur with his revulsion at his grandfather's behavior.

This lesson guides students through the process of writing about the theme of a work of fiction. The lesson reinforces the textbook's instruction on theme and the way in which other literary elements, such as plot, characterization, setting, point of view, and tone, all help illuminate the theme of a work. You may want to teach this lesson in conjunction with the fourth section in the Short Story unit, Stories About Personal Values, in which two Literary Focus features highlight theme. Since the lesson uses examples from "Salt," you may want to assign that story before you teach this lesson. Under Assignments on the following page, you will find a cross-reference to a Composition assignment in this textbook that focuses on theme.

LESSON 6: *Writing About Theme*

The **theme** of a literary work is its underlying central idea or the generalization it communicates about life. The theme expresses the author's opinion or raises a question about human nature or the meaning of human experience. At times the author's theme may not confirm or agree with your own beliefs. Even then, if skillfully written, the story will have a theme that illuminates human experience.

CONCEPTS TO REMEMBER

1. A piece of literature may have both a subject and a theme. The subject is the specific topic of the selection. The theme is the generalization about life at large that the specific selection leads you to see. For example, "baseball" may be the subject of a short story, but the theme goes beyond a one-word label such as "baseball." The theme of a story about baseball may be "Teamwork is particularly important when pressure builds."

2. A long work—for example, a novel—may contain not just one theme but several.

3. Sometimes the theme may be clearly stated. More often, the theme is implied or suggested through other elements. In fact, you can determine the theme by looking closely at characterization, setting, events, point of view, and tone.

TYPICAL ESSAY QUESTION

When you are asked to write about the theme of a selection, you are often answering an essay assignment such as the following:

Some common themes in literature are

- Growth is achieved only through taking risks.
- Faithfulness to oneself is the ultimate law.
- Petty concerns may blind one to life's riches.

Select a piece of literature that presents one of these themes, or think of a work that reveals another truth about life. Write an essay in which you identify a piece of literature, state its theme, and then show how the author illuminates the theme through characterization, setting, plot, point of view, and tone.

PREWRITING

1. Identify the subject of a selection that you have read. The selection may have more than one subject, but select only one. For example, the subject of "Salt" (page 130) is the interaction between a husband and wife as they encounter and overcome obstacles during a crisis.

2. Keeping the subject in mind, ask yourself the following questions so that you can get beyond the subject of the selection to its theme.

   a. What do various characters think, say, and do regarding the subject?
   b. What are the main character's key traits? Does the character change at all during the course of the selection?
   c. How do the time, place, clothing, and other details of setting serve as a suitable background for the work's subject, or topic?
   d. What do the particular conflicts of the selection have to do with the selection's subject matter?
   e. What do the work's climax and resolution have to say about the subject matter of the selection?
   f. What does the point of view make us realize about the subject matter?
   g. What is the author's tone, or attitude, toward the subject as revealed by the author's word choice and other details?

3. Prepare a chart on which to record your answers to the questions in Prewriting Step 2. The chart on the opposite page is a sample prepared for "Salt."

4. Examine the completed chart, and try to formulate a statement of the theme. For "Salt" you might state the theme as follows: When people are nourished by ethnic identity and reminded of their cultural ties, they will often help one another and try to overcome oppression.

WRITING PARAGRAPH BY PARAGRAPH

1. Begin your introductory paragraph with a thesis statement, which restates the main idea of the

602 *Writing About Literature Handbook*

ELEMENTS ILLUMINATING THEME
SELECTION: "Salt"
SUBJECT OF STORY: the interaction between a husband and wife
as they encounter and overcome obstacles during a crisis

CHARACTERIZATION	SETTING	PLOT
Marit: Shrewd and stubborn, she refuses to be bullied into signing away her and her husband's land. *Heikki:* Without his salt, he is nasty to Marit though he knows she was right not to sign. *Change in Heikki:* When after her meeting, Marit tells him of the spirit of Finnish nationalism, they are reconciled and together plan the community's future.	Bare fields and icy forests in grim, gray winter weather. Warmth in interior setting as the two, on the couch, talk of reviving Finnish traditions.	*Conflict with authorities:* Marit wants to trade for salt and seeds but will not sign away her property. *Conflict with Heikki:* Marit deals with his frustration at being deprived of salt. *Climax:* Marit has learned, and tells Heikki, that her instinct in refusing to sign was right. For the first time he admits to her that she was right. *Falling action and resolution:* The two see that the revival of Finnish tradition is the spiritual nourishment, the salt of life, that they and the others in their community crave. Now, with all in perfect harmony, neighbors bring a gift of salt.

POINT OF VIEW	TONE	
Omniscient: The story includes some presentation of Heikki's thoughts; however, the main focus is on Marit's feelings and thoughts.	*Sympathy and empathy:* Author is appealing to reader's sense of pride in heritage and the universal need to resist oppression.	

assignment. Indicate what the theme of the selection is, being certain to state the theme in terms of a generalization about human nature or experience. Then indicate that the theme is illuminated through other elements of the selection.

Example: The theme of "Salt" is that, when nourished by a sense of their ethnic identity and reminded of their cultural ties, people unite and try to overcome oppression. All the story's elements—characterization, setting, plot, point of view, and tone—heighten the tension and release that the couple and others in the community feel as they work their way from the threat of oppression to a joyful embrace of their cultural heritage.

2. In the next paragraph focus on how the characters, the settings, and the events reveal the generalization about life.

3. In the next paragraph focus on how the point of view and tone illustrate the theme.

4. Finally, restate your thesis statement. Explain whether the story led you to understand a theme new to you or to renew a prior awareness.

■ REVISING AND EDITING
See Lesson 1 for detailed reminders about improving your writing.

■ ASSIGNMENTS
1. Use the chart for "Salt" to write about theme. How do characterization, setting, events, point of view, and tone illuminate the theme that people help each other and fight oppression when they feel a sense of their ethnic identity and are reminded of their cultural ties?

2. Do the assignment called "Writing About Theme" for "Like the Sun" (page 144). Or, write on the theme of another story in this book. Show how that theme is illuminated through characterization, setting, events, point of view, and tone.

LESSON 7: *Writing About a Symbol*

The first chore in writing about a symbol is proper identification of a person, object, or event as symbolic. Too often, readers who have learned about symbolism try to label anything and everything as a symbol. This lesson will review the characteristics of symbols and demonstrate how to write a coherent composition about symbolism.

CONCEPTS TO REMEMBER

1. A **symbol** is something that stands for itself but also for something larger than itself. It may be a person, an animal, an inanimate object, or an action. A writer often uses a concrete object to express an abstract idea, a quality, or a belief. A symbol may also appeal to a reader's emotions and can provide a dramatic way to express an idea, communicate a message, or clarify meaning.

2. There are conventional symbols and private symbols. A conventional symbol is one that is widely accepted and used by many writers; for example, a nightingale is a symbol for melancholy, a dove for peace, a rose for beauty, and red for danger. A private symbol is one that an individual writer creates for a particular work of literature.

3. An object is a symbol only if it seems to be representative of something of *another kind.* For example, you would not say that the Hope diamond is symbolic of all magnificent diamonds; it is merely representative of all magnificent diamonds. You might, however, say that the Hope diamond is symbolic of wealth; a diamond is a concrete mineral, whereas wealth is something *of a different kind*—an abstract term.

TYPICAL ESSAY QUESTION

When you are asked to write about the symbol in a work, you are often answering an essay question like the following:

Select a central symbol from a work of literature. State what the symbol reveals about the characters and the theme.

PREWRITING

1. To identify a symbol, ask yourself the following questions:

   a. Is some person, place, animal, object, or action emphasized in this work and repeatedly mentioned to the extent that it seems to mean more than itself?
   b. What else could it stand for besides itself?

   Example: In "The Doll's House" (page 105) the "exquisite" little amber lamp on the dining room table in the doll's house is mentioned several times. It could stand for the qualities of hope, warmth, friendliness, enlightenment.

2. Trace your candidate for a symbol throughout the work to see if it symbolizes something consistently or if it gathers new meaning from beginning to end.

   Example: At the beginning the lamp's symbolic values are shown in the context of the doll's house. Later these values are extended to include the society in which the characters live.

   - *page 105, column 2, paragraph 1:* To Kezia the lamp is the most real and perfect object in the doll's house. Its appeal to her foreshadows her sense of awareness and compassion.
   - *page 108, column 1, paragraphs 3-4:* Until Kezia reminds her, Isabel does not mention the lamp when she describes the doll's house. To her the lamp is just another object.
   - *page 108, column 1, paragraph 5:* The lamp's importance to Kezia is reiterated by Kezia herself who describes it as the "best of all" to the group.
   - *page 110, column 2, paragraph 3:* By the story's end the lamp has extended its warmth and light to our Else's imagination. Having seen the lamp, and like Kezia, having felt its meaning, our Else unexpectedly expresses her joy at having had this experience.

3. Analyze what the symbol reveals about the *character.* Identify the character's key traits and underlying motivation.

Example:

Kezia is perceptive and instantly recognizes the little lamp as the only source of warmth and friendliness in the doll's house.

Kezia is courageous, publicly criticizing Isabel for forgetting to describe the lamp. She also shows courage in letting the Kelveys see the doll's house.

Kezia herself, warm, friendly, and caring, reflects those qualities in the little lamp that appeal to her.

Explain how the symbol reveals the character's key traits, which you have listed.

Example: In "The Doll's House" the lamp, a symbol of light and warmth, reveals the warmth and brightness of Kezia's character. Although she is the "baby" of the family, only she sees the lamp as that element in the doll's house that makes it a home. Later she rejects the cold and unenlightened attitude of her society toward the Kelveys by inviting them to see the doll's house.

4. Analyze what the symbol reveals about *theme.* Identify the theme of the selection.

Example: It is cruel to exclude people from the companionship of society, leaving them out in the cold and dark because they have less social status or money than the majority.

Then determine how the symbol summarizes or illustrates the theme.

Example: The little lamp symbolizes companionship, warmth, and, ultimately, hope. Those within its circle—its golden light—are part of the group. Kezia grasps this concept intuitively. Isabel, who forgets to mention the lamp and snubs the Kelveys, does not. By having the courage and kindness to show Lil and our Else the doll's house, Kezia enables them to enter the closed circle and belong, however briefly.

WRITING PARAGRAPH BY PARAGRAPH

1. Begin the introductory paragraph with a thesis statement that addresses the major points in the essay question.

   Example: The lamp in "The Doll's House" by Katherine Mansfield is a central symbol, which reveals a great deal about the main character and, at the same time, illustrates the theme.

   Finish the introductory paragraph by stating in general terms what the symbol tells you about the character and perhaps by actually stating the themes of the story.

2. In the next paragraph explain in more detail how the symbol and the character connect. Use your thoughts from Prewriting Step 3 here.

3. In the next paragraph explain in more detail how the symbol and the theme connect. Use your thoughts from Prewriting Step 4 here.

4. In the final paragraph restate in other words the thesis statement from the introductory paragraph. You might conclude by discussing the suitability of the symbol. For example, what is there in the nature of a lamp that suits it for symbolizing all that it does in "The Doll's House"?

REVISING AND EDITING

See Lesson 1 for detailed reminders for improving your writing.

ASSIGNMENTS

1. Use the examples from the Prewriting steps to prepare a brief composition that explains what the lamp in "The Doll's House" reveals about the main character and the theme of the story.

2. Do the assignment called "Writing About a Symbol" on page 151 for "Hastrman" or use another story that you have read in this book. Choose a central symbol and state what that symbol reveals about the characters and the theme of the work.

LESSON 8: *Writing About Nonfiction*

A piece of nonfiction may be only a few paragraphs long or book length. It may be a biography, an autobiography, or an essay. When you write about any kind of nonfiction, however, you can use the same approach. Specifically, you can comment on the author's purpose in writing the piece and then show how the author achieved that purpose.

■■■ CONCEPTS TO REMEMBER

1. The **purpose** of a piece of nonfiction is the central idea, or general statement about life, that the author wants to express.

2. To communicate the purpose, the author uses various techniques such as sensory details, facts, statistics, examples, and opinions.

■■■ TYPICAL ESSAY QUESTION

When you are asked to write about a piece of nonfiction, you are often answering an assignment such as the following:

Select a piece of nonfiction that you have read. An author always has a purpose for writing nonfiction. To accomplish this purpose the author may use various techniques such as sensory details, facts, statistics, examples, and opinions.

What is the purpose of the piece of nonfiction that you have read? Cite with examples the particular techniques that the author uses to accomplish the purpose of the piece.

■■■ PREWRITING

1. To determine the author's purpose in writing a work of nonfiction, ask yourself the following questions:

   a. What, if anything, does the title suggest about the author's opinion of the subject of the biography, autobiography, or essay?
   b. What opinion about the subject of the work or about life in general is suggested by the experiences that the author relates?
   c. What opinion about the subject of the biography or autobiography or about people in general is suggested by details of behavior?
   d. What ideas about the world in general are suggested by details of setting?
   e. What tone, or attitude, toward the subject is revealed by the author's style?

2. Based on your answers to the preceding questions, prepare a statement of the author's purpose, and, on a chart like the one on the opposite page, record the techniques that the author uses to achieve that purpose. The filled-in chart represents an analysis of V. S. Naipaul's essay "The Crocodiles of Yamoussoukro," impressions of a visit to the Ivory Coast in West Africa (page 431).

■■■ WRITING PARAGRAPH BY PARAGRAPH

1. Begin the introductory paragraph with a thesis statement, which should specify the author's purpose and the techniques used to achieve it.

   Example: In "The Crocodiles of Yamoussoukro" the author's use of sensory details, facts, statistics, examples, and opinions communicates that, despite vigorous European cultural and economic influence, many aspects of African values, traditions, and power remain strong.

2. In each of the following paragraphs, show how the author uses one technique to make the purpose clear.

3. In the concluding paragraph restate the thesis in other words.

■■■ REVISING AND EDITING

See Lesson 1 for detailed reminders about improving your writing.

PURPOSE AND TECHNIQUES OF NONFICTION
SELECTION: "The Crocodiles of Yamoussoukro"

PURPOSE: To show that African values, traditions, and power remain alive in the Ivory Coast, as elsewhere in Africa, even in the midst of intense European modernization and influence.

SENSORY DETAILS	EXAMPLES	FACTS
"...the black mud of a fetid lagoon..."	*Of traditions:* "...the authority of the chieftaincy—moral, or spiritual, or magical authority—was not forgotten."	"With independence in 1960—the bush returned with alterations to its people—he began to rule the Ivory Coast. And he has ruled ever since."
"For square mile upon square mile mangoes, avocados, or pineapples grow in straight lines...."	*Of values:* "...turtles and man-eating crocodiles have been introduced. These are totemic, emblematic creatures...."	"There were no crocodiles in Yamoussoukro before."
"...and the scarred, empty spaces so forbidding, that only people with cars can...go...."	"This element of sacrifice, this protracted display of power and cruelty, is as unsettling as it is meant to be...."	"Where once were African fields, unused common land, and wild trees there are now ordered, mechanized plantations."
"The feeding ritual takes place in the afternoon, in bright light."	*Of power:* "But to all Africans they speak at once of danger and of the president's, the chief's, magically granted knowledge of his power as something more than human, something emanating from the earth itself."	"To house the visitors, there is a twelve-story Hotel President, one of the French Sofitel hotel chain."
		"...the president's totemic crocodiles are fed with fresh meat every day."

OPINIONS	STATISTICS	
"He has ruled well."	"Labor immigration, as much as natural increase, has raised the population from three million in 1960 to nine million today."	
"Extravagant and sometimes brilliant... buildings have been set down...."		
"To the man from outside, whatever his political or religious faith, Africa can ...seem...in a state of becoming."	"And one hundred and fifty miles inland, at the end of an auto-route that would not disgrace France itself...Yamoussoukro has been transformed."	
"And even the success of the Ivory Coast induces a kind of anxiety."		

▬ ASSIGNMENTS

1. Use the chart for V. S. Naipaul's essay "The Crocodiles of Yamoussoukro" (Prewriting Step 2) to write an essay about the author's purpose.

2. Do the assignment called "Writing About Autobiography" for "The Snake and the Goldsmith" (page 391) or for "The Iguana" (page 422). Or select another piece of nonfiction you have read in this book and answer the following: What is the purpose of this nonfiction work? Cite with examples the particular techniques, including sensory details, facts, statistics, examples, and opinions, that the author uses to accomplish the purpose of the piece.

This lesson guides students through the process of writing about a poem. The lesson reinforces the textbook's instruction on the speaker, sound devices, imagery, and figurative language. You may want to teach this lesson in conjunction with the Poetry unit in this textbook. Since the lesson uses examples from "The Horses," you may want to assign that poem before you teach this lesson. Under Assignments on the following page, you will find cross-references to Composition assignments in this textbook that focus on poetry.

LESSON 9: *Writing About Poetry*

The pleasure experienced in listening to or reading poetry comes from the interrelationship of all the literary techniques that the poet uses to present the sense, or meaning, of the poem: choice of speaker, sound, imagery, and figurative language. When you write an essay about a poem, you will do well to show the connection between the techniques of the poem and its meaning.

CONCEPTS TO REMEMBER

1. The **speaker** of the poem is the voice of the poem. Sometimes the speaker is the poet himself or herself; sometimes the speaker is a character or thing created by the poet.

2. Among the sound devices that a poet may use are **onomatopoeia** (a word or phrase that actually imitates or suggests the sound of what it describes), **alliteration** (the repetition of initial consonant sounds), **consonance** (the repetition of similar consonant sounds preceded by different accented vowels), and **assonance** (the repetition of vowel sounds).

3. Other aspects of sound in poetry are **rhyme** (the repetition at regular intervals of similar or identical sounds) and **rhythm** (the pattern created by arranging stressed and unstressed syllables).

4. A poem's **images** appeal to one or more senses.

5. **Metaphor** is a figure of speech in which two unlike things are compared without the use of *like* or *as;* **simile** is a comparison using *like* or *as;* **personification** is a figure of speech in which an animal, object, or idea is described as having human form or characteristics.

TYPICAL ESSAY QUESTION

When you are asked to write about poetry, you are often answering an assignment like this one:

Select a poem that you have read. What is the meaning of the poem? What techniques does the poet use to reveal this meaning? Techniques include the selection of speaker, sound, imagery, and figurative language.

PREWRITING

1. Use the following questions to help you determine the meaning of the poem.

   a. Does the poem focus on the actions of a character?

   b. Does the poem describe a person, place, or thing?

   c. Does the poem focus on an idea? A feeling?

   d. What emotional response does the poem seem to call up in you?

   e. After your immediate emotional response, on what does the poem cause you to reflect?

2. Prepare a chart on which to record your statement of the meaning of the poem and your observations about the techniques of the poem. The chart on the opposite page represents an analysis of "The Horses" (page 308). Each column deals with one of the poetic techniques.

WRITING PARAGRAPH BY PARAGRAPH

1. Begin your introductory paragraph with a thesis statement, which should restate the main points of the assignment. Indicate that the various techniques used by the poet all serve to enhance and present effectively the underlying meaning of the poem.

   Example: In "The Horses" Pablo Neruda uses the speaker, sound devices, imagery, and figurative language to describe the powerfully uplifting effect that Nature's beauty and vibrancy can have on the human spirit.

2. In each of the following paragraphs discuss one or two of the techniques that the poet uses to underscore the poem's meaning. Show how each technique enhances the poem's overall meaning.

3. In the next paragraph develop your interpretation of the poem's meaning.

4. In the concluding paragraph restate your thesis in other words. You might discuss further your interpretation of the poem and describe in a bit more detail the poem's emotional impact on you.

THE MEANING AND TECHNIQUES OF A POEM
SELECTION: "The Horses"

MEANING: When the world seems empty and life meaningless, the splendor of Nature, represented here by a group of spirited horses, can transform darkness into light and despair into joy.

SPEAKER	SOUND	IMAGERY	FIGURATIVE LANGUAGE
First-person speaker: confidential, sharing, presumes the reader will understand	*Rhythm:* long, cadenced unrhymed lines *Alliteration:* "salt-spumed waves"; "dirty, disorganized"; "rumps were round"	*Extensive color images:* "air . . .white," "color. . .honey, amber, fire," "golden dance"	*Similes:* "white like fresh bread" "like fire" "like ten gods" "like salt-spumed waves" "round as. . .oranges" "necks . . .like towers" "energy, like a prisoner" *Metaphors:* "Their color was honey, amber, fire;" ". . .those intense horses became blood, became rhythm. . ." "this was the fountain, the golden dance, the fire that lived in beauty." *Implied metaphor:* "a ring bitten in snow by the teeth of winter."

ASSIGNMENTS

1. Use the chart for "The Horses" to write an essay about poetry. What is the meaning of the poem? What techniques does the poet use to reveal this meaning?
2. Do the assignment called "Writing About Poetry" that follows "Street Cries" (page 328), or "The Window" (page 355), or "The Monument" (page 367). Or select another poem that you have read in this book and answer the following: What is the meaning of the poem? What techniques does the author use to reveal this meaning? Techniques include selection of speaker, sound devices, imagery, and figurative language.

This lesson guides students through the process of writing about the total effect of a work of fiction. The lesson reinforces the textbook's instruction on how various literary elements interact in producing a particular effect on the reader. You may want to teach this lesson in conjunction with the final section of the Short Story unit, Stories About Cultures and Conflicts. Since the lesson uses examples from "The Guest," you may want to assign that story before you teach this lesson. Under Assignments on the following page, you will find a cross-reference to a Composition assignment in this textbook that focuses on the total effect.

LESSON 10: *Writing About the Total Effect*

Like the conductor of an orchestra calling in each of the instruments on cue to create a magnificent symphony, the author of a skillfully crafted piece of literature orchestrates all the key literary elements—plot, character, setting, point of view, tone, theme, symbol, and irony—to achieve a specific emotional response on the part of the readers. Although we, the readers, immediately sense the impact of the literary work, we often have to analyze just *how* this effect is achieved.

▄▄ CONCEPTS TO REMEMBER

1. When discussing total effect, we often use the term *impact*. A selection makes an impact on a reader because of its theme and the skill with which all the other elements support this theme.

2. Consult the lessons dealing with writing about the various literary elements individually, and review the definitions and concepts in each lesson.

▄▄ TYPICAL ESSAY QUESTION

When you are asked to write about the total effect of a selection, you are often answering an essay question such as the following:

What is the total effect of the selection? That is, what is its impact on the reader? How does the author use each of the following elements to achieve this effect: plot, character, setting, point of view, tone, theme, symbol, and irony?

▄▄ PREWRITING

1. Ask yourself the following questions as you reflect on the piece of literature:

   a. What is the impact of the work? Specifically, does the work delight you, irritate you, sadden you?

   b. Which literary element dominates?

   c. How do the other literary elements support or relate to the dominant element?

2. Prepare a chart on which to record your answers to the questions in Prewriting Step 1. For Albert

Camus's "The Guest" on page 209, a chart might look like the one on the opposite page.

▄▄ WRITING PARAGRAPH BY PARAGRAPH

1. Begin the first paragraph with a thesis statement. The thesis statement should indicate the total effect of the work on the reader and note that all the key literary elements work together to create this impact.

   Example: The dominant literary element of "The Guest" is character, but all the elements work together to create the total effect of the piece—a sense of the loneliness and hopelessness of human existence and of peoples' inability to communicate and sympathize with one another.

2. In the next paragraph focus on the dominant literary element, and show by the inclusion of details how it contributes to the total effect.

3. In the subsequent paragraphs discuss additional literary elements, and show by the inclusion of details how each element supports or relates to the dominant element.

4. In the concluding paragraph remind your audience that the elements mentioned in the preceding paragraphs work together to produce the total impact on the reader.

▄▄ REVISING AND EDITING

See Lesson 1 for detailed reminders about improving your writing.

▄▄ ASSIGNMENTS

1. Use the chart for "The Guest" to write about the total effect of the work. How does the author use the key elements of plot, character, setting, point of view, tone, theme, symbol, and irony to achieve this effect?

2. Do the assignment called "Writing About the Total Effect" for "The Shoes" (page 225). Or choose another selection in this book, and describe its overall impact.

610 *Writing About Literature Handbook*

ANALYSIS OF THE TOTAL EFFECT
SELECTION: "The Guest"

QUESTION	ANSWER	DETAILS
A. WHAT IS THE IMPACT OF THE WORK?	The reader is overcome with a sense of the loneliness and hopelessness of human existence and of peoples' inability to communicate and sympathize with each other.	*Details creating sense of loneliness and lack of communication:* The sense of loneliness is created by the three insignificant figures in the vast and barren landscape; the problems of communication are heightened by political and cultural conflicts.
B. WHAT IS THE DOMINANT LITERARY ELEMENT?	*Character:* Daru's beliefs and actions determine the shape and outcome of the story.	A decent man, Daru is against French domination in Algeria and refuses to surrender the Arab to French authorities. Yet he is repelled by the Arab's crime and is therefore less sympathetic to him.
C. HOW DO THE OTHER LITERARY ELEMENTS SUPPORT THE DOMINANT ELEMENT?	*Plot:* At odds with the French authorities for his uncooperative attitude and saddled with an Arab national accused of murder, Daru is on his own. He alone must decide how to deal with the prisoner.	The major conflicts are Daru's external one—his lonely struggle against the rules of colonial authority—and the internal mental struggle over what to do with the prisoner.
	Setting: The harsh and empty landscape underscores the fierceness of the struggle for existence of the Algerians and evokes the barrenness of the lives of those who live there.	"...progress in the snow, among the stones, on the vast expanse of the high, deserted plateau." "...the earth shriveled up little by little, literally scorched...."
	Point of View: Camus uses limited third-person point of view. The reader knows only what Daru is thinking.	No details of thoughts or feelings of Balducci or the Arab are given; the reader feels both sympathy and anger with Daru. He acts positively by freeing the Arab but acts negatively at the end by refusing to listen to him. Had he done so the prisoner might not have turned himself in.
	Tone: matter-of-fact, unemotional tone	The severe landscape blends in with the self-disciplined personalities of Daru and the Arab. Only the Corsican, Balducci, is both colorful and vital.
	Theme: No member of a society can avoid the consequences of that society's struggles if he or she wishes to remain a part of that society.	The result of Daru's efforts to stay above the conflicts around him is that he becomes the enemy of both sides.
	Symbol: Each of the three men can also be seen as a symbol: Daru as the intellectual who tries to stay above the conflict; Balducci as a member of the colonial presence; and the prisoner as the hopeless victim of colonialism.	Each acts out his role in this drama.
	Irony: Situational irony at the end surprises the reader who has not expected Daru to be threatened by those whose "brother" he aided.	Daru, caught between two violent forces, is threatened not only by those he opposes but also by those he helps.

Writing About Literature Handbook **611**

This handbook lists alphabetically the literary terms taught in this anthology, as well as other important terms. Each entry defines a term and then briefly discusses it, elaborating with examples from the selections. Cross-references at the end of most entries indicate the pages on which the term is taught and, in some cases, indicate related entries in this handbook.

LITERARY TERMS HANDBOOK

ALLITERATION   *The repetition of sounds, most often consonant sounds, at the beginnings of words.* This line from Sarojini Naidu's "Street Cries" contains an example of alliteration:

And *f*asting men go *f*orth on hurrying *f*eet,

See page 328.

ALLUSION   *A reference in a work of literature to a well-known character, place, or situation from another work of literature, music, or art or from history.* For example, *Matusalén* is Spanish for the word *Methuselah,* the name of a biblical figure said to have lived for nine hundred years. By naming the town Matusalén, the author emphasizes the unusual relationship between the town and time.

See page 156.

ANALOGY   *A comparison made between two things to show how one is like the other.* In "The Iguana" the author draws a subtle analogy between wearing an inappropriate bracelet and committing an "injustice" or suppressing "a truth."

ANECDOTE   *A brief account of an event, usually intended to entertain, to explain an idea, and to reveal personality through a person's actions.* In "Two Memories of Sido" the author describes her mother's morning rituals. This brief story illustrates Sido's willful, independent personality.

See page 397.

ANTAGONIST   *A person or force that opposes the **protagonist,** or central character in a story or drama.* In "The Piece of String" Malandain is an antagonist, opposing Hauchecome. In "Dead Men's Path" traditional values are the antagonist, or force, that opposes the main character.

See also CONFLICT.

ARGUMENT   *That kind of writing in which reason is used to influence people's ideas or actions.* "Pericles' Funeral Oration" is an example of an argument.

See also PERSUASION.

ASIDE   *In a play a comment made by a character who is heard by the audience but not by the other characters on stage.* Because other characters are on stage at the time, the speaker turns to one side, or "aside." Asides reveal what a character is thinking and feeling. For example, in the following line from Act III of *Cyrano de Bergerac,* Roxane expresses her delight that her beloved Christian will stay in Paris while De Guiche goes to battle:

ROXANE: Go! [*Aside.*] And Christian will stay.
[*To* DE GUICHE.] I want you to be heroic. . . .

ASSONANCE   *The repetition of vowel sounds, especially in a line of poetry.* For example, the *i* sound is repeated in this line from "Summer Is Dying":

Casting an *eye* and a s*igh* after the fl*ight*

See page 328.

ATMOSPHERE   *The emotional quality, or mood, of a story.* In "Lingkuan Gorge" a family's spirit of commitment and dedication to hard work inspires the main character to accomplish his task.

See page 128.
See also SETTING.

AUTOBIOGRAPHY   *The story of a person's life written by that person.* "By Any Other Name" by Santha Rama Rau is an autobiography.

See page 378.

BALLAD   *A short, musical, narrative poem.* **Folk ballads,** or popular ballads, were passed on by word of mouth over generations before being written down. **Literary ballads** are written in imitation of folk ballads. "The Lorelei" is a literary ballad.

See page 349.

BIOGRAPHY   *The account of a person's life written by someone other than the subject.* Biographies can be short or book-length. "Two Memories of Sido" is a short biography.

See page 397.

BLANK VERSE   *Poetry written in unrhymed **iambic pentameter,** which is a meter made up of five iambic feet to a line of verse, each foot containing one unstressed* ($\smile$) *and one stressed* ($\prime$) *syllable.* Shakespeare wrote his plays in blank verse.

See also FOOT, METER, RHYTHM.

CHARACTER *A person in a literary work.* Characters who reveal only one personality trait are called **flat.** Edla in Lagerlöf's "The Rat Trap" is a flat character because the reader sees only her kind and compassionate qualities. Characters who show varied and sometimes contradictory traits are called **round.** The peddler in "The Rat Trap" is a round character because he displays a variety of conflicting emotions and personality traits such as bitterness, regret, dishonesty, cleverness, and dignity. A **static character** remains primarily the same throughout the story, as the ironmaster does in "The Rat Trap." A **dynamic character** changes during the story. The peddler is a dynamic character because he changes as a result of the story's events.

See pages 71, 510.
See also
CHARACTERIZATION.

CHARACTERIZATION *The methods a writer uses to develop the personality of a character.* In **direct characterization** the writer makes direct statements about a character's personality, as in this line from "The Kabuliwallah": "Mini's mother is unfortunately a very timid lady." In **indirect characterization** the writer reveals a character's personality through the character's words and actions and through what other characters say and think about the character. For example, the narrator's behavior in "The Kabuliwallah" shows that he is sensitive and compassionate. Indirect characterization requires readers to interpret the character's words and actions.

See page 43.
See also
CHARACTER.

CLIMAX *The point of greatest emotional intensity, interest, or suspense in a narrative.* Usually the climax comes at the turning point in a story or drama, the point at which the resolution of the conflict becomes clear. In "The Winner" the climax occurs when Pius' feelings for Sarah change after he sees her reaction to some unexpected news.

See page 10.

COMEDY *A type of drama that is humorous and usually has a happy ending.* A comedy may entertain by exposing human weaknesses in an amusing way. Although it is essentially a tragedy, *Cyrano de Bergerac* has comedic elements because it relies on the characters' weaknesses for humorous situations.

See also TRAGEDY.

CONCRETE POEM *A poem that stresses the visual appearance of the words and lines on the page.*

CONFLICT *The struggle between two opposing forces that lies at the center of a plot in a story or drama.* An **external conflict** exists when a character struggles against some outside force, such as another person, nature, society, or fate. In "You Need to Go Upstairs" the blind girl experiences an external conflict with the environment as she makes her way through the garden and the house. An **internal conflict** exists within the mind of a character who is torn between opposing feelings or goals. The blind girl is engaged in an internal conflict as she strives to overcome her fears.

See pages 17, 22.
See also PLOT.

CONNOTATION *The unspoken or unwritten meanings associated with a word beyond its dictionary definition, or* **denotation.** In "On the Way to School" the poet speaks of the "heavy shining animals" that pull carriages. Because readers may associate machinery with the words *heavy* and *shining,* they apply those associations to the poem and perceive the horses as sleek and massive.

See page 343.
See also DENOTATION,
FIGURATIVE LANGUAGE.

COUPLET *Two consecutive lines of poetry that rhyme.* For example, these two lines from Dickinson's "How Happy Is the Little Stone" form a couplet:

How happy is the little Stone
That rambles in the Road alone,

See page 299.
See also RHYME, SONNET.

DENOTATION *The literal or dictionary meaning of a word.* **Literal language** seeks to convey denotation, or exact meaning.

See also CONNOTATION.

DESCRIPTION *Any carefully detailed portrayal of a person, place, thing, or event.* While description is the writer's primary aim in the descriptive essay, this kind of writing is also used in stories and biography.

See page 422.
See also EXPOSITION,
NARRATION, PERSUASION.

DIALECT *A variation of language spoken by a particular group, often within a particular region.* Dialects differ from standard language because they contain different sounds, grammatical forms, and meanings. The conversational language in "The Actor" represents the dialect of Yorkshire, England, in the twentieth century. For example, Albert uses nonstandard terms and pronunciations when he says: "This lad an' his brother are havin' a row, see."

See page 38.

DIALOGUE   *Conversation between characters in a literary work.*

See page 452.

DRAMA   *A play performed before an audience by actors and actresses on a stage.* Most drama before the modern period can be divided into two basic types: **tragedy,** a play in which the main character suffers unhappy circumstances, and **comedy,** a humorous play in which the characters enjoy a happy outcome. The two basic parts of a drama are its script, which includes **dialogue** and **stage directions,** and the staging, which prepares the play to be performed.

See also COMEDY,
NO THEATER,
STAGE DIRECTIONS,
TRAGEDY.

DRAMATIC CONVENTION   *A device that a playwright uses to present a story on stage and that the audience accepts as realistic.* Shakespeare's audience, for example, accepted the convention of boys playing the roles of women.

DRAMATIC MONOLOGUE   *A form of dramatic poetry that presents only one speaker, who addresses a silent listener.*

See also DRAMATIC
POETRY.

DRAMATIC POETRY   *Poetry in which one or more characters speak to other characters, to themselves, or to the reader.* In "Politics," for example, Yeats addresses himself.

See page 289.
See also DRAMATIC
MONOLOGUE, SPEAKER.

EPIC   *A long narrative poem that traces the adventures of a hero.* Epics intertwine myths, legends, and history, reflecting the values of the societies in which they originate. In epics gods and goddesses often intervene in the affairs of humans. Virgil's *Aeneid,* the famous epic poem glorifying Rome's origins, was written to be read as well as recited.

See page 268.
See also EPIC HERO.

EPIC HERO   *A legendary, larger-than-life figure whose adventures form the core of the epic poem.* The hero embodies the goals and virtues of an entire nation or culture. For example, Aeneas in the *Aeneid* functions as an epic hero because he is a courageous warrior who fulfills his people's destiny by founding a new city.

See page 274.

ESSAY   *A short piece of nonfiction writing on any topic.* The purpose of the essay is to communicate an idea or opinion. The **formal essay** is serious and impersonal, such as "The Crocodiles of Yamoussoukro." The **informal essay** entertains while it informs; it usually takes a light approach to its subject and uses a conversational style. The personality of the author often shines through the informal essay. *Platero and I* is a collection of informal essays.

   Narrative essays, such as Isaac Bashevis Singer's "Shosha," relate true events, usually in chronological order. **Descriptive essays,** such as "The Iguana" by Isak Dinesen, describe actual people, places, or things. **Persuasive essays,** such as "Pericles' Funeral Oration," aim to convince the reader of an opinion. **Expository essays,** such as "The Crocodiles of Yamoussoukro," present information and explain ideas.

See pages 408, 422, 433.

EXPOSITION   *An author's introduction to the characters, setting, and the situation at the beginning of a story, novel, or play.* For example, in *The Jewels of the Shrine,* the exposition soon reveals that Okorie feels his grandsons do not respect him.

   The term *exposition* also refers to the **expository essay,** in which the writer presents facts or explains ideas. "The Crocodiles of Yamoussoukro" by V. S. Naipaul consists largely of exposition.

See page 10.
See also PLOT.

FABLE   *A very brief story told to teach a lesson.* Themes are usually stated explicitly, as in Aesop's fables. Aesop's "The Fox and the Grapes" reveals how people belittle what they cannot have.

See page 241.
See also MORAL, PARABLE,
THEME.

FALLING ACTION   *In a play or story the action that follows the climax.* In "Salt" the falling action comes when Marit is visited by her neighbors who give her salt and assure her that she was right to not surrender ownership of her land. In "Federigo's Falcon," Monna's decision to marry Federigo is part of the falling action.

See page 10.
See also PLOT.

FICTION *A prose narrative in which situations and characters are invented by the writer.* Some aspects of a fictional work may be based on fact or experience, such as the historical setting of "Lingkuan Gorge." Fiction includes both short stories and novels.

> See also NOVEL, SHORT STORY.

FIGURATIVE LANGUAGE *Language used for descriptive effect, often to imply ideas indirectly.* Expressions of figurative language are not literally true but express some truth beyond that literal level. For example, in "The Rat Trap" the author uses figurative phrases to describe the iron forge when she writes that "the big bellows groaned" as coal was shoveled into "the maw of the furnace." Figurative language emphasizes the forge's dominating presence. Although it appears in all kinds of writing, figurative language is especially prominent in poetry.

> See pages 43, 310.
> See also FIGURE OF SPEECH, LITERAL LANGUAGE, METAPHOR, PERSONIFICATION, SIMILE, SYMBOL.

FIGURE OF SPEECH *A specific device or kind of figurative language such as* **metaphor, personification, simile,** *or* **symbol.**

> See pages 151, 310.
> See also METAPHOR, PERSONIFICATION, SIMILE, SYMBOL.

FOIL *A character who is used to contrast with another character.* In the adventures of *Don Quixote,* Sancho Panza, who is practical and realistic, is a foil for Don Quixote, who is impractical and idealistic. The author points out how different the two characters are by contrasting their behavior in several situations.

> See page 166.

FOOT *The basic unit in the measurement of rhythm.* A foot usually contains one accented syllable (´) and one or more unaccented syllables (˘).

˘ ´ ˘ ˘ ´ ˘ ˘ ´ ˘ ´
It was/ that ve/ry day/ on which/ the sun

—Sonnet 3

> See also METER, RHYTHM.

FORESHADOWING *The use of clues by the author to prepare readers for events that will happen in a story.* In "The Winner" the author hints at the story's outcome when she has Pius remark that he "could not help but admire the way Sarah took things in her stride."

> See page 10.

FRAME STORY *A plot structure that includes the telling of a story within a story.* The frame is the outer story, which usually precedes and follows the inner and more important story. For example, in "Autumn Mountain," narration by Wang Shih-ku and his friend introduces, concludes, and appears within the frame story.

> See page 187.

FREE VERSE *Poetry that has no fixed pattern of meter, rhyme, line length, or stanza arrangement.* Vicente Aleixandre uses free verse in "On the Way to School":

I hurried past on my bicycle and smiled . . .
and I remember perfectly
how I folded my wings mysteriously on the very
    threshold of the school.

> See page 334.
> See also RHYTHM.

IAMBIC PENTAMETER *A specific meter in a line of poetry composed of five feet (pentameter), most of which are iambs.* The iamb consists of one unstressed syllable (˘) followed by a stressed syllable (´). This line from Shakespeare's Sonnet 29 exemplifies iambic pentameter:

˘ ´ ˘ ´ ˘ ´ ˘ ´ ˘ ´
And look/ upon/ myself/ and curse/ my fate,

> See page 331.
> See also BLANK VERSE, FOOT, METER.

IMAGE *A reference to something that can be experienced through one of the five senses of sight, hearing, smell, taste, or touch.* Note the images of sight and touch from Rilke's "Spanish Dancer":

One upward glance and she ignites her hair
and, whirling faster and faster, fans her dress
into passionate flames, till it becomes a furnace

> See page 306.
> See also FIGURATIVE LANGUAGE, IMAGERY.

IMAGERY *The collection of sense images that helps a reader visualize scenes, hear sounds, feel textures, smell aromas, and taste foods described in a work.*

> See page 306.
> See also FIGURATIVE LANGUAGE, IMAGERY.

IRONY *A contrast between reality and what seems to be real.* **Situational irony** exists when the actual outcome of a situation is the opposite of someone's expectations. In "Air des Clochettes," for example, we expect Péralbe to end his relationship with Arabella. Instead, she breaks off the romance because she learns that he was seen following another woman.

Verbal irony exists when a person says one thing and means another. For instance, in "The Beggar" Lushkoff's praise for his former employer's kind deeds is an example of verbal irony because he admits that he truly owes his recovery not to the employer but to the employer's cook.

Dramatic irony occurs when the audience has important information that characters in a literary work do not have. In "The Actor," for example, the reader's special knowledge that Albert sincerely wants to express himself makes his thwarted attempt to act even more disappointing.

> See pages 28, 38, 494.

LITERAL LANGUAGE *Language that means nothing more than exactly what it says.*

> See FIGURATIVE
> LANGUAGE.

LOCAL COLOR *A technique of writing that uses specific details to evoke a particular region.* Local color re-creates the language, customs, geography, and habits of the area. In "Tuesday Siesta" the author uses local color to describe a stifling Latin American village.

LYRIC POETRY *Poetry that expresses a speaker's personal thoughts and feelings.* Lyric poems are usually short and musical. With just a few words the speaker expresses how precious her daughter is in "Fragment of a Lullaby."

> See pages 289, 292.

MAXIM *A short, concise statement expressing practical advice or a widely held truth.* Confucius' sayings, or maxims, outline moral behavior. La Rochefoucauld's elegant maxims examine human motives.

> See page 402.

METAPHOR *A type of figurative language used to compare or equate seemingly unlike things.* In these lines from "Spanish Dancer," for instance, the author compares a dance with fire:

Her *dance* begins to flicker in the dark room.

And all at once *it* is completely *fire.*

> See pages 310, 314.
> See also FIGURATIVE
> LANGUAGE, SIMILE.

METER *A regular pattern of stressed and unstressed syllables that gives a line of poetry a predictable rhythm.* Note the pattern of stressed and unstressed syllables

in these lines from Emily Dickinson's "How Happy Is the Little Stone":

And independent as the Sun

Associates or glows alone,

> See page 331.
> See also FOOT,
> RHYTHM.

MONOLOGUE *A long speech by a character in a play.* The "nose speech" in Act I of *Cyrano de Bergerac* is a monologue.

> See also SOLILOQUY.

MOOD *The emotional quality or atmosphere of a story.*

> See page 306.
> See also ATMOSPHERE,
> SETTING.

MORAL *A practical lesson about right and wrong conduct, often in an instructive story such as a fable or parable.*

> See page 241.

MOTIVATION *The stated or implied reasons that characters in a literary work behave as they do.* In "The Kabuliwallah," for example, the narrator's comments suggest that he is moved by compassion to give the Kabuliwallah money to return home to his daughter.

> See page 55.
> See also CHARACTER.

MYTH *An anonymous traditional story that relies on the supernatural to explain natural phenomena, human behavior, or mysteries of the universe.* "The Bat" is a myth told by the Zapotec people to explain the ugly appearance of bats.

> See page 236.

NARRATION *The kind of writing or speech that tells a story.* Narration is used in novels, short stories, and narrative poetry. Narration can also be an important technique used in biographies, autobiographies, and essays.

> See also DESCRIPTION,
> EXPOSITION, PERSUASION.

NARRATIVE HOOK *The point in a story or novel at which the author catches the reader's attention by presenting an interesting problem or situation.* In "The

616 *Literary Terms Handbook*

Winner" the narrative hook is Sarah's arrival and actions at Pius' house.

See page 10.
See also PLOT.

NARRATIVE POETRY   *Verse that tells a story.* The narrative poem is generally more selective and concentrated than the prose story. Tu Fu's "The Emperor" is a narrative poem.

See page 289.
See also BALLAD.

NARRATOR   *The person who tells a story in a work of fiction.* In some cases the narrator is a character in the story—for example, Wang Shih-ku in "Autumn Mountain" or the boy in "The Snake and the Goldsmith." In other cases the narrator stands outside the story, as in "The Glass of Milk."

See page 160.
See also
POINT OF VIEW.

NONFICTION   *Factual prose writing.* Nonfiction deals with real people and experiences. Among the categories of nonfiction are **biographies, autobiographies,** and **essays.** "Two Memories of Sido" is a biography. "Shosha" by Isaac Bashevis Singer is an autobiographical selection in which Singer remembers his youth. "The Iguana" by Isak Dinesen is an essay.

See also
AUTOBIOGRAPHY,
BIOGRAPHY, ESSAY,
FICTION.

NO THEATER   *A traditional form of Japanese drama that combines poetry, music, and ritual dance with elaborate, symbolic staging and costumes.* In the No play *The Dwarf Trees* an old couple is visited by a stranger whose visit leads to a surprising revelation and good fortune for the couple.

See page 462.

NOVEL   *An extended fictional prose narrative.* The novel has more scope than a short story in its presentation of plot, character, setting, and theme. Because novels are not subject to any limits in their presentation of these elements, they can encompass a wide range of narrative content and styles.

See also FICTION, SHORT
STORY.

ONOMATOPOEIA   *The use of a word or phrase that actually imitates or suggests the sound of what it describes.* For example, in each of the following lines

from "All That Dances," the sound of the animal mentioned is imitated at the end of the line:

The fish does . . . *hip!*
The bird does . . . *viss!*
The monkey does . . . *gnan!*

See page 323.

PARABLE   *A simple story from which a lesson should be drawn.* The biblical story of "The Prodigal Son," for example, is a parable.

See also FABLE, MORAL.

PARALLELISM   *The use of a series of words, phrases, or lines that have similar grammatical form.* Parallelism emphasizes the items that are arranged in the similar structures and adds a sense of unity to a piece of writing. Sarojini Naidu uses parallelism in "Street Cries" to draw attention to India's vibrant street life. For example, she begins each stanza with *When* and a clause that describes the activity on the street, and ends the stanza with a phrase that tells the vendors' cries. The repeated phrases echo the day's rhythms and connect the stanzas together.

See page 328.
See also REPETITION.

PERSONIFICATION   *A figure of speech in which an animal, object, or idea is given human form or characteristics.* In "Traveling in the Alcarria," the author gives a pine tree human features when he writes that it "has a graceful and aristocratic air and seems like an old ruined nobleman."

See page 317.
See also FIGURATIVE
LANGUAGE.

PERSUASION   *A type of writing that aims to make the audience accept an opinion.*

See page 429.
See also ARGUMENT,
DESCRIPTION,
EXPOSITION,
NARRATION.

PLOT   *The sequence of events in a story, novel, or play, each event causing or leading to the next.* The plot begins with **exposition,** which introduces the story's characters, setting, and situation. The plot catches the reader's attention with the **narrative hook.** The **rising action** adds complications to the story's **conflicts,** or problems, leading to the **climax,** or point of highest emotional pitch. The **falling action** is the logical result of the climax, and the **resolution** presents the final outcome.

See pages 10, 526.

POETRY *A concentrated kind of writing in which imagery, figurative language, rhythm, and often rhyme combine to create a special emotional effect.* Poetry is usually arranged in lines and groups of lines known as **stanzas.** Types of poetry include **narrative poetry,** which tells a story, **lyric poetry,** which expresses emotion, and **dramatic poetry,** which presents a character.

See page 289.

POINT OF VIEW *The relationship of the narrator, or storyteller, to the story.* In a story with **first-person point of view,** the story is told by one of the characters, referred to as "I." The reader generally sees everything through that character's eyes. "A Handful of Dates," for instance, has a first-person narrator.

In a story with a **limited third-person point of view,** the narrator reveals the thoughts of only one character but refers to that character as "he" or "she." "On the Ferry," told from Mr. Lopez's perspective by a third-person narrator, is an example of limited third-person narration.

In a story with an **omniscient point of view,** the narrator reveals the thoughts of several characters. "The Quarry" is told from an omniscient point of view.

See pages 82, 90, 103.
See also NARRATOR, TONE.

PROTAGONIST *The central character in a story or drama.* Generally the audience is meant to sympathize with the protagonist. For example, the reader of "The Glass of Milk" suffers with the youth as he struggles to maintain his dignity and self-reliance. In *The Jewels of the Shrine* Okorie is the protagonist, and because he is neglected by his grandsons, the audience sympathizes with him.

See ANTAGONIST,
CONFLICT.

REPETITION *The recurrence of sounds, words, phrases, lines, or stanzas in a speech or piece of writing.* Repetition increases the feeling of unity in a work. When a line or stanza is repeated in a poem, it is called a refrain. For example, each stanza of Mistral's "Rocking" concludes with the line "I rock my son," which has a rhythmic, calming quality in the poem.

See page 323.
See also PARALLELISM.

RESOLUTION *The part of the plot that concludes the falling action by revealing or suggesting the outcome of*

the conflict. The resolution in "The Piece of String" comes when Hauchecome, his spirit broken by public ridicule, falls ill and dies.

See page 10.

RHYME *The repetition of sounds in words that appear close to each other in a poem.* **End rhymes** occur at the ends of lines. The following lines from Goethe's "The Erl-King" exemplify end rhyme:

"O father, my father, and did you not *hear*
The Erl-King whisper so low in my *ear*?"

Slant rhymes occur when words include sounds that are similar but not identical. Slant rhyme usually involves some variation of **consonance** (the repetition of consonant sounds) or **assonance** (the repetition of vowel sounds). For example, the following lines from Mistral's "Rocking" contain an example of slant rhyme:

The wind wandering by nigh*t*
rocks the whea*t*.

Night and *wheat* form a slant rhyme because they include the same final consonants but different vowel sounds.

See pages 299, 302.
See also REPETITION,
RHYME SCHEME.

RHYME SCHEME *The pattern of rhymes formed by the end rhyme in a poem.* Rhyme scheme is designated by the assignment of a different letter of the alphabet to each new rhyme. For instance, the rhyme scheme of the first four lines of "Lot's Wife" is *abab:*

The just man followed then his angel guide	a
Where he strode on the black highway, hulking and bright;	b
But a wild grief in his wife's bosom cried,	a
Look back, it is not too late for a last sight	b

See page 299.
See also SONNET.

RHYTHM *The pattern of beats created by the arrangement of stressed and unstressed syllables, particularly in poetry.* Rhythm gives poetry a musical quality that helps convey its meaning. Rhythm can be regular, with a predictable pattern, or meter, or irregular. Note the regular rhythm in these lines from Dickinson's "How Happy Is the Little Stone":

Fulfilling absolute Decree
In casual simplicity—

See page 331.

RISING ACTION *The part of the plot that adds complications to the plot's problems and increases reader* *interest.* For example, in "The Glass of Milk" the rising action occurs as the main character is driven by agonizing hunger to find food at any cost.

See page 10.

ROMANCE *A story concerning a knightly hero, his exciting adventures, and the pursuit of love.*

SATIRE *A form of writing that ridicules abuses for the sake of remedying them.* In the adventures of *Don Quixote* Cervantes mildly satirizes the romantic and idealistic ways of Don Quixote in order to draw attention to old-fashioned ideas.

SCANSION *The analysis of the rhythm of a line of verse.* To scan a line of poetry means to note stressed and unstressed syllables and to divide the line into its feet, or rhythmical units.

See also FOOT, RHYTHM.

SETTING *The time and place in which the events of a story, novel, or play occur.* The setting often helps create an atmosphere or mood. For example, the prairie in "Hoodoo Valley" is a flat, harsh land, peopled with strangers "carried away by . . . madness." The bleak mood of the prairie emphasizes the difficult conditions the characters first face and contrasts with the inviting valley they later find.

See pages 128, 218, 538.
See also SETTING.

SHORT STORY *A brief fictional narrative in prose.* Elements of the short story include plot, character, setting, point of view, theme, and sometimes symbol and irony.

See page 218.

SIMILE *A figure of speech using* like *or as to compare seemingly unlike things.* For example, author R. K. Narayan says that "truth . . . is like the sun" to describe truth as dazzling and powerful.

See pages 268, 310, 314.
See also FIGURATIVE
LANGUAGE, METAPHOR.

SOLILOQUY *A long speech spoken by a character who is alone on stage.* The speech usually reveals the private thoughts and emotions of the character.

SONNET *A lyric poem of fourteen lines, almost always written in iambic pentameter and usually following strict patterns of stanza divisions and rhymes.*

The **Shakespearean,** or **English, sonnet** consists of three **quatrains,** or four-line stanzas, followed by a **couplet,** or pair of rhyming lines. The rhyme scheme is usually *abab, cdcd, efef, gg.* The rhyming couplet often presents a conclusion to the issues or questions presented in the three quatrains. Sonnet 29 is a Shakespearean sonnet.

In the **Petrarchan,** or **Italian, sonnet** fourteen lines are divided into two stanzas. The first eight lines, called an **octave,** usually present a situation, an idea, or question. The remaining six lines, or **sestet,** provide a resolution, comment, or answer. The rhyme scheme for the octave is usually *abbaabba;* for the sestet the rhyme scheme is usually *cdecde.* Sonnet 3 is a Petrarchan sonnet.

See page 302.
See also COUPLET, RHYME
SCHEME, STANZA.

SPEAKER *The voice of a poem, sometimes that of the poet, sometimes that of a fictional person or even a thing.* The speaker's words communicate a particular *tone,* or attitude toward the subject of the poem. In "Summer Is Dying" the speaker's tone is mournful as he notes the season's passing.

See page 295.
See also TONE.

STAGE DIRECTIONS *Instructions written by the dramatist to describe the appearance and actions of characters, as well as sets, costumes, and lighting.*

See pages 452, 510.

STANZA *A group of lines forming a unit in a poem.* "Lot's Wife" has four stanzas.

See page 299.

STREAM OF CONCIOUSNESS *A technique of writing that imitates the way the human mind works by providing a continuous flow of thoughts, feelings, images, observations, and memories.* Unlike stories with conventional plots, stream-of-consciousness stories may change topic suddenly in order to imitate the way the mind suddenly shifts from one thought to another. "Air des Clochettes" is a stream-of-consciousness story.

See page 179.

STYLE *The author's choice and arrangement of words in a literary work.* Style can reveal an author's purpose in writing and attitude toward his or her subject and audience. For example, in "Old Man at the Bridge" Hemingway's style is simple and subtly reveals the tragedy of war.

See page 196.

SYMBOL *Any object, person, place, or experience that means more than what it is.* Kezia and our Else in "The

Doll's House," for example, are entranced by the little lamp that symbolizes the kindness and compassion needed to overcome the ignorance and cruelty of the story's characters.

See pages 151, 355.

THEME *The main idea of a story, poem, novel, or play, usually expressed as a general statement.* Some works have a **stated theme,** which is expressed directly and explicitly. More often works have an **implied theme,** which is revealed gradually through such other elements as plot, character, setting, point of view, symbol, and irony. In "Salt" the implied theme is that ethnic pride can spiritually nourish and unite a community.

See pages 133, 139, 352.

THESIS *The central idea or purpose in a work of nonfiction.* Often the thesis is expressed in a **thesis statement.** For example, in "Freedom to Breathe" Solzhenitsyn states that "the freedom to breathe freely" is "the single most precious freedom that prison takes away." Sometimes the thesis is not stated but rather is implied in the work. For example, *Platero and I* has an implied thesis: Jiménez wants the reader to experience his beloved burro's gentle but sturdy personality.

See page 433.

TONE *The attitude taken by the author or speaker toward the subject of a work.* The tone conveys an emotion or several emotions. For example, in Li Po's "Taking Leave of a Friend" the tone is sad, while the tone of "Waltzing Matilda" is lighthearted and rousing.

See pages 111, 196, 339.
See also NARRATOR,
POINT OF VIEW, SPEAKER.

TRAGEDY *A play in which a main character suffers a downfall or other unhappy circumstances.* That character is often a person of dignified or heroic stature. The downfall may result from outside forces or from a weakness within the character, which is known as a **tragic flaw.** Tragedies often celebrate human dignity in the face of defeat. Cyrano, in *Cyrano de Bergerac,* accepts with dignity his tragic failure at love.

See also COMEDY, DRAMA.

WORD CHOICE *The selection of words in a piece of literature to convey meaning, suggest attitude, and create images.* In "The Guitar," for example, the translators chose specific words to create a melancholy mood and suggest the rhythms of a guitar.

See page 343.
See also CONNOTATION.

GLOSSARY

The following Glossary lists words that are from the selections but may be unfamiliar to you. Although many of the words have several different meanings, they are defined only as they are used in the selections. Some words may be familiar to you in other contexts but may have unusual meanings in the text.

Each Glossary entry contains a pronunciation, a part of speech, and a definition. Some words are used in more than one way in the textbook and therefore have more than one definition and occasionally more than one part of speech. Related words are often combined in one entry: The main form (for example, the verb *abet*) is defined, and another form (for example, the noun *abbetor*) is run on after the main definition. Adverbs ending in *-ly* are usually run on after the definition of the adjective form.

Occasionally an unfamiliar idiomatic expression is used within a selection; in such cases, the main word of the expression is listed, followed by a definition of the idiom. The following abbreviations are used in this Glossary:

n.	noun	*conj.*	conjunction
v.	verb	*prep.*	preposition
adj.	adjective	*interj.*	interjection
adv.	adverb	*pl.*	plural
pron.	pronoun	*n. pl.*	plural noun

A key to pronunciations may be found in the lower right-hand corner of each right-hand page of the Glossary.

A

abate [ə bāt'] *v.* to ease or lessen in severity.
ablution [ə bloo' shən] *n.* ceremonial cleansing.
abode [ə bōd'] *n.* home; dwelling place.
abysmal [ə biz'məl] *adj.* very deep.
acacia [ə kā'shə] *n.* tree of the mimosa family.
acquaintance [ə kwānt'əns] *n.* person whom one knows but who is not a close friend.
acquire [ə kwīr'] *v.* to get by one's own efforts.
adjudge [ə juj'] *v.* to deem; consider.
adversary [ad'vər ser'ē] *n.* enemy; opponent.
affable [af'ə bəl] *adj.* friendly.
air [âr] *n.* 1. manner. 2. melody. —**airs**, *n. pl.* pretense of superiority.
alight [ə līt'] *v.* to land.
allusion [ə loo'zhən] *n.* a casual or indirect reference.
ally [ə lī'] *v.* to combine or unite.
aloof [ə loof'] *adj.* remote; reserved.
amputate [am'pyə tāt'] *v.* to cut off (a limb, etc.).
anemic [ə nē'mik] *adj.* pale.
antechamber [an'tē chām'bər] *n.* entrance room.
anvil [an'vəl] *n.* steel or iron block on which softened metals are hammered into various shapes.
aplomb [ə plom', ə plum'] *n.* poise; self-confidence.
appal *or* **appall** [ə pôl'] *v.* to horrify.
apparel [ə par'əl] *v.* to dress.
apposite [ap'ə zit, ə poz'it] *adj.* appropriate.
appraise [ə prāz'] *v.* evaluate the quality of.
apprehensive [ap'ri hen'siv] *adj.* worried about future events. —**apprehensively**, *adv.*

arable [ar'ə bəl] *adj.* fit for cultivation.
arid [ar'id] *adj.* having a dry climate.
aristocracy [ar'is tok'rə sē] *n.* 1. upper class. 2. group that is regarded as superior.
array [ə rā'] *v.* to adorn.
artful [ärt'fəl] *adj.* clever; cunning.
artillery [är til'ər ē] *n.* mounted firearms capable of shooting projectiles.
ascent [ə sent'] *n.* act of going up or climbing.
ascribe [ə skrīb'] *v.* to attribute.
assurance [ə shoor'əns] *n.* certainty.
astray [ə strā'] *adj.* wandering; off the correct path.
atone [ə tōn'] *v.* to make amends.
attest [ə test'] *v.* affirm to be true.
auspicious [ôs pish'əs] *adj.* promising; favorable.
avid [av'id] *adj.* eager. —**avidly**, *adv.*
avowal [ə vou'əl] *n.* straight declaration.

B

banter [ban'tər] *n.* playful jesting. —*v.* to tease; joke. —**bantering**, *adj.* —**banteringly**, *adv.*
baptize [bap tīz', bap'tīz] *v.* to initiate into a Christian church by ceremony.
base [bās] *adj.* low; dishonorable.
beacon [bē'kən] *n.* guiding light.
behindhand [bi hīnd'hand'] *adj.* late.
belabor [bi lā'bər] *v.* to thrash; beat soundly.
belfry [bel'frē] *n.* tower containing a bell, often part of a church or other structure.
belligerent [bə lij'ər ənt] *adj.* eager to fight. —**belligerently**, *adv.*
benevolent [bə nev'ə lənt] *adj.* kindly.
berate [bi rāt'] *v.* scold.
beseech [bi sēch'] *v.* to plead. —**besought**, past tense and past participle of **beseech**.
bestow [bi stō'] *v.* to give.
bide [bīd] *v.* to wait or stay.
billet [bil'it] *n.* small stick of wood.
blaspheme [blas fēm', blas'fēm] *v.* 1. to speak irreverently of sacred matters. 2. to curse.
bower [bou'ər] *n.* area enclosed by branches.
bravado [brə vä'dō] *n.* pretended bravery, especially when it is boastful.
brazen [brā'zən] *adj.* bold. —**brazenly**, *adv.*
bridgehead [brij'hed'] *n.* a secured position established by one force in the territory held by its enemy.
burble [bur'bəl] *n.* a bubbling sound.

---

at; āpe; cär; end; mē; it; īce; hot; ōld; fôrk; wood; fool; oil; out; up; ūse; turn; ə in ago, taken, pencil, lemon, circus; bat; chin; dear; five; game; hit; hw in white; joke; kit; lid; man; not; singer; pail; ride; sat; shoe; tag; thin; this; very; wet; yes; zoo; zh in treasure; KH in loch, German ach; N in French bon; œ in French feu, German schön

Glossary **621**

GLOSSARY

In the Glossary you will find the more difficult words in the selections, along with pronunciations and definitions of each word as it is used in the selection.

You will also find the Glossary words for each selection listed in the selection's Teaching Notes section of your *Teacher's Classroom Resources* and in this *Teacher's Annotated Edition.*

The short pronunciation key at the bottom of each right-hand Glossary page applies not only to pronunciations given for Glossary words but also to all pronunciations that appear in footnotes throughout the anthology.

C

callow [kal′ō] *adj.* immature; inexperienced.

calumny [kal′əm nē] *n.* slander.

camellia [kə mēl′yə, kə mē′lē ə] *n.* fragrant flower with pink, red, or white petals.

candelabrum [kand′əl ä′brəm, a′brəm] *n.* a large candlestick with holders for several candles.

carcass [kär′kəs] *n.* animal's dead body.

cassock [kas′ək] *n.* ankle-length, close-fitting garment worn by the clergy.

caterwaul [kat′ər wôl′] *v.* to make a screech or shrill sound like that of a cat.

cavalier [kav′ə lēr′] *n.* **1.** knight. **2.** gallant man.

chagrin [shə grin′] *n.* distress caused by frustration or disappointment.

chandelier [shand′əl ēr′] *n.* a lamp that has holders for a number of candles or lightbulbs and hangs from the ceiling.

chaste [chāst] *adj.* pure; modest; virtuous.

cherub [cher′əb] *n.* innocent child.

chide [chīd] *v.* to reproach.

churlish [chur′lish] *adj.* surly. —**churlishness,** *n.*

cinder [sin′dər] *n.* speck of ash.

clamor [klam′ər] *n.* noisy outcry.

cleave [klēv] *v.* **1.** to stick to. **2.** to remain devoted or faithful to.

coax [kōks] *v.* to persuade.

collaborate [kə lab′ə rāt′] *v.* to work together.

collide [kə līd′] *v.* to crash into something, usually moving.

colonnade [kol′ə nād′] *n.* a row of columns.

commodity [kə mod′ə tē] *n.* product; item of trade.

commotion [kə mō′shən] *n.* bustle; confusion.

compensate [kom′pən sāt′] *v.* to repay.

comply [kəm plī′] *v.* to act in accordance with a command or request.

compound [kom′pound′] *n.* enclosed area containing buildings.

concussion [kən kush′ən] *n.* the shock of a blow or collision.

confederate [kən fed′ər it] *n.* accomplice.

confirm [kən furm′] *v.* to admit to full membership in a Christian church by ceremony.

congeal [kən jēl′] *v.* to solidify or thicken.

conjecture [kən jek′chər] *n.* guess.

conscientious [kon′shē en′shəs] *adj.* ruled by one's conscience.

consolation [kon′sə lā′shən] *n.* something that comforts someone who is sad or disappointed.

consolidate [kən sol′ə dāt′] *v.* to combine.

constitutional [kon′stə tōō′shən əl, kon′stə tū′shən əl] *n.* exercise, often a walk, taken to benefit one's health.

constrict [kən strikt′] *v.* to make narrower or smaller.

contralto [kən tral′tō] *adj.* relating to the lowest female voice.

converge [kən vurj′] *v.* to come together.

coquettish [kō ket′ish] *adj.* flirtatious.

corrupt [kə rupt′] *v.* to destroy the morality of.

countenance [koun′tə nəns] *n.* face.

covetous [kuv′it əs] *adj.* excessively desirous; greedy. —**covetousness,** *n.*

critique [kri tēk′] *n.* critical assessment or evaluation.

curtail [kər tāl′] *v.* to shorten.

cut [kut] *n.* passage.

D

dalliance [dal′ē əns] *n.* wasting of time.

debauch [di bôch′] *v.* to corrupt.

decimate [des′ə māt′] *v.* to destroy a large number of.

declaim [di klām′] *v.* to recite or speak in a dramatic or artificial manner.

defile [di fīl′, dē′fīl′] *n.* narrow passageway in a mountain region.

degradation [deg′rə dā′shən] *n.* state of being lowered in character or status.

deign [dān] *v.* to condescend.

demur [di mur′] *v.* to object.

denigrate [den′ə grāt′] *v.* to belittle.

denounce [di nouns′] *v.* to condemn publicly.

denude [di nōōd′, di nūd′] *v.* strip bare.

deplorable [di plôr′ə bəl] *adj.* extremely bad.

deportation [dē′pôr tā′shən] *n.* ejection of a foreign person from a country.

depot [dep′ō] *n.* place where military supplies are stored.

depravity [di prav′ə tē] *n.* state of being corrupt.

deprecate [dep′rə kāt′] *v.* to belittle. —**deprecatory** [dep′rə kə tôr′ē], *adj.*

destitute [des′tə tōōt′, des′tə tūt′] *adj.* impoverished.

devoid [di void′] *adj.* lacking.

dexterous [deks′trəs, deks′tər əs] *adj.* skillful. —**dexterously,** *adv.*

diabolic [dī′ə bol′ik] *adj.* fiendish; cruel. —**diabolical,** *adj.*

diffident [dif′ə dənt] *adj.* shy.

dilatory [dil′ə tôr′ē] *adj.* inclined or intended to cause delay or gain time.

dimension [di men′shən] *n.* measurable extent.

diminutive [di min′yə tiv] *adj.* of an extremely small size; tiny.

discern [di surn′, di zurn′] *v.* to recognize.

discomfit [dis kum′fit] *v.* to confuse; disconcert.

discreet [dis krēt′] *adj.* showing prudence or extra care about what is done. —**discreetly,** *adv.*

disdain [dis dān′] *v.* to scorn.

disheveled [di shev′əld] *adj.* not well groomed; messy.

dissimulate [di sim′yə lāt′] *v.* to disguise feelings; pretend.

distillation [dist′əl ā′shən] *n.* concentration of something.

disquieting [dis kwī′i ting] *adj.* causing uneasiness; disturbing.

divine [di vīn′] *v.* to prophesy; discover or interpret by supernatural means. —**diviner,** *n.*

domain [dō mān′] *n.* area under one government.

dormant [dôr′mənt] *adj.* **1.** sleeping. **2.** inactive.

drove [drōv] *n.* a crowd.

drudgery [druj′ər ē] *n.* tedious or menial work.

E

edification [ed′ə fi kā′shən] *n.* improvement or enlightenment.

effusive [i fū′siv] *adj.* expressing excessive feeling or emotion. —**effusively,** *adv.*

elasticity [i las′tis′ə tē] *n.* quality of being able to adapt to various circumstances; flexibility.

elation [i lā′shən] *n.* great happiness.

elocution [el′ə kū′shən] *n.* art of public speaking.

eloquence [el′ə kwəns] *n.* vivid, expressive speech.

emaciated [i mā′shē āt′id] *adj.* very thin.

622 *Glossary*

emanate [em′ə nāt′] *v.* to issue or come forth from a source.

embankment [em bangk′mənt] *n.* a long mound of earth, stones, etc., used to stop water or hold up a road.

emblematic [em′blə mat′ik] *adj.* acting as a symbol or representation of something else.

emigrate [em′ə grāt′] *v.* to go from one country to another.

emulation [em′yə lā′shən] *n.* attempt to equal or surpass.

enact [i nakt′] *v.* to put into effect, as a law.

encampment [en kamp′mənt] *n.* camp.

enchant [en chant′] *v.* to charm; bewitch. —**enchantment,** *n.*

encircle [en sur′kəl] *v.* to surround.

enclave [en′klāv, än′klāv] *n.* a territory surrounded by another territory.

encounter [en koun′tər] *v.* to find; meet; come upon.

endow [en dou′] *v.* to provide with some quality.

engender [en jen′dər] *v.* to cause to be; create.

enigmatic [en′ig mat′ik, ē′nig mat′ik] *adj.* puzzling; mysterious.

entangle [en tang′gəl] *v.* to catch in a tangle.

entice [en tīs′] *v.* to tempt.

entourage [än′too räzh′, än′too räzh′] *n.* group of companions.

entrails [en′trālz, en′trəlz] *n. pl.* bowels; inner organs.

eradicate [i rad′ə kāt′] *v.* to do away with.

espousal [es pou′zəl] *n.* advocacy.

ether [ē′thər] *n.* a supposed substance once thought to fill outer space.

ethereal [i thēr′ē əl] *adj.* light and delicate.

euphemism [ū′fə miz′əm] *n.* mild or polite word used in place of a harsher one.

ewer [ū′ər] *n.* wide-mouthed, large pitcher.

exalt [ig zôlt′] *v.* to esteem; glorify. —**exalted,** *adj.*

exertion [ig zur′shən] *n.* effort.

exhilaration [ig zil′ə rā′shən] *n.* excited condition.

exigency [ek′sə jən sē] *n.* situation calling for immediate action or attention.

expedient [iks pē′dē ənt] *adj.* appropriate.

exploit [eks′ploit, iks ploit′] *n.* heroic feat or deed.

extremity [iks trem′ə tē] *n.* condition of great need.

exultant [ig zult′ənt] *adj.* rejoicing; triumphant.

F

fabrication [fab′rə kā′shen] *n.* lie; false statement.

facetious [fə sē′ shəs] *adj.* joking, sometimes inappropriately.

falter [fôl′tər] *v.* to stumble; move unsteadily.

fancy [fan′sē] *v.* to imagine.

fatuous [fach′ōō əs] *adj.* foolish.

faze [fāz] *v.* to bother; disturb; disconcert.

fervent [fur′vənt] *adj.* having great emotional intensity.

fetid [fet′id, fē′tid] *adj.* stinking; foul-smelling.

fetter [fet′ər] *v.* to bind with chains.

filial [fil′ē əl] *adj.* befitting a son.

flag [flag] *v.* to lose vigor; grow weak.

flamboyant [flam boi′ənt] *adj.* showy. —**flamboyantly,** *adv.*

fogy [fō′gē] *n.* old-fashioned person.

foreboding [fôr bō′ding] *n.* premonition; feeling that something will happen, usually something bad.

foredoom [fôr dōōm′] *v.* to condemn in advance.

forestall [fôr stôl′] *v.* to thwart.

forfeit [fôr′fit] *v.* to lose; give up.

forge [fôrj] *n.* blacksmith's workshop.

formidable [fôr′mi də bəl] *adj.* inspiring awe; impressive.

fortune [fôr′chən] *n.* the way events turn out, especially when favorable; luck.

fraternize [frat′ər nīz′] *v.* to associate with someone else in a friendly way.

frivolity [fri vol′ə tē] *n.* **1.** condition of being of little importance. **2.** silliness; playfulness.

frivolous [friv′ə ləs] *adj.* unimportant.

furrow [fur′ō] *n.* narrow groove in the ground.

furtive [fur′tiv] *adj.* done in a sneaky manner. —**furtively,** *adv.*

G

gallery [gal′ər ē, gal′rē] *n.* theater balcony.

garrulous [gar′ə ləs, gar′yə ləs] *adj.* talkative.

genealogy [jē′nē ol′ə jē, jē′nē al′ə jē] *n.* study of a person's or a family's ancestry. —**genealogical** [jē′nē ə loj′i kəl], *adj.*

ghastly [gast′lē] *adj.* terrible; horrible.

gibberish [jib′ər ish, gib′ər ish] *n.* nonsense; obscure language.

gird [gurd] *v.* to fasten with a belt.

goblet [gob′lit] *n.* drinking glass.

gorge [gôrj] *n.* narrow opening between steep sides.

gospel [gos′pəl] *n.* **1.** the account of the life of Jesus given in the first four books of the New Testament. **2.** the teachings or message of Jesus.

grandiloquent [gran dil′ə kwənt] *adj.* using flowery and important-sounding but empty language.

grave [grāv] *adj.* serious.

grievous [grē′vəs] *adj.* serious; causing grief.

grouse [grous] *n.* fowl-like game bird.

gruff [gruf] *adj.* rough and deep.

guileless [gīl′lis] *adj.* candid; not sly or crafty.

gumption [gump′shən] *n.* courage; initiative.

guttural [gut′ər əl] *adj.* with a rasping quality.

gyration [jī rā′shən] *n.* circular motion.

H

hallucination [hə lōō′sə nā′shən] *n.* perception of something that is not really there.

hamlet [ham′lit] *n.* small village.

hawser [hô′zər] *n.* a heavy rope for moving or anchoring a ship.

headmaster [hed′mas′tər] *n.* head of a school.

hearten [härt′ən] *v.* to encourage. —**heartening,** *adj.*

herald [her′əld] *v.* to announce; proclaim.

hie [hī] *v.* to hurry.

hobgoblin [hob′gob′lin] *n.* mischievous elf.

---

at; āpe; cär; end; mē; it; īce; hot; ōld; fôrk; wood; fōōl; oil; out; up; ūse; turn; ə in ago, taken, pencil, lemon, circus; bat; chin; dear; five; game; hit; hw in white; joke; kit; lid; man; not; singer; pail; ride; sat; shoe; tag; thin; <u>th</u>is; very; wet; yes; zoo; zh in treasure; KH in loch, German ach; N in French bon; œ in French feu, German schön

---

homage [hom′ij, om′ij] *n.* respect; honor; reverence.
hoodoo [hoo′doo′] *n.* **1.** bad luck. **2.** thing or person that brings bad luck.
hulking [hul′king] *adj.* massive.

I

ignominy [ig′nə min′ē] *n.* dishonor.
imbue [im bū′] *v.* to pass through; fill.
immeasurable [i mezh′ər ə bəl] *adj.* unable to be measured.
immunity [i mū′nə tē] *n.* protection from harm.
impassive [im pas′iv] *adj.* not showing or feeling emotion; calm.
impeccable [im pek′ə bəl] *adj.* without fault or flaw; perfect.
impenetrable [im pen′ə trə bəl] *adj.* unable to be passed through.
imperious [im pēr′ē əs] *adj.* domineering.
impertinence [im purt′ən əns] *n.* rudeness or offensive boldness.
impetuous [im pech′oo əs] *adj.* rash; impulsive.
implacable [im plak′ə bəl, im plā′kə bəl] *adj.* relentless; unchanging.
implore [im plôr′] *v.* to beg.
incantation [in′kan tā′shən] *n.* words spoken to cast a spell.
incessant [in ses′ənt] *adj.* going on without interruption.
incomprehensible [in′kom pri hen′sə bəl] *adj.* unable to be understood.
incredulous [in krej′ə ləs] *adj.* unbelieving.
increment [ing′krə mənt, in′krə mənt] *n.* a small amount of growth, such as a salary increase.
indignant [in dig′nənt] *adj.* full of anger about supposed injustice. —**indignantly,** *adv.*
indiscriminate [in dis krim′ə nit] *adj.* not making distinctions or noting differences; random.
indolent [ind′əl ənt] *adj.* lazy.
induce [in doos′, in dūs′] *v.* to bring about.
indulgent [in dul′jənt] *adj.* characterized by leniency. —**indulgently,** *adv.*
ineffable [in ef′ə bəl] *adj.* difficult to express in words.
inert [i nurt′] *adj.* unmoving.
infectious [in fek′shəs] *adj.* tending to spread among people.
infest [in fest′] *v.* to spread over; fill; overrun.
ingenuity [in′ jə noo′ə tē] *n.* cleverness in accomplishing something.
ingratiate [in grā′shē āt′] *v.* to bring oneself deliberately into another person's favor. —**ingratiating,** *adj.*
innumerable [i noo′mər ə bəl, i nū′mər ə bəl] *adj.* too many to count.
inscrutable [in skroo′tə bəl] *adj.* not easily understood; mysterious.
insidious [in sid′ē əs] *adj.* characterized by deceitfulness or sly treachery.
insular [in′sə lər, ins′yə lər] *adj.* narrow-minded.
interment [in tur′mənt] *n.* act of burying.
interminable [in tur′mi nə bəl] *adj.* endless or seeming to last forever.
interrogation [in ter′ə gā′shən] *n.* questioning.
intimacy [in′tə mə sē] *n.* state of close friendship.
intimidate [in tim′ə dāt′] *v.* to make fearful.
intrigue [in′trēg, in trēg′] *n.* underhanded plot.

inveterate [in vet′ər it] *adj.* habitual.
invoke [in vōk′] *v.* call on; pray for.
iridescent [ir′ə des′ənt] *adj.* showing changing colors.
irrepressible [ir′i pres′ə bəl] *adj.* unable to be restrained.
irresolute [i rez′ə loot′] *adj.* without determination. —**irresolutely,** *adv.*

J

jasmine [jaz′min, jas′min] *n.* a plant with sweet-smelling yellow, white, or red flowers.
jeer [jēr] *v.* to shout at in a derisive or scornful manner.
jovial [jō′vē əl] *adj.* full of good humor; jolly. —**jovialness,** *n.*
judicious [joo dish′əs] *adj.* showing good judgment.
juncture [jungk′ chər] *n.* point in time.

L

lackey [lak′e] *n.* a servant.
laggard [lag′ ərd] *n.* a slow individual; one who lags behind.
languid [lang′gwid] *adj.* sluggish; without energy.
lave [lāv] *v.* to wash.
lavish [lav′ish] *adj.* extravagant.
legacy [leg′ə sē] *n.* something left in a will.
lethargic [li thär′jik] *adj.* sluggish; without energy.
list [list] *v.* to tilt.
listless [list′lis] *adj.* without energy or enthusiasm. —**listlessly,** *adv.*
loathe [lōth] *v.* to hate.
lodge [loj] *v.* to give someone a place to stay on a temporary basis.
lofty [lôf′tē] *adj.* towering; of great height.
low [lō] *v.* moo.
lute [loot] *n.* a stringed instrument with a pear-shaped body.
luxuriant [lug zhoor′ē ənt, luk shoor′ē ənt] *adj.* abundant or thick.

M

malaria [mə lār′ē ə] *n.* disease characterized by chills, fever, and shaking.
malice [mal′is] *n.* ill will.
mangy [mān′ jē] *adj.* squalid and dirty in appearance.
marrow [mar′ō] *n.* innermost part.
martial [mär′shəl] *adj.* relating to war.
meager [mē′gər] *adj.* thin.
meditate [med′ə tāt′] *v.* to think deeply.
mendicant [men′di kənt] *n.* beggar.
menial [mē′nē əl, mēn′ yəl] *adj.* degrading.
meritorious [mer′ə tôr′ē əs] *adj.* deserving praise.
metamorphosis [met′ə môr′fə sis] *n.* change or transformation.
meteorite [mē′tē ə rīt′] *n.* a body from space that has fallen to Earth.
milestone [mīl′stōn′] *n.* stone on a roadway that shows the distance in miles to or from a specific place.
mime [mīm] *n.* art of pantomime.
mingle [ming′əl] *v.* to join.
mirage [mi räzh′] *n.* visual illusion.
mischance [mis chans′] *n.* bad luck.
misgiving [mis giv′ing] *n.* feeling of doubt, fear, or worry.
moderation [mod′ə rā′shən] *n.* state of avoiding extremes.

624 *Glossary*

monotony [mə not'ən ē] *n.* unvaried, tiresome sameness.

morose [mə rōs'] *adj.* gloomy.

municipal [mū nis'ə pəl] *adj.* of the city.

munificent [mū nif'ə sənt] *adj.* lavish.

muse [mūz] *v.* to think in an idle way. —**musings,** *n. pl.*

mystify [mis'tə fī] *v.* to puzzle; bewilder.

N

nebulous [neb'yə ləs] *adj.* not clear; hazy.

niche [nich] *n.* **1.** a recess in a wall, used to place an ornament. **2.** a suitable place.

nocturnal [nok turn'əl] *adj.* having to do with or happening at night.

nuptials [nup'shəlz, nup'chəlz] *n.* wedding ceremony.

nurture [nur'chər] *v.* to nourish.

O

oblivion [ə bliv'ē ən] *n.* state of forgetfulness.

obscurity [əb skyoor'ə tē] *n.* quality of being not well known.

obsequious [əb sē'kwē əs] *adj.* overly humble, attentive, and obedient.

ordinance [ôrd'ən əns] *n.* law.

overture [ō'vər choor', ō'vər chər] *n.* proposal meant to bring about some action; offer.

ovation [ō vā'shən] *n.* enthusiastic demonstration of public acclaim.

P

pagan [pā'gən] *adj.* pertaining to a religion that worships many gods. —*n.* person who is not religious.

pagoda [pə gō'də] *n.* in the Far East, a multistoried tower, often pyramidal in form.

palatial [pə lā'shəl] *adj.* like that of a palace.

pall [pôl] *v.* to become boring; lose appeal.

pallid [pal'id] *adj.* pale; of an unhealthy color.

paltry [pôl'trē] *adj.* unimportant.

pander [pan'dər] *n.* one who helps others yield to base deeds or desires.

parapet [par'ə pit, par'ə pet'] *n.* a wall, sometimes on top of a large mound of earth, to protect soldiers from attack.

parasitic [par' ə sit'ik] *adj.* living at another person's expense.

parish [par'ish] *n.* district containing its own church.

parlor [pär'lər] *n.* living room or room where guests are received and entertained.

parry [par'ē] *v.* to turn aside; fight off.

patriarch [pā'trē ärk'] *n.* old man who is given great respect.

paunch [pônch, pänch] *n.* a belly that sticks out.

pedestal [ped'əst əl] *n.* support for a statue.

peevish [pē'vish] *adj.* cross; ill-tempered; irritable.

pensive [pen'siv] *adj.* thoughtful.

penurious [pi noor'ē əs, pi nyoor'ē əs] *adj.* stingy; miserly. —**penuriously,** *adv.*

peremptory [pə remp'tər ē] *adj.* not permitting argument or delay; commanding.

permeate [pur'mē āt'] *v.* to spread through.

perpendicular [pur'pən dik'yə lər] *adj.* at right angles to the line of the horizon; vertical.

perpetual [pər pech'oo əl] *adj.* eternal; endless.

perplexity [pər plek'sə tē] *n.* state of confusion.

pervade [pər vād'] *v.* to spread through.

pivotal [piv'ət əl] *adj.* of central importance.

placid [plas'id] *adj.* calm. —**placidity** [plə sid'ə tē], *n.*

plagiarist [plā'jə rist] *n.* someone who presents another person's writing as his or her own.

plaintive [plān'tiv] *adj.* sad; mournful.

plumage [ploo'mij] *n.* coat of feathers of a bird.

poignant [poin'yənt] *adj.* touching; evoking emotions.

ponderous [pon'də rəs] *adj.* heavy and clumsy. —**ponderously,** *adv.*

poplar [pop'lər] *n.* tree of the willow family.

posterior [pos tēr'ē ər, pōs tēr'ē ər] *n.* the buttocks.

potent [pōt'ənt] *adj.* powerful; strong.

prattle [prat'əl] *n.* idle talk.

precarious [pri kãr'ē əs] *adj.* uncertain; dependent on chance.

prefiguration [prē'fig yə rā'shən] *n.* something that foreshadows.

prescribe [pri skrīb'] *v.* to direct.

pretext [prē'tekst'] *n.* excuse; false reason.

prickle [prik'əl] *n.* sharp point.

primer [prim'ər] *n.* elementary book on any subject.

prodigy [prod'ə jē] *n.* extremely talented or gifted person, usually a child.

profane [prō fān', prə fān'] *v.* treat something regarded as sacred with disrespect or contempt.

profound [prə found'] *adj.* **1.** felt intensely. **2.** characterized by deep understanding.

profuse [prə fūs'] *adj.* abundant. —**profusely,** *adv.*

propitiate [prə pish'ē āt'] *v.* to appease; pacify.

prosaic [prō zā'ik] *adj.* commonplace.

protestation [prot'is tā'shən, prō'tes tā'shən] *n.* serious affirmation.

protract [prō trakt'] *v.* to extend in time.

protrude [prō trood'] *v.* to stick out.

protuberance [prō too'bər əns, prō tū'bər əns] *n.* something that sticks out; bulge.

provisions [prə vizh'ənz] *n.* supplies.

provocative [prə vok'ə tiv] *adj.* tending to stir up emotion.

prowess [prou'is] *n.* **1.** bravery. **2.** ability; skill.

prudent [prood'ənt] *adj.* exercising caution; using good judgment.

Q

quake [kwāk] *v.* to shake.

quench [kwench] *v.* to satisfy.

querulous [kwer'ə ləs, kwer'yə ləs] *adj.* inclined to complain or find fault. —**querulously,** *adv.*

quest [kwest] *n.* search to find something or achieve a goal.

quintessence [kwin tes'əns] *n.* basic or most essential part of something. —**quintessential** [kwin'tə sen'shəl], *adj.*

---

at; āpe; cär; end; mē; it; īce; hot; ōld; fôrk; wood; fool; oil; out; up; ūse; turn; ə in ago, taken, pencil, lemon, circus; bat; chin; dear; five; game; hit; hw in white; joke; kit; lid; man; not; singer; pail; ride; sat; shoe; tag; thin; this; very; wet; yes; zoo; zh in treasure; KH in loch, German ach; N in French bon; œ in French feu, German schön

Glossary **625**

rabble [rab'əl] *n.* a mass of people, usually regarded as being of a low class.

radiate [rā'dē āt'] *v.* to shine out.

rancor [rang'kər] *n.* strong hate or spite.

ravine]rə vēn'] *n.* deep valley in the earth.

rebuff [ri buf'] *v.* to reject bluntly.

rebuke [ri būk'] *v.* to reprimand.

recollection [rek'ə lek'shən] *n.* remembrance.

recompense [rek'əm pens'] *v.* to repay.

reiterate [rē it'ə rāt'] *v.* to say or do repeatedly.

remorse [ri môrs'] *n.* feeling of sorrow or guilt for past behavior. —**remorseful,** *adj.*

rendezvous [rän'də vōō', rän'dā vōō'] *n.* arranged meeting, especially when done in secret.

repose [ri pōz'] *n.* rest.

reprieve [ri prēv'] *n.* release from something unpleasant; relief.

reproach [ri prōch'] *v.* to blame.

resolute [rez'ə lōōt'] *adj.* having determination. —**resolutely,** *adv.*

resolve [ri zolv'] *n.* steadfast resolution. —*v.* to be determined.

resound [ri zound'] *v.* **1.** to be full of sound. **2.** echo; reverberate.

respite [res'pit] *n.* interval of relief.

resplendent [ri splen'dənt] *adj.* shining brilliantly; gleaming.

retail [rē'tāl, ri tāl'] *v.* to retell or repeat.

revelation [rev'ə lā'shən] *n.* a sudden or striking disclosure.

rimy [rī'mē] *adj.* covered with frost.

rosary [rō'zər ē] *n.* a string of beads used by Roman Catholics in praying.

rudimentary [rōō' də men'tər ē, rōō' də men'trē] *adj.* very basic or elementary.

ruinous [rōō'i nəs] *adj.* tending to bring disaster.

rustic [rus'tik] *n.* a person from the country, especially when regarded as unsophisticated.

rustle [rus'əl] *n.* soft sound.

sallow [sal'ō] *adj.* having a pale or sickly yellowish complexion.

saunter [sôn'tər, sän' tər] *v.* to stroll.

scabbard [skab'ərd] *n.* a case for the blade of a sword.

scarab [skar'əb] *n.* gem cut in the shape of a beetle.

scavenger [skav'in jər] *n.* one who searches through refuse for useful things.

scintillate [sint'əl āt'] *v.* to give off flashes of light.

score [skôr] *v.* to write out parts of a musical composition for various instruments.

scrupulous [skrōō'pyə ləs] *adj.* paying strict attention to what is right; careful. —**scrupulously,** *adv.*

scuttle [skut'əl] *v.* to move with short, rapid steps.

sedate [si dāt'] *adj.* calm. —**sedately,** *adv.*

semblance [sem'bləns] *n.* outward appearance, especially a false one.

serenity [sə ren'ə tē] *n.* state of being calm or peaceful.

shamble [sham'bəl] *v.* to shuffle.

sharper [shär'pər] *n.* cheat.

sheepish [shē'pish] *adj.* embarrassed or bashful. —**sheepishly,** *adv.*

shirk [shurk] *v.* to avoid.

shroud [shroud] *n.* cloth covering for a dead body. —*v.* to cover; conceal.

sickle [sik'əl] *n.* tool with a crescent-shaped blade attached to a short handle that is used for cutting weeds, grass, and other growing things.

siege [sēj] *n.* sustained attack involving cutting off an enemy from sources of supplies.

siegeworks [sēj'wurks'] *n. pl.* barricade set up by a force surrounding an enemy.

silhouette [sil'ōō et', sil'ōō et'] *n.* dark shape seen against a lighter background; outline.

sinewy [sin'ū ē] *adj.* powerful; strong.

skein [skān] *n.* bundle of yarn or thread.

slipshod [slip'shod'] *adj.* careless.

slither [slith'ər] *v.* to move with a gliding motion. —**slithery,** *adj.*

sojourn [sō'jurn, sō jurn'] *v.* to live somewhere on a temporary basis.

sordid [sôr'did] *adj.* filthy; squalid.

sot [sot] *n.* one who drinks too much by habit.

spawn [spôn] *v.* to bring into existence; produce.

speculate [spek'yə lāt'] *v.* to think about something and come to a guess. —**speculation,** *n.*

spew [spū] *v.* to vomit.

splay [splā] *v.* spread out.

spry [sprī] *adj.* nimble; lively; active.

squabble [skwob'əl] *v.* to quarrel or argue noisily.

stalwart [stôl'wərt] *n.* one who is physically or morally strong or brave.

steep [stēp] *v.* to saturate.

stint [stint] *n.* limitation.

stupefy [stōō'pə fī, stū'pə fī] *v.* to astonish; bewilder. —**stupefaction** [stōō'pə fak'shən, stu'pə fak'shən], *n.*

sullen [sul'ən] *adj.* sulky; gloomy. —**sullenly,** *adv.*

sully [sul'ē] *v.* to dirty; soil; dishonor.

superannuated [sōō'pər an'ū ā'tid] *adj.* too old for work or use.

supercilious [sōō'pər sil'ē əs] *adj.* arrogant; disdainful. —**superciliously,** *adv.*

supine [sōō pīn'] *adj.* lying on one's back.

suppliant [sup'lē ənt] *n.* one who asks for something humbly.

surmise [sər mīz'] *v.* to guess.

swagger [swag'ər] *v.* to walk in a bold or superior fashion.

symmetrical [si met'ri kəl] *adj.* exhibiting correspondence of opposite parts in size, shape, and position.

taciturn [tas'ə turn'] *adj.* very quiet.

talon [tal'ən] *n.* bird's claw.

tankard [tang'kərd] *n.* large mug with a lid.

tedium [tē'dē əm] *n.* state of being wearisome or boring; unchanging dullness.

temper [tem'pər] *v.* to soften; moderate.

temperate [tem'pər it, tem'prit] *adj.* moderate.

tenacity [ti nas'ə tē] *n.* state of being inclined to hold firmly.

terrain [tə rān', te rān'] *n.* region of land, especially with regard to its features.

threshold [thresh'ōld, thresh'hōld'] *n.* point of entry; beginning.

timorous [tim'ər əs] *adj.* showing a lack of courage.

tortoise [tôr'təs] *n.* a land turtle.

626 *Glossary*

trace [trās] *n.* a strap or chain connecting an animal's harness to a vehicle being pulled.

traipse [trāps] *v.* to walk around aimlessly.

transcendent [tran sen′dənt] *adj.* surpassing all others; superior.

transgress [trans gres′, tranz gres′] *v.* to go beyond a proper limit. —**transgression** [trans gresh′ən, tranz gresh′ən], *n.* sin.

transition [tran zish′ən] *n.* passage from one condition or state to another.

transmit [trans mit′, tranz mit′] *v.* to send or communicate.

transpire [tran spīr′] *v.* to happen.

tremolo [trem′ə lō] *n.* a wavering or trembling sound.

trifle [trī′fəl] *n.* something unimportant. —**a trifle,** *adv.* somewhat.

trudge [truj] *v.* to walk laboriously.

tweak [twēk] *v.* to pull sharply.

U

uncanny [un kan′ē] *adj.* strange and mysterious; eerie.

undaunted [un dôn′tid] *adj.* not discouraged.

unpretentious [un′pri ten′shəs] *adj.* not showy or affected; modest.

unshriven [un shriv′ən] *adj.* not having received confession and absolution.

unwonted [un wôn′tid, un wōn′təd] *adj.* unusual.

usurp [ū surp′, ū zurp′] *v.* to take unjustly.

V

vagabond [vag′ə bond′] *n.* wanderer; tramp.

vainglory [vān′glôr′ē, vān glôr′ē] *n.* great vanity.

valet [val′it, val′ā] *n.* servant who cares for a person's clothes.

vapor [vā′pər] *n.* **1.** cloudy or gaseous matter. **2.** something insubstantial.

variegated [vâr′ē ə gā′tid, vâr′ə gā′tid] *adj.* streaked or marked with different colors.

veranda [və ran′də] *n.* an open porch, which may be roofed.

veritable [ver′i tə bəl] *adj.* actual.

vicissitude [vi sis′ə tōōd′, vi sis′ə tūd′] *n.* change in a situation.

visor [vī′zər] *n.* front part of a helmet that lowers to cover the top part of the face.

vista [vis′tə] *n.* view, particularly one seen through a long passage.

vivacity [vi vas′ə tē, vī vas′ə tē] *n.* liveliness.

voluble [vol′yə bəl] *adj.* speaking easily and rapidly; talkative. —**volubly,** *adv.*

vulnerable [vul′nər ə bəl] *adj.* able to be harmed.

W

wag [wag] *n.* one who jokes.

waif [wāf] *n.* homeless person, especially a child.

wan [won] *adj.* **1.** pale; sickly. **2.** weak; faint. —**wanly,** *adv.*

ware [wâr] *n.* item for sale.

wayfarer [wā′fâr′ər] *n.* traveler, usually on foot.

wrath [rath] *n.* rage; extreme anger.

wrest [rest] *v.* to extract by exerting great effort.

Z

zeal [zēl] *n.* great enthusiasm.

---

at; āpe; cär; end; mē; it; īce; hot; ōld; fôrk; wood; fōōl; oil;
out; up; ūse; turn; ə in ago, taken, pencil, lemon, circus;
bat; chin; dear; five; game; hit; hw in white; joke; kit; lid;
man; not; singer; pail; ride; sat; shoe; tag; thin; this; very;
wet; yes; zoo; zh in treasure; KH in loch, German ach;
N in French bon; œ in French feu, German schön

Glossary **627**

Continued from page iv

Chatto and Windus Ltd.
VIRGIL: Excerpt from the *Aeneid* translated by C. Day Lewis. Reprinted by permission of the Executors of the Estate of C. Day Lewis and Chatto and Windus Ltd.

Judith Ciardi
DANTE ALIGHIERI: Excerpt from *The Inferno* translated by John Ciardi. Copyright 1954 by John Ciardi. Copyright © renewed 1982 by John Ciardi. Excerpt from *The Divine Comedy* translated by John Ciardi. Copyright © 1961, 1965, 1967, 1970, 1977 by John Ciardi. Both used by permission of Mrs. Judith Ciardi.

Rosica Colin Limited
GIOVANNI BOCCACCIO: "Federigo's Falcon" (Fifth Day, Ninth Tale) from *The Decameron* translated by Richard Aldington. © Catherine Guillaume. Used by permission of Rosica Colin Limited.

N. J. Dawood
N.J. DAWOOD: "The Second Voyage of Sindbad the Sailor" from *Tales from the Arabian Nights*. Retold from the Arabic by N. J. Dawood. Translations copyright © 1978 by N. J. Dawood. Used by permission of the translator.

Editions La Decouverte
CHARLOTTE H. BRUNER: "The Story of the Chest" from *Unwinding Threads*. Originally published as "Le grain magique" by Marguerite Amrouche. Copyright Librairie Maspero, 1966 Paris. Reprinted by permission of Editions La Decouverte.

Joan Daves
HEINRICH BÖLL: "The Laugher" from *18 Stories,* translated by Leila Vennewitz. Copyright © 1966 by Heinrich Böll.
GABRIELA MISTRAL: "Rocking" from *Selected Poems of Gabriela Mistral* translated and edited by Doris Dana. Copyright © 1961, 1964, 1970, 1971 by Doris Dana. Both are reprinted by permission of Joan Daves.

Delacorte Press/Seymour Lawrence
JORGE LUIS BORGES: "Afterglow" from *Jorge Luis Borges: Selected Poems 1923–1967* edited, with an Introduction and Notes, by Norman Thomas Di Giovanni. Copyright © 1968, 1969, 1970, 1971, 1972 by Jorge Luis Borges, Emece Editores, S. A. and Norman Thomas Di Giovanni. Reprinted by permission of Delacorte Press/Seymour Lawrence and Emece Editores S. A.

Devin-Adair Publishers, Inc.
SEAN O'FAOLAIN: "The Trout" from *The Man Who Invented Sin.* Copyright 1948, 1976 by Devin-Adair, Inc., 6 North Water Street, Greenwich, Connecticut 06830. All Rights Reserved. No portion of this book may be quoted without permission of the publisher. Used by permission.

Doubleday & Company, Inc.
CHINUA ACHEBE: "Dead Men's Path" from *Girls at War and Other Stories.* Copyright © 1972, 1973 by Chinua Achebe.
HAROLD G. HENDERSON: Excerpts from *An Introduction to Haiku.* Copyright © 1958 by Harold G. Henderson.
HOMER: Excerpt from the *Iliad* translation copyright © 1974 by Robert Fitzgerald. Excerpt from the *Odyssey* translation copyright © 1961, 1963 by Robert Fitzgerald. Used by permission.

VIRGIL: Excerpt from the *Aeneid* translation copyright © 1980, 1982, 1983 by Robert Fitzgerald. Used by permission. All are used by permission of Doubleday, a division of Bantam, Doubleday, Dell Publishing Group, Inc.

Duke University Press
ANTONIO MACHADO: "Winter Sun" from *Solitudes, Galleries and Other Poems.* Reprinted by permission of the publisher.

The Ecco Press
CZESLAW MILOSZ: "Encounter" from *The Collected Poems: 1931–1987.* Copyright © Czeslaw Milosz Royalties, Inc. First published by the Ecco Press in 1988. Reprinted by permission.

Editorial Extemporáneos S. A.
GERARDO MARÍA: "Matusalén, the Village Without Time" from *Y después de Dios . . . y otros cuentos.* Reprinted by permission of the publisher, Editorial Extemporáneos S. A., Mexico.

Espasa Calpe, S.A.
GABRIEL GARCÍA MÁRQUEZ: Excerpt from *Cien Años de Soledad.* Copyright © 1973 by Selecciones Austral, Espasa Calpe, S.A.

Farrar, Straus & Giroux, Inc.
COLETTE: Excerpts from *Earthly Paradise,* translated and edited by Robert Phelps. Copyright © 1966 by Farrar, Strauss & Giroux, Inc.
CAMARA LAYE: "The Snake and the Goldsmith" from *The Dark Child.* Copyright © 1954, 1982 by Camara Laye.
FRANCOISE MALLET-JORIS: "Air Des Clochettes" from *Cordelia and Other Stories.* Copyright © 1965 by Françoise Mallet-Joris.
NELLY SACHS: "The Swan" from *O the Chimneys.* Copyright © 1967 by Farrar, Straus & Giroux, Inc.
ISAAC BASHEVIS SINGER: "Shosha" from *A Day of Pleasure.* Copyright © 1963, 1965, 1966, 1969 by Isaac Bashevis Singer.
ALEKSANDR SOLZHENITSYN: "Freedom to Breathe," "The Duckling," and "A Storm in the Mountains" from *Stories and Prose Poems.* Translation copyright © 1970, 1971 by Michael Glenny. All are reprinted by permission of Farrar, Straus & Giroux, Inc.

Florence Feiler Literary Agency
ISAK DINESEN: "The Iguana" from *Out of Africa.* Copyright 1937 by Random House, Inc. and renewed 1965 by Rungstedlundfonden. Reprinted by permission of Florence Feiler Literary Agency.

Carl Fischer, Inc.
A. B. ("BANJO") PATERSON: "Waltzing Matilda" is copyright © 1936 by Allan & Co., Prop. Ltd., Melbourne. Copyright © 1941 by Carl Fischer, Inc., New York. International Copyright Secured. All Rights Reserved. Reprinted by permission of Carl Fischer, Inc., New York.

Foreign Language Press
TU PENG-CHENG: "Lingkuan Gorge" from *Sowing the Clouds.* Published by Foreign Languages Press, Beijing, China. Second Edition 1964. Reprinted by permission of the publisher.

N. V. M. Gonzalez
N. V. M. GONZALEZ: "On the Ferry" from *Modern Stories from Many Lands* edited by Charles Angoff. Used by permission of the author.

Grove Weidenfeld
SEAMI MOTOKIYO: "The Dwarf Trees" from *The Nō Plays of Japan* by Arthur Waley. Copyright 1922 by Arthur Waley, copyright renewed. Reprinted by permission of Grove Weidenfeld.

Harcourt Brace Jovanovich, Inc.
C. P. CAVAFY: "Che Fece . . . Il Gran Rifiuto" from *The Complete Poems of Cavafy,* Expanded Edition, translated and copyright © 1961 by Rae Dalven.
HEINRICH HEINE: "The Lorelei" (originally titled "The Loreley") translated by Louis Untermeyer in *Heinrich Heine: Paradox and Poet, The Poems.* Copyright 1937 by Harcourt Brace Jovanovich, Inc. and renewed 1965 by Louis Untermeyer. All are reprinted by permission of Harcourt Brace Jovanovich, Inc.

Harper & Row, Publishers, Inc.
GABRIEL GARCÍA MÁRQUEZ: "Tuesday Siesta" from *No One Writes to the Colonel & Other Stories.* English language translation copyright © 1968 by Harper & Row, Publishers, Inc.
SANTHA RAMA RAU: "By Any Other Name" from *Gifts of Passage.* Copyright © 1961 by Vasanthi Rama Rau Bowers; copyright © renewed 1989 by the author. Reprinted by permission of Harper & Row, Publishers, Inc.

William Heinemann Ltd.
THOMAS WOLFE: "The Far and the Near" from *From Death to Morning.*

The Hispanic Society of America
FEDERICO GARCÍA LORCA: "The Guitar" translated by Elizabeth du Gué Trapier from *Translations from the Hispanic Poets.* Copyright 1938. Used by permission of the Hispanic Society of America.

Holmes & Meier Publishers, Inc.
JOSÉ MARTÍ: XXXIX from *José Martí, Major Poems* (a bilingual edition), translated by Elinor Randall and edited by Philip S. Foner (New York: Holmes & Meier, 1982), p. 95. Copyright © 1982 by Holmes & Meier. Reprinted by permission of the publisher.

Houghton Mifflin Company
E. POWYS MATHERS: "Tu Fu: The Emperor" from *Colored Stars.*

Indiana University Press
OVID: Excerpt from "Midas" from *Metamorphoses* translated by Rolfe Humphries. Copyright 1955 Indiana University Press and reprinted with their permission.

George Kearns
PABLO NERUDA: "The Horses" translated by George Kearns. Translation copyright © 1974 George Kearns. Reprinted by permission of the translator.

Barbara Kimenye
BARBARA KIMENYE: "The Winter" from *Kalasanda.* Copyright © 1965 by Barbara Kimenye. Reprinted by permission of the author.

Kodansha International Ltd.
MATSUO BASHŌ: Haiku from *A Haiku Journey* translated and introduced by Dorothy Britton. Copyright © 1974 by Kodansha International Ltd. Reprinted by permission of the publisher.

Las Americas Publishing Company
ANDRÉS HENESTROSA: "The Bat"
MANUEL ROJAS: "The Glass of Milk"
Both are from *Short Stories of Latin America* edited by Arturo Torres-Rioseco, translated by Zoila Nelken. Copyright 1963 by Las Americas Publishing Company. Reprinted by permission of the publisher.

Lemon, Unna & Durbridge, Ltd.
STAN BARSTOW: "The Actor" from *The Desperadoes and Other Stories.* Copyright 1961 by Michael Joseph, Ltd. Used by permission of Lemon, Unna & Durbridge, Ltd.

Little, Brown and Company
GEORGE SEFERIS: "I Am Sorry" from *Poems, 1960* translated from the Greek by Rex Warner. English translation © Rex Warner 1960. Reprinted by permission of Little, Brown and Company.

McClelland and Stewart Limited
GABRIELLE ROY: "Hoodoo Valley" from *Garden in the Wind.* Copyright 1977. Used by permission of the Canadian Publishers, McClelland and Stewart, Toronto.

McGraw-Hill Book Company, Inc.
MIGUEL DE CERVANTES: "Don Quixote" from *Some Adventures of Don Quixote,* translated by George Kearns. Translation copyright © 1974, 1963 by the McGraw-Hill Book Company, Inc.
VICTOR HUGO: "June Nights" translated by George Kearns. Translation copyright © 1974, 1963 by the McGraw-Hill Book Company, Inc.
JEAN DE LA FONTAINE: "The Fox and the Crow" translated by George Kearns. Translation copyright © 1974, 1963 by the McGraw-Hill Book Company, Inc.
JAIME TORRES BODET: "The Window" translated by George Kearns. Translation copyright © 1974, 1963 by the McGraw-Hill Book Company, Inc.

Macmillan Accounts and Administration Ltd.
RABINDRANATH TAGORE: "The Kabuliwallah" (originally titled "The Cabuliwallah") from *The Hungry Stones and Other Stories.* Copyright 1916. Reprinted by permission of Macmillan, London and Basingstoke.

Macmillan Publishing Company
JOSEPH (IOSIP) BRODSKY: "The Monument" from *Selected Translations 1948–1968* by W. S. Merwin. Copyright © 1968 by W. S. Merwin. Reprinted by permission of Atheneum Publishers, an imprint of Macmillan Publishing Company.
GRAZIA DELEDDA: "The Shoes" translated by Alethea Graham (pp. 260–264) in *The Copeland Translations.* Copyright 1934 by Charles Townsend Copeland, copyright renewed © 1962 Charles F. Dunbar. Reprinted with permission of Charles Scribner's Sons, an imprint of Macmillan Publishing Company.
ERNEST HEMINGWAY: "Old Man at the Bridge" from *The Short Stories of Ernest Hemingway.* Copyright 1938 by Ernest Hemingway, renewal copyright © 1966 by Mary Hemingway. Reprinted with permission of Charles Scribner's Sons, an imprint of Macmillan Publishing Company.
ALAN PATON: "The Quarry" from *Knocking on the Door.* Copyright © 1975 by Alan Paton. Reprinted with permission

Acknowledgments **629**

of Charles Scribner's Sons, an imprint of Macmillan Publishing Company.

RABINDRANATH TAGORE: "The Cabuliwallah" from *The Hungry Stones and Other Stories.* Copyright 1916 by Macmillan Publishing Company, renewed 1944 by Rabindranath Tagore and Henry L. S. Polak.

THOMAS WOLFE: "The Far and the Near" from *From Death to Morning.* Copyright 1935 by International Magazine Company, Inc., renewal copyright © 1963 by Paul Gitlin. Reprinted with permission of Charles Scribner's Sons, an imprint of Macmillan Publishing Company.

WILLIAM BUTLER YEATS: "Politics" from *The Poems of W. B. Yeats: A New Edition* edited by Richard J. Finneran. Copyright 1940 by Georgie Yeats, renewed 1968 by Bertha Georgie Yeats, Michael Butler Yeats, and Anne Yeats.

The Tagore and Yeats selections are reprinted by permission of Macmillan Publishing Company.

Sarojini Naidu

SAROJINI NAIDU: "Street Cries" from *The Sceptered Flute.* Copyright © 1956 by Sarojini Naidu and originally published by Dodd, Mead & Company, Inc.

New Directions Publishing Corporation

JORGE CARRERA ANDRADE: "Reaping the Barley" translated by Muna Lee de Muñoz Marín from *Anthology of Latin-American Poetry* edited by Dudley Fitts. Copyright © 1942, 1947 by New Directions Publishing Corporation.

FEDERICO GARCÍA LORCA: "The Guitar" translated by J. L. Gili and Stephen Spender from *Selected Poems of Federico García Lorca.* Copyright 1955 by New Directions Publishing Corporation.

LI PO: "Taking Leave of a Friend" from *Personae* by Ezra Pound. Copyright 1926 by Ezra Pound.

OCTAVIO PAZ: "Wind and Water and Stone" from *The Collected Poems of Octavio Paz, 1957–1987* edited and translated by Eliot Weinberger. © 1979 by Octavio Paz and Eliot Weinberger. Reprinted by permission of New Directions Publishing Corporation.

Harold Ober Associates, Inc.

CHINUA ACHEBE: "Dead Men's Path" from *Girls at War and Other Stories.* Copyright © 1972, 1973 by Chinua Achebe. Reprinted by permission of Harold Ober Associates, Inc.

Deborah Owens Ltd.

JAN NERUDA: "Hastrman" from *Tales of the Little Quarter* translated from the original Czech by Edith Pargeter. Reprinted by permission.

Oxford University Press

BJØRNSTJERNE BJØRNSON: "The Father" from *Slaves of Love and Other Norwegian Short Stories* edited and translated by James McFarlane (1982).

LADY ŌTOMO OF SAKANOYÉ: "My Heart, Thinking . . ." from *Japanese Poetry: "The Uta"* translated by Arthur Waley (1919).

THUCYDIDES: "Pericles' Funeral Oration" from *The History of the Peloponnesian War* edited and translated by Sir Richard Livingstone (1943).

All are reprinted by permission of Oxford University Press.

Paragon Book Reprint Corp.

LI PO: "On a Quiet Night" from *The Works of Li Po the Chinese Poet* translated by Shigeyoshi Obata. Published in 1965 by Paragon Book Reprint Corp.

The Paris Review

ANNA AKHMATOVA: "Lot's Wife" from *Walking to Sleep* translated by Richard Wilbur. Copyright © *The Paris Review,* Inc. Reprinted by permission.

Penguin Books Ltd.

YEVGENY YEVTUSHENKO: "Colors" from *Yevtushenko: Selected Poems* translated by Robin Milner-Gulland and Peter Levi, SJ (Penguin Books, 1962), copyright © Robin Milner-Gulland and Peter Levi, 1962. Reprinted by permission of Penguin Books Ltd.

Penguin USA

EDMOND ROSTAND: From *Cyrano de Bergerac: A Heroic Comedy in Five Acts* translated by Lowell Bair. Copyright © 1972 by Lowell Bair. Reprinted by permission of New American Library, a division of Penguin USA, Inc.

Persea Books, Inc.

NAZIM HIKMET: "The World, My Friends, My Enemies, You, and the Earth" from *Things I Didn't Know I Loved.* Copyright © 1975 by Randy Blasing and Mutlu Konuk. Reprinted by permission of the publisher.

Peters, Fraser & Dunlop, Ltd.

VIRGIL: Excerpt from the *Aeneid* translated by C. Day Lewis. Reprinted by permission of the Peters, Fraser & Dunlop Group, Ltd.

Princeton University Press

ROBERT P. GOLDMAN: Excerpt from *The Ramayana of Valmiki: An Epic of Ancient India,* Vol. I: "Balakanda." Introduction and translation by Robert P. Goldman. Copyright © 1985 by Princeton University Press. Used by permission of the publisher.

Random House, Inc.

ALBERT CAMUS: "The Guest" from *Exile and the Kingdom,* translated by Justin O'Brien. Copyright © 1957, 1958 by Alfred A. Knopf, Inc. Reprinted by permission of the publisher.

FRANÇOIS DE LA ROCHEFOUCAULD: Excerpts from *The Maxims of La Rochefoucauld* translated by Louis Kronenberger. Copyright © 1959 by Random House, Inc.

ISAK DINESEN: "The Iguana" from *Out of Africa.* Copyright 1937 by Random House, Inc. and renewed 1965 by Rungstedlundfonden.

THOMAS MANN: "The Infant Prodigy" is copyright 1936 and renewed 1964 by Alfred A. Knopf, Inc. Reprinted from *Stories of Three Decades* by Thomas Mann translated by H. T. Lowe-Porter. Reprinted by permission of Alfred A. Knopf, Inc.

KATHERINE MANSFIELD: "The Doll's House" is copyright 1923 by Alfred A. Knopf, Inc. and renewed 1951 by John Middleton Murray. Reprinted from *The Short Stories of Katherine Mansfield* by permission of Alfred A. Knopf, Inc.

V. S. NAIPAUL: Specified excerpt from "The Crocodiles of Yamoussoukro" from *Finding the Center, Two Narratives* by V. S. Naipaul. Copyright © 1984 by V. S. Naipaul. Reprinted by permission of Alfred A. Knopf, Inc.

RAINER MARIA RILKE: "Spanish Dancer" from *The Selected Poetry of Rainer Maria Rilke* translated by Stephen Mitchell. Copyright © 1982 by Stephen Mitchell.

All selections not otherwise identified are reprinted by permission of Random House, Inc.

630 *Acknowledgments*

David Ray
CHIYO: "After a Long Winter" translated by David Ray. This appeared originally in *A Book of Women Poets from Antiquity to Now* edited by Barnstone and Barnstone, Schocken Books.

Fonds Gabrielle Roy
GABRIELLE ROY: "Hoodoo Valley" from *Garden in the Wind.* © Fonds Gabrielle Roy. Reprinted by permission.

Tayeb Salih
TAYEB SALIH: "A Handful of Dates" from *The Wedding of Zein,* translated by Denys Johnson-Davies. © 1968 Tayeb Salih and Denys Johnson-Davies.

The Seal Press
ÅSTA HOLTH: "Salt" from *An Everyday Story: Norwegian Women's Fiction.* Translated and edited by Katherine Hanson. Copyright © 1984 by The Seal Press. Reprinted by permission of the publisher.

Society for Promoting Christian Knowledge
SWAHILI TRADITIONAL: "The Hare and the Lion" from *Swahili Tales,* collected and translated by Edward Steere, LL.D. Published in 1928 by the Society for Promoting Christian Knowledge.

Third Press/Joseph Okpaku Publishing Co.
OSWALD MBUYISENI MTSHALI: "Sunset" from *Sounds of a Cowhide Drum.* Copyright © 1972 by The Third Press Joseph Okpaku Publishing Co., Inc.
LÉOPOLD SEDAR SENGHOR: "For Khalam" from *Nocturnes.* © Editions du Seuil. Translation copyright © 1971 John Reed and Clive Wake.

Three Continents Press, Inc.
NAGUIB MAHFOUZ: "A Tale of Our Quarter" from *Fountain and Tomb.* Translated by James Kenneson. Copyright James Kenneson © 1988. Published by Three Continents Press, Washington, D.C. and reprinted with their permission.

Jaime Torres Bodet
JAIME TORRES BODET: "The Window."

Charles E. Tuttle Co., Inc.
AKUTAGAWA RYŪNOSUKE: "Autumn Mountain" from *Modern Japanese Stories* edited by Ivan Morris. Published by Charles E. Tuttle Co., Inc. and used with their permission.

University of Alabama Press
FRANCESCO PETRARCA (PETRARCH): "It Was That Very Day on Which the Sun" (No. III) from *Petrarch: Selected Poems* translated by Anthony Mortimer. Copyright © 1977 by the University of Alabama Press. Reprinted by permission of the publisher.

University of Baroda Press
G. H. BHATT: Excerpt from *The Valmiki-Ramayana,* Book I, the "Balakanda," edited by G. H. Bhatt. Published in 1960 by the University of Baroda Press.

University of California Press
SAPPHO: "Fragment of a Lullaby" from *Sappho: A New Translation* translated by Mary Barnard. Copyright © 1958 by the Regents of the University of California, © renewed 1984 Mary Barnard. Reprinted by permission of the University of California Press.

University of Chicago Press
HORACE: Ode excerpted from *The Odes and Epodes of Horace* translated by Joseph P. Clancy. © 1960 by the University of Chicago. Reprinted by permission of the University of Chicago Press and the translator.

University of Colorado
BORIS PASTERNAK: "My Pictures Swing" from *Boris Pasternak: Poems* translated by Eugene M. Kayden. Reprinted by permission of the University of Colorado.

University of Texas Press
JUAN RAMÓN JIMÉNEZ: Excerpt from *Platero and I,* translated by Eloise Roach. By permission of University of Texas Press.

University of Wisconsin Press
CAMILO JOSÉ CELA: "Traveling in the Alcarria" from *Journey to the Alcarria,* translated by Frances M. López-Morillas. Copyright © 1948 by Camilo José Cela. Copyright © 1984 by the Regents of the University of Wisconsin. Reprinted by permission of the publisher, the University of Wisconsin Press.

University Press of New England
JOÃO CABRAL DE MELO NETO: "Weaving the Morning" from *An Anthology of Twentieth-Century Brazilian Poetry.* Copyright © 1972 by João Cabral de Melo Neto. Reprinted by permission of University Press of New England.

Viking Penguin, Inc.
RUMER GODDEN: "You Need to Go Upstairs" from *Gone, A Thread of Stories.* Copyright 1940, 1944, 1947, 1948, 1953, 1954. © 1959, 1968 by Rumer Godden.
R. K. NARAYAN: "Like the Sun" from *Under the Banyan Tree and Other Stories.* Copyright © 1985 R. K. Narayan. Both are reprinted by permission of Viking Penguin, Inc., a division of Penguin USA

Weidenfeld (Publishers) Ltd.
GABON PYGMY TRADITIONAL: "All That Dances" from *Primitive Song* by C. M. Bowra.

Editions YMCA Press
ALEKSANDR SOLZHENITSYN: "Freedom to Breathe," "The Duckling," and "A Storm in the Mountains" from *Stories and Prose Poems.* Translation copyright © 1970, 1971 by Michael Glenny.

Map Credit: Joe Le Monnier

Photo Credits: AKG, Berlin, pp. 145, 204, 335t. Art Resource: pp. 27 Thyssen-Bornemisza Collection, Switzerland/Nimatallah; 41 Turnley; 107, 110 Scala; 146 National Gallery, Prague; 163 Musée de Saint-Denis, France, © ARS NY/Spadem; 228-229 Tutino; 230 Scala; 237 Alinari; 269 Giraudon; 275 Scala; 277 Biblioteca Marciana, Venice, Giraudon; 300 Scala; 360 Archaeological Museum, Delphi; 366 © 1986 Scala; 401, Rodin Museum, Paris. ARS NY/Spadem: 423, 545t Scala; 424 Alinari; 434 Bodleian Library, Oxford/Bridgeman; 436-437 Scala; 544b Vatican Museum, Rome/Scala; 546-547b National Museum, Belgrade/Scala; 547b

National Museum, Naples/Scala; 549t Christie's, London/ Bridgeman; 551b Uffizi, Florence; 552b Cooper-Hewitt Museum, Smithsonian Institution; 557t Prado, Madrid/Scala; 557b Musée Picasso, Antibes, ARS/Spadem; © 1990 The Art Institute of Chicago, All Rights Reserved pp. xxviii-1, 395, Helen Birch Bartlett Memorial Collection. Australian Overseas Information Service, p. 356. The Baltimore Museum of Art: pp. 99, 221, The Cone Collection, formed by Dr. Claribel Cone and Miss Etta Cone of Baltimore, Maryland. The Bettmann Archive: pp. 44, 48, 167, 188, 193, 261, 288t, 270, 294, 307t, 330t, 359, 400, 420, 463. Bettmann / Hulton, p. 311. Courtesy of Hayyim Nahman Bialik, p. 315t. The Brooklyn Museum: pp. 93 in memory of Dick S. Ramsay; 315b purchased by special subscription; 410 Museum Collection Fund; 449 The Caroline A.L. Pratt Fund, Frederick Loeser Fund, and Carll H. deSilver Fund. Lee Boltin: p. 231, 235, 284-285, 563b, 573b. The Boston Museum of Fine Arts, Massachusetts: pp. 183, 265 Perkins Collection; 375 gift of John Goelet. The Bridgeman Art Library, London: pp. 67 Musée D'Orsay, Paris; 78 Chester Beatty Library and Gallery of Oriental Art, Dublin. Brown University, Providence, R.I.: pp. 191 Anne S.K. Brown Military Collection, Brown University Library; 351 John Carter Brown Library. Bulloz, Paris, p. 304b Musée D'Orsay. © Nancy Crampton: pp. 345, 403. Dallas Museum of Art, p. 327 The Wendy and Emery Reves Collection. Detroit Institute of Arts, Michigan, p. 61 bequest of Dr. Wilhelm R. Valentiner. Leo de Wys: pp. 282 Steve Vidler; 307b Rocky Weldon; 551t V. Lefteroff; 553t Jean Paul Nacivet; 560 Steve Vidler; 565t J. Messerschmidt; 568r Steve Vidler; 577t. The Fine Arts Museums of San Francisco, California, p. 168 Achenback Foundation for Graphic Arts, gift of Mr. and Mrs. John D. Rockefeller III. The Forbes Collection, New York, p. 571b. Foreign Languages Press, p. 72. Courtesy Galería Arvil, Mexico, p. 199. Courtesy of N.V.M. Gonzalez, p. 83. Courtesy Grace Borgenicht Gallery, New York, p. 155. Courtesy Graham Modern, New York, p. 217. Solomon R. Guggenheim Museum, New York, p. 571t gift, Solomon R. Guggenheim, 1937. Gyldendal Norsk Forlag, p. 129. © George Hallett/Heinemann International, p. 77. Helsingborgs Museum, Sweden, p. 69. Michael Holford, London: pp. 322, 577b Museum für Völkerkunde, Berlin; 439, 441, 576b British Museum. The Image Bank: pp. 84 Harald Sund; 348 Hans Wolf. The Image Works: pp. 18, 29, 296t, 305, 308 © Topham; 140 © PPA Archives; 353 Margot Granitsas Archives. INBA, Mexico, p. 414. Israel Museum, Jerusalem, p. 368. Courtesy Glenn C. Janss Collection, p. 35. Courtesy Japan Society, p. 180. © Clems Kalischer, p. 365. Keystone Photos, p. 252. Kobal Collection, p. 540. Magnum Photos, p. 194 Robert Capa. © Lucy Maxym, *Russian Lacquer Legends and Fairy Tales, Volume II*, p. 568l. McClelland & Stewart Publishing, p. 120 John Reeves. Marion Koogler McNay Art Museum, San Antonio, Texas, p. 311 gift of the estate of Tom Slick. Ann Münchow, Aachen, Germany: p. 444 Rautenstrauch-Joset Museum, Cologne. The Metropolitan Museum of Art: pp. 52 Rogers Fund; 143 gift of Alice E. Getty, 1946; 243, 290 The Alice and Nasli Heeramaneck Collection, gift of Alice Heeramaneck, 1985; 287 Fletcher Fund, 1927; 290, 293 bequest of Mrs. H. O. Havemeyer, 1929, The H. O. Havemeyer Collection; 319 bequest of Benjamin Altman, 1913; 337b gift of Mrs. Henry-George J. McNeary, 1971; 344b gift of Lila Acheson Wallace, 1983; 370-371 (Detail) gift of Mrs. John H. Ballantine, 1947; 457 purchase, Joseph Pulitzer Bequest, 1932; 461 The Harry C.C. Packard Collection of Asian Art, gift of Harry C.C. Packard and Purchase, Fletcher, Rogers, Harris Brisbane, Dick and Louis V. Bell Funds, Joseph Pulitzer Bequest and The Annenberg Fund, Inc., Gift, 1975; 548t gift of Mrs. Evelyn Start, 1974; 549b Roger Lehman Collection, 1975; 564 gift of Helen C. Lanier, 1981; 565bl gift of R. Thornton Wilson, in memory of Florence Ellsworth Wilson, 1950; 575 (Detail) Winifred Foundation gift, 1970, The Helena Woolworth McCann Collection; 580b Rogers Fund, 1925; 583t The James F. Ballard Collection, gift of James F. Ballard, 1922; 583b gift of Charles B. Hoyt, 1932. The Museum of Modern Art, New York: pp. 175 (Detail) *The Park,* c. 1910, Gustav Klimt, Gertrud A. Mellon Fund; 341 *Guitar,* 1912-13, Pablo Picasso, gift of the artist. National Gallery of Art, Washington, D.C.: 123 gift of Dr. Margaret I. Handy; 137 Alisa Mellon Bruce Fund; 158 Chester Dale Fund; 288b, 555 Chester Dale Collection; 301b Andrew W. Mellon Collection. National Gallery, Oslo, Norway, p. 46. National Museum of African Art, Washington, D.C., p. 380 Eliot Elisofon Archives. New York Public Library, p. 259 The Music Division, New York Public Library at Lincoln Center, Astor, Lenox and Tilden Foundations. Office of India Library, London, p. 324b. Oronoz, Madrid, p. 563t Museum of Modern Art, Madrid. Phillips Collection, Washington, D.C.: pp. 316b, 335b. Photo Researchers: pp. 87 © Soames Summerhays; 357 Bill Bachman; 556 © Paolo Koch; 559, 572b © Carl Purcell; 573t © Marcello Bertinetti; 581t Lionello Labbri. Piccadilly Gallery, London, p. 396 and courtesy of the artist. Private Collection, p. 56. Max Polster Archive: pp. 238, 240, 249. Rebus, Inc., p. 313 Museum für Völkerkunde, Berlin. The Regis Collection, Minneapolis, Minnesota, p. 333. Doran H. Ross, Los Angeles, pp. 226, 385, 431. Arthur M. Sackler Museum, Harvard University, Cambridge, Massachusetts, p. 244 private collection. Saint Louis Art Museum, Missouri, p. 12 museum purchase. Sherry French Gallery, New York, p. 330b. Collection Luciana and Michael Solomon, Los Angeles, California, p. 418. Sovfoto: pp. 298, 364 Tass. Städtische Galerie im Lenbachhaus, Munich, Germany: pp. 309, 567. The Stock Market: pp. 548b © Ken Straiton; 552t © Davil Ball; 553b © Bill Wassman; 565br © Hans-Peter Merten; 569 © Robert Semeniuk; 572t © R. Ian Lloyd; 580t © David Bell. Studio Museum in Harlem, New York: pp. 5, 42. Martha Swope: pp. 464-536 American Shakespeare Festival, Stratford, Conn. The Turku Art Museum, Finland, p. 115. Courtesy of UNESCO, Paris, p. 354. UPI/Bettmann Newsphotos: pp. 112, 157, 197, 291, 332, 344t, 362, 372, 409, 413. Roger Viollet, Paris: pp. 23, 63, 161, 172, 208, 257, 290t; 134 Alinari-Viollet; 11, 104, 239t, 304t, 340 © Harlonique-Viollet; 239, 324t Lapi-Viollet; 337t, 392, 398 Collection Viollet. Virginia Museum of Fine Arts, Richmond, p. 21 collection of Mr. and Mrs. Paul Mellon. Walker Art Center, Minneapolis, p. 206 art center acquisition fund, 1983. H.C. Weng/Collection Wan-go, p. 75. Werner Foreman Archive, London: pp. 296b, 576tl; 579 Museum für Völkerkunde, Berlin. Wide World Photos: pp. 39, 91, 96, 219, 301t, 316t, 338, 347, 350, 399, 417, 430. Woodfin Camp & Associates: pp. 544t © W. Hubbell; 545b © Robert Frerck; 561b © Bob Nickelsberg; 561t © Loren McIntyre; 581b © Geoffrey Clifford. Yivo Institute for Jewish Research, New York: pp. 404, 407.

632 *Acknowledgments*

INDEX OF SKILLS

Page numbers in boldface italics indicate entries in the Writing About Literature Handbook. Page numbers in italics indicate entries in the Guide to Literary Movements and the Literary Terms Handbook.

LITERARY SKILLS

Aestheticism, *584*
Allegory, 281
Alliteration, 328, **608,** *612*
Allusion, 156, 166, *612*
Analogy, *612*
Anecdote, 397, *612*
Antagonist, *612*
Apostrophe, 361
Argument, *612*
Aside, *612*
Assonance, 302, 328, **608,** *612*
Atmosphere, 128, *612*
Autobiography, 378, *612*

Ballad, 349, *612*
  folk, 349, *612*
  literary, 349, *612*
  popular, 349, *612*
Biography, 397, *612*
Blank verse, *612*

Character, 43, 55, 71, 166, 218, 510, 538, **596,** *613*
  in drama, 510, 538
  dynamic, 71, **596**
  flat, 71, **596**
  motivation, 55, **596,** *616*
  round, 71, **596**
  in short story, 55, 71, 218
  and staging, 510
  static, 71, **596**
Character foils, 166, *615*
Characterization, 43, *613*
  direct, 43, *613*
  indirect, 43, *613*
Classical literature, *584*
Climax, 10, 526, **594,** *613*
  in drama, 526
  in short story, 10
Comedy, 463, *613*
  heroic, 463
Concrete language, 422
Concrete poem, *613*

Conflict, 17, 22, 526, *613*
  in drama, 526
  external, 17, 22, *613*
  internal, 22, *613*
  in short story, 17, 22, 133
Connotation, 343, *613*
Consonance, 302, **608**
Couplet, 299, *613*

Denotation, *613*
Description, *613*
Dialect, *613*
Dialogue, 452, *614*
Diction, 343
Drama, 452, 453, 462, 494, *614*
  No theater, 453, 462, *617*
Dramatic convention, *614*
Dramatic monologue, *614*

Enlightenment, *584*
Epic, 268, 274, *614*
Epic hero, 274, *614*
Epithet, 268
Essay, 408, 422, 433, *614*
  descriptive, 422, *614*
  expository, 433, *614*
  narrative, 408, *614*
  persuasive, *614*
Exposition, 10, 526, **594,** *614*

Fable, 241, *614*
Falling action, 10, 526, **594,** *614*
  in drama, 526
  in short story, 10
Fantasy, 156
Fiction, 156, *615*
  fantastic, 156
  realistic, 156
Figurative language, 43, 310, 419, *615*
Figures of speech, 310, 419, *615*
Foil, 166, *615*
Folk song, 358
Folk tale, 256, 257
Foot, *615*

Foreshadowing, 10, *595, 615*
Frame story, 134, 187, *615*
Free verse, 334, *615*

Hero, epic, 274, *614*

Iambic pentameter, 331, *615*
Image, 306, **608,** *615*
Imagery, 306, *615*
Imagism, *585*
Impact, **610**
Irony, 28, 38, 207, 218, 494, 538, *615*
  dramatic, 38, 494, *616*
  situational, 38
  and surprise endings, 28
  verbal, *616*

Legend, 251
Literal language, *616*
Local color, *616*

Magic Realism, 152, *585*
Maxim, 402, *616*
Medieval literature, *584*
Metamorphosis, 233
Metaphor, 310, 314, 419, **608,** *616*
  implied, 310
  extended, 314
Meter, 331, *616*
Modernism, *585*
Monologue, *616*
Mood, 128, 306, *616*
Moral, 241, *616*
Motivation, 55, **596,** *616*
Myth, 230, 233, 234, 236, *616*
Mythology, Greek and Roman, 230, 233, 361

Narration, *616*
Narrative hook, 10, **594,** *616*
Narrator, 82, 160, *617*
Naturalism, *585*
Neoclassicism, *584*
Nonfiction, **606,** *617*
Novel, 161, *617*

This index lists the skills examined in the study aids that follow each selection. In this index the following headings are used: Literary Skills (for Literary Focus), Composition Skills (for Composition), and Vocabulary Skills (for Language Study). The index identifies the pages on which the skills are taught or reinforced. Page numbers in boldface italics indicate entries in the Writing About Literature Handbook. Page numbers in lightface italics indicate entries in the Guide to Literary Movements or the Literary Terms Handbook.

Ode, 361
  Horatian, 361
Onomatopoeia, 323, **608, 617**

Parable, *617*
Parallelism, 328, *617*
Personification, 317, **608,** *617*
Persuasion, 429, *617*
Plot, 10, 133, 218, 526, 538, **594,** *617*
Poetry, 289, 292, 295, 320, 349, **608, 614, 616, 617,** *618*
  dramatic, 289, *614*
  haiku, 320
  lyric, 289, 292, *616*
  narrative, 289, 349, *617*
  speaker in, 295, **608**
Point of view, 82, 90, 103, 218, **600,** *618*
  first-person, 82, **600**
  limited third-person, 90, **600**
  omniscient, 103, **600**
Protagonist, *618*
Proverb, 43
Purpose, 378, 422, 429, **598, 606**
  in autobiography, 378
  in essay, 422
  in nonfiction, 606
  in short story, **598**
  in speech, 429

Realism, *585*
Realistic fiction, 156
Refrain, 323, 358
Renaissance literature, *584*
Repetition, *618*
Resolution, 10, **594,** *618*
Rhyme, 299, 302, **608,** *618*
  end, 299
  slant, 302
Rhyme scheme, 299, 302, 303, *618*
Rhythm, 331, **608,** *618*
Rising action, 10, 526, **594,** *618*
Romance, *619*
Romanticism, *584*

Satire, *619*
Saying, 402
Scansion, *619*
Sensory language, 412
Setting, 128, 218, 538, **598,** *619*

and atmosphere, 128
Short story, 207, 218, 225, *619*
  elements of, 218, 225
  single effect, 207
Simile, 268, 310, 314, 419, **608,** *619*
  epic, 268
  extended, 314
  Homeric, 268
Single effect, 207
Soliloquy, *619*
Sonnet, 302, 303, *619*
  Petrarchan, 302, *619*
  Shakespearean, 303, *619*
Speaker in a poem, 295, **608,** *619*
Speech, 429
Stage directions and staging, 452, 510, *619*
Stanza, 299, 302, 303, 349, *619*
  ballad, 349
  couplet, 299, 303
  octave, 299, 302
  quatrain, 299, 303, 349
  sestet, 299, 302
  in sonnet, 302
Stream of consciousness, 179, *619*
Style, 196, 218, *619*
Surprise endings, 28
Symbol, 151, 218, 355, 538, **604,** *619*
Symbolism, 355, *585*

Theme, 133, 139, 218, 352, 538, **602,** *620*
  in drama, 538
  implied, 139
  in poetry, 352
  in short story, 133, 139
  stated, 139
  unstated, 139
Thesis statement, 433, **592,** *620*
Tone, 111, 196, 218, 339, *620*
  in poetry, 339
  in short story, 111, 196
Topic sentence, **593**
Total effect, 225, 538, **610**
  in drama, 538
  in short story, 225
Tragedy, *620*
Translation, 343

Word choice, 343, *620*

COMPOSITION SKILLS

ANALYTICAL
Writing *about* the following:
Autobiography, 391
Character, 22, 47, 62, 71, 166, 256, 539, **596**
Comparison/contrast, 38, 71, 76, 111, 119, 133, 139, 151, 196, 225, 241, 256, 289, 292, 295, 303, 306, 310, 314, 317, 320, 331, 339, 343, 346, 355, 367, 402, 416, **596**
Drama, 539
Epic, 268
Essay, 416, 419, 433
Fantasy and reality, 156
Irony, 207
Nonfiction, 391, 402, 416, 419, 433, **606**
Plot, 17, **594**
Poetry, 260, 295, 297, 299, 303, 306, 314, 328, 331, 334, 336, 343, 346, 349, 355, 363, 367, **608**
  figurative language, 314, 336, 346
  free verse, 334
  imagery, 306, 336, 346
  lyric poem, 297
  poetic techniques, 349, 367
  sonnet, 303
  speaker in, 295
  translations, 343
Point of view, 82, 95, 103, 119, **600**
Purpose, 260, 416
Quotation, 90
Sensory details, 22
Setting, 133, 156, 160, **598**
Symbol, 151, 363, **604**
Theme, 144, 355, **602**
Title, 171
Tone, 111, 203
Total effect, 225, **610**
  in short story, 225

CREATIVE
Writing the following:
Advertisement, 207
Article, 260, 349
Autobiographical account, 378
Biographical sketch, 397
Description, 22, 103, 128, 160, 187, 336, 346

of character's experience, 22
of childhood experience, 160
of movement, 336
of process, 103
of setting, 128
of unreal experience, 346
of work of art, 187
Dialogue, 55, 218
Diary entry, 151, 171, 299
Drama, 38, 452, 539
Epic hero, 274
Epitaph, 203
Essay, 297, 408, 416, 422
    descriptive, 422
    about heritage, 297
    narrative, 408
    about nonfiction, 416
    about purpose, 416
Fable, 241, 245
Fantasy, 156
Folk tale, 256
Imagery, 306
Interviews, 268
Letter, 62, 171, 192, 303, 331, 363
    from character, 171, 192
    to poet, 331
    between sonnet speakers, 303
    with symbols, 363
    of thanks, 62
Narrative, 28, 76, 119, 139, 156,
    160, 166, 179, 233, 236, 251,
    256, 281
Poem, 292, 295, 297, 306, 314, 317,
    320, 323, 334, 336, 339, 343,
    346, 352, 355, 358, 361, 367,
    412, 416, 462
    about a cycle, 317
    about emotional incident, 339
    with extended simile or
        metaphor, 314

in free verse, 334
haiku, 320, 462
about heritage, 297
with imagery, 306
with invented speaker, 295
lullaby, 292
about movement, 336
about music, 343
about personal convictions, 352
political, 367
prose poem, 412, 416
as response to poem, 361
song, 323, 358
with symbolism, 355
about unreal experience, 346
Point of view, 82, 95, 119, 236
    different, 82, 236
    limited third-person, 95
    omniscient, 119
Reaction of character, 171
Report, job-related, 43
Response to poet, 361
Review of music, 144
Sequel, 179, 251
    to a legend, 251
    stream-of-consciousness, 179
Setting, 128, 156
Song, 323, 358
Speech, 429, 539
Symbolism, 355
Tone, different, 196

VOCABULARY SKILLS

LANGUAGE STUDY
Allusions, 166
Cognates, 47
Dialect and Anglicisms, 38
Dialect and slang, 358
Foreign titles, 179

French and Middle English, 17
French expressions, 397
Indo-European language family, 245
Jargon, 62
Name origins, 192
Proverbs and figurative language,
    43
Romance languages, 139
Shakespearean English, 303
Terms from ancient history, 292
Transliteration, 28, 76
Word origins
    African languages, 391
    Arabic, 251
    Celtic languages, 95
    Chinese, 187
    French, 17, 397, 538
    German, 336
    Greek, 241, 346, 429
    Greek and Roman mythology,
        233, 361
    Hebrew, 317
    Indian languages, 55, 378
    Italian, 225
    Japanese, 187, 462
    Latin, 274
    Malayo-Polynesian languages, 90
    Middle English, 17
    Native languages of Mexico,
        South America, Caribbean, 236
    Old English, 260
    Place names, 144
    Scandinavian languages, 71
    Spanish, 203
    Turkish, 352
    Various languages, 128
    Yiddish, 408
Words for musical instruments, 297
Writing systems and transliteration,
    28, 76

INDEX OF FINE ART

Cover	Japanese lacquer writing box, early nineteenth century
xxviii	*Sunday Afternoon on the Island of La Grande Jatte,* Georges Seurat
5	*Mr. and Mrs. Nyanga,* El Anatsui
12	*The Auvers Stairs with Five Figures,* Vincent van Gogh
21	Detail. *Camille at Her Window, Argenteuil,* Claude Monet
27	*La Casa Grigia,* Marc Chagall
35	*Quantrell II,* Judy North
41	*Sculpture of Man,* Felix Eboigbe
42	*The Garden Imagined,* Ablade Glover
46	*Nordlandsgutt* ("Boy from Norland"), Jean Heiburg
52	Indian glass bottle, eighteenth century
61	*Evening by the Sea,* Karl Schmidt-Rottluff
67	Detail. *Interior of a Factory* ("Une Forge"), Fernand Cormon
69	*Christmas at Sanborn,* from *The Christmas Triptych,* Carl Larsson
75	*Winter Landscape,* Wang Jian
78	*The Great Mosque at Medina,* manuscript
93	*Jumping Trout,* Winslow Homer
99	*Mont Sainte-Victoire Seen from the Bibemus Quarry,* Paul Cézanne
107	*Doll House from Nuremberg,* seventeenth century
110	Detail. *Doll House from Nuremberg,* seventeenth century
115	*Grand Piano,* Cawen
123	*Snow Flurries,* Andrew Wyeth
137	*Ginevra de'Benci,* Leonardo da Vinci
143	*Two vinas (stringed instruments),* Indian
146	*Castle in Prague,* Oscar Kokoschka
155	Detail. *Burro and Peddler,* Milton Avery
158	*La Palme* ("The Palm"), Henri Matisse
163	*Don Quixote and Sancho Panza,* Pablo Picasso
168	*Railroad in Spring,* Charles Burchfield
175	*The Park,* Gustav Klimt
183	*Mt. Omei of Ssuch'uan,* Chang Yuan
191	*Prussian Guard Drum-Major,* G. Oudry
199	*El Reto* ("The Challenge"), David Alfaro Siqueiros
206	*I,* Francesco Clemente
217	Detail. *August Moon,* Paul Resika
221	*A Pair of Boots,* Vincent van Gogh
226	Fante chief's figurative cloth, Ghana
228	African ceremonial masks, Ivory Coast, Ghana, and Sierra Leone
231	Scythian gold helmet, fourth century B.C.
235	Zapotec clay urn, Oaxaca, c. fifth to eighth century
238	*The Fox and the Grapes,* illustration from an early German edition of *Aesop's Fables*
240	*The Fox and the Crow,* illustration from an early German edition of *Aesop's Fables*
243	Detail from an Indian painting, Mughal Period
249	Detail. Illustration depicting Sindbad the Sailor from an early German edition of *The Thousand and One Nights*
259	Frontispiece for sheet music for Franz Schubert's ballad "Erlkönig"
265	*Kalyx Krater,* attributed to the Tyszkiewicz Painter
270	*The Trojan Horse,* print after a painting by Henri Motte

Index of Fine Art **637**

This index lists, in the order in which they appear, the many examples of fine art included in this textbook. By examining the list and turning to the pages on which each work of art appears, students can attain a better understanding of the achievements and diversity of artists from all over the world.

277 *Encounter of Dante and Beatrice,* Venetian School, fourteenth century
282 Machu Picchu, Peru
284 Gold ear spools inlaid with turquoise, Mochica, Peru
287 Detail from a Chinese painting, Ming Dynasty
288 *Woman with Red Hair,* Amedeo Modigliani
290 *Girl with Pigeons,* grave relief from Island of Paros
293 Woodblock print, Suzuki Harunobu
296 Baule mask, Ivory Coast
301 *Portrait of a Youth,* Filippino Lippi
304 Detail. *La Pie* ("The Magpie"), Claude Monet
309 *Blaues Pferd I,* Franz Marc
311 *From the Plains I,* Georgia O'Keeffe
313 Benin brass rooster
315 *Gourds,* John Singer Sargent
316 *From the White Place,* Georgia O'Keeffe
319 *Spring Landscape with Blossoming Cherry Tree and Waterfall,* lid from a Japanese writing box
322 Carved and painted prow, Douala, Cameroun, nineteenth century
324 *Fish Seller and Sweet Meat Maker and Seller with Their Wares,* Shiva Dayal Lal
327 *Sheaves of Wheat,* Vincent van Gogh
330 *The Trail to Champney Falls,* Robert Jordan
333 *Kids on Bikes,* David Park
335 Detail. *Ballet Espagnol,* Edouard Manet
337 Detail from an eight-panel Chinese screen, eighteenth century
341 *Guitar,* Pablo Picasso
344 *Le Coeur,* Henri Matisse
351 *World Map,* Battista Agnese
360 Greek two-handled drinking cup, fifth century
366 *Monument to Bartolomeo Colleoni,* Andrea del Verrocchio
368 Initial word panel of the Book of Psalms featuring King David playing his harp. Detail from the *Rothschild Miscellany* illuminated manuscript, fifteenth century
370 Chinese embroidered silk banner, nineteenth century
375 Indian fabric, design of Gopis in a garden, seventeenth century
380 Gold rings of the Mawerehene, Ashanti, Ghana
385 Ornament from African ceremonial state sword, early twentieth century
395 *Madame Roulin Rocking the Cradle,* Vincent van Gogh
396 Detail. *Auriculas in a Basket,* John Morley
399 Confucius, woodblock print
401 Detail. *The Thinker,* Auguste Rodin
410 *Apple Blossoms,* John William Hill
411 *Overhanging Cloud in July,* Charles Burchfield
414 *The Little Mule,* Abraham Angel
418 *Jeune fille à l'éventail,* Henri Lebasque
424 Pericles, possibly by Kresilas
431 Ornament from African ceremonial state sword, early twentieth century
434 Marco Polo arriving in the Court of Kublai Khan, thirteenth century
436 *The View of Ducal Palace and the Piazzeta San Marco,* Canaletto
439 Bead-embroidered staff, Yoruba
441 Ife head, Yoruba, fourteenth or fifteenth century
444 Stool-throne carved with crocodiles, Cameroun
449 African beaded headdress
457 *Detail* from a No robe, seventeenth century
461 *The Old Plum,* attributed to Kano Sansetsu

638 *Index of Fine Art*

544 Parthenon, Athens
544 Greek amphora
545 Statue of Augustus Caesar
545 Colosseum, Rome
547 Fresco from Pompeii, first century B.C.
547 Roman coin, fourth century B.C.
548 Violin, Nicolò Amati, seventeenth century
548 Tower of Pisa, Tuscany
549 *St. Mark's Square, Venice,* Canaletto
549 Majolica pottery, sixteenth century
551 *David,* Michelangelo
551 *Head of a Woman,* Leonardo da Vinci
552 Faience dog, Emile Gallé
552 Palace of Versailles
553 Louvre Museum, Paris
553 Cathedral of Notre Dame, Paris
555 *Boulevard des Italiens, Morning, Sunlight,* Camille Pissarro
556 Alhambra, Court of the Lions, Granada
557 *The Bull,* Pablo Picasso
557 *Infanta Margherita d'Austria,* Diego Velázquez
559 Casa Batlló, Antonio Gaudí
560 Chichén Itzá, Mexico
561 Chimú gold mask, Peru
561 Guatemalan cloth
563 *Flower Vendor,* Diego Rivera
563 Nazca vessel, Peru
564 German harpsichord, eighteenth century
565 Meissen porcelain, eighteenth century
565 Neuschwanstein castle, Bavaria
567 *Reflection,* Gabriele Münter
568 Russian lacquered chest
568 Cathedral of St. Basil, Moscow
569 Ukrainian Easter eggs
571 *Coronation Egg,* Fabergé
571 *Green Violinist,* Marc Chagall
572 Great Wall of China
572 Forbidden City, Beijing
573 *Bird Catcher,* Okinomo
575 Chinese ceramic platter, nineteenth century
576 Lion, Royal Palace of Benin
576 Ashanti stool, Ghana
577 Bird scupture, Ivory Coast
579 Ngindo stool sculpture, Tanzania, nineteenth century
580 Indian album leaf, Khem Karan, sixteenth century
580 Taj Mahal, Agra
581 Pyramids at Giza
581 Stained glass window for Hadassah Hospital, Jerusalem, Marc Chagall
583 Iranian star tile, thirteenth century
583 Turkish carpet, Bursa tribe, sixteenth century

Index of Fine Art **639**

INDEX OF AUTHORS AND TITLES

Page numbers in italics indicate biographical material.

A Note on Alphabetization of Names:

Spanish and Portuguese surnames (family names) are often compounds including both the father's family name and the mother's family name. In such cases, the author is indexed under the first word of the compound. For example, *Jorge Carrera Andrade* is indexed under *C.*

In Oriental names the surname traditionally precedes the given name. These authors are indexed under the surname. For example, *Tu Peng-cheng* is indexed under *T.*

Achebe, Chinua, *39,* 40
Actor, The, 30
Aeneid, from the, 270
Aesop, *237,* 238
After a Long Winter, 318
Afterglow, 345
Air des Clochettes, 173
Akhmatova, Anna, *298,* 298
Akutagawa Ryūnosuke, *180,* 181
Aleixandre, Vicente, *332,* 332
All That Dances, 321
Amrouche, Marguerite, *252,* 253
Analects, The, Sayings from, 399
And We Shall Be Steeped, 296
Arabian and Persian
   Traditional, 247
Autumn, 318
Autumn Mountain, 181

Bamboo Hut, The, 329
Barstow, Stan, *29,* 30
Bashō, *318,* 318
Bat, The, 235
Beggar, The, 24
Bialik, Chaim Nachman, *315,* 315
Bjørnson, Bjørnstjerne, *44,* 45
Boccaccio, Giovanni, *134,* 135
Böll, Heinrich *204,* 205
Borges, Jorge Luis, *345,* 345
Brodsky, Joseph, *365,* 365
By Any Other Name, 373

Cabral de Melo Neto, João, *312,*
   312
Camus, Albert, *208,* 209

Carrera Andrade, Jorge *326,* 326
Cavafy, C. P., *353,* 353
Cela, Camilo José, *417,* 418
Cervantes, Miguel de, *161,* 162
Che Fece . . . Il Gran Rifiuto,
   353
Chekhov, Anton, *23,* 24
Chiyo, *318,* 318
Colette, *392,* 393
Colors, 294
Confucius, *398,* 399
Crocodiles of Yamoussoukro, The,
   431
Cyrano de Bergerac, 464

Dante, *275,* 276
Daudet, Alphonse, *188,* 189
Dead Men's Path, 40
Deledda, Grazia, *219,* 220
Dickinson, Emily, *330,* 330
Dinesen, Isak, *420,* 421
Divine Comedy, The, from, 276
Doll's House, The, 105
Don Quixote, from, 162
Dwarf Trees, The, 454

Emperor, The, 286
Encounter, 338
Erl-King, The, 258

Far and the Near, The, 168
Father, The, 45
Federigo's Falcon, 135
Fox and the Crow, The, 240
Fox and the Grapes, The, 238
Fragment of a Lullaby, 290

Gabon Pygmy Traditional, 321
García Lorca, Federico, *340,* 340
García Márquez, Gabriel, *197,* 198
Glass of Milk, The, 57
Goatherd and the Wild Goats, The,
   238
Godden, Rumer, *18,* 19
Goethe, Johann Wolfgang von, *257,*
   258
Gonzalez, N. V. M., *83,* 84

This index is an alphabetical listing of all the selections and authors included in this anthology. Page numbers in italics indicate the pages on which there is biographical information about the author listed.

Notice that authors with Spanish and Portuguese compound family names are listed under the first word of the compound; for example, Brazil's João Cabral de Melo Neto is listed under *C.* Authors with Asian names in which the family name precedes the given name are listed under the family name; for example, Japan's Akutagawa Ryūnosuke is listed under *A.*

Guest, The, 209
Guitar, The, 340

Handful of Dates, A, 78
Hastrman, 146
Heat, 318
Heine, Heinrich, *347,* 347
Hemingway, Ernest, *193,* 194
Henestrosa, Andrés, *234,* 235
Henshaw, James Ene, *438,* 439
Hikmet, Nazim, *350,* 350
Holth, Åsta, *129,* 130
Homer, *261,* 262
Hoodoo Valley, 121
Horace, *359,* 359
Horses, The, 308
How Happy Is the Little Stone, 330
Hugo, Victor, *305,* 305

I Am Sorry, 344
Iguana, The, 421
Iliad, from the, 262
Indian Traditional, 243
Infant Prodigy, The, 113
It Was That Very Day on Which the Sun, 300

Jewels of the Shrine, The, 439
Jiménez, Juan Ramón, *413,* 414
Jōsō, *318,* 318
June Nights, 305

Kabuliwallah, The, 49
Kabyle Traditional, 253
Kimenye, Barbara, *2,* 3

La Fontaine, Jean de, *239,* 240
Lagerlöf, Selma, *63,* 64
La Rochefoucauld, François de, *400,* 401
Last Lesson, The, 189
Laugher, The, 205
Laye, Camara, *379,* 380
Like the Sun, 141
Lingkuan Gorge, 73
Li Po, *337,* 337
Lorelei, The, 347
Lot's Wife, 298

Machado, Antonio, *304,* 304
Mahfouz, Naguib, *157,* 158
Mallet-Joris, Françoise, *172,* 173
Mann, Thomas, *112,* 113
Mansfield, Katherine, *104,* 105

María, Gerardo, *152,* 153
Martí, José, *362,* 362
Matusalén, the Village Without Time, 153
Maupassant, Guy de, *11,* 12
Maxims, from, 401
Message to Siberia, 364
Metamorphoses, from the, 231
Milosz, Czeslaw, *338,* 338
Mistral, Gabriela, *291,* 291
Monument, The, 365
Mtshali, Oswald Mbuyiseni, *311,* 311
My Heart, Thinking, 293

Naidu, Sarojini, *324,* 325
Naipaul, V. S., *430,* 431
Narayan, R. K., *140,* 141
Neruda, Jan, *145,* 146
Neruda, Pablo, *308,* 308
Nguyen Trai, *329,* 329

Ode: Better to Live, Licinius, 359
O'Faolain, Sean, *91,* 92
Old Man at the Bridge, 194
On the Ferry, 84
On the Way to School, 332
Ōtomo, Lady, *293,* 293
Ovid, *230,* 231

Panchatantra, from the, 243
Paterson, A. B. ("Banjo"), *356,* 356
Paton, Alan, *96,* 97
Paz, Octavio, *316,* 316
Pericles' Funeral Oration, 424
Petrarch, *300,* 300
Piece of String, The, 12
Platero and I, from, 414
Politics, 288
Pushkin, Alexander, *364,* 364

Quarry, The, 97

Rat Trap, The, 64
Rau, Santha Rama, *372,* 373
Reaping the Barley, 326
Rilke, Rainer Maria, *335,* 335
Rocking, 291
Rojas, Manuel, *56,* 57
Rostand, Edmond, *463,* 464
Roy, Gabrielle, *120,* 121

Sachs, Nelly, *307,* 307
Salih, Tayeb, *77,* 78

642   *Index of Authors and Titles*

Salt, 130
Sappho, *290,* 290
Sayings from *The Analects,* 399
Seami Motokiyo, *453,* 454
Seferis, George, *344,* 344
Senghor, Léopold S., *296,* 296
Shakespeare, William, *301,* 301
Shiki, *318,* 318
Shoes, The, 220
Shosha, 404
Singer, Isaac Bashevis, *403,* 404
Snake and the Goldsmith, The, 380
Solzhenitsyn, Aleksandr, *409,* 410
Sonnet 3 (Petrarch), 300
Sonnet 29 (Shakespeare), *301*
Spanish Dancer, 335
Story of the Chest, The, 253
Street Cries, 325
Summer Is Dying, 315
Sunset, 311
Swan, The, 307

Tagore, Rabindranath, *48,* 49
Taking Leave of a Friend, 337
Tale of Our Quarter, A, 158
Thousand and One Nights, The,
    from, 247
Three Prose Poems, 410
Thucydides, *423,* 424

Torres Bodet, Jaime, *354,* 354
Traveling in the Alcarria, 418
Trout, The, 92
Tuesday Siesta, 198
Tu Fu, *286,* 286
Tu Peng-cheng, *72,* 73
Two Memories of Sido, 393

Versos Sencillos, from, 362
Virgil, *269,* 270

Waltzing Matilda, 356
Weaving the Morning, 312
When, in Disgrace with Fortune and
    Men's Eyes, 301
Wind and Water and Stone, 316
Window, The, 354
Winner, The, 3
Winter, 318
Winter Sun, 304
Wolfe, Thomas, *167,* 168
World, My Friends, My Enemies,
    You, and the Earth, The, 350

Yeats, William Butler, *288,* 288
Yevtushenko, Yevgeny, *294,* 294
You Need to Go Upstairs, 19

Zapotec Traditional, 235

E. Dickinson William Faulkner Tom Wolfe

Gerard M. Hopkins S.J. Mark Twain Rudyard Kipling

Gwendolyn Brooks Randall Jarrell Joseph Conrad

Stephen Spender R. M. Rilke C Brontë Virginia Woolf

John Keats Arthur Conan Doyle Sidney Lanier

W. Shakespeare Robert Burns A Bradstreet William Shakespeare

A Lincoln Henry W. Longfellow Marianne Moore

James Joyce F. Douglass W Blake J. Austen

Wallace Stevens Robert Burns Phillis Wheatley

C Brontë James Thurber F Scott Fitzgerald